1 MONTH OF
FREE
READING

at

www.ForgottenBooks.com

By purchasing this book you are eligible for one month membership to ForgottenBooks.com, giving you unlimited access to our entire collection of over 1,000,000 titles via our web site and mobile apps.

To claim your free month visit:

www.forgottenbooks.com/free885629

ISBN 978-0-265-75938-7
PIBN 10885629

PUBLICATIONS

OF THE

ODERN LANGUAGE ASSOCIATIO

OF

AMERICA

EDITED BY

CHARLES H. GRANDGENT

SECRETARY OF THE ASSOCIATION

VOL. XXI

NEW SERIES, VOL. XIV

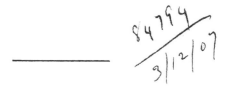

PUBLISHED QUARTERLY BY THE ASSOCIATION

PRINTED BY J. H. FURST COMPANY

BALTIMORE

1906

CONTENTS.

		PAGE.
I.—Three "Lapland Songs." By FRANK EDGAR FARLEY,		1
II.—Friedrich Schlegel and Goethe, 1790–1802: A Study in Early German Romanticism. By JOHN WILLIAM SCHOLL,		40
III.—Nash and the Earlier Hamlet. By JOHN W. CUNLIFFE,		193
IV.—The English Fabliau. By HENRY SEIDEL CANBY,		200
V.—Montaigne: The Average Man. By RALPH W. TRUEBLOOD,		215
VI.—Italian Fables in Verse. By KENNETH McKENZIE,		226
VII.—The Character Types in the Old French *Chansons de Geste.* By WILLIAM WISTAR COMFORT,		279
VIII.—Gismond of Salerne. By JOHN W. CUNLIFFE,		435
IX.—On the Date of *King Lear.* By ROBERT ADGER LAW,		462
X.—The Duration of the Canterbury Pilgrimage. By JOHN S. P. TATLOCK,		478
XI.—Chaucer's *Prioresses Tale* and its Analogues. By CARLETON F. BROWN,		486
XII.—Parataxis in Provençal. By WILLIAM PIERCE SHEPARD,		519
XIII.—The Vows of Baldwin: A Study in Mediæval Fiction. By EDWIN A. GREENLAW,		575
XIV.—The History of *ai* and *ei* in French before the Dental, Labial, and Palatal Nasals. By JOHN E. MATZKE,		637
XV.—Impressionist *versus* Judicial Criticism. By IRVING BABBITT,		687
XVI.—New Mexican Spanish. By E. C. HILLS,		706
XVII.—Professor Child and the Ballad. By WALTER MORRIS HART,		755
XVIII.—A Literary Link between Thomas Shadwell and Christian Felix Weisse. By ALFRED E. RICHARDS,		808
XIX.—Legends of Cain, especially in Old and Middle English. By OLIVER F. EMERSON,		831
XX.—Goethe's Essay *Über Laokoon.* By WILLIAM GUILD HOWARD,		930

APPENDIX.

PAGE.

Proceedings of the Twenty-third Annual Meeting of the Modern Language Association of America, held at Haverford College, Haverford, Pa., and at the University of Wisconsin, Madison, Wis., December 27, 28, 29, 1905.

THE ASSOCIATION MEETING.

Address of Welcome. By President ISAAC SHARPLESS. - - iii

Report of the Secretary, - - - - - - - - iv

Report of the Treasurer, - - - - - - - - iv

Appointment of Committees, - - - - - - - vi

1. A Low German Account of the Voyage of Columbus. By DANIEL B. SHUMWAY, - - - - - - vi

2. *Patelin* in the Oldest Texts. By RICHARD T. HOLBROOK, vi

3. On the Date of *King Lear*. By ROBERT ADGER LAW, - vi

4. The Vows of Baldwin in *The Avowing of Arthur*. By EDWIN A. GREENLAW, - - - - - - vii

5. The Raven Banner. By ARTHUR C. L. BROWN, - - vii

The Address of the President of the Association. By FRANCIS B. GUMMERE, - - - - - - - - vii

6. Chaucer's Relation to Old French Love-Vision Literature. By W. OWEN SYPHERD, - - - - - - vii

7. *Beatrijs*, a Netherlandish Romance of the Early Fourteenth Century. By HAROLD DEW. FULLER, - - - viii

8. American Speech. By LEIGH R. GREGOR, - - - viii

9. The Chronology of Boccaccio's First Stay in Naples. By E. H. WILKINS, - - - - - - - - viii

10. Gismond of Salerne. By JOHN W, CUNLIFFE, - - - viii

Report of the Committee of Five, - - - - - - ix

11. Some Notes on the Short Story. By H. T. BAKER, - - xv

12. The Structure and Interpretation of the *Widsith*. By W. W. LAWRENCE, - - - - - - - - xvi

13. Jean Paul Richter and E. T. A. Hoffmann. By ROBERT H. FIFE, Jr., - - - - - - - - xvi

14. Furetière as a Satirist. By ISABEL BRONK, - - - xvii

CONTENTS.

15. Wordsworthian Borrowings in Descriptions of External Nature. By Lane Cooper, - - - - -   xvii

Report of Auditing Committee, - - - - - -   xvii

Report of Nominating Committee, - - - - - -   xvii

Resolutions and Votes, - - - - - - - -   xviii

16. The Relation of Dryden's *State of Innocence* to Milton's *Paradise Lost* and Wycherley's *Plain Dealer*: an Inquiry into Dates. By George B. Churchill, - - -   xix

17. The Prosody of Walt Whitman. By F. N. Scott, - -   xix

18. The English *Fabliaux*. By Henry S. Canby, - - -   xx

19. Ben Jonson's *Alchemist* and Bruno's *Candelaio*. By C. G. Child, - - - - - - - - - -   xx

20. Margaret Fuller's Criticism of Goethe. By Karl D. Jessen, - - - - - - - - - -   xx

21. Three "Lapland Songs." By Frank Edgar Farley, -   xx

22. American Theories of Poetry. By Clyde B. Furst, -   xxi

23. Chaucer's *Litel Clergeon*. Carleton F. Brown, - -   xxi

Papers read by Title, - - - - - - - -   xxi

The Central Division Meeting.

1. Möser and the doctrine of the Diversity of Nature. By J. A. C. Hildner, - - - - - - - -   xxvi

2. *Los Pastores*, the Mexican Shepherd Plays. By Arthur Llewellyn Eno, - - - - - - - -   xxvi

3. The Historic Drama before Grabbe. By Louise M. Kueffner, - - - - - - - - - -   xxvii

4. The Literary Personality of José M. de Pereda. By Ralph Emerson Bassett, - - - - - -   xxvii

5. Adam Daniel Richter, Nachricht von J. Wimpflings Deutschland zur Ehre der Stadt Strassburg, etc., mit einigen Anmerkungen zu der teutschen Sprache, 1752. By Ernst Voss, - - - - - - - -   xxviii

6. The Language of Tennyson's early Poems, with reference to the Influence of his Predecessors. By James F. A. Pyre, - - - - - - - - - -   xxviii

Address of Welcome. By Edward Asahel Birge, - -   xxviii

Address of the Chairman of the Division:

A Neglected Branch of the Teaching of English. By Francis Adelbert Blackburn, - - - -   xxix

Appointment of Committees, - - - - - - - xxix

7. Paul Bourget, the Novelist. By MORITZ LEVI, - - xxix

8. Friedrich Heinrich Jacobi's Home at Pempelfort. By OTTO MANTHEY-ZORN, - - - - - - xxx

9. Symbolism of the early German Romanticists. By PAUL REIFF, - - - - - - - - - xxx

10. Some misinterpreted Passages in *Godefroi de Bouillon*. By HUGH ALLISON SMITH, - - - - - - xxx

11. German Sources of Ruskin. By CAMILLO VON KLENZE, - xxx

12. Some Technical Elements in Donne's Verse. By HENRY MARVIN BELDEN, - - - - - - - xxxi

13. Luther's Study of the Social Conditions of Germans as a Preparation for the Translation of the Bible. By WARREN WASHBURN FLORER, - - - - - - xxxi

14. The Source and Composition of *Ille et Galeron*. By JOHN E. MATZKE, - - - - - - - - xxxii

Departmental Meetings :—

English, - - - - - - - - - xxxii

Romance Languages, - - - - - - - xxxii

Germanic Languages, - - - - - - xxxiii

15. The Thames Fitting. By GEORGE HEMPL, - - - - xxxiii

16. Sebastian Mey's *Fabulario*, a forgotten Collection of Spanish Stories (Valencia, 1613). By MILTON A. BUCHANAN, xxxiv

17. German Literature in American Magazines from 1800 to 1845. By S. H. GOODNIGHT, - - - - xxxiv

18. The Relative Dates of the Canterbury Tales. By ELEANOR P. HAMMOND, - - - - - - - xxxiv

19. English Translations of Modern German Literature—a statistical Study. By A. BUSSE, - - - - xxxv

20. A Study of Obsolete Words and Grammatical Forms in the Prologues of the French Mysteries of the Fifteenth Century. By DAVID H. CARNAHAN, - - - xxxv

21. The Source of Weisse's *Richard III*. By F. W. MEISNEST, xxxv

Report of the Auditing Committee, - - - - - xxxvi

Report of the Nominating Committee, - - - - xxxvi

Report of Committee on Place of Meeting, - - - xxxvi

List of Officers, - - - - - - - - xxxviii

The Chairman's Address :—

A Neglected Branch of the Teaching of English. By
FRANCIS ADELBERT BLACKBURN, - - - - xxxix

The Constitution of the Association, - - - - - - lxx

List of Members, - - - - - - - - - lxxiv

List of Subscribing Libraries, - - - - - - - cx

Honorary Members, - - - - - - - - - cxii

Roll of Members Deceased, - - - - - - - cxiii

PUBLICATIONS

OF THE

Modern Language Association of America

1906.

| VOL. XXI, 1. | NEW SERIES, VOL. XIV, 1. |

I.—THREE "LAPLAND SONGS."

The second antistrophe of *The Progress of Poesy* opens, it will be recalled, with a rather striking allusion to the beneficent visitations of the Muse in the far North:

> In climes beyond the solar road,
> Where shaggy forms o'er ice-built mountains roam,
> The Muse has broke the twilight-gloom
> To chear the shiv'ring Native's dull abode.

In the second edition of the poem (1768), this tolerably lucid passage was somewhat obscured for future generations by one of those notes in which Gray compromised his "respect for the understanding of his readers":

> Extensive influence of poetic Genius over the remotest and most uncivilized nations: its connection with liberty, and the virtues that naturally attend on it. (See the Erse, Norwegian, and Welch Fragments, the Lapland and American songs.) [1]

The "Erse, Norwegian, and Welch Fragments" are of

---

[1] Phelps, *Selections from the Poetry and Prose of Thomas Gray*, Boston, 1894, p. 29.

course the publications of Macpherson, Evans, and Percy, together with certain experiments by Gray himself. By "American Songs" Gray meant various productions, current in his day and later, in which the American Indian was represented as giving lyrical expression to amorous desire, scorn, or spiritual aspiration.[1]

The present paper endeavors to trace the history of three once famous lyrical compositions of the type known to Gray and his contemporaries as "Lapland songs."

To Johan Scheffer, for many years Professor of Law and Rhetoric in the University at Upsala, undoubtedly belongs the credit of having reproduced the first specimens of Lappish poetry ever printed. The volume in which they appeared, Scheffer's *Lapponia*, is an extraordinarily entertaining account of an expedition into Lapland undertaken by the author at the instance of the Swedish government, published originally in Latin at Frankfurt in 1673, and before the expiration of a decade successively translated into English (Oxford, 1674),[2] German (Frankfurt and Leipzig,

---

[1] See *Scandinavian Influences in the English Romantic Movement*, by F. E. Farley (*Studies and Notes in Philology and Literature*, vol. IX, Boston, 1903, pp. 66 f., n. 2).

[2] A copy of this edition is owned by the Boston Public Library. The title page reads: *The History of Lapland wherein are shewed the Original, Manners, Habits, Marriages, Conjurations, &c., of that People. Written by John Scheffer, Professor of Law and Rhetoric at Upsal in Sweden. At the Theatre in Oxford*, MDCLXXIV. The preface explains that this version is abridged from the Latin.

Another English version, a copy of which is owned by the Harvard College Library, was published in London in 1704. It purports to be "done from the last Edition in the original *Latin*, and collated with a French translation Printed at *Paris*, which contains several *Addenda* that the Translator had from the Author, all which are here taken in." To the Translation of *Lapponia* are added in this edition, "The Travels of the King of *Sweden's* Mathematicians into *Lapland*: The History of *Livonia*, and the Wars there: Also a Journey into *Lapland*, *Finland*, &c. Written by Dr. *Olof Rudbeck* in the Year 1701."

1675), French (Paris, 1678), and Dutch (Amsterdam, 1682). The two lyrics in question are found in a chapter "Of their Contracts and Marriages." I quote from the English version of 1674;[1] the author is describing the conduct of the Lapland lover during the period of courtship:

In this interval he ever and anon makes a visit to his Mistress, to whom while he is travelling he solaces himself with a Love Song, and diverts the wearisomness of his journy. And 'tis their common custom, to use such kind of Songs, not with any set tune, but such as every one thinks best himself, nor in the same manner, but sometimes one way, sometimes another, as goes best to every man, when he is in the mode of singing. An ensampel of one they use in the Winter season, communicated to me by *Olaus Matthias*, a *Laplander*, I here annex :

> *Kulnasatz niraosam œugaos joao audas jordee skaode*
> *Nurte waota waolges skaode*
> *Abeide kockit laidi ede*
> *Fauruogaoidhe sadiede*
> *Ællao momiaiat kuekan kaigewarri.*
>   [There are eleven lines more.]

The meaning of this song is this,

> *Kulnasatz* my Rain-deer
> We have a long journy to go ;
>   The Moor's are vast,
>   And we must hast,
> Our strength I fear
> Will fail if we are slow,
>   And so
> Our Songs will do.

> *Kaigè* the watery Moor
>   Is pleasant unto me,
>   Though long it be ;
> Since it doth to my Mistriss lead,

The Catalogue of Printed Books in the British Museum records a third translation into English, abridged, published in London, 1751. Throughout the eighteenth century, allusions to Scheffer are very common in the works of English writers on Scandinavian subjects.

[1] Pp. 111 ff.

Whom I adore ;
The *Kilwa* Moor,
I nere again will tread.

Thoughts fill'd my mind
Whilst I thro *Kaigè* past.
   Swift as the wind,
   And my desire,
Winged with impatient fire,
My Rain-deer let us hast.
So shall we quickly end our pleasing pain :
   Behold my Mistresse there,
With decent motion walking ore the Plain.

Kulnasatz my Rain-deer,
   Look yonder, where
   She washes in the Lake.
See while she swims
The waters from her purer limbs
   New cleerness take.[1]

This is a love Song of the *Laplanders*, wherewith they incourage their Rain-deers to travell nimbly along. For all delay, tho in it self short, is tedious to lovers. They use too at other times to entertain themselves with such Sonnets, when at some distance from their Mistresses, and therein to make mention of them, and extoll their beauty. One of this kind I received of the said *Olaus*, and seeing we have lit upon this subject, I here set it down :

Pastos paiwa Kiufwresist jawra Orre Iawra
Ios kaosa kirrakeid korngatzim
Ia tiedadzim man oinœmam jaufre Orre Jawra
Ma tangast lomest lie sun lie
               [and so on for twenty-six lines farther].

The sense of this Song is thus,

-----

[1] Scheffer's Latin version of this song (*Lapponia*, ed. 1673, p. 283) is as follows : Kulnasatz, rangifer meus parvus properandum nobis iterque porro faciendum, loca uliginosa vasta sunt, & cantiones nos deficiunt. Nec tamen tædiosus mihi palus kaige es, tibi palus kailvva dico vale. Multæ cogitationes animum meum subeunt, dum per paludem kaige vehor. Rangifer meus simus agiles levesque, sic citius absolvemus laborem, eoque veniemus, quo destinamus, ubi videbo amicam meam ambulantem. Kulnasatz rangifer meus prospice ac vide, utrū non cernas eam se lavaatem.

With brightest beams let the Sun shine
  On *Orra Moor*,
    Could I be sure, .
That from the top o'th lofty Pine,
I *Orra Moor* might see,
I to his highest bow would climb,
And with industrious labor try,
    Thence to descry
My Mistress, if that there she be.

Could I but know amidst what Flowers,
  Or in what shade she staies,
    The gaudy Bowers
With all their verdant pride,
  Their blossomes and their spraies,
    Which make my Mistress disappear ;
And her in Envious darkness hide,
I from the roots and bed of Earth would tear.

Upon the raft of clouds I'de ride
  Which unto *Orra* fly,
O'th Ravens I would borrow wings,
And all the feathered In-mates of the sky :
  But wings alas are me denied,
The Stork and Swan their pinions will not lend,
    There's none who unto *Orra* brings,
Or will by that kind conduct me befriend.

Enough enough thou hast delaied
  So many Summers daies,
The best of daies that crown the year,
  Which light upon the eielids dart,
    And melting joy upon the heart :
But since that thou so long hast staied,
· They in unwelcome darkness disappear,
    Yet vainly dost thou me forsake,
    I will pursue and overtake.

What stronger is then bolts of steel ?
  What can more surely bind ?
    Love is stronger far then it ;
Upon the Head in triumph she doth sit :
    Fetters the mind,   ·
    And doth controul,
    The thought and soul.

A youths desire is the desire of wind,
  All his Essaies
  Are long delaies,
No issue can they find.
Away fond Counsellors, away,
  No more advice obtrude :
  I'le rather prove,
The guidance of blind Love ;
To follow you is certainly to stray :
  One single Counsel tho unwise is good.[1]

No attempt seems to have been made to give these songs a better English rendering until 1712. The issue of *The Spectator* for April 30 of that year (No. 366) contained a communication beginning :

The following verses are a translation of a Lapland love-song, which I met with in Scheffer's history of that country. . . . The numbers in the

---

[1] Scheffer's Latin runs as follows : "Sol, clarissimum emitte lumen in paludem Orra. Si enisus in summa picearum cacumina, scirem me visurum Orra paludem, in ea eniterer, ut viderem, inter quos amica mea esset flores, omnes sucscinderem frutices recens ibi enatos, omnes ramos præsecarem, hos virentes ramos. Cursum nubium essem secutus, quæ iter suum instituunt versus paludem Orra, si ad te volare possem alis, cornicum alis. Sed mihi desunt alæ, alæ querquedulæ, pedesque, anserum pedes plan[tæ]ve bonæ, quæ deferre me valeant ad te. Satis expectasti diu, per tot dies, tot dies tuos optimos, oculis tuis jucundissimis, corde tuo amicissimo. Quod si longissime velles effugere, cito tamen te consequerer. Quid firmius validiusve esse potest, quam contorti nervi catenæve ferreæ, quæ durissime ligant? Sic amor contorquet caput nostrum, mutat cogitationes & sententias. Puerorum voluntas, voluntas venti, juvenum cogitationes, longæ cogitationes. Quos si audirem omnes, omnes, à via, à via justa declinarem. Vnum est consilium, quod capiam, ita scio viam rectiorem me reperturum."

Revisions of the Lappish text which seem to establish the authenticity of Scheffer's two songs, are printed in Otto Donner's *Lieder der Lappen*, Helsingfors, 1876, and in Richard Bergström's monograph, *Spring, min Snälla ren!* (Nyare Bidrag till kannedom om de Svenska Landsmålen ock svenskt Folklif, v, 4 [Stockholm, 1885]). Of Scheffer's Lappish version of the Orra Moor song Donner writes (p. 115) : "Die ortografie ist sehr inkorrekt, wodurch einige wörter gar nicht zur ermitteln sind, besonders da bei dem mündlichen vortrage gewisse silben, wie es scheint, wiederholt wurden." Scheffer's Latin version, he adds, though "überhaupt treue . . . . leidet doch an einigen fehlern." See below, p. 9, n. 2.

original are as loose and unequal, as those in which the British ladies sport their Pindarics; and perhaps the fairest of them might not, think it a disagreeable present from a lover: but I have ventured to bind it in stricter measures, as being more proper for our tongue, though perhaps wilder graces may better suit the genius of the Lapponian language. . . . [Then follows this new version of the Orra Moor song. It will be observed that the name "Orra Moor," properly, of course, the designation of a locality, here, and in some later versions of the song, answers for the name of the Lappish damsel:]

Thou rising sun, whose gladsome ray
Invites my fair to rural play,
Dispel the mist, and clear the skies,
And bring my Orra to my eyes.

Oh! were I sure my dear to view,
I'd climb that pine-tree's topmost bough
Aloft in air that quivering plays,
And round and round for ever gaze.

My Orra Moor, where art thou laid?
What wood conceals my sleeping maid?
Fast by the roots enraged I'll tear
The trees that hide my promised fair.

Oh! I could ride the clouds and skies,
Or on the raven's pinions rise:
Ye storks, ye swans, a moment stay,
And waft a lover on his way.

My bliss too long my bride denies,
Apace the wasting summer flies:
Nor yet the wintry blasts I fear,
Not storms or night shall keep me here.

What may for strength with steel compare?
Oh! love has fetters stronger far:
By bolts of steel are limbs confined,
But cruel love enchains the mind.

No longer then perplex thy breast,
When thoughts torment the first are best;
'Tis mad to go, 'tis death to stay,
Away to Orra, haste away.[1]

---

[1] I quote from Aitken's edition, London, 1898, v, 249 ff. In Aitken's *Life of Richard Steele*, London, 1889, II, 385 f., may be found a musical

This experiment aroused emulation; in No. 406 of *The Spectator* (printed June 16, 1712) appeared a paraphrase of the other Scheffer song :

The town being so well pleased with the fine picture of artless love which nature inspired the Laplander to paint in the ode you lately printed [writes the author], we were in hopes that the ingenious translator would have obliged it with the other also which Scheffer has given us; but since he has not, a much inferior hand has ventured to send you this . . . [and a new version of the reindeer song follows :]

> Haste, my reindeer, and let us nimbly go
> Our amorous journey through this dreary waste :
> Haste, my reindeer, still, still thou art too slow,
> Impetuous love demands the lightning's haste.
>
> Around us far the rushy moors are spread :
> Soon will the sun withdraw his cheerful ray ;
> Darkling and tired we shall the marshes tread,
> No lay unsung to cheat the tedious way.
>
> The watery length of these unjoyous moors
> Does all the flowery meadows' pride excel ;
> Through these I fly to her my soul adores ;
> Ye flowery meadows, empty pride, farewell.
>
> Each moment from the charmer I'm confined,
> My breast is tortured with impatient fires ;
> Fly, my reindeer, fly swifter than the wind,
> Thy tardy feet wing with my fierce desires.

---

rendering of this song "set for the German Flute" by C. Smith, Jr., cir. 1750.

A note in modern editions of *The Spectator*, which may be traced back at least as far as the edition of 1797 (v, 281), ascribes this paraphrase to Ambrose Philips, though I cannot find that Philips ever acknowledged it. Philips contributed to No. 12 of *The Tatler* (May 7, 1709) the well known lines written from Copenhagen, beginning :—

> From frozen climes, and endless tracts of snow,
> From streams that northern winds forbid to flow ;
> What present shall the muse to Dorset bring ;
> Or how, so near the pole, attempt to sing ?

Our pleasing toil will then be soon o'erpaid,
And thou, in wonder lost, shalt view my fair,
Admire each feature of the lovely maid,
Her artless charms, her bloom, her sprightly air.

But lo! with graceful motion there she swims,
Gently removing each ambitious wave;
The crowding waves transported clasp her limbs:
When, when, oh when, shall I such freedoms have!

In vain, you envious streams, so fast you flow,
To hide her from a lover's ardent gaze:
From every touch you more transparent grow,
And all revealed the beauteous wanton plays.[1]

The *Spectator* version of the reindeer song was printed, without acknowledgment, in *The Hive, a Collection of the Most Celebrated Songs* (4th ed., London, 1732, I, 13).

Among the *Miscellaneous Works in Prose and Verse of Mrs. Elizabeth Rowe*, London, 1739, appeared a third English rendering of the Orra Moor song which seems to have been received with more enthusiasm in Germany than at home.[2] Mrs. Rowe's stanzas run as follows:

---

[1] Quoted from Aitken's edition, VI, 52 f. This version, signed "T," is usually attributed to Steele.

[2] I, 92 f. Theodor Vetter, author of a eulogistic biography of Mrs. Rowe entitled *Die Göttliche Rowe*, Zürich, 1894, makes special mention (pp. 13 f.) of this translation and calls attention to the other versions in the Oxford edition of Scheffer and in *The Spectator*. Vetter adds, "Das kleine Liedchen hat übrigens in der deutschen Literatur seine Geschichte" and goes on to cite the very free paraphrase of Mrs. Rowe's version made by Kleist in 1757 (cf. Kleist's *Werke*, ed. Sauer, Berlin, 1880–81, I, 107 f.), upon which Lessing commented in *Briefe, die neueste Litteratur betreffend* (No. 33—cf. Lessing's *Sämtliche Schriften*, ed. Lachmann-Muncker, VIII, 75, Stuttgart, 1892), together with Herder's more literal rendering (1771). Herder also translated the reindeer song (cf. Herder's *Volkslieder*, Leipzig, 1778–79, I, 264; II, 106). Herder's translations are printed in Donner's *Lieder der Lappen*, Helsingfors, 1876, together with another German version of the Orra Moor song. Donner also mentions the Finnish poet Franzén's Swedish version of the reindeer song, "Spring, min snälla ren," which Richard Bergström has made the subject of a monograph

A Laplander's Song to his Mistress.

Shine out, resplendent God of day,
    On my fair *Orramoor ;*
Her charms thy most propitious ray,
    And kindest looks allure.

In mountain, vale, or gloomy grove,
    I'd climb the tallest tree,
Could I from thence my absent love,
    My charming rover see.

I'd venture on a rising cloud,
    Aloft in yielding air,
From that exalted station proud,
    To view the smiling fair.

Should she in some sequester'd bow'r,
    Among the branches hide,
I'd tear off ev'ry leaf and flow'r,
    Till she was there descry'd.

From ev'ry bird I'd steal a wing
    To *Orramoor* to fly ;
And urg'd by love, would swiftly spring
    Along the lightsome sky.

Return, and bless me with thy charms,
    While yet the sun displays
His fairest beams, and kindly warms
    Us with his vital rays.

Return before that light be gone,
    In which thou shouldst appear ;
Unwelcome night is hast'ning on
    To darken half the year.

In vain, relentless maid, in vain
    Thou dost a youth forsake,
Whose love shall quickly o'er the plain,
    Thy savage flight o'ertake.

(*Spring, min snälla ren !* [Stockholm, 1885]). Bergström prints the English versions published in the Oxford edition of 1674 and in *The Spectator,* together with Franzén's Swedish and Kleist's German versions. See above, p. 6, n.

> Should bars of steel my passage stay,
> They could not thee secure :
> I'd thro' enchantments find a way
> To seize my *Orramoor.*

Of course nothing printed in *The Spectator* could altogether escape the attention of any generation of English readers, but the Lapland songs seem not to have aroused any very general interest until the changing literary fashions of half a century all at once gave them an unexpected significance. The publication of Macpherson's Ossianic fragments (1760), Percy's *Five Pieces of Runic Poetry* (1761), Evans's *Specimens of the Antient Welsh Bards* (1764) and Percy's *Reliques* (1765) marked the beginning, as everybody knows, of a new attitude toward the literature of half-civilized races. These attempts to popularize the folk poetry of Great Britain and Scandinavia led to a widespread curiosity in England with regard to the habits of our northern ancestors, and to countless experiments in "runic" and "Welsh" songs, pseudo-archaic "ballads" and Ossianic prose.[1] "Odin," "Thor," and "Taliessin" became names to conjure with, and the fastnesses of Wales, the highlands of Scotland, and the "frozen North" were imbued with a romantic significance unfelt in any previous age.

Lapland had long been the subject of vague and sporadic allusions in the polite literature of England, from which we may gather that Englishmen, in common with most other Europeans, looked upon it merely as an uncanny tract whose barbarous inhabitants, like the followers of Odin, were

---

[1] See *Scandinavian Influences in the English Romantic Movement*; also Schnabel's *Ossian in der schönen litteratur England's bis 1832 (Englische Studien,* xxiii, 31 ff., 366 ff.). I do not know that any special study has been made of English imitations of "Welsh" poetry, but one has only to turn over the leaves of any considerable number of eighteenth century magazines and collections of fugitive verse to realize that here lies a fruitful field for investigation.

reputed skillful in the practice of the black art. Hence Shakspere's "Lapland sorcerers," [1] Marlowe's "Lapland giants" [2] and Milton's "Lapland witches." [3]

[1] *Comedy of Errors*, IV, 3, 11.
[2] *Faustus*, sc. i, l. 127, ed. Gollancz.
[3] *Paradise Lost*, ii, 665.

Scheffer has a chapter on the magic arts practiced by the Laplanders which begins, "There is scarce a Country under the Sun, whither the Name of *Lapland* has reach'd by Fame or otherwise, which does not always look upon this Nation as greatly addicted to Magick" (*Lapponia*, translation of 1704, p. 119). The authorities cited by Scheffer in this particular, run back well toward the beginning of the sixteenth century ; among them are Olaus Magnus, whose *Historia de Gentibus Septentrionalibus* appeared at Rome in 1555 (see Lib. iii, Cap. 16), his friend the Portuguese historian Damiano de Goes, and Jacob Ziegler, a German mathematician and theologian who died in 1549. An English translation of a tract by Ziegler with the picturesque title "Of the Northeast frostie sea" is included in Eden and Willes' *The History of Trauayle in the West and East Indies*, London, 1577 : I quote from fol. 280 (*recto*) where Ziegler writes of "Gronelande" ; the inhabitants of this country, he says, are "geuen to magicall artes. For it is sayd that they (as also the people of *Laponia*) do rayse tempestes on the sea with magicall inchauntmentes, and bryng such shyps into daunger as they entend to spoyle." Ziegler touches here upon a specific branch of magic in which about all the northern races were held to be more or less proficient,—the power to control winds and bad weather. Saxo Grammaticus, whose *Historia Danica* was finished very early in the thirteenth century, attributes this power to Danes, Norwegians and Permlanders (cf. ed. Holder, pp. 32, 128 ; Elton and Powell, pp. 39, 156). Trevisa's translation of Bartholomew's *De Proprietatibus Rerum*, made in 1397, charges the inhabitants of "Wynlandia" with selling winds to mariners. "Wynlandia," he explains, "is a countree besydes ye moun-. tayns of Norwey towarde the eest. and stretchyth vppon the clyf of Occean ... The men of that countree ben straūge and somwhat wylde and fyers. And occupyen themselfe wyth wytchecrafte. And so to men that saylle by theyr costes : and also to men that abyde wyth theym for defawte of wynde they proffre wynde to sayllynge. and so sell wynde. And thei vse to make a clewe of threde and make dyuers knottes to be Joyned therin. And holdeth to drawe ont [*sic*] of the clewe thre knottes other moo : other lesse as he woll haue ye wynde more soft or strange. And for theyr mysbyleue fendes moue the ayre and areyse stronge tempeste other softe as he draweth of ye clewe more or lesse knottes. And somtyme they meue the wynde soo strongly : that wretches that byleue in suche doyng

It is probable that no specimens of Lappish literature, with the .exception of Scheffer's songs, were in existence. These songs, however, were so accessible in the *Spectator* version, that they were inevitably called to mind by the "northern" pieces which were repeatedly appearing in English literary periodicals and miscellanies during the last third of the eighteenth century. Presently "Lapland songs" shared the popularity of "runic odes," and Scheffer's lyrics acquired a vogue they had never before known. The following citations—which might, no doubt, be considerably extended by further search—will gave some idea of the extent to which Scheffer's songs were reprinted and paraphrased.

In 1763 Hugh Blair mentioned the *Spectator* songs and printed Scheffer's Latin version of the Orra Moor song in his *Critical Dissertation on the Poems of Ossian.*[1]

---

are drowned by ryghtfull dome of god" (Wynkyn De Worde's ed., West-minster, cir. 1495, Lib. xv, Cap. clxxi). This information is repeated in *Batman vppon Bartholome*, London, 1582 (fol. 248, *recto*). See also Burton's *Anatomy of Melancholy* (1621), ed. Shilleto, I, 161, 218, and Scheffer, ed. 1673, pp. 144 ff. Pierre Martin de la Martinière, author of a very popular volume called *Voyage des Pais Septentrionaux* which appeared first at Paris in 1671 and was later reprinted and translated into English, relates that the captain of the vessel in which he was sailing actually pu.chased three winds in a Lapland port at which they touched. The price paid was the equivalent of twenty French livres in money, with the addition of a pound of tobacco. The winds were confined in three knots tied into a woolen rag which was nailed to the masthead. De la Martinière disclaims belief in magic, but the experiment, he says, proved only too successful; for when the third knot was loosed, such a terrible tempest arose that the vessel nearly foundered, and the superstitious crew, who looked upon the storm as a judgment from Heaven, were beside themselves with fear. See the first edition, Paris, 1671, pp. 28 ff., and the English translation, *A New Voyage to the North*, London, 1706, pp. 22 ff. This business of selling winds came after a while to be regarded as rather a specialty of the Laplanders.

I am indebted to Dr. Alfred Cope Garrett for a part of the above information.

[1] P. 13, n.

Samuel Bishop's *Feriæ Poeticæ: sive Carmina Anglicana Elegiaci Plerumque Argumenti Latine Reddita* .... London, 1766, contains[1] both songs, properly credited, together with an original Latin translation of each, arranged in stanzas. Bishop's version of the Orra Moor song begins:

> Tu, sol, lætifico qui lumina spargis ab ortu,
> Pulchellamque meam ad ludicra pensa vocas,
> Pelle, precor, tenebras, et nubila discute coelo,
> Stetque oculis præsens ORRA videnda meis.

The opening stanza of the reindeer song is as follows:

> I, cerve, I, propera; rapiamur præpete cursu
> Quà deserta adeo per loca ducit iter:
> I, cerve, I, propera; quin jam, jam, tarde, moraris;
> Vincere præcipitans fulgura debet amor.

In his *Sketches of Man*, London, 1774, Henry Home, who refers several times to Scheffer, quotes, as an instance of the "mutual esteem and affection" which "naturally take place · .... in every country where the women equal the men," the English version of the two songs which appeared in the Oxford translation of *Lapponia*, 1674.[2] The reindeer song

---

[1] Pp. 1 ff.

[2] Second ed., Edinburgh, 1778, I, 487 ff. Anna Seward wrote to Court Dewes, March 9, 1788 (*Letters of Anna Seward*, Edinburgh, 1811, II, 65 ff.): "You remember the beautiful translation in the Spectator of the Lapland odes! I was once shewn a close translation of them, and copied it. There was much richer matter to work upon in the Lapland poems; yet the author of the Spectator-paraphrases found it advantageous, if not necessary, to strengthen into visibility those ideas which, in a version nearly literal, are seen but as through a glass darkly; and also to add some thoughts and images, of which no trace can be found in the originals, however exquisitely in keeping with the Lapland character, soil, and climate, as they appear to us in the ruder and faithful translations, which you will find enclosed." The editor of Miss Seward's correspondence explains that "The translations here mentioned are printed in Lord Kames's [Henry Home's] Sketches on Man."

as Home prints it was reprinted without acknowledgment in the *London Magazine* for August, 1774.[1]

Charles Theodore Middleton observes in his *New and Complete System of Geography*, London [1778] :

> When a [Lapland] lover goes to pay a visit to his mistress, during his journey through the fenny moors, he usually diverts himself with a song, which he addresses to his rein-deer. [Then follows, properly credited, "professor Scheffer's *Laplander's Song to his Rein deer.*" This translation, the editor informs us,] is taken from the Spectator; to which we shall subjoin a Laplander's love-song, the original having been procured by professor Scheffer, from the same Olaus Matthias, a native of Lapland. The translation, however, has never before appeared in print, and is the performance of a nobleman lately deceased, whose genius, politeness, and literary accomplishments, were the admiration of all the courts in Europe. His heir having obliged the authors of this work with a copy of this elegant poem, they thought it their duty to lay it before the public, both for the entertainment of their readers, and to honour so distinguished a character, who very recently adorned the British court.[2]

This unnamed nobleman[3] paraphrases the Orra Moor song in thirteen fervid stanzas which constitute probably a unique contribution to geographical lore :

A Laplander's Love Song.

Source of my daily thoughts, and nightly dreams
    Whose captivating beauties I adore,   •
O may the radiant sun's refulgent beams,
    Shine on the charms of lovely Orra Moor.

I'd climb the summit of the lofty pine,
    Could I my *Orra Moor* at distance view ;
No labour, danger, care, would I decline,
    To see my charmer, and to find her true.

Could she be wafted to terrestrial bow'rs,
    And there in pleasant shades induc'd to stay ;
Or range enamell'd fields of sweetest flow'rs,
    Charm'd by the birds that warbled on each spray.

---

[1] P. 402.   [2] II, 31.   [3] Chesterfield?

Enrag'd, those pretty birds I would destroy,
  Pluck up the flowers that beauty [1] the fields,
Cut down the bow'rs that rob me of my joy,
  And from my view my *Orra's* beauties shields.

O that I could but soar into the sky,
  And wing my passage thro' the ambient air,
Swift as the feather'd race could I but fly,
  I'd soon be with my captivating fair.

But vain, alas! my wishes are in vain,
  No stork, nor raven will a pinion lend;
Fated to feel unmitigated pain,
  With scarce a hope my passion to befriend.

So long my bliss can *Orra Moor* delay?
  Reflect, the summer's sun now brightly gleams;
Short are our summers—haste, then haste away,
  And, with thy love, enjoy his glad'ning beams.

Alas! unkindly you delay the time;
  Our short-lived summer wears away apace:
You've tortur'd me, and dally'd with your prime,
  'Till frowning winter shews his rugged face.

Still, still my lovely charmer I'll pursue,
  And scorn all danger to reveal my pains;
For what can love, all-pow'rful love subdue;
  He laughs at tempests, and despises chains.

Love! mighty victor, triumphs o'er mankind,
  Brings ev'ry thought beneath his own controul,
Enslaves the heart, puts fetters on the mind,
  And captivates the haughty human soul.

But, hark! stern reason whispers in my ear,
  Friend, you are wrong, thus to pour oil on fire,
Rashly to follow what you ought to fear,
  And rush into a whirlwind of desire.

A thousand things advise you to desist,
  A thousand dread examples bid you view
The fate of those whom love's delusive mist
  Hath slily blinded, sadly to undo.

[1] *Sic.*

Reason, avaunt ! to passion I submit,
And will not hear thy disimpassion'd tone ;
Others, thy thousand counsellors may fit,
But I'll attend the voice of love alone.

J. W. Holder includes the *Spectator* version of the Orra Moor song, properly credited and set to music, in his *Favorite Collection of Songs*, London, 1778.[1]

Both songs appeared in the *Spectator* version, but without acknowledgment, in *The Charmer, a Collection of Songs*, Edinburgh, 1782,[2] and in the *Vocal Library*, London, n. d.[3] Ritson printed them in the *Historical Essay on National Song* prefixed to his *Select Collection of English Songs*, London, 1783,[4] and attributed them, with a query, to Steele. He commends the "remarkable elegance" of one of them, presumably the Orra Moor song. Vicesimus Knox includes both songs in his *Elegant Extracts of Useful and Entertaining Passages in Poetry*, London, 1809,[5] and ascribes them, without query, to Steele.

The Orra Moor song, which proved, deservedly, the more popular of the two, appeared in the *Spectator* version, but without credit, in *The Charms of Melody*, Dublin [cir. 1800],[6] and again in a song-book called *The Syren*, Wilmington, Delaware, n. d.[7]

Familiar, however, as Scheffer's songs became in England, they had to compete for popularity, before the end of the eighteenth century, with a third famous "Lapland song" which possesses a curious history. In May, 1786, a party

[1] I am indebted to Lewis Edwards Gates, Esq., for this information.

[2] I, 11 f., 302.

[3] Pp. 24, 134. This collection of songs seems to have been compiled early in the nineteenth century.

[4] I, 216, 223. Cf. xxxix, n.

[5] II, 919.

[6] P. 94.

[7] Pt. 2, p. 5. The book appears to have been printed early in the last century. See, further, below, p. 21.

of Englishmen under the leadership of Sir Henry George Liddell, Bart., of Ravensworth, in Durham, made an expedition to certain northern countries, from which they returned in the following August, bringing with them two Lapland women. The women were exhibited for some months in various parts of England, where they attracted considerable attention, and were finally sent back home with a little money and numerous presents.

Very soon after their arrival in England, these women were entertained at a certain tavern in Newcastle, where they were induced to sing some of their native songs. On the 2d of September the following anonymous letter appeared in the *Newcastle Courant:*

To the Printer of the Courant, Sir,—

The public curiosity having been excited by the appearance of the musical Lapland females in this country, a specimen of Scandinavian poetry may, probably, afford some little amusement to the many. In my youth, a propensity to travel led me through many a rude, uncivilized region ; and in August of 1761, I sat me down in Lapland at a place called Trorian, about 150 miles to the north-west of Torne : there I lived through the winter. I was kindly treated by the hospitable owner of the cottage, and however inclined the polished natives of Europe may be to treat the inhabitants of the arctick region with derision, let it be remembered that happiness is to be found on the cliffs of Torne, and that hospitality spreads its unadorned table to the wanderers on the cold shores of Lulhea. I have joined in the song, and capered in the dance, and oft, when the storm pattered loudly without, the face of chearfulness and content was to be seen round the fire in the hut of the Laplander.

Curiosity led me to see the Lapland wanderers, at present in this country, and, to my great satisfaction, they sang me a song, to which I had often listened, with pleasure, at Trouan, and which I now offer to you, in an English dress, confident that it will afford some amusement to the readers of your excellent paper.

I am,

SIR,

Your very obedient servant,

T. S.

Newcastle, August 28th, 1786.

LAPLAND SONG.

Ouk fruezen tharanno el Torne van zien ;
Zo fruezen Lulhea thwe zarro a rien :
Thwe zarro a rien pa Lulhea teway,
Zo fleuris erzacken par ette octa.

        [There are three more stanzas, after which follows this
        English version :]

The snows are dissolving on TORNE'S rude side,
And the ice of LULHEA flows down the dark tide !
Thy dark streams, O LULHEA ! flow freely away,
And the snow-drop unfolds her pale beauties to day.

Remote, the keen terrors of Winter retire,
Where the North's dancing streamers relinquish their fire ;
Where the Sun's genial beams swell the bud on the tree,
And ENNA chaunts forth her wild warblings with glee.

The rein-deer, unharness'd, in freedom shall play,
And safely o'er ODON'S steep precipice stray :
The wolfe to the forest's recesses shall fly,
And howl to the moon as she glides thro' the sky.

Then haste my fair LHEA ; ah ! hast to the grove ;
And pass the sweet season in rapture and love :
In youth let our bosoms with exstacy glow,
For the winter of life ne'er a transport can know.[1]

The issue of the *Courant* for October 21 of the same year
(1786) contained another communication, signed " U. V."
from a correspondent who alleges an acquaintance with the
Lappish tongue, and who criticizes in detail the translation
of the Lapland song which has just been quoted. The
translator, he avers, has quite mistaken the meaning of the
original, and by way of correction he offers the following
version from his own pen :

---

[1] Lewis Edwards Gates, Esq., had the kindness to transcribe this letter
and the accompanying verses for me from the British Museum copy of
*Poetry Fugitive and Original by the late Thomas Bedingfeld, Esq. and Mr.
George Pickering*, Newcastle, 1815. I also owe to Mr. Gates several other
items of information with regard to this song.

O Torno ! the snows on thy summit we see,
　　Shall dissolve ; and the stream that sleeps frozen below
Again from its fetters of ice shall be free ;
　　And the snow-drop, now wither'd, with beauty shall glow.

The terrors of winter shall fly far away,
　　And the sun o'er the north shed his influence again,
And warm into bloom the sweet blossom of May,
　　And wake, through fair Enna, the wild warbling strain !

The rein-deer, now harness'd, shall quit with delight
　　His car, and o'er Odon in freedom shall fly ;
And the mist that now veils the pale ruler of night,
　　Shall pass, while unclouded she glides through the sky.

But for me ! wretched me ! since my Luah's no more,
　　Thro' my season of sorrow no changes can roll ;
My summer of joys and of rapture is o'er,
　　And winter for ever must chill my sad soul.

The second of these versions—that signed "U. V."—
seems, for all its author's assumption, to have fallen straightway into oblivion; but the first—by "T. S."—became
extraordinarily popular.　For some inexplicable reason this
poem was almost immediately attributed to Sir Matthew
White Ridley, the second baronet of the name, at that time
member of Parliament for Newcastle-upon-Tyne.　Among a
collection of miscellaneous tracts bound together in a single
volume owned by the British Museum, and all, according to
a MS. note on the fly-leaf, from the press of Fowler, of
Salisbury, is one consisting of a single sheet, octavo, upon
which is printed the "T. S." version under the title *Lapland
Song by Sir M. W. Ridley.*　The sheet bears no imprint, but
the British Museum Catalogue of Printed Books supplies a
conjectural date, " [Salisbury, 1785 ?] ".　I do not know the
authority for this date but it is certainly at least one year
too early.

In the July number of the *European Magazine* for 1787

this song was printed,[1] credited to "Sir W. M. Ridley," and strangely enough dated "Newcastle, June 9, 1787." In October, 1789, it was printed in the *Gentleman's Magazine*[2] and the name of the author was given as "Sir Matthew White Ridley." The same year, 1789, the piece appeared in the third volume of the London *Asylum for Fugitive Pieces*[3] credited again to Ridley. The next year it was set to music and published as *The Laplander's Song. The words written by Sir Matthew White Ridley. Set to Music, with Accompanyments By J. Relfe.* London, [1790].[4]

In 1789 an account of Liddell's northern expedition was prepared by one of the party and published in book form with the title, *A Tour through Sweden, Swedish-Lapland, Finland and Denmark. In a series of letters illustrated with engravings. By Matthew Consett, Esq.* London, 1789. In the course of his dissertation Consett observes:[5]

> The language of the Laplanders is a harsh and unintelligible Jargon derived from their neighbors the ancient Inhabitants of Finland. Their voices however are musical and they never require much entreaty to oblige. The few specimens which we possess of Lapland Poetry, give you a favorable impression of their *taste*, and taste most certainly it is, uncorrupted by foreign Ideas, and entirely the production of nature. In the Spectator you have two elegant Odes translated from the language of Lapland. . . . I shall make no apology for adding a third.

Then, under the title *A Lapland Song*, follows the Ridley poem without a word, however, to indicate that it is not Consett's own composition. In fact it was later attributed, naturally enough, to Consett by William Lisle Bowles.[6]

[1] P. 58. [2] P. 939. [3] P. 92.
[4] The date is supplied in the British Museum Catalogue.
[5] Pp. 63 f.
[6] See below, p. 29. Facing p. 148 Consett has a picture of "Sighre and Aniea," the two Lapland women brought to England by Liddell; the Appendix to the book describes them at length. Arthur de Capell Brooke, author of *A Winter in Lapland and Sweden*, London, 1826, declared that these women were not Lapps, but Finns. The Scheffer songs "which have

The next allusion I find to this song was occasioned indirectly by the publication, in Dr. Currie's edition of Burns's *Works*, Edinburgh and London, 1800,[1] of a letter written by Robert Burns to George Thomson, the musical composer. It seems that Thomson, who was then compiling his collection of Scottish airs with the assistance of Burns, had come upon an anonymous song in Johnson's *Musical Museum*[2] which so struck his fancy that he asked if Burns were not the author. Burns replied, in a letter dated October 19, 1794, "Donocht head is not mine: I would give ten pounds it were. It appeared first in the Edinburgh Herald; and came to the Editor of that paper with the Newcastle post-mark on it." Currie prints the poem in a foot-note, and adds, "The author need not be ashamed to own himself." Shortly after the publication of Currie's work the following communication, dated August 10, 1800, appeared in the *Monthly Magazine*:[3]

been admired, and not without reason, in the shape in which they have appeared in the Spectator," he thinks "cannot be mistaken for anything but the production of a Finlander," and the song printed by Consett he would "here give if my limits allowed me to present any specimens of Finland poetry." But he concludes, rather shrewdly, "It signifies indeed little if the words be but pretty and the air agreeable, whether the numerous Lapland compositions which now make their appearance, were the production of some tender Lap, breathing out his soul in amorous sighs and passionate love-strains beyond the Polar Circle, or have owed their birth to some ingenious wight, whose travels northward have not extended beyond his own country" (pp. 377 f.). Brooke probably did not know the history of the verses reproduced by Consett, but he may have guessed it. Liddell's Lapland women are also mentioned by Ch. Gottlob Küttner, whose *Travels Through Denmark, Sweden,* [etc.] . . . . in 1798–99, *Translated from the German*, are published in the first volume of a *Collection of Modern and Contemporary Voyages and Travels*, London, 1805, I, 35 ff. (second numbering). Boswell alludes to Liddell (*Life of Johnson*, ed. Hill, New York, 1891, II, 193, n.).

[1] IV, 175.

[2] *The Scots Musical Museum*, by James Johnson, vol. IV, Edinburgh, 1792, p. 388. Burns, it will be remembered, had furnished a good deal of material for this work.   [3] For October, 1800, p. 208.

To the Editor of the Monthly Magazine, SIR,

The fragment of which ROBERT BURNS said,[1] 'DONOCHT HEAD *is not mine: I would give ten pounds it were,*' was written by a Mr. GEORGE PICKERING, then of Newcastle upon Tyne, and who is, I believe, though not there, yet living. The amiable, but unfortunate *Mr.* BEDDINGFIELD (whose poems, surreptitiously printed,[2] are known to few, but by those few admired) was at the time his coadjutor and friend. There are, Mr. Editor, several gentlemen, and among those a worthy baronet, whose knowledge and elegant taste might enrich your publication with authentic and interesting memoirs of PICKERING and of BEDDINGFIELD : that tribute, due to genius nearly allied to that of BURNS, cannot, alas ! be paid, and must not be attempted by

ALBOIN.

The hint took effect. In the March number of the *Monthly Magazine* for 1801,[3] was printed a reply to "Alboin" signed "Georgii Amicus" and dated "Newcastle, Feb. 1." The communication embodies, curiously enough, a reprint of the Lapland song so often ascribed to Ridley, together with the alleged improvement upon that rendering which had appeared, under the signature "U. V.", in the *Newcastle Courant* of October 21, 1786. Pickering and Bedingfield, declares "Georgii Amicus," "were the real authors" of these two songs, "though it is known to very few."

The writer of this [he continues] was in the particular intimacy of the former [*i. e.,* Pickering]. To use his own words of the Laplanders, whose language, he imitated as below, 'I have joined (with him) in the song, and capered (with him) in the dance,'[4] the night has often passed by unheeded, and the morning has been brought on with our songs—but my friend has departed, and I know not what has become of him ! the witty, the worthy, but deluded Pickering, the sharer of my mirth, and the partner in my vagaries, perhaps, like his own Gaberlunzie man, now wanders through a Wreath o' Sna ! I needed not the promptings of Alboin in [regard to] Donocht Head ; often have I seen it in the writing of my friend ; frequently have I heard it, when his voice increased its melody.

---

[1] A foot-note refers to Currie, *loc. cit.*

[2] *Poems by T. B—g—d, Esq. of the Inner Temple* [London, 1800].

[3] Pp. 141 f.

[4] Cf. the letter of "T. S." to the *Courant* quoted above, p. 18.

Then the writer goes back to the Lapland song. He tells of Liddell's northern expedition and of the Lappish women he brought back to England.

An account of this voyage and those females [he proceeds] was given to the public by Matthew Consett, esq. in which he most mistakenly introduces the song of my lamented friend as *an original Composition of Laplandic Genius!* But why need we be astonished? the poems of Rowley have had their Chatterton, and those of Ossian, a Macpherson; need we wonder then, that a similar genius should impose upon a Consett? These Lapland females had been at a large tavern in Newcastle, and Pickering had the fortune to hear them sing. He went home, recollected the sounds of the words as well as he could, wrote the following letter to the Printer of the Newcastle Courant, introducing the accompanying *jeu d'esprit* as one of the songs he had heard; and I know also, that it was the occasion of a meeting of a good many of the orthodox priests of that town to judge of its genuineness, who decidedly pronounced in the affirmative! !

The letter of "T. S." to the Courant, reproduced above, follows. Pickering sent a copy of this letter, we learn, to Bedingfield (or rather Bedingfeld) with the suggestion that the latter make the criticism and revision which were afterwards printed under the signature "U. V." in the *Courant*.

'Tis at the request of several gentlemen [explains "Georgii Amicus" in conclusion] acquaintances of theirs, (after I had informed them of the real authors) that I send you the above. Your inserting it in your very valuable Magazine, will oblige many of your friends here, and be paying some little tribute of respect to so much ingenuity.

There is no reason to doubt the accuracy of this anonymous explanation in regard to the authorship of the Lapland song hitherto attributed to Ridley. George Pickering is not an important figure in the annals of our literature; he had clearly been pretty well forgotten by the year 1800, and had it not been for these two communications in the *Monthly Magazine* and the pious care of a member of the rather obscure literary coterie to which he belonged, he would have fallen entirely into oblivion. As it is, he is still remembered by local historians of the district about Newcastle-upon-Tyne as the perpetrator of the Lapland hoax, and by collectors of Scottish songs as the author of one lyric that had the good fortune to be praised by Burns.

Little is known in regard to Pickering's life.[1] He was born in Simonburn, North Tyne, in January, 1758. His father was a land steward, in charge, at various times, of important estates in the vicinity. The boy received an ordinary grammar-school education, and at the age of eighteen entered the employ of Thomas Davidson and Sons, attorneys, in Newcastle-upon-Tyne. Here he formed an intimate acquaintance with two fellow clerks, Thomas Bedingfeld and James Ellis, and the three young men presently began to occupy themselves with certain "literary diversions" in which we are told that "while Mr. Bedingfeld played the learned philosopher, and Mr. Ellis the sentimental swain, Pickering was the jovial and convivial poet of the set, who kept them all in good humor. He had," we learn further, "a keener sense of wit than his companions, a wider range of style, and a faculty of imitation which sometimes bordered upon plagiarism."[2] He is said to have been frequently entertained "at good tables" and to have fallen early into intemperate habits. Not long after the perpetration of the Lapland hoax he left Newcastle and for many years "drifted aimlessly about," no one knows where. In his declining years he returned to the north of England, where he died, obscurely, at his sister's house in

---

[1] He has not been deemed worthy an article in the *Dictionary of National Biography*, though he is mentioned in connection with Bedingfeld and Ellis, who are entered there. Ellis's *Poetry, Fugitive and Original* . . . . Newcastle, 1815, contains an unsatisfactory memoir of Pickering, which seems to have furnished the basis for later biographical notices in M. A. Richardson's *The Borderer's Table Book*, Newcastle, 1846 (III, 331 f.) and in R. Welford's *Men of Mark Twixt Tyne and Tweed*, London, 1895 (III, 267 ff.). My information is derived from all three of these sources.

[2] Welford, III, 268.

Kibblesworth in July, 1826. In 1815 Pickering's comrade, James Ellis, edited and published at Newcastle a volume entitled *Poetry, Fugitive and Original, by the late Thomas Bedingfeld, Esq. and Mr. George Pickering. With notes and some additional pieces by a Friend.* A collection of Bedingfeld's poems had already appeared, published surreptitiously, it is said,[1] after the author's death : *Poems by T. B—g—d, Esq. of the Inner Temple* [London, 1800].

The only composition of Pickering's, apart from the Lapland song, that attracted general attention, was his *Donocht Head*—the poem Burns would have given ten pounds to have written,—a fragment of two and a half stanzas, the first of which is as follows :

> Keen blaws the wind o'er Donocht-Head,
>   The snaw drives snelly through the dale,
> The gaberlunzie tirls my sneck,
>   And, shivering, tells his waefu' tale.
> 'Cauld is the night, oh let me in,
>   And dinna let your minstrel fa',
> And dinna let his winding-sheet
>   Be naething but a wreath o' snaw.'

This poem was originally communicated to the Edinburgh *Herald*—we are not told the date—and accompanied by a characteristically mystifying letter :

To the Printers,

The little poem, or rather the remnant of something that must have been looked upon as valuable formerly, and which I now enclose you, lately fell into my hands, in looking through the papers of a deceased friend. If in the heterogeneous mass, that I am informed you are possessed of, in antique line, you can favour the world with the remainder of the production, it would, perhaps, add to the 'harmless stock of public pleasure.' I do not remember to have seen it either in Percy's, or any other collection of Scottish poetry. The fragment appears to be the hand-writing of a lady, and though the idiom is preserved, the orthography is certainly erroneous.

I am, your's, &c.

P. Q.[2]

---

[1] See above, p. 23.   [2] From *Poetry, Fugitive and Original*, p. 55.

In 1792 the poem, as we have seen, found its way into Johnson's *Museum*, and since that date it has been repeatedly reprinted. Scott knew the piece, we are told, and was able to recite it from memory.[1]

[1] For a long time there was a good deal of uncertainty with regard to the author's name. Burns could not give it in 1794, neither could Currie in 1800. In October, 1800, a correspondent of the *Monthly Magazine*, ascribed the poem to George Pickering. In vol. iv, p. 186, of the folio edition of George Thomson's *A Select Collection of Original Scottish Airs* [1805] the author is said to be "Mr. Pickering." In 1815 appeared Ellis's *Poetry, Fugitive and Original*, which contained a reprint of *Donocht Head* and an introductory note in which the editor explains that Walter Scott assures him "it is now attributed by the literati of Scotland to Pickering." The editor adds that "this is stated as a positive fact by a correspondent of the Monthly Magazine," an assertion which would seem to indicate—though it may be designedly misleading—that Ellis himself was not the author of either of the communications to the *Monthly Magazine* which we have already quoted. Ellis adds that Scott recited the piece to him from memory.

In 1838 David Laing published an annotated edition of Johnson's *Museum* which embodied a number of notes compiled by William Stenhouse before 1820. One of these notes (Laing, ed. of 1853, iv, 348) ascribes *Donocht Head* to "Thomas Pickering," and in this connection Stenhouse presents the reader with the text of "another specimen of Mr. Pickering's poetical talents, A LAPLAND SONG." Stenhouse adds that "this song [*i. e.*, the Lapland song] was arranged as a glee for three voices by Dr. Horsley." This explains the "Thomas," for on the title-page of Horsley's glee (London, 1803, see below, p. 28), the author appears as "Thos. Pickering, Esq."

R. A. Smith printed the song in *The Scotish Minstrel*, Edinburgh, 1821–24, iii, 96, and ascribed it to "Pickering."

In *The Scottish Songs Collected and Illustrated by Robert Chambers*, Edinburgh, 1829, the author is said to be "William Pickering" (ii, 507), and is further described as "a poor North of England poet, who never wrote anything else of the least merit." Chambers ekes out Pickering's fragment with an additional stanza and a half composed by Captain Charles Gray.

In the edition of Burns's works published by Hogg and Motherwell in 1834–36 the poem is printed in connection with Burns's letter to Thomson, with the information, "It was written, we believe, by a gentleman of Newcastle named Pickering, now deceased" (ed. of 1850, iii, 172, n.). Chambers's edition of Burns, published in 1838, likewise reprints the poem

The popularity of Pickering's Lapland song did not cease with the explanation of its authorship made by the *Monthly Magazine* in 1801. In 1803 it was set to music a second time, in this instance by William Horsley, a celebrated composer of glees. Horsley's title-page reads: *A Lapland Song for Three Voices, the Poetry by Tho! Pickering, Esq., the Music Composed and inscribed to Miss Stapleton, Miss Mary, Miss Mellisina Stapleton, by W. Horsley, Mus. Bac. Oxon.*, London [1803].[1] The words of the song were copied by William Stenhouse, apparently from Horsley's publication, and again credited to "Thomas" Pickering, in a note appended to Pickering's *Donocht Head* and printed in 1838 in David Laing's revision of Johnson's *Museum*.[2]

In 1810 Scott printed the *Lapland Song* in his *English Minstrelsy*,[3] where the name of the author is given as

and substantially repeats Motherwell's information (see ed. of 1852, IV, 99, n.). Wallace adds nothing in his edition (1896) of Chambers.

George F. Graham printed the poem, with Captain Gray's addition, in his *Songs of Scotland*, Edinburgh, 1848–49, II, 140, and assigned it to "George Pickering" on the strength of the information contained in Ellis's *Poetry, Fugitive and Original*.

John D. Ross also includes Pickering's piece, with Captain Gray's addition, in *Celebrated Songs of Scotland*, New York, 1887, p. 120. He gives the author's name correctly and adds approximate dates of his birth and death.

There seems to be no good reason for questioning the assertion with regard to Pickering's authorship of *Donocht Head*, made by the anonymous correspondents of the *Monthly Magazine*. It may be worth noting that the letter quoted above which accompanied the poem upon its first appearance in print was signed "P. Q.," and that, though the resemblance may of course be accidental, the communications sent to the Newcastle *Courant* by Pickering and Bedingfeld bore the signatures "T. S." and "U. V.," respectively.

[1] The date is supplied in the British Museum Music Catalogue, where a note explains that "The words of this song have been erroneously attributed to Sir M. W. Ridley."

[2] See the edition of 1853, IV, 348. See also above, p. 27, n.

[3] II, 100.

"Pickering." In 1815 the poem appeared in Ellis's *Poetry, Fugitive and Original*, with a lengthy explanation of the circumstances under which it was composed. Ellis's book is fortified with this interesting dedication : "To Walter Scott, Esquire, this Collection of Poetry, which in a great measure owes its existence to a wish expressed by him, is inscribed, with sentiments of high admiration, and sincere regard, by the Editor." Scott had already shown his interest in Pickering by committing *Donocht Head* to memory and by including the *Lapland Song* in his *English Minstrelsy*. Furthermore he had assured the apparently somewhat doubtful Ellis, that in the opinion of "the Edinburgh literati," *Donocht Head* was the work of Pickering.[1] No doubt the wish alluded to in the dedication was not altogether perfunctory, but partly due to a genuine desire to make Pickering better known.[2]

Finally, among the works of William Lisle Bowles is a poem called *The Laplander's Song*, which begins,

[1] See above, p. 27, n.
[2] Ellis was tolerably well acquainted with Scott. In 1850 a tract of thirty-one pages was published at Newcastle, *Letters between James Ellis, Esq. and Walter Scott, Esq.*, containing one letter from Ellis to Scott, dated 22 February, 1812, and two from Scott to Ellis, dated respectively 27 February, 1812, and 3 April, 1813, with some introductory matter and notes. The letters relate to the site of the Battle of Otterburn and other matters of local historical interest ; Pickering is not mentioned. It appears from the editor's introduction (p. 10) that "Mr. Ellis practiced as an attorney for several years in Newcastle, maintaining an unblemished respectability of character, and afterwards retired to his estate of Otterburn Castle, where he cultivated his literary and antiquarian taste, and closed his honourable career on the 25th March, 1830 [æt. 67]."

In September, 1812, Scott spent a night with Ellis at Otterburne castle while on his way to Rokeby to visit J. B. S. Morritt, to whom the poem "Rokeby," upon which Scott was then engaged, was dedicated. The next morning Ellis showed Scott some objects of antiquarian interest in the neighborhood and gave him other information which Scott later incorporated into his poem.

> 'Tis now mid winter's reign,
> O'er the unmoving main
> The ice is stretch'd in dead expanse.

A note by the author reads: "I fear there is not much *nature* in this, considering the general character of the Laplanders; but I must leave it to the indulgence of the reader. He will, however, recollect the beautiful ballad so excellently translated by Conset," whereupon Pickering's *Lapland Song* is quoted entire, with the comment, "The whole song is as delicate in sentiment as it is striking in poetical beauty."[1]

Between 1786 and 1838, then, Pickering's *jeu d'esprit* was printed in at least thirteen separate publications, and very likely in others. During this period its authorship was variously ascribed to Sir Matthew White Ridley, Matthew Consett, Thomas Pickering, and George Pickering, but it seems fairly certain that the poem was the work of George Pickering. "Thomas Pickering" was, of course, a mere blunder, and it is easy to see why Bowles attributed the poem to Consett, but persistent investigation has so far failed to show why its composition came to be attributed to Ridley. The Sir Matthew White Ridley in question was the second baronet of the name. He was born in 1746 and succeeded to his uncle's title in 1763. At the time when the Lapland hoax was perpetrated he was forty years of age, governor of the Merchants' Company of Newcastle—an office which he held for thirty-five years—and member of Parliament, where he represented Newcastle from 1774 to 1812. He was three times mayor of the city, for fifteen years colonel of the Newcastle Associated Volunteer Infantry, and seems to have been a serious-minded and altogether model citizen.[2]

---

[1] See the *Poetical Works of Milman, Bowles, Wilson and Cornwall*, Paris, 1829, p. 148.

[2] See the obituary notices in the *Gentleman's Magazine* for 1813, vol. 83,

So far as I can discover, his name is nowhere mentioned in connection with Pickering or his circle, nor is there anything to indicate that he was particularly interested in literature or that he would have found Pickering a congenial companion. Pickering's friends are all reticent in regard to this matter. The correspondent of the *Monthly Magazine* who signed himself "Georgii Amicus" was "in the particular intimacy" of Pickering, and recalled the fact that Consett was taken in by the hoax; Pickering's secret was known, he says, "to very few," but he does not hint that the poem was ever ascribed to another hand. Ellis, who must have known the history of the poem as well as anybody, notes[1] that the song was "set to music, and . . . . published as having been sung by the female Laplanders at Ravensworth Castle, the seat of Sir Henry George Liddell;" he mentions its publication in Consett's volume, and observes that it was "copied from thence into several of the London magazines"; but he does not allude to the fact that the London magazines and the musical composer (assuming that he means Relfe) ascribed the song to Ridley.

"Alboin," the author of the communication to the *Monthly Magazine* which was the direct occasion of the article by "Georgii Amicus," mentions, it will be recalled, "a worthy baronet" who is one of "several gentlemen . . . . whose knowledge and elegant taste might enrich" the magazine "with authentic and interesting memoirs of Pickering." This at once suggests Ridley; but Ellis, writing in 1815, quotes the above passage and adds, "The present editor sincerely regrets that the imperfect sketch, now offered, has not been anticipated by the authentic and interesting memoirs

pp. 397, 671, and the *Monthly Magazine*, vol. 35, p. 459; Richardson's *Borderer's Table Book*, vol. III, *passim*; Welford's *Men of Mark Twixt Tyne and Tweed*, III, 322 f.

[1] *Poetry, Fugitive and Original*, p. 128.

thus suggested; and he peculiarly laments that the suggestion
failed of its effect on the highly-respected Baronet alluded to,
whose acknowledged taste and abilities would have rendered
a publication, like this, more interesting and more complete. He begs leave, however, to offer that gentleman his
grateful acknowledgements, for the trouble he politely took
to examine his papers, in the hope of finding more of
Mr. Bedingfeld's poems, and for information respecting
him of which the editor has availed himself in this
memoir." [1] Ridley had been dead two years when Ellis's
book was published; Ellis, therefore, evidently alludes to
someone else. Scott, the only other baronet [2] mentioned in
connection with Pickering, was not gazetted, of course, until
1820. For the present, Ellis's baronet must remain unidentified; but whoever he may have been, it is probably
safe to assume that he was responsible for one of those
numerous "good tables" which proved to be poor Pickering's undoing.

The popularity of Pickering's Lapland song, as well as
of the songs transcribed by Scheffer, was due, as I have
already suggested, to something more than merely the
sentiment which they conveyed—the "amorous sighs and
passionate love-strains" at which Brooke caviled—however
acceptable those strains may have been to eighteenth-century
ears. In view of the "runic" and "Ossianic" vagaries of
the half century following 1760, we can hardly avoid the
conclusion that the pleasure which the "numerous Lapland
compositions" [3] gave, arose largely from the romantic suggestiveness of the background. Lapland was thought of merely

---

[1] *Poetry, Fugitive and Original*, p. xvi.

[2] Except Sir Henry George Liddell who, obviously, need not be considered.

[3] Brooke's phrase in 1826. See above, p. 22, n.

as an extension of Odin's domain, a gruesome, remote, ice-bound region where the Scandinavian gods had been worshiped [1] and magic had been practiced for centuries, and in some literary circles allusions to the barbarous North, to Odin, Thor, and the cauldron of the Lapland witches, excited a peculiar kind of thrill which the effete "machinery" of the Homeric age had long since ceased to arouse. Into the love-songs under discussion neither the heathen gods nor the cauldron are obtruded, to be sure; but the ice, the reindeer, and the bleak moors are there, and *Orra, Lulhea, Torne, Enna, Odon,* and *Lhea* doubtless had an enticingly romantic sound. Above all, the name Lapland itself made a peculiar and generally-recognized appeal to the imagination which bears out my contention. As an illustration of the nature of this appeal I append, in conclusion, a list of scattered allusions to Lapland which I have happened upon in the course of my reading and which, I need not add, makes no pretension to anything like completeness. It will be observed that several of these allusions may be traced directly to Scheffer.

1695.

In his *Prince Arthur, An Heroick Poem in Ten Books,* London, 1695, Sir Richard Blackmore makes Lucifer

> On *Fiœl* Light,
> Of *Lapland Alpes,* chief for amazing Height;
> Where *Thor* resides, who heretofore by Lot,
> The Sovereign Rule o'er Winds and Tempests got. [2]

1726.

> Not such the sons of *Lapland:* wisely they
> Despise th' insensate barbarous trade of war.

---

[1] Scheffer's *Lapponia* (p. 105, Latin ed.) contains a picture of the idol Thor, as it was worshiped by the Laplanders, which was copied in various English books.

[2] 3d ed., 1696, p. 6.

Thomson's *Winter*. See his *Works*, London, 1788, I, 168.
Thomson also alludes (p. 170) to "Tornéa's lake." This
lake is the source of the river Torneå, which flows into the
Gulf of Bothnia at the extreme northern end. Compare the
first line of Pickering's *Lapland Song*.

1733.

In the *Gentleman's Magazine* for April, 1733, appeared
(p. 206) a poem with the title, *A Gentleman in Lapland to
his Mistress in England*. It contains an imaginary description of Lapland scenery.

1745.

> What though beneath thy gloom the sorceress-train,
> Far in obscured haunt of Lapland-moors,
> With rhymes uncouth the bloody cauldron bless.

Thomas Warton's *Pleasures of Melancholy*. In Dodsley's
Collection, IV, 228.

1746.

> As, where, in Lapland, Night collects her reign,
> Oppressive, over half the rounded year
> Uninterrupted with one struggling beam ;
> Young Orra-Moor, in furry spoils enroll'd,
> Shagged and warm, first spies th' imperfect blush
> Of op'ning light, exulting.

William Thompson's *Sickness*, Bk. iv. See Chalmers, XV,
51.

1765.

> In a dark corner of the cave he view'd
> Somewhat, that in the shape of woman stood ;
> But more deform'd than dreams can represent
> The midnight hag, or poet's fancy paint
> The Lapland witch, when she her broom bestrides,
> And scatters storms and tempests as she rides.

Thomas Lisle, *The History of Porsenna, King of Russia*, Bk. i. See Dodsley's Collection, VI, 199.

1773.

> Ere from *Norwegia's* desolated shores,
> The *Danish* navy wafted o'er the main
> This storm of arms, from *Lapland's* frozen climes
> I summon'd ev'ry hell-devoted mage,
> Whose incantations bound th' imprisoned winds.

G. E. Howard, *The Siege of Tamor*, Act II, sc. iii. Dublin, 1773, p. 25. In Act I, sc. iii of this play, one of the characters invokes

> Eternal Woden! mighty God of battles!
> Whom on the cloudy top of *Torneo's* hill
> In thunder oft we've heard.

1789.

A part of the action of Richard Hole's *Arthur, or the Northern Enchantment, A Poetical Romance in Seven Books*, London, 1789, takes place in Lapland.

1798.

> Mid Lapland's woods, and noisome wastes forlorn,
> Where lurid hags the moon's pale orbit hail :
> There, in some vast, some wild and cavern'd cell,
> Where flits the dim blue flame,
> They drink warm blood, and act the deed of hell.

Dr. Nathan Drake, *Ode to Superstition*. See Drake's *Literary Hours*, London, 1804, I, 150.

1799.

Thomas Campbell's *Pleasures of Hope* has a line (*Poetical Works*, Boston, 1854, p. 29),

> Cold as the rocks on Torneo's hoary brow,

which moved Bayard Taylor to observe (*Northern Travel*, New York, 1872, p. 77) that Campbell here shows "the same disregard for geography which makes him grow palm trees along the Susquehanna River."

Campbell also alludes in his *Ode to Winter* (*Works* as above, p. 189) to the "Lapland drum" used in incantations.

1804.

> Uprose the fiend of Gaul with speed
> And seized his fiery footed steed.
> And over sea and land he flew,
> Till near the witches' den he drew.
> The lofty rock, the gloomy cave,
> Echoed to Finland's roaring wave ;
> And far within the fiend's abode
> That rules the blasts and vex [1] the flood,
> 'Give me a wind, the demon cry'd,
> To sweep the broad Atlantic side,
> And drive away the British train,
> That block our ports and guard the Main.'

These are the opening lines of *The Witch of Lapland, Written before a late Storm. Partly an Imitation of Gray's 'Descent of Odin.' By Henry Boyd.* The poem is dated Rathfryland, Jan., 1804, and was printed the same year in the *Gentleman's Magazine* for April (p. 352), the *European Magazine* for March (p. 223), the *Poetical Register* (p. 246), and the *Annual Register* (p. 905).

Before 1807.

Among the *Poems by Anne Bannerman, A New Edition,* Edinburgh, 1807, is one called *The Fisherman of Lapland* (pp. 166 ff.).

---

[1] *Sic.*

1813.

And quhan we cam to the Lapland lone
  The fairies war all in array ;
For all the genii of the north
  War keipyng their holeday.

The warlock men and the weird wemyng,
  And the fays of the wood and the steip
And the phantom hunteris all war there,
  And the mermaidis of the deip.

And they washit us all with the witch-water,
  Distillit fra the muirland dew,
Quhill our beauty blumit like the Lapland rose
  That wylde in the foreste grew.

James Hogg, *The Queen's Wake; Night the First; The Witch of Fife.* See Hogg's *Poetical Works*, 5 vols., Edinburgh [? 1838], I, 47 f.

1818.

Then there's a little wing, far from the Sun,
Built by a Lapland Witch turn'd maudlin Nun.

Keats to Reynolds, March 25, 1818. See *Letters of John Keats*, ed. Colvin, London, 1891, p. 92.

?

No more, as horror stirs the trees,
The path-belated peasant sees
Witches adown the sleety breeze,
  To Lapland flats careering.

David Macbeth Moir's *Disenchantment.* See his *Poetical Works*, Edinburgh and London, 1852, II, 285. A note reads, "For some reason, not sufficiently explained, Lapland was set down as a favourite seat of the orgies of the 'Midnight Hags.'" The note also quotes the passage from Hogg given above.

1823.

A London periodical called *The Mirror of Literature, Amusement, and Instruction* printed early in 1823 a series of articles on Lapland which were inspired by the exhibition of a family of Laplanders in Egyptian Hall, Piccadilly. The article in the number for January 4 ends as follows :

We cannot perhaps better close this account of a singular and interesting people than by giving a literary curiosity—a Lapland Ode.

> What mean these tedious forms and ways,
> That still, by fresh and fresh delays,
>   Protract a lover's pain ?
> Five years I've woo'd my Orra fair,
> Five years my sighs have filled the air,
>   But woo'd and sigh'd in vain.
>
> Of brandy-kegs almost a score,
> Of beavers' tongues a hundred more,
>   I've giv'n her kin by turns ;
> But neither kegs their hearts can warm,
> Nor tongues prevail, to sooth the charm
>   With which my bosom burns.

There are four more stanzas. The "ode" is based on information originally given by Scheffer, but incorporated into various later accounts of Lapland. I quote two passages from the chapter "Of their Contracts and Marriages" in the English version of 1674—the second of which is surely quaint enough to justify its reproduction at some length. Scheffer is writing of the Lapland lover: "Next he makes her a present of the rarest delicacies that *Lapland* affords, the *Rain-deers* tongue, the Beavers flesh, and other dainties" (p. 111).—"As they come to visit their Mistresses, they are necessitated to bring along with them some spirit of Wine, as a singular and most acceptable present, and Tobacco too. But if in the mean while, as it often falls out, the father intends not to bestow his daughter upon the man that hath made pretensions to her, he seldom refuses them [*sic*], but defers the positive answer till the year following, that he may the oftener entertain himself with the spirit of Wine the Suiter brings along with him. And thus he delaies his answer from one year to the other, till the Suiter perceive himself cheated, and be constrained to require at his hands his charges made to no purpose. There is then no other remedy to be taken, then bringing the business before the Judg, where the Maids Father is sentenced to refund either the entire sum, or half of it, as the case stands. Wherewithal we must observe this, that the expences made by the Suiter on the Spirit of Wine, at his first arrival, do not fall under this compensation, but he alone stands to the loss of that. But if after the downright refusal of the Maid, he of his own accord will show his liberality, he may try what luck he will have at his own peril " (p. 116).

FRANK EDGAR FARLEY.

II.—FRIEDRICH SCHLEGEL AND GOETHE,
1790–1802 :

A STUDY IN EARLY GERMAN ROMANTICISM.

INTRODUCTION.

a. STATEMENT OF PROBLEMS.

Friedrich Schlegel, youngest son of Johann Adolf Schlegel, was born at Hannover on March 10, 1772, just three months after Goethe had finished the first version of his first great work, *Götz von Berlichingen.* His literary career begins in 1794 with the publication of *Von den Schulen der Griechischen Poesie.* At this time he is as old as Goethe was when writing the *Götz.*

In the meantime Goethe has written many great works, passed through several cultural stages, been enriched by varied experiences, and in the great general aspects of his character as also in the essentials of his *Weltanschauung* become a *developed* man. Life will deepen, knowledge widen with the coming years, but the Italian journey (September 3, 1786–June 18, 1788), with its revolutionary influences, is past, and twenty years (since November, 1775) of responsible public service in great little Weimar by the side of his devoted friend, the Duke, whom he loved and praised,[1] have had their sedative influence upon the stormy genius of the period of *Götz* and *Werther.* The unique literary friendship with Schiller, who has been at Weimar and Jena since 1787, is just beginning with the establishment of the *Horen.*

On the other hand Schlegel is but little beyond the first

---

[1] *G Wke.* *v.* Venetian Epigrams, No. 35.

stadia of his intellectual progress. He has scarcely begun a development which is to be conditioned to a remarkable degree by the great minds of the period and by certain great thinkers and writers of the past, and will result in an almost complete reversal of his attitude toward all problems of literature, philosophy, and life. These great influences are Plato, the Greek dramatists, the Platonizing Hemsterhuis, Winckelmann, Herder, Kant, Fichte, Schiller, and Goethe. Personal relations will exist with the last three. The relative force of these influences will vary widely at different stages of his progress. The Hellenizing influence is based in a general way upon Winckelmann, but stands in the closest relations to the doctrines and practice of the Weimar classicists. Kant's critical philosophy, supplemented by Fichte and modified by Schiller, is a second powerful moment and becomes more and more important toward the close. Goethe's works (this can hardly be overemphasized) are influential from first to last. They are the atmosphere in which Schlegel as a literary student breathes. They are the concrete examples of all possible literary excellence since the Greeks. Their author is the acknowledged leader of Weimar culture when Weimar is the center of German letters. Schlegel as a literary aspirant knows no higher goal than the approval of this genius whom he is soon to glorify with extravagant daring as "Gott, Vater."[1]

Friedrich's attitude toward Goethe had, however, materially changed before 1804, about which time many evidences of the alteration exist. The least arbitrary date near this period is naturally the date of Schlegel's departure for Paris, the date of the final dispersion of the older Romantic school. Since the earliest known sources of information concerning Friedrich[2] begin in 1791, we may select the year of student

[1] *RDBr.*, Bd. 1, p. 36.   [2] *WSBr.*

life at Göttingen in company with August Wilhelm as the
beginning of his development. The most important years
of his activity are thus included between 1790 and 1802.
These limits are further favored by the second great source
of our knowledge of Friedrich's early career, *Friedrich
Schlegels prosaische Jugendschriften, 1794–1802,* edited by
Minor.

No complete statement of Friedrich Schlegel's personal
and literary relations to Goethe exists. Much work has
been done upon certain phases of the dependence, but even
here contributions may be made. Statements have been made
recently that Goethe learned much from the earlier romanticists, but few definite evidences are produced in their support.
It has seemed advisable therefore *to collect into one complete
statement, so far as possible, what is certainly known of the
relationship of Friedrich Schlegel to Goethe during the period
above fixed.*

b. Relations as Seen in Later Life.

Goethe published his correspondence with Schiller in
1828–9, just as Friedrich's unfortunate career was drawing
to its close. The severe judgments of Schiller upon the
character, accomplishments, and pretensions of both Schlegels, with the contemporary assent of Goethe in all essential
points, were given to the public unaccompanied by the least
hint of Goethe's own disapproval of their sharpness and
with no disavowal of his own present belief in Schiller's
correctness. August Wilhelm, mindful of his outwardly
pleasant relations with Goethe during those fruitful years
in Jena, was surprised and pained at such revelations. To
defend himself and his brother against these criticisms an
edition of the Goethe-Schlegel correspondence was planned.
But it did not appear. The surviving brother vented his

feelings, however, in print. His attack appeared in Wendt's *Musenalmanach* for 1832, issued in the fall of 1831. To the shame of August Wilhelm, his harshest thrusts were aimed at the dead friend Schiller and not at Goethe.[1] Zelter calls Goethe's attention to these "galligwässrige" attacks in a letter of October 15, 1831. To this circumstance we owe the latest, completest, and most positive expression of Goethe's views of the character of the Schlegels and especially of his relations with them.[2]

This letter is too well known to need quotation, though almost every line of it is important for our problem. The relations of Goethe to the Schlegels, according to this direct testimony, were (a) universal tolerance, not hearty favor, (b) the furthering of that which he himself did not approve, (c) an effort to keep up a sort of social relation with them, though (d) he stood outside of the romantic circle and would have been extinguished by them, but for his own solid worth, and (e) he did not trouble himself about others while following out his own designs. Schiller's hatred is justified as right, and their accomplishment in all fields except the oriental is discredited.

Such statements roundly deny any real sympathy with the romantic doctrines and practises of the Schlegels and imply a degree of artistic and literary isolation incompatible with *mutual* influence.

This letter cannot be credited to momentary bitterness at August Wilhelm's attack on Schiller in Wendt's *Almanach*. If bitterness dictated it, it was a settled bitterness of a quarter of a century. Many utterances of Goethe from 1804 until his death seem to show that the bitterness was a part of the settled consistent judgment of all his riper years.

---

[1] *BXen.*, Bd. II, p. 285 ff.

[2] *GZBr.*, Bd. VI, pp. 315 f. and 318 ff. ; Goethe an Zelter, October 26, 1831.

In a conversation with Sulpiz Boisserée, May 25, 1826, he charges the Schlegels with dishonesty and an evil influence upon free investigation.[1] In 1819, in conversation with an anonymous person (F. A. Wolf?) he charges them with attempting to throttle him with friendly words, rob him of himself, and make him other than himself; they were thus his worst enemies.[2] Another conversation with Boisserée shows that Goethe called Friedrich a "Schelm" in spite of all the artist's defense of his friend. Boisserée explained this language as due to envy and pride of faint-hearted old age, etc.[3] Several very important facts are omitted from Boisserée's report, which would have given a key to Goethe's full meaning. We do not learn what arguments were presented by Sulpiz in favor of Friedrich's honesty, the truth of which might be granted without involving a denial of the appearance of dishonesty. Perhaps *irony* was urged, that unconscious accompaniment of a life without inward fundamental convictions. We must admit that Friedrich's conduct toward Goethe and his works had every appearance of insincerity, if one assumes in his character that fixity of opinion which marks the ripened man. It was no forced inference when Goethe concluded that the Schlegels had a dishonest purpose in their praise of him. We should further like to know what statements of Goethe were considered well-grounded and what were concordant with things which must be admitted. Thus we should be in condition to judge whether the "chief point" rested merely upon personalities, and also to estimate the degree of justice in Sulpiz's reference of Goethe's words to motives of envy and pride. Without these further facts we have here simply a confirmation of Goethe's usual attitude accompanied by an interpretation

[1] *BGG.*, Bd. v, p. 290, No. 1038.
[2] *Ibid.*, Bd. viii, p. 357, No. 1531.
[3] *Ibid.*, Bd. iii, p. 14, May 9, 1811.

equally liable to personal coloring, for the Boisserées were loyal disciples of Friedrich, and Goethe had every opportunity to know the character and capacity of Schlegel at first hand and as accurately as they.

Several years earlier we have a number of utterances which are in point. On May 17, 1808, Goethe is angry at Schlegel's imputation to him of Voltaire's principles. This is interpreted as an attempt to discredit him while using his name for financial advantage.[1] To this period belongs also the report of a conversation by Falk in which the claims of the Schlegels to literary dictatorship are satirically disposed of. Goethe is resigned to the prospective loss of his imperial mantle, since it does not involve the loss of his head too, and expects to die in peace in his bed beside his beloved Ilm.[2] Several days later Goethe again attacked the literary anarchy of Germany, this time "mit dreimal kaustischer Lauge" and directed a volley at Friedrich Schlegel as the self-styled Hercules of German literature.[3]

Goethe brought out an edition of his collected works in 1808. Friedrich reviewed them for the romantic organ, the *Heidelberger Jahrbücher*. The former sworn eulogist of Goethe could not break entirely with his past and appear in his true attitude before the world while his former utterances were so readily accessible. He could now no longer praise with a full throat, so we have a carefully toned-down repetition of much that he had already said. Whoever compares this performance with previous reviews becomes at once aware of the whole vast change in personal relations.[4] Goethe could say complacently that he was content, he understood how the review had been produced, but as an

[1] *Ibid.*, Bd. ɪɪ, p. 144 ; Bericht von Frl. Schopenhauer.

[2] *Ibid.*, Bd. ɪɪ, p. 202 ff., No. 357, April 18, 1808.

[3] *Ibid.*, Bd. ɪɪ, p. 208, No. 357b.

[4] *FSWke.*, Bd. vɪɪɪ, p. 117 ff.

artist he was not content with a mere historical account of
how his works came to be.[1] On April 6, 1808, Goethe
declares that the judgment of Schlegel rests upon the principle of the game of dominoes in which each one praises the
piece to which he can play his own to advantage.[2]

So far we have a consistent attitude on the part of Goethe,
now jesting, now in bitter earnest, but always condemnatory. The charge of dishonesty, overweening assumption of
authority, the use of his name and fame for self-advance-
ment, etc., constantly recurs. If we consider a word of
wisdom from the Goethe of almost fourscore, " überall lernt
man nur von dem, den man liebt," we must admit little
probability that anything for which Friedrich Schlegel stood
would find acceptance because he stood for it, or would be
influential with Goethe in this long closing period of his life.

That this dislike was heartily returned by Friedrich is
equally certain, though recorded utterances are rarer. A
sort of reflection of this feeling of dislike is found in the
correspondence of his wife Dorothea, though she is doubtless
more radically outspoken than he. Her utterances may be
found in a letter to Caroline Paulus from Cologne, 1804,
also July 13, 1805.[3] He has no " Gemüt," no love, is
" versteinert," and his whole artistic and personal life is
"Sächsisch-weimarisches Heidenthum."   Only the first part
of *Faust* awakens enthusiasm in 1808, but even here Tieck's
Genoveva and Calderon's dramas are the standards by which
Goethe is judged. Goethe's *Rhein und Main Buch* is the
object of her violent denunciation in letters to Boisserée in
1810[4] and to her sons in 1816.[5] She charges Goethe with
an evil purpose in ignoring the merits of Friedrich Schlegel
as a pioneer in this field of German art. The much admired

---

[1] *BGG.*, Bd. II, p. 209.   [2] *BGG.*, Bd. II, p. 201, No. 356.
[3] *RDBr.*, Bd. I, pp. 143 and 155 f.
  Ibid., p. 428.   [5] *Ibid.*, Bd. II, p. 355 ff. .

Wilhelm Meister has become the object of contempt by 1810.[1]
Friedrich may not have gone to such lengths in adverse
judgment, but he shared them to a certain extent at least,
and for somewhat the same reason. It was his entrance into
the Roman fold. In a postscript to one of her letters to
Caroline Paulus in 1806 he writes: "Meine ehemaligen
sogenannten Freunde, als Calvinische, Lutherische, Herrn-
hutische, — theistische, atheistische und idealistische mit
eingerechnet, haben sich, meines einzigen leiblichen Bruders
ausgenommen, der aber auch ein sehr schlechter Calviner
ist, sämmtlich als wahres Zigeunergesindel gegen mich auf-
geführt." [2] Goethe must be included in one or more of the
above categories.

Looking at the whole matter of the breach between Goethe
and the Schlegels, and the consequent relations among them
for a quarter of a century, we see at its center the question
of religious affiliation. But this was not all. An honest
Catholic either by birth and training or by genuine conversion was not an object of dislike to Goethe. Friedrich's
entrance into the Roman church after a period of uncompromising individualism and after his efforts to establish a
new religion on the basis of Goethe's culture and Fichte's
idealism, his entrance into the service of a reactionary
monarchy after his enthusiastic essay on Republicanism,
whose tone was too democratic to find favor with Goethe,[3]
his doctrine of romantic poetry and his preference for
northern and oriental literatures after an excessive exaltation
of Hellenism, his assumption of dictatorial office in the
realm of German letters and his subsequent degradation of
Goethe's works after having declared them the canon of all
German poetic art, all these things seemed to Goethe to

---

[1] *Ibid.*, Bd. i, p. 262; Aus Dorothea's *Tagebuch*, Nos. 38, 39.
[2] *Ibid.*, p. 166.   [3] *HRS.*, p. 337.

signify that Friedrich Schlegel was unsound and false, dishonest at bottom, or, if not, then at least so variable and unreliable that nothing could be made of him. The Schlegels seem to have wished to force Goethe into following their aesthetic leading and acknowledging their supremacy in the field of sound criticism. Goethe would not follow them into their romantic region of whimsy and arbitrariness of fancy, and they turned from him. Goethe was the sound realist with steady purpose and clear insight, Schlegel the unripe brilliant vagarist. August Wilhelm knew this as well as anyone.[1] No permanent friendly relations with such a being were possible. His own brother could not endure it to the end.

Feeling always colors the judgment. However, its demonstrated existence during later life must not lead us to assume an exaggerated degree of friendliness and even a sort of discipleship earlier.

Goethe himself seems to admit that mutually helpful relations existed. Two passages are of especial importance, though we could wish in them more detail and less vagueness. In a conversation with Eckermann, on March 12, 1825, he tries to account for certain advantages due to his peculiar relations to the older men, Lessing, Winckelmann, and Kant, and to the younger men, Schiller, the Humboldts, and the Schlegels. He says: "Es sind mir daher unnennbare Vortheile entstanden." This may apply to the influences of the whole group, or if it be taken to apply only to the latter, as is possible, it must refer chiefly to the prosodic aid received from Wilhelm von Humboldt and August Wilhelm Schlegel.[2] Again, in Goethe's posthumous essay, *Einwirkung*

---

[1] *AWSWke.*, Bd. VIII, p. 292; Brief an Windischmann, December 29, 1834.

[2] *GGE.*, May 12, 1825.

der neuern Philosophie, written about 1817,[1] he refers to the influence of Niethammer in clarifying his conceptions of philosophy, and hints vaguely at certain advantages accruing from similar efforts on the part of the Schlegels. This, of course, can apply only to Friedrich Schlegel, whose conversations on idealism were contemporaneous with Niethammer's *colloquia.* We could wish that Goethe had found opportunity to indicate in some way, however briefly, what kind and degree of influence he attributed to the various persons mentioned. But all is left vague and undeterminable.[2]

FRIEDRICH SCHLEGEL'S CAREER.

A. To Publication of *Von den Schulen.*

1. *Göttingen.*

There are no contemporary records of Friedrich's life in Göttingen in 1790–1. He studied under Heyne, busied himself with philology and æsthetics, as well as jurisprudence, for which he came to the university. He was associated with August Wilhelm and a small group of friends.

According to his own later testimony, Plato, the tragedians and Winckelmann formed the atmosphere of his life about this time. His seventeenth year would be 1789, or the year preceding the Göttingen period.[3] In this same year he saw the collection of antiquities in Dresden for the first time. Did this atmosphere continue at Göttingen? Certain testimony in later letters seems to involve an affirmative answer.

On January 1, 1794, when collecting materials for his first Greek publications, he says that he has not yet "*reread*"

---

[1] *Goethe und Kant,* Karl Vorländer, *G.-Jahrb.,* xix, pp. 180 ff.
[2] Goethe's *Nachlass,* Bd. x, p. 54.
[3] *FSWke.,* Bd. vi, pp. iv ff.

the works of Aristophanes and Euripides, nor yet completely
worked through Aeschylus, etc.[1] The first reading must
have antedated the earliest letter to August Wilhelm, since
we have in this correspondence a most complete record of
Friedrich's intellectual interests, and no Greek reading is
mentioned until about September, 1793, from which time
forward it is a marked feature.

That this first reading was not *thorough* is proved by the
immense difficulty which he has in 1793–4. It must also
seem strange that an *absorbing* study carried on *in spite of
parental purposes to the contrary,* should have sunk so completely into the background of his interests during his first
two whole years at Leipzig, as will appear from an examination of his letters.

On February 10, 1794, he declares that it was his inclination to investigate art where it was *indigenous,* and that it was
necessary to his very life to begin his career with the study
of art. He adds : " Du erinnerst Dich einiger mitgeteilten
Plane in Göttingen. *Sie sind nicht vergessen, und enthielten
den Keim meiner jetzigen Absicht."* [2] When we compare this
statement with his contemporary work, we might assume
that some embryonic Hellenic project had begun to stir in
the mind of Friedrich at Göttingen. A more definite notion
of what his present purpose is can be gained from a letter of
December, 1793, where he names such essays as *Über die
Moralität der Griechischen Tragiker, Über die Nachahmung
der Griechischen Dichter, Apologie des Aristophanes;* also a
translation of *Orestes* and the *Eumenides* of Aeschylus. The
register then proceeds : " Bei dem was ich Dir in Hannover
ankündigte, bleibt's." This refers certainly to the meeting
of the brothers in the summer of 1793, when Caroline was
on the way to her retreat at Lucka, and not to their short

---

[1] *WSBr.*, p. 158.   [2] *Ibid.*, p. 165.

stay in Hannover before August Wilhelm's departure for Amsterdam in May, 1791. To what it refers is not known. It may have been a promise to concentrate his energies upon some self-supporting work of a literary nature. It is clear that this whole definite plan is *recent* and only the *germ* of it is referred to Göttingen.[1]

A complete characterization of Greek literature and life, especially of Greek poetry, seems to hover before Schlegel's eyes, such a characterization as he once proposed to August Wilhelm with respect to Roman literature, such a characterization of the Greeks as he once planned for himself concerning the Germans, or such as he tried to make of several individual great poets. However, if the *germ* of any such plan did exist as early as 1790 it was incapable of development and fell completely out of sight for two whole years of intellectual foraging in various fields. If not *forgotten*, it was so *overwhelmed* by other interests that it never came to expression in one of the most intimate correspondences ever conducted, even when poetic art and art criticism were his special themes.

It is conceivable that a youth of eighteen in the dominantly classical atmosphere of the circle of Heyne's pupils should find Hemsterhuis delightful and Winckelmann inspiring, should follow the best minds of the day in their gropings for the light of Greek antiquity, and thus vaguely dream of some great work for himself to do in this new and fruitful field. But the plan, or dream, dropped out of sight completely.

That it dropped out of sight must have its explanation, and it seems most probable that his classicism at Göttingen *has been simply overrated.* His whole interest is not even in the classics, especially not in the Greeks. He devoted much

[1] *Ibid.*, pp. 148–9.

time to current German literature and was more moved by
Goethe and Klopstock than by all other Hellenizing forces
combined.

At his parting from his brother in Hannover, the words
of Goethe's *An Schwager Chronos* come into their minds.
This and the *Prometheus*, as contrasted with Herder's poems,
have a magic force: "An ein solches Wort heftet sich so viel
Erinnerung ehemaligen Entschlusses und Genusses—so dass
es plötzliches Licht in die Finsternis bringt." [1]   In the very
first letter from Leipzig we see the enthusiastic Goethe-
worshipper, full of the echoes of the Faust fragment.   His
motto is the quatrain beginning

"Die Geisterwelt ist nicht verschlossen."

The slight inaccuracy of quotation here, as also in the case,
of *An Schwager Chronos* on another occasion, is the best
possible evidence of the power which the *Faust* of 1790 and
Goethe's lyrics had upon him. [2]   Schlegel has the deepest
sympathy with the "Himmelsstürmer" Faust who is in
search of the absolute.   He turns to Nature, which is
infinite, and will use her for sublime contemplation, like
Faust, and find strength and healing in her.   The *Faust*,
if completed, would surpass Shakespeare's *Hamlet*.   But
enough for the present that this supreme interest in Goethe
antedates his Leipzig university career and is contemporaneous with any then existing Hellenism.   It must have been
a very essential part of his intellectual atmosphere, if not
the dominant one as in the years immediately following.

If we consider Friedrich Schlegel's character as a whole
at this time, all doubt as to his real inclinations must vanish.
Haym has admirably collected the materials which are
scattered throughout the early letters: "Wenn wir die

[1] *Ibid.*, p. 3.   [2] *Ibid.*, pp. 1 and 4.

Summe der brieflichen Selbstbekenntnisse des jungen Mannes ziehen, so tritt uns darin ganz jener Geist der Selbstüberspannung, jenes unklare, titanische Streben, jenes zuchtlose Spiel mit leidenschaftlichen Einbildungen entgegen, welches seit den siebziger Jahren in unserer Litteratur so vielfach Aùsdruck gefunden hatte," etc.[1] This careful and most just estimate makes it perfectly clear that any sympathy with the Greeks at this time must have been conditioned greatly by Storm and Stress motives.

One suspects that Goethe's *Werther*, *Prometheus*, and *Faust* have contributed not a little to strengthen this element in Friedrich's character. Titanic revolt against tyranny, contest of the individual against Fate, coarse strength, and indomitable will are the positive elements that appeal to him, and these are far removed from that "edle Einfalt und stille Grösse"[2] which Winckelmann saw in Greek art. Storm and Stress elements were dominant over all others in Göttingen. They were primary in point of time also, and Schüddekopf is in error when he asserts that the critical leaders of romanticism do not start from Storm and Stress, but from the Forster circle.[3]

For Friedrich the most prominent representative of the movement is Goethe. At first Klopstock is a close second. At a greater distance stand Schiller and Herder.

2. *Leipzig, Dresden.*

a. Utterances about Goethe.

After arriving in Leipzig conditions remain little changed for some time. Goethe stands in the midst of all his interests,

---

[1] *HRS.*, Ergänzungen und Berichtigungen, No. 3, pp. 873 ff. The whole passage should be carefully considered in connection with this subject. Cf. letters in *WSBr*.

[2] *WGed.*, pp. 24, 26, 29, etc.   [3] *GuR.*, Bd. I, p. xvi.

as may be seen from the frequent utterances in regard to
him. First comes his *Wahlspruch* from *Faust* (May 18,
1791) and then the contrast of Herder and Goethe, to the
latter's great advantage (June 4). · This is followed by a
considerable passage from *An Schwager Chronos,*

> Sieh, die Sonne sinkt, etc. (July 21),

which is pointed with a question : " Was könnte wohl eher
die *Sonne* des Lebens genannt werden als der Enthusiasmus
oder die Liebe ? Ich wüsste nicht zu was ein Alter ohne
sie lebte, als etwa seinen Geist stückweise abfaulen zu sehen."
This reminds us of the despairing old scholar Faust with the
words on his lips :

> "Es möchte kein Hund so länger leben," etc.

On August 26, he has found one person in Leipzig with an
appreciation for poetry—a merchant who enjoys Goethe's
Prometheus and *Schwager Chronos*.[1]   On November 8, Goethe
is classed with Frederick the Great, Klopstock, Winckelmann,
and Kant, as the greatest Germans known to fame, whose
greatness he calls "ursprünglich Deutsch."   Such men are
rare in all generations, and these have some qualities that no
people known to us have had a presentiment of.   Klopstock
belongs to this class on moral grounds, not literary.   In
fact, Friedrich's judgments here are decidedly preclassic.
Aesthetic interests are completely subordinated to the moral.
Poetry is an ornament of life, and has as yet no justification
within itself for its existence.[2]

On February 11, Friedrich tries to encourage August
Wilhelm by showing that what the latter condemned in
himself as simply "Übersetzertalent" was the most admirable quality of Goethe, the power of entering into the

---

[1] *WSBr.*, p. 13.   [2] *Ibid.*, pp. 36 and 125.

innermost recesses of a great soul and interpreting it. August was right, however, for there is a vast difference between interpreting the *Divina Commedia* or *Romeo and Juliet* and the creation of a Götz, a Tasso, or a Faust. Yet Friedrich's sophistry shows that Goethe was considered the great interpreter of human life.[1] We have also a comparison of Goethe's *Faust* with Klinger's, with a decided preference for the former; also a notice of Goethe's portrait by Lips: "ein herrlicher Kopf," etc.[2]

Two months later, April 13, 1792, Schlegel finds the *Gross-Cophta* lifeless. He sees in the recent works of Goethe an unpardonable falling off from the excellence of earlier works.[3] The *Cophta* must have been written during sleep, as Caroline said. At least Goethe's *genius* had not kept awake.

Again, a little later, in the same critical strain but more specific: "Der Inbegriff seiner Werke (*i. e.*, the recent ones) ist der Abdruck einer eigennützigen, kaltgewordenen Seele." *Götz, Werther, Faust, Iphigenie, Prometheus*, and *Schwager Chronos* were the beginnings of a great man, but the poet soon became a courtier, no longer a Storm and Stress leader. Here, too, even Goethe's best works are blamed for their *intentional* truth, "peinlich gelernte Wissenschaft, nicht angebornes Wesen."[4] Friedrich is out of touch with the Goethe of Weimar.

In May, 1793, there is a brief reference to Reichardt's music for *Erwin und Elmire*.

In the following letter, No. 25, undated, where a first attempt is made to formulate æsthetic ideas, Goethe's *Götz*, Shakespeare's *Hamlet* and *Romeo*, and Schiller's *Don Carlos* are the only illustrative materials. The complaint occurs here: "man darf fordern dass die Werke des Dichters nicht

---

[1] *Ibid.*, p. 36.
[3] *Ibid.*, p. 43.
[2] *Ibid.*, p. 39.
[4] *Ibid.*, p. 59.

kleiner sind, als er selbst, wie man Goethen Schuld giebt." [1]
In poetic *truth* Schlegel demands *depth* and *similitude to
nature*. In respect to these qualities Goethe and Klopstock
are paired and placed above Schiller but beneath Shakespeare. The character of a poet is defined as "Trieb zur
Darstellung." A poet's perfection is "die allgemeine Fähigkeit *alles* gut darzustellen." "Und es scheint dies Goethens
Absicht gewesen zu sein." [2] Even Goethe and Klopstock
have erred, e. g., in. *Götz* and the *Barditen*, but the day is
breaking upon the Germans, and when it breaks it will be a
great day. It is no great step from this to Schlegel's proclamation of Goethe as the "Morgenröthe echter Kunst."

On June 2, 1793, Goethe is classed with Kant, Klopstock,
Hemsterhuis, Spinoza, and Schiller as a great man whose
spirit Friedrich has sought to fathom; a testimony to that
carefulness and frequency of reading necessary to the profound formative influence assumed.[3]

With the exception of one brief mention of Reichardt's
music, we have no further reference to Goethe until September
29, when Schlegel is in the midst of his studies of Greek
tragedy. In connection with Aeschylus and Sophocles only
Shakespeare and Goethe are mentioned. The best Greek
tragedy represents a contest of the human heart with fate,
in which the heart is the "victorious God." The effect
of such tragedy is the highest exaltation. Shakespeare's
Richard III is of this class. Goethe's *Faust*, if completed,
would perhaps attain to the same rank. His other dramas
simply end well; exaltation is impossible from their very
nature. *Götz* leaves too much bitterness behind, though this
is only a tentative judgment.[4]

On October 23, occurs one of the most remarkable of
Friedrich's critical judgments. His doctrine is that humanity

[1] *Ibid.*, p. 88.   [2] *Ibid.*, pp. 87 f.
[3] *Ibid.*, p. 91.   [4] *Ibid.*, pp. 118 f.

is the supreme thing and that art exists only for its sake.
Not only Schiller and Bürger place art above nature, "ja
selbst der grosse Goethe ist im Alter zu dieser Selbstver-
götterung herabgesunken. Er scheint selbstgefällig seinem
Genius zu lauschen, und ich erinnre mich dann wohl an
Mozart's Musik, die in jedem Laute Eitelkeit und weibliche
Verderbtheit athmet." [1]

In November Friedrich finds in the *Allg. Litt. Zeit.* a
review of Goethe's writings by Huber. Schlegel's comments
are of some length. He finds many things well said, but
the great question is unanswered "warum Apelles jetzt nur
Linien malt." The "morality" of *Werther, Stella,* and *Faust*
is too obscurely defended, and the last is inadequately described. "Ist es nicht fühllos und armselig ein erhabenes
Gedicht so zu beschreiben? Er sage was es ist, für ihn und
für das Verhältnis für welches er es beurtheilt, und wenn er
kann, wie es wurde." [2]

On December 11, Schlegel would exchange all of Bürger's
poems for Goethe's *Amor als Landschaftsmaler*. Goethe
is "volksmässig genug," while Percy's *Reliques* belong to
learned literature. Goethe is popular in the same sense as
the Athenian poets.[3] He defends Schiller's character against
the attacks of August Wilhelm, but, to leave no doubt of
his attitude, adds: "*Ich bewundre eigentlich keinen deutschen
Dichter als Goethe.*" "Und doch ist er vielleicht nicht
gerade durch Übermacht des Genies so unendlich weit über
jene beiden (*i. e.,* Klopstock and Schiller) erhaben, als durch
etwas andres. Etwas das er doch nur *beinahe* hat, was allein
den Griechischen, vorzüglich den Atheniensischen Dichtern
eigenthümlich ist." [4] Goethe and the Greeks are now the
key-note of Friedrich's æsthetics.

---

[1] *Ibid.*, p. 125.
[2] *Ibid.*, p. 139.
[3] *Ibid.*, pp. 150 f.
[4] *Ibid.*, p. 152.

On December 15, he writes a long letter with frequent reference to Goethe. Goethe and Raphael only among moderns show the antique spirit, "und Goethe scheint es nur zu besitzen." Although the flatness of some later works is mentioned, the whole tone is not apologetic but frankly commendatory. Modern poets are of two classes, the musical and the plastic. Goethe inclines to the latter; Bürger, Klopstock, even Schiller, to the former. Shakespeare is the most musical of all poets. Goethe is a Greek.[1]

From Dresden he writes, on February 27, 1794: "Das Problem unsrer Poesie scheint mir die Vereinigung des Wesentlich-Modernen mit dem Wesentlich-Antiken ; wenn ich hinzusetze, dass Goethe, der erste einer ganz neuen Kunstperiode, einen Anfang gemacht hat sich diesem Ziele zu nähern, so wirst du mich wohl verstehen."[2] Goethe is thus elevated to the rank of ideal modern poet. As this passage is from the same letter in which Schlegel reports the reading of Goethe's *Iphigenie* by Caroline, we may associate this drama with the ideal above formulated and refer the new insight into Goethe's classic manner to the same brilliant interpreter.

Other notices of greater or less importance occur from time to time. He notes the announcement of *Reineke Fuchs* (April 5, 1794); the announcement of the *Horen* to succeed the *Thalia;* Goethe's Epistles, Epigrams, and Elegies are to appear in the first issue, this would be a good medium for August Wilhelm's Essays, etc. (December 7, 1794). The presence of *Goethe* and Herder in Weimar is urged as a reason for August Wilhelm's settlement at Jena (November 18, 1794). Schiller wants a characterization of Goethe, but Körner refuses to undertake it. Could not August Wilhelm do it and so gain entrance to the *Horen* and the Weimar

---

[1] *Ibid.*, pp. 154 ff.   [2] *Ibid.*, p. 170.

circle? (April 28, 1795). Goethe is working upon a "*Prometheus Unbound*" (*Ibid.*).

But we have already passed the threshold of Friedrich Schlegel's public career. His essay *Von den Schulen* appeared in the *Berliner Monatschrift* before the close of 1794.

More than a score of references to Goethe and his works, most of them important and very few of them depreciatory, show how large a space he occupied in the interests of Schlegel. Klopstock is noticed but half so often, many times barely mentioned. Herder has about the same attention as Klopstock, but is never placed above second rank. Lessing is almost absent from this early period. Winckelmann has but half a dozen unimportant notices. Wieland has scarcely more. Bürger has a dozen, mostly condemnatory. Shakespeare himself has but a dozen. Dante rivals Goethe in the number of references, owing to August Wilhelm's essays and translations, but they are often mere references. Schiller alone of all the great spirits of the period receives more frequent mention than Goethe. This is due to the brothers' quarrel over Schiller's review of Bürger, and to Schiller's position as editor of the journals *Thalia* and the *Horen*. Schiller is esteemed as a man and critical genius, but not as a poet. No clearer proof could be desired to establish the contention that Goethe and his works were the *dominant literary interest of Friedrich from this earliest period.*

Yet this interest was neither uniform nor stationary. At first there was an unconditional enthusiasm for the Storm and Stress Goethe, then a period of more or less outspoken criticism because the poet's product fell below his own greatness, or was not the spontaneous gush of genius, then finally a revival of enthusiasm for Goethe *the artist* in his classic manner. *This revival falls in the late summer of 1793.*

β. Occupations.

If we compare Schlegel's intellectual occupations for the same three years, we find an equally remarkable change at the same season, *viz.* late in the summer of 1793.

On August 26, 1791, we have an account of Friedrich's arrangements at Leipzig. No Hellenism is shown. He is interested somewhat in æsthetics and philosophy, but the center of his interest is Roman civilization. He is using Montesquieu, Ferguson, and Middleton as sources. He hopes to produce a work of art which shall characterize the whole nation in the life of one of its heroes in one of its great catastrophes. This was to be a dramatic work, a sort of Roman *Götz*. Friedrich had thought of this plan in Göttingen, and he intended to treat several nations in the same way. Perhaps Herder's *Ideen* were a second incentive to the formation of these plans. The essential point is, they were not connected with the Winckelmann movement at all as yet, were to be *not investigations* but *works of art*, and *dramatic* in form.[1]

We next get a glimpse of a plan to characterize Voltaire, and his method is outlined in some fulness. It is the method which he later applied to Lessing, Forster, and Jacobi, the construction of the poet out of his works and the known facts of his life, in the process of becoming. This shows the influence of Herder. Such works are more elevating, he adds, than the Ideal Beauty of the arts.[2]

In October, 1791, in reply to August Wilhelm's question whether he has not a desire to become a writer, he confesses to having certain plans for it. Among these projects are an *allegory*, probably in the manner of Hemsterhuis, but of which nothing further is known, and a "*Gespräch über die*

---

[1] *Ibid.*, p. 14.   [2] *Ibid.*, p. 16.

Poesie," which, as we know, has nothing to do with the poetry of the Greeks, nor with his essay of the same name in vol. III of the *Athenäum*. It was to be a sort of sketch embodying his views of art at their present Germanic stage.[1]

He now proposes to treat Rome in a series of historical plays like those of Shakespeare, since a single drama like *Götz* is inadequate to the larger theme. The history of the king of Prussia would be a good subject for such an historical play, he thinks. But his interests are not wholly artistic. He proposes historical works for August Wilhelm's productive leisure, a history of knightly poetry, or of Greek poetry, the latter as yet considered no more important than the former.[2]

On November 8, he is trying his critical steel upon *Hamlet*, making those wonderful subjective interpretations which are to appear later in published essays. Incidentally, he mentions that if he attempts a *Gespräch* his wish will be to draw it wholly from native sources, "aus der immensen Eigenthümlichkeit unsrer Nation." He would not attempt a genuine Greek one. The Greeks are too distant from us, and it is best to represent excellently those things first which are round about us and in us.[3]

Here, too, we see how far Schlegel is from Winckelmann's canon of art. There is a greatness and beauty for every climate, even for the north pole, and for every race, however degenerate.

Again he places *Deutschheit* above *Griechheit* when considering the character of the Germans.[4]

In letter No. 6, undated, Friedrich is glad of his brother's intention to write a history of Greek poetry, but warns him of the difficulties in grasping the real inner life of such a

---

[1] *Ibid.*, p. 18.
[2] *Ibid.*, p. 19.
[3] *Ibid.*, p. 26.
[4] *Ibid.*, footnote.

distant people. He himself is immersed in German imperial history.[1] When August Wilhelm drops the plan, Friedrich shows no desire to take it up himself, but suggests with apparently equal interest historical works, a history of Florence, of knighthood in Germany, of the rise and fall of the power of cities, of modern culture, of the Reformation, of the reign of the King of Prussia, of the Seven Years' War, or biographies of Wallenstein, Bernhard von Weimar, Mansfeld, Luther, Eugen, Friedrich II. No more thoroughgoing Germanism could well be imagined. He wants something "was dem deutschen Volke am nächsten liegt." [2]

On July 5, 1792, a passage of uncertain significance occurs. Comparing Garve (much to his disadvantage) with various great moderns, as Voltaire, Rousseau, Shaftesbury and Kant, he proceeds: "und vieler andrer, *aller Alten nicht zu gedenken.*" The vague generality suggests a pious afterthought in accord with contemporary scholarly traditions. If there is any specific reference intended, the Roman historians and moralists are meant, and not the Greeks.[3]

On November 21, 1792, his time is devoted chiefly to law and metaphysics, with medical studies to fill up his leisure.[4]

Early in 1793 he proposes a correspondence on poetic art, but cannot begin until after Easter, because pressed with other things, a little jurisprudence (his specialty), but a great deal of earnest work in morals, theology, physiology, Kantian philosophy, and politics. His enthusiasm for these side lines shows that his prosecution of them is no "Frohndienst." [5]

Not until June does he begin his æsthetic project. Here occurs the record (June 2): "Im Studium des Shakespeare und Sophocles ward ich unterbrochen." The context does

---

[1] *Ibid.*, pp. 28 f.   [2] *Ibid.*, p. 37.   [3] *Ibid.*, p. 51.
[4] *Ibid.*, p. 68.   [5] *Ibid.*, p. 74.

not explain this fragmentary indulgence in Sophocles. It is not the dawn of his Hellenism however, for in his wide readings at this time he has but *one purpose*, one *earnest undertaking*,—the investigation of the German spirit and the German tongue.[1]

By September 29, he is at last busy with the Greek authors Aeschylus and Sophocles. Aristophanes has not yet appeared within his circle, and the supremacy of Sophocles, as poet, is affirmed with great caution. To feel how gradually the Hellenic element grows, the student should read the correspondence in its entirety for the next two years. It finds frequent expression, but study of the Greek dramatists is as yet merely an *avocation*. Friedrich's chief study is political, for he intends to produce a history of Germany as soon as he removes to Dresden.[2]

By December 11, the Hellenic element has increased to such an extent that he affirms, as if without fear of successful challenge, that the Greeks were the only people who had *taste*.[3] Four days later the panegyric continues. Their greatness was not a sense for art, nor high culture, nor sublimity, nor understanding, but a something which includes all these.[4]

This must not blind us to the fact that other interests are still strong. History and political science are no insignificant part of his life-plan, as seen at this time. Since the disturbing events at Mainz and the fall of the Clubbists his dearest recreation is the study of Rousseau, the only political writer worthy of exhaustive study, as he says, and a type of thought is developing in him which it would be folly not to conceal. To this interest we owe his later essay on *Republicanism* in answer to Kant's "zum ewigen Frieden."[5]

[1] *Ibid.*, pp. 91 f.   [2] *Ibid.*, p. 146.   [3] *Ibid.*, p. 154.
[4] *Ibid.*   [5] *Ibid.*, p. 128.

On November 10, Friedrich plans to continue gathering
materials for two months yet, then to go to Dresden and
concentrate his powers upon the composition of his treatise.
Then correspondence and political studies shall cease. Yet
January 1 finds him with the works of Euripides and
Aristophanes and Aeschylus still unfinished.

Early in January, 1794, Schlegel removes to Dresden and
begins with redoubled energies the task of mastering the
Greek literature and Greek spirit. Now he consults the
Greek writers upon grammar, for here as elsewhere they are
"Menschen κατ' ἐξοχήν."[1] He seems wholly absorbed in
Greek studies, but it is from the midst of these very studies
that he announces the problem of German poetry to be the
union of the antique and the modern, as begun by Goethe.
One suspects that the apparent exclusiveness of Friedrich's
Hellenism is due wholly to an effort to earn a decent living
with his pen. Caroline's inspiration was helpful, but August
Wilhelm was especially interested to escape the burden of
his financial support.

But how far from exclusive his Hellenism was is seen
from a vast project mentioned April 5, 1794. He has been
brooding over a course of lectures on Kant's philosophy, to
be delivered in 1794–5, but now postpones it for a year.
Only a month later, however, the course is to be exchanged
for one in the practical philosophy of the Greeks from
Socrates to Carneiades, on Greek history, politics, antiquities,
art, etc.[2]

There is a contest going on within him between two
forces, the modern philosophical and historical tendency,
and the classic tendency. The latter has now gained the
ascendency, but has not conquered. To satisfy it he projects
a great work, a characterization of the Greeks from the

[1] *Ibid.*, p. 164.   [2] *Ibid.*, pp. 174 and 182.

whole of their literary remains in connection with their own grammatical, rhetorical, and philosophical commentaries, and their remaining sculptures. As he looks at this great work he can say with some decision: "Das Alterthum wird meine Heimat bleiben. Habe ich mir in diesem Fache nur erst einen Namen gemacht, so hoffe ich manche schöne Wünsche wirklich zu machen, und das Studium der Alten wenigstens in Deutschland neu zu beleben." [1] At first he hopes to devote himself wholly to this task, and promises by Michaelis, 1795, three volumes of Greek Essays. "Dann wird eine Pause gemacht," he says: "die zu etwas andres bestimmt." It is not clear just what. Certainly not translations and other hackwork. Possibly the execution of his " Ergänzung, Berichtigung oder Vollendung der Kantischen Philosophie " mentioned January 20, 1795,[2] or the history of Germany planned for composition in Dresden, or his *Geist der neuern Geschichte* or *Kritik des Zeitalters* or *Theorie der Bildung.* The pause is devoted to the modern interests, and even in the classic studies he has a modern tendency and recognizes a union of his conflicting interests as the ideal. He could scarcely foresee that the modern would regain the ascendency in less than two years and that the product of his brief devotion to the Greeks would remain so like a heap of ruins. After two years of hard study he declares positively, July 31, 1795, that he has more culture in the philosophic field than in that of Greek letters, and almost if not equal original inclination for it.[3]

In looking over these four years we find first a complete absorption in German problems: history, philosophy of history, politics, metaphysics, ethics, theology, physiology, medicine, even mathematics, and current German literature in large doses. These fill up his whole time,—by free choice,

[1] *Ibid.*, p. 211.   [2] *Ibid.*   [3] *Ibid.*, p. 229.

too, for his time should have been spent on the *Corpus juris*.
In the late summer of 1793 the first definite practical interest
in the Greek classics appears. It does not at once become
absorbing, but has become predominant by the end of 1793.
That this record is correct appears not only from the completeness and intimacy of the confessions of the letters, but
also from a direct statement of December 11, 1793 : "Eine
Übersetzung des Ganzen (*i. e.*, Aeschylus' works) gehört *seit
einem Vierteljahre, so lange ich mich mit diesen Gegenständen
beschäftige,* unter meine grossen Plane." [1]   Three months
from December 11 is the middle of September, which coin-
cides with the date of the first notices of Greek studies in
the letters.   Before September, 1793, Hellenic interests were
completely in abeyance.

We must now note that the revival of enthusiasm for the
classic Goethe falls in the same summer, probably in the
same month with Schlegel's dawning interest in Greek
tragedy. This circumstance is probably not accidental. A
causal connection may exist, yet it may assume one of two
possible forms : (1) A deeper insight into Greek tragedy
may have opened the eyes of Schlegel to the beauties of
Iphigenie, Tasso, etc., and (2) it is equally possible that a
new insight into Goethe's classic manner may have awakened
in a Goethe-worshipper like Friedrich a desire to drink
inspiration from the same fount of art or bring an appreciation of its excellence to his countrymen. The latter
seems more consistent with his subsequent career, for
Schlegel's *Studium der Griechischen Poesie* was, after all,
as we shall see, produced in support of Weimar classicism.
He begins with the dramatists, and the very poet to which
the *Iphigenie* points.

---

[1] *Ibid.*, p. 149.

γ. *Influences.*

Two events occurred in September, 1793, either or both of which may have affected Schlegel's activities: the death of his father on the 16th, and the appearance of Caroline Böhmer in her retreat at Lucha, near Leipzig, where Friedrich came for the first time under her direct personal influence.

a. Father's Death.

It might be assumed that Friedrich kept up his pretense of studying jurisprudence, and purposely avoided classic studies though actually preferring them, because his father wished it and furnished him the financial support. We might then associate the sudden appearance of Greek studies in September, 1793, with this release from parental restraint. This assumption seems even to have some support in the letters. On May 8, 1793, he declares that his parents must give up a plan which they have forced upon him and which has such slight prospects.[1] On February 11, 1792, he calls his legal studies "Frohndienste," but finds it conducive to mental soundness to have this regular work.[2] He realizes that the elder brother's career is not for him, and a professorship seems out of the question, so he has chosen a career in the civil service, apparently in full rational consent to his parents' wishes.[3] When August Wilhelm's literary prospects brighten, the career of Hofmeister seems tempting, and this is the plan which he wishes to substitute for his father's.

This can in no wise be used as a proof of Friedrich's desire to have leisure for classic studies. As we have seen, he neglected jurisprudence and took up with genuine enthusiasm various other things, none of which were even remotely

---

[1] *Ibid.*, p. 84.   [2] *Ibid.*, p. 38.   [3] *Ibid.*, pp. 9 f.

connected with the Greeks. This avoidance of all "trockene Sachen" improves his health and spirits, and his enthusiasm does not indicate submission to a forced lot. The only hateful thing to Friedrich is the prospect of subordination and routine, which must be unendurable to a man whose ideals smack of Prometheus and Faust. "Die lichte Bahn des Ruhmes" is his only course.[1] When his father dies, that important event leaves but the slightest record in the letters; nothing about release or change of plans. He will simply receive less money from home and will expect more from August Wilhelm. That is all. One feels that the change from a civil to a literary career would have been made in spite of his father's wishes. Further, it seems probable that the Greek studies were begun somewhat before the news of the death arrived in Leipzig. Financial straits due to dissipation compel the removal from Leipzig to Dresden, and the Dresden environment, the art collections, and the library favor classic interests.

b. Caroline Böhmer.

The appearance of this gifted lady at Lucha is an altogether different matter. She is one of the remarkable women of all time, if we may trust contemporary judgment and the opinion of that ripe scholar, Haym.[2] All men whom she met were brought under her spell.

Friedrich's interest in her dates from the spring of 1791, when he learns of her through August Wilhelm, who is then in love with her. We cannot follow the growth of this interest in detail as reflected in the correspondence of more than two years. She is to him a great riddle to whose solu-

---

[1] *Ibid.*, p. 86.

[2] Ein deutsches Frauenleben aus der Zeit unsrer Litteraturblüte, R. Haym, *Preuss. Jahrb.*, Bd. 28, pp. 457 ff., November 1871.

tion he turns again and again. He reads extracts from her letters, and is astonished at her greatness. He blames her for oracular speech, a tendency to make her superiority felt, and " sich huldigen zu lassen." But ere long she has become " ein Phantom dessen wirkliches Erkennen mir gefährlich sein könnte." It is his pleasure " das grosse Ganze ihres Geistes zu errathen." " Welches Weib! Du Glücklicher!" he exclaims, on another occasion. The actual meeting only heightens these impressions. " Der Eindruck, den sie auf mich gemacht hat, ist viel zu ausserordentlich als dass ich ihn selbst schon deutlich übersehen und mittheilen könnte." [1] At first he feels in danger of expressing himself "schwärmerisch." " Die Überlegenheit ihres Verstandes über den Meinigen habe ich sehr früh gefühlt;" he writes, but can scarcely believe in her frankness, in such artlessness and greatness in a woman. He had not expected to find such " Einfachheit," such " Göttlicher Sinn für Wahrheit." One cannot know her without loving her. Her society is a rich return for what he loses by remaining away from classic Dresden.[2] At first she was an inexhaustible source from which he learned.[3] They talked of literature. As was inevitable, they talked of Goethe. She read *Iphigenie* to him. " B's Urtheile über Poesie sind mir *sehr neu und angenehm*. Sie dringt tief ins Innre, und man hört das auch aus ihrem Lesen, wie die *Iphigenie* liest sie herrlich. Wenn ihr Urtheil *rein* (i. e., impersonal, objective) wäre, so könnte es vielleicht nicht so unaussprechlich wahr und tief sein." " Sie findet Lust an den Griechen, und ich schicke ihr immer einen über den andern." [4] On November 24 he is enthusiastic in the hope of a triple alliance " Du, Caroline und Ich" which, however, was not to be realized for several

[1] *WSBr.*, p. 98.   [2] *Ibid.*, p. 114.
[3] *Ibid.*, p. 159.   [4] *Ibid.*, p. 119.

years. After the separation Friedrich writes about her from
Dresden : "Carolines Meinung ist seit der letzten Zeit von
grossem Werth für mich gewesen ;" "Carolines Theilnahme
und Rath ist mir sehr nützlich gewesen, kann es weit mehr
sein. Mein Zutrauen zu ihr ist ganz unbedingt. Sie ist
nicht mehr die Einzige, die Unerforschliche, von der man nie
aufhört zu lernen, sondern die Gute, die Beste, vor der ich
mich meiner Fehler schäme." [1] About a month later there
is another reference to the *Iphigenie:* as she read it, it
approached the melody of the Greeks. "Ich gestehe Dir,
dass die Musik dieses Werkes mir der geflügelten Fülle und
der kräftigen Zartheit der Alten *nahe zu kommen* scheint." [2]

We must admit therefore that Caroline exerted a powerful
influence upon Friedrich Schlegel. She strengthened his
character and moulded his thought. She was a Goethe-
worshipper, and remained so when his public had turned
from him. She was at one time almost the only Goethe
enthusiast in Germany, the only person who appreciated the
classic Goethe. It was the *Iphigenie* which she interpreted
to Schlegel, and the *new views* of poetry were developed
during the interpretation. She identified herself with the
heroine "das Land der Griechen mit der Seele suchend"
and Schlegel felt all the force of its artistic beauty. It
would be no marvel if he too began, from that moment, to
seek "das Land der Griechen" in his way.

We have one positive testimony to this influence, though
it is embodied in a romance and gains significance only in
connection with the whole preceding argument. In Schlegel's
Lucinde we find a passage beginning : "Die Vergötterung
seiner erhabenen Freundin (here certainly Caroline) wurde
für seinen Geist ein fester Mittelpunkt und Boden einer
neuen Welt," etc. The paragraph, which is important in its

---

[1] *Ibid.*, p. 159.   [2] *Ibid.*, p. 171.

entirety, contains the specific confession : " Er vergass sein
Zeitalter, und bildete sich nach den Helden der Vorwelt,
deren Ruinen er mit Anbetung liebte." [1] Julius is Schlegel
himself, and this is a scarcely disguised literary confession
of his personal relations to Caroline at Lucha.

To sum up, Caroline opened Schlegel's eyes to the superiority of the classic Goethe over the earlier Storm and Stress
Goethe. This directed his attention to the Greeks as a
source of inspiration for all great art, especially for modern
German art. He now saw that his scholarship might enlist
itself in the service of Weimar classicism and produce fruitful results. To be sure he could read Greek already, and
had been affected by the general classical movement of
Winckelmann and Shaftesbury. The new desire, having
been awakened, all these dormant elements must become the
basis of his work. He takes advantage as far as possible
of the chief works of others. He rereads Herder's *Kritische
Wälder*, and Barthélemy's *Anacharsis*, and doubtless Winckelmann. In this way the new ambition drives him on to
acquire a mass-knowledge of the Greeks never attained in
Germany before his time.

δ. *Traces of Goethe.*

Whether the preceding argument be sound or not, we
know that Schlegel had a very deep interest in Goethe's
works. His acquaintance with them was very intimate.
An interest so intense cannot fail to affect a young man in
his formative period.

Such influence is shown in frequency of quotation from
most of the great works. How much of Schlegel's interest
in German history and the history of Roman law was due
to the inspiration of Goethe's *Götz* is not directly determin-

[1] *Luc.*, p. 56.

able. He is particularly interested in Luther, the Reformation, the Peasant Wars, etc. Friedrich's Roman drama was doubtless planned after *Götz*. Schlegel's "daily" thoughts of suicide might be associated with the reading of *Werther*, though the causes may have lain in his own unfortunate mental and physical organization. However his "inner dissonance" is a genuine and definite Wertherian symptom. Possibly, too, the Goethean terms "Fülle" and "Harmonie," used so often in *Werther, Faust, Stella, Tasso*, etc., for ideal excellence of all kinds, may have suggested to Schlegel these æsthetic watchwords. Haym refers them to the Plato studies, but they occur for the first time, and suddenly, upon his first study of the Greek dramatists and Goethe's *Iphigenie*.

In further consideration of this whole problem we must remember that (1) Friedrich did not come into personal contact with Goethe until the second Jena residence after his æsthetic theories had been formulated in the *Athenäum;* that (2) Goethe was not a *theorist* in his art until after 1794 when he had come under Schiller's influence; that (3) no utterances of Goethe on art or literary criticism, *except as contained in his dramas and novels*, were published after about 1773 until the date of the inception of the *Propyläen*, if we neglect the three essays, a notice of Moritz's *Nachahmung des Schönen* made up wholly of excerpts (July, 1787), *Litterarischer Sanskulottismus* (1795), and Mme. de Stael's *Versuch über die Dichtungen* (1796), the first of which only can have fallen into Schlegel's hands in time to affect his views.[1] Thus any direct influence of Goethe upon Schlegel's views of art, philosophy, life, must come from reading and

---

[1] This does not exclude the possibility of access to the *Frankf. Gel. Anzeiger* essays and reviews, and the derivation of earlier Storm and Stress ideas from them and from *Von Deutscher Art und Kunst*, though we have no direct testimony to such access.

rereading the published literary works. The results will naturally be less specific than those in the case of Kant, Schiller, and Fichte.

Schlegel read carefully, with an eye to the character of the poet, and constantly tried to reconstruct him from his confessions. The works of Goethe were constantly used for the purpose of deriving æsthetic laws. These two facts are patent.

Another source of influence, secondary and but slight, was correspondence, rumor from mouth to mouth, etc. In Leipzig Schlegel stood in relations with Göschen, and we know that this was a source of much literary information. In Dresden he was intimate with Körner, who was in constant correspondence with Schiller and Humboldt. Schlegel was not lacking in impertinent curiosity, and Körner told him many things, even showed him letters from both authors. Schiller's letters often contained hints of Goethe's artistic principles, which might have become fruitful in Friedrich's thought.

Schlegel's own personality will therefore condition the form in which Goethean influences appear.

One of the most striking things in Goethe's early works is his treatment of *Nature*. In *Werther* it is unavoidable. We know that this feature impressed Schlegel deeply.[1] For him it was *Werther's* chief characteristic.[2] In *Faust* he was impressed by the treatment of *Nature*,[3] especially its Spinozism, its tendency to mysticism. There is enough in *Werther*, *Faust*, and the lyrics to force a recognition of nature in any system of æsthetics derived from them as concrete models. Compare the passage beginning " Das volle warme Gefühl meines Herzens an der lebendigen Natur," etc. (*Werther*, August 18). How he grasps " das innre

---

[1] *MS.*, Bd. II, p. 82.   [2] *Ibid.*, p. 378.   [3] *WSBr.*, p. 1.

glühende heilige Leben der Natur" in his own warm heart!
How he feels the breath of the "Geist des Ewigschaffenden"
that rejoices in the minutest forms of life! How he longs
to feel in his bosom one drop of the bliss of the being "das
alles in sich und durch sich hervorbringt!" Or compare
the passage beginning "Kannst du sagen: *Das ist*" (*Ibid.*).
This all-creating, rejoicing nature takes on its destructive
aspect as an "ewig-verschlingendes, ewig-wiederkäuendes
Ungeheuer."

The mood of sympathy between the soul and nature finds
noble expression in the Faust-fragment of 1790. "Erhab-
ner Geist, du gabst mir, gabst mir alles warum ich bat,"
etc.[1] The pantheistic element is present also in this scene.
Faust speaks of "dieser Wonne, die mich den Göttern nah
und näher bringt."[2] Mephisto joins both elements in his
satires.[3] For the pantheistic element, especially for the
identification of God and man, compare the catechetic scene,[4]
or the words of the *Geist* "In Lebensfluthen," etc.[5] For
the organic nature and harmony of the universe we have the
famous passage from which Schlegel's motto was taken:
"Wie sich alles zum Ganzen webt," etc.[6]

Dr. Alfred Biese, who discusses Goethe's *Naturanschauung* in this early period, using the lyrics also as materials,
sums up in substance as follows: (1) It was a pantheistic
identification of the fulness of nature with God; (2) a
sympathy of nature with the human soul, both being profoundly in harmony, so much so indeed that there is nothing
in the one which has not its answering counterpart in the
other; (3) Goethe's attitude toward nature is not predomi-
nantly the idyllic one of escape from the corruptions of

---

[1] Faustfragment of 1790, ll. 1890–1912.   [2] *Ibid.*, ll. 1914–5.
[3] *Ibid.*, ll. 1955–64.   [4] *Ibid.*, ll. 1734–61.
[5] *Ibid.*, ll. 148–156.   [6] *Ibid.*, ll. 94–106.

culture and artificiality, but the more profound one of self-identification with nature and God, since these and man are at heart *all one*. According to Biese this is the *distinctive* feature in Goethe's treatment of nature, his *advance* upon Rousseau and Klopstock, the two highest representatives of the nature cult preceding him.[1] Dilthey vindicates the view of nature as a *living organic whole* as Goethe's special contribution to the *Weltanschauung* of his own and succeeding generations.[2]

But Goethe's works were full of nature, life. Every character was alive, as if stolen bodily from nature. They were not mere outlines of being, mere abstractions given a sort of rhetorical life by personification, but concrete products with all the fulness of reality. They could be intuited. They formed a picture for the imagination and in this respect were a remarkable advance upon all previous poetic art of recent times.

Besides, Goethe's works are not wanting here and there in expressions of artistic principles which illumine his apparent practices. Compare *Werther* (May 10), the passage beginning "Ich bin so glücklich, mein Bester," etc. When his soul is full of nature, full of God, he is a great painter, though he could not sketch a line, and he exclaims : "Ach ! könntest du das wieder ausdrücken, könntest dem Papier das einhauchen, was so voll, so warm in dir lebt, dass es würde der Spiegel deiner Seele, wie deine Seele ist der Spiegel des unendlichen Gottes ! " Or again (May 26), when Werther sketches the children in a natural group : " Das bestärkte mich in meinem Vorsatze, mich künftig allein an die Natur zu halten. Sie allein ist unendlich reich, und sie allein bildet den grossen Künstler." This is also true of poetry, he says elsewhere (May 30), but adds the

[1] *Preuss. Jahrb.*, Bde. 59-60.   [2] *DLS.*, pp. 96 and 170.

necessary warning that nature is not always *artistic:* she is not typically perfect at every moment in all places : " Es ist nur, *dass man das Vortreffliche erkenne* und es auszusprechen *wage."* He has just seen such an instance, which "rein abgeschrieben" would be the most beautiful idyl in the world (*Ibid.*). Compare also the famous *dicta* of Faust.[1] The art which compels all hearts must come with an inner necessity out of a glowing heart, and without any artificial restraints.

We have seen that Goethe's realism keeps clear of mere naturalism. The selection of typically perfect scenes from nature, "das Erkennen des Vortrefflichen," is idealization. This selective treatment was also accorded to historic themes and persons, as is patent to all in *Götz, Egmont,* and *Tasso,* That such personalities were often used as mouthpieces for the poet's own thought and feeling, his own deepest problems and firmest convictions, was equally apparent in the " Faust-fragment" and the *Prometheus.*

Let us now turn to Friedrich Schlegel's utterances in the letters. We have first his profession of interest in nature, and his conversion from a previous distaste for it, made in connection with a quotation from *Faust.*[2] But he is too subjective to maintain long any great enthusiasm for external nature. He turns rather to human problems, to history, philosophy, art, and we shall find Goethe's influence greatest here. Nevertheless one remarkable passage occurs : " Grosse Männer! Lasst euch zu der hellen Einsicht herunter, und verständigt sie, was nennt ihr Natur? Etwa alle einzelne Dinge, so vorhanden sind? Oder *die Seele des Alls?* Das mächtige Leben, das in allem, was entsteht und untergeht, seine eigene, unendliche Fülle, in wechselnder Liebe und wechselndem Kampfe mit sich selbst, ewig verschlingt?

---

[1] Faust fragment of 1790, ll. 181–92 and 197–8.
[2] *WSBr.*, p. 1.

Ihr ahndet im heiligen Dunkel nicht ein unendliches Nichts,
sondern *ewige Quellen vergänglichen Lebens?* *Wir auch!*
Oft scheint es, als meintet ihr alle Regungen des Menschlichen Herzens in ihrer Üppigkeit und Ausschweifungen.
Wir brauchen aber unsrer edelsten Kraft nicht zu entsagen.
Wir dürfen auch ohne das innere Eintracht hoffen? Ist
denn Vernunft etwas andres als höheres Leben?" [1]

The first portion of this passage is a condensed scheme
of Goethe's *Anschauung* with all warmth of feeling omitted.
The latter is a confused recognition of the parallelism of
man and nature with *Vernunft* as the unifying, harmonizing
principle in man, as the *Seele des Alls* is the unifying element in Nature.

Beauty is *nature*, not human *selection*. Thus he begins
his first æsthetic treatise, May, 1793 : — [2]

"In einem dichterischen Kunstwerke muss die *Ordnung*
richtig und schön sein, der *Stoff* wahr, und die *Ausführung*
gut."

"Es giebt nur zwei *Gesetze* für die Dichtkunst. Eines
derselben ist—das Mannigfaltige muss zu *innrer Einheit
notwendig* verknüpft sein. Zu einem muss alles hinwirken,
und aus diesem einem, jedes andren Dasein, Stelle, Bedeutung notwendig folgen." This unity is often deep hidden.
In *Hamlet* it is the prince's mood, his whole view of the
purpose of man. In *Götz* it is the German knightly
spirit, its last effort to rise before it is extinguished. With
Götz dies ancient virtue and the age of heroes. Shakespeare's *Romeo* has unity, but our critic has not yet been
able to investigate it. In *Don Carlos* he has sought in
vain for it.

"Ohne *Natureinheit* und *Vernunfteinheit* ist die höchste
Schönheit der Ordnung unmöglich." No chaotic subject

---

[1] *Ibid.*, p. 118.　　　　　[2] *Ibid.*, pp. 86 ff.

can be really unified, but even naturally unified subject matter can become an artistic unity only through the free activity of the *Vernunft*. This is doubtless a derivative from Goethe's practices as we have seen. The *Vernunft* also decides upon the lesser divisions of a work of art. These lesser divisions should flow together like waves and not disturb the continuity of the whole. This is really directed against all types of regular stanza, a series of which cannot form a natural organic whole. This is to be associated with Friedrich's marked preference for Goethe's free rhythms.

Truth requires *depth* and *likeness to nature*. To the first Goethe, Schiller, and Klopstock (he recognizes no others) have equal claims. Their relations to the second are unlike. "Ehe der Geist mit der Natur eins ist" (intended to characterize Goethe) "wirkt es zu sehr nur *aus sich* und aus *seinen Begriffen;* weiss nicht sich *dem Wirklichen anzuschmiegen.*" This is Schiller's condition. "Wenige nur vernehmen den leisen Gang der Natur in der Zeit." This is Goethe's excellence. He knows the world and several passions well. Klopstock is especially successful in catching the notes of the inner life.

The characteristic of the poet is "Trieb zur Darstellung," but it must be a representation of poetic materials. His perfection is "die allgemeine Fähigkeit alles gut darzustellen." He adds specially that this seems to have been Goethe's intention. Indeed, Schlegel insisted later that some of Goethe's poems were products of this form-instinct alone, pure form-poems without content.

But a poem, to deserve the praise of those who alone are competent judges, must be more than *formally* perfect, it must have "einen grossen Gehalt." Only the self-active human spirit and its deeds have worth in themselves. "Je menschlicher, je würdiger" is Schlegel's *dictum*, and we know that Goethe's poems are for him the great examples of perfect form with great content. Greatness of heart was ascribed to Werther, and Faust was a great man in contrast to Klinger's *Faust*.

It is hardest to judge of the content of a poem. There is, however, only one unconditional law, " *Vernunfteinheit*," ideal unity, or as he formulates it, "dass der freie Geist stets siege über die Natur." This is difficult, he admits, at the close of epic or dramatic works.

There is not only a type of poetry for each age, people, rank, but for each individual. Yet the more individual, the less intelligible to the world at large. The poets generally compose only for themselves, and yet for the great number of them it remains an eternal truth, "wer für die Welt lebt, in dessen Herzen muss Raum sein für eine Welt." This must be compared with the later claims of universality for Goethe's poetry.

Only Shakespeare, Goethe, Klopstock, Schiller, and Wieland are considered in this first aesthetic sketch. It is apparent that he is working out his principles from the works of these authors, among whom Goethe bears the chief part.

This sketch was intended merely as a statement of the most general laws of poetry, according to which a critic might pass valid judgments upon any given poem. For the poet himself "giebt's keine Gesetze." [1] He is a creative genius, and a law unto himself. This is still Storm and Stress. These laws are only for the critic.

A passage in reply to certain restrictions of August Wilhelm brings out more fully Friedrich's conception of the artistic unity of a poem. The *Seele* or *Herz* of a poem is what we call *Geist* in man, *Gott* in creation, *i. e.*, "lebendigster Zusammenhang"—organic unity. Here occurs also

---

[1] *Ibid.*, p. 110.

a passage remarkable for its relation to Moritz's thought. "Es giebt nur ein wirkliches System, die grosse verborgene, die ewige Natur, oder die Wahrheit." [1]

This represents the height of Schlegel's aesthetics before his meeting with Caroline and his entrance upon Greek studies. In the following December utterances occur which show a change. The "Vernunfteinheit" which he now calls "poetische Sittlichkeit" is the product of the poet alone, a demand of art, not a gift of nature. The definition of the nature of the poet is now changed to "Harmonie innrer Fülle," which accords well with a deepened insight into *Iphigenie* and *Tasso*. The essential attitude of the poet is an instinct for the consciousness of this inner fulness in harmony. The external manifestation is as before: "Trieb zur Darstellung." Shortly after this the influences of Kant and especially of Schiller make themselves felt in his essays.

When Schlegel goes to the Greeks, it is to the *dramatists*, not to Homer. This is in accordance with our assumption that he proceeds from the *Iphigenie*, but is explainable perhaps equally well on other grounds. Yet it remains psychologically impossible for Schlegel to have gone to the study of the Greeks without taking with him pretty fully developed notions of the drama. These were formed chiefly from Goethe's practice. Hence we are somewhat justified in suspecting a transference of Goethean qualities into the Greeks when Friedrich finds perfect harmony in Sophocles, and declares that tragedy best where "das Herz der siegende Gott ist," in the contest with fate.

Few other traces remain to be noted. Friedrich's masterly sophistic defense of lying [2] may be a reminiscence of

---

[1] *Ibid.*, p. 111.   Cf. also *MNach.*, p. 14, *et passim.*
[2] *Ibid.*, p. 62.

Mephisto's sophisms.[1] His notions of Genius and its relation to rules and regulations of life not only are akin to Goethe's Storm and Stress ideas, but their expression shows close similarity : " wir verstehen aber denke ich darunter (*i. e.*, Fehlerlosigkeit) ein mittleres Mass an allen Seelenkräften, ein Mensch, der es besitzt, lebt recht ordentlich und anständig, ist ziemlich liebenswürdig, ziemlich klug, und thut das, was die Menge mit Verehrung nennt. Er schweift also nirgends sehr ab, stösst nie an ; mit einem Worte, er hat so etwas der Tugend Ähnliches, in kritischen Fällen muss ihm der liebe Gott helfen. Er ist alles, was ein gewöhnlicher Mensch sein kann. Die Bildner der Menschen haben ihre Einrichtungen, als Staaten und Religionen, und in kleinen Kreisen, Gewohnheiten und Cursivmoralen, an die man glaubt durch Ehre und Schande, nach den allgemeinen Eigenschaften der Klasse recht sehr gut gemacht, nur die Menschen unschädlich, und doch auch ein klein wenig gut zu machen. Für gewöhnliche Menschen verdient daher der Inbegriff dieser Eigenschaften, welchen du Fehlerlosigkeit oder Rechtlichkeit nennen kannst, alle mögliche Empfehlung, und lass uns ja *das Genie nicht machen wollen*. Das wahre Genie kann sich nicht in diesen fremden Massstab fügen, bald überspringt es ihn weit, bald bleibt es zurück." [2]

When he adds that genius is the *æterna fons* of life, and that the few geniuses are a class of beings who have nothing in common with other mortals, he has certainly Goethe's personality in mind. But compare the above passage with that of *Werther* (May 26), " man kann zum Vortheile der Regeln viel sagen," etc., and the kinship is at once apparent.

Hence, of this first period we may say : (1) until the summer of 1793, Schlegel was dominated by Storm and Stress ideas ; (2) Goethe and his works were the dominant influ-

---

[1] Faust fragment of 1790, ll. 1464–1500.   [2] *WSBr.*, p. 5.

ence; (3) through the personal influence of Caroline Böhmer his taste and appreciation for Goethe's classic manner were awakened September, 1793; (4) this induced Friedrich to turn to the Greeks in support of Weimar classicism; (5) he carried into the study of the Greeks subjective elements derived from Goethe; and (6) this study of the Greeks reacted upon his estimate of Goethe and caused him to place the latter in the center of all ideal poetry, and made his works the canon of all poetic art.

B. 1794–1802.

1. *Dresden, Publications.*

Friedrich Schlegel's public career began in November, 1794. The first recorded recognition of him by the Weimar poets is in a letter of Schiller to Goethe, August 8, 1796. He writes, "Schlegel's Bruder ist hier: er macht einen recht guten Eindruck und verspricht viel." To this Goethe makes no reply. Goethe could have had access to the journals in which Friedrich's essays appeared, but we have no record of his reading them or caring to read them.

The essays here meant are the following: "Von den Schulen der Griechischen Poesie," *Berlin. Monatschrift,* November, 1794; "Über die Weiblichen Charaktere in den Griechischen Dichtern," *Leipzig. Monatschrift für Damen,* October and November, 1794; "Vom æsthetischen Werthe der Griechischen Komödie," *Berlin. Monatschrift,* December, 1794; "Über die Grenzen des Schönen," Wieland's *Teutscher Merkur,* May, 1795; "Über die Diotima," *Berlin. Monatschrift,* July and August, 1795; review of Condorcet's "Esquisse d'un tableau historique," etc., Niethammer's *Journal,* III, 2, 1795; review of "Schiller's Musenalmanach für 1796," *Deutschland,* June, 1796; review of "Schiller's

Horen, Stücke II–V," *Deutschland*, July, 1796 ; "Goethe, ein Fragment" from his *Studium*, also selected passages from his *Studium der Griechischen Poesie*, a work which he hoped soon to lay before the German public.

The most important of these was perhaps the first, which shows the influence of Winckelmann, Herder, Humboldt and Schiller.[1] The tendency to look upon Greek life and poetry as a natural organic whole may be referable to Goethe.[2] The other essays do not betray Goethe's influence noticeably. Dr. Carl Alt[3] has shown that they are æsthetic decendants of Schiller's earlier essays. They are thus pendants of Weimar classicism in a large sense, but not directly related to Goethe. The *Diotima* alone makes reference to Goethe. Here Goethe and Shakespeare are mentioned as the greatest masters in the delineation of feminine characters. Their women are richer for the understanding but not more beautiful ·or delicate than those of Homer, the "Ionic Bard."

To most of these essays we shall pay no attention. They are easily accessible in Minor's edition and their contents are analyzed by Haym. We shall consider only those which offer materials for the problem in hand.

We must, however, note the personal relations of Friedrich. He needed a publisher in order to live. His ambition was scarcely satisfied with less than the best organ, which at that time was Schiller's *Horen*. But two things stood in the way. The need of this journal for classic contributions was already supplied by Wilhelm v. Humboldt, and Schiller was pleased neither with Schlegel's character, whom he called "einen unbescheidnen kalten Witzling,"[4] nor with his literary ability, about which anyone might be justly scepti-

---

[1] *HRS.*, p. 187 ff.   [2] *DLS.*, pp. 96 and 170.
[3] Alt. *Schiller und die Brüder Schlegel.*   [4] *WSBr.*, p. 45.

cal. One essay was refused and there now seemed to be no other opportunity of entering the charmed circle of the organ of the Weimar classicists. Schlegel turned to Reichardt, whose *Deutschland* was opened to him. Now Reichardt happened to be in a feud with Goethe and Schiller, and gladly made Schlegel the cat's paw in taking revenge. The latter was already unfriendly to Schiller, and had been rendered more so by Caroline, the dominant spirit of the Jena circle which he was soon to enter. The purpose of this Jena coterie seems to have been to separate the great poet friends, to reduce Schiller, to place Goethe on the highest pinnacle of fame, and to establish its members as literary dictators. Such a program pleased Friedrich and he readily lent himself as the foremost instrument in carrying it out.

The first blow in this campaign was the review of Schiller's *Musenalmanach für 1796*. Having developed from Schiller his theory of objectivity as the essential of all art,[1] he now makes application of it to concrete cases. He has no respect for persons. With dictatorial mien he assumes the judge's chair, and the higher the master the sterner and more searching the criticism. He has not yet provided himself with the *Filzschuhe* of his later years. He does not shrink from insult if it only seem witty enough.

In the review praise and blame are mingled, but in un equal proportions. The epigrams are so numerous and excellent, he says in substance, that a complete theory of this kind of poetry might be developed from them. Schiller's *Kolumbus* is one of the finest. *Der Tanz* is too long, and too earnest. It has no poetic unity and combines the prolixity of Ovid with the heaviness of Propertius. The elegy is not at all adapted to Schiller's quick fire and terse strength. Schiller in his prime knew better how to choose

---

[1] Alt, pp. 25 f.

and strike the proper tone than now since his long sojourn in historical and philosophical fields. Would he have pardoned himself such a work as *Pegasus* then? For comic poems are uninteresting unless they have original joyousness, wit, grace, and urbanity. So many phrases, so many offenses. But, he adds, this must not disturb any one's satisfaction in Schiller's return from the subterranean vaults of metaphysics into the light of day as a poet. The *Ideale* will win him friends. The *Macht des Gesanges* is disfigured by incorrect figures of speech. The *Würde der Frauen* is monotonous and wholly lacking in taste. It is not a poem at all. It gains by reading it strophe by strophe backwards. The characters are not realistic, but idealized downwards beneath the truth. " Männer wie diese müssten an Händen und Beinen gebunden werden ; solchen Frauen ziemte Gängelband und Fallhut." [1] The more detailed analysis of the *Ideale* merely brings out personal abuse of Schiller.[2]

The treatment of Goethe is quite different. *Der Besuch* pleases Schlegel best. *Meeresstille* is very attractive, but must be read in connection with the text from which it is taken, in order to have its due effect. " Die Epigramme, in denen *der grösste Dichter unsrer Zeit* unverkennbar ist, sind in der That eine Rolle reichlich mit Leben ausgeschmückt, voll der lieblichsten Würzen." This spice resembles most the fresh salt found only too sparingly in Martial. In one of the epigrams " athmet eine zarte Griechheit, und überall jener echtdeutsche, unschuldige, gleichsam kindliche Mutwillen, von dem sich in einigen epischen Stücken der Griechen etwas Gleiches findet." The chief point of the whole review, however, is summed up in a paragraph which compares Goethe and Schiller, but denies the justice of making such a comparison.

The review of the *Horen II–V* was less insulting to

---

[1] *MS.*, Bd. II, p. 4.   [2] *Ibid.*

the editor but less favorable to the contents. August Wilhelm's contributions are generously praised, while Schiller's aesthetic essay is barely mentioned. Goethe's translation of *Benvenuto Cellini* is too long and monotonous for such a journal. The chief attention of the reviewer is devoted to Shakespeare's *Hamlet*. The exegesis in *Wilhelm Meister* had pleased the elder brother very highly, but Friedrich himself had brooded over *Hamlet* and reached other results. Goethe was in part mistaken. A critic must not be merely an exegete, must not merely account for the existence of a work of art, but must pass upon its merits as art. The critic must not merely appreciate the beauties of a piece, but be able "gültige Grundsätze richtig anzuwenden." This was Goethe's fault. He took licenses with *Hamlet*. "Goethe schwelgt zu sehr im Genusse seines vollendet schönen Selbst, als dass er die schreienden Härten, die empörenden Nacktheiten des zu aufrichtigen Shakespeare ertragen könnte und sich nicht verhüllen müsste. *Er ist auch wohl zu sehr Dichter,* als dass er sich seiner Schöpferkraft ganz entäussern und mit der treuen Enthaltsamkeit eines bescheidenen Forschers die Werke eines andern Dichters erklären könnte."[1] No critic is more unsafe than a poet himself. Goethe's harmonious soul could hardly understand the sublime despair of Hamlet. "Wie Goethe den *Werther* schrieb, da ersetzte jenen Mangel die Jugend, ihre wehmüthigen Ahnungen, ihre weissagenden Thränen. Nachher liess ihn das Geschick, zu nachsichtig, mit seinem Genius allein."

Faust and *Hamlet* are now compared. The passage is too long for citation, but indicates a purely Storm and Stress conception of *Faust*. It closes: "Hamlet muss seiner Natur nach langsam vergehen, und wie von selbst aufhören; Faust

---

[1] *Ibid.*, Bd. II, p. 11 f.

hingegen muss mit Krachen zur Hölle hinabstürzen. Das ist denn freilich prächtiger und auch poetischer." But "um die Ausführung Klopstockisch zu vergleichen, so dürfen wir, wenn wir die Kraft und Kunst, welche den Hamlet vollendete, auf hundert schätzen, die, welche den Faust entwarf, *nicht wohl über sieben ansetzen.*"

This must have proven a fine introduction into the good graces of Goethe, but fortunately a more extraordinary essay had preceded it. This was *Goethe, ein Fragment*, which had immediately won for its author the reputation of an unconditional and blinded eulogist of Goethe's poetry. It begins: "Der Charakter der æsthetischen Bildung unseres Zeitalters und unsrer Nation verräth sich selbst durch ein merkwürdiges und grosses Symptom. Goethens Poesie ist die Morgenröthe echter Kunst und reiner Schönheit," etc.[1] Few extracts can be made from all Schlegel's writings in which such extravagant and sustained eulogy occur. The central idea is that the beautiful is the true standard of Goethe's work. Its character is objectivity. And yet the poet is not strictly objective but stands midway between the objective and the characteristic. For this reason he is the artist of the future. "Dieser grosse Künstler eröffnet die Aussicht auf *eine ganz neue Stufe der æsthetischen Bildung.*" The objective, the beautiful, is no empty illusion, but a reality, because here realized.

The whole panegyric contains little else than what we have already seen in the correspondence of Friedrich. The increased enthusiasm is due to the appearance of Goethe's recent brilliant performances, his Roman elegies, Venetian epigrams, and *Wilhelm Meister*. The letters are full of expressions of it. "Was sagst Du zu den Göttlichen Elegien?" "Was sagst Du zum Göttlicben Wilhelm?" "Sage und singe mir ein schönes, feines und langes Lied

---

[1] *Ibid.*, Bd. I, p. 114 ff.

davon."[1] Other expressions of interest in Goethe occur.
"Ich freue mich herzlich auf deine Ergiessungen über
Shakespeare und Goethe."[2] This refers to the essay on
Shakespeare and Wilhelm Meister reviewed later by Fried-
rich in *Deutschland*. "Ich habe grosse Lust ein paar
Blätter über die harmonische Ausbildung und Goethe und
Politik hineinzugeben" in the opposition papers against the
reviewers of the *Horen*, I and II, which contained Goethe's
elegies, epigrams, and epistles.[3] "Das Stück Künstlerroman
(Benvenuto Cellini), welches man deinem Shakespeare zuge-
sellt hat, gefällt mir köstlich. Goethe muss die Hände im
Spiel gehabt haben. Es gefällt mir millionenmal besser als
Märchen und Ausgewanderte."[4] "Über alles bin ich auf
deine Bekanntschaft mit Goethe begierig."[5] "Sehr schön
ist's, dass Du mit Goethe so gut bist, und alles, was Du von
ihm schreibst, hat mich höchlich ergötzt."[6]

All in all, then, we are not forced to assume that the
public praise of this "Fragment" was overwrought for
the purpose of lifting himself and establishing a school.
Friedrich's admiration of Goethe is of too early origin, and
exaggeration too firmly ingrained in his nature, to compel
such a conclusion. But it is not impossible, nor improbable,
that he considered it a most fortunate situation to be able to
turn his honest enthusiasm to literary profit. He had always
desired to stand well with Goethe, though his admiration
had not been wholly unmixed. "Ihr seid so wunderlich,"
he writes to the Jena circle, December 23, 1795, "dass ihr
mich dahin bringen könntet, eine Satire wider Goethe zu
schreiben;" and a little earlier: "Auch Goethe's Leichtig-
keit ist oft die Frucht von unsäglichem Fleiss und grosser
Anstrengung."[7] Of late, however, this tendency to finding
fault had been overcome.

---

[1] *WSBr.*, p. 231. [2] *Ibid.*, p. 270. [3] *Ibid.*, p. 275. [4] *Ibid.*, p. 276.
[5] *Ibid.*, p. 279. [6] *Ibid.*, p. 280. [7] *Ibid.*, p. 234.

2. Jena.

a. Xenienkampf.

When now Friedrich arrived in Jena, in August, 1796, Goethe and Schiller had already nearly completed the preparation of those remarkable distichs, the *Xenia*, which were soon to interest and alarm the whole literary and journalistic world of Germany. The plan, suggested by Goethe, December 23, 1795, and approved at once by Schiller, began as a reply to the enemies of the *Horen*, a simple satirical volley at the various journals of the day, but grew larger and more inclusive from time to time, until it promised to become a vast manifesto of a thousand distichs against all tendencies not in harmony with Weimar classicism.

It is no part of our task here to follow this development in detail. The production of *Xenia* continued up to the last moment before the last sheets of the *Musenalmanach für 1797* went to press. Goethe and Schiller were together in daily conference from the middle of August until the first week in October. During this period the collection received its final form, was reduced to half its volume, and published.

During this period of daily coöperation Schlegel's review of their *Almanach* came to the eyes of Goethe and Schiller. There appeared also selected passages from Friedrich's *Studium*, with their paradoxes and exaggerations. We have no record of the reception of the works, and no comment upon their contents, for the correspondence ceased in August. A most valuable index of Goethe's attitude toward Schlegel is thus wanting. All is left to inference.

Schlegel had begun to regret his folly before he set out for Jena, but Körner's letter to Schiller in Friedrich's behalf arrived too late with its assurances that the poet had no greater admirer than this same foolhardy young critic. The

excuses, moreover, were insufficient. The public praise of
Goethe and degradation of Schiller seemed an effort to alienate the friends. At any rate it was an unwarranted piece
of insolence from a mere upstart in letters. It was also a
type of literary and æsthetic mischief which deserved a
heavy hand. There was still time to remember the belated
guest with a due number of the spiciest gifts.

The Schlegels had already been remembered by two
distichs, *Frage* (484)[1] and *Antwort* (485), which recognized
their services in the contest against Nikolai and the Philistines.
These were now given an unfavorable turn before publication. Their bolts fall still upon the Trojans, but often
also "blind ins Blaue hinein."

Another *Xenion* (501) of the great *Underworld Cycle* was
now given the title *Pure Manier* to satirize Friedrich's published *dictum* that Shakespeare is "nie objectiv," but
"durchgängig manieriert."[2] Possibly No. 500, with its
Geschrei der Tragöden and *Hundegebell der Dramaturgen*
around the shade of Shakespeare may apply to Friedrich,
though more probably only to the earlier Shakespearians,
J. E. Schlegel, Böttiger, Wieland, and Eschenburg.

The real attack upon Friedrich begins with No. 826
(302), *Neueste Kritikproben*, and consists of an unbroken
series to No. 844 (331), in all nineteen epigrams, including
the following titles: *Eine Zweite, Eine Dritte, Schillers
Würde der Frauen, Pegasus von demselben, Das unglückliche
Verhältnis, Neugier, Die Zwei Fieber, Griechheit, Warnung,
Übertreibung und Einseitigkeit, Neueste Behauptung, Griechische und Moderne Tragödie, Entgegengesetzte Wirkung, Die
höchste Harmonie, Aufgelöstes Rätsel, Gefährliche Nachfolge,
Geschwindschreiber,* and *Sonntagskinder,* most of which left
little doubt in regard to the victim.

[1] These all refer to the numbers in *SSXen.*
[2] *MS.*, Bd. I, p. 109.

The first three are examples of Goethe's proposed manner of self-characterization. They would say of themselves simply what "die albernen Burschen" say of them.[1] No. 826 refers to Schlegel's brutal comment on Schiller: "die einmal zerrüttete Gesundheit der Einbildungskraft ist unheilbar."[2] No. 827 is a similar paradox in defense of Herder's *Epigrams*.[3] No. 828 is a reproof of Schlegel's statement that Goethe was always natural even at the risk of becoming trivial and uninteresting.[4] The following two apply the same method to individual poems unjustly censured by Schlegel. Nos. 831 and 832 contrast the unproductivity or bad literary quality of the Schlegels with their dictatorial assumptions. The next nine distichs bring into ludicrous juxtaposition a number of Schlegel's utterances on the nature of Greek art, its contrast to modern art, etc., etc., charge him with "Graecomanie," with utter failure to appreciate the "Masz" and "Klarheit" of the Greeks, warn him from making the cause of classicism a laughing-stock through his excesses, and point out several instances of grossly incorrect judgment in his essays. Finally the desire of the brothers to become teachers at once, before they have had time to become masters, is sternly rebuked.

The great number of these *Xenia*, only exceeded by those of Reichardt and Nikolai, has been readily explained by some as due to Schiller's personal animosity. Schiller was offended, and justly, too, but there is another side to this question. Schlegel's works were *programmatic*. They outlined a vast work in a most promising field in the most immediate relations with Weimar classicism. They made vast promises which would assure their author an honorable place in the world of scholarship and letters, if *well* fulfilled. If *ill* done, these works might cast reproach upon the whole

---

[1] *GSBr.*, December 30, 1795.
[2] *MS.*, Bd. II, p. 6.
[3] *Bern.*, Bd. II, pp. 224 ff.
[4] *MS.*, Bd. II, p. 6.

classic movement. Schiller saw this, felt that Schlegel would play a leading *rôle*, if at all possible, and therefore decided upon a thorough castigation of his earliest follies and imper-tinences. It was as the type of literary revolution that Schlegel was attacked.

What now is Goethe's share in all this? These *Xenia* have been attributed with remarkable unanimity to Schiller. Goethe cannot be proved to be the author of any one of them. Schiller's style seems manifest in most of them, but this alone is no safe criterion. Even if we assume that Goethe is not the author of any single *Xenion* against Friedrich, the following facts are still to be considered: 1) Goethe and Schiller intended to keep the authorship *secret*; both intended that each should republish the whole collection *as his own work*. This demonstrates Goethe's intention to accept responsibility for the whole; he subscribed to the Schlegel satire as readily as Schiller to the Reichardt cycle: 2) Schiller constantly urged Goethe to strike out mercilessly any *Xenion* which *for any reason* might seem inadvisable, and Schiller performed the same office for Goethe. Certainly this mutual criticism did not cease while the poets were in daily conference during August and Sep-tember. The retention of a score of blows at Schlegel in the final collection, when over half the original number were condemned to privacy, seems to imply a mutual belief in their justice and importance: 3) Goethe's statement to Eckermann that he often furnished the idea and Schiller the expression and *vice versa*, that he sometimes composed the hexameter and Schiller the pentameter and *vice versa*, has always been regarded as excellent testimony.[1] But when can this have occurred if not when both poets were in *daily personal communication*? The correspondence shows nothing but exchange of masses of *Xenia, complete* and having the

---

[1] *GGE.*, December 16, 1828.

single authorship of Goethe or Schiller. Those against Schlegel were composed at a time favorable to such mutual composition : 4) Goethe urged that nothing should be published which might give offense in *their own circle.* Thus Herder and Wieland escaped, though there was occasion enough to satirize both. Hence the Schlegels could not have been recognized as of their circle : 5) finally those distichs were not all directed against sharp treatment of Schiller, but two of them at least were against equally senseless treatment of Goethe. The majority were against ridiculous passages in Schlegel's essay, which, if unchallenged, might react against the good cause of classicism, which Goethe had more at heart than had Schiller himself.

β. *Results, Continued Reviews.*

Friedrich was stung. He attributed the whole attack to Schiller, and considered it an expression of personal hatred. Goethe was wholly exonerated. To Böttiger he likened the poets to a giant walking arm in arm with a dwarf, and Schiller especially to lame Hephaestus attempting to imitate the natural movements of Hebe. As late as 1802 (April 1) he sent five pitifully absurd epigrams against Schiller to Rahel in Berlin for private circulation,[1] while he sang Goethe's praises in private and in public.

Friedrich's utterances were not confined to private circles, however. He gave the *Xenienalmanach* a spicy review in Reichardt's *Deutschland*, in which the *Xenia* figured as like that Vergilian monster " fama, malum qua non aliud velocius ullum," etc. The reviewer chooses a simple device to let them characterize themselves, by quoting about a dozen distichs in immediate succession without comment. Here follows a characteristically Schlegelian passage in which the

[1] *BXen.*, Bd. II, p. 226.

Xenia figure as "klassische Grobheiten" not wholly in place, sometimes betraying base hatred, and not even sparing the grave of a noble unfortunate. Friedrich takes up the challenge to the *Chorizonten*, "*Die Aufgabe*," and declares it is Schiller's voice, who rejoices in the fact that in his anonymity he can be mistaken for Goethe. The passage ends with the prophecy "Heuer spanisches Pfeffer, übers Jahr *asa foetida*." [1]

In all this Friedrich assumes a very knowing attitude, as if he had certain knowledge not accessible to less favored persons. This manner was favored by his reputation outside Jena and Weimar as the herald of Goethe's preëminence in art. To those who did not know better Schlegel seemed to enjoy the most intimate personal acquaintance with his idol. His utterances must therefore have a sort of *ex cathedra* authority in the world of letters. Ridiculous enough, but certainly true. Goethe complained of it to Schiller, and explained it to Wieland as inevitable. Fräulein von Schimmelmann could not believe in Goethe's moral character because of this assumed intimacy with the Schlegels. When Friedrich assured Reichardt that Goethe had not written the *Xenia* against him, he believed it unquestioningly and wrote Schiller at once demanding information respecting their authorship.

All this supposed intimacy has absolutely no foundation at this date, as shown by the above blunder in respect to Reichardt and by his error in solving the *Aufgabe*, which is by Goethe himself. Schlegel played the *rôle* of "Gelehrter Geck" in his review. As a prophet he was equally unsuccessful, for it was Schiller who opposed a repetition of the attack and proposed to shame their adversaries by publishing the beautiful *Balladenalmanach* for 1798, and

---

[1] *MS.*, Bd. II, p. 32.

then excluded from it *Oberon und Titaniens Hochzeit* with its literary satires.

It may be noted in passing that the distich became a favorite form of epigram for Friedrich,[1] though their contents smacked more of the *Sudelköche* than of the *Xenia*.

The essay on *Georg Forster* was called out by the *Xenia*. Its democratic tone, as we have noted, wrote its author completely out of favor with Goethe.

However, there were other things beside the *Xenia* in the *Musenalmanach* for 1797, and these offered excellent opportunity for paying off old scores. It contained no less a masterpiece than *Alexis und Dora*. Friedrich greets this with an unbounded enthusiasm which excuses all imperfections or turns them into supreme excellences. It is an idyl in the true Greek sense, with a mingling of " epischer Fülle und lyrischer Glut." " Das Gedicht athmet den ganzen Frühling, oder vielmehr, es athmet zugleich das frische Leben des Frühlings, die mächtige Glut des Sommers, und die reife Milde des Herbstes."

However this is not mere public glorification. His private words are even more enthusiastic. " Gestern war ein Götterfest für mich," he writes, June 15, 1796 : " Ich las die *Idylle*. Nur einmal, aber wenn es auch das einzigemal bliebe, so würde sie nie aus meinem Gedächtnis verlöschen. Es hat mich mit Entzücken durchdrungen. Das *Ewig* ging mir durch Mark und Bein. Eine wollüstige Thräne fiel auf das Blatt. Wie zart ist nicht die Rede des Mädchens ! Es ist mir lieber als alles was Goethe je über Liebe metrisch gedichtet hat." He does not set it above the Mariane scenes in *Wilhelm Meister*. " Eine kleine Unschicklichkeit fühlte ich gleich darin, dass Alexis noch so nahe am Ufer redend eingeführt wird, und doch mit so ruhiger Sorgfalt

---

[1] *WSBr.*, pp. 460 and 509.

ausmalt, wie das Gleichnis vom Rätsel und das bequeme
Bette. Die Mischung des Weisen und Sinnlich-Süssen mit
der Leidenschaft, deren Brand halte ich dem Gedichte für
wesentlich, seine eigenthümliche Schönheit. Nur gegen die
Wahrheit scheint mir jenes ein kleines Verstoss. Ich er-
kläre es mir daraus, was Körner mir sagte, es hat erst sollen
eine Heroide werden, dann ist es in diese Form umgegossen.
Er hat übrigens sehr Recht es eine Idylle zu nennen. Es ist
wirklich eine, nur nicht im modern Schiller'schen Sinn,
sondern im Griechischen. Doch versteht sich's, dass sie
mehr werth ist als alle Theokritischen und dergleichen.
Wer so dichten kann, ist glücklich wie ein Gott! Gehe hin
und thue desgleichen." [1]

Other poems of Goethe are favorably mentioned in the
review, though much less warmly than this supreme work.
Der Chinese zu Rom has the charm of Horace. *Die Eisbahn*
is praised equally. The *tabulae votivae*, however, are not all
so excellent. Some are mere versified antitheses and commonplaces, deserters from the van or rear of some philosophical discourse. These are of course from the hand of
Schiller. A number of them, evidently taken to be from
Goethe, are selected and praised as little masterpieces. Of
those dedicated to *Einer* Schlegel makes two collections, one
chaplet in the manner of Goethe's Roman elegies, whose
worthiest praise is a thankful silence, the other chaplet—
well, he does not wish to disturb anyone else in the enjoyment of it.

With the excuse that a critique cannot take note of everything in such a rich collection of works of genius, Schiller's
product gets but slight attention. August Wilhelm's *Pyg-
malion* gets twice the space and more unstinted praise than
all of Schiller's works together. This review appeared in
October.

[1] *Ibid.*, p. 284.

In August, October, and December reviews of the *Horen* continued to appear. They were in general unfavorable. The *Briefe auf einer Reise nach dem Gotthard* form a notable exception. The reviewer must have felt sure of their author in spite of their anonymity. A few pages of well-chosen excerpts, mingled with almost unqualified praise, are devoted to them. In December he writes: "jetzt scheint für die stets wechselnden und oft von ihrer Bahn abweichenden *Horen* die *Periode der Übersetzungen* gekommen zu sein." He justifies this by estimates, though he admits that the *Cellini* could not have fallen into better hands than Goethe's. This attack was ungracious, seeing that the elder brother derived good profit from some of those very translations. The *Horen*, he says further, is an example of the usual fate of undertakings brilliantly begun, but too great for the capacity of their editors. Here occurs also Schlegel's review of *Agnes von Lilien*, the supposed work of Goethe. This is the most significant and most attractive original contribution which has appeared in the *Horen* for a long time. It has, however, extravagant and squinting expressions, one poem in it is below freezing, and another is obscure. When the concluding portions appear, he greets them with an "alas!" for the lovely Agnes has now approached the mediocre and commonplace. The situations are never used with true artistic spirit and the unity is obscured by disconnected masses of petty detail, etc.

As a last blow the reviewer returns to the subject of translations, and says: "Man hat vortreffliche, mittelgute, und auch schlechte Originale aus dem Französischen, Englischen, Italienischen, Lateinischen, und dem Griechischen, vortrefflich, auch mittelmässig, und auch schlecht übersetzt."

Such treatment reached a point beyond which Schiller could endure it no longer. At first we hear but little of it. When Reichardt is coming to take Friedrich Schlegel to his

7

residence at Giebichenstein, Schiller calls it "*vom Teufel geholt*" and the anger against the publisher is greater than that against the contributor.[1]

A little later Schiller reports Jacobi's anger at Schlegel's review of *Woldemar*, but no word escapes him to indicate personal dislike to Friedrich. On December 6, Schiller writes with satisfaction of the success of *Agnes von Lilien*, and reports the astonishing news that the Schlegels consider it a work of Goethe's genius, that Caroline's conception of Goethe had been broadened by it, that Goethe had never created a purer and more perfect feminine character. Schiller had not been able to resolve to destroy the illusion as yet.[2] Goethe replies in good humor : " Lassen Sie mir so lange als möglich die Ehre als Verfasser der *Agnes* zu gelten." In earlier times, he adds, a large library might have been gathered about his name.

The next utterance of Schiller concerns Schlegel's *Deutscher Orpheus*. The latter had published a defense of Kant against Schlosser, Goethe's brother-in-law. What Friedrich said was true enough in its way, but his youth, as compared with Kant and Schlosser, and the whole manner in which he wrote justified Schiller in calling his expressions "*Impertinenzen.*" This essay was delayed in reaching Schiller, for it is May 16, 1797, before he reads it. He comments particularly upon the evil purpose and mere party-spirit of the essay. And then he proceeds to retail a piece of literary news in which his bitterness finds its first vent : " Es wird doch zu arg mit diesem Herrn Friedrich Schlegel." The latter had told Humboldt that he had reviewed the *Agnes* severely, but was sorry now that he had learned that it was not Goethe's work. Schiller proceeds : " Der Laffe meinte also, er müsse dafür sorgen, dass Ihr Geschmack sich nicht verschlimmre.

[1] *GSBr.*, November 2, 1796.   [2] *Ibid.*, December 6, 1796.

Und d'iese Unverschämtheit kann er mit einer solchen Unwissenheit und Oberflächlichkeit paaren, dass er die *Agnes* wirklich für Ihr Werk hielt." [1]

Goethe replies next day: "Fast bei allen Urtheilen waltet nur der gute oder der böse Wille gegen die Person, und die Fratze des Parteigeistes ist mir mehr zuwider als irgend eine andre Carrikatur." [2] There is no absolute express agreement with Schiller and no trace of feeling in respect to the error of the Jena critics. It is an appropriate characterization, however, of Schlegel's whole career as reviewer. It is entirely gratuitous to see in this brief, quiet answer a rebuke of Schiller's own tone. Goethe's friendship for Schiller continued to deepen. Whatever his attitude toward Friedrich may have been, it was not altered much.

Two weeks after this, May 31, Schiller wrote the famous letter to August Wilhelm, which severed all literary and personal relations with the whole Schlegel family. August Wilhelm made a last effort to excuse himself from any responsibility for Friedrich's offenses, and pleaded for a continuance of friendly relations. But the effort was based on falsehood and personal advantage on August's part, and friendly relations with a household, of which the chief offender was a member, was too uncertain, or, rather, too certain, for Schiller's straightforward character, and the appeal was vain. As a concession to Goethe the literary relations were partially restored, for August completely repudiated Friedrich's reviews and Greek essay, and professed to accept the castigation of the *Xenia* as just.

This disruption brought about a triangular relationship which affects the problem in hand. Goethe's relations to both parties put him into a peculiar attitude, one of the following possible attitudes, either (1) tolerant silence toward

---

[1] *Ibid.*, May 16, 1797.　　　　[2] *Ibid.*, May 17, 1797.

both with possible offense to both, or (2) a choice between the two, or (3) a mediatorial attitude between the two, or (4) a double-dealing with one or both. Goethe's character is guaranty against the last. That he was expected to play the *rôle* of mediator with respect to August Wilhelm is clear from a letter of Goethe to Schiller of March, 1798.[1] But though a year had elapsed, Schiller's resolution remained unaltered, and the mediation failed. That Goethe should choose one party to the exclusion of the other, except for most urgent reasons, such as literary and artistic incompatibility, is contrary to his own universality of interest, even if he had had no hopes of spreading his artistic creed through the agency of these younger professed disciples, or if he had had the energy to make a firm stand against the importunity of their friendship. Goethe did the only thing compatible with his nature. He clung to both parties with a large tolerance for their personal antipathies. This does not imply indifference to one party, nor, on the other hand, does it imply equal regard for both. Goethe's friendship for Schiller overshadowed every other relationship for more than ten years. The Schlegels recognized this fact themselves, at last, and seemed to become resigned to it, though with inward vexation. Dorothea reported from Jena that Goethe visited no one but Schiller. Friedrich advised against the establishment of a Musenalmanach so long as Schiller had Goethe, and August Wilhelm vetoed the *Athenäumsfragmente* against Schiller, because their publication would involve the alienation of Goethe from themselves—a sacrifice too great to make for the satisfaction of revenge.

In the essays that appeared from time to time during this period almost nothing of interest to us occurs. Goethe's treatment of Nature in *Werther* is contrasted with Jacobi's

---

[1] *Ibid.*, March (day uncertain), 1798.

in *Woldemar.*[1] A charge of coldness, made by Herder in his *Humanitätsbriefe* is repelled by Friedrich. Coldness is a necessary *seeming* of all classic art, but Goethe is not "gefühllos" at all. He is simply perfectly plastic.[2] One essay appears, however, which is important to us—*Über die Homerische Poesie.* It is important because Goethe read it and expressed his opinion of it.

γ. Die Homerische Poesie.

Of course Homer must be a great figure in a complete history of Greek life and art, such as Schlegel planned. Accordingly, we find him early at work upon the problem. In October, 1794, he is in search of an hypothesis concerning the age of Homer. In November he inclines to the English view as against the German, but has not yet finished reading the Iliad and Odyssey. He finds it incredible that the two epics have come from different or various sources. He cites the opinion of the Greeks that one ἀοιδός excelled all others in genius. But this singer was an Achaean, not an Ionian as he formerly supposed. Two months later he is reading Homer, Apollodorus, and Strabo, and the English view falls of itself. About six months later these desultory investigations receive a powerful impulse through the appearance of Wolf's *Prolegomena ad Homerum,* which Friedrich considered one of the greatest books of the period, the peer of Lessing's Greek essays and Kant's *Kritik der reinen Vernunft.* In fact no single book seems to have taken deeper hold upon Schlegel, excepting only *Wilhelm Meister* and Fichte's *Wissenschaftslehre.*

Schlegel's essay now becomes an attempt to explain Homer from Homer himself, to picture the times in which

[1] *MS.*, Bd. II, p. 82. [2] *Ibid.*, p. 47.

it was produced and outline the development of the poems
into their present form. It is to be a literary analogue to
Wolf's philological work. In addition it is to be essentially a treatise on epic poetry. This doctrine of the *epic*
is what chiefly concerns us here.

Goethe had just finished his *Hermann und Dorothea* and
was revolving in his mind a second epic, this time on a
purely classic subject, the death of Achilles. Goethe and
Schiller were together attempting to define and establish the
differences between the drama and the epic. They wished
to deduce laws for the epic and the drama, which should
aid them in their own poetic production. On the whole their
interest in the problem of the epic was *practical*, not *historical*. Schlegel's essay is first of all *historic* and then *theoretic*.
He says:

"Die *epische Dichtart* ist unter allen die einfachste. Sie
ordnet eine unbegrenzte Vielheit möglicher, aüssrer, durch
ursachliche Verknüpfung verbundene Gegenstände, durch
Gleichartigkeit des Stoffes und Abrundung der Umrisse zu
einer *bloss sinnlichen Einheit.*" The harmony of the epic is
exactly opposite to that of the drama; the former is "eine
unbestimmte Masse poetischer Begebenheiten," the latter
"eine poetische Handlung." The drama must have one
principal action and one hero, the epic has many, each of
which becomes in turn the center of the whole.

These ideas were derived from Goethe's *Wilhelm Meister*
rather than from Homer himself. This would be apparent
enough on comparison with Goethe's differentiation of the
drama and the *Roman*,[1] even if August Wilhelm had not
directly acknowledged the debt in his review of *Hermann
und Dorothea*.[2]

---

[1] *Wilhelm Meister*, Bch. v, Kap. 7, *G Wke.*, Abt. i, Bd. 22, p. 178 ff.
[2] *A WS Wke.*, Bd. iv, p. 139.

The epic is infinite, because every event is a member of an infinite series. "Jedes echt epische und harmonische Gedicht . . . . fängt . . . . in der Mitte an." "Die reine dichterische Erzählung . . . . *kennt ihrem Wesen nach weder Anfang noch Ende.*" "Gebt dem epischen Dichter Raum und Zeit, er wird nicht eher enden, als bis er seinen Stoff erschöpft, und eine vollständige Ansicht der ihn umgebenden Welt vollendet hat, wie sie die Homerische Poesie gewährt."

A poem with unity such as Goethe demanded does and must awaken certain definite expectations in respect to the movement and close of the action. But Homer, Schlegel says, "erregt keine bestimmte Erwartung *nach der Entwickelung eines Keimes,* der *Auflösung eines Knotens,* der *Vollendung einer Absicht,* oder auch nach *einer bestimmten Art des Stoffes,* sondern eine durchaus unbestimmte und also ins Unendliche gehende Erwartung blosser Fülle überhaupt." This may be a true characterization of Homer's epics, or it may not; but it practically denies the possibility of *any modern epic,* the very thing sought for by Goethe in all his Homeric studies.

Lest we might still suppose that this judgment was meant to apply only to Greek art, and so left hope for some modern analogue of more artistic character, Schlegel assures us that such an epic is "wirklich ein vollständiges Urbild der epischen Dichtart" because the Greeks themselves are "das Urbild des rein Menschlichen" and necessarily furnish us "den reinen Gesetzen und Begriffen der Vernunft entsprechende Anschauungen." Furthermore Homer is not only *classic* but *perfect.* A work is classic if it is the most perfect expression extant of even a crude stage of culture. To be perfect, it must be the highest art form of the most perfect stage of culture. Therefore Homer's epics are "eine vollständige Anschauung für den reinen Begriff" of epic poetry, and contain "die Gesetze einer ursprünglichen Dichtart."

Goethe read this essay in April, 1797. On the 28th he writes to Schiller: "Haben Sie Schlegel's Abhandlung über das epische Gedicht im 11ten Stück *Deutschland* vom vorigen Jahr gesehen? Lesen Sie es ja! Es ist sonderbar, wie er, als ein guter Kopf, auf dem rechten Wege ist, *und sich ihn doch gleich wieder selbst verrennt.* Weil das epische Gedicht nicht die *dramatische Einheit* haben kann, weil man eine solche absolute Einheit in der Ilias und Odyssée nicht gerade nachweisen kann, vielmehr nach der neuern Idee *sie noch für zerstückelter angiebt als sie sind;* so soll das epische Gedicht keine Einheit *haben,* noch *fordern,* das heisst, nach meiner Vorstellung: es soll aufhören ein Gedicht zu sein. Und das sollen reine Begriffe sein, *denen doch selbst die Erfahrung, wenn man genau aufmerkt, widerspricht.* Denn die Ilias und Odyssée, und wenn sie durch die Hände von tausend Dichtern und Redakteurs gegangen wären, zeigen die gewaltige Tendenz der poetischen und kritischen Natur nach Einheit. Und am Ende ist diese neue Schlegel'sche Ausführung doch nur zu Gunsten der Wolfischen Meinung, die eines solchen Beistandes gar nicht einmal bedarf. Denn daraus, dass jene grossen Gedichte erst nach und nach entstanden sind, und zu keiner vollständigen und vollkommenen Einheit haben gebracht werden können (obgleich beide vielleicht weit vollkommener organisiert sind als man denkt) folgt noch nicht, dass ein solches Gedicht auf keine Weise vollständig, vollkommen und Eins werden könne noch solle."[1] ·

This amounts to a complete denial of the practical and theoretical value of Friedrich's essay. Schiller himself could hardly have been severer. To Goethe the *canon* of art is not the Greeks as they were, but the Greeks as they

---

[1] *GSBr.*, April 28, 1797.

would have been had they realized the perfect intention of their art. Schlegel's *canon* for all ages and times is what the Greeks *realized* in art.

Schiller seems not to have replied directly, but in a few days we find him reading, at Goethe's suggestion, Aristotle's *Poetics*, which had been discredited in Schlegel's essay. He finds the Stagyrite most excellent, "ein wahrer Höllenrichter für alle, die entweder an der äussern Form sklavisch hängen, *oder die über alle Form sich hinwegsetzen.*" [1]

These studies do not lead Goethe to look more favorably upon Schlegel's ideas. He writes to Schiller, May 16 : "Ich bin mehr als jemals von der Einheit und Untheilbarkeit des Gedichts überzeugt, und es lebt überhaupt kein Mensch mehr, und wird nicht wieder geboren werden, der es zu beurtheilen im Stande wäre." Goethe and others are constantly forced back upon their subjective judgments. "'Die Ilias erscheint mir so rund und fertig, man mag sagen was man will, dass nichts dazu und nichts davon gethan werden kann." [2]

Goethe now drops the subject for a time, and does not go over the ground again until after the appearance of August Wilhelm's review of *Hermann und Dorothea*. He thinks he has made some good discoveries. He embodies these in an essay, *Über epische und dramatische Dichtung*, which he appends to a letter to Schiller on December 23, 1797. Minor goes too far in assuming that Schlegel's review gave Goethe his insight into the principles which he there lays down.[3] Goethe read the review, and found there that Friedrich's ideas had been modified in *one most essential point*. August Wilhelm attempts to strip the epic of all that is local to the Greek people, the Greek subject, and Homer's age, and now applies this conception of pure epic poetry to

[1] *Ibid.*, May 5, 1797. [2] *Ibid.*, May 16, 1797.
[3] *CuR.*, p. 216 f.

Hermann und Dorothea. This simply raises once more for Goethe the old question : What is the nature of the epic *per se?* The manner of attacking the problem shows no dependence upon the review, and the results do not show dependence upon the principles there applied. As regards the Homeric epic August Wilhelm accepts Friedrich's idea of the divisibility and infinite extensibility of it, and denies all other unity than that of the separate songs of the various rhapsodists. Goethe's essay demands first of all *Einheit* and *Entwicklung* as the basic principles of all art whatsoever.[1]

As late as April 28, 1798, Goethe is still more convinced of the unity of the Homeric poems. "Indessen muss man alle Chorizonten mit dem Fluche des Bischofs Ernulphus verfluchen, und wie die Franzosen, auf Leben und Tod, die Einheit und Untheilbarkeit des poetischen Werthes in einem feinen Herzen festhalten und vertheidigen."[2]

But Goethe had received and read another of Friedrich's works before he came upon the above earlier essay in *Deutschland.* This was the fragmentary volume *Die Griechen und Römer* with its introductory essay, *Über das Studium der griechischen Poesie.* It appeared early in 1797, though it had been sent to press as early as December, 1795. We shall constantly refer to this essay as the *Studium* for sake of brevity.

δ. *Studium der Griechischen Poesie.*

The briefest analysis of this essay must suffice. It begins with an almost complete denial of the æsthetic worth of all modern poetry. There are individuals who stand out like rocks jutting from the fog in a distant landscape. Such are Dante, Shakespeare, and *Goethe.* Even these were moralists

---

[1] *V.* whole review. *A WS Wke.,* Bd. II, pp. 183 ff.
[2] *GSBr.,* April 28, 1798.

rather than poets. They were more interested in laying upon the altar of humanity the best which they knew and thought and strove for, than in producing perfect art-works from the standpoint of the *Beautiful*, which is here Schlegel's æsthetic watchword.

There is no settled public taste, no settled public morals out of which an aesthetic tradition might grow. Even the great aesthetic thinkers have had no influence upon the formation of taste. *Theory*, drawn from the current poetic practice, lost all credit with the public, and chance became the unlimited despot of a realm of confusion. Each successful favorite is hounded to disfavor or oblivion by a host of pitiful imitators. Germany is especially unfortunate because of this plague of imitators. Her poetry represents " ein beinahe vollständiges geographisches Naturalienkabinett aller Nationalcharaktere jedes Zeitalters und jeder Weltgegend." In the midst of all this disharmony the aesthetic faculty, like Faust, "taumelt von Begierde zu Genuss, und im Genuss verschmachtet nach Begierde," and in unsatisfied longing and vain striving is driven almost to despair.

This chaos must be explainable in some manner. Schlegel naturally chooses the historic method of clarification. To explain how it became is to hint at what it must become. To note its past course of development is to prophesy its future course. To discern its present movement is to foretell its future goal.

Perhaps the universal despair itself will give birth to a great confidence for the future. Anarchy is the mother of beneficent revolutions. There are signs of a catastrophe which may inaugurate a better era. What these signs are will appear later.

After all, we are assured that there is no such thing as absolute "Charakterlosigkeit." Modern life is in fact a vast unity, heterogeneity being merely one of its most striking elements. Mutual imitation among modern nations, their common imitation of antiquity from lack of originality, the coexistence of a higher and a lower type of art in all these nations, these are elements of unity. The preponderance of the *characteristic*, and the insatiable striving after the new and *piquant*, are still other elements. Therefore there must be some *inner unity* of modern art.

Schlegel tries to show by the very nature of culture that modern life and art had to become what it did. All life is activity, and all activity brings culture. But life is a contest between the individual and environment. "Nur das Gemüth, welches von dem Schicksal hinlänglich durchgearbeitet worden ist (sc. Goethe?) erreicht das seltene Glück selbständig sein zu können." In all other cases either the individual will (Freiheit) or environment (Natur) must give the determining impulse to action. In one case the result is *artificial* culture, in the other *natural.* Experience shows that the natural precedes the artificial in all nations. The natural is harmonious and lasts until *instinct* disturbs it. The earliest stages of European culture already show traces of artificiality. These increase with time. Rhyme, which Schlegel disliked and declared unjustifiable, which only a great artist like Goethe could render harmless, as in *Faust,* was a common element of mediæval art.

The *Christian religion,* with its insistence upon the relative worthlessness of the flesh and the world, compared with spirit and eternal life, was the germ of all this artificial culture, and the essential cause of the unity among modern nations.

The progress of this religion brought about corruption and confusion in which only one guide remained, the authority of the ancients. The critical faculty was not developed sufficiently to formulate independent law out of itself, and hence was forced to rely upon imitation of *fixed models.* This led to complete individualism in art as opposed to earlier *schools* of art.

The *reason,* in its first efforts to overcome the errors of false imitation, actually adds to the confusion by commingling the various arts, as music and poetry, or the various kinds of a single art, as the drama and the lyric, the drama and the epic, the epic and the lyric, etc. Here Schlegel stands squarely upon the platform of Weimar classicism.

Out of didactic poetry, so characteristic of the moderns, grows, through the activity of the *Vernunft,* true philosophic poetry as contrasted with beauty poetry,—to the *philosophic* tragedy of Shakespeare with its "highest disharmony" as opposed to the *beauty* tragedy of Goethe and Sophocles with its "highest harmony."

In an excursion on *Hamlet, the* philosophic tragedy, Schlegel praises in high terms Goethe's analysis in *Wilhelm Meister,* but repeats his previous restrictions in the terms, "nur vergesse man nicht was er (Hamlet) war."

The one hopeful element in all modern art is the constant striving for an *æsthetic maximum.* This can be found only in the *universal,* the *permanent,* the *necessary, i. e.,* in Friedrich's terminology, the *objective.* This argues that the *interesting* must be only a crisis, a transition stage in the development of modern art.

Schlegel admits that there may be retrogression through all degrees of badness to the complete extinction of taste, but insists that under *proper conditions* progress will be made to the *objective.* These conditions are great moral force and firm independence.

But the *objective,* being fixed, is a never attainable goal of art, the continued approach to which must rest upon devoted efforts of all true lovers of poetry. In these efforts wise leadership alone is needed. The imitation of all *nationalities* must be turned into a preparation for German *univer-*

sality, and the evil will be destroyed. Indeed the crisis is already passing favorably. "Der Charakter der aesthetischen Bildung unsres Zeitalters und unsrer Nation verräth sich selbst durch ein merkwürdiges und grosses Symptom. Goethens Poesie ist die Morgenröthe echter Kunst und reiner Schönheit, etc." Goethe's poetry, characterized throughout several pages of extravagant eulogium, is the demonstration that the *objective* is attainable, at least approximately.

To confirm this happy revolution several prejudgments must be set aside. Poetry must not be considered the peculiar gift of early or crude peoples, nor the necessary victim of civilization and scientific progress. Its organ, the imagination, is a permanent element of the soul and cannot be destroyed by true culture. The golden age lies ahead and not behind. Schlegel finds it truly wonderful how a belief in the beautiful is awakening again, how the need of the *objective* is being felt everywhere. The moment is ripe for an aesthetic revolution. If we try to conceive this revolution as Friedrich conceived it, we find first Schlegel's proclamation of Goethe's poetry as *objective* art, and second the proclamation of his own and August Wilhelm's critical judgments as *objective* criticism. When these two are accepted as the law and its fulfilment, the aesthetic heteronomy of Germany will be ended.

Objective criticism implies a *true theory* of art. This is difficult in itself, yet is of itself insufficient. The true theory needs an *Anschauung,* which is a universal natural history of art. This necessary *Anschauung* is furnished by Greek art as a whole.

One naturally expects to find following this a careful consideration of the spirit, the principles of Greek art, and perhaps a fine characterization of the masterpieces which make up this proposed "gesetzgebende Anschauung," but confusion holds carnival in the remainder of the essay, which

Greek art. Homer and Sophocles are eulogized later on in the essay, but no serious effort is made to characterize in brief the whole Greek spirit, though this rather than the practice of individual authors is the canon of art.

A few ideas here and there are worthy of note in this connection. As a condition of objectivity Friedrich demands " Versinnlichung des Allgemeinen " and " Nachahmung des Einzelnen "—a demand which belongs primarily to Goethe's artistic creed. Objectivity itself is merely " das gesetz-mässige Verhältnis " between these two principles. No special degree of perfection is required in either term of the ratio, but the ratio itself is fixed by absolute law. Objec-tivity thus turns out to be a useless and pernicious abstraction, for Schlegel can now commend every work of Greek art from the prehomeric crudities down to the last product of the corrupt Alexandrian school as a model on the mere ground of objectivity.

Here a characterization of Goethe's style as a mixture of the styles of Homer, Euripides, and Aristophanes is introduced with no very apparent excuse.

Certain objections to this Greek program for modern art are now taken up. The Greeks are defended against charges of immorality on the ground that decency has no right to dictate in matters of poetry. To the objection that imitation has been tried, he replies that it has never been tried *rightly.* The poet must know the whole mass of Greek literature before he can truly imitate its spirit. " Nur der ahmt sie *wirklich* nach, der sich die Objectivität der ganzen Masse, den schönen Geist der einzelnen Dichter, und den voll-kommenen Styl des goldenen Zeitalters zueignet." The Olympian of Weimar must have smiled when he noted this passage, with its boundless demand of erudition on his part, before he could reach his goal.

Another error in previous efforts at imitation is the failure to separate the *local* from the *objective* or *universal* in Greek art. This is difficult, *but must be done.* Local forms are the *didactic*, which has no justification except in the age of myth, and the *epic*, which has no justification except in the age just preceding the rise of the drama and of authentic history. While these observations are doubtless true in a proper sense, we must note again in passing how fundamentally different this view is from Goethe's, according to which a modern epic is justified if it fulfils the conditions of a perfected Greek epic.

We are told that all modern imitations of Homer have failed (Goethe's *Hermann* has not yet appeared), from Tasso to Wieland.

The *mythic* element is *local* and impossible in a modern drama, because the myth itself must needs be explained first to the beholders. One might even doubt the possibility of a "beauty drama" in modern times, were it not for the existence of an almost perfect one—*Don Carlos.*

This is a decided note of dishonesty. The praise of Schiller's play as objective, as a beauty drama in a Greek sense, was either bitter irony in the midst of an otherwise wholly serious essay, or it was an effort to conciliate Schiller by an awkward and transparent sham.

Goethe is now criticised for his improper treatment of Homer in earlier years. This was a tendency to modernize him : " Wer den Homer nur interessant findet, der entweiht ihn. . . . Der ursprüngliche Zauber der Heldenzeit wird in dem Gemüthe, welches mit den Zerrüttungen der Misbildung bekannt ist, ohne doch den Sinn für Natur ganz verloren zu haben, unendlich erhöht; und ein unzufriedener Bürger unsres Jahrhunderts kann leicht in der Griechischen Ansicht jener reizenden Einfalt, Freiheit und Innigkeit alles zu finden glauben, was er entbehren muss. Eine solche

Werther'sche Ansicht des ehrwürdigen Dichters ist kein reiner Genuss des Schönen, keine reine Würdigung der Kunst."

To imitate the Greeks truly, one must bring to their study an objective philosophy of history, and an objective philosophy of art. This is practically a demand for the dictatorship of an erudite critic, such as Schlegel felt himself to be. He demands specifically that the dictatorship of Aristotle, even as reinterpreted by Lessing, shall end.

The three great periods of modern literature are now reviewed in order. The third and last, the immediate future, is to see the conquest of *objective* theory, *objective* taste, *objective* creative art, as well as *objective* imitation. Kant and Fichte are establishing the first, August Wilhelm Schlegel is wielding the sceptre of objective taste, Goethe is creating objective poetry, and Friedrich Schlegel is hereby announcing an objective history of Greek art which shall be the firm basis of all the preceding objectivities.

In this revolution Germany is to lead. All other nations must first learn of Germany an *objective theory* before they can share in the movement. "Welchen weiten Weg haben unsre einzigen bedeutenden Nebenbuhler, die Franzosen, noch zurückzulegen, ehe sie es nur ahnen können, wie sehr sich Goethe den Griechen nähere."

If now we take a view of this essay as a whole we see that Schlegel is not deeply interested in the Greeks *per se*, as was Winckelmann. His primary interest is in contemporary art. In fact this interest is overwhelming. For him there is no doubt that Germany is to be the intellectual leader of Europe and the world in all fields. In German intellectual life the highest and best thing is *art, poetic art*. "Die einzige, eigentliche reine Kunst ohne erborgte Kraft und fremde Hülfe ist Poesie." [1] In poetic art only one

---

[1] *MS.*, Bd. I, p. 37. Cf. Lyceums fragment No. 7. *Ibid.*, Bd. II, p. 184.

name stands out as worthy of highest praise, that of Goethe.

If we wish to realize what were Schlegel's purposes in his Hellenic studies, we have to consider such facts as these. Friedrich knew the conditions of German literature. He knew that Goethe's and Schiller's art looked to Greece for its inspiration and stood in open conflict with the rationalism and Philistinism of Nikolai, *et al.* Goethe's practise in recent times was so exclusively Greek and his utterances on Greek art in the Roman elegies, etc., so extremely favorable that Schlegel must have known his general position, even if we leave out of account all other sources of information, as correspondence, rumor, and the news retailed in public prints. One might easily discern a greater partiality for the Greeks on Goethe's part than on Schiller's. Schlegel chose to lead a literary life. He had no originality and force to create a new movement, and he realized it. He had to ally himself with parties already existing. Weimar classicism represented that revolt against Philistinism with which his whole nature sympathized. He elected to become an auxiliary of this movement. His most hopeful, indeed only opportunity lay in criticism. The imperfect knowledge of Greek literature then current gave him a fruitful suggestion and he made vast plans to contribute a broader and more critical basis to Goethe's Hellenizing effort in behalf of German art. This essay is merely programmatic, setting forth his aims and methods as an aesthetic lawgiver.

At the earliest moment a volume is sent to Goethe for his judgment. On March 13, 1797, Goethe records in his journal : "Nachmittag, Schlegel's *Griechen und Römer* ; " again, March 15, "Mittag, zu Schiller, nachher an Klopstock und Schlegel weiter gelesen ; " March 19, "dazu Schlegel ; " March 20, "Nach Tische, Schlegel's *Griechen und Römer*." [1] These

---

[1] *GWke.*, Abt. III, Bd. 2, pp. 63 ff. *Tagebuch.*

are the only direct testimonies of Goethe with respect to the *Studium*. He does not mention it in letters to Schiller nor in his other correspondence. We can only infer his opinions and attitude.

That Goethe must have been interested in the theme needs no mention, for he was at the height of his classicism. He recognized in the midst of its confusion an essential kinship with Schiller's æsthetic doctrines.[1] He had been himself an enthusiast on the exclusive canonicity of the Greeks before Schiller's æsthetic doctrine was fully formulated.[2]

Furthermore Goethe found here in most emphatic form his own conception of art as an organism. Much more pronounced than in the *Schulen* is the idea of the naturalness and organic unity and growth of all Greek life, with its expression in an equally organic literature. "Aber jenes höchste Schöne ist ein gewordnes *organisch gebildetes Ganzes*, welches durch die kleinste Trennung zerrissen, durch das geringste Übergewicht zerstört wird." "Die Einheit seiner Dramen ist nicht mechanisch erzwungen, sondern *organisch entstanden*." "Ihre Zusammensetzung ist durchaus gleichartig, rein und einfach wie der *Organismus der plastischen Natur*, nicht wie der Mechanismus des technischen Verstandes." "In ihr ist der ganze Kreislauf der *organischen Entwickelung* der Kunst abgeschlossen und vollendet." Many other passages occur. One has a close resemblance to *Faust*, "Wenn der kritische Anatom die schöne Organisation eines Kunstwerkes erst zerstört, in elementarische Masse analysiert, und mit dieser dann mancherlei physische Versuche anstellt, aus denen er stolze Resultate zieht; so täuscht er sich selbst auf eine sehr handgreifliche Weise : denn das Kunstwerk existiert gar nicht mehr."[3]

[1] *GGE.*, March 21, 1830.
[2] *Einwirkung der neuern Philosophie*, Goethe's *Nachlass*, Bd. 10, p. 53.
[3] Cf. Faust fragment of 1790, ll. 415–18.

If Dilthey be correct we have here a Goethean contribution to Schlegel's thought.[1]   Haym seems to accept the view that this idea of organization, organic development, and unity of art comes originally from Goethe.[2]   If so, it may have been mediated to Schlegel through Herder's *Ideen* which he read as early as 1791.   The idea did not become prominent in his essays until after the reading and rereading of *Wilhelm Meister* in the early months of 1795, while the *Studium* was in progress.   The *Meister* seemed to him a complete treatise on art, and its utterances on *Hamlet* and its development, as well as other passages on other phases of art, may well have stimulated the development of the idea of organization in art to the prominence which it finally attained.   Pichtos refers this conception of art to Goethe and Kant, both of whom Schlegel studied carefully.[3]   Special investigation would be necessary to determine the source and course of development of this æsthetic doctrine, even if it should not prove finally to be one of those conceptions which are in the air, whose origin is not ascribable to any one leading thinker in particular.   In any case this attitude toward Greek art was a commendable feature in the eyes of Goethe.

Another   recommendation,   according   to   Schüddekopf, Hehn, and others, was the unstinted praise of Goethe's poetry, which must have proved refreshing in the midst of almost universal apathy, or hostility or misunderstanding. Haym remarks that Goethe's tolerance of the Schlegels "sich reichlich bezahlt machte."   On the strength of these undoubted facts we are assured that Goethe must have been either more or less than human, not to have welcomed this

---

[1] *DLS.*, p. 170–6.

[2] *HLH.*, Bd. II, pp. 203, 208, 222, 233, etc.   The whole discussion of Herder's dependence upon Goethe is in point.

[3] *PAesth.*, pp. 18 and 28.

praise as a sign of his spreading influence. Possibly, but we must hardly assume that Goethe's character was petty enough to be greatly moved by extravagant praise. It is probable that he felt at this time, as later, that the Schlegels were offering him adulation that was not due, "das mir nicht zukam," as he says. He excused it all to Wieland as beyond his control: "Man muss sich das ebenso gefallen lassen, als wenn man aus vollem Halse getadelt wird." [1]

It is certain from Goethe's letters that he had no hopes of influencing the older generation, and that he looked to the representatives of the younger, the Humboldts, the Schlegels, etc., for recognition and propaganda of his ideas and principles. In such cases he could overlook minor differences and hope for growing harmony unless the differences tended to become greater. As disciples Goethe tolerated the Schlegels, and not as incense offerers.

The faults of obscurity and the utter lack of organization of the *Studium* must have repelled Goethe as they did Schiller. A man "dem die Natur ein offenes Auge verliehen hatte, alles was ihn umgiebt, rein und klar und gleichsam mit dem Blick des Naturforschers aufzunehmen, der in allen Gegenständen des Nachdenkens und der Empfindung nur *Wahrheit* und *gediegenen Gehalt* schätzt, und vor dem kein Kunstwerk, dem nicht *verständige und regelmässige Anordnung*, kein Raissonnement, dem nicht *geprüfte Beobachtung*, keine Handlung besteht, der nicht *consequente Maximen* zu Grunde liegen," [2] must have been wonderfully tolerant to remain silent.

Goethe's silence is rather to be interpreted as meaning that he considered the castigation of the unripeness, the paradoxes and follies of this essay in Schiller's *Xenia* an appropriate and final comment.

[1] *BGG.*, Bd. I, pp. 280 f.
[2] *HWke.*, Bd. 4, pp. 143 ff. *Über Hermann und Dorothea.*

A certain exchange of ideas with Schiller shortly after this time has reference to the contents of the *Studium.* The latter writes under date of July 7, 1797 : " Es wäre, däucht mir, jetzt gerade der rechte Moment, dass die Griechischen Kunstwerke *von Seiten des Charakteristischen* beleuchtet und durchgegangen würden ; denn allgemein herrscht noch immer der Winckelmann'sche und Lessing'sche Begriff, und *unsre allerneuesten Aesthetiker,* so wohl über Poesie als Plastik, *lassen sich's nicht sauer werden,* das Schöne der Griechen von *allem Charakteristischen* zu befreien, und *dieses* zum Merkzeichen des Modernen zu machen. Mir däucht dass die neuen Analytiker durch ihre Bemühungen, den Begriff des Schönen abzusondern und in einer gewissen Reinheit aufzustellen, ihn beinahe ausgehöhlt und in einen leeren Schall verwandelt haben, dass man in der Entgegensetzung *des Schönen* gegen das *Richtige* und *Treffende* viel zu weit gegangen ist, und eine Absonderung, die bloss der Philosoph macht, und die bloss von einer Seite statthaft ist, viel zu grob genommen hat." [1]

In reply Goethe secures for the *Horen* an essay by Hirt on the *Laokoon,* in. which the characteristic in Greek art is emphatically shown. This essay was not exactly what either Goethe or Schiller wanted, but it had the merit of calling attention to the presence of the characteristic even in the best Greek sculptures. Goethe's part in this matter is clearly stated in his letter to Kunst-Meyer of July 14, 1797 (*q. v.*). It was a misunderstanding of the beautiful to make it exclude the characteristic. To set Weimar classicism in a correct light with respect both to Hirt's essay and to Schlegel's *Studium,* Goethe wrote his *Laokoon,* which likewise brings the characteristic in Greek sculpture to a much greater prominence than does Lessing's work. Goethe planned a whole series of such essays for the same purpose.

[1] *GSBr.,* July 7, 1797.

Hirt's essay was felt by the Schlegels to be a direct attack upon the position of Friedrich in the *Studium*. This is shown by the long critical notice of it in the *Litterarischer Reichsanzeiger* of the *Athenäum*, vol. ii, No. 2, and by *Fragment*, No. 310. We cannot say then with Minor[1] that Goethe allied himself with the Schlegels against Hirt in favor of Winckelmann's idea of beauty. His *Laokoon* is a polemic against both, and distinctly agrees with Schiller that the new æsthetic critics had *misunderstood* the idea of beauty when they made it exclude the characteristic.

ε. *Lyceumsfragmente.*

About this time there appeared in Unger's *Lyceum der Schönen Künste* a series of one hundred and twenty-seven *Kritische Fragmente*. We have seen that Schlegel's interests were modern and German from the start, that under special influences he turned to the study of the Greeks to find a critical basis for a sound judgment of modern literature, and a mode of imitation which might perfect modern German literary creations. We have seen that for a time this secondary movement seemed to absorb all his energies, but it was merely seeming. The original nature of Friedrich Schlegel was so insistent that it burst through all this constraint and found expression in its most appropriate form—practical formlessness—in fragments.

The essential thing discussed in the Lyceum fragments is the *Roman*. The *Roman* is the Socratic dialogue of modern times (26),[2] a compendium or encyclopædia of the spiritual life of a man of genius (78). All the novels of any single author are in one sense only *a single Roman*, and it is

---

[1] *CuR.*, p. 217.

[2] Numbers refer to those of the fragments in *MS.* Bd. ii, pp. 183 ff.

superfluous to write more than one, unless the author has become a new man (89).

Though they name neither Goethe nor any of his works, these fragments were written during the time in which Goethe's *Wilhelm Meister* seemed the greatest product of all recent literature, and are so many fragmentary characterizations of it. However, we are not left without direct evidence that these are chips from the workshop of a man who is carving out æsthetic doctrines from the materials of Goethe's novel.

In No. 124, Friedrich defines rhyme as "symmetrische Wiederkehr des Gleichen," and names as an example the scene in *Wilhelm Meister* where the old Barbara sets the bottle of champagne and three glasses on the table before Wilhelm.

In No. 120 occurs the famous dictum: "Wer Goethens *Meister* gehörig charakterisierte, der hätte damit wohl eigentlich gesagt, was es jetzt an der Zeit ist in der Poesie. Er dürfte sich, was poetische Kritik betrifft, immer zur Ruhe setzen."

No. 20, with its statement that a classic product must never be fully intelligible, refers specifically to *Wilhelm Meister*. Other fragments refer to Goethe's other works, or to himself as an artist. One defends him against charges of metrical carelessness (6). Another refers to him as a "Kunstwerk der Natur" (1). Nothing is more *piquant* than a genius who has mannerisms, that is, provided they do not possess him—which is often affirmed of Goethe (88). "Welches ist denn nun die poetische Poesie?" he asks in No. 120, and certainly implies the answer, "Goethe's."

Of all modern poets Goethe alone is mentioned with favor in the whole collection. Bodmer is jested at. Lessing is mentioned twice. The rest are passed over in silence.

But Friedrich's position in Jena had by this time become *impossible*. Berlin, with its small "Goethe-gemeinde" in the midst of overwhelming rationalism, seemed the most favorable spot for his further activities. He would beard the lion in his den, attack the "Aufklärungs-Berlinismus" and its representative, Nikolai, in its own stronghold. Before leaving Jena, he had the great honor of meeting Goethe. We find in Goethe's journal under date of June 10, "Mit Friedrich Schlegel spazieren." But the two did not enter into relations approaching in degree of familiarity even the rather exoteric friendliness which existed in 1800.

3. *Berlin.*

a. *Athenäum,* Vol. I.

All in all the first Jena period was one of personal failure and of no adequate literary success on Friedrich's part. His choice of Reichardt as publisher would not have recommended him in Weimar and Jena, if he had published nothing but Greek studies. That he became his publisher's ready tool in attacking the classic poets, and published those ill-advised reviews of the *Musenalmanache* and the *Horen,* led to a complete rupture with Schiller, which closed the columns of the *Horen* to August Wilhelm and made open friendly relations with Goethe impossible. Goethe and Schiller soon had the satisfaction of seeing Friedrich at odds with Reichardt—a fulfilment of their prophecy.

As a result, our literary and critical dictators were placed in a difficult situation both financially and in respect to a medium for their ideas. Friedrich was especially hurt by the loss of a publisher. August Wilhelm had still the *Jen. Lit. Zeitung* for his short critical reviews, but there existed no medium so profitable or so exclusive and select as the *Horen* to which he might turn for his more pretentious literary efforts. Under these circumstances it is not strange that they thought seriously of founding a new journal. Since Friedrich's situation was the more galling, it was but natural that he should be the leading spirit in urging on the enterprise, determining its character, and, in fact, editing it after it was founded.

The first of August, 1797, finds Friedrich Schlegel in Berlin. He is soon introduced into the best literary society. He meets Schleiermacher, who is also an exponent of radicalism and reform in the spirit of Berlin enlightenment. Through this friend Schlegel gets an introduction into the salon of Henriette Herz and is thus brought into contact with the celebrities of the day. Friedrich's personal appearance had something imposing in it, and his erudition and wit, and his reputation as a eulogist of Goethe soon made him the acknowledged leader and spokesman of the "Goethegemeinde" in Berlin. This social round and dining-out was unfavorable to literary production. Financial pressure made it impossible to continue his Greek works to completion. Besides he had now a decided distaste for them. Therefore he rounded them off perfunctorily and published them as fragments, in order to devote himself to the new journal.

After almost interminable discussion, the nature of the journal, its size and frequency of issue, the rate of payment, the mutual power of veto, the advisability of admitting other contributors, etc., etc., are determined, and whether it shall see the light as an accomplished fact, depends largely upon Friedrich's capacity to produce sufficient literary material himself or to stimulate August Wilhelm to its production. This new *Hercules* of the literary world, a mere *Schlegeleum* in substance, is to appear before the public with the presumptious title of *Athenäum*.[1]

---

[1] All these names were proposed and considered before finally adopting the last.

The literary position of the *Athenäum* for the time being is clearly shown by the materials which are to fill the first two numbers. There is to be a *Characterization of Wilhelm Meister*; a mass of *Fragments* full of Goethe and *Universalpoesie*; an essay on Goethe's lyric poetry and *Reineke Fuchs*;[1] Novalis' *Blütenstaub* is to appear with its proclamation of Goethe as "der wahre Stadthalter des poetischen Geistes auf Erden;" August Wilhelm is to proclaim Goethe's *prose style* and his "goldenes Märchen" or "Märchen *par excellence*," also Goethe's mediatorial function in German studies of Shakespeare. It is plain that the *Athenäum* was intended to establish a literary school on the basis of Goethe's poetry.

This relation to Goethe is further shown by various passages in the letters of Friedrich to August Wilhelm. The latter fears that Goethe may take offense at certain fragments, but Friedrich replies that Goethe's feelings cannot be considered if they are to remain true to their fundamental principle. They might be silent, but unfortunately the offending fragment is already printed.[2] August Wilhelm's marginal notes to the collection of Friedrich's fragments are significant. "Goethe wird lächeln," "Goethe wird die Stirn runzeln," etc. But Friedrich will not strike out a fragment from such motives.[3]

Minor calls attention to the prominent influence which Goethe's *Propyläen* had upon the form and substance of the *Athenäum*, and especially points out Goethe's fondness for the form of correspondence, conversation, etc., and the *Kunstnovelle*, as the inspiration to similar forms in the *Athenäum*.[4] We need only add that these influences scarcely affect the first two numbers.

---

[1] *WSBr.*, p. 353.

[2] *Ibid.*, pp. 361 f., also p. 372.   Cf. Preface to *Ath.*, vol. 1.

[3] *Ibid.*, p. 373.   [4] *CuR.*, p. 218.

a. Fragmente.

If we except the prose comments on his brother's translations of fragments of Greek elegies, the *Fragmente* are Friedrich's first contribution.   Their anonymity, their joint authorship, the intention of the brothers to assume the responsibility jointly (since they enjoyed the right of mutual veto), their effort to establish a school by polemic against *Aufklärung*, all point to direct kinship with the *Xenia*.   If Friedrich had had poetic talent, there is little doubt that these fragments would have become a collection of elegiac distichs.   We shall accept as Friedrich's contributions those fragments not credited to any other contributor by Minor.[1]

Goethe is not directly mentioned in many places.   In one fragment his world-historic position is fixed : "die Französische Revoluzion, Fichte's *Wissenschaftslehre*, und Goethes *Meister* sind die grössten Tendenzen des Zeitalters" (216).[2]   In another Goethe is ranked with Dante and Shakespeare, and all three are "der grosse Dreiklang der modernen Poesie."   Goethe's poetry is "reine poetische Poesie" and "die vollständigste Poesie der Poesie" (247).   In No. 228 *Transcendentalpoesie* is defined in terms that are plainly derived from Schiller.   It begins as *satire* with the absolute difference of the ideal and the real, hovers as *elegy* in the middle, and ends as the *idyl* with the absolute identity of both the ideal and the real.[3]   But to this it must add a constant self-characterization, "eine schöne Selbstbespiegelung," as in *Wilhelm Meister* particularly.   Goethe alone

---

[1] In *MS.* those fragments known to be from other authors than Friedrich are printed in smaller type.

[2] Numerals refer to numbers in *MS.* Bd. II, pp. 203 ff.

[3] Cf. Schiller's *Naïve und Sentimentalische Dichtung*, paragraphs on the Satire, the Elegy, and the Idyl.

among moderns produces this *Transcendentalpoesie.* Goethe's ballads, especially the *Braut von Korinth,* are made the text of a long fragment on the poetic *Märchen,* which must be infinitely bizarre, yet bewitch the mind and charm the soul (429).

These are all the direct utterances, unless No. 193 is the joint product of the brothers.

But before we discuss the æsthetic doctrines contained in the rest of these fragments, we must consider Friedrich's essay on *Wilhelm Meister,* which, as we saw, was to be in itself a sort of æsthetic compendium.

b. Wilhelm Meister.

Friedrich follows the development of the first and second books with a deep interest in the scenes and characters, but he keeps a keen eye for the poet's mysterious purposes, of which there are many more than we commonly think.

The whole work is *organic.* Not a pause is accidental or insignificant, he says. Everything is means and goal. Thus the first part can be considered as a unit in itself. Its subject-matter is *art.* It is "poetische Physik der Poesie," and was originally intended to be a didactic poem on art. The drama is selected as its central theme, because it alone of all the arts is social and many-sided enough to form the basis of a *Roman.* Nevertheless, it is not merely an historical philosophy of art, but in itself "reine hohe Poesie." Its author is at the same time a divine poet and perfect artist, and every slight feature of even secondary parts seems to enjoy an independent objective existence even to the extent of contradicting the laws of probability. And such wonderful prose! And everywhere golden fruits are offered in silver vessels.

One must not assume that the poet is not in earnest because he scarcely ever mentions his hero without irony

and because he seems to smile down upon his own masterpiece from the serene heights of his spirit. In fact one must
not judge by ordinary standards "*dieses schlechthin neue und
einzige Buch, welches man nur aus sich selbst verstehen lernen
kann.*" It cannot even be reviewed like an ordinary book.
It must be read and *felt.*

It disappoints the ordinary expectations of unity as often
as it fulfills them, but it has a living personality for him
who has "Sinn für das Universum." The deeper his investigations, the more spiritual unity it has.

However, the beginning and the end are not completely in
harmony, however deeply studied. Credit what one may to
the justifiable effect of "das Göttliche der gebildeten Willkür" there still remains something isolated in the *Roman.*
"Es fehlt eben die letzte Verknüpfung der Gedanken und
der Gefühle."

This is no serious fault. Like the Iliad, *Wilhelm Meister*
is a great whole made up of lesser wholes whose unity is
greater than that of the entire work. It is a mistake to
demand unity in the whole and to lose one's self in the infinitely little in studying the faulty articulation of the parts.
Each book opens a new scene and a new world, elaborates
the materials of the preceding and contains the germs of the
succeeding.

In the third book everything is comic. "Die Ironie
schwebt über dem ganzen Werke." Schlegel mentions also
"ein sich selbst belächelnder Schein von Würde und Bedeut-
samkeit." Other instances of irony are Jarno's want of
imagination and Aurelia's lack of judgment and sense of the
appropriate. These "Verstandesmenschen" are shown in
their limitations to indicate that the whole book is not a
mere eulogy on the "Verstand," as it might seem at first.

The *Hamlet* criticism represents an essential step in Wilhelm's artistic development. The striking adaptability of

the characters to assume the various *rôles* of *Hamlet* is emphasized, but the whole fifth book sinks below the level of the whole *Roman*, with the exception of *Mignon* in the *rôle* of Mænad.

Even the "*Bekenntnisse einer schönen Seele*," in spite of the unexampled arbitrariness of Goethe in inserting them as a chapter, are justified by Schlegel.   They are the history of an actress who decks out her *Gemüt* and plays all parts before the mirror of conscience.   They form a picture of the inner life contrasted with the outer life of other portions, and are therefore necessary to the universality of the work.   They represent religion becoming an art, and so accord with the spirit of the whole.   Besides, the "schöne Seele" herself belongs to the ancestral stock of the family with which Wilhelm is to be allied.

This whole chapter so resembles a portrait that Schlegel wishes to rescue it from the charge of unideality, by asserting that all characters of the *Roman* are similarly drawn, all being objective and realistic, but that at the same time all are fundamentally *allegoric*·and *universal*.

In the fourth volume, he says, the *Roman* comes of age. It passes from a mere treatise on the theatre into the great drama of humanity itself, from a mere treatise on art into the art of all arts, "die Kunst zu leben," and gives us the solid results of a philosophy founded upon a noble spirit and a striving for the sublime universality of human forces and arts.   Wilhelm's apprenticeship is now over, he resigns his will, and "Natalie wird Supplement des Romans."

The women, Natalie and Theresa, are examples from which a perfect theory of womanhood might be derived, namely by combining the two into one personality, and then characterizing her.

Schlegel excuses as a poetic license on a grand scale the employment of the secret society as an agency in Wilhelm's development.

The principal characters are now treated.   The uncle and
the *abbé* are the two mighty pillars upon which rests the
heaven-piercing cupola, Lothario, the one perfect character.
These three architectonic natures embrace and sustain the
whole edifice.   The other characters are mere images and
decorations of the temple.   They interest the intellect, but
for the *Gemüt* they are mere allegorical puppets.   Not so,
however, Mignon, Sperata, and Augustino, " die heilige
Familie der Naturpoesie, welche dem Ganzen romantischen
Zauber und Musik geben, und im Übermass ihrer eigenen
Seelengluth zu Grunde gehen."

Thus in brief what Schlegel saw in *Wilhelm Meister* at this
time.   Only in his characterizations of Goethe and Sophocles
in the *Studium* and in his review of *Alexis und Dora* does
he approach this fine enthusiasm, this high tone of unmixed
eulogy, this warmth and partisanship which justifies even
grave artistic faults and weaknesses.   Everything appears
here " göttlich, gelassen und rein."

I. *Theories of Romantic Art, etc.*

We now turn to the romantic doctrines as propounded in
more or less chaotic fashion in the Fragments of the *Athenäum*.   Haym has worked out this problem with considerable
fulness and essential correctness.[1]

A fundamental change of attitude has been produced by
the constant reading of *Wilhelm Meister*.   Just as Friedrich
went from Goethe's *Iphigenie* to the study of the Greeks, so
now he is brought face to face with a new problem of art in
Goethe's *Roman*.   All Hellenistic ideas of purity of form are
contradicted by this book.   It is a new creation of genius.
It could not occur to our critic to condemn the new work

---

[1] *HRS., Drittes Kapitel*, pp. 235 ff.

because of its transgression of old rules. Goethe's genius
was above rules. Hence this book was a new *fact* in art, a
new species of literature, and its rules must be deduced from
a study of itself (*v. supra*). In No. 252 the position of the
Roman is made to correspond with Schiller's ideal of the final
perfected sentimental poetry, or with Schlegel's own conception of the union of the essentially antique with the essentially modern. The *Roman* represents the final harmony of
Kunst and *Natur*.

The absorbing study of *Wilhelm Meister* led soon to the
identification of the *Roman* with poetry *per se*. This was
but a step. Assuming once that the *Roman* represents the
final triumph of modern art in its progress toward objectivity,
classicism, nature, this type of art must be greater than the
classics, greater than the modern masterpieces. It must be
all-inclusive, and supersede all lesser, partial forms of art,
however justifiable at stages preceding the *Roman* era.
Hence a proper characterization of the *Roman*, especially
of *Wilhelm Meister*, the great original of the class, must
result in a complete doctrine of poetry itself.[1] Many of the
Athenäum fragments are simply parts of this necessary
characterization. Compare Nos. 111, 116, 118, 139, 146,
216, 238, 252, 255, 297, 434, and 451.

No. 116 is the classic programmatic fragment for the
æsthetic doctrines of Friedrich Schlegel. "Die romantische
Poesie ist eine progressive Universalpoesie." "Romantische
Poesie" is simply *Roman* poetry.[2] If the *Roman* is once
identified with the final harmony of *Kunstpoesie* and *Naturpoesie* it becomes an absolutely unattainable ideal goal. All
art must constantly approach it. Hence the term *progressiv*.
There will be perhaps "ein unübersteiglich fixes Proximum"
somewhere. For Friedrich this is temporarily *Wilhelm Mei-*

---

[1] *V. supra.*, *Lyc. Frag.*, No. 120.   [2] *HRS.*, p. 252.

ster. But he dreams of advances even beyond this.   If its genius had found perfect expression everywhere, if the pure spirit of *Wilhelm Meister* had attained a perfect form, that would have been absolute poetry.   Since the absolute can have no varieties, no national subdivisions, no racial differentiations, no temporal modifications, this absolute poetry must be *Universalpoesie.*

What follows in this fragment is at the same time a characterization of *Wilhelm Meister* and a deduction from the ideal universal poetry.   "Ihre Bestimmung ist nicht bloss alle getrennten Gattungen der Poesie wieder zu vereinigen, und die Poesie mit der Philosophie und der Rhetorik in Berührung zu setzen.   Sie will und soll auch *Poesie und Prosa, Genialität und Kritik,* Kunstpoesie und Naturpoesie bald mischen, bald verschmelzen, *die Poesie lebendig und gesellig,* und *das Leben und die Gesellschaft poetisch* machen, den Witz poetisiren, und die Formen der Kunst *mit gediegenem Bildungsstoff jeder Art* anfüllen und sättigen, und *durch die Schwingungen des Humors* beseelen.   Sie *umfasst alles, was nur poetisch ist,* vom grössten wieder mehre Systeme in sich enthaltenden Systeme der Kunst bis zu dem Seufzer, dem Kuss, den das dichtende Kind aushaucht in kunstlosem Gesang.   Sie kann sich so in das Dargestellte verlieren, dass man glauben möchte, *poetische Individuen jeder Art zu charakterisieren sei ihr eins und alles :* und doch giebt es keine Form, die so dazu gemacht wäre, *den Geist des Autors vollständig auszudrücken :* so dass manche Künstler, die nur auch einen *Roman* schreiben wollten, von ungefähr sich selbst dargestellt haben." [1]

Unity of spirit as against unity of form, unity of lesser parts as against unity of the whole are qualities common to Homer's epic and Goethe's *Roman,* as we have seen.

---

[1] Cf. also *Lyc. Frag.,* p. 89.

Romantic poetry alone can become a mirror of the world and the age. This is a third Homeric element of the new doctrine, and is also brought in *via Meister*. But the philosophic, reflective character of ideal poetry separates it heaven-wide from the Homeric epic. This is formulated into a demand for "Potenzierung der poetischen Reflexion." No. 255 likewise insists : "Der Dichter muss über seine Kunst philosophieren." Nothing is more apparent than that this is derived from Goethe's practice in *Wilhelm Meister*, and however absurd the demand that this involution shall proceed to such lengths that the work of art becomes an infinite series of mirrors of itself and its mirrorings *ad infinitum*, it is meant to find its justification in Goethe's *Roman*. This is clear from the characterization of Goethe's poetry as "Poesie der Poesie" (247), which is the first stage of "Potenzierung." Schlegel's peculiar habit of reflecting and then reflecting upon the reflection, and upon this second reflection, etc., until all feeling was dead and forgotten, is responsible for most of the fantastic folly of the romantic doctrines. Fichte had furnished a philosophy of philosophy, Goethe a poetry of poetry, and Schlegel himself a critique of criticism. Haym finds in this involution doctrine a transference of Fichte's philosophy into romantic æsthetics, but Goethe's poetry is always the "Anschauung" which gives fulness to the "Begriff." Fichte's philosophy may be a secondary influence, but self-reflection of poetry, as a doctrine, rests primarily upon Goethe's practice in the *Roman*.

All parts of a romantic whole must be capable of infinite development not only from within but from without. It need only organize the parts similarly, and like the Homeric epic and the Goethean *Roman* it has thereby a prospect of "grenzenlos wachsende Klassizität." In fact, the great advantage of romantic poetry is that it is always "im Werden," and never, like other kinds, "fertig." It is inexhaustible by any theory, infinite, free, and its first law is "dass die Willkür des Dichters kein Gesetz über sich leide." This is just what is definitely affirmed in the *Übermeister* of the author of *Wilhelm Meister*. The poet's *Willkür* is his highest law.

Other fragments contain parallels to these doctrines, or are partial characterizations of Goethe's works, or are suggested by them. When Friedrich demands that everything in a poem shall be both end and means, he has the *Meister* in mind as his ideal (117). No. 297 was written with the hero of this *Roman* in mind. It is Meister's education which is characterized. The list of fragments closes with an ideal of universality which seems an attempt at climax, a proclamation, not merely of the harmony of *Kunstpoesie* and *Naturpoesie* which he found in Goethe's art, but of the final synthesis of poetry and philosophy which is elsewhere expressed as the synthesis of Goetheanism and Fichteanism.

II. *Ironie.*

One other doctrine of the new school may as well be considered here—the doctrine of *Irony*. Here again Haym has given us the essentials in respect to the development of the theory, and its place in romantic æsthetics. He shows in the use of this term a development parallel to that of the term *romantic*, and refers the latter stages of the development to the influence of Fichte's idealism. We need only add the caution that these philosophic influences should not be assumed as beginning very early. They were scarcely felt while Schlegel wrote his *Übermeister*, for the use of the term *irony* is there generally in accordance with the ordinary significance of the word. Yet the thing which is afterwards called *irony* is felt and expressed in different terms. For the time being Goethe's *Meister* is the great *Anschauung* which led Schlegel to develop the idea of irony in the æsthetic field, and Goethe himself is the great art-Proteus, whom he idealizes in the fragment which characterizes the cultured man as able to put himself into any mood at will (*Lyc. Frag.* 55). When he says that the only philosophy remaining for the poet is "der schaffende," which originates in freedom and the belief in freedom, which shows that the human spirit impresses its law upon all things, and that the world is its art-product, he is thinking as much or more of the poet Goethe than of the philosopher Fichte. Schlegel says that *irony* has its home in philosophy. This is an afterthought. But for Goethe's poetic product, it is doubtful whether the developed doctrine of irony would ever have left the strict confines of its "home" and become colonized in "poetics." The earlier phases of this doctrine are distinctly literary, and are developed from Goethe's *Meister* and the dialoges of Socrates.

c. Goethe's Reception of the Athenäum.

The first number of the *Athenäum* was to be sent by Vieweg to Goethe on April 29. Goethe seems not to have left any record of the receipt of this copy, though he certainly received it in due time. Schiller received his copy on May 15, but did not look through it at once.[1] Goethe expresses no opinion of this first number. Its contents were almost wholly from the pen of August Wilhelm, and showed him in no radically new light. The reviews had a note of independence due to the fact that he was writing for his own journal. The literary quality was above the average and the whole stood quite plainly "im Zeichen Goethes." However, it was not likely to make any stir in the literary world.

---

[1] *GSBr.*, May 15, 1798.

The second number of the *Athenäum*, which was to be issued simultaneously with the first, was delayed until July. Schiller received a copy late in the month. On the 23rd he writes to Goethe: "Was sagen Sie zum neuen Schlegel'schen *Athenäum*, und besonders zu den *Fragmenten?* Mir macht diese naseweise, entscheidende, schneidende und einseitige Manier physisch wehe."[1]

Two days later Goethe replies in favorable terms: "Das Schlegel'sche Ingredienz in seiner ganzen Individualität scheint mir denn doch in der *olla potrida* unsres deutschen Journalwesens nicht zu verachten. Diese allgemeine Nichtigkeit, Parteisucht fürs äusserst Mittelmässige, diese Augendienerei, diese Katzenbuckelgebärden, diese Leerheit und Lahmheit, in der die wenigen guten Produkte sich verlieren, hat an einem solchen Wespenneste, wie die Fragmente sind, einen furchtbaren Gegner .... Bei allem was Ihnen daran mit Recht misfällt kann man denn doch den Verfassern einen gewissen Ernst, eine gewisse Tiefe, und von der andern Seite Liberalität nicht ableugnen. Ein Dutzend solcher Stücke wird zeigen wie reich und wie perfektibel sie sind."[2]

On the 27th Schiller admits the earnestness and depth, but declares that the good loses its worth and utility by mixture with egotistical and repulsive elements. It is incredible that such persons as the Schlegels can have any real appreciation for Goethe's works, while their own show nothing but "Dürre, Trockenheit und sachlose Wortstrenge," "herzlose Kälte." They are not to be defended on the ground that they are fighting the enemies of Weimar classicism, because their excesses, their folly "wirft auf die gute Sache selbst einen fast lächerlichen Schein."[3]

---

[1] *Ibid.*, July 23, 1798. [2] *Ibid.*, July 25, 1798.
[3] *Ibid.*, July 27, 1798.

'On the following day Goethe refers all further discussion to conversation. He would like to go through the Fragments with Schiller and discuss them.[1] This wish was fulfilled. In Goethe's journal under date of August 1, 1798, we find the record: "Bei Herrn Hofrath Schiller, über litterarische und poetische Angelegenheiten, besonders die Schlegel betreffend." No record tells us what the nature of this colloquy was or with what understanding it closed. It did close the incident, however, for no reference to the Schlegels occurs in their letters until March, 1799, when *Athenäum*, Vol. II, came to hand.

Goethe's interest in the *Athenäum* is testified to in the correspondence of Caroline,[2] who reports Goethe's efforts in behalf of the new Journal. These efforts were due to Böttiger's attempt to discredit the *Athenäum* on its first appearance.[3] Goethe felt justified in preferring the Schlegels' journalistic method to that of his old enemy *Ubique*; and Friedrich professed to be content.[4]

β. *Athenäum*, Vol. II.

The second volume, No. 1, is largely the product of August Wilhelm, Caroline, and Hülsen. Friedrich contributes only *Über die Philosophie: an Dorothea*, and some notices of Schleiermacher's *Reden über die Religion* and Tieck's translation of *Don Quixote*. The latter do not concern us here.

In the opening essay, *Über die Philosophie*, Friedrich makes his first public utterances on philosophy and religion in somewhat more connected form. Certain fragments had treated Christianity as a form of religion, some had insisted upon the necessity of uniting philosophy and poetry in order to realize the highest culture, the eternal unity of life. But

---

[1] *Ibid.*, July 28, 1798.   [2] *WCBr.*, Bd. I, pp. 215 f.
[3] *GSBr.*, July 25, 1798.   [4] *WSBr.*, p. 396.

now for the first time does the religious idea assume importance and demand a place in his system. This is the first fruit of his association with Schleiermacher.

The form of the essay is that of a letter addressed to Dorothea Veit, who was soon to become the consort of Friedrich, the muse of the *Lucinde,* and the faithful sharer of the wanderings and burdens of his checkered existence.

His first thesis is that the only *virtue* of woman is *religion.* This can be attained only through *philosophy.* Religion is, however, simply an instinct for divinity.

The works of Goethe shimmer through here and there. Almost in the beginning we have an earnest protest against *moral* education *à la* Goethe's old Italian in *Wilhelm Meister,* and then with conscious (?) characterization of the career of Meister, he adds : " Die Tugend lässt sich nicht lehren und lernen, ausser durch Freundschaft und Liebe mit tüchtigen und wahren Menschen und durch Umgang mit uns selbst, mit den Göttern in uns."

The world's idea of manhood and womanhood is like that of Sophie in the *Mitschuldigen.* " Es ist ein schlechter Mensch, allein es ist ein Mann." The true ideal of man and woman should subordinate sex characteristics to the higher elements of humanity. Man should become " sanft," and woman " selbständig."

In woman divinity and animality are perfectly blended. It is her function to bring harmony into life. This faculty of bringing harmony into life's discords is the faculty of religion, or rather *religion* itself. Here again Friedrich's words assume a strong likeness to the catechetic scene in *Faust.* " Wenn man göttlich denkt und dichtet und lebt, wenn man voll von Gott ist, wenn ein Hauch von Andacht und Begeistrung über unser ganzes Sein ausgegossen ist," then is one truly religious, and acts no longer from a sense of duty, but from love, because the God within him commands, and he wills it because God commands.

Poetry and philosophy are the paths which lead to this communion with the *Universe*. Dorothea stands like Hercules, or Wilhelm Meister at the parting of the ways, doubtful which to choose.

She does not enjoy pure poetry. She makes it a complement of life, enjoys the godlike thoughts and not the beauty *per se*. In reading Goethe's works she seeks this great content and not pure poetic form.[1] The purpose of poetry is to make our spirit at one with nature, philosophy is related to God. Poetry is concrete, philosophy abstract. Abstractions are divine because purified from all earthly reference. By abstraction the gods were made out of men. We see in the background of these contrasts Goethe and the Greeks for poetry, Fichte and Plato for philosophy. And when Schlegel adds, "Poesie und Philosophie sind ein untheilbares Ganzes, ewig verbunden," we have an expression of his highest humanitarian ideal, the union of Goetheanism and Fichteanism, which is *religion*.

Of course woman *has* poetry, and therefore *needs* philosophy as her only means of attaining the highest life. Schlegel proposes himself as a popular interpreter and complementer of all past and extant philosophical systems. His philosophy he calls a philosophy for *Humanity*, and it has three cardinal principles: (1) The infinity of the human spirit, (2) the divinity of all natural things, and (3) the humanity of the gods. This betrays again the Goethean and Fichtean elements, though other systems contribute elements to the proposed hodge-podge of ideas.

Goethe's only reference to this number of the *Athenäum* is in a letter to Schiller, March 9, 1799, in which he expresses in general terms considerable interest.[2] This number contained the fine *Gemäldegespräche* by August Wilhelm, and

---

[1] *RDBr., Tagebuch für 1802.*   [2] *GSBr.*, March 9, 1799.

it was this which so held the poet's interest, for Goethe thanked the elder brother in person at Jena for this number.[1]

Goethe had no sympathy with the idea of womanhood in Friedrich's essay. He had no sympathy with the elevation of abstractions above concrete ideals, of philosophy above poetry. Elements of attraction there were without doubt. The emphatic individualism was perhaps one. As Goethe greeted Schleiermacher's *Reden* with favor, so he may have felt an interest in the similar tendency of Schlegel's essay. The bold proposal to interpret all systems of philosophy may have led to the few *colloquia* of the following year.

On August 10, the fourth number was sent to Jena, thus completing the volume for 1799. On August 16, Schiller writes to Goethe calling attention to the *Reichsanzeiger* (which was modeled on the *Xenia*), blaming the whole tone and especially the abuse of Schlegel's own friends. "Man sieht aufs neue daraus, dass sie im Grunde doch nichts taugen." August Wilhelm's *Elegy to Goethe* is a good but not faultless work, etc.[2]

Goethe's reply of the next day runs: "Wegen des Schlegelschen Streifzugs bin ich ganz Ihrer Meinung." We will not quote the whole, but two passages are particularly important. "Leider mangelt es beiden Brüdern an einem gewissen innern Halt, der sie zusammenhalte und festhalte. Ein Jugendfehler ist nicht liebenswürdig als insofern er hoffen lässt, dass er nicht Fehler des Alters sein werde." This passage can have no point unless Goethe felt that the faults of the Schlegels were fundamental and incorrigible. "Uebrigens lässt sich auch im persönlichen Verhältnis keineswegs hoffen, dass man gelegentlich ungerupft von ihnen wegkommen werde. Doch will ich es ihnen lieber verzeihen,

---

[1] *GWke.*, Abt. IV, Bd. 14, p. 54; Goethe to A. W. Schlegel, March 26, 1799.

[2] *GSBr.*, August 16, 1799.

wenn sie etwas versetzen sollten, als die infame Manier der Meister in der Journalistik." [1]   This passage has reference to past reviews of Friedrich as well as to present and prospective impertinences, and shows again the ground of preference for the *Athenäum* over Böttiger's journal, etc. This is thus an example of Goethe's "Beförderung dessen, was ich nicht mochte." [2]   More than a feeling of militant comradeship against common foes can hardly be inferred from the above passages.

That Schiller was correct in assigning the *Xenia* as the model for the *Anzeiger* is clear.   That they were models for satiric fragments of *Athenäum*, vol. I, is shown by August Wilhelm's fears lest they provoke parodies on all hands, by Friedrich's designation of the fragment on Wieland as *Xeniastisch*, and by August's characterization of them all as "eine sthenische Diät" and "gepfefferte Kritiken." [3]

a. Religion and Morals; Ideen.

Before leaving Berlin to return to Jena, Friedrich took on a new phase of thought, the religious one, which remained with him more or less to the end of his life.

Friedrich Schlegel was not naturally and temperamentally religious.   His earliest expressions show him to be *practically* atheistic.   All conventional conceptions of God are given up.   His ideal is to be his own God.   Culture of the individual, "sich ausleben," is his ethical ideal.   Morals of a revolutionary kind find occasional expression, but religion receives scarcely a word of mention in all his early correspondence.   This fact is recognized by Haym, and by

---

[1] *Ibid.*, August 17, 1799.
[2] Goethe to Zelter, *v. supra*, note 2, p. 43.
[3] *WSBr.*, p. 349 ; *Xenien*, Nos. 364, 365 ; *RNBr.*, p. 97.

Dilthey. Even Ricarda Huch, the enthusiastic interpreter
and apologist of romanticism, admits that self-interest and
not conviction led Friedrich to the Roman fold.

His earliest religious convictions are mere theories about
religion, received from Kant and Fichte, and the religious
confessions of the poets, chiefly of Goethe. We can affirm
without hesitation that a natural undisturbed evolution of
Schlegel's soul would never have produced a system of
religious convictions or led to a life of religious observances.
The same may be said of several external influences, his
Hellenism, and Goethe-worship. Even Fichte can have
aroused only a *theoretic* interest in conceptions of God. But
now Friedrich was brought into intimate association with
two men who were to affect romanticism profoundly, Hardenberg and Schleiermacher. To Schleiermacher's personal
influence and his *Reden* may be accorded the primacy in this
revolution. Hardenberg's naïvely religious soul influenced
him secondarily.

The philosophic aspects of the religious problem and its
practical bearings on the whole romantic movement had
been already impressed upon the brothers by the difficulties
of Fichte in Jena. In the spring of 1799,[1] Friedrich feels
that Fichte's cause is theirs also, and proposes to write a
brochure in order to prove that Fichte had *discovered
religion*. August Wilhelm encourages him,[2] but a restraining force is the fear that such a publication might affect
unfavorably his position in Jena, so near to Weimar, and to
Goethe, whose influence had been paramount in the acceptance
of Fichte's resignation.[3] By May 7, 1799, we have the
remarkable passage in which Friedrich proposes *to found
a new religion*, which is to be the greatest birth of modern
times, a movement which shall swallow up the French

---

[1] *Ibid.*, p. 416. [2] *RNBr.*, January 12, 1799.
[3] *WSBr.*, p. 416.

revolution, as primitive Christianity engulfed the Roman empire.[1]

To a man gifted with so fertile a "Theorieneierstock," who considered world-revolutions as possible as a general change of opinions in himself, this seemed probable enough.

Hardenberg, the born mystic, *had* religion, and was to be the *Christ* of the new religion. Schleiermacher and Goethe were the concrete examples of its ethical counterpart, and Schlegel himself assumed the office of *Paul* of the new propaganda.

There were various reasons why Schlegel should choose this part, (1) his mere love of theorizing, (2) his need of fruitful literary materials, and (3) his overweening desire of leadership in the *whole* romantic movement, which at this moment began to include religion as well as philosophy and aesthetics. Friedrich proposed to produce a Bible for the new evangel, but in this he became utterly unintelligible to his *Christ*, and his fragmentary nature overcame his resolution.

In the meantime a series of fragments must constitute the new religious doctrines, just as the preceding *Athenäum* fragments were to constitute the æsthetic doctrines of a new school. These *Ansichten* (afterwards published as *Ideen*) were begun in August, 1799.

How the problem appeared to Schlegel at this time may be seen from his correspondence with Hardenberg. His Bible was to be "klassische Urbilder" such as the Greeks were for poetry, according to Goethe's practice. The new religion was not to swallow up philosophy and poetry. These *Urkünste* were to remain independently existing, justified in thus existing, though it was time they should exchange many of their qualities. The chief merit of Kant and

---

[1] *Ibid.*, p. 421. Cf. also *Ideen*, No. 94; *Ath.*, III, 1800.

Fichte is that they lead philosophy merely to the threshold
of religion and then stop. Goethe's culture enters into the
Propyläen of the temple from the opposite side. How
unite them? By religion which enters the temple itself.
"Giebt die Synthesis von Goethe und Fichte wohl etwas
anders als Religion?" Their separation in life is purely
personal and due to the improper relations of both to their
age.[1]

But to see further how he conceives this synthesis of
Goethe and Fichte we must examine the *Ideen* of *Athenäum*,
vol. III, for 1800, though it seems to involve a violation
of our chronological study.

"Die Religion ist die all-belebende Weltseele der Bildung, das vierte unsichtbare Element zur Philosophie,
Moral und Poesie" (4).[2] These four elements are inseparable, but not of equal rank (89). Philosophy and poetry
must recognize their subordination to religion (42), for they
are but different factors of religion (46). Poetry contributes
to religion *Fülle der Bildung*, and philosophy *Tiefe der
Menschheit* (57). Morals are also subordinate to religion
(173). Religion and morals are symmetrically opposite,
just as theory and *Anschauung* (67) or as human and divine
things (110). Like religion, morals depends upon philosophy and poetry (62). Philosophy gives the *theory* of
humanity, poetry the *intuition* of life in its fulness and
ideal harmony. Religion is simply the pure theory of ideal
humanity become fact in concrete life, with all its attendant
feeling.

Philosophy is pure idealism. Poetry possesses the only
realism. Until these are united there are no perfectly
cultured individuals and no true religion (96). Religion
cannot be induced by destruction of either of its elements.

---

[1] *RNBr.*, December 2, 1788. Fr. Schlegel to Novalis.
[2] Numerals refer to the numbers of the *Ideen* in *MS*.

Destruction of the philosophers and poets destroys religion itself (90).

"Jede Beziehung des Menschen aufs Unendliche ist Religion, nämlich *des Menschen in der ganzen Fülle seiner Menschheit*" (81). Here is a distinct Goethean element, this demand for the whole man. Schlegel's God is not Fichte's moral order of the universe, but "das Unendliche in jener Fülle gedacht, ist die Gottheit" (81). The deity is still "gedacht." The reality of the universe is the reality which results from its inherent necessity in the subject, as with Fichte. As with Fichte, too, the world of the great poets of Weimar-Jena is the fullest and most original expression of the universe so posited,—the best example of "das Unendliche in jener Fülle gedacht." But unlike Fichte, Schlegel has no moral rigorism.

Different imperfect individuals will have different types of religion (137). "Der religiöse Zustand des Poeten ist leidenschaftlicher und mitteilender." Compare *Faust*, catechetic scene, admired also by Fichte. To get a perfect individual we must blend individualities, as for example, all members of a family, male and female, young and old. But as this is impracticable, we must go still to the great poets. "Es giebt keine grosse Welt als die Welt der Künstler. Sie leben hohes Leben." They must be supplemented by philosophy. Nothing more can be done so long as philosophy and poetry are sundered. "Also ist die Zeit nun da beide zu vereinigen."

The essential kinship of these doctrines with Schleiermacher's religious views is apparent. The great difference theoretically is that Schlegel has a positive genius for confusion, and thus emphasizes the wholeness of the universe, the wholeness of humanity, at the expense of a clear perception of the parts and their relations. All things flow together in one and lines of demarcation are blotted out. The greatest difference from Schliermacher, however, is the insistence upon Goethean culture of the individual as an essential element of religion.

γ. *Lucinde.*

Yet another product belongs to the period in Berlin—the notorious *Lucinde.*

Schlēgel was at work upon a *Roman* as early as December, 1798. This was simply incredible to his most intimate friends. Hitherto he had been a critic and philologist, and had shown no inclination or capacity for creative art. Nevertheless the first portion of a *Roman* was sent to Jena, in January, 1799, for Caroline's critical inspection. By February 5, *Treue und Scherz,* a new chapter, is completed. Friends consider this a distinct falling off from the opening portions. This opinion does not entirely discourage him, and on March 2 he is able to announce to Schleiermacher the body of the *Roman* proper, *Lehrjahre der Männlichkeit.* By March 26, a considerable portion is already printed, but must be done over to reduce the cynicism, which Caroline found too pronounced. The first volume is complete in May, 1799. A second part is planned, but the harsh reception of the first, or his own want of talent, or a revulsion of feeling against his previous cynicism, or a combination of such causes, leads to its abandonment. Some poems, about fifty-nine in all, were produced for this second part, but the work itself never was completed. Thus we have only the fragmentary Part I of *Lucinde.*

Wilhelm Meister had been recognized as the highest type of modern art. A characterization of it had seemed equivalent to a treatise on art *per se.* Goethe had expressed approval of Friedrich's attempt to characterize it. Furthermore, a whole body of æsthetic doctrines had been derived by him from Goethe's *Roman*, and these seemed to be creating a new æsthetic school which looked to Goethe as its *god.* Friedrich felt that he had founded this school on the side of *theory*, but he himself had demanded more of a real leader. Such a leader must be both *creative* and *critical.* He must prove himself such. Hence nothing is more natural, in spite of his utterly unpoetic nature, than that he should attempt to exemplify his own doctrines in creative art. This was all the easier, since the greatest arbitrariness was permitted the poet, and since the affair with Madame Veit had awakened his enthusiasm and given his life new meaning.

Didactic poetry had been condemned in the *Studium* as purely local, like the epic, and thus unjustifiable in modern times; but the Schlegels were never anything else than didactic themselves. This led them to emphasize the didacticism of all Goethe's works, and especially of *Wilhelm Meister.* The only limitation upon didacticism in the new æsthetics, is that it must be the spirit of the whole work.[1]

The *Lucinde*, then, was first of all to be didactic. It was to found a new system of morals, just as the *Meister* of Goethe was a treatise on *Lebenskunst.*[2]

Goethe's objectivity is marked : " Er lässt die Menschen walten und hat seine Freude daran." [3] The great realist Goethe is tolerant in his morals, and pictures scenes in social life in the most daring way, without expressing any judgment upon the characters or their actions. Vischer will have it that here and there Goethe oversteps the limits of the æsthetically permissible from his delight in sexual scenes.[4] Schlegel had too distinct a theory concerning the proper sex-relations of men to women (cf. *Diotima, An Dorothea*, review

---

[1] *V. Ath. Fragment*, No. 111.   [2] *D WM.*, p. 80.

[3] *Ibid.*, p. 84.

[4] Vischer, *Kleine Beiträge zur Charakteristik Goethes. G. Jahrb.*, Bd. IV, pp. 30 ff.

of Schiller's *Würde der Frauen*, etc.) not to feel that Goethe had left here unanswered a vital problem of any true *Kunst zu leben*.[1]

The name *Lehrjahre* confesses a direct relation to Goethe's *Meister*. The new evangel is also Goethean in a general sense—*Natur*. Not in the large sense, of Nature, however. *Natur* in sex-relations is the specific theme of the *Lucinde*.

There was at that time a strong feeling among certain choice spirits that the marriage-bond, as a civil and canonical institution, was oppressive, unnatural, and altogether evil. Great laxity existed in the marriage relations at court and in all the best literary circles. The burning question was: "What is the true natural sex-relation?"

Schlegel undertook to answer it, and "das hohe Evangelium der ächten Lust und Liebe zu verkündigen." Schleiermacher's *Vertraute Briefe* give us the best insight into the intentions of the work. It is a book "wo die Liebe bis in ihre innersten Mysterien aufgesucht wird." "Die Liebe ist dem Werke alles in allem." "Die Liebe soll auferstehen . . . . und die leeren Schatten vermeinter Tugenden verdrängen." Still more definitely in a long passage in which sensuality is defended as an integral part of love, and not a necessary evil to be endured through resignation to the will of God, nor "geistlose Libertinage" to be refined and humanized. Love need not be rescued in marriage, but its parties should dare to live on with no other bond than their own "sublime geistige Gemeinschaft." The *Lucinde* fulfils Schleiermacher's yearning "die göttliche Pflanze der Liebe einmal ganz in ihrer vollständigen Gestalt abgebildet zu sehen." "Hier hast du die Liebe ganz und aus einem Stück, das geistigste und das sinnlichste . . . in jedem Zuge aufs innigste verbunden."[2]

---

[1] *DWM.*, p. 85.

[2] *SVBr.*, especially first letter to Ernestine.

Friedrich Schlegel was much pleased at his friend's fine apology, but others were still inclined to think that the *Lucinde* had merely put "*geistvolle* Libertinage" in place of the "*geistlose.*"

As a polemic against the restraints of love by the civil marriage-bond, this work was only too liable to exalt sensuality, to maintain, as Schleiermacher did in his apology, that "der Zustand des Genusses und der herrschenden Sinnlichkeit hat auch sein Heiliges," which demands equal respect with the condition of quiet reflection.

This excess of sensuality was favored by the nature of Schlegel himself. "Sinnlich bin ich sehr," he admits, but will not yield to gratification.[1] "Die Wollust liegt so tief in meiner Seele dass sie bei jeder Liebe sein wird. . . . Eine Liebe unter steter Entsagung wäre mir Qual." etc.[2] "Vielleicht bin ich *reiner* Liebe nur gegen Männer fähig."[3] Consider, too, Friedrich's sympathy with the Greek "ἑταῖραι," his boundless delight in the most sensual works of the Greeks, the loves of Daphnis and Phyllis, commented upon in *Ath.*, vol. II, his profession of love for the *man* Shakespeare on reading the *Adonis* and *Sonnets*, simply because of their erotic character,[4] his enthusiasm for Goethe's *Roman Elegies* chiefly for their erotic content.   Add to this Grillparzer's testimony, with its final charge: "Dieser Mensch könnte jetzt noch einen Ehebruch begehen, und sich völlig beruhigt fühlen, wenn er dabei nur symbolisch an die Vereinigung Christi mit der Kirche dächte."[5]

The ethical doctrine of the *Lucinde* had to suffer from this defect of its author, for he was a subjective idealist who substituted for Goethe's "das Subject *scheint* Recht zu

---

[1] *WSBr.*, p. 10.   [2] *Ibid.*, p. 63 f.   [3] *Ibid.*, p. 66.
[4] *HTBr.*, Bd. 3, p. 313 ; *Fr. Schlegel an Lud. Tieck*, July 27, 1798.
[5] *Grillparzer*, 1822, cited *BLittgesch.*, Bd. II, pp. 86 f.

haben" the positive principle "Das Subject hat Recht," namely his *own* subject, however unideal and undisciplined.

In the study of *Wilhelm Meister*, Friedrich had evolved the doctrine that all novels are *personal confessions*. The *Lucinde* is to be such also. It cannot be so complex as *Wilhelm Meister*, but it does give genuine confessions of Friedrich's experiences with a Leipzig woman, with Caroline Böhmer, Dorothea Veit, and Schleiermacher.

To do this he had to overcome personal aversion to such revelations. He was the very opposite of frankness. He objects to all this "geheime Dichtkunst." He says: "aber ich für mein Theil würde nie im Stande sein, mein *innerstes Ich*, gleichsam als eine Naturseltenheit, die in einem Naturalienkabinett verwahrt wird, den Liebhabern vorzuzeigen."[1] In a *Lyceumfragment* he had said: "Sapphische Gedichte müssen wachsen und gefunden werden. *Sie lassen sich weder machen, noch ohne Entweihung öffentlich mittheilen.* Wer es thut, dem fehlt es zugleich an Stolz und an Bescheidenheit. An Stolz: indem er sein Innerstes herausreisst aus der heiligen Stille des Herzens, und es hinwirft unter die Menge, dass sie's angaffen, roh und fremd; und das für ein lausiges *Da Capo*, oder für *Friedrichs d'or*. Unbescheiden bleibt's immer sein selbst auf die Ausstellung zu schicken wie ein Urbild. . . . Nur Cyniker lieben auf dem Markte."[2]

Schlegel needed the *Friedrichs d'or*, and the applause of the crowd would have been welcomed, despite his scorn of them, but such motives are not the whole cause of the violation of this demand of sacred silence with regard to his affair with Dorothea Veit. The *example of Goethe* was most prominent among all the motives of it.

The Schlegels never doubted that the *Roman Elegies* were

---

[1] *WSBr.*, pp. 27 f.
[2] *Lyc. Fragment*, No. 119; *MS.*, Bd. II, p. 200.

so many disguised experiences of Goethe in Rome. *Der Gott und die Bajadere* was to them a confession of Goethe's relations to Christiana Vulpius, and they called him "Mahodöh" thereafter.[1] If Goethe's best works were such direct personal confessions of the most outspoken *erotic* character, why should not Schlegel's passion be detailed for the public enjoyment and admiration. His friends recognized this relation to Goethe. Novalis warned him that the public would say : "Aus Venedig ist Berlin geworden."

The *Roman* is to be a mixture of all literary forms. The *Lucinde* exemplifies this principle in the extreme. An introductory letter of Julius to Lucinde is followed by a dithyrambic fancy concerning the most beautiful situation, and this in turn by a characterization of little Wilhelmine. Now follows an allegory on impudence, an idyl on idleness, and sensual chitchat called *Treue und Scherz*. The *Roman* proper, a simple narrative, *Lehrjahre der Männlichkeit*, is abruptly broken off and gives place to more allegory in the form of *Metamorphosès*. Hereupon follow two letters, the first a mere series of fragments without visible unity. After these comes a reflection, as if there had not been enough of it and to spare already, then two polemic letters, a dialogue, and finally *Tändeleien der Phantasie*. Nothing is absent but *lyric verse* and genuine poetry. The second part would have furnished abundance of the former had it been completed.

A *Roman* must be reflective and contain comments upon its own art, just as *Wilhelm Meister*. It is only a high degree of this quality, when Julius is interrupted in the middle of his first letter in order to permit the writer (who of course is the hero) to reflect upon the manner of his confession and deliver a treatise on romantic confusion. The dithyrambic fancy is simply a reminiscent reflection upon

---

[1] *GuR.*, Bd. I, p. 7. A. W. Schlegel to Goethe, September 24, 1797.

imagined feeling in a situation conceived by tasteless wit. It is not necessary to *prove* the reflective character of the *Lucinde,* nor its character as an art-treatise.

The *Lucinde* was a practical fulfilment of all the doctrines derived from *Wilhelm Meister,* so far as it lay in Schlegel's power to fulfil them. There were, however, supplemen-tary influences traceable to Tieck's *Sternbald* and Cervantes' *Novelas* and *Don Quixote.* Not only on the æsthetic side is this *Roman* arbitrary and fantastic, but ethically as well. Arbitrariness and fantastic opposition to all law and established custom are its whole spirit and tenor.

Here, too, Goethe is one of Schlegel's models. All in all, we can scarcely avoid the conviction that Goethe's free existence in the Weimar circle, his superiority to narrow convention in his domestic establishment, the tolerant morals of his poems and novels are the concrete examples which give fulness to Schlegel's ethical conceptions, as shown in the *Lucinde.*

Let us now examine this *Roman* for minor traces of Goethe's works. Donner finds it probable that Philline's character was influential upon the development of *Lisette.* He quotes a considerable passage beginning : " Ihr naïver Witz," etc.,[1] and calls it a characterization of Philline as she appears in Goethe's *Roman.* But even if this be so, he declares that a second model for *Lisette* must be assumed. Dilthey refers in general terms to " einem schlechten französischen *Romane.*" [2] Julian Schmidt is more specific and refers to Prévost's *Manon Lescaut* as the second model.[3] Yet Schmidt recognizes in *Lisette's* suicide because of Julius' unfaithfulness, the necessity of a third influence. As the Leipzig lady who was the object of Schlegel's violent passion

---

[1] *DWM.,* p. 96.   [2] *DLS.,* p. 491.
[3] *SLittgesch.,* Bd. I, p. 395.

did not furnish this element, and as we know of nothing else in his earlier career to suggest it, it seems probably referable to some as yet unearthed literary source. Perhaps the tragic turn in Goethe's *Gott und die Bajadere* (which to Schlegel seemed a pure invention of the imagination injected into an actual experience of the poet, simply for artistic effect) or perhaps the tragedy in *Die Braut von Korinth*, which "made a new epoch in poetry," was enough to suggest a tragic end of some sort. Then again the *Bajadere* is elevated out of her class by *Mahodöh*, as *Lisette* by *Julius*.

Treue und Scherz is an attempt to reproduce the night scenes of Philline and Wilhelm, says Donner, and he rightly considers the *Idylle über den Müssiggang* as directly due to the passive nature of Wilhelm, who reaches the goal of culture by a complete surrender to external influences. The general resemblance of Julius to Wilhelm, however, is but slight and elusive.

Other Goethean influences shimmer through here and there. In the characterization of little Wilhelmine we have an example: "Und nun sieh! diese liebenswürdige Wilhelmine findet nicht selten ein unaussprechliches Vergnügen darin, auf dem Rücken liegend, mit den Beinchen in die Höhe zu gesticulieren, unbekümmert um ihren Rock und um das Urtheil der Welt. Wenn das Wilhelmine thut, was darf ich nicht thun, da ich doch, bei Gott! ein Mann bin, und nicht zarter zu sein brauche, wie das zarteste weibliche Wesen." Compare *Venetian Epigrams:*

39.

Kehre nicht, liebliches Kind, die Beinchen hinauf zu dem Himmel,
Jupiter sieht dich, der Schalk, und Ganymed ist besorgt.

40.

Wende die Füsschen zum Himmel nur ohne Sorge! wir strecken
Arme betend empor; aber nicht schuldlos, wie du."

When Julius says to Lucinde: "Ich weiss auch du würdest mich nicht überleben wollen, du würdest dem voreiligen Gemahle auch im Sarge folgen, und *aus Lust und Liebe* in den *flammenden Abgrund* steigen, in den ein rasendes Gesetz die *indischen Frauen* zwingt, und die zartesten Heiligthümer der Willkür durch grobe Absicht und Befehl entweiht und zerstört," we are clearly reminded of the *Bajadere*.

> "Bei der Bahre stürzt sie nieder,
> Ihr Geschrei durchdringt die Luft.
> *Meinen Gatten will ich wieder*
> *Und ich such' ihn in der Gruft.*
> Soll zu Asche mir zerfallen
> Dieser Glieder Götterpracht?
> Mein! Er war es, mein vor allen!
> Ach nur eine süsse Nacht!
> . . . .
>
> Höre deiner Priester Lehre:
> Dieser war dein Gatte nicht.
> *Lebst du doch als Bajadere,*
> *Und so hast du keine Pflicht.*
> . . . .
>
> Und mit ausgestreckten Armen
> *Springt sie in den heissen Tod.*"

When *Lisette* is described as "beinahe öffentlich" and her chief charms summarized as "ihre seltene Gewandtheit und unerschöpfliche Mannigfaltigkeit in allen verführerischen Künsten der Sinnlichkeit," we have a summary of the first three stanzas of the above poem. When Friedrich adds: "sie vergass beinahe der Kunst" when any man pleased her "und verfiel in eine hinreissende Anbetung der Männlichkeit," we have the fourth and fifth stanzas:

> "Und des Mädchens frühe Künste
> Werden nach und nach *Natur.*
> . . . .
>
> Und sie fühlt der Liebe Qual."

In the *Allegorie von der Frechheit* we find a passage which seems at first a direct reference to *Wilhelm Meister*. Wit says to Julius: "Ich werde ein altes Schauspiel vor dir erneuern : einige Jünglinge am Scheidewege. Ich selbst habe es der Mühe werth gehalten, sie in müssigen Stunden mit der göttlichen Phantasie zu erzeugen. *Es sind die echten Romane vier an der Zahl und unsterblich wie wir.*" From the descriptions which follow we are tempted to try to determine what they are. The one which chose *Frechheit* for its muse is certainly the *Lucinde*. We might guess Goethe's *Meister* for that one which stood "mitten unter den Damen" and was "einer von denen, wie man sie gegenwärtig sieht, *aber viel gebildeter;*" "er unterhielt die Gesellschaft, und schien sich für alle (*i. e.* Sittlichkeit, Bescheidenheit, Decenz, Schöne Seele, and Frechheit) zu interessieren." What to make of the *Knight* and the *bathing Youth* is more doubtful, if we assume that they have already an objective existence, as the *Lucinde* and *Meister*. They would have to be symbols for Tieck's *Sternbald* and some work of Cervantes. If, however, Schlegel's own interpretation (as reported by Haym[1]) is correct, and the only genuine *Romane* are four of his own projected works (a piece of colossal egotism hardly credible even in a Schlegel), then the problem is easier. The *Lucinde* is certain. The Knight with his mediæval catholicism and gigantic form, is Schlegel's *Faust*, which was to complete the *Faustfragment of 1790*, just as the *Lucinde* was to supplement the *Wilhelm Meister*. The third was to be a complete *Bildungsroman* of the type of *Wilhelm Meister*. The bathing youth is too vaguely sketched to suggest any definite content.

"Glaube mir," Julius says: "es ist mir bloss um die Objectivität meiner Leibe zu thun." Compare Goethe's *Roman Elegies* as a single poem, objectivizing Goethe's love experi-

[1] *HRS.*, p. 497.

ences in Rome, as the Schlegels believed. "Und weil es
mir versagt ist *meine Flamme in Gesänge* auszuhauchen,
muss ich *den stillen Zügen* das schöne Geheimnis vertrauen."
The *Lucinde* must be all prose, though elegiacs had been
more fitting. And if Julius must think of some world
while making his confessions, "so sei es am liebsten die
Vorwelt. Die Liebe selbst sei ewig neu und ewig jung,
aber ihre Sprache sei kühn, nach alter klassischer Sitte,
*nicht züchtiger wie die römische Elegie und die edelsten der
grössten Nation.*" Compare *Roman Elegies*, XIII, where
Amor says:

> "Die Schule der Griechen
> Blieb noch offen, das Thor schlossen die Jahre nicht zu.
> *Ich*, der Lehrer, *bin ewig jung*, und liebe die Jungen,
> Altklug lieb' ich dich nicht! Munter! Begreife mich wohl!
> War das Antike doch neu, da jene Glücklichen lebten!
> Lebe glücklich, und so lebe die *Vorzeit* in dir!
> Stoff zum Liede wo nimmst du ihn her? Ich muss dir ihn geben,
> Und den höhern Styl lehrt die Liebe dich nur!'"

When Schlegel speaks of woman's love as follows: "Kein
Linnée kann uns alle die schönen Gewächse und Pflanzen im
grossen Garten des Lebens classifizieren und *verderben*,
und nur der eingeweihte Liebling der Götter versteht ihre
wunderbare Botanik; die göttliche Kunst, ihre verhüllten
Kräfte und Schönheiten zu errathen und zu erkennen, wann
die Zeit ihrer Blüthe sei, und welches Erdreich sie be-
dürfen," etc., he has reference to Goethe, the great master of
delineation of woman's character.

The passage in *Treue und Scherz:* "Wirst du nicht
wenigstens erst den Vorhang niederlassen?—Du hast Recht,
die Beleuchtung wird *so* viel reizender. *Wie schön glänzt die
weisse Hüfte in dem rothen Schein!* . . . . Warum so kalt,
Lucinde?—Lieber, setze die Hyacinthen weiter weg, der
Geruch betäubt mich.—*Wie fest und selbständig, wie glatt
und wie fein! Das ist harmonische Ausbildung.*—O nein,

Julius! lass', ich bitt' dich; ich will nicht.—*Darf ich nicht fühlen,* ob du glühst, wie ich," etc., is a part of the fifth Roman elegy broken into prose dialogue:

> "Und belehr' ich mich nicht, indem ich des lieblichen Busens
> Formen spähe, die Hand leite die Hüften hinab?
> Dann versteh' ich den Marmor erst recht," etc.

Julius' fatherhood and his enjoyment in being with his child are sharp reminders of Wilhelm Meister's relations to Felix.

The meeting of Julius and Lucinde is strikingly like the recognition scene in *Alexis und Dora.* Their feelings are awakened by music, the specifically romantic art, and their confession is brought about by this melodious exchange of feeling. "Er konnte nicht widerstehen, er drückte einen schüchternen Kuss auf die frischen Lippen und die feurigen Augen. *Mit ewigem Entzücken fühlte er das göttliche Haupt der hohen Gestalt auf seine Schulter sinken,* die schwarzen Locken flossen über den Schnee des vollen Busens und des schönen Rückens, *leise sagte er: Herrliche Frau; als die fatale Gesellschaft unerwartet hereintrat.*"

The situation and succession of events is exactly parallel to those of *Alexis und Dora:* (1) the recognition; (2) the embrace and kisses; (3) the "leise sagte er: Herrliche Frau" and "Ewig! sagte sie leise;" (4) the entrance of the company, and that of the ship's boy. We have seen how deep the impression was which Goethe's *Idylle* made upon him. This scene is the fruit of it.

If Schlegel had felt able to write verse, *Sehnsucht und Ruhe* would doubtless have taken the form of Goethe's "*der neue Pausias und sein Blumenmädchen*" instead of its present prose form.

The *Lucinde* was greeted with a great cry of indignation

from people of all schools, whether they had read it or not. Even the romantic circle condemned it. Goethe heard these condemnations, but seems not to have thought it worth while trying to form a closer acquaintance. Schiller is the first to give him a nearer knowledge of its nature and content. Schiller expresses his disappointment in finding none of the simplicity of the Greeks in it, after all Schlegel's *Rhodomontaden von Griechheit.* On the other hand it is "eine höchst seltsame Paarung des Nebulistischen mit dem Charakteristischen," "der Gipfel moderner Unform und Unnatur." He urges Goethe to read it for curiosity's sake. "Das Werk ist übrigens nicht ganz durchzulesen, weil einem das hohle Geschwätz gar zu übel macht." [1]

Goethe replies next day: "Ich danke Ihnen dass Sie mir von der wunderlichen Schlegel'schen Produktion einen nähern Begriff machen; ich hörte schon viel darüber reden. Jederman liest's, jederman schilt darauf, und man erfährt nicht was eigentlich damit sei. *Wenn mir es einmal in die Hände kommt,* will ich's auch ansehen."

Goethe made no haste to gratify his curiosity. Not till two months later, September 19, 1799, do we find a record in his journal: "Abends *Lucinde* und Schelling's *Naturphilosophie.*" And then he left no record of his impression in diary or correspondence. If he expressed an opinion orally, no one has recorded it for us. It is safe to assume that Goethe had and could have no sympathy whatever with its form or content, its purpose or tendency. His most tolerant attitude must be "eine gesunde Abneigung." Perhaps he reserved his opinions for public expression, possibly in the *Faust* satires.

---

[1] *GSBr.*, July 19, 1799.

4. Jena. Second Period.

a. Social Relations, etc.

Friedrich's stay in Berlin had been rendered unpleasant by the publication of the *Lucinde* and by differences with the rigoristic moralist, Fichte. Tieck, the poet *par excellence* of the romantic school, was intending to leave Berlin for Jena. It seemed possible now to reassemble the scattered school in Jena. So Friedrich arranged to return.

Goethe made frequent visits to Jena to escape the confusion of his domestic life and the demands of society in the Duke's capital, and to enjoy the quiet of the university town. One of these visits extended from September 17, 1799, to October 13. Goethe worked upon the translation of *Mahomet*, but found time for certain walks and occasional intercourse with others than Schiller. In his journal we find: "September 28, Nachmittags, Herr Friedrich Schlegel," and "October 12, Harland und Schlegel d(er) J(üngere)." The nature and purpose of these visits are not stated here or elsewhere. Dorothea writes in deep disappointment that he goes only to Schiller's, and others do not invite him, though the Schlegels see him every day at his old castle. She is inconsolable at her failure to see Goethe.[1] If we run through Goethe's diary of the period, this news is confirmed. August Wilhelm came to discuss the Roman elegies and the epigrams, and "Versmass" in general. Schelling came still oftener to discuss empiricism and idealism, and explain his own views of philosophy. The object of all visits by Schiller, August Wilhelm, and Schelling are clearly stated. The colorless mention of Friedrich Schlegel's presence on two occasions must imply that their chief meaning was a satis-

---

[1] *RDBr.*, to Schleiermacher, October 28, 1799.

faction of his own personal ambitions. They were of no consequence to Goethe.

Another visit to Jena occurred between November 11, 1799, and December 9. In the journal we have the record of one visit: "November 23, Friedrich Schlegel." Goethe was busied with his *Farbenlehre*. On Schiller's removal to Weimar, Goethe lived in almost absolute solitude in the quiet of Jena. This was broken only by a visit from Mellish, an evening at Loder's, and a reading of *Genoveva* by Tieck. Goethe discussed the *Natürliche Tochter* with August Wilhelm. We have again the same colorless mention of Friedrich. Before Schiller's departure many walks were taken, but no particulars are recorded in the diary of Goethe. On the other hand we have mention of this visit by Dorothea in a letter of November 15 to Schleiermacher. She reports meeting Goethe while on a pleasure walk "im Paradies." At the end of a long paragraph about Goethe's courtesy and her own pride she adds: "An Friedrich machte er auch ein recht auszeichnendes Gesicht, wie er ihn grüsste." To Rahel Levi she writes of the same circumstance, calling it "ein heller Punkt in meinem Lebenslauf."[1]

In these two letters we have an expression of the boundless enthusiasm of the romanticists, the deification of the master Goethe, and the intense delight of the disciples in the least nod of recognition from Olympus. It is the feeling which Caroline expressed with respect to Goethe's *Propyläen*, "Was brauchen wir die Vorhöfe, da wir das Allerheiligste selber besitzen. Er lebt alleweil mitten unter uns."[2] But on Goethe's part there is nothing but an instance of his formal courtesy in this meeting. There is no trace of social intimacy. The meeting was forced upon him by a manœuvre

[1] *Ibid.*, November 15 and November 18, 1799.
[2] *RNBr.*, Caroline Schlegel an Novalis, November 15, 1798.

of the Schlegels. In the same letter we learn that Caroline gave out her intention of giving a "*Soupé*" which she hoped Goethe might attend. No evidence exists that such an invitation was ever accepted.

About this time two products of opposite character came into the hands of the Schlegels for publication in the *Athenäum*. These were Schelling's *Widerporst* and Novalis' *Christenheit oder Europa*. The authors were members of the inner circle of romanticism. The editors were in straits for want of manuscripts. The censorship, however, was strict, and doubts arose concerning the advisability of publishing such essays. All were in favor of publication except Dorothea, then August began to doubt, and finally Goethe was made umpire. The choice was appropriate, because Goethe knew the whole situation, the attitude of his government and the temper of the public since the affair with Fichte. Goethe's decision was against publication.[1]

In rendering this decision he may have had other motives than those of mere prudence. He certainly opposed the whole spirit of the *Europa*, and probably felt it a prostitution of his power and position as well as a compromise of himself to permit such a glorification of mediæval catholicism and absolutism to see the light in a journal whose every third word was Goethe and Goethean art.

This decision was probably rendered on November 27, when Goethe records a talk with August Wilhelm on the relations of their society to the public. "Vivat Goethe!" Dorothea cries; "der ist . . . . nach Weimar gereist, kommt aber in acht Wochen wieder, und hat gesagt, nun sie ihn so öffentlich und geradezu als Haupt einer Partei ausschreien, wollte er sich auch auf eine honette Weise als ein solches zeigen."[2]

---

[1] *RDBr.*, December 9, 1799. [2] *Ibid.*

This promise of Goethe, here alone recorded, seems a direct recognition of the members of the romantic school as his disciples. In the absence of any evidence to show that Goethe really fulfilled such a promise, we may consider it as a misinterpretation on Dorothea's part of Goethe's courteous generalities, or an expression of a transitory hope on Goethe's part that he might help this party to steer clear of outer dangers, modify and restrain their false tendencies in art, etc., and so bind together all elements of opposition against the dominant Philistinism. He felt that the romanticists ought to be maintained as a fighting corps, though irregular.

Goethe kept up some sort of communication with Jena during the winter. He sent his poems in classic meters for August Wilhelm's criticism and suggestions, and adopted some of the latter. On one occasion Goethe expressed an interest in the intellectual output of August Wilhelm's *Geistesverwandten*, chiefly Tieck and Schelling.

The promised visit to Jena was delayed about seven months, and did not take place until July 22, 1800. In the meantime, however, Friedrich made several visits to Weimar. On April 10 he took the *Athenäum* containing August Wilhelm's satire on Schmidt, Matthison, und Voss, and read it to Goethe.[1] On April 28 Dorothea reports to Schleiermacher and Rahel a visit to Goethe: "Friedrich der Göttliche ist diesen Morgen zu Vater Goethe oder Gott dem Vater nach Weimar gewandert."[2] He started at five in the morning, in order to reach Goethe before his departure for Leipzig, where he arrived by four in the afternoon. The nature of these visits is not known, for they are not mentioned by Goethe in his journal, or in correspondence. On July 12, a visit is planned for Friedrich at his brother's request, as we learn, "um ein paar Stunden mit Ihnen schwatzen zu können."[3]   Goethe

---

[1] *Ibid.*, April 10, 1800.   [2] *Ibid.*, April 28, 1800.
[3] *GuR.*, Bd. I.   A. W. Schlegel an Goethe, July 12, 1800.

expresses his willingness to grant the favor on the following Wednesday, but we have no record of any such visit on that date or any other near it.

Friedrich seems to have waited until the third day after Goethe's arrival in Jena, when a call is noted in Goethe's diary with the usual simplicity. Every morning of this visit is devoted to *Tancred*, the afternoons are devoted to visits, etc. Almost a score of persons are mentioned in his diary. Among these Friedrich Schlegel is recorded three times, on the 28th, on the 30th, and on the 31st. On the 25th he had a long talk with Goethe, mostly literary and personal chitchat.[1] On the 28th he took one of his poems to Goethe, also *Aushängebogen* of the *Athenäum*.[2] We know nothing of the remaining visits.

Goethe's next visit to Jena was from September 3 to October 4, 1800, with the exception of a trip to Rossla from the 6th to the 10th. Two interests absorb Goethe's attention at this time, the Helena episode of *Faust*, and the philosophy of Kant and his successors. August Wilhelm is not in Jena. Humboldt is also absent. Hence Goethe turns to Friedrich instead for information regarding iambic trimeters and the meters of the Greek chorus. Philosophy is represented by Niethammer, at first a Kantian and later a Fichtean, now professor at the university, and by Friedrich Schlegel, who as "Privatdozent" has announced a course of lectures on philosophy. Fichte is permanently absent in Berlin, and Schelling temporarily so in Bamberg. It is to be noted that Goethe turns to Friedrich only because his trusted counselors are not at hand.

These interests bring Schlegel into Goethe's presence a number of times during the next several months. On the 5th of September he made a call. The diary records visits

---

[1] *WSBr.*, p. 431.   [2] *GSBr.*, July 29, 1800.

11

on September 20, September 25, September 30, October 3, and
November 11. These visits are the subject of correspondence
on both sides. On September 16, September 23, and September
28, Goethe reports progress in his philosophical *colloquia* with
Niethammer, and from these reports we have no reason to
suppose that Schlegel has been consulted as yet on such subjects.[1] But on September 30 Friedrich Schlegel is mentioned
as an exponent of transcendental idealism in these discussions.
November 18 the muses are still in danger from the philosophers, but Goethe takes all the blame upon himself, for he
has invited the gentlemen and set them to answering questions. By December 17, the philosophers are banished and
the muses are again in favor.[2] The relative importance of
Niethammer and Schlegel in this series of conversations may be
seen in the ratio of the numbers of their conferences, *viz.*:
17:3.

Dorothea reports on September 30, 1800 : " Goethe ist noch
hier. Er scheint nun mit Ernst etwas lernen zu wollen :
er ist sehr fleissig, lässt sich ein Privatissimum nach dem
andern lesen. Übrigens ist er auch sehr lustig und Friedrich
hat neulich den Abend tête-à-tête mit ihm gespeist."[3] These
privatissima of course are not those of Friedrich alone, but
those of Niethammer and the physicist Ritter as well.
Friedrich notes on November 24 that Goethe had consulted
him about the Greek name for his *Paleophron und Neoterpe*,
and on Greek trimeters, etc. "Er hat einigemal recht viel
darüber mit mir gesprochen, indessen habe ich mich doch
nicht überwinden können, zu fragen nach dem Sujet."[4]
Goethe does not voluntarily confide in him, but uses his
special knowledge of the Greek language and meters, and

---

[1] *Ibid.*, on dates mentioned in text.
[2] *Ibid.*, on dates mentioned in text.
[3] *RDBr.*, Dorothèa an A. W. Schlegel, September 30, 1800.
[4] *WSBr.*, pp. 446 f.

the impertinent Friedrich has not felt himself privileged to inquire directly. Compare this with Goethe's free discussions of the Helena episode with Schiller in contemporary letters.

Goethe came to Jena again in December. Friedrich called on him to present him August Wilhelm's *Ehrenpforte für Kotzebue*, which Goethe praised "durch alle Kategorien."[1] Goethe sent this work to Schiller with the comment: "es ist nicht zu leugnen dass es brillante Partien hat."[2]

The next visit recorded is February 28, 1801, after Schlegel has taken the degree of Doctor of Philosophy. Schiller gives Goethe an account of the scandal on that occasion, and Goethe expresses the hope that Friedrich may have some advantage from the contest, "denn freilich habe ich seine Gabe als Dozent, auch von seinen besten Freunden, nicht rühmen hören."[3]

Why should Goethe deliver this hearsay opinion, if those consultations in philosophy were of any importance? Why not his own personal judgment—to Schiller, at least?

A call on May 29 seems to have been the last personal meeting of the second Jena period.

If we examine these meetings as a whole, we note the complete reserve of Goethe as compared with his manner toward Schiller and Meyer, and even toward Humboldt, Knebel, Schelling, etc. There is nothing to contradict Schiller's letter of November 23, 1800, to Charlotte, Gräfin von Schimmelmann. This summary of Goethe's character is so sound and wholesome, so sober, so earnest, so unmixed with personal feeling, that it carries conviction in those parts also which deal with the Schlegels. Among other things Schiller says: "*Dies Verhältnis ist durchaus nur ein litte-*

---

[1] *Ibid.*, p. 452.   [2] *GSBr.*, December 22, 1800.
[3] *Ibid.*, March 18, 1801.

rarisches und kein freundschaftliches wie man es in der Ferne beurtheilt. Goethe schätzt alles Gute, wo er es findet, und so lässt er auch . . . dem philosophischen Talent des jüngern Schlegels Gerechtigkeit widerfahren : . . . . an der lächerlichen Verehrung, welche die beiden Schlegels Goethe erweisen, ist er selbst unschuldig, er hat sie nicht dazu aufgemuntert, er leidet vielmehr dadurch, und sieht selbst recht wohl ein, dass die Quelle dieser Verehrung nicht die reinste ist : denn diese eitlen Menschen bedienen sich seines Namens nur als eines Paniers gegen ihre Feinde, und es ist ihnen im Grunde nur um sich selbst zu thun. *Dieses Urtheil, das ich Ihnen hier niederschreibe, ist aus Goethes eigenem Munde, in diesem Tone wird zwischen ihm und mir von den Herren Schlegel gesprochen.* . . . . Insofern aber diese Menschen und ihr Anhang sich dem einreissenden Philosophie-Hass, und einer gewissen kraftlosen, seichten Kunstkritik tapfer entgegensetzen, ob sie gleich selbst in ein andres Extrem verfallen, insofern kann man sie gegen die andre Partei, die noch schädlicher ist, nicht ganz sinken lassen, und die Klugheit befiehlt zum Nutzen der Wissenschaft ein gewisses Gleichgewicht zwischen den idealistischen Philosophen und den Unphilosophischen zu beobachten." [1]

In respect to Goethe's philosophical interests, we find that he considered himself without the proper organ for speculation. The Kantian philosophy, however, had to be reckoned with. Schiller's friendship brought to him a system of æsthetics based on Kant, and the affair with Fichte brought him into practical contact with the whole movement. Gradually he yielded to the tendency to theorize, and began a course of reading in philosophy, which included the works of Kant, Fichte, and Schelling, among contemporaries. He consulted the personal representatives of the various systems

---

[1] *JSBr.*, Bd. VI, p. 219 f.

in order to obtain fuller explanations of technical terms and to ply them with questions.

At first Goethe's interest is chiefly æsthetic, and he finds little good to hope for from the new philosophy, and is positively opposed to idealism.[1] The most important thing for the philosophers is to reunite object and subject. Until that shall be effected, he will employ a rational empiricism as his own working theory.[2] In September, 1799, he complains of the insuperable limitations of the new school. "Sie kauen sämmtlich ihren eigenen Narren beständig wieder, ruminieren ihr *Ich*."[3] To Schelling's *Naturphilosophie* Goethe is more attracted. It seems an attempt to reunite object and subject, but he is not ready to pass final judgment as yet on September 27, 1800, when beginning the *colloquia* with Niethammer.[4]

The conversations with Niethammer and Schlegel seem to have shown the more clearly the inner dissensions of the school, as is seen in a letter to Schiller in which he says: "Ich fürchte nur die Herren Idealisten und Dynamiker werden ehester Tages als Dogmatiker und Pedanten erscheinen und sich gelegentlich einander in die Haare gerathen;"[5] and in another to Humboldt where he complains: "Schade dass die kritisch-idealistische Partei, *der wir schon so viel verdanken*, in sich selbst nicht einig ist, und das Grundgute ihrer Lehre, das ohnehin so leicht misgedeutet werden kann, mit Übermuth und Leichtsinn zur Schau stellt."[6] These are references to the Schlegel-Niet-

---

[1] *GSBr.*, November 25, 1797, and January 6, 1798.

[2] *Ibid.*, February 21, 1798.

[3] *GWke.*, Abt. IV, Bd. 14, p. 179. Goethe an Wm. von Humboldt, September 16, 1799.

[4] *Ibid.*, Bd. 15, p. 117. Goethe an Schelling, September 27, 1800.

[5] *GSBr.*, September 16, 1800.

[6] *GWke.*, Abt. IV, Bd. 15, p. 147. Goethe an Wm. von Humboldt, November 19, 1800.

hammer and possibly to Schlegel-Schelling contests, which seemed so inexcusable to Goethe.

Goethe seems to have hoped for an ultimate unity among philosophers upon a system which should recognize the unity of object and subject. Compare the Baccalaureus scene of *Faust*, Part II, which was composed at this period of Goethe's activity. This scene is hardly a representation of mere youthful insolence in general, and certainly not a mere fulfilment of Mephisto's promise that the young fellow should become "sicut deus." The reference to Fichte's philosophy is too specific to admit of any doubt:

> "Original, fahr' hin in deiner Pracht!
> Wie würde dich die Einsicht kränken;
> Wer kann was Dummes, wer was Kluges denken,
> Das nicht die Vorwelt schon gedacht?
> *Doch sind wir auch mit diesem nicht gefährdet,*
> *In wenig Jahren wird es anders sein:*
> *Wenn sich der Most auch ganz absurd gebärdet,*
> *Es giebt zuletzt doch noch e' Wein."*

There is a conservative tendency in all Nature's activities. The youth, and the young philosophical revolution, will both settle into soberness and sense with years. How much of this hope of returning clearness and sanity was based on Friedrich Schlegel's vague system of real idealism, as known to Goethe, is at present indeterminable. Probably but little, if any, for his hopes seem to have lain rather in a clarification of Schelling's *Naturephilosophy*.

β. *Athenäum,* Vol. III.

a. *Gespräch über die Poesie, etc.*

Schlegel's literary work of the Jena period consisted of his *Gespräch über die Poesie,* a poem *An Heliodora,* a parting word to his critics, *Über die Unverständlichkeit,* and

Herkules Musagetes; the first three appearing in the *Athenäum* for 1800, and the last in *Charakteristiken und Kritiken.*

The poem *An Heliodora* does not concern us at all. The *Gespräch* is most important. It is modeled upon Goethe's manner in the *Propyläen,*[1] and consists of *Epochen der Dichtkunst, Rede über die Mythologie,* a *Brief über den Roman,* and a *Versuch über den Verschiedenen Styl in Goethes frühern und spätern Werken.*

The *Epochen* attempts to do over again, what had been done so confusedly and imperfectly in the *Studium, viz.,* to show the relations of modern poetry to the ancient, and trace the development of the former. The great change from the position taken in the *Studium* is shown in the fuller treatment of the modern periods and the unstinted praise of certain modern poets, as Dante, Shakespeare, Cervantes, and *Goethe.* The latter is still the only German poet to be named with Shakespeare and Dante. Goethe's universality is emphasized.

The moderns are now superior to the ancients, even the poets of Athens, because the union of poetry and philosophy has introduced a new period of development in art. The Germans need only employ these means, and follow the models of Goethe, and seek the spirit of German art in the *Niebelungen-Lied,* etc., in order to attain the highest possible art.

But poetry needs a *Mythology.* It is time to make a new one. It is to be born out of the deeps of the soul itself. Fichte's idealism is to be its basis, and Ritter's *Transcendental Physics* is to help in its development. Out of idealism must eventually come an infinite realism. But philosophy can not express this realism. Poetry alone can. In fact, all beauty, though concrete, is likewise symbolic. We seem to have here again an instance of the union of Fichtean-

---

[1] *CuR.,* pp. 218 f.

ism and Goetheanism, but Schlegel is passing beyond that *stadium*. Goethe is not mentioned at all, but Friedrich longs for access to the mythology of the orient—the true home of fantasy and mysticism. This is the burden of the *Rede*.

The *Brief über den Roman* is a supplement to the aesthetic fragments of *Athenäum*, vol. i. In these fragments already Tieck's *Lovell* and *Sternbald*, Jean Paul's *Siebenkäs*, and Cervantes' *Don Quixote* and *Novelas* were considered, though all were subordinated to the one overshadowing *Roman*, *Wilhelm Meister*.

In a sort of defense of Jean Paul, Friedrich gives a formal definition of the romantic: "*nach meiner Ansicht und nach meinem Sprachgebrauch ist eben das romantisch was uns einen sentimentalen Stoff in einer fantastischen Form darstellt.*"

The *sentimental* is a spiritual feeling whose source is love. "Der Geist der Liebe muss in der romantischen Poesie überall unsichtbar sichtbar schweben." All of this love must be simply "eine Hindeutung auf das Höhre, Unendliche, Hieroglyphe der einen ewigen Liebe und der heiligen Lebensfülle der bildenden Natur."

This is a new order of poetry which has left the *Wilhelm Meister* lagging far behind. The "*organ*" of this new art is the "Phantasie" which strives to utter in riddles the ineffable divinity of life. This art makes no distinction between play and earnest, semblance and truth; it rests on historic grounds almost entirely, including personal confessions in the term historical grounds, and permits, nay demands, free play of the author's own personality, his humor and reflection. It is purely *subjective*. In this respect, too, it has abandoned Goethe's views.

Again, this art does not look to the *future* for its perfection, as Schlegel proclaimed, when he characterized Goethe's art as the "Morgenröthe echter Kunst." Its ideal is now the art of the *elder* moderns, of Shakespeare, Cervantes, Dante, Tasso, Ariosto, Petrarca, Boccaccio, Calderon, and Lope, and that "Zeitalter der Ritter, der Liebe und der Märchen, aus welchem die Sachen und das Wort selbst (romantisch) stammt." This is the only modern period to be compared with Greece, and the romantic movement with this specific ideal is the only justifiable modern art, unless we return to antiquity itself. Goethe is thus justified in his classicism, but really excluded from the new school.

The romantic is not a *genus* of poetry, but an *element* in *all* poetry. A *Roman* then is simply "ein romantisches Buch,"—a thing to be read, not seen as a drama nor heard as an epic. A *Roman* in this narrow sense is "ein ange-wandter *Roman*" in the wider sense. Its unity is spiritual only. It involves a mingling of all forms, as shown by the practice of Cervantes.

The fundamental forms of romantic art are the *Novelle* and *Märchen*, and Friedrich wishes that some genuine artist might create a number of these, so that he might deduce their laws.

Romantic criticism should partake of romantic confusion in the highest degree, and become a *Roman* itself.

In this whole letter Goethe's name is not mentioned, nor is that of any one of his works. The *Wilhelm Meister* is scrupulously, even studiously avoided, while a year earlier it would have been dragged in under every slightest pretext. Goethe is outgrown. The scales have fallen from Schlegel's eyes. *Wilhelm Meister* no longer appears the divine example of "progressive Universalpoesie." It has been surpassed already by Tieck's *Sternbald*, which is "der erste *Roman* seit Cervantes, *der romantisch ist, und darüber weit über Meister*." [1] Tieck's style is romantic and superior to Goethe's splendid prose. Friedrich has gone so far in his progress toward the

[1] *WSBr.*, p. 414.

modern that August Wilhelm now seems "gar zu teufel-
mässig antik."

We must not omit to note in passing that Schlegel's
production of the *Lucinde* seems to be reflected in his high
praise of the fantastic and the confusion of the *genera*.

Such are the facts of this revolution in respect to Goethe.
What are its motives?

First, Schlegel's original disposition to domineer. This
was held in check by prudential motives until Goethe's
patronizing tolerance seemed to be a recognition of his rising
importance, and his position as spokesman of the new school
seemed assured. His original imperiousness returned and
Goethe had to be quietly shoved aside.

Secondly, Schlegel had published the *Lucinde*, which
turned out to be more fantastic and lawless than he himself
anticipated. Since no one else defended it, it seemed best to
defend it himself by enunciating æsthetic doctrines which
it did truly exemplify.

A third consideration was the fundamental unity and
clearness in Goethe's works, the constant dominance of the
artistic purpose. Goethe's intensified interest in the plasticity of poetry was really foreign to Friedrich Schlegel's
mental constitution. It was as inevitable that Schlegel
should forsake the classic Goethe as that he should forsake
the Greeks. His course lay toward the mystic *orient*.

But Goethe's works are still a fascinating problem. His
universality is still amazing, and, though his life-work is not
yet finished, Friedrich proposes to apply the historic method
of criticism to Goethe's works, so far as known. This he
does in his *Versuch*.

The extreme differences between Goethe's earlier and later
works are noted as exceptional. Goethe has passed through
three stages of development. *Götz* is the type of the first,
Tasso of the second, and *Hermann und Dorothea* of the third.

All are highly objective. *Werther* has admirable details, excludes everything accidental, moves direct to the goal, but sinks below *Götz* with its German knights and its formlessness. *Werther's* "Ansicht der Natur" prophesies the future naturalist Goethe. *Faust* is a revelation of Goethe's self, and so belongs to all periods. It belongs "zum Grössten, was die Kraft des Menschen je gedichtet hat." The *Clavigo* and other lesser works are remarkable as examples of self-limitation for artistic purposes.

The *Iphigenie* is a transition from the first period to the second.

In *Tasso* everything is antithesis and music, and the fine smile of court life lights up all. Everything rests upon an ideal of harmonious life and harmonious culture. *Egmont* is a pendent to *Tasso*. "Auch hier unterliegt eine schöne Natur der ewigen Macht des Verstandes." The *Claudine von Villa Bella* represents in Rugantino the romantic life of a gay vagabond. *Egmont* is a study after Shakespeare's Roman plays, and *Tasso* a study after Lessing's *Nathan*; just as *Wilhelm Meister* is a study after a host of *Romane*, which taken jointly and severally had no validity. Friedrich hastens to assure us that such imitation is eminently proper. In fact no true work of art can exist without it. The model is simply an incentive to more complete individualization of the artist's thought. This seems like an intentionally inserted excuse of the *Lucinde*, or of this whole "Gespräch" itself.

Wilhelm Meister has qualities of both earlier periods, but above all it has the classic spirit of the third. The inner antiquity of *Reineke Fuchs* places it in the third also. The *Elegies, Epigrams, Idyls*, and *Epistles* make one poetic family, or one poem characterized by antique form, but having as their principal charm their lyric quality.

In the first period the subjective and objective are thoroughly blended; in the second the execution is thoroughly objective, but the content shows reference to a distinctive individuality; in the third the works are wholly objective. What seems naturalness in them is purely a product of conscious art.

In concluding, Friedrich reverts to the *Wilhelm Meister*, and emphasizes once more the combination of the antique and the modern in it. "Diese grosse Combination eröffnet eine ganz neue endlose Aussicht auf das was die höchste Aufgabe aller Dichtkunst zu sein scheint, die Harmonie des Classischen und Romantischen." Here is the motive to Schlegel's unfortunate *Alarkos*.

Goethe, Shakespeare, and Cervantes are alike in universality, but Goethe alone lives in an age favorable to the founding of a school. German spirit must take a direction toward this goal; and Schlegel hopes that poets will not be wanting to follow Goethe's models. If these can make Goethe's "universelle Tendenz" and "progressive Maximen" their own and apply them in art, "*wenn sie wie er das Sichre des Verstandes dem Schimmer des Geistreichen vorziehen*," then Goethe shall become the head of a new school, the dominant spirit of our age, as Dante was for the middle ages. This sound peroration was, however, *irony*, or worse, in the mouth of Friedrich Schlegel, for it does not represent his real convictions. The whole tone of this essay, as well as its more enthusiastic praise of Goethe, seems to indicate that it was written much earlier than the *Brief über den Roman*, in fact, about the period of the *Übermeister*, or shortly thereafter, before he wrote the *Lucinde* and became fully committed to the fantastic and formless. A notable feature already is the attempt to treat Goethe historically rather than as a *canon* of present art.

Schlegel's *Athenäum* had provoked attack on account of

its unintelligibility. This was no serious objection in Friedrich's eyes, for language is too imperfect to express all the shades of thought and feeling in men who are exploiting the *chiaro oscuro* of the German *Gemüt,* who are cultivating the hitherto neglected fallow-ground of the unconscious. Moreover the reader himself must have a certain experience and training in order to understand his author. So Friedrich satirizes the critics mercilessly, reminds them that Goethe's poetry and Fichte's idealistic philosophy are the two centers of German culture, that these facts are known to every body, but cannot be too often repeated. "Goethe und Fichte" is the formula for all offense given by the *Athenäum,* But these names will have to be named over and over again. To make a beginning Friedrich inserts his brother's sonnet,

"Bewundert nur die feingeschnitzten Götzen," etc.,

with its ingenious play upon the name Goethe, in other respects a work without a spark of divine fire in it, but which shows-perhaps better than anything else could-the immeasurable gulf fixed between the master and the professed disciple.

The doctrine of irony is redefended, and progress is predicted to a point of vantage from which every reader will find the *Lucinde* innocent, Tieck's *Genoveva* protestant, and August Wilhelm's didactic elegies too easy and transparent. This progress is conditioned upon the outbreak of "viel verborgene Unverständlichkeit," such as that of the *Athenäum.* Goethe could hardly have been particularly delighted to find the obscurities and inconsistencies of the *Athenäum* credited wholly to himself and his literary movement. But then Schlegel was desperate in defeat.

γ. *Poetical Activities.*

a. *Herkules Musagetes.*

Herkules Musagetes is a personal confession dating from the Jena period. It is written in elegiac verse, modelled on that of Goethe's *Roman Elegies,* for a casual comparison of its structure, metrically considered, reveals its kinship with Goethe's *Hexameters* rather than those of stricter schools.

This bit of verse is a declaration of the coming of age of the romantic school. Lessing and Winckelmann left their legacy to Goethe, and Goethe, though a great living representative of German culture, is withdrawn to a solitary Olympus. Tieck, Novalis, August Wilhelm Schlegel, Schleiermacher, Fichte, Ritter, these are now the "treue Pilaster der Kunst." Friedrich expresses his joy in his own recently discovered creative (?) talent. Books and the midnight lamp are the foundations of art, and Friedrich himself, as aesthetic lawgiver as well as creator, assumes the leadership of the school in the *rôle* of *Herkules Musagetes.*

Spanish poetry, French knightly poetry, and oriental hyperbole, have assumed a much wider place in his arttheories. In like proportion the sober Goethe has sunk to a secondary place in the romantic circle.

Not only in this literary work do we find evidence of this change. Even more occurs in contemporary letters. One suspects that Goethe has shown himself too little responsive to the new leadership to suit the wishes of our overweening dictator. The old critical attitude has come back. Goethe is too prosaic. Goethe's *Propyläen* are now privately branded as harmful to art.[1] Tieck's style is superior to Goethe's, because of its music in contrast to the plasticity of the latter.

---

[1] *Ibid.,* p. 464.

Tieck's *Ein schön kurzweilig Fastnachtsspiel vom alten und neuen Jahrhundert* is composed in accordance with better principles than Goethe's *Paleophon und Neoterpe*, etc.[1]

b. Alarkos, etc.

Through the experiments in verse-making, such as *An Heliodora, Herkules Musagetes,* and the fifty-nine pieces of verse intended for the second part of *Lucinde,* Friedrich is convinced that he possesses poetic powers of a high order. He is very glad, for whatever he may have declared about the equality of the critic with the creative artist, it was never his genuine conviction, even in the period of disbelief in his own creative powers. Now criticism must be subordinated to production. His motto is, "*nulla dies sine linea.*" He indulges in *terza rima,* sonnets, trochaics, elegiacs, iambics, everything which may be attained by a purely formal "Verstalent," all of which posterity has generously forgotten or forgiven.

One work was destined to make a ripple in the dramatic world—his *Alarkos.* The leader of the new school ought to show such universality as the old leader, Goethe. He had shown himself productive in the *Roman,* the *elegy,* the *lyric,* and the *epigram.* It yet remained to rival Goethe in the *drama.* Or rather outdo him? He would make a drama according to the true romantic recipe. It should surpass anything hitherto seen upon the stage, because it was to avoid the onesidedness of the purely classical drama or of the purely romantic. Goethe's *Wilhelm Meister* was a modern subject filled with the antique spirit. The *Iphigenie* was an antique subject, in antique form, but filled with the modern spirit. The new drama, which was to be a perfect harmony of the classic and romantic, must go even further.

[1] *Ibid.,* p. 462.

The subject should be modern with antique spirit, and the form should be a mingling of all forms, lyric, epic, and dramatic.

The result was *Alarkos*, a Spanish subject, tragic in the antique sense according to the early type of Aeschylus, but tricked out in a motley dress of antique-modern cut.

August Wilhelm had produced *Jon*, a simple modernization of Euripides' *Jon*, in this respect a more or less clearly recognized imitation of Goethe's *Iphigenie*. Friedrich's *Alarkos* was stimulated by Goethe's drama, but just as the *Lucinde* was to be a corrective or supplement to *Wilhelm Meister*, so the *Alarkos* was to supplement the *Iphigenie* by showing the complete harmony of the ancient and the modern.

Early in 1802 Goethe had the *Alarkos* in hand and was preparing to bring it out on the Weimar stage. To August Wilhelm he praises its *Gedrängtheit* and prefers it to Tieck's *Genoveva*.[1] On May 3 additions are asked for from the author, and two days later stage-director Kirms assigns the parts.[2]

The preparation falls chiefly to the lot of Schiller, while Goethe is in Jena. Schiller foresees certain defeat in this attempt to put *Alarkos* on the boards. The opposing party will be given an opportunity to deride them. "Einen Schritt zum Ziele werden wir durch diese Vorstellung nicht thun, oder ich müsste mich ganz betrügen." He will consider themselves lucky if they escape "eine totale Niederlage."[3] Goethe replies at once: "*Über den Alarkos bin ich völlig Ihrer Meinung; allein mich dünkt, wir müssen alles wagen, weil am Gelingen oder nicht-Gelingen nach aussen gar nichts liegt. Was wir dabei gewinnen scheint mir hauptsächlich das zu sein, dass wir diese äusserst obligaten Sylben-*

---

[1] *G Wke.*, Abt. IV, Bd. 16, p. 75.   Goethe an A. W. Schlegel.
[2] *Ibid.*, p. 74.   [3] *GSBr.*, May 7/8.

masse sprechen lassen und sprechen hören. Übrigens kann man auf das stoffartige Interesse doch auch was rechnen." [1] Schiller promises to do his best, but is by no means reassured.[2]

The play was finally produced on May 29, and would have been laughed off the stage, if Goethe's personal presence and vigorous efforts had not subdued the audience. Goethe's own utterances in the *Tag- und Jahreshefte für 1802* is as follows: " Über alles Erwarten glückten die Vorstellungen von *Jon* (January 4), *Turandot* (January 30), *Iphigenie* (May 15), *Alarkos* (May 29). Sie wurden mit grösster Sorgfalt trefflich gegeben : *letzter konnte sich jedoch keine Gunst erwerben.* Durch diese Vorstellungen bewiesen wir, dass es Ernst sei alles was der Aufmerksamkeit würdig wäre einem freien reinen Urtheil aufzustellen." If Goethe was thinking clearly of the inclusion of Schlegel's *Alarkos* in this group of plays which succeeded beyond all expectation, his last statement above is somewhat remarkable in view of the acknowledged suppression of all opposition to both *Jon* and *Alarkos.*[3]

The Countess of Egloffstein reports the occurrences at the representation of *Alarkos.* At a certain passage a wild laughter burst out so that the whole theater trembled with it. " Aber nur einen Moment. Im Nu sprang Goethe auf, rief mit donnernder Stimme und drohender Bewegung : 'Stille! Stille!' und das wirkte wie eine Zauberformel. Augenblicklich legte sich der Tumult, und der unselige *Alarkos* ging ohne weitere Störung, aber auch ohne das geringste Zeichen des Beifalls zu Ende." [4] Genast reports that Goethe expressed himself as satisfied with the representation, but one could see that he was in ill-humor.[5] Goethe himself

[1] *Ibid.*, May 9.   [2] *Ibid.*, May 12.
[3] *GWke.*, Abt. I, Bd. 35, p. 120.   *Tag- und Jahreshefte.*
[4] *BGG.*, Bd. I, pp. 234 f.   [5] *Ibid.*, p. 235.

excused the whole affair to Madame de Staël in 1804 as simply a "Kunstversuch." [1] Schiller wrote to Körner, July 5, 1802: "Mit dem *Alarkos* hat sich allerdings Goethe compromittiert: es ist seine Krankheit, sich der Schlegels anzunehmen, über die er doch selbst bitterlich schimpft und schmählt. Das Stück ist aber hier nur einmal und völlig ohne allen Beifall gegeben worden." [2]

Goethe's behavior was considered an evidence of active support and friendship of the greatest practical value by Friedrich himself, possibly by others. From this distance of time, and with the records before us, the favor of Goethe for the *Alarkos* looks more like the reflex of Goethe's hatred of Kotzebue and Co., than real approval of Schlegel. Compare the account of the whole affair given by the Countess of Egloffstein.[3]

GENERAL MATTERS.

C. Faust: *Walpurgisnacht* Satires.

The *Walpurgisnacht* scenes were written from the fall of 1800 to the spring of 1801. ms. dates are November 5, 1800, to February 8/9, 1801.[4] The *Walpurgisnachtstraum*, a continuation of the *Xenia*, was produced in its first form June 4/5, 1797.[5] By December 20, this increased to double its size.[6] There is no reason to suppose that additions were not made from time to time as occasion for satires arose. Additions were made at the very last moment.

We must examine these works carefully for any satires on Friedrich Schlegel. No other contemporary works of Goethe give occasion to introduce literary satire.

---

[1] *Ibid.*, p. 258.
[2] *JSBr.*, Bd. VI, p. 400. Schiller an Körner, July 5, 1802.
[3] Goethe's *Cours d'amour.* *G. Jahrb.*, Bd. VI, pp. 65 ff.
[4] *MF.*, Bd. II, p. 236.   [5] *Ibid.*, p. 259.   [6] *Ibid.*, p. 260.

Minor's *Faust* is the latest scholarly attempt to interpret these satires. Baumgart's *Faust, als einheitliche Dichtung* contains another attempt. Veit Valentin's *Goethes Faust-dichtung* attacks the same problem, and Witkowski's *Wal-purgisnacht* treats the scene as a whole in its formal aspects, but gives little attention to exegesis. Earlier commentators are in general superseded.

Demonstration is generally out of the question when we seek distinct personalities under any of the allegorical masks of the *Walpurgisnacht* proper. The *Kranich* is Lavater, the *Proktophantasmist*, Nikolai, the *Orthodoxe*, Stolberg, the *Idealist*, Fichte or a Fichtean, the *Autor*, probably Wieland or Herder, and the *Genius der Zeit* Henning's Journal of that name. But all attempts to find such personalities behind the *Dudelsack, Irrlicht, Halbhexe, Windfahne*, etc., must remain very uncertain. Goethe himself has said about them : " Was darin von Piquen vorkommt, habe ich so von den besonderen Gegenständen abgelöst und ins allgemeine gespielt, dass es zwar dem Leser nicht an Beziehungen fehlen, aber niemand wissen wird, worauf es eigentlich gemeint ist." [1] We shall be lucky if we escape the Goethean condemnation of " was unterzulegen " in our attempt " alles auszulegen."

In the *Traum*, however, which is a continuation of the *Xenia*, we must suspect distinct personalities under most of the allegorical masks.

Did Friedrich Schlegel and the tendencies with which he was identified find a place on the Blocksberg?

If Baumgart is correct, Goethe intended to characterize the evil principle in its entirety, and disposed his materials in three great groups: the first, *Evil* in its absolute opposi-tion to moral law ; the second, *Evil* in more specialized form

---

[1] *GGE.*, March 21, 1830 = *BGG.*, Bd. vii, p. 276.

as the essence of corruption in society and State; and third, *Evil* as falsity and perversity in art, science and literature. The great primal sources of corruption, *Mammon*, and *Frau Baubo*, gold and sex, the catholic misuse of absolution, and the protestant degeneration, fill the whole of Goethe's poem up to the point where Faust and Mephisto step aside into the circle of campfires "in die kleine Welt." In this little world Goethe describes a decadent society. Instead of going into details the poem strikes at the single root of the whole evil, the tendency to cling to the old. To give concrete expression to this principle certain typical individuals are made to utter their opinions, *e. g.*, the General and the Minister who grumble at innovations, the Parvenu who wishes innovations to cease when he is at the top, the author, who, like Herder, stands fretfully aside and carps at the new classicism, or Wieland, who sees the golden age of German literature rise and decline with his own fame. This *Beharren beim Alten* is further symbolized by the *Trödelhexe* who collects and preserves all old instruments of crime and corruption. But the chief instrumentality of destruction for the society is frivolous lustfulness symbolized in Lilith and her disciples, the young witch and the old witch, who pair off with Faust and Mephisto for the dance.

The scene is broken up by the escape of a red mouse from the mouth of the young witch, by the vision of Gretchen's *Idol*, and the sudden appearance of the rationalistic *Proktophantasmist*.

Thus Baumgart, whose exegesis is certainly attractive in its exclusion of the frivolous and meaningless in these scenes. If we accept it as correct, there is no place for Friedrich Schlegel in this portion of the *Walpurgisnacht*.

Witkowski and Valentin, though differing widely from Baumgart in other essential respects, both agree with him that contemporary satires are confined to the group of personages in the "little world." The only possible reference to Schlegel, then, is the implied recognition of youthful energy and progress. This is too general, and applies better to Weimar classicism than to the rising romanticism.

Minor disagrees with these three scholars and finds considerable contemporary satire in the *Walpurgisnacht* proper. The *Halbhexen* are symbolic of the half-natures, and half-talents, who seem to succeed by imitation, etc. If this is correct, then we are entitled to be more specific, for there is no better example of such half-talent in German literature in 1800 than the author of the *Lucinde,* with his jubilant confidence in his skill to produce elegiacs, iambics, trochaics, etc., on models of Goethe, August Wilhelm Schlegel, and the Spanish poets.

Whatever scholars assume as the aesthetic function of the *Traum,* whether it is the third part of a three-fold symbolic representation of evil in its entirety (Baumgart) or a *dilettanti* theater for the amusement of Faust and the extinction of impressions made by the *Idol* of Gretchen (Valentin), or an Intermezzo before the final ascent of the Brocken (Witkowski) or a part without organic connection introduced without sufficient aesthetic justification (Minor), all agree that we have here contemporary satire. Here we must seek for expressions in regard to the romanticists and their doctrinaire leader Friedrich Schlegel. But first let it be said that the *paralipomena* to this part, as well as to the whole scene, are so clearly not applicable to our problem that they need no consideration.

First of all, according to Baumgart, the stanza,—

> "Fliegenschnauz und Mückennas
> Mit ihren Anverwandten,
> Frosch im Laub und Grill' im Gras,
> Das sind die Musikanten."

is "eine wahrhaft köstliche Symbolik" for the whole assembly

on the German Parnassus, which Goethe and Schiller had
called into being with their lyre.   This must thus include
the romanticists.[1]

In the fivefold group which now passes by we have
representatives of creation and criticism.   Baumgart applies
this group directly to the romanticists and refers particularly
to unpleasant relations between Goethe and Tieck, which
were due wholly to the Schlegels' efforts to elevate Tieck
above Goethe.   He refers to Schlegel's critical castigation
of Goethe in the reviews of the *Horen* and *Musenalmanache*,
and declares that the feelings so aroused determined Goethe
to remember Friedrich upon the Blocksberg.   This is readily
conceivable in 1797, yet a more kindly feeling supervened
before 1800.   This was again followed by bitterness before
1802.   The *Lucinde*, however, was perversity enough in
itself to deserve a diabolic translation to the Brocken, even
without the persistence of earlier vexations.

> "Seht, da kommt der Dudelsack !
>   Es ist die Seifenblase.
>   Hört den Schneckeschnickeschnack
>   Durch seine stumpfe Nase."

This represents the emptiness of romantic criticism with
its vast pretensions.   Romantic poetry, made in accordance
with Schlegel's recipe, is described in the stanza,—

> *Geist der sich bildet.*
>
> Spinnenfuss und Krötenbauch
>   Und Flügelchen dem Wichtchen !
>   Zwar ein Tierchen giebt est nicht,
>   Doch giebt es ein Gedichtchen.

Baumgart's language, almost identical with that of Schiller's
characterization of the *Lucinde* shows that he must have had
Schlegel distinctly in mind, though he does not say so.[2]

---

[1] *BF.*, Bd. i, p. 372.
[2] *Ibid.*, p. 376. Cf. *GSBr.*, July 19, 1799.

The stanza,—

Pärchen.

"Kleiner Schritt und hoher Sprung
Durch Honigthau und Düfte ;
Zwar du trippelst mir genung
Doch geht's nicht in die Lüfte"

signifies " die in Süssigkeit schwelgende Inhaltslosigkeit, die schwungvoll sich gebärdende Unkraft der verschwommenen Lyrik" in the Schlegel-Tieck *Musenalmanach* of 1802. When we consider that the next following attacks are upon the older representatives of rationalism, the conclusions of Baumgart have much in their favor. We know that Goethe stood between the two extremes of romanticism and rationalism, and condemned both as æsthetically perverse.

Minor is very reserved. The *Dudelsack* represents the half-talents, the *Geist der sich bildet*, inorganic poems in general, the *Pärchen*, possibly the brothers Stolberg. But these guesses make Goethe's satires more pointless and less individual than is usual with the poet elsewhere in the *Intermezzo* and in the *Xenia*, to which these stanzas properly belong.

The next group for consideration is that of the *Nordischer Künstler*, who is preparing for the Italian journey. The *Purist* is a representative of that class who branded the classicism of Weimar as "lüderliche Licenz," who could not see " die edle Wahrheit keuscher Natur" in Goethe's *Roman Elegies*. The dressed and powdered matron and the stark-naked young witch are symbols of the two extremes, "anständig thuende Prüderie" and " freche Schamlosigkeit," between which Goethe's poetry stands as a golden mean.[1]

Minor agrees in general with Baumgart in respect to the meaning of the *Purist*, but sees reference to a definite literary

[1] *Ibid.*, pp. 378 f.

phenomenon in the nude young witch. "Man kann bei ihr an die *Lucinde* von Friedrich Schlegel denken, wenn man einen spätern Zusatz annehmen will." [1]

The whole orchestra is brought to confusion by the witch's appearance. Shall we see here the confusion brought into the whole romantic circle by the *Lucinde*, a fact in full accord with Minor's assumption, and at the same time confirmatory of Baumgart's identification of the choir with the romantic school? Or shall we see in it the general licentiousness of the romantic school, which left such blots on the *Lucinde* and the first version of Tieck's *Sternbald*, etc., a fact likewise confirmatory of Baumgart's view?

After the *Aufklärer* have received due attention, a new chorus enters:

> "Da kommt ja wohl ein neues Chor,
>   Ich höre ferne Trommeln.
> Nur ungestört! Es sind im Rohr
>   Die unisonen Dommeln."

It seems more in accord with Goethe's own views, and with the almost immediate appearance of a chorus of typical philosophers, to find here, with Minor, "das eintönige Schulgezänk der Philosophen" rather than droning "Frömmelei" in poetry. Goethe looked upon the disagreements within the single group of transcendental idealists at Jena as a lamentable defect. If Minor is right, then we must have here a reflection of the philosophic *colloquia* with Niethammer and Friedrich Schlegel.

When the philosophers do appear, we find among them the *Idealist*, who has to confess that, if the scenes on the Blocksberg are the product of his own ego, he surely must be insane. Fichte is the best representative of this type, but since these *are* types and not individuals, we may justly

---

[1] *MF.*, Bd. II, pp. 268 f.

make this stanza include Friedrich Schlegel, who, in spite of vague beginnings of realism, was in all essentials a Fichtean, especially at the time this scene was written.

On the whole, Friedrich seems to have been richly remembered on the Blocksberg, as richly as in the *Xenia*, though in less transparent guise, because of Goethe's more symbolic manner of writing.

D. INFLUENCES UPON GOETHE.

We have not interpreted our problem to include an examination of Goethe's writings from 1802 to his death, for the purpose of finding materials traceable to the teachings of Friedrich Schlegel anterior to his departure for Paris.

Goethe's later approaches to romanticism in the second part of *Faust* are already guaranteed in Schiller's *Naïve und Sentimentalische Dichtung* and his private correspondence with Goethe upon *Faust*. Any further influence is due to the *creative* work of the school rather than the *critical*. Friedrich Schlegel's influence upon Goethe during his later life would doubtless be found to be a vanishing quantity.

But if we confine our inquiry to the period preceding 1802, any contribution of Schlegel to Goethe must be sought in one or more of three fields,—helpful knowledge, fruitful æsthetic theory, or models for imitation.

In the first field we know that Friedrich was of service. Goethe consulted him in regard to the name for *Paleophron und Neoterpe*, in regard to Greek trimeters and choric measures while working on the *Helena*, and in regard to *Margites*. Other instances are doubtless unrecorded. Schlegel's historic works, like the *Griechen und Römer*, were contributions to Goethe's knowledge of the subjects treated. More doubtful are his contributions to Goethe's understanding of idealistic philosophy. But contributions of this sort have very little value, and may be passed by with mere mention.

When we consider Schlegel's career as a *theorist*, we may divide it into three periods;—a first *eclectic* period influenced by current æsthetic views of all schools, but growing more decisively dependent upon Schiller's teachings and coming more and more fully under the spell of Goethe's classic manner, its close being marked by independent study of the Greeks; a second period, the *earliest romantic* period, completely dominated by Goethe's poetry, especially *Wilhelm Meister* and by Fichte's *Wissenschaftslehre*; a *third* period, when the romantic literatures of France, Italy, and Spain have begun to modify and complete his aesthetic doctrines.

Any real influence upon Goethe must of course come from the independent studies of the Greeks in the first period, or from his wider studies of the third. Otherwise we should have merely a reaction of Goethe upon Goethe.

Minor holds that Goethe obtained his doctrine of the epic from Friedrich Schlegel through August Wilhelm, but we have seen that Goethe never really accepted the Schlegel view. We have seen also that the Schlegels were led to formulate their doctrine of the epic more from an elaboration of Goethe's doctrine of the *Roman* found in *Wilhelm Meister* and his Schiller correspondence (which Körner undoubtedly brought to the eyes of Friedrich) than from independent studies of Homer. When Goethe says that he shall excuse the lack of unity in *Faust* upon the principle of the epic promulgated by the new school, it is so manifestly in jest, that it is incomprehensible that any scholar should consider it an earnest adoption of Schlegel's doctrine. Goethe sought to bring unity into his *Faust*, such unity as Homer's *Iliad* would have possessed, had its "gewaltige Tendenz zur Einheit" attained its goal. But the Gothic and the Greek elements refused to blend. Goethe, therefore, called the whole a *monstrous birth,* and could scarcely bring himself to undertake a further development of it. Schiller's urgency and encouragement overcame this reluctance and Goethe proceeded. And then it was that Goethe jestingly remarked that he would have to avail himself of the new epic theory of the harmony of the parts and partial disharmony of the whole. But he never ceased trying to reduce the disjointedness.

Schlegel's doctrine of the *Roman* in the *Gesprach, Ath.,* III, seems to have had no influence upon Goethe's practice. Indeed, it could not. Nor had the *Ideen* any appreciable effect upon Goethe's moral and religious conceptions as they are laid before us by Harnack.[1]

Goethe's use of trochaïcs in the *Walpurgisnacht* is referred in general to Friedrich Schlegel's experiments in that measure.[2] But there is a long road to traverse from a mere *post hoc* to a *propter hoc.* Goethe became interested in the Spanish literature through August Wilhelm Schlegel, and especially through Tieck. He read the Spanish poets at first hand. It seems almost incredible that the *Machwerke* of an unpoetic and purely formal imitator could have had any influence upon Goethe's metrical practice, not to mention a greater influence than the originals. August Wilhelm's practice had influence, for he had remarkable formal skill in the sonnet, in *terza rima, ottava rima,* and iambic pentameter, but Friedrich had no real skill as a versifier.

On the whole, almost any other member of the romantic circle could establish greater claims to influence upon Goethe than Friedrich Schlegel himself.

---

[1] *HG.,* Zweiter Abschnitt, pp. 17 ff.
[2] *MF.,* Bd. II, p. 239.

SUMMARY.

To sum up very briefly, Friedrich Schlegel was overwhelmingly dependent upon Goethe for the subject matter of literary work, materials for æsthetic and moral theory, and for models of imitation, while his own influence upon Goethe is exceedingly slight.

Schlegel passes through an æsthetic revolution comprising roughly the following stages: (1) Storm and Stress Germanism with Goethe as its idol; (2) theoretic Hellenism in support of Goethe's classicism; (3) romanticism based upon *Wilhelm Meister*, accompanied by a reduction of Greek models from their formerly accepted canonicity for German art; (4) romanticism based upon romance writers of early modern times, especially Cervantes.

All changes but the last were brought about by new insight into Goethe's art. Even the last may have been induced by a discovery of the essential sanity and unity of Goethe's works, and the latter's failure to respond to the dictatorial leadership of Friedrich.

Schlegel's personal relations with Goethe were never intimate. Goethe was patronizing and tolerant, and did not throw him over to please Schiller, but he never shared Goethe's personal or literary confidences. Goethe found it prudent to support the brothers against Nikolai, *et al.*, in journalism, and against Kotzebue and Co. in the theater, but he never approved their extreme romantic views and practices.

In conclusion, I wish to acknowledge that the foregoing essay owes its inception and much of what value it may possess to the suggestion and constant interest of Professor Max Winkler of the University of Michigan.

JOHN WILLIAM SCHOLL.

BIBLIOGRAPHY.

The following works have been carefully studied in the preparation of the above essay. The general histories whose chapters on the classic and romantic movements have been consulted are not here mentioned. The abbreviation used in referring to any work in the notes stands at the left of its title.

LITERARY WORKS.

MS. Friedrich Schlegel, 1794–1802, seine prosaischen Jugend-schriften, hrsg. von Jakob Minor, Wien, 1882, 2 Bde.

Luc. Lucinde, Ein Roman von Friedrich Schlegel, ed. Reclam.

FSWke. Friedrich Schlegels Sämmtliche Werke, Zweite Original Aus-gabe, Wien, 1846.

Ath. Athenäum, Eine Zeitschrift von August Wilhelm Schlegel und Friedrich Schlegel, Berlin, 1798–1800.

GWke. Goethes Werke, hrsg. im Auftrage der Grossherzogin Sophie von Sachsen. Abt. I.

AWSWke. August Wilhelm von Schlegels Sämmtliche Werke, hrsg. von Edward Böcking, Leipzig, 1846, 12 Bde.

HWke. Wilhelm von Humboldt's Werke, Berlin, 1841, 7 Bde.

CORRESPONDENCE.

WSBr. Friedrich Schlegels Briefe an seinen Bruder August Wilhelm, hrsg. von Dr. Oskar F. Walzel, Berlin, 1890.

GSBr. Briefwechsel zwischen Schiller und Goethe, vierte Auflage, Cotta, Stuttgart, 1881, 2 Bde. Contents found also in *GWke.*, Abt. IV, and *JSBr.* under corresponding dates.

JSBr. Schillers Briefe, hrsg. und mit Anmerkungen versehen, von Fritz Jonas. Kritische Gesammtausgabe. Deutsche Verlags-anstalt, 1892, 7 Bde.
Goethes Briefe, Abt. IV, in *GWke.*

RDBr. Dorothea von Schlegel, geb. Mendelssohn, und deren Söhne Johannes und Philipp Veit, Briefwechsel im Auftrage der Familie Veit, hrsg. von Dr. J. M. Raich, Mainz, 1881, 2 Bde.

HTBr. Briefe an Ludwig Tieck, ausgewählt und hrsg. von Karl von Holtei, Breslau, 1864, 2 Bde.

RNBr. Novalis' Briefwechsel mit Friedrich und August Wilhelm, Charlotte und Caroline Schlegel, hrsg. von Dr. J. M. Raich, Mainz, 1880.

GZBr. Briefwechsel zwischen Goethe und Zelter in den Jahren 1796 bis 1832, hrsg. von Dr. Friedrich Wilhelm Riemer, Berlin, 1834.

GuR. Goethe und die Romantik. Briefe mit Erläuterungen, hrsg. von Carl Schüddekopf und Oskar Walzel, Weimar, Verlag der Goethe-Gesellschaft, 1898, 2 Bde.

WCBr. Caroline, Briefe an ihre Geschwister, ihre Tochter Auguste, die Familie Gotter, F. S. W. Meyer, A. W. und Fr. Schlegel, J. Schelling, u. a. Hrsg. von G. Waitz, Leipzig, 1871, 2 Bde.

GGE. Goethes Gespräche mit Eckermann, contained also in *BGG.* under corresponding dates.

BGG. Goethes Gespräche. Herausgeber, Woldemar, Freiherr von Biedermann, Leipzig, 1889, 10 Bde.

TREATISES.

HRS. Die Romantische Schule, Ein Beitrag zur Geschichte des deutschen Geistes von R. Haym, Berlin, 1870.

HRomB. Blütezeit der Romantik, von Ricarda Huch, Leipzig, 1901.

HRomV. Ausbreitung und Verfall der Romantik, von Ricarda Huch, Leipzig, 1902.

Alt. Schiller und die Brüder Schlegel, von Dr. Carl Alt, Weimar, 1904.

PAesth. Die Aesthetik August Wilhelm Schlegels in ihrer Geschichtlichen Entwickelung, von Nicklaus M. Pichtos, Berlin, 1894.

Bern. Schriften zur Kritik und Litteraturgeschichte von Michael Bernays, Stuttgart, 1895, 5 Bde.

BXen. Schiller und Goethe im Xenienkampf, von Edward Boas, Stuttgart und Tübingen, 1851, 2 Bde.

SSXen. Xenien, 1796, Nach den Handschriften des Goethe und Schiller Archivs, hrsg. von Erich Schmidt und Bernard Suphan. Mit einem Facsimile. Weimar, Verlag der Goethe-Gesellschaft, 1893.

MF. Goethes Faust, Entstehungsgeschichte und Erklärung von Jakob Minor, Stuttgart, Erster Band, 1901, Zweiter Band, der erste Teil, 1901.

WFW. Die Walpurgisnacht im ersten Teile von Goethes Faust, von Georg Witkowski, Leipzig, 1894.

VF. Goethes Faustdichtung in ihrer künstlerischen Einheit, von Veit Valentin, Berlin, 1894.

BF. Goethes Faust als Einheitliche Dichtung, von Hermann Baumgart, Königsberg i. Pr., 1893, 2ter Band, 1902.

HG. Goethe in der Periode seiner Vollendung (1805–1832). Versuch einer Darstellung seiner Denkweise und Weltbetrachtung, von Dr. Otto Harnack, Leipzig, 1887.

HGed.꞉ Gedanken über Goethe, von Viktor Hehn, Berlin, 1887.

SVBr. Vertraute Briefe über die Lucinde, Schleiermachers Sämmtliche Werke, Abt. III, Bd. 1, pp. 421 f.

DLS. Aus dem Leben Schleiermachers, von Wilhelm Dilthey, Bd. I, Berlin, 1870.

HLH. Herder, nach seinem Leben und seinen Werken dargestellt von R. Haym, Berlin, 1880.

WGed. Gedanken über die Nachahmung der Griechischen Werke in der Malerei und Bildhauerkunst, von J. J. Winckelmann, Deutsch. Litt. Denk. d. 18 u. 19 Jahr. in Neudrucken, hrsg. v. Bernard Seuffert, No. 20, Heilbronn, 1885.

MNach. Über die bildende Nachahmung des Schönen, von Karl Philipp Moritz, Neudrucke, No. 31, Heilbronn, 1888.

DWM. Der Einfluss Wilhelm Meisters auf den Roman der Romantiker, von J. Donner, Berlin, 1893.

SLittgesch. Geschichte der deutschen Litteratur seit Lessings Tod, von Julian Schmidt, Leipzig, 1858, 3 Bde.

BLittgesch. Geschichte der deutschen Litteratur, von Adolf Bartels, Leipzig, 1901-2.

ARTICLES.

Biese. Die Aesthetische Naturanschauung Goethes in ihren Vorbedingungen und in ihren Wandlungen. Dr. Alfred Biese. *Preuss. Jahrb.*, vol. 59, pp. 542 ff. and vol. 60, pp. 36 ff., 1887.

CuR. Classiker und Romantiker. Jakob Minor. *G. Jahrb.*, Bd. X, pp. 212 ff.

Goethe und Kant. Karl Vorländer. *G. Jahrb.*, Bd. XIX, pp. 180 ff.

Ein deutsches Frauenleben aus der Zeit unsrer Litteraturblüte. R. Haym. *Preuss. Jahrb.*, Bd. 28, pp. 457 ff., November, 1871.

Kleine Beiträge zur Charakteristik Goethes, von Friedrich Vischer. *G. Jahrb.*, Bd. IV, pp. 3–50.

TABLE OF CONTENTS.

INTRODUCTION.
  a. General.
  b. Relations as seen in later years.

CAREER.
  A. PRIVATE. 1790 TO PUBLICATION OF *VON DEN SCHULEN IN* 1794.

    1. *Göttingen.*
    2. *Leipzig and Dresden.*
       a. Utterances about Goethe, etc.
       β. Intellectual occupations.
       γ. Personal factors.
          a. Father's death.
          b. Caroline Böhmer.
       δ. Traces of Goethe.

  B. Public, 1794 to 1802.
    1. *Dresden, Publications.*
    2. *Jena, first period.*
       a. Xenienkampf.
       β. Results, Continuation of Reviews, etc.
       γ. "Die Homerische Poesie."
       δ. "Das Studium der Griechischen Poesie."
       ε. "Lyceumsfragmente."
    3. *Berlin.*
       a. Athenäum, vol. I.
          a. Fragmente.
          b. Wilhelm Meister.
             I. Theories of Romantic Art, etc.
             II. Irony.
          c. Goethe's reception of the Athenäum.
       β. Athenäum, vol. II.
          a. Religion and Morals, "Ideen."
       γ. Lucinde.
    4. *Jena, Second Period.*
       a. Social Relations, etc.
       β. Athenäum, Vol. III.
          a. "Gespräch über die Poesie," etc.
       γ. Poetical activities in general.
          a. "Herkules Musagetes."
          b. "Alarkos" and its reception.

GENERAL MATTERS.
   C. "Walpurgisnacht" Satires.
   D. Influences upon Goethe.

SUMMARY.

NOTES.

BIBLIOGRAPHY.

TABLE OF CONTENTS.

The sceptical reconsideration of accepted theories is often of advantage in revealing weak points and establishing strong ones; Professor Jack's paper on *Thomas Kyd and the Ur-Hamlet* in the last issue of the *Publications* will no doubt be of service in both these ways; but it does not seem likely that his interpretation of the well known passage from Nash's prefatory epistle to Greene's *Menaphon* will displace that "all but universally accepted by scholars." It is, however, ingenious enough to merit careful examination from the conservative point of view. On the broader issue Mr. Jack has raised, it is to be remembered, in the first place, that this passage is by no means the only evidence of an earlier *Hamlet*. The entry in Henslowe's *Diary* under date June 9, 1594, and the reference in Lodge's *Wit's Miserie* (1596) to "the ghost, which cried so miserally at the theator, like an oisterwife, *Hamlet revenge*" prove conclusively the existence of a play on the subject of Hamlet at a date when Shakspere's tragedy was unknown, if we are to be guided by its omission from the Meres list and the unanimous opinion of Shaksperean critics. The general resemblance of the earlier *Hamlet*, so far as it can be divined, to the type of revenge-play of which *The Spanish Tragedy* is the most conspicuous example, must also be borne in mind;[1] but these are considerations familiar to students of the Elizabethan drama, and need not be urged here. Let us turn to the new interpretation of Nash's

---

[1] On this point Professor Thorndike's contribution to the *Publications* of 1902 is of capital importance; there are some additional details in Otto Michael's *Der Stil in Thomas Kyds Originaldramen* (Berlin Doctoral Thesis, 1905).

reference to contemporary literature, and see how far it is
borne out by the text. To begin with, I confess I attach
little importance to what Mr. Jack calls the "unifying
theme" of Nash's prefatory epistle; that "biting satirist"
was wont to follow the vagrant fancies of a facile pen, and
cannot be tied down to any rules of rhetoric. I am willing,
however, to accept Mr. Jack's view of the purpose of the
opening paragraphs, at the end of which the passage in
question occurs. "A plea for the kindly reception of the
Menaphon on the part of the students at the Universities.
A plea is necessary because its simple style and originality
will not at once be attractive to those whose habits and
tastes have recently been spoiled by the ' vain glorious tragedians.' " Let us examine the matter, however, a little more
closely, and allow Nash to speak for himself. Explaining,
in his first paragraph, why he appeals " to the Gentlemen
Students of both Universities," he writes :—

I am not ignorant how eloquent our gowned age is growen of late ; so
that everie mœchanicall mate abhorres the english he was borne too, and
plucks with a solemne periphrasis, his *ut vales* from the inkhorne ; which
I impute not so much to the perfection of arts, as to the servile imitation
of vainglorious tragœdians, who contend not so seriouslie to excell in action,
as to embowell the cloudes in a speach of comparison ; thinking themselves
more than initiated in poets immortalitie, if they but once get *Boreas* by
the beard, and the heavenlie bull by the deaw-lap. But herein I cannot
so fully bequeath them to follie, as their idiote art-masters, that intrude
themselves to our eares as the alcumists of eloquence ; who (mounted on
the stage of arrogance) think to outbrave better pens with the swelling
bumbast of a bragging blanke verse. Indeed it may be the ingrafted over-
flow of some kilcow conceipt, that overcloieth their imagination with a
more than drunken resolution, beeing not extemporall in the invention of
anie other meanes to vent their manhood, commits the digestion of their
cholerick incumbrances, to the spacious volubilitie of a drumming decasil-
labon. Mongst this kinde of men that repose eternity in the mouth of a
player, I can but ingrosse some deepe read Grammarians, who having no
more learning in their scull, than will serve to take up a commoditie ; nor
arte in their brain, than was nourished in a serving mans idlenesse, will
take upon them to be the ironicall censors of all, when God and Poetrie

doth know, they are the simplest of all. To leave these to the mercie of their mother tongue, that feed on nought but the crummes that fal from the translators trencher, I come (sweet friend) to thy *Arcadian Menaphon* . . . .

Now obviously we have here a direct reference to the stage—first, to the actors, who are corrupting popular taste by mouthing bombastic speeches, full of classical allusions; next, to the writers of these bombastic tragedies in blank verse, who, without skill or learning, "feed on nought but the crummes that fal from the translators trencher."[1] Nash goes then to his immediate purpose, the extolling of the "extemporall vaine" of his friend Greene; and in the next paragraph (I use Grosart's edition of Greene in the Huth Library), returns to his attack upon the "undescerning judgement" of the age :—

Oft have I observed what I now set downe; a secular wit that hath lived all daies of his life by what doo you lacke, to bee more judiciall in matters of conceit, than our quadrant crepundios, that spit *ergo* in the mouth of everie one they meete : yet those & these are so affectionate to dogged detracting, as the most poysonous *Pasquil*, anie durtie mouthed *Martin*, or *Momus* ever composed, is gathered up with greedinesse before it fall to the ground, and bought at the deerest, though they smell of the friplers lavander halfe a yeere after : for I know not how the minde of the meanest is fedde with this follie, that they impute singularitie to him that slanders

---

[1] Professor Churton Collins in his new edition of Greene, which came into my hands after the above was in type, says in his General Introduction (p. 41), in a discussion of Nash's Epistle from an altogether different point of view, viz., its bearing on the chronology of Greene's plays : "The plain object of the whole discourse is to pour contempt on Marlowe, and the *Tamburlaine* circle, and to contrast them to their disadvantage with the illustrious scholars associated with Saint John's College, Cambridge, and with such translators and poets as Gascoigne, Turberville, Golding, Phaer, Watson, Spenser, Atchelow, Peele, and Warner. It is an attempt to rally what may be called an Academic party against Marlowe and his partisans, who were now on the flood-tide of the popular success of *Tamburlaine*, and to exalt Greene's novels with their scholarly elaboration and their *temperatum dicendi genus* over 'kill-cow conceits and the spacious volubilities of a drumming decasyllabon.'"

privelie, and count it a great peece of arte in an inkhorne man, in anie
tapsterlie tearmes whatsoever, to oppose his superiours to envie. I will not
denie but in scholler-like matters of controversie, a quicker stile may passe
as commendable ; and that a quippe to an asse is as good as a goad to an
oxe : but when an irregular idiot, that was up to the eares in divinitie,
before ever he met with *probabile* in the Universitie, shall leave *pro & contra*
before he can scarcely pronounce it, and come to correct Common weales,
that never heard of the name of Magistrate before he came to *Cambridge*,
it is no mervaile if every alehouse vaunt the table of the world turned
upside down ; since the childe beats his father, & the asse whippes his
master. But least I might seem with these night crowes, *Nimis curiosus in
aliena republica*, I'le turne backe to my first text, of studies of delight ; and
talke a little in friendship with a few of our triviall translators.

Now at this point, at the very threshold of the crucial
passage, Mr. Jack, as it seems to me, goes astray. After
quoting the last sentence, he writes :—

In the 3rd paragraph of the Epistle, Nash has said that these "vain
glorious tragedians" feed on "nought but the crummes that fall from the
translators trenchers." Surely the natural interpretation here will identify
the "translators" of the 3rd paragraph and the "trivial translators" of
the 8th, as Nash distinctly says he will "turn back" to them.

No, Nash does not say he will turn back to the translators.
What he says is, "I'le turne backe to my first text, of
studies of delight ; " and his reference immediately before,
as quoted above, to the Marprelate controversy, makes it
clear that he is contrasting these theological subjects—an
alien realm into which he professes his unwillingness to
enter—with the lighter literature, aiming at pleasure rather
than profit, with which he began his Epistle. His earlier
theme was the work of those ignorant dramatists who "feed
on nought but the crummes that fal from the translators
trencher : " to them he will now return, and he will also
"talke a little in friendship with a few of our triviall
translators." That, at least, is my view of Nash's meaning
in the sentence quoted ; and there is nothing to show that
these "triviall translators" are the same as the translators

from whom, in his opening paragraph, he accuses the dramatists of borrowing.   These latter translators, as Mr. Jack says, "must have been translators of the ancient classics, most likely translators of Seneca:" the fundamental error of his position is that he assumes these translators to be the same as those Nash goes on to attack.   If we examine the passage we shall see that the "triviall translators" are the very dramatists and plagiaries whom Nash has already scourged, and that to identify them with the classical translators of the earlier passage would be to make Nash accuse them of borrowing from themselves.   The quotation, broken off at the words "triviall translators," runs on as follows :—

It is a common practise now a daies amongst a sort of shifting companions, that runne through every arte and thrive by none, to leave the trade of *Noverint* whereto they were borne, and busie themselves with the indevors of Art, that could scarcelie latinize their necke-verse if they should have neede ; yet English *Seneca* read by candle light yeeldes manie good sentences, as *Bloud is a begger*, and so foorth : and if you intreate him faire in a frostie morning, he will affoord you whole *Hamlets*, I should say handfulls of tragical speaches.   But ô griefe ! *tempus edax rerum*, what's that will last alwaies ?   The sea exhaled by droppes will in continuance be drie, and *Seneca* let bloud line by line and page by page, at length must needes die to our stage : which makes his famisht followers to imitate the Kidde in *Æsop*, who enamored with the Foxes newfangles, forsooke all hopes of life to leape into a new occupation ; and these men renowncing all possibilities of credit or estimation, to intermeddle with Italian translations wherein how poorelie they have plodded, (as those that are neither provenzall men, nor are able to distinguish of Articles,) let all indifferent gentlemen that have travailed in that tongue, discerne by their twopenie pamphlets : & no mervaile though their homeborn mediocritie be such in this matter ; for what can be hoped of those, that thrust *Elisium* into hell, and have not learned so long as they have lived in the spheares, the just measure of the Horizon without an hexameter.   Sufficeth them to bodge up a blanke verse with ifs and ands, & other while for recreation after their candle stuffe, having starched their beardes most curiouslie, to make a peripateticall path into the inner parts of the Citie, & spend two or three howers in turning over French *Doudie*, where they attract more infection in one minute, than they can do eloquence all dayes of their life, by conversing with anie Authors of like argument.

Mr. Jack's interpretation of this passage will be found in full on pp. 746–7. He takes Nash's attack as directed against the translators of Seneca. "Even these hack translators themselves feel their work to be so poor that they see Seneca will soon lose his vogue on the English stage. In anticipation of this they (hack writers) are turning from the translation of Latin to the translation of Italian."

A glance at the classical scholarship of the translators of Seneca will show how improbable this interpretation is to begin with. Studley was educated at Westminster School and afterwards a scholar of Trinity College, Cambridge. Nuce was a fellow of Pembroke. Nevyle took his M. A. at Cambridge, wrote works in Latin, and is thus described by Warton: "He was one of the learned men whom Archbishop Parker retained in his family, and at the time of the archbishop's death, in 1575, was his secretary." Heywood was a fellow of All Souls and Professor of Theology at Dilling, in Switzerland. Newton was educated at Oxford and Cambridge, and "quickly became famous for the pure elegance of his Latin poetry," for which indeed he is commended by Nash in this very Epistle (p. 22). "The laudable authors of Seneca in English," as Webbe calls them, were held in very high esteem, and their classical attainments were such as to make it positively absurd for Nash to revile them as "a sort of shifting companions . . . . that could scarcelie latinize their necke verse if they should have neede." As a matter of fact, he did nothing of the kind. All that he says of them is that they were stolen from by ignorant dramatists. Nash's first reference to "studies of delight" was to the drama; the drama is still his theme. "Seneca let bloud line by line and page by page, at length must needes die to our stage." In what reasonable sense would Seneca be "let bloud line by line and page by page," if the meaning is merely, as Mr. Jack suggests, that the translation has been so badly done that

Seneca will lose his vogue on the English stage? Obviously the accusation made against the dramatists is that they have borrowed lines and even pages from the translation of Seneca—"whole *Hamlets*, I should say handfulls of tragical speaches." But as this process of plundering Seneca cannot go on for ever, his "famisht followers" (the writers of bombastic tragedies) are driven into a new occupation—that of translating from the Italian, wherein from their ignorance they renounce all possibility of gaining credit or estimation.

I think I have gone far enough in the elaboration of the obvious. I shall, therefore, not attempt to controvert Mr. Jack's assumption that if Kyd is referred to in paragraph 8, Nash must again be speaking of him in paragraphs 11 and 12. Any one with half an hour to spare and the text at hand may decide this issue for himself. Nor shall I discuss the suggestions that "thrust Elisium into hell" may be paraphrased "transformed good Latin into wretched English," and that "whole *Hamlets* .... of tragical speaches" does not necessarily refer to a tragedy. It may be admitted that some of the explanations Mr. Jack challenges are not as satisfactory as could be wished : but they are more probable than his substitutes for them. I should be inclined on the evidence of the passage Mr. Jack quotes to arrive at a twofold conclusion exactly opposite to his :—(1) Nash had a dramatist or dramatists in mind in this paragraph ; (2) it is perfectly clear that Nash knew of a Hamlet drama, and this paragraph does throw some light upon its authorship." Professor McCallum, who devoted some time to a sceptical review of the evidence a few years ago, concluded : "The obvious and natural explanation of the passage is that the author of *Hamlet* tried his hand at the translation of Italian tracts ;" and this conclusion remains unshaken.

JOHN W. CUNLIFFE.

IV.—THE ENGLISH FABLIAU.

One feels inclined, like Bédier in *Les Fabliaux*, to apologize, at the beginning of this discussion, for dealing heavily with a light subject. Andrew Lang, to be sure, has spun the fabric of primitive imagination out of story threads from our simplest fairy tales. But there are no remnants of primitive thought to be discovered in the *fabliaux*, and few vestiges of ancient myth discernible in their narratives. One's only justification for approaching these *contes à rire* with anything but laughter must be a desire to search into the qualities which make "lewed peple loven tales olde," and especially the nature of the humor which preserves those called *fabliaux* from age to age. But a brief consideration of the nature and origin of the *fabliau* must precede an attempt to discover the characteristic quality of the English contribution to this literary form.

If one divests a *fabliau* of its minor qualities, such as verse, local color, and the depiction of character, there remains simply a humorous story. In the majority of *fabliaux*, and in all the best ones, this is not merely a jest, a quip, or a play upon words. It is usually a plot, simple, and often trivial enough, but depending for success, in part upon the true relation between its action and some quality of human nature, in part upon the originality and the excellence of that action. The deceit of wives, the gullibility of husbands, the greed of all mankind, vanity which blinds the best of us—such is the groundwork of its plots, and its episodes are humorous, not as a pun is humorous, but because they spring from and illustrate true qualities and true tendencies in universal human nature.

For example, the famous story of *La housse partie* tells

200

of the grandson who kept for the old age of his father one-
half of the sack which that ingrate had ordered bestowed
upon the poor and much-wronged grandfather. And *The
Reeve's Tale* of Chaucer relates how the proud miller was
himself beguiled by the two clerks whom he had wronged.
In the first of these stories the moral points itself, in the
second it is notably lacking; in the one the plot is not easily
to be forgotten, in the other it is of little value apart from
its local color and the characters which move through it; yet
both have this in common, that human nature as it is, betraying itself in some characteristic fault, is the groundwork of
each. This seems to be typical of nearly all the stories
which we call *fabliaux*, as well as of many more which, for
various reasons, cannot be distinguished by that title. And
more than anything else it is this quality, perhaps, which
makes these jesting narratives valuable and worthy of a
literary treatment. For in them, as through colored glass,
we see humanity in an aspect which more serious literature
cannot supply to us.

With these humorous stories the fable and the apologue
have at least this in common, that a reflection upon human
nature lies behind their narratives. If so, since the power
to observe and to generalize is not acquired in the earliest
stages of primitive man, they are, presumably, less ancient
than the folk tale; and, since a certain kind of insight is
common to all three, they may be said to spring from much
the same soil. The fable and the apologue, to be sure, point
a moral, while the writer of real *fabliaux* can seldom be
accused of a serious aim, yet the difference is only in point
of view. One has observed that again and again man comes
to grief through his own greed. Shall he point the moral?
He may do so by a little fable of the *Disciplina Clericalis* in
which the fox persuades the wolf to come down the well for
the full moon cheese. Or shall he make fun of it and let

the moral take care of itself? A dozen suitable stories come to mind, but see how in the Middle English beast *fabliau* of *The Vox and the Wolf* this same little fable gets the bit in its teeth, runs away with the moral, and becomes a good story and brilliant satire upon contemporary society.

Thus it might be said that from the same observation one man has made fun, another sermons. And since these plots may be shifted from apologue or fable to *fabliau* or back, according to the purpose of the writer, the relationship among these three forms is even closer than this statement implies. It is not uninteresting to note that this has always been recognized by those who seek illustrative stories. There are few fable collections which do not contain some *fabliau* plots, and few mediæval sermon books or *exemplum* collections not enriched in the same manner.

But although we agree that the *fabliau* has sprung, like the fable, from an observation taken upon human nature we have not yet arrived at a definition which will be valuable in the consideration of a particular literature. For the study of a given literature the thousand little plots which make most of our fables and apologues, and are often the germ cells of the *fabliaux*, can scarcely be useful. Upon nothing has the race spirit and the *Zeitgeist* made less impression. Told over countries, preached in the churches, gleaned from manuscripts, carried over sea in ships, these little stories pass from tongue to tongue and under the eyes of many races. They are called anecdotes, good stories, fables, *exempla*, at will. Rolling stones, birds of passage which go from clime to clime and owe allegiance to no one of them, they often come from a region above and beyond any national peculiarity and localism, while, compared with theirs, the anonymity of the rest of mediæval literature is almost personal. Their ranks are swelled by additions from the brains of each generation, but, unless some master writer enshrines them in literature, the condition for the immortality of these newcomers is that they shall lose their traits of race and time. Formless, without setting and without character, such stories have no more reference for one land than for another, and no significance for the literature in which they appear. And yet the land of their birth or their adoption may become the scene of their action. They may be given a local habitation and a name, while men of the period, with all that distinguishes the abstract from the concrete character, move through their story. Only when this happens do these tales become material for literary, rather than psychological, historical, or sociological, criticism.

With the fable this seldom occurs, for the actors are animals and the point is the moral; yet we have had a La Fontaine. With the apologue it is less infrequent. But with the stories told mainly for the humor of the side lights which they threw upon old human nature this was a process easy and much to be desired. It happened to a notable extent in Italy, and the *novella* literature resulted. In France, where invention was quicker, it gave us at an earlier period the fine *fabliaux* from which we take a convenient name for the verse form. In England the stories which resulted were fewer but of a quality by no means inferior.

In estimating them, and in attempting to discover what distinctive literary quality they possess, we shall readily eliminate all rolling stones whose moss of localism has not yet gathered. But the real *fabliaux* which remain we must value for something more than originality in plot, or be negligent of the just discussed nature of the form. For, since the *fabliau* is the offspring of the talk of the roads and of the inns, it is a doubtful business to praise plot alone, when it is probable that the best plots are ages old and have acquired their polish by long handling. Narrative skill in adaptation and expansion, good expression, good setting, all

should get their meed of praise. But must we not also heed
an art which develops and makes more effective the reflective nature of the *fabliau*, and adds this to the attraction
which a good story well told must always possess? The
French, for example, are witty, inventive enough in the
matter of stories, good plot handlers, thoroughly conscious
of the satiric power of the *fabliau* story, yet often the
character study suggested by the plot they have used so well
finds no adequate expression. One seldom suspects, with
them, that the *fabliau* is an apologue with a different point
of view. The lemon, it seems, is well squeezed, but not
squeezed dry.

The defects and merits of the English work can be made
clear in a brief survey.

If the Anglo-Saxons had a taste for the humorous, it was
dormant, with other good pagan qualities, in the monkish
writers. One scarcely expects to find a *fabliau* in Old
English. But not even a fable rewards careful searching.
With a few borrowed narratives of a type called by the
French *contes dévots*, the short story feebly begins its career,
but there is no contribution to reflective narrative, much less
to *fabliau*, by its literature.

Middle English is as rich in reflective stories as Anglo-
Saxon is poor. Yet the majority of them are fables,
apologues, and *fabliau* plots, which are not valuable for the
attempt to discern the quality of the English *fabliau*, because
they offer no grasping points. Their narrative is usually a
direct translation. Their story has not been referred to
English conditions, and they have taken no advantage of the
reflective possibilities of their plots except to add sometimes
a far-fetched moral. They are cosmopolitan, not racial, and
they have little interest except to the student of comparative
literature, and the indefatigable collector of the ubiquitous
parallel.

The real English *fabliaux* are better than the contemporary narratives of the last group because their authors tell them either as their own stories or in their own way. No longer mere birds of passage, feathered alike in all climes, they have been caught and domesticated, or are natives to the soil itself. They fall into two strata, one in the 13th and early 14th centuries, the other in the late 14th.

From the first stratum many must be lost. But it is represented in our literature by several excellent stories, which present, however, nothing that was not done as well, and usually at an earlier period, in France. Genuine *fabliaux* certainly, and certainly of this period, are *Dame Siriz, The Pennyworth of Wit,* and, in spite of its best actors, *The Vox and the Wolf.* To these may be added a few more from the homily collections and elsewhere by those more generous in their attribution of date or originality.

Dame Siriz[1] was written probably in the Southwest and perhaps in the latter half of the 13th century. It is the old story of the woman beguiled by a procuress who puts pepper into the eyes of a dog to make it weep. The unknown source is probably a Latin *exemplum* rather than a French *fabliau.* But there is no doubt of the essential originality of the English version in everything except plot. The very spicy, colloquial dialogue is proof of this, and the homely realism of the details. The story, moreover, is localized in England by a reference to Botolfston. Yet there is no quality which might not be duplicated in the earlier work of the French *jongleurs,* and the poem, when compared with their best, is crude in rhythm and expression.

A much more finished production is *The Vox and the Wolf,*[2] written in the dialect of Kent or Sussex, also in the latter half of the 13th century. It is the familiar tale of the

---

[1] Ed. Mätzner, *Altenglische Sprachproben,* I, pp. 103 f.
[2] Ed. Mätzner, *Altenglische Sprachproben,* I, pp. 130 f.

well with buckets into which the guileful Reynard lures the
trusting Isengrym.   Nothing in all the branches of the great
animal *epos* is more delightful than the shriving of Isengrym
at the well head before he is permitted to enter into the
paradise which Reynard says is below.   This is in all the
French versions, while the excellent little dialogue in the
hen yard seems to be in the English alone.   Come down and
be bled, says Reynald to Chauntecleer.   "For almes sake"
I have "leten thine hennen blod;" and unless he does the
same for him the cock may "sone axe after the prest."   Up
to the scene at the well head the unique variant of Branch
4, preserved in MS. 3334 of the Bibliothèque de L'Arsénal,
is the closest analogue, while the ordinary version, as presented in Méon, t. I, p. 240, is nearer the latter half of
the poem.   In short, the English author can be tied down
to no existing French original, and adds an episode found in
no one of them.   If he could write,

> "Him were levere meten one hen
> Than half an oundred wimmen,"

he could rearrange the narrative without assistance.   So we
grant him originality in plot handling, as well as the power
to readapt French wit for English hearers, and to add spice
of his own.   Yet no one will claim that his poem is noticeably better than the French versions.   It certainly possesses
no characteristic definitely English or definitely new.

An old apologue idea is preserved in the Southeast Mid-
land poem *A Pennyworth of Witte*,[1] preserved in a manuscript
of about 1330.   It is the story of a husband who tested
wife and leman and found the former true.   Kölbing too
readily asserts that this is a French *fabliau* Englished.[2]   The
only French version of the story which we possess is quite

---

[1] Ed. by E. Kölbing, *Englische Studien*, VII, pp. 111 f.
[2] See Kölbing, *op. cit.*

different in detail, and the resemblances are those which oral tradition or memory would supply. In both English stories (for there is a later version) the localization in France is avoided, and the scene is moved so that the husband travels into France instead of away from it. Furthermore, the villain is much blacker, the heroine more noble than in Jehans D'Aubepierre's *De la bourse pleine de sens*. But, as with *The Vox and the Wolf*, one can claim no distinguishing quality for the English *fabliau*. The writer reaches the level of the French, but he adds nothing which may be accredited to his race.

A history of the English *fabliaux* would have to make more of these poems. Though it is true that models existed for them in the French, though the earliest is in a barbarous tongue, and the latest somewhat pedestrian, yet, if their average be that of the time, the French art of story telling had been well learned. And yet, at the best, here are only imitators, imitators who express the individuality of their race only by a somewhat unhappy trait ; for if they tell the tales as well, they allow some of the bubbling Gallic wit, the *esprit gaulois*, characteristic of the true *fabliau*, to escape in the reworking. The English have not yet put their imprint upon the *fabliau*.

The step forward which English narrative took, in common with all English literature of the 14th century, is best exhibited perhaps in the religious literature. The flowering forth of the beautiful *contes dévots* from the mould of saints' legend can there be seen in all its stages. But so little of the *fabliau* literature was written down and preserved unto our day that we cannot say, here it was developing, here retarded. We must deal with individual works and with individuals. To this period of literary advance belongs the second stratum of *fabliaux*. It contains a number of those story microcosms which we have agreed to neglect. Gower's

work remains, in certain specimens to which the name fossil
may be fitly applied, but all that is valuable for this inquiry
is Chaucer's.

There are seven stories in the Canterbury Tales which
may be fairly called *fabliaux,* and four others that belong in
the same gallery. The praise of these stories fills a shelf of
publications, but criticism is not lacking. They are unoriginal,
write some French scholars; they are rambling, digressive,
planless, cry the authors of manuals on short story writing.
That. they are unoriginal can be maintained only by a
foreigner who employs convenient plot digests. Like all
good story writers, Chaucer used the best available plot.
His originality lies elsewhere, and it will be enough to show
that he never spoiled the plots which were given to him.
As for digressions, are there to be no more cakes and ale?
Must we be held to the bare plot? May we have no
humorous side issues, no apt "ensamples," no foraging by
the way? Because a child will have the story and nothing
but the story does a man require of a novel nothing but the
plot? No master of "rethorike sweete," I suppose, was
ever so "unenlumyned" as to desire much amputation or
extraction in any of these stories. Yet Chaucer, like Shakespeare, has been charged with bad technique. Since the
object of technique in narrative is to secure that excellence
of total effect which no one denies him, a defence is unnecessary, but a closer inspection of the abused and delightful
digressions which called forth the criticism will reveal an
artistic purpose behind them, and help to define the distinctive characteristic of the English *fabliau.*

Let us put *The Merchant's Tale* upon the operating table
and dissect it in the German fashion. The poem consists
of 1174 lines. The first twenty-two begin the story much
in the manner of a French *fabliau:* "Whilom ther was
dwellynge in Lumbardye a worthy knyght that born was

of Pavye." But with the twenty-third line, and before the plot has begun to unfold, the poet drifts off into a deliciously ironical praise of wiving, which lasts until the 148th line. And now we return to the hero, but the wordy battle which wages over his choice of a wife has nothing to do with the plot. It is, rather, ironical dialogue which illustrates the character of the old knight and the quality of his folly. Only with line 446 does the plot begin to move. Then, with the bit in his teeth, Chaucer rides merrily through the remaining 728 lines, pausing only for brief and characteristic appeals to Fortune, to Ovyde, and to Salomone. Thus the story proper is in 750 lines, while humor, wit, moralizing, and suggestion of character employ 424.

Is this bad art? Consider first the story told in the 750 lines. The young wife loves the squire of her old, blind husband. Their love affair is discovered when, in the midst, sight is granted to the husband. Boccacio in the ninth *novella* of the seventh day tells very much the same story. He indulges in no introduction, and in no digressions,—in the absence of the latter resembling Chaucer more than at first appears, for, once started on the plot proper, the English poet keeps at his muttons until the end. Two differences between the two stories remain : one lies in the introduction to the English narrative ; the other is this, that, throughout, Chaucer's story is made real by every probable circumstance, and particularly by all the personality which dialogue can give to his characters, whereas, with Boccacio, the plot's the thing, and it moves gracefully, but unreally, to its conclusion.

When one considers the nature of the *fabliau*, that it is based upon human nature and must deal with real humanity, this seems a very noteworthy difference. But a yet greater one lies in the substance of the remaining 445 lines of the story, Chaucer's introduction, which has no counterpart in the Italian *novella*.

14

Like all *fabliaux*, this famous little story of the pear tree
is based upon the error of human nature, here just the universal weakness of man, whose self-conceit blinds him to his
own infirmities, and whose silly optimism makes him think
that the images his sentimental fancy paints for him are true
copies of bliss to come.   It is this universal quality which
makes the story something more than a rather spicy practical
joke, and this, too, made it profitable for story mongers to
bear the tale from race to race.   Without it the narrative
would have just the value which would appertain to *The Ass
in the Lion's Skin* if men ceased to clothe themselves in .
virtues not their own, or were no more unmasked when
so doing.

Now a consideration of the 445 introductory lines just
mentioned shows that they are devoted to an exposition and
illustration of just this human error which lies beneath the
story, namely, of the folly of the man that believes all matri-
mony to be " parfit bliss," and the folly of the old husband
who cannot see that his age may be a disability in the eyes
of his young wife.   These twin follies are born in one mind,
that of January, the hero of the piece, and most of the
so-called digression consists of his own discourse on matri-
mony, whereby Chaucer convicts him out of his own mouth.
This comment upon the text,—for although Chaucer is not
moralizing, so it may figuratively be called,—is what chiefly
distinguishes his work upon this story from the Italian's,
and, to go further afield, sets apart his method from that of
Italian story-tellers and French jongleurs.

For it seems that Chaucer, with an instinct for spirit
stronger than the feeling for form which keeps the Latin
races to the story, has apprehended the true potential value
of this plot.   For him it is not just a good tale to be retold
in the French style.   Pondered more deeply, it is a treatise
upon humanity ; it is a specimen from which the living

creature may be reconstructed. And to reconstruct is his work, in which, for method, he chooses to bring back personality through life and speech into the bare bones of the narrative. And not content with this, by parading the love-sodden January upon his stage, he makes so much the more vivid the succeeding action, and the keen reflection upon human nature which it implies. Something in unity of narrative impression suffers of course. His work lacks the perfect structure of the simple *lais* of Marie of France. But the comparison between his work and hers is the old one between Shakespeare and Racine, between Kipling and Maupassant. We will decide, forever, I suppose, according to the land we were born in, but in this case at least that Chaucer better appreciated the nature and the possibilities of the *fabliau* story seems to be susceptible of demonstration.

If space permitted, this characteristic quality of Chaucer's work might be illustrated by an analysis of all his *fabliaux*. But a brief review will be sufficient to indicate how thoroughly he realized the nature of his material and how different was his method from the less discerning art of his French rivals.

For example, the Sumnor's tale of the begging friar, when stripped of its character study, is a mere anecdote. Chaucer uses it to satirize the greed of friars, and to put in the pillory a hypocritical beggar. His method is to expand the begging speech of the friar until it becomes the principal part of the first 384 lines. By a careful realism he makes the "frere" a lively personation, and succeeds in describing him by his own tongue. An Italian or French jongleur would presumably have begun the story near the point where the friar ends his sermon.

The Reeve's Tale is a practical joke story of a type very common in the French *fabliau*. It could be told simply for the humor of the adventure of the "clerkes tweye." So, indeed, does Jean de Boves tell it in *De Gombert et des deux clers*, which Leclerc praises as Chaucer's original. But the Englishman, getting his plot there, no doubt, adds his famous description of the proud miller and his well born wife, to the effect that we shall see that it is pride which is getting a fall here, and yet recognize the characters as individuals and not types.

To analyze all of these stories would be to savor of Chaucer's favorite vice, for he too seldom is like Justinus of whom it is said, "for he wolde his longe tale abregge, He wolde noon auctoritee allege." Yet while all are not equally susceptible of development for reflective purposes, from all may be drawn evidence to illustrate this point. Subtract, for example, from the 625 lines of *The Nun's Priest's Tale* that part which corresponds to the thirty-five lines of the fable of Marie of France, and consider the purpose and effect of Chaucer's padding. Or note *The Manciple's Tale*, in which, since the characters of the fable were not attractive subjects for development, the poet has tried to make his story reflective by adding example and moralizing, failing this time, because he emphasizes woman's weakness and not the point of the story. In no case, when some quality of human nature is to be illustrated by the story, does he depend, like Gower, upon plot alone.

Nor, in this connection, must we omit to notice that digression for the sake of character development is, in the shorter stories, typical only of the *fabliaux*. Sandras noted many years ago[1] that Chaucer departed very little from his original in legends, and only to bring in classical allusions, or for the purpose of satire in his *lais*, while in his *fabliaux* he became a creator by his added details, by the eloquence of his personages, and by his truth to character. And since his method springs from the nature of his material, this is just what we should expect.

[1] E. G. Sandras, *Étude sur G. Chaucer considéré comme imitateur des trouvères.*

Thus to discover a really original characteristic in the English *fabliau* it has been necessary to eliminate all merely cosmopolitan stories from the discussion, and afterwards to set aside the genuine *fabliaux* of the earlier English stratum. The sought-for quality seems to appear in Chaucer. In him, it was the art to discover and employ the reflective power of a *fabliau* story, but in praising his genius one must not forget that this desire to moralize, to seek spirit rather than form, is characteristic of the English mind. If it does not appear in other English *fabliaux*, where race spirit has not been allowed to mould the foreign material, it may be discovered elsewhere, even in this comparatively unoriginal period. Langland possessed it, and so did Robert Manning of Brunne. Its result in Chaucer is not typical of all English *fabliaux*, but in him, at least, it is a typical English spirit working upon the *fabliau* form.

This is illustrated, by converse, in the unoriginal work of Gower. It does not seem that Gower is inferior to Chaucer in the art of handling a plot. In arrangement of incident and in proportion he is certainly his equal, and sometimes his superior. He has little traffic with the pure *fabliau*, perhaps because of the nature of his poem, perhaps because, as I have tried to show, the *fabliau* seldom has a ponderable value unless it is a character sketch, and Gower sought the ponderable, and could not develop character. But in the *Confessio Amantis* he employs a number of apologues which give him just the opportunity that was Chaucer's in, say, *The Nun's Priest's Tale*. Indeed, he retells the story of Phebus and Cornide, which was given to the Manciple among the Canterbury pilgrims. But in these narratives he takes no advantage of the reflective possibilities. And, co-ordinately, he makes no use of any art which might spring from the temperament of his own race, and indeed of no art whatsoever except the art of simple tale-telling, which he must be allowed to possess. And, consequently, his stories, like the *fabliaux* discussed in the earlier part of this paper, possess no more of the characteristic quality of the English *fabliau*, than do the novels of Charles Brockden Brown of the characteristic quality of American fiction. He is at best a teller of correctly told stories, and to Chaucer we must return for proof of originality in the *fabliau*.

After the 14th century English literature lost, for a while, any original impulses that it may have possessed. But the English *fabliau*, as a literary form, had already been established and been given an individual and characteristic form. Chaucer was like a scientist who applies for great results a law whose implications had been only imperfectly realized by its framers. He borrowed a form from his French masters and infused it with a new, a proper, and what seems to be a more profitable spirit. Not forgetting to allow for the power of genius, which knows no race, perhaps we may recognize in the result the impress of the English mind upon the *fabliau*, and the contribution of the race to that literary form.

HENRY SEIDEL CANBY.

V.—MONTAIGNE: THE AVERAGE MAN.

We are accustomed to associate with the names of the great men of all times and in all lines of activity, certain dominant characteristics and traits of personality, which, though usually merely coincident and contributing factors, serve none the less as the tangible facts whereby the mind is enabled to grasp and gauge their power. It is a criterion whose insufficiency becomes evident only in the isolated instances wherein such natural indices of character are made conspicuous chiefly by their absence. There are characters in history upon which the test of time has set its seal of greatness, but which, considered abstractly and apart from their achievements, seem merely negative and colorless. Their work remains as the tangible evidence of their genius, yet any effort to establish the relation of cause and effect between that work and the intrinsic personality of its author is uniformly unsatisfactory in its results.

The *Essays* of Montaigne present the somewhat unique spectacle of an author who has undertaken the task of laying before his readers the dissection of himself; who, with the high standard of litéral and intelligent accuracy ever before him, has set himself to discover, with impartial hand and unsparing judgment, the entirety of his personality, to its smallest detail, and from as many different viewpoints as a life of considerable variety enabled him to assume.

And yet, with the study of this labored self-analysis, inevitably comes the disquieting if unacknowledged thought that the intrinsic worth of its subject does not warrant such elaboration. Assembling and regarding, as a whole, the different phases of the personality which is laid before us in such faithful detail, we cannot but be struck by its icono-

215

clastic mediocrity; should one endeavor to sum up that abstract personality in a single terse adjective, he would perforce term it merely "ordinary."

Montaigne lived in a time of political and religious upheaval, whose turbulence and tumult was inevitably reflected in the moral degeneracy and vicious licentiousness of its society; aside, however, from a certain degree of moderation and self-restraint, and at least a realizing sense of the depravity of the social state, he does not seem to have noticeably differentiated himself from the spirit of his age. His private life presents nothing more than the extreme of the commonplace;—evidently the life of a hundred others of his own rank and time. His virtues were the virtues of a gentleman; his vices at least no worse than the ordinary; of distinctive individuality and positive force of character the available evidence indicates no more than the average amount. Moreover, the verdict to which we are thus apparently forced, he has anticipated by himself affirming its truth :—

"For my part," he says, "I am but a man of the common sort . . . . I propose a life ordinary and without lustre : 'tis all one; all moral philosophy can as well be applied to a common life as to one of richer composition." [1]

Naturally, however, this arbitrary classification of the author does not coincide with the facts which even the most casual reader of the *Essays* must feel to exist. We must insist that, if his character, *per se*, identifies him with the common rank of men, it becomes necessary to seek elsewhere the elements which differentiate him from them. For the solution of the problem one turns naturally to the *Essays*— at once the most celebrated and permanent of Montaigne's literary productions, and, of course, the immediate source of

[1] *Essays*, III, 2.

his fame. Yet when one reads and analyses these *Essays* with the purpose of discovering therein something higher and worthier than their author expressed in his daily life— something whose loftiness shall redeem his personal insufficiency—one is speedily undeceived, and obliged to admit the force of that which the essayist everywhere insists upon and reiterates with monotonous persistence : that his book and himself are one and identical, that his central idea and dominant aim is to portray himself, fully and accurately, without adornment and without artifice. In his very preface he warns us that, should we seek to glorify him, we must seek justification elsewhere than in his book. So far from pluming himself upon his literary achievements, he mocks the efforts of his amiable critics to reduce to tangible expression the secret of his charm, by himself elucidating, emphasizing, dragging to the light his own defects and those of his work. If we seek an ulterior motive for the *Essays*, we are told that Montaigne wrote them to " shame the chimeras and fantastic monsters of his mind ; " if we impute to him logical and connected purpose, he calls them a " rhapsody," a " hodge-podge, wild and extravagant in design ; " if we would admire the forceful beauty of his style, and the delicate coquetries of his pen, he gives us the lie with the naïve remark :—" All I write is rude ; polish and beauty are wanting . . . . my language has nothing in it that is facile and polished ; 'tis rough, free, and irregular," [1] and so on indefinitely.

Much has been said and written concerning the literary influence which the essayist exerted upon the writers of his own and later times. As a pioneer in a new school of letters and morals, the great share which his mind had in emancipating literature from the narrow rut of a stilted and imitative artificiality is beyond question. Nor is it to be denied

---

[1] *Essays*, II, 17.

that the freshness and originality of his style, the unexampled frankness with which his views are presented, constitute a no inconsiderable share of the charm of his *Essays*, his own disparaging statements to the contrary notwithstanding. But to maintain that these factors, in themselves, comprise the total operative assets of Montaigne's work, is a theory whose inadequacy is at once apparent. For that class of ordinary readers —necessarily greatly in the majority—who do not trouble themselves particularly concerning the literary influence or descendance of an author ; who are not perhaps in a position to adequately appreciate the artistic and technical beauties of a style, but who read Montaigne for the pleasure which they find in it—what is there in such a theory for them?

We have seen that the author voluntarily identifies himself with the "common sort" of men. Consistent, therefore, with his preconceived purpose of making "himself the matter of his book," he naturally elects to relegate the *Essays* to a similar position :—

"Were these Essays of mine considerable enough to deserve a critical judgment, it might then, I think, fall out that they would not much take with common or vulgar capacities, nor be very acceptable to the singular and excellent sort of men—the first would not understand them enough, and the last too much ; and so they may hover in the middle region." [1]

It is in these words, in my opinion, that is to be found the real secret of the enormous popularity of Montaigne. Whatever other contributing influences may exist, the one thing above all else which must consciously or unconsciously appeal to us, is that everywhere he consistently represents and personifies the viewpoint of that great "middle region" of mankind to which the majority of his readers belong. It is in this sense, and with reason, that it has been said that there is of Montaigne in all of us. We insensibly feel, in reading his *Essays*, that we are listening to the conversation

[1] *Essays*, I, 54.

of a man, rather than of a philosopher, whose thoughts are our own, who regards the affairs of life from our own standpoint, who has placed himself upon the intellectual plane of the commonplace and every day, insomuch that his judgments are formulated without a labored effort to construct, upon that basis, an intricate and abstruse philosophy.

One ordinarily associates with the idea of philosophy a doctrine whose tenets advocate a continual striving toward a goal beyond the limits of the average moral constitution; we are apt to regard philosophers as a class apart, as the embodiments of the reason which exempts itself from the ordinary foibles of men by dint of an extraordinary exercise of will. To such a preconceived conception, Montaigne's doctrine of life comes as a unique and refreshing novelty. There is nothing in his philosophy to inspire in his readers a desire to elevate and ennoble themselves; he never preaches to us; he never poses as an infallible arbiter of right and wrong, nor arrogates to himself the privileges of superior virtue or intelligence. In the midst of a literature of strained enthusiasm and frenetic aspiration toward an ill-defined higher state, whose expression was, for the most part, mere glittering generality, Montaigne stood alone as the mouthpiece of the less pretentious ideals and aims of those who, in the obscurity of comparative mediocrity, had hitherto remained unrepresented, even in their own chronicles.

As the embodiment of the philosophy of the majority of humanity—the average people—the *Essays* are unique in the history of literature. In the social system whose aristocracy is the arbitrary product of mere chance of birth, wealth, and social rank, every degree of society is adequately represented in the world's letters; but in the truer aristocracy of intellect and talent, the great majority are condemned to eternal silence by their very inability to force the world's hearing. It is of these that Montaigne has constituted him-

self the voluntary representative—it is by their verdict that
he maintains an enduring position in the literature of all
time.   He rigidly differentiates himself from the ordinary
procedure of philosophic discourse by speaking, not to his
audience as from a higher plane, but for them, from a position among themselves.   It is just this fact that has won for
him a degree of popularity which far profounder writers have
failed to attain.

It is evident, however, that, should we stop here, our own
facts may be adduced to disprove our theory.   Obviously
Montaigne was not, essentially and by nature, of those whose
spokesman he made himself.   The mere fact that he possessed the ability to represent that class as none of them had
ever been able to do before or has done since, necessarily
places him on a higher level than themselves.   His attitude in
identifying himself with them would seem, therefore, to assume
more the aspect of a voluntary choice than of a necessity;
whence our principal concern is reduced to a question of his
probable motives for such a choice.

The most ordinary and commonly accepted conception of
the essayist seems to be essentially that of M. Huet; he is
to be arbitrarily classified in the category of the merely idly
passive, who, lacking the talent and ambition to play an
active and useful part in the world, are content to lead a
calm and peaceful life in the repose of their own thoughts.

There is doubtless a certain amount of truth in this
conception; but, in my opinion, there is even more of
inaccuracy and injustice to the author.   For it contends
necessarily that this negative sort of existence was the
natural result of his inherent instincts; that he accepted
those instincts as he found them, without putting them to
the test either of practical utility, or of abstract philosophy;
that he would probably not have tried to combat them, even
had he found them insufficient to such standards.   Is it not

an attitude a trifle unworthy of one who made the study of himself the principal object of his life? We are told by certain critics that Montaigne was merely a writer and nothing more—the idle dreamer of a philosophy which he never removed, or wished to remove, from the narrow domain of letters to put it to the proof of practicality. It is interesting to note his own words in this connection :—

"Such as I am, I will be elsewhere than on paper ; my art and industry have been ever directed to render myself good for something ; my studies to teach me to do, and not to write. I have made it my whole business to form my life—this has been my trade and my work. I am less a writer of books than anything else. . . . How I should hate the reputation of being a clever fellow at writing and an ass and an inanity at everything else!" [1]

From the evidence which we possess of Montaigne's political status, and of the ability which he displayed in his short career as a public man, there can be little doubt that he could have greatly augmented, by that means, the scanty credit accorded him for his literary productions, had he chosen to realize his possibilities. It is true, as has been frequently pointed out, that he had but little use for the world's applause ; but to conclude from this that his disdain was merely the expression of a temperament naturally passive and indifferent, is to presume too far upon his words. In fact, he assures us to the contrary :—

"I sometimes feel rising in my soul temptations to ambition, but I resolutely cling to the contrary. . . . I whet my heart for patience and weaken it on the side of desire." [2] . . . . "Against such affections, I say, I struggle with all my strength." [3]

It may be maintained that he suppressed his executive talents and refused to profit thereby, only to seek, in another manner, that glory apparently scorned ; that is, by means of his *Essays*. Did he, perhaps, foresee their great popularity,

---

[1] *Essays*, II, 37.   [2] *Essays*, III, 7.   [3] *Essays*, III, 10.

and the influence which they were to exert on the world's literature, long after his death? If it be so, he must have possessed a foresight indeed extraordinary;—the frigid reception which the *Essays* met with, in his own time, would naturally have made him believe the contrary. Moreover, his own words regarding the stability of his work scarcely display any such degree of foresight:—

"I write my book for few men and few years. Had it been a matter of duration, I must have put it into more stable language." [1]

In the light of these facts, that theory so little flattering to Montaigne, the man, loses some of its justification to the profit of a motive more worthy of Montaigne, the philosopher; his disinclination to profit, personally, by his abilities, appears rather the product of philosophic conviction than that of a nature too sluggish to make practical use of its own native talents.

And yet, what sort of a philosophy may this be, which demands of its disciples that they condemn themselves to mediocrity by their own voluntary suppression of their most natural abilities and desires? Montaigne was far too acute of perception not to realize the apparent inconsistency of such a sacrifice, and the imperative necessity of justifying his position to the world.

In the essay entitled, curiously enough, the *Apologie de Raymond Sebond*, he devotes a considerable space to an apparently irrelevant discussion of the actual differences existing between man and the brute creation, taking up in turn the various reasons ordinarily given to account for the former's superiority: *i. e.*, his reason, sensibility, power of speech, etc.; and each of them he rejects in turn, as being qualities shared in a greater or less degree by all creatures. By this process of elimination he ultimately arrives at the

[1] *Essays*, III, 9.

conclusion that the only definite and essential difference is
the result of what he terms the "elasticity" of the human
mind.[1] For, while the limits of the domain of the lower
animals are sharply defined by their merely corporeal needs
of nutrition and reproduction, man was created a being absolutely unlimited in his needs, his possibilities and his desires.
Neither by nature, nor by his own reason, are limits prescribed to his infinity :—

"In nothing is man able to limit himself to his actual necessities; of
pleasure, of riches, of knowledge, he grasps at more than he can hold; his
greed is incapable of moderation." [2]

For the essayist, at least, the corollary is obvious. Since
this appetite for knowledge and self-aggrandizement, coupled
with the ability to satisfy it in a greater or less degree, is,
in no case, more than simply a natural and inherent instinct,
small credit shall it be to him if he blindly obey that
instinct; for in so doing, he merely places himself on the
level of the unreasoning brutes, and sets his own vaunted
powers of reason and will at naught. The highest and only
test of his superiority must therefore lie in his ability to
dominate and master his natural heritage of ambition and
curiosity; consistent moderation, expressed by the voluntary
repression of his most cherished aims, must constitute his
sole claim to credit at the hands of true philosophy :—

"The virtue of the soul does not consist in flying high, but in walking
orderly; its grandeur does not exercise itself in grandeur but in mediocrity;
. . . . nor so much in mounting and pressing forward, as in knowing how to
govern and circumscribe itself . . . . demonstrating itself better in moderation than in eminence." [3]

Much has been said and written of the "scepticism" of
Montaigne; it has often been pointed out that, alone among

[1] E. Faguet, Seizième Siècle (Études Littéraires).
[2] Essays, III, 12.   [3] Essays, III, 13.

the philosophical writers of his epoch, he refused to share
their spirit of enthusiastic positivism and speculative abandon
in what they fantastically styled the Quest of Truth; that
the Essays everywhere represent the extreme of cautious
conservatism and incuriosity which declines to ally itself
with any specific doctrine, or to commit itself to any positive opinion regarding the problems which are ordinarily the
natural prey of the philosopher.

But to go a step farther and maintain that this spirit of
incuriosity was the elemental characteristic of his mind, is to
incur the possibility of serious inaccuracy. From his intimate knowledge of the philosophy of all ages, the essayist
assembles the essential points of their speculative theories;
he considers and compares them with due care, and, finally,
finding them inadequate, he rejects them;—to the reader,
then, who demands his own explanation, he replies simply
" que sais-je? "

It is not the expression of an inability, or even of a
reluctance to formulate a theory as satisfactory to his reason
as those which he rejects; it is rather the expression of
a higher conception of the uselessness of such an effort; and,
to the discriminating reader, must also, I think, convey a
conviction of the voluntary suppression, on the author's part,
of that " greedy curiosity of knowing " which constitutes so
primary an element of all minds.

For this reason, whether we accept it or not, we can
scarcely reproach Montaigne with having formulated a merely
altruistic and impracticable philosophy. The doctrine which
he laid down in his *Essays* was the doctrine which formed
the concrete basis of his own life; and by its interpretation
the many apparent inconsistencies and eccentricities of his
character are readily explained.

The practical aspect of that doctrine is a matter which lies
altogether without our present province; yet that it does

possess a practical value, as applied to the affairs of our own day, is not to be disputed. In the modern era of the strenuous life, when the purely materialistic extreme of existence is coming to be more and more emphasized ; when the true perspective of things is being submerged by the radical instincts of a merely personal ambition, it is not inconceivable that the world might learn, with profit to itself and to its future, that lesson of moderation and self-restraint which Montaigne sought to teach and to embody in his own life.

RALPH W. TRUEBLOOD.

VI.—ITALIAN FABLES IN VERSE.

Before the revival of Greek learning in the fifteenth century, the Æsopic fables of classical antiquity were known in Europe through Latin collections derived from Phædrus. Two of these collections were particularly well known; one which goes under the name of Romulus, written in prose in the tenth century; and a metrical version of the larger part of Romulus, written in the twelfth century. This metrical collection, called in the Middle Ages *Esopus*, is now ascribed to Walter of England, but is often called *Anonymus Neveleti*. Another metrical version of Romulus was made a little later by Alexander Neckam, and the fables of Avianus, also, were known to some extent. These collections, with numerous recensions and derivatives in Latin, and translations into many different languages, form a body of written fable-literature whose development can for the most part be clearly traced. At the same time, beast-fables were extensively employed in school and pulpit, and were continually repeated for entertainment as well as for instruction. Thus there was current all over Europe a great mass of fable-literature in oral tradition. The oral versions came in part from the written fable-books; others originated as folk-tales in medieval Europe; others had descended orally from ancient Greece, or had been brought from the Orient. Many are still current among the people in all parts of Europe, and beyond. From this mass of traditional material, heterogeneous collections of popular stories, including beast-fables, were reduced to writing in Latin and in other languages. An example of this process is found in the *Esope* of Marie de France, the earliest known fable-book in a modern vernacular, which was translated into French in the twelfth

century from an English work which is now lost. Forty of
Marie's fables, less than two-fifths of the whole number,
came from a recension of the original Romulus called *Romulus Nilantii;* the others from popular stories of various kinds.
Similarly, the important *Æsop* of Heinrich Steinhöwel contains the Romulus fables in four books, followed by seventeen
fables called *Extravagantes,* others from the recently published
Latin version of the Greek fables, from Avianus, from the
Disciplina Clericalis of Petrus Alphonsus, and from Poggio,—
in all, nine books, printed in Latin with a German translation about 1480, and speedily translated into many languages
(including English, by Caxton in 1484, from the French
version). The *Extravagantes,* like other collections, and like
the episodes of the beast-epic (little known in Italy), came
from popular tradition. Many writers show by incidental
references that they were familiar with fables, although they
may not have regarded them as worthy of serious attention,—
writers like Dante, and his commentator Benvenuto da Imola.
Moreover, the animal-lore of the bestiaries and of works like
the *Fiore di Virtù* is closely akin to that of the fables. It is
evident, then, that the collections descended from Phædrus,
important though they were, represented but a fraction of
the fable-literature that was current in the Middle Ages.

The best work now available on the history of fable-
literature in Italy up to the end of the fifteenth century, is
the Introduction to Dr. Brush's edition of the *Isopo Laurenziano,*[1] which is based in part on the works of Ghivizzani,[2]
Hervieux,[3] and de Lollis.[4] But no work yet published gives

[1] M. P. Brush, *The Isopo Laurenziano,* Columbus, 1899 (Johns Hopkins
dissertation).
[2] G. Ghivizzani, *Il Volgarizzamento delle Favole di Galfredo,* Bologna, 1866.
[3] L. Hervieux, *Les Fabulistes latins,* vol. I, Paris, 1883 ; 2d ed., 1893.
[4] *L'Esopo di Francesco del Tuppo,* Firenze, 1886 (selections, with introduction by C. de Lollis).

anything like an adequate treatment of the subject; in particular, statements that have been made about the fables now published for the first time are inaccurate and misleading.[1] It will be well, then, in order that we may properly determine the place of this collection of fables, to give a brief account of the other Italian collections belonging to the same period.

In the first place, we have several translations of the fables of Walter of England. The best known is called *Esopo volgarizzato per Uno da Siena*, belonging to the fourteenth century, with sixty-three fables in prose. Dr. Brush enumerates fifteen manuscripts of this translation, and I am able to add to the list one more,—Cod. Riccardiano 1185.[2] The text was printed in 1496, again in 1778, and many times during the nineteenth century.[3] Another prose translation of the fourteenth century, with sixty-two fables, is contained in the Cod. Riccardiano 1338, from which it was published in 1866 by Ghivizzani.[4] The Cod. Vaticano 4834 contains, with other writings of the fourteenth century,

---

[1] Cf. K. McKenzie, *An Italian Fable, its sources and its history*, in *Modern Philology*, vol. I, no. 4 (April, 1904), pp. 497–524.

[2] Under this number are included six volumes; the first volume contains 44 folios, written in the 15th century; ff. 1a–2b, "Le beleze di merchato vechio" (by Antonio Pucci); ff. 3a–36b, the fables, without title; ff. 37a–38b, "Epistola di santo bernardo;" ff. 39a–41a, "Anoie" (Le Noie di Antonio Pucci; published in his *Poesie*, vol. IV, pp. 275–285); ff. 41b–44b, "Chalendario" and arithmetical problems. The fables, each one illustrated by a picture, originally numbered 63; but eight folios have been lost, carrying with them, in whole or in part, some fourteen fables. The remaining folios are numbered continuously.

[3] In 1496 in connection with the translation in sonnet form by Accio Zucchi: see Brush, *op. cit.*, p. 31. In 1778 at Florence from the Cod. Farsetti (Brush, no. 26); in 1811 at Padova from the Cod. Mocenigo (Brush, no. 25); in 1864 at Florence from the Cod. Laurenziano (Brush, no. 3). These are the important editions, the others being mere reprints. A thorough study of the MSS. and a critical edition are much to be desired.

[4] *Op. cit.*

twenty-three of Walter's fables translated into verses.[1] In the fifteenth century three more translations appeared, which are now little known; one in sonnets by Accio Zucchi (or Zuccho), one by Francesco del Tuppo, and one by Fazio Caffarello. The translations of Zucchi and Tuppo, each containing sixty-five fables, went through several editions, but have not been reprinted in modern times.[2]

But the fables of Walter of England were not the only ones that found favor in Italy. A translation of a part of the collection of Marie de France is represented by five manuscripts of the fourteenth and fifteenth centuries; three of these manuscripts have been published, not including, however, the one with the largest number of fables.[3] Another collection was translated into Tuscan in the thirteenth century, as a part of the bestiary called il Libro della Natura degli Animali; its sixteen fables are found in full or in part in seven of the dozen or more manuscripts that contain the bestiary, and their text has only recently been printed in full, although parts of the collection have appeared at various

[1] Published by E. Monaci, *Apologhi verseggiati in antico volgare reatino,* Roma, 1894 (*Rendiconti della R. Accademia dei Lincei*).

[2] See Brush, Hervieux, and de Lollis, works cited. I know nothing about Caffarello except what is stated by de Lollis, p. 15; and by Zambrini, *Opere volgari a stampa,* 3d edition, p. 71 (with quotation), 4th ed., p. 209.

[3] Cod. Laurenziano 649, which is called by Brush *Laur. ii* (with 57 fables, of which three are not from Marie); Cod. Palatino 200 in the Biblioteca Nazionale at Florence is likewise unedited. Cod. Riccardiano 1088 was published by Rigoli, *Volgarizzamento delle Favole di Esopo,* Firenze, 1818 (54 fables); Cod. Palatino 92 già Guadagni, by S. Bongi and others, *Favole di Esopo in volgare,* Lucca, Giusti, 1864 (46 fables); Cod. Laurenziano XLII. 30 by Brush, *op. cit.* (46 fables). Some of these fables were reprinted by Ghivizzani, *op. cit.,* and by L. del Prete, *Favole Esopiane raccolte dai Volgarizzamenti,* Milano, 1869. See also Mall, *Zur Geschichte der mittelalterlichen Fabellitteratur,* in *Zeitschrift f. Rom. Philol.,* IX; and Warnke, *Die Fabeln der Marie de France,* Halle, 1898.

times.[1] The Latin original has been lost, but a descendant of it preserves fragments of the bestiary and twelve of the fables.[2] The first six of the fables are found in Avianus; the rest seem to have come from popular tradition, and for some of them no parallels have yet been pointed out. In addition to these collections, single fables, or references to them, are occasionally found; for instance, the fable of the crow in borrowed feathers appears in a sonnet by Chiaro Davanzati (whose source was probably the bestiary just mentioned), and in a poem ascribed to Dante,[3] and it is one of several fables in a Venetian example-book.[4] The *Fiore di Virtù* and the *Novelle antiche* each contain one fable.

We now come to a number of fables which were put into verse in the last part of the fourteenth century or the beginning of the fifteenth, probably at Florence; eleven of them are in *sonetti caudati* of seventeen lines each, seven in *terza rima*, and two in *ottava rima*. The chief purpose of this paper is to present the text of those in *sonetti* and in *terza rima*; as the two in *ottava rima* have been published, I do not reprint them here, but they may appropriately be considered in connection with the others.[5] It is not to be assumed,

[1] For the text of the fables and full bibliographical information, see K. McKenzie, *Unpublished manuscripts of Italian Bestiaries*, in *Publications of the Modern Language Association*, vol. xx, pp. 380–433 (1905). A Venetian version of the bestiary, with eleven of the fables, and an account of about half of the manuscripts, were published by Goldstaub und Wendriner, *Ein Tosco-Venezianischer Bestiarius*, Halle, 1892.

[2] Cod. Hamilton 390, now in Berlin, containing a collection of examples published by Tobler, *Lateinische Beispielsammlung mit Bildern*, in *Zeitschrift f. Romanische Philologie*, xii, 57–88.

[3] See article cited, *Pub. of Mod. Lang. Assn.*, xx, pp. 385, 431.

[4] *Trattati religiosi e Libro de li Exempli*, ed. Ulrich, Bologna, 1891, no. 36; also in *Romania*, vol. xiii.

[5] See P. Fanfani, *Scritti inediti: una lettera di A. Lancia e due favole di Esopo*, in *L'Etruria*, vol. i, pp. 103–121 (1851). Fanfani copied the fables from a 14th century ms. in the Riccardiana, but he does not give its number; he ascribes them to Boccaccio, but without any convincing reason.

however, that the twenty fables were necessarily composed as a collection. They were all anonymous except two of the sonnets (nos. 9 and 10) which have already been printed; these are ascribed both to Antonio Pucci and to Burchiello, though in most manuscripts they too are anonymous. No. 10, which differs from the others in having absolutely no close analogues, has been regularly printed with the poems of Burchiello from the edition of 1490 on; but I have found no manuscript authority for the ascription. No. 9 is given to him by a manuscript of the Ambrosiana, but it has been pointed out that two of the other manuscripts which have this sonnet are too old to contain anything by Burchiello.[1] The particular form of these sonnets with coda of three lines—a seven-syllable line rhyming with the fourteenth line of the sonnet, followed by two hendecasyllables rhyming together,—is the form regularly used by Burchiello and the other burlesque poets of his time, but it was also used in the fourteenth century, by Antonio Pucci and various others.[2] Considering, then, that Pucci was in the habit of turning stories of different kinds into verse, using *sonetti caudati*, *terza rima* and *ottava rima*; that writings of his frequently occur in the manuscripts in connection both with these and with other fables; and, finally, that one manuscript definitely ascribes two of the fables to him, it is surely natural to conclude that he wrote at least some of these fables in verse.

Of the manuscripts that we have to consider, the most important is one written on paper in the fifteenth century, stamped on the binding *Zibaldone di Rime diverse*, and pre-

---

[1] See Frati, *Indice delle Carte di P. Bilancioni*, in *Propugnatore*, xxv, ii, pp. 279–301. This useful index mentions only these two of our fables, and does not cite the MSS. from which I have copied the text; it does cite a number of MSS. that I have not seen, and it ascribes these sonnets to Pucci.

[2] See L. Biadene, *Morfologia del sonetto*, in *Studj di Filologia Romanza*, iv, pp. 72–77; and *Poesie di Antonio Pucci*, vol. iv, pp. 286–92, Firenze, 1775 (= *Delizie degli Eruditi Toscani*, tom. vi).

served in the Biblioteca Nazionale at Florence, with the
shelf-mark Cod. Magliabechiano VII. ix. 375; it contáins
ten of the fables in sonnets, and five of those in *terza rima;*
the latter alone have been mentioned by previous writers.[1]
I shall refer to this manuscript as "M." There are 129
folios, about 21 x 14 cm. in size, of which ff. 3 and 102b–
129 are blank, and ff. 1–2 contain the *Rubriche.* The text
includes miscellaneous poems, a few pieces of prose, and
some tables "for finding Easter," etc. Among these various
pieces a few may be noted: f. 15b, "Sonetto che mando
andrea piccholuomini dassiena a Francho Sacchetti;" f. 16a,
"Risposta di Francho Sacchetti;" ff. 16b–20a, "Lauda
lamentativa doñ Zenobiù" (206 verses; there are several
sonnets, also, by don Zenobio); f. 46b–51b, "Delle bellezze
di merchato vecchio" (by Antonio Pucci; found in several
MSS., and published in his *Poesie,* IV, 267; also in *Raccolta
di Rime antiche toscane,* Palermo, 1817, III, 305); ff. 55a–
60a, "Le noie d'Antonio Pucci" (*Poesie,* IV, 275); ff. 61a,
"Memoria chome adi xvii di giennaio MCCCCVIIXXX venne per
tutto quello mese di grandi neuazzi;" ff. 66b–74a, after a
blank half-page, nineteen sonnets, including the ten fables, most
of them with the heading "Sonetto di," but no name.[2] Then

---

[1] See works already cited: Ghivizzani, p. clxxi; Hervieux, 2d ed., I,
641; Brush, pp. 15, 39; and also *Una Favola Esopiana in versi del secolo
xv,* Livorno, 1870 [published by O. Targioni-Tozzetti, *per nozze*]. Cf. K.
McKenzie in *Modern Philology,* I, p. 497.

[2] Aside from the fables, these sonnets are as follows:

f. 69b	Florenza benchio sia menipossente
69b	Figliolo mio facche tussia leale
70a	Non fa maggiore more sabato santo
70b	Senpre si disse chun fa danno acciento
73a	Sonetto di petrarcha
	Rotto e lalta cholonna el verde lauro
73b	I fra minori della povera vita
73b	I priegho idio chellunga e buona vita
74a	Itirimeno il piu nobile ronzino

follows: "*Le bellezze di firenze fatte per Antonio Pucci*,"
being the 91st and last canto of his *Centiloquio*, the versification of Villani's chronicle in *terza rima*; this canto (*Poesie*,
IV, pp. 177–87), which is found by itself in several manuscripts, begins thus (ff. 74b–79b):

> Mille trecento sessantatre chorrendo
> mi ueggio uecchio e non mi dicie il quore
> poter piu oltre sequitar volendo . . . .

This is followed by: ff. 80a–89b, "lo giudicio," in *ottava
rima*; ff. 90a–92a, *canzone* and *sonetto*;[1] and ff. 92b–102a,
the five fables in *terza rima*, the last one being left unfinished.
In the *Rubriche* each of these five fables has a title beginning thus:

> Vna fauola dilisopo la quale chonta. . . .

In publishing the text, I leave the fables in the order in
which M gives them, adding from two Riccardian MSS. of
the fifteenth century two more in *terza rima* and one sonnet.
Cod. Riccardiano 2971 is a volume containing five separate
manuscripts; the second of the five, being ff. 76–140 of the
whole volume, contains some well-known poems by Antonio
Pucci, three "Favole disopo," and other pieces in prose and
verse.[2] The fables are three in number, beginning with the

---

[1] The *canzone* is thus described in the *Rubriche*: "Sonetto cioe una chan-
zone chome uno confortava i fiorentini quando avevano la guerra chol ducha
di melano;" it begins: "Firenze mia io temo chetti rincrescha." The
sonetto (f. 92a) begins: "Sio avessi saputo quelo chio so."

[2] This manuscript, which we may call "R," begins with a poem in *ottava
rima*, of which the first three ff. have been lost; the first line preserved
(f. 76a, also marked "4") is:

> E dettogli la dama questo motto.

The poem ends on f. 93b: "finito e libro doriente e fatto fu per ant°
pucci." Another begins immediately:

> Chominca la nobilta di firenze fato per deto ant°
> Settantatre milletrecento chorrendo
> mi veggio vecchio e non mi dicie il chore. . . .

one left incomplete in M; the secònd is a sonnet which is
not in M, but is in another manuscript (Ma; see below);
the third is in *terza rima*, but it stops short after the fifteenth
verse, without having told enough to show what fable it is.[1]
Another fable in *terza rima* is found in Cod. Riccardiano
1939, a paper manuscript of the middle of the fifteenth
century, containing miscellaneous prose and verse.[2] Several
of these fables are in other manuscripts also, but I have
found no others which can be appropriately grouped with
them, although some of the sonnets of Burchiello have a
certain resemblance to fables.[3] Nos. 9 and 10 of the *sonetti*

In spite of the different date given, this is the same canto of the *Centiloquio*
that we found in M. It ends thus on f. 98b: "Finito le belezze di firenze
inchomincano le nobilta di merchato vecchio fatte per ant° pucci detto,"
and the following poem, which also is in M, ends on f. 102a. Then follow
two *sonetti caudati*, in form like the fables; the first one,

La femina fa luom viver chontento,

being by Pucci (see A. D'Ancona, *Una Poesia ed una Prosa di Antonio Pucci,*
Bologna, 1870, pp. 58–61). Ff. 103a–106a, a poem about the flood at
Florence in 1333; ff. 106b–109a, "Favole disopo," followed by pieces of
prose and verse; first after the fables is a sonnet (f. 109b; also in M,
f. 15b):

Chon gran verghongna rimase longnaffe.

[1] Erroneous descriptions of these three fables are given in the works
already cited,—Ghivizzani, p. clxvi; Hervieux, I, p. 638; Brush, pp.
21, 39.

[2] There are 145 folios, written with two columns to the page. The fable
comes on f. 130a. It is preceded by "Trionfi fatti per f. pretarcha," and
followed by "Sonetti fatti per l'auuta di Pisa." On ff. 28a–46b is: "La
scriptura di tutti i papi . . . ." The last pope mentioned is "Eugenio papa
quarto . . . . e finalmente a di 23 di febraio 1446 il detto papa eugenio
mori in roma . . . ." This text I call "Ra."

[3] For instance, one describing a fight between a cat and a kite, beginning:

Un ghatto si dormia insun un tetto,
e un nibbio a chui parea che fosse morto
gli die di piglio . . . .

This is found, *e. g.*, in Ma (f. 175b; see below); in Doni's edition of the
Rime del Burchiello, 1553, p. 190, it is accompanied by the comment that
Burchiello often wrote verses on very trivial subjects.

are found in several MSS. that I have not been able to examine,[1] and it is quite possible that more real fables of the same kind will come to light. I have found No. 9 in Cod. Palatino 200 (f. 46a), already mentioned as containing the Italian translation of Marie de France;[2] in Cod. Magliabechiano II. i. 157 (p. 91), with other sonnets following the *Teseide* of Boccaccio (this MS. I will call "Mb"); and in Cod. Magliabechiano VII. vii. 1168 (f. 104a), which I will call "Mc." In Cod. Magliabechiano II. iv. 250, a badly written fifteenth century manuscript, there are, with many sonnets by Burchiello and others, three of the fables: No. 10 (f. 188a), no. 11 (f. 196b, with the heading "No*n* di burchiello"), and no. 8a (*i. e.*, the first one of the two sonnets that comprise the fable; f. 196b, with the heading "No*n* so lautore"); this text I call "Ma."

Beside the manuscripts already mentioned, only Cod. Riccardiano 2873, so far as I know, contains any of the fables in *terza rima*; it has on ff. 74b–76a the fourth, "Fauola del topo e delione." It is a paper manuscript, dated 1432, originally of 165 folios. Together with several religious pieces, it has a number of narrative poems in *terza* and *ottava rima*, several of which are by Antonio Pucci; some of these poems are found nowhere else, and most of them have been published.[3]

---

[1] See notes with the text, below.

[2] This MS. of 116 ff. is dated at the end: "Finis Deo gratias Die xxvi ianuarij hora tertia iam preterita. M. cccc. lxxiij." The 14 fables from Marie (unedited from this text) are on ff. 31a–34b (cf. Brush, *op. cit.*), followed by several blank pages.

[3] This manuscript, which I call "Rb," was mentioned by Targioni-Tozzetti in the edition of the only one of the fables in *terza rima* (no. 2) which has hitherto been published: *Una Favola Esopiana in versi del secolo xv*, Livorno, 1870, p. 15. It was described by Pio Rajna in editing two of the poems contained in it: *I Cantari di Carduino giuntovi quello di Tristano e Lancielotto*, Bologna, 1873 (*Scelta di Curiosità*, 135). From it have also

Having, then, described the manuscripts, I now give a list of the fables, indicating the manuscripts that contain each one. While reserving a fuller discussion of the sources until later, I also indicate when the same fable is found in the other early Italian collections: *Esopo volgarizzato per Uno da Siena*, Padova, 1811 (referred to as S); the texts edited by Ghivizzani (G), Monaci (Mon), Rigoli (Rig), and Brush (B). The Palatino text (Lucca, 1864) corresponds to that of Brush. The references for the Siena collection hold good also for the collections of F. del Tuppo and Accio Zucchi. For the two Bestiary-fables, the references are to my edition, already cited; in Goldstaub-Wendriner they are nos. 11 and 6. The fables already printed are marked *

I. *Sonetti.*

1. Sheep, Goat, Cow and Lion (Lion's share). M.
   (S. 6; G. 6; Rig. 11, 12; B. 10; Bestiary-fables, 15.)
2. Pet-dog and Ass. M.
   (S. 17; G. 20; Rig. 17; B. 15; Mon. 17.)
3. Lion sick. M.
   (S. 16; G. 19; Rig. 6; B. 6; Mon. 8.)
4. Lion and Fox (Lion's breath). M.
   (Rig. 35; B. 35.)
5. Fox and Cat (one trick better than many). M.
   (Marie, but not in Italian.)
6. Lion and Ass. M.
   (Rig. 43; B. 44.)
7. Fly and Bald Man. M.
   (S. 33; G. 32; Mon. 19.)
8. { a. Fox, Wolf and Ass (Confession). M, Ma.
     { b. [Same, continued.] M.
*9. Grass-hopper and Ant. M, Mb, Mc, Pal, etc.
    (Rig. 20; B. 18; Bestiary-fables, 6.)
*10. Ant and Skull. M, Ma, etc.
11. Fox, Wolf and Mule (reading name on hoof). Ma, R.
    (*Novelle antiche.*)

---

been published *La Lusignacca* (*Scelta*, 10); *Cantare di Madonna Leonessa* (*Scelta*, 89); and Pucci's *Gismirante* (by F. Corazzini, *Miscellanea di cose inedite*, Firenze, 1853, pp. 275 ff.). Cf. Volpi, *Il Trecento*, pp. 217, 271.

II. *Terza Rima.*

1. Lion and Man. M.
*2. ˏ Fox and Wolf in well. M.
3. Fox, Lion, Wolf and Sheep (Lion's share). M.
    (See no. 1, *Sonetti.*)
4. Lion and Mouse. M, Rb.
    (S. 18; G. 21; Rig. 18; B. 16; Mon. 18.)
5. City Mouse and Country Mouse. M, R.
    (S. 12; G. 12; Rig. 9; B. 8; Mon. 4.)
6. Ant. R [unfinished].
7. Eagle, Tortoise and Crow. Ra.
    (S. 14; G. 13; Rig. 13; B. 11; Mon. 6.)

III.

To these may be added the two fables in *Ottava Rima :*
*1. Lion sick. (Cf. no. 3, *Sonetti.*)
*2. Dog and Sheep before Judge.
    (S. 4; G. 4; Rig. 3; B. 3.)

The only case of real duplication in this list is that of "Lion sick," the subject of *Son.* 3 and *Ottava rima* 1. The two versions of "Lion's share," though coming from the same ultimate source, give different forms of the fable; *Son.* 1 corresponds closely to the version in Walter of England (S., G., Bestiary-fables); while *Terza rima* 3, with its double division of the prey, is analogous to the version of Marie and Rigoli, but probably came from an oral version. The sources of *Son.* 8 and *Terz.* 1 and 2 were also probably oral; while *Son.* 11, which does not appear in other Italian fable-collections, was known through the *Novelle*. *Son.* 10 was probably original, though its author may have found a suggestion in the Latin fables. *Son.* 1, 2, 3, *Terz.* 3, 4, 5, 7, *Ott.* 1, 2 are found in the Italian translations both from the Latin of Walter and from the French of Marie. *Son.* 7 is found in the translations from Walter, but not from Marie. *Son.* 4, 6, 9 are in the translation from Marie, but not from Walter; while *Son.* 5 is in the original French of Marie, but not in the translation. *Terz.* 6 starts like *Son.* 10, but its subject is a matter of conjecture. The writers of the fables in verse took a certain amount of liberty in treating their subjects, and yet it seems probable that they knew the Italian versions which had then been recently made; for some of the fables, however, if not for all, they depended either on written versions now lost, or, more probably, on oral tradition. I reserve a more detailed discussion of the separate fables and their sources for the notes following the text.

The text as here printed follows the orthography of the manuscripts faithfully, except as indicated in the foot-notes. I have put abbreviated letters in italics, separated words, and introduced punctuation; but have left the capitalization as in the manuscripts. I have added a few explanatory notes, but have not attempted emendation except in obvious cases. The language in general calls for little remark, although a number of interesting linguistic phenomena occur. Metrically the lines are usually correct, but final syllables must occasionally be cut off in scanning. My object in printing these fables is not so much to offer linguistic material as to make them accessible to all students of folk-lore and of literature. Dr. Brush was kind enough to place at my disposal his copy of the fables in *terza rima* while I was making my own copy; and I should not have under-taken to publish them but for his declaration that he did not intend to do so.

I. SONETTI.

1.

SONETTO DI.

La pechora e lla chapra cholla uaccha
 feciono vn di chonpangnia chol lione
 e andorono alla chaccia inn un uallone.
 presono vn cierbio e per tutti s'attacha.
5 poi il lione in quatro parti il fiaccha,
 e disse, "l'una mi toccha a ragione,
 l'altra uoglio perch'io son uostro chanpione,
 la terza perch'io chorro piu di straccha ;
 l'altra tolgha chi vuole." e per paura,
10 niuno la tolse ; sicch'egli ebbe il tutto,
 perche si seppe far buona misura.
Chosi diuien d'alchun maluagio e brutto
 che ssi fa buona parte e non si chura
 perche il chonpangno rimangha asciutto ;
15 che per se vuole il frutto,
E al chonpangno vuole assengnar danno ;
 ma poi giustizia il pagha dello 'nghanno.

M, f. 66b.
8 *di straccha* in its modern meaning would make no sense here ; in the
14th century it meant "violently, impetuously," and it is so used, *e. g.*,
by A. Pucci, *Centiloquio* (see Petrocchi, *Novo Dizionario universale*).

2.

SONETTO DI.

Vn abate avea vn suo bel chatellino,
 che per suo trastullar molto l'amaua,
 e dauagli di cio ched esso mangiava
 la parte sua da ssera e da mattino.
5 l'asino suo, veggiendo il sonaglino
 chome ciaschuno di chasa il uezzegiaua,
 penso che ttutto l'anno someggiava
 e mai no gli era serbato vn lupino ;
E disse : "i' uo uedere s'i' so saltare."
10 trouando in sul pratello dormire l'abate,
 saltogli adosso chome il chane solie fare.
 se ll'abate il senti, or lo sappiate :
 chome lione chomincio a mughiare,

onde il miccio ebbe molte bastonate.
15 pero non u'inpacciate
di uolere fare quel ch'a uoi non s'aviene ;
lasciatel fare a cchui piu si chonuiene.

M, ff. 66b–67a.

1 *Catellino, catello,* Latin *catellus,* little dog. 14 *miccio,* a playful equivalent for *asino.*

3.

SONETTO DI.

Nel tenpo che 'l lione era infermato,
ongni animale lo schocchoueggiaua ;
il porcho gli toglieua quel che mangiaua,
e 'l toro chol chorno il pungieva dal lato,
5 e dall' asino era schalcheggiato,
e 'l lupo la sua morte disiaua ;
e lla uolpe chogli altri ragionaua :
" se ssi morisse, miglioremmo stato,
E fuor saremmo di sua tirannia,
10 che uo' sapete chom' egli e ferocie
verso di noi, per la sua gran balia."
Chonsidera, lettor, ch'ongni mal nuocie,
pero quand' ai alchuna singnoria
aquista amici, che 'l chontrario quocie ;
15 vedi la mala bocie
Che gli animali dauano al lione,
e cchi aueua il torto e cchi ragione.

M, f. 67a.

2 *scoccoveggiare,* a word equivalent to *burlare,* used by Poliziano, Varchi,
etc. 14 *quocie* is *cocere* in the sense of bringing trouble.

4.

SONETTO DI.

Disse alla uolpe lo lione pregiato :
" non son' io bel singnore ? " ed ella schoccha :
" singnor mio, si ; ma puteui la boccha ; "
di che il lione si fu forte turbato.
5 apresso po' quand' egli era malato,
disse la uolpe, mostrandosi iscioccha :
" molto mi pesa del male che vvi toccha,
ma uo' parete molto migliorato."
Ed e' rispuose : " i' son guarito ommai,

10 ma lla parola che ttu mi diciesti
   m' ando al quore e non si parti mai.''
   e lla uolpe : "messere, vo' non douresti
   crucciarui del mio dir, ch'io non pensai
   che uui turbassi chome uoi faciesti.''
15 de, inprendi da questi
  E ffa ch'ongni tuo dir sia buono e bello,
   che 'l maldire va doue no ua 'l choltello.

M, f. 67b.

3 *putevi*, *vi pute*, from *putire* (*puzzare*). 12 *douresti*, 14 *faciesti*, plural,
for *-ste*, to rhyme with *diciesti* (10). The syntax of 14 is odd : *uui = vi*.

5.

Sonetto di.

  La uolpe si trouo vn di chol ghatto,
   e domandollo quel che sapie fare ;
   ed e'rispuose che sapie saltare,
   ed ella disse : "allora tu sse' vn matto.''
5 sentendo il ghatto i chani, al primo tratto
   salto in su vno alber per chanpare ;
   veggiendosi la uolpe seguitare,
   nonn aspetto di far triegua ne patto.
  Disse il ghatto, ueggiendola fuggire :
10   "o tu che sse' chosi sauia e ssentita,
   che no stai ferma e llasciagli uenire?''
  Disse la uolpe : "i' uo chanpare la uita ;
   se i chani sapesser chome ttu salire,
   tu non saresti oue tu sse' salita.''
15 allora fu assalita
  Da' chani, che lla stracciaron tutta quanta ;
   chosi diuengna a cchi troppo si uanta.

M, ff. 67b–68a.

6.

Sonetto di.

  Disse il miccio al leon : "singnor leale,
   se ttu sapessi chom'io son temuto
   dagli animali, tu m' auresti tenuto
   piu che ttu non m'ai a cchapitale.''
5 chome fu nella selua, aperse l' ale,
   sono ragghiando e pendendo il liuto,
   e que' che noll' aueuano chonosciuto
   tutti fugien per paura mortale.

16

Disse il miccio al lèon : "che tte ne pare?"
10　　　e llo leon : " parmi che stu faciessi
　　　　que' modi a me che io ti ueggio fare,
Ch' io fuggirei s' i' non ti chonosciessi ;
　　　　ma sso che sse' da ssi pocho chontare
　　　　che men ti churei chom' io piu diciessi."
15　　　o chome sono spessi
　　　　minacciatori ch' anno maggior paura
　　　　che quelli a cchui e' fanno tale ingiuria.

M, f. 68a.
3-4 *tenere a capitale* = *fare stima di* ; *stu* = *se tu.* 11 *a me,* MS. *anme.*

7.

SONETTO DI.

Vna moscha a un chaluo faciea noia,
　　　　e cchome piu cholle mani s' arrostaua,
　　　　piu si fuggiua e poscia ritornaua,
　　　　chom' ella avesse del trafiggier gioia.
5　　　disse l' uon chaluo : " e' chonuien che ttu muoia
　　　　p*er* le mie mani ; " e sulla guardia staua.
　　　　chom' ella del tornar s' assichuraua,
　　　　in sul chapo le fe lasciar le quoia.
Questo si dicie p*er* molti che ffano
10　　　tanta ingiuria ad altrui che quelle sorte
　　　　tornano a lloro chon uerghongna e chon danno,
　　　　e p*er*donar si vuole ma qui sta chorte,
　　　　e cchi ua chon malitia e chon inghanno,
　　　　ispesse uolte fa sentir la morte.
15　　　p*er* le parole storte
Chonprender puoi che 'l fare altrui ingiuria
　　　　indugiar puo, ma no gli mancha furia.

M, f. 68b.
2 *arrostarsi* = *scacciar le mosche con rosta, affaticarsi* (Petrocchi).

8a.

SONETTO DI.

La uolpe e 'l lupo e ll' asino pregiato
　　　　insieme fecier legha e cconpangnia,
　　　　e nauichando per merchatantia,
　　　　il mar si fu crudelmente turbato.
5　　　" questo ci auiene p*er* lo nostro pecchato,

disse la uolpe ; chonfessianci pria,
eppoi iṇ qual si truoua piu follia,
in mare subitamente sia gittato.
Chonfesso ch'io o mangiato alchun pollo."
10. e 'l lupo fu a sseguitarlo acchorto :
"e io mi sono di pechore satollo."
L' asino disse : "i' o roso nell' orto
il prezemolo, e anchor non mollo,
quand' i' posso chon esso mi chonforto."
15 "e ttu debb' essere morto,
disse la uolpe chome molto falsa,
ch' ai roso quel di che l' uon fa la salsa."

M, f. 68b–69a ; Ma, f. 196b.

1 Ma *spregiato.* 2 Ma *Facciendo insieme.*   4 Ma *fu chon lor molto crucciato.* 5 Ma *Disse la uolpe queste.* 6 Ma *Allora illupo de chonfessianci inpria.* 7 Ma *Et cholui in chui.* 9 Ma *Dicie la uolpe io. o. preso alchun.* 12 M *nellotro.*   13 Ma *Del prezemolo assai sanza alchun crollo.*   16 Ma *Chome rea e.* 17 Ma *Tu ai mangia chonche si fa.* The readings of M are better, especially in 5 and 6, for in other versions it is always the fox who proposes confession. With 13 and 17 cf. a sonnet by Antonio Pucci, printed in *Rivista critica d. lett. ital.,* I, 120 (1884), of which the first four lines read as follows :

A far la salsa si come smiraglio
e' vi vuol salvia e ancor sermollino,
con petrosello, menta e ramerino
e prezzemolo e pan secco coll' aglio. . . .

8b.

L' asino disse : "vna grazia ui chieggio,
che in pria che in mare uoi mi gittiate
de' ferri ch' i'o in pie non mi schalzate,
po' che patir siffatta morte deggio."
5 disse la uolpe allora : "ben lo ueggio ;"
chorse all' un pie chon molta sichurtate,
ed e' le diede vn chalcio, or lo sacciate,
nel cieffo tal che ffe de' denti scheggio.
E 'l lupo disse alla uolpe : "che ffu?"
10 allora la uolpe si turo la boccha,
e disse : "va, schalza l'altra pie tu."
e cchom' el s'apresso, l'asino schoccha
e diegli tale che nel mare ando giu,
ed e' rimase padron della roccha.

15   allora si mostro scioccha
La uolpe, e disse al miccio chon amore :
  "de, chome be' gli sta a quel traditore l''
    Amen.

M, f. 69a (following previous sonnet without break).
1 MS. *ghieggio.*

9.

SONETTO DI.

Manchando alla cichala che mangiare
  di uerno chiese del grano in prestanza
  alla formicha che nn'auea abondanza,
  ed ella disse : "i' non te ne vo' dare ;
5 Che ttu intendevi senpre mai a cchantare
  per gli alberi menando il chulo a danza
  nel chaldo tenpo che ciaschuno avanza
  per potersi nel freddo nutrichare.
Non faccian chosi noi ; a piu fiate
10   portiamo a rischio charicha la spalla,
  e molte ne son di noi schalpitate.
  vatti chon dio, che 'l pensiero ti falla ;
  avessine *probato* nella state ;
  il uo' per me, se tu sai ballar, balla ;
15   quando stai bene, tu mi dai dell' ala ;
  or mi lusinghi perche il chaldo chala.''

M, f. 72b ; Mb, p. 91 ; Mc, f. 104a ; Palatino, f. 46a ; printed from Cod.
Laurenziano XL, 46, by A. M. Salvini in the annotations to *La Fiera,
commedia di Michelagnolo Buonarruoti il Giovane,* Firenze, 1726, p. 448 (note
on the word *cicale*) ; and from a Cod. Ambrosiano by A. Mai, *Spicilegium
Romanum,* tom. I, Romæ, 1839, p. 686, under the name of Burchiello.
According to the *Carte di Bilancioni, loc. cit.,* it is ascribed in Mc to A.
Pucci, and is found also in MSS. at Bologna and Parma. According to
R. Sabbadini, *Frammenti di poesie volgari,* in *Giornale Storico d. lett. ital.,*
XL, 272, it is also in a MS. at Domodossola. I give the text of M, emended
by comparison with Pal. and Laur. Variants : 4 Pal *uo prestare* (this
makes the line too long).   5 Pal, Laur *Pero chettu attendeui achantare.*
7 M *tempo quando eglie vsanza.*   8 M *fedro* ; Laur *riposare.*   11 M *e
son di noi molte schapitate* ; Pal *e molte son di no schalpistate.*   12 Pal, Laur
hondio ti dicho chel.   13 Pal, Laur *pensato.*   14 M omits *tu* ; Pal *chiluo
per me stussai ballar si balla* ; Laur *ch io l vo per me e se sai cantar balla.*
15 M *che quando tu ai buon tenpo simmi dai dellalia* ; Pal *Che quando tu stai
bene mi dai dellala.*

It is seen that in the text of M, lines 11 and 14 are too short metrically, and 15 too long; 7 and 12 read as in no other MS. Furthermore, in these three MSS., the coda has only two lines, and the whole sonnet, 16. The expression *dar dell' ala a uno* (15) is equivalent to *levarselo di torno* (Petrocchi). In three other MSS., however, there is a regular 3-line coda, as follows (Mb, cf. Mc, Amb) :

15 Tu fai come farfalla
    Che la state si pasce d'ogni fiore
    Poi quando uiene il freddo e ella muore.

Other variants (those of Mc due to the kindness of Prof. Pio Rajna ; those of Amb from Mai, *loc. cit.*) :

2 Mc *il uerno.* 4 Mb *no tel uo prestare.* Amb *ed ella a lei non te ne vo prestare.* 5 Mb *Pero che tu ai preso a cantare* ; Mc *Pero chettu atendj.* 8 Mb, Mc, Amb *riposare* (cf. Laur). 11 Mb *scalpitate* ; Mc *schalpicciate* ; Amb *iscapitate.* 12 Mb, Mc, Amb *ondio ti dicho.* 13 Mb, Mc *pensato* ; Amb *procacciato.* 14 Mb *Chio iluo per me e se tu sai ballar balla* ; Mc *esesui chantare balla* ; Amb *Si che se sai cantare or canta e balla.* 15 Amb *Fa come la farfalla.* 17 Amb *E come tocca il verno ella si muore* ; Mc *il uerno uiene.*

I do not attempt to decide on the original text of this sonnet, partly because I have not seen all the manuscripts which contain it. In regard to the coda, I should be inclined to regard the 3-line form as original, were it not for a curious circumstance which seems to favor the 2-line form. There is in the Cod. Laur. another sonnet, rhyming throughout with this one, and containing the moral of the fable. Salvini prints it, *loc. cit.*, with lines 5–8 missing; but it is also found standing by itself in Cod. Magliab. VII. viii. 1145, f. 80a, from which Prof. Pio Rajna very kindly copied it for me.

   Dalla formica si uuol imparare
    spirituale e temporale usanza ;
    in questo mondo non prender baldanza
    ma serui a dio per altro aquistare.
   Quando se' sano procaccia d'auanzare,
    si che nel difetto non abbia mancanza ;
    nell' altrui bene non auere speranza,
    che ciascun ama se, piu che 'l compare.
   Pero quando se' in giouentate
    procaccia si che se 'l tempo t' aualla
    non ti ritruoui uecchio in pouertate.
   Che tal con teco d'allegreza galla,
    non che ti dessi danari o derrate,
    non ti darebbe del loto della stalla.
   Ma se da tte arai nell' altrui scala,
    non ti fia detto come alla cicala.

(Salvini : 3 *vita non pigliar.* 4 *per altrove.* 9 *giovane etate.* 13 *desse.*
14 *il loto.* 15 *avrai per.*)

These two sonnets recall the fact that Accio Zucchi gives each of his fables in a *sonetto materiale* (with coda), followed by a *sonetto morale*; he does not make the two sonnets rhyme together, however; and his collection does not include this particular fable. But it is not necessary to conclude that in this case the moral was composed contemporaneously with the fable, and hence the 3-line coda may after all be the one written by the original author.

10.

Andando la formicha alla uentura,
 si ariuo inn un teschio di chauallo,
 il quale le parue sanza niuno fallo
 vn palagio reale chon belle mura.
5 Et quanto piu cerchaua sua misura,
 le parea piu chiaro che 'l cristallo,
 *diciendo : "quest' e 'l piu bello stallo
 ch' al mondo ma' uedessi criatura."
 Ma quand' ella fu molto agirata,
10 di mangiare le uenne gran disio,
 e non trovando che, si fu turbata ;
 Ond' ella disse : "anchora e meglio ch' io
 mi torni al bucho ou' io mi sono vsata
 che morir qui di fame, e gir mi uo' chon dio.
15 chosi vo' dire io ;
 La stanza e bella, auendoci viuanda,
 ma qui nonn a chi non ci recha o manda."

M, f. 73a ; Ma, f. 188a. Published in *Rime del Burchiello comentate dal Doni*, Vinegia, 1553, p. 52 ; *Sonetti del Burchiello*, Londra, 1757, p. 113 ; *Lirici Antichi serj e giocosi* (with *La Bella Mano* di Giusto de' Conti), Venezia, 1784, p. 325. According to the *Carte di Bilancioni, loc. cit.*, also found in the 1490 edition of Burchiello ; in Mc (ascribed to A. Pucci) ; and in Cod. Laur. SS. Annunz. 122.

The text follows M except in line 5, where I give the reading of Ma ; this line in M reads :

 Ecchome piu cierchaua dentro sua misura.

Variants of Ma, to which the printed text corresponds. 2 *giunse dovera un.* 7 *E si dicea eglie piu.* 8 *trovassi.* 9 *Ma pur quando si fu assai girata.* 11 *trouando ela si fu.* 12 *E si dicea egle pur meglio.* 14 *Che morte aver pero mi uo.* 17 *non a salchun non cene manda.*

11.

La volpe e 'l lupo andando per vn prato
Si ssi schontraro inn un mul viandante.

Dicie la volpe : "chi se' tu, brighante?
Dicci il tuo nome et nol tener celato."
5 Rispuose il mulo ; "io l'o dimentichato,
Ma ssempre il porto scritto nelle piante.
Chi sa leggiere di voi facciasi avante."
E vn de' pie di drieto ebbe levato.
Quando la volpe s'avide del ferro,
10 Disse : "io non so leggier, char chompagno,
Ma il lupo legiera, se io non erro."
E' fessi innanzi e ebe del chalcagno
Vna nel muso, che grido chom' un verro,
Et poi si diparti chon molto lagno.
15   E del suo mal ghuadagno
Disse la uolpe : "megl' e non saper leggiere
Che per tal modo vedersi chorreggiere."

Ma, f. 196b : *Non di burchiello.*
R, f. 109a : *della gholpe e dellupo.*
The text follows Ma. In R the fourth line was misplaced, but the
proper order is indicated by figures : 1, 2, 3, 5, 6, 4, 7, 8.

2 R *furon schontrati.*   3 R *la uolpe disse ove uatu brighante.*   4 R *dimi
. . . non mel.*   5 R *ede rispuose.*   7 R *si facca.*   9 R *La mastra volpe
quando vidde il ferro.*   10 R *so gramaticha.*   11 R *ellupo disse si. io.*
12 R *fecesi innanzi ettoccho.*   13 R *nel ceffo che mughio chome verro.*   14 R
e uia chesseneva chon un gran lagno.   15 R *O charo mio chonpangno.*
16 R *Alchuna volta e meglo non.*

II. TERZA RIMA.

1.

M, f. 92b.   QUESTA SI E LA FAUOLA DEL LIONE E DELL' UOMO.

Io priegho il mio singnore uisto e ueracie
      che mi dia grazia ch'io possa rimare
      vna Fauola bella e molta audacie,
Per dare diletto a cchi uorra ascholtare
5   e cchi leggier uorra perfettamente,
      non uolendo alchuno vizio seguitare.
Parla l'isopo, se 'l mio dir non mente,
      ch'andandosi il lione per la foresta,
      ebbe trouato vn cierro di presente,
10 ·Dall' uno lato partito molto a sesta,
      e dentro in quella parte vn chonio u'era,

sicchome questa storia manifesta.

Il gran lione, ueggiendo sua maniera,
 inchomincio chon quello chonio a ruzare,
15 chon amendue le branche, quella fiera,

E ccholl' una brancha il chonio n'a chauare,
 e ll'altra misse per quella fessura,
 onde quel chonio forte ebe a sserrare.

Preso quello lione per tale misura,
20 e mughiar chomincio per la gran pena,
 pero che di morire a gran paura.

Istandosi il lione in chotal pena,
 che da quello cierro non si puo partire,
 sicche gli batte il polso cholla vena ;

25 Ecchoti in quella parte l'uomo uenire
 e ueggiendo il lione qual era preso,
 ebe di lui gran tema, a non mentire.

Giacieua in terra quel lione disteso,
 pero ch' egli era molto dibattuto,
30 e di quello cierro sentiua gran peso.

f. 93a A quell' uomo disse : "tu ssia il benuenuto.
 prieghoti che tti piaccia, singnor mio,
 ch'a questo punto mi dia qualch' aiuto ;

Ischanperami da ttormento rio ;
35 anchora potrebbe per chaso uenire
 ch' io te ne meritere', o singnor mio."

Rispuose l' uomo : "al tuo grieue martire
 tanto m' increscie ch' io ti uoglio atare ;
 non uo' che ssi vilmente abia a morire."

40 E prese il chonio sechondo il rimare,
 e misselo in quel fesso, onde il lione
 di subito la brancha n' a acchauare.

Inuer dell' uomo parlo per tal sermone :
 "di questo fatto m' ai molto guarito,
45 ma ben e uero ch' i' o altra chagione ;

Io sono per la gran fame si auilito
 ch' io non mi posso quasi sostenere,
 e ueramente io sono a mal partito.

Pero ti priegho che tti de' piaciere
50 ch' io ti possa mangiare, chonpangno mio,
 sicch' io chontenti tutto il mio volere."

16 With this use of *a* and the infinitive cf. similar expressions in lines
42, 105, 187 ; Fable 2, l. 22 ; etc.

Rispuose l'uomo : "el tuo e átto rio ;
si t'o atato, e ttu mi vuoi dare morte,
onde io mi richiamo al alto idio.
55 Da tte voglio vna grazia, lione forte,
che lla quistione si dicha a tre animali,
se ttu mi de' mangiare gitta le sorte."
Disse il lione : "queste sono chose iguali :
ora andialle a trouare, ch' io son chontento ;
60 ma uo' che noi cierchiamo de' piu lealj."
f. 93b Pella selua ongnuno n'andaua attento.
principalmente si schontrar nel chane,
e lla quistione gli dissono, chom' io sento.
Rispuose Ioro il chane quello . . . .
65 "or mi mirate chom' io son magretto,
perch' io mi fido delle gente uane.
Io era di quest' uomo molto suggietto
inn abaiare e pigliare chacciagioni,
al mio potere gli dava gran diletto.
70 Chom' io fu uecchio mi muto quistioni ;
perch' io no gli era buono, mi chaccio via,
onde io uoglio distinguere uostre quistioni.
Se uui atterete alla parola mia,
dicho che ll' uomo deb' essere mangiato ;
75 chi altro dicie si parla bugia,
Pero che ss' e di me si mal portato
che ffu dengno di morte gia ffa piu anni ;
e questo per sentenzia i' o chiosato."
Rispuose quel lione sanz' altri affanni :
80 "tu odi bene, buon uomo, quel ch' egli a detto ;
abian gia chi a chiosati i tuoi danni."
E dal chane si parte sanza sospetto,
e 'l sechondo animale giua cierchando,
e ffurono ariuati sopra vn bretto.
85 Trovarono vn chauallo cierchando andando,
e ssi gli dissero tutta la quistione
ch' era tra lloro, sanza nulla manchando.
Detta la tema, rispuose e rroncione :
"i' mi posso dell' uomo molto dolere,
90 e cchonterouui tutta la ragione.
f. 94a Io il soleua portare al suo piaciere,
e spesse volte la soma portaua

---

64 The final word is omitted in MS. ; possibly *mane?*   88 MS. *erroncione*
= *il roncione* (*ronzone*).

e ffaciea di lui il suo volere ;
Ed egli a mme molto orzo mi donaua,
95   e ffieno assai perch' io lo ne seruia,
e anche spesse volte mi streghiaua.
Quando fu uecchio, ed e' mi chaccio via,
e uo pasciendo per questa riuera,
magro, dolente per malinchonia ;
100 Ond' io uo' sentenziare sentenzia uera :
dicho l' uomo che ttu 'l dei mangiare
sechondo mia sentenzia giusta e uera."
Vdendo quel lione chotale affare,
a quello huomo disse : "tu ai bene vdito
105   quel che questo chauallo a ssentenziare."
Gia era l'uomo tutto sbighottito,
perche della sentenzia a gran paura ;
e di quel locho ciaschuno s'e partito.
Chosi andando per quella pianura,
110   si furono nella gholpe rischontrati,
la falsa lima fuori d'ogni misura.
Chon grande amore si furono salutati ;
dopo le gran chareze il lion dicie
la quistion tutta di primi merchati.
115 Disse la gholpe : "lion mio filicie,
io non sentenzierei se primamente
non uegho dalla cima alla radicie ;
Io vo' uedere il fatto di presente,
doue tu staui, lion mio sovrano,
120   ch' io non dicha sentenzia falsamente."
f. 94b Disse il lione : "i' son chontento, andiano ;"
e ttutti e tre quindi si partiro,
e a quel cierro arriuaro ciertano.
La falsa gholpe, ch' a ccio a miro,
125   al lione disse : "metti qui la brancha
la doue prima sentisti il martiro ;
Alla sentenzia poi non saro stancha,
ueggiendo il fatto chome staua apunto,
si cch' io sia tenuta leale e francha."
130 Dalla malizia fu quel lion giunto ;
fidossi della gholpe maliziata,
onde alla fine si truouo difunto.
Nella fessura la brancha a cchacciata,
e a llei disse : "io staua a questo modo
135   quando l'uomo mi trouo quella fiata."

Disse la gholpe: "i' non ci diro frodo,
senonche cchome staui, chosi stea,
che di uederti preso molto ghodo,
Poi che lla malizia tua fu ssi rea
140   chontra l'uomo che ttanto liberamente,
e poi mangiare mi pare che ttu 'l uolea."
Parla l'isopo molto giustamente
di quello lione, che ffu chotanto ingrato
chontra quell' uomo che gli fu si seruente;
145   Sicchome inprima rimase incierrato
per uolersi mangiare il chonpangnone;
pero chi 'nganna rimane inghannato.
Or uolendo tornare al mio sermone,
disse la gholpe all' uomo: "i' t'o seruito,
150   chanpato t'o delle mani del lione."

f. 95a Rispuose l'uomo a ssi fatto partito:
"da tte chonoscho la uita e ll'auere
ch'era quasi del mondo transito;
E pero tutto sono al tuo piaciere.
155   or mi chomanda chom'a seruo charo,
arditamente, sanza alchun temere."
Disse la gholpe: "solo per mio riparo,
eppoi per fare la uita mia piu lungha,
vo'da tte vn gran seruigio charo,
160 Che mai da tte, da presso o dalla lungha,
isgridata non sia inn alchuno atto,
se cchaso viene ch' alchuno pollaio agiungha.
Se ttutti i polli tuoi quasi in un tratto
i' ne portassi, non gridar gianmai;
165   tu uedi bene quello ch' i' o per te fatto."
Rispuose l'uomo: "i' o de polli assai;
vienti per essi, gholpe, al tuo diletto;
da me isgridata gianmai non sarai."
Rispuose quella gholpe con sospetto:
170   "i' ne uo' charta, sicch' io sia siqura
ch' adrieto non ritorni quel ch' ai detto."
E ll' uomo ch' era fedele a ccio procchura,
alla gholpe rispuose: "i' son chontento,
falla roghar cholla buona uentura."
175   Allo spinoso n'andar, chom' io sento,
e ffene fare la charta e lla chiarezza,
e ppoi chonpiere fecie al suo talento.

152 MS. *uito.*

E quindi si partir chon alegrezza,
　　　E cciaschuno si ritorna a ssua amagione,
180　　　chome l'isopo parla per ciertezza.
f. 95b　Or viene poi che lla gholpe vna stagione
　　　chon suoi figlioli si misse in chanmino,
　　　a quell' uomo se n'ando alla magione,
　　E uolendo pigliare vn polastrino,
185　　　e' polli chominciarono a schiamazare,
　　　onde ciaschuno l'a gridata a tale latino :
　　"Alla fina, alla fina," anno a gridare ;
　　　ella fuggiendo forte cho' figliuoli
　　　vn de' suoi figli chomincio a parlare,
190　E dicie alla sua madre chon gran duoli :
　　　" chauate fuori la charta, madre mia,
　　　che noi ci difendiano a questi stuoli."
　　Rispose la madre che ffugia :
　　　" non ci e chi 'l legha, non ci e chi cc' intenda,
195　　　sicche fuggianci giu per questa via."
　　I' priegho te lettore che qui chonprenda
　　　el dire che ffecie quella falsa lima,
　　　sicch' a ben fare merito ti renda.
　　L' isopo chiaro del lione fa rima,
200　　　che ffu inghannato per altrui inghannare,
　　　e ritornossi alla pena di prima.
　　Di quella gholpe ui uo' dichiarare
　　　ch' a buona fine non die la sentenzia,
　　　propio la die per lo lion chonsumare ;
205　E ppoi la die perch' ell' avie credenza
　　　auersi di quell' uomo le sue ghalline,
　　　e lla charta fe ffare a quella intenza.
　　Onde isgridata fu dalle uicine
　　　e no lle valse niente lo 'nghanno ;
210　　　cho' suoi figlioli porto discipline.
f. 96a　Quando tu serui ciaschuno chon affanno,
　　　brighati di seruire liberamente,
　　　non chon malizia chome molti fanno ;
　　Che questo vuole il singnore 'nipotente,
215　　　che quel che serue ne de' esere meritato
　　　se ggia di quel seruigio non si pente.
　　Se cchosi tosto non se' prezolato,
　　　non ti marauigliare, che tenpo uene
　　　che doppiamente se' guidardonato
220　Dal singnor nostro, che parte non tene.
　　　　　finita amen—

2.

M, f. 96a   FAUOLA DELLA GHOLPE E DEL LUPO.

Parla l'isopo per asenpro dare
   ch'una uolta la gholpe frodolente
   le uenne uizio volersi bangnare.
A vn pozzo arriuo, se 'l dire non mente,
5   doue due secchie stauano appicchate
   chom' e vsanza potere bere la giente.
Giungnendo iui la gholpe chon setate,
   nell' una secchia subito entraua
   la falsa sopra l'altre maliziate.
10   Chome dentro vi fu, nell' aqua andaua,
   peroch' ell' era grassa e di gran peso ;
   la secchia ch' e disotto in su tornaua.
La gholpe stando chom' avete inteso,
   chon gran pensier per paura di morte,
15   sol di tormento sentiua gran peso.
f. 96b   Andando il lupo per lo chanmino forte,
   per la chaldana gli ueniua sete ;
   a quel pozzo ariuo per chotal sorte.
Vide le secchie quale vdite auete ;
20   in quella stanza si fermo per bere ;
   vidde la gholpe ch' era nella rete.
Guato nel pozo, e quell' era a ssedere
   in quella secchia la qual ui chontai
   l'altra fiata nel mio profferere.
25   Disse il lupo alla gholpe   "che cci ffai?"
   ella rispuose : "pescho chon diletto
   e piglio molti pesci sanza lai."
E 'l lupo le rispuose a ttale effetto :
   "se io potessi de' pesci mangiare,
30   alla mia uita ti sare' suggietto."
Disse la gholpe : "charo mio chonpare,
   entrate nella secchia pianamente ;
   di molti pesci vi faro mangiare."
Vdendo il lupo dire chotal chonuenente,
35   in quella secchia entro sanza dimoro ;
   alla malizia gia non puose mente.

4 MS. *nonnerra* (corrected by Targioni-Tozzetti in the edition of this fable
already cited. Variants marked "T-T").   16 T-T *cammin.*   34 T-T
dir tal.

D' ongni suo danno quiui ebbe ristoro,
  che cchome fu in quella secchia intrato,
  inuer dell' acqua va per tal tenoro.
40 La gholpe, che va su, l' ebbe schontrato ;
  il lupo, che va giu, si maraviglia,
  e 'nuer di lei in tal guisa a parlato :
  "O doue ne va' tu, o chara figlia ?
   di' cch' io uengha pe' pesci, e poi te ne vai !"
45 la gholpe inuer di lui a parlare piglia :
f. 97a "Chonpangno charo, i' non so se ttu sai
  che questo mondo e ffatto a schale ;
  credo che per adrieto vdito l' ai.
  Alchuna volta chi sciende, chi sale.
50 piglia de' pesci omai quanto ti piacie,
  che mai nonn esci, chonpangno leale."
  Del pozo vsci quella gholpe mordacie,
  e 'l lupo si rimase doloroso
  nell' aqua fredda, il tristo chontumacie.
55 Partendosi la gholpe chome io chioso,
  si rischontro nel chane per lo chanmino,
  che da cchacciare venia tutto gioioso.
  La gholpe il saluto per tal latino :
   "tu ssia per mille volte il ben trouato !"
60 e 'l chane a quella gholpe fecie inchino.
  "Or sappi, chane, ch' i' o diliberato
  ched i' o morto il lupo tuo nimicho ;
  i' l'o lasciato inn un pozo affoghato."
  E 'l chane le rispuose molto osticho :
65 "tu fosti senpre gholpe maliziosa,
  ma la malizia tua non uarra vn ficho.
  Vdit' o dire per anticho vna chiosa
  e di peruerbio, che llo 'nghannatore
  piangie lo 'nghanno che per lui si chiosa.
70 Ond' io voglio essere qui prochuratore
  del lupo ch' afoghasti chon inghanno,
  benche sia mio nemicho a ttutte l'ore.
  Se fosti maliziata, ti fia danno ;
   di questo inghanno ti chonuien morire."
75 per la ghola la prese sanza affanno.

---

40 ms *cheuua*. 41 ms *cheuua*. 44 T-T *ten*. 47 The line is too short ; T-T inserts *nostro* before *mondo*. 61 T-T *can, ch' i' l'o*. 73 T-T *maliziosa ti sia*.

f. 97b   La morte le dono chon gran martire ;
      del lupo volle far giusta uendetta,
      alla diritta ragion volle seguire.
    Pero nessuno a inghannare si metta,
80   che que' che inghanna rimane inghannato
      di quel che uedi chonprare astetta.
    Chi usa chon diritto suo merchato,
      senpre n'ariua bene, vuole idio,
      quale a tut' ore sia senpre ringraziato,
85   E cchi a di seguirlo alchun disio/amen.

3.

M, f. 97b FAVOLA DELLA GHOLPE, DEL LIONE E LUPO E PECHORA.

    Dicie l'isopo per esenpro dare,
      ciaschuno che non chorreggie sua persona
      chon grand' uomo non si deba achonpangniare.
    E ssottilmente in tal guisa sermona
5   che 'l gran lione faciea chonpangnia
      chon cierte bestie, chome si ragiona.
    La prima fu la gholpe falsa e ria,
      il sechondo fu 'l lupo al mio parere,
      la pechora fu terza, vmile e pia ;
10   E questo fe per aquistare auere.
      disse il lione : " andiamo a guadagnare,
      accioche noi possiano senpre ghodere.
    Ciaschuna chosa ch'aremo a pigliare
      la partiro per quarto, se ui piacie,
15   accioche 'n amore possiamo stare."
    Ongnun di loro diciea : " singnore veracie,
      noi sian chontenti di chotale effetto."
      la pechorella chome vile si tacie.
f. 98a   La gholpe staua senpre chon sospetto
20   nonn essere inghannata dal lione ;
      di tale affare non a molto diletto.

78 T-T *servire.*   81 T-T suggests :

    di quel che vedi, e di campare à stretta,

which he interprets : " Colui che inganna rimane ingannato di ciò che vedi (come tu vedi), ed è condotto ad avere stretta (pericolo) di campare." 82 T-T *E cui fa con diritto.*

Chome sapete egli e uecchio sermone
    che quello che inghanna rimane inghannato,
    che cholto no gli sia adosso chagione.
25 Insieme si metteano per la pianura
    per trouar qualche preda al lor talento,
    onde di ben cierchare ciaschuno procchura.
Andando per la selua ongnuno attento,
    nel mezogiorno vn cierbio ebon trouato,
30   onde il lione gli fe assalimento.
Chorrendogli dirieto l'a pigliato ;
    quando l'a preso ciascheduno gli ataua,
    subitamente l'anno schortichato.
Il gran lione in tal guisa·parlaua,
35   disse alla gholpe : "insegnami partire."
    se ella in chotal guisa sermonaua :
"Se ttu mi crederai, charo mio sire,
    la prima parte fia grande e chonpiuta,
    per te la terrai, che nn'ai disire ;
40 E lla sechonda fa viepiu minuta,
    e donerala al lupo, se tti pare,
    magli si fa sechondo mia paruta.
La terza parte de no la lasciare,
    darala a me peroche schifa sono ;
45   danmi buon cibo charo mio chonpare.
Di questa pechorella non ragiono ;
    dare di quel dentro ongni ciuanza,
    peroche lle sue pari da ppocho sono."
f. 98b   Vdendo quel lione chotale stanza
50   disse alla gholpe : "tu sse troppa ingrata,
    ma io terro chon uoi vn altra vsanza."
Subitamente la cierbia a squartata,
    e ffenne quatro parti molto a sesta ;
    poi per tal modo inpose su' anbasciata ;
55 "La prima parte mi toccha di questa,
    chome ciaschuno vna parte de' auere,
    e pero me la tolgho sanza resta ;
La sechonda mi toccha, al mio parere,
    perch' io sono re di tutti gli animali,
60   sauio, gientile, e pien d'ongni sapere ;
La terza perch' io il giunsi a passi iguali ;

23 Cf. fable 2, l. 80, and fable 1, l. 147.   45 MS. *anme.*   46 MS. *ragiona.*   53 Cf. fable 1, l. 10.

,· sappiate bene ch' io il presi soletto,
    da uoi non ricieuetti brigha o mali.
La quarta parte tanto v' inprometto,
65   che cchi lla tocchera fia mio nimicho.
    noti ciaschuno di uoi quel ch' i' o detto."
E gli animali vdendo tale obligho,
    ciaschuno si tira adrieto per paura,
    per rimanere di quel lione amicho.
70 O tu che lleggi a questo dir, proqura
    e non ti acchonpangniare chon tuo maggiore
    quando metterti uuoi per la uentura,
E non far mai soperchio a tuo minore,
    che sse chonosci te, chonoscierai
75   che 'n questo mondo se' gran pecchatore.
E peroche ttu pari senpre vsvrai,
    fa quello altrui che vuoi ch' a tte sia fatto
    e nella fine bene ariuerai.
f. 99a Sopra tutte le chose, a ongni patto
80   polla speranza nel ueracie idio,
    che lla morte de' sonare vn tratto ;
Tutt' altre chose non uagliono vn ficho. amen.

4.

M, f. 99a   FAUOLA DEL LIONE E DEL TOPO.

Sichome 'l sauio isopo ne' suoi uersi
    fauoleggio del topo e del lione,
    chosi in quest' abici potra uedersi,
Auengna gia nel suo dire menzione
5   tra sse faciessi chome gli animali
    fra llor parlasson chome le persone.
Ben parlo che ssi dissor que' chotali
    perche ciaschuno sapesse me chonprendere
    chatuni di loro e ppose que sengnali.
10 Chol mio proporre mi uoglio omai distendere,
    peroche ttenuta e persona stolta

The text is given according to M, occasionally emended by comparison
with Cod. Riccard. 2873, ff. 74b–76a (Rb); all significant variants of Rb
in foot-notes.

· 3 Rb *chosi questd uisi.* abici (M) = A-B-C (cf. Petrocchi, s. v. *abbicci*).
5 Rb *trasse e fecie.*   9 Rb *ciaschuno.*

   cholui che 'ndarno vuole suo tenpo spendere.
  Di state pon l' isopo ch' una uolta
   s' era posto vn lione a dormir suso
15 vn frescho erbaio inn una selua folta ;
  E ppone ch' egli era si di sopra chiuso
   ch'essendo il sole nella magior montata
   vn razo iscieso non ui sarie giuso.
  Forse a quel luogho presso a una gittata
20 piu topi andauan, dandosi piaciere,
   facciendo l' uno choll' altro gran ruzata.
  Girando intorno a quello bello possedere
   doue dormia il lion quella cinaglia,
   lo uiddono in lor chorrere a giaciere.
f. 99b 25 Or truouo, se 'l uedere qui non m'abaglia,
   si tosto chome 'l uiddono, tutti quanti
   furogli adosso cho' crudele battaglia.
  I topi intorno gli pareano gioghanti,
   si gran busso faciean, poi vn le sanne
30 gli ficcho si che par che 'l chor gli si schianti.
  Chaccia via il sonno allora piu di sei channe
   i topi a quel lione, onde crucciandosi
   uno inbrancho choll' una delle spanne.
  La ciurma uenne allora dilunghandosi
35 e 'l chattiuello che rimaneua preso
   veniua forte a llui rachomandandosi.
  Ma ll' ira l'auea si fforte chonpreso
   che quasi nulla li ualea il dire,
   si ffortemente si tenea offeso.
40 "Non ti piaccia, lione, farmi morire,'
   gli diciea il topo chon parole schorte,
   "che gran uerghongna puoi per me salire.
  Tu al mondo tenuto se 'l piu forte
   di tutti gli animali, e io il piu tristo ;
45 spregierai poi quant' io se mi dai morte."
  Poi ueggiendo ch' a ragione l'auea chonquisto,
   disse il lione : "tu m'ai piu che chontento

---

  14 Rb *ilione.* 18 M *vn rezo ;* Rb *urazo scieso non sarebe.* (*razzo* = *raggio,*
Petrocchi). 19 M omits *presso.* 20 Rb *andauano dandosi ;* M *andandosi
dando.* 23 Rb *nela boschaglia.* 25 Rb *sel uer dir.* 26 Rb *tutti auanti.*
28 *gioghanti* (Rb *giughanti*) = *giganti.* 31 Rb *Vagli uia* . . . . *se spanne.*
33 M omits *uno ;* Rb *uno ne piglia choluna dele branche.* 43 Rb *Oue al.*
45 Rb *ispregierati se tue mi dai la morte.* 46 M *chonpreso.* 47 M *tunmai.*

chol tuo benedire ; ora va al nome di Christo.''
Qui spari il topo, e 'n quel tenpo ben ciento
50   chacciattori uennono per pigliare il lione ; onde
preso che ffue chol suo arghomento,
Resta a gridare, non ne sperando altronde
aiuto auere, fortemente a mughiare
chon forte strida altissime e profonde ;
f. 100a 55   Sicche quel topo che lascio andare
tosto chonobbe il lione alla bocie
ched e' facieua nel suo gran mughiare.
Tosto chome strale ch' escie di nocie
si mise per atallo sanza forse,
60   per ischanpallo dalla crudele focie.
Velocie chome 'l uide a llui si porse
e salutollo, ma e' no gli rispuose,
anzi uerso chulacci il chapo torse.
Christiani non taglierebbono chome rose
65   subitamente tutte quelle funi,
tanto inber seruillo si dispuose.
Islacciato che ffu, "fa che tti sproni,"
gli dicie il topo parlandogli dopo ;
"esci chostinci e andianciene amenduni."
70   Zuccharo tutto melato parie 'l topo,
e 'l lione si 'l lecchaua dolciemente,
posi dapparte, e qui gli lascia isopo.
Per uolere fare piu l'anime chontente
chonuiensi or qui chiarir chon prouedenza
75   si ben ch' altri chonprenda nella mente.
O tu che nell' altissima potenzia
del mondo siedi al quanto reggi 'l bello,
dicie qui il sauio e pieno d'intelligienzia,
I' dicho che non sia neuno tanto fello
80   che 'l menomo chattiuo suo minore
gianmai l'offenda chon crudele maciello ;

---

48 Rb *bel dire.*   50 Rb *pigliare lui.*   51 Rb *e preso lanno choloro.*
52 Rb *Prese amughiare non isperando aiuto.*   53 Rb *e forte mente incho-*
mincio amughiare ; M *mughiando.*   54 Rb *alte istrida.*   56 Rb *si richonobe.*
61 M *si proferse* (which spoils both rhyme and metre ; the acceptance of
Rb here involves l. 63 also, to avoid repetition of *porse* in rhyme).   63 Rb
inuerso i lacci. M *porse.*   64 Rb *Cristiano non taglierebe.*   73 Rb *qui.*
75 Rb *chongnun.*   76 M *chellaltissima.*   77 Rb *e alquanto.*   79 Rb *chio
non so niun si fello.*

Che ttanto quanto l'uomo e piu maggiore,
 e nuocie a que' che no gli puo far danno,
 chotanto piu acquista disinore.
f. 100b 85 Anchora se 'l puoi trarre fuor d' un grande afanno,
 sicchome il topo il gran lione ne trasse,
 essendo chosi uile chome piu sanno.
Che noi ueggiamo che molte alteze basse
 venute sono, e spende lor grandeza,
90 perche fortuna e 'l mondo la frachasse.
E 'l menimo e ssalito in sull' alteza
 di quello albero che pocho basta intero,
 perche piu ssu che idio non ci a fermeza ;
E qui pensi ciaschuno si dicho il uero.
  Amen deo grat/amen.

5.

LA FAUOLA DEL TOPO CITTADINO E DEL TOPO CHONTADINO/

M, f. 100b Qualunche d' una Fauola d' isopo
 vuol trarre saper, chostume e gran diletto
 chonprenda quello che gli diro qui dopo,
Chon libero volere tutto perfetto,
5 sicche quel frutto che di sopra istilla
 chon gran profondita gli passi il petto.
Leggiendo il libro suo quasi alla squilla,
 trouian sicchome insieme fecion chonpangnia
 vn topo cittadino chon un di uilla.
10 Dicie ch' auendo vn topo della spangnia
 piu volte inteso, standosi in cittade,

84 Rb *piu e si fa.* 85 Rb *Anche.* 89 Rb *ma spento lor mateza.* 90
M *la frasse.* Rb *almondo gli frachasse.* 93 Rb *piu so.*

For lines 1–114 of no. 5, the text follows M, ff. 100b–102a, emended by
comparison with R, ff. 106b–108b, with variants in the foot-notes ; from
115 to the end there is only the text of R. The two texts differ much more
than those of the preceding fable ; neither one is derived from the other,
and the original reading is sometimes evidently preserved in M, sometimes
in R ; while sometimes neither is satisfactory.

TITLE R *Fauole disopo.* 1 R *Qualunque vna fauola.* 2 M *vul* ; R
auoler trarsi chostumi chon diletto. 3 M *chi seguiro.* 4 R *Del libro suo
voler tanto.* 5 R *il feruto dire di.* 6 R *vi passi.* 8 R *truouasi chome.*
9 M *a vno chontadino.* 10 R *Andando disse il topo.* 11 R *chome piu
volte.*

chome lla uilla era si mangnia,
Disse : "per cierto tanta dengnitade
chonuien ch' io ueggia quando il mio singnore
15   andera per uedere quelle chontade."
Vide il singnore in chasa far sentore,
diciendo : "domattina voglio andare
nella tal uilla a ttal lauoratore."
Sentendo il topo villa richordare
20   ch' era iui presso, disse : "ora aro io
quel ch' i' o voluto al mio desiderare."
In tutta quella notte non dormio
per non perdere l'andata di quel giorno
che chontento ciaschuno suo disio.
25 In prima 'l singnore chon piu dintorno
in villa chaualcho chol lunghi passi,
po 'l topo drieto loro sanza soggiorno.
Dicieua andando il topo : "s' io trouassi
bel chacio grattugiato, o fine charne,
30   vn passo nonn istarei ch' io nonn andassi."
Gunto ciaschuno doue douea andare,
dove ser ghodingnano staua apunto
chon tutte fine chose da mangiare.
Essendo il topo in quello paese giunto,
35   inchomincio a cchorrere per le chase,
ma che ui trouasse migha d'unto.
Trouandole chosi d'ongni bene rase
dicie : "qui pare che ss' usi star digiuno ;
ma non doue quel tesoro rimase."
40 Poi tosto uenne in questo dire quell' uno
topo villano, chol pel chome spinoso ;
vi giunse magro e secco chom' un pruno.

12 R vdi dir chella chosa di villa era mangna.   13 R Certo e chonvien
che tanta.   14 R io si vegha.   15 R chontrade.   16 R singnor so ;
M fe sentore.   17 R e disse.   19 R Udendo ; M ragionare.   20 M
chenunpresso disse ordaro io.   21 M peruersini tal mio.   23 M infino che
giorno.   25 M chel singnore ; R La mattina ilsingnore.   26 M chaual-
chando.   28 R Andando disse que.   29 R del . . . . della charne. (With
chacio grattugiato cf. Pulci, Morgante, xxv, 266.)   32 R ser ghodiglano.
33 R di tutte buone chose.   35 R la chasa.   36 R non che ui trouasse
micha punto dunto.   37 R Trovandola . . . . rasa.   38 R disse.   39 R
la doue il mio tesoro rimaso.   40 R Inmantanente in quel dir.   41 R il
topo chontadino chome spinoso.   42 R piu chun pruno.

In questo il cittadino si die riposo,
    e disse al chontadino : "dio ti dia pacie."
45   egli rispuose tutto grazioso.
Dopo rispondere disse : "se tti piacie
    vienti a pposare mecho, che sse' lasso,
    in quello albergho doue per me si giacle.
Mangiare e bere darotti molto masso."
50   egli accietto, allor quel uillan sorcho
    nel meno secho la sott' un gran sasso.
Quiui gli aparecchio sicchome al porcho
    fauuce secche, e per dormire la notte
    la ppaccia molle, e disse : "qui mi chorcho."
55 E que' ch' usaua auere le chose ghiotte
    disse : "i' son pur qui mal arivato ;"
    e di quel cibo giu per fame inghiotte.
Dicie mangiando que' di uilla nato :
    "chome ti pare stare, charo chonpangno?"
60   dicie : "pur bene, che dio ne sia Iodato."
Pareva al uilan fare il ghoder mangno,
    e 'l cittadino diciea fra sse stessi :
    "se 'l singnor ne va, non ci rimangno."
E ppoi dicieua a llui : "se ttu sapessi
65   chom' io staua per l'anpio ond' io uengno,
    diresti bene che qui stare non uolessi."
"De," disse que', "che dio ti faccia dengno !
    di tanto benificio dimmi il modo,
    che quasi della uoglia son gia prengno."
70 Rispuose il cittadino : "sappi ch' io ghodo
    farina, fichi secchi, e llardo uieto,
    salsiccia e olio e pane molle nel brodo
Chon altre chose assai, sicche stu drieto
    vora' tenermi quand' io andro via,
75   tu ssi potrai, e io ne saro lieto."
"De," disse quel, " de, dolcie la uita mia,

43 R *In quello.*   45 R *egli gli.*   47 R *iuo che uengha mecho.*   53
M *fauore* ; R *fauuce* (from *fava*).   54 R *lo spazzo* ; M *loppaccia* (=
paglia?) M *cholcho.*   55 R *Quel che solea auer.*   56 M *infino aqui
malprochaciato.*   58 R *Poi gli dicieva quel.*   60 R *e rispose bene cheddio
senia lodato.*   61 R *a quel di villa fa ghodere.*   62 R *stesso.*   63 M
nemai neua singnor mio io non rimangno.   70 R *Dicieua.*   71 R *in charne
in chacio in lardo uieto.*   72 R *e dopo questo pan tinto nel brodo.*   73 R *E
altre . . . chessettu dietro.*   74 R *vorai venir quando me nandro via.*   75
R *potrai venire.*   76 R *quegli si dolce.*

ch' io sento dire chosa da no starci,
    e anche di' che vuoi mia chonpangnia.''
"Si,'' disse que', "ma qui tanto aspettarci
80 chonuien, fratello, che 'l mio singnore gradito
    vada alla terra, allora potremo andarci,
Peroche de' far tosto vn gran chonuito.''
    po' uenne che non molto entro in chanmino
    el gientile huomo chol suo volere fornito.
85 Allora disse il topo cittadino :
    "vienne, chonpangno, e non far piu dimoro.''
    "ve' cch' io ne uengho,'' disse il chontadino.
Giunto ciaschuno nel mangno territoro,
    subito 'l chasaiuol quel uillan secho
90 meno ueggiendo ongni magiore tesoro.
Diciendo : "qui ti sta, fratello, chomecho,
    e ghoderemo insieme per ragione.''
    ed e' rispuose :. "al tuo uolere son techo.''
E in quel tenpo que' della magione
95 fe gran chonuito chome auea speranza
    di nobile giente e d'ongni inbandigione.
E ssicchome in tal luogho e ssenpre vsanza
    che' rimanente si pon fuori del cierchio
    per piu belleza e mangna chostumanza,
100 Chosi ripuose quiui si 'l soperchio
    daparte sanza guardia, e que tanfuri
    subito su di loro vi fer choperchio.
E mentre che mangiauan piu sichuri,
    ed e' vi s'abatte vn balughante ;
105 chi s'era, non bisongnia ch' io perchuri ;
Veggiendouegli stare su cholle piante,
    tolse vn bastone e giuro d'amazargli.

77 R *i sento dirti.*   79 R *Andianne tosto eppiu nonnaspettarci.*   80 R *e disse e chonvien chel mie singnor ghuarito.*   82 R *Perche e tosto facea.*   83 R *or vien che molto tosto.*   84 R *quel chaualier.*   85 M *topo al cittadino.* 86 M *fare qui piu.*   87 R *ve. chenne vengho.*   88 R *Gunti che furon;* M *territorio.*   89 R *il topo chasalingho a quel di villa seccho.*   90 R *menol mostrando dongni magor.*   91 R *Poi disse fratel mio or tista mecho.*   92 R *se ghoder vuogli senpre per.*   93 R *e e disse vedi al.*   94 R *Venne tenpo che que.*   95 R *feggia chonvito chome ve per usunza.*   96 R *dorrevoli.* 97 R *E chome inn ongni luogho e per usanza.*   98 R *vada fuor.*   100 M *rispuose quiui esil;* R *Da parte si ripuose il superchio.*   101 R *e iui sanza eque.*   102 R *damendue dilor vi furon su.*   105 R *chie. enon bisongna chil misuri.*   107 R *damazagli.*

vdite se ffu bene ghagliardo fante.
Quel che sapea l'amaror degli agli
110   subitamente si misse inn aringho,
che 'l balughante allora non pote dagli.
Ma 'l topo moggio, lento, non guardingho,
alchuna bastonata gli fu porto,
ma ppur fe ssi che ttorno al chasalingho//
115 Gunto che fu, egli dicea : "chonsorto,
quel baston mi gunse qua in sull' anche ;
se non che io ben chorsi, i' era morto. ·
Chosi 'lueghio squartare in sulle panche
quel che cci a tolto il manichar de' polli,
120   ma ss'egli se ne va, tornereno anche ;
De, va stu uedi persona che ssi crolli."
e iui immantanente quel ranocchio
indietro ritorno chon passi molli.
Intorno intorno gira a ciaschun occhio,
125   eppoi gli disse : "vieni, ch' anima nata
non ci a intorno quasi che io occhio."
E' disse : "ua, torna, e me' righuarda ;
al fiuto par ch' i' senta il mio nimicho."
ed e' ui ritorno l'altra fiata,
130 E disse : "vieni, ch' altri non ci a, ti dicho,
se non vna tal bella personcina
che non inpedira il valer d'un ficho."
"E chom' e fatta ?" e que' dicie : "piccina
angnel pare, si sta mansueto,
135   e stassi in cenere chome tu in farina."
"Ome, vien qua, e statti cheto,
ch'ell' e la ghatta mia nimicha ; mentre
ch'ella dorme sta mecho sagreto,
Cha sse ttu t'abbattessi illei ni scentre,
140   metterebbeti tra gl'altri scharafaggi ;
di tutti ch' ella gungnie senpre il uentre

---

108 R *or odi.*   109 R *Or ne che sapeua.*   110 M *subito si misse in* (rest of line blank).   111 R *e chorse piu che que non pote dagli.*   112 *moggio* is probably for *mogio* (slow, dull) ; R *El villan magro ellente e non.* 114 R *ma tanto fe che giunse al.* The text of M ends with this line. 115 This is in the middle of f. 108a in R.

141 This line is followed immediately in R by line 148, without indication that anything has been lost ; but the rhyme-scheme shows that six lines originally intervened, which are here counted as lines 142–7. A few lines may have been lost after 165, also, as the end of the fable comes somewhat suddenly.

. . . . . . -aggi
. . . . : . .
. . . . . . -aggi .
145 . . . .
. . . . . . -ingni
. . . .
O ella mostra gl' atti si beningni
    ella si e rea, ella par si onesta,
150   che cci vanno vnque cholor che sta malingni.
Vivi tu senpre, dimmi, in tal tenpesta?"
    "mai si, di chostei, ma niuuo altro churo
    di chasa che mmi possa dar molesta."
"Or dunque e meglo a mangar sichuro
155   la faua seccha la dove si zappa,
    che nnon e in tuo luogho tanto schuro.
Or fa sano, ch' i' me ne vo, e tu ti pappa
    questi bocchoni grassissimi e tementi."
    e qui veste la fauola altra chappa.
160 Poi che uersi del ciesto sono spenti,
    chonvienmi fare il mio disporre sifatto
    ch' i' faccia gl' uditori tutti chontenti.
Dicie l' isopo : prendi per quel ghatto
    qualunque vna ipocrita persona,
165   ch' e rea dietro e par buona nell' atto.

6.

DELLA FORMICA.

R, f. 109a Volendo modo reghola e dottrina
    per dar diletto isopo al seme vmano,
    vna formicha in fauola dicrina,
Al qual fauolegiar pongho la mano,
5   dando al Iettore anchor molta faticha
    per dimostrar suo dir quant' e sourano.
Brieue parlando, e' pon ch'una formicha
    s'andaua fuori vscita d'vn gran cerro
    per vna selua ch'era molta anticha ;
10 Cierchando quiui andando, s'io nonn erro,
    viuanda per riporre per auer quando
    al tenpo quasi fa dell' aqua freddo.
Dice ch'andando qua ella cerchando
    per quella selua chome sua natura
15   chome le da la uita mendichando . . . .

3 *dicrina* = *narra* (Petrocchi says so used by Pucci).   12 *freddo* in
assonance, not rhyme.

7.

Vna favola d'Isopo della testuggine.

In versi.

Ra, f. 130a Per mutar gusto e pasto agli afamati,
   dir cose nuoue, e seguitro lo stile
   del poeta alleghierj ne' suoi trattati.

   Acoio che lla mia rima non sia vile,
5   choluj che naque indella e fe la Ioda
   mi tuffi in elichon, fonte gentile ;

   Accio ch' io innarj e ciascun di uoi m' oda
   il debito permesso, o catedrante,
   i' si 'ncomincero alla tua Ioda.

10 Era nel tauro febo rutilante,
   e di sotterra vsciuano le bizzughe
   a ppascer l'erbe fresche e uirizante,

   E molte n' auen fuorj delle lor buche,
   quando l'ucciello di gioue ardito e forte
15   vna ne uide fra l'altre si stuche,

   Inver la quale aprendo l'alie acorte,
   trassela in alto con suoi crudi artiglj,
   dandogli morsi per donargli morte.

   Ma ttu, bizzugha, che dentro t' agrouigli,
20   e collo ossuto schudo tuo couerta,
   e molti colpi incolumi ripigli.

   Allora la cornachiella, in fraude sperta,
   all' aquila parllo : "somma reina,
   di quel ch' io dicho renditi certa.

25 Tu porti techo vn' escha molto fina
   e d' essa non potraj auer contenta

3 The reference to Dante Alighieri may concern simply the use of *terza rima*, or perhaps also the inclusion of literary allusions, such as do not occur in the other fables. The text is evidently corrupt in places. 6 Helicon (*Elicona*) is spoken of as a fountain by Dante, *Purg.* xxix, 40, using the name of the mountain instead of the names of the streams that flow from it. Cf. *De Vulg. Eloq.*, ii, 4. 10 The sun enters Taurus in April. Dante mentions Tauro : *Purg.* xxv, 3, and *Par.* xxii, 111 ; he does not use Febo or Phoebus in his Italian works, but the Latin form occurs in a quotation from Boethius in *De Monarchia*, ii, 9. According to Petrocchi, *Diz.*, the word *rutilante* (*risplendente*) is "termine letterario e non senza affettazione." 14 Dante, *Purg.* xxxii, 112, calls the eagle *l'uccel di Giove.*

se tu non-ronpi la dura catina.
Pero parrebbe a me, secondo ch' io senta,
    che tu portassi chotesto van peso
30   verso le stella migli piu di cento,
E poi che inn alto tanto l' arai oppeso,
    lascialo cadere, et quel ch' io dicho intendi :
    in terra il trouerrai morto steso."
Per seguire il consiglio l' alie stende
35   lo 'nperiale vcciello, et ogni monte,
    le nugole oppacie si transciende.
Aprendo il rostro, quel animale insonte
    come fulgur da ciel ruina a tterra ;
    ruinando si tronccha insun uno ponte.
40 Vdite trandimento sanza guerra
    che fe la consultrice con quel pasto :
    in vna folta macchia si diserra.
Se ffusse tempo i' ui direi il contasto
    che fe la difraudata aquila, quando
45   vide quel teschio uoto esser si guasto.
M' accio ch' io non rincrescha, troppo stando
    nelle mie rime rozze il dolze frutto,
    diro brieuemente i duo versetti rimando :
Il parllar fitto et pien d' inganni
50   suol dare altrui spesse volte di grandi affanni.
        finita deo gratias

SOURCES AND PARALLELS.

In the notes that follow I have no intention of giving
complete lists of parallels, but only such as seemed important
for fixing the position in fable-literature of the text here
offered. Many additional references can be found for the
fables that occur in La Fontaine in Robert, *Fables inédites
des* xiiₑ, xiiiₑ *et* xivₑ *siècles et Fables de La Fontaine*, Paris,
1825 ; and the *Œuvres*, edited by Regnier (*Grands Ecrivains
de la France*) ; for those in Waldis, in the notes to the edi-

---

27 *catina*, probably for *catino*.   37 *insonte*, harmless.   43 *contasto* =
contrasto (Petrocchi).   48 *due versetti*,—an unusual ending for a poem
in *terza rima*.

tion by H. Kurz, Leipzig, 1862 ; for those in Marie de
France, in K. Warnke, *Die Quellen des Esope der Marie de
France*, in *Festgabe für H. Suchier*, Halle, 1900 ; for those
in Steinhöwel and his descendants, in Joseph Jacobs, *The
Fables of Aesop as printed by Caxton in 1484*, London, 1889
(often inaccurate). Other references for special fables below.
In regard to the Italian collections, the references to Brush,
Isopo Laurenziano, hold good also for the Cod. Palatino,—
Favole di Esopo in volgare, Lucca, 1864 ; those to "Siena"
hold good also for Accio Zucchi and Francesco del Tuppo.

Son. 1. Lion's share ; sheep, goat and cow, hunting in company with
lion, capture a stag ; the lion claims all four of the parts into which the
prey is divided. In Romulus, I, 6, the animals are *leo, vacca, capella, ovis*
(so in Phædrus, ed. Müller, I, 5), and the lion's reason for claiming the
third share is *quia plus vobis cucurri* ; so in the sonnet, and likewise in the
Bestiary-fables, no. 15 (ed. McKenzie ; no. 11, ed. Goldstaub and Wendriner), the animals are *pechora, chapra, vaccha*, and one of the lion's
reasons is : *chorro più.* . . . . These exact features occur in only one other
Latin version known to me, that by John of Sheppey (Hervieux, IV, p.
418, no. 4). Cod. Hamilton (no. 19, in *Zeitschrift f. R. P.* XII, p. 70) is
apparently a condensed form of the Latin source of the Bestiary-fable, and
says simply : *leo qui forcior erat omnibus totam partem abstulit aliis.* Neckam
(no. 9 ; in Du Méril, *Poésies inédites du Moyen Age*, Paris, 1854) and
Walter of England (no. 6) have nothing about the lion running faster. In
Walter the animals are *ovis, capra, juvenca*, and in the translation by Uno
da Siena (no. 6) and in Ghivizzani (no. 6) they are *pecora, capra, giovenca.*
Marie de France (ed. Warnke, no. 11) gives two versions as one fable ; the
second version (lines 27–40) begins :

> Une altre feiz ot li leuns
> el bois od lui plus cumpaignuns ;
> la chievre e la berbiz i fu.

Rigoli's manuscript, the only one giving this part of Marie's fable in
Italian, has *capra, pecora, e molti compagni* (no. 12 ; the first part of Marie's
fable is no. 11 in Rigoli). It would seem, then, that the writer of the
sonnet knew either the Bestiary text, or its source, or Romulus.

Son. 2. The ass which tries to imitate the pet dog,—a very familiar
fable, here told with some original features ; the master is an *abate*, he is
lying asleep in a field when fawned upon by the ass, and he roars like a
lion. There are numerous versions in Greek (ed. Halm, no. 331 ; Babrios,

ed. Schneidewin, no. 131) and Latin (not preserved in Phædrus, but in Romulus, ed. Oesterley, I, 16; Neckam, no. 5; Steinhöwel, Caxton, Walter of England, no. 17), and there are Oriental analogues (cf. Benfey, *Pantschatantra*, I, 110, 494; II, 339). Italian versions, Siena, 17; Ghivizzani, 20; Monaci, 17; from Marie de France (no. 15): Rigoli, 17; Brush, 15. The fable is found in the *Gesta Romanorum* (ed. Oesterley, no. 79), Jacques de Vitry (ed. Crane, London, 1890, no. 15), La Fontaine, IV, 5. In Spain it was known in the 14th century; see Juan Ruiz, *Libro de buen amor* (ed. Ducamin, Toulouse, 1901, p. 257), and C. P. Wagner, *The Sources of El Cavallero Cifar*, Paris, 1903, p. 74 (reprinted from *Revue Hispanique*, tome X). Franco-Italian version in the fragmentary text published by P. Rajna, *Estratti di una raccolta di Favole*, in *Giornale di Filologia Romanza*, I, p. 36 (1878).

Son. 3. The sick lion is insulted and struck by *porco, toro, asino, lupo, volpe*; moral: make friends while you have the opportunity. Other versions have different animals, but are sufficiently like the sonnet to have been its source: Romulus, I, 15 (Steinhöwel 16; from Phædrus, I, 21), with *aper, taurus, asinus, leo senex*; Walter, 16, same animals; Siena, 16, and Ghivizzani, 19: *porco, toro, asino*; Monaci, 8: *porco, asino, cervo*. In Marie, 14, followed by the Italian translation (Rigoli, Brush, Pal. 6), and by the *Promptuarium exemplorum*, 8 (published by Warnke in his edition of the *Fabeln*), and the first fable of Berachiah ha-Nakdan, the animals are different (cf. Warnke, *Quellen*). The fable is told by Jacques de Vitry, 184, La Fontaine, III, 14, and Waldis, I, 12. There is no close parallel in the beast-epic or in Greek, although the germ may be in a fable of the fox which mocks a lion in a cage (Halm, 40).

It is interesting to find the same fable in *ottava rima* (*L'Etruria*, I, 107; see above); an idea of the florid style of this version may be given by quoting one of its nineteen stanzas:

> Or la volante fama ch' è veloce
> Vie più che altra cosa con su' ale,
> Volando, sparge del lion la voce,
> Sì che notizia è a ciascuno animale
> Come vecchiezza e miseria gli nuoce;
> Onde col toro l'asino e cinghiale,
> Lor disponendo dell' antica ingiuria
> Di vendicarsi, mossonsi con furia.

Like the sonnet, this poem, in spite of expansion, belongs to the Romulus tradition.

Son. 4. When told by the fox that his mouth has a bad odor, the lion is offended, and refuses to accept an apology. This seems to be a feeble reminiscence of the fables in which the lion asks various animals about the odor of his breath, and kills them whatever they reply. In Romulus, III,

20, the monkey gives an evasive answer; the lion feigns illness, and demands monkey's flesh (not in Waltér, Siena, etc.). Similarly in Marie, 29, except that the wolf has taken the place of the lion; in the Italian translation (Rigoli, Brush, 35), the monkey has a cold and cannot smell. In Rigoli (not in Marie or Brush) the fox is one of the animals killed. In other versions, the fox gives the evasive answer and escapes; see Warnke, *Quellen*; La Fontaine, VII, 7; Du Méril, *Poésies inédites*, p. 29; P. W. Harry, *A Comparative Study of the Æsopic Fable in Nicole Bozon*, Cincinnati, 1905, pp. 25–29; Braune, *Die Fabeln des Erasmus Alberus*, no. 36. The closest parallel to our sonnet is an African story of a lion and a woman; see Benfey, *Pantschatantra*, I, p. 354. The evil smell of the lion's breath is spoken of by Brunetto Latini (*Il Tesoro*, Italian translation, vol. II, p. 209: "la bocca gli pute molto malamente.")

Son. 5. This fable of the fox with many tricks and the cat with one, must have been widely current in popular tradition in the Middle Ages. It does not belong to the collections of the Romulus family, but is found in the *Extravagantes*, no. 5 (Steinhöwel, Caxton, etc.); Odo of Cheriton, no. 39 (in Hervieux, vol. IV, p. 212); Marie, 98 (not in the Italian translation); in "The Owl and the Nightingale" (lines 807 ff., in Mätzner, *Altenglische Sprachproben*, I, 43); *Der Fuhs und diu Katze* (in Grimm, *Reinhart Fuchs*, Berlin, 1834, p. 363; cf. pp. cliii, clxxxviii, 421); La Fontaine, IX, 14; Waldis, II, 21; Grimm, *Kinder- und Haus-Märchen*, no. 75,—in these and still other versions, as in our sonnet (the only Italian version that I have found), the cat's trick is to climb a tree and thus escape the dogs, while the too clever fox is caught. The ancient Greeks had a proverb: The fox knows many things, the hedgehog one big thing. The fable undoubtedly came down to the Middle Ages by oral tradition. In the original form, preserved in folk-tales in Greece and among the Slavs, the hedgehog's one trick was to feign death, and in some oral versions the cat also uses this trick. In India a similar story is told about a crow which can fly in a hundred ways, while a flamingo knows but one way, and yet escapes (see Benfey, *Pantschatantra*, I, 312 ff.). For further references and discussion, see K. Krohn, *Eine uralte griechische Tierfabel*, in *Am Urquell*, III, p. 177 ff. (1892); K. O. Petersen, *On the Sources of the Nonne Prestes Tale*, Boston, 1898, p. 18; Warnke, *Quellen*, no. 98; Sudre, *Sources du Roman de Renart*, p. 273; Robert, II, 549; and other works already cited.

Son. 6. This fable of the ass terrifying other animals by braying, while the lion says that he too would be afraid if he did not know who it was, is a close parallel to Romulus, IV, 10 (= Phædrus, I, 11; not in Walter and descendants). There are several Oriental and Greek fables containing the same idea; see Benfey, I, 101, 107, 462, II, 308; Halm, nos. 248, 259, 323, 333; Ribezzo, *Nuovi Studi sulla Origine e la Propagazione delle Favole indo-elleniche*, Napoli, 1901, p. 191. The version of Romulus is slightly modified in Marie, 35, followed by Rigoli, 43, Brush, 44. See Grimm,

Reinhart Fuchs, pp. cclxxv, 383–7, for German version. Cf. La Fontaine, II, 19, Neckam, 8, etc.

Line 6 of the sonnet is not quite clear. Can it be a reminiscence of the proverbial *asinus ad lyram?* Cf. the first lines of a fourteenth century sonnet (published by Gigli, *Sermoni evangelici ed altri scritti di F. Sacchetti*, Firenze, 1857, p. 252):

> Come a l' asel s' avvien sonar la lira,
> Così a me cantar le rime snelle. . . .

Cf. Ribezzo, *op. cit.*, p. 170.

Son. 7. This version of the fly annoying the bald man is probably derived from some version of the Romulus family,—Romulus, II, 13 (= Phædrus, V, 3); Steinhöwel, II, 12; Walter, 32; Siena, 33; Ghivizzani, 32; Monaci, 19. Also in Neckam, 19; Jacques de Vitry, 190; Waldis, II, 99. Cf. Halm, 425; and for discussion of possible Oriental parallels, see Ribezzo, *op. cit.*, p. 183; Benfey, I, 292; Jacobs, *Fables of Æsop*, p. 64. Not in Marie or La Fontaine. Franco-Italian fragment, see P. Rajna, *loc. cit.*

Son. 8. The kernel of this fable is the confession, in which the more guilty animals are excused, while the comparatively innocent one is condemned. Although the general idea may possibly have been suggested by an Oriental story (see Benfey, I, 230, II, 80; Jacobs, *Fables of Bidpai*, p. 153; etc.), in this form the fable seems to have originated in Germany in the thirteenth century. A Latin poem of that period, *Pœnitentiarius* (published by Grimm, *Reinhart Fuchs*, pp. 397–409, cf. p. clxxxv) begins as follows:

> Instabat festiva dies; animalia bruta
> conveniunt, culpas depositura suas:
> et lupus et vulpes capitolia proxima jungunt,
> additur his asinus nulla sinistra ratus.

The wolf and the fox confess that they have eaten various animals; the ass confesses some trifling offences, and is killed by the others. From about the same period are two German poems: *Diu Betevart* (Grimm, p. 391) and *Diu Bihte* (in H. Trimberg's *Der Renner*; Grimm, p. 392, cf. p. clxxxi). At the beginning of the sixteenth century, *Diu Bihte* was turned into Latin prose by Heinrich Bebel (*Facetiarum Henrici Bebelii libri tres rursus redditi*, Tubingæ, 1544; lib. ii, fol. 33), with a moral:

> Sic equidem faciunt potentes . . . . ut bene novit Juvenalis in satyra secunda, "Dat veniam corvis, vexat censura columbas," atque huius fabulae autor, Hugo scilicet Trimpergius, egregius in vernacula lingua poeta.

Bebel was probably the source of Waldis, IV, 1, and of French versions by Haudent and Larivey (Haudent, *Apologues d' Esope, reproduits d' après l' édi-*

tion de 1547, Rouen, 1877, livre II, no. lx; also in Regnier, II, 485; Larivey inserted the fable, in a prose version, in place of one of the original stories, in his translation of Straparola's *Piacevoli Notti*, 13, 1; see *Facétieuses Nuits*, Paris, 1857, I, p. li). In these versions the fox, the wolf and the ass confess to one another while on a pilgrimage; light penance is imposed on fox and wolf, while the ass is either killed or severely beaten. Erasmus Alberus knew the version of Bebel, but the chief source of his version, no. 11, was Luscinius, *Ioci ac Sales*, no. 126, printed in 1524 (see A. L. Stiefel, *Zu den Quellen der Erasmus Alberschen Fabeln*, in *Euphorion*, IX, 609–11). Here, and in the version of Gueroult (reprinted from edition of 1550 by Regnier, II, 489), the lion asks the wolf and the ass to confess; lion and wolf excuse one another's sins, but condemn the ass for having eaten a little straw. In several Latin versions the lion summons his subjects to confession, with the usual result (*Promptuarium*, ed. Warnke in *Fabeln der Marie*, no. 3; Nicole Bozon, no. 1, in Hervieux, IV, p. 256; Raulin, *Itinerarium Paradisi*, 1524, quoted by Regnier, II, 484). In Odo of Cheriton (no. 81, Hervieux, IV, p. 255; Voigt, *Kleinere Lat. Denkmäler der Thiersage*, p. 138) the fox and the ass confess to the wolf. For other versions in Latin and German, see Stiefel, *loc. cit.*; Regnier, II, 88 ff.; K. Goedeke, *Deutsche Dichtung im Mittelalter*, 2te Ausg., Dresden, 1871, pp. 617–27; Hervieux, III, pp. 167, 349. An Italian version, not hitherto cited in this connection, is found in a sermon, dated 1427, by San Bernadino da Siena: Lion, imitating monks, orders confession; he absolves goat, fox and wolf, but has ass and sheep soundly beaten (see D'Ancona e Bacci, *Manuale della Letteratura Italiana*, vol. II). In La Fontaine, *Les Animaux malades de la Peste* (VII, 1; the chief source was probably Gueroult), the reason for confession is the prevalence of the plague; the lion confesses first, followed by others, and finally by the ass, which is killed.

Nearer to our Italian sonnets is a fable by Filelfo, published in 1480 (French version in *Esope en belle humeur*, Hambourg, 1750, p. 273, the only edition that I have seen; cf. Regnier, *loc. cit.*). Here the wolf, the fox and the ass go out in a boat and are beset by a storm. The fox thinks some one must have committed a crime, and proposes confession; he has eaten hens, the wolf has eaten sheep and calves, the ass once ate some flour from the load he was carrying. The wolf and the fox decide that the storm has come on account of this sin, and throw the ass overboard. According to P. A. Becker, in *Literaturblatt f. germ. u. rom. Philol.*, 1905, col. 373–5, a story corresponding to this was told in Bohemian by Pelbart in the fifteenth century. A similar but more elaborate version is found in a Greek poem of the fifteenth century; see A. C. Gidel, *Etudes sur la littérature grecque moderne*, Paris, 1866, pp. 331 ff.; Goedeke, *op. cit.*, p. 625; Grimm, *Sendschreiben an Karl Lachmann*, Leipzig, 1840, pp. 68–106. Here the fox and the wolf persuade the ass to set sail with them for the Orient; the fox is troubled by dreaming of a storm, and invites the others to confess. The ass has eaten a leaf, and is condemned to death. He says, however, that he has a talisman on his hoof, and the wolf, wishing to see it, is kicked overboard, the fox following from fright. As in the Italian sonnets, we find here, instead of the usual ending of the confession story, another tale, which was no doubt added in oral transmission. A similar combination is found in several folk-tales in North Africa ; for instance, in this Berber tale : A lion, a jackal and a mule, traveling together, are hungry. They draw lots to see which one shall be eaten, and the lot falls to the mule. He asks the others to wait until they reach a certain place, the name of which is written on his hoof ; the jackal can read only at a distance, but the lion comes close to the mule, and is killed by a kick. See R. Basset, *Nouveaux contes berbères*, Paris, 1897, no. 83 ; cf. no. 73. In another Berber story, R. Basset, *Contes populaires d'Afrique*, p. 25, the animals, plotting against the mule, decide to eat the one who will not tell the name of his father ; the mule says the name is written on his hoof, and kicks the lion who tries to read it (cf. also Rivière, *Recueil de contes populaires de la Kabylie*, Paris, 1882, p. 141). In all these cases, reading on the hoof of the mule or ass is combined with the confession ; see below, notes on *Son.* 11. As for the particular pretext used by the ass in *Son.* 8,—begging his enemies not to do the very thing that he wishes them to do,—it does not occur elsewhere in this connection ; cf. Brer Rabbit begging the fox not to throw him into the brier-patch, J. C. Harris, *Uncle Remus, his Songs and his Sayings*, New York, 1892, chap. 4.

Son. 9. The familiar fable of the grass-hopper and the ant, known in many Greek and Latin versions : Halm, 401, 401b, 295 ; Babrios, 137 ; Romulus, ed. Oesterley, IV, 19, in Steinhöwel and Caxton, IV, 17 ; Avianus, 34 ; Cod. Hamilton, 15 ; not in Phædrus or Walter. The version in the Italian Bestiary, no. 6, is probably one of several fables in that collection that were derived from Avianus. On a Franco-Italian fragment, and on derivatives from Avianus in general, see article by P. Rajna already cited, in *Giornale di Fil. Rom.*, I, pp. 13–42 (no. 26). Text of Avianus and derivatives in Hervieux, tome III. Other Italian versions from Marie, 39 : Rigoli, 20, Brush, 18. Marie and Brush do not have the taunt : *Se estate cantasti, hieme salta* (Romulus) ; but it is in Rigoli : *Se cantasti d'estate balla di verno*, as well as in the Bestiary. Cf. notes in editions cited, and also La Fontaine, I, 1. The fable is inserted by Benvenuto da Imola in his comment on Dante, *Inf.* III, 30 (Florence, 1887, vol. I, p. 111).

Son. 10. The ant find a horse's skull, and thinks it a fine palace, but empty. I know of no exact parallel, unless it be the unfinished no. 6 in *terza rima* ; but the fable of the fox or wolf and the mask is similar. The very short version of Phædrus, I, 7 (cf. Halm, 47) is as follows :

Personam tragicam forte vulpes viderat ;
O quante species, inquit, cerebrum non habet.

18

Romulus, II, 15 (Steinhöwel II, 14), followed by Walter, 34, Siena, 35, Ghivizzani, 34, substitutes the wolf for the fox. Walter further changes the tragic mask to *caput arte superbum*, which in Ghiv. is *uno capo d' uomo intagliato e formato di marmo;* in Siena, however, the fable begins : "Andando il Lupo a diletto per uno campo, trovò uno capo d' uno *uomo morto partito dallo imbusto.*" For other versions, see Waldis, I, 28 ; La Fontaine, IV, 14 ; Du Méril, *op. cit.*, p. 227, note ; Benfey, *op. cit.*, I, 132 ; II. 21.

Son. 11. This fable of the wolf reading something supposed to be written on the mule's hoof was medieval in origin ; it was current in Italy from the end of the thirteenth century on, in one of the *Novelle antiche*, which I believe was the source of the sonnet: *Le Ciento Novelle antike*, Bologna, 1525 (ed. Gualteruzzi), no. 94 ; *Libro di Novelle e di bel parlar gentile*, Fiorenza, 1572 (ed. Borghini), no. 91 ; Biagi, *Le Novelle antiche*, Firenze, 1880, no. 130 ; and in other editions ; cf. D'Ancona e Bacci, *Manuale*, vol. I ; D'Ancona, *Le Fonti del Novellino*, no. 94, in : *Studj di Critica e Storia letteraria*, Bologna, 1880. This medieval fable probably grew out of a classical fable ; in the Greek versions (Halm, 334b, 334 ; Babrios, 122) the ass either has or pretends to have a thorn in his foot, and kicks the wolf who comes to extract it. This is not in Phædrus ; but in Romulus, III, 2, the horse, when the lion passes himself off as a physician, pretends to have a thorn in his foot, asks the lion for help, and kicks him ; so in Neckam, 24, Walter, 42, Siena, 43, Ghivizzani, 42 (also La Fontaine, V, 8, and Waldis, I, 32, but not in Marie). A medieval version based on popular tradition is found as a part of the long tenth fable of the *Extravagantes* (Steinhöwel, ed. Oesterley, p. 212 ; Caxton, etc.; also in Grimm, *Reinhart Fuchs*, p. 429 ; cf. Robert, *Fables inédites*, I, p. xcviii). Here the wolf, having a good omen for the day, refuses to touch common food ; he proposes to eat a colt which is grazing with its mother ; the mare consents, but begs the wolf to extract a thorn from her hoof, and kicks him ; whereupon the wolf goes off to meet with still more disastrous adventures. More or less similar versions in various poems of the Reynard cycle (cf. Grimm, p. cclxiii). In the *Roman de Renart* (ed. Martin, branche 19 ; cf. Sudre, *Sources du R. de R.*, ᴾ. 332) the mare asks the wolf to pull a thorn from her foot, and kicks him ; in *Reineke* and *Reinaert* the mare says the price of her colt is written on her hoof ; in *Reinardus* (Grimm, p. lxxv) and *Ysengrinus* (ed. Voigt, Halle, 1884, pp. lxxxiii and 329 ff.) the circumstances are still different ; while in *Renart le Contrefait* (Robert, II, p. 365) the mare consents to give up her colt if the fox and the wolf will let it first be baptized ; she has the name on her hoof, and the wolf tries to read it, with the usual result, Renart excusing himself on the plea of sore eyes. In another of the *Extravagantes*, no. 1, we find the mule grazing ; the fox asks who he is ; the mule says he is *bestia* ; his uncle was the horse. The fox insists on knowing his name, and the mule says it is written on his left hind foot. The fox persuades his enemy the wolf to try to read the name, and the mule kicks. Here we find the reading on hoof combined, just as in the African stories mentioned under *Son.* 8, with the mule's sensitiveness as to his family ; the latter episode often appears by itself (e. g., in Petrus Alphonsus and in the fragmentary Italian translation, P. Papa, *Frammento di un' antica versione toscana della Disciplina Clericalis*, Firenze, 1891, p. 50 ; Halm, 157 ; Babrios, 62 ; La Fontaine, VI, 7. Benvenuto da Imola, commenting on *Purg.* III, compares Manfred to the mule which, when asked by the lion whose son he was, said : *Sum nepos equi*). Baldo, *Alter Æsopus*, no. 27 (Du Méril, p. 257), has the fable almost as in *Extrav.* 1. The latter is probably connected with the source of our Italian versions, through oral transmission. It is also, in my opinion, the chief source, through the French translation of Steinhöwel's *Æsop* by J. Machault, of La Fontaine, XII, 17 : *Le Renard, Le Loup et le Cheval.* Regnier, *Œuvres de La F.*, III, pp. 292, 404, and Robert, I, p. ccxl, propose as La Fontaine's source the third *Satire* of Mathurin Regnier, in which the mule's victim is the lioness, while the wolf takes the place of the fox ; La Fontaine probably took some features of his fable from this *Satire*, and changed the mule of Regnier and *Extrav.* 1 to the horse. The fable of the wolf wishing to eat the mare's colt is found as a modern folk-tale ; see Kuhn, *Märkische Sagen und Märchen*, Berlin, 1843, p. 299 ; Haupt und Schmaler, *Volkslieder der Wenden*, Grimma, 1843, Th. II, p. 161. In Russia the mare says she has a certificate of safety on her hoof, and kicks the wolf when he tries to read it ; see Gerber, *Great Russian Animal Tales*, in these *Publications*, vol. VI, no. 2, 1891 ; tale 40, with further references on p. 80.

Terza rima 1. The lion, liberated by the man, proves ungrateful ; three arbitrators ; the fox puts the lion in his original predicament, and is promised hens as a reward, but does not receive them. For a discussion and bibliography of this highly interesting fable, see my paper entitled *An Italian Fable, its Sources and its History*, in *Modern Philology*, vol. I, no. 4 (April, 1904). The story probably originated in India some time before the eleventh century, substantially in the form in which it occurs in the *Panchatantra* : a man carries a crocodile to a river in his bag, and the crocodile tries to pull him under water ; the man demands arbitrators, two of whom decide against him, while the fox persuades the crocodile to get into the bag again, and kills it with a stone. This is the oldest version now known. The story became modified in various ways, and spread over Asia, Africa, and all parts of Europe ; it is found in innumerable versions, written and oral, sometimes simplified by the omission of all the judges except the fox, sometimes amplified by combination with other stories. The earliest version having the lion is the fable in *terza rima*, of which the text is now published for the first time ; this is also the earliest version with the hen-episode. In the first half of the following (sixteenth) century we find several German versions which have the hen-episode, but instead of the lion a dragon or serpent. For additional discussion of these German versions, see two articles by A. L. Stiefel, which I had not seen when I wrote my paper; one on Alberus, already cited, p. 616; the other: *Zu den Quellen des 'Esopus' von B. Waldis*, in *Archiv f. d. Studium d. neueren Sprachen*, CIX (1902), pp. 271–77. It appears from these articles that the source of Alberus, 48, was a *Schwankbuch* of 1545, the version in which was derived from Camerarius; and that the sources of Waldis, IV, 99, were Camerarius, *Merces anguina*, and Sebastian Franck's *Sprichwörter*. Stiefel does not mention the version quoted by Regnier, III, 359, from the 1568 edition of Luther's *Tischreden*, which I have not been able to find in any edition of the *Tischreden* accessible to me. For further discussion and parallels, see Carnoy, *Contes d'animaux dans les Romans du Renard*, Paris, 1889, p. viii; the brief review of my paper in *Revue des Traditions Populaires*, XIX, 319 (R. Basset); and especially R. Basset, *Nouveaux Contes Berbères*, Paris, 1897, pp. 191–202.

Terza rima 2. The fox, having descended into a well in one of the two buckets, persuades the wolf to get into the other bucket and so pull him up. This fable, which is found in various forms, appears to be medieval in origin, and to have no connection with the classical fable of fox and goat in well (Halm, 45; Phædrus IV, 9; La Fontaine, III, 5; Steinhöwel, Caxton, *Remicius* 3; not in Romulus; cf. Sudre, *Sources*, p. 226). The pretext by which the fox persuades the wolf to get into the bucket varies; in the version of Odo of Cheriton, just as in the Italian, the fox pretends to be eating fish (no. 19, Hervieux, *op. cit.*, IV, p. 192; also John of Sheppey, *ibid.*, p. 441). Precisely the same story, with the usual shifting of rôles, is told by Uncle Remus; Brer Rabbit in the well tells Brer Fox that he is fishing, and Brer Fox pulls him out by getting into the other bucket (J. C. Harris, *Uncle Remus, his Songs and his Sayings*, chap. 16). In the *Roman de Renart* (ed. Martin, *branche* IV, cf. Voretzsch, in *Zeitschrift f. R. P.*, XV, 352 ff., and Sudre, *Sources*, p. 226) the fox sees his reflection in the well, and supposes it is his wife; he tells the wolf he is in paradise. So in *Renart le Contrefait* he describes to the wolf the delightful country at the bottom of the well (see Robert, II, pp. 300–307; *Poètes de Champagne antérieurs au XVI*e *siècle*, Paris, 1851, p. 62). In an English poem of the thirteenth century, *The Vox and the Wolf*, (in Mätzner, *Altenglische Sprachproben*, I, 130), the fox tells the wolf he is in paradise. In the *Disciplina Clericalis* the story is combined with another which originated in northern Europe: a farmer, angered by the slowness of his oxen, wishes that the wolf might get them, and the wolf thereupon claims them; the fox, to whom the farmer promises hens, persuades the wolf to take instead of the oxen a cheese, which turns out to be the reflection of the moon in a well; the fox goes down in one bucket to get it, but says it is too heavy, and so the wolf pulls him up by going down in the other bucket.

This story is in Steinhöwel's *Æsop*, in the section derived from Petrus Alphonsus, no. 9 (*De lupo, rustico, vulpe et caseo*; also in Caxton, etc. In the
Disciplina, no. 21 in the edition of Paris, 1824, and in Migne, *Patrologia
Latina*, vol. 157; ed. Schmidt, Berlin, 1827, no. 24. For further references, see McKenzie, *An Italian Fable*, p. 17; Grimm, *R. F.*, p. cclxxviii,
H. Sachs, *Fabeln*, ed. Goetze, bd. ii, Halle, 1894, no. 202). The fable of
the fox showing to the wolf the reflection of the moon as a cheese, and thus
being pulled up by the two buckets, in Waldis, iv, 8; La Fontaine, xi, 6.
In Marie de France, 58, the fox mistakes the reflection of the moon in a
pool for a cheese, and attempts to drink up the water in order to get it (see
Warnke, *Quellen*). The ending in the Italian version,—the dog kills the
fox to avenge the wolf,—I have not found elsewhere.

Terza rima 3. Lion, fox, wolf and sheep hunt together and catch a stag;
lion askes fox to divide it; fox offers large share to lion, small shares to
herself and wolf, and the refuse to the sheep. The lion is dissatisfied,
makes four equal parts, and claims them all for himself. This is evidently
not the simple fable of the Romulus tradition which we have discussed
under *Son.* 1, in which the lion alone divides the booty, and his companions
are entirely passive. Neither does it belong to the group of versions represented by Odo of Cheriton and by various poems of the Reynard cycle
(Odo, no. 20, in Hervieux, iv, p. 193; J. of Sheppey, *ibid.*, p. 418;
Jacques de Vitry, no. 158; *Roman de Renart, br.* xvi; *La Compagnie
Renart*, in Robert, i, p. 32; Du Méril, p. 420; Sudre, pp. 124 ff.; Grimm,
p. cclxii; Górski, *Die Fabel vom Löwenantheil*, Berlin, 1888, pp. 52–80).
Here the animals are usually lion, wolf, fox; the wolf first divides, giving
a share to each, and is wounded or killed by the lion; the fox then divides,
giving all or nearly all to the lion, and saying that he learned the proper
method by observing the experience of the wolf. In Marie de France, 11,
are two separate fables, counted by Warnke as one; but both belong to the
first group of versions, with the lion alone dividing. First the lion hunts
with buffalo and wolf; they catch a stag, and the wolf asks how it shall be
divided; the buffalo refers the division to the lion. Again (*une altre feiz*)
the lion hunts with goat, sheep and others (see Górski, p. 16; Warnke,
Quellen). The two parts of Marie's fable are given separately in Rigoli,
11, 12; in 11 the lion asks: "Chi lo partirà?" and the wolf replies:
"Siate il partitore pur voi;" the third animal is the bear instead of the
fox. This is also in Brush, no. 10, but Rigoli, 12, is not. On Nicole Bozon's
version, cf. Harry, *op. cit.*, pp. 50–4. The fable in *terza rima* seems to be
a weakened version of the Reynard type, modified by oral transmission and
by influence of the Romulus type; thus the lion does not strike the fox,
but simply reproves her, and then makes his own division. The inclusion
of the sheep is probably due to some version of the Romulus type, to
which, however, the double division by the same animals is foreign.

Terza rima 4. The classical fable of the lion sparing the life of the

mouse, and later, when caught by hunters, released by the mouse. Halm,
256; Babrios, 107; Romulus, ed. Oesterley, I, 17, Steinhöwel, I, 18; Walter, 18; Marie, 16; Waldis, I, 14; J. de Vitry, 145; Neckam, 41; Baldo,
24 (Du Méril, pp. 210, 254); La Fontaine, II, 11. In Italian: Siena, 18';
Ghivizzani, 21; Monaci, 18; Brush, 16; Rigoli, 18. Brugsch gives a
version purporting to come from ancient Egypt (see R. Basset, *Contes populaires d'Afrique*, p. 1), but according to Wiedemann, *Popular Literature in
ancient Egypt*, London, 1902, pp. 14–18, this version comes from the Greek
period. There are, however, striking Oriental parallels; see Benfey, I,
324–30; Ribezzo, p. 155. This fable is alluded to in a long poem ascribed
to Fra Jacopone da Todi (Nannucci, *Manuale*, I, pp. 401, 409):

> Perchè gli uomini dimandano
> Detti con brevitate,
> Favello per proverbii
> Dicendo veritate . . . .
> Se puote picciol sorice
> Leon disprigionare . . . .

On the version by Nicole Bozon, cf. Harry, *op. cit.*, p. 47.

Terza rima 5. A very much expanded version of the city mouse (*topo
cittadino*) and country mouse (*topo di villa, chontadino*), which may come
from Romulus, I, 12; Walter, 12; Siena, Ghivizzani, 12. The fable in
Marie, 9; Rigoli, 9; Brush, 8, is slightly different. Versions in Monaci,
4; Waldis, I, 9; Er. Alberus, 8; La Fontaine, I, 9; in Greek, Halm,
297; Babrios, 108; in Latin, Horace, *Sat.* II, 6, etc. The cat is specifically mentioned by Odo of Cheriton, no. 16 (Hervieux, IV, p. 190), and in
Renart le Contrefait (Robert, I, 48–53; *Poètes de Champagne*, p. 151); very
probably the fable was familiar in oral as well as written versions.

Terza rima 7. Here also we find an elaborated version of a familiar
fable,—the eagle, on the advice of the crow, drops a tortoise on the
rocks to break its shell. In Phædrus, II, 6 (cf. Halm, 419), followed by
Romulus (ed. Oesterley, I, 13; Steinhöwel, I, 14); Walter, 14; Siena, 14;
Monaci, 6; the eagle shares the meat with the crow as a reward for the
advice. But in at least two descendants of Walter the crow carries off the
meat before the eagle can get to it, as in the *terza rima*; these are Ghivizzani, 13; Ysopet I, no. 14 (in Robert, II, p. 453); cf. Waldis, I, 10;
Alberus, 28. So also in Marie de France, 12, followed by Rigoli, 13; Brush,
11, the crow carries off the meat (cf. Warnke, *Quellen*). In the version in
Ghivizzani the shell-fish is *testuggine*; in Rigoli and Brush, *pescie scaglia*;
in our text, *bizzugha*, but *testuggine* in the title.

KENNETH McKENZIE.

PUBLICATIONS

OF THE

Modern Language Association of America

1906.

VOL. XXI, 2.   NEW SERIES, VOL. XIV, 2.

VII.—THE CHARACTER TYPES IN THE OLD FRENCH *CHANSONS DE GESTE.*

INTRODUCTION.

"Le moyen âge forme un anneau indispensable dans la chaîne de la transmission littéraire à travers les siècles."—Gaston Paris, *Cosmopolis*, Sept., 1898.

Three-quarters of a century has elapsed since the mediæval epic literature of France first attracted the attention of scholars. This interval has been marked by an uninterrupted succession of texts discovered and edited. The value of these texts to the student of language is great; their value to the historian of politics and society is considerable;[1] but their literary bearing has not been sufficiently emphasized. To this day the general public has but a vague idea of the character and significance of that national epic of which the *Chanson de Roland* is the highest expression

---

[1] Cf. P. Meyer, *Bull. annuaire de la Soc. de l'hist. de France*, v. xxvii, pp. 82–106; G. Paris, *Romania*, v. xxii, p. 145; Charles Potvin, *Nos premiers siècles litt.*, v. i, p. 26.

and which Léon Gautier strove so bravely to render popular.[1] The mediæval literature of France has not yet completely recovered from the reputation of vulgarity given to it by the Renaissance.

Ticknor, in speaking of the *Poema del Cid*, remarks that we read it "for its living pictures of the age it represents and for the vivacity with which it brings up manners and customs so remote from our own experience that when they are attempted in formal history, they come to us as cold as the fables of mythology."[2] These words express admirably the charm exercised by the old French *chansons de geste* upon the mind of the student who wanders at will among their treasures. These poems, at first sight so monotonous and so crude, are really the living expression of the society which produced them. They throb with the pulse of the changing political, social, and literary conditions of the twelfth and thirteenth centuries. When we recall the importance of these centuries in the pre-Renaissance literature of France, we marvel that so little has been written to make clear the place of the epic poems in the evolution of French literature. If "the Middle Age is an indispensable link in the chain of literary transmission," surely we should seek in the national epic some reflection of the development of French nationality and literary art.

With this end in view scholars have made many detailed studies of individual poems and of certain historical characters therein treated. These studies have been of a historical and critical rather than of a literary nature. Now that a considerable number of *chansons de geste* have been edited in a fairly definitive form, the time has come for a comprehensive appreciation of their value conceived from a purely

[1] Cf. *Revue des Questions hist.*, v. ii, p. 329; *Bibliothèque de l'Ecole des Chartes*, v. LX (mars-juin, 1899).

[2] Ticknor, *History of Spanish Literature*, v. i, p. 15.

literary point of view. We have a right to ask what was the message of these long poems to their age, and what is the literary inheritance they have left to us in these latter days. Truly contemporary with the age which produced them they surely are. Yet, in spite of the wide gulf of changed conditions which separate us from them, we recognize in the *dramatis personae* of the *chansons de geste* men and women of like passions with ourselves, trusting in the same eternal forces which make for goodness, and tempted by the same evils which assail mankind in all generations.

The human interest of the French epic poems, as revealed in the actors in these mediæval dramas, has never been lost from sight in the writing of the following pages. Our study is not philological in any sense; it is historical only in a broad sense; it does, however, seek to throw fresh light upon the literary ideals and execution of our mediæval ancestors. The method to be followed, then, will clearly be of an expository character. The poems themselves will be allowed to present the evidence; we shall but draw the patent conclusions. Much will be taken for granted, as requiring no further proof beyond that already adduced by experts in the neighboring field of historical criticism. But an earnest effort will be made to get nearer to the mind and art of feudal society in its last phase, to determine the forces at work which produced this rich literature, which enabled it to hold its popularity for three centuries, and which finally account for its failure as an expression of contemporary ideals.

Such an exposition as we here anticipate would have little bearing upon our knowledge of the literary sense of the Middle Age, were it not that we assume the mediæval poet-historian to have been in close contact with his audience. Between the *jongleur* and his auditors there was a perfect understanding. His livelihood depended upon his

success as a purveyor of acceptable entertainment, in which
each auditor might feel his share. Thus, whatever the
original subject of the poem, the treatment of it was a
response to contemporary taste and requirements. Only so
could perfect harmony exist between the story-teller and his
audience. Moreover, the former's appeal in these poems is
not to the romantic and the marvelous, but to the historical
and the true. Our *jongleur* angrily disclaimed the reputation of a wonder-working magician, but insistently asserted
his devotion to veracity. It is intended, then, here to study
the literary art of the Middle Age from a new view-point;
more specifically, to watch the *trouvère* as he handles the
traditional epic material.

The new view-point has been found in the characters
which figure in the *chansons de geste*. Their conventionality
and unvarying recurrence enable us, without violence, to
divide them conveniently into types. Each type of character will be studied chronologically, so far as possible, and
the significance of its evolution will be noted. With the
belief that such an exposition along six different lines will
contribute to our knowledge of the mediæval man in his
relation to literary expression, we pass to our examination
of the poems themselves.

THE KING.

It is not our purpose under this heading to reconsider
the facts so carefully exposed by Gaston Paris in *L'histoire
poétique de Charlemagne*. But the figure of the great Emperor dominates to a great degree the whole body of the
poetry which occupies our attention. It is with his epic
personality and with his far-reaching activities that other
persons and events are brought into relation. A study of
the personages in the French epic necessarily begins with
Charlemagne.

It was the purpose of Gaston Paris to trace the poetic history of Charlemagne through the epic poetry not only of·France, but of those countries into which the French epic material penetrated. He has classified the legends, many of them of local origin, which grew up in regard to the birth, marriage, conquests and pilgrimages of the Emperor. These were the matters of prime interest to a feudal audience, and it was upon these events that the imagination of the *trouvères* loved to dwell. " Les milieux populaires ne s'intéressent aux affaires publiques que par rapport à leur côté individuel et personnel. C'est le héros qui passionne le peuple, ce ne sont pas les destinées nationales dont il a la responsabilité, ni les graves intérêts qui reposent sur sa tête." [1] In spite, however, of the vagaries and palpable inaccuracies resulting from popular treatment, one is astonished in reading *L'histoire poétique* by the general accord of history and legend. This, too, is the conclusion recorded by Paris at the close of his long study.

The accord of history and poetry interests us, however, very little just now. For it is not of Charlemagne as an historical personage that we are thinking. It is rather of a king as an impersonal figure and of the rôle that is assigned to him in a body of poetry which supposedly expresses very accurately the sentiments of the public for whom it was cast into shape. If in this poetry the king is exalted far above the people, if he dwells in an atmosphere almost exclusively his own, it may be supposed that in fact the ideal of a king at that period was held in sufficient reverence to permit such a literary presentation. If, on the other hand, the figure of the king is not at all.epic in character, if his arm is shortened, his prerogatives scorned and his majesty only unwillingly admitted, we must suppose the influence of the

---

[1] Kurth, *Histoire poétique des Mérovingiens*, p. 226.

great vassals at work. The literary elevation or humiliation of the king considered relatively to that of his great vassals forms the interest of a study of the royal personage. For, as Luchaire has said : " L'histoire politique de la France pendant la plus grande partie du moyen âge peut se résumer dans la lutte soutenue par le pouvoir royal contre la féodalité." [1]

Rajna [2] and Kurth [3] have proved that tradition had busied itself with some of the Merovingian kings. But by the time when our literary period opens the Carolingian dynasty had taken to itself all the traditions of former times. With the exception of Clovis in *Floovant*, we meet only the names of Charles, Pepin and Louis as applied to the king of France. The latter two names owe their distinction respectively to the father and the son of Charles the Great. So absorbing was the personality of the great Emperor that all other Charles' became confounded with him,[4] just as Pepin the father of Charlemagne absorbed Pepin the father of Charles Martel, and Louis the son of Charlemagne caused the oblivion of all the other Louis'. This process of centralization is one of the most familiar features of popular poetry. The author of *Doon de Maience* felt the confusion of identity to which it gave rise when he wrote :

> "Segnurs, vous savés bien, et je en sui tous fis,
> Que plusors Kalles ot (chà arrier) à Paris,
> A Nerbonne la grant ot plusors Aymeris,
> Et à Orenge rot maint Guillaume marchis,
> Et si rot maint Doon à Maience jadis."
>
> *Doon de Maience*, p. 201.

It is not necessary to account for Charlemagne's promi-

---

[1] A. Luchaire, *Histoire des Institutions Monarchiques de la France sous les premiers Capétiens, 987–1180;* vid. *Préface.*

[2] *Origini dell' epopea francese.*

[3] *Histoire poétique des Mérovingiens.*

[4] Cf. Rajna, *Origini*, p. 199 f.

nence in the epic poetry of the Middle Age.   His learning, his imperial dignity, his defense of the Church against Mahometan invasion,—all these qualifications guaranteed for Charlemagne first rank among his country's rulers.   Of· these three historical qualifications, the first, naturally, left hardly a trace in the epic treatment of the Emperor.   It is an exceptional note,—that of Charles the mediæval scholar :

> " L'ampereor troverent an son palais marbrin.
> L'apostoilles li conte la vie Saint Martin,
> Et devise la letre et espont le latin."
> *Chanson des Saisnes,* v. i, pp. 64, 65.

So also *Renaus de Montauban,* p. 161.   To his claim as political organizer, as divinely protected Roman Emperor, however, full justice was done.   The memory of the impe-rial power of the historical Charlemagne contributed potently to the original majesty of the epic king of France.   But it was Charles the warrior, the right arm of the Church, the valiant defender of Christendom against pagan and Infidel invasion that comes most prominently into view.[1]   For the attention of a society which made fighting its principal occupation was necessarily devoted almost exclusively to the battlefield and to those heroic contests which the Emperor and his faithful vassals waged in the defense of France and of Christendom.   This is the scene displayed when the curtain goes up in the *Chanson de Roland,* the earliest *chanson de geste* that has been preserved.

Before turning to the poems themselves for evidence, it should be stated here what we intend to show : that there were three distinct treatments of the royal personage in the epic poems.   Whether he be called Charles, Pepin or Louis,

---

[1] For the literature based upon Charles' personal religious enthusiasm cf. G. Paris, *Hist. poét.,* and Gerhard Rauschen, *Die Legende Karls des Grossen im xi und xii Jahrhundert.*

the king undergoes a literary transformation,—a degeneration,—which we must explain in advance upon historical
and literary grounds.

We shall see that in the earliest poems the king's rôle is
grandiose and epic to the full. Somewhat more than man,
he is less only than God. Through the rallying of his
Christian knights he is God's agent upon earth for the casting down of the strongholds of anti-Christ. Full of dignity
and protected by divine favor he assists at the deeds of his
undaunted and trusty vassals,—trusty all save one who shall
betray him. To these vassals he is in almost the relation
of father to son, and to him all give the affection and
reverence which is his due.

To produce this primitive conception of the royal person
the Church writers contributed in common with the part
actually played by Charlemagne in the defense of Europe
against the Saracens. The Church writers had their own
reasons for emphasizing the reputed piety of the great
Emperor and for elaborating it into a sort of saintly example
which the later sovereigns should follow. On the other
hand, even after all danger in Western Europe had long
passed away and the fierce hatred against the followers of
the Prophet was appeased, the epic poems continue to represent the Emperor as the divinely appointed bulwark of
Christianity against the Infidels. These two influences,
then, working contemporaneously, the one ecclesiastical and
the other distinctly popular, combined to develop that conception of the king as viceroy of God in the conflict of the
French with the Saracens which is in progress in the *Roland*.

We come now to the second manner of treatment. The
primitive conception of the king, at once noble and naïve,
inevitably underwent an alteration. When one considers
how small and relatively mean were Charles' successors
until the Capetian house waxed strong and flourished, it is

not surprising that the literary portrait of the king lost in grandeur and dignity. In this second period interest centres in the increasingly strained relations of the king to the great vassals. The process of centralization is going steadily forward. The Capetian monarchs are strengthening their position at the expense of the ancient feudal prerogatives. Now, the sentiment of the feudal lords is directly reflected in the poems of this second period. Political and social problems are regarded almost exclusively from their point of view. From this point of view, hostile to the monarch, the latter is sometimes a king in deed; but more often he is recognized as but the nominal head, subject in all respects to the opinion of his powerful vassals and depending upon them for material aid. Henri Martin,[1] in some remarks upon the *Chanson de Roland* has explained this, at first unexpected, discrepancy between the historical facts and the literary treatment. As the king's power and the Capetian idea of centralization supported by the newly awakened *bourgeoisie* took root during the twelfth and thirteenth centuries, so the jealousy of the great feudal lords increased. This natural feeling is vividly manifested in the literary treatment accorded to the king in the poems of the second period. The king is now often represented as a tottering old man no longer able to defend his possessions, or as a young upstart whose inexperience makes him the laughing-stock of his more tried advisers. Artistically considered, this is a sad degeneration. One regrets the masterful epic traits of the *Roland.* But this very critical and often scornful vein in the later poems proves what is of essential importance: that the king was ever human; that he was tempted even as other men are tempted; and that he was criticised for incompetence or unfaithfulness in the perform-

[1] *Histoire de France,* v. iii, p. 345.

ance of those duties imposed upon the head of a feudal state. With the possible exception of that first exalted note in the *Roland* there is perhaps no trace of that spirit which tends to raise the king above his people and to make him one of those favored creatures who occupy the middle space between man and the gods. Nowhere is the French epic more intensely human, more historically accurate, when trespassing upon dangerous ground than in its conception of the leader of the people.[1]

The middle of the twelfth century in France saw the introduction of the Breton cycle, soon to be made popular throughout Europe by the romances of Chrestien de Troyes. One result of the Celtic influence was that the songs of national achievement were converted into biographies of individual heroes. This entailed the banishment of the king to a still more obscure position in the latest epic poems. The shadow of a Frankish king, however, is still there, and the events narrated in even the late poems are uniformly brought into touch with the great epic family of the king and his Peers. The latest poems do not offer us much material for a historical study of the monarchy. The interest in the struggle of king and vassal weakens before the charm of personal adventure and chivalric sentiment. The king in these poems is nothing more than a political necessity. From a literary point of view his importance is *nil.* He is only a fixed point of support, on which the leading characters in the story are made to lean,—a lay figure about whom the action moves without involving him.

This much having been said of the literary suppression of the king, we may now turn to the poems themselves for confirmation of the fact.

---

[1] Chè io non so se vi sia cosa più notevole nella nostra epopea di quel suo carattere schiettamante storico ed umano, che pare accentuarsi viepiù quanto più si risale addietro."—Rajna, *Origini,* p. 455.

. The first appearance of the king is in the well-known scene in the *Roland* where *Carles li reis, nostre emperere magnes* receives the Saracen ambassadors.   The scene is in every way worthy of this epic personage :

> " Desuz un pin, delez un eglentier,
> Un faldestoed i out fait tut d'or mier,
> Là siet li reis qui dulce France tient ;
> Blanche ad la barbe e tut flurit le chief,
> Gent ad le cors e le cuntenant fier.
> S'est qui l' demandet, ne l'estoet enseignier."
>
> *Roland,* 114–119.

This is the picture of the mature dignity of the King surrounded by his Peers uniformly presented in this poem. These Peers, better known as destroyers of the Infidel, form as well a body of advisers, without whose counsel even the great Charles takes no measure of state.   Thus, when the proposition of Marsile is under consideration :

> "Li empereres s'en vait desuz un pin,
> Ses baruns mandet pur sun cunseill fenir."
>
> *Id.,* 168-169.

The method of procedure is somewhat strange.   Free expression was given to all opinions, whether good or bad, whether trustworthy or treacherous.   Although the King was bound to follow the best sense of his counsellors, of whom Naimon was the chief, yet he could suppress any individual at will.   Thus when *Turpins de Reins en est levez del renc* (v. 264) it might be expected that the King would listen with deference to the archbishop's proposition.   On the contrary, he cuts him off :

> " 'Alez sedeir desur cel palie blanc ;
> N'en parlez mais, se jo ne l' vus cumant.' "
>
> *Id.,* 272-273.

Important for the personal character of the epic king

are the words of Ganelon in reply to Marsile's curiosity. Ganelon, who was never prompted by personal animosity to the King, resented the insinuation of old age and general weakness made against Charles by Marsile. He replied:

> " ' Carles n'est mie tels.
> N'est hum qui l' veit e conuistre le set,
> Que ço ne diet que l'emperere est ber.
> Tant ne l' vus sai ne preiser ne loer
> Que plus n'i ad d'onur e de bontet.
> Ses granz valurs qui s' purreit acunter?
> De tel barnage l'ad Deus enluminet,
> Mieilz voelt murir que guerpir sun barnet.' "
>
> *Id.*, 529–536.

As for Charles' valor, Ganelon has already confided to the crafty Blancandrin:

> " ' Itels est sis curages ;
> Jamais n'iert hum qui encuntre lui vaille.' "
>
> *Id.*, 375–376.

The personal relation which existed between the King and his warriors, mentioned in v. 536, is well illustrated in the following passage:

> " ' Seignur barun, jo vus aim, si vus crei ;
> Tantes batailles avez faites pur mei,
> Regnes cunquis e desordenet reis !
> Bien le conuis que gueredun vus dei
> E de mun cors, de terres e d'aveir.
> Vengiez voz filz, voz freres e voz heirs
> Qu'en Rencesvals furent ocis hier seir !
> Ja savez vus cuntre paiens ai dreit.' "
>
> *Id.*, 3406–13.

It is not strange that in a time of great danger Charles should be visited by dreams which warn him. Since he is the servant of God, he is cared for by the divine agents (v. 717 f. ; v. 725 f. ; v. 2525 f. ; v. 2555 f.). But if the King received warning as a privileged individual, he soon rued his carelessness like an ordinary mortal. The description of his grief upon leaving Roland behind emphasizes his human weakness and despair which must have forcibly impressed his followers:

> "Li emperere s'en repairet en France,
> Suz sun mantel enfuit la cuntenance."
>
> *Id.*, 829–830.

His sorrow is contagious among his emotional followers:

> "Carles li magnes ne poet muer n'en plurt,
> C. milie Franc pur lui unt grant tendrur,
> E de Rollant merveilluse poür."
>
> *Id.*, 841–843.

When Charles hears the mighty blast blown by Roland in his agony, he at once recognizes the danger of his nephew. But Ganelon fearlessly says:

> " 'De bataille est nient.
> Ja estes vus vieilz e fluriz e blancs,
> Par tels paroles vus resemblez enfant.' "
>
> *Id.*, 1770–72.

These last words of Ganelon are significant, because they betray a reaction against the majesty of the king's character, which reaction must have been tacitly admitted even before the *Roland*. There can be hardly any doubt that the earliest songs about the great Emperor represented him as quite faultless and heroic in every way. But owing to feudal jealousy under later kings this sentiment was early undermined, and a mental condition bordering upon that of Shakespeare's seventh age was occasionally ascribed even to Charlemagne. This reputation of the Emperor was current also among his enemies, as evidenced by Marsile's inquiries (v. 522–528). One is inclined to see even in this, the oldest and most heroic remnant of the royal cycle, the influence of the great vassals at work. It is no other than Ganelon, the brother-in-law of his sovereign, who addresses him with the scornful and belittling language just quoted. In the later poems this tendency is carried much further. This is but the first note of the change, and jars upon the otherwise unbroken paean of praise to the defender of Christendom.

Allusion has been made to the divine protection accorded to Charles in the *Roland.* Similar cases of divine interposition by miracles or dreams are offered by later poems.[1] But with all this, the humanity of the king is emphasized to a gratifying extent. He appears primarily in the *Roland* in his proper place, that of the leader of the people. When the plan of vengeance for the death of the Peers has been once decided upon, Charles

> "Mult fierement tute sa gent reguardet,
> Puis si s'escriet à sa voiz grand e halte :
> 'Barun franceis, as chevals e as armes !'
> Li empereres tuz premerains s'adubet,
> Isnelement ad vestue sa brunie,
> Lacet sun helme, si ad ceinte Joiuse."
>
> *Id.*, 2984–89.

It is the Emperor in person who gives the orders, draws up the battle array and commands the first three divisions (v. 3015 f., v. 3035 f.). This glimpse of the king at the head of his troops is worth noting, for such scenes are rare. Rarely in the later poems is to be found this conception of the king as the active general-in-chief. More and more he is relegated to his palaces,—a victim of intrigue, and content to let the fighting be done by his vassals.

Returned to Aix, in what Gautier has well termed the last act in the tragedy, Charles appears in two more characteristic scenes. In the former, where the question of Ganelon's guilt is considered, Charles finds his authority

---

[1] Cf. *Anseïs de Carthage, Gui de Bourgogne, Chanson des Saisnes.* G. Paris treats the whole subject in *L' hist. poét. de Charlemagne.*

paralysed by the failure of his barons to return a verdict of guilt in the council. The unexpected verdict in favor of pardon having been returned, Charles was at a loss what to do:

> "Quant Carles veit que tuit li sunt faillid,
> Mult l'en enbrunchet e la chiere e li vis,
> Al doel qu'il ad si se claimet caitifs."
>
> *Id.*, 3815–17.

And it was only the personal attachment of Tierry which saved the Emperor's cause and honor.

We have seen the royal council discussing the king's policy on the field of battle (v. 168 f.), and again we have seen it render a decision on a question of purely feudal bearing (v. 3742 f.). Finally, at the close of the poem, a matter of religious import is handed over to an ecclesiastical council as being outside the royal jurisdiction. It concerns the baptism of the captive wife of Marsile. Even this detail Charles may not decide:

> "Si 'n apelat les evesques de France,
> Cels de Baviere e icels d'Alemaigne."
>
> *Id.*, 3976–77.

It is these bishops who authorize the baptism.

Other conventional traits of the king in the *Roland* are his riches and his power:

> "Le riche empereur" (v. 2199).
>
> "Li reis poestéifs" (v. 2133).

It would be interesting to note how identically the same traits are assigned to Charles in the *Voyage de Charlemagne*. Just as the assumed date of this remarkable poem brings it into close proximity with the *Roland*, so the two poems represent the same grandiose portrait of the king. A few quotations, to be compared with those already made from the *Roland*, will show this clearly. At the very outset:

> "Un jorn fut li reis Charles al saint Denis mostier,
> S'out prise sa corone, en croiz seignat son chief,
> Et at ceinte s'espee dont li ponz fut d'or mier.
> Dus i out et demeines, barons et chevaliers."
>
> *Voyage de Charlemagne*, 1–4.

For the treasure he takes with him:

> "'Set cenz chameilz menrez d'or et d'argent trossez,
> Por set anz en la terre ester et demorer.'"
>
> *Id.*, 73–74.

And for his escort:

> "Or vait li emperere od ses granz compaignies.
> Devant el premier chief furent oitante milie."
>
> [.] *Id.*, 98–99.

Arrived at Jerusalem, the King is worthy to sit upon the throne in the *mostier* of sacred memory with his Peers in a scene that is highly impressive (v. 115–131).[1] King Hugo from afar knows of Charles' fame:

> "'Bien at set anz et mielz
> Qu'en ai oït parler estranges soldeiers
> Que issi grant barnage nen ait nuls reis soz ciel.'"
>
> *Id.*, 310–312.

Later, when an angel arrives most opportunely to assure Charles of success in the accomplishment of the *gabs*, we must say with the poet:

> "Deus i fist grant vertut por amor Charlemaigne."
>
> *Id.*, 791.

These few verses suffice to show the portrait of royalty as it is regarded in the eleventh century poetry. In the second

[1]An analogous idea was still current when a Spanish dramatist named Luis Velez de Guevara († 1644) wrote a play entitled *De la mesa redonda*. Of this Schack says: "Carlomagno personifica á Jesucristo; Flor de Lis á la Iglesia; Rolando á San Pedro; Durandarte á San Juan Evangelista; Montesinos á San Juan Bautista, y Garcelón á Judas;" Vid. *Literatura y arte dramático en España*, 5 vols., Madrid, 1886–88; vol. III, p. 307.

and third periods respectively, the influence of feudal hostility is more pronounced, and the spirit of the *romans d'aventure* contributes to relegate the king to a minor rôle by substituting the career of a chivalric knight. In the following chapters these later periods of the epic poetry bring some welcome innovations. The tendency of this literature, being, as already explained, just the opposite of the political tendency, the movement is toward individualism and away from national unity of action. The interest centres in the fortunes of a feudal family or of a single hero. It is no longer exclusively the nation against a foreign foe ; and, when it is so, it is the fortune of the individual warrior in the national struggle that compels the attention. To the royal personage this tendency was fatal. A steady degeneration in the literary treatment of royalty is remarked. In the typical poems of the feudal, as compared with the royal epic, some hesitation will be felt in the rôle of the king as an individual,—a hesitation which doubtless reflects vacillation in popular estimation. Yet, the tradition of Charlemagne's majesty still asserts itself, and the king as a feudal conception always implies certain prerogatives and privileges.

Raoul de Cambrai, whose historical basis is evident,[1] throws interesting light on the bearing of the feudal lords before the king. The motive of the poem is the misguided award of a fief made by the *fort roi Loeys* to the prejudice of his own nephew Raoul. Such conventional epithets as *drois empereres* should not mislead us. The spirit of the poem is in open revolt against the policy of an unjust king. Raoul's uncle Guerri does not mince his words in addressing Louis :

> " ' Et vos, fox rois, on vos en doit blasmer :
> Vos niés est l'enfes, nel deüssiés penser,
> Ne sa grant terre vers autrui delivrer.' "
> *Raoul de Cambrai,* 304–306.

[1] Cf. Paul Meyer in *Bulletin annuaire de la Société de l'histoire de France,* **XXVII**, pp. 82–106.

2

After Raoul's death, his mother Alix thus wards off the King who wishes to embrace her:

> " ' Fui de ci, rois, tu aies encombrier !
> Tu ne deüses pas regne justicier.
> Se je fuse hom, ains le sollelg couchier,
> Te mosteroie a l'espée d'acier
> Q'a tort iés rois, bien le pues afichier,
> Qant celui laises a ta table mengier
> Qi ton neveu fist les menbres trenchier.' "

Id., 5226–32.

The king is nominally head of the council of his vassals called after Raoul's death. *Loeys au vis fier* (v. 4820) *tint i. baston de pommier* (v. 4846) in this tumultuous gathering of passionate vassals. But no one is afraid of these conventional expressions of authority. Guerri sums it up when he says:

> " ' Drois empereres, ci a grant mesprison :
> Se Dex m'aït, ne valez i. bouton.' "

Id., 4865–66.

And again:

> " ' Drois empereres, ne vos en qier mentir ;
> Trestos li mons vos en devroit haïr.' "

Id., 4879–80.

Guerri reaches the height of insolence a little later when he exclaims:

> " ' Cest coart roi doit on bien essillier,
> Car ceste guere nos fist il commencier,
> Et mon neveu ocire et detranchier.' "

Id., 5425–27.

In the Provençal poem of *Girart de Rossillon*, devoted to the adventures of that proud vassal whom Paulin Paris called "le seul adversaire digne du roi,"[1] we find the hero in constant and open revolt against the king,—here Charles Martel. In his strong city of Roussillon, with his four nephews, he mocks at the king's pretentions :

---

[1] *Hist. litt. de la France*, xxii, p. 305.

> " ' Li castels è bien fors el murs de caire
> Neu ne le tien de lui nen sui bauzaire
> Ne nen sa chevaler regun retraire
> Catre nebous ai proz qui tuit sunt fraire
> Li sordere len pout fulie faire
> Seu vuel a monleum a son repaire.' "
>
> *Girart de Rossillon* (Ox. ms.), 838–843.

Two verses at the outset show Charles Martel in a conventionally unattractive light :

> "Soz toz omes est carles reis enviious
> Hanc ne vistes negun tan orgeillous."
>
> *Id.*, 680–681.

The great cycle quoted usually under the title of *Les Loherains* presents the same state of affairs as *Raoul de Cambrai*. In their present form these poems give us a vivid picture of the turbulent feudal society.[1] There is a fierce untamed spirit in the heroes of this cycle which is well depicted in the vigorous verse. The king, here the weak Pepin, son of Charles Martel, is again represented as giving fiefs to those attached to him :

> "Un riche don l'empereres li fist
> Tote Gascoigne li dona a tenir."
>
> *Li Romans de Garin le Loherain*, i, p. 64.

Other passages show that the king controlled the marriage of his great vassals. But in all this he should follow the advice of his council. No king can afford to neglect this council, if he expects to preserve his land and honor. Bernart says to Pepin :

> " ' Vos estes jones et chevalier meschins,
> Sé ciaus déchasses qui te doivent servir,
> Tu en verras tes regnes apovrir ;
> Sor toi venront Paien et Sarrasin,

---

[1] Cf. G. Paris in *Romania*, xvi, p. 581.

> Ne te porront Loherenc garentir.
> Que ne te fassent tes bons chatiaux croissir.' " [1]
>
> *Id.*, i, p. 281.

The opening of the last poem in this cycle, *La Mort Garin*, presents an interesting scene at the court of Pepin. At a grand assembly of the two opposing factions Pepin presides in person and announces that he will decide all disputes : [2]

> " ' Je jugerai, ce dit li rois Pepins,
>   Par tel convent com vos porroiz oïr ;
>   Que s'il i a escuier ne meschin,
>   Ne chevalier tant soit de riche lin,
>   Sé a mon dit met nesun contredit,
>   J'en combatrai orendroit, sanz respit,
>   Trestos armés sor un cheval de priz.' "
>
> *Mort Garin,* p. 36.

Some quotations from another cycle will suffice for this period.   In the opening verses of *Le Couronnement de Louis*, which belongs to the cycle of Guillaume d'Orange or Guillaume *au court nez*,[3] the *trouvère* thus recalls the past glories of France :

> "Quant Deus eslist nonante et nuef reiames,
>   Tot le meillor torna en dolce France.
>   Li mieldre reis ot nom Charlemagne ;
>   Cil aleva volentiers dolce France ;
>   Deus ne fist terre qui envers lui n'apende ;
>   Il i apent Baviere et Alemaigne,
>   Et Normandie, et Anjou, et Bretaigne,
>   Et Lombardie, et Navare, et Toscane."
>
> *Le Couronnement de Louis,* v. 12–19.

This souvenir makes only more apparent the weakness of

---

[1] For the political situation described in *Les Loherains* cf. Charles Potvin, *L'Epopée des Ducs de Lorraine et de Brabant* in *Nos premiers siècles littéraires,* v. i.

[2] "Au point de vue de sa fonction sociale le roi Capétien remplit une double mission : il était juge et législateur." Luchaire, *Institutions monarchiques,* Préface.

[3] The introduction of Langlois' edition of the poem (Anc. Textes) presents an elaborate study of its historical basis.

Charles' successor Louis,—the personification of the tottering, vacillating king who throughout the poem needs the strong support of the faithful Guillaume.   Louis calls upon him thus :

> " ' Hé! gentilz cuens, por Dieu l'esperitable,
> Veez mon pere de cest siecle trespasse :
> Vielz est et frailes, ne portera mais armes,
> Et je sui jovenes et de petit eage ;
> Se n'ai secors, tot ira a damage.' "

Id., 256–260.

In *Le Charroi de Nimes* reference is made to the feeble condition of Louis upon Charles' death.   Guillaume refers to this time, when Louis' rights to the throne were almost waived, in saying :

> " ' François le virent que ne valoies gaire :
> Faire en voloient de toi ou moine ou abe,
> Ou que tu fusses en aucun habitacle,
> En un moustier ou en i. hermitage.' "
> *Le Charroi de Nimes* (Meyer, *Rec.*
> *d'anciens textes*), 167–170.

This poem also shows Louis in his conventionally ungrateful attitude towards the faithful, determined Guillaume, who is the real hero of the *geste*.   When other vassals have been rewarded, Guillaume, who has done the most in the campaigns in Italy, is sent empty-handed away :

> " ' Einsi vet d'ome qui sert a male gent :
> Quant il plus fet, n'i gaaigne neant,
> Einçois en vet tot adès enpirant.' "

Id., 302–304.

In *Aliscans*, of the same cycle, should be noted the appearance of this same Guillaume at the court of Louis, his brother-in-law.   Furious that the King has sent no aid to his distressed vassals in the South, Guillaume strides into the audience chamber with no uncertain words :

" 'Jhesu de gloire, li rois de paradis,
    Save celi de qui je fu nasquis,
    Et mon chier pere dont fui engenuis,
    Et tos mes freres et mes autres amis,
    Et il confonde cel mavais roi faillis,
    Et ma serour, la putain, la mautris,
    Par qui je fui si vieument recuellis
    Et en sa cor gabés et escarnis.
    Quant descendi sous l'olivier foillis, ·
    Ainc de ses hommes n'i ot grant ne petis
    Ki me tenist mon destrier arabis ;
    Mais, par les sains ke Diex a benéis,
    Ne fust mes pere ki lés lui est assis,
    Ja le fendisse del branc dusqe el pis.' "
                                Aliscans, 2637–51.

No wonder the King trembles at such a threat !

These quotations from the feudal epic, all dating from a period when the *trouvères* still felt a certain respect for tradition, reveal, as has been seen, a hesitancy of treatment. The individual king may be weak and despicable ; he may be unjust and cowardly. But there is no open hostility against the *idea* of royalty. The king's literary rôle, though it has lost much of its original majesty, is still sufficiently prominent. The king, indeed, was an essential feature of feudalism, without which the social and political structure could not have existed. The cap-stone would have been lacking. No wonder the want of a strong, unified, respect-compelling figure in sympathy with his vassals, like Charlemagne, was often regretted. Nor is it any wonder that the memory of his just and all-victorious reign should long continue to be the feudal ideal. The fact that it was the feudal ideal accounts for the glory always ascribed to the rule of the great Emperor even when this glory is pushed far beyond the bounds set by history. This traditional halo about the name of Charlemagne shed something of sanctity even about his successors, and, we believe, saved the epic king for a time from the literary oblivion or disrepute into which a hostile feudal poetry tended to sink him.

The passages just quoted show that the complaint against the king in the feudal epic was based upon his injustice. This point will be made clearer when we come to consider the *traitors* as the givers of evil counsel at the court. To these *traitors* the king too often listened ; and, as a result, he was charged with ungratefulness, favoritism, moral weakness, avarice, cowardice and injustice.

Our main point has already been made. An idea of the king's rôle in the national and feudal epic has already been gained. It is neither a brilliant nor a prominent rôle. But it is indispensable, and it is attended with certain heroic features of dignity and majesty. In the poems of the third period,—those ascribed to a date subsequent to the close of the twelfth century,—the sense of historical accuracy was steadily losing ground. The poems become diverting recitals, and, though they are most important for the general matter of this study, they bear little fruit for the study of the king's rôle. A few random quotations from these later poems will indicate the liberties taken with the once august figure of the king, and will show how he was occasionally travestied. With this will be found cropping up now and again the tradition of the heroic Emperor and his Peers.

In *Doon de Maience* we find a typical example of this mingled scorn and respect for the sovereign. When Charles first hears the audacious proposition of Doon to win Vauclere from the Saracens in order that Doon may marry the beautiful Flandrine, Charles trembles at the very thought :

> "Lors regarde entour li, de paour va tremblant ;
> N'i voit home dez siens qui ja li port garant."
> *Doon de Maience*, p. 193.

But he recovers at once and defies Doon to compel him to take part in any such hare-brained expedition, while staking his life on the result of the single combat. Though the

excuse for this combat seems a paltry one, and though every
effort is made to prevent it (p. 202) and to stop it (p. 218),
yet, the result long remains in doubt.   Doon may safely
trust in God's protection :

> "Qui Dex aime de cuer ne se doit esmaier ;
> Ja honni ne sera, pour qu'il voist droit sentier."
>
> *Id.*, p. 202.

Doon angrily expresses his intention of killing Charles
(p. 211), but in his better mood, which doubtless represents
the attitude of the poet and his audience, he hopes he may
do the King no harm (p. 206), and twice later, when he fears
he has mortally wounded Charles, he cries out to the Queen
of Heaven :

> "'Glorieuse du chiel, roïne couronnée !
> Gardez moi mon seignor l'ame n'en soit alée.'"
>
> *Id.*, p. 210.

The barons too cry out in horror:

> "'Do, ne l'ochirre pas! mar l'oseras penser.'"
>
> *Id.*, p. 214.

But each combatant is so obstinate that God himself must
stop the fight, not desiring the death of either hero.   The
poet states as a matter of fact:

> "Mez Dex gari le roy, qui tous jors l'avoit chier."
>
> *Id.*, p. 212.

The interfering angel bids Charles to accede to the reasonable request of Doon, threatening him with death, if he
refuses :

> "'Et iras en enfer, en la meson puant
> Où déables t'atendent, qui t'iront tormentant.'"
>
> *Id.*, p. 221.

In *Fierabras*, while Oliver is fighting with the Saracen
giant, Charles relapses into a most unworthy frame of mind.

The poet does not hesitate to put into his mouth sacrilegious words which would divert the audience:

> " 'Sainte Marie dame, dist Karles au fier vis,
> Garisiés Olivier qu'il n'i soit mors ne prins;
> Car, par l'arme mon pere, se il estoit ochis,
> Ja en moustier de France ni en tout les païs
> Ne seroit clers ne prestres à nul jour revestis;
> Trestous feroie abatre auteus et crucefis.'
> 'Sire, ce dist dus Naimes, laisiés ester vos dis;
> Li hons qui si parole sanble du sens mendis;
> Mais priés pour le conte le roi de paradis,
> Qu'il li soit en aïe par ses saintes merchis.' "

Fierabras, p. 28.

A harder thrust home than that given by Ogier to Charles in *Gui de Bourgogne* could hardly be imagined. The accusation of the *fainéant* kings is all there:

> " ' On dit que Karlemaines conquiert tous les reniez;
> Non fait par Saint-Denis! vaillant iiii. deniers,
> Ains les conquiert Rollans et li cuens Oliviers,
> Et Naimes à la barbe, et je qui sui Ogiers.
> Quant vos estes soef en vostre lit couchiez,
> Et mangiez les gastiaus, les poons, les ploviers,
> Lors menaciez Espaigne la terre à essillier;
> Mais vos n'en ferrés ja en escu chevalier.
> Damedieu me confonde, qui tout a à jugier,
> Se g'estoie là fors, montés sor mon destrier,
> Et fuisse de mes armes mult bien aparilliez
> Se je ne vos prenoie par mon cors prisonier.' "

Gui de Bourgogne, 37–48.

Elsewhere it is Roland himself who says to the Emperor:

> " ' Ce n'est pas grant merveille se vous estes felon;
> Cent ans i ad premier que cauchastes speron:
> Puis que li hons vit trop, il n'a sens ne raison.' "

Jehan de Lanson (vid. Hist. litt., xxii, p. 572).

In *Macaire*, when that arch-traitor seeks to seduce the queen in the garden, he uses that most artful of all methods to accomplish his foul purpose; he tells the queen that her husband, the king, is not good enough for her :

> " ' Et ce est bien uns grans pechiés mortés
> Quant un tés hom vos a à governer.' "
>
> *Macaire*, p. 9.

None of the later poems better than *Gaydon* shows the type of perfect knight and vassal opposed to the king surrounded by his traitor council. This long poem is the recital of this long conflict with intercalations of an adventurous character. There is no rôle too ridiculous for the Emperor to play. Charles himself says it is two hundred years since he first put on his spurs and is angry at being baffled in his siege of Gaydon. He lowers himself to take a disguise and thus with Naimon seeks to gain admittance into Gaydon's strong place :[1]

> " Charles li rois à la barbe chenue
> Avoit sa robe maintenant desvestue ;
> Une esclavinne, qui fu noire et velue,
> Vest en son dos sans nulle arrestéue.
> Son vis a taint de suie bien molue,
> Prent i. chapel de grant roe tortue,
> Et i. bordon dont la pointe iert aigue,
> L'escharpe au col qui bien estoit couzue.
> Fransois en rient, quant l'ont apercéue.
> Naynmes s'adoube par autel connéue."
>
> *Gaydon*, p. 294.

Disguised as a pilgrim, Charles finds difficulty in containing himself when one of the barons, referring to Charles himself, boasts in his presence :

> " ' Par la foi que doi Dé,
> Se gel tenoie en cest palais pavé,
> Ja li auroie le sien grenon plumé,
> Car nus plus fel ne fu de mere nés.
> Tant a traïtres entor lui à plenté
> Que loiaus hom n'i puet iestre escoutez.' "
>
> *Id.*, p. 298.

[1] For similar disguises adopted by Charles cf. *Doon de Maience*, p. 224, and the *Pseudo-Turpin*, cap. **ix.**

In spite of this disrespect, another late poem suggests the epic king :

> " Karles dedanz son tref sist en i. chaiere
> Tote de blanc yvoire, d'uevre subtile et chiere ;
> Delez lui se seoit dus Naymes de Baviere,
> iiii. roi et x. contes vestu à lor baniere."
>
> *Chanson des Saisnes*, i, p. 83.

Another note of confidence, though it seems rather a dying gasp of the epic king, is found in the *Roman d'Aquin* or *La Conqueste de la Bretaigne*, dating probably from the end of the twelfth century. The king has been wounded in fighting the Saracens (*i. e.*, Normans),[1] and his condition fills his followers with dismay. But with his old-time confidence Charles reassures them :

> " ' Ne saiez esmayé,
> Ge gariray et vendré en santé.' "
>
> *Aquin*, 2816.

The only post-mortem mention we have found of Charles personally is in *Les Narbonnais*. The tradition here represents him majestic in his solitary grandeur :

> "A Es l'an portent anterrer hautement :
> En la chaere l'ont assis an seant,
> O encore est ; bien le sevent alquant
> C'ont esté en la terre."
>
> *Les Narbonnais*, 5327–30.

Such are the general aspects under which the epic poetry of the eleventh to the thirteenth century treats the figure of royalty. By whatever name he might be called, the epic king shows unmistakable traces of the beneficent influence of the long cherished respect for Charlemagne. But the illustrations have shown how the tendencies of contemporary feudalism undermined the grandiose position of the king in

---

[1] Cf. G. Paris, *Romania*, ix, p. 455 ; *Aquin* (ed. Anc. Textes), Introd., p. xxxix.

the earliest poems. Of his final insignificance it has been difficult to present testimony, for the simple reason that the king is merely named as an existing personage and then left in the background. The predominance of other types in our later chapters will tacitly explain the literary oblivion which overtook the king.

In reality the *trouvères* expended but little effort upon the monarch. There is in all literature something hopelessly uninteresting about a king *as* king. Perhaps we feel the impossibility of his measuring up to the requirements of his exalted place. Perhaps his royalty detracts from his humanity. The poets of all time have chosen their heroes among the warriors or from the middle classes of society. It has been truly said : "Les grands hommes perdent plus qu'ils ne gagnent à passer par le prisme de l'épopée, et Charlemagne, comme l'a fort bien montré M. Léon Gautier, est incontestablement plus grand dans l'histoire que dans tous les poèmes de la *geste de France*." [1] So as time went on, first the feudal vassal rose into prominence ; then, the chivalrous hero in search of adventure and of the love of a woman; and, finally, the *bourgeoisie* of the thirteenth century cities announces itself with no uncertain sound. In the succeeding chapters we shall for the first time find strength and vitality of character-drawing, high ideals in domestic as well as in national life,—in fine, that living incarnation of the nation in the individual which makes of the French epic a chapter in the history of French civilization. [2]

---

[1] Kurth, *Hist. poét. des Mérovingiens*, pp. 316, 317.

[2] For an excellent summary of the treatment of the king in the late poems cf. G. Paris, *Hist. poét. de Charlemagne*, p. 357.

· THE HERO.

Having disposed of the impersonal and somewhat uninteresting type of monarch as described in the *chansons de
geste*, we come now to consider those heroes upon whom the
whole skill of the *trouvères* was expended. A glimpse has
already been caught of the Twelve Peers[1] struggling at
Ronceval in defence of the Emperor and of the ideas of
Christian chivalry for which he stood.[2] They were originally few in number, these heroes devoted to the person
of the Emperor with an unquestioning personal attachment,
and with an unwavering execution of duty, whatever might
be the sacrifice. They were singularly simple characters,
capable of being summed up in a single epic epithet,—the
incarnation of such plain but noble qualities as appealed to
the unsophisticated audience which delighted in the *Roland*.
A single phrase sufficed to recall the moral aspect conventionally ascribed to each individual hero.

It would seem that in the earlier part of our period the
conception of the *trouvères* divided all vassals into two
categories : first, those who were faithful to the king and to
the Christian cause ; these were their heroes ; and second,
those who were traitors to this same cause, and who correspond to the villains in a play. Upon the latter the vials
of their wrath are generously discharged.

Such a simple system of dividing the good from the bad
is surely indicative of a very limited amount of artistic
ability. The time very soon came when the reality in feudal
relations belied such a summary fashion of treating those in
opposition to the king. The great vassals of illustrious

---

[1] Cf. Ferdinand Lot, *Quelques mots sur l'origine des pairs de France* in
Revue historique, jan.-avril, 1894.

[2] Cf. Kurth, *Hist. poët. des Mérovingiens,* pp. 462, 463.

lineage who were opposing the progress of the royal power naturally objected to figuring in the *chansons de geste* as traitors. Self-aggrandizement and armed opposition to the king were perfectly compatible with the highest heroism and the noblest qualities of character. Such is the simple explanation of the noble but disloyal characters we meet in *Raoul de Cambrai, Ogier de Danemarche, Gaydon, Girart de Rossillon, Quatre Fils Aymon,* &c. Thus, instead of treating under this head the faithful vassal only, we must use the broader word : the *hero.*

From an artistic point of view the progress herein indicated is considerable. Charles himself, Turpin, Roland and Oliver indeed stand out grandly and majestically with their simple devotion. But they are not human. They are the impersonation of an ideal ; and, like any exaggerated type, they finally become tiresome. The change that came in the twelfth century poems is, then, to be welcomed. The *trouvère* sought to make his hero, whether faithful or rebel, more human. To accomplish this implied the substitution of the individual for the nation. The heroes of the poems of this second period are painted from life. There is a satisfying quality of humanity about Raoul de Cambrai, Garin and Begon, Guillaume *au court nez* and Girart de Rossillon which is lacking in the older heroes.

It has been frequently remarked that the heroes in the *Roland* are rather personifications of ideals dear to the spirit of the time than men of changing mind and mood like ourselves. As a natural man and from a psychological point of view, Ganelon is the only satisfying figure in the *Roland,* and he must be reserved for the next chapter. Roland, Oliver, Turpin and Naimon are men who can be counted upon. Once given their moral shade of character, it will not change. The late poems unvaryingly refer to them as the highest types of certain moral qualities. It has become

a commonplace for us also, since Gautier first made the
Roland known in an appreciative edition,[1] to speak of
Roland as the personification of youthful unreflecting ardor,
of Oliver his companion as no less brave but more wise,
of Naimon the old giver of good counsel as always ready to
speak a word for justice and fairness, and of Turpin as the
Christian warrior, not disdaining to join the temporal arm
with the power of the Spirit in the fight for his Lord and
his Emperor. These are the four characters who, with
Ganelon and the Emperor, occupy the foreground in the
poem and upon whom the action turns. Anyone familiar
with the poem feels that they alone are responsible for its
high tone, its lofty ideals of patriotism, of faithful service,
of personal honor untarnished, and of an unbroken faith in
that bliss of a future existence to which nothing is to be
preferred. High indeed are these ideals; eloquent and
inspiring are the pages which two modern critics have
written on such a text.[2]

What then, judging from these types in the earliest
chansons de geste, are the essential traits of a hero to an
eleventh century audience? Upon what qualities did such
an audience insist before a character could be altogether
admirable?

    i. Trust in God.
    ii. Loyalty, in a broad sense.
    iii. Bravery and jealousy of honor.

What is important to notice and what is clear in the poems
themselves is that these three qualities of the hero remain
constant throughout the period of popularity of the *chansons
de geste*. Other qualities are only grafted upon these. In

---

[1] First edition, Tours, 1872.

[2] Cf. Léon Gautier *passim;* and G. Paris, *La poésie du moyen âge:* pre-
mière série, pp. 87–118.

the feudal epic, to be sure, loyalty to the king as an individual gives way before loyalty to family, to friends, or to
some ideal of justice and equity. But the essential idea
of loyalty to some cause is constant in the hero, just as one of
the traits of the traitor is his fickleness, his underhand deal-
ings, his frequent change of front. This being so, it will not
be necessary to consider the poems by periods as was done
in the preceding chapter. All that need be noticed is the
filling in of the detail, the rounding out of the character in
the twelfth and thirteenth century poems. The base features
remain the same, but the result is more real, more human.

This trust in God as the Giver of every good and perfect
gift is a very real thing in the minds of these heroes, and is
one of the first lessons taught to a young man by his parents
or sponsors. When that good and gentle man Guillaume
d'Orange came to give his nephew Vivien the *accolade*, he
charged him with these words:

> " ' Va t'en biaus nies diex qui fist moisant
>   Te donst proesce honor et hardement
>   De foi garder ton seignor lealment
>   Et de confondre celle gent mescreant'
> 'Amen biaus honcles' l'anfes vait respondant."
>   *Les Enfances Vivien* (MS. 1448), 5173–77.

These farewell pieces of advice given to the youthful heroes
as they were about to embark on their adventurous careers
are usually long affairs,—too long to permit quotation here.

Intermixed, especially in the later poems, with the
inculcation of religious duty, we find a series of practical
injunctions, — *chastiements* or *enseignements* as they were
called,—some of which are remarkably modern in tone.[1]
They reveal a very different conception of duty, they con-

---

[1] For an exhaustive collection of *chastiements* in the French epic poems cf.
Eugen Altner, *Ueber die Chastiements in den altfranzösischen chansons de geste*,
Leipzig, 1885.

tain elaborate formulae of conduct for circumstances in which we cannot imagine one of the older heroes with his simplified code. This innovation and refinement of conduct seems to be directly traceable to the softening of feudal manners and to that complication of daily life which was contemporary with the invasion of Provençal etiquette combined with the literary conventions of the Breton poems. The following passage, where Elie sends his son Aiol to the king, is a perfect manual of behavior :

> " ' Or en irés, biaus fieus, al congiet Dé :
> Jhesus vos i laist faire par sa bonté
> Dont li rois mieus vous aint et son barné.
> As eskiés ne as tables, fieus, ne jués :
> Celui tient on a sot qui plus en set,
> Car se li uns les aime, l'autre les het,
> Lors commenche grant guerre sans nul catel.
> N'aiés cure d'autrui feme enamer,
> Car chou est un pechiés que Dex moult het,
> Et se ele vos aime, laissiele ester.
> Si vos gardés molt bien de l'enivrer,
> Et sachiés bien qu' ivreche est grant vieutés.
> Se vous veés preudome, si le servés,
> Se vous seés en bant, si vous levés ;
> Les grans et les petis tous honorés ;
> Gardés que nul povre home vos ne gabés ;
> Ançois i poriés perdre que conquester.'
> ' Ce ferai jou, biaus pere,' che dist li ber."
>
> *Aiol*, 162–179.

Most interesting is the scene in *Les Narbonnais* where Aymeri dismisses his sons in search of adventure and a living. He urges them to be gone quickly, lest he suspect they delay for some evil purpose :

> " ' Volez i fere oltraje ne folie
> Ne les puceles prandre par esboutie
> Ne les borjoises honir par vilanie ? ' "
>
> *Les Narbonnais*, 283–285.

As for the youngest, upon his head the father puts all the responsibility of guarding Narbonne :

3

" ' Dormir porré en ma sale hautaingne
 Entre les braz Hermanjart ma compaingne ;
 N'avrai poor que Sarrazins m'i praigne
 Filz, por vostre barnage !' ' "
Id., 236–239.

When their father is dead it is their mother who gives
parting counsel to the two *dolant orfelin*, Huon de Bordeaux
and his brother Gerart :

" ' Enfant, dist ele, vous alés cortoier
 Je vous requier, pour Diu le droiturier,
 Que n'aiés cure de malvais losengier ;
 As plus preudommes vous alés acointier.
 A sainte glise pensés du repairier,
 Portés honnor et amor au clergié.
 Donnés du vostre as povres volentiers ;
 Soiiés courtois et larges vivendiers,
 Si serés plus amés et tenus chiers.' "
Huon de Bordeaux, p. 18.

In the same strain are the following : *Doon de Maience*,
pp. 74, 75 ; *Gaufrey*, pp. 8, 9 ; *Chanson des Saisnes*, p. 86.
The standard of social etiquette in some of these latter
poems closely reflects that in vogue among the Provençal
poets who speak much of measure, generosity, courtesy and
frankness.

 Needless to say, his trust in God goes everywhere with
the hero. With God all things are possible, and the warrior
in a critical juncture does well to call upom Him. God,
however, has his own favorites whom he aids without waiting to be addressed. This divine aid is available for any
end. Just preceding the passage already quoted from *Aiol*,
his mother regrets to see her son start out so slimly equipped
financially. But Aiol is of good cheer and laughingly cries
out :

" ' Se vos n'avés avoir, Dieus a assés,•
 Qui del sien me donra a grant plenté.' "
Aiol, 159, 160.

When Aymeri de Narbonne offers to stay behind and guard Narbonne for Charlemagne, the Emperor bids him remember that he is poor and will need much money.   He replies:

> " ' N'est encor Dex la sus el firmament,
>   Qui est puisanz toz jorz sanz finement?
>   Je croi en lui molt bien veraiement
>   Qu'il m'aidera, ce cuit, prochienement.' "
>
> *Aymeri de Narbonne*, 762–765.

When Gaydon is about to engage in single battle with the traitor Thiebaut, Riol comforts Gaydon by assuring him:

> " ' Je sai de voir que voz Thiebaut vaintrez,
>   Car Dex et drois sera vostre avoez.' "
>
> *Gaydon*, p. 28.

This, of course, is the theory of the judicial trial by arms.[1] It is the true note of Christian confidence expressed by Guibert, when he is restored to his baptized Saracen bride Agaiete and when in reply to her anxious questions about the future, he replies:

> " ' Dame, c'est au Déu de lassus.' "
>
> *Prise de Cordres*, 2529.

More mystic is the faith of the thoroughly religious Naimon who, when hard pressed by the Saracens, assures his men:

> " ' En paradis Damme Dé nous atant,
>   Je ouay les anges qui cy nous vont gueraint
>   De nous touz vont les armes attendant.' "
>
> *Aquin*, 1573–75.

Also the ecstatic words of Vivien:

> " ' En Paradis Damedex nos atant.
>   Ge oi les angles par desoz nos chantant.
>   Dex ! por quoi vif, que ge ne sui morant,
>   En cele joie que je désirre tant
>   Fust la moie ame avec les innocenz !' "
>
> *Li Covenans Vivien*, 1560–64.

---

[1] Cf. *Gaydon*, pp. 42, 43 ; *Doon de Maience*, p. 79.

One is tempted to see in such expressions as these and others,[1] especially of the Crusade cycle, the influence of the Mahometan belief in the reward of those who fell in battle.

Instances could be multiplied to show this belief in the constant participation of the divine with the human. That the religion of the Middle Age was closely bound up with every activity of life is evident in every monument, artistic and literary, that we have of the period. Hence, it is not surprising to find in the epic that the heroes were uniformly men of God, valiant defenders of Christianity as an ideal, above all mighty men of prayer. These prayers constitute to the last one of the features of the epic poems.[2] Often of great length, in the form of an address to God, to Christ, to the Virgin, and in the later poems to the saints as well, they sum up the *trouvère's* off-hand recollection of incidents gathered from the Old and New Testaments. When a prayer is to be made, time is no object. The battle stands still, the enemy holds off until the hero shall have finished his orisons. One of these prayers resembles another so much that that of Oliver made in the midst of his combat with Fierabras may serve as a type:

> " ' Glorieus Sire peres, qui formastes Adam
> Et Evain sa moullier, dont li pules sunt grant,
> Tout lor abandonastes par le vostre commant,
> Fors le fruit d'un pumier dont ne fuissent goustant ;
> Eve l'en fist mengier par le dit du serpent,
> Paradis en perdirent trestout de maintenant,
> Labourer les convint, dont moult furent dolent ;
> Puis furent li dyable en après si poissant,
> Qui n'estoit saint ne sainte, tant fuissent bienfaisant,
> Ne convenist aler en ynfer le puant.

[1] Cf. *Roland*, 1134–35 ; *Doon de Maience*, p. 316 ; *Chanson d'Antioche*, v. i, pp. 113, 162 ; *Cov. Vivien*, 778–780 ; *Chancun de Willame*, 344–346.

[2] Cf. *Bauduin de Sebourc*, v, 134–163. The whole subject has been treated by Johann Alton, *Gebete und Anrufungen in den altfranzösischen chansons de geste*, Marburg, 1883.

Pités vous en prinst, Sire, quant souffert eustes tant ;
Par saint Gabriel l'angle fu fais l'anoncement
Que en la sainte Virge prenderiés naissement.
Trestoute créature en fu reléechant,
Grant joie en demenerent bestes, oisiel volant.
Li troi roi d'autres teres vous alerent querant,
Tout lié vous aourerent quant vous vinrent devant ;
Vo destre main tendistes, à vous furent offrant,
Et par estraignes teres furent puis repairant
Pour le felon Herode qui les aloit cercant ;
Puis decola pour vous maint innochent enfant,
Desquels les ames sunt en joie permanant.
Puis alastes par tere vos amis préechant,
Le bien leur demonstrates et alas pourcachant.
En la crois vous pendirent li felon mescréant.
Quant Longis vous feri de la lance trenchant,
Il n'avoit ainc véu en trestout son vivant ;
Li sans li vinst par l'anste juques as ex coulant,
Il en terst à ses ex, tantost en fu véant.
Merchi vous cria, Sire, sa poitrine batant,
Et vous li pardonnastes sans point de mautalent.
El sepucre fus mis après nonne sonnant,
Au tierc jour en après éus suscitement ;
En infer en alastes, si en jetas Adan
Et tes autres amis qu'en furent desirant.
A saintismes apostres fustes apparissant,
Commandas que ton nom alaissent préechant ;
Puis montastes ou chiel, trestout lor ex véant.
Si voirement, biax Sire, com jou i sui créant,
Et c'est voirs que j'ai dit, si me soiés aidant,
Ke je cest paien faice de bataille taisant,
Et ke il croie en vous, ains qu'il soit recréant.' "

Fierabras, pp. 29, 30.

No wonder Fierabras

"Olivier apela, si li dist en riant :
'Biaus amis Oliviers, ne me va pas celant,
Quele orison est ce que as devisé tant ?
Volentiers l'ai oïe, par mon diu Tervagant.' "

Id., p. 30.

Next in importance as an essential feature of the hero's character is his loyalty to his king or to those toward whom

he is in some peculiar relation of mutual faith. Of this
loyalty there is no lack of examples. The *Roland* is impreg-
nated with this grand spirit of unflinching loyalty. Just
before the battle Roland says to Oliver :

> " ' Bien devuns ci ester pur nostre rei ;
>   Pur sun seignur deit hum sufrir destreiz,
>   E endurer e granz chalz e granz freiz,
>   Si'n deit hum perdre e del cuir e del peil.' "
>
> *Roland*, 1009–12.

Again :

> " ' Pur sun seignur deit hum susfrir granz mals,
>   E endurer e forz freiz e granz chalz,
>   Si'n deit hum perdre del sanc e de la char.' "
>
> *Id.*, 1117–19.

Turpin says :

> " ' Seignur barun, Carles nus laissat ci,
>   Pur nostre rei devum nus bien murir ;
>   Chrestientet aidiez à sustenir ! ' "
>
> *Id.*, 1127–29.

The reward of this loyalty is certain :

> " 'Amis Rollanz, Deus metet t'anme en flurs
>   En paréis entre les glorius ! ' "
>
> *Id.*, 2898–99.

> " Morz est Turpins li guerreiers Charlun.
>   Par granz batailles e par mult bels sermuns
>   Cuntre paiens fut tuz tens campiuns.
>   Deus li otreit sainte benéiçun ! "
>
> *Id.*, 2242–45.

When Garin tries to dissuade Oliver from risking himself
in battle for the king's cause, Oliver replies :

> " ' Qui son droit signeur faut, il n'a droit de parler.
>   Puisque je voi Franchois fuïr et trestourner,
>   Se je ensi le fac, où se puet mes fier ?
>   Au besoing puet on bien son ami esprouver.' "
>
> *Fierabras*, pp. 7, 8.

This last verse constantly recurs throughout our poems as
the expression of loyalty between friends. The oath taken

by young Vivien upon two occasions brings out the combination of personal bravery and zeal for the good cause :

> " La jura l'enfes oant tot le barne
> Que jà mais ne fuiroit por Turc ne por Escler
> Demie lanche ne ii. pies mesure."
>
> *Les Enfances Vivien* (MS. de Boulogne), 2206–08.

And again :

> " ' Oncle Guillaume, dist Viviens li frans,
> Par tel covent me ceigniez hui le brant,
> Que ne fuirai jamès en mon vivant
> Por Sarrazin, por Turc né por Persant
> Plain pié de terre selonc mon escient :
> Tant le met-ge vers Deu en covenant,
> Le glorieus, le pere roiament.' "
>
> *Li Covenans Vivien,* 40–45.

Nor are those of humble birth, as will be seen in another chapter, always behindhand in their expressions of loyalty (cf. *Doon de Maience,* p. 276). But by none is the idea so beautifully expressed as by Guillaume d'Orange :

> " ' Mal soit de l'arbre quel vergier est plantes
> Ki son seignor ne donne ombre en este.' "
>
> *Les Enfances Vivien* (MS. de Boulogne), 335–336.

But there were other objects of loyalty besides the overlord. The sentiment of family or personal honor, as well as that of friendship, equalled, if it did not triumph over, this sentiment of feudal loyalty. Roland and Oliver have become types of friends, bound together by this *compagnonnage* or *fraternité d'armes* of which Flach has made such an interesting study.[1] In the *Chanson d'Antioche* of the Crusade cycle we read :

> " Par dedens Antioche furent doi chevalier
> Qu'estoient compaignon, moult tint l'uns l'autre chier."
>
> *Chanson d'Antioche,* v. ii, pp. 187, 188.

---

[1] *Le compagnonnage dans les chansons de geste* in *Etudes romanes dédiées à Gaston Paris* (Paris, 1891). Reviewed in *Romania,* xxii, 145.

This *compagnonnage* usually dates from early youth and seems to be based chiefly upon a mutual liking between two young chevaliers. Such are Beuve d'Antone and Gui d'Aspremont in *Daurel et Beton* and Ami and Amile in the poem of that name. In *A'ye d'Avignon* Garnier, son of Doon de Maience, quarrels with his *compagnon* Berengier, son of Ganelon, *por une pucele*. Based upon a generous recognition of good qualities in an enemy is the friendship, though not technical *compagnonnage* of Ogier and Karahuel the Saracen in the *Enfances Ogier*. In the *Mort Garin* we find this idea of mutual aid among allied vassals :

> " ' Cuidiez-vos ore que je soie si pris,
>   Sé a moi viénent li mien charnel ami,
>   Que je lor viée, ne mon pain, ne mon vin,
>   Ne mes chastiax, ne mes viles ausi ? ' "
>
> *Mort Garin,* p. 80.

No sacrifice, however, was ever so great as that made by Amile for his friend Ami. Amile discovers that by the blood of his two little sons alone can his friend Ami be healed. It is the fearful sacrifice of a father's love and pride to a friend's duty supported by the promise of God,— a motive that would have pleased Corneille. Note the last two verses especially of Amile's consent :

> " ' Mais que santé voz poïsse donner,
>   Tost le feroie, ge'l voz di sans fausser ;
>   Car au besoing puet li hom esprouver
>   Qui est amis ne qui le weult amer.' "
>
> *Amis et Amiles,* 2854–57.

The poet hastens to justify the sacrifice :

> " Mais tout ce fu par l'amonestement
>   Jhesu le pere qui touz les biens consent."
>
> *Id.,* 3161–62.

The editor Hofmann is quite right in saying of this legend which has had such popularity through the ages : " Der moralische Sinn der Sage ist, dass Freundestreue bis zur Aufopferung des eignen Lebens Gott wohlgefällig sei."[1] Speaking of a similar sacrifice in *Daurel et Beton* (1062–64) M. Paul Meyer writes: "L'idée du serviteur poussant jusqu'à ses plus extrèmes limites le dévouement à son seigneur est un des lieux communs de la littérature féodale et se présente sous des formes variées."[2]

No less vital than the importance of his duty to others is the responsibility of the hero to preserve his own fair name untarnished. The *Roland* is full of this solicitude for reputation:[3]

> " ' Or guart chascuns que granz colps i empleit,
> Male cançun ja chantée n'en seit.
> Paien unt tort e chrestien unt dreit.
> Malvaise essample n'en serat ja de mei.' "
>
> *Roland*, 1013–16.

> " Respunt Rollanz : ' Jo fereie que fols,
> En dulce France en perdreie mun los.' "
>
> *Id.*, 1053–54.

> " Respunt Rollanz : ' Ne placet damne Deu
> Que mi parent pur mei seient blasmet,
> Ne France dulce ja chieet en viltet ! "
>
> *Id.*, 1062–64.

> " ' Mielz voeill murir que me vienget viltance.' "
>
> *Id.*, 1091.

> " ' Se jo i moerc, dire poet ki l'avrat,
> Que ele fut à nobilie vassal.' "
>
> *Id.*, 1122–23.

> " ' Male chançun n'en deit estre cantée. ' "
>
> *Id.*, 1466.

> " ' Pur Deu vus pri que ne seiez fuiant,
> Que nuls pruzdum malvaisement n'en chant ! ' "
>
> *Id.*, 1473–74.

[1] Vid. Hofmann's Introduction to his edition of the poem, p. viii.
[2] Vid. *Daurel et Beton*, Préface, p. xxiv.
[3] Cf. F. Settegast, *Der Ehrebegriff im altfranzösischen Rolandsliede* in *Ztsch. für rom. Phil.*, ix, p. 204 f.

> " ' Mielz voeill murir que hunte jo'n retraie.' "
>
> *Id.*, 1701.

Numerous parallels are offered by later poems. The sentiment of honor forbids Guillaume to give ear to a dishonorable
proposition made to him by the king:

> " ' Que ja diroient cil baron chevalier :
> Vey la G., le marchis au vis fier,
> Comme il a ore son droit seignor boisié ! ' "
>
> *Charroi de Nimes* (Meyer Rec.), 406–408.

In *Garin et Begon* it is Isori who rising from bed to fight
says :

> " 'Ains mangeroie mon auferrant de pris
> Que de ma bouche nuns mauvais plais issit.' "
>
> *Romans de Garin le Loherain,* v. i, p. 279.

In the same spirit :

> " 'Signeur, ce dist Ogiers, france gent honnerée,
> Gardés male canchons n'en soit de nous cantée,
> K'il n'i ait couardie faite ne pourparlée.' "
>
> *Fierabras,* p. 162.

More forcible still are the words of a proud vassal who,
when summoned to surrender, casts back this defiance from
the walls :

> " ' Por néant l'avez dit ;
> Se je tenoie l'ung pié en paradis
> Et l'autre avoie au chastel de Naisil,
> Je retrairoie celui de paradis
> Et le mettroie arrier dedans Naisil.' "
>
> *Romans de Garin le Loherain,* v. i, p. 232.

Vivien's words on the battlefield of Aliscans show there is
more glory for a young man than for him who is old in
dying on the field. He strikes the same note as Roland at
that other great defeat at Ronceval :

> " 'Ore est einsi alé :
> Tenu nos fust toz jorz mès a vilté,
> A nos parenz fust toz jorz reprové.

Mielz nos vient-il einsi avoir erré
Que nos fuison à tel honte eschapé ;
Se nos morons en cest champ hennoré
S'aurons vers Deu conquise d'amisté.
Quant li homs muert en son premier aé,
Et en sa force et en sa poesté,
Adont est-il et plaint et regreté ;
Mais quand il muert dedenz son viel aé,
Jà ne sera né plaint né regreté.' "

Li Covenans Vivien, 680–691.

To the same effect are the words of Aymeri as he comforts his wife for the supposed loss of their son in battle :

" ' Nostre linage l'a en eür ainsi,
Q'an cemetire n'en a nul enfoï.
Mes en bataille et en estor forni,
Qui la morra, par Dieu qui ne menti,
Vilain reproche ne sera dit de lui
Au grant jor do joïsse.' " [1]

Les Narbonnais, 4390–95.

[1] To a note may be relegated the mention of another primitive Teutonic trait of the hero's character,—that of vaunting his own prowess in public or before an adversary with whom he is about to engage. Every poem presents examples of this obligation incumbent upon the hero to do a certain amount of blustering and boasting before undertaking a task. Sometimes it takes the form of indulging in innocent *gabs*, as did the French in King Hugo's palace (vid. *Voyage de Charlemagne*) ; more often it is a confident assertion that one's adversary is doomed to a deservedly speedy annihilation (vid. *Aymeri de Narbonne*, 1108–1119). This was particularly a fault of young knights, and we are glad to come upon a passage in which the voice of authority reproves this habit, so opposed to our ideas of becoming modesty. Charles says to his young knights disputing one another's prowess :

" ' Mès de vostre aventure vos volez trop prisier,
Vostre chevalerie fait trop à resoignier,
Trop an volez parler le soir contre foier.
L'an ne doit sa proece mentevoir ne prisier ;
Assez est qi dira : ' Vez là bon chevalier.' "

Chanson des Saisnes, v. i, p. 225.

Too suggestive to pass unnoted in this connection are the words with which Aymeri's men present themselves to the king of Pavia :

Very closely allied to this pride in the maintenance of an irreproachable honor is that feverish love of vengeance which characterized the feudal ages. There is an element of gentleness and courteous consideration in much of the religious and chivalric literature which is a very plain evidence of how much the Church did to moderate the passions and refine the manners of the Middle Age. But these feudal heroes were of different stuff. Their religion did not include a very broad interpretation of brotherly love. It was usually a question of honor that was at the root of all these feudal and religious wars. To maintain his own honor was as incumbent upon the mediæval fighting man as to defend the honor of his God. The preservation of each made for the same qualities of character. Just as in the *Roland* the Twelve Peers, representing Charles' vassals, were all present to a man to defend the honor of the Christian Emperor against the Infidel, so in the feudal epic are the *vavassours* at the disposal of their overlord's interests. The claims of land and of honor are the loudest claims upon those involved in the complicated chain of the feudal system.

In the *Roland*, when the loss of the rear-guard is known, vengeance is the cry of the herald angel in person :

> " ' Charles, chevalche ! car tei ne falt clartet.
> La flur de France as perdut, ço set Deus ;
> Vangier te poez de la gent criminel.' "
>
> *Roland*, 2454–56.

> " ' Si m'eist Dex, li rois de paradis,
> No somes tuit duc et conte et marchis
> N'i a celui qui n'ait riche pais.
> Ca nous envoie le preuz cuens Aymeris
> Li mieudre princes qui el monde soit vis.' "
>
> *Aymeri de Narbonne*, 2340–44.

Six centuries later M. Edmond Rostand struck the same Gascon note in the lines wherein Cyrano de Bergerac presents to De Guiche the *cadets de Gascogne.*

And Turpin makes Roland in his *Passion* cry out : " Quotiens per te aut Iudaeum perfidum aut Sarracenum peremi, totiens Christi sanguinem, ut puto, vindicavi." [1] The avenging of the death of the Peers at Ronceval was destined to be a long story. So great was this insult to Christendom that throughout our period the *trouvères* represent their heroes as engaged in the congenial task of making the pagans drink to the dregs the cup of repentance.

This wreaking of vengeance, whether it be upon Saracen or feudal rival, fills the pages of the *chansons de geste* with scenes of cruelty and bloodshed. The best example is offered by *Raoul de Cambrai*, which to mention is sufficient; for an inextinguishable hatred and an unsatisfied thirst for blood runs through the whole of this impressive poem. The poets themselves seem to have felt the monotony of this motive, judging from an exclamation at the close of the *Mort Garin :*

> " Grans est la guerre qui onques ne prist fin ;
> Sainte-Marie ! mervoille est a oïr,
> Qu'apres les peres la reprenent li fil."
>
> *Mort Garin*, p. 146.

It is quite evident that it is the unhappy Ganelon turning over in his mind some means of retaliation upon Roland, and upon Roland only, that brings on the whole catastrophe at Ronceval.

Presumably this passion for vengeance met with a severe rebuke at the hands of the Church, pledged as it was theoretically to submission, to forgiveness and to charity. When the sons of Aymon are incensed against Yon for his treatment of them, Renaut alone, remembering Yon's past kindness to them, preaches the doctrine of returning good for evil :

---

[1] *Pseudo-Turpin*, cap. **xxii.**

" ' Contre sa felonie li doi rendre bonté.
Si le dist l'escristure et li bon clerc letré,
Que ensi le doit faire qui a le cuer sené.' "
                                    Renaus de Montauban, p. 228.

Such, again, seems to be the lesson in the reproof administered
to Guy, Count of Maience and father of Doon. Guy is
promising himself the pleasure of putting an end to the
machinations of the traitor Herchembaut.   He is consumed
by this idea of revenge; so much so

"Que i. angre du chiel contreval devala ;
Devant le conte vint, ainc mot ne li sonna,
Mez de la grant clarté le bon quens aveugla,
Et li angre du pié si grant coup li donna
Que trestout estendu à terre le porta. . . .
Qui goute ne véoit, ne jamès ne fera
Se Dex n'i fet vertu, qui le poveir en a."
                                    Doon de Maience, p. 58.

The *procédé* is likely borrowed from the blindness of Saul
of Tarsus on the way to Damascus.   This strife among
vassals brought all the horrors of intestine war in its train.
To close with what is at once a sad picture and a piece of
vivid description, read this passage from one of the older
poems.   The country has been ravaged by forty thousand
Germans engaged in the feudal wars of the *Lorrains* against
the king :

"Tex siz jornées alast uns pelerins,
Qu'il n'i trovast, ne pain, ne char, ne vin ;
Encontre terre gisent li crucefi ;
Sor les autex puet on l'erbe coillir ;
Ne gentis homs n'i plaide a son vesin.
La o estoient li champ et li maisnil,
Les beles viles, et li borc seignori,
Croissent li bois, ronces et aubespin,
Et li boschaje grant, et fier et antif.
Nus homs n'i ose aler par le paiz,
Qu'il ne soit mors, o desrobis, o pris."
                            Romans de Garin le Loherain, v. ii, p. 139.

We can judge from the passages quoted the emphasis laid upon the three features of our heroes' character as they have been mentioned. If any differentiation were attempted between the heroes of the earlier and those of the later poems, it would consist in this : the heroes of the later poems are less passionate, less fiery, less implacable; they feel the softening influence of woman and of many of those principles of Christian charity which the later Middle Age included in the terms *chevalerie* and *courtoisie*. After 1150 the feudal code of ethics weakens before the chivalric code, though most poems offer a combination of the two. The great body of the thirteenth century epic poems present the chivalric ideal grafted upon the old feudal heroes who still preserve many of their primitive ear-marks. But it is to be noted that the hero of even the latest *chansons de geste* is not quite the same man as the hero of a contemporary romance of adventure. There remains in him an unmistakable trace of his genealogical connection with the paladins of Charlemagne. In spite of his love adventures, and the lorn maidens, and the kind fairies, his mind harks back to his old-time foe, the Saracens, and to his·duty toward God. If we are not mistaken, this undercurrent of sturdy faith, this seriousness of purpose, was just the quality which was sought by a portion of the public as a contrast to the more imaginative, fantastic and *vain* heroes of the Breton cycle. Had it not been for the traditional reverence unconsciously felt for this primitive Christianized Teutonic hero, the Gawains and the Lancelots would perhaps have sooner driven out the more serious Guillaumes and Ogiers.

Bearing in mind, then, that the poet sometimes takes familiar liberties with a character for whom he feels a certain traditional reverence, we shall find the result to be less clear-cut as a type, but more tangible, more human, more appealing to our sense of reality.

Some scattered references to a poem, probably of the twelfth century, will bring this out in a variety of ways. When Oliver *incognito* goes out to fight Fierabras, the giant Saracen asks him what sort of a man the far-famed Roland is. Oliver unrecognized compares his *compagnon* thus with himself:

> " ' Rollans est i. peu menres de li en son estant,
> Mais trop par a le cors hardi et combatant.
> Onques Dius ne fist homme, tant soit de haute gent
> Se Rollant s'i combat, ne faice recréant ;
> Oliviers ne vaut mie encontre lui i. gant.' "
>
> *Fierabras*, pp. 17, 18.

Oliver himself still maintains as of old :

> " ' Miex vaut mesure à dire que ne fait sorparler.' "
>
> *Id.*, p. 18.

Roland's rashness is again brought out when the Peers, taken prisoners, are sent to parley with the Saracen *amirant*. Naimon is in despair :

> " ' A Diex, ce dist dus Namles, qui en crois fus penés,
> Rollans nous fera tous ocirre et afoler ;
> Quel Cm diable l'ont o nous amené?' "
>
> *Id.*, p. 77.

This same Naimon, the traditional adviser of the king, this mediæval Nestor, this uncompromising advocate of Right against Might, is the most unchanging figure among the heroes. He is the embodiment of good sense, moderation and justice. In the present poem there is a touch given him which is as amusing as it is rare. When the *amirant* boasts :

> " ' Mauhomet me maudie, qui j'ai mon cief voé,
> Se je jamais menguë tant comme vis serés.'
> ' Se Diex plaist, dist dus Namles, assés jéunerés.' "
>
> *Id.*, p. 79.

When later at the dinner Floripas, the beautiful daughter of the *amirant,* appears, Naimon becomes quite gallant and renews his youth to such an extent as to surprise the young knights :

> "Et respondi Rollans : 'Onques mais n'oï tel ;
> Trop par avés ce poil et kanu et mellé ;
> Quel L. dyable vous font d'amours parler?'
> 'Sire, ce dist dus Namles, je fui ja bacelers.'"

Id., p. 84.

We should be passing over one of the most attractive sides of the heroes' character if, after showing them in their conventional aspects, we should fail to note their attitude toward women.   Early mediæval literature affords us very little material for a study of the sentimental relations of man and woman.   The literature of the clerks had little to say of woman that was good.   When the great change of attitude came over Christian Europe, when woman was raised upon an ideal literary pinnacle which she was far from actually occupying in society, and when woman-service became a vogue in chivalric society,—then it was natural that her part in love-making should be the major part.   A discussion of this subject will be taken up in the chapter devoted to woman.   We may simply note here what we should expect to find,—that the growing prominence of woman as a compelling agent and as an object to be won, during our period profoundly affects the aims and purposes of the hero.   Woman is no longer merely a lesser incident in the career of a hero, hardly worthy of notice.   Under the influence of Provençal and Breton literary forces working together, she emerges into the foreground, and especially in the later poems is to be carefully considered.

Where there are no women, however, there can be no love-making, and in the early poems the women very rarely appear.   The Puritan Aude must be mentioned later in her proper place.   The betrothal of Berneçon in the second part of *Raoul de Cambrai* brings out some interesting features,

4

but manifestly of a later period than the first part of the
poem. The *Lorrains* cycle offers in general only the Germanic type of woman. Thus, one comes naturally in these
few remarks, as in the chapter devoted to woman, to a later
period when the influence of the Breton cycle has already
made itself felt. The whole period from the eleventh to the
fourteenth century presents an unsettled opinion of woman's
value and of her place in society. Occasional exceptions to
the contrary, and in spite of her conventional position as
mistress of man's affections and dictator of his service, one
has difficulty in admitting her moral and social equality with
man in the literature preceding the Italian Renaissance.
What is said here is from the point of view of the heroes.

When Guillaume d'Orange hears of the beauty of Orable,
the Saracen princess of Orange, he describes thus the well-
known effects of his reflections :

> " ' Ne puis dormir par nuit né someillier,
> Né si ne puis né boivre né mengier,
> Né porter armes né monter sor destrier,
> N'aler à messe, né entrer en moustier.' "
>
> *Prise d' Orange*, 372–375.

And a little later, when Guillaume finds her in her palace :

> " ' Diex ! dist Guillaumes, Paradis est céanz ! ' "

No scene in that masterpiece of the talented Adenet is more
beautiful than the finding of the unhappy Berte by the King
Pepin. The King is here down on the level of an ordinary
mortal, indeed is *incognito*. The King, upon learning of the
innocence of Berte and after putting away Aliste, uses
every means to discover if his real wife be alive in obscurity.
He confesses :

> " ' S'aucune chose en ai, par la Virge honnorée,
> De li ou de la robe que ele en ot portée,
> Sachiez, je l'ameroie assez plus que riens née,
> Et si la baiseroie et soir et matinée.' "
>
> *Berte aus grans piés*, 2468–71.

Shortly after this the King comes upon Berte praying at a chapel in the wood, as is her wont. Without recognizing her after three years of separation, Pepin is struck by her beauty :

> "De son cheval à terre tout maintenant descent,
> Et Berte remest coie, qui nul mal n'i entent,
> Et li rois assez tost entre ses bras la prent.
> Et quant Berte voit ce, moult ot grant marement.
> Damedieu reclama, qui maint ou firmament."
>
> *Id.*, 2670–74.

The King, furiously in love, now declares :

> " 'O moi venrez en France, la terre noble et gente,
> Ja n'i veriez jouel, tant soit de chiere vente,
> Que je ne vous achatte se il vous atalente,
> Et si vous asserai ou pays bele rente,
> N'aura home en la terre qui de riens vous tormente.' "
>
> *Id.*, 2680–84.

The reply of Berte is charmingly naïve :

> " 'Frans hom, fait ele au roy, pour Dieu, laissiez m'ester,
> Trop me faites ici longuement demorer,
> Car mes oncles Symons doit assez tost disner,
> Pour ce k'apres mengier s'en doit au Mans aler
> As gens le roi de France, por vitaille porter."
>
> *Id.*, 2690–94.

It would be hard to find in modern poetry a courting-scene where the artist's hand is more delicately shown than this scene by the thirteenth century poet just quoted. But there were other conceptions of the subject. In *Fierabras*, when the Christian knights are at the mercy of the Saracen Floripas, it is she who controls the situation and dictates the terms. She is determined to have Guy for her lover and swears by Mahomet :

> " 'Se vous ne me prenés,
> Je vous ferai tous pendre et au vent encruer.' "
>
> *Fierabras*, p. 85.

This argument is evidently unanswerable and Floripas has her

way. More women of her type will be met later. Then, there
is scorn for the seduction of youthful beauty, and praise for
the good homely housewife and companion of years. An
amusing passage in *Gaydon* offers this view artistically contrasted with the chivalric love of Gaydon and Claresme.
When one of Claresme's handmaidens seeks to seduce old
Gautier, he breaks out in a wholesome rage with *tel parole
qui ne fu mie bele:*

> " ' Dame, dist, il, par saint Pol de Tudelle,
> A moult petit m'est de vostre favelle.
> Alez voz ent aval celle praelle,
> Enmi cel pré, à une fontainnelle,
> Desoz cel aubre dont la foille ventelle ;
> Clere en est l'eve, et clere la gravelle.
> S'avez trop chaut, si i alez, pucelle.
> De vostre amor ne m'est une escuielle,
> Car moillier ai et plus cointe et plus bele ;
> Quant il m'en membre, trop li cuers me sautelle.' "
>
> *Gaydon,* pp. 269, 270.

And thus he regrets his absence from his own faithful
spouse :

> " 'Ahi ! Lorance, dame bien conéue,
> Gentil moillier, toz jorz vos ai éue ;
> Se me perdez, ce est chose séue,
> Tote joie est de vostre cors issue.
> Vos soliez venir à la charrue   .
> Aporter moi la grant crote cornue,
> En la toaille la grant tarte fessue.
> Quant vos véoie, s'iert ma joie créue,
> Puis vos tenoie au vespre tote nue ;
> La vostre paie n'estoit pas à créue.
> J'ai por mon sire fait grant desconvenue,
> Quant j'ai laissié ma terre et ma charrue,
> Et ma moillier por coi li cuers m'arguë ;
> Por soie amor la guere ai maintenue.' "
>
> *Id.,* p. 274.

Then, there are countless examples in the later poems
of the sort of amorous encounters related in the *romans*

d'aventure. In these the knights fall easy victims to the charms of some maiden in distress and serve her under the most impossible circumstances. An instance of this treatment is furnished by Doon's meeting with the youthful Nicolette who, we are told, has reached but the inexperienced age of eleven years and one month! This does not prevent Doon, who is but fifteen, from falling the easiest of victims to *amours qui tout vainc.* The following verses, describing the youthful lovers at table, deserve to be quoted:[1]

> "Au mengier sunt assis, qui longuement dura,
> De beisier savereus i. entremes i a,
> Que à chascun morsel li i. l'autre donna.
> Du mestier sunt nouvel, mès Dex les enseigna
> Et destreiche d'amours, qui si souspris les a."
>
> *Doon de Maience,* p. 117.

Such are some of the aspects in which the heroes appear before the feminine element in the epic poems. Beginning with the undemonstrative love relegated to the background in the earliest *chansons de geste,* we soon get to the period where love plays a leading rôle. A more detailed examination would only further prove how profoundly the chivalric conception modified the original epic treatment of the relation of the sexes in literature. Yet, in the epic the hero is first and last a fighting-man; only as a diversion or by chance is he interested in woman. His dearest companions throughout are his horse and his sword; only from time to time do we hear of his wife, his mother or his sweetheart. The essential point to retain from the foregoing exposition is this: woman appears with increasing frequency as our period advances, and the hero's treatment of her reflects the influence of chivalric ideals.

One object, though necessarily a minor object, of this

---

[1] With this passage cf. the love of Garin de Montglane. Vid. *Analyse de Garin de Montglane* in Gautier, *Epopées,* iv, pp. 126–171.

study is to show the French *trouvères* at their best as literary
artists, as creators of characters.   Enough has already been
said to indicate in general the chief features of the epic
hero's character.   But some poets got beyond the stage of
following a type and created an individual, something more
than a wooden man to put through a series of bloody
conflicts or a succession of romantic adventures in which
events alone were emphasized.   To this class belong Aiol,
Vivien, Roland, Oliver (in *Fierabras*), Girart de Rossillon,
Begon in the *Lorrains* cycle, Berneçon in *Raoul de Cambrai*,
Gaydon and Guillaume.   It is with reason that Gautier has
devoted the whole of his fourth volume to the remarkable
geste of which Guillaume is the central figure.   With its
many *branches* it penetrates the whole body of the epic
poetry from the primitive style to the *romans d'aventure*.
Throughout Guillaume preserves certain characteristics which
make of him not only a hero, but what is more interesting,—
a man.   After some acquaintance with these figures of the
Past, perhaps a preference for Guillaume may be permitted
and supported.   A few passages from *Aliscans* will serve to
show Guillaume at his best.[1]   We have already seen him in
the *Prise d'Orange* wooing the Saracen Orable who was
destined to become his wife under the new name of Guibourc.
Aliscans lands us squarely *in medias res*.   The battle is on,
and Guillaume finds his horse Baucent is weakening.   Now,
all depends upon the horse when the odds are so great, and
the hero addresses these words of cheer and comfort to his
weary mount :

> " ' Cheval, dist il, moult par estes lassez ;
> Se vous fussiez iiii. jorz sejornez,
> Ja me refusse as Sarrasins mellez,
> Si m'en vengasse, quar à tort sui navrez ;

---

[1] The newly discovered *Chancun de Willame* represents Guillaume in an
equally attractive light.

Mès or voi bien qu'aidier ne me poez.
Si m'aïst Dex, n'en dois estre blasmez,
Quar tote jor moult bien servi m'avez.
Petit fu ore ne fussiez galopez
Et coréuz, poinz et esperonez :
De ton service te rent merciz et grez.
S'estre péusses à Orenge menez,
N'i montast sele devant xx. jorz passez,
N'i mengissiez d'orge ne fust purez,
ii. fois ou iii. o le bacin colez,
Et li fourages fust jentil fein de prez
Tot esléuz et en seson fenez ;
Ne béussiez s'en vessel non dorez ;
Le jor fussiez iiii. fois conréez
Et de chier poile trestoz envelopez.
Se en Espaigne es des paiens menez,
Si m'aïst Dex, moult en serai irez.' "

Aliscans, pp. 16, 17.

It is no wonder after this that Baucent arches his neck, whinnies, paws the earth and starts off refreshed. Another scene on the battlefield : this time his nephew Vivien is dying and asks for confession and absolution. No priest is at hand; but with what solemn dignity Guillaume replaces the man of God :

"A s'amosniere mist Guillaumes sa main,
Si en traist fors de son benoït pain
Ki fu sainés sor l'autel Saint Germain.

. . . .

'En lieu de Dieu serai ton capelain,
A cest bautesme vuel estre ton parin,
Plus vos serai ke oncles ne germain.' "

Id., p. 26.

The whole scene, which treats of Guillaume's return to Orange and of Guibourc's refusal to receive the defeated warrior who claims to be her husband, has been fully appreciated by Gautier.[1] When it is decided that Guillaume shall go to King Louis to demand his aid, the poet intro-

[1] *Epopées*, iv, p. 496 f.

duces this charming scene between this childless couple
(*Aliscans*, pp. 60, 61):

> "Od le Guillames, Guiborc va enbraçant.
> Par grant amor se vont entre acolant,
> Li uns por l'autre va de dolor plorant."

His wife begins to try Guillaume :

> " ' Or t'en iras en France l'alosée,
> Or me lairas dolante et esgarée
> Entre tel gent dont ne sui pas amée,
> Et tu iras en la terre asasée.
> Mainte pucele i venras coulorée
> Et mainte dame par noblece acesmée ;
> Je sai très bien tost m'auras obliée,
> Tost i sera vostre amors atornée.' "

Guillaume embraces and comforts his wife, promises temper-
ance in everything, and most important:

> " ' Ne ja ma bouce n'ert à autre adesée,
> S'iert de la vostre basie et savorée
> En cest palais dont la cors est pavée.' "

We have already seen with what high words Guillaume
dared address the king and queen at Paris.   But he did not
forget the host and his wife who alone had received him
kindly.   Generosity was one of his traits, as it is everywhere
of the ideal hero.   At the close of the poem, when the
warriors take final leave of Guillaume and Guibourc at
Orange, the affection of all the host for this lovable couple
takes the form of a general regret:

> "Congié demandent à Guillame au cort nés ;
> Li quens leur done, ses a molt acolés
> Dame Guibors les a baisiés assés.
> Aval par l'ost ont leur grailles sonés ;
> Lors s'apresterent, s'ont leur harnas trossés.
> Defors Orenge fu grans li deus menés ;
> Mains chevaliers s'i pasme."

Id., p. 252.

The *Lorrains* cycle offers two death scenes which may fittingly bring the study of the epic heroes to a close. The first to die is Begon who falls, treacherously shot by a traitor, while hunting with his dogs :

> "Hulent et braient et mainent grant tempier,
> Toutes ses plaies li corurent lichier ;
> Diex ne fist home qui n'en préist pitié . . . .
> Gentis homs fu, moult l'amoient si chien."
> *Romans Garin le Loherain*, v. ii, p. 244.

The other to die is his brother Garin who also meets a violent death in a church at the hands of the opposite party. Even in death he towered above his foes :

> "Autresi gist Garins entr'ax ocis
> Com fait li chasnes entre les bois petis."
> *Mort Garin*, p. 219.

The preceding pages, though not exhaustive, have presented the hero of the French epic in various lights : as warrior, as vassal, as husband, as father, as son, as chevalier. The qualities of Christian faith, loyalty and courage everywhere distinguish the hero,—qualities of a warrior sternly trained in a society dominated by the feudal ideal. Upon these three virtues as a basis there was built by the *trouvère* a superstructure of character which became more varied as time went on. The later poems relate the life-story of an individual hero whose personal doings invest the narrative with interest. This latter-day hero is no longer simply a personified virtue : he is a man with psychological processes of his own, for whose divers triumphs and failures we feel a human sympathy. The literary development of the hero from Roland to Aiol, Hugues Capet and Bauduin de Sebourc registers the contemporary evolution in the ideals of mediæval society.

The Traitor.

Of all the characters presented in the *chansons de geste* there is none whose origin is so obscure and whose persistence is so remarkable as that of the traitor. The epic king, as has been seen, is an historic personage with epic traits; the heroes are the embodiment of the feudal virtues; the rise of woman and of the bourgeoisie in the twelfth century poems is in accord with the social evolution of the time; the presence of the Saracens as the conventional enemies of Christendom is accounted for by tradition and by the contemporary influence of the crusades. But how account for this Ganelon? Does he spring fully armed with his wiles from the head of the unknown author of the *Roland*, or is he the mere personification in literature of a type already current in popular tradition?

Few attempts have been made hitherto to at once account for the appearance of the traitor in popular tradition and to explain the rare favor with which the epic poetry maintained him. Although the question of origins does not primarily concern this study, where we are considering the written literature only, yet a suggestion may not be out of place.

To begin with, the word *traître* in old French has two meanings: one, a restricted meaning applied to a person who, like Ganelon or Judas Iscariot, has betrayed his over-lord or master; the second is a derived and extended meaning applied to anyone who fails to observe the feudal code of ethics. In the latter sense *traître* is the equivalent of *felon, gloz, pute gent, mauvais recréant,* or any of the general abusive epithets bestowed by the *trouvères.* Innumerable instances could be cited from mediæval Romance literature, in which no definite act of *lèse-majesté* is ascribed to the traitor. Here at the outset, in considering the possible origin of the traitor as a familiar spirit in French popular tradition, it is only the traitor in a restricted sense that we mean.

No one has gone farther than Osterhage in seeking in nature-worship the origin of certain phenomena of the Northern *sagas*.[1] The same method is employed in his study of the Ganelon *mythos*. We may borrow from Osterhage's theory what he seems to have satisfactorily proved and reject its vagaries. Take this sentence: "Auch aus dem Rolandsliede lässt sich also der Kern eines Mythos, der den Stiefsohn verfolgende und tötende Stiefvater, heraus-schälen, und ich gelange auch hier zu dem Resultat dass der Verräther ein den Lichtgott tötender Dämon der Finsterniss und des Winters ist."[2] The first part of this statement seems well founded: there is evidently something back of Ganelon, something profoundly intimate and real which had maintained itself in the popular mind because it touched closely the reality of life. This something real is furnished by the enmity which in all time has existed between step-parents and children as the result of second marriages. That this suspicion of animosity, of which individuals in this relationship are sensible, should have developed into an epic motive is plausible. But when Osterhage, following in the footsteps of Grimm, begins to talk about the *Lichtgott tötender Dämon*, we are not only on dangerous ground, but very far from Ganelon in whom we have the first recorded traitor. We cannot follow Osterhage with his hypothesis into the realms of Germanic mythology. But limiting our confidence to his remarks upon the strife bred between parents and children as the result of second marriages, there

---

[1] Vid. Osterhage's further series of articles entitled *Anklänge an die germanische Mythologie in der altfranzösischen Karlssage* in *Ztsch. für rom. Phil.*, xi, 1–21 ; xi, 185–211 ; xi, 327–344 ; xii, 365–380.

[2] Vid. *Ztsch. für rom. Phil.*, x, 260.

are passages in the *Roland*, in *Amis et Amiles*, *Daurel et Beton*, *Doon de Maience*, *Aye d'Avignon*, *Gui de Nanteuil*, *Les Enfances Ogier* and *Bauduin de Sebourc* which lend a strong color of likelihood to his theory.

Quite as primitive as the step-father idea is another, much easier to grasp,—that of attributing a defeat to the machinations of a traitor. This idea is so familiar both in history and in literature that it need not be developed here. As Lamartine has said, speaking of the people: "Ce qu'il retient, ce sont surtout les grandes chutes et les belles morts." [1] But the people is also inclined to account for defeat and the death of its heroes: the traitor is created to bear the blame.

But there were two other special reasons why the traitor as a type should have been brought into special prominence in the popular poetry that concerns us. First, the prominence of Judas as the betrayer of Christ naturally suggested the seeking of a corresponding figure in the *entourage* of Charlemagne, himself so often represented in the rôle of Christ.[2] In the legend there were twelve Peers just as there were twelve Disciples. Who should be the Judas but he who already had evil in his heart and cherished bitter hatred against his own kith and kin? Granted that there was well founded belief in the enmity existing between step-parents and children, upon whom could the rôle of Judas in this mediaeval Passion be more reasonably grafted than upon Ganelon? The scope for the activity of such a traitor within the family was limited. The dominating figure of Charlemagne attracted him. There is nothing new in this thought: even Uhland was struck by the parallelism which here exists and notes the twelve Peers as armed

---

[1] Lamartine, *Graziella*.

[2] For Ganelon in the rôle of Judas cf. *Pseudo-Turpin*, cap. xi; *Chronique rimée de Philippe Mouskes*, 6773–74.

Apostles and Ganelon as the Judas among them.[1] At the close of this chapter will be found a few extracts showing how widely Judas and Ganelon were recognized as partners in the crime of treachery. When one recollects the influence of the Church upon the popular poetry, and the rôle assigned to Charlemagne as the result of this influence, no further proof is needed to show that the position of Ganelon as arch-traitor was assured.

So much explains the rôle of Ganelon not only in the *Roland* but in the whole cycle of poems which have their point of departure in the defeat at Ronceval. But there is a final and immediate reason for the continued popularity of the traitors. It has been seen that there is another and broader signification universally given to the word *traître*. This concerns us especially in the later poems, when the field for digression offered by the defeat at Ronceval had become too circumscribed. The strife of the great vassals and the Crown had as a result in the epic poems a division of the characters into families or *gestes*. On the one hand, there were those who were faithful to the king and who naturally desired his welfare; and on the other hand, there were those who were in reality hostile to him and poured into his willing ear the most treacherous of counsels. Now, it frequently happened that these wicked, self-seeking vassals were very near to the royal person and profited by the royal favor to gain their own ends. This naturally aroused the indignation of the loyal vassals against these evil counsellors and against the king who was foolish enough to heed them.[2] The type of king, then, was bound to lose in dignity, as we have seen, just in proportion as the rôle of the traitor

---

[1] Vid. Uhland, *Schriften*, iv, p. 331.

[2] These court counsellors under the Capetians were called *palatini, curiales, familiares, consiliarii*, and replaced the *comitat* of the Merovingian kings. Cf. Luchaire, *Institutions monarchiques*, i, p. 197.

developed. There is a whole series of poems, including *Ogier le Danois, Girart de Rossillon, Les Quatre Fils Aymon* and *Gaydon,* in which feudal heroes who would naturally be the sturdiest defenders of the Crown are forced to take arms against it as a result of the traitors' machinations. To sum it up, the actual presence in feudal times of a class of men among the king's counsellors who for selfish ends were hostile to the best interests of the nation, as represented by the king and his true well-wishers, is the real explanation of the hold which this idea of a traitor in an extended sense took upon the feudal mind. There we must seek, in history again as in every case, the explanation of the traitors' rôle in the French epic.

One more phase in the development, this time literary, of the traitor, and we shall have done. The *trouvères,* rarely gifted with originality of treatment, and finding themselves confronted with the presence of the traitor, naturally kept him in an important rôle. Even as early as the *Roland* one may see what an elaborate, what an artistic and absorbing treatment was expended upon Ganelon. The literary possibilities of the traitor were early evident. But as the poems turned more and more into lighter vein and the element of fiction asserted itself, the figure of the traitor as villain became more appreciable. From this point of view someone has spoken of the traitor as " ce personnage sacrifié, dont tout poète a besoin pour faire valoir davantage par le contraste son héros de prédilection." [1] This is certainly the light in which most of the later poets regard the traitor. He is not always mean and despicable. On the contrary, he is often noble and heroic like Milton's fallen angels, and in his fate the poet awakens our keenest interest. As it

---

[1] Siméon Luce, *Le génie français dans la Chanson de Roland* in *Revue contemporaine,* 28 février, 1867.

often transpires in a play, so in many a poem it is the villain and not the hero who has the leading part.

They are, then, in every sense worthy of attention, not only for their own traits but for the artistic service they render in bringing out the other personages. There is an element of fate about their sad lot. For when the mania for genealogies set in, the traitor *geste* was set apart by itself. Then not only was every independent traitor connected by the poet with this family or *geste*, but every member of this family was *ipso facto* a traitor born. The odious seal was set even upon generations yet unborn. Gautier has gathered in a note three passages from *Girard de Viane*, *Doon de Maience* and *Jourdains de Blaivies* which indicate how completely this division of the epic personages into three *gestes* was felt and practised.[1]

The traitor, then, in the broad sense of the word had his place in a great number of poems,—in fully one-half of the poems in the bibliography which accompanies this study.

The first, the best and the most interesting of the whole race is unquestionably Ganelon. Not only to our way of thinking, but to the mediæval poets as well, his figure dominates all his successors. To him, then, we must devote a special study; for in so doing we shall come upon one of the best character sketches in the epic poetry. Let us follow step by step the poet's development of Ganelon's character.

Ganelon, who is the brother-in-law of Charles (v. 294), first appears in the *Roland* (v. 217) with sound advice in favor of accepting Marsile's peace overtures. Even Naimon, the conventional exponent of wisdom and the unwearied destroyer of traitorous counsels, unreservedly advocates Ganelon's advice (v. 230–242). It is Roland (v. 277) who frankly recommends his step-father for the important mission

---

[1] *Epopées*, i, p. 409, note.

to the Saracens, and the confidence of Charles and of the other counsellors in him is complete :

> "Dient Franceis : 'Car il le poet bien faire ;
> Se lui laissiez, n'i trametrez plus saive.' "
>
> *Roland,* 278–279.

Ganelon is clearly the best man for the commission. But his outburst of indignation against Roland can be explained only by the supposition that bad blood was already known to exist between them. Ganelon then, naturally suspicious, thinks Roland is seeking his death instead of his honor by naming him for this dangerous mission. The following verses lead a strong probability to Osterhage's theory already considered :

> "Dist à Rollant : 'Tut fols, pur quei t'esrages ?
> Ço set hum bien que jo suis tis parastres ;
> Si as jugiet qu'à Marsiliun alge.
> Se Deus ço dunet que jo de là repaire,
> Jo t'en muvrai un si tres grant cuntraire,
> Qui durerat à trestut tun edage.' " [1]
>
> *Id.,* 307–312.

The supposition of preëxistent enmity may be inferred from verse 308.[2] But this is all that the poet has borrowed from tradition in the drawing of his character. The whole conception of the poem indicates a new and original treatment of a familiar matter :

> "Guenes i vint, qui la traïsun fist.
> Dès or cumencet li cunseilz que mal prist."
>
> *Id.,* 178–179.

---

[1] Pseudo-Turpin and Philippe Mousket offer the same treatment of this episode. The latter contains the significant explanation :

> "Mais, moult à loi d'ome parastre,
> Maneçoit Rollant, son fillastre."
>
> *Chronique rimée,* 6542–43.

[2] Graevell in *Die Charakteristik der Personen im Rolandsliede,* p. 122, accounts for Ganelon's hatred of Roland by pointing out that Roland is his step-son and that Ganelon is envious of the young knight.

These verses indicate that Ganelon was already known as the traitor of Ronceval. Other songs had doubtless related his treachery. But the form that we know of the *Roland* seems to owe nothing to earlier treatments. The portrait of Ganelon is original and complete in itself.

Whatever may have been the complexion of the primitive Ganelon, he appears first in the *Roland* as a hero, one of the best and most trusted servitors of the Emperor, tainted only by a family quarrel with his step-son, the *preux* Roland. From the time that he makes up his mind to fulfil the commission, he is turning over some dire means of retaliation upon Roland. This is the psychological interest of Ganelon: to watch how his heart is corroded by this desire for vengeance. The intimacy of Blancandrin and Ganelon as they ride along on their way is a most subtle appreciation of the suggestive influence of one man upon another. Ganelon in a communicative frame of mind, brim full of dire projects, cannot disguise his personal animosity for Roland, upon whom the conversation turns. The upshot of their intimacy is:

> "Tant chevalchierent Guenes e Blancandrins
> Que l'uns à l'altre la sue feit plevit,
> Que il querreient que Rollanz fust ocis."
>
> *Id.*, 402–404.

Blancandrin is not slow to apprize his king of what a handy tool they have in Ganelon. What a picture of the moral downfall of a man is presented in these simple words:

> "Guenelun prist par la main destre as deiz,
> Enz el vergier l'en meinet jusqu'al rei.
> La purparolent la traïsun seinz dreit." [1]
>
> *Id.*, 509–511.

Ganelon renders full justice to the prowess of Roland

---

[1] *Pseudo-Turpin* makes of Ganelon a mere barterer, a second Judas. Vid. cap. xxi.

5

(v. 557) and scouts the idea that the Saracens could harm the united strength of the Christian army commanded by Charles in person.   It is only by a ruse that the death of Roland can be compassed, and that ruse Ganelon's influence with Charles is strong enough to insure.   Note especially that this is all that Ganelon contemplates.   He does not see, as Marsile does, the far-reaching consequences of his treason. He does not admit even at his trial that he has transgressed the bounds of legitimate revenge in causing Roland's death. That is all which occupies him now :

> " ' Bels sire Guenes, ço dist li reis Marsilies,
>   Cunfaitement purrai Rollant ocire ?'
>   Guenes respunt : 'Ço vus sai jo bien dire.' "
>
> *Id.*, 580–582.

The psychological interest is vastly increased by this limited purpose of the traitor.   The treasonable pact is solemnly made between Marsile and Ganelon, who has now sold himself body and soul like Judas Iscariot (v. 603–660).

To follow the narrative in its later details is unnecessary. The critical moment in the evolution of Ganelon's character has been indicated.   Charles does not like his advice to leave Roland in charge of the rear-guard :

> "Si li ad dit : 'Vus estes vifs diables ;
>   El cors vus est entrée mortel rage.' "
>
> *Id.*, 746–747.

But nevertheless he follows the advice.   Later, when the treason has become evident, Ganelon is arrested and kept in confinement until Charles reaches Aix.   It is the moment of the trial which again interests us.   Ganelon, charged with the betrayal, affirms in perfect good faith :

> "Dist Guenelun : 'Fel seie, se jo l' ceil !
>   Rollanz me forfist en or e en aveir,
>   Pur que jo quis sa mort e sun destreit ;
>   Mais traïsun nule n'en i otrei.' "
>
> *Id.*, 3757–60.

The sympathy of the poet and of his audience has not yet entirely deserted Ganelon :

> "Devant le rei là s'estut Guenelun ;
> Cors ad gaillard, el vis gente colur ;
> S'il fust leials, bien resemblast barun."
>
> *Id.*, 3762-64.

Again, in the presence of all he stoutly maintains that he has only taken vengeance upon Roland :

> "'Vengiez m'en sui, mais n'i ad traïsun.'"
>
> *Id.*, 3778.

We know how it ended : the proven traitor was torn asunder by four horses, and this or an equally ignominious death by hanging became the conventional reward of the traitor. Not only is Ganelon torn asunder, but his thirty hostages are hung. And this is just :

> "Qui traïst hume, sei ocit e altrui."
>
> *Id.*, 3959.

> "Qui traïst altre, nen est dreiz qu'il s'en vant."
>
> *Id.*, 3974.

Such is the Ganelon of the *Roland* : at the outset a brave warrior and a sage counsellor ; but when corroded by hatred, flattery and bribes he is capable of treachery. He maintains his dignified bearing to the last, and is by all odds the most living figure in this poem.

If his rôle was not already fixed, the *Roland* indicated the treatment to the poets who came after. The later poets simply contented themselves with the remark that their traitor was *of the race of Ganelon*. The natural thing to do, as Gautier has shown,[1] was to provide ancestors for Ganelon. It is curious to notice that the later poets were evidently in the same predicament as ourselves about Ganelon's ancestors. Was he the first traitor of the family, or did he inherit his

---

[1] *Epopées*, i, pp. 399-415.

tendencies? A few quotations will best indicate this hesitancy. The author of *Gaufrey* sets the seeds of treachery back one generation in the character of Ganelon's father Grifon de Hautefeuille.[1] It is with him, genealogically speaking, that the earmarks of the traitor are first visible. Of the twelve sons of Doon de Maience this Grifon alone was the black sheep. This at once suggests that the number of the twelve Disciples has again here counted for something, and also that the traitor *geste* might be properly called the *geste* of Grifon de Hautefeuille:

> "En France ot i. linage, cui Damedex maldon!
> Ce fu Griffon d' Autefueille et son fil Guenelon,
> Beranger, et Hardré, et Hervi de Lion,
> Antiaumes li felon, Fouques de Morillon."
>
> *Les Quatre Fils Aymon*, p. 46.

In *Gaufrey* this Grifon is of a jealous and plotting disposition throughout, and thus sums up his programme:

> " 'Que ja n'amerai homme qui fache loiautés,
> Mez tous jours traïson et fine faussetés,
> Icheus seront tous jours mi dru et mi privés.' "

The poet adds:

> "De chen a il dit voir, le traitre prouvés;
> Que de li issi puis Guenelon et Hardrés,
> Milon et Auboin, et Herpin et Gondrez,
> Pinabel de Sorenche et Tiebaut et Fourrés,
> Et Hervieu du Lion, qui sot du mal assés,
> Et Tiebaut d' Aspremont, qui fu moult redoutés.
> De li issi tel geste dont Kalles fu irés
> Et tous les xii. pers ochis et decoupés,
> Que Guenelon vendi, oï l'avés assés."
>
> *Gaufrey*, p. 121.

The closing lines of the poem leave no doubt of the author's intention to give Grifon the place of honor as head of the traitor family.

---

[1] Cf. Kr. Nyrop, *Storia dell' epopea francese*, p. 159; *Les Quatre Fils Aymon*, p. 46.

In *Fierabras* again, where the action in Italy is supposed to precede the defeat at Ronceval, Ganelon is represented as already tainted and all his *parent* (pp. 10, 136). Ganelon is *faus provés*, but he will not yet, even at the bidding of his more unprincipled family, raise his hand against the person of the Emperor :

> " ' Ne plaice Dieu, dist Guenes, le pere onipotent,
> Que ja vers mon signeur faice traitrement ;
> Trop serai recréans se je sa mort consent.
> De lui tenons nos teres et nos grans casement,
> Si li devons aidier et bien et loiaument ;
> N'i a celui ne soit à lui par serement.' . . .
> ' Mils aim avoir le teste et les menbres caupés
> Que mon pooir ne face, ja n'en serai blamés.' "
>
> *Fierabras*, p. 151.

Gui de Bourgogne, likewise pretending to antedate the events narrated in the *Roland*, represents Charles as vacillating between the treacherous counsels of Ganelon and Hardri on one side, and of Naimon on the other. In general it may be said that the poets who have represented Ganelon or any of his pseudo-ancestors as taking part in events previous to the tragedy at Ronceval have all taken for granted Ganelon's rôle in the *Roland*. Ganelon seems to have long been given the benefit of extenuating circumstances, and to have been regarded as the best of a bad family. The *cycle du roi* in general retains some of the good points in his character, and thus differs from the latest poems, like *Macaire*, wherein the traitor is altogether despicable. One amusingly crude effort to connect Ganelon with the traitors of antiquity is offered by one of the Italian versions of the *Roland*, cited by Müller[1] in a note :

> "Ses ancesur firent ingresme fellune,
> E fellonie tut or ave in costume ;
> In capitoille de Rome ça'n fe une,

[1] Vid. *Roland* (ed. Müller), p. 193, note.

> Jullio Çesar onçient il per ordure
> Pois oit il malvase sepolture,
> Chi in fogo ardent et angosos mis fure." [1]

The ridiculous genealogies which were invented by the late poets for their traitors as well as for their heroes became so involved that they drive us, as Gautier admits, to despair : "Autant de poëmes, autant de généalogies différentes." [2] It evidently simplified matters to agree that the heads of the three principal *gestes*, Charles, Doon and Garin were all born on the same day ; thus, the three families made a fair start ! [3]

The trouble over Ganelon was far from settled when Charles had put him and thirty of his kin to death.[4] From what has been seen of the essential principle of revenge in the feudal code, the activity of Ganelon's surviving relatives is not surprising. Only by the spilling of more blood can the insult done to their family be wiped out. On the other hand, the loyal vassals are ever ready to go one step farther in stamping out this dangerous brood. The following words of Aymeri de Narbonne, left behind after the Spanish expedition as a bulwark against the Saracens, beseech Charles to show no mercy to Ganelon when he shall be tried. He ought to be punished in a way—

> " ' Si que trestuit, li grant et li menor
> L'oient conter jusqu'en Inde major,
> Et que poor en aient traitor,
> Si que jamès vers lor lige seignor
> N'osent panser einsi grant desennor.' "
>
> *Aymeri de Narbonne*, 1283–87.

---

[1] In the *Chanson des Saisnes*, v. ii, p. 66, for the exigency of the rhyme, Cain is made of the same lineage as the traitors opposed to Charles !

[2] *Epopées*, i, p. 127, note.

[3] Vid. *Doon de Maience*, p. 162.

[4] G. Paris in writing of *Le Roman de la Geste de Monglane* has reprinted the detailed description of Ganelon's death in one of the two prose redactions of *Galien*. Vid. *Romania*, xii, pp. 10, 11.

In *Gaydon*, where the traitors play such an important rôle in their successful efforts to alienate Gaydon from the king, they contemplate nothing less than vengeance upon Charles' person. When Aulori sees the success of his poison :

> " ' Par Deu, dist il, nos puisons viennent bien ;
> S' or en menjüent li rois ne li princier,
> Ainz la complie sera Ganes vengiez.' "
>
> *Gaydon*, p. 7.

In *Huon de Bordeaux* Amauri hopes to kill Charles and possess the crown for himself :

> " ' Damedix doinst que Karlos soit ocis,
> France ert sans oir, si tenrai le païs ;
> Ains que l'ans past, arai Karlon mordri.' "
>
> *Huon de Bordeaux*, p. 21.

In *Macaire* the traitor's efforts are devoted to seducing Charles' queen :

> " Segnur, or entendés e siés certan
> Qe la cha de Magançe, e darer e davan,
> Ma non ceso de far risa e buban ;
> Senpre avoit guere cun Rainaldo da Mote Alban,
> Et si traï Oliver e Rolan,
> E li doçe pere e ses compagna gran.
> Or de la raine vole far traïman ;
> Par son voloir elo non reman
> Q'elo non onischa l'inperer K. man."
>
> *Macaire,* p. 18.

It will be remembered that the cause of the popularity of the traitors in the epic was found in the relations between the monarch and his great vassals in the twelfth and thirteenth centuries. At the time when the Capetian monarchy was already strong and casting off the shackles imposed by the great feudal lords, these latter still retained great power and flattered their pride with reminiscences of the earlier feudal period when their word had been law. To these retrospective sentiments the *trouvères* catered ; at first, with

quasi-historical poems; later, with series of adventures which
had scant foundation upon fact. It seems certain, after the
studies of Kurth and Rajna, that under the late Carolingians
there had existed plotters around the monarch. We know
also of the tendency among the feudal poets to ascribe the
events under discussion to an antecedent period,—that of
Charlemagne and of his immediate successors. The traitors,
then, as a type may represent the hostile vassals of the
degenerate Carolingian monarchs seen with the eyes of men
governed by the later feudal and chivalric ideals. But
the rigor and bitterness of the accusations made against the
traitors in some of the poems seem to indicate that they
were very real persons to an audience of the twelfth century.
The passages that follow are hard to account for except upon
the hypothesis that such self-seeking individuals were at
court working against the interests of the feudal lords. In
other words, there must have been traitors in contemporary
politics as well as in the poetical history of Charlemagne.
Garin speaks of these evil counsellors as of those

> " ' Qui le sejour aiment et repouser,
> Et au couchier le vin et le claré.
> Jà par tels gens en pris ne monterez.' "
> *Romans de Garin le Loherain*, v. i, pp. 80, 81.

In the *Chanson des Saisnes*, after a quarrel between Charles
and his proud vassals, one of the latter tells the King that
all the trouble comes from his heeding his evil counsellors :

> " ' Sire, dist Salemonz, i. don querre vos os :
> Li felon nos feront desserver par lor los
> Qui à vos nos meslerent ; mar i furent si os :
> Trancherons lor les testes et les nés et les os.' "
> *Chanson des Saisnes*, v. i, p. 76.

This seems to be the echo of some particular grudge and of
the desire to get even with the king's favorites. Again, in
Aiol no specific charge is made against the traitors. They

are mar-alls at court and in general opposed to honesty and fairness as represented by the heroes :

> "A Loeys resmest li tere et li pais.
> Li traitor de France l'ont de guere entrepris :
> Loeys ne set mie u se puisse vertir,
> N'en quel de ses chastieus il se puisse garir
> Enfressi que al jor que vos poés oir
> Que il sa serour done a un conte gentil :
> Il ot a non Elies, molt fu preus et ardis,
> Ainc mieudre chevaliers nen ot auberc vestis ;
> Quant il ot espousee la seror Loeys,
> Son droiturier signor par qui il ert cheris,
> Les traitors de France par armes acoilli
> La ou il les pot prendre, ainc raençon n'en prist
> Ne avoir ne loier onques n'en requelli :
> Del prendre et de l'ochire estoit cascuns tous fis,
> Et con plus ert haus hom, plus grant justice en fist ;
> Ainc n'espargna le grant nient plus que le petit.
> Ançois que li ans fust passés ne acomplis,
> Ot il si bien le roi aquité son pais
> Que il n'avoit nul home qui guerre li fesist."

Aiol, 25–43.

Judging from the twelfth and thirteenth century poems, envy, lust, lying, sometimes cowardice and even blasphemy were the badge of all this tribe. Time and again we find the traitors accomplishing their ends by bribes. It evidently took a strong man to resist temptation thus offered, and the king himself was frequently a victim. He who wrote these words was probably right :

> "'Avarisce est de tous péchiés commenchemens." [1]

Envy and jealousy caused by the bestowal of fiefs or by the contraction of feudal marriages was a frequent cause of alienation.[2]

But all the traitors were not equally dignified figures. In *Gaydon* and in *Parise la Duchesse* they are downright

---

[1] *Roman de Mahomet* (ed. Reinaud et Michel), p. 26.
[2] Cf. *Raoul de Cambrai; Les Loherains; Daurel et Beton.*

cowards, employing poisons and ambushes to accomplish their objects. Grifon in *Gaufrey* (pp. 94, 110) is a coward, while Archambaut in *Doon de Maience* (p. 137) is the incarnation of all that is base and mean. Further, he is brutal and lascivious (*Doon de Maience*, p. 6). Nothing, indeed, the poet can say is too bad for this Archambaut. When he finds himself defeated by Doon in single combat he is so *forsené* that he denies God himself:

> " 'Dex, je te renoi chi et les tieues bontés.
> Jamès jour n'amerai ne toi ne tes privés ;
> Que quant plus je t'aour et serf, et plus me hés,
> Et plus me vient ennui, mort et maléurtés.'
> Ainsi le desloial Damedieu renoia.
> A li méisme dist et Damedieu jura
> Que jamez hermitain en bois ne trouvera
> Que il ne meite mort, tantost que le verra,
> Ne moine ne rendu il n'i espargnera,
> Toutez rendations à tous jours destruira
> Et moustiers et yglises trestous combruisera,
> Crucefix et ymages ja n'i deportera."
>
> *Doon de Maience*, p. 154.

Such violence of treatment is rare. As a rule, the traitors are Christians like other normal people. Only the Saracens are accustomed to deny their gods of wood and of stone. The wicked Macaire in *Aiol* completes his ignominy by turning Saracen, but his conversion is rather introduced as a comic feature.[1] Even the Saracens suspect the motives of his action and blame him. He is finally quartered in the conventional way befitting a traitor (*Aiol*, 10903).

In *Parise la Duchesse* the traitors play the same rôle as in the first part of *Doon de Maience*. They are leagued together for the undoing of the Duchess, who they fear will give birth to an heir. The following verses show two of these devils plotting her ruin:

[1] In *Aye d'Avignon* (p. 51) the traitor Berenger, urged by desire of vengeance, embraces the cause of the Saracens.

" ' Madame est eschapée, à malaïçon Dé !
  Elle est grosse d'anfant, bien lo m'a l'on conté ;
  Tex oirs en puet issir et croitre et emender
  Qui nos fera touz pendre i an aut encroer.
  Qui or saroit consoil qu'il la peust destorber,
  Il ne le devroit mie ne covrir ne celer.'
' Seignor, dist Aumauguins, ja fui je fiz Herdré,
  Qui ainz de traïson ne puet estre lassé ;
  Moult par savoit mes peres traïson desmener ;
  Dont seroit ce merveille se j'an sui esgarez.' "

Parise la Duchesse, p. 6.

The verses just quoted show what a change had come over the traitors since the noble figure of Ganelon was traced. Personal initiative is dispensed with. Men are traitors now in spite of themselves, thanks to the family influence, and no form of crime is too base to be practised by them. There is a passage in *Gaydon* which sums up the complete programme of their wickedness. The following is the parting advice given by a traitor bishop to his nephew :

" Dist a Guiot : ' Biau niés, or entendez :
  Se voz volez faire mes volentez
  Et mon commant, la bataille vaintrez.
  Et tout avant à Dammeldeu voez
  Que ja à home ne tenras loiautez ;
  Vo seignor lige ja foi ne porterez,
  Les loiaus homes traïssiez et vendez,
  Le mal hauciez et le bien abatez.
  Se voz à home compaingnie prennez,
  En devant lui tout adez le loez,
  Et en derrier à la gent le blasmez.
  Les povres gens laidengiez et gabez,
  Les orphenins à tort desheritez,
  Les vesves dammes lor doayres tolez,
  Les murtrissors, les larrons souztenez.
  Et sainte eglise adez deshonorez,
  Prestres et clers fuiez et eschievez,
  Rendus et moinnes, par tout les desrobez,
  Et cordeliers et jacobins batez.
  Petits anfans en la boe gietez,
  Et coiement les prennez et mordez ;

S'on ne voz voit, as mains les estrainglez.
Les vielles gens empoingniez et boutez,
Ou an visaiges au mains les escopez.
Les abéies escilliez et gastez,
Et les nonnains toutes abandonnez.
En touz lez lieus là où voz esterez
Hardiement mentez et parjurez,
Que ja vo foi nul jor ne mentirez
Devant ice que voz la main perdrez.
Se voz ce faitez que voz oï avez,
Ja à nul jor desconfiz ne serez.'
' Oïl, dist il, encore pis assez.' " [1]

Gaydon, pp. 194, 195.

Here is the same code more briefly expressed :

" ' Je te chastoi, biaus filleus Aulori,
Que n'aiez cure de dammeldeu servir,
Ne de voir dire, se ne cuides mentir.
Se vois preudomme, panse de l'escharnir,
De ta parole, se tu puez, le honnis.
Ardez les villes les bors et les maisnils,
Metez par terre autex et crucefix,
Par ce serez honorez et servis.' " [2]

Amis et Amiles, 1625–32.

These passages, conventional as they are, give an interesting catalogue of feudal vices. When compared with the very different advice given to the young heroes, they give a clear idea of what a feudal audience esteemed and loathed. There is such a note of genuineness and reality in these passages that we must admit the familiarity of a feudal audience with such cruelty, perjury, disloyalty, injustice and sacrilege in order to explain their significance.

The traitor has been seen to be in general true to his primitive rôle. In no case can we better employ the word *type*. If we should examine in detail the *motifs* of such

---

[1] A parallel is offered by *Le Miracle de Théophile* in *Théâtre français au moyen âge* (ed. Monmerqué et Michel), pp. 145, 146.

[2] Cf. *Bauduin de Sebourc*, chant I, 582–591 ; chant I, 666–669.

poems as *Les Loherains, Huon de Bordeaux, Les Quatre Fils Aymon, Gaydon* and *Amis et Amiles* we should find the traitors at the court of the king or of some great vassal always seeking their own ends. The only difference is that in the older poems they employ more worthy and fair means to obtain those ends; while in the later poems like *Gaydon, Macaire, Berte aus grans piés* or *Parise la Duchesse* no means are too despicable for them. Cowardice and treachery are always blamed, but simple brutality and cruelty of the kind we find in *Les Loherains* and *Raoul de Cambrai* were certainly not discountenanced in the early feudal period. So intractable are these fierce vassals until their thirst for revenge is satisfied, that no gentle arguments of the peace-maker availed :

> "Grans est la guerre qui onques ne prist fin ;
> Sainte Marie ! mervoille est a oir,
> Qu'apres les peres la reprenent li fil."
>
> *Mort Garin*, p. 146.

Notwithstanding the general adherence to the type, there will be felt to be a wide difference between the Ganelons and the Fromonts of the early poems and the Macaires and Archambauts of the later poems. As a dignified and sympathetic figure the traitor degenerates. But one should read *Berte aus grans piés* and the Franco-Italian poem of *Macaire* to realize what good literary use a skilful poet could make of this contrast between the evil and the good.[1] These poems have all the traits of a modern novel and are marvelously interesting from the psychological point of view. But, as said at the outset, no traitor stands out more clear-cut and more dignified in his treason, no sinner among them enlists our interest and our sympathy more than Ganelon.

To express their abhorrence of the traitor the *trouvères*

---

[1] It has been frequently remarked that the Italian court epic poets especially developed the traitor characters and episodes.

were ever ready. Their conventional spokesman was old
Naimon of Bavaria. Had it not been for his indefatigable
efforts in suppressing violence and exposing fraud, the
epic king would have been drawn to ruin by the traitors.
Naimon is a curious embodiment of justice and clear-
sightedness. He lacks any human traits (with rare exceptions as in *Gui de Bourgogne* and *Fierabras*), but appears
rather as a mechanical check upon evil. His counsels are
always just, and, when not followed, evil results. Two verses
in *Gaufrey* epitomize Naimon's rôle in the epic:

> " Naimez son conseiller est si endoctriné
> Et si het plus traitres que homme qui soit né."
>
> *Gaufrey*, p. 147.

When he has exposed his plan for arriving at any truth,
Charles acquiesces:

> " ' Certes, dist Karles, vous avés bien parlé ;
> Je le ferai, puisqe le me loés.' "
>
> *Huon de Bordeaux*, p. 285.

There is a comforting belief apparent in the ultimate
triumph of right:

> "Tous jours vont traïtours à male destinée ;
> U en près ou en loing, jà n'i aront durée."
>
> *Fierabras*, p. 188.

> " ' Traïs soit il en fin qui à traïr entent !
> Nus traïtre ne peut pas vivre longuement
> Et, se il longues vit, che est honteusement.' "
>
> *Doon de Maience*, p. 234.

> " Bien avez oï dire mainte fois et retraire
> Que traison et murdre convient k'en la fin paire."
>
> *Berte aus grans piés*, 1663–64.

But it is in their death, above all, that the wicked are
separated from the just. The devils then claim their own.
The manner of their death is as humiliating as its consequences are sure. The hermit in *Girart de Rossillon* seems
to voice the Church sentiment:

> "Que la devinitaz e li autor
> Nos mostrent en la lei au redemptor
> Qual iustise on deit faire de tracor
> Desmenbrar a cheval ardre a chalor
> La poudre de celui lai o chai por
> Ja pois ni creistera erbe ne labor
> Arbres ne rins qui traie a verdor."
>
> *Girart de Rossillon* (Ox. MS.), 7505-11.

The disgrace of the traitor's death compared with the bliss of the just soul as it is borne away upon angels' wings is well brought out in the following passages from *Doon de Maience*. When the good hermit dies a violent death:

> "Tout estendu l'a jus à la terre versé;
> Es vous venir lez angres, qui l'ame en ont porté."
>
> *Doon de Maience*, pp. 3, 4.

When the traitor Salemon has killed one of the three little sons of Guy, the innocent child

> "Mort quéi tout envers, onques ne souspira,
> Et li angre du chiel l'esperit emporta
> Comme d'un innocent, qui ainc mal ne pensa."
>
> *Id.*, p. 11.

Compare these with the following:

> "Salemon est noiez à sa maléurée.
> Li déable d'enfer en ont l'ame portée
> En enfer le puant, où ele est embrasée,
> Dont jamez nen istra: si sera comperée
> La mortel traïson que il a demenée."
>
> *Id.*, p. 15.

> "En la plache revint, où le glouton trouva,
> A i. cheval courant partout le traïna;
> Et quant l'ot traïné, ens u feu le geta,
> Qui grant estoit espris et fierement flamba.
> Quant il fu ens u feu et la vie en sevra,
> Le déable d'enfer l'esperit emporta,
> Bruiant de grant ravine, que chascun l'avisa;
> U parfont puis d'enfer là le tourmentera."
>
> *Id.*, p. 159.

One traitor about to die humorously remarks:

> " ' Se je vois en enfer, selon m'entencion,
>   Je trouverai laiens mon oncle Ganelon
>   Pinabel de Sorence, et mon parent Guion ;
>   Nous seron moult grant geste en cele region.' "
>
> <div align="right"><i>Aye d' Avignon</i>, p. 22.</div>

A few passages quoted without comment from late mediæval authors will serve to show the wide literary currency of the traitors as familiar spirits in the Middle Age:[1]

> . . . . " l'us de traitour
>   Que bien sevent li plusour
>   Que Judas fist son seignour
>   Et Guenes l'emperaour."
>
> <div align="right"><i>Chansons du Chât. de Coucy</i>, iii^e chanson.</div>

> "As gladly doon thise homicydes alle,
>   That in awayt liggen to mordre men.
>   O false mordrer, lurking in thy den !
>   O newe Scariot, newe Genilon ! "
>
> <div align="right"><i>The Nonne Preestes Tale</i> (ed. Skeat), 4414–17.</div>

> " 'And but I do, god take on me vengeance
>   As foul as ever had Geniloun of France ! ' "
>
> <div align="right"><i>The Shipmannes Tale</i> (ed. Skeat), 1383–84.</div>

> " Este tiene dos hijos : el mayor, heredero de su estado y al parecer de sus buenas costumbres, y el menor no sé yo de que sea heredero, sino de las traiciones de Bellido y de los embustes de Galalón."
>
> <div align="right"><i>Don Quijote</i>, Part I, ch. 28.</div>

> " Pedroso cita un auto en que Carlo-Magno se lanza a conquistar la Tierra Santa, donde Galalón le vende por treinta dineros, y Carlo-Magno muere crucificado."
>
> <div align="right">Menéndez y Pelayo, <i>Calderón y su teatro</i>, p. 122.</div>

> " Gianni de' Soldanier credo che sia
>   Più là con Ganellone e Tribaldello."
>
> <div align="right"><i>Inferno</i>, xxxii, 122.</div>

----

[1] For three curious nineteenth century oral traditions bearing on the matter treated in this chapter vid. Henri Carnoy in <i>Romania</i>, **xi**, pp. 410–13.

WOMAN.

The three most essential character types of the *chansons de geste* have already been treated. The king, the faithful vassal and the traitor are certainly in the early poems the personages upon whom the attention is fixed and upon whose relations the action turns. Before leaving the Christian ranks and passing to a study of the Saracens who belong also among the most venerable creations of the French epic, there remain two categories of personages who cannot longer be neglected : woman and the *bourgeois* or *vilain* hero.

The appearance of woman and of the *bourgeois* hero in the rude masculine epic becomes a perfectly natural phenomenon when we recollect the great social changes of the twelfth century. Woman cult, which was the result partly of a literary fashion and partly of a more intimate association of woman in the in-door *château* life of the period, is especially reflected in the French *romans d'aventure*. In this chapter of our study we shall clearly see how profoundly the spirit of the chivalrous *romans d'aventure* permeated the primitive warlike spirit of the *chansons de geste*. In the next chapter we shall see the different forces which brought the *bourgeoisie* into literary prominence. It is sufficient to remember in regard to woman how completely her social status changed during the period covered by the *chansons de geste*. That she does not figure prominently in the earliest epic poems is no proof that she was not revered and respected in the eleventh century. Indeed, the sparse references we have to woman in the earliest poems depict her possessed of dignity and authority. But she had no place in a purely heroic poetry,—in poems devoted exclusively to the narration of warlike deeds upon the field of battle. When, however, the literary scene changes with the gradual

6

shifting of interest from the battlefield to the *foyer*, even the heroic poems inevitably become at once more domestic and more sentimental.

Not until the twelfth century did woman take her place in mediæval literature as an end in herself, as a subject worthy of description and of detailed analysis. In the literature anterior to that period she is introduced, if at all, as an incident or as an accident. She rarely emerges from the obscurity in which society confines her. We shall first take up the older poems in order the better to understand the development of woman's literary importance as our period advances. One familiar with the various lights in which woman was regarded during the later Middle Age will not be surprised at the contradictory testimony as to her social and moral status. We shall study the poems as they represent her in her various spheres and activities: as maid, as young wife, as the mature wife and counsellor, as the mother of warriors.

Here, as before, the *Roland* is the point of departure. It is the unique figure of Aude in the Christian ranks that interests us and that interested the audience of the eleventh century. One always thinks of Aude in connection with Roland and Oliver; for she was the *fiancée* of the one and sister of the other. The old legend of her presence at the fierce combat outside of Vienne and of her betrothal to Roland may be read in the thirteenth century poem of *Girart de Viane*. But her treatment in the *Roland* is much more primitive, though it supposes the knowledge of her betrothal before Roland's departure with Charles into Spain. This is all the poet says of her; it is evidently of minor importance, but gains by its very simplicity. When Charles without Roland has returned to Aix:

"As li venue Alde, une bele dame ;
Ço dist al rei : ' U est Rollanz li catanies,

Qui me jurat cume sa per à prendre?'
Carles en ad e dulur e pesance,
Pluret des oilz, tiret sa barbe blance :
'Soer, chiere amie, d'hume mort me demandes.
Jo t'en durrai mult esforciet eschange,
Ço est Loewis, mielz ne sai jo qu'en parle :
Il est mes filz e si tendrat mes marches.'
Alde respunt : 'Cist moz mei est estranges.
Ne place Deu ne ses sainz ne ses angles
Après Rollant que jo vive remaigne !'
Pert la culur, chiet as piez Carlemagne,
Sempres est morte.''

Roland, 3708–21.

There are several points to notice in this simple appearance
of Aude : instead of a description of her charms as Bertrand
of Bar-sur-Aube at a later period would have detailed, she
is dignifiedly styled *une bele dame;* again, she aspires to be
the *per,* the equal of the man to whom she has given her
heart; moreover, she has the right and the independence to
refuse *Loewis* as a substitute for Roland. There is no possibility of replacing Roland in Aude's broken heart. The
type of fidelity, she has nothing to do but die. It would be
a mistake to credit the poet of the *Roland* with the charm
which his allusion to Aude has for us. The episode of her
grief and sudden death is too soon passed over to permit us
to think that it made much impression upon the audience.
Aude's death was but one of many sad consequences of the
death of Roland,—perhaps the least important to an eleventh
century audience eager rather to hear of the punishment
meted out to Ganelon. Faithfulness was expected not only
in the wife but in the betrothed maiden by the men who had
done them the honor to ask for their hand. Remaining at
home in the secluded life of the feudal *château,* the women
must have had time to develop traits of character very
different from those engendered by the more intimate and
frivolous relations between the sexes in the thirteenth
century. To be sure, when Aude falls lifeless *Franceis barun*

en plurent, si la plaignent (v. 3722); but they are hardly surprised at this display of Aude's depth of feeling and devotion. Before leaving this poem, note that at its close, when the Saracen Bramimunde is converted, an excellent opportunity for a romantic marriage is neglected, and the baptism alone is emphasized.

The feminine element is practically lacking in the *Voyage de Charlemagne*. There seems implied, however, the primitive idea of equality in the opening lines:

> "Charles li emperere reguardet sa moillier;
> Ele fu coronee al plus bel et al mielz." [1]
>
> *Voyage de Charlemagne*, v. 5–6.

After her intended pleasantry at the King's expense, she begs forgiveness:

> " ' Emperere, dist ele, mercit por amor Deu!
> Ja sui jo vostre femme, si me cuidai joer.' "
>
> *Id.*, 32–33.

But to no purpose. Charles with a touch of perhaps primitive brutality twice threatens to cut off her head if she does not reveal the name of the monarch who exceeds him in glory.

Passing over these early mentions of woman, we find her in a new light in the oldest poems of the feudal cycle. Luchaire has shown that though the Roman system of female inheritance was opposed to the Germanic system of exclusion, the fact that the former was favored by the Church led to its final adoption toward the end of the twelfth century. In the meantime, usage was not fixed and woman's claims needed to be vigorously presented. Her importance as a feudal personage, involved in the transfer of fiefs, is well illustrated in such poems as *Raoul de Cambrai* and *Les*

---

[1] "Un mariage royal pouvait être considéré comme une véritable association à la couronne."—Luchaire, *Institutions monarchiques*, v. i, p. 145.

Loherains. She was to be reckoned with in politics; she was to be depicted in her true rôle in the poetry.[1]

It is as counsellor in feudal matters that Aalais, mother of Raoul, first appears in *Raoul de Cambrai.* She has the right to give advice, since it is through her fiefs as sister of the king that Raoul is one of the great vassals. This is the way the reckless son treats his mother's counsels:

> " ' Maldehait ait, je le taing por lanier,
>   Le gentil homme, qant il doit tornoier,
>   A gentil dame qant se va consellier !
>   Dedens vos chambres vos alez aasier :
>   Beveiz puison por vo pance encraissier,
>   Et si pensez de boivre et de mengier ;
>   Car d'autre chose ne devez mais plaidier.' "
>
> *Raoul de Cambrai,* 1100–06.

Likewise when the wife of Beuve d'Aigremont begs her husband to take her advice on a matter of feudal service, he repulses her with coarse brutality (*Les Quatre Fils Aymon,* p. 17). This note of brutality between men and women of the same family is heard more than once in the older poems. It seems as though it were intended to banish woman back to her apartments from which she had temporarily emerged to take her part in state matters. To return to *Raoul de Cambrai,* the scene does not end where we left it; it has a more human outcome. Aalais, hot-headed like her son, curses him :

> " ' Et qant por moi ne le viex or laisier,
>   Cil Damerdiex qi tout a a jugier,
>   Ne t'en ramaint sain ne sauf ne entier !' "
>
> *Raoul de Cambrai,* 1131–33.

Then, still more unhappy than before, she goes into a church and, kneeling before the crucifix, offers this mother's prayer:

[1] Cf. Luchaire, *Manuel des Institutions françaises,* pp. 166–169.

" ' Glorieus Diex qi en crois fustes mis,
    Si com c'est voirs q'al jor del venredi
    Fustes penez qant Longis vos feri,
    Por pecheors vostre sanc espandi,
    Ren moi mon filg sain et sauf et gari.
    Lasse dolante ! a grant tort l'ai maldi.
    Ja l'ai je, lase ! si doucement norri ;
    Se il i muert, bien doit estre gehi,
    Ce iert mervelle s'a coutel ne m'oci.' "
                                    Id., 1141–49.

The same coarseness and brutality, contrasting strongly with
most of the later thirteenth century poems, crops out in the
scene (*Raoul de Cambrai*, 1300–33) preceding the burning
of the convent of Origny.   This vivid scene shows us
Raoul hurling the most insulting epithets at the Mother
Superior of the convent.   When Raoul was killed shortly
after this by the bastard Bernier, once the companion squire
of Raoul, his dead body was borne back to Cambrai upon a
shield.   Then the mother's grief begins anew :

" ' Mieudres ne fu Rolans ne Oliviers
    Qe fustes, fix, por vos amis aidier !
    Qant moi remenbre del traitor B.
    Qi vos a mort, j'en quit vive erragier ! '
    Lors chiet pasmée ; on la cort redrecier.
    De pitié pleure mainte franche mollier."
                                    Id. 3551–56.

Coupled with the natural grief of the mother is that of the
parent left without an heir,—a serious matter in feudal
times :

" ' Diex ! dist la dame, cum est mes cuers maris !
    Se l'eüst mort un quens poesteïs,
    De mon duel fust l'une motiés jus mis.
    Qui lairai je ma terre et mon païs ?
    Or n'i ai oir, par foi le vos plevis.' "
                                    Id., 3596–3600.

The grief of Raoul's *fiancée* is even more touching, and,
though much more elaborated than the tragic grief of Aude,

the scene still retains some primitive traits.   When Heluïs
arrives upon the news of her lover's death :

> " El mostier entre comme feme esmarie ;
> Isnelement a haute vois escrie :
> ' Sire R., con dure departie !
> Biax dous amis, car baisiés vostre amie.
> La vostre mors doit estre trop haïe . . . .
> Mors felonese, trop par fustes hardie
> Qi a tel prince osas faire envaïe !
> Por seul itant qe je fui vostre amie,
> N'avrai signor en trestoute ma vie.' . . .
> ' Sire R., dist la franche pucele,
> Vos me jurastes dedens une chapele.
> Puis me reqist Harduïns de Nivele
> Qi tint Braibant, cele contrée bele ;
> Mais nel presise por l'onnor de Tudele.
> Sainte Marie, glorieuse pucele,
> Porquoi ne part mes quers soz ma mamele
> Qant celui per cui devoie estre ancele ?
> Or porrira cele tenre maissele
> Et cil vair oel dont clere est la prunele.
> La vostre alaine estoit tos jors novele.' "

Id., 3665–93.

She tells the mother Aalais to go seek repose, and she insists
upon watching alone (3701–15).   And when it is all over :

> " En Pontiu va Heluïs au vis fier ;
> Molt la reqierent et haut home et princier,
> Mais n'en vost nul ne prendre ne baillier."

Id., 3729–31.

Thus, disdaining social prestige and feudal alliance, Heluïs
rested true to the memory of Raoul.   The author, while
preserving in the first half of his poem the rude spirit of the
primitive version, has consciously developed this scene of
inconsolable sadness.   Just enough is said ; the rest is
suggested.   Nowhere in these poems has the grief of a lover
been drawn so sympathetically and so naturally.

Les Loherains presents another example of this devotion,

likewise simple and natural. When Beatrix hears the news
of the death of her husband Begon :

> " La dame l'ot, à la terre chaï,
> Quant se redresce, si a gieté un cri ;
> Vient à la biere, si a signor pris,
> Ele li baise et iels et bouce et vis,
> Si le regrete com jà porrez oïr."
>
> *Romans de Garin le Loherain*, v. ii, p. 267.

It will be remembered that this was the hero of whom it
was said :

> "Gentis hons fu, moult l'amoient si chien,'

and on his tomb they carved :

> " Ce fu li mieuldres qui sor destrier séist."
>
> *Id.*, v. ii, p. 272.

The prominence of the queen at court and her part in
intrigues is clearly evidenced also in *Les Loherains*. Throughout these poems the queen sympathizes with the Lorrains
and uses her influence to incite the weak Pepin to encourage
the quarrels among the Bordelais who are the antagonists
of the Crown. It is in policy and in feudal supremacy that
this queen is interested. For example, in the *Mort Garin*
when this same Blancheflor hears from Rigaut how he has
killed the four sons of the traitor Fromont, she exclaims
with more frankness than charity :

> " ' Pléust a Deu, qui en la croiz fu mis,
> Li remanans fust ore tot ainsi ! ' "
>
> *Mort Garin*, p. 70.

And again in the same connection :

> " Ot le la dame, de rire esbofi."

This heartlessness in woman did not shock the sensibilities
of the audience. But there is place even in these cruel
poems for tender feelings. Hear this lament of a mother
over her two sons :

> " ' Li mien enfant, com iestes hui emblée !
> Lasse! dolente, com sui en grant nerté l
> Mon fier lignaje et mon grant parenté
> Voi en cest siégle durement tormenter ;
> Terre, car euvre ; lairai moi enz coler :
> Po pris ma vie, ma joie et ma santé.' "
>
> *Id.*, p. 97.

Already in a poem of this cycle is found that conventional detailed description of a young girl's beauty which became one of the favorite themes with the later *trouvères*. It seems out of place with the sternness of the rest of the poem, and offers a charming relief after the bitterness and bloodshed of the preceding narrative. It is Blancheflor who is brought to Paris to be given in marriage to Garin. (The subsequent poems relate how the King Pepin appropriated her instead) :

> " Et la pucelle est entree en Paris
> Moult richement, o li dux Auberi.
> Desafublée en fut en un samis ;
> Li palefrois sor quoi la dame sist
> Estoit plus blans que n'est la flor de lis ;
> Li lorains vaut cent mars de parisis,
> Et la sambue nuns plus riche ne vit.
> La dame ert gente et de cor et de vis,
> Bouche espessete et les dens ot petis,
> Il sunt plus blans qu'ivoire planéis ;
> Hanches bassetes, blans et vermeil li vis,
> Les ieus rians et bien fais les sorcis ;
> C'est la plus belle qui onques mais naquit.
> Sor ses espaules li gisent si blon crin :
> En son chief ot un chapelet petit
> D'or et de pieres qui mout bien li avint.
> Toutes les rues emplissent de Paris ;
> Dist l'uns à l'autre : ' Comme belle dame a ci !
> Elle devroit un roiaume tenir.' "
>
> *Romans de Garin le Loherain*, v. i, pp. 297, 298.

This description enumerates the details of youthful beauty in a woman which became conventional after the popularity of the Breton poets. Such a passage as that just quoted alone would warrant Gaston Paris in assigning the poem as it stands to the last part of the twelfth century. This slender fair-haired type was produced in French literature as soon as woman in herself became worthy of detailed description.[1] The moment people began to hear about and to read about beautiful women it became necessary to describe her outward features in some detail. This literary type was produced, then, once for all as the ideal of France, and it is doubtful if it has changed since the twelfth century.

But before considering the type of young maid and her relations to the hero, it will be well to look more closely at woman as wife and mother. By so doing we shall get a truer idea of the mediæval conception of woman's duty. Krabbes[2] has rightly noted that the devotion of wives to husbands is an essential feature of the early poems and of those which were afterwards modelled directly upon them. This characteristic has already been noted in more than one of the preceding quotations. Not only is the bond between husband and wife, but between mother and son, very strong. There is no reason to doubt of a strong family affection, if reliance be placed in these epic poems.

Les Enfances Vivien offers one of the most beautiful *regrets* of a mother over her son, to serve as an example, and the Swedish editors of the poem have done well to call attention to it. The Saracens demand little Vivien, then only seven years old, as ransom for his father Garin whom they hold captive. The whole passage expressing the grief of the mother at parting from her son is worth quoting. Note especially the twelfth *tirade* for the familiar details upon which the mother's love lingers :

[1] Cf., *e. g.*, in other *genres: Floire et Blancheflor* (ed. Elz.), pp. 107–109 ; *Erec et Enide* (ed. Förster), 411–441, 1554 f. ; *Cliges* (ed. Förster), 770 f. ; *Aucassin et Nicolette* (3rd ed. Suchier), p. 16.

[2] Theodor Krabbes, *Die Frau im altfranzösischen Karlsepos.*

XI.

" ' Filz Vivien, ce dist la gentis dame,
Ne vos envoi, bels filz, por armes prendre,
Ne por halberc, por escut,' ne por lance,
Mais por la mort dont ge suis a fiance.
Filz Vivien, por ce vas en Espaigne ;
Li Sarrazin en prenront la vengence,
Filz Vivien, de vos belles enfances,
Qui molt estoient dolces et avenantes.

XII.

" ' Filz Vivien, or prenrai de ton poil.
Et de ta char des ongles de tes dois,
Qui plus sont blanc que ermine ne nois,
Enpres mon cuer les lierai estroit,
Les reverrai as festes et as mois.
Encore me membre, bels filz, del mot cortois
Que me deïstes, n'a mie encor un mois ;
Dedens ma chambre seïstes ioste moi,
Cant ge ploroie dan Garin le cortois,
Vos me deïstes : ' Belle mere, tais toi,
La mort mon pere que me ramentevois,
Se ge vif tant que porte mes conrois,
Parmi Espaigne ne porra remanoir
Que la vengence tote prise n'en soit.'
Lors oi-ge ioie, bels filz, adont me toi.

XIII.

" ' Filz Vivien, la gentis dame dist,
Tu fais ansi con l'aignelet petit
Que laist sa mere, cant voit lo louf venir,
Et il i trueve si tres male merci
Qu'il le mengue et met tot a declin.
Or vendra pasques, une feste en avril,
Cil damoisel sont chaucie et vesti,
Vont en riviere por lor gibier tenir,
En lor poinz portent falcons et esmeris ;
Ne te verrai ne aler ne venir.
He mort! car rien, si me pren et oci !
Duel et domage est or mais, cant je vif.' ''

Les Enfances Vivien, tirades xi, xii, xiii.

In the same strain of tender affection compare the *regret* of

Eremborc in *Jourdains de Blaivies*.   She is the wife of the
faithful vassal Renier to whom little Jourdain has been
confided for safe-keeping.   Rather than betray their charge,
these parents hand over to the traitor Fromont their own
son :

> " ' Or revenront cil biau jor en esté,
>   Que m'en irai desor ces murs ester,
>   Ces dammoisiax verrai de ton aé
>   Par devant moi et venir et aler,
>   A la quintaine et à l'escu jouster
>   Et corre as barres et luitier et verser ;
>   Lors referai si mon cuer replorer,
>   Molt m'esmervoil se ne l'estuet crever.' "
>
> *Jourdains de Blaivies*, 656–663.

These passages, which might be multiplied, leave no doubt
as to the kind of affection which the feudal mother had for
her son.[1]   As wives, too, the women are usually models of
constancy, love and self-sacrifice.   For illustrations there is
an embarrassment of choice.   Let us take Guibourc, wife
of Guillaume d'Orange, Ermengard, wife of Aymeri de
Narbonne and Berte, wife of Girart de Roussillon ;—these
three from the feudal epic ; and Parise, wife of Raymond,
Duke of Saint-Gilles, the latter from a poem which is almost
a *roman d'aventure*.

As for Guibourc, *La Prise d'Orange* relates how Guillaume, son of Aymeri, wooed and won the fair Saracen
princess Orable.   But in the poem of *Aliscans* she appears
in a less romantic guise as the childless wife of the hero
of the Guillaume cycle.   When speaking of this Guillaume
in a preceding chapter reference was made to the parting
between the devoted couple when the husband left Orange to
demand help from Louis at Paris.   Orange was in great
straits and Guibourc was left behind to defend the city.

---

[1]An interesting scene, too diffuse for quotation, is found at the close
of *Les Quatre Fils Aymon* where the four sons take leave of their mother.

Note the vigor and confidence of her determination to guard well the place :

> " ' Je remanrai en Orenge le grant
> Aveuc les dames, dont il a céenz tant.
> Cascune aura le hauberc jaserant
> Et en son cief le vert elme luisant,
> Et à sa coste aura chaint le bon branc,
> Au col l'escu, el poing l'espie trenchant.
> Si sont chaens chevalier ne sai quant
> Ke delivrastes de la gent Tervagant ;
> Deseur ces murs monterons là devant,
> Bien desfendrons se Turc vont assaillant.
> Jou ere armée à loi de combatant.
> Par saint Denis, que je trai à garant,
> N'i a paien, Sarrasin, ne Persant,
> Se je l'ataing d'une piere en ruant,
> Ne le convingne chaiir de l'auferrant.' "
>
> *Aliscans,* 1948–62.

It is not credible that under any condition the defense of a strong place was confided to women, though we have more than one instance of their personal bravery in times of stress.   It is important, however, to notice the rôle of dignified heroism assigned here to woman as sharer in the projects and dangers of her warrior husband.

Not less complete is the active association of Ermengard in the deeds of Aymeri de Narbonne.   When the old hero is laid out upon his death-bed, as they think, it is his wife who watches over him *en la sale maior* and who does not lose hope :

> " Ovri les euz li quens, si esgarda
> Et vit plorer mil chevaliers loials ;
> Devant lui fu as piez dame Hermenjarz,
> Toz ses chevex ronpi et descira
> Et Aymeri son seignor regreta . . . .
> ' Sire, por Deu, dist ele, respasez,
> Et si ne morez mie.' "
>
> *La Mort Aymeri de Narbonne,* v. 267 f.

However, Aymeri is reserved for more prodigies of valor.

He recovers, and when a great army of Saracens appears
before Narbonne, he calls for his arms and mounts his steed.
His last words are of comfort to Ermengard :

> " Torne la resne, si s'en va galopant
> A Hermenjart au coraje vaillant :
> ' Franche contesse, dist Aymeris li frans,
> Or sont entré Sarrazin en mal an.
> Mar issirent d' Espaigne.' "
>
> *Id.*, 769–773.

And as Aymeri fights with Corsolt it seems that he is constantly thinking of his wife (*Id.*, 1113–19). Later, when
Aymeri is taken prisoner and is about to be burnt alive by
the Saracens, it is again Ermengard who calls from the walls
that she will surrender the city on her own responsibility, if
her people be allowed to keep the Christian religion. When
finally, at the end of the poem, Aymeri is killed by the
outlandish *Saietaires* in a scene that seems like a foretaste
of Ariosto, we are told that a year afterward Ermengard
died also of sorrow.

Paulin Paris, in a delicate appreciation, has said of the
wife of Girart de Roussillon : "Sa femme a, comme lui,
changé plusieurs fois de nom ; c'est tantôt Berte, tantôt
Ermengarde, et tantôt Emmeline ; mais toujours c'est une
épouse courageuse, sage, dévouée, dont la mission est de
cicatriser les plaies, de calmer les fureurs de son orgueilleux
époux, et de le ramener à des sentiments de loiauté, de
désintéressement et de piété." [1] It was, indeed, during the
twenty-two years of penitence imposed upon him by the
hermit that Girart found Berte to be the uncomplaining
sharer of his miseries. Broken in spirit and spent physically he let himself be guided in his wanderings by her.
When she hears of the price that Charles had put upon his
head, it is Berte who assumes the direction of their affairs :

---

[1] *Hist. litt. de la France*, xxii, p. 305.

"Seiner dis la contesse quer me creaz
Eschiven les castels e les citaz
E toz les chevalers e les poestaz
Que la felnie es granz el cobeitaz
Car seiner vostre non car o caniaz
E el li respondet si com vos plaz."

Girart de Rossillon (Ox. MS.), 7605–10.

The whole scene of exile is vivid and natural, despite the visible influence of the lives of saints. When the poor Count, rising from his sick bed, realizes his misery and destitution, it is his wife who comforts him :

" E sa bone mullers lo cap li ders
' Car seiner laisse estar lonor que pers
Quar si mal cuelz en grat mellor conquers.
Pois li despont des saumes david tes vers
E contet lui de iop qui fun deu sers."

Id., 7664–68.

When the wretched couple in their poverty become the sport of lewd fellows who mock them, Berte courageously comes to the defense of her husband against these brazen calumniators : .

" Seiner mercet por deu e por saint pere.
Trobet mei orfenine pauche bergere
E me prest a muller deus lo li mere
E pois me fes aprendre a costurere
Non sai plus gentil ome de lui o quere
Quel non est de ca mar diste ribere
Ni a un tan felun de male terre
Assa duce razon nol conquere."

Id., 7722–29.

These quotations will suffice to show the justice of Paulin Paris' estimate of Berte's character.[1]

In the poem of *Parise la Duchesse* the theme of *Berte aus grans piés* and of *Macaire* again recurs. It belongs to the Carolingian cycle only by courtesy, and after the fourth

---

[1] To these examples of conjugal devotion might be added that of Beatrix in *Hervis de Metz.*

verse there is no more question of Charlemagne. Our interest centres in Parise, the young wife accused of murdering the Duke's brother. She is apparently spared because she is pregnant (pp. 19, 22); but she is driven into exile from which she returns only after years. It may be permitted to note the delicate psychological treatment of this episode. When Raymond hears the accusation made against Parise he is furious and, almost another Othello, stays his hand from his right to murder her on the spot only because she is with child. Now, there is a traitor Milon who treacherously offers to defend Parise in a judicial combat. According to agreement with the traitor crew who are plotting Parise's discomfiture, he lets himself be defeated. But Raymond does not know he is a traitor, and he is so angry that Parise's guilt should thus be proven that he hangs Milon for not winning the trial by arms. Jealous, moreover, for his wife's innocence, even against the evidence, he burns the traitor bishop who asserts falsely that Parise has confessed her crime. The swift execution belongs to a by-gone age; but the inconsistency of Raymond is perfectly natural. He cannot bear to hear anyone speak evil of his wife. If she is guilty, and he believes she is, he reserves for himself the right to punish her. No other hand is worthy. Parise, for her part, is concerned only for the child yet unborn. Her pleas that she be spared until the child be born, and that Raymond then kill her, are at last heard and she is sent into exile. She begs her husband to remember :

> " ' Quele part que ge aille, que m' en remanra orez :
> De vos sera li anfes qui de moi sera nez.' "
>
> *Parise la Duchesse,* p. 22.

There is a beautiful devotion in the midnight scene of her departure from the castle, as she goes out into exile :

> " Et apres la mienuit issirent de l'ostel.
> La dame vit la tor o norri ot esté ;

Dist à sez compaignos : 'Un petit m'atendez,
Tant que mon seignor aie véu et esgardé.'
'Dame, disent si home, merci por amor Dé !
Se li dus le savoit, n'an porron eschaper ;
Maintenant nos fera toz les mambres coper.'
Et respondi la dame : 'Il ne puet estre el.'
Ele se Iaise à terre de la mule coler,
Et trespassa la dame les chevaliers membrez,
Qui gisent ou palais es couches lez à lez,
Puis vint elle ou palais où li dus Raimons ert.
Tant a ploré li dus toz an fu agrevez ;
Par devant lui ardirent dui grant cirge alumé.
Atant e vos la dame au gent cors honoré ;
Elle ne l'ose mie esveillier ne boter ;
An la face lo baise coiement et soé,
Puis prist andeus ses ganz qui sont à or paré,
Après, leva sa main, si l'a de Deu seigné :
'Sire dus de Saint Gile, de Deu soiez sauvez !
Or somes moi et toi à doleur desevré,
Que jamais à ma vie des ieuz ne me verez !'
Devant l'uis de la chambre ne pot sor piez ester ;
Li cuers li est paumez, si s'en torne arier.''

Id., pp. 23, 24.

In reading the *chansons de geste* one feels that as time
went on the centre of interest shifted more and more from
the married woman to the maid. We know that the Celtic
romances and the Provençal *courtoise* poetry were popular
in the North of France from the middle of the twelfth
century, a date anterior to the composition of the greater
number of the epic poems as we have them. It is natural,
then, that many of these poems should have felt these two
new influences, especially that of the romances of adventure,
in the treatment of woman. How, then, account for the
fact that many even of the twelfth and thirteenth century
poets adhered to the old style? The explanation is that
these poets intentionally maintain the conventional epic
tradition by the subordination of woman to an unromantic
rôle. The poems that represent woman as the companion
of man, as his spouse, as his constant helper and adviser

7

even in military and political matters, rather than as a
romantic object of diversion during his idle moments or as
the end of adventurous quests,—these poems represent the
persistence of the primitive feudal ideal of woman. By
some poets, sticklers for this national tradition, the *chansons
de geste* were evidently considered an improper place for the
introduction of the heroine who dictated the conduct of
the once proud warrior and who claimed his service. Such
poets essentially assert that neither Provençal woman-worship
nor Breton woman-service has any place in the vigorous
songs of deeds which these poets were called to sing. This
satisfactorily explains the survival of the warrior hero's
popularity and the subordination of woman even in poems
composed long after the Breton and Provençal influences
were supreme in feudal society.

The poems now to be examined have, for the most part,
felt the force of the new literary demands for a new sort
of woman,—a passionate heroine who shall occupy in the
narrative a place equal, if not superior, in importance to that
of the hero. While adhering to the *cadre* of the epic and
avoiding the domain of the *romans d'aventure*, the poets
contrived to bring the young woman into prominence and to
develop her rôle.

The second part of *Raoul de Cambrai*, beginning at *tirade*
CCL, offers a striking example of this grafting on of a new
style. In the first part, it will be remembered, Aalais and
Heluïs were hardly more than incidental personages happily
introduced as devoted to Raoul. The second part lands us *in
medias res* with the passionate love of the daughter of Guerri
for Bernier. Notice that it is his beauty and bravery that
win her, without his even thinking of love. When he
arrives as her father's guest, she says to herself:

> " ' Lie la dame qe isil aroit prise,
> Car molt a los de grant chevalerie !

> Qi le tenroit tot nu soz sa cortine.
> Miex li valroit qe nule rien qi vire.' "
>
> *Raoul de Cambrai*, 5591–94.

She takes the initiative and lays plans at once to capture him. The scene no longer passes in the open air or in the great hall of the feudal castle, but in the privacy of the lady's boudoir. There is an air of intimate secrecy and intrigue. She sends her chamberlain to Bernier :

> " ' Di li par moi salus et amistié,
> Et q'en mes chambres ce vaigne esbanoier
> Et as eschès et as tables joier.' "
>
> *Id.*, 5623–25.

Once in possession of Bernier she loses no time :

> " Il n'ont or cure d'autres blés gaaignier.
> La damoisele a parlé tout premier."
>
> *Id.*, 5678–79.

She does not hesitate to rehearse her charms :

> " ' En non Dieu, sire, ains estes mes amis.
> Pren moi a feme, frans chevalier eslis . . . .
> Veés mon cors com est amanevis :
> Mamele dure, blanc le col, cler le vis ;
> Et car me baise, frans chevalier gentis ;
> Si fai de moi trestot a ton devis.' "
>
> *Id.*, 5695–5702.

It is not necessary to insist upon the distance we have come from Aude and Heluïs !

To the same class of passionate young women belong Claresme in *Gaydon*, Galienne in *Garin de Montglane*,[1] Belissant in *Amis et Amiles*, Lusiane in *Aiol*, Floripas in *Fierabras*, Letise in *Anseïs de Carthage*, Rosamonde in *Elie de S. Gille*, and others. Of these Floripas, Rosamonde, together with the lovely Mirabel, will be more extensively treated in the chapter devoted to the Saracens. Though

---

[1] Vid. Gautier, *Epopées*, iv, p. 139.

there is little to distinguish them from the Christian women just referred to, yet they properly belong in another category. We shall see the tendency in the later poems was to introduce the Saracens rather as a romantic element, and it was thus that the Saracen princesses were brought into connection with the Christian knights.

Another instance of the grafting of a new style upon old matter is offered by Jean Bodel's *Chanson des Saisnes*. The romantic features are introduced well on in the poem, when the Christian army is encamped on the Rhine. The meeting of the French knights under Baudouin with the Saxon ladies accompanying Sibyle is the first part of a plot to ensnare the former. It is urged that the beauty of the Saxon women will lure the French knights across the river to their death. But the women do not take the plot very seriously, and welcome the chance to become acquainted with their opponents :

> " ' Dame, dist la roine, or somes bien an voie
> De veoir les François, se aucuns s'an cointoie.
> Qui or a son ami, qu'ele ne le fauvoie ;
> Mès sovant an sa tante se deduise et donoie :
> Que vaut biautez de dame, s'an jovant ne l'amploie?'
> ' Dame, dist Marsebile, qi joste li s'apoie,
> Bien ait ore maistresse qi si bien nos maistroie ! ' "
> *Chanson des Saisnes*, v. i, pp. 108, 109.

As the intrigue, all too successful, progresses, and Sibyle really gains the love of Baudouin, it is amusing to note that her waiting-maid Helissant in like manner ensnares Berart, the ' second-man.'

Another poem in which the two spirits exist side by side is *Anseïs de Carthage*. There are numerous female characters in this poem. During her father's absence to demand a wife for the young Anseïs, Letise arranges to anticipate the as yet unknown rival and lie with the king herself. Anseïs disdains her proffered love and Letise plots a ven-

geance worthy of such a passionate woman. Upon her
father's return she accuses Anseïs of attempted rape. Ysoré
espouses his daughter's cause and from that beginning dates
a long conflict. Later Anseïs marries Gaudisse, as intended.
After a battle he returns to the palace where the radiant
Gaudisse awaits her lord and one of his vassals says :

> " 'Sire rois, esgardes !
> En vo castel est li solaus Ieves.'
> Ot le li rois, si a ii. ris getes." [1]
>
> *Anseis von Karthago,* 7561–63.

In spite of the psychological interest which they sometimes present, it may be permitted to hurry over this type
of forward women of whom a brief list has been already
given. They are not attractive morally and could not
have existed as a standard in any conceivable state of
society. Their characters are interesting only as they show
the imagination of the poets drawing away from the primitive type, elaborating the rôle of woman in modern fiction.

With Aude, Heluïs, Ermengard, Berte, Guibourc and
Parise in mind, one must admit that the same qualities
which we admire in woman to-day already in the twelfth
century constituted her glory : beauty, love, constancy, intelligence and companionship. It is quite certain that by the
thirteenth century these virtues in woman were held as high
as they are to-day. The foregoing passages have shown
how profoundly the literary presentation of woman changed
between the eleventh and the fourteenth century. The contrast that exists, for example, between the first and second
parts of *Raoul de Cambrai* or between the *Roland* and *Parise
la Duchesse* reveals the growing interest in a psychological

---

[1] Cf. " De sa tres grant biauté fu toute enluminée
La chambre où nostre gent fu trestoute assemblée."
Doon de Maience, p. 239.

treatment of woman. She has changed from the incidental rough-hewn but deep-feeling woman of the early poems into a delicately refined creature, capable of elaborate literary treatment.

It would be a mistake to close this chapter without a glance at the reverse side of the medal. The bad women in the epic poetry are rare. There are two poems, however, in which these she-devils, these *traitors* bear an important rôle; and these two poems, regarded as psychological novels, happen to be among the best we have. It is undeniable that the artistic portrayal of the evil in human nature is impressive. *Berte aus grans piés* and *Amis et Amiles*, of all the poems we know, approach most closely in plot and psychological interest to the modern novel. They easily distance the greater number of monotonous modern variations of the eternal theme of alienated affections.

Passing over mythological hypotheses, which do not interest us here, and speaking from a literary point of view, *Berte aus grans piés* is Adenet le Roi's [1] artistic treatment of a well-known *motif*,—of how the wiles of a wicked but clever woman enable her to usurp the place of the timid, virtuous wife, and how the latter finally triumphs and regains her rights. By the artifice of the plot and the skilful handling of contrasted characters this poem indicates the last gasp of the national poetry on the point of turning into another *genre* of vaster possibilities : the novel.

Again, in *Amis et Amiles*, we have a character who is fascinating by her very villainy. Lubias is thoroughly cold, crafty and pitiless. She is the type of wife who is hopelessly incompatible with her husband. The contrast between this treatment and that of the same familiar *motif* in the satiric literature reveals the superiority of the former.

---

[1] Cf. the excellent pages of Paulin Paris on Adenet le Roi in *Hist. litt. de la France*, xx, pp. 701–706.

The author of our poem is, indeed, of no mean versatility.
Now a Maupassant in the bed-room scene between Amile
and Belissant (662–722), he is as religious at the close as
the author of the *Saint Alexis* and apparently quite as sincere
(3472–3504). The poem has for its theme the beauty of
self-sacrifice, a lesson which the story of Lubias' villainy
serves to make more effective by contrast. What is to be
insisted upon is this constant preoccupation of the poet with
this matter of eternal interest in French literature : the intimate relations of men and women. This poem should be
studied as presenting an early chapter in the evolution of
social literature in France.

The slanders upon woman so common in the popular
literature of the Middle Age are rarely met with in the epic
poems. These poems breathe a nobler spirit. They are
free from the petty annoyances of *bourgeois* life. They
breathe a purer air, where woman as a rule occupies a
worthy place. An occasional concession is made in the later
poems to that settled mediæval conviction that woman is to
blame for all the evil in the world. But such concessions
are out of spirit with the context and are generally quoted
as a proverb or with some saving clause :

> " ' Voir dist, ki dist icheste prophesie :
>   Par feme esmuet sovent grans deablie."
>
> > *Anseïs von Karthago,* 9021–22.

> " Quar de famme ne sera vuil homme amé,
>   Qui ne la peut bien servir à son gré ;
>   Vuil hom fredist quant il est an aé,
>   Et geune famme pour dire verité
>   Soupvent eschauffe, telle est sa qualité,
>   Qui sont à paine els deux à ung gré."
>
> > *Aquin,* 915–920.

> " Souvent voit on grant mal par fame alever. . . .
>   Maint preudomme äi véu à mal par fame aler."
>
> > *Fierabras,* p. 63.

> " Tant par est fox qui mainte fame croit
> Et qui li dist noient de son consoil.
> Or sai je bien, Salemons se dist voir :
> En set milliers n'en a quatre non trois
> De bien parfaitez, qui croire les voldroit."
>
> *Amis et Amiles*, 1218–22.

> " Plus soit honis mâles, qui croit famele
> Que les traitres, qui hom en cort apele ! "
>
> *Fouque de Candie*, p. 29.

It will be felt that such expressions do not harmonize with the spirit of the *chansons de geste* nor with the society for which they were originally composed.

Three conclusions may be drawn from what has preceded : I. The earliest poems, and those that imitate them, reflect a natural and perfectly attainable ideal of woman as maid, wife and mother, the equal and companion of man. But since her existence is common-place and monotonous she rarely emerges from obscurity in poems intended for an audience whose main interest was fighting.

II. The poems composed as we have them after the middle of the twelfth century reflect, but do not totally appropriate, the spirit of the Celtic romances. Under the influence of the latter, the later epic poems introduce woman for her own sake, indeed, but never give her the first place in the story nor make her the motive force of the action.

III. Finally, here and there crops out as an excrescence the theory of woman's moral inferiority to man. Here she is infinitely crafty, and brutish in her passions, the cause of man's first disobedience. We do not believe that an early aristocratic feudal audience would have any sympathy for this attitude toward woman. It was only when the *bourgeoisie* began to compose poems and to listen to them in the public squares, that this feature of the *bourgeois* philosophy finds expression.

In no period of French literature,—neither in the *romans*

d'aventure, nor in the society literature of the *grand siècle*, nor in the emancipated treatment of the modern novelists,— is woman more attractively and more truthfully, albeit often naïvely, portrayed than in the *chansons de geste.* Here the respectful but rough Teutonic conception is agreeably tempered by the Celtic chivalric conception. It is proper, then, to speak of the epic type of woman. It is a type distinct from the contemporary romantic, pastoral, and satiric types. Affected especially by the romantic presentation of woman in the romances of adventure, as will be seen in the chapter upon the Saracen women, the epic poems nevertheless reflect a type of woman which is more natural, more many-sided, less exaggerated in her traits than is the case in any of the contemporary *genres.*

As for the artistic treatment of woman, we think it much more advanced than others have held. One must not be misled by conventional descriptions of beauty. There was but one type of feminine beauty and the poets had not enough ingenuity to vary the details to any extent. Gaston Paris, speaking of Renier's *Il tipo estetico della donna nel medio evo,* writes: "Le conventionalisme pur de presque toutes les descriptions de beauté féminine du moyen âge y est parfaitement mis en lumière, et c'est un trait qui a son importance pour l'appréciation intellectuelle artistique et morale de cette époque." [1]   But this conventionalism is only on the outside. Considering that we are dealing with an essentially unimaginative form of poetry, the examples we have quoted surely offer a considerable variety of treatment, and show the *trouvères* seeking to express the truth about woman as they saw her and as they wished her to be. The coloring given to woman in a given poem depends upon the period and the *milieu* for which it was composed. But

---

[1] *Romania*, xiv, p. 316.

an accurate observation, a knowledge of woman's heart, and an attempt to analyse her motives as a social creature, are already noticeable, and bind these poems closely to later French literature by the very preoccupation with the relation of the sexes.

NOTE.—Only twice, in *Gui de Bourgogne* and in the *Chanson des Saisnes*, have we found women in the train of the Christian armies. Only the author of the *Pseudo-Turpin* was apparently thinking of lewd camp-followers, where he explains the Christians' defeat (cap. XXI).

BOURGEOIS AND VILAIN.

The characters treated thus far have all belonged to the upper classes of society. The king, the great vassals, the young knights, the noble ladies, the Saracen princesses,— these are the personages who played the leading part in the French epic poetry. This was natural; for this poetry was originally intended for the upper classes, and we assume the *dramatis personœ* to have accurately mirrored forth the sentiments of the audience. It has been pointed out by M. Rajna that some of the great seigneurial families of the North of Italy even flattered themselves that they were descended from the very heroes who aided Charlemagne against the Saracens.[1] There is an echo of this pride of lineage in *La Chanson d'Antioche* where, while quarreling for supremacy at the capture of Antioch, Godefroi de Bouillon boasts himself to be *del lignage Charlon* and the Duc de Normandie replies: *Dont ne sui-je del lin Renart le fil Aimon?*[2] In assisting at the recital of a *chanson de geste*, then, one might listen in some sense to a chapter of family history. It was natural that the chief personages of such a body of poetry should be of noble, if not of royal, birth.

[1] Vid. Pio Rajna, *Le fonti dell' Orlando Furioso*, 2nd ed., Florence, 1900, pp. 13, 14.
[2] *La Chanson d'Antioche*, v. ii, p. 178.

But beneath these upper classes and separated from them by many a round on the social ladder, lived and toiled the working classes in varying degrees of dependence. The peasants of Wace's day say :

> "Nus sumes homes cum il sunt ;
> Tex membres avum cum il unt."
>
> *Roman de Rou* (ed. Pluquet), 6027–28.

It is known how from humble beginnings a *bourgeoisie* developed, how with royal favor it became a great political and social power, how it lifted up its head and overthrew the Bourbons. The narrative of this evolution is one of the most important chapters in the annals of France.

We are to consider now the rôle of the *bourgeois* and the appearance of his ideals in the epic poems. If our thesis be true, that the epic poetry reflects accurately the contemporary social evolution, we shall find in literature as in history the lower classes emerging from obscurity.

It is of something more, however, than the occasional appearance of the *bourgeois* and *vilain* in the epic poems that we must speak. The *bourgeois* or *vilain* hero is, indeed, sometimes introduced in good faith for his own worth ; but more often as a contrast, as a conscious artistic device of the *trouvère* to enhance the interest of his poem. Félix Brun, speaking of the treatment accorded to the *vilain* in the *chansons de geste*, says : " Elles n'ont pas toujours mal parlé des vilains. Elles leur ont même donné parfois, peutêtre pour amener un curieux contraste, une place qui n'est pas sans importance ; elles les ont revêtus de couleurs sympathiques."[1] In some of these characters we shall find the grotesque element, which would raise a laugh even in a refined audience, to be the dominant trait. Serious and

---

[1] Félix Brun, *La vie privée des paysans au moyen âge et sous l'ancien régime*, p. 56.

solemn as the epic poetry conventionally remains, occasional bursts of fun are by no means rare in the later poems. Though a touch of humor may be given to the narrative by any grim warrior or romantic maiden, it is mainly these heroes of low degree who are responsible for the intrusion of the *esprit gaulois* upon the stately gravity of the French epic. To borrow a phrase from Mr. Chandler's *Romances of Roguery*, we should call such a jolly fellow as Galopin, Rainouart and Robastre the *anti-hero*, charged with presenting a contrast to his nobler prototype and, at the same time, answering the demands of a more democratic public.

We find the *bourgeois* element as a social class already in the *Roland*. It is a mere mention, in passing, of the townspeople of Saragossa :

> " Tant chevalchierent qu'en Sarraguce sunt,
> Passent x. portes, traversent iiii. punz,
> Tutes les rues, ù li burgeis estunt.
> Cum il aproisment en la citet amunt,
> Vers le palais oirent grant fremur.''
>
> *Roland*, 2689–93.

This is the early feudal conception : the townspeople huddled in the narrow streets of the lower town, within the enclosure of the fortifications, but living apart from the fighting-men who kept to the citadel, the *citet amunt*. This bare mention of the *bourgeois* element in a town is to be noted chiefly for its complete failure to serve as an artistic back-ground. It never occurred to the *trouvère* of the *Roland* to narrate what the *bourgeois* of Saragossa were doing at the time, and how they received the Christian messengers. Indeed, such a description of a crowd of common people, as we soon find in *Aiol*, would have had no interest for this audience.

Not till the end of the twelfth century does the *bourgeoisie* appear in all its glory as a part of the artistic setting of the poem. The heroes still move about on a higher plane, but the *bourgeoisie* at times receives all the attention. For example, the spirit of raillery and jest has taken complete possession of the poet in the two famous scenes in *Aiol* where the hero with his wretched old-fashioned accoutrement is jeered at and mocked by the people of Poitiers and of Orléans. At Poitiers Aiol and his horse Marchegai, after arousing the wonder and curiosity of people along the streets, are assailed by a drunken man :

> " E vous i. lecheor corant venu :
>   D'un celier ist tous ivres, qu'il ot beu,
>   Et ot jué as deis, s'ot tout perdu ;
>   Corant vint a Aiol, si l'arestut,
>   Par le frain le sacha par grant vertu.
> ' Maistre, dist li lechieres, estes venus?
>   Qu'avés tant demoré al boin eur ?
>   Mi compaignon vos beent, tout ont perdu.
>   Cis chevaus est moult maigres et confondus :
>   Il estera anqui al vin beu,
>   Et cele lance roide et cis escus.
>   Qui vous dona che frain a or batu ?
>   Les resnes en sont routes, mais molt boins fu.' "
>
> *Aiol*, 911–923.

Marchegai, as well as Aiol, resents this familiarity so common in drunken men, and kills the intruder with a well-directed kick. The bystanders are delighted with this, and incite Aiol to further violence by comparing Marchegai with one of King Arthur's horses, and Aiol's antiquated arms with those of *dant Esau, quives qui par eage c. ans u plus*. Many and varied are the coarse jests which they hurl at the poor knight and his jaded mount. The whole scene should be read to realize the importance of the rôle played by the citizens. Poitiers seems well furnished with men who love good cheer not wisely but too well. Another scene (vv. 1021–33) with a drunken man follows close upon that already quoted. Here, again, Marchegai quiets the *glouton* without Aiol soiling his hands in the matter. The hero's

gentle courtesy is everywhere effectively contrasted with the
vulgarity of these lewd fellows.   At last Aiol finds a kind
host who cares for him and apologizes for the rudeness of
his fellow-townsmen :

> " ' François sont orgellous desmurés.
>   Et si sont coustumier de lait parler : [1]
>   Laidengier vos vauront et ranproner.' "
>
> <div align="right"><i>Id.</i>, 1157–59.</div>

We follow Aiol to Orléans where, in the market-place, a
similar scene is described :

> "Aiols li fieus Elie a tant alé
> Qu'al grant marchiet d'Orliens en est entrés :
> Borgois et macheclier l'ont molt gabé,
> Des pomons de lor vakes l'ont il rué :
> ' Voiéns, compere Pieres, che dist Eldrés,
> E Dieus ! cis avoit ore trop demoré !
> S'il ore avoit ja fors l'estor trové
> Il ne donroit mais trieves devant Noel ;
> Car fust chi Hageneus li enivrés
> Et Hersent, sa mollier al ventre lé !
> Toutes gens set lait dire et reprover ;
> Chele ne voit nul home par chi passer
> Que maintenant ne sache un gab doner ;
> S'ele avoit son coutel grant acheré
> Son ronchi li aroit ja escoué,
> Dont seroit il plus biaus a amener.' "
>
> <div align="right"><i>Id.</i>, 2579–94.</div>

The above-mentioned Hersent is not slow to appear.   Note
the *trouvère's* slur at the *bourgeoisie parvenue :*

> "Atant evos Hersent al ventre grant ;
> Ch'ert une pautoniere molt mesdisant,
> Feme a un macheclier d'Orliens le grant :
> Né furent de Borgonge la (de) devant ;
> Quant vinrent a Orliens la chité grant,
> Ni aporterent il, mien ensiant,
> De tous avoirs en tere v. sous vaillant ;
> Ains estoient kaitif et mendiant,

---

[1] Cf. *Le Français, né malin* of Boileau (*Art Poétique,* ii, 182).

> Dolant et mort de fain et pain querant :
> Mais par lor esparenge fissent il tant
> Que xx. sous de deniers vont espargnant,
> A monte et a usure si vont prestant :
> Ainc que fuissent passé plus de v. ans
> Les vont si li diable montepliant
> Ces xx. sous de deniers qu'il vont prestant,
> Un si trés grant avoir vont amassant
> Que les ii. pars d'Orliens vont engagant,
> Fours, molins et rechès vont acatant
> Et vont tous les frans homes desiretant.
> Quant il furent venu en l'avoir grant
> Qu'il sont venu a auques de droit niant,
> Lors ceullent un orgeul de maintenant,
> Ne laisoient durer home vivant."

Id., 2656–78.

After she has had her jest like the others, Aiol gets even with her thus :

> " ' Dame, dist (li) li valès, laisieme atant :
> Vous m'avés bien gabé, s'en sui dolant ;
> Mais (i)che me va auques reconfortant
> Que vous avés cel cors mal avenant :
> Hideuse estes et laide et mal puant,
> Et le vostre serviche pas ne demanc.
> Molt vous aiment ches mousques par Dé le grant,
> Car vos estes lor mere, mien ensiant :
> Entor vos trevent merde, j'en sai itant,
> Que a molt grans tropiaus vos vont sivant.' "

Id., 2704–13.

Hersent is discomfited by being answered in kind, and makes her escape through the jeering crowd. Thus, even our hero Aiol had been infected by his surroundings. His conventional knightly behavior gave place to the vulgarity of the natural man.

This contrast of the knight and the *bourgeois* is again brought out in *Les Enfances Vivien*, a thirteenth century poem. Vivien, a captive in Spain at the age of seven, was bought by a merchant's wife and kindly treated by her. She presents him to her husband, from whom she has long

been separated, as her son, and such the husband believes
him to be. They plan a mercantile career for Vivien when
he shall be old enough to assist them at the great fairs.[1]
But the knight's son soon speaks out :

> " ' Dist W. de folie paroles
> De marchandise ne donroie je i. denier
> Mais i. destrier me faites amener
> Et ii. brakes me faites delivrer
> i. espervier me faites aporter
> Par ces montaignes m'en irai deporter
> Prendrai de quailles et des pertris asés.' "
>   *Les Enfances Vivien* (MS. de Boulogne), 855–861.

As his initial commercial transaction Vivien betrays his
unpractical turn by paying one hundred *deniers* for a crippled
old horse. Here the intentional contrast is between the careful money-hoarding merchant and the open-handed young
knight.[2] The *bourgeois* is properly scandalized at hearing
his supposed son talk about laying siege to cities and castles,
hiring *soudoiers* and spending money recklessly for arms.
He tries to persuade Vivien to be sensible and become his
successor :

> " ' Je suis mais viex et kanus et ferrant
> Si me deuses reposer sor mon banc.' "
>   *Id.*, 1173–74.

Vivien calls such business usury and continues to spend
money confided to him upon dogs and *esperviers*. Finally,
put in charge of a convoy of merchants bound to a distant
fair, he sells all the goods, arms his followers, and attacks
the caravan of a Saracen merchant whose plunder he sends
back to the delighted Godefroi. The rest of the poem
assumes the character of a *chanson de geste*. We are glad to

---

[1] Cf. *Les Narbonnais*, 301 f. The *borjois riches* say :

> " ' Marcheant somes, qui ne finom d'errer
> Par plussors terres por avoir conquester.' "

[2] Cf. *Hervis de Metz*, 324 f., for an identical situation.

hear that, when it is in his power, Vivien rewards the old merchant couple for all the trouble he had caused them.

Parise la Duchesse gives us a picture of the *bourgeoisie* under arms at the siege of Cologne:

> "Par de desus la vile sont issuz li archier,
> As murs et as escrimes sont li arbelestier ;
> Devant la maitre porte sont li borjois à pié,
> Qui portent bones armes et jusarmes d'acier,
> Et grant targes raondes, fandues de carter."
>
> *Parise la Duchesse*, p. 57.

One of the principal figures in this scene is *Richiers li maires*! The rôles have changed since the *Roland*, but they are still fighting.

Hugues Capet, of the fourteenth century, represents the literary triumph of the *bourgeois* spirit in our *genre*. It is not necessary to give a *résumé* of this poem in which the hero, the son of a Parisian butcher's daughter, breaks the hearts of all the ladies, marries the daughter of King Louis, and finally becomes king of France. No more satisfactory example of new matter put into an old mould could be desired than this pseudo-*chanson de geste*. Of one of the numerous bastard sons of Hugh we shall speak later. More important to remark is the *bourgeois* spirit personified in Hugh's rich uncle Simon the butcher. It is the sordid spirit of Philistinism in this uncle which is contrasted with the more chivalric conception of Hugh, whose father, indeed, was a knight. The uncle wants his nephew to be his apprentice and successor:

> " ' Or demorez chéens, sy vous aprenderon
> A tuer ung pourchiel, ou buef, ou i. mouton,
> Et s'en serez marquans, waingnerez à ffoison.
> Se trez bien vous portez, quanquez vaillant avon
> Arez aprez me mort ; je n'ay oir se vous non.'
> ' Biaulz onclez, ce dist Huez, j'ai aultre opinion.' "
>
> *Hugues Capet*, pp. 5, 6.

8

Seeing that he can do nothing to convert the roving tendencies of his nephew:

> "Tout pensis, sans mot dire, s'assist sur i. tonniel.
> Quant assez ot pensé, s'alla à son huchiel,
> ii° florins a pris en sen plus grant monchiel,
> A Huon lez donna en ung petit saquel."
>
> *Id.*, p. 7.

What a picture this is of the careful hoarding Parisian
bourgeois! Hugh then begins a tour of France, during
which his principal occupation is the undoing of all the
damoisellez and *pucellez* along his route. For he had taken
his motto from Ovid:

> " 'Que ly ons doit avoir des amiez pluseurs.
> Je lairay ceste cy, s'en refferay ailleurs.' "
>
> *Id.*, p. 10.

While Hugh is away, business goes well with the butcher,
and on Hugh's return the uncle makes new propositions:

> " 'J'ay, puis que ne vo vy, gaingnié si largement
> Qu'à Paris n'a bourgois, biaus niez, certainement,
> Qui ait autant de meublez, de rentez ne d'argent.' "
>
> *Id.*, p. 23.

Hugh shall have money enough to live in grand style, and
moreover:

> " 'Se vous querons aussy ung biau mariement.' "

Hugh is willing enough to do all but marry:

> " ' Je demoray o vous car mez cuers s'y assent ;
> Mais de moy marier n'ai ge mie tallent,
> Si ce n'est à tel dame, sachiez certainnement
> Dont onneur et riquesse me viegne hautement,
> Car à lui marier a grant peril souvent :
> Il y quiet jallousie ou pire argüement . . . .
> Dont di ge que d'amours servir tout ligement
> Vienent grace et éurs, car, tant ly hons se prent
> De amer, il doit estre de bel esbatement.
> Riens ne doit esparnier, ains doit songneusement

Rouver mercy partout où ces cuers ly aprent.
Se ly une reffuse, ly autre s'y assent.
En tel estat veul je user le mien jouvent,
Car c'est drois paradis à homme qui s'entent.' "
Id., pp. 23, 24.

We may imagine how Chrétien de Troyes and Jean de Meun respectively would have been variously affected by this frank expression of material love.   But the *bourgeois* Simon was not scandalized by these ideas of his progressive nephew. He was rather proud of this emancipated upstart :

"Ly bourgois souffisant doucement en rioit ;
Hue retint o lui, qui grant estat menoit."
Id., p. 24.

The prominence of the *bourgeoisie* as a political factor is interesting to notice in this poem.   When it is a question of giving her daughter in marriage, the Queen Blancheflor says that the consent of the Peers of France is not sufficient ; she wishes the expression of *bourgeois* opinion as well :

" 'Et ly bourgeois oussy de che roiaulme chà ;
Me fille à leur volloir du tout obéyra.' "
Id., p. 27.

Even the princes who favor the enterprise of the Count Savari bow before the *franc bourgois de ceste cité.*   The battle fought against the Parisians by the allied princes is a combat between the chivalric nobility on one side, and the allied monarchy and *bourgeoisie* on the other.   At first, the leader of the royal forces disdains the support of his *bourgeois* troops :

" 'Mais entre vous, bourgois au fourré capperon,
Estez devant voz huis trop noble campion,
Et cant vient en bataille, n'i vallez i. bouton.' "
Id., p. 48.

But soon afterward, his life having been saved by Hugh
and his *bourgeois* troops, the *connétable* begs pardon.   Hugh
says :

> " ' Connetablez, par Dieu de paradis,
> Mestier avez éu dez bourgois de Paris,
> De cellui proprement qui de vous fu laidis !
> Ly hons n'est mie saigez de blamer sez amis.' "
>
> *Id.*, p. 52.

And the *connétable* replies :

> " ' Frans vassaus postaïs,
> Ne say c'estez bourgois, du cuer estez gentis,
> Et de tous conbatans estez superlatis . . . .
> Pardon vous en requier, car j'aroie mespris.' "
>
> *Id.*, p. 52.

It is Hugh who deals the great blows in this fight and who
is the strength of the royal forces.   The *connétable* fully
recognizes his prowess (p. 55), and in giving an account to
the queen, it is in these words that he speaks of Hugh :

> " ' J'ay moult oy lower Rolant et Olivier,
> Et Guillame, vo frere, et le danois Ogier ;
> Mais je croy que cil iiii. que m'oés prononchier,
> Ne Judas Maquabeus, ne Alixandre le fier,[1]
> Ne peurent tant de bien en yaus amanagier
> Qu'à cestui se péussent de proesche apairier.' "
>
> *Id.*, p. 58.

More brave than Roland and Oliver, than Ogier and Judas
Maccabeus, worthy to marry the king's daughter (p. 55) !
For what greater triumph could the butcher's nephew wish ?
The spirit of social equality in this poem is epitomized in
the words of the queen's brother :

> " ' Car certez il vault bien qu'il ait i. tel destin,
> Car il est biaulz et bons, et s'il n'est de hault lin,
> Au vrai considerer, et tout pauvre meschin

---

[1] For these heroes as types of chivalry cf. Paul Meyer in *Bull. annuaire
de la Société des anciens textes français*, 1883, pp. 45–54.

Sont tout estrait d'Adam et Bilart et Justin ;
Mais orguelz nous aprent à dire faulz latin.' "

Id., p. 126.

We have had to do thus far with the population of the towns, and we have seen how the *bourgeoisie* took hold of the epic poems during the period which elapsed between the *Roland* and *Hugues Capet*. More rarely do the poems speak of the rural population. The peasant rarely appears, though never with scorn or disdain, in the poems of the *trouvère*. *Li Charrois de Nymes* offers a scene of a jovial character, in which a countryman and his children are returning home from the town with a load of salt. The thrifty peasant with his ox-cart is still to-day a familiar sight on the high-roads of the *Midi :*

"Vient de Saint Gile où il ot conversé,
A iiii. bués que il ot conquesté,
Et iii. anfanz que il ot engendré.
De ce s'apensi li vilains que senez,
Que sel est chier el règne dont fu nez.
Desor son char a un tonel levé,
Si l'ot empli et tot rasé de sel.
Les iii. enfanz que il ot engendrez
Jeuent et rient et tienent pain assez :
A la billete jeuent desus le sel.
François s'en rient, que feroient-il el ?"

Li Charrois de Nymes, 877–887.

The incessant wars must have frequently reduced the country population to a state of intense suffering, to which was added misery induced by over-taxation. Their destitute condition is touched upon with a sympathetic hand in the following passages : *Li Charrois de Nymes*, 570–580; *Mort Garin*, p. 139; *Berte aus grans piés*, 1758 f.; *Roman de Rou*, 5975 f.

It remains to speak under this heading of the heroes of low degree, of those who rose from the ranks to an equality with the old-time heroes. Just how far this literary evolution was a mirror of the actual state of feudal society is not easy to determine. The poets, addressing themselves to an aristocratic audience, certainly often deprecate the raising of low-born men above their station to places of responsibility (cf. *Girart de Rossillon*, 940–942 in *Rom. Studien, Couronnement de Louis*, 204–207). On the other hand, Paulin Paris cites the following interesting passage from *Aspremont* which argues eloquently for the democratic spirit of the times. It is Charles himself who is speaking :

> " 'Chevalier ert qui estre le voudra ;
> Chascuns de ceus qui les armes penra,
> Se Dex me maine iluec où je fui jà
> Il aura terre, dont chevaliers sera !' . . .
> Chevaliers fist de gent de maint lignage ;
> Por qu'il i sache proesce et vasselage,
> Auques n'i ot aconté nul parage ;
> Se il est serf, quites ert de servage,
> Ne donra mais, en trestot son eage,
> Ne por sa terre, ne tréu ne pasage."
> *Aspremont* (Summary in *Hist. litt. de la
> France*, v. xxii, pp. 300–318).

Everything indicates that under the late feudal system a man could raise himself socially by extraordinary talents or by rendering a signal service to those to whom he was nominally subject. Warnings against such presumption would naturally be uttered by those jealous of social and political encroachment ; but these warnings did not stem the tide of advance of the *people* into prominence.

We maintain, however, that the introduction of these heroes of the middle and lower classes was due to something more than to social and political encroachment from below. In many cases the *trouvères* were conscious literary artists and had a clear conception of how to obtain an artistic effect. It is incredible that it should have been otherwise in a *genre* which reigned supreme for over a century and then shared the popularity of the *romans d'aventure* for a century and a half more.   To keep abreast of popular demands in a period of changing taste, innovations were necessary.   There is every reason to believe that the introduction of these vulgar heroes dates from an early period, the purpose being to vary the monotony of the recital and to effect a contrast with the eternally recurring type of feudal and chivalric hero.   That this innovation was fostered by the contemporary rise of the *bourgeoisie* into prominence is certain.   But it seems equally certain that this type of the popular hero possessed from the outset of our period a literary value which the *trouvères* exploited more and more as time went on.   There need be no surprise at finding, in the quotations that follow, the heroic and the burlesque side by side.   For, as Guessard has said : "Le principe de la séparation des genres, si fort contesté de nos jours, était, selon toute apparence, inconnue du moyen âge, et lorsqu'il était appliqué, c'était pour ainsi dire, par la force des choses."[1]   At an early date in the French epic literature there was a modest revolt against the perfect hero, whether epic or romantic.   The changing public was doubtless gratified with an occasional Galopin, Raynouart or Robastre, because these figures, more real themselves, are the incarnation of the real and the practical,—the expression of the Sancho Panza there is in every man who would, in his best moments, be a Don Quixote.

The first sign of humor in the grim poem of *Garin et Begon* is presented by Menuel Galopin, whose very name puts him without the pale of heroism.   It is Hervi who finds this pot-house cousin of Begon :

> "Iluec trouva Menuel Galopin
> Les le tonnel, en sa main trois dés tint
> Et trois putains, tels estoient ses délis ;

---

[1] Vid. Préface of *Aliscans*, p. lxi.

> Quatre ribaus ont les mustiaus rostis.
> Hervis le voit, si l'a à raison mis :
> 'Et Diex te saut! Menuel Galopin!'
> Et il respont : 'Diex bénéie ti!
> Venez séoir et si getez au vin.'
> Et dit Hervis : 'Onques por ce n'i vins ;
> Begues vous mande, vostre germains cousins,
> Vos parens est, ne li devez faillir.'
> Dist Menués : 'Onques ne m'apartint,
> Je n'ai mestier de si riche voisin ;
> Mieus aims taverne et le soulas dou vin,
> Ces demisieles que vous véez par ci,
> Que je ne fais duchés à maintenir.'"
> *Li Romans de Garin le Loherain*, vol. ii, pp. 99, 100.

It is only with the greatest trouble that Hervi can rouse this reprobate, whose figure would be sympathetic and familiar to even a feudal audience.

When the bastard sons of Hugh Capet meet by chance in the tavern at Senlis, they fall to discussing the reception which their father will give them. One of them predicts that each will receive a comfortable berth and reserves for himself that of *boutillier* :

> "'Je ly demanderay cez clez de sen cellier,
> Car c'est trez bon office que d'estre boutillier.'"
> *Hugues Capet*, p. 101.

When they arrive at Paris, one of the brothers, more practical, suggests the advisability of attending to the inner man before embarking on any other enterprises :

> "'Alons nous desjuner par amour tout devant,
> Car sachiez que ly cuers me va de fain faillant,
> Et je n'ay mie apris certez à juner tant.
> Il n'est si bon' armeure que de ce vin friant
> Et de cez patez là qui vont souez flairant.
> Allez où il vous plaist, car, par Saint Guineman,
> Ains seray desjunez que voise plus avant ;
> Car qui aroit vestu lez armez roy Priant
> Et s'éuist fain et soif, ne vauroit il ung gant. . . .
> Signeurs, ce dist Richiers, par le Verge absollue,

Une deffaute au cuer m'est maintenant venue
Qu'il convient vrayement que je boive et menjue.
J'oy grant presse laiens, le vendenge y est drue ;
On se doit desjuner à premiere venue.' ''

Id., p. 103.

The same contrast of the heroic and practical is amusingly illustrated in *Aspremont,* where the young Roland and
his boy-companions beg the *portier* to let them out of Laon
to join the Christian army as it marches past. The *portier*
takes no interest in their proposals, for he is satisfied with
his own uneventful existence :

> '' 'Tassiez vous, losengier,
> Je n'ai que faire que soie chevaliers,
> Car on i boute moult laidement et fiert ;
> Je aim moult miels caiens le sommillier ;
> Fors vous garder, n'ai soing d'autre mestier,
> Car l'arcevesque m'en dona bon loier.
> N'en isterez, laissiez vostre plaidier.
> Alez deduire laiens en cel vergier,
> De vos faucons pensez d'aplenoier.' ''

Aspremont in *Hist. litt. de la France,*
v. xxii, pp. 300–318.

It is not surprising after this self-satisfied declaration that
the *portier* falls a victim to the blows of these ambitious
young knights. We may recognize in the scene the two
philosophies, that of the ideal, and that of the material.

There are, however, two popular heroes, whose operations
are not confined to a single scene, but who share the honors
of an entire poem : Rainouart and Robastre. It is impossible to relate here all the achievements of these grotesque
creatures who came to jostle such heroes as Guillaume
d'Orange and Gaufrey in the popular interest. Just enough
will be said to indicate their complexion and their artistic
value.

Rainouart,[1] who first appears in *Aliscans* at verse 3140,

[1] For an extended analysis of his rôle, vid. Gautier, *Epopées,* iv, devoted to
the *geste de Guillaume.*

has been bought by Louis of some merchants. Thus, he
was only a Saracen captive and served in the royal kitchen
as cook's boy. His gigantic proportions and unconventional
manners at once distinguish him. He devours the king's
dinner without ceremony, punishes summarily the cooks who
worry him, and is, in short, an *enfant terrible*. From the
moment that Rainouart sees Guillaume at the court, he is
fascinated by this noble man. From this time begins,
though slowly, his moral awakening. He begs to join
Guillaume's expedition against the Saracens. He gets
drunk, however, on the eve of the departure, and has to
follow as best he can armed only with his *tinel*,[1] the conventional weapon of this type of hero. Having rejoined
the army, he is unmanageable for all save Guillaume and
his niece Aelis. He is inseparable from his *tinel* and rejoices
in his self-confidence. One night when he is drunk again,
they jestingly tell him that he should go with them to
Aliscans. His confident answer, with the tenacity of a
drunken man for one idea, is perfect :

> " ' Par foi molt le desir ;
> Et moi et aus laissiés moi convenir,
> Mais ke mon tinel aie.' "
>
> *Aliscans*, 4324–26.

Drunk again the night before the army leaves Orange,
Rainouart forgets his *tinel*. It has to be fetched for him in
a cart ; once again in possession of it, he is content :

> " En la quisine va Rainouars couchier
> Joste le fu, dalés i. grant brasier.
> De son tinel a fait son oreillier ;
> Adont s'en dort à aise."
>
> *Id.*, 4750–53.

His moral aspect changes, as he moves now in better society.

---

[1] Such a club, variously called *tinel, massue, cuignie* is the conventional
weapon of the *vilain* in mediaeval court poetry.

In defeat he compels the coward leaders to return to the battle. When the French are hard pressed, it is he who is the strength of the Christian forces :

> "Mien ensientre, n'en peust i. escaper
> Se Diex ne fust et Rainouars li ber,
> Ki en fist grant machacle."
>
> *Id.*, 5687–89.

The height of fun is reached when Rainouart tries to mount a horse. One can imagine how this description would amuse an audience of people who spent much of their time in the saddle :

> "Del chevaucher n'estoit pas costumiere,
> De la cuisine connoist mielz la fumiere.
> Quant du monter, ainz n'i quist estriere,
> Saut en la sele tot ce devant deriere,
> Devers la queue a tornée sa chiere.
> Et li chevas s'en fuit comme levriere
> Tot contreval, parmi une bruiere."
>
> *Id.*, 6154–60.

After a temporary rupture with Guillaume when he thinks he has been insulted, Rainouart returns to Orange where he is recognized as the brother of Guibourc, sometime the Saracen princess Orable. He still prefers the kitchen and stables to the great hall, *car forment li anoie*. When Guillaume wishes to baptize him and indulges in quite a sermon upon the subject, Rainouart raises a laugh by exclaiming :

> " 'Sire Guillames qui savés de sermon,
> Vous déusiés avoir un pelichon
> Lonc traïnant desci ke au talon,
> Et puis le froc, el chief 'le caperon,
> Les grandes botes forrées environ,
> Et le chief rés et corouné en son,
> Et sesisiés tous dis sor un leson,
> En cel moustier fesisiés orison,
> Et éusiés à mangier à fuison
> Blans pois au lart, formage de saison,
> A la foïe pitance de poison.' "
>
> *Id.*, 7885–95.

When he is baptized it takes eleven men to lift him in and out of the font. Then he is knighted and marries Aelis, the king's daughter. Thus, in mere outline, we have assisted at the moral and social uplift of this brute of a kitchen-boy to high honors, fit to be placed with Guillaume and Godfrey in Dante's Paradise (*Par.*, XVIII, 46).[1]

This second part of *Aliscans* presents only a marked case of this spirit of fun entering the serious heroic poems. Many less conspicuous examples of the same tendency are noticeable in the later poems. Guessard points out rightly that the solemn tone of the *Roland* is an almost unique exception to the generality of the poems, which introduce comic features into the epic material.[2] Our own idea for *Aliscans*, as for the whole body of the epic poems, is that the purity of the heroic spirit originally native to such poetry was early contaminated by this laughter-provoking *esprit gaulois*. The poems as we have them do not represent the original spirit of heroic poetry. All show the mark of the later age in which the extant versions were invented or made over. The comic and grotesque element, though foreign to the primitive spirit of the French epic, is a common adjunct of it in the poems as they stand to-day.

Less interesting than Rainouart, because less natural, is Robastre, who figures in the *geste* of Doon de Maience. He is to be found in *Doon de Maience*, in *Gaufrey*, and in *Garin de Montglane*. He is introduced well on in the narrative of the first of these poems as a great, honest, merry fellow, a follower of Garin's who must have his own way, and who puts himself at the services of the Christians against the pagan *Danois*. He is at once less interesting to us because

---

[1] Two late poems, *Loquifer* and *Moniage Rainouart*, continue the story of Rainouart in comic vein. Cf. G. Paris, *Litt. du moyen âge*, 2nd ed., pp. 68, 69.

[2] Vid. Préface of *Aliscans*, pp. lxi f.

born in unnatural circumstances.[1] Hence, his prodigious deeds savor rather of *féerie* than of the comic. He is as independent and confident with his *cuignie* as is Rainouart with his *tinel* (*Doon de Maience*, p. 248). In *Gaufrey* we are warned at the outset that this Robastre is to be one of the central figures. After outlining the subject of the poem, how the Saracen king Gloriant harassed Doon and Garin, the poet adds:

> "Et si comme Robastre en prist puis vengement,
> Et comme il ochist puis le fort roi Gloriant."
>
> *Gaufrey*, p. 9.

In another place the poet relates how this Robastre was the son of a *luiton* Malabron,[2] who like the Celtic fairies has the power to change his form. This fairy father stands by Robastre in the numerous adventures wherein he distinguishes himself. Gautier, in speaking of Robastre's rôle in *Garin de Montglane* where he is the hero of the siege, says: "Il représente la force corporelle et sans intelligence au service d'une bonne cause."[3]

The conclusion to which one is led as regards these individual heroes of the Rainouart-Robastre type is that they were introduced for the sake of contrast, and incidentally to please a certain class of persons in the mediæval audience. They have certainly their value from this point of view, and still serve to-day to break the monotony of the conventional narrative of *hauts faits d'armes* performed with sword and lance. Even in the *Chanson d'Antioche* we find Peter the Hermit representing the rough element in the crusade as contrasted with the gentle mien and orderly

---

[1] Vid. *Doon de Maience*, p. 249, which recalls the fairy origin of characters in the Breton poems. Cf. *Yvain* (ed. Förster), 5269–73.

[2] *Gaufrey*, p. 161. Cf. Osterhage, *Ztsch. für rom. Phil.*, xi, pp. 1–21.

[3] *Epopées*, iv, p. 148.

equipment of the French knights. The man with a plain club is a positive relief!

Enough has been said to prove the importance of these *bourgeois* and unnoble types in the *chansons de geste*, whether they be regarded in a mass as in the passage from *Aiol*, or as individuals. They represent a spirit originally foreign to this poetry, but which, under the strain of social changes and the consequent demand for literary variety, necessarily gained in importance until it became one of the causes of the decline of the *genre* into vulgar commonplace.

NOTE.—Throughout the French epic poems the Lombards are ridiculed for their cowardice. They so appear in *Gaufrey*, pp. 186, 268 ; *Chevalerie Ogier de Danemarche*, vv. 916, 4980 ; *Hervis von Metz*, vv. 1410–13, 2520–21 ; *Girart de Viane*, p. 23 ; *Aymeri de Narbonne*, 3440–45 : *Les Narbonnais*, 1608–11 ; *Renaut de Montauban*, p. 231. G. Baist (*Zeitsch. für rom. Phil.*, ii, 303–306) attributes their reputation for cowardice to jealousy of the rise of the Lombard cities in the twelfth century. He cites passages in which the Lombards are represented as fighting against snails, a curious notion upon which Adolph Tobler has thrown light (*Zeitsch. für rom. Phil.*, iii, 98–102) by quoting a passage from Giovanni Villani (ix, 110). The passages referred to indicate that the cowardice of the Lombards was a widespread joke. Of the character and flavor of this mediaeval communal humor Dr. F. B. Gummere says : "It was a thing not of individuals but of classes, guilds, cities, towns, villages, countries,—collective altogether." (*Beginnings of Poetry*, p. 160.)

THE SARACENS.

No proof of the important part played by the Saracens in the epic poetry is needed. There are barely half a dozen poems out of some two score in which the Saracens under one of their divers captions do not enter. Since the French epic poetry and the Italian court epic inspired by it contain the only considerable popular reference we have to the Saracens in Western Europe outside of Spain, it will be worth while to account for their presence in French tradition before going further.

The historical basis for the conflicts between Christians and Saracens in France is as follows.[1] The first invasion of Spain and of the region about the Eastern end of the Pyrennees dates from 711 ; but this first invasion left no permanent traces on French soil. More important, though unsuccessful, was the siege of Narbonne by the Saracens in 721. Established in Spain, however, and as yet undisturbed by intestine strife, the following years saw frequent raids of the Saracens into French territory. According to Arab writers Arles was attacked about 730. These raids were swift and destructive. The Saracens burned and pillaged everywhere, rifling monasteries and convents. Meanwhile, the Saracen khalif was preparing a more serious invasion of France. When in 732 the Infidels crossed the frontier in great numbers, Eudes was unable to stop them at the Dordogne. They penetrated as far as Tours before Charles Martel, defender of the weak Chilpéric II, could get to meet them. The battle was fought between Tours and Poitiers and was decisive ; for the schism in Barbary and the consequent intestine strife in Spain prevented the organization of any subsequent invading force on an equally grand scale. Charles Martel was succeeded by Pepin as Mayor of the Palace. From 752 to 759 the latter was in the South, where he succeeded in winning back Narbonne which the Saracens had captured some time before. It is to be noted that Narbonne, on account of its maritime importance, is as prominent in the historical as it is in the legendary account of these wars. The important date of the fall of Narbonne closes the first period of Saracen conquest as conceived by Reinaud. It had been one of high hope to the Saracens, of expectation and determination to win the rich kingdom of the Franks.

[1] Cf. Reinaud, *Invasions des Sarrasins en France;* E. Mercier, *La bataille de Poitiers,* &c. in *Revue hist.,* Mai, 1878 ; L. von Ranke, *Weltgeschichte* v. Theil, i, ii, Abtheilung ; L. Gautier, *Epopées,* iv. p. 84 f.

The second period is less rosy for the Saracens, who are now a prey to the process of disintegration and disaffection. It was the rivalry among certain Saracen chiefs in Spain that accounts for Charlemagne's expedition in 778. His aid had been called for by certain Saracen ambassadors at Paderborn in 777 in favor of their cause. Pampelune was taken by siege, but Saragossa resisted (cf. *Roland*), and Charlemagne was called back to the Rhine by a fresh Saxon insurrection instigated by Witikind. During the retreat occurred the incident developed in the *Roland* and of which Eginhard has left us a brief description. L. von Ranke points out that in spite of the numerous negotiations and frequent contact between Christians and Saracens, especially as represented in Charlemagne and Haroun-al-Raschid, in reality no permanent good feeling was possible. Religious motives were at the bottom of the hostility,—a permanent stumbling-block in the way of peace.

The Saracens were, in fact, recruiting their forces at this time, and invaded the South of France in 793. Charlemagne was near the Danube at the time, and Guillaume, Count of Toulouse, led the Christian army at the disastrous battle of Villedaigne. But the Saracens were ultimately forced across the mountains, and in 801 even Barcelona was regained by the Christians.

It was not until after Louis' death that the Saracens and Normans alike profited by the divisions in the Empire to renew their piratical invasions of French soil. In 846 the Saracens were before Rome, while their devastating hordes a century later penetrated into Lombardy, Provence, and even Savoy. Popular uprisings, in which St. Bernard figured prominently,[1] in the Dauphiné and in Provence finally expelled the Saracens, and after 1050 their operations were

[1] Cf. *Le Mystère de S. Bernard de Menthon* (ed. Lecoy de la Marche, Paris, 1888), Introd., pp. ix–xii.

confined to piracy on the high seas, a trade originally totally foreign to this people of the desert.

After this brief review of the historical conflicts between the Saracens and the French in the early centuries of the French monarchy, we are better able to account for the omnipresence of the Saracen type in the *chansons de geste.*

There is no doubt that at least the older epic poems rest upon lost heroic songs which treated, in the fashion of communal poetry, episodes in the military history of the nation and its chiefs. After the Franks had become assimilated with the Christian Gallo-Roman population and were ready to devote their freshly aroused enthusiasm to this defense of the Christian faith, there was one series of conflicts in which, above all, their enthusiasm was called into play. The Saracens seem to have been considered the especial charge of the French. It was the inhabitants of the territory comprised in Cæsar's Gaul and in the *Provincia romana* who formed the bulwark against the Southern invasion of the Unbelievers. Judging from its after-effects, it is reasonable to suppose that the full significance of that check which the Saracens received at Tours from Charles Martel was perfectly realized by the national poets. In spite of Huns, Saxons and Normans, who at different times troubled the borders of the kingdom, it was the Saracens who continue to represent the typical enemy, the uncompromising foe of the true God and of the French warriors alike. For the French feudal audience the only conflict worth telling about is that between the French under the great Emperor Charlemagne and the Saracens. For the French epic is essentially a war epic, in which difference of religion furnishes the *motif.* The idea of a strife between two peoples of different religion seems to have been originally inherent in the French epic. As Gaston Paris has put it: " La grande idée qui a présidé à la formation de notre épopée . . . . peut se définir ainsi ; la lutte de

9

l'Europe chrétienne contre les Sarrasins sous l'hégémonie de
la France." [1]   Basing itself upon historical facts, popular
tradition singled out the Saracens to represent the permanent
enemies of the French.   Stray local traditions may account
for a poem in which are narrated deeds which have nothing
to do with the real Saracens.   But so great was the tendency
toward assimilation and absorption that Jean Bodel, writing
toward the end of the twelfth century his *Chanson des
Saisnes,* fell quite naturally into the habit of calling these
northern pagans *Sarrasins.* [2]   Down to the very close of our
period there are two great camps of personages : the Christians
and the *Sarrasins.*

All the types that we have treated thus far have belonged
in the Christian ranks ; we have now to deal with the Saracens, and see to what literary use they were put by the
authors of the extant poems.   That old uncompromising
bitterness of the *Roland* will be found to have largely disappeared.   As time passed, the vividness of the eighth and
ninth century conflicts must have faded.   The twelfth century witnessed a fresh contact between the old enemies.
Under different circumstances and in far more romantic
surroundings the French knight now met his opponent,—
quite civilized, but still professing the hated faith.   Resisting
a foreign invader at Tours was a different matter from a
courteous exchange of hostilities at Acre and Jerusalem.
What effect the comparatively refined contact had upon the
Saracens depicted in the *chansons de geste,*—upon the epic
Saracens,—will be seen in the following pages.   It is important to recollect, in this connection, that the Saracens as

---

[1] *Hist. poét. de Charlemagne,* p. 16.

[2] So also are the Saxons spoken of in *Ogier de Danemarche;* the Normans
in *Aquin* (vid. Nyrop, p. 109) and in *Le Roi Louis,* where they are called
ceus d'Islande; the Danes in *Chron. de Phil. Mouskes;* the Albigenses in
Garin de Montglane.

we find them in most of the epic poems are not the Saracens of Charlemagne's time. Nowhere in the poems that have come down to us do we find a perfect echo of that barbarian shock of arms with its accompanying slaughter that took place in 732. As regards even the *Roland*, the general truth of the remark made seventy years ago is evident: "La guerre contre les Mussulmans est uniquement considérée sous le point de vue des croisades. Malgré ce qui leur reste encore de dur et de barbare, les héros de Roncevaux sont en tout de véritables chevaliers, tels que les avaient faits les premières croisades : ce ne sont plus les féroces compagnons de Charlemagne." [1] The *Roland* offers the most naïve, the most primitive picture of this Christian-Saracen contact. But relations are already refined, the warriors are already delicate and courteous to such a degree that the tone of chivalry is already foreshadowed.

Thus, the crusades brought fresh life to the old poetry, while they changed its spirit. The Saracens still figured in great prominence. But increased familiarity produced less hatred, less bitterness, more respect. Consider the experience of any individual French *chevalier* who took part in the twelfth century crusades. Not only were his eyes opened in the East to a new world of oriental magnificence far exceeding his own, but he was inevitably thrown into personal relations with Infidels who were not a whit behind him in dignity, bravery and courtesy. There were fair maidens, too, usually princesses indeed, who held the Christian knight enthralled, and who gave an air of amorous adventure and romance to the expedition perhaps so prayerfully undertaken. It will be seen, then, what consequences followed upon the continued prominence of the Saracens. The following pages will show them alternately as the

---

[1] H. Monin, *Dissertation sur le Roman de Roncevaux* (Paris, 1832), p. 87.

worthy antagonists of the Christian knights, as a laughing-stock introducing the comic element, as the romantic
characters surrounded by an exotic perfume which often
served to turn the head of the French *chevalier*. But
throughout the religious distinction is maintained. Faith
is the touchstone.[1] There are certain limits which religion
interposes, and these limits are respected.

This difference in religion is a very important item when
the poet is describing a Saracen hero. It will be remembered
that the Christian heroes already in the *Roland* are imbued
with the spirit of a Richard Cœur de Lion or a Godefroi de
Bouillon, embodying the chivalric code of faith, courage and
loyalty. A feudal audience could not conceive a hero who
was faithless to these ideals. Even the Saracen hero, then,
was distinguished from his Christian prototype only by his
religion. The familiar cry of the *trouvère* in despair is
repeated throughout all the epic poems. No higher expression can be given to his admiration for a Saracen warrior
than this :

> "Deus ! quels vassals, s'oüst chrestientet ! "
>
> *Roland*, 3164.

It is quite unnecesrary to insist upon the type of Saracen
hero represented in the *Roland*. Barring the difference in
religion, King Marsile is a miniature Charlemagne, and
Blancandrin and Ganelon as they ride along together are in
congenial company. In their essential traits and in their
ethical code Christians and Saracens are identical. Nevertheless, the *trouvères* made good use of the unbelieving
Saracens for other purposes. When there is need of any
local color, of any exotic or grotesque element, it is the
Saracens who do duty. Upon a foundation of fact the
trouvères developed a conventional superstructure of which

---

[1] Cf. Johann Alton in *Ausgaben und Abhandlungen*, No. 9, p. 29.

the following passages give us an idea.   Note in the *Roland*
the naïve description of

> " Ethiope, une terre maldite ;
> La neire gent en ad en sa baillie,
> Granz unt les nes e lées les orilles,
> E sunt ensemble plus de cinquante milie." [1]
>
> *Roland*, 1916–19.

Or again of the scene—

> " Quant Rollanz veit la cuntredite gent,
> Qui plus sunt neir que nen est arremenz,
> Ne n'unt de blanc ne mais que sul les denz. "
>
> *Id.*, 1932–34.

So also much later, in *Les Narbonnais*, the same conventional
trait is forthcoming :

> " ' Granz ont les cors et noirs com arrement,
> Longues eschines et cortes par devant.
> Les eulz ont roges come charbon ardant,
> Les groinz aguz et les danz bien tranchanz
> (Pire est lor mordres que i n'est d'un sarpant),
> Tetes menues et les oreilles granz.' "
>
> *Les Narbonnais*, 3803–08.

This grotesque trait in the portrayal of the African type
will be met again, applied to individuals, as also that other
scene often repeated by the *trouvères*, in which the Saracens
show their violent disgust for their own gods.   This latter
procédé, as old as the destruction of the gods of Baal, could
never have failed to divert a Christian audience.   When
Marsile returns wounded after his defeat at the hands of
Charles, Bramimunde the queen and with her *plus de xxx
milie humes* make a sudden raid upon their faithless gods and
images :

---

[1] Cf. also *Roland*, 979–983, for the country of Valneire whence comes
Chernuble.

"Ad Apolin current en une crute,
Tencent à lui, laidement les despersunent . . . .
Puis si li tolent sun sceptre e sa curune,
Par mains le pendent desur une culumbe,
Entre lur piez à terre le tresturnent,
A granz bastuns le batent e defruissent.
E Tervagan tolent sun escarbuncle,
E Mahumet enz en un fosset butent,
E porc e chien le mordent e defulent." [1]

Roland, 2580–91.

This is simple farce, and has no other object than to hold
up to ridicule the gods in whose images the Saracens, so
sensible in most respects, are foolish enough to place their
trust.   It is a common resort of the poets when they wish to
raise a laugh.   The coarse joke practised upon Macaire in
Aiol (9630 f.) has already been referred to in a previous
chapter.   This childish impatience at the failure of their gods
to give them material help is frequently observed.   It is the
counterpart of the firm belief that the God of the Christians
is a God of battles and a very present help in time of
trouble.   Thus in *Fierabras* one disgusted Saracen cries out:

" ' Lor diex veille pour aus, moult les a bien gardez ;
Mais li nostre dieu sont caitif et enivré :
Ne se pueent aidier pieça ne furent né.' "

Fierabras, p. 113.

Again the *amiral* Balant is so disgusted with the success of
Charles' advance that he curses his gods:

"Une machue voit, à ii. mains l'a saisie,
Tous dervés vint courant à la mahommerie,
iii. cos en a donné Mahomet lés l'oïe,
La teste li pechoie et le col li esmie."

Id., p. 156.

After one of the battles in *Mainet* as many as ten thousand

---

[1] For this vulgar tradition of Mahomet's death vid. *Floovant*, 373 ; *Gaufrey*,
3582 ; *Couronnement de Louis*, 846 ; *Conquête de Jérusalem*, 5546 ; *Aiol*, 10090.
(Cf. D' Ancona in *Giornale storico della Lett. ital.*, xiii, pp. 199–281.)

Syrians are baptized Christians after having had sad experience of the inefficacy of their gods, their reason being:

> " ' Car li dieus ou il crot est et bons et honestes
> Qui les honors li done et maintient et gouverne,
> Et fait croistre les blés, raverdir la verde herbe :
> Mahons et Tervagant ne valent une astele ;
> Qui les croit et aoure bien en doit honis estre. . . .
> Fai nos baptisier, sire, crestien volons estre,
> Et si creons en Diu le glorious celestre
> K'en Belleem fu nés de le virge pucele.' "
>
> Mainet, vid. Romania, iv, p. 330.

So much for the semi-grotesque light in which the populace
loved to regard the idolatry of the Saracens.   Like Vergil,[1]
Mahomet suffered a somewhat different treatment in the
Middle Age at the hands of the clerks and of the popular
poëts.   D'Ancona[2] and Renan[3] have written interesting
pages upon this development of the ecclesiastical and popular legend of Mahomet.   Renan thus sums up the various
phases in which the Prophet appears in the mediæval
writers : "Mahomet fut à la fois un sorcier, un infâme
débauché, un voleur de chameaux, un cardinal qui, n'ayant
pu réussir à se faire pape, inventa une nouvelle religion
pour se venger de ses collègues."[4]

The faith of the Saracens, however, was not always a
subject for jest.   By opposing warriors in battle, the comparative merits of the two religions are freely discussed, and
the Saracen is neither slower nor less eloquent than his
Christian rival in coming to the defense of his gods.   These
wordy encounters, out of place as they usually are in a battle
scene, none the less indicate the absorbing interest taken in
this question of religious faith.   Paltry and petty as his

---

[1] Cf. Comparetti, *Virgilio nel medio evo.*
[2] *Loc. cit.*
[3] *Etudes d'histoire religieuse,* 2nd. ed.
[4] Renan, *op. cit.*, p. 224.

reasonings are, owing to the ignorance of the *trouvères*, more
than once the Saracen carries off the palm of eloquence.
The following passages will illustrate the preoccupation of
the *trouvères* with this question of religious difference. *Le
Couronnement de Louis* offers one of the best of these battlefield controversies. We are here with Guillaume and the
Christian army before Rome, whither they have been summoned by the pope to defend him against King Galafre and
the Saracens. It is finally agreed that instead of a general
battle the giant Corsolt shall represent the Saracens, while
Guillaume shall represent the cause of the *sire al chaperon
large,* as Galafre wittily styles the pope. The scorn of
Corsolt for the God of the Christians is Miltonic in its
grandeur :

> " ' Quant je la sus ne puis Deu guerreier,
> Nul de ses omes ne vueil ça jus laissier,
> Et mei et Deu n'avons mais que plaidier :
> Meie est la terre et siens sera li ciels.' "
> *Couronnement de Louis,* 534–537.

In reply to Corsolt's insulting words Guillaume retorts :

> " ' Que Mahomez, ce sevent plusor gent,
> Il fu profetes Jesu omnipotent ;
> Si vint en terre par le mont preechant.
> Il vint a Mesques trestot premierement,
> Mais il bu trop, par son enivrement,
> Puis le mangierent porcel vilainement.
> Qui en lui creit il n'a nul buen talent.' "
> *Id.,* 847–853.

Similarly in *Aliscans* it is the adversary of Guillaume who
voices the same conviction that the Christians' God has
nothing to do with terrestrial affairs :

> " ' Diex est lassus deseur le firmament ;
> Il n'a chà jus de terre plain arpent,
> Ains est Mahon à son commandement.
> Iciex nous done et l'orage et le vent ;
> Lui doit on croire et faire son talent.' "
> *Aliscans,* 1223–27.

That model of Saracen knighthood Karahuel, in *Enfances Ogier*, after he becomes the bosom friend of Ogier still obstinately refuses to turn Christian. As they ride along together a pretty scene shows the two warriors discussing the faith to which each will remain true in his own way. Karahuel fully understands the position of Ogier :

> " ' J'oi bien que vous pensés,
> Miex vorriez estre par pieces decoupés
> Que li vos Diex fust de vous adossés.'
> 'Voir, dist Ogiers, ce est certainetés.' "
>
> *Enfances Ogier*, 4453–56.

In response to the efforts made to convert him, Karahuel thanks the Christians but cannot be moved :

> "Ains leur a dit Sarrazins remanra
> Tout son vivant et Sarrazins morra. "
>
> *Id.*, 7118–19.

More fiery and ending in the swift death of the Saracen king Florian, is the interview between him and Aiol (*Aiol*, 10080–98). Finally, in *Chevalerie Ogier de Danemarche*, after Ogier and his Saracen adversary have blackguarded each other and their respective gods, the Saracen says :

> " ' Fols ! que c'est qe tu dis ?
> Ja ne querrai nul jor que soie vis
> En vostre Deu que penèrent Juis ;
> Il te tuèrent, puis ne fu surrexsis :
> Ki en lui croit, il ert plus faus que bris,
> Tos ses pooirs ne vaut deus parisis.' "
>
> *Chevalerie Ogier*, 11316–21.

In these disputes the point to notice is that each party seizes upon the weakest point in the sacred personage that his opponent is defending. Thus, the Saracens emphasize the ignominious death of Christ upon the Cross ; to which the Christian retorts, while granting the mission of the Heaven-sent Prophet, that Mahomet dissipated his energies in riotous living and died a drunkard. In truth, D'Ancona[1] brings out the interesting fact that in the opinion of the Middle Age Mahometanism was a heresy of Christianity, the resemblance discovered between the New Testament and the Koran by the Christian scholars being considered to indicate that the latter was a surreptitious corruption of the former.[2]

From the vigor of the individual attempts at conversion some idea has been gained of the religious fervor which attended in the popular mind these racial conflicts. The same vigor is remarked in dealing with the masses of the Saracen armies. When they are defeated no quarter is given unless they consent to be baptized. This wholesale conversion and baptism of Saracens, in which the number of converts handled at one time fills us with amazement, is a constantly naïve feature of their portrayal in the epic poems. In the *Roland* when Charles has won the battle and taken Saragossa :

> "A mil Franceis fait bien cercer la vile,
> Les sinagoges e les mahumeries ;
> A mailz de fer, à cuignées qu'il tiendrent,
> Fruissent les murs e trestutes les idles ;
> N'i remaindrat ne sorz ne falserie.
> Li reis creit Deu, faire voelt sun servise,
> E si evesque les eves benéissent.
> Meinent paiens entresqu'al baptistirie.
> S'or i ad cel qui Carle cuntrediet,
> Il le fait pendre o ardeir o ocire.
> Baptiziet sunt asez plus de C. milie
> Veir chrestien, ne mais sul la réine ;
> En France dulce iert menée caitive :
> Ço voelt li reis par amur cunvertisset."
>
> *Roland,* 3661–74.

[1] *Giornale storico, &c.,* xiii, pp. 199–281.

[2] Cf. further G. Schiavo, *Fede e superstizione nell' antica poesia francese* in *Ztsch. für rom. Phil.,* vol. xi ff., and R. Schroeder, *Glaube und Aberglaube in den altfranzösischen Dichtungen,* Erlangen, 1886.

This conquest, followed by conversion of the Unbelievers to the true faith, is the main object in view in the *Roland*. No mercy is shown except to the queen; and the poet hastens to explain that Charles made an exception in her favor because he wished to convert her *par amur*. The same unique condition of peace recurs throughout the epic poems, but with this difference: the sword does not so swiftly descend upon the recalcitrant Saracen; some chance is given to him to reflect and be converted rationally. The women, following perhaps the lead of the *Roland*, are always treated kindly and, after being carried off captive, usually consent to be baptized and to marry the Christian hero. We shall see presently how systematically the romantic Saracen princesses become converted, usually of their own free will. For their scruples, after all, are but skin-deep and never stand in the way of the heart's affections. Note, finally, that poetic justice is uniformly done to every Saracen hero, for whose personality and fate the sympathy of the audience has been aroused, by converting him at the close of the poem. The poet could confer no greater benefit upon his Saracen hero than to depict him as repenting of his obstinate folly and acknowledging the omnipotence of *Damnedieu* as revealed in his suffering Son.

We have seen how completely the religious interest in the epic poetry depended upon the contact of Christian and Saracen. Without the Saracens there would have been no objective point upon which to apply the religious faith and zeal of the all-conquering hosts of Charlemagne. Yet, if one were to consider the *chansons de geste* chronologically, nothing would be more striking than the gradual effacement of the intensely vital religious and warlike spirit before the spirit of romance. We still find the long prayers of the heroes, the interminable descriptions of individual combats between Christian and Saracen. But the spirit has changed,

and these are only the outward finery inherited from the old
songs.   The pessimistic lament of Adenet le Roi, familiar as
it is in the mediæval poets of all classes, is worth quoting in
this connection :

> " En ce roiaume avoit adont tel gent
>   Qui pas n'amoient tant or fin ne argent,
>   Ne nul avoir, k'a guerroier souvent
>   Ceaus qui n'amoient le roi omnipotent,
>   Mais cis usages va or moult malement,
>   Car ce a faire laissent legierement
>   Grant et petit partout coumunaument,
>   Dont c'est pitiez, ce sachiez vraiement,
>   K'es plusours n'a meillour entendement."
>
> *Enfances Ogier*, 7712–20.

Ruteboeuf reproaches his generation in similar strains for
religious inactivity in his *Complainte d' Outremer*.   It is not
surprising, then, to find the Saracens in the late poems presented rather in a grotesque, marvelous or romantic light.
The fierce rudeness of the religious epic being no longer
considered sufficient, other means were taken to stimulate
curiosity and interest.   In the general literary reform of
personages necessitated by the change of ideals regretted by
Adenet and Ruteboeuf, the Saracens of course bore their
part.   The rôle of the Saracens changes from that of the
traditional enemy of Christianity to that of the grotesque or
romantic personage.   This is particularly true of the crusade
cycle.   M. Paul Meyer has written of those " merveilleux
récits, dans lesquels les Sarrasins étaient représentés non plus
comme des mécréants indignes de vivre, mais comme des
émules, parfois comme les auxiliaires des chrétiens." [1]   This
change is partly attributable to the general change in literary
taste in the twelfth century, but more especially as it affected
the Saracens, it is due to the increased familiarity and respect
between the two peoples in the Orient.

---

[1] Vid. *Daurel et Beton*, Préface, p. xx.

As one might expect in popular poetry, the numbers of fighting-men are vastly exaggerated. This is especially true of the Saracens. Jean Bodel expresses the general opinion when he makes Baudouin say of the *Saisnes* (Saracens):

> " 'Sire, dist Baudouins, Saisne ont molt grant foison ;
> N'an savons tant ocire que plus en i trovon.' "
> *Chanson des Saisnes*, v. ii, p. 130.

Very pleasing is the simile in *Anseïs de Carthage* where we are told of the Saracens :

> " Des tentes issent aussi espesement
> Come li pluie, quant le cachent li vent."
> *Anseïs von Karthago*, 6658–59.

The *trouvères* doubtless exaggerated their numbers in order to produce a contrast. The Saracens come down upon Christendom in hordes, and have no less audacious pretensions than the possession of St. Denis and the subjugation of the French. To an audience of the eleventh and twelfth century this audacity could not fail to seem preposterous. In the *Roland* at the council of the Saracen kings, one of them boasts :

> " ' Carles li vielz à la barbe flurie,
> Jamais n'iert jurns qu'il n'en ait doel e ire.
> Jusqu'à un an avrum France saisie,
> Gesir porrum el burc de Seint-Denise. "
> *Roland*, 970–73.

Similarly *Gaufrey*, p. 35 ; *Les Narbonnais*, 3692–94 ; *Aiol*, 4064–72.

In the preceding chapter we noticed certain grotesque traits which belong to the heroes of the Rainouart-Robastre type. Physically different from the latter is the grotesque Saracen type occasionally met. Here there is added an element of awful hideousness. Take the portrait of the giant Corsolt in the *Couronnement de Louis:*

"L'en li ameine le rei Corsolt en pié,
    Lait et anché, hisdos come aversier ;
    Les uelz ot roges com charbon en brasier,
    La teste lee et herupé le chief ;
    Entre dous ueilz ot de lé demi pié,
    Une grant teise de l'espalle al braier ;
    Plus hisdos om ne puet de pain mangier."
                        Couronnement de Louis, 504–510.

So also Tornebeuf in *Aiol* (3983–88) and Tabur in the
Chancun de Willame (3171–75). But the most detailed
portrait is that of the *mal paien Nasier* in *Gaufrey:*

"xiiii. piés avoit en estant l'aversier,
    Et de large ot la toise à i. grant chevalier,
    La teste avoit plus grosse assez d'un buef plenier,
    Et si estoit plus noir que meure de meurier ;
    Les iex avoit plus rougez que carbon en brasier,
    Le cheveus herupés, pongnans comme esglentier ;
    Qui bien l'esgarderoit, bien devroit esragier.
    En une des narines du nés, lés le joier,
    Pourroit on largement un oef d'oue muchier ;
    En sa bouche enterroit i. grant pain de denier ;
    Bien menjast i. mouton tout seul à un mengier ;
    Et je que vous diroie? ch'estoit i. aversier."
                        Gaufrey, p. 90.

Last to make their appearance in a leading part are the
Saracen women. The Saracen maid does not differ essentially from her Christian sister. The *trouvères* were no more
able to imagine a Saracen type of female beauty and charm
distinct from that of the Christian than they were able to
create a Saracen hero who should not be identical with a
Christian chevalier. Yet, the introduction of Saracen women,
in the poems of the thirteenth century especially, is significant. The conviction has already been expressed that the
treatment of the Saracens in the epic poems as we have them
was affected by the contact of the two races in the East rather
than in the West. From the first the Saracens had a place
reserved for them in the conventional scheme of the epic

poets. It was understood that they were to represent the conventional enemies of Christendom. In the early poems we have seen that the feminine element was either totally neglected or relegated to a minor position. Hence, we find only warriors among the Saracens as among the Christians. But the audiences of the late twelfth and thirteenth centuries were no longer satisfied with combats alone and with heroic deeds from which the feminine element was completely absent. The cult of chivalry required that the bravery and devotion of man should be expended and consecrated in favor of some woman.

Given the rôle of the Saracens in this poetry from the outset, it is not surprising to find in the late poems the Saracen women occupying a prominent place. In fact, there was a special reason why it should be so. The change in life and literary taste had introduced in the middle of the twelfth century an interest in romance and adventure, while increased commerce with and knowledge of the Eastern world induced a craving for what the Romantic School has since called *l'exotisme*. To both of these new literary demands a well elaborated episode between a Christian hero and a Saracen princess perfectly responded. How interesting to the unpampered literary taste of the period was an adventure in which the lovers met and wedded under such romantic circumstances! The breach between the old and the new style of *chanson de geste* is very considerable, and the difference depends almost entirely upon the growing importance of woman in the hero's life.

To better realize this, we need only recall the stray references to Saracen princesses in the earliest poems. They are the proper ancestors of the later Flordépine, Floripas and Rosamonde. In the *Roland* all we are told of Bramimunde is that she figured among the prisoners taken by Charles (3680–81). At a later date we should have had

the bravest of the French knights woo and wed her. When
Ganelon has been put out of the way, Charles' mind again
reverts to the captive queen :

> "La baptizierent la réine d'Espaigne,
> Truvet li unt le num de Juliane.
> Chrestiene est par veire conuissance."
>
> *Roland*, 3985–87.

The last verse contains the important information. We are
not told that she married any Christian peer. Again, in the
Voyage de Charlemagne we may consider the daughter of the
Emperor Hugo a Saracen princess for our present purpose.
Oliver wins, to be sure, the love of this Jacqueline ; but no
point is made of it. The poet absolutely fails to develop the
romantic episode. The accomplishment of Oliver's *gab*
(705–726), though not without a certain graceful gallantry,
redounds entirely to his own prodigious valor as a wooer.
The two later passages (822–826; 852–857) in which the
girl is mentioned are strikingly undeveloped.

With these primitive undeveloped portraits of Saracen
women in mind, we can better gauge the significance of their
treatment in the later poems.

It is easy to understand now why the *trouvère* devoted
himself almost exclusively to the Saracen maiden, and to her
as princess. No other type could have consorted with the
type of Christian hero already given. They are all paragons
of beauty, they are usually more forward in their amorous
declarations than we would have them, and they end regularly by being baptized and marrying the hero. In a word,
they may be thus described. But the *trouvère* expended all
his talent upon these foreign beauties ; and to fill out one's
ideas of the *trouvère's* literary skill and of his response to
contemporary taste, one is bound to glance at some of these
Saracen women. It will be seen that they are distinguished
from some of the women described in a preceding chapter
only by their religion.

First among the Saracen women, judging from the charming character elsewhere attributed to her as Guibourc the wife of Guillaume, is Orable.   In the *Prise d'Orange*, composed to throw light upon the early history of Guillaume, there is an early illustration of this shifting of interest from the heroic to the romantic.   Guillaume falls in love with Orable by hear-say[1] and risks his life to see her and talk with her.   It is Orahle who saves Guillaume's life when his ruse is discovered, and protects him until his companions arrive from Nîmes and take the city.   Orable, of course, becomes a Christian and marries Guillaume, according to rule.   It is not hard to see that, though the epic *moule* is preserved, it is the wooing of Guillaume and Orable, not the taking of Orange, that forms the interest of the poem.   The poet was fully aware of the transformation he had wrought in the heroic figure of Guillaume in making him a wooer, when he says:

> " ' L'en soloit dire Guillaume Fièrebrace,
>   Or dira l'en Guillaume l'amiable.
>   En ceste vile par amistié entrastes.' "
>
> *Prise d'Orange*, 1562–64.

No less attractive than Orable is Mirabel, once a Saracen but easily converted under Aiol's tutelage.   Their adventures are of an improbable nature, but the poet has made a very flesh and blood creature of Mirabel.   She is quite remarkable for her virtue, humility, courage and humanity. Like a few other women in this mediæval poetry she was something of a scholar:

> " Ele sut bien parler de xiiii. latins :
>   Ele savoit parler et grigois et hermin,
>   Flamenc et borgengon et tout le sarrasin,
>   Poitevin et gascon, se li vient a plaisir."
>
> *Aiol*, 5420–23.

[1] So Garin with the Christian Mabile in *Garin de Montglane*, and frequently in the *romans d'aventure*.

10

The account of their wanderings together, of their hunger and privations, is well done. It is the more natural because it is Aiol who carries off the. girl, in this case against her will :

> " ' O moi venrés en Franche en la terre garnie,
> Puis vous prendrai a feme, se Dex le me destine.' "
>
> <div align="right"><i>Id.</i>, 5404–05.</div>

Such proximity was likely to produce a change in the young woman's way of thinking; for Aiol was brave and fair :

> " Bien avés oi dire et as uns et as autres
> Que feme aime tost home qui bien fiert en bataille :
> Ele li escria, qu'il l'entent en l'angarde :
> ' Sire, venés vous ent qui preus estes as armes ;
> Por vous querra je Dieu le pere esperitable.' "
>
> <div align="right"><i>Id.</i>, 5596–5600.</div>

And, in fact, a little later (6240–71) she delivers herself of a prayer to *Sire Abraham* which would do credit to a life-long Christian. But Mirabel is human, and the poet is happy in giving the dialogue of the young pair in their destitution :

> " La pucele fu lasse, se li greva li caus ;
> Ele vint a Aiol, si l'en araisona :
> ' Gentieus damoiseus sire, et de moi que sera?
> Je ne mengai her soir ne hui trois jors i a ! '
> ' Bele, che dist Aiols li preus et li loials,
> Ne vos ai que doner, foi que doi saint Tumas !
> Vés la tere gastee et le pais tout ars.' "
>
> <div align="right"><i>Id.</i>, 5622–28.</div>

The close of this long poem, which relates the triumph of an ideal knight over a series of difficulties, shows Aiol and Mirabel and their two sons reunited after years of separation. Then it is that Mirabel, like Guibourc in *Aliscans*, asks her husband if he has been true to her :

> " ' Sire, vous fustes fors de la cartre perine,
> Et Dieus vous en geta, li fiex sainte Marie.
> Vous avés or, je quic, autre feme reprisse,

U vous avés piecha faite novele amie.'
'Bele, che dist Aiols, vous parlés de folie.
Je vous plevis par foi et jure sainte Marie,
Puis que parti de vous, n'oc feme a compaignie.' ''

Id., 10951–57.

Another of the same type is Rosamonde in *Elie de Saint Gille*. Very poetically conceived is the scene in which she first sees and succors the Christian hero Elie. The latter, wearied with fighting against the Saracens, goes with his squire Galopin to rest in an orchard hard by. At daybreak Rosamonde, already more than half disposed to embrace Christianity, is at her balcony breathing in the fresh morning air :

" Rosamonde s'estut sus el palais autor
Et vint a la fenestre por oir la douchour
Des oissellons menus qui chantoient al jor ;
L'euriel et la merle ot chanter sor l'aubor,
Le cri del rousingol, se li sovient d'amor :
'Vrais Dieus, dist la pucele, con tu es presious !
Tu fais croistre les arbres, porter foilles et flors,
Et le blé nous fais sourdre de la terre en amour,
Et en la sainte viergene presis anonsion,
Biaus sire, et sanc et char i presistes por nous.
Aussi con chou est voirs, biaus sire glorious,
Desfendés le Franchois de mort et de prison.' ''

Elie de Saint Gille, 1365–76.

When she catches sight of Elie :

" Tous les degrés avale, si est venue a tere
Et desfreme i. guicet d'une fauce posterne,
Par u ele sieut issir et les soies pucheles,
Quant vient el mois de mai, por colir la florete.
Venue est a Elye qui se pasme sor tere,
Son cief li a lor mis par desous son brac destre,
Puis l'en a apelé la cortoisse puchele :
'Qui es tu chevalier ?' ''

Id., 1404–11.

After Elie has been promptly healed with precious herbs, Rosamonde leads him away to her own apartments where she bathes and dresses him :

"Rosamonde la bele par les flans l'enbracha,
    Sor i. lit l'a asis geteis a cristal ;
    XL. fois li baisse et le vis et la char.
    Cil li guenchi la bouche, que el n'i adesa :
'Galopin, dist Elies, vois quel feme chi a ?
    U roialme de Franche si gente nen avra.'"
                                        Id., 1468–73.

The Saracen princesses are certainly not lacking in vigor
when they have set their mind upon a Christian knight for
their lover. The latter must have possessed every recommendation to have produced such an immediate effect upon
the hearts of those who were separated from them by the
great barrier of religion. In *Gaufrey* the beautiful Flordépine is willing to do anything for the Christians provided
she can win Berart for her lover :

"'Et par la foi que doi nostre Dieu Baraton,
    Se vous povez tant fere que j'aie le baron
    Berart du Mont Didier a la clere fachon,
    (On dit qu'il n'a si bel en Franche le roion),
    Vous serés delivré hors de cheste prison,
    Que je l'aim si forment, ja ne le cheleron,
    Que pour l'amour de li deguerpiroi Mahon,
    Et si crerrei en Dieu qui souffri passion.'"
                                Gaufrey, pp. 57, 58.

Flordépine will not allow the caresses of her Saracen lover
(pp. 59, 60), for her one idea is to win Berart.

A relief in the tedious poem of *La Prise de Cordres et de
Sebille* is offered by the Saracen princess Nubie who, won by
the beauty of Bertran, plans the delivery of the Christians.
She too will change her faith out of love for her new master :

"'E ! Deus,' dist elle, 'li filz sainte Marie,
    Por vostre amour recevrai baptistire,
    Mais que me rent dan Bertran a delivre.'"
                    La Prise de Cordres et de Sebille, 751–53.

A variation of the conventional situation is Gloriande in
Les Enfances Ogier. She is betrothed to that excellent

Saracen knight Karahuel, the friend of Ogier. We are expecting Gloriande's affections to shift in favor of Ogier. But here Adenet surprises us by keeping Gloriande faithful to her first lover, whom she finally marries (7601–31). And Adenet says that nothing more is surely known of them, but that if ever anyone deserved God's blessing it is this pair of Saracen lovers :

> " Et Diex le vueille par sa douce amisté,
> Et s'il ainc fist gent paienne bonté,
> Plaire li vueille que il d'aus ait pité,
> Car se valoir i povoit loiauté,
> Estre devroient devant Dieu corouné."
>
> *Enfances Ogier*, 7642–46.

Another of the same type as Flordépine is Floripas in *Fierabras*. Here, again, the king's daughter is in league with the Christian knights, whose lives she spares because of her love for Gui de Bourgogne :

> " ' Or voel que tout ensamble vos fois ne plevirés
> Que vous ferés mon boin sans nul point de fauser,
> Et de ce m'aiderés que je vorrai rouver.' "
>
> *Fierabras*, p. 84.

She has no trouble in persuading them to gratify her, since she controls the situation. It is to Roland she speaks of her love for Gui :

> " ' Je aim en douce France i. leger baceler.'
> ' Dame, comment a nom? ' ce dist Rollans li ber.
> Et respont la puciele : 'Ja le m'orrés nommer ;
> Guis a nom de Borgoigne, moult i a bel armé.'
> ' Par mon cief, dist Rollans, à vos ex le véés ;
> N'a pas entre vous deus iiii. piés mesurés.'
> ' Sire, dist Floripas, cel voel quel me donnés.'
> ' Par mon cief, dist Rollans, à vostre volenté.' "
>
> *Id.*, p. 85.

Gui has scruples about engaging his faith without Charles' permission. But Floripas swears by Mahomet :

> " ' Se vous ne me prenés,
> Je vous ferai tous pendre et au vent encruer ! ' "
>
> *Id.*, p. 85.

This argument is conclusive, and Floripas readily consents to be baptized and believe in Jesus (pp. 85, 86). Then she puts her arms about his neck, but does not kiss him :

> " Pour ce k'ele est paiene, il est crestiennés."
>
> *Id.*, p. 86.

This last verse suggests the last observation to be made in regard to the treatment of the Saracen women. However fiery and uncontrollable may appear the passion of a Christian knight for a Saracen woman, or *vice versa*, one rule was generally observed : there is no intercourse between them until the woman has been baptized. Intercourse with an Unbeliever is universally discountenanced. No great inconvenience resulted, however, as the Saracen woman was more than ready to make the slight sacrifice required. It was only necessary to perform the prescribed rites of the Church. The relations of Aiol and Mirabel offer a typical instance. After Aiol has rescued Mirabel and carried her off, the moment of temptation comes. The poet dilates upon the beauty of the maiden as she lay on the greensward beside her lover :

> "Aiols li fieus Elie le prist a regarder,
> Ens en son cuer le prist forment a enamer :
> Ja le vausist baisier s'eust kerstienté,
> Mais por chou qu'ert paiene, ne le vaut adeser :
> La loi au roi Jesu ne voloit vergonder,
> Ançois le voloit faire baptisier et lever,
> Si le prendroit a feme, a mollier et a per."
>
> *Aiol*, 5452–58.

Such a naïvely delicate scene as this shows how vital was the force of religion in controlling the passions and appetites of this age when, in most matters, might made right. Rarely was it that the poets dared to go against this popular demand for continence between persons of different creeds.

An instance of this conviction, though no longer strong enough to be effective, is found as late as the fourteenth century in *Li Bastars de Buillon*. Though Bauduin is already married, the Saracen Synamonde determines to have him for her lover. His reasons for at first resisting her overtures are that he is already married and *que ne doi abiter a dame sarrasine* (2568 f.). The first reason had little effect in these degenerate days of the French epic, and the second scruple is quashed by Synamonde claiming that she is a Christian at heart. This sudden discovery on the part of Synamonde nicely settles the knotty question of conscience, and accounts for the appearance in the crusade cycle of the *Bastart de Buillon*.

But two notable infringements of this law have been remarked. One is in *Anseïs de Carthage* (5031 f.) in a passage similar to that in the *Chanson des Saisnes* (vol. i, p. 107 f.) and in *Beuves de Commarchis* (2680 f.). In all of these the women take the initiative. In *Anseïs de Carthage* it is the very wife of King Marsile who, with her maids, sends at night for the Christian Raimon and two of his knights to come and do their pleasure. This they do, apparently without compunction.

The other case of exception is that in the strange poem of *Huon de Bordeaux*. Here Esclarmonde burns for Huon, this brazen Christian who, in the execution of his orders from Charlemagne, stops at no adventure. At first he is faithful to his conviction:

> " ' Dame, dist Hues, laisiés tot çou ester ;
> Sarrasine estes, je ne vous puis amer.
> Je vous baisai, çou est la verités,
> Mais je le fis por ma foi aquiter,
> Car ensi l'oi à Karlon créanté.
> Se devoie estre tos jors emprisonés
> En ceste cartre tant con porai durer,
> Ne quier jou ja à vo car adeser.' "

> *Huon de Bordeaux*, p. 175.

In spite of this good resolution, the little fairy Auberon
knows Huon's weakness and forbids all intercourse with
Esclarmonde until they shall have been married in Rome
(p. 200). Once on the sea Huon's passions run away with
him, and with his eyes open he sins. Straightway, in accordance with mediæval superstition, a tempest breaks upon the
sea and the two lovers are cast upon a solitary island (p.
202). The poet has tried to excuse this breach of the conventions by an allusion to the all-consuming passion of
Tristram and Iseult. Huon tries to comfort Esclarmonde
thus :

> " 'Acolons nous, se morrons plus soef.
> Tristrans morut por bele Iseut amer,
> Si ferons nous, moi et vous, en non Dé.' "
>
> Id., p. 203.

They do not die ; but many a misfortune comes to Huon for
having disobeyed the advice of Auberon.

To conclude, we have shown that any traditions of the
Saracens in France which may have been current before
the eleventh century, have been completely recolored subsequently by the contact of the two races in the Orient.
Moreover, the poets failed to distinguish perceptibly between
the Christian and the Saracen character. Finally, there is
distinctly traceable a change of function in the Saracen
regarded as a literary type. Coming to view in the *Roland*
as an unbelieving chevalier, the uncompromising enemy of
the Christians' God, he ends by embodying together with his
daughter, the conventional princess, all that the *trouvère*
could imagine of a romantic and exotic nature. In other
words, the Saracens conform to the new literary demand of
the twelfth and thirteenth centuries. No longer exclusively represented as the enemies of the Most High, to be
slaughtered or converted on a grand scale, they are to be
respected and converted if possible, in any case to be met on
equal terms. It is perhaps not too much to say that the

change in the rôle of the Saracens stands for that weakening of the religious conscience and the birth of a more generous humanity which followed upon the crusades in Western Europe.[1]

CONCLUSION.

An attempt has been made in the preceding pages to trace, by simple expository methods, the development which the *chansons de geste* passed through during the period of their greatest popularity. A study of the personages offers, as has been seen, the best opportunity to penetrate the spirit of the poems. For the personages readily group themselves into types. It is especially true of the older poems that "the great emotions and convictions are presented in types and symbols; multitudes of persons are represented by colossal figures, the range and compass of whose lives create an impression of universality."[2]

We have had, then, nothing to prove. The general truth is known in regard to the transformation which took place in the *chansons de geste* as the result of contemporary changes in social, political, and literary ideals. The division of the personages into types is, we believe, original; it is hoped that by this division clearness has been gained in determining how far and in what way the spirit of the national epic was altered.

The value of the *chansons de geste* as literary monuments depends upon their origin, and upon the peculiar society whose ideals they express. Of all the literary currents which contributed to form the distinctive product known as French literature, the *chansons de geste* alone in the

---

[1] Cf. Alfred Nutt, *Celtic and Mediæval Romance,* p. 15.
[2] Hamilton Mabie, *Essays in Literary Interpretation,* p. 1.

Middle Age represent the Teutonic current. Other features of French literature find their sources in the classic
tradition, in the native *gaulois* residue, in the Celtic innovations, as the case may be. The heroic note, the epic note
of self-sacrifice and religious devotion harks back to the
Frankish ancestors of those feudal lords who applauded the
Chanson de Roland. Of Teutonic inspiration, the *chansons
de geste* are yet profoundly national, profoundly French.[1]
They are the vigorous literary assertion of the new nationality formed by the contact of two civilizations. Shaking
itself free from its Germanic *impedimenta*, the French spirit
reveals itself on tip-toe ready to strike out its own course.
To the historian of literature this is the strongest claim for
recognition put forward by the French *chansons de geste.*
In closing we may revert to the words of Gaston Paris
placed at the head of this study : " Le moyen âge forme
un anneau indispensable dans la chaîne de la transmission
littéraire à travers les siècles." [2]

WILLIAM WISTAR COMFORT.

BIBLIOGRAPHY.

TEXTS OF *CHANSONS DE GESTE* READ FOR THIS STUDY.

1. *Aiol.* Pub. par Normand et Raynaud.   Paris, 1877.   Soc. des anciens
     textes.
2. *Aliscans.* Pub. par Guessard et Montaiglon.   Paris, 1870.   Anciens
     Poètes de la France.
3. *Amis et Amiles.* Ed. by Konrad Hofmann. 1st ed. Erlangen, 1852.
4. *La Chanson d'Antioche.* Pub. par Paulin Paris. 2 vols. Paris, 1848.
     Romans des douze Pairs.
5. *Anseïs von Karthago.* Ed. by Johann Alton. Tübingen, 1892. Bibl.
     des litt. Vereins in Stuttgart CXCIV.

---

[1] Cf. Kurth, *Hist. poét. des Mérovingiens,* p. 487.

[2] *Cosmopolis,* September, 1898.

6. *Aquin.* Pub. par F Joüon des Langrais. Nantes, 1880.
7. *Aspremont.* Summary of Paulin Paris in *Hist. litt. de la France*, xxii, 300–318.
8. *Aye d'Avignon.* Pub. par Guessard et Meyer. Paris, 1861. Anciens Poètes de la France.
9. *Aymeri de Narbonne.* Pub. par Demaison. 2 vols. Paris, 1887. Soc. des anciens textes.
10. *La Mort Aymeri de Narbonne.* Pub. par J. Couraye du Parc. Paris, 1884. Soc. des anciens textes.
11. *Li Bastars de Buillon.* Pub. par A. Scheler. Bruxelles, 1877.
12. *Bauduin de Sebourc.* Pub. par Boca. 2 vols. Valenciennes, 1841.
13. *Berte aus grans piés.* Pub. par A. Scheler. Bruxelles, 1874.
14. *Beuves de Commarchis.* Pub. par A. Scheler. Bruxelles, 1874.
15. *Le Charroi de Nîmes.* Fragment pub. by Paul Meyer in *Recueil d'anciens textes, &c.* 2 vols. Paris, 1877.
16. *Li Charrois de Nymes.* Vid. *Guillaume d' Orange.*
17. *La Chanson du Chevalier au Cygne et de Godefroi de Bouillon.* Pub. par C. Hippeau. 2 vols. Paris, 1874.
18. *Le Couronnement de Louis.* Pub. par E. Langlois. Paris, 1888. Soc. des anciens textes.
19. *Daurel et Beton.* Pub. par P. Meyer. Paris, 1880. Soc. des anciens textes.
20. *Doon de Maience.* Pub. par A. Pey. Paris, 1859. Anciens Poètes de la France.
21. *Elie de Saint Gille.* Pub. par Raynaud. Paris, 1879. Soc. des anciens textes.
22. *Fierabras.* Pub. par Kroeber et Servois. Paris, 1860. Anciens Poètes de la France.
23. *Floovant.* Pub. par Guessard et Michelant. Paris, 1858. Anciens Poètes de la France.
24. *Foulque de Candie.* Pub. par Prosper Tarbé. Reims, 1860.
25. *Li Romans de Garin le Loherain.* (Consists of selections from four poems of this cycle. Passages in the text are quoted under this general title.) Pub. par P. Paris. 2 vols. Paris, 1833. Romans des douze Pairs.
26. *Mort Garin le Loherain.* Pub. par E. du Méril. Paris, 1845. Romans des douze Pairs.
27. *Garin de Montglane.* Vid. Analysis of L. Gautier in *Epopées*, 2nd ed., iv, 126–171.
28. *Gaufrey.* Pub. par Guessard et Chabaille. Paris, 1859. Anciens Poètes de la France.
29. *Gaydon.* Pub. par Guessard et Luce. Paris, 1862. Anciens Poètes de la France.
30. *Gérard de Rossillon.* Pub. par F. Michel. Paris, 1856.

31. *Girart de Rossillon* (Ox. MS.) in *Rom. Studien*, 1880.
32. *Girard de Viane.* Pub. par Prosper Tarbé. Reims, 1850.
33. *Gormund et Isembart* (*Le Roi Louis*). Fragment pub. in *Rom. Studien*, 1878.
34. *Gui de Bourgogne.* Pub. par Guessard et Michelant. Paris, 1859. Anciens Poètes de la France.
35. *Guillaume d' Orange* (contains *Couronnement Looys, Li Charrois de Nymes, Prise d' Orange, Li Covenans Vivien, La Bataille d' Aleschans*). Pub. par W. J. A. Jonckbloet. 2 vols. La Haye, 1854.
36. *Hervis von Metz.* Ed. by E. Stengel. Dresden, 1903.
37. *Hugues Capet.* Pub. par La Grange. Paris, 1864. Anciens Poètes de la France.
38. *Huon de Bordeaux.* Pub. par Guessard et Grandmaison. Paris, 1860. Anciens Poètes de la France.
39. *Jourdains de Blaivies*, Ed. by Konrad Hofmann. 1st edition. Erlangen, 1852.
40. *Macaire.* Pub. par Guessard. Paris, 1866. Anciens Poètes de la France.
41. *Mainet.* Fragments pub. by G. Paris in *Romania*, iv, 305–337.
42. *Les Narbonnais.* Pub. par H. Suchier. 2 vols. Paris, 1898. Soc. des anciens textes.
43. *La Chevalerie Ogier de Danemarche.* Pub. par J. Barrois. 2 vols. Paris, 1842. Romans des douze Pairs.
44. *Les Enfances Ogier.* Pub. par A. Scheler. Bruxelles, 1874.
45. *Orson de Beauvais.* Pub. par G. Paris. Paris, 1899. Soc. des anciens textes.
46. *Parise la Duchesse.* Pub. par Guessard et Larchey. Paris, 1860. Anciens Poètes de la France.
47. *La Prise de Cordres et de Sebille.* Pub. par Densusianu. Paris, 1896. Soc. des anciens textes.
48. *Prise d' Orange.* Vid. *Guillaume d' Orange.*
49. *Raoul de Cambrai.* Pub. par Meyer et Longnon. Paris, 1882. Soc. des anciens textes.
50. *Renaus de Montauban.* Ed. by H. Michelant. Stuttgart, 1862. Bibl. des litt. Vereins in Stuttgart, lxvii.
51. *La Chanson de Roland.* Ed. by Müller. 2nd ed. Göttingen, 1878.
52. *La Chanson des Saisnes.* Pub. par F. Michel. 2 vols. Paris, 1839. Romans des douze Pairs.
53. *Li Covenans Vivien.* Vid. *Guillaume d' Orange.*
54. *Les Enfances Vivien.* Pub. par C. Wahlund et Hugo von Feilitzen. Upsala and Paris, 1895.
55. *Voyage de Charlemagne* (*Karls des Grossen Reise, &c.*). Ed. by E. Koschwitz. 3rd ed. Leipzig, 1895.
56. *La Chancun de Willame.* London, 1903.

VIII.—GISMOND OF SALERNE.

This tragedy was presented before Queen Elizabeth by the Gentlemen of the Inner Temple in 1567–8. In its original shape it remained in MS. until published a few years ago in Brandl's *Quellen des weltlichen Dramas in England;* but a recast by Robert Wilmot was printed in 1591 under the title *Tancred and Gismunda* and included in Dodsley's *Collection of Old English Plays.* From the initials appended to each act in this later version it has been concluded that Henry Noel wrote Act II, Christopher Hatton Act IV, and Robert Wilmot Act V; the authors of Act I (Rod. Staf.) and Act III (G. Al.) are as yet unidentified. Before examining the play it will be well to glance at the literary and dramatic influences under which it was produced. A notable beginning in English classical tragedy had been made at the Grand Christmas of the Inner Temple in 1561–2 by the performance of *Gorboduc,* which was repeated before the Queen at Whitehall a few weeks later: an unauthorized edition of the play was printed in 1565. In 1564 the Queen saw at King's College, Cambridge, "a Tragedie named *Dido,* in hexametre verse, without anie chorus," and "an English play called *Ezechias,* made by Mr. Udall." At Christmas, 1564, a tragedy by Richard Edwards (probably *Damon and Pythias*) was acted at Whitehall, and in 1566 his *Palamon and Arcyte* was presented before the Queen in the hall of Christ Church, Oxford, as well as a Latin play, called *Marcus Geminus.* At Gray's Inn the same year Gascoigne's *Supposes* (translated from Ariosto) and the *Jocasta* were performed: the last purported to be taken from Euripides, but was really a translation of Lodovico Dolce's adaptation, itself made probably not from

the Greek but from the Latin.   Dolce adhered in the main
to the model of Seneca, whose tragedies he had translated :
English translations of eight out of the ten had also been
published during the ten years before 1566, so that Elizabethan tragedy came under Senecan influence at first, second,
and third hand.   The learned dramatists of the Inner Temple
no doubt had recourse to the original text, but like their
fellows of Gray's Inn of a year or two before, they turned
to Dolce as their immediate model, and they made an important step in advance by taking their plot from Boccaccio.
It is true that Arthur Brooke in the preface to *The Tragicall
Historye of Romeus and Juliet* (1562) said that he had seen
the same argument "lately set foorth on stage," but the play
referred to is now to be found only at second-hand in a
Dutch version, *Romeo en Juliette,* written about 1630.[1]
Gismond of Salerne is the earliest extant English tragedy
founded upon an Italian novel.

I.

THE DEBT TO BOCCACCIO.

A comparison of the text with that of the First Novel
of the Fourth Day of Boccaccio's *Decamerone* shows that
the English authors went to the original Italian and did not,
as has been hitherto assumed, use the translation in Painter's

[1] I am indebted for this information to Dr. Harold de W. Fuller of Harvard University, whose article on the subject will be found in the July
number of *Modern Philology.*   Hunter (New Illustrations of *Shakespeare,*
II, 130) and Courthope (*History of English Poetry,* IV, 100), suggest that
Brooke referred to a Latin tragedy among the Sloane MSS. in the British
Museum, but Dr. Fuller finds that this was based entirely on Brooke, and was
probably written by a Cambridge student about 1605.   Dr. Fuller thinks that
the English original on which the Dutch play was founded was written about
1560, since, to judge from the Dutch version, it constantly echoed the
phraseology of Boisteau's novel, which was first published in 1559.

Palace of Pleasure, which had just been published. As the play had five authors, it is necessary to establish this point for each act. In the first, little use is made of the original source, the purpose of this act being to present Gismond's grief at the loss of her husband, which Boccaccio does not even refer to, contenting himself with the statement that after a short married life she became a widow, and returned home to her father. But the English tragedian found that a line or two which Ghismonda uses in the original about her lover might be transferred in application to her husband. She says of the soul (*anima*) of Guiscardo : " Io son certa, che ella è ancora quicentro, e riguarda i luoghi de' suoi diletti, e de' miei : e come colei, che ancor son certa, che m'ama, aspetta la mia, dalla quale sommamente è amata." In I, ii, 30–1, we read :

> Thy sprite, I know, doth lingre herabout,
> and lokes that I pore wretch shold after come.

The evidence here is slight, but the two lines bear a closer resemblance to the Italian than to Painter's : "Truly I am well assured, that it is yet here within, that hath respecte to the place, aswell of his owne pleasures, as of mine, being assured (as she who is certaine, that yet he looveth me) that he attendeth for myne, of whom he is greatly beloved."

In Act II we have again a tedious dialoguizing of considerations which Boccaccio expresses in a few lines, and again borrowings from another part of the novel, in themselves of no great moment, but pointing to the Italian text rather than to Painter as the authority on which they rest. Here are the passages in question :—

(1.)

"Sono adunque, sicome da te generata, di carne, e sì poco vivuta, che ancor son giovane : e per l'una cosa, e per l'altra piena di concupiscibile desiderio : al quale maravigliosissime forze hanno date l'aver già, per essere stata maritata, conosciuto qual piacer sia a così fatto desidero dar compimento."

Gismond.   No, no, sutch hap shold not so long forwast
               my youthfull dayes ; which bringes me greater grefe,
               when I somtime record my pleasure past.

                                                    (II, i, 38–40.)

"I am then as you be, begotten of fleshe, and my yeres so few, as yet but yonge, and thereby full of lust and delight. Wherunto the knowledge which I have had alredy in mariage, forceth me to accomplishe that desire."

                                (2.)

"Esser ti dovè, Tancredi, manifesto, essendo tu di carne, aver generata figliuola di carne, e non di pietra, o di ferro : e ricordar ti dovevi, e dei, quantunque tu ora sii vecchio, chenti, e quali, e con che forza vengano le leggi della giovanezza."

Lucrece.   Such passions hold her tender hart in presse,
               as shew the same not to be wrought of stele,
               or carved out of the hard and stony rock,
               that as by course of kinde can nought desire,
               nor feleth nought but as a senselesse stock.
               Such stern hardnesse ne ought ye to require
               in her, whoes gentle hart and tender yeres
               yet flouring in her chefest lust of youth
               is led of force to feele the whote desires
               that fall unto that age.   (II, ii, 19–28.)

"You ought deare father to knowe, that your selfe is of fleshe, and of fleshe you have engendred me your doughter, and not of Stone or Iron. In likewyse you ought, and must remember (although now you be arrived to olde yeares) what yonge folkes bee, and of what great power the lawe of youth is."

In Act III the writer's direct reference to Boccaccio is more obvious :—

"Guiscardo il prese ; ed avvisando costei non senza cagione dovergliele aver donato, e così detto ; partitosi, con esso sene tornò alla sua casa. E guardando la canna, e quella trovando fessa, l'aperse."

Guisharde.   Assuredly it is not without cause
                 she gave me this : somthing she meant thereby :
                 for therewithall I might perceive her pause
                 a while, as though some weighty thing did lye
                 upon her hart, which she conceled, bycause
                 the bystanders shold not our love espie.

> This clift declares that it hath ben disclosed :
> parhappes herin she hath something enclosed.
> (He breakes the cane and findes a letter enclosed.)

(III, iii, 41–48.)

"Guiscardo toke it, and thought that shee did not geve it unto him, without some special purpose went to his chamber, and loking upon the Cane perceived it to be hollowe, and openyng it founde the letter within whiche shee had written."

Painter mistranslated *fessa* (split) by the word "hollowe:" the dramatist had a keener eye for the significance of the original. "This clift declares," &c. The writer of the argument was equally alive to the point: "a letter subtilely enclosed in a cloven cane."

In Act **IV** the following passages lead to the same conclusion. In the first instance it is Tancredi who speaks :—

(1.)

"Ghismonda, parendomi conoscere la tua virtù, e la tua onestà, mai non mi sarebbe potuto cader nell' animo (quantunque mi fosse stato detto) se io co' miei occhi non l'avessi veduto, che tu di sottoporti ad alcuno huomo, se tuo marito stato non fosse, avessi, non che fatto, ma pur pensato."

> No, no : there stayed in me so settled trust,
> that thy chast life and uncorrupted minde
> wold not have yelded to unlawfull lust
> of strayeng love, other than was assigned
> lefull by law of honest wedlockes band,
> that, if these self same eyes had not behold
> thy shame, that wrought the woe, wherin I stand,
> in vain ten thousand Catoes shold have told,
> that thow didst ones unhonestly agree
> with that vile traitor Counté Palurine,
> without regard had to thy self, or me,
> unshamefastly to staine thy state and myné.

(IV, iii, 17–28.)

" 'Gismonda, I had so much affiaunce and truste in thy vertue and honestie, that it coulde never have entred into my mynde (althoughe it had bene tolde me, if I had not sene it with mine owne propre eyes) but that thou haddest not onely in deede, but also in thought, abandoned the companie of all men, except it had bene thy husbande.' "

11

(2.)

"Al quale Guiscardo niuna altra cosa disse, se non questo. Amor può troppo più, che nè voi, nè io possiamo."

> But greater lord is love, and larger reigne
> he hath upon eche god and mortal wight,
> than yow upon your subjectes have, or I
> upon my self.
>
> (IV, iv, 36–39.)

"To whom Guiscardo gave no other aunswere, but that Love was of greater force, than either any Prince or hym selfe."

Two passages in Act V make it abundantly clear that they were independently translated from Boccaccio, not taken from Painter :—

(1.)

"Il tuo padre ti manda questo, per consolarti di quella cosa, che tu più ami, come tu hai lui consolato di ciò, che egli più amava."

> "Thy father hath here in this cup thee sent
> that thing to joy and comfort thee withall
> which thow loved best, even as thou weart content
> to comfort him with his chefe joy of all."
>
> (V, i, 201–4.)

" 'Thy father hath sent thee this presente, to comforte thy selfe with the thing, which thou doest chieflie love, as thou haste comforted him of that which he loved most.' "

The *di* of the last line, which the dramatist translated " with " and Painter " of," seems to mean " concerning, with respect to, for;" and here Painter comes nearer the original than R. W.; but the divergence is none the less significant.

(2.)

"Ahi dolcissimo albergo di tutti i miei piaceri, maladetta sia la crudeltà di colui, che con gli occhi della fronte or mi ti fa vedere. Assai m'era con quegli della mente riguardarti a ciascuna ora. Tu hai il tuo corso fornito, e di tale, chente la fortuna tel concedette, ti se' spacciato. Venuto se' alla fine, alla qual ciascun corre. Lasciate hai le miserie del mondo, e le fatiche, e dal tuo nemico medesimo quella sepoltura hai, che il tuo valore ha meritata. Niuna cosa ti mancava ad aver compiute esequie, se non le lagrime

di colei, la qual tu, vivendo, cotanto amasti : le quali, acciocchè tu l'avessi,
pose Iddio nell' animo al mio dispietato padre, che a me ti mandasse : ed
io le ti darò (comechè di morire con gli occhi asciutti, e con viso da niuna
cosa spaventato proposto avessi) e dateleti, senza alcuno indugio farò, che
la mia anima si congiugnerà con quella, adoperandol tu, che tu già cotanto
cara guardasti.''

> Ah pleasant harborrow of my hartës thought.
> Ah swete delight, joy, comfort of my life.
> Ah cursed be his crueltie that wrought
> thee this despite, and unto me such grefe,
> to make me to behold thus with these eyes
> thy woefull hart, and force me here to see
> this dolefull sight.   Alas, did not suffise
> that with my hartes eyen continually
> I did behold the same?   Thow hâst fordone·
> the course of kinde, dispatched thy life from snares
> of fortunes venomed bayt : yea thou hâst ronne
> the mortall race, and left these worldly cares,
> and of thy foe, to honor thee with all,
> received a worthy grave to thy desert.
> Nothing doeth want to thy just funerall,
> but even my teres to wash thy bloody hart
> thus fouled and defaced, which to the end
> eke thou might have, Jove in the mynde putt soe
> of my despitefull father for to send
> thy hart to me. and thow shalt have them loe,
> though I determed to shede no tere at all,
> but with drye eyes and constant face to dye,
> yea though I thought to wett thy funerall
> only with blood, and with no weping eye.
> This doen fourthwith my soule shall come to thee,
> whome in thy life thow did so derely love.
>
> (V, ii, 25–50.)

" 'Oh sweete harboroughe of my pleasures, cursed be the crueltye of
him that hath caused mee at this time to loke uppon thee with the eyes
of my face : it was pleasure ynoughe, to see thee every hower, amonges
people of knowledge and understanding.   Thou hast finished thy course,
and by that ende, which fortune vouchsafed to give thee, thou art dispatched, and arrived to the ende wherunto all men have recourse : thou
hast forsaken the miseries and traveyles of this world, and haste had by the
enemy himselfe such a sepulture as thy worthinesse deserveth.   There
needeth nothing els to accomplishe thy funerall, but onely the teares of
her whom thou diddest hartelye love all the dayes of thy lyfe.   For

having wherof, our Lord did put into the head of my unmercifull father
to send thee unto me, and truly I will bestow some teares uppon thee,
although I was determined to die, without sheading any teares at all,
stoutlie, not fearefull of any thinge. And when I have powred them out
for thee, I will cause my soule, which thou hast heretofore so carefully
kepte, to be joyned wyth thine.' "

R. W., in line 32, correctly translates "con quegli della
mente" which Painter woefully misunderstands; and in the
last line quoted, the sense of "che tu già cotanto cara
guardasti" is more closely rendered by the dramatist than
by the professed translator.

The evidence, therefore, entitles us to reject the conclusion
arrived at by Sherwood (*Die Neu-Englischen Bearbeitungen
der Erzählung Boccaccios von Ghismonda and Guiscardo*)
and adopted by Brandl that Painter was most probably
used: it is manifest that Painter was not followed: if used
at all, his translation was carefully checked and corrected
by comparison with the original. But as I shall show that
the dramatists made use of an Italian play which had not
been translated, there seems no reason to suppose that they
would need anything beyond Boccaccio's text, which they
obviously understood better than Painter himself. Indeed,
famous as the latter's versions of Italian novels are, it must
be confessed that in the instance under consideration, his
efforts are not particularly happy. *E. g.*, in Ghismonda's
death scene he translates "stringendosi al petto il morto
cuore" *strained the dead hart harde to her stomacke!*

II.

THE DEBT TO DOLCE.

I happened to pick up in a second-hand book shop at
Florence a copy of Dolce's *Didone* (1547) and on reading
it I was at once struck by the close resemblance of the
opening lines to those of *Gismond of Salerne.* The parallel

seems to have escaped most of the historians of the drama
except the omniscient Creizenach, who mentions it in passing. The indebtedness of the English to the Italian tragedy,
however, is found on examination to go much further than
this. Not only is the supernatural machinery taken from
Dolce's play, but the whole conception of Gismond, the
grief-stricken widow a second time the victim of Love,
is due to the Italian tragedy, and not to the novel, for
Boccaccio's heroine is presented in a very different light.
The forces to which his Ghismonda yields are natural forces.
Speaking on his own behalf in the Introduction to the
Fourth Day, Boccaccio says: "Carissime donne .... io
conosco, che altra cosa dir non potrà alcun con ragione, se
non che gli altri, ed io, che v'amiano, naturalmente operiamo.
Alle cui leggi, cioè della natura, voler contrastare, troppo
gran forze bisognano, e spesse volte, non solamente in vano,
ma con grandissimo danno del faticante s'adoperano." The
obedience of his heroine to this law of nature is conscious
and deliberate : "si pensò di volere avere, se esser potesse,
occultamente un valoroso amante." Her plea to her father
in her own defence is to the same effect—that she is made
of flesh, and not of rock or iron—a plea which the English
dramatist has weakened by placing it not in her mouth, but
in that of the Aunt, Lucrece, and putting it before, not after,
the event. At the end of the novel, the lovers' fate is
lamented, but they are felt to be objects of envy as well
as compassion. "Il Re con rigido viso disse. Poco prezzo
mi parebbe la vita mia a dover dare per la metà diletto di
quello, che con Guiscardo ebbe Ghismonda." The writers
of the English tragedy took a very different view. R.
Wilmot, in his preface to *Tancred and Gismunda*, protests
that his purpose "tendeth only to the exaltation of virtue
and suppression of vice," and compares the tragedy with
Beza's *Abraham* and Buchanan's *Jephtha*, apologizing for

any defects on account of the youth of his coadjutors. "Nevertheless herein they all agree, commending virtue, detesting vice, and lively deciphering their overthrow that suppress not their unruly affections." Accordingly the Chorus in *Gismond of Salerne* hold up "worthy dames" such as Lucrece and Penelope as "a mirrour and a glasse to womankinde," and exhort their hearers to resist Cupid's assaults and be content with a moderate and virtuous affection (Choruses II, III, IV). The Epilogue assures the ladies in the audience that such disordered passions are unknown "in Britain land :"

> Nor Pluto heareth English ghostes complaine
> our dames disteined lyves.   Therfore ye may
> be free from fere.   Suffiseth to mainteine
> the vertues which we honor in yow all :
> so as our Britain ghostes, when life is past,
> may praise in heven, not plaine in Plutoes hall
> our dames, but hold them vertuous and chast,
> worthy to live where furie never came,
> where Love can see, and beares no deadly bowe.

It was, therefore, to Dolce's Dido and to the Phaedra of Seneca and Euripides that the English dramatists turned for an example of the victim of guilty passion they wished to present. Dolce in the prologue to *Didone* introduced Cupid as the evil influence which worked the Queen's ruin. The original suggestion came perhaps from Vergil (for in Dolce's prologue Cupid appears in the form of Ascanius) perhaps from a Latin translation of the *Hippolytus* of Euripides, where Aphrodite speaks the prologue, but so far as the English dramatists are concerned it is obvious that not only the idea, but the words, were taken directly from Dolce :—

> Io, che dimostro in viso,
> A la statura, e à i panni,
> D'esser picciol fanciullo,
> Si come voi mortale :
> Son quel gran Dio, che'l mondo chiama Amore.

Quel, che pò in cielo, e in terra,
Et nel bollente Averno ;
Contra di cui non vale
Forza, ne human consiglio :
Ne d'ambrosia mi pasco,
Si come gli altri Dei,
Ma di sangue, e di pianto.
Ne l'una mano io porto
Dubbia speme, fallace, e breve gioia ;
Ne l'altra affanno, e noia,
Pene, sospiri, e morti.

                              (*Didone*, 1-16.)

The beginning of *Gismond of Salerne* is a translation, with slight omissions and a little rearrangement, of the above lines :—

                        Cupide.

Loe I, in shape that seme unto your sight
a naked boy, not clothed but with wing,
am that great god of love that with my might
do rule the world, and everie living thing.
This one hand beares vain hope, short joyfull state,
with faire semblance the lover to allure :
this other holdes repentance all to late,
warr, fiër, blood, and paines without recure.
On swete ambrosia is not my foode,
nor nectar is my drink, as to the rest
of all the Goddes.   I drink the lovers blood,
and eate the living hart within his brest.

The next four lines :—

The depe Avern my percing force hath knowen.
What secret hollow do the huge seas hide
where blasting fame my actes hath not forth blowen?
To me the mighty Jove him self hath yeld,

might be suggested by *Didone*, II, i, 27-29 :—

Dio piu ch'altro possente ;
Dio, che disprezzi le saette horrende
Del gran padre d'i Dei ;

but are more probably taken direct from Seneca, with whom this thought is a commonplace.   See *Phaedra*, 191-2, and

Octavia, 566–8, and compare the references in the following
lines to Mars and Troy with *Phaedra*, 193, and *Octavia*,
832–3.   Lines 61–4 of the prologue :—

> This royall palace will I entre in,
> and there enflame the faire Gismonda soe,
> in creping thorough all her veines within,
> that she thereby shall raise much ruthe and woe

resemble a passage in Dolce's prologue (27–34) :—

> Con quella face ardente,
> C'hò nel mio petto ascosa
> Il che subito i fei
> Ch'ella mi strinse al seno
> Sotto imagine falsa
> Del pargoletto mio nipote caro :
> Et d'occulto veneno
> L'hebbi il misero cuor colmo e ripieno.

But the resemblance may be due to a common origin in
Seneca's *Medea*, 823–4 :—

> imas
> urat serpens flamma medullas.

Gismond's lament, which follows, reveals one or two
parallels with that of Dido in Dolce, V, i :—

(1.)

> Oh vaine unstedfast state of mortall thinges !
> Whoe trustes the world doeth leave to brittle stay.
> Such fickle frute his flattering blome forth bringes ;
> ere it be ripe it falleth to decaye.
> The joy and blisse, that late I did possesse
> in weale at will with one I lovëd best,
> disturnëd now into so depe distresse
> hâth taught me plaine to know our states unrest.
>
> (I, ii, 1–8.)

> Et tu volubil Dea, che'l mondo giri
> Calcando i buoni, e sollevando i rei :
> Che t'hò fatto io? che invidia ohime t'ha mosso
> A ridurmi à lo stato, in ch'io mi trovo?

Quanto mutata m'hai da quel ch'io fui,
Che in un sol punto m'hai levato, e tolto
Tutto quel, che mi fea viver contenta.

(V, i, 37–43.)

(2.)

But yet abide : I may perhappes devise
some way to be unburdened of my life.

(I, ii, 33–34.)

Però è ben tempo di provar s'io posso
Finir le pene mie con questa mano.

(V, i, 55–56.)

The Chorus which closes Act I is identical in thought with that which closes Act II in Dolce, but as both are mere tissues of Senecan commonplaces, this similarity does not necessarily prove indebtedness. One or two resemblances in phraseology may, however, be noted :—

(1.)

No raunsom serves for to redeme our dayes.
If prowesse could preserve, or worthy dedes,

(9–10.)

In van contra di lor nostro intelletto
Opra l'alta virtù d'i doni suoi.

(16–17.)

(2.)

But happy is he, that endes this mortal life
by spedy death, whoe is not forced to see
the many cares, nor fele the sondry grefe,
which we susteine in woe and miserie.

(33–36.)

Beato chi piu tosto s'avicina
Al fine, à cui camina
Chi prima è nato, ò nascera giamai.

(25–27.)

The last three lines were probably taken by Dolce from *Hercules Œtœus*, 104–111 :—

Par ille est superis cui pariter dies
et fortuna fuit. mortis habet uices
lente cum trahitur uita gementibus.
quisquis sub pedibus fata rapacia

> et puppem posuit liminis ultimi,
> non captiua dabit bracchia uinculis
> nec pompae ueniet nobile ferculum.
> numquam est ille miser cui facile est mori.[1]

But they might have been suggested by a Latin translation of Sophocles :—

> μὴ φῦναι τὸν ἅπαντα νικᾷ λόγον· τὸ δ᾽, ἐπεὶ φανῇ,
> βῆναι κεῖθεν ὅθεν περ ἥκει πολὺ δεύτερον ὡς τάχιστα.
>
> (*Œdipus Colonœus*, 1225–8.)

or by Cicero's " Non nasci bomini longe optimum esse, proximum autem quam primum mori " (*Tusc.*, 1, 48, 115). The thought was taken by Sophocles from Theognis, but with the latter writer, Dolce, who knew no Greek, was probably unacquainted.

In Act II the parallels are fewer and less striking. Gismond indeed reflects :—

> For if I should my pleasant yeres neglect
> of fresh grene youth frutelesse to fade away :
> whearto live I?   (II, ii, 26–28.)

in much the same terms as Dido :—

> Et ch'a l'incontro era sciochezza grande
> A consumar il fior de' miei verd' anni
> Senza gustar alcun soave frutto.

---

[1] This passage was translated by Dolce as follows :—

> Colui, ch' eguale è ai Dei,
> A cui il giorno fu par con la fortuna
> Sottoposto è ancor' egli
> A la pallida morte.
> La lunga vita spesso
> Ci da causa di pianto ;
> Onde chi tosto corre
> Al nostro ultimo fine,
> Non temerà di gire
> In servitù d'altrui :
> Ne misero è colui,
> Che disprezza la morte.

And the comparison of a wave-beaten ship with which Gismond closes this speech (II, i, 53–58) is used by Æneas in *Didone* (II, ii, 87–94), but this is a favorite Senecan metaphor (see *Medea*, 945–51, and *Agamemnon*, 139–144).

In Act III I observe no parallels with *Didone* worth noting; but the author of Act IV (undoubtedly Christopher Hatton, who was Master of the Game at the Grand Christmas of 1561–2, when *Gorboduc* was performed) evidently kept an eye on the Italian play. Megaera, who opens the act, is no doubt derived ultimately from Seneca's *Thyestes*, where she drives the ghost of Tantalus to curse his own descendants. He comes unwillingly :—

> Quid ora terres uerbere et tortos ferox
> minaris angues? quid famem infixam intimis
> agitas medullis? flagrat incensum siti
> cor et perustis flamma uisceribus micat.
> sequor.

In *Didone* the ghost introduced is that of Sichæus; the serpents and other torments are applied, not to the bearer, but to the victim of the curse. Cupid says in the Prologue :—

> Però discendo al fondo
> De l'empia styge, e del suo cerchio fuora
> Vò trar la pallid' ombra
> Del misero Sicheo
> (Che ben impetrerò de Pluto questa
> Gratia degna, et honesta)
> Et vò, ch'à Dido ella si mostri inanzi :
> Tolto prima d'Abysso
> Una de le ceraste ;
> Che in vece di capei, torte e sanguigne
> A le tempie d'intorno
> Ondeggiano di quelle
> Furie spietate e felle,
> Che sogliono voltar sossopra il mondo,
> Et questa i vò, che tutto l'empi il core
> Di sdegno, e di furore,
> Fin ch'à morte trabbocchi,
> Et turbar vegga gli occhi

> De la sirocchia altera
> Di quei, che move il sole, e ogni sphera.

In *Didone*, II, i, Cupid brings the snake on to the stage :—

> Che in tanto io le porrò su 'l bianco petto
> Questo serpe sanguigno, horrido, e fiero,
> C'hò divelto pur' hora
> Dal capo di Megera,
> Il quale il cor di lei roda e consumi.

We learn later (III, i, 79–83) that the serpent was actually seen on Dido's neck :—

> Fu posto à lei da non veduta mano
> Un serpe al collo, che con molti nodi
> Lo cinse errando, e sibillando pose
> La testa in seno ; e la vibrante lingua
> Quinci e quindi lecò le poppe e'l petto.

Hatton spared the English audience some of the details, but he gave them two snakes instead of one, and added a characteristic moral turn.   His Megaera says :—

> Loe, I will throwe
> into her fathers brest this stinging snake,
> and into hers an other will I cast.
> So stong with wrath, and with recurelesse woe,
> eche shalbe others murder at the last.
> Furies must aide, when men will ceasse to know
> their Goddes : and Hell shall send revenging paine
> to those, whome Shame from sinne can not restraine.
> (VI, i, 37–44.)

The Gentlemen of the Inner Temple were apparently fond of these grisly sights, for in the Dumb Show before the Fourth Act of *Gorboduc* three Furies were brought on the stage "clad in blacke garments sprinkled with bloud and flames, their bodies girt with snakes, their heds spread with serpents instead of heare, the one bearing in her hande a snake, the other a whip, and the thirde a burning fire-brande." [1]

---

[1] See also Chorus at end of Act IV, 12–15.

III. The Debt to Seneca.

The divergence in the development of the plot between *Didone* and *Gismond* made Dolce of little service to our authors for the latter part of their play, and they turned to the unfailing fount of early Elizabethan tragedy—Seneca. In the character and extent of their borrowings they come half-way between the general imitation of *Gorboduc* and the exact and wholesale copying of *The Misfortunes of Arthur*, which was presented to her Majesty by the Gentlemen of Gray's Inn in 1588. Some of the Senecan parallels in the earlier acts of the play have already been quoted. In the Chorus at the end of Act I, there appear to be reminiscences of *Thyestes*, 596–622, *Octavia*, 933–5, *Œdipus*, 1010–11, *Agamemnon*, 57–70, *Hercules Furens*, 376–382, *Phaedra*, 1132–52, *Octavia*, 915–18, in the order given; but the resemblance is in no case very close. One may serve as an example for all :—

> Loke what the cruël sisters do decree,
> the mighty Jove himself can not remove.
>
> (29–30.)
>
> non illa deo uertisse licet
> quae nexa suis currunt causis.
>
> (*Œdipus*, 1010–11.)

The author of Act II (probably Henry Noel) either had not learnt the lesson one admirer of Seneca's tragedies used to teach his pupils—"how and wherein they may imitate them, and borrow something out of them"—or he preferred to rely on his own efforts. His imitations of Seneca are as few and faint as of the *Didone*. The chorus was, no doubt, suggested by *Octavia*, 298–312 and 689–95. The only other parallel I have thought worth noting is this :—

> Suffiseth this, good niece, that you have sayed.
> Full well I see how sondry passions strive

in your unquiet brest : for oft ere this
your countenance half confused did plainly showe
some clowdy thoughtes overwhelmed all your blisse.

(II, i, 59–63.)

Regina Danaum et inclitum Ledae genus
quid tacita uersas quidue consilii inpotens
tumido feroces impetus animo geris ?
licet ipsa sileas, totus in uultu est dolor.

(Agamemnon, 126–9.)

Act III is much richer in allusions. The author quotes
Chaucer (III, ii, 1) : —

> Pitie, that moveth everie gentle hart,

and Cupid's " Now shall they know what mighty Love can
do " reminds one of Aphrodite's Prologue in the *Hippolytus*
of Euripides ; but this is probably a mere coincidence.
Seneca's *Phaedra* is, however, obviously copied in the following scenes and Chorus. Lines 105–8, 368–94, 649–51
should be compared with scene ii, and the beginning of scene
iii ; and lines 621–4 with the end of scene iii. In the
Chorus the following may be noted :—

(1.)

Full mighty is thy power, o cruel Love,
if Jove himself can not resist thy bowe :
but sendest him down even from the hevens above
in sondry shapes here to the earth belowe.

(1–4.)

> Quid fera frustra bella mouetis ?
> inuicta gerit tela Cupido.
> flammis uestros obruet ignes,
> quibus extinxit fulmina saepe
> captumque Iouem caelo traxit.

(*Octavia,* 820–4.)

> et iubet caelo superos relicto
> nultibus falsis habitare terras.

(*Phaedra,* 299–300.)

(2.)

Then how shold mortal men escape thy dart,
the fervent flame, and burning of thy fire ?
sins that thy might is such, and sins thow art
both of the seas and land the lord and sire.

(5–8.)

Sacer est ignis, credite laesis,
nimiumque potens.
qua terra mari cingitur alto
quaque ethereo
candida mundo sidera currunt.

(*Phaedra*, 336–340.)

(3.)

For Love assaultes not but the idle hart :
and such as live in pleasure and delight,
he turneth oft their glad joyes into smart.

(17–19.)

uis magna mentis blandus atque animi calor
amor est. iuventae gignitur luxu otio,
nutritur inter laeta fortunae bona.

(*Octavia*, 573–5.)

(4.)

Whoe yeldeth unto him his captive hart,
ere he resist, and holdes his open brest
withouten warr to take his bloody dart,
let him not think to shake of, when him list,
his heavy yoke. Resist his first assaulte :
weak is his bowe, his quenched brand is cold.

(33–38.)

extingue flammas neue te dirae spei
praebe obsequentem. quisquis in primo obstitit
pepulitque amorem tutus ac uictor fuit,
qui blandiendo dulce nutriuit malum
sero recusat ferre quod subiit iugum.

(*Phaedra*, 136–140.)

quem si fouere atque alere desistas, cadit
breuique uires perdit extinctus suas.

(*Octavia*, 576–7.)

(5.)

But he geves poison so to drink in gold.

(41.)

uenenum in auro bibitur.

(*Thyestes*, 453.)

The opening of Act IV is doubtless imitated from the opening of the *Thyestes*, but the same examples of the pains of hell occur in *Octavia*, 631–5, and *Didone*, IV, i, 126–133. The invocation of Jove's thunder at the beginning of scene ii was probably suggested by *Phaedra*, 679–90, or

Thyestes, 1081–1100;[1] this stock device of Seneca was to become no less familiar · in Elizabethan tragedy.   It had already been used in *Gorboduc* (end of III, i) :—

> O heavens, send down the flames of your revenge ;
> Destroie, I saie, with flashe of wrekeful fier
> The traitour sonne, and then the wretched sire !

The original passage in the *Phaedra* was quoted—or rather misquoted—in *Titus Andronicus*, IV, i, 81–2 :—

> Magni Dominator poli,
> Tam lentus audis scelera ? tam lentus vides ?

Shakspere possibly had it in mind when he made Lear say (II, iv, 230–1) —

> I do not bid the thunder bearer shoot,
> Nor tell tales of thee to high-judging Jove.

It is in the First Scene of Act V that the imitation of Seneca is most extensive and most obvious.   Renuchio is the regular Senecan messenger, the detailed horror of his story is quite after Seneca's manner, and there are many lines translated, with slight alterations, from the narratives of the *Thyestes* and other plays :—

(1.)

> O cruel fate ! o dolefull destinie !
> O heavy hap ! o woe can not be told !

(1–2.)

> O sors acerba.   (*Phaedra*, 1000.)
>
> O dira fata saeua miseranda horrida.
>
> (*Troades*, 1066.)

(2.)

Chor.   What newes be these ?

---

[1] It came originally from Sophocles, *Electra*, 823–6 :

τοῦ ποτε κεραυνὸι Διὸs, ἢ ποῦ φαέθων
Ἅλιos, εἰ ταῦτ' ἐφορῶντεs κρύπτουσιν ἔκηλοι ;

Renu.   Is this Salerńe I see?
What? doeth king Tancred govern here, and guide?
Is this the place where civile people be?
or do the savage Scythians here abide?

Chor.   What meanes this cruel folk, and eke this king,
that thus yow name? Declare how standes the case?
and whatsoëver dolefull newes yow bring
recompt fourthwith.

Ren.   Where shall I turne my face?
or whether shall I bend my weryed sight?
what ever way I seke or can devise,
or do I what I can to ease my plight,
the cruel fact is ever in myne eyes.

Chor.   Leave of this wise to hold us in such maze
of doutfull drede what newes yow have to show.
For drede of thinges unknowen doeth allway cause
man drede the worst, till he the better know.
Tell therfore what is chaunced, and wherunto
this bloody cuppe thus in your hand yow bring.

(21–38.)

Chor.   quid portas noui?
Nunt. Quanam ista regio est? Argos et Sparte inpios
sortita fratres et maris gemini premens
fauces Corinthos, an feris Hister fugam
praebens Alanis, an sub aeterna niue
Hyrcana tellus, an uagi passim Scythae?

Chor.   quis hic nefandi est conscius monstri locus?
effare et istud pande quodcumque est malum.

Nunt. Si steterit animus, si metu corpus rigens
remittet artus. haeret in uulta trucis
imago facti. ferte me insanae procul
illo procellae ferte, quo fertur dies
hinc raptus.

Chor.   animos grauius incertos tenes.
quid sit quod horres effer, autorem indica.
non quaero quis sed uter. effare ocius.

(*Thyestes*, 626–640.)

(3.)

although my minde so sorrowfull a thing
repine to tell, and though my voice eschue
to say what I have seen :   (40–2.)

uocem dolori lingua luctifica negat.

(*Phaedra*, 1004.)

12

(4.)

The description of the tower and dungeon (45–68) is modelled upon *Thyestes*, 641–79,[1] with a possible reminiscence of the tower in the *Troades* (630–1), from which Astyanax leaps "intrepidus animo."

(5.)

Cho.   O cruel dede.

Ren.   why? deme ye this to be
the dolefull newes that I have now to show?
Is here (think yow?) end of the crueltie,
that I have seen?

Cho.   Could worse or crueller woe
be wrought to him, than to bereve him life?

Ren.   What? think yow this outrage did end so well?
The horror of the fact, the greatest grefe,
the cruëltie, the terror is to tell.

Cho.   Alack, what could be more?   They threw percase
the dead body to be devoured and eate
of the cruel wilde beastes.

Ren.   O me, alas,
wold god it had ben cast a dolefull meate
to beastes and birdes.   But loe that dredfull thing,
which even the tygre wold not work, but to
fulfill his hongre with, that hath the king
withouten ruthe commaunded to be do,
only to please his cruel hart withall.
Oh, happy had ben his chaunce, to happy alas,
if birdes had eate his corps, yea hart and all.

                                                     (149–167.)

Chor.   o saeuum scelus.

Nunt.   exhorruistis? hactenus non stat nefas,
plus est.

Chor.   An ultra maius aut atrocius
natura recipit?

Nunt.   sceleris hunc finem putas?
gradus est.

---

[1] Copied also in Giraldi's *Orbecche*, IV, i, 59–62 :—

Giace nel fondo di quest' alta torre,
In parte sì solinga, e sì riposta,
Che non vi giunge mai raggio di Sole,
Un luoco dedicato a'sacrificii.

Chor.   quid ultra potuit? obiecit feris
laniauda forsan corpora atque igne arcuit.
Nunt.   utinam arcuisset. ne tegat functos humus,
ne soluat ignis, auibus epulandos licet
ferisque triste pabulum saeuis trahat.
Votum est sub hoc, quod esse supplicium solet.

(*Thyestes*, 743–752.)

(6.)

The warme entrailes were toren out of his brest
within their handes trembling not fully dead :
his veines smoked : his bowelles all to strest
ruthelesse were rent, and throwen amidde the place :
all clottered lay the blood in lompes of gore,
sprent on his corps, and on his palëd face.
His hart panting out from his brest they tore.

(182–188.)

erepta uiuis exta pectoribus tremunt
spirantque uenae corque adhuc pauidum salit.

(*Thyestes*, 755–6.)

(7.)

O haynous dede ! which no posteritie
will ones beleve.   (207–8.)

O nullo scelus
credibile in aeuo quodque posteritas neget.

(*Thyestes*, 753–4.)

The imitations of Seneca were made, so far as I have
been able to judge, from the original, and not from the
English translation. The latter reveals occasional similarities of phrase, as in No. 1 of the last series of quotations,
where the translators render Seneca's lines :—

O heavy happe . . . .

O dyre, fierce, wretched, horrible,
O cruell fates accurste.

But these might well be mere coincidences ; and such
instances of the use of the same words are rare. In most
cases the version of the Gentlemen of the Inner Temple
gives every evidence of independence of the English trans-

lation.   A fair idea of the relation of the two to the original
text is given by comparing quotations 5, 6 and 7 with
Heywood's rendering of the same lines in his translation
of the *Thyestes* :—

Chor.   O heynous hateful act.
Mess.   Abhorre ye this? ye heare not yet the end of all the fact,
           There followes more.
Chor.   A fiercer thing, or worse then this to see
           Could Nature beare?
Mess.   why thinke ye this of gylt the end to be?
           It is but part.
Chor.   what could be more? to cruel beastes he cast
           Perhappes their bodyes to be torne, and kept from fyres at last.
Mess.   Would God he had : that never tombe the dead might over hyde,
           Nor flames dissolve, though them for food to foules in pastures wyde
           He had out throwen, or them for pray to cruell beastes would flinge.
           That which the worst was wont to be, were here a wished thing.
           That them their father saw untombd : but oh more cursed crime
           Uncredible, the which denye will men of after tyme :
           From bosomes yet alive out drawne the trembling bowels shake,
           The vaynes yet breath, the feareful hart doth yet both pant and quake.

IV. Traces of Originality.

When due deductions are made for what the authors
borrowed from Boccaccio, Dolce, and Seneca, what, it will
naturally be asked, remains of their own? Not a great
deal, it must be acknowledged. The intrinsic interest of the
theme is much superior to that of *Gorboduc* or *Jocasta,* and
they had the great advantage of a well-told story on which
to found their plot; but it cannot be said that they added
much to it, or showed any great skill in adapting it to the
tragic stage. Of the characters not found or implied in
Boccaccio's novel, Cupid is taken from Dolce, Renuchio,
Megaera and the Chorus from Seneca, Lucrece and Claudia
are the conventional confidantes of classical tragedy. In
the early part of the play, where they had to develop the

story for themselves, they borrowed scraps of speeches from later scenes in Boccaccio or imitated Senecan commonplaces. The following dialogue, though not taken directly from the Roman tragedies, is an obvious attempt to imitate Senecan steichomutheia :—

> Gism. Oh sir, these teres love chalengeth as due.
> Tanc. But reason sayeth they do no whitt availe.
> Gism. Yet can I not my passions so subdue.
> Tanc. Your fond affections ought not to prevaile.
> Gism. Whoe can but plaine the losse of such a one?
> Tanc. Of mortall thinges no losse shold seme so strange.
> Gism. Such gemme was he as erst was never none.
>
> (I, iii, 53–9.)

The elaborate setting forth of Gismond's disconsolate widow-hood, to which the whole of the first act is given up, is a poor preparation for the part the heroine is to play later. Tan-cred's refusal of the plea for a second marriage, which occupies Act II, has more to do with the main interest of the play, but here too the progress of the action is slow and languid. The author of Act III contributed little of his own except Gismond's love-letter, which is not found in Boccaccio. Almost the whole of the action—the discovery, Guishard's capture and execution, and Gismond's suicide—is crowded into Acts IV and V. The order of events is in the main that of the novel, though a noteworthy change is made in that after the discovery Tancred sends for his daughter before he meets her lover—with this disadvantage, that at the time of the interview Gismond is not made aware of Guishard's imprisonment and impending fate. This it is which gives point to the magnificent speech of Boccaccio's heroine in defence of her fame and defiance of her father's tyranny. The English tragedians were able to make little use of this truly dramatic scene, partly because of the weak-ened situation, as they had planned it, partly because of their different conception of Gismond's character; the altered

position of Guishard, who is no longer "un giovane val-
letto" but "the Counté Palurine," takes away the occasion
for some of the reproaches urged by Tancredi against his
daughter in the original, but this is a change of less moment.
The last meeting between the heroine and her father is more
effectively managed, though she is finally dismissed somewhat perfunctorily with the stage direction "Gismond dyeth."
The death of Tancred (added by the dramatists to Boccaccio's
story) is only announced as an intention in the action, but
we are informed parenthetically in the Epilogue that he
"now himself hath slayen."

The various rhymed measures substituted by the dramatists for the blank verse of *Gorboduc* and *Jocasta* are ill-
suited to tragedy and are not managed by them with any
great success. But in spite of these obvious defects, *Gismond
of Salerne* is in some respects an advance upon its predecessors. Cupid and Megaera are an improvement on the old
dumb shows in that they are speaking persons, intimately
connected with the action of the play. The episodical treatment of the plot, though poorly contrived, is characteristic
of the English romantic drama, which aims at presenting the
whole course of the action, in its inception, development, and
consequences, rather than a particular situation or crisis, as
was the custom in Senecan tragedy and its Italian imitations.
There is accordingly no attempt to observe the unity of time,
though the scene is restricted to the court of Tancred's palace
and the chamber of Gismond lying immediately behind it—
the chamber "within," which was afterwards to become a
habitual resource of the popular stage. Cupid comes down
from heaven, and Megaera up from hell, so that we have
here the beginnings of stage machinery. But these are after
all matters of detail. The substantial merit of *Gismond of
Salerne* is that it endeavoured to present a romantic subject
with something of the gravity and dignity of classical trag-

edy. From the latter point of view, its superiority to its immediate predecessors, *Damon and Pythias* and *Horestes*, is abundantly manifest; and in both interest of theme and manner of treatment it surpasses the earlier and more academic models. *Gorboduc* is overweighted with political considerations, and the plot loses itself in abstractions. *Jocasta* has the double disadvantage of a time-worn theme and frigid manner of presentation. *Gismond of Salerne* struck out a new path in which later dramatists followed with infinitely greater art. It seems a far cry from Gismond and Guishard to the "pair of star-cross'd lovers" of Shakspere's first Italian tragedy; but the Gentlemen of the Inner Temple at least attempted what he achieved—to present the problem of human passion *sub specie eternitatis*. What Courthope[1] says of *Romeo and Juliet* is true in a general way of *Gismond of Salerne* : "The power of the human will in this play counts for little; it is swept away by the tide of passion and fatè. An image of the world is presented to us as a whole, and in the vein of reflection pervading the prologue to the play, the chorus before the second act, and the occasional speeches of Friar Laurence, we observe the Greek tragic doctrine of moral necessity blended with the mediaeval doctrine of human vanity." The authors of *Gismond of Salerne* did not succeed in reconciling these conflicting elements; but by bringing them together, however blindly and ineffectively, they at least suggested that they were not irreconcilable.

JOHN W. CUNLIFFE.

[1] *History of English Poetry*, IV, 100.

IX.—ON THE DATE OF *KING LEAR*.

Within certain limits the date of composition of Shakspere's tragedy of *King Lear* is well defined. It must have been written no earlier than 1603, when Harsnet's *Declaration of Egregious Popish Impostures* was published,[1] and no later than December, 1606, when the play was presented before "the kinges maiestie at Whitehall." [2]

A further limitation is suggested in Malone's famous *Attempt to Ascertain the Order in Which the Plays of Shakspere Were Written* (1778) as follows:

"It seems extremely probable that its first appearance was in March or April, 1605, in which year the old play of *King Leir* that had been entered at Stationers' Hall in 1594, was printed by Simon Stafford for John Wright, who, we may presume, finding Shakspere's play successful, hoped to palm the spurious one on the publick for his." [3]

Malone's theory that the older anonymous play was reprinted in 1605 in order to palm it off as Shakspere's for many years met with general acceptance on the part of the critics.[4] Recently, however, two Shaksperean scholars on

[1] This discovery is due to Theobald. Cf. Furness, *Variorum Shakspere, King Lear*, (Philadelphia, 1880), pp. 186–7.

[2] So the original entry of the "book" in the Stationers' Register informs us. See below.

[3] *Variorum of 1821*, ed. Boswell, II, 404–5. Cf. Furness, p. 377. Malone's further argument based on the substitution of "British man" for "Englishman" in a well-known line in the play, seems not to have been well founded.

[4] It has been more or less definitely accepted by Eschenburg, *Ueber W. Shakspere* (Zurich, 1787), p. 270; Nathan Drake, *Shakspere and his Times* (London, 1817), II, 458; Collier, *Works of Shakspere* (London, 1843), VII, 352; Hudson, *Works of Shakspere* (Boston, 1856), IX, 391; Dyce, *Works of Shakspere* (London, 1857), I, clxxxvi; Staunton, *Plays of Shakspere* (London, 1860), III, 56; Ulrici, *Shaksperes Dramatische Werke* (Berlin, 1871), XI,

reviewing the evidence for this hypothesis, have found it insufficient and have proposed a later date for the tragedy. It is the purpose of this paper to examine the problem once more in the effort to bring forth new evidence on the subject. The general plan will be to note carefully the circumstances of the publication of each of these plays.

I.

Shakspere's tragedy was entered at Stationers' Hall, November 26, 1607, in the language below:

"Nathaniel Butter John Busby

Entred for their copie vnder th[e h]andes of Sir George Buck knight and Th[e] wardens A booke called Master William Shakespeare his 'historye of Kinge Lear' as yt was played before the kinges maiestie at Whitehall vppon Sainct Stephens night [26 December] at Christmas Last by his maiesties servantes playinge vsually at the 'Globe' on the Banksyde .... vj^d." [1]

4; Delius, *Shaksperes Werke* (Elberfield, 1872), II, 427; von Friesen, *Shakspere-Studien* (Wien, 1876), III, 79; Eidam, *Ueber die Sage von König Lear* (Würzburg, 1880), p. 13; Fleay, *Life and Works of Shakspere* (London, 1886), p. 237; Adee, *Bankside Shakspere* (New York, 1890), X, vi; Wendell, *Wm. Shakspere* (New York, 1894), p. 288; Boas, *Shakspere and His Predecessors* (New York, 1896), p. 438; Ward, *History of English Dramatic Literature* (London, 1899), II, 174; Herford, *Eversley Shakspere* (London, 1899), IX, 7; Gollancz, *Temple Shakspere* (London, 1900), X, preface to *Lear* (pages not numbered). Doubtless this list could be much extended. On the other hand the theory has been received with disfavor by W. A. Wright, who in the *Clarendon Press Series, King Lear* (Oxford, 1879), p. xvii, dates it late in 1605, ignoring Malone; by Furness, *Variorum King Lear*, p. 378; by Lee, who adopts a later date for the play in his *Life of Shakspere* (London, 1898), p. 241; by Craig, *King Lear* (London, 1901), p. xx; and by Perrett, *Story of King Lear* (*Palæstra*, XXXV; Berlin, 1904), pp. 97–9.

[1] Arber's *Transcript*, III, 366.

In the following year appeared two quartos of the play "printed for Nathaniel Butter" under the title:

"M. William Shak-speare: | HIS | True Chronicle Historie of the life and | death of King LEAR and his three | Daughters. | *With the vnfortunate life of* Edgar, *sonne* | and heire to the Earle of Gloster, and his | sullen and assumed humor of | TOM of Bedlam: | *As it was played before the Kings Maiestie at Whitehall vpon* | *S.* Stephans *Night in Christmas Hollidayes.* | By his Maiesties seruants playing vsually at the Gloabe | on the Bancke-side," etc.[1]

The emphasis put upon Shakspere's name in both the Register and the quartos is striking.[2] Even those who discredit Malone's hypothesis to-day admit that we have here a tacit reference to the older play of *King Leir*,[3] which had been printed by Stafford and Wright three years before 1608, and had *not* been written by "M. William Shakspeare." The details connected with its publication are not easily made clear to the reader.

In April, 1594,[4] as we learn from Phillip Henslowe's *Diary*, a play of "kinge leare" was on the English stage, being presented by "the Quenes men & my lord of Susexe to geather."[5] Presumably it was this same play which was entered the very next month at Stationers' Hall:

---

[1] I here follow the *fac-simile* title-page given by Prætorius in his reprint of Quarto 1 (London, 1885), p. 1. The few variations in wording between the two quartos do not concern us.

[2] Scarcely less striking in each case is the carefulness of the publisher to note the company which is presenting the play. Moreover on his title-page he specifically mentions the Gloster subplot and the death of Lear—two details which distinguish Shakspere's play from its predecessor.

[3] So Mr. Aldis Wright, p. xiv of his edition of the *Lear*.

[4] Not April, 1593, as sometimes stated. Henslowe, to be sure, marks it 1593 in one place, but a close examination of the entries in this connection will convince every reader that what is meant is the year beginning with January, 1594, according to modern usage.

[5] Henslowe's *Diary*, ed. Collier (London, 1845), pp. 33–4; ed. Greg. (London, 1904), I, 17.

Adam Islip. |
Edward White. |

"xiiij^{to} die Maij. | . [1594.]

Entred alsoe for his Copie vnder th[e h]andes of bothe the wardens a booke entituled | The most famous Chronicle historye of Leire kinge of England and his Three Daughters .... vj^dC | ." [1]

On the same day were entered to White, with Islip's name again written and crossed out, as above, *the Historye of ffryer Bacon and ffryer Bungaye, A pastorall plesant Commedie of Robin Hood and Little John,* and two other plays of the time.[2] Of these five "bookes" the *Friar Bacon and Friar Bungay* is the only one which White published in 1594 that is extant to-day.[3] But the book with which we are now concerned, the *Leir*, or else another play of the same name, was printed, we have seen, in the year 1605 by Stafford and Wright. The 1605 entry of this play in the Stationers' Register follows:

Simon Stafford

"8 Maij

Entred for his Copie vnder th[e h]andes of the Wardens a booke called 'the Tragecall historie of kinge Leir and his Three Daughters, &c.' As it was latelie Acted .... vj^d.

---

[1] Arber's *Transcript*, II, 649. It has been suggested that Islip's name was first written and then crossed out because he was the printer and White the publisher. White does not seem to have done his own printing. It is on record that Islip printed for him de Guevara's *Mount of Calvary*, Pt. I, 1595, Part II, 1597 ; and *The Key to Unknown Knowledge*, 1599. See Ames, *Typographical Antiquities* (ed. Herbert, London, 1786), II, 1200.

[2] Peele's *David and Bethsabe*, and a lost play of *John of Gaunt*.

[3] See title-page in Greene's *Plays and Poems* (ed. Collins, Oxford, 1905), II, 15. The earliest extant copy of the *David and Bethsabe* was printed by Islip in 1599. The *Robin Hood and Little John*, with the *John of Gaunt*, seems to have perished.

John Wright.

" Entred for his Copie by assignement from Simon Stafford and by consent of Master Leake, The Tragicall history of kinge Leire and his Three Daughters | Provided that Simon Stafford shall have the printinge of this book | | . . . . vj^{d}." [1]

Several copies of this work printed by Stafford for Wright are still extant. On them the title is not "the tragical history," but runs :

" The | True Chronicle Hi- | story of King Leir, and his three | *daughters, Gonorill, Ragan,* | *and Cordella.* | As it hath bene divers and sundry | times lately acted. | London, | Printed by Simon Stafford for John | Wright, and are to bee sold at his shop at | Christes Church dore, next Newgate | Market, 1605." [2]

This is not the place to enter upon any lengthy discussion as to whether or not *The true chronicle history of King Leir,* published in 1605, is the same play as *The most famous chronicle history of King Leir,* registered in 1594. Absolute

---

[1] Arber's *Transcript,* III, 289. Arber adds in a note, "It is evident that *King Lear* was printed by S. Stafford before the 8th of May, 1605, though not entered until it was assigned on that date." This statement Perrett, *op. cit.,* p. 98, justly questions. Rather, if we already have a suspicion of fraud in this transaction, the immediate assignment of the book to another publisher, might tend to strengthen the suspicions. Halliwell-[Phillips], *Works of Shakspere* (London, 1865), XIV, 353, observes that it would seem from the second entry "that Leake had some interest in the work." But Leake was then one of the wardens and probably his consent to the transfer was merely official.

[2] Not having seen a copy of the quarto, I follow here the title as given in Capell's *Shakspere* (London, 1767–8?), I, 55. In Steevens's reprint the title-page differs slightly in spacing, but not in reading. A careful collation of the reprints made respectively by Steevens in *Wm. Shakspere, Twenty of His Plays,* IV (pages not numbered), by Nichols in *Six Old Plays,* etc., II, 377 ff., and by Hazlitt in *Shakspere's Library,* II, 307 ff., has brought forth differences of no importance whatever.

proof on this point is wanting and will probably always be. But there is not lacking internal evidence in the play of 1605 to show that it was written many years before that date and quite as early as 1594.[1] Those who are most positive in rejecting Malone's charge of fraud do not hesitate to say that it is "extremely probable" that the two plays are identical.[2] We shall not go far astray in making this assumption at the outset.

All these matters must have been known to Malone when he wrote the sentence quoted in the beginning of this article, and they have been the common property of students of Shakspere since that time. For convenience let us summarize the evidence just adduced in a form which would not be questioned by any of those who have examined it:

(1). It is probable that the anonymous play registered in May, 1594, by Edward White as *The most famous Chronicle historye of Leire kinge of England and his Three Daughters*, was on the stage in April, 1594.

(2). What is believed by practically every one to be again the same play was registered on May 8, 1605, by Stafford and Wright as *the Tragecall historie of kinge Leir and his Three Daughters*, and published by them that year as *the True Chronicle History of King Leir, and his three daughters*, without the name of the author.

(3). Shakspere's play was written between 1603 and 1606, inclusive.

(4). Shakspere's play was first entered by Butter and Busby late in 1607 as *Master William Shakespeare his 'historye of Kinge Lear,'* and published by them in 1608 as

---

[1] This evidence concerns the style, versification and technique of the play, and its relation to certain others of the 1590–95 period. Much of this matter is discussed at length by Perrett in his *Story of King Lear;* other evidence I hope to put into print later.

[2] For example, Craig, *King Lear*, p. xvii, and Perrett, p. 97.

M. William Shakspeare, HIS True Chronicle Historie of the life and death of King Lear and his Three Daughters.

(5). The peculiar phrasing of this title must have been adopted for the purpose of distinguishing Shakspere's work from the anonymous play published three years before.

II.

Malone's suspicion of fraud in Stafford and Wright's 1605 publication may have been aroused by the fact that these men apparently were only reprinting an old play which had been put on the market by another publisher eleven years before. Did they reprint the old anonymous *Leir* with a slight change of title because the public just at that time was particularly interested in another play on the same subject, and with a very similar name? Perhaps the reader will be more ready to answer this question as Malone did if it can be shown beyond a reasonable doubt that this publication was piratical on the part of Stafford and Wright, and that the copyright to this play not only in 1605, but years after, belonged to the family of White, the publisher of the 1594 *Leir*.

Evidence on the subject is found in two entries in the Stationers' Register. Both these entries have long been known to students of the drama, but their significance has either been overlooked or misunderstood.[1] The first is on June 29, 1624, when some twenty books are assigned to "master Aldee"[2] from the estate of "mistris White."

---

[1] Cf. Fleay, *Life of Shakspere*, p. 353, stating that the "Leire . . . . was not the old play, but a prose history now lost,"—a remark probably based on what Halliwell-Phillips says, *op. cit.*, XIV, 362.

[2] Probably Edward Aldee, who printed for White the earliest extant edition of Kyd's *Spanish Tragedy* (cf. W. W. Greg, *List of Plays*, etc., p. 61) ; *The Rare Triumphs of Love and Fortune*, 1589 (Greg, p. 123) ; three editions of *Soliman and Perseda* (mentioned in the 1624 entry as transferred

This list of books includes *Leire and his daughters, Fryer Bacon and frier Bungay*, and *Robin Hood and little John*.[1] These same three books, we remember, had been entered together on May 14, 1594, by Edward White, and "mistris White" is evidently his widow.[2]

The second entry serves only to confirm the first. On April 22, 1640, "Master Oulton" enters for his copies twenty books "which lately did belong to Mistris Aldee his mother in Law deceased."[3] Among these twenty works again are *Lear and his 3. daughters, ffrier Bacon and ffrier Bungey, Robin Hood and little John*, and four other books whose names appeared in the 1624 entry. If now the copyright to these three books belonged to Edward White in 1594, and to his widow in 1624, the suspicion grows strong that the copyright to the *Leir* belonged to White also in 1605, and that the edition printed that year by Stafford for Wright was piratical. But it is not easy to see why

to Aldee), 1599, and another edition undated (Greg, p. 123). On June 25, 1600, Aldee and Wm. White were fined for printing, and Edward White for selling "a Disorderly ballad," Arber, II, 831. Again, on April 14 and May 30, 1603, Aldee was fined for printing, and Edward White for selling the *Basilicon Doron*, Arber, II, 835–6.

[1] Arber, IV, 120.

[2] Arber, V, cix, makes her the widow of Edward White, Jr., who was publishing just before 1624, but an examination of the entry will show, I believe, that every one of the books on the list had been originally entered by the older White, and not one by the younger.

[3] Arber, IV, 507. Mrs. Aldee is Elizabeth, widow of Edward. Halliwell-Phillips in his *Shakspere*, XIV, 363, speaks of still another assignment of the play: "In April, 1655, the copyright of this play was entered to William Gilbertson 'by vertue of an assignment under the hand and seale of Edward Wright.'" Unfortunately Arber's *Transcript* does not extend beyond 1640, but Halliwell-Phillips gives a *fac-simile* of this entry, *op. cit.*, XIV, facing p. 361. It is a coincidence that in 1655 was also published the third quarto of Shakspere's *Lear*. Edward Wright, as stated below, was the younger brother of John Wright, and probably inherited his interest in the *Leir* printed in 1605.

these two printers should join together at that time to bring out a piratical edition of a play eleven years old unless in the year 1605 there was a revival of interest in the Leir story, or some special opportunity for the sale of their fraudulent work.[1] Such an opportunity might readily have come from a presentation of Shakspere's tragedy on the stage.

If the book was printed by White in 1594, a copy might have been easily obtained by Stafford or Wright, but it is very doubtful if Wright had even to go to the trouble of purchasing one. Long before 1605 he must have become acquainted with the *Leir*, and had an excellent opportunity of obtaining a copy in the shop of the original publisher. On the revival of public interest in the theme his mind would naturally turn to this play copyrighted, and probably printed eleven years before by Edward White. For this information we are again indebted to the Stationers' Register, which tells us under date of "25 Junii," 1594, that "John Wright son of Thomas Wright of Bugbrook in county Northampton yoman, hath put him self an apprentise to Edward White citizen and Staconer of London for Eight yeres from Sainct John baptist Last past [24 June, 1594]."[2] When his eight years of apprenticeship are ended, it is under the patronage of "Master White" that "John Wright" is "sworne and admitted a freman of this company."[3] He probably went into business almost immediately,[4] but the first book on record[5] as copyrighted by him is this *Tragicall*

---

[1] For a suggestion here I am indebted to Professor Kittredge, though he is not to be held responsible for inaccuracies in the form of the statement.

[2] Arber, II, 194. It was May 14, 1594, when White entered *Leir*. Probably the printing was done some weeks later while Wright was in the shop. So Shakspere's *Lear* entered November 26, 1607, was printed 1608.

[3] Arber, II, 732.

[4] On August 6, 1604, he takes as apprentice Edward Wright, "sonne of Thomas Wright," and evidently his brother. Arber, II, 282.

[5] Arber, v, cxi.

history of kinge Leire, which Stafford transferred at the same time as he entered it for himself May 8, 1605. It will be noted that this business connection serves to join definitely the 1594 *Leir* with that of 1605.

That Wright's character would not forbid our putting such an interpretation on his act, may be surmised from one incident in his career. When Thorpe printed in 1609 his surreptitious edition of Shakspere's sonnets, John Wright was one of the two men who sold the book, and his name and place of business appear on the title-page of "half the edition." [1] The man who in 1609 would be ready to assist Thorpe in a piratical edition of sonnets written by Shakspere would probably not have scrupled in 1605 to assist, or get the assistance of, Stafford, in a piratical edition of the *Leir,* supposed to have been written also by Shakspere.

But what of Simon Stafford, his partner in this venture? Mr. Fleay long ago pointed out that Stafford "had to do" with the surreptitious edition of *Pericles* in 1611. [2] That he was regarded by his fellow-printers with suspicion as early as 1602, seems to be implied elsewhere in the stationers' books. On September 27 of that year, two books are entered in which "Jas. Shawe" is interested. Of these the first is entered jointly by Shawe and Stafford with the express statement, "Symond Stafford with Jas. Shawe in this first history onely;" while the second is no less distinctly marked, "James Shawe properly to hym selfe." [3] Those familiar

---

[1] Lee, *Life of Shakspere,* p. 90. If one is disposed to question the authority of Mr. Lee concerning the Sonnets, one may refer to Rolfe, *Life of Shakspere* (Boston, 1904), p. 334, where Mr. Lee's general position is strongly combated, but Thorpe's edition is pronounced piratical.

[2] Cf. Furness, p. 381. Of Mr. Fleay's further statement that Stafford's *Edward III* was surreptitious, I am not so sure. On the *Pericles* see Halliwell-Phillips's *Shakspere,* XVI, 72.

[3] Arber, III, 217. On the next page Stafford enters a book "not to be printed til he have gotten better authority for yt."

13

with the Register know that such language is unusual on its pages. The conclusion is inevitable that before 1605 Stafford was regarded in some quarters as an unscrupulous tradesman.

Summing up now the evidence in reference to these stationers, and their relations to each other, we find :

(1). That the copyright to the anonymous *Leir*, entered by White in 1594, belonged to a member of his family as late as 1624.

(2). That in all likelihood, therefore, the book was White's property in 1605, and the edition published that year by Stafford and Wright must have been piratical.

(3). That Wright probably became acquainted with the play soon after its original entry in May, 1594, since he was an apprentice in White's shop for eight years commencing June 24, 1594.

(4). That this connection between White and Wright confirms the opinion already formed that the two *Leir* plays copyrighted by them in 1594 and 1605 respectively were identical, and so strengthens conclusion (2).

(5). That Wright assisted in selling a piratical edition of Shakspere's *Sonnets* in 1609.

(6). That Stafford was engaged in 1611 in publishing a piratical edition of the *Pericles*, which he ascribed to Shakspere, and long before that time was regarded, at least in some quarters, with suspicion.

The cumulative effect of these bits of evidence must surely tend to make more reasonable Malone's theory that the publication of the anonymous play by Stafford and Wright in 1605 was for the purpose of deceiving a public that desired to read Shakspere's tragedy. What follows does not relate particularly to this fraud, but concerns the date of the Shaksperean *Lear*.

III.

In the Folio of 1623 the *King Lear* is entitled a tragedy, but as already observed, it was called a history on the entry of the quarto in 1607, and on its publication next year bore the name, *M. William Shak-speare, HIS True Chronicle History*. About twenty years ago Mr. Fleay,[1] arguing in support of Malone's suggestion, called attention to the fact that the 1605 anonymous *Leir* was entered on the Register as *the Tragecall historie*, but was on publication likewise entitled *The True Chronicle History*.

Mr. Fleay argued that the use of the word "Tragecall" in the entry of the anonymous play, which has a happy, not a tragical, ending, was a palpable attempt on the part of Stafford to mislead the public into buying the play for Shakspere's, but that Wright in publishing the play "had not the impudence" to put Stafford's phrasing on his title-page. The similarity in the titles of these two printed plays Mr. Fleay accounted for as due to the desire of Butter to mark his as the genuine Shaksperean work.

Mr. W. J. Craig and Dr. Wilfrid Perrett have recently been at much pains to confute Mr. Fleay's reasoning as to the use of the word "Tragecall." Mr. Craig shows[2] that the anonymous *Leir* is really tragical in a certain sense, and that the term might be applied to a play with a happy ending. Dr. Perrett[3] accepting Mr. Craig's arguments ridicules the contention of Mr. Fleay on the reasonable ground that an effort to deceive the public by the use of this word would be "remarkably ineffectual," if that effort were confined "to the private papers of the company of Stationers."

---

[1] In an article on this subject in Robinson's *Epitome of Literature*, quoted by Furness, *Variorum Lear*, p. 381.

[2] *King Lear*, p. xix.

[3] *Story of King Lear*, p. 97.

But it is rather surprising that in all this discussion apropos of the term "Tragecall," apparently no one has gone back to the original entry in the Stationers' Register to examine the word there.   Fortunately those of us to whom the identical entry is inaccessible will not have to depend on Arber's printed *Transcript* for our knowledge of it, since a *facsimile* reproduction of the same was published in Halliwell's edition of Shakspere [1] just forty years ago.   A close examination of this entry will, I think, convince any one that the word in question is due to a scribal error partially corrected.   What the scribe has done is first to write "Tragedie," and then change it to "Tragecall historie." [2] It seems probable that this error alone is responsible for the use of the word in the entry ; perhaps neither Stafford nor Wright thought of employing the adjective till after the mistake was made. [3]

This fact seems to dispose of Mr. Fleay's ingenious argument, but how does it affect his main contention that Shakspere's tragedy was already on the stage when this entry was made ?   The scribe apparently first wrote "Tragedie of kinge Leir," and afterwards corrected his own mistake, perhaps at the express desire of the stationer who was then entering the book.   But why should he fall into this error

[1] xiv, facing p. 354. Even Dr. Perrett seems to have overlooked this reproduction, although on p. 94 of his *Lear Story* he quotes from Halliwell-Phillips, xiv, 354.

[2] The loop of the "d" is plainly visible.   Under the last three letters of "Tragecall," appear certain other letters, probably "-die," while the word "historie" has been written above the line.   All these corrections are in the same handwriting as the original entry.

[3] Professor Kittredge suggests to me that this accounts for the spelling of "Tragecall."   Since this suggestion was made I have come upon the word very frequently in Elizabethan literature, but have yet to find another instance of it spelled with an -e.   When the scribe is obliged to repeat the title just below, in transferring the play to Wright, it will be noted that he uses "Tragicall."

at all?[1] The most plausible explanation is that there was a certain tragedy of that name already in existence with which the scribe was acquainted.[2] If this be admitted it will scarcely be doubted that the tragedy was Shakspere's, the only tragedy known to have been written on the subject.

It is possible that Shakspere's *King Lear* was at this date sometimes called a tragedy, and sometimes the "True Chronicle History." Like *Richard III* the play would be fairly entitled to either name.[3] Certain it is that the quartos of the *Lear* use one term, and the folios the other. The employment of the second title by Stafford and Wright in what we have already found reason to believe was a fraudulent edition of the older play, would tend to show that both names were given as early as 1605 to Shakspere's *Lear*. If their intention was to deceive the public the piratical publishers would hardly have adopted new nomenclature.[4]

IV.

In this severely technical discussion of facts relative to the publication of the genuine tragedy of *King Lear* and its predecessor, it has been deemed necessary frequently to

---

[1] The arguments of Mr. Craig and Dr. Perrett that the *Leir* could be called a "tragical history" are scarcely convincing. To prove that it could be termed a tragedy would be more difficult still. Mr. Fleay is partially right. If Wright and Stafford intended to call the play a "tragical history," there must have been some reason why they did not use that phrase on their title-page.

[2] I shall not attempt to say whether or not the scribe was actually led by the printers to believe that the play they were entering was the genuine tragedy which he had heard of. Possibly he had the tragedy in mind beforehand.

[3] One must not forget that to the Elizabethans the story of Leir was veracious history, or that Shakspere's play was in part founded on Holinshed's Chronicle.

[4] This is at variance with the theory of Mr. Fleay, as above, that the phrasing was first adopted by Stafford and Wright, and afterwards imitated by Butter. I do not feel quite sure that Mr. Fleay is in error.

recapitulate the points in the argument for the sake of clearness. There remain to add only a few words now summarizing the evidence and stating the general bearings of the discussion.

Assuming Malone's hypothesis to be true we have found confirmation of it in several directions. First of all it seems reasonably clear that the *Leir* of 1594 never belonged to Stafford and Wright, but that they printed a piratical edition of it in 1605. Evidence on this point is strengthened by the discovery that Wright had been an apprentice of the original publisher for eight years, beginning with 1594, and that the *Leir* of 1605 was the first book which bore Wright's name as publisher. Wright again appears a few years later engaged with Thorpe in the piratical publication of Shakspere's *Sonnets*, while Stafford, his partner in the *Leir* transaction, is known to have published a piratical edition of the *Pericles* bearing Shakspere's name. Finally it has been pointed out that in the entry of this anonymous *Leir* in May, 1605, the scribe first wrote "*Tragedie of kinge Leir,*" an error which seems to point to the existence of a genuine tragedy of that name at the time. Adding these facts to what is already known as to the actual date of Shakspere's *Lear*, and the curious phrasing of its title on the quartos, we find Malone's theory at least more plausible. To reject it now we shall have to explain away a set of very striking coincidences. If we accept it we must date *King Lear* some time before May, 1605.[1]

---

[1]Arguments for a later date based on internal evidence are far from convincing, and have convinced almost none of the editors of the play. Mr. Aldis Wright's inference from Edmund's allusion to "these eclipses" (cf. Furness, p. 379 f.) that "Shakspere did not begin to write *King Lear* till towards the end of the year 1605," when occurred a great eclipse of the sun, following an eclipse of the moon, cannot have much weight in determining the question. It is not accepted by Furness (p. 381), or by Craig (*op. cit.*, p. xxii), although both these last are inclined with Wright to

Tò certain questions in regard to the date and the author-ship of the anonymous play I hope to return later.[1]

ROBERT ADGER LAW.

a later date than Malone's. Even less may be said in favor of the supposed allusion to the Gunpowder Plot of November, 1605, in the same speech. Mr. Craig's suggestion (p. xxiv) that the *Lear* was probably a new play when presented at Whitehall in December, 1606, "the plays selected on such occasions being seldom or never old plays," deserves more considera-tion. An answer to this argument is found in the court performance of *The Tempest* at the nuptial festivities of Princess Elizabeth and the Elector Frederick, May, 1613. *The Tempest* was one of nineteen plays performed on that occasion. "But none of the other plays produced seem to have been new; they were all apparently chosen because they were established favorites at Court and on the public stage. . . . But 1613 is, in fact, on more substantial ground far too late a date to which to assign the compo-sition of *The Tempest*" (Lee, *Life of Shakspere*, p. 254).

[1] For much more in this paper than can be acknowledged in detail, I am indebted to Professor George P. Baker of Harvard University, under whose direction the study was originally undertaken.

X.—THE DURATION OF THE CANTERBURY PILGRIMAGE.

The question as to how many days Chaucer conceived his Canterbury pilgrimage as occupying is of interest for a number of reasons. The consideration of it takes us more familiarly into the time and place where we may behold

> "the nine and twenty ride
> Through those dim aisles their deathless pilgrimage,
> Lady and monk and rascal laugh and chide,
> Living and loving on the enchanted page."

But the matter may also throw welcome light on such questions as how thoroughly Chaucer planned out the *Canterbury Tales* and how far their present shape is due to his conscious design. Tyrwhitt[1] accepted, though with some misgivings, the primitive and impossible assumption that the journey lasted but one day, which till within a generation or so was the usual view.[2] A duration of two days has been occasionally suggested, but never seriously advocated, I believe. Dr. Furnivall[3] in 1868 suggested the four-days (or three-and-a-half-days) journey, which has since been generally accepted.[4] Only Dr. John Koch, so far as I know, has advocated a three-days journey, a scheme rejected earlier

---

[1] Vol. IV, 328–9 (London, 1830) ; p. 206 (Routledge, 1871).

[2] Professor Skeat admits its possibility in his *Chaucer*, vol. V, p. 132, but denies it in III, 375, and V, 415. Cf. also W. Hertzberg in his German translation of the *Canterbury Tales* (Hildburghausen, 1866), pp. 666–7.

[3] *Temporary Preface*, pp. 41–3.

[4] See Skeat, III, 376 ; Mr. George Shipley, *Modern Language Notes*, **x**, columns 265–6 ; Mr. A. W. Pollard, *Globe Chaucer*, p. **xxviii**.

478

by Furnivall,[1] with the lodging-places Rochester and Ospring. This scheme, with Dartford and Ospring as lodging-places, I propose now.

Chaucer had been absolutely familiar with the entire route for years, it must be remembered; I do not believe there is the least indication of a connection between the *Canterbury Tales* and any pilgrimage of Chaucer's own, but he had been over the road again and again in his journeys between London and the Continent. So it is fair to assume that he would not have violated what was usual in real journeys between London[2] and Canterbury, at any rate without in some manner showing the eccentricity of his conception; and on this subject I am fortunate in having some light which these who have formerly treated this subject had not, mostly supplied by Professor Ewald Flügel and Dr. Furnivall.[3] Disregarding several journeys on which nothing can be based, either because they occurred as late as the 16th century or were very much interrupted, we may consider the records of thirteen journeys in the 14th and 15th centuries. Of these, three took only one day, but with modifying circumstances in each case; one was achieved in 1381 by

---

[1] *The Chronology of Chaucer's Writings* (Chaucer Society, 1890), 59, 63; *Pardoner's Tale* (Berlin, 1902), p. xxi; *Temp. Pref.*, 39.

[2] Sometimes Eltham, for persons connected with the court; but it makes no difference, for these travellers all stopped over night at Dartford.

[3] See *Anglia*, XXIII, 239–241; *Temp. Pref.*, 14–15, 119–132, and corrections and additions to p. 15 (the citation from Froissart is the same as Flügel's fifth case; see Froissart's *Chronicles*, edited by Kervyn de Lettenhove, XVI, 221); Koch, *Chronology*, 79–80 (a note by Furnivall on 16th century royal journeys, which I do not consider; given again in *Notes and Queries*, 8 Ser., I, 474); Furnivall in *Academy*, L, 14; E. A. Bond in *Archæologia*, XXXV, 453–469. See also *Notes and Queries*, 8 Ser., I, 522–3, and Henry Littlehales, *Notes on the Road between London and Canterbury* (Ch. Soc., 1898). For an interesting essay on roads and travel in the Middle Ages, see F. S. Merryweather, *Glimmerings in the Dark* (London, 1850), pp. 40–63.

the dowager Princess of Wales in mortal terror of Jack Straw's rebels, and two by several citizens of Canterbury, men, and from London to Gravesend were by water. Three took two days; two of them by these same men (once partly by water), and the other apparently by men only.[1] Four took three days; one by two knights,[2] the other three by large companies of people (one of them by Queen Philippa on her first entry into England). Three took four days;[3] two of these journeys were pilgrimages by the dowager Queen Isabella, "the She-wolf of France," in 1357 and 1358, and the other was by King John of France, in 1360, who took four days from Eltham, where he had gone the day before from London.[4]

The four-days journeys are of the less value as parallels to Chaucer's, because it is pretty clear that they were more of the nature of royal progresses[5] and strictly religious devotions than of ordinary pilgrimages; both King John and Queen Isabella heard masses and gave copious alms on the way, and clearly travelled in much state. Isabella's journeys are especially non-significant, though they have been the ones most quoted as offering parallels. She was far advanced in

[1] See *Academy*, L, 14, and *Angl.*, XXIII, 240. Froissart curiously says that the latter went "à petites journées."

[2] See Flügel's quotation from Froissart; Professor Skeat is somewhat mistaken here (I, xix).

[3] *N. and Q.*, l. c., p. 523; *Temp. Pref.*, 120–130.

[4] It does not seem that time of year made very much difference, as has sometimes been suggested. One of the 1-day journeys was in June, and two in October; two of the 2-days in October and the other in March; of the 3-days, one was in April, one in December or January, and the other two seem to have been in winter, though this is not certain; the 4-days journeys were in June, October and July. This suggests that the state of the road was not very variable, and this that it cannot have been so bad after all; or else that three days was the usual time when the roads were in their worse state, and that, when they were best, people might either rush things, or else linger in order to enjoy themselves.

[5] So with the 16th century journeys that have been adduced.

years, and so was the Countess of Warren, who accompanied her.[1] More than this, she was in very poor health.[2] Should two old women, one of them a sick queen-dowager, set the pace for Chaucer's pilgrims?

It is interesting also to notice the stages of the journey, and where these various travellers spent the nights. The distance from Southwark to Canterbury is 57 miles or over; to Dartford is 15 miles, to Rochester 15 more, to Ospring 17 and over, and to Canterbury a little over 9. Eltham is 7 miles from Southwark. On the two-day journeys the travellers slept once at Rochester and once at Gravesend (because they took boat there and probably had to wait for the tide); on the three-day journeys, at Dartford and Rochester three times, and at Dartford and Ospring once; on the four-day journeys, always at Dartford, Rochester and Ospring.[3] These are the only lodging-places found in these records.[4]

[1] And appears to have been a friend of her youth (*Archæologia*, xxxv, 456). The Countess was a granddaughter of Edward I., and was married in 1305. Isabella was born in 1292, so was nearly seventy.

[2] "Respecting Isabella's death, she is stated by chroniclers to have sunk, in the course of a single day, under the effect of a too powerful medicine, administered at her own desire. From several entries, however, in this account [the document from which all this information is gained contains many entries as to medicines and physicians for the queen, the latter, apparently, sometimes summoned in haste] it would appear that she had been in a state requiring medical treatment for some time previous to her decease" (*Arch.*, xxxv, 462), which took place 22 August, 1358 (*ib.*, 455), two or three months after her second pilgrimage. Considering all this, her two elaborate pilgrimages within nine months, her death shortly after, and St. Thomas' repute as a healer, it seems pretty clear that she was seeking his help against a lingering and fatal disease. In this case we should expect her to travel slowly.

[3] Isabella stopped here on her return, which thereafter followed a different route. Froissart himself did the same (*Angl.*, xxiii, 241). On a different journey she went from Leeds Castle to Rochester in one day, thence to Dartford in a second, thence to London in a third (*Arch.*, xxxv, 462). Leeds is 10 m. S. E. of Rochester. Froissart, with Richard II. and his suite, went from Leeds Castle through Rochester and Dartford to Eltham in two days or less (*Chronicles*, tr. by T. Johnes, iv, 65–6).

[4] King John, and the citizens of Canterbury on their four journeys, dined

Now for Chaucer's pilgrims. We may reject the idea of a one or two-days journey;[1] not only is it inharmonious with what the records and good sense alike show must have been usual for such bodies of people, but it seems clear that the poem itself indicates two nights passed *en route*. In the first place, if we accept as Chaucerian the arrangement of either the modern editions or of the manuscripts, it is nearly certain that a night intervened between Group A and the Man of Law's Prologue, as is the general view.[2] In the Reve's Prologue, 3906-7, the pilgrims are near Greenwich at (say) half-past seven o'clock; in the Man of Law's Prologue, 14, it is only ten, yet four or five tales later they are near Rochester (Monk's Prol., 3116), nearly thirty miles farther. Though we must not assume that Chaucer's notes of time were all carefully studied with reference to each other, such quick going is a presumption against putting all this on one day. But more than this, it seems to me that Chaucer, if he thought what he was about when he wrote the Man of Law's Prologue, meant it to open the day's story-telling. In lines 17-19 the Host warns the rout that the fourth part of the day is gone, and exhorts them to lose no time; in 32-38 he urges them not to mould in idleness, and reminds the lawyer of his contract. Here again, of

---

at Sittingbourne, 11 miles from Rochester and 6 or 7 from Ospring. The Sumnour had promised to make the Friar wince before they came "to Sidingborne" (D, 847). So when he ends

"My tale is doon, we been almost at toune,"

this may refer, as Furnivall opines (*Temp. Pref.*, 42), to such a stop. Or if Chaucer did not go into such minutiae—and it is easy to exaggerate the minor realisms of the poem—it may refer to the arrival at Ospring, which it can be shown must have come between Groups D and E, not (as is usually assumed—cf. *Temp. Pref.*, p. 43) between E and F.

[1] So Shipley, *Mod. Lang. Notes*, x, 264-6; *Temp. Pref.*, 38-41 (though Furnivall leaves the 2-days journey a faint possibility); Skeat, III, 375-6.

[2] See, *e. g.*, Skeat, III, 376-7; *Temp. Pref.*, 42.

course, we cannot be sure that the passage was not written
without regard to a time-scheme; but if they had had at
least four tales before ten o'clock, and two since half-way
prime, the pilgrims certainly deserved no warning to *carpere
diem* or rebuke for moulding in idleness; and the charge to
the Man of Law sounds like a reminder, after a few hours
of general talk, of an agreement made a day or two before.
It certainly seems best so far to put one night at Dartford, a
place clearly indicated by the records, where all the three and
four days travellers slept.   As to the last night, Skeat[1]
shows conclusively by the Canon's Yeoman's Prologue, 555–
6, 588–9, that it must have been passed at Ospring,[2] a
conclusion also favored by the records.

Since a five-days journey is not to be thought of, the
question is between three and four.   Although the latter and
usually-accepted view, with a third stop at Rochester, is not
impossible, I believe that the evidence, both internal and
external, strongly favors the former.   In the first place,
there is distinct if not decisive evidence that Chaucer did not
conceive the party as stopping at Rochester.   In the Monk's
Prologue (3116–7) the Host says to him:

> "Lo! Rouchestre stant heer faste by!
> Ryd forth, myn owene lord, brek nat our game."

This no more suggests a stop at Rochester than the "Lo
Depeford!", "Lo Grenewich!", of the Reve's Prologue,
3906–7, suggest stops at these places.   It certainly means
that they were very close to Rochester; yet nobody objects
when the Monk proposes to deliver a selection from his
hundred tragedies, perhaps followed by a Life of St. Edward.
When he is choked off, after nearly 800 lines, the bells are

---

[1] Vol. v, 415.

[2] Which is, precisely as Chaucer says, somewhat under five miles back
from Boughton.   A writer in *Notes and Queries* (8 Ser., i, 523) suggests
Feversham, which seems unlikely and comes to the same thing as regards
distance.

still clinking on his bridle (3984–5); then follows the tale
of the Nun's Priest, after which the Host even calls on
someone else. Does not this indicate that the pilgrims
passed Rochester without stopping, at all events for any
length of time? And, in the second place, the three-days
journey is distinctly confirmed by the records; we have seen
that, out of the thirteen journeys, the number of those which
occupied three days is larger (four), and the travellers more
like Chaucer's, than is the case with any of the others.

This strongly confirms the view that the first night was
spent at Dartford. Since the records indicate no other
lodging-places than these two on the London side of Ospring,
the pilgrims must have slept at Dartford unless they went 47
miles the first day and only 9 the second. This point is
particularly important because my conclusion will not be
invalidated by the view, which I believe, and shall hope to
support on a later occasion, that the arrangement of the
groups in the manuscripts is not due to Chaucer. Against
securing a two-days journey by putting the Man of Law's
Prologue and Tale after Group F or Group G, which there
is not the slightest reason to do, there is the argument that
the Squire's "pryme" (F, 73) indicates the second day and
that, as we have seen, the Man of Law's Prologue seems to
indicate that on that day nothing had preceded it. But,
above all, this view will not invalidate the main premises,
that a night was spent at Ospring, and none at Rochester.

The only possible objection to this scheme is that stopping
only at Dartford and Ospring divides the journey into very
unequal stages, 15, 32 and 9 miles, and puts short distances
into the first and last days, when we know the party made
an early start or travelled long. But we have seen that just
these stops were made in an actual journey, in which case
the division was still more uneven, for the first stage was
only eight miles, from Eltham. And in the other cases of a
three-days journey, by considerable bodies of people, it was

little less uneven,—26, 15 and 8 (in one case 15) miles for each day respectively. It is clear that the only places where there were satisfactory accommodations were Dartford, Rochester and Ospring, and if people wished to take only three days they had no choice but to make things uneven; it would have been less uneven to have travelled from Rochester to Canterbury on the third day, but the only certain stopping-place we have found is Ospring, so this we know Chaucer's pilgrims did not do. There is certainly no ground for believing that, on one of the most travelled roads in England, it would be difficult for a collection of able-bodied people, even including a Prioress and a Shipman and some persons with indifferent mounts, to travel thirty-two miles in one day.[1]

The conclusion which I have suggested seems more perfectly than any other to follow from the evidence, both internal and external, and to involve fewer incongruities. It involves no actual inconsistencies. What improprieties there are, such as crowding tales into the early mornings and the unequal assignments to the several days, are due mainly to the unfinished state of the work, a condition which deserves frequent emphasis. If Chaucer had in mind any definite scheme at all, which there is no sufficient reason to deny, we seem justified in concluding that the days of his pilgrimage were three.

JOHN S. P. TATLOCK.

University of Michigan.

---

[1] They started at a good rate (Prol., 825). Cf. *New English Dictionary:* "*Canterbury pace*—supposed originally to designate the pace of the mounted pilgrims"; "*Canter*. A Canterbury gallop; an easy gallop." Furnivall casts aspersions on the road (*Temp. Pref.*, 15–17), but the slough may have been only at the side (*ib.*, Corr. and Add.). My scheme agrees well with 16th century customs. "Twenty miles a day in winter, and thirty in summer, were in the sixteenth century reckoned in official accounts a day's journey. Members of Parliament were paid on this basis." E. Porritt, *The Unreformed House of Commons* (1903), p. 157.

XI.—CHAUCER'S *PRIORESSES TALE* AND ITS ANALOGUES.

It is now thirty years ago that three stories, more or less closely related to the *Prioresses Tale*, were printed in the Chaucer Society's *Originals and Analogues*. Since that time but little new light has been thrown on the source used by Chaucer for this Tale. The general opinion has been that Chaucer followed some version of the legend not now known, though Professor Skeat in his most recent discussion of the subject takes the view that the *Prioresses Tale* is the result of a combination, probably by Chaucer himself, of two miracles of Our Lady related by Gautier de Coincy : that of the boy killed by the Jew, and that of the wicked cleric in whose mouth after death a miraculous flower was found.[1]

It is the purpose of the present article to bring together a number of additional analogues to ´Chaucer's story in an attempt to define a little more closely than has hitherto been possible the form of the legend which he must have had before him. For—if I may anticipate my conclusions to this extent—I believe that Chaucer's immediate source was a version of the legend still unknown to us.

The analogues which follow are arranged, so far as possible, in chronological succession. For the sake of completeness I have inserted in their proper order references to the versions already published in *Originals and Analogues*.

1. Cæsarius of Heisterbach, *Libri VIII Miraculorum*, Ed. A. Meister, Römische Quartalschrift, Rom 1901, pp. 189-91.

---

[1] *Academy*, London, Sept. 1, 1894, p. 153, and Sept. 15, p. 195 ; cf. *Oxford Chaucer*, Vol. V, p. 491.

Lib. III, No. 67. De scholari, quem iudaei pro cantu de sancta Maria occiderunt, quem beata Maria iterum vivificabat.

Quidam scholaris diligebat multum beatam virginem Mariam, qui consuetus erat de ipsa cantare, quidquid dulcius invenire poterat. Qui habebat hanc consuetudinem : Quotiens de scholis rediens vel ad scholas veniens quod stare solebat ante domum unius iudaei, "Salve regina" vel sequentiam "Ave praeclara" cantabat. Quod iudaeus supra modum aegre ferens et valde iratus scholarem pro cantare durius arguebat et saepius increpabat rogans puerum, ut a domo sua recederet et consuetum dimitteret. Quod puer omnino recusans saepius cantum, "Salve regina" "Ave Maria" iterabat. Tempore parvo transacto dum scholares etiam hieme in crepusculo noctis de schola venerunt et ad propria tecta regressi sunt, scholaris ille solus domum vadens et socios suos deserens ante domum praefati iudaei transiens et more solito cum magna laetitia coepit cantare "Salve regina" cum sequentia "Ave praeclara." Iudaeus vero ad iram provocatus domo exiens scholarem accepit et cum amicis suis hunc puerum interficere voluit. Qui iudaeus collum pueri ita stringens in captione, quod puer clamare non poterat, iudaei vero in vicino commorantes ad domum praefati iudaei convolantes consilium inierunt, quomodo puerum interficere possent. Qui puerum accipientes et in secreto loco super tabulam postea eum posuerunt et cum funibus eum ligaverunt dicentes ei, si cessare vellet a cantu, ipsum non interficerent. Puer irridens dixit, quamdiu viveret, a cantu beatae Mariae virginis non cessare posset, et hoc etiam iudaeis dixit, quod si possibile esset, quoniam membra verterentur in linguas, matrém misericordiae vellem cum cantu laudare. Iudaei hoc audientes furore repleti linguam suam absciderunt. Corpus vero suum ubi equi stare solebant, ibi sub fimo sepelierunt. Hoc facto mater vero pueri de mane ad scholas veniens puerum suum requirens, magister vero cum scholaribus ei responderunt se nihil de puero scire, tandem unus scholaris dixit, quod omni fere nocte solebat stare ante ianuam unius iudaei et ibi "Salve regina" cum "Ave Maria" solitus cantare. Tunc magister coepit cogitare, quod iudaei puerum interemissent, statim sine mora ad iudicem, ad consiliaros aggrediens et eis mentionem de puero faciens. Qui statim omnes ad domum iudaei euntes ei de puero, quoniam ad ianuam suam devote "Salve regina" cum "Ave Maria" consuetus cantare erat, mentionem facientes, iudaei vero cum iuramento de puero se excusabant. Illi vero verbis iudaeorum non credentes domum intrant et diligenter investigant. Scholares [nec] non cum civibus civitatis puerum adclamabant. Puer vero sub fimo illis respondebat. Illi vero statim puerum extraxerunt, in vultu roseo quasi inter lilia bene redolentia sedentem eum invenerunt. Post hoc vero puer recitavit eis per ordinem, quomodo beata virgo Maria eum custodivit et ipsum in omnibus membris suis sanavit et a periculo mortis liberavit.

14

Iudaei vero ǫe tanto miraculo stupefacti omnes sunt baptizati et ad fidem
Christi conversi.   Gratias egerunt deo et beatam virginem Mariam cum
magno tripudio de sua misericordia laudaverunt.[1]

2. Gautier de Coincy, *Miracles de la Sainte Vierge*, cf.
   Originals and Analogues, pp. 251 ff.
3. Paris Bibl. Nat., MS. lat. 18,134 (fol. 108 ff.)
   No. 31 (fol. 142 dorso) :—
   Exemplum de puero qui frequent*er* cantabat scilicet
   Gaude maria.

Fuit quidam puer qui clericus erat *et* beatam u*ir*ginem magno affectu
diligebat.   Paup*er* erat *et* paup*er*em matrem habebat.   *Sed* canonici multa
bona ei *et* mat*ri* eius p*ro*pt*er* Ch*ris*tum faciebant.   Optime *enim* cantabat *et*
fere ab omnib*us* libenter audiebatur.   Responsum aut*em* de beate u*ir*gine
scil*icet* Gaude maria libentissime cantabat.   Quadam *ergo* die c*um* illud
responsum p*er* uic*um* que*n*dam cantaret eundo.   Iudeus qui in illo uico
manebat audiens eum b*eat*am u*ir*ginem attollentem *et* iudeos in suo simil*iter*
cantu increpantem, sicut *in* illo *responso* continetur ultra modum iratus est.
Et uocans in domum suam illum puerum qui sic cantabat securi eum
p*er*cussit in capite *et* occidit eum.   Et post h*ec* c*um* in domo sua eum
sepeliss*et* ostium suum a*per*uit tamq*uam* nich*il* mali feciss*et*.   *Sed* c*um* ma*ter*
filium suum uespere no*n* uidiss*et* ad se sicut solebat reuertentem mirata est
ubi ess*et*.   Et eadem die cum filium *per* diu*er*sa loca quereret uenit in illum
uicum ubi filius suus occisus fuerat.   Et cum ante ostium illius iudei ma*ter*
predicta cum m*u*ltis amicis suis ad querend*um* filium suum transiret audiuit
puer*um* suum clara uoce cantantem *responsum* illud Gaude maria.   E*t*
introeuntes quesierunt a iudeo ubi puer ille erat.   Et c*um* iudeus negaret
illum ibi ess*e* fodit mat*er* *et* amici eius t*er*ram et puerum sub terra uiuu*m*
reppereru*n*t.   Et c*um* ma*ter* int*er*rogaret eum, fili quid faciebas sub terra?
dixit ei quom*od*o iudeus ille eum occid*er*at *et* sub terra posu*er*at.   *Sed* q*uad*am
pulcra do*m*ina, inqu*it*, ad me uenit que matrem dei se *esse* dicebat *et* rogauit
me q*uod* *responsum* suum cantarem sicut solebam.   Ad q*uam* uocem ego
cepi cantare Gaude maria et me uiuu*m* *et* sanum repperi.   Hec cum
audiss*et* mater de*um* *et* ma*t*rem eiu*s* laudauit.   Et c*um* p*ro*positi ciuitatis
istum casum audissent, illum iudeum q*ui* hoc fecerat int*er*fecerunt et om*nes*
alios iudeos de illa ciuitate expulerunt.[2]

---

[1] Attention was first called to the fact that this *Libri* VIII *Miraculorum*
contained an analogue to the Prioresses Tale by Professor Max Förster
(Herrig's Archiv. Vol. 110, 1903, p. 427).

[2] This transcript has been made for me through the courtesy of M. Mario
Roques.
Paris MS. lat. 18,134 is of the thirteenth century (cf. as to date and con-

4. Thomas Cantimpré, *Bonum universale de Apibus*, Lib. II, cap. XXIX, sect. 13 (Ed. G. Colvener, Douay, 1605, p. 289; in the edition of 1597 this story is added by Colvener among his notes, p. 542).

De puero a Iudaeis iugulato, & sub lapide sepulchrali recondito, qui postridie viuus est inuentus.

Dum quidam puer Scholaris, sicut Fratrum Praedicatorum fidelissima relatione didicimus, in odium Iudaeorum per plateas de vespere saepe cantaret: *Erubescat Iudaeus infelix qui dicit Christum ex Ioseph semine esse natum*,[1] Iudaei nocte quadam comprehendentes puerum, iugularunt & in cœmiterio sub cuiusdam sepulchri lapide absconderunt. Mane autem facto, cum mater filium perdidisset, & cum vicinis eum per diuersa loca quaereret, transiens per cœmiterium eiulando clamaret: Fili carissime, vbi te perdidi, vbi quaeram te; puer de sub lapide, alta voce clamauit: *Erubescat Iudaeus infelix*, &c. Ad cuius vocem stupefacti quaerentes,

---

tents of this MS. *Bibl. de l'ecole des chartes*, Vol. XXXI, 1870, p. 543). This story is summarized by Mussafia, "Studien zu den mittelalt. Marienlegenden," *Sitzungsberichte der phil. hist. Classe der kaiserl. Akad. der Wissensch.*, Wien, 1886, p. 984, who, however, erroneously registers it as No. 28 in the collection. As to the contents of this collection, Mussafia remarks in his third paper (*Akad. der Wissensch.*, 1889, p. 62): "Ebenfalls für sich steht Par. lat. 18,134, das sich nur im Beginne an SV. (*i. e.*, Paris MS. lat. 14, 463, of the twelfth century), anschliesst, bald aber eine grosse Reihe von Wundern vorführt, von denen manche, trotzdem sie in lateinischen Handschriften—wenigstens in den mir bisher bekannten—selten oder gar nicht vorkommen, in die Vulgärdichtung eindrangen."

[1] This line, *Erubescat Iudaeus infelix*, identifies the response sung by the young scholar with the *Gaude Maria* mentioned in other versions. The full text of this response is given by Mr. G. F. Warner in his edition of Mielot, and I avail myself of his note: "The complete response, which is said to have been composed by Robert II, King of France (997–1031), is as follows:—

> Gaude Maria virgo cunctas hereses sola interemisti
> Quae Gabrielis Archangeli dictis credidisti
> Dum Virgo Deum et hominem genuisti
> Et post partum Virgo inviolata permanisti.
> *Versus:* Gabrielem archangelum scimus divinitus te esse affatum;
> Uterum tuum de Spiritu sancto credimus impregnatum;
> Erubescat Judaeus infelix, qui dicit Christum Joseph semine esse natum."

circumspexerunt, & tandem de sub lapide puerum aduertentes, viuum & incolumem sustulerunt.[1]

5. Egerton MS. 1117 (fol. 176 b).

Puer quidam clericus, filius cujusdam pauperculae, cantans peroptime et saepius, cantabat istud responsum Gaude Maria virgo et laetantur. Et quia dicebat Erubescat Iudaeus infelix, ideo Iudaei invidebant sibi. Accidit quodam die ut transiret ante domum Iudaeorum. Iudaei eum acceperunt et eum jugulaverunt et sub fimo posuerunt in stabulo. Cum mater vero puerum suum quaereret et ante domum Iudaeorum transiret, ita loquebatur ad beatam virginem : 'O beate virgo, ubi est nunc cantor tuus qui dicebat Gaude Marie virgo cum affectu cordis?' Tunc subito puer qui fuerat mortuus, de domo Iudaeorum exiens, dixit : 'Ecce ego sum hic, mater ; noli flere.' Et requisitus ubi fuerat, ait : 'Iudaeus ille, invidens me quia cantabam de beata virgine, jugulavit me et in suo stabulo me sepelivit, sed beata virgo, matris meae commota lacrimis, me modo suscitavit de stabulo.'[2]

6. Vernon MS., The Paris Beggar-Boy, about 1375 A. D. Cf. *Originals and Analogues*, pp. 277 ff.

7. Paris Bibl. Nat., MS. lat. 14,857 (fol. 104 ff.), No. 13 (fol. 110 dorso) :—

Presbiter eximiam solitus laudare mariam
Sueuit cantare gaude maria scolare
Versum cantante gabrielem uoce sonante
Iudeus in uilla prediues mansit in illa
5 Se reputans dominum quia sciuit forte latinum
Infelicem se esse per uersum putat esse
Non hoc portare potuit cantante scolare
Insidias* tendit quem quondam uespre pendit
Quem demembrauit et sub trabe frusta locauit
10 Nulli scire dedit malefacta sed inde recedit
Cantat in ecclesia consuetum gaude maria

---

[1] Thomas Cantimpré compiled his Bonum universale de Apibus between 1256 and 1263 (cf. Elie Berger, *Thom. Cant. Bonum univ. de Apibus quid illustrandis saeculi XIII. moribus conferat*, Paris, 1895, pp. 15–6).

[2] I am under obligations to Dr. H. de W. Fuller of Harvard University for copying this text.

This is a MS. of the fourteenth century. It is printed by Warner in his edition of Mielot, p. xvi.

* MS. *insididias.*

Quod solito more *uersumque* scolaris ab ore
Pro dulci uoce quem dem*em*brauit a*troce*
Quod miser occidit pu*erum* bene viu*ere* vidit
15　Admirando satis timet acta sue f*er*itatis
Eius tecta subit abscondita me*m*bra req*ui*rit
Vt signu*m* tale clarescat sp*iritu*ale
Qu*o*d pia stella maris fecit nox ip*sa* scolaris
Plebano dixit na*m* s*ic* de morte *re*uixit
20　Et pr*o*bat hoc verum tunc p*re*sbi*ter* undique clerum
*C*onuocat *et* laycos actus res*er*rauit iniquos
Iudei miseri quem iudex vult cito q*ueri*
Queritu*r* inuentus reus est in morte retentus
Sig*na* cicatricum pueri dampnant i*n*imicum
25　Dum sic *con*uictus iudeus ait benedictus
Sis Iesu Christe q*uoniam* viuit puer iste
Quem dem*em*braui tantum pro uoce suaui
De genetrice dei qua*m* detestantu*r* hebrei
Quam credo vere super omne iuuame*n* hab*ere*
30　In *Christum* credo simu*l* et seruu*m* sibi me do
Hoc pr*opter* signum tam claru*m* tamque benignum
Tam bona tam*que* pia nunc constat virgo m*aria*
Quod dememb*ratum* sic reddere sic e*st* reparatum
Sic sibi vita datur et sacro fonte lauatur
35　Baptismu*m* q*uero* de *Christi* nomine vero [1]
Et secum multi sunt *Christi* nomine fulti. [2]

8.　Hague Kon. Bibl. MS. X 64 (new number 70, H 42). Fol. 48 c. :

"Het was een scolier, die woende bi eenre straten, daer Ioden in woenden, ende als hem sijn ouders om bier ende om broet sende[n], soe

---

[1] One suspects that v. 35 originally followed v. 30.

[2] This transcript was made for me under the direction of M. Mario Roques, who took much pains in deciphering this difficult MS.

MS. 14,857 is of the end of the fourteenth century (Cf. as to date and contents of this MS. *Bibl. de l'ecole des chartes*, Series VI, Vol. V, p. 53). Mussafia (*Akad. der Wissensch.*, Wien, 1889, p. 13) remarks as to the character of this miracle collection: "Auf die vielfachen Berührungspunkte mit Cæsarius möge noch einmal hingewiesen werden ; es liesse sich vielleicht daraus irgend ein Anhaltspunkt für die Ermittlung der Heimat der kleinen Sammlung gewinnen." This metrical version is found also in Metz MS. No. 612 (fourteenth to fifteenth century) and in Vatican MS. No. 4318, fifteenth century).

ghinc hi voerbi die Iodenhuus ende sanc dat vers, hoe Gabriël Mariën boetscapte, dat si overmits cracht des heilighen gheest den soen Gods ontfinc, ende dan soe sanc hi : 'Scaemt u, onsalighe Ioden, die segt, dat Ihesus van Ioseph sade gheboren is.' Die Ioden, die daer woenden, die hadden daer grote onghenoechte in ende wachteden dat kint bi avont, ende een Iode riept in, ende doe hijt in sijn huus hadde, doe stac hi hem die keel ontween ende bedalft in sijn huus."

De ouders gingen zoeken en hoorden bij het huis van den Jood "hoers kints stemme," want "het sanc noch dat selve vers, daert lach onder die aerde." Toen het levend in het huis van den Jood was opgegraven, en nog bovendien een litteeken overtuigend bewees, dat er een misdaad gepleegd was, werden de Joden "vanden ghemeenen recht veroerdelt totter doet, mer overmits dat mirakel so begheerdense kersten te worden, ende men lietse leven." [1]

9. Johannes Herolt, *De Miraculis beate Virginis* (printed as a third part in his *Sermones de Tempore, cum promptuario exemplorum*, Ed. 1492).

Scholarem a iudeis occisum resuscitavit virgo Maria. Exemplum LXVI.

Scholaris quidam in ecclesia ubi statutum est quod responsorium Gaude Maria quotidie cum versu Gabrielem, in quo est Erubescat iudeus, etc., iussus est propter vocis sue dulcedinem decantare. Iudei ergo ad vineas suas ante ecclesiam transitum facientes, et ex verbis erubescentiam sustinentes scholarem caute abducunt et in vineis perimunt.

Nox, illis abeuntibus, gloriosa virgo Maria puerum resuscitans, iubet eum suam laudem cum fiducia decantare. Iudei, iterum eandem vocem cognoscentes et audientes, admiratione percussi, secrete perquirunt a puero. Respondit si quidem se ab eis occisum sed per reginam sum pristine vite restitutus. Hoc cognito, iudei non parvo numero convertunt ad gloriose virginis Marie gloriam.[2]

---

[1] As given in somewhat condensed form by Dr. W. A. van der Vet, *Het Biënboec van Thomas van Cantimpre en zijn Exempelen*, 's-Gravenhage, 1902, pp. 223–4. This MS. is of the fifteenth century.

[2] I am under obligations to Dr. Robert A. Law of Harvard University for transcribing this exemplum and also for cheerfully looking up other references.

This story is noted by Mussafia, III, p. 50.

In regard to Herolt and his works, cf. the extract from Warton reprinted in *Originals and Analogues*, p. 104. Herolt is there said to have flourished about 1418. He was a Dominican friar of Basel.

10. Alphonsus a Spina,[1] *Fortalicium Fidei*, 1459, Story of *Alfonsus of Lincoln* (Cf. *Originals and Analogues*, pp. 108 ff.)

11. Miracles de Nostre Dame, Collected by Jean Mielot. Reproduced for John Malcom of Poltalloch with Text, Introduction and Annotated Analysis by George F. Warner, M. A., Westminster, 1885 (Roxburghe Club), pp. 14–15.

XIX. Dun jeusne clerc qui bien chantoit et hault Erubescat Judeus, le quel la vierge Marie preserua de mort.

En la cite de Anice, que lon nomme orendroit Le Puis, en Auuergne, fut jadiz vne coustume en leglise quilz aloyent tous les samedis de lan a procession entour leglise de la glorieuse vierge Marie. En alant a celle procession ilz faisoyent par deux jeusnes filz chanter vng respons qui se commence *Gaude Maria virgo cunctas hereses*, etc., ou quel respons est contenu *Erubescat Judeus infelix*, etc. ; et est cest *Erubescat* de moult hault chant. Entre les autres enfans de celle eglise il en y auoit vng qui auoit moult bonne voix et haulte, le quel par coustume chantoit ce respons. Or doncques auprez de celle eglise estoit vne rue, en la quelle demouroyent adoncques les Juifz. Et aduenoit tousiours, que la clause de ce respons la ou il dit *Erubescat Judeus*, etc., venoit tousiours a point destre chantez en celle procession droittement quant les enfans passoyent au bout de la rue des Juifz, qui les ouoyent ainsi chanter a leur grant vitupre. Auoyent grant dueil et haissoyent mortellement les enfans qui communement chantoyent ce respons. Auprez dicelle eglise et de la rue des Juifz auoit vng puits grant et parfont, la ou en prenoit et puisoit de leaue pour le service de celle eglise. Entre les Juifz de celle rue estoit vng Juifz qui bien entendoit lattin, et qui mortelement hayssoit ce jeusne filz qui chantoit si bien ce respons, si quil proposa en soy mesmes quil tenroit le jeusne filz sil pouoit, par quelque voye, et contendit pluiseurs foiz de trouuer son point de occire et tuer le jeusne filz. Or aduint a vng matin, que ce jeusne clerc deult aidier vng prestre a dire messe en celle eglise ; et lors, pour ce quil nauoit point deaue, il ala a ce puis pour puisier de leaue. Le [page 15] Juifz maluaiz et felon, qui veit lenfant a ce puis, qui [quil] hayssoit plus que

---

[1]Alphonsus a Spina, a member of the Franciscan order, was bishop of Orense, Spain. Of the printed editions of the *Fortalicium Fidei* the earliest bearing date appeared at Nuremberg in 1485. According to the British Museum Catalogue, earlier editions were printed at Strasburg (1471?) and at Basel (1475?).

personne du monde, regarde entour luy et ne veit personne. Il se approucha
de lenfant hastiuement et le reuersa dedens ce puis si secretement que nulz
nen sceut riens. Le puis auoit bien de iiii^{xx}, a c. pas de parfont. Les
amis de lenfant, le prestre et les voisins furent les plus esbahis du monde
quilz ne le veoyent plus et ne scauoyent quil estoit devenu. Ilz le feirent
querir et demander en pluiseurs villes, mais trouuer ne le pouoyent. Le
prestre morut tantost aprez. Or doncques, quant vint droittement en fin de
celle annee, au jour meismes lan reuoulut, que la procession aloit entour
leglise, ainsi comme elle lauoit accoustume et quil y auoit vng enfant ou
lieu de laultre qui chantoit ce respons, quant vint a monter celle clause,
Erubescat Judeus, il ne le peult chanter si hault comme il appartenoit.
Lors dist le maistre des enfans, "Dieu," dist il, "veuille auoir lame de
ton compaignon. Se il fust icy maintenant, il eust bien le respons entonne
et chante plus hault que tu ne le puez faire." A pou eust le maistre sa
parole finee, quant tous ceulz de la procession ouyrent lenfant dedens le puis,
qui chantoit la clause de ce respons tout hault, ainsi comme il le souloit faire.
Ilz le congneurent tout incontinent a sa voix, et lui aualerent vne forte
corde et longue et au bout de la corde vne grande seille. Lenfant entre
dedens la sielle et fut tirez a mont. Ilz trouuerent que lenfant auoit la
teste toute fendue, et quil estoit forment bleciez et tout chargie de sang en
pluiseurs lieux, si quil auoit pluiseurs playes mortelles, dont il fut mort, se
celle ne len eust preserue, qui vng an entier le garda vif dedanz le puis.
Lon luy demanda comment il cheut en ce puis; il leur respondit, "Je
vins ores au matin pour tirer de leaue pour aidier vng tel chappellain a
dire messe. Ainsi comme je me fuiz abaissiez pour puisier de leaue, vng
tel Juifz (qui [quil] leur nomma) se approucha de moy et me reuersa
dedans le puis." Tous ceulz qui lenfant ouyrent parler furent merueil-
leusement esbahiz tant pour ce quilz le veoyent ainsi naure mortellement,
et si nauoit nul quelconque semblant de doleur, comme pour ce quil ne
cuidoit auoir este dedans le puis que demi jour seulement, et il ly auoit vng
an entier. Le Juifz fut prins, son cas confessa tout incontinent et la cause
pour quoy il auoit eu gette lenfant dedens le puis. Son proces fut fa.t,
et fut ars, ne tarda gaires aprez. Quant lenfant fut gairis, il demoura
tousiours depuis deuots a la vierge Marie, si que, aprez le trespas de
leuesque de celle cite, il en fut euesque par le merite de la vierge Marie.[1]

---

[1] Transcribed for me through the courtesy of Dr. H. deW. Fuller.

Mielot's Collection is found in Douce MS. 374, of which the date of
writing was probably not earlier than 1467, a matter which is more or less
satisfactorily decided by the frontispiece in the MS. The figure represents,
most likely, Charles the Bold, and the arms which he bears indicate that
he was then duke—which he became at the date mentioned above. Mielot
was secretary to Philip the Good (1396–1467).

12. Speculum Exemplorum, Ed. Strassburg, 1487, Ex Vitis Sanctorum, Distinctio octava, cap. LIX.

Contigit post multa tempora circa hoc idem responsorium 'Gaude maria' aliud quoddam mirabile miraculum. Nam habitabat in confinio cuiusdam capellule iudeus quidam incarnationis dominice sed precipue (sicut et sunt omnes iudei) virginitatis marie extremus inimicus. Erat autem eodem tempore in eadem parrochia scolaris quidam eidem virgini gloriose valde devotus, qui ad honorem dei genitricis, sed precipue in confusionem et opprobrium illius improbi iudei integritatem virginis nequiter impugnantis, hoc duxit in consuetudinem vt inter cetera devotionis exercitia quibus eam venerabat singulis diebus in capellam illam ingressus coram ipsius imagine hoc responsorium flexis genibus decantaret devote.

Audiebat hoc iudeus quotidie et quoniam clericus erat verba intelligens in sui derisum composita ingenti tabescebat invidia. Stridensque in illum dentibus suis observabat si quando solum illum posset invenire quatenus hoc suum opprobrium ipsius occisione terminaret. Et ecce die quadam iuvenem hunc ingressum capellulam iudeus persecutus est et solum illum considerans. 'Nunc,' inquit, 'tante tue insolentie mihique diu iniurie exhibite finem imponam.' Arripiensque iuvenem discidit in frusta sicque per singula membra discisum sub ipsius capelle gradibus sepelivit.

Sed virgo beata, que misericordie sue officium ingratis atque peccatoribus exhibere consuevit, huic fideli suo famulo et martyri in tribulatione non defuit. Sed corpus pro sibi impenso obsequio in frusta discisum recolligens rursus misericorditer vivificavit, precipitque iam vivo ut solitum obsequium exhiberet ei tanto devotius quanto pro exhibito famulatu copiosius se sensisset adiutum. Mox iuvenis ad altare rediit et idem responsorium solito multo devotius decantavit. Tum autem ad verba illa pervenisset. 'Erubescat iudeus infelix,' cum multa cordis fiducia secundum altitudinem notarum vocem altius plus solito elevabat, ut scilicet altitudine vocis exprimeret magnitudinem gratiarum actionis; et iudeus qui ad delendum marie obsequium et in sue invidie remedium eum occiderat audiens rursum canentem quem credebat occisum amplius veretur, quod et factum est. Nam iudeus audiens illum canentem alium quendam nunc esse suspicatus. Verum tamen venit ut videret atque si alius esset rursus illum occideret. Sed videt et stupet, quia quem ipse se sciebat sepelisse, iam resurrexisse videbat atque ideo se frustra tantum facinus commississe.

Tunc iuvenis ne tam gloriosum miraculum suo silentio celaretur vadens ad pastorem parrochianum singula illi per ordinem narravit, ostendens eidem cicatrices tanquam signa quedam in singulis incisionum locis pro confirmatione miraculi derelicta. Pastor autem pro mirabili hoc divulgando miraculo populum convocavit eisque de dei genitricis misericordia egregium sermonem fecit. Pro cuius confirmatione sermonis iuvenem produxit in medium, et quod circa eum contigisset per singula patefecit. Quod omnis

plebs ut vidit dedit gloriam deo et laudem gloriose virgini matri eius que
sibi devotos in sua tribulatione non deserit. Verum cum iudici ciuitatis
hoc idem esset recitatum miraculum comprehendens iudeum pro commisso
latrocinio condemnavit, in mortem. Sed iudeus Christianum se fieri toto
corde desiderauit, et sic vitam obtinens eius virginitatem studuit conatu toto
defendere quam noscebat pruis impie et pertinaciter impugnasse. Legitur
in historia annunciationis beate virginis.[1]

13. Pelbartus de Themeswar, *Stellarium Corone beate virginis*,
Lib. XII, pars ultima, cap. 1 (Fol. cxxxvi dors. in ed.
Hagenaw, 1511).

Secundum miraculum de responsorio Gaude Maria virgo,
etc.

Quidam etiam puer fertur quod cum in scholis didicisset istud responsorium
Gaude Maria virgo cunctas hereses solas interemisti, etc., quod responsorium
cantatur in festo purificationis beate virginis. Et cum pulcra voce per plateas
et ciuium portas hoc decantaret: porrigebantur sibi plurime elemosyne et
ciborum reliquie. Iudei autem (quare plurimi in illa ciuitate commora-
bantur) cum audirent puerum canentem multum dolebant: eoquod matrem
Iesu laudaret et iudeos per responsorium hunc confunderet dicens Erubescat
iudeus infelix qui dicit christum ex Ioseph semine esse natum. Stomachatus
igitur in vicinatu platee: vnus iudeorum cum puerum talia canentem audiret
pluries: accessit et vocauit quasi aliquid pomum vel simile se daturum
asserendo; et sic promissionibus ac exenijs fructuum ipsum in domum suam
aduocauit tanquam si cantum istum ab eo audire, puer simplicitate perditus:
secutus est promittentem iudeum. Et mox iste habita opportunitate ipsum
puerum in gutture cultro cedendo occidit.

Cumque mater eius vidua paupercula diutius quesitum non inueniret:
dictum est a conuicaneis quod visus est a plurimis portas illius iudei intrasse.
Sed quid fuerit vel utrum sanus inde exierit: nullus testimonium poterat
ferre. Mater ergo iudicem adijt et iudex iudeos coegit, et facta lite: cum
probatio incumberet ipsi matri pueri: eoquod contra eam iudei insurrexis-
sent: nec probare quicumque de hac re mater posset: anxia pro filio
perdito: in hoc se obligauit quod requirerentur omnes domus iudeorum: etsi
inueniretur apud eos suus filius deperditus omnes iudei comburerentur. aut
si non: mulier ipsa calumnie conuicta comburetur. Quod cum placuisset

---

[1] I have been unable to identify the *Historia Annunciationis B. V.* here
referred to as the source of this version. I suspect that it was a fifteenth
century compilation similar in character to Franciscus de Retza's *Historia
Conceptionis B. M. V.*, otherwise known as the *Defensio immaculatae conceptionis B. M. V.*, printed in 1470.

iudeis et iudices approbassent. Ecce *quesitione* facta : nullibi *compertus* est *apud* iudeos puer occisus : qui *tamen* sub modio iacebat *occultatus* in *conclaui*. Tunc *mulier* lata *sententia* ad cremandum *ducitur* ab *omni populo*. exult*ant* iudei. compatiunt*ur* et dolent noti chr*istiani* ac vicini. *scilicet*. mulier*is* illius. pl*urimum* qu*oque* plorat ipsa qu*are* perdito filio : seipsam etiam amiserit.

Cum*que* nullum ha*beret* refrigerium qu*are* i*n*sult*antibus* iudeis tan*que* victorib*us* ; ad i*n*cendium duci cogebatur. sic educendo cum prope ecclesiam *beate virginis* peruenisset : atq*ue* recordata de beata *virgine* inuocaret ipsam lachrymabil*iter* : cepit audire dulces sonos acsi filius su*us* cantaret illud res*p*onsorium solitum. *scilicet*. Gaude Maria *virgo*, etc. Cepit*que* *protendere* collum et po*pulum* commonere si audirent. Et ecce omnes audientes populi cantum : commoti su*nt* et illuc accesserunt ubi audiebatur vox sonare. Et sic comperer*unt* qu*are* in domo illi*us* iudei sub modio absconsus fuerat puer occisus. subleu*antes* modium : videru*nt* puer*um* in gutture cruentatum cum angelis pl*uribus* dulciter illud res*p*onsorium concinentem. Quo viso miraculo et puero interrogato ac *omnia* facta enarrante *per* ordinem. *scilicet*. quo*modo* *per* beatam *virginem* fuerit sanat*us* i*n* gutture vulnerato : et dulci*ter* inter angel*orum* agmina fot*us*. Ecce *omnes* in laudem *beate virginis* chr*istiani* *proruperunt* : et iudeos *combusserunt* : ac puer*um* sanum *matri* restituer*unt*. Sic*que* *precibus* et merit*is* beate *virginis* saluata *est* *mulier* et fili*us*.[1]

14. *Magnum Speculum Exemplorum*, B. Maria Virgo, Exemplum xxx (Ed. Colvener, 1611, p. 650).

This version is a reprint of that in the *Speculum Exemplorum*, with the alteration of scarcely a word. I have not thought it necessary, therefore, to give the text here.

15. J. Collin de Plancy, Légendes des Saintes Images de Notre Seigneur de la Sainte Vierge et des Saints, Paris, 1862. "L'Enfant de Choeur," p. 218 ff.

The author says that this miracle (which he selects from a great number of similar wonders) occurred at DuPuy in the year 1325. For lack of space I must content myself with

---

[1] Pelbartus was a Hungarian friar of the Franciscan order. The full title of his book runs : *Pomerium Sermonum de beata virgine dei genetrice, vel Stellarium Corone beate virginis pro singularum festiuitatum eiusdem predicationibus coaptatum*. The earliest edition, according to Hain, was printed at Hagenaw, 1498.

giving an abstract of the story.[1]   There was a choirboy in
the cathedral of Notre Dame who was devoted to the Virgin
and sang her anthems so sweetly that all rejoiced to hear.
On Christmas Eve, leaving the church at the close of the
services, he disappeared and could not be found.   His
parents, the clergy, and the citizens searched for him in vain.
He had been seized and murdered while passing through a
dark street, by a Jew who had been angered at hearing his
song of the birth of Christ.   The body was buried by the Jew
with all secrecy.   On Palm Sunday, as the boys of the choir
were marching through the streets in procession, chanting
Hosannas, the slain child suddenly emerged from the grave
and took his place among them.   He told the story of the
murder and pointed out the assassin, who was forthwith
stoned by the mob.   Report of the miracle came to the king,
Charles the Fair, who made an investigation and as a consequence expelled the Jews from DuPuy.

Lydgate's story [2] (Harl. MS. 2251, fol. 70), printed under
the title, " The Monk who Honoured the Virgin," [3] is not at
all an analogue of the Prioresses Tale, but is a distinct
legend, found in many collections of miracles of Our Lady.
Lydgate takes the story, as he tells us himself, from the
Speculum Historiale of Vincent de Beauvais (Lib. VII, cap.
116).

Though these narratives—I do not include Lydgate, of

---

[1] The full text has been copied for me through the kindness of Dr. Fuller.

[2] Horstman is doubtless right in thinking that this poem by Lydgate,
written in the same metre as the *Prioresses Tale*, was an imitation of
Chaucer's poem.   Hoccleve likewise paid the *Prioresses Tale* the tribute of
an imitation.   Curiously enough in one manuscript of the Canterbury
Tales (Christ Church MS. CLII) Hoccleve's legend of the Virgin and her
sleeveless garment has been fitted out with a prologue and introduced into
the fellowship of the Canterbury company as the *Ploughman's Tale* (*A New
Ploughman's Tale*, Ed. A. Beatty, Chaucer Soc'y, 1902).

[3] *Originals and Analogues*, pp. 286-8.

course—present a wide variety of setting and detail, we have recorded in each the murder of a boy by the Jews because he sang an anthem in praise of the Virgin, and the miracle which our Lady wrought in his case. This constitutes the kernel of the story, and this serves to distinguish this legend from the host of others in the collections of Marian miracles.

Four of the versions in the foregoing list date from the thirteenth century. But the starting-point of the legend must be placed still earlier. For these thirteenth-century versions, when compared, exhibit such wide divergence that it is impossible to regard any one of them as the original of the others. Moreover, the question of dates forbids us to fix upon any of the versions before us as the common original. Thus, take the two which head the list: Gautier de Coincy wrote his *Miracles de la Sainte Vierge* while he was Prior of Vic, an office which he held from 1214 to 1233. But Caesarius of Heisterbach began his collection as early as 1225[1], and the mention of the *Libri VIII Miraculorum* in 1237, in the *Epistula Catalogica* of his works, would indicate that by that time the collection was already completed.[2] These two versions are thus so nearly synchronous that unless there were explicit evidence of dependence one would hesitate to assume that either author knew the other's work. A comparison of the two versions, however, fails to disclose any direct relationship between them; and, on the other hand, there are many important differences.

The origin of the legend, then, we must refer to some version earlier than any yet discovered—a version which can hardly have been later than the twelfth century. The home of the legend may be fixed with some probability either in Germany or in the Netherlands. The geographical distribu-

---

[1] Cf. Lib. I, No. 16, Ed. Meister, p. 25.

[2] For discussion of the date of the *Lib. VIII Miracul.* see further Meister, pp. xxxvi-vii.

tion of such versions as are known certainly points in this direction. One of the earliest is that of the German Cistercian, Cæsarius of Heisterbach, who, as Mussafia remarks, seems to have gathered his materials in large part from local tradition.[1] Thomas Cantimpré wrote his *Liber de Apibus* at the Dominican priory in the suburbs of Louvain, and definitely localizes many of his stories in Flanders. Coming to some of the later versions, our legend is found in the library at Metz, in a manuscript of the end of the fourteenth century; it occurs again in the collection of miracles in Netherlandish of the fifteenth century; it was also related in the fifteenth century by Herolt, the Belgian Dominican, and by the Hungarian Franciscan, Pelbartus. On the other hand, the collections of Marian legends made in France afford few versions of this story until a comparatively late date; and in England I cannot find evidence of it before the fourteenth century.

With this conjecture as to its probable home, I leave the question of the genesis of the legend. The wide variety of setting which meets us even in the versions of the thirteenth century makes it impossible to work out their exact relation to the parent version. Indeed, these changes of incident and detail suggest that the authors of these thirteenth century collections became acquainted with this legend through oral transmission. Certainly this miracle in its shifting form is in striking contrast to others which travelled through the legendaries and example-books with the variation of scarcely an incident.

Let us turn now to the subsequent history of the legend,

---

[1] "Die meisten jedoch sind ihm eigen ; sie tragen mehr den Charakter localer Sagen und fanden in die vulgären Literaturen keinen Eingang " (II, p. 57). Mussafia is here referring, it is true, to the Marian legends in the *Dialogus*, another work by Cæsarius. But his remark is of equal importance in considering the sources of the *Libri VIII Miraculorum*.

with the particular purpose of tracing its development to the form of the story told by Chaucer.

On comparing these versions it will be seen that they fall at once into two distinct groups. According to the first, which I shall designate Group A, the story ends happily. After being revived by Our Lady, the boy continues to live. Though nothing is known of his later life, Gautier tells us, it is to be presumed that both he and his mother continued to serve the Virgin devoutly. Mielot says that he grew up to be a bishop. To this "happy-ending group" belong all the versions except the *Paris Beggar-Boy*, the *Prioresses Tale* and *Alfonsus of Lincoln*. In these three, which I call Group B, the story ends tragically. The whole scene, after the discovery of the body, is funereal. Though by a miracle the child continues to sing, yet he is placed on a bier, and the mother follows weeping. Indeed, in the *Paris Beggar-Boy* and *Alfonsus of Lincoln* the boy was not actually restored to life at all; it was his corpse which sang.[1] Chaucer does not go so far; the clergeon testifies:

> And as by wey of kynde,
> I sholde haue deyed, ye, longe tyme agoon.

But in all three of these versions the miracle did not result in the young saint's restoration. As soon as the magical stone, or grain, or flower, was removed from the boy's mouth the song ceased forever and the corpse was buried with the honors appropriate to a martyr.

There are still other significant differences which separate these two Groups. In each of the versions of Group B, the miracle is effected by means of a magical object which the

---

[1] Note particularly *Paris B. B.*, vv. 128, 132, and 141. Cf. also *Alfons. of Linc.*: "Nec vnquam cessabat a cantu illo dulcissimo, licet mortuus foret." Again, in the boy's account of the miracle: "Vt non cessaret mortuus ab eius laude."

Virgin places in the mouth of the corpse. In Group A, on the other hand, no mention is made of any magical object. Moreover, the anthem which the child sings is the *Alma Redemptoris* in each version of Group B, but in none of the versions of Group A.

There can be no doubt that the "happy-ending" story of Group A represents the earlier form of the legend. This conclusion—inherently probable on the ground of greater simplicity—is established by the fact that, whereas several versions of this group are found in the thirteenth century, no version of Group B appears until the second half of the fourteenth century.

Having observed the distinct line of cleavage between the two groups, we may now proceed to consider a little more closely the relations between the several versions of Group A. Without entering upon a tedious comparison of minute details, it is evident, I think, that these "happy-ending" versions arrange themselves in several clearly defined subdivisions.

In the first place, MS. 14,857, John Herolt, and the *Speculum Exemplorum* are linked together by certain features of the story not found elsewhere.

1. The mother of the young saint is not even mentioned. In all the others (except the two French prose versions, which will be discussed presently) she is a conspicuous figure.

2. Our Lady, reviving the child, sends him back to the church to sing her anthem as before his murder. The Jew hears the song again from the church, and on investigation, is astounded to find his victim alive and well as ever. Thus in their account of the discovery of the miracle these versions differ radically from the others.

Such striking peculiarities warrant the grouping of these versions in a separate class. To this class also belonged, no doubt, the story in the *Historia annunciationis B. V.*, from which the account in the *Speculum Exemplorum* was taken. We may suppose, then, that Herolt and the author of the *Historia annunciationis* depended more or less directly upon the version in MS. 14,857.[1]

Another branch of Group A is represented by Gautier de Coincy, MS. 18,134, and Pelbartus. According to each of these versions the boy receives alms from those who hear him singing in the streets. This is a detail not found elsewhere in Group A.[2] The relation of these three versions to one another is particularly interesting. Let us first compare Gautier's French poem with MS. 18,134, to which it clearly stands in close relationship of some sort. If we leave out of account the characteristic elaborations of Gautier's narrative, it will be seen that the French poem corresponds to the Latin text incident for incident. One even finds that in these two, though in no other version, the boy is killed with an axe. These correspondences may be explained in two ways: MS. 18,134 may be regarded as a condensed version of Gautier, or, on the other hand, one may take the Latin text as representing essentially the source on which Gautier based his amplified poetical rendering of the story.[3] The latter view, in my opinion, is more likely. In the first place, Gautier is known to have gathered the material for his *Miracles de la Sainte Vierge* from various Latin compilations.[4] Again, Gautier's narrative is in some points confused and involved,

---

[1] Not necessarily, of course, upon this particular MS. It will be remembered that several MSS. of this version are still in existence.

[2] It occurs also in the *Paris Beggar-Boy*, but I defer the consideration of this until I come to speak of Group B.

[3] It is not necessary, according to this hypothesis, to suppose that Gautier used this identical manuscript. MS. 18,134, though of the 13th century, is probably not old enough for that. The date of the MS., however, is no obstacle to the supposition that it preserves essentially the version which Gautier used as his source.

[4] G. Paris, *La Litt. Française au Moyen Age*, 1890, p. 206 ; cf. G. Servois, *Bibl. de l'ecole des chartes*, series IV, vol. III, p. 41.

15

whereas the Latin text is direct and consistent throughout. Note, for example, that in Gautier's poem the mother hysterically denounces the Jews as the murderers of her child before the crime has been discovered. The French poet, moreover, shows a tendency to multiply wonders. When the child is recovered, wrapped about his head is found a paper containing a convenient account of the miracle—an absurd detail absent from the Latin version. Finally, it may be pointed out that though there are repeated cases in which this legend passed from Latin to the vernacular, this would be the only instance in which the process was reversed. MS. 18,134, then, we may conclude, gives us a form of the story older than the French poem, and represents essentially the source used by Gautier.

This conclusion is confirmed when we turn to Pelbartus. Though this fifteenth century Latin version clearly belongs in this class, it entirely lacks the elaborations added to the legend by Gautier. Instead, it reads like an expansion of the account in MS. 18,134. Pelbartus introduces a new incident: the mother's peril. To secure an order from the justice for the search of the Jew's house, she is obliged to put her own life in jeopardy in case the child should not be found there. But, aside from this device to heighten the interest of the story, the version of Pelbartus corresponds closely enough to the thirteenth-century Latin text. We have, then, in Pelbartus another descendant from the Latin version on which Gautier based his poem.

We come at length to the third class of Group A, represented by Caesarius, Egerton MS. 1117, and possibly also the Hague MS. The version of Cæsarius is most important for our purpose inasmuch as it approaches in some striking details the form of the story found in the *Prioresses Tale*. These agreements will be more fully considered when we come to examine Group B. By Cæsarius the story

is much more definitely connected with a school. The boy
sings his anthem on his way to and from school; the mother
goes first to the school to search for him; it is the school-
master who first suspects the Jew of the murder and lays information before the authorities. None of these details are
found in any other version of Group A. Moreover, in
Cæsarius the body is buried in a stable under the manure.
(Cf. the "jakes" of Group B).

In the Egerton MS. the story is condensed to such an extent
that details are for the most part excluded. But here, as in
Cæsarius, the body is buried beneath the manure of the
stable. This is sufficient, I think, to establish the connection
of this version with that of Cæsarius. As to the source of
the account in the Hague MS., I am by no means certain.
The fragment of the text which I have before me does not
afford any decisive test, though it seems to resemble Cæsarius
rather than any of the other early versions. Therefore I
classify it here, though doubtfully.

The extremely brief version of Thomas Cantimpré seems
to belong in a class by itself. It differs from all others in
describing the child as buried in a cemetery. The author
tells us that he had the story by word of mouth. This may
account for his variation from the usual setting. But since
no other account shows any trace of dependence on Cantimpré
the question of his source is not an important one.

We have now completed the examination of all the versions
of Group A except the two French prose accounts: one by
Mielot in the fifteenth century, the other by Collin de Plancy
in the nineteenth. Both these depart so widely from all other
versions that it is difficult to classify them. Nor does de
Plancy seem to have derived his account from Mielot, for
the latter says that the boy was killed by being tumbled into
a well, whereas de Plancy, in this particular, adheres to the
older form of the story. According to both, the boy was

discovered months after his murder, on the occasion of a great
fête.   The fact that neither version introduces the mother of
the child into the scene would seem to relate them to the MS.
14,857-Herolt-*Speculum* group rather than to the others.
One may conjecture perhaps that they have been derived—
perhaps through several intermediaries—from the form of
the story represented by MS. 14,857.   But for our purpose it
is unnecessary to inquire into the sources of these late French
versions.   They may be dismissed as variants which stand
in no direct relation to the versions with which we are concerned.

To sum up the results of our examination of Group A,
the probable relationship of the several versions may be indicated by the following diagram.   It should be understood
that connecting lines drawn between versions are not intended
to imply immediate dependence, but only to indicate relationship.   In many cases, doubtless, there were other inter-
mediary versions.

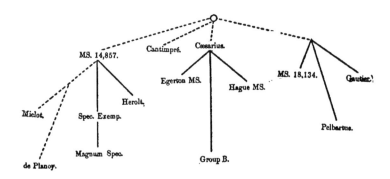

We are ready now to examine the versions of Group B,
in which the legend has been modified by substituting the
tragic ending.   At once we are confronted by the question:

How came this tragic ending to be introduced into the story? The explanation is found, I believe, by supposing that in Group B the legend of the boy put to death for singing anthems has been affected by the well-known story of Hugh of Lincoln.

In origin, of course, the two stories were quite distinct. The martyrdom of Hugh—always localized at Lincoln—is recorded by Matthew of Paris and by the annalists of Burton and Waverly as occurring in the year 1255,[1] a quarter of a century later than the earliest versions of the other legend. Moreover, the two stories differ most essentially :

1. The story of the boy killed for singing anthems belongs to the cycle of miracles of the Virgin. Hugh of Lincoln, on the other hand, is not—at least in its essence—a miracle at all ; nor does the Virgin play any part in it.

---

[1] One can't help suspecting that the martyrdom of little Hugh is after all only a second edition of the similar story of William of Norwich which sprang up in 1144 (Cf. A. Jessopp, "St. William of Norwich," *Nineteenth Century*, XXXIII, 1893, pp. 749 ff., and the *Nova Legenda Anglie*, Ed. C. Horstman, Oxford, 1901, II, p. 452). How the story arose is not, however, a matter which concerns us here. For our purpose the essential point is that the story of Hugh of Lincoln was well known in the 13th and 14th centuries ; it is related in the *Annales de Waverleia* (Rolls Series, pp. 346-8), in the *Annales de Burton* (Rolls Series, pp. 340-5), by Matthew Paris (*Chronica Majora*, Rolls Series, v, pp. 516-9), and by John of Tynemouth in his *Sanctilogium Angliæ, Scotiæ et Hiberniæ*, written shortly before 1350 (Tynemouth's collection was afterwards incorporated in Capgrave's *Nova Legenda Anglie*, recently edited by Horstman. The story of Hugh will be found in Vol. II, p. 39). It was also the subject of an Anglo-French poem, *Hugues de Lincoln*, (Ed. F. Michel, Paris, 1834).

For further bibliography in regard to Hugh of Lincoln and similar stories the reader is referred to Professor Child's introduction to the Ballad of the Jew's Daughter (*English and Scottish Popular Ballads*, No. 155, vol. III, pp. 235 ff.). Professor Child recognizes in the mention of "Our Lady's draw-well," in one version of the ballad, "a mixing, to this extent, of the story of Hugh with that of the young devotee of the Virgin who is celebrated in Chaucer's Prioresses Tale." But he does not enter into the question of the relationship of the Prioresses Tale to the story of Hugh of Lincoln.

2. In both the motive for the murder and the method of
its accomplishment, the two narratives are unlike. Hugh
was slain without any provocation, merely in accordance
with the custom of the Jews (so it was believed) of capturing
from time to time a Christian child and putting him to death
in mockery of Christ's passion. And thus Hugh, according
to all the versions, was crucified. In the other legend, on
the contrary, the method of death is never crucifixion.

3. In none of the accounts of Hugh of Lincoln is he
represented as singing anthems.

4. The discovery of the body of the murdered child is
effected by different means in the two stories.

5. Finally, Hugh of Lincoln was never revived after his
murder.

But though there are such wide differences between the
two legends it will be seen that they possess certain common
features which made it easy for one to affect the other. In
the first place, both were stories of the murder of a Christian
child by the Jews. Again, both stories presented the same
situation of a distracted mother, who searches for her child,
and at length learns that he was last seen entering the house
of a Jew.

These striking similarities of situation, then, led to the
introduction of certain elements from the Hugh story into
our legend. In Group B practically the whole scene after
the recovery of the child's body has been taken over from the
legend of Hugh. The body is laid on a bier, the mother
weeps, a solemn procession, headed by the bishop, bears the
corpse to the cathedral; finally, the remains of the young
martyr are enclosed in a splendid tomb of marble. It will
be observed also that the rigorous punishment of the Jews,
which in Group B follows the discovery of their crime,
closely parallels the vengeance taken upon them for the murder
of Hugh. According to Cæsarius and the majority of ver-

sions of Group A, on the other hand, the Jews are converted as a result of the miracle, and their lives are spared.

The Hugh of Lincoln story, then, enables us to account satisfactorily for the changed form of our legend as we meet it in Group B. It is necessary now to inquire as to the relationship between the three versions of this group. An independent variation of these versions from the form of the story found in Group A is clearly out of the question. That they agree in substituting the tragic ending, in adding the incident of the magical object placed in the boy's mouth by the Virgin, and in changing the anthem which the boy sang from *Gaude Maria* to *Alma Redemptoris* can only be explained by supposing, either that one of the three versions of this group served as the original of the other two, or that the three depended on a common source. Let us first consider the former of these alternatives.

It would be pleasant if the student of Chaucer might regard the tragic ending (as Professor Skeat apparently does)[1] as Chaucer's own substitution for the "inartistic ending" of the earlier versions. But against this is the fact that the tragic ending is found in the *Paris Beggar-Boy*, which according to universal opinion is earlier than the *Prioresses Tale*. On the basis of dates, then, the only existing version which could be credited with first introducing the elements borrowed from Hugh of Lincoln is the *Paris Beggar-Boy*. But a closer examination of this version makes it clear, I think, that it was not the source upon which Chaucer and the author of *Alfonsus of Lincoln*[2] depended. It will perhaps suffice to note here a single point

---

[1] *Academy*, Sept. 1, 1894, p. 153.

[2] In a later note (P. 512, note 1) I call attention to the extreme improbability that Alphonsus a Spina took his story from a version in English. What is there said against his dependence on Chaucer would apply, perhaps with greater force, to the possibility that he borrowed from the Vernon MS.

of difference. In the *Prioresses Tale* and *Alfonsus of Lincoln* the hero is a school-boy;[1] in *Paris Beggar-Boy*, on the other hand, he is a street-singer. This is more than a casual difference of detail, for it carries with it an important change in the setting of the story. Moreover, Chaucer and the author of *Alfonsus*, in making the hero of their story a school-boy, are in agreement with the majority of the versions of Group A, particularly that of Cæsarius. From this it seems to follow that they were not depending on the *Paris Beggar-Boy*. As the common source of Group B, therefore, we are obliged to suppose a version no longer extant, or at least not now known, which for convenience I shall call X_i.

This X_i, I conceive to have been a Latin version written in England. In the first place, the introduction of features borrowed from the Hugh of Lincoln—which according to hypothesis is to be credited to X—would point toward England. Again, all three versions of Group B are in one way or another attached to English soil. Two of them are in English; and the third, *Alfonsus of Lincoln*, though written in Spain, is placed in an English setting, for it is introduced into the *Fortalicium Fidei* in connection with an account of a persecution of the Jews in England.[2] That X was a Latin version may be inferred with even greater confidence. For only through the medium of Latin would the

---

[1] In a recent article ("Chaucer's Litel Clergeon," *Mod. Philol.*, vol. III, 1906, p. 468) I endeavored to make it clear that the hero of the *Prioresses Tale* was not a chorister but an ordinary school-boy. This is confirmed by comparing Chaucer's account on this point with the older versions of the legend.

[2] This account, it may be remarked, strikingly resembles the persecution which, according to the monastic chroniclers, followed the martyrdom of Hugh of Lincoln. This has some significance, it seems to me, as a further indication that in X (the source of *Alfonsus*) there was a fusion of elements from the two legends.

story have been at all likely to come into the hands of Alphonsus a Spina.

Inasmuch as version X was the immediate source used by Chaucer, it becomes a matter of some importance to determine as closely as possible the form of the story which it presented. And, having now before us, on the one hand the earlier versions of Group A, and on the other the three versions derived from X, it ought to be possible to reconstruct in outline the missing version.

To begin with, to X may be assigned features of the story which are preserved in all three versions of Group B. At the risk of repetition, I recapitulate the more important of these : The body of the murdered child was thrown into a "jakes ; " the Virgin appeared to the child and placed in its mouth a magical object—whether flower, stone, or grain, will be considered later—at the same time bidding him sing her anthem ; the body on being drawn up was placed on a bier, and carried in solemn procession to the abbey or cathedral ; on the removal of the magical object the song ceased ; the corpse was interred in a marble tomb with great ceremony ; finally, the Jews were apprehended and punished with great severity.[1] Moreover, in X the anthem sung must have been the *Alma Redemptoris,* instead of the *Gaude Maria* of the earlier versions.

Thus far the reconstruction is easy for we are dealing with incidents common to the group. Let us pass on now to details in which the versions of Group B differ.

In the first place, shall we suppose that in X the hero was a schoolboy as in the *Prioresses Tale* and *Alfonsus,* or a street-singer as in *Paris Beggar-Boy*? If we refer to Group A it

---

[1] *Alfonsus of Lincoln,* as printed in *Originals and Analogues,* does not include this. But in the *Fortalicium Fidei* the account of the punishment of the Jews immediately follows the extract printed.

will be seen that the street-singer tradition appears only in
Gautier and the Latin versions, MS. 18,134 and Pelbartus.
On the other hand, the boy is a "scholaris" in Cæsarius,
Cantimpré, Herolt and the *Speculum Exemplorum;* a "clericus" according to Egerton MS.; a "scolier" in Hague MS.;
a "jeusne clerc" in Mielot. Moreover, in Cæsarius, as I
have already pointed out, the school is prominently introduced into the setting of the story, in a manner which at
once suggests the *Prioresses Tale* and *Alfonsus*. The appearance of this setting in these two versions of Group B is
most easily accounted for by supposing that it stood in the
source X.[1]

How, then, shall we explain the street-singer in the *Paris
Beggar-Boy*? If we compare this English version again
with the MS. 18,134-Gautier-Pelbartus group we shall see
certain other agreements in details not found outside this
group. For example, the murderer entices his victim into
his house in order to slay him—a touch which is lacking in
the *Prioresses Tale* and *Alfonsus*. This is a trifling detail,
it may be granted, yet it serves to emphasize the peculiar
dependence of the *Paris Beggar-Boy* on this group, as shown
in the matter of the street-singer. We are thus driven to
the supposition that the author of the poem in the Vernon
MS. was acquainted with two forms of the legend—version X
and either Gautier or, more probably, a Latin version belonging to the Gautier group—and that he has combined features

---

[1] I may say at this point that I am unable to accept the view of Professor
Skeat that the author of *Alfonsus of Lincoln* was depending on Chaucer's
tale. The agreements between the two versions, to be sure, are in many
points striking, but they can be explained equally well on the hypothesis of
a common source. Furthermore, as I shall proceed to show, the form of
the story in the *Fortalicium Fidei* seems more primitive than that in Chaucer.
But, above all, is it likely that a Spanish ecclesiastic of the fifteenth century
knew the Canterbury Tales, or could have read the language in which they
were written?

from both.   This is an hypothesis which is always distasteful
to one engaged in tracing the filiation of versions, though it
is not in itself at all unreasonable.   Furthermore, to judge
from his workmanship, the unknown author of this Vernon
collection was a person perfectly capable of making such
combinations.   Of his collection of miracles of Our Lady,
only a fragment has been preserved in the Vernon MS.   But
the chapter - headings in the index at the beginning show the
scope of the work and testify to the extensive acquaintance
of the author with saints' legendaries.   Finally, there is
another instance, as I shall show in the next paragraph, in
which the author of the *Paris Beggar-Boy* appears to have
combined in his narrative an incident drawn from an outside
source.

We come next to the matter of the stone, or grain, or
flower placed in the boy's mouth.   Though here the versions
of Group B differ, yet they agree in placing some magical
object in the child's mouth—a detail of the story not found
outside of Group B.   Clearly, then, X must have contained
this incident in some form.   But was it the stone, the grain,
or the flower?

According to the *Paris Beggar-Boy* there was found in
the child's mouth a lily on which was written in golden
letters, "Alma redemptoris mater."[1]   This is a familiar

---

[1] Professor Skeat makes a slip here.   Referring to the account in the
Vernon MS., he says: "In this version, it is not the grain that is found in
the child's mouth, but the original rose ; or rather, the original rose multiplied by five.   For one fresh red rose was found in his mouth, two in his
eyes, and two in his ears!   We now know whence these roses sprang."
(*Academy*, Sept. 1, 1894, p. 153; cf. also Oxford Chaucer, Vol. v, p.
491).   But this is not the story of the Vernon MS., which gives us neither
one rose nor five, but a lily.   Professor Skeat has accidentally turned the
page of his copy of *Originals and Analogues* to Lydgate's miracle, "The
Monk who Honoured the Virgin."   Accordingly his attempt to derive
this incident in the Vernon MS. from the rose legend of Gautier de Coincy
comes to nothing.

story in the collections of miracles of Our Lady, but nowhere except in the Vernon MS. is it connected with the story of the boy killed by the Jews. Cæsarius of Heisterbach relates this miracle—exactly as in the Vernon MS., except that the lily bore the words " Ave Maria "—of a certain knight who became a Cistercian,[1] and it is borrowed from Cæsarius without change in the *Legenda Aurea*.[2] Moreover, elsewhere the author of *Paris Beggar-Boy* related this very story of a monk, this time with " Ave Maria " inscribed on the lily.[3] It is clear, therefore, that we are to regard the lily with the legend " Alma redemptoris mater" as a feature borrowed from another Marian legend and adapted to its present setting in the *Paris Beggar-Boy*. I think it altogether likely that the introduction of this feature is to be credited to the author of the Vernon collection himself, who, as we have seen above, shows independence in combining material drawn from more than one source.

Let us turn next to the *Prioresses Tale*. According to Chaucer, Our Lady placed a grain upon the boy's tongue. This is an incident which, so far as I am aware, cannot be paralleled in any Marian legend. But, as Professor Skeat has already pointed out,[4] Chaucer may easily have taken the suggestion for this detail from the legend of Adam and Seth.[5] Chaucer, then, as well as the author of *Paris Beggar-Boy*, has chosen to insert in the story at this point an incident borrowed from a foreign source.

But why should both authors have wished to substitute something else for what they found in their text? The answer to this question is obvious if we assume that, in this

---

[1] *Libri VIII Miraculorum*, p. 195.   [2] Cap. LI.

[3] Cf. *Originals and Analogues*, p. 279, No. 16.

[4] *Academy*, ut supra.

[5] Cf. *Legends of the Holy Rood*, E. E. T. S., p. 70 ; *Early South Engl. Legendary*, E. E. T. S., p. 7 ; *Cursor Mundi*, E. E. T. S., vv. 1369-76.

matter, *Alfonsus of Lincoln* represents the form of the story which stood in *X*. The device of inserting a precious stone in place of the tongue which had been cut out is not a happy one, even though it may have been intended to account for the sweetness of the young martyr's song. Now the author of *Paris Beggar-Boy*, as Horstman points out, was by no means lacking in literary art. Both he and Chaucer were dissatisfied with this crude device; each, therefore, in his own way, replaced this objectionable detail by an incident originally foreign to the story.

In supposing that *Alfonsus of Lincoln*, in the matter of the gem-tongue, preserves essentially the reading of X, there is a difficulty which I will not evade. The bestowal of the precious stone in place of the tongue necessarily supposes that the tongue had been cut out. But if this was the form of the story in *X*, how comes it that neither Chaucer nor the author of the Vernon MS. represents the boy's tongue as cut out, but tell us instead that his throat was cut? In this difficulty, of course, there is nothing inherently insuperable. A whole series of possible hypotheses might be devised to solve it.[1] But to such speculations without further facts to support them, one might well reply:

> This is *ignotum per ignotius*.

The authority of *Alfonsus of Lincoln*, however, is not the only consideration which inclines me to believe that the tongue-cutting actually stood in X. This very detail, it will be remembered, occurs also in the version of Cæsarius of Heisterbach, which of all the early versions approaches most

---

[1] If anyone should be disposed to argue that Chaucer had the Vernon MS. before him, I should not dispute such a possibility. On this, however, I insist : that the *Paris Beggar–Boy* alone will not account for the form of the story told by the Prioress. In that case, how does it happen that Chaucer agrees with the other versions in making his hero a school-boy?

closely the form of the story which Chaucer must have had before him. The miracle collections of Cæsarius enjoyed the widest popularity, in England as well as on the Continent, down to the fifteenth century.[1] There is nothing unlikely, therefore, in the supposition that the author of X used Cæsarius as his source. Moreover, in that case we may even find a reason for the addition in X of the object placed in the young martyr's mouth. "How was it possible," pondered this rationalistic recorder of miracles, "for the boy to sing after his tongue was gone?" Accordingly, Our Lady appears to him and inserts a precious stone in place of the tongue!

In the course of our attempt to reconstruct the form of the story in the missing X, we have had occasion more than once to note the fact that the account by Cæsarius supplies a parallel to Group B in details which are found in no other early version. Still other parallels may be noted here. In Cæsarius the child sings his anthem as he passes through Jewry on his way to and from school (Cf. *Prioresses Tale* and *Alfonsus*); the body is buried under the manure of the stable (Cf. the "jakes" of Group B); the mother waits all night for her missing child and in the morning goes first to the school to inquire for him (cf. *Prioresses Tale* and *Alfonsus*). Indeed, Cæsarius + Hugh of Lincoln will account for every element of the story in X, except the placing of the magical object in the boy's mouth, and this may have been added in X for the reason suggested above.

That between Cæsarius and X there may have been inter-

---

[1] Thus in Part I. of the 15th century treatise known as *Jacob's Well* (E. E. T. S., 1904) I count no less than nineteen miracles expressly quoted from Cæsarius. And in the *Alphabet of Tales* (E. E. T. S., 1904–05) out of 801 stories, 133 are taken from Cæsarius—a far larger number than from any other single author. Compare also the stories from Cæsarius in English treatises which have been ascribed to Richard Rolle (*R. Rolle of Hampole*, Ed. Horstman, vol. I, pp. 157, 192, 193).

mediate versions, I would not deny. I affirm merely that we are not required to assume any intermediate version in order to account for the development of the story to the form which it assumes in Group B. Cæsarius's collections of miracles enjoyed wide popularity; there is nothing improbable, therefore, in supposing that the author of X was acquainted with them at first hand. And, generally speaking, the simplest explanation which will account for the facts is to be preferred.

Let me sum up the conclusions in regard to the versions of Group B by resorting again to a diagram:

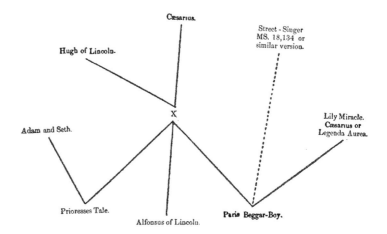

The result of this examination of the legend told by the Prioress exactly accords with what one would expect from observing Chaucer's methods in the case of other Tales. Practically nothing in the plot of the legend is his own invention. But no one, I trust, will so far misunderstand my intentions in pointing out this fact as to accuse me of assailing the poet's originality. It did not require originality of a very high order to invent a saint's legend, as everyone must feel after ploughing through the huge collections of mediæval miracles.   Chaucer's originality was of an altogether different kind.   And nothing, in my opinion, helps us better to appreciate exactly in what this contribution of his own genius consisted, than to compare the *Prioresses Tale* with such a story as *Alfonsus of Lincoln*, which, as we now see, corresponds essentially to the form of the legend which he used as his source.   One is the skeleton, complete in every limb ; the other is flesh and blood.

CARLETON F. BROWN.

PUBLICATIONS

OF THE

Modern Language Association of America

1906.

| VOL. XXI, 3. | NEW SERIES, VOL. XIV, 3. |

XII.—PARATAXIS IN PROVENÇAL.

Comparative philologists have long since recognized that the logical relation of mental concepts need not find expression by means of words. Viewed from the standpoint of pure logic a sentence like "I think he will come" contains a subordination; but the student of historical grammar rightly regards it as exhibiting two independent, if not unrelated, sentences. It is altogether likely that such a method of juxtaposing concepts was the only one that prevailed in remote antiquity and that in the course of time such a loosely connected sequence of clauses developed into one organic whole. The fact of parataxis is now established for all branches of the Indo-European family, and Hermann[1] has proved that grammatical subordination was unknown in the "Ursprache," being developed in the daughter tongues by means of the specific determinants of the originally independent sentence. Notwithstanding these results, there is still a plentiful lack of agreement among scholars in regard

[1] Kuhn's *Zeitschrift*, xxxiii, 481–535.

519

to the definition of the term parataxis and to the degree of extension to be ascribed to it.

The best recent discussion of the question is that by Morris in his important work on Methods in Syntax.[1] He demonstrates that psychologically there is no such thing as complete independence among successive groups of concepts. Contiguous sentences, to the normal mind, imply relation-ship; and its non-existence is an indication of mental disorder. It seems, then, advisable to avoid psychological definition of the speech-structure in question and to consider it solely as a phenomenon of language, to be defined by its linguistic characteristics. For practical purposes in the following paper, I adopt Morris' definition :[2] parataxis is any form of sentence structure in which two finite verbs are brought into close connection without a subordinating word to define their relation.

The various forms of the paratactic sentence have been much studied of late, especially in the Classical and Teutonic languages.[3] Its existence in the Romance dialects has also long been recognized. Diez[4] pointed out that in certain cases the conjunction *que* or the relative pronoun can be dropped. The theory of ellipsis as an explanation of para-taxis is now practically obsolete. In regard to the Romance languages especially, Gröber[5] showed that Diez's explanation

---

[1] *Principles and Methods in Latin Syntax*, New York, 1901, chap. VI, pp. 113–149.

[2] *Op. cit.*, p. 146.

[3] Cf. especially Morris, *The Independent Subjunctive in Plautus*, Amer. *Journ. of Phil.*, XVIII, 133–167, 275–301, 383–401 ; Becker, *Beiordnende und unterordnende Satzverbindung bei den altrömischen Bühnendichtern*, Metz, 1888 ; Hentze, *Die Parataxis bei Homer*, Göttingen, 1888–91 ; Behagel, *Germania*, XXIV, 167 ff. ; Delbrück, *Vergleichende Syntax der indogermanischen Sprachen*, III, 416–423.

[4] *Grammatik*, 1012, 1040, 1042, 1057.

[5] *Grundriss*[1], I, 226.

is untenable and proved that in the older stages of the various dialects the logical relation of two contiguous sentences was often left to the hearer to determine, and that the new conjunctions arise out of the adverbial modifiers of an independent sentence. The only complete study of parataxis in a single Romance dialect that we possess is that of Dubislav.[1] The classification adopted in this paper is purely functional; the author arranges the different categories of paratactic sentence-structure in accordance with the grammatical function which one or the other of the sentences would have if subordinate. Dubislav's conclusions were accepted and extended to the other Romance languages by Meyer-Lübke,[2] whose classification is that of the earlier author. The disadvantages of this method are obvious and have been pointed out by Morris. Classification by grammatical function is uncertain even in the case of strictly subordinate clauses; in parataxis, where the relation is only suggested, not expressed, it becomes still more difficult. Take a case in Provençal like *Non sai hom tan sia e dieu frems* . . . . *cum sia vas cella de cui can* (Dan. 14, 25). Is the second sentence here " objective," depending on *sai*, or " adjectival," modifying *hom*? Or in *Tals la cug' en baisan tener non a mas l'ufana* (Ba. Ch. 5220) does the second sentence correspond to a consecutive or a relative clause? In view of the uncertainty in these and similar cases, I believe it advisable to give up the older classification by apparent functional relation and to adopt one which seems more in accord with the observed facts and more apt to elucidate speech development. I shall follow, therefore, Professor Morris, who arranges the paratactic material in Latin according to the means used to indicate relation and the forms of sentence

---

[1] *Satzbeiordnung für Satzunterordnung im Altfranzösichen*, Berlin, 1888.
[2] *Grammatik*, III, §§ 535–541.

resulting therefrom. According to him, a relation between concepts, apart from subordinating conjunctions and pronouns, may be indicated: *a*, by mere contiguity; *b*, by means of single words, adverbs, pronouns, etc.; *c*, by contrast; *d*, by word-order; *e*, by a defining parenthesis. Of course, these different methods are never kept entirely separate and distinct; two or more are often combined. It should be premised also that in Provençal word-order is practically never employed to indicate relation by itself alone, but only in combination with some other method. The foregoing scheme must be regarded, therefore, as only approximate; I arrange each example according to what seems to me its prevailing characteristic and according to the usual tendencies of the language.

The purpose of the following pages is to present a view of the different types of paratactic sentence structure in Old Provençal, arranged according to the foregoing method. Examples are taken only from trustworthy critical texts. Latin forms have been cited for comparison only when there seems to exist a genuinely genetic relation between Latin and Provençal types. These Latin examples are mostly taken from the already cited paper of Professor Morris. To show the persistency of the type in Late Latin, I give also some instances from Gregory of Tours.[1] And to show further the extension of the typical forms in Romance, I cite for comparison a few examples from early Italian authors. These are taken from the lyric poets in Monaci's *Crestomazia*,[2] from Fra Guittone d'Arezzo,[3] Dante,[4] and Dino Compagni.[5]

---

[1] Taken from Bonnet, *Le Latin de Grégoire de Tours*, Paris, 1890.

[2] Monaci, *Crestomazia italiana dei primi secoli*, Città del Castello, 1889–97.

[3] Edition Pellegrini, Bologna, 1901.

[4] Oxford edition.

[5] Del Lungo, "Edizione scolastica," Florence, 1902.

I. Parataxis by Contiguity.

The simplest way of denoting relation arises when two sentences, each containing ‚a common concept, are juxtaposed without any other method being employed to indicate the connection between them. The spoken language often hints at relation more or less strongly by means of tone or stress, but such means do not ordinarily find expression in written speech. Personal pronouns sometimes assist in carrying the thought forward. When in more developed stages of language such a relation comes to be expressed in words, it is generally by the use of a coördinating conjunction or a relative pronoun. The latter means is mostly preferred to-day, and that is why I have ventured to introduce such sentences as the following into this discussion: they may be interpreted as exhibiting either subordinating parataxis or asyndetic coördination. They all show a juxtaposition of two verbs, united by a common noun concept: Crois. 1800, *E lo coms de Cumenge, segon mon eseient, I perdec a l'estorn un cavaer valent, R. at de Castelbo*: *plaints fo de mainta gent*; Barra 4688, *E pres at si X‹ companhos*: *Trestug eran filh de baros*; In. Par. 122, 7, *En un deves prop d'un cortil Trobey pastor' ab cors ysnel*: *Vestida fon d'un nier sardil Ab capa grizeta ses pel*; S. Fe 133, *Vell vos vengud inz en Agen. Aqo fo hom*: *non ag bon sen*: *Tals obras va per tot fazen, Per que sabem qe Deu offen*; cf. also Denkm. 275, 90; Ap. Ch. 110, 95; Ba. Ch. 17, 29; 340, 9; 366, 35; Sord. 23, 25; Gav. 5, 8.[1] How easily such juxtaposition may become coördination by conjunctions is shown by

[1] Cf. for Italian, Guit. Sonnet 117, 4, *Il tuo affare m' è tanto amoroso Ch' ogni preghero fai prendo in comando ;* Dino, I, 21, *Con lui era uno figliuolo d'uno affinatore d'ariento, si chiamava il Nero Cambi ;* and for Old French, Dubislav, 5, 6 ; and Tobler, *VB*, III, 66.

two neighboring passages in *Girartz de Rossillon,* Ap. Ch. 1, 31, *La mollers· Girart ac une enviiose, De sa cambre s'ancele, ville diose* : *Pres les claus de la porte, la cobeitose, E det les au porter, cui fun espose,* and *ibid,* 1, 24, *Lainç ac un porter maleureu, Faus crestian felun plus d'un iudeu, E gardet l'une porte en lat' en feu.* In both instances a modern writer would prefer a relatival connection.

Such juxtapositions must have been common in popular Aryan speech at all epochs. They are frequently preserved in modern ballad poetry of all nations. Compare, for example, the French ballad of *La Courte Paille* :[1] *Le maître qu'a parti les pailles, la plus courte lui a resté. S'est écrié : O Vierge Marie! sera donc moi: sera mangé,* with the Spanish *Conde Alarcos* :[2] *Porque en todos los mis reinos Vuestro pro igual no· había, Sino era el conde Alarcos: Hijos y mujer tenía,* and the Scottish *Lady Maisry* :[3] *O out it spake a bonny boy: Stood by her brother's side.*

Occasionally a personal or demonstrative pronoun repeats the concept previously expressed, thus forming a closer union between the two verbs : Ap. Ch. 1, 457, *Trobet mei orfenine, pauche bergere, E me prest a muller* : *deus lo li mere* ; Ba. Ch. 21, 38, *C'aisso sui remazutz Sai senes totz ajutz Per vos, e n'ai perdutz Mains dons* : *qui voillals prenda.* In both these cases we find a " wish " subjunctive attached paratactically to a preceding sentence and containing a pronoun which carries forward the thought. Another type is found in phrases like Biog. 20, *El vescoms de Segur, so fo lo vescoms de Lemoges* ; *ibid,* 21, 59, etc. Here we have an explanatory addition to the preceding sentence tacked on by means of a demonstrative, thus repeating what was probably the first stage in the evolution of the relative pronouns.

---

[1] Doncieux, *Romancéro populaire de la France,* XVII, 6.
[2] Wolf und Hoffmann, *Primavera y Flor de Romances,* II, 112.
[3] Child, No. 65, A, 19.

Sometimes such contiguous sentences express a locative or temporal relation, as for example: Ap. Ch. 1, 251, *Girarz iac en l'arvol*: *n'i a servent Fors sa muller quil sert molt bonament*; Ba. Ch. 21, 38 (Boëce), *Car la lissos es de vertat*: *Non hy a mot de falsetat*; Crois. 92, *El preguec Domni Deu, vezent tota la jant, Qu'el perdo sos pecatz a cel felo serjant, Cant el fo comenjatz, en la ves lo gal cant.*[1] In such cases the thought is carried forward by adverbs, *i, en la ves.*

In the preceding examples, the relation of the second sentence is mostly attributive to some element of the first; the old ellipsis theory would supply a relative. In other cases the relation may be one of cause or result. So in Ap. Ch. 1, 498, *Girartz respondet*: *bens es que diz, E eu lai m'en irai*: *toz sui garniz*, the last sentence is purely causal. In the following we find a consecutive clause merely juxtaposed, without the relation being indicated grammatically in any way: Ba. Ch. 23, 20, *Quant an auzida la raso E conogro que vencut so, D'ira lor enflan li polmo*: *Las dens croissen cuma leo*; Crois. 2115, *Per l'escut le feri, trauquet li los brazos El perpunh e l'ausberc, que dareir pels arsos Li mes uns trotz de l'asta*: *sancnens fo lo penos*; ibid, 3072, *Qui fug sa, qui fug la*: *us no s'es defendutz.*

More frequently a subjunctive wish-sentence is juxtaposed in a similar manner to express a desired result, just as if *tan* or *tal* had been inserted in the preceding sentence: In. It. 19, 390, *Talanç de domna gais Met son cor en pantais De tota ren a faire, De son preç sia maire*; ibid, 21, 467, *Gardaz vostre garnir*: *non puosca hom mal dir*; Ap. Ch. 104, 14, *Sest mal c'an fach perdona lor*: *Non aion pena ni dolor*; Ba. Ch. 23, 25, *Ar escoutatz*: *nous sia greu, Que sus lo cel*

---

[1] Cf. in Italian, Dino, I, 2, *E ordinorono ucciderlo il dì menasse la donna; e così feciono.*

ubert vei eu; ibid, 279, 29, *Sejaç me defenderis: L'anemic non aja part En me per negun esguart.*[1] The last four examples are uncertain in so far as they can also be explained as mere asyndetic coördination of wishes. It seems to me, however, that in each case a vague idea of result is present in the mind of the speaker, such as would ordinarily find expression by means of *tal . . . que, tan . . . que,* or a similar subordination.

II. Parataxis by Single Words.

In rapid narration it often happens that two actions of which one is the result of the other, are mentioned in succession, without the speaker explicitly stating that the second is a consequence of the first, as in "I ran fast: I fell." If the speaker desires to impress this result-concept upon the hearer's mind, an adverb of degree may be inserted in the first sentence, and this adverb points forward to the action of the second sentence so vividly that a relation of sequence necessarily arises: "I ran so fast: I fell." If the order of the two sentences be inverted, as in "I fell: I ran so fast," the second sentence assumes a causal relation to the action expressed in the first. In neither case does colloquial English demand a grammatical expression of this two-fold relation, although "that" or "because" may be inserted in slower speech. This type of parataxis, by means of adverbs which point forward or back, is richly represented in Provençal, giving rise to many kinds of consecutive or causal clauses. In Latin authors, this type is not frequent, though somewhat similar examples do occur, as for example

---

[1] Cf. in Italian, Dino, I, 4, *E chiamoronsi Priori delle Arti, e stettono nella torre di Castagna appresso alla Badia acciò non temessono le minaccie de' potenti.* For Old French, Dubislav, 10, 11.

Plautus, Poen. 909, *ita dei faxint*: *ne apud lenonem hunc serviem*; Terence, Heaut. 783, *ita tu istaec miscete*: *ne me admisceas*; Cicero, ad Att. XIII, 21, 5, *tantum aberat ut bino* (*libros*) *scriberent*: *vix singulos confecerent.* The Romance languages show, however, that this type must have been abundant in popular speech.[1]

The adverbs or indefinite adjectives used to indicate this kind of relation in Provençal are those derived from *tantus, sic, talis* and their compounds. I consider first those sentences which have the indicative in both parts. So far as the concept-relation is concerned, it is unimportant whether the pointing particle be adjective or adverb in function. More worthy of notice is the fact that a further indication of relation is often introduced by means of the word-order, the particle being placed at the head of the sentence. The examples fall then into the following groups :

1. Paratactic consecutive clauses with *tan.*

A. With *tan* in the interior of the sentence: C. M. 5, 21, *Qand eu vas mi donz vir l'esgar Li sieu beill huoill tant ben l'estan: Per paura mi teing car eu vas lieis mon cor*; Ap. Ch. 6, 118, *E porto un' ascona tan fera e tan estranha : Ja res no la vira quel bratz destre nos franha*; ibid, 105, 42; 105, 162; 105, 229 ; Born 11, 51, *Mas eu hai tant ensenhador: Non sai, per Crist, lo mielhs chausir*; ibid, 28, 31 ; Dan. 11, 40, *Per qu'ieu sui d'est prec tant espertz : Non ai d'als talen neis magre*; Crois. 3510, *E en tantas maneiras s'en es fort entremes: Non es dreitz ni razos c'om ara loilh tolgues*; ibid, 4283, 7065, 7248, 8303 ; Flam. 4012, *Perdutz fos qui bendas fes primas, Quar hom non las poc far tan primas: La vista d'ome non afollen*; Monk 2, 31 ; Rom. 2, 3 ; 2, 20 ; Gav. 2, 21 ; 7, 42 ; 7, 56, etc.[2]

---

[1] See Meyer-Lübke, § 538 ; and for Old French, Dubislav, 12 ff.

[2] For Italian, cf. Monaci, 35, 2, 22, *Di tanto bello sete: Non è donna ki sia alt' a si bella pare; Dino, II, 20, Il padre loro gli disse che . . . gli darebbe tante delle sue terre sarebbe sodisfatto.*

B. With *tan* at head of sentence : Ba. Ch. 62, 21, *Tant
ai mon cor plen de joja* : *Tot me desnatura*; *ibid*, 94, 25 ;
214, 16 ; Ap. Ch. 96, 45 ; Blac. 1, 28, *Tant m'es avinen
Qand ab midons cui ador Puosc jazer sotz cubertor* : *Ren als
no m'es tant plazen* ; Born 6, 60, *Tant etz falhit el rei e en sa
mort* : *Laig razonar fai en cort vostre tort* ; *ibid*, 37, 3 ; Dan.
3, 52 ; 9, 22 ; Crois. 1802, 4218 ; Monk 15, 18 ; Sord. 40,
125 ; Flam. 1711, 6960 ; In. Par. 26, 41 ; Dicht. IV, 2 ;
Capd. 17, 43 ; Gav. 2, 26 ; Denkm. 211, 20, etc.

When the order of the two sentences is inverted, the
concept first in point of time being placed last to indicate
the cause, the word-order is invariable, *tan* always heading
the sentence.   The only exception that I have noted appears
in Mont. 2, 50, *E ieu, las, a cui mas platz Mueir, quan vei
vostre cors gens* : *D'enveia tan mi destrenh.*   This type of
parataxis is extraordinarily frequent in Provençal, and is
still in common use in the modern Romance dialects, save
Roumanian.[1]   I cite only a few examples : Born 8, 4, *Bem
platz car trega ni fis Non reman entrels baros, Qu'ades plantavon boissos* : *Tant aman ortz e jardis* ; Dan. 15, 7, *Ades ses
lieis dic a lieis cochos motz, Pois quan la vei non sai* : *Tant
l'ai que dire* ; cf. also Ba. Ch. 29, 22 ; 31, 5 ; 34, 3 ; 60,
30 ; Mont. 1, 20 ; 6, 5 ; Crois. 249, 2699, 4945 ; Monk 4,
44 ; Rom. 7, 55 ; Alam. 9, 3 ; Sord. 10, 24 ; 23, 6 ; 33, 2 ;
Zorzi 7, 36 ; Flam. 1705, 3081 ; Barra 500, 883 ; In. It.
15, 289 ; In. Par. 7, 29 ; 14, 1 ; 22, 4 ; Capd. 20, 23 ; 27,
15 ; Vid. 17, 7 ; 21, 43 ; 30, 18 ; Biog. 24, 42 ; Gesta 245,
etc.[2]   Instead of *tan* we find its compound *aitan* in one
instance : C. M. 35, 22, *Dire mel farez a enuiz, Mas non
puosc* : *aitant sui iraz.*

---

[1] See Tobler, *VB*, I², 134.
[2] For Italian, cf. Monaci, 26, 2, 30, *E certa bene ancoscio, k'a pena mi
conoscio, Tanto bella mi pare.*

2. Paratactic consecutive sentences with *si* or *aissi*. These are much rarer than those with *tan*. No examples with inversion of the two sentences to indicate cause are found.[1]

A. With *si* in the interior : Ba. Ch. 96, 33, *Can som remembral cors nim ditz, Adonc remanc si esbaitz* : *No sai on vauc ni on me venc* ; *ibid*, 95, 21, *El desiriers de vezer vos Me ten aissi lo cor aissos* : *Cen vetz prec deu la noit el jor Quem do mort o la vostre amor* ; Crois. 591, *E poiches de vitalha i ac si a plantatz* : *Donec om XXX pas per I denier monedatz*.[2]

B. With *si* at head of sentence : Dan. 11, .36, *Si m'al sen desirs forz duich* : *No sap lo cors trep ois duoilla* ; Crois. 1233, *Car aisi lor es pres* : *no i a cel nol maldia* ; In. It. 34, 52, *Asim nafret gent s'amors* : *Non sai con m'estia* ; Ap. Ch. 6, 177, *Aissi veiras dels mortz encombrat lo gravier* : *No sera delhiuratz en tot un an entier*.

3. Paratactic consecutive sentences with *tal* or *aital*. Here examples are somewhat more numerous than with *si*, and, as with *tan*, the order of the sentences may be inverted.

A. With *tal* in the interior : Ap. Ch. 6, 173, *Al baissar de las lansas penran tal destorbier* : *Ja us non atenra ni par ni companer* ; Gav. 8, 50, *Elh era assis en tal banc* : *Ja no saupra mals ques fora* ; In. Par. 191, 11, *Mas ieu ai pres tal usatge* : *totz jorns chant* ; Dan. 5, 25, *Ai un tal ver dig adug* : *Re no sai que mentirs espel* ; Crois. 1770 ; In. Par. 74, 8, etc.[3]

B. With *tal* at head of sentence : Brun. 2, 50, *Quan sa gran beutat remir, Tal joy ai: nom sai nim sen* ; Crois. 1296 ; Flam. 8084. When the relation indicated by the second sentence is causal, *tal* always stands at the head : Born 13, 2, *D'un sirventes nom cal far lonhor ganda* : *Tal talan ai quel*

---

[1] Such occur however in Italian : Monaci, 26, 5, 87, *Lo mio core non insomma se non scietto, si m'à stretto Pur di voi, madonna*.

[2] For Italian, cf. Guit. canzone 7, 107, *Temevi si: non osa mettersi 'n voi.*

[3] Cf. for Italian, Guit. sonnet 15, 13, *Seraggio tal: non credo esser blasmato.*

diga e que l'espanda ; Zorzi, 5, 15, *Estiers ai certanza Qu'eu
aurai pen' eternal Enfernal* : *Tal son fag tuit mei jornal* ; *ibid*,
6, 89 ; Barra 1033, 3179 ; Capd. Un. 5, 37 ; Vid. 37, 8 ;
Ap. Ch. 3, 247, etc.[1]

By contamination with the relative-contiguous type of
parataxis already discussed, there arise such constructions as
the following, in which the relation of the second sentence
to the first is attributive. The presence of the indefinite *tal*
in the first sentence, however, pointing forward as it does to
the second concept of result, entitles us to consider such
cases under the general head of parataxis by single words.
The particle *tal* here may be either an adjective or a substantive, and the second sentence may contain as common
concept either the subject or the object of the first. I have
found only one example of the second sentence coördinated
with the subject of the first : Ba. Ch. 52, 20, *Tals la cug en
baisan tener* : *Non a mas l'ufana.* Examples relating to the
object are more numerous : Ba. Ch. 177, 26, *Car tals n'i a* :
son tan esquiu Que pois non tornon a cel viu ; *ibid*, 313, 28,
Tals n'i a : *neus del araire Lur levols buous, non dreg gardan* ;
Crois. 2128, *Tals C n'i laissan mortz* : *ja no veiran nadal, Ni
lor fara contraria caresma ni carnal* ;[2] Sord. 22, 36, *Tal don
deman* : *ni estre non deuria* ; Daur. 719, *Al filh del duc an
fache tal maio* : *Dedins non a lata ni cabiro.* As in the case
of simple juxtaposition, the sentence foreshadowed by *tal*
may express a locative or temporal relation : Flam. 6073,
Tal ora fon : *non siam certas De sa vida* ; In. Par. 74, 8,
*Car s'ieu agues lo mieu sen per folia, Domna, camjat, en tal
loc fuy ab vos* : *Ja no fora marritz ni doloiros.*

---

[1] Cf. for Italian, Monaci, 39, 15, *Io perciò nom lasso d'amarla, oi me lasso,
Tale mi mena orgoglio ;* Dante, Inf. 9, 8, *Pure a noi converrà vincer la punga,
cominciò ei ; se non . . . tal ne s'offerse.*

[2] Note how the concept is carried forward by *lor* in the second paratactic
sentence.

A peculiar shift of meaning occurs in some sentences which otherwise would show simply a causal relation with the inversion of sentence-order 'already noted. Whereas in the cases cited above the paratactic causal sentence containing the adverb of degree is positive, in these it is negative and indicates that the preceding concept is thought of as unlimited in space or time. The *tan*-sentence is still explanatory of the foregoing, but acquires in this way, somewhat of a concessive force.[1] Such sentences may often be completed in thought by a following consecutive clause in the subjunctive. Thus when Guiraut de Bornelh says (Ba.. Ch. 83, 27) *Anc nom vi ni ja non veirai, Tan non irai, D'un sol ome tan bel assai*, it is tolerably certain that the thought is not fully expressed; we may supply, after *irai*, **que jol veia*. Cf. further Crois. 324, *E cela ost jutgero mot eretge arder E mota bela eretga ins en lo foc giter, Car convertir nos volon, tan nols podon preier* (sc. **que convertiscan*); ibid, 1518, *Mas contra la ost de Crist no a castel dureia Ni ciutatz que ilh trobon*: *tan no es enserreia* (sc. **que aia dureia*); ibid, 3146; Daur. 340, *Ferrem lo porc, senher, et ieu e vos, El tombara*: *non er tan vigoros* (sc. **que non tomb*); Denkm. 242, 32, *Per o aissom conorta, car dieus es tan lials Q'ab lei trobam merce, tant non em vilh ni fals* (sc. **que non trobem merce*); ibid, 273, 46; Capd. 12, 3, *Si com sellui c'a pro de valledors En la sasson qu'es desaventuratz Li faillen tuich*: *ja non er tant amatz* (sc. **que non li faillan*), *Mi faill midons.*

When the subjunctive appears in similar paratactic consecutive or causal sentences, the fundamental conception is different. Provençal ordinarily puts side by side two independent statements of fact: *jo sui tan faz*: *sai triar lo meillor*. The real connection between these two propositions

---

[1] For similar sentences in Old French, see Dubislav, 21 ff. ; and cf. Tobler, *VB.*, I, 131 ff.

is left to the hearer, whose mind is already prepared for the
second statement by the adverb of degree in the first.   But
it is the second sentence which contains the main element
of the utterance.   If now this main element be conceived as
hypothetical or desired, it is put naturally in the subjunctive,
and the first sentence generally contains a negation, together
with the adverb of degree.   This is exactly what Guillem
de Poitou does (Ba. Ch. 29, 5), *E sim partez un joc d'amor,
No sui tan faz*: *No sapcha triar lo meillor D'entrels malvatz.*
The subjunctive cannot, I think, be considered as establishing
a subordination, for the two sentences are as grammatically
independent as in the preceding cases.   Cf. also Rud. 1, 22,
Anc tan soven no m'adurmi: *Mos esperitz tost non fost la*: *Ni
tan d'ira non ac de sa Mos cors*: *ades no fos aqui*; Dan. 1,
45, *Ja non saubra tant de gandilh*: *Noil compisses lo groig el
cilh*; In. Par. 119, 12, *No sai tan dir de laus*: *Sa valors no
fos plus granda*;[1] *ibid*, 276, 20, *Quan bem albir sa valor,
Non aus dir tan de ricor*: *De mi denhes penre patz*; Capd.
11, 28, *Hom non a tan dur cor*: *si la ve, Noill port honor*;
ibid, 23, 26; Ap. Ch. 1, 462; 1, 496; In Flam. 2997,
Adonc' si levet someillos, Mais ges non fon si nuaillos: *Non
anes la fenestr' ubrir*, the degree is expressed by *si*.[2]

In many cases the subjunctive sentence, foreshadowed by
the adverb of degree, is related as an attribute to a substantive in the preceding.   I regard such sentences as a
modification of the paratactic double negative, to be discussed
later as a variety of defining parataxis, contaminated to a
certain extent by the type just considered.   Such a contamination appears, for example, in: Flam. 5272, *E non sai tan*

---

[1] With the var. lect. *que sa valors*.   The *que* must be rejected on account
of the metre; but the variant shows how easily the subordinating conjunction could be introduced.

[2] Cf. for Italian, Guit., sonnet 8, 10, *Tanto de dolzor meve donate ch'amorti
lo venen si: non m'aucida.*

fort malanconi: *Nom portes d'aisso testimoni*; *ibid*, 7193, *Messages mand' a totas partz Que ja non sia tan coartz Negus cavalliers*: *non remainna*; In. Par. 5, 50, *No cug fossetz tan avara*: *Non acsetz qualque dolor al cor*; Denkm. 157, 12. *Non ha sotz cel home tan bon, Si vas dieu ha s'entencion, E mes tot un pauc a parlar*; *Sempres no comens a plorar*; Ap. Ch. 1, 444, *N'i a donne tan riche*: *no la requiere*; Ba. Ch. 37, 23, *Noi a ta fort escut*: *non escantel, No fenda o no pertus o no arcel, Asta reida de fraisser que no astel, Noi a ta fort ausberc*: *no desclavel.* The last passage is noteworthy through the introduction of the relative *que* in the third line; it shows therefore that to the writer the paratactic and hypotactic constructions were practically equivalent and he places them in correlation here with perfect freedom. The sentence, Mont. 7, 59, *Mas d'aissous prec sius plazia, Dompna, que s'ieu ren dizia Queus fos plazen ni benestan Que de vos n'aja sol aitan*: *Mi voill' onrar vostre gens cors*, does not properly belong here. I regard it as an example of defining parataxis, the utterance *de vos n'aja sol aitan* being parenthetical and defining the attitude of the speaker's mind to the following wish.

In the examples lately discussed it is an adverb of degree which serves to indicate the relation between the two paratactic sentences. In other cases a temporal adverb may subserve the same purpose. Of these adverbs the most common are *pos* and *tro*. It must, I think, be admitted that these words have in Provençal assumed nearly the function of true conjunctions. The original adverbial force of *pos* and *tro* may, however, still be recognized in many sentences, where for practical purposes editors punctuate the texts as if a true subordinating effect were inherent in these words. So, for example, in Zorzi 3, 5, *Pois fui en vostra comanda, ab petit de jauzimen, Humil et obedien, Amors, m'avetz retengut,* the sense would permit a full stop after *jauzimen* and allow us to translate *pois* as "then" or "afterwards." The adverbial force of *tro* is likewise evident in sentences which contain a wish subjunctive, juxtaposed with a preceding independant utterance, as in Born 6, 60, *Aragones, nous fassatz plus iratz, Troi diga mais, mas tant vuolh que sapchatz*, where the sense likewise would permit a full stop after *iratz*.

Examples of this usage of *pos* and *tro* are very common in all the texts, the simple form being rather more frequent than the compound hypotactic *posque, troque.* For *pos*, cf. Ap. Ch. 94, 13, *Pois me plages, no cuit q'eu vos desplaia*; Mont. 7, 17, *Quascuna, pus ve son amador, Fi ses error, falh si l'alonga mais*; Dan. 3, 18, *Bona es vida Pos joia la mante*; Crois. 8627; Monk 1, 37; Vid. 40, 32; Alv. 9, 32, etc. For *tro* with the indicative, cf. Vaq. 1, 40, *E cujem lor a totz gent escapar, Tro silh de Piza nos vengron assautar*; Crois. 1288; 4354; 5069; Capd. 2, 28, etc. With the subjunctive, Rom. 9, 58, *A dieu prec per sa doussor Que nos fassa tan d'onor Quens guart de mortal aguag Tro son plazer ajam fag*; Gesta 1915, *E Karles disx li que nos iria encara, tro aguessen fayta batalha am Matran et am Borrelh e qu'elh fos ondradament senhatz per abbat*;[1] Ba. Ch. 154, 17; Brun. 4, 23; Crois. 2019, 2831; Flam. 2243; Vid. 26, 22, etc.

I have noted also one similar example of adverbial *ans* used to indicate the paratactic relation: Crois. 1896, *Ni us cuh que n'ichis: ans vindreit lo pascor.*[2]

The transition from the temporal to the causal conception of relation between sentences is common in most languages, and was easily effected in Provençal in the case of *pos.* Most of the sentences containing this adverb express a cause, as in Ba. Ch. 83, 26, *Cabra joglar, Non posc mudar,*

---

[1] Note the *que* in the second sentence, correlated with *tro*.

[2] This use of *ante* is not infrequent in Italian; cf. Monaci, 46, 143, *Esto fatto fare potevi inanti scalfi un uovo;* Dino, I, 29, *Io Dino Compagni, desideroso di unità e pace fra' cittadini, avanti si partissero, dissi.*

Q'eu non chan, pos a mi sap bon; Brun. 2, 19, *E doncx, e quem volon dir Siey huelh*? *ni quem van queren*? *Pus ma dolor' non enten Ni mos precx non vol auzir*; Born 1, 14; Mont. 2, 21; Dan. 6, 33; Crois. 1978; Monk 2, 31; Rom. 3, 118; Alam. 20, 9; Sord. 8, 19; Vaq. 1, 113; Flam. 277; In. Par. 8, 30, etc.[1]

In the case of "causal" *tant* and *pos* we have in Provençal a good example of the origin of conjunctions. These words possess in the language of the troubadours all their original adverbial force. When used to express a relation between two contiguous sentences, they still have all the vagueness characteristic of such relation-concepts. It is possible, as we have seen, to treat many sentences with *tan* or *pos* as entirely independent utterances, and in most cases it is impossible to say whether they possess subordinating or coördinating force. The Old Provençal speech was in this respect wholly unfixed. No sharp distinction was ever made between words expressing relation and words which correspond to concepts of space or time. It shows too how a language can use elements of many different sources to denote like ideas. The distinction in meaning between a sentence like Born 8, 4, (*Los baros*) *plantavon boissos, tant amon ortz e jardis*, and the variant *pois amon ortz e jardis* is extremely slight. If the adverbial use of both words had died out, it would now be as impossible to trace their earlier history as it is to trace that of Latin *ut* or *enim*.

Another instance of conjunction-making can be observed in Provençal in the case of the adverb *mais*,[2] which seems to be employed in certain passages to replace *poisque*. Cf. Ba. Ch. 51, 14, *Quar li melhor de tot est mon Vos van servir*,

---

[1] Cf. for Italian, Monaci, 32, 11, *Lo partir non mi vale; Ch'adesso mi reprende Amor ch'en omo asende, Poi li piace*; Dante, Canz. x, 136, *Di radica di ben altro ben tira, Poi suo simile è in grado.*

[2] Cf. Diez, p. 1021, note, and Kolsen, note to Guiraut de Bornelh, I, 20.

2

mais a vos platz; ibid, 306, 25; Sord. 22, 6, *E mas nolh
plai, farai hueymais mon chan Leu a chantar e d'auzir
agradan;* Daur. 123, *Bem podes enrequir mas vos ve per
plazir;* In. Par. 116, 27, *E mas ben vuelh, ben auray;* Vid.
24, 49, *Domna, mas no m'en posc sofrir, Deus e chauzimens
mi valgues, Quem vengues de vos qualsque bes;* Flam. 1942,
*Ben segrai vostra volontat E so qu'aves acostumat, So dis
Guillems, mais tan vos plas; ibid,* 2927, 3542, 4307, 5383,
6289; Born. 1, 20, etc. I interpret all these cases as contiguous parataxis, with a conceptual relation of cause,
reinforced by an adverb signifying "but," "moreover."
The first example from Flamenca is instructive, the causal
relation being further strengthened by *tan.* In all, *mas*
indicates that the causal conception is, to a certain extent,
self-evident.

III. PARATAXIS BY CONTRAST.

A fruitful source of subordinate clauses in all languages
arises from the contrast of two concept-groups by some
similarity in sound, structure or meaning.[1] Generally in
the written language some hint is given, by word-order,
repetition or correlation, of the relation existing between
the two concepts. Sentences of this sort may range greatly
in extent, from those consisting of verbs only to long
rhetorical periods. In Provençal the types which are of
especial interest are those in which the contrasted concepts
imply either a comparison or a condition.

When two subject-concepts are contrasted by means of
some quality inherent in each, the simplest way of expressing this relation is by balancing a positive and a negative
sentence: "He is rich. I am not rich." If now a word

---

[1] See Morris, pp. 124–131.

denoting a greater or less degree of the quality be inserted
in either sentence, the type remains unchanged grammatically, though the two parts acquire a closer relationship.
Thus arises the form we find in Provençal, as, for example,
Capd. 23, 13, *Car fis amans Li sui trop meills Non fo d'Iseut
Tristans*. The word-order in this and similar sentences
leads me to suspect that the original type was: *Fis sui :
meills non fo Tristans*, i. e., that the comparative belonged in
the second sentence. On the whole it seems most probable
that the position of the comparative depended on the place
of the *I*-concept; the speaker takes his own condition, act
or quality as the basis of comparison with another, who
exercises the act or possesses the quality to a greater or less
degree. From this stage to the acquirement of complete
grammatical subordination by the insertion of a conjunction
equivalent to Latin *quam* is but a step. But while taking
this step, as the example shows, the language also cast about
for another means of reinforcing the idea of relation and
found it in the word-order. The Provençal examples all
show a well-marked tendency to shift the verb of the second
sentence to the head. In fact, whenever a subject is
expressed in the second part, it invariably follows the verb,
which is generally a *verbum vicarium, far* or *esser*. I
arrange the examples in two classes ; A, those in which no
direct conclusion as to order is possible, owing to the lack
of an expressed subject; B, those with inversion of subject
and verb.

A. No inversion; with *plus* or an organic comparative :
Ba. Ch. 124, 16, *Aissi com prez' om plus laida peintura de
lonh* : *no fai quand es pres vengutz* ; Ap. Ch. 1, 323, *E as
plus homes morz* : *non saz retraire* ; *ibid*, 115, 122 ; Flam.
125, *Non sai d'aici en Alamainna Negun baron que jai
remainna Qu'a cesta cort non venga tost Plus volontiers* : *non
farì' en ost* ; In. Par. 91, 16, *E joys qui tost si desrazigua
Fai piegz, quant hom lon ve anar* : *No fetz de be al comensar*.

With *mais*: Ba. Ch. 37, 30, *Mais en a remasutz en plan estel*: *Non a ni vius ni mortz dedins Bordel*; *ibid*, 175, 2; Born 32, 35, *Del rei tafur Pretz mais sa cort e son atur*: *Non fatz cella don fui trahitz*; Alam. 6, 47, *Ieu am trop mais lo glatz*: *No fas las flors dels pratz*; Flam. 1231, *Mais am ieu la mieua folleza*: *Non fas lo sieu sen tan prion*; Denkm. 330, 14; Vid. 9, 46.

B. Subject inverted; with *plus* or an organic comparative: C. M. 22, 20, *Plus soven vens castels e domejos*: *No fai velha gallinas ni capos*; Dan. 3, 46, *Ieu plus ai de joia*; *Non ac Paris d'Elena, cel de Troia*; *ibid*, 14, 49; Sord. 32, 15, *Ad amar prec no voilla un sol auzir Qel vius trai peiz*: *no fai l'autre al morir*; S. Fe 367, *Aqell angels qe i es venguz Aujaz qual deintad i aduz, Corona d'aur qe plus reluz*: *Non fal soleilz quand es creguz*; Denkm. 338, 48; Vid. 33, 20; Capd. Un. 5, 43, etc.

With *mais*: Dan. 15, 11, *Mais la vol*: *non ditz la bocal cors*; Monk 4, 16, *Cel qu'aitals es val mais mon escien Ad obs d'amar*: *Non fai ducs ni marques*; Alam. 5, 57, *Per qe pes' en la balansa Mas le mals qes hom en dis*: *No fal le bes ni l'onransa*; Rog. Un. 292, 30, *Mais val d'amor, quant hom n'es enveios Uns bons plorars*: *No fan quatorze ris*; In. Par. 113, 33; Capd. 6, 43; Dicht. 2, 2, 11; 2, 3, 14, etc.[1]

An exactly similar construction, but with the greater degree indicated by a multiplicative, is found in C. M. 34, 1, 38, *Per qem fan que dur dos tans Un mes*: *Non fazi' us ans Qan reignava dompneis ses trahizo.*

I have found only one case of the use of the subjunctive in such contrasted paratactic sentences: Denkm. 333, 24, *Assatz n'a mais drutz de son benvoler Quant de sidonz pot vezer la semblanza, Lo douz esgar, la simpla contenanza*: . . .

---

[1] For similar sentences in Old French, see Dubislav, 24, 25; Meyer-Lübke, § 538; for Italian, cf. Guit. sonnet, 24, 4, *Tu paghi più l'om sua disianza*: *Non fa quello que tene in signoria.*

Ja en cellat non sia reis de Fransa. Here the second contrasted concept is posited as purely hypothetical, hence the subjunctive.

That this originally paratactic construction explains the retention of so-called " expletive " *non-ne* in the later stages of the Romance languages, has already been proved by Dubislav and Tobler.

A second variety of parataxis by contrast is found in those sentences which indicate a concessive or conditional relation. This form has been much studied in the classical languages, and it is generally considered as the source of protasis and apodosis and of the *dum*-clause in Latin. In authors of all periods this type of the paratactic sentence is preserved, the so-called concessive subjunctive being in common use at all epochs. The conceptual association which is the basis of such constructions is the following: the speaker posits as hypothetical or willed a certain relation of subject and predicate, which determines the relation of another subject to another predicate. The contrast is always present implicitly in the thought, but contrasted words do not always appear in the sentences as stated. The most primitive form is, therefore, to be sought in such sentences as Cicero, Tusc. 11, 5, *Ne sit summum malum*: *malum certe est*; Tacitus, hist. 4, 58, *sane ego displiceam*: *sunt alii legati*; or in Provençal: Alam. 5, 60, *Mas tot o revenra lieu*: *sol li faig non syon grieu*; Capd. Un. 7, 18, *Bona dompna, de totz aips complida, Ja no m'ames*: *tostemps vos amarai*. In these sentences the contrast finds complete expression in the correlated words *summum malum—malum certe, ego—alii, lieu—grieu, no ames—amarai*. In the majority of cases, however, the fundamental contrast is less clearly indicated, though an analysis of the thought always reveals it.

In form, one element of such combinations is prevailingly an optative subjunctive, which may have a jussive force, as in Ap. C. 110, 15, *Ja lun hom no vuelas dampnar, Ans lor vuelas ben dir e ffar*: *Enaychi tu seras amatz*. Occasionally, however, the determining concept is put in the form of an independent imperative or indicative sentence,[1] as in Born 4, 46, *Quan seras lai, no t'enoja, Tu li diras que, s'ar nolh valh ab bran, Elh valrai tost, silh rei nom van bauzan;* Biog. 40, *Richa domna so, em voill maridar. Donc eu dis que aver mi podetz, o voletz per druda o voletz per molher; e conselhatz vos per cal me voletz.*[2]

The interest of the Provençal examples however lies in the means employed by the language to indicate the relation. The contrast residing in the mere juxtaposition of opposing concepts rarely suffices; it is generally heightened by word-order or by the use of single words, adverbs or indefinite pronouns, or by both combined. When the relation is not indicated by an adverb, and frequently when it is, inversion of subject and verb occurs. The sole example I have found with subject expressed and not inverted is Gesta 82, *Donc en per amor d'aysso el aja tantz turmentz per nos suffertatz . . . en per amor d'aysso devem suffertar per Jhesu Christ.*[3] The contrast is here fully expressed by repetition. The remaining examples fall naturally into the following groups:

A. Without adverb, no subject expressed: Ba. Ch. 77, 2, *En baizan, nius plagues*: *Ja no volgram solses; ibid*, 389, 33, *Seignor, dis el, no vos sia greu, Per sert ieu acosselharia, Si conoisses que be fag sia, Davant Josep nos non anem;* Aug. 6, 59, *E cug, sia Que m'enbria Doncs fadia, M'en partria, S'ieu podia.*

B. Without adverb, with subject inverted: Flam. 2862, *Ara sia queus voill' amar, Vos nous poires de mi aizir Ni eu*

---

[1] Cf. the French *Dis-moi qui tu hantes, je te dirai qui tu es.*

[2] Cf. for Italian, Dino, II, 10, *Signori, volete esser consigliati, fate l'uficio nuovo, ritornate i confinati a città.*

[3] In the Latin original: *cum igitur . . . passus sit.*

de vos nulz tems gausir; Ap. Ch. 3, 588, *Car tant de pretz e de valor Avetz que beus deu dar s'amor Tota domna*: *sia quis voilla*; Sord. 40, 215, *Quex deu de totz bos aibs usar Tan quan pot, quar fi prez ni car Non aura ja*: *lausel quis vol*; *ibid*, 11, 6, *Fos qui m'o enseignes, ben me conortaria*;[1] Ba. Ch. 127, 26, *Perqu' eu am mais, s'a lui ven a plazer, Morir de lai que sai vius remaner En aventura*: *fos mi' Alamanha*; Crois, 2559, *Retengutz fora e pres en aicela sazon*: *No fos W. d'Encontre, cui Domni-Dieus ben don*; Rog. Un. p. 65, 41, *Pel ben quem n'es escazegutz, Jamais nom n'avengues salutz*: *Li dey tostemps estar als pes.*[2]

C. With adverbs. The chief words employed in Provençal to indicate this relation are *sol, ja, tant*, more rarely *tal, mais, pur, ancara*.

1. *With sol*, and normal order: C. M. 27, 8, *E cals queus n'atalen Vencerai vos*: *sol la cortz leials sia*; Mont. 6, 7, *Pro n'ai ieu*: *sol midons m'ampar*; In. Par. 282, 24, *No vuel plus en aquèst mon*: *Sol dieus mi gart del segon*; Capd. 4, 45, *Apres l'ira m'eschaja Tals jois quem deing plazer*: *Sol fin' amors non traja.*

2. *With sol*, no subject expressed: Born 32, 42, *El bons reis navars, cui dreitz es, Cobraral ab sos Alanes*: *Sol s'i atur*; Zorzi 6, 44, *Perqu' eram guida alegriers, Car il m'autreja e coventa So don serai parliers*; *Sol de ben far nois repenta*; Vid. 32, 45, *Chanso, vai t'en al bon rei part Cerveira, Que de bon pretz non a el mon egansa*: *Sol plus francs fos ves mi dons de Cabreira*; Ba. Ch. 49, 1; 124, 23; 154, 7; 360, 1J; Flam. 173, 218, 997, 2024, 2534, 2633, 3795, 7602.

---

[1] This type of parataxis, with indefinite subject formed by a relative clause, goes back to Latin; cf. Plautus, Pers. 373, *Dicat quod quisque volt: ego non demovebo.*

[2] For Old French, see Dubislav, 16, 17; for Italian, cf. Guit., canzone 20, 93, *Gentil mia donna, fosse in voi tesoro Quanto v'è senno in cor, la più valente Fora ver voi neente;* but without inversion, Dino, III, 5, *facendo noi pace, e Pistoia rimanesse a'nostri avversarii, noi saremo ingannati.*

3. With *sol*, and inverted order : Ap. Ch. 102, 9, *Sil vuelh ofrir Lai don venir Me pot complid' aiuda* : *Sol nom si' irascuda La maire dieu* ; Sord. 19, 33, *Sol creza leis, en cuy ay m'esperansa, Qu'ieu si' arditz, Bertran, ab gaug entier Viurai tostemps* ; Zorzi 17, 46, *Car sol fos faitz en lieis aitals acortz, Aissi cum es senes par sa beutatz, Volria amors c'a mi vengues la sortz D'esser de joi senes par aondatz* ; Dan. 15, 40.

4. With *ja*,[1] no inversion : Monk 6, 19, *E ja de leis bes nom veigna Tos temps li serai aclis* ; *ibid*, 15, 20, *Mas gaps avetz be ad egual d'un rey* : *Ja us vers non sia* ; Flam. 7831, *E cil qui es joves no i eira* ; *Ja veilla no sia, o quiera* ; In. It. 66, 3, *Lo plus fis drutz q'anc nasqes Seri' eu, s'ami' ages, Qe, ia plaiser nom feses, Ben fora sos hom ades* ; In. Par. 226, 65, *Tan val sa lausors saupuda De bon pres sauput Q'a liei m'autrei per retengut, Gia nom fos tenguda* ; Capd. *Perqu'eu vos am, ja autre pro noi aja, Tan fianmen que d'al re nom sove* ; *ibid*, 18, 26.[2]

5. With *ja*, and inversion : In. It. 24, 554, *Ja non ajas vos re, Vostre noms n'er saupuz* ; Bornelh 1, 18, *Ja siatz vos, donsela, bell' e blonda, Pauc d'iraus notz e paucs jois vos aonda* ; *ibid*, 1, 63, *Beus eu valrai* : *ja l'ai' eu mantenguda, Si mais nous i mesclats* ; Rog. 3, 60, *E vuelh mais morir ad estros* : *Jal sapcha negus hom mas vos* ; Biog. 40, *Vos etz mot gentil hom* : *ja siatz vos canorges*.

6. With *tan*.[3] Here the contrast-relation is sometimes difficult to distinguish from that of defining parataxis here-after to be considered. Take for example a sentence like

---

[1] For examples in Old French, see Dubislav, 17.

[2] In late Provençal, the locution *ja sia so que, ja sia aisso que*, has become a conjunction, like French *jaçoit que* ; cf. Ap. Ch. 109, 7 ; Gesta 73, 660, 1455, 2019, etc.

[3] The latest study of such sentences is that by Ebeling, in the *Festschrift für Adolf Tobler*, Braunschweig, 1905. Cf. the remarks by Tobler, *Archiv f. neueren Sprachen*, cxv, 244, and Dubislav, 18–20.

Sord. 33, 2, *El mon non es domna, tan sia pros, Ques defendes de mos dos precs plazens.* It is obvious that the relation of subject to predicate in the main utterance is contingent on the hypothetical relation in the second sentence only in so far as it is conceived by the speaker to fall short of universal validity in respect to some stated quality; "no lady,—let her possess to the highest degree the quality *pros,*—can defend herself from my sweet words." That the essential element of the paratactic relation is still one of contrast, is often indicated by the repetition or correlation of single words, as in Sirv. Jog. 14, 22, *Anc ab armas non sab valer Hom meinz, tant s'en volgues guabar,* where *meinz* and *tant* express the full force of the opposition in thought. Cf. also C. M. 5, 24, *Anc non fo cors mieills taillatz ni depens Ad ops d'amar: sia tant greus ni lens;* Ap. Ch. 105, 92 (Boeci), *Hanc no fo om; ta grant vertut agues, Qui sapiencia compenre pogues; ibid,* 105, 178, *Hanc no vist omne; ta grant onor agues, Sil forfez tan dont ellas rancures, Sos cors ni s'anma miga per ren guaris;* Sirv. Jog. 15, 22, *E non aves senhoril: Tant aut son dur cor apil, Que jaius trobon en plan mil Per quem pren de vos pezansa.*

7. With other adverbs or indefinite pronouns. Of exactly similar nature are the following examples with *tal, pur, mais, ancara:* Dan. 7, 40, *L'us conseilla e l'autre brama, Per queis desmanda Amors, tals fora granda;* Denkm. 313, 73, *Ni non ai tan coral amic Qu'eu nol tengue per enemic, Dompna: pur vos m'ordenisses,[1] ibid,* 31, 1054, *Senhors, aujas que vos direm; Ja sol un motz no mentirem. Cant venc a nueg, a mieja nueg, Mays nous ho tengas ad enueg, Tota la terra si crollet;* Ap. Ch. 1, 166, *Ia mais ne li estot sofraite aver: Mas pur face iustise e die ver;* Ba. Ch. 301, 16, *E egalment devunt tuit partir las causas del mort, ancara*

---

[1] Cf. for Italian, Monaci, 41, 5, 6, *Pote omo fare tal movimento, Pur asgio n'agia.*

non i sia negus que non aja ben en autra guisa;[1] *Ibid,* 301, 25.

It is evident, however, that even with these aids of word-order or adverbial determinants Provençal did not make much progress toward grammatical subordination. The occasional use of the coördinating conjunction *e* to introduce such hypothetical conditional sentences, shows that they were regarded as independant concepts. Cf., for instance, Capd. 21, 20, *Mas en midonz ve que nos faill en re Nim pot aver tort, e volgues m'aucire*: Flam. 4145, *Quar esquerns vers enuja plus, E ja non sia neis mais us, Que non farion C messongier*; In. Par. 62, 55, *Que bos volers, e ja le faitz noy fos, Si deu per fag contar totas sazos.*

A last variety of parataxis by contrast is furnished by what Dubislav calls the disjunctive concessive form.[2] In this type the validity of a statement is conditioned by two correlated wish-sentences, independent in form, which, by positing two contradictory hypotheses, tend likewise to establish the universality of the main utterance. Sentences of this type may be arranged in the following two divisions.

A. With two or more verbs in the wish-sentence: Ba. Ch. 59, 26, *E l'amarai, be li plass' o belh pes, Qu'om no pot cor destrenher ses aucire*; *ibid*, 59, 28; 392, 30; Brun. 1, 34, *Ab dous semblans, vuelh' o non denh', Pren los uns els autres destrenh*; Crois. 5004, *Baro, so ditz lo coms, o vos plassa o vos pes, Desgarnitz o garnitz o en lonc o en tes, Intrarei en la viala, e verei ben qui es*; Monk 8, 32, *Cossi que vos en captengnatz, Vos amarai: ous plass' ous pes*; Rom. 13, 74, *O muer' o viu, a vos mi ren*; Barra 844, *Que luns hom, per lunha razo, Dins lo camp non auses intrar Ni als campios ajudar: Fos crestias o fos sarrazis*; Vid. 24, 3, *Nuls*

---

[1] Cf. for Italian, Monaci, 36, 2, 18, *Par k'eo n'agia avante Si kom om ke si crede Salvarsi per sua fede, Ancor non vegia avante.*

[2] See Dubislav, 22.

om nos pot d'amor gandir, Pos el seu senhoriu s'es mes: *O tot li plas' o tot li pes, Sos talens l'avem a seguir.*

B. With single verb, but double predicate: Ap. Ch. 14, 12, *E fassa caut o freidura, Trastot m'es d'una mezura Amors e joys, d'eyssa guiza*; *ibid*, 84, 11, *La nueg el jorn mi ven en pessamens Qu'ieu cavalgue ab totz mos valedors Dreyt a Sant Pos, sia sen o folhors*; *ibid*, 95, 47; Crois. 8315, *Car per la crotz sanctisma, sia sens o foldatz, Nos irem per la gata si vos o comensatz*; Sord. 23, 3, *Sa vidas trai, venha l'en mals o bes, Quar per quascu mor, languen, de dezire*; In. Par. 113, 28, *Pus aissim suy acordatz*: *Fassa mi amor o no*; *ibid*, 121, 5; 191, 11; Capd. 16, 20, *Car el mon non es res*: *Sia senz o follors, Qu'eu pensses queill plagues*: *Nom fos gaugz o douçors*; S. Fe 450, *S'ad ella ven hom cegs o muz*, ... *Pos devant ella n'er tenduz, O sia jovens o canuz, Si de peccaz es peneduz, Semprel venra gaujz e salutz.*

IV. PARATAXIS BY DEFINITION.

Following Professor Morris, I have ventured to employ this somewhat ambiguous term to denote that variety of parataxis which arises when a verb is inserted parenthetically into a longer sentence to express a thought which comes to the speaker's mind and which he utters at once without waiting to finish the statement in process of utterance.[1] The parenthetical thought is not necessarily parenthetical in grammatical expression; it may be, and quite often is, prefixed or appended. It may be recognized in that it adds no new element to the original concept, but merely defines the attitude of the speaker's or hearer's mind to it. When the Provençal said "eu cug: vendra," the verb *cug* served simply to define his own position in regard to the main statement *vendra*.

[1] See Morris, *Methods in Syntax*, pp. 126, 132.

This kind of paratactic relation is richly represented in Early Latin, where it has been exhaustively studied by Morris.[1] It recurs likewise abundantly in the mediæval Romance dialects, so that it seems justifiable to assume a genetic relation between the Plautine *mercator credost* (Poen. 1016) and the Provençal *sas plazens dolors cre l'auciran* (Ap. Ch. 84, 28), which show exactly the same incorporation of the parenthetical verb into the main utterance; or between the Plautine *ergo animum aduortas uolo* (Capt. 383) and the Provençal *nostre reis aragones que val mais de totz los pros vuelh renovelh vostr' arnes* (Sirv. Jog. 8, 23). Nor is it possible to explain the construction in either language by the ellipse of a conjunction. *Volo abeas* does not stand for *volo ut abeas*, nor does *vuelh venha* represent a hypothetical original *vuelh que venha*. The two sentence-forms, it is evident, are genetically related, and both go back to a time when conjunctions were not in use. The Plautine type reappears in the later Latin authors who affect a more colloquial speech; cf. Varro, r. r. 1, 2, 26, *est satius dicas*; Petronius, Cena Tri. 129, *crede mihi non intellego*; St. Cyprian, ep. 8, 3, *sed et vos petimus memores sitis*. And it is abundantly represented in the works of Gregory of Tours:[2] hist. fran. 3, 13, *et credo ob illius causa fuerit ipsum castrum in manibus traditum iniquorum*; conf., p. 753, *velim diceris quid vidisti*. A continuous tradition between Early Latin and the Romance languages may easily be established.

With this general agreement between early Latin and Provençal, there are to be observed several noteworthy differences. Parataxis in questions, with an inserted verb of mental action or will to express the attitude or the desire of the hearer, is very common in Plautus.[3] My material in

---

[1] In *Amer. Journ. of Phil.*, XVIII, especially pp. 202–301.

[2] See Bonnet, pp. 666 ff.

[3] Cf. Rud. 1269, *censen hodie despondebit eam mihi, quaeso?* Epid. 584, *quid loquar vis?*

Provençal has thus far afforded only a single case of this type: Ap. Ch. 5, 225, *Non sabies degues venir*? This I believe to be due, partly at least, to chance. Direct questions of any kind are not common in lyric poetry; if we possessed a true dramatic literature we should doubtless find this type of sentence well represented. On the other hand, the very common Provençal type *non cug venha* seems to be sparingly if at all represented in Latin. Cf., however, Gregory of Tours, hist. fran. 5, 14, *credo acceptum non fuisset deo*, which would undoubtedly become in Provençal, by attraction of the negation, *non cre fos retengutz per deu*. In addition, the generalized double negative sentence, of the type *non es om non venha*, is unknown to Latin authors of all periods. Keeping in mind these differences, I shall adopt Morris' classification in treating these forms of parataxis.

1. Sentences showing insertion of a verb of mental action to indicate the attitude of the speaker or hearer to the main utterance, which is always in the indicative. Type: *cre venra*.[1] In Latin such verbs are always in the first person singular, but in Provençal they occur also in the second person, the parenthetical *sapchatz* "know ye" being especially common. Originally such verbs stood in the middle of the phrase, but later they came to be prefixed or appended. They generally consist of a simple finite verb-form, sometimes with an added pronoun or adverb intensive in meaning. Not infrequently the thought may be carried over by a personal or demonstrative pronoun object of the verb of mental action, which serves to sum up the main concept already expressed or at least present in the mind. So, for example, Ba. Ch. 249, 21, *Don enueja mout a Jaufre E a Brunessen mais, so cre*, where the *so* sums up all the preced-

---

[1] For Old French, see Dubislav, 4–5, but the author's treatment of these forms is brief.

ing statement; Crois. 2633, *Aicels de Savardu lor tolol vin el pan, E no vendemieren, so cug, mais a d'un an*; Capd. Un. 4, 22, *La genser es que anc nasques de maire E la meilhs, so aug a totz retraire*; Crois. 1449, *Bochart, so li a dit, vos estes, ben o sai, De mot granda natura e proz om e verai*; ibid, 1560, *Que ja nulhs hom del segle, so sapchatz de vertat, No partira de leis entro agues manjat*; Monk 4, 20, *Aitals vos son ab ferm voler, Bona dompna de fin cor, so sapchatz*; Sord. 24, 17, *Ilh fai orguelh, ben o sai, Quar l'am*; Vid. 24, 30, *E non o dic eu, so sapchatz, Per so quem fassa mortz paor, Mas quar ilh pert son amador*; ibid, 29, 30. But the majority of cases are without any single word to indicate the relation.

1. With inserted verb of thinking: C. M. 3, 18, *Que s'abans anam a la mort D'aut, eu cug, aurem alberc bas*; Zorzi, 1, 57, *Per qu'eu cui dregz Non pot cobrar pidanza*; Flam. 2138, *Na Tor, fai s'el, bell' est defor, Ben cug dedins est pur' e clara*; Dan. 10, 23, *Ab trop voler cug lam toli S'om ren per ben amar pert*; Ap. Ch. 84, 28; Crois. 3146, 1248.[1]

2. With inserted verb of knowing: Mont. 14, 25, *Sordel, mais val veramen, Sapchatz, lo cor e il talen*; Daur. 1620, *Ben per ver sapiatz Noil farai mal, ans sera be gardatz*; Ba. Ch. 122, 23, *Pero ben sai mos lauzors pro nom te*; Crois. 5392, 5764, 7727; Flam. 7029; In Par. 62, 55; 70, 38; 76, 5; Ap. Ch. 60, 44, etc.[2]

3. With inserted verb of saying or promising: Ba. Ch. 198, 10, *Pero beus dic, totz temps serai clamos*; S. Fe 333, *Jur vos, perls deus d'aqest clocher E per aqelz cui eu profer, Car comprarez est reprober*; In Par. 156, 40, *Pograi dir als fis amadors, Mos fis joys part totz creys e sors*; Vid. 41, 24,

---

[1] For Italian, cf. Guit., sonnet 2, 12, *Ben credo la vorresti altro servire.*

[2] For Italian, cf. Guit., canzone 20, 30, *Al qual donna saven* (= *suppiamo*) *meglio contende.*

De mi dic ben, si pel marques no fos, No pretz cinc marcs una rota camiza; Crois. 2985; Rom. 6, 43, etc.

When the parenthetical verb is in the third person, as sometimes happens, it indicates in a similar manner the mental attitude of the person to whom the main utterance is directed, as in Capd. 17, 33, *Pus del tot li sui mentire, Sivals aitan sapcha nol men*; or more commonly it shows the attitude of the person whose utterance is reported, as in Crois. 1854, *Be sabon e lur cor no lor poiran durar*; *ibid*, 2605, *Mas el lor a jurat per los sants d'outra mar Non laisara a vida un solet escapar*; *ibid*, 4236; Daur. 402; Flam. 4339, etc.[1]

An increasing tendency in the language, which led eventually to complete grammatical subordination, appears in some sentences. The inclination was persistent to regard the main utterance as depending on the inserted verb. This tendency is shown in the attraction exercised by the parenthetical verb, as in Ap. Ch. 1, 1, *Carles veit de Girart, nel pout trobar A plane terre en camp, si com sol far*, where the object of the chief proposition is attached as an adverbial modifier to the defining verb, and also by the fact that sometimes a second coördinated sentence is introduced by *que*, as in Crois. 2284, *Per tot fan entender: Frances son descofit E quel coms de Montfort s'en es de noit fugit.*

A peculiar variety of this kind of parataxis arises when the speaker makes a declaration and then by means of an independent wish-sentence, generally introduced by *sic*, solemnly attests its truth. I regard this adjuration or prayer as an after-thought, which determines or defines the relation of the speaker to the main utterance, much as an intercalated *eu cre* or *eu dic* would do. It closely approximates, however, the form of parataxis by contrast, already considered, as the wish-sentence is so far conditional that

---

[1] For Italian, cf. Dino, I, 22, *Uno masnadiere de' Donati, il quale si disse fu Piero Spini.*

the absolute validity of the main utterance depends upon it. Often a wish of this kind is intercalated parenthetically into the main proposition,[1] as in Vid. 8, 27, *Mas ma Lob' am si conques Que: si m'ajut deus ni fes: Al cor m'estan sei dous vis; ibid, 28, 40, E s'eu li pogues mal voler: Si deus m'ampar: de mon poder, Li for' eu mals et orgolhos.* Cf. also Ba. Ch. 250, 19, *O ieu, que anc non l'ac major, Dis Jaufres: sim sal dieus ni fes;* Biog. 101, *Domna, sim vailla dieus, de l'ora en sai que fui vostre servire, nom poc entrar en cor nuls pessamens que non fossetz la mielz qu'anc nasques; ibid,* 102, *Guillem si dieus e fes vos vailla, avetz domna per cui cantatz?* In Par. 75, 44, *Ieu nulh temps no faria Forssadamen so qu'ieu dezir: Aissi dieus gui lo caiteus doloiros;* Crois. 1035, *Perqu'ieu: si m'ajud fes, no m'en fas meravelha, Si om be los confon;* Vid. 37, 17, *Si m'ajut deus, peccat fai criminal Ma bela domna, can ilh nom socor.*

B. Sentences showing insertion of a verb of mental action to indicate the relation of the speaker (rarely of the hearer) to a hypothetical statement. Type: *non cre venha.* This type is a fruitful source of subjunctive clauses in all the Romance languages. The main points of interest connected with it are the questions as to whether the use of the subjunctive implies subordination of thought, and as to the original position of the negation. The meaning of the independent potential subjunctive in Latin varied widely, but it often expressed the conviction of the speaker in regard to an action in a supposed case, as in Plautus, Ba. 1184, *quem quidem ut non hodie excruciem, alterum tantum auri non meream;* M. G. 736, *qui deorum consilia culpet, stultus inscitusque sit.* Though no verb of mental action is present, the thought is essentially the same as it would be in Provençal *non cre miera tan d'aur.* Occasionally, even in

---

[1] Similar Latin wish-subjunctives in Plautus, often containing the name of a god, are given by Morris, *Subjunctive,* p. 150.

Latin, such potentials were accompanied by a verb of mental action, as in Asin. 465, *Sauream non novi. At nosce sane. Sit, non sit: non edepol scio.* If now in such expressions the verb of mental action be prefixed or intercalated, we get the Provençal type fully developed, as in Dan. 11, 36, *Si m'al sen desirs fors duich, No sap lo cors trep ois duoilla.* The parenthetical defining character of the inserted verb is still more apparent in cases like Ba. Ch. 261, 28, *E portatz lim aquest angel, Qu'el mon non cug n'aya pus bel.* In my opinion, it is the hypothetical negative sentence which is original and which contains all the essential elements of the thought. Then, some time before the earliest Provençal literary monuments, it must have become customary to insert in such sentences, generally at the beginning, a verb of mental action to indicate more clearly the speaker's attitude toward the supposed action. Next, the negation was displaced by attraction, and formed an ever closer union with the inserted verb. The attraction did not, however, always take place, as is apparent from a consideration of such sentences as Flam. 1011, *De lui si partol cumpanho E cujon ben non sia sas*; S. Fe 531, *S'aichi fos Judas Machabeus, . . . O Josue oll paucs Zacheus, Czom cuid, no foss totz lo jogs seus,* which are clearly analogous to such Late Latin constructions as Greg. Tur. Mart. 490, *putavi quasi vas esset effractum*; hist. franc. 8, 20, *quod credo providencia dei fecissit.* After the attraction, the next step would be the insertion of the subordinating conjunction *que*, and the reduction of the originally independent sentence to an object clause would be accomplished.[1] An example like Cerc. 6, 27, *Cist serven fals fan a plusors gequir Pretz e joven e lonhar ad estros, Don proeza non cug que sia mais, Qu'escarsetatz ten las claus dels baros,*

---

[1] If the main utterance be thought of as actually existing, the indicative is used, as in Rud. 7, 27, *Grailles e fresca ab cor plazen, E non cre gensser s'enseigna,* which is otherwise of the usual type. Such cases are very rare.

3

shows how easily the main utterance became subordinate grammatically, even though the inserted verb retained its parenthetical character.

Of sentences of this type[1] by far the most common are those which contain a verb of thinking, *cuidar* or *creire*, in the first person: Ba. Ch. 54, 17, *L'segles non cuit dure gaire, segon qu'escriptura di*; Ap. Ch. 77, 52, *A totas gens dic e mon serventes Que, si vertatz e dreitura e merces Non governon home en aquest mon, Ni sai ni lai no cre valors l'aon,*[2] *ibid.,* 85, 41; 105, 42; Aug. 7, 17, *E ges non ay crezensa, Per nulha ren que sia, Puesca querir, s'eu no complisc lo joc*; Born 29, 27, *Eu non cuich lais Caorz ni Caiarc Mos Oc e Non*; *ibid.,* 28, 34; Sirv. Jog. 3, 38, *Tu es joglaretz novels, Ogan no cre recepchas Draps entiers envoutz de pels*; *ibid.,* 23, 21; 23, 48; Crois. 184, *Quant lo coms de Tolosa e li autre baro El vescoms de Bezers an auzit li sermo Que los Frances se crozan, no cug lor sapcha bo*; Alv., p. 142, 17, *Mas ieu no cre pros dompna denh Far drut molherat gelos brau*; Rog. 4, 32, *Fas ton talen, mas ieu no cug ni cre Tan quan vivras n'ayas nulh jauzimen*; Gav. 1, 48, *E nom pes negus m'en desmenta*; *ibid.,* 4, 7; 6, 48; 8, 38; Sord. 40, 115; In. It. 82, 10; Vid. 5, 30; Blac. 5, 33; Flam. 6974, etc.[3]

The attraction exercised by the defining verb is clearly shown by a sentence like Born 28, 27, *Del senhor de Mirandol Qui ten Cruisa e Martel, No cre, ogan se revel.* Here the subject of the main statement becomes by attraction an adverbial modifier of the inserted verb.

Much less frequently we find the defining verb in the second person: Ap. Ch. 22, 34, *Puois sui per lui aissi ausartz*

---

[1] Cf. Dubislav, 4, 5; Meyer-Lübke, § 557.

[2] In this sentence the hypothetical character of the subjunctive *aon* is clearly indicated by the preceding protasis.

[3] For Italian, cf. Guit., canzone 12, 21, *Mai de servir lei non credo penta*; Dante, sestina III, 13, *non credo fosse mai virtute in erba Di tal salute.*

Que nous cuidetz lanssas ni dartz M'espaven, ni aciers ni fers;
Flam. 1186, *Et on plus hom a lui o chanta, Nous cujes sos
mals cors l'eschanta;* In. Par. 42, 10, *En dos amicx, pus que
y es fin' amors, Ja nous cugetz loncx respiegz s'i emprenda.*
In these cases the inserted verb expresses the relation which
the hearer is to assume toward the hypothetical concept in
question. Similarly, when the verb is in the third person,
it indicates the attitude to be assumed by the third party. I
have found only one example: Ba. Ch. 123, 25, *Pero nos
cuit, si bem sui irascutz, Sitot me dic en chantan ma rencura,
Jal diga ren que si' outra mezura.*

Sentences in which the main utterance is affirmative are
much less common. In such cases the potential character of
the subjunctive often shades off into an expression of desire.
So in In. Par. 13, 19, *Estra lur grat cre jois m'alberc,* the
original concept *jois m'alberc* is clearly a wish, to which a
determinant is added by the defining verb *cre.* Cf. also In.
It. 82, 10, *D'amor mor eu plangen tot l'an; Si pens fassan
li autre fin aman;* Gav. 5, 20, *Dombridieus cre m'o appa-
relh; ibid.,* 9, 20, *Tant an d'erguelh sils q'a tuatz Q'els cujol
mons lui si' aclis;* Ap. Ch. 105, 202 (Boeci), *Tant a Boecis
lo vis esvanuit Que el so pensa uel sien amosit;* Crois. 2279,
Ans segon lur esmansa cujan sian (li crozatz) vencut; ibid,
6281; Denkm. 70, 2321, *Car pessaron Messias sia Que
atendo, e fan follia;* Daur. 621; Flam. 990, 3840, 6916;
In. Par. 60, 3.

All the sentences thus far studied contain the present
subjunctive. The use of the imperfect subjunctive is not
so frequent, although many examples are at hand. By
some,[1] the shift of tense is considered a sign of partial subordination, but it is difficult to trace such a distinction in
Provençal. The verb of mental action seems to be just as

---

[1] Cf. Schmalz, *Lateinische Syntax*[3], § 267.

much of an addition, an afterthought, as in the instances already considered. Where the imperfect appears, its employment seems to be determined by a protasis, either actually present or implied in the thought. That it is original in the main utterance, and not determined by the tense of the defining verb, is shown by such examples as the following, where the insertion is in the present: Flam. 2172, *Aitals plazers esperitals, Ben cug valgues unas daneras*; *ibid.*, 4884; Ba. Ch. 224, 20, *E membram be, cals c'os disses, E cug fos n'Arnautz de Maruelh*; *ibid*, 264, 42; Ap. Ch. 9, 90, *Ni no me puesc pessar per re Aquel effan fag o agues*; *ibid.*, 38, 38, *Mas s'ilh auzis con li sui fis E leials ses tot cor vaire, Non crei sufris C'aissi languis Fins amanz e mercejaire*; Dan. 18, 28, *Tant fina amors cum cella qu'el cor m'intra Non cuig fos anc en cors non eis en arma*; Crois. 497, *E los clercs auzician li fols ribautz mendics E femnas e efans, c'anc no cug us n'ichis*; *ibid.*, 1291, 1302; In. Par. 5, 50, *No cug fossetz tan avara Non acsetz qualque dolor al cor*; Monk 5, 89; Flam. 738, 7485.

In the other cases, the defining verb is in the conditional (a) or the preterite (b): a, Ba. Ch. 108, 18, *Qu'eu vi l'or' e vos la vitz, Non cuidera res amiranz mi mogues*; *ibid*, 222, 10; Crois. 1770, *E fan aital chaplei, Quin volia ver diire cujeratz fos gabei*; Monk 4, 18, *Sa ricors cujarial valgues*; Flam. 5230, *Ben cujera Jupiter fos O alcus dels dieus amoros*; *ibid.*, 5636; b, Ba. Ch. 250, 20, *Diable cugiei aguesson pres*; Crois. 1007, *E eu cugei aguessan fait patz e establida*; Capd. Un. 3, 33, *A, com cuidei fos*[1] *dinz d'aital color Co m'aparec deforas per semblan*; Vid. 21, 3, *Eu cugei acsetz conquiza La gensor e la plus gaja.*

The insertion of other verbs of mental action than those of thinking or knowing is rare in Provençal. I have noted

---

[1] This subjunctive is clearly optative.

it only with verbs of promising, as in Ap. Ch. 1, 644, *E iurava sor sains, com om leiaus, Ia mais tan com el fust vis om cárnaus, Ne vos venges per lui noise ni maus*; ibid., 30, 12, *E sim sentis lo cor ferm Quel plagues, bel fauc fermansa: Ja mos chantars tritz ni braus Non fos ni de razon brava*; Flam. 2046, *E jam promessest vos l'autrier A bona fem cossellasses*.

C. In sentences which express some of the various shades of meaning denoted by the term jussive, all in the subjunctive, a verb is inserted indicating more definitely the relation of the speaker, hearer or a third person to the main utterance. Such sentences may be either positive or negative; but in the latter case the negation is mostly attracted to the inserted verb, though the union is never so strong as in the case of the Latin *nolo amet*. The Provençal types are thus: *vuelh venha* and *non vuelh venha*. The verb of the main utterance is nearly always in the second or third person. The only cases with the first person which I have found are the following: In Par. 52, 58, *Seguros ses espaventalh Vuelh fassam d'els tal esparpalh Que sial camps per nos retengutz*; Flam. 7738, *E vol per pres a vos mi renda*; Cerc. 2, 37, *S'elha nom vol, volgra moris Lo dia quem pres a coman*; Rom. 7, 31, *Ben volgr' aguessem un senhor Ab tan de poder e d'albir Qu'als avols tolgues la ricor*; In. Par. 117, 25, *Lo jorn volgra fos part Roais*; Ba. Ch. 361, 14, *Mi dons . . . que de lonc temps no avia volgut fossem ensemps*; ibid., 389, 36, *Senher, dis el, no vos sia greu, Per sert ieu acosselharia, Si connoisses que be fag sia, Davant Josep nos non anem*; Sirv. Jog. 3, 2, *Joglaretz, petit Artus, si vols t'enjoglarisca, Ni vols segre aquest us, Dreitz es qu'ieu t'en garnisca*; Flam. 6845, *Cant mi dises Qu'ieu de vos mi parta voles*; In. It. 5, 41, *Mezuram ditz no si' escas, Ni ja trop d'aver non amas*; Cerc. 1, 10, *E quin diria m'en partis Fariam morir des era*. Of these, all but the last four examples follow the usual type, the verb of willing, advising or ordering being clearly parenthetical. The whole gist of the statement lies in the subjunctive wish-concept, and the inserted verb serves only to make more definite the attitude of the speaker to his own wish. The last four, however, show a shift of person, due to the fact that they are really reported wishes, but preserve otherwise the original form. For example, what Artus really said was (Sirv. Jog. 3, 2): *vuelh m'enjoglariscatz.* This is reported by the Dalfin in the form: *si vols t'enjoglarisca.* Such examples show what may be called a partial subordination.

In all other cases, the main utterance is in the second or third person, and the defining verb in the first person, rarely in the second or third. With the verb in the second person we have for example, C. M. 23, 36, *Uns cans enrabjatz No voillaz ja venga,* which shows clearly the nature of the inserted verb. *Venga* alone would have conveyed the speaker's wish; *voillaz* defines the hearer's duty in relation to it. As in the familiar Latin *nolo*-type, the negation is attracted to the intercalated verb. So for the third person: Dan. 11, 49, *Arnautz vol sos chans sia ofertz Lai on doutz motz mou en agre.* Here, as before, the subjunctive sentence is complete in itself; the prefixed *Arnautz vol* expresses the defining relation of the poet to his own wish.

Sentences containing the imperfect subjunctive do not differ in essentials from those with the present. The device of denoting a non-realizable wish by the past tenses of the mood[1] had long been in existence, and the proper definition is then indicated by the insertion of a verb, mostly conditional in form: Ba. Ch. 62, 16, *Tot arma crestiana volgra agues tal jai Cum eu agui et ai;* Born 19, 7, *E degram estar soau C'aitan volgra volgues mon pro Na Lana Cum lo senher de Peitau;* Vid. 20, 50, *Na Viern', en patz Volgra fos castiatz.*

---

[1] See Meyer-Lübke, §§ 118–19.

Omitting then these differences of person and tense, I distinguish the following types of defining parataxis in jussive sentences :

1. With verb inserted parenthetically into the subjunctive sentence. a. With verb of willing : Sirv. Jog. 8, 23, *Nostre reis aragones Que val mais de totz los pros Vuelh renovelh vostr' arues* ; Sord. 5, 29, *Et apus vuelh del cor don om al rey navar* ; Daur. 920, *Mos amicx vuelh siatz* ; *ibid*, 1222, 1510 ; Mont. 14, 42, *Perque mon fin cor qu'ieulh ren, Vuelh sapch' on qu'ilh estia* ; Ba. Ch. 83, 21 ; 269, 42 ; Ap. Ch. 89, 3 ; 89, 5 ; Flam. 5433, 6781 ; Born 8, 25 ; 8, 33 ; 31, 31 ; Dicht. 2, 2, 37.[1]

b. With verbs of ordering and advising : In. Par. 25, 23, *Mas sil drutz premers l'enguana, Enguans, si floris, non grana, Lai felnei, Ses mercei, Mas ben gart no s'en sordei* ; Rud. 1, 34, *E sel que de mil apenra, Gart nol franha ni nol pessi.*

c. With verbs of asking : Ap. Ch. 9, 213, *Senher Josep, per dieu vos prec, L'effant Jhesus me mostrasses* ; Sord. 10, 12, *Per quel compte voill pregar non li pes S'ab lui non pas* ; In. Par. 65, 26, *Perqu'ieus prec me valgues Ab vos, domna, fin' amors e merces.*

2. With verb prefixed to the subjunctive sentence.

a. With verb of willing : C. M. 35, 14, *Demandaz cum? voill o sapchaz* ; Born 35, 65, *Volh sapchal reis et aprenda De son grat e fassa chantar Mos sirventes al rei navar* ; Flam. 758, *Eu voil sian franc tut vostre fieu* ; Mont. 5, 15, *Be volri' agues enveya Le reys qu'ab Frances mogues tenza.*

b. With verb of ordering : Ba. Ch, 111, 32, *El' a fait per tot mandar, eya, Non sia jusqu'a la mar, eya* ; Flam. 6143, *Amiga, vai, e digas li Non sa entre, que pause mi* ; Ba. Ch. 56, 3, *Gardatz s'en ben bedoi* ; Rom. 3, 8, *Bels dous amics, e guarda not trics, Si vols que mortz non sia* ; Ap. Ch. 1, 227,

---

[1] For Italian, cf. Monaci, 46, 16, *Ke 'l nostro amore ajungasi non voglio m' atalenti ;* Dino, III, 12, *Il re di Francia non volea si partisse di là.*

Monge, di a Girart, gar, no li mence; Cerc. 1, 10, *E quim diria m'en partis, Fariam morir des era.* (These Provençal sentences with *gardar*, "take care," seem to present an exact parallel to the Latin clauses with *cave, fac, facito*; cf. Plautus, Most. 854, *age canem istam a foribus aliquis abducat face*; Rud. 1219, *et tua filia facito oret*; Capt. 431, *caue tu mi iratus fias.*)[1]

c. With verbs of asking: Aug. 4, 22, *Per merceius prec, bella dousset' amia, Si cum yeus am, vos me vulhatz amar*; Ba. Ch. 245, 7, *E prec, si plaz, nom ochaison*; Flam. 5210, *E prega las a bona fe La cosselhon*; In. Par. 4, 25, *E prec li nom mostr' erguelh No guart vas mi sa ricor*; Gav. 3, 61, *E prec merce m'ajatz.*[2]

3. Sentences containing an attraction of some part of the subjunctive sentences to the defining verb. The commonest form of this type contains a verb of willing with the negation, equivalent to the Latin *nolo amet*; Ba. Ch. 83, 21, *Autre jois no m'er dous ni bos, Ni non volh jam sia promes*; *ibid.*, 77, 2, *En baizan, nius plagues, Ja non volgram solses*; *ibid.*, 103, 9; 170, 15; Born, 2, 13, *E non vuolh sia mieus Doais Ses la sospeisson de Cambrais*; *ibid.*, 33, 7; 33, 36; Dan. 3, 33, *No vueill s'asemble Mos cors ab autre amor*; Rom. 6, 20; Flam. 2954, 3506; Alam. 2, 38.

In the following sentences we find a more violent attraction, generally of the subject or object of the subjunctive sentence: C. M. 39, 3, *En Nicolet, d'un sognie qu'ieu sognava Meravillios, una nuit quan dormiva, Voil, m'esplanez*; Flam. 2905, *Non voil pas d'aital cavallier Moria per mi sil puesc' estorser*; Born, 13, 27, *Conselh vuolh dar el son de n'Alamanda Lai a'n Richart, sitot no lam demanda: Ja per son*

---

[1] For Italian, cf. Monaci, 46, 18, *Guarda non t'argolgano questi forti corenti.*

[2] For Italian, cf. Monaci, 26, 3, 16, *Eo prego l'amore, a cui pregha ogni amante, Li miei sospiri e pianti Vi pungano lo core.*

fraire sos homes non blanda; *ibid.,* 37, 60, *E prec a'n Golfier
de la Tor Mos chantars nolh fassa paor*;[1] Ap. Ch. 102, 15,
Mas sa gran merce prec, sil platz, la mi fass' apaguada; In.
Par. 38, 10, *Dieu prec, non prenda dan tan grieu*; Capd.
22, 68, *N'Audiartz, chascun dia prec dieu a rescos*: *Gart la
comtess' e vos e midons na Maria.*

4. Sentences which show a shift of person, generally
through being reported by another, and hence may be
considered as partially subordinate in thought: Barra 5051,
*Van contar Le respost del rey de la Serra E cum volia patz
ses guerra E mosenhor G. tornes E son ric castel que cobres.*
(Here with colloquial freedom a substantive, a *que*-clause and
the paratactic subjunctive *tornes* are employed as exactly
parallel constructions; cf. the similar Latin sentence : Plautus, Amph. 9, *uti bonis uos uostrosque omnis nuntiis me
adficere uoltis, ea adferam, ea uti nuntiem.*); Alam. 14, 40,
*Per que mielz ama la dompna per un cen Que sos amanz vol
muera honradamen D'armas, sin muor, que cil que ten en fre
Lo seu, que vol viva aunitz per jase*; Flam. 332, *E gardet si
al plus que poc Noil fassa mal on que la toc*; *ibid.,* 1065,
2013, 7091, 7120, 7789.

5. A special type of these paratactic jussive sentences in
Provençal is constituted by expressions of fearing. It is
now generally recognizèd that the Latin form *timeo ne veniat*
consisted originally of an independent prohibition with a
defining verb.[2] In Vulgar Latin the full negation *non* seems
to have been substituted for *ne*, but otherwise the type
remained unchanged.[3] Provençal examples which show the
primitive relations without any shift are: Dan. 18, 12, *Tal*

---

[1] Here the attracted object is repeated by a personal pronoun in the
subjunctive sentence.

[2] See Schmalz, § 211.

[3] Tobler has shown how out of this originally paratactic construction is
to be explained the "expletive" *ne* in French *je crains qu'il ne vienne.*

paor ai nol sia prop de l'arma; Born 42, 37, *Dir non aus mon cor, Tal espaven mi pren de vos, Nous fezes desplazer*; In. Par. 155, 18, *Tal paor ay plazer nom cuelha Del sieu gen cors*; Ap. Ch. 1, 220, *E tem noil face torre la genitance*; Ba. Ch. 349, 29, *Per qe ai paor non prenas deisonor Per cesta gent avols e sens valor.*[1]

In case the original wish was affirmative, then the defining expression of fearing became negative, as in Gav. 6, 9, *Que ja per autre nos jungra Locx que non tem folhs deparca.* But the two original types, *tem non venha* and *non tem venha* were not kept rigidly distinct; only by contamination can we explain such sentences as the following: Capd. Un. 5, 37, *Eu nom˙posc d'una pessa mover Tal paor ai nom vailla chauzimens* (the original wish, if stated independently, must have been *mi vailla chauzimens*); Vaq. 1, 3, *Que paor ai tornes a mal estar A nos quels autres deuriam chastiar* (the original wish was *non torn a mal estar*); Flam. 6760, *E d'aisso era lui temensa Guillems vengues, e mal estera* (original wish: *non venga G.*); In. Par. 133, 45, *Don ai temor M'arma sia en tristor* (original wish: *m'arma non sia en tristor*).

Occasionally an originally potential subjunctive sentence contains an intercalated expression of fearing of a similar type. Such is, for example, In. Par. 65, 7, *Mas qui joven-sella Mi comandava bella Paor ai piuzella No fos al cap del an.* Here the subjunctive *no fos* is determined by the preceding protasis *qui comandava* (= *si om comandava*) and cannot be explained as a primitive wish-concept, but the defining verb of fearing is still purely parenthetic. The sentence is a good illustration of the impossibility of sharply distinguishing between the potential and the optative meanings inherent in the subjunctive form.

---

[1] For Italian, cf. Dante, canzone XII, 29, *Chè più mi trema il core, qualora io penso di lei in parte, ov' altri gli occhi induca, Per tema non traluca Lo mio pensier;* Dino, I, 19, *Sentendolo messer Niccola, ebbe paura non si palesasse più.*

D. In an independent sentence of fact, hypothesis or wish, an impersonal expression is inserted to define more exactly the idea of the principal verb. Type: *es obs venha.*

When such a definition is intercalated in an indicative sentence, the effect is the same as in the first form of defining parataxis already considered. The impersonal *mi par* has precisely the same force as *eu cre*; it defines the attitude of the speaker to the main utterance. So, for example: Crois. 8815, *Senh' en Br. bem sembla s'aisils avem giquitz, Vos meteis e nos autres avetz vius sebelhitz*; Sord. 17, 27, *En Andrieus, sitot s'aucis, Noi gazaingnet ren, som par*; Vid. 28, 21, *Mas car sui de celar ginhos, Degr' esser melhs mos pretz, som par*; Denkm. 249, 242, *E qui vai ad encontre e pueiss noss' en repent, Certz es, son plait perdra ses tot restaurament*; Flam. 3427, 3626; Ba. Ch. 161, 17.

In most cases, however, such impersonals are introduced into a subjunctive sentence, to define more closely the vague meaning of the persons of that mood. The subjunctive may be either potential, in which case an expression of seeming, *mi par, es vejaire, es vis*, is intercalated to strengthen the subjective character of the assertion: or optative, in which case an expression of necessity or fitness, *es obs, val mais, es dreitz, mi plai, mielhs es*, is introduced to elucidate the precise meaning of the mood. This construction was already prevalent in Latin; cf. for instance, Plautus, Asin. 448, *nunc adeam optumumst*; Poen. 1244, *pro hoc mihi patronus sim necessest*; and for Late Latin, Gregory of Tours, hist. franc. 4, 32, *Melius sibi fieri esset inter monachos occultus*; patr. 125, *contigit ad urbem Toroniam veniret.* Here, I may distinguish the following types:

1. With the impersonal inserted parenthetically into the subjunctive sentence: Born 35, 55, *Reis que badalh ni s'estenda, Quant au de batalha parlar, Sembla, o fassa per*

vanejar O qu'en armas no s'entenda ;[1] Ba. Ch. 105, 21, *E pos si ficha ses somos, Semblail failla pans e maisos ;* Ibid., 389, 25 ; Ap. Ch. 38, 8, *Non o sai ; mais l'entreseinha M'esmaia, con ques captanha D'una qu'aissim par m'estreignha Quel cor mi frainh' e m'estregna ;* Sord. 40, 727, *Qui vol regnar ab sen verai, Obs l'es de conoisser si poign Totz jorns lo segle e s'en don soign ;* In. Par. 75, 30, *Per que aisi com ieus am ses bauzia, es obs a mi segatz la semblan via.*[2]

2. With the impersonal prefixed or appended to the subjunctive sentence : Born 8, 6, *Semblais gardon d'anssessis ;* ibid., 12, 50, *A mon Mielhs-de-ben deman Son adreich, nou cors prezan, De que par a la veguda La fassa bon tener nuda ;* Sord. 40, 258, *Bem pes, e par sia vertatz, Qu'el nasquet en desaventura ;* Flam. 1818, *Ben fa parer l'aia trobat Solet quant tan fort lo combat ;* ibid., 2606, *Vejaire l'es tot lo mon aia E mai res noil posca falhir ;* ibid, 4598, 6339 ; Capd. Un. 3, 36, *E con val mais gardes genseis s'onor ;* Denkm. 44, 1522, *Bem pot esser, cest angels fos Jhesus que n'es al cel pojatz ;* Dan. 2, 25, *Dreitz es lagram Et arda e rim Qui 'ncontra amor janguoilla ;* Capd. 1, 14, *Ar es sazos facham son mandamen ;* Gav. 1, 26, *Qual queus parletz, yeus dic eus man Que mielhs fora tug fossetz nug ;* Daur. 351, *Un pauc fil ai, vuelh vos merce clamar, Queus plassa, senhe, lo m'anes bategar ;* Barra 2416, 3746 ; In. Par. 32, 16 ; 38, 30 ; 161, 18 ; 198, 39 ;[3] Ba. Ch. 180, 33 ; 202, 30 ; Born 24, 6 ; Ap. Ch. 110, 63 ; Crois. 2966. In Denkm. 142, 644, *Mas li valgra fos degolatz O fos son cors en foc crematz O que estes*

---

[1] Here the paratactic subjunctive sentence is correlative with a *que*-clause, as in other cases already considered.

[2] For Italian, cf. Guit., sonnet 24, 3, *La cosa ch'altrui par venen sia, È sola medecina al mio dolore.* Dino, II, 20, *Messer Carlo di Valos signore di grande e disordinata spesa, convenne palesasse la sua rea intenzione.*

[3] For Italian, cf. Guit., canzone II, 15, *Certo che ben è ragione Me sia noios' e spiacente ;* Dante, sestina III, 10, *E sento doglia che par uom mi colli.*

en cros penden, we find the same correlation of a paratactic sentence and a *que*-clause already noted.

3. With the subjunctive sentence affected by the attractive influence of the impersonal. The attracted part is generally the simple negation, as in Ba. Ch. 105, 29, *E quis fai del autrui cortes, Pos del seu sera sobravars, Ges nom es vis aport razos C'a lui repairel guizerdos*; Sord. 7, 9, *Om que nuill temps non fetz colp ni pres plaja No m'es semblan pogues far nuill faich bon*; Zorzi 14, 36, *Pero dels tres nom par respos s'eschaja*; Rog., p. 92, 3, *No sembla sia coralz amicx*; S. Fe 259, *Ellal respon si que non ment*; *Ja deu non placzu folz me tent*; Vid. 21, 41, *Pos nolh platz bes m'en eschaja, Peitz trai de mort*; Flam. 2047, *Non auri' obs m'o tradesses*; Capd. 12, 36, *Ja no m'agr' obs fos faitz lo miradors, On vos miratz vostre cors bel e gen*; Mont. 3, 24, *En tal sonalh An mes batalh Don non tanh pretz los vuelha*; Alv. 15, 20, *E non es obs, n'an delitz Per oltracujat vejaire.*

More rarely the subject or object of the subjunctive sentence is attracted to the impersonal, in the form of an adverbial modifier: Born 1, 16, *Mas d'aquest mon nom par aja sonh* (*mon* is the logical subject of *aja sonh*); *ibid.*, 31, 40, *E valgra mais, per la fe qu'ieu vos dei, Al rei Felip, comenses lo desrei Que plaidefar armatz sobre la glesa*; Sord. 40, 826, *Quar, segon la humanitat, D'ome cove, faza foldat*; Ba. Ch. 141, 1, *No s'eschai d'ome savai Li venga tan d'onors.*

E. To a potential sentence is prefixed a general denial, which negatives the possibility of the hypothesis posited in the main utterance. Type: *non es om non venha.* This form of sentence, which reappears in the early Teutonic dialects,[1] has been much discussed, and the various explanations proposed are by no means in accord. Diez[2] explained

---

[1] Cf. Otfried, 1, 17, 1, *Nist man nihein in uuorolti thaz saman al irsageti;* 1, 3, 21, *burg nist thes uuenke.*

[2] *Grammatik,* 1043.

the type as consisting of originally consecutive sentences with ellipse of the conjunction *que* and considered it as a parallel construction to the Latin *quin*-sentence (*nemo est quin non veniat*). This explanation is rejected by Meyer-Lübke[1] and Dubislav,[2] who see in such forms two paratactic independent sentences. They think that the first proposition is determined by the second and that the connection is so evidently emphasized by the negation that the speaker does not consider it necessary to indicate it by a single subordinating word like a relative. The Teutonic forms have been especially studied by L. Tobler[3] and Behagel,[4] who explain them as asyndetic parataxis. This solution is doubted by Delbrück,[5] who however proposes no other explanation in its stead. Paul[6] accepts the paratactic theory and suggests that such sentences need not necessarily be traced back to a common Indo-European form, but that they may have arisen spontaneously in later epochs.

It seems to me that the type *non es om non venha* cannot be separated from the other forms of defining parataxis already considered. It is most closely related to the type *non cre venha*. Just as in the latter the speaker defines his attitude to a hypothetical statement by the addition of a verb of mental action originally foreign to the thought, so here the mental attitude of the speaker is defined by the addition of a generalizing negation. The definition is there subjective, here objective. It seems furthermore likely that the type originated in question and answer. First a speaker made a hypothetical or repudiating question,[7] *om non venha*? To this the generalized negative answer *non es* was given. If now this dialogue be united into a single utterance and

[1] *Grammatik*, § 540.
[2] *Op. cit.*, pp. 6–7.
[3] *Germania*, XVII, 257 ff.
[7] Cf. Morris, *Subjunctive*, pp. 287–92.

[4] *Ibid.*, XXIV, 167 ff.
[5] *Vergl. Syntax*, III, 381–85.
[6] *Principien*[2], 115.

the order of the parts be inverted, we get the perfect type already formulated.

I have considered as the normal type of this variety of defining parataxis the generalized negation of being. That is, the existence of the subject of the main hypothetical· utterance is denied by the defining addition. The chief proposition, when it is made grammatically subordinate, becomes a relative clause. If, however, not the non-existence of a particular subject, but the non-performance of a particular act, be the afterthought of the speaker, we get generalized negative parataxes which, if subordinate, would become objective or subjective clauses. Thus I would explain, for example, sentences of the type *non pot esser non venha, non posc mudar non venha.* Here what is denied by the defining addition is merely the possibility of the hypothetical act posited in the main utterance.[1] Such sentences are less common in Provençal than the other type. I class here the following: Born 14, 66, *On venran tal cinc cent armat Que, quan serem tug ajustat, Non er, Peitieus no s'en planha*; ibid., 23, 32, *E non pot esser remasut, Contra cel non volon tronco E que samit e cisclato E cendat noi sion romput*; Ba. Ch. 93, 15, *E pos tota res terrena S'alegra quan folha nais, Non posc mudar nom sovena D'un amor per qu'eu sui jais*; ibid., 176, 28, *Quil fer en gauta, quil en col, El non pot mudar nos degol*; Ap. Ch. 1, 500, *Non laiserai per ren, par man non leu*; ibid., 3, 437, *Totz m'atendretz mos covinenz, O ia, per dieu, aurs ni argens Nous garra, non siatz perduts*; Born 29, 1, *Non puosc mudar, un chantar non esparga*; Crois 3514, *Baro, ditz l'apostolis, no pos mudar, nom pes, Car ergolhs e maleza es entre nos ases*; Alv. 7, 15, *E pero non puesc mudar, De mos enemics nol gar*; Flam. 4550,

---

[1] Cf. the common Old French "cheville," *ne poet muer n'en plurt, Roland*, 826.

Margarida nos pot tener, Non dig' un pauc de som plazer;
Dicht. 11, 2, *Bona domna, tan vos ai fin coratge, Non puesc
mudar, nous cosselh vostre be* ; Capd. 20, 29, *Eu non ai poder,
rompa ni franha L'amor qu'ieu l'ai.*

Returning now to the more usual type, *non es om non
venha,* there remain to be considered the various modifications of this primitive form brought about in the development of the language. As already stated, it is generally
the subject of the subjunctive sentence which is defined
by the preceding negation ; but two cases at least are found
in which the defining negation affects the object of the main
utterance : [1] Ap. Ch. 85, 43, *Ni anc no fo res meinz prezes
Daitals joglars esbaluiz* ; Flam. 4340, *Res non es amors non
ensein.* In Born, 43, 8, *Aissi cum un confraire, No i es uns
nol poscatz tondr' e raire,* the object-concept is carried
forward by a personal pronoun in the subjunctive sentence.

In all other cases, however, the "missing relative," to use
a convenient expression, is subject : Ap. Ch. 6, 112, *Que se
el t'acosego, la perda er tamanha, Tro a Maroc lo gran non er
selh no s'en planha; ibid.,* 96, 17, *Mas non es hom en tot lo
mon pietz traya Com selh cuy ditz quascus: "paya me, paya ;"*
Flam. 376, *Ni de Baiona ni de Blaya Non fon pros hom
letras non aia; ibid.,* 1427, *E non es cavalliers ni clergues
Adonc pogues ab leis parlar; ibid.,* 1768, *Non fon res el mon
tan grieus, A leis non paregues trop leus;* [2] *ibid.,* 5980, 7777 ;
In. It. 26, 625, *Car non es nuills destrics Ni messions, no i
tagna;* In. Par. 67, 11, *Uey non es Nulhs om pogues la falseza
Que a en si; ibid.,* 181, 24, *Car entre totz los corals amadors
Non fo us miels ames ses falsura Con ai amat.*[3]

---

[1] Similar constructions are of doubtful recurrence in Old French ; cf.
Dubislav, p. 7.

[2] This sentence may be considered as a contamination of two types of
parataxis, the contrasted and the defining.

[3] For Italian, cf. Guit., sonnet 33, 8, *Omo non è già sì fermo 'n sua fede,
non fallisse, ant' eo ver vostro amore;* ibid., canzone 13, 13, *Altro non è sì ben
cominci e sovri En tutto ciò dove donna altra s' ovri.*

When this type was fully established, it was inevitable that shiftings and attractions should occur, tending to develop a closer union between the two elements. Even in the sentences already considered, it may be questioned whether the subjects *om*, *res*, etc., do not belong really to both sentences, according to the construction called ἀπὸ κοινοῦ. In all other varieties of this type, this ἀπὸ κοινοῦ is more apparent; the subject is attracted out of the main subjunctive utterance and associated with the defining negative. The simplest kind of attraction is seen in such examples as Cerc. 1, 17, *Anc res no fo no s'umelis Vas amor, mas ill n'es fera*; In. Par. 113, 22, *Anc hom mais pres no fo, No volgues esser desliuratz*. That however even in this case Provençal did not regard the subjunctive sentence as subordinate is shown by such a passage as In. Par. 194, 27, *Quar anc princeps negus melher no fo El nostre temps de sa ni de la mar, Ni tant aya fach sobre la gent canha*, in which it is introduced by the coördinating conjunction.

The next step toward subordination was taken when for the general negative *non es* another negative verb was substituted, with which the subject of the subjunctive sentence was associated. The original condition with such verbs is shown by such an example as Dan. 14, 25, *Non sai hom tan sia e dieu frems, Ermita ni monge ni clerc, Cum ieu vas cella de cui can*, in which the attraction has not yet taken place.[1] This example proves also the close connection which once existed between "relative" sentences of this type and those discussed under type C. Canello translates: "*non conosco alcuno che sia tanto devoto a Dio;*" but a translation: "*non so che alcuno sia tanto devoto*" is equally possible.

Ordinarily, however, the subject of the main utterance

---

[1] That *om* is here the late analogical accusative form is unlikely. Arnaut Daniel keeps faithfully to the old declension *om—ome*; cf. 14, 17 and 17, 29.

4

becomes the subject or object of the defining negative verb. The chief varieties of this attraction are :

a. The subject of the subjunctive sentence is object of impersonal *non a* : Ba. Ch. 32, 14, *Non i a negu de vos jam desautrei* ; *ibid.*, 371, 30, *Non ac negun non menes gran dolor* ; Ap. Ch. 5, 447, *Anc non ac en la cort baro, Cavalier donsel ni donzela, Sesto ni sest, ni sel ni sela, De las novas nos azautes E per bonas non las lauzes* ; Brun. 1, 3, *E no y a ram no s'entressenh* ; Born. 34, 45, *Noi aura un no veja son arnes* ; Dan. 17, 30, *El mon non ha home de negun nom Tant desires gran benenansa·aver Cum ieu fatz lieis* ; *ibid.* 18, 10 ; Crois. 429, 1233, 5205, 7366 ; Flam. 533 ; Denkm. 80, 2656 ; 157, 12.

b. The subject of the subjunctive sentence is object of a transitive verb : Ap. Ch. 1, 18, *Non laisse aver en Fransa bon car ne leu, Ni rente en sa anor, cenz ne tonleu, Tot nos face venir aiqui o seu* ; *ibid.* 6, 45, *Anc no vi fautz en bratz ni falco montargi Tant be cas per usatie ni segua la perdris* ; *ibid.* 22, 19, *Ni anc Bordeus Non ac seignor tant fos gaillartz Cum ieu* ; *ibid.* 105, 178, (Boeci), *Anc no vist omne ta grant onor agues, Sil forfez tan dont ellas rancures, Sos corps ni s'anma miga per ren guaris* ; Born. 17, 3, *Pero non hai ni senhor ni vezi, D'aquest afar aja cor ni talan Ni vuelha ges qu'en chantan lo casti* ; Dan. 2, 51, *Anc no vim Del temps Caim Amador meins acuoilla Cor trichador* ; Crois. 288, *Anc dieus no fe nulh clerc per punha que i mezes, Los pogues totz escriure e dos mes o en tres* ; *ibid.* 3365, *E no as en ta cort cardenal ni abat Agues millor crezensa e la crestiandat* ; Monk 4, 26, *Anc mais no fi ardit tan bem vengues* ; Vid. 12, 33, *Anc no vist nulh arquier Tan dreg ni tan prim traisses* ; Flam. 143, 1150, 1193 ; Dicht. 2, 2, 26.

In a few sentences of this type the defining negation is not actually expressed, but implied by *pauc* or a similar word : In. Par. 33, 22, *Si duerm trop, non er quim revelh,*

Ans si penran tug a gabar ; *E s'istau tot jorn al solelh, Pauc trobarai m'an covidar* ; Flam. 1193, *Ben pauc ne sai gelos non fossan.*

c. The subject of the subjunctive sentence is subject of the defining verb : Alv. 9, 44, *Anc om no nasquet de maire, Tan beus posca valer* ; Rom. 13, 71, *Eu non cre que negus fo naz Con tan bel glavi fos navraz*; Flam. 2000, *Ja nuls om non s'avenra Tan destreitz non garisqu' els bainz* ; Denkm. 225, 355, *Vergena de las verges, francha res e grazida, C'anc no nasquet de carn d'aquesta nostra vida Nulha fila de femna tan ben fos establida.*

. Whether out of this type sentences could be formed which seem to show a relative-locative relation, as in Zorzi 14, 31, *Anc no preiron Venecian conten Non aguesson lauzer al fenimen* : Sirv. Jog. 12, 10, *Anc un bon mot non fezes Non i agues dos malvas,*[1] is doubtful. I prefer to regard these sentences as exhibiting parataxis by contrast ; the subjunctive sentence is conditional in character.[2]

Dubislav[3] has shown that in this negative defining parataxis, in Old French, the indicative may occasionally be used (*ni a celui ne se claime chaitis*). The difference in mood depends of course on the subjective attitude of the speaker ; if he think that the proposition which he defines by negation is valid in point of fact, the indicative is naturally chosen. In Provençal the use of the indicative is also probable, but the only example of this form which I have found occurs in " Daurel et Beton," a poem whose language is too mixed to permit a definite conclusion : Daur. 645, *Tuh la regardo li*

---

[1] Cf. also Ba. Ch. 167, 12, where the relation is still more complicated.

[2] For Old French, see Dubislav, 25. In Italian, however, we find sentences of this locative character which present the pure type of defining parataxis ; cf. Guit., canzone 16, 52, *Nel mondo non è loco ne canto, No li portasse pietanza e doglia.*

[3] *Op. cit*, p. 7.

gran e li menor, Non i a un nois plore de dolor. In Ba. Ch.
182, 18, *Pero si negun n'i a Mais ne saubes e meills dizia
Ja nos pense que m'enoges*, the indicative *dizia* is correlated
with a subjunctive, *saubes*; but is evidently employed for
the sake of the rhyme.

F. In an utterance of fact, an independent sentence is
intercalated to indicate a time-relation of the main thought.
Type: *ieu vinc un an a.* The relations here are so simple
and this type of parataxis is so well known, being still
preserved in most of the Romance languages that I shall
content myself with a citation of the principal examples.
The verbs used in the defining sentence in Provençal are
impersonal *aver, esser* and *passar*; Ap. Ch. 3, 136, *E fora
bellazor dos tans, Mas non fo, prop a de set ans*; ibid., 84,
23; Born 28, 4, *Assaut ni cembel Nom vin, mais aura d'un
an*; Crois. 3633, *Aicels de Savardu lor tolol vin e pan, E no
vendemieren, so cug, mais a d'un an*; Gav. 4, 30, *Lonc temps
a degra remaner La foldatz que vos mantenetz*; Barra, 4953,
Mosenh' en G. aytals es Cum era huey a XIII ans; Born 4,
14, *Eu fora lai, ben ha passat un an*; Barra 4761, *Que
lunhas novas non ausem, Ni fem, ben a passatz XX ans*;
Biog. 13, *Lo joglars demandet an Arnaut si avia fag, en
Arnautz respos que oc, passat a III jorns*; Gesta 837, *Alcus
reys e princeps, que avia faitz jurar, pessa avia*; ibid., 1428,
1846; In. Par. 13, 24, *Mas, pel senhor qu'en crotz fo mes,
Sa colors fresqu' e vermeilla Camja mon sen, tal ora es.* Such
time-definitions go back undoubtedly to Vulgar Latin speech-
forms. Sentences not very dissimilar appear occasionally in
the classical authors; cf. Cicero, ad Att. 2, 15, 3, *nondum
plane ingemueram: salve, dixit Arrius.*

The preceding pages illustrate the remarkable abundance
of the paratactic type of sentence structure in Provençal.
It will be seen that nearly every relation ordinarily expressed
by means of subordinating conjunctions and pronouns may

also be indicated by parataxis. Provençal in this respect evidently remains in the earlier stage of a literary language struggling to free itself from the primitive method of stringing concepts together without unity. Nevertheless the fondness of the language for parataxis must not be over-estimated. Beside every form of sentence-structure with parataxis there existed another form with hypotaxis and the latter are numerically the more important. To illustrate this difference, I shall take that typical troubadour of the golden age, Bertran de Born. A count of the first twenty *cansos* of Stimming's edition shows that Bertran employed parataxis to indicate a relation of concepts in about 16 % of all the sentences which clearly are subordinate in thought. In all remaining instances, he employs a subordinating word, conjunction or pronoun.

Vossler[1] has lately pointed out that languages used by races in lower stages of culture prefer the paratactic type of sentence structure, those more advanced the hypotactic. Vossler uses the term parataxis in a more extended sense than I have done, but even restricting it in accordance with the definition given above, a comparison of Provençal with Old French on one hand and Early Italian on the other proves the justice of his general principle. Notwithstanding the diversity of the paratactic types in Provençal, a glance at Dubislav's program[2] shows that in Old French the variety is still greater. And that in numerical frequency Provençal is also inferior may be proved by a comparison of two works of like literary character, such as *Orson de Beauvais* and the *Chanson de la Croisade contre les Albigeois*. In the 3,600 lines of the former I have counted 95 unmistakable cases of "subordinating" parataxis, while a like number of lines in the latter contained only 60. In Italian

---

[1] *Sprache als Schöpfung und Entwicklung*, p. 131.

[2] For Old French forms lacking in Provençal, see Dubislav, p. 7, 9.

on the other hand parataxis is comparatively rare, much rarer than in Provençal.[1] The significance of these results from Vossler's "cultur-historisch" standpoint cannot be mistaken.

In the Old Provençal language itself a progressive tendency toward hypotaxis is quite evident. The best proof of this is afforded by a comparison of the two romans d'aventure, *Flamenca*, written probably about 1234,[2] and *Guillaume de la Barre*, dated 1318. The former contains, in 5,300 lines, 94 examples of parataxis, while the latter has only 32. The difference is striking, and proves the existence of a real progress in the language.

Another noteworthy fact is the relative scarcity of parataxis in prose literature. In those prose monuments which are mere translations of Latin originals, this is not surprising, but it is equally manifest in the Biographies of the Troubadours. The same fact, however, is noticeable in Old French. Villehardouin,[3] for instance, contains only three examples of defining parataxis. The explanation must, I think, be sought partly in the subservience of the prose authors to existing Latin models, and partly in their more deliberate habit of thought, so different from the emotional energy and rapidity of the lyric poets.

WILLIAM PIERCE SHEPARD.

---

[1] Except with Dino Compagni, whose short-hand style is evidently peculiar to himself.

[2] See Revillout, *Revue des langues romanes*, VIII, pp. 5–18.

[3] See Greving, *Studien über die Nebensätze bei Villehardouin*, Kiel, 1903.

LIST OF TEXTS CITED, WITH ABBREVIATIONS.

Ap. Ch. : Appel, *Provenzalische Chrestomathie*, Leipzig, 1895.

Ba. Ch. : Bartsch, *Chrestomathie provençale*, 5ᵉ éd., Berlin, 1892.

C. M. : Crescini, *Manualetto provenzale*, Verona, 1892.

Denkm. : Suchier, *Denkmäler provenzalischer Literatur und Sprache*, Halle, 1883.

In. Par. : Appel, *Provenzalische Inedita aus Pariser Handscriften*, Leipzig, 1890.

In. It. : Appel, *Poésies inédites tirées des manuscrits d'Italie*, Paris, 1898.

Dicht. : Schultz, *Die provenzalischen Dichterinnen*, Leipzig, 1888.

Sirv. Jog. : Withoeft, *Sirventes joglaresc*, Marburg, 1891.

Alam. : Salverda de Grave, *Le Troubadour Bertran d'Alamanon*, Toulouse, 1902.

Alv. : Zenker, *Die Lieder Peires von Auvergne*, Erlangen, 1900.

Aug. : Müller, *Die Gedichte des Guillem Augier Novella*, Zs. f. rom. Phil., XXIII, 47–78.

Barra : P. Meyer, *Guillaume de la Barre, par Arnaut Vidal de Castelnaudari*, Paris, 1895 (Soc. des anc. textes fr.).

Biog. : Chabaneau, *Les Biographies des troubadours en langue provençale*, Toulouse, 1885.

Blac. : Soltau, *Die Werke des Trobadors Blacatz*, Zs. f. rom. Phil., XXIII, 201–248.

Born : Stimming, *Bertran de Born, sein Leben und seine Werke*, Halle, 1879,

Bornelh : Kolsen, *Guiraut von Bornelh, der Meister der Trobadors*, Berlin, 1894.

Brun. : Appel, *Der Trobador Uc Brunec*, in *Tobler-Abhandlungen*, Halle, 1895, pp. 44–78.

Capd. : Napolski, *Leben und Werke des Trobadors Ponz de Capduoill*, Halle, 1880.

Cerc. : Dejeanne, *Le Troubadour Cercamon*, Toulouse, 1905.

Crois. : P. Meyer, *La Chanson de la croisade contre les Albigeois*, Paris, 1875 (Soc. de l'hist. de France).

Dan. : Canello, *La vita e le opere del trovatore Arnaldo Daniello*, Halle, 1883.

Daur. : P. Meyer, *Daurel et Beton, chanson de geste provençale*, Paris, 1880 (Soc. des anc. textes fr.).

S. Fe : J. Leite de Vasconcellos, *Cançāo de Sancta Fides de Agen*, Romania, XXXI, 177–200.

Flam. : P. Meyer, *Le Roman de Flamenca*, Iᵉ éd., Paris, 1865.

Gav. : Jeanroy, *Poésies du troubadour Gavaudan*, Romania, XXXIV, 498–539.

Gesta : Schneegans, *Gesta Karoli Magni ad Carcassonam et Narbonam*, Halle, 1898 (Rom. Bibl. xv).

Monk : Philippson, *Der Mönch von Montaudon*, Halle, 1873.

Mont. : Coulet, *Le Troubadour Guillem Montanhagol*, Toulouse, 1898.

Rog. : Appel, *Das Leben und die Lieder des Trobadors Peire Rogier*, Berlin, 1882.

Rom. : Zenker, *Die Gedichte des Folquet von Romans*, Halle, 1896 (Rom. ʼBibl. XII.)

Rud. : Stimming, *Der Troubadour Jaufre Rudel, sein Leben und seine Werke*, Halle, 1873.

Sord. : de Lollis, *Vita e Poesie di Sordello di Goito*, Halle, 1896 (Rom. Bibl. XI). .

Vaq. : Schultz, *Die Briefe des Trobadors Raimbaut de Vaqueiras an Bonifaz I*, Halle, 1893.

Vid. : Bartsch, *Peire Vidals Lieder*, Berlin, 1857.

Zorzi : Levy, *Der Troubadour Bertolome Zorzi*, Halle, 1883.

Ba. Ch., Denkm., In. Par., In. It., Biog. are cited by page and line, all the others by number of piece and line.

The abbreviation Un. signifies that the citation is to be found among the "unechte Lieder," included in the respective editions of the troubadour cited.

XIII.—THE VOWS OF BALDWIN.

A Study in Mediæval Fiction.

Although one of the most interesting of Middle English romances, the *Avowing of Arthur* has been singularly neglected. The story is told with the gratifying freshness which marks *Gawain and the Green Knight* and the other poems of the Northern school. The incidents of which the story is composed are fitted into the general framework with rare skill. Even more striking is the. vividness of the characterization. The ordinary romance character is a dummy upon which are hung splendid clothes tagged with catalogues of all the virtues. Dealing with these personages is often like handling the bits of cardboard stamped "sugar," "tea," "potatoes," with which students in commercial colleges play. But in this romance there is sharp distinction between Arthur, genial, brave, a practical joker, and Baldwin, a man of few words, cynical without being bitter, nonchalant, a man of deeds; between Kay, impulsive, always getting into scrapes, inclined to jeer at others, a great boy with a boy's love of adventure, and Gawain, the courteous knight, equally ready to aid beauty in distress and to assist a comrade in time of need. The story is crowded with incidents, and the verse is vigorous and effective.

The literary relations of this romance are interesting and important. With the possible exception of a political poem entitled the *Vows of the Heron*, we have in it the best example in English of the singular custom of "gabbing," while it is certainly not inferior to the more famous French romance of boastful vowing, the *Pèlerinage Charlemagne*. The hunting of the boar seems to be a late popular redaction of one of the most elaborate of Celtic tales. The stories of Gawain and Kay, while of the stock type, are given with new vivacity by this Northern poet and introduce some of the most interesting characteristics of chivalric romance. The three vows of Baldwin, against jealousy, lack of hospitality, and cowardice, with the adventures which follow upon his keeping of them, indicate a relationship of structure between this romance and an extremely widespread class of popular fictions. Finally, in the vow against jealousy and the test to which Baldwin is subjected the romance is brought into connection with a class of tales with which Shakspere's *Cymbeline* is pretty certainly related. Other incidents have sources less interesting, while as a document which throws considerable light upon English life in mediæval times this romance is not unimportant. All in all, it would be difficult to find a Middle English romance with literary relations more significant and varied.

Nevertheless, the poem has been rarely referred to by scholars and no extended investigation has been published. The text has been printed but once, by Robson, for the Camden Society, in 1842. Brandl has a brief comment in Paul's *Grundriss*,[1] and another note was given by the late Gaston Paris.[2] Professor Kittredge some years ago noted a Latin "tragedy" in the *Poetria* of Johannes de Garlandia containing a story similar to that of the soldiers and the women.[3] At another time I hope to discuss the boar-hunt, with its custom of vowing upon an animal and the possible relations of the romance to the famous *Kilhwch and Olwen*, and also the curious jumble of materials drawn from conventional chivalric romances. The aim of the present article is to discuss the vows of Baldwin and several problems which the last half of the poem suggests.

---

[1] I, 665.

[2] *Hist. Litt. de France*, xxx, 111 ff.

[3] *M. L. N.*, viii, 251.

It will be remembered that upon hearing of the terrible depredations wrought by an immense wild boar, Arthur, who 'with his knights is at Carlisle, resolves to kill the monster. He takes with him Gawain, Kay, and Baldwin. After an unsuccessful attempt to kill the beast, Arthur vows to encounter him single-handed, and calls upon the others to make their vows. Gawain will watch all night by the tarn, Kay will ride up and down the forest ready to do battle should occasion present. Baldwin, who is characterized throughout the romance as a man of extreme taciturnity, given to deeds rather than words, and with a strong tinge of cynicism, makes three vows instead of one, and these are of a very peculiar character. His vows, made merely " to stinte oure stryfe," are never to be jealous of his wife; never to be afraid of death, and never to refuse his hospitality to any who may call upon him. Our interest is aroused (1) by the fact that he makes three vows, not one, as was the case in such ceremonies;[1] (2) by the striking differences between his vows and those of his companions. It will be noted that the vows made by Arthur, Gawain, and Kay each involved some deed of knighthood which was to be actually performed. But Baldwin had no wild beast to slay, no mysterious tarn to watch, no forest paths to guard. Again, his vows were apparently forgotten as soon

---

[1] For an excellent example of the custom of vowing upon an animal, cf. *The Vows of the Heron*, Wright, *Polit. Poems and Songs*, pp. 1 ff. That a considerable formality was observed in Arthurian romance finds abundant evidence, notably in *La Queste del Saint Graal* (ed. Furnivall, pp. 14 ff.) In general, it may be said that when some unusual event took place, or when some especially dainty dish was served at meat, it was the custom of Arthur to make a vow, and it became at once obligatory upon the chief knights to follow with their vows. As for vowing upon the boar, in particular, we may also cf. the Hervar Saga, in which we are told that men used to lead the Soma-boar before the king and men laid their hands on his bristles to make their vows. (*Corp. Poeticum Boreale* I, 405–406.)

as uttered. We have no indications that he thought it necessary for him to alter his ordinary course of life, or that he even remembered his vows, until in the *dénouement* he explains how he came to make such vows. Thus the vows relate not to deeds which he swears to perform but to a philosophy of life which he has already long held. That this is true is made evident in the closing scene, where the philosopher-knight explains the time and the occasion which led him to come to each conclusion. A certain happening many years previously determined him that it was of no use to be jealous of a woman. Other experiences brought the conclusion that it is foolish to refuse hospitality and useless to fear death. Then it is evident that these were no new rules of conduct but were the statements of certain guiding principles of Baldwin's life, phrased as one may phrase New Year's resolutions. Thus the attitude of Baldwin toward the ceremony of vowing becomes very interesting. He listens with entire good humor while the king makes the somewhat foolish vow to attack the beast single-handed, and while the others make vows which will necessitate their spending a disagreeable if not a perilous night; then he satisfies the etiquette of the occasion by phrasing three principles constituting his philosophy of life. Having done this, he immediately forgets that he has vowed anything at all; a fact to be insisted on, because the vows, once made, become practically *geasa* upon him in that if he fails to observe the restrictions which they place upon his conduct he will be subject to ridicule and a certain disgrace.[1] Thus

---

[1] Celtic literature is full of references to *geasa*, or tabus, which were laid upon various heroes and became matters of life or death to them. Sometimes the heroes knew of these *geasa;* sometimes not. It was *geasa* for Diarmaid to hunt wild boars; his enemy knew this and craftily laid a trap by which Diarmaid was induced to hunt a monstrous boar. After a desperate fight the hero was slain. Professor Kittredge cites an Irish tale in

it is clear that Baldwin was subjected to three tests of his knighthood, though these tests were quite different from those' usually found in Arthurian romance. He was unconscious that he was being tried; if he had failed in any of the tests he would have been held up to the ridicule of the court.

By this time, the peculiar structure of this part of the romance should be evident. In seeking an explanation, one must keep in mind not only the fact that he makes three vows, vows of an unusual type, instead of one, but that he is characterized throughout the story as a man given to sententious speech, that these vows are in reality maxims underlying his philosophy of life, and that while he is unconscious of the tests, failure to keep his vows will bring disaster.

THE "THREE COUNSELS" TYPE.

The number three, like the number seven, has long been sacred. Every reader of fairy tales knows how common are stories involving three wishes. In the Celtic poets songs frequently are constructed in a similar manner. For ex-

which a young champion defeats Morraha in a game of cards and says: "I lay on you the bonds of the art of the druid, not to sleep two nights in óne house, nor finish a second meal at the one table, till you bring me the sword of light and news of the death of Anshgayliacht." (*Harv. Stud. and Notes*, VIII, 163.) Every man who entered Fenian ranks had four *geasa* laid upon him. "The first, never to receive a portion with a wife, but to choose her for good manners and virtues; the second, never to offer violence to any woman; the third, never to refuse any one for anything he might possess (*i. e.*, refuse *to* any one); the fourth, that no single warrior should ever flee before nine (*i. e.*, less than nine) champions." (Hyde, *Lit. Hist. Ireland*, p. 373.) This account of the conditions on which a hero was admitted to Fenianship is interesting because two of the *geasa* coincide with Baldwin's vows against cowardice and inhospitable action, and also because the four *geasa* form practically a code of morals, a statement of the qualities of the ideal knight.

ample, Caeilte sings of three things in great plenty, three
sorts of music, three noises, three fruit crops, three sons, etc.[1]

In the wisdom literature of the oriental peoples aphoristic
sayings are grouped in the same fashion; the number three
being the usual basis. A familiar example is found in the
book of Proverbs.[2] Here the author uses the number three,
but immediately changes to four by a fixed formula. "There
be three things which are too wonderful for me, yea, four
which I know not: the way of an eagle in the air, the way
of a serpent upon a rock, the way of a ship in the midst of
the sea, and the way of a man with a maid." The same
type of construction is used to explain the three (four) things
that are never satisfied; the three (four) things for which the
earth is disquieted; the four things which are little upon
the earth, but are exceeding wise; and the three (four) things
which are comely in going. Other examples in Hebrew
wisdom literature are not hard to find.

If we turn to such Eastern books of wisdom as the Fables
of Bidpai we note the same form for presenting maxims and
aphorisms. Love of friends, we are told, is increased by
three things: (1) that one should go to his friend's house;
(2) that he should see his friend's wife and children; (3)
that he should eat and drink in his friend's company.[3]
Again, "a wise man has said that there are three things
with which only a madman of weak discernment will meddle,
and whoever meddles with them shall in no wise escape from
them. One of them is approach to a prince, the second,
confidence in women concerning matters which are secret
and terrible, and the third the conduct of the man who took
deadly poison to try or test it."[4]

---

[1] *Silva Gadelica*, II, 111. A similar song is given on p. 124 of the same
volume.

[2] Ch. 30.   [3] Keith-Falconer ed., p. 161.   [4] *Ibid.*, p. 8.

From this practise of combining wise sayings into groups
of three sprang a stock type of constructing tales. How
this came about may be realized if one observes how effectively stories might be introduced to explain the aphorism.
In the example from the book of Proverbs cited above, how
easy it would be to illustrate "the way of a man with a
maid" by a story. Or, in the case of the three things which
disquiet the earth, stories might be told to emphasize the bad
influence of a servant who is put on the throne, or of a fool
who is filled with meat, or of an odious woman when she is
married, or of an handmaid that is heir to her mistress.
Even better suited to such a treatment would be the three
warnings found in the Indian fables; and the second, regarding putting one's trust in women, has in fact been illustrated
by scores of stories, and is an element in the philosophy of
Baldwin.

Thus there developed a new type of construction. Sometimes the stories are obviously meant to drive home the
lesson taught by the aphorism. The great collections of
exempla are illustrations of this use, though each *exemplum*
commonly deals with one aphorism, not three. In other
cases the didactic element is almost lost sight of, and the
three counsels or maxims simply supply a convenient frame
to which may be attached a series of otherwise unrelated
stories. The popularity of this form of construction was
immense. The mere bibliography of the subject is formid-
able, and includes tales in almost every language known.
The favorite form of the story is as follows: Three counsels
as to one's conduct are obtained by a person either as a wage
for work performed or as a purchase; afterwards the life
of the fortunate possessor of these maxims is saved by his
observance of them in time of peril; or, in case he forgets
them, he suffers the loss of property or of life. Without
attempting anything like an exhaustive account of this

story-cycle, it will be useful to examine some representative stories, and to try to organize the material under the several forms most frequently met.

Typical Forms of Construction.

A study of the stories which belong to this cycle shows that there are five important types.   In the first, three rules of life are given, with no stories based upon them and with but little story element, if any, even in the statement.   In the second, a king purchases three maxims and his life is saved by observing them.   In the third, a poor man, or a youth just leaving home, engages as a servant; at the expiration of his term of service he is given his choice between receiving his pay or in place of it three maxims; he chooses the wise sayings, and afterwards has occasion to be thankful that he did so.   In the fourth, the king appears as a wise teacher, who sells or gives three counsels to certain pupils.   In the fifth and last, a man who is poor but wise pays for some service done him by giving three advices in place of money.

Type I. Three rules of life are stated; no application made.

This is the primitive form of the cycle.   An example has already been cited from the Fables of Bidpai; the teaching is that one should not approach a prince (with presumption), or place confidence concerning important matters in a woman, or take poison in order to test it.   Another example, from the same book, is as follows : " It has been said by the wise that a man who follows after the fear of God ought not (1) to withhold questions from ascetics, since they can bring him near to God; nor (2) to withhold from princes anything that may help them to fight against their enemies and bring them to rest and the peace of their army; nor (3) to withhold from his friend anything that may console his trouble and relieve his distress."[1] Of the same character is the account of the three things essential to the wise man. "(1) Let him examine what profitable and what harmful things he is doing, so that he may beware of the harmful and pursue the profitable. (2) Let him be watchful so that he may not suffer hurt, and beware lest his good things be snatched from him. (3) Let him discern with the clear eye of the mind what good things he expects to receive, that he be active and eager to get them and afraid of the harmful things lest they touch him."[2]

The way in which the development from a mere statement of maxims to a story took place is illustrated by some versions of Bidpai's fables in which it is expressly said that the fables are intended to illustrate the counsels. In one version,[3] fourteen maxims are given for the guidance of kings. Among them are several repeatedly met elsewhere, such as, "When you have once acquired what you have diligently sought, preserve it carefully;" "do not be too hasty, but weigh and examine what you plan to do;" "never be disturbed at the accidents of the world." The fables which follow emphasize the importance of these counsels.

But the most famous example of a story of this type, where there is only the slightest narrative element, with no development of illustrations, is the *exemplum* of the nightingale. There are countless versions of it, in many languages. As good a case as any is that given by Jacques de Vitry.[4] A man catches a nightingale, which tells him that if he will

---

[1] P. 164 (Keith-Falconer ed.).   [2] P. 21 (Keith-Falconer ed.).
[3] *The Fables of Pilpay*, London, 1818. The editor's name is not given.
[4] *The Exempla of Jacques de Vitry*, ed. for F. L. S. by Thomas F. Crane, No. 28.

release her she will teach him wisdom which will prove of great benefit to him. He assents, and after the bird has reached a safe place, she says: " Numquam apprehendere coneris que apprehendere non possis, et nunquam de re perdita doleas, quam recupare nequeas, et verbo incredibili numquam fidem adhibeas." Whether the peasant immediately grasped the application of these advices to his own release of the bird in hand, is not explained. Neither are we told whether the peasant found any use for the counsels or not, nor what the occasion was. This *exemplum*, therefore, represents a primitive form of the type. The next step was to use the incident as a basis for developing a complex story.[1]

It is not essential to the present discussion to make a complete collection of versions of this *exemplum*. It is found in *Barlaam and Josaphat*, under slightly different form, and in *Legenda Aurea*. Lydgate has a version of it, under the title of "The Chorle and the Byrde."[2] In the *Gesta Romanorum* it is told of the emperor Boemius.[3] An Old French version is given in Le Grand's collection under the title "Le Lai de l'Oiselet."[4] In Petrus Alphonsus, the order of the counsels is different, and the second one reads, "Quod tuum est habe semper, si potes."[5] This is also the counsel found in "Le Lai l'Oiselet,"—"Ce que tu tiens dans tes mains ne le jette pas à tes pieds." Greek and Latin parallels have also been found.

---

[1] Here, as elsewhere, I am not speaking of the chronology of these stories as a matter of centuries or years. I am dealing with types, with reference to their primitive or developed forms. Of course a primitive type may be preserved long after the cycle has taken a more complicated form.

[2] Printed in Ashmole, *Theatrum Chemicum*.

[3] Ed. *Oesterley*, No. 73.

[4] *Fabliaux ou Contes*, v, 27 ff.

[5] Ed. Schmidt, No. 23. Schmidt's note (p. 150) is very valuable and contains an extensive bibliography.

Type II. A king purchases three counsels, which are the means at a later time of saving his life.

This is one of the most important forms of the cycle.[1] The purchase of the counsels forms the introduction to the story, and the main interest is centered in the plot made against the king's life and the way in which the three advices deliver him. The most widely known example of this type is found in the *Gesta Romanorum*.[2] A merchant has for sale "*tres sapiencias*," and the emperor purchases them. They are: (1) Quicquid agas, prudenter agas, et respice finem. (2) Numquam viam publicam dimittas propter semitam. (3) Numquam hospicium ad manendum de nocte in domo alicuius accipias, ubi dominus domus est senex et uxor iuvencula." For these the emperor gives a thousand florins, but they are worth the price, for afterwards on three separate occasions his life is saved by his observance of them.

Somewhat similar is an account in Etienne de Bourbon of a king who pays a great price for the counsel "In

---

[1] It is impossible to consider all the tales belonging to this and the following types. Some idea of the extent of the cycle may be gained from Oesterley's note in his edition of the *Gesta* (p. 727), where he cites Plutarch, de Garrulitate, 14; P. Alphonsus, 19; Dialog. creaturar, 93; Vincent Bellovac, Spec. mor. 3, 1, 10, p. 907; Bromyard 9, 14; Specul. Exem. 5, 97; Pelbartus, 21; Mart. Polon. ex. 8, N.; Arnoldus de Hollandia, 1, 8, 5, 2; Baldo, 3; Liber Apum, 2, 43, 3; Lucanor, 48; Bibl. des romans, p. 197; Fuggilozio, 158; Libro di nov. 18, p. 41; Boner, 100; H. Sachs, 1, 4, 383; Eyering, 2, 51; Forty Viziers, p. 235; Egenolf, 114; Memel, p. 360; Acerra philolog. 4, 39; Abraham a S. Cl. Lauberhütt, 1, 259; Zeitverkürzer, 498; Haupt's Zeitschr. 1, 407; Massmann, Kaiserchr. 3, 74. Other versions are found in Archivio per le Tradizioni Popolari, III, 98; in Mélusine, IV, 166, and in Museon, 1884, pp. 552–560; Straparola, Night 1, Tale 7, is another example. I am indebted to Professor Kittredge for some additional parallels. Dunlop has a brief bibliographical note in Hist. Fic., I, 76. René Basset, in his Contes Populaire Berbères (p. 227) has an excellent bibliography.

[2] Ed. Oesterley, pp. 431 ff.

omnibus factis tuis considera antequam facias, ad quem finem inde venire valeas." [1]   By following this advice the king's life is saved in a time of great peril.   The resemblance between this advice and the first one in the story from the *Gesta* will be noted.   There is an Arabian story in which the same maxim figures: "Let him who begins a thing consider its end." [2]   This saves the life of the king when a wicked surgeon who has plotted his death comes to bleed him.   Both these stories are evidently closely allied to the parable of Kulla Panthaka in Buddhaghosha's *Parables*, where a youth who had received from his teacher the charm, "Why are you busy?   I know what you are about," sold it to the king for a thousand pieces of gold.   The prime minister, meanwhile, had made a plot against the king by which the barber was to murder him.   While the king was being shaved, however, he kept repeating these words over and over, all unconsciously, which so terrified the barber that he confessed all. [3]

Type III.   A poor man, or a youth just leaving home engages as a servant; at the ᵃd of the term of service he is offered either his wages or three counsels; he chooses the latter, and, in the adventures which follow, these save his life.

[1] No. 81 (ed. Lecoy, p. 77).   Cf. also article by Th. de Puymaigre in *Archivio per le Tradizioni Popolari* for 1884 ; and also Clouston, *Pop. Tales and Fictions*, II, 317.

[2] Beloe, *Oriental Apologues*, cited by Clouston, *op. cit.*, p. 318.   Clouston calls attention to similar stories in the Turkish romance of the Forty Vazirs ; in several collections of Italian Tales, and in Gonzenbach's *Sicilianische Märchen*.

[3] Another version of this last story relates that the charm was "Do I not know why you rub your neck against the rock," which also means, "Do I not know why you whet your razor."   This charm is given the king by the stupid attempts of a favorite but illiterate minister to write a complimentary verse in accordance with a test proposed by jealous companions who thought such a verse would arouse the king's anger.   The *dénouement* is the same in both cases and the story is practically the same as that which illustrates the first maxim in the *Gesta*.   (Clouston, *op. cit.*, II, 491.)

Stories belonging to this type are very numerous. A good example is the tale of Ivan, which is a Celtic version, though the type is probably of Eastern origin.[1] Ivan is very poor, so he leaves his wife and travels far toward the East until he reaches a farmer's house; here he engages for three years, his wages to be 3℔. At the end of the year, his master offers him the amount due but proposes that he take a piece of advice instead. To this Ivan consents, though unwillingly; so he is told, "Never leave the old road for the sake of a new one." At the end of the second year, the same scene is enacted, and the counsel Ivan receives is, "Never lodge where an old man is married to a young woman." At the end of the third year the advice is, "Honesty is the best policy." Ivan now returns to his wife, carrying with him as a present from his former master a cake. He meets many adventures on the way, and would have lost his life but for the three counsels he had received, each of which is the basis for a thrilling experience. When he at last reaches home, he finds his three years' wages in his cake.[2]

Another story of the same type is told of the Baker of Beanly.[3] A poor widow's son leaves his mother in order to look for work. He finds a situation, and soon falls in love with his master's daughter; the night of their marriage he leaves her to find a better place. He binds himself to a baker for seven years; at the end of the term the master commends him and promises better pay for another seven years. This term, likewise, is completed, and the baker

---

[1] Jacobs, *Celtic Fairy Tales*, p. 195 ff.

[2] Jacobs's note cites *Archaelogia Britannia*, 1707, ed. Lluyd; *Blackwood's Magazine*, May, 1818; and Lover's tale, *The Three Advices*. He also shows that the tale was popular in Cornwall and Wales.

[3] Clouston, W. A., *The Baker of Beanly*, *Folk Lore*, III, 183 ff. The Gaelic text is printed by Alex. McBain in the *Celtic Magazine*, July, 1887.

renews his offer. At the end of twenty-one years the baker asks him if he prefers the wages or three advices. He chooses the counsels, which are: (1) Keep the proper roundabout road. (2) Do not stay in the house with a young and beautiful wife who has an old, surly husband. (3) Think thrice before you ever lift your hand to strike anyone. The remainder of the tale is of the stock type, telling how each of these counsels saves the life of the hero. The adventures are not the same as those found elsewhere, an admirable proof that the three-counsels type of construction was well-known at the time the tale was put together, and that it was used simply as the framework on which to hang new and really unrelated incidents.

Of the same character is a Mingrelian tale of a poor orphan who in his utmost extremity met a fair stranger who said that if he would bind himself to his service for three years he would receive three counsels of the greatest value.[1] At the end of the first year, the clever man said to the youth, " Whatever thou seest outside thy yard, throw it into thy yard." At the end of the second year, the counsel was, " Lend nothing to anybody unless thou art much pressed to do so." At the end of the last year, when the youth was ready to depart, he was advised, " Tell not thy secret to a woman." A little variation is introduced into the remainder of the tale. The youth observes the first counsel, and meets with good fortune; the second and third he disregards, and disaster is the result. It will be observed how persistent is the construction of these tales by means of the three counsels, and how the main part of each story consists in the account of the perils which the hero avoided if he kept the counsels in mind, while bad fortune was his if he forgot them.

[1] Wardrop, *Georgian Folk-Tales*, p. 110.

The most elaborate tale belonging to this type is *Ruodlieb*, which involves twelve counsels instead of three.[1] Here the hero serves a king, and at the expiration of his term is given the usual choice. He prefers to have the counsels, and receives twelve advices, of which the most interesting are the following: (1) Trust no red-beard. (2) Leave not the highway for the byway. (3) Avoid lodging where there is an old man with a young wife. (4) Never hitch a mare with foal to a harrow, otherwise you may lose the colt. (5) Don't visit a dear friend too often; rarer visits bring higher regard. (6) Don't take even a beautiful *eigenmagd* as a wife; she will prove too proud. (7) Seek a wife only where your mother advises it; when you win her, treat her well, but remain her master; don't trust secrets to her. (8) Keep your anger and delay revenge at least over night. (9) Do not contend with your master. (10) Don't leave the church until mass is all said. The remainder of the story is quite conventional; a series of experiences involving these counsels is found.

Many other examples belonging to this type might be cited. There is a Cornish *märchen*, in which Hans leaves his wife and serves three years; at the end of the time he receives three advices and a cake: (1) Don't leave the old way for the new; (2) Don't lodge where is an old husband with a young wife; (3) Do not strike in anger.[2] The use of these counsels is conventional. In a West Cornwall tale the same advices are given, together with the counsel: " Never swear to any body or thing seen through a glass." [3] The story is also applied to men who come from other countries to England. In one version, a Highlander spends

[1] Ed. F. W. E. Seiler, Halle, 1882.

[2] Cited by Seiler in his *Ruodlieb*, p. 52.

[3] Bottvell, *Traditions and Hearthside Stories of West Cornwall*, 2nd Series, p. 77 ff.

three years thus and is paid in advices of the conventional type.[1] An Irishman has a similar experience, in another tale, but carries away two cakes instead of one.[2] Sometimes the three years of service become forty, as in a Sicilian tale,[3] but the usual three counsels follow. There are Spanish, Italian, and German versions of tales belonging to this type.[4]

Type IV. Three counsels are obtained from a king (a) by purchase; (b) by living for a time under his instruction. In some cases a monk or a friend takes the place of the king.

This type is not so clearly defined as the one just treated. It is the opposite of Type II, where the king is the purchaser. In the stories belonging to this type the king is famed for his wisdom. The story may even be ascribed to Solomon, as in a Jewish version cited by M. Lévi.[5] Three brothers study with Solomon for three years; then they resolve to go home. The king asks them whether they prefer three hundred pieces of gold or three counsels, and they choose the gold. On the way home, however, they are induced by the youngest brother to return to the king and ask for the counsels instead of the money. This done, they set out once more. The youngest brother, who keeps the maxims in mind, prospers exceedingly; the others disregard them and are killed.

---

[1] Seiler's *Ruodlieb*, p. 52. The story is in Cuthbert Bede's *The White Wife*, London, 1868, p. 141.

[2] Also cited by Seiler, who points out Spanish and Italian parallels.

[3] Gonzenbach, *Sicilianische Märchen*, II, 133.

[4] Cf. Mistral, *Lis Isclo d' Or* (Avignon, 1876); Gradi, *La Vigilia di Pasqua di Ceppo*; Trueba, *Cuentos Populares*; *La Enciclopedia* (May, 1879); Jecklin, *Volkstümliches aus Graubünden* (I, 116–118); Zingerle, *Lusernisches Wörterbuch* (p. 69); Hahn, *Contes Populaires Grecs* (p. 222); Lutolf, *Sagen, bräuche und legenden aus Luzern* (p. 85).

[5] In *Mélusine*, III, 514 ff. Cf. also *Revue des Etudes Juives*, t. XI, pp. 50–74.

More interesting than this is the story told in the Irish Odyssey, *Merugud Uilix Maicc Leirtis.*[1] In their wanderings, the heroes landed at a place where they were told that the Judge of Right (Solomon) was lord, and that every man who got instruction from him would reach his native land at once. It was necessary to pay thirty ounces of gold each day for the instruction. To this they agreed, and at the end of the first day were advised, "Do not kill your enemy until you have had three counsels with yourself about it." At the end of the second day, the precept was, "Do not follow a by-path but follow the main road." The third, "Let none leave his place or dwelling, however impatient he may be, till the sun has reached the place where he is now." They were then dismissed with the king's blessing, and were given a box which they were forbidden to open until they got home; this box, of course, contained the ninety ounces of gold they had paid the king.

A Norse variant of this tale has been found.[2] Haco takes service with the king of Denmark, who instructs him in the arts of the silversmith, of the goldsmith, and finally in architecture. At the end of each year he asks of the king some piece of advice. At the expiration of the three years he had learned, besides the arts he studied, (1) never to trust a little man or a man with red hair; (2) never to leave church, no matter how great the haste, until mass has ended; (3) if angry to say the Lord's prayer three times before attacking one's enemy. The remainder of the story has the conventional adventures, with the great service of the counsels duly emphasized.

A variant of the type is seen in two stories in which some one else is substituted for the king. In one, an

---

[1] Ed. K. Meyer, from an early 14th century MS.
[2] Clouston, W. A., in *Folk Lore*, III, 556 ff.

oriental tale, a poor widow's son marries a princess; they live in great poverty because the girl is exiled with her husband. She advises her husband to visit a wise monk and get his counsel. This is done and the youth is given three maxims which afterwards saved his life: (1) She whom one loves the best is the most beautiful; (2) patience leads to safety; (3) there is good in every patient waiting.[1] Another variant is more complicated, and is also oriental.[2] A youth is about to travel and is given three counsels by a friend. The first one, "Give not thy heart to the love of the world and riches," is illustrated by a story somewhat like that told about Joseph and Potiphar's wife; it is very complex and narrates many adventures. The second advice, "Do not trust implicitly in persons whose character is neither known nor tested," is also followed by a long tale made up of many short ones and covering about twenty-five pages. The third advice, "Be provident and do not despise the counsel of friends," is followed by another set of stories. Altogether, these three advices, with the stories for which they serve as frame, occupy about eighty-five pages. Thus the romance is an admirable example of the use to which this stock type was put after it had been fully developed.[3]

---

[1] Seklemain, *The Golden Maiden*, pp. 141 ff.

[2] Clouston, *Eastern Romances*, pp. 11 ff.

[3] In Hazlitt's *Early Popular Poetry*, I, 200 ff., is an interesting account of how a merchant, being away from home on a trading expedition, bought many rich gifts for a courtesan of whom he was enamoured, and at last, thinking of his rather plain and sober-minded wife, purchased as a present for her a "peny worth of witt." An old man sold him this counsel, which was to the effect that if he would return from a journey dressed vilely and apparently ruined, he would learn that which would profit him. He followed this advice. The courtesan spurned him, now that his money was gone, but the faithful wife was true and said that she would go out and work for him. Naturally, he reformed his method of living.

Type V. Counsels are used in place of money in paying for small services.

This type differs from III in that the element of choice is not introduced; the money is not concealed in a cake or a loaf; the person who gives the advices is too poor to make payment in any other way. The type is interesting because it proves that at one time advice had a market value and could be bought and sold like tea or sugar. Very few shoe-makers would nowadays accept three pieces of advice in payment for some repairing work; yet there is an oriental story based on this very odd business transaction.[1] A young cobbler mends the shoes of a darivesh and gets in payment three counsels: (1) Set not out on a journey until you have found your fellow traveler; (2) light not in a waterless place; (3) enter great cities when the sun is rising. The cobbler follows these advices, and they save his life. The facts are that in those days, if one offered counsels instead of money it was not safe to refuse, for nobody knew when some dire peril would come upon a man who had just had such an opportunity to get wisdom. Neither history nor litera-ture records the sad fate of those who dared refuse proffered advice. In some cases it was accepted unwillingly, as we have seen. In all recorded cases, however, it was accepted, though sometimes it was straightway forgotten and then swift destruction overtook the careless one.

Evidence of the money value of advice is given by a story of a Brahman whose wife, having been deserted by him, tells him she is in need.[2] He gives her a paper con-taining four bits of advice. These she does not need for personal use, so she sells them for a lach of rupees. This

---

[1] Gibbs, J. W. (tr.), *Hist. of the Forty Vazirs*, No. 18.
[2] Knowles, *Folk-Tales of Kashmir*, p. 33. A similar tale is in *North Indian Notes and Queries*, III, 327.

is the introduction to a very long tale of how the purchaser of the counsels several times saved his life by following them. The substance of the counsels was : (1) Let one beware of sleeping in a strange place ; (2) a man may test his friends if he is in need, but if he is not in need let not his friends try him ; (3) a married sister will receive a man well or ill according as he comes in state or in poverty ; (4) a man must not depend on others to do his work.

This lengthy classification of the types under which the tales belonging to this cycle may be placed, will be closed by a reference to a humorous form of type V, which tells how an impecunious trickster tried to deceive a porter.[1] The cheat bought a box of glasses and sought a porter to carry it. He offered the servant his choice between the usual fee and three counsels. This was a safe proposition, since, according to the etiquette of such occasions, the porter could do nothing else than to accept the bits of advice. When one-third of the way had been traversed, the porter said that the box was heavy, so he begged for one of the words to inspirit him. The rogue replied, " If any one tells you that slavery is better than freedom, don't believe him." The porter realized that his employer was making game of him but said nothing. When two-thirds the distance had been passed, he asked once more for his word of wisdom, whereupon he was given the advice, " If any one tells you that poverty is better than riches, don't believe him." At the end of the journey he secured the third advice before he set the box down. It was, " If any one tells you that hunger is better than fulness, don't believe him." Where-upon the porter let the box fall, so that all the glass was broken, saying, " If any one tells you that there is one glass in this box not broken, don't believe him."

---

[1] Steere, *Swahili Tales*, pp. 413–414.

The story last mentioned has a significance deeper than the mere humorous treatment of a common type. It is a prose parody of the story-type; it bears evidence to the extreme frequency with which this form of structure was used. It is important to note that we have in this story-cycle a type of construction as marked and as popular as the type represented by the *Seven Wise Masters* or by the *Decamerone*. Just as the individual stories told in the *Seven Wise Masters* vary in the different versions, while all preserve the same frame, so with the individual stories used in different versions of this cycle.

We have therefore a very large and important class of fictions, apparently oriental in origin but permeating every nation of Europe. In structure, the tale belonging to the cycle consists of an introduction telling how some student or some poor man or youth obtained three counsels. To get these, he had to give up the wages which he had served years to earn; three years in most cases, twenty-one in others, forty in at least one. This stock device serves as an introduction to a series of adventures which befall the hero, generally on his return from the place where he has been bound to service. By the means of these counsels, he is saved from disgrace or death.

One more observation remains before we pass to the next topic : the source of these tales is undoubtedly popular. We are in an atmosphere quite different from that of courtly romance. These are stories born of the people. There are cautions against hasty temper, cautions against the dangers of travel, cynical remarks about women, emphasis on the homely virtues. Before drawing any comparisons between the cycle and the Baldwin episode in the *Avowing* it is necessary to develop this last point a little more fully.

Virtues Illustrated by these Tales.

A little observation will show that the counsels which occur most frequently in the tales examined fall under one or another of five heads. In the first class, counsels which illustrate the virtue of caution, the following examples have been cited in the pages immediately preceding: (1) Before you do anything, consider well the consequences (Etienne de Bourbon; *Gesta Romanorum*; Bidpai's *Fables*; *The White Wife*; Arabian, Spanish, and Italian *märchen*). (2) If you spend a night in a strange place, don't sleep, lest you be slain (Folk Tales of Kashmir). (3) Don't spend the night in a house where there is a beautiful young wife with an old husband (*The White Wife; Ruodlieb; Baker of Beanly; Gesta; Celtic Folk Lore;* Cornish *märchen*). (4) Keep the proper road, don't leave the highway for the byway (*Beanly*; Greek *märchen; Gesta;* Irish *Odyssey;* Italian and Cornish *märchen; Celtic Folk Lore*). (5) Don't set out until you have a fellow traveler; light not in a waterless place; enter a great city while the sun is rising (*The Forty Vazirs*). (6) Don't trust apparent submission of enemy (Bidpai). (7) Don't trust a red beard (Story of Haco; *Ruodlieb*). (8) Don't trust persons whose character is not known (*East. Romances*). (9) Lend nothing unless compelled (*Georgian Tales*).

In the second class, in which the virtue of controlling the temper is illustrated, we have such counsels as the following: (1) Think thrice before lifting the hand to strike (*Beanly*). (2) Don't kill thy enemy until thou has held three counsels with thyself about it (Irish *Od.*). (3) Be mild, and of an affable temper (Bidpai). (4) Keep thy anger and delay revenge over night (*Ruodlieb*; Cornish, Sicilian, Greek *märchen*).

Illustrations of the third class, in which cynical views

about women are expressed, are as follows : (1) Trust nothing to a woman (Jewish *Counsels of Solomon*). (2) If a man has a married sister and visits her in pomp, she will receive him for the sake of what she can gain, but if he comes in poverty she will disown him (*Folk Tales of Kash.*). (3) Tell not thy secret to a woman (*Georgian Tales*). (4) Place no reliance on a woman's love, for it changes on every frivolous fancy (Bidpai). (5) A wise man places no confidence in women on matters secret and terrible (Bidpai).

As to patience, (1) Don't be disturbed at the accidents of the world (Bidpai). (2) Don't weep over that which is lost (*Nightingale*, etc.). (3) Patience leads to safety (*Golden Maiden*). (4) There is good in every patient waiting (*Ibid.*).

Some other virtues, chiefly those pertaining to the simple philosophy of humble lives, are illustrated : Don't contend with thy master (*Ruod.*) ; honesty is the best policy (Celtic F.) ; she whom one loves best is most beautiful (*Golden Maiden*) ; don't leave the church until mass is said (F. L. III : 556 ; *Haco; Ruod.*) ; don't withhold from thy friend anything that increases his happiness (Bid.) ; when you have acquired what you have sought, preserve it (Bid. ; *Nightingale*, etc.) ; never decline good counsel and prudence (Bid.) ; seek not what is below your dignity (Bid., etc.).

RELATION OF THIS CYCLE TO THE BALDWIN EPISODE.

We are now ready to inquire as to the relation between this cycle of stories based on three counsels and the Baldwin episode.

1. Attention has already been called to the fact that the part of the romance dealing with Baldwin's vows is very different from what precedes. There are three vows, not one, as in the case of the others ; and this, too, in the face of the fact that only one vow was expected of a knight on the

occasion of such ceremonies. Again, Baldwin's vows necessitate no action on his part.

2. The vows once made, they become practically *geasa* for him. Although he apparently does not make them with any idea that his words will necessitate any particular action on his part, and though he evidently does not know that he is being tested until the king explains the joke, yet he would have suffered disgrace if he had failed to observe them. He was, therefore, compelled to live up to these vows or pay a severe penalty. It is noteworthy, also, that two of his vows are practically identical with two of the four *geasa* which every candidate for Fianship had laid upon him : the vow not to fear death, and the vow pledging hospitality.

3. But all this is the ideal of the story-cycle of the three counsels. There is a marked resemblance between the Celtic *geasa* and the counsels which the poor man received in lieu of a wage, or which the king bought from some merchant. In the case of the counsels, each becomes a maxim governing the life of the recipient. If he keep them, he will prosper ; if he fail to keep them, disaster will come upon him ; thus they are practically *geasa*.

4. Again, in the story-cycle of the three counsels there is a certain philosophy of life. The counsels, with the stories depending on them, illustrate some of the prevailing ideals of manhood. The fact that in so many cases *caution* was dwelt on as a cardinal virtue speaks of a time when traveling was exceedingly dangerous, and when man could rarely trust his neighbor. The restrictions of a system of caste and the inharmonious relations between masters and servants find a reflection in the oft-repeated emphasis on patience. The same might be said of the virtues of self-control and foresight and those homely virtues so often insisted upon. The view of woman, also, is indicated in some of these tales as clearly as in the fabliaux.

5. The same tendency to illustrate with stories the virtues considered important to any age is shown in mediæval literature generally. The great collections of *exempla* illustrate it. In secular literature, too, an elaborate code was drawn up for the government of lovers. Stories emphasizing such a virtue as patience were eagerly sought by a people whose life at its best was too hard. As to the ideal man, Pertelote says,

> "We alle desyren, if it mighte be,
> To han housbondes hardy, wyse, and free." [1]

And it is noticeable that in this list of the virtues considered of paramount importance in the ideal husband, two are the subjects of Baldwin's vows. For the knight was assuredly "hardy," as is shown by his conduct when attacked by Kay and his fellow-conspirators; while that he was "free" is sufficiently attested by the lavish hospitality which he dispensed at his castle. Possibly his views on women were proofs of his wisdom.

6. In the Baldwin episode we find this characteristic method of emphasizing cardinal virtues which was the underlying motive of the cycle of the three counsels, as well as of such mediæval tales as the story of Griselda and her patience. There is a philosophy of life: the ideal knight must be a man above petty jealousies, above the fear of death, above niggardliness. The vows of Baldwin are in reality maxims of life merely cast into the form required by the general character of the piece. One might easily construct a story of the conventional type, thus: A king is approached by a poor merchant, who tells him that he wishes to sell three counsels of great value. After consulting with the ministers, the king decides to pay the price demanded, whereupon he receives the following three advices: "(1) Never, under any

---

[1] *Nonne Prestes Tale*, ll. 93–94.

6

circumstances, be jealous of your wife. (2) Do not fear death, even though attacked by many foes. (3) Do not refuse your bounty to any who apply, no matter how unworthy." The remainder of the tale, according to the conventional type, would be taken up with accounts of adventures in which the king was saved from death or disgrace by following the advice contained in the three wise counsels. The author adopted this plan as a frame work. He used illustrative incidents to suit himself. As already noted, different versions of the *Seven Wise Masters* cycle show that among the various nations many different stories have been fitted into this frame. Similarly, in the *Avowing*, three virtues are emphasized, and this introduction prepares the way for the author to tell some favorite stories. He uses the form of vows rather than that of counsels, merely in order to connect this episode with what has preceded.

7. That this episode is tacked on, and bears no organic relation to the preceding incidents in which Arthur and the other knights perform their vows, is abundantly proved (*a*) by the entirely different nature of the vows; (*b*) by the fact that these vows not only differ from the vows of Arthur and the other knights but also differ from the vows made in other romances on such occasions; (*c*) from the fact that it was not at that time good etiquette to make more than one vow, thus there is a deviation from the normal type of avowing: (*d*) from the fact that this episode is strongly unified.

In the Baldwin episode, therefore, we have the virtual creation of a character. This Baldwin is not the Bawdewyn or the Beduer of the romances; neither is he the Baldwin of the other Northern tales. In the presentation of his story, recourse is had to a very famous device, that of the three counsels. This device is entirely new in the English romances; it springs from the popular literature and not from the court literature of the day. Thus the episode possesses rare interest for those who wish to study the beginnings of characterization and the reachings toward originality manifested by the connection of conventional types not elsewhere found in conjunction. It will now be our duty to examine in greater detail the three tests to which Baldwin was subjected.[1]

THE TESTING OF BALDWIN.

Looked at a little more closely, it will be observed that the Baldwin episode possesses a unity quite unknown in the story cycle of the three maxims. In the popular tales cited above, there was no necessary connection between the virtues which were represented ; there was certainly no connection between the adventures which tested the steadfastness of him who possessed the three counsels. When we turn to the story of Baldwin, however, the conditions are quite different. For one thing, there is evident arrangement towards climax : the second test is more severe than the first, while the last is even more difficult than the second. Moreover, the unconcerned manner which Baldwin displays when confronted with seemingly absolute proofs of his wife's infidelity is so startling that it shocks us. To a modern reader it is inconceivable that any man should act, under such circumstances, as Baldwin is said to have acted.

---

[1] Of course the making of vows which represent one's ideals of righteous living have been known from Hebrew times down to last New Year's Day. An interesting example is found in Schiefner's *Tibetan Tales* (tr. by W. R. S. Ralston, Boston, 1882, p. 306). A king learns of the prosperity attending those who take the five vows and adopts the same plan. The vows are not to take the life of any living creature ; not to steal the property of others ; not to enter into unlawful unions ; not to lie ; not to drink intoxicating liquors. These five vows the king takes, and his wives, and the princes, ministers, warriors, townspeople, and country folk ; all live in conformity with them. We are also informed that the tributary kings, with their people, did the same.

To review the story briefly at this point, it will be remembered that after Arthur has killed the boar and Kay has been rescued from the inevitable disaster which in the later romances always attends his exploits, the joke-loving king turns his attention to the testing of Baldwin. The vow never to fear death is put to the test by a surprise planned by Kay: Baldwin has no difficulty in putting to flight the six knights who set upon him. Next, Arthur sends his minstrel, under disguise, to Baldwin's castle, where he is to remain forty days and to report if in that time any man go meatless away. The minstrel finds that there is no porter to warn men away; all is merry and free. When, later, the king expresses surprise, the knight philosopher responds succinctly that God has a good plough. Thus, all unconsciously, Baldwin has met the second test. Next, the king commands the knight to go hunting. Precautions are taken to keep him away all night. Arthur then goes to the room of Baldwin's wife, taking with him a young knight. The king orders the youth to get into the bed, but not, on pain of his life, to touch the lady. The king remains in the room all night, the lady's attendants also being present, and when Baldwin returns, at dawn, he is summoned to the chamber, where Arthur explains that he thought best to keep the lady and her supposed lover in this compromising position until the husband should return. The knight makes no comment. Arthur asks, "Art thou wroth?" "By no means," responds Baldwin; "if any man came to her thus, it was at her own will." The king expresses utter amazement, whereupon Baldwin explains by telling a story of five hundred soldiers and three women, the upshot of which is that whether a woman be virtuous or not will be as she pleases. The joke is revealed, and Baldwin then explains why he does not fear death and why he never begrudges meat to any, relating an experience which fits each case.

It is clear that the most interesting problem at this point is as to the significance of the vow against jealousy. The other situations we can readily understand, but not even the fact that the romance may reflect some of those cynical views about women which are to be found in the literature of an age when women and priests were the favorite butts for ridicule in minstrel songs and fabliaux will sufficiently explain the astonishing behavior of Baldwin. The story cycle of Griselda may assist us toward a solution.

It will be remembered that Griselda is expressly required by her husband to pledge herself never to disobey him in any respect. She thereupon takes what is practically a vow:

> "And heer I swere that never willingly
> In werk ne thoght I wil yow disobeye,
> For to be deed, though me were looth to deye." [1]

The remainder of the story relates how she is put to three tests. At first her infant daughter is taken from her; she makes no complaint, and is as meekly obedient when, a little later, her husband causes to be carried away her little son. This first test of her faithfulness to her vow having been successfully endured, the husband resolves on a more severe trial. She is told that a younger and fairer woman will be brought to the castle as the new wife, and that she must return to her former conditions of poverty. This trial of her ability to endure the ignominy of being thrust out of her place as wife is withstood as bravely as the former test. The supreme trial comes last: she is commanded to return to her husband's castle, this time in the guise of a servant, and to perform the most menial tasks for her successor, on no higher footing than the crowds of slaves who had once been at her call. Having passed this ordeal

---

[1] *The Clerkes Tale*, ll. 362–364.

with the same faithfulness to her vow which had characterized her entire life, her husband declares it is enough, reveals
his purpose and the tricks which have been performed, and
joy reigns supreme.

Now in this story the virtue of patience is emphasized to
an extent which to modern readers seems not only revolting
but immoral.[1] That even Chaucer felt this exaggeration is
shown by one of those famous exclamations which endear
him to the modern reader :

> " Grisilde is deed, and eek hir pacience." [2]

We have precisely the same feeling when we read of Baldwin's behavior when put to the test of his vow against jealousy,—his action is not to be understood when judged by
any modern standards. We should expect him to tear the
unlucky knight limbmeal, in precisely the manner which
more human if more violent men are repeatedly represented
to have used in the other stories which, we shall see presently, belong to the cycle of which this is a part. Let us
note, now, the correspondence between the tests to which
Baldwin was subjected and such stories as that of Griselda,
stories in which some cardinal virtue is exalted even to the
extent of immorality.

1. It is evident that the supreme characteristic of Baldwin is his self-control. This is the cardinal virtue which
includes freedom from fear, freedom from resentment even
when grossly imposed upon, freedom from jealousy. It is

---

[1] For this suggestion that the story of Griselda is an illustration of a
tendency to carry the praise of a virtue to immoral excess, and that this
was a common feature of mediæval literature, I am indebted to a paper
read by Professor Kittredge before the Modern Language Conference of
Harvard University, in October, 1903. Professor Kittredge did not, however, make any reference to the Baldwin story or to the fact that the story
of Griselda may be considered as the story of a vow and its fulfillment.

[2] *The Clerkes Tale*, 1. 1177.

manifested in the nonchalant manner in which he brings about the discomfiture of Kay and his fellows; it is manifested in his laconic inquiry as to whether they wanted any more; it is also manifested in his failure to say anything to Arthur about his adventure. Even more pronounced is it in the test of his hospitality, where he is imposed upon most shamelessly. He does not fail in any respect; this virtue he possesses beyond others; the king is utterly astonished by what he sees. The tendency to carry the virtue to an immoral excess, so patent in the case of Griselda and her patience, is certainly marked in the test of his power to resist jealousy. When he is confronted with seemingly absolute proofs of his wife's infidelity, only to make no word of complaint, to show no sign of anger,—here we have the virtue of self-control carried to Griselda-like lengths. Thus it may be said that the purpose of the author was to exalt supreme self-control as the cardinal virtue; to do this he treats the three virtues most certainly proofs of self-control; as a means of so doing, he chooses the frame made universally popular through the story-cycle of the three counsels.[1]

This hypothesis explains the order in which the tests are described in the *Avowing;* it explains the astounding coolness with which Baldwin receives the news of his wife's apparent infidelity. As to the manner in which the tests were carried out, only the third need detain us long. The test of courage refers to the fundamental virtue of good knighthood: the chief merit of the incident in the *Avowing* consists less in the evidence which it gives of Baldwin's valor than in the

---

[1] It may not be out of place to note that in less important respects, also, there is a suggestion of the Griselda story in this part of the *Avowing.* In each case, the remainder of the story relates how the steadfastness of the one who has taken the vow is tested; the tests are arranged in climactic order, the last being exaggerated to an immoral degree; there are three tests in each case; the *dénouement* is happy.

raciness with which the account is presented. As to the hospitality test, the elements will be observed to be as follows: (1) The usual limit of three days for the entertainment of a stranger is not observed; (2) in the entire forty days no one who applied, whether prince or beggar, was refused, and no distinction in the class of entertainment was made; (3) in all this time, no matter how severely he was imposed upon, Baldwin showed his self-control by manifesting no resentment.[1] Of particular interest in the fact that Baldwin keeps no porter.[2]

THE VOW AGAINST JEALOUSY.

Thus Baldwin, all unconsciously, satisfied the requirements which his first two vows placed upon him. If he had failed in any respect, he would have suffered a certain disgrace. Only one thing remained; to test his third vow, Arthur prepared an elaborately diabolical plot, the outline of which has already been given.[3] Incidents similar to this

---

[1] On the importance of hospitality as a chief virtue in the mediæval period, cf. Wright, *Hist. of Domestic Manners and Sentiments in England*, pp. 328, 329; Craigie, *Scandinavian Folklore*, p. 15; Guest, *Mabinogion*, p. 59; *Silva Gadelica*, II, 154, 239; and many others.

On the disgrace involved if one's hospitality was rejected, much interesting material may be found in Kittredge, *Arthur and Gorlagon* (*Harv. Stud. and Notes*), VIII, 210 ff.

On the function and privileges of the minstrels, one may consult Chambers, *Mediæval Stage*, I, *index;* Wright, *op. cit.*, 178 ff. and 333.

[2] For illustrations of the importance of the porter in the middle ages, see Skene, *Four Anc. Bks.*, I, 261; Guest, *Mabin.*, pp. 20, 220, 243, etc. There are frequent references to the "proud porter" in the ballads, *e. g.*, *King Estmere* (Percy, *Rel.*, ed. 1840, p. 18; Child, II, 54).

[3] The Arthur of this incident, it will be noted, is quite a different person from the Arthur of Malory. In the early part of the poem we have simply the brave king of the primitive romances. Here the treatment is more original. The king is jovial, ready to play a practical joke upon a friend, and, as Robson observes, has a shade of cunning. This view of Arthur's

story of Arthur, the knight, and the lady are not uncommon in the romances. Frequently a knight was tested as to his chastity by subjecting him to the seductions of a beautiful woman, as in *Gawain and the Green Knight*, *Ider*, etc. Sometimes the woman played only a passive part, the knight being compelled by her husband to pass the night with her, or to get into her bed while the husband stands by. A case in point is the *Carle of Carelyle*, in which Gawain is compelled to share the bed of the carl's wife.[1] But such stories as these, while involving incidents very similar to the one in the *Avowing*, belong to an entirely different type. Here we have not a test of a knight's faithfulness to his vow of chastity, but a plot designed to make the husband believe his wife unchaste, the lady, nevertheless, being innocent.

THE CYCLE OF "THE WOMAN FALSELY ACCUSED."[2]

Our investigation of the large number of tales belonging to this cycle will be facilitated if we distinguish two impor-

---

character is occasionally met elsewhere, though not in the courtly romances. In the *Mule sans Frein, e. g.*, when Kay returns in disgrace from the quest so boldly claimed by him, Arthur goes out to meet him and, with a fine show of ceremony, seeks to lead the seneschal to claim the rewarding kiss. Others fall in with the jest, and salute Kay with great reverence; the poor blusterer is speechless for a time, then hurries from the hall in shame.

[1] The test lasts only a few minutes, and the carl is present. Professor Kittredge thinks that in the original version the test was for the entire night and that the husband was not present.

[2] No complete study of this cycle has yet been published. Professor Child discusses *Sir Aldingar* and its variants, but attempts no history of the plot and does not speak of the wager-group or the oriental versions. The late Gaston Paris (*Romania*, t. 32. pp. 481 ff.) discussed the wager-group, but said nothing of such very representative romances as the *Erl of Tolous*, *Sir Aldingar*, *Octavian*, etc., which are indubitably connected with the cycle we have now under consideration. My indebtedness to the last-named article will be apparent, and is always noted by the citation "Paris," with the page.

tant groups, which agree in that the motive really actuating
the accusation is chagrin because of the rejected advances of
a gallant.   In the first group, however, the accuser pretends
to have enjoyed the favors of the lady, presenting as proofs
an intimate knowledge of her room and of her person, as well
as a jewel or other treasure.   In the second, the accuser
makes no such boasts, but alleges that the lady has been
guilty of sin with another man.   In general, the course of
the plot is as follows :

A. A woman, either a wife or a maiden sought in marriage by a king or a noble, is as famed for her virtue as for
her beauty.   His knowledge of her may come from the
boasts made by her brother ; [1] or by her husband. [2]   Such an
introduction naturally leads to the proposal of the wager and
is thus peculiarly characteristic of that group.

B. An attempt is made, without success, on the honor of
the heroine.   This characteristic belongs to all the tales.   At
times little is made of it because in the wager group a slight
difference in emphasis may serve to obscure it in order to
gain interest for the stratagem by which the proofs are to be
obtained.   In most of the tales belonging to the group examined by M. Paris, in his article " Le Cycle de la Gageure,"
the attempt is inspired not merely by passion but by the
gambling instinct.   If one turn from this group to such
romances as the *Erl of Tolous, Aldingar, Oliva, Gaudine*, etc.,
the emphasis upon the accuser's passion for the lady is more
noticeable.   In every case the attempt is made and is, of

---

[1] *Guillaume de Nevers ; Guillaume de Dole ; Nouvelle de Sens, Eufemia*, etc.
(Paris, pp. 487-491.) In the *Erl of Tolous*, the hero asks his captive to
describe the wife of the emperor to whom the captive is subject ; smitten-
with love for her, the earl departs forthwith to seek her favor.

[2] *Cymbeline*, with the tales closely connected in plot, such as the French
miracle play ; *Roman de Violette ; Comte de Poitiers ;* fishwife's tale in *West-
ward for Smelts.*

course, indignantly repelled. The next thought of the rejected gallant is of revenge.

C. In the tales belonging to the wager type the idea of revenge is more or less obscured by the desire of the repulsed suitor to get more tangible evidence to use in proof of his accusation. This may be considered a deviation from the type, due to the influence of the wager *motif*. It is noticeable that of the many tales cited by M. Paris, the great majority are Italian and are of no very great age. On the other hand, the form in which the suitor's passion turns to bitter hate, a hate which he strives to satisfy by contriving that the lady shall be found by her husband in a compromising position, is frequent in oriental versions of undoubted age. It is probable that the wager *motif* was a later development of an old and very popular type which is best preserved in such romances as the *Erl of Tolous*, *Aldingar*, etc.

D. Of the three means by which evidence is secured against the woman, (1) information gained from a maid or a friend; (2) concealment of accuser in the lady's chamber; (3) placing another man in her bed; the last is more primitive and marks group II., while the first two especially characterize the wager type, and mark group I.

Since our present inquiry is mainly concerned with group II., marked by the strange bedfellow, the treatment of the first two methods may be somewhat summary.

1. M. Paris cites a number of tales in which the gallant does not even see the woman against whom he makes an accusation.[1] By bribing some one, he secures a minute description, noting some mark on her body, and also secures a jewel or other token.

2. In some cases the accuser contrives that he be concealed in the chamber, where he makes careful note of the

[1] Pp. 487–498.

room and of the lady's person, and carries away with him a jewel or a crucifix. This is the situation in *Cymbeline*, and in a large number of other cases.[1]

It will be observed that this device of concealment in the chamber is similar to the third method in that it involves the actual presence of a supposed lover in the woman's room. In *Cymbeline*, Iachimo induces Imogen to assume charge of a chest presumably containing costly plate. The same situation obtains in the *Decamerone*. M. Paris notes an anonymous Italian novel contained in a fourteenth century manuscript,[2] and also a German version of the same story first printed in 1489 at Nuremberg.[3] In two of these versions (*Decamerone* and the German tale) the accuser remains three nights in the chest before he observes anything useful as evidence; in both these versions, also, the lady does not sleep alone, but with a servant or a little girl. Another German tale, *Der Pfiffigste*, contains a similar incident; the chest is taken into the room by a servant on the plea that it contains *économies*;[4] the situation is the same in a tale "The Chest" printed by Campbell in his Tales of the West Highlands.[5] In all these cases it will be observed that (1) the man is actually present in the chamber; (2) he proves his knowledge of the room and of the lady's person; (3) this is counted sufficient proof by the husband.

---

[1] The important element is the description of a mark on the woman's person. There is a curious story in Schiefner's *Tibetan Tales* (tr. Ralston, p. 230 ff), in which, it should be noted, the woman actually loves and is not falsely accused. Súsroni, the beautiful wife of King Brahmadatta, is accused of improper behavior with a young lute player, Asuga by name. The king summons Asuga and says, "If it be said that thou hast looked in sinful fashion on my dear Súsroni say then what marks her body bears." With astonishing promptness, Asuga replies: "On her thigh is the svastika. Her breast is spiral; over her spread wreaths of Timira blossoms." In anger the king gives the woman to her lover and both are banished.

[2] P. 500.   [3] P. 501.   [4] Paris, p. 518.

[5] II, 1 ff; cited by Paris, p. 519.

3. We now come to the very large class of fictions in which a man is actually found in the woman's bed. This strange bedfellow is (a) a leper, cripple, or dwarf; (b) a "kitchen knave;" (c) a young knight. The order of development from (a) to (c) is probably chronological.

At first thought, it would seem that the choice of some repulsive person as the alleged object of the wife's affections would either defeat its own end or would indicate that the rejected suitor, in his hatred, desired to fix on the woman not only the sin of adultery but the added disgrace of an unnatural affection for a loathsome leper or a hideously deformed dwarf. In the later tales, no doubt, the latter motive crept in; in the original versions, however, no surprise or repulsion was felt by those who listened. That women in oriental tales are frequently represented as loving such creatures a few examples will prove.

The most interesting of these is the famous story of Kanakaratha.[1] A prince named Kanakaratha lived in a city in Bharata. "In him 'abode these virtues: he was munificent, simple, the essence of courtesy, handsome, and able to assume what shape he pleased." He went to another land to find out if it was true, as a song said, that everywhere the enjoyer enjoys. To do away with any fortuitous advantages, he assumed a very hideous shape, that of a deformed man with both eyes streaming, with nose and lips gone. The king of the country, Támrachúda, was looking at the beauty of the city from his seven-storied palace, and was puffed up with importance. He said, "You courtiers, by whose favor do you enjoy such a fortune of rule?" They said, servilely, "King, all this springs from your favor." Then the princess, Madanamanjarí, laughed a little, after which she became silent. The king asked why, and she said, "My

---

[1] Tawney, *The Kathákoca*, pp. 184–191.

father, these servants of yours said what is not true ; for that reason I laughed." Again he asked why, and was told, "Every man fares according to his own actions." When the king heard this, he flew into a passion and said, "Come! come! bring some poor leper, afflicted with disease, and very wretched, as a fit bridegroom for my daughter, in order that she may be given to him, so that she may reap the fruit of her own actions." So they searched everywhere for such a man, and soon found the prince who had assumed the loathly form. The leper was dragged to the king, protesting all the way that it was not proper for a crow to marry a female swan. The irate father wedded the two, however, and dismissed them.[1] We are told that Madanamanjarí "bowed before the feet of her father and mother, and, with her lotus-like face full of joy, went out of the palace." When they were walking together, her husband fell in the main street and could not rise, whereupon the princess begged him not to be unhappy but to get upon her back and let her carry him. A straw hut was built for them by the king's servants, and in this they lived. The leper tested his wife in every way ; he described the loathsome disease that would come upon her, and advised her to seek the protection of her mother. She refused this, saying, "Women born in a good family do not do such things, even when the world is coming to an end. . . . To excellent women husbands are deities." Thus the husband was convinced of her worth ; and the Griselda-like story ends with accounts of palaces of pure gold forty stories high, with the leper transformed into a splendid monarch who receives the homage of his father-in-law.[2]

[1] The curious similarity between this situation and the story of Cordelia and Lear is suggested by Tawney, op. cit., p. 485, note.

[2] Other stories of the love of women for a leprous or deformed person are frequently met. One is cited by Dunlop (Hist. Fiction, II, 39 ; Les Trois Bossus) and tells of a wife and her humpbacked husband. It is true that

There are some indications that for a leper to occupy the bed of a married woman was thought in mediæval times to presage a miracle.[1] Sir Aldingar induces the lazar to get into the queen's bed on the promise that by his doing so a miracle would be wrought. The fact that this seems to have been considered by the leper a sufficient excuse for his action indicates that such a belief was well-known. This opinion is strengthened by an *exemplum* of Jacques de Vitry.[2] A noble lady whose husband loathed lepers and would not permit them in his house, received one in his absence and had him placed in her bed. The husband returned suddenly, but when he entered the chamber, he found only a sweet odor. The wife, who had feared the leper's death rather than her own at the hands of the angry husband, confessed the truth. The husband was converted and henceforth lived as exem-

she married him because he had money, but when three other humpbacks come to the castle they are royally entertained by the lady. In Schiefner's *Tibetan Tales* (tr. Ralston, p. 292) is the story of a woman who loves a cripple with neither hands nor feet, and who kills her husband (as she supposes), in order to enjoy her lover. She carries the cripple on her back, begging food from place to place. In the *Panchatantra* (IV, 5) is an account of a woman's love for a cripple who had a beautiful voice. Although her husband had recently given half his life to bring her back from the dead, she deprived him of even the small part of his existence remaining to him by pushing him into a well and setting out with her deformed lover. Other similar tales may be found in Jacobs' *Hindoo Tales*, p. 261, and in Ralston's tr. of *Tibetan Tales*, intro., p. 62. See also Kittredge, *Arthur and Gorlagon*, p. 188, and note.

[1] In the romance of *Nuller et Amys* (summarized in Dunlop, ed. Wilson, I, 317 ff.) is an incident relating how Amys, being smitten with leprosy was driven from his own castle by his wife, "who appears to have been ignorant of the value of a husband of this description." In a note to p. 320 it is said, "Contrary to modern medical opinion, lepers were in the Middle Ages popularly credited with great sexual vigor. Women who were willing to do so were permitted to marry lepers by the Gregorian Decretals."

[2] No. xcv. See notes (ed. Crane) p. 174 for bib. The *exemplum* occurs in several collections.

plary a religious life as his wife. The action of the wife in
causing the leper to be put in her bed is puzzling unless it
be interpreted as indicating, in the original form of the story
at least, a belief on her part that by so doing a miracle would
be wrought.

Two points seem made clear by the investigation of the
leper-type just concluded : (1) the introduction of this element proves the incident to be of great age and hints at an
oriental origin ; (2) in early forms of the story the placing of
a leper or deformed person in a lady's bed in the effort to
convict her of sin, did not necessarily indicate any marked
addition to the disgrace. This also helps to explain why in
so many later tales the loathly bedfellow was introduced.
In some versions, as in the *Erl of Tolous* and the *Avowing*,
a young knight is the instrument.

It remains only to note some important mediæval romances in which the strange bedfellow is found. In *Sir
Aldingar*, a leper is put in the queen's bed ; the same conditions obtain in numerous variants of the tale, as we shall
find later. In *Oliva*, a black beggar ; in numerous Charlemagne romances a leper, beggar, or other mis-shapen person ;
in *Octavian*, a kitchen knave with a loathly face ; in *Gaudine*,
a dwarf; in the *Erl of Tolous* and the *Avowing*, a young
knight.

E. Only a few words need be said on the bringing of the
accusation before the husband. In romances belonging to
group I. the accuser merely displays a knowledge of the
lady's person and of her room. In group II. the husband
is brought to the chamber and is allowed to look upon his
wife in the embraces of a deformed or diseased man, a
knave, or a young knight. It is to this group that the
Avowing belongs. At times the incident is very badly mud-
dled. In a group of Northern poems shortly to be examined,
no other proof is given than the assertion of a steward that

the wife has mis-behaved. Sometimes the steward swears that he has seen a man lying with the queen and has slain the traitor.[1] The husband at times does not wait for proof, as in the ballad of the "Emperour and the Childe,"[2] in which a Greek emperor marries a French princess and lives happily with her until a Bishop tries to seduce the wife. He is denied with scornful words, and the Bishop, whose passion has turned to anger, denounces her to the emperor. He says he can prove that she has been unfaithful, but the monarch does not wait for proofs; he banishes her at once. The original probably contained the usual account of the securing of proof.

F. This topic might more exactly be divided into two: the punishment of the woman, and the vindication. This will be done in the examination of the group of representative romances soon to engage our attention. For the present it is sufficient to map out the subject in broad outlines. The first type of vindication is characteristic of those tales belonging to group I. in which the accuser does not in reality see the woman. Several such tales have already been cited; the accuser rests his charge on the minute description of the lady which he has gained from a corrupted servant. Often the accused woman causes some property belonging to her to be placed in the rooms of the man who charges her with wrong-doing. She thereupon lodges against him a counter charge of robbery, appearing to him in the trial for the first time, he swears he never saw her before, thus forcing a confession of his false charge. Examples are the story of Guillaume de Nevers;[3] *Guillaume de Dole*;[4] *Nouvelle de Sens*;[5] *Eufemia*;[6] *Justa Victoria*;[7]

---

[1] *Sir Triamour.*   [2] Percy MSS., II, 393 ff.
[3] *Manuscrit de Tours*, 468, 33, cited by Paris, p. 487.
[4] Ed. Servois; cited by Paris, p. 487.
[5] Paris, p. 490.   [6] *Ibid.*, pp. 490–491.   [7] *Ibid.*, p. 492.

7

La Pianella ;[1] *Les deux enfants du prince de Monteleone* ;[2] with some additional Italian versions cited by M. Paris,[3] and the German version, already referred to, in Simrock's *Deutsche Märchen*. It will be noted that the usual situation in romances of this group is that the lady is unmarried and is thus not subject to punishment; she sets out for the court where dwells the man who has boasted of having seduced her, and puts him to confusion in the manner described.

In a second group, the lady is a wife and is either banished or sentenced to death by her husband. If the latter punishment is ordered, the servant charged with her execution permits her to go free, and tells his lord that he has exposed her body to the wild beasts of the forest. She often assumes male attire, and is finally in a position where she can force a confession from the man who wrongfully charged her with crime. This is the situation in *Cymbeline* and in the group of tales, already cited, which have plots closely similar to it.[4] The point worth noting here is the period of exile in which the woman is forced to wear a man's clothes. M. Paris cites a number of tales, in addition to the *Cymbeline* group, in which the conditions are similar.[5] The English romances of *Triamour*, *Octavian*, and the *Erl of Tolous* should also be noted.

The third group is sharply differentiated from the two just considered by two characteristics: (1) The tales belonging to it are practically all Northern,[6] while those of the first two groups are practically all French and Italian ; (2) the essential element is the trial by combat, rarely the ordeal. A typical example is the ballad of *Sir Aldingar*,[7] in which

---

[1] *Raccolta di novelle del P. Atanasio da Verrocchio*, Paris, p. 494.

[2] Gonzenbach, op. cit., I, 70 ; Paris, p. 495.

[3] Pp. 496–8.   [4] The exile and return formula.   [5] Pp. 515 ff.

[6] In *La Royalle Couronne des Roys d'Arles*, the accuser proclaims himself ready to support his charge by combat.

[7] Child, II, 33 ff. (No. 59).

the lady claims the right of trial by battle and is vindicated. Professor Child cites eleven Scandinavian versions, in all of which the trial by combat is found. In the romance of *Oliva*, the queen asks to be tried by ordeal, to be put naked into a copper vessel over a hot fire, or thrown from a high tower upon sword and spear points, or taken in a boat out of sight of land.[1] The *Erl of Tolous* makes use of the same method; this is a composite tale, however, introducing the southern elements of the strange bedfellow and the period of banishment.

Important Representatives of the Cycle.

We have now to consider a group of romances whose relation to the subject of our inquiry is very important. All of them show the general characteristics of the cycle; all are related in important respects; several are the chief representatives of groups in which a large number of closely related tales are found.

1. The *Erl of Tolous* (T.) runs as follows: The earl asks his prisoner, a knight in the service of an emperor, about the emperor's wife; her beauty is praised; the earl promises to free his prisoner if the knight will lead him to see her. The earl visits the lady and tries to win her love; he is repulsed, though with courtesy; she forgives him readily and they part as friends. There is a break in the story at this point, the earl dropping out for a time. Two knights appear on the scene; both fall in love with the lady; one makes an attempt upon her and is scornfully repulsed. The knight, terrified by her anger, protests that his purpose was merely to prove her virtue, whereupon he is at once forgiven. The attempt of the second is not more successful; as a

---

[1] Summarized by Child, II, 39.

result, they plot the lady's ruin. A young knight, carver to the lady, is induced to creep behind the curtain in her chamber. By "the game" he is first to cast off his clothing; he is not to move until called. Suspecting nothing, the lady enters and retires. After a little time the knights raise an alarm, and, with others, rush into the room. The innocent knight is promptly killed; the lady is seized and imprisoned. Next morning, the emperor returns; he is given seemingly absolute proofs of her guilt; she is banished. After many perils, the lady is reunited to her husband, through the instrumentality of the Earl of Tolouse, who vindicates her as her champion in a trial by combat.[1]

2. In *Sir Aldingar*[2] (Al.) we have a ballad which Professor Child considered very old, although it was written down about the middle of the seventeenth century. Sir Aldingar is the steward of King Henry; he falls in love with the queen and seeks her favors; she repulses him with bitter words. In order to get revenge, he places a lazar in her bed, promising the fellow that a miracle will be wrought. He then summons the king, who sentences both the queen and the lazar to death. But the queen sees the hand of Aldingar in all this (she has been warned by a dream), and claims the right of trial by battle. She is vindicated, and the story ends happily. This tale has many variants, especially in Scandinavian (eleven versions) and Scotch. None of these versions, however, has the strange bedfellow · incident; the steward, when repulsed, merely accuses the lady of having misbehaved with a bishop or with some other person. The trial by combat is preserved in all cases.

3. A miracle play, *Miracle de la Marquise de Gaudine*

---

[1] The striking parallel between this romance and *Cymbeline* is apparent, and has not, to my knowledge, been pointed out.

[2] Child, II, 33 ff.

has a story very similar to the type.[1] By reason of enmity
caused by rejected love, a dwarf is hidden by the suitor in
the lady's chamber. The knights rush in and kill him, as in
the *Erl of Tolous*, and then accuse the lady to her husband.

4. The story of *Oliva*[2] is even more striking in its correspondence to the type. Oliva is the sister of Charlemagne
and is Hugo's wife. The husband goes on a hunt, leaving the wife in charge of a steward named Milon. This
steward approaches the lady with the usual proposal; is
spurned; and goes home in chagrin. He soon reappears,
bearing a drink; telling the queen his object had merely
been to test her virtue, he proposes that she signify her forgiveness by drinking with him. To this the amiable lady
readily assents; the cup has been drugged; the lady is soon
unconscious. The steward now gives the same drink to a
black beggar, and puts both in the lady's bed with arms about
each other's necks. The king returns, and is conducted by
the steward to the chamber. In a rage, he kills the beggar
and would have dispatched the queen but for the fact that
every drop of blood which falls from the beggar turns into
a burning candle. The queen awakes; is confronted with
the charge; asks for the ordeal. She is fully vindicated,
and is reunited to her husband. This romance combines the
northern feature of the trial with the southern and oriental
strange bedfellow type.[3] Other versions of the tale are
found: a Spanish prose romance of Oliva and a *chanson de
geste* of *Doon l'Alemanz*.[4] In these versions a youth and
not a leper or beggar is put into the bed; the trial by ordeal
is the means of vindication. Another version attaches the

---

[1] Ed. G. Paris, in *Miracles de Notre Dame*, II, 121 ff.

[2] Summarized by Child, II, 39.

[3] Child (p. 39) says it is tr. from an English copy brought home by a
Norseman resident in Scotland in 1287.

[4] Child, p. 40.

tale to Sibilla, wife of Charlemagne, who was repudiated by her husband because an ugly dwarf was found in her bed. Professor Child cites many other versions in Spanish, Dutch, French, German, in almost all of which the ugly dwarf is introduced. It is noticeable how completely this element disappears in the northern versions : as an illustration, the tale of Sisibe is interesting ; the more so because the heroine is the daughter of a Spanish queen.[1] In this story, the plot is very similar to the type, with the exception that no dwarf or knight appears. When the king returns, the queen's accusers swear that she has been entertaining a handsome thrall ; this thrall evidently disappeared somewhere on the journey from a southern original to a northern home.

5. *Sir Triamour* (Tr.), an English romance, is of this type also ; the queen is left in the steward's care during the husband's absence on a crusade. When repulsed, the steward maintains that he has only been testing her. On the return of the king, he claims to have seen a man lying with the queen and to have slain the traitor. The queen is banished. It is evident that in some process of making over, *Sir Triamour* lost the important incident of the strange bedfellow ; all that remains is the mere assertion of the steward.

6. The romance of *Octavian*[2] (O.) differs from all others belonging to the type in that the actuating motive is not hatred caused by rejected love, but the envy of the mother-in-law. The empress Florence gives birth to twin sons ; the mother of the emperor insists that this is a proof of the wife's infidelity ; she soon prefers the charge of having seen the new wife with a lover, and offers to prove this to the husband's satisfaction. Upon being challenged to do so she goes to a boy with a loathly face, who is called also a

---

[1] *Ibid.*, p. 41.   [2] *Octavian Imperator*, Weber, III, 161 ff.

" cokes knave," and tells him that he must sleep with queen
Florence, by her son's order, and that he will be advanced.
The knave is expressly ordered not to touch the lady,
though this precaution was dictated solely by the danger
which would result to her plan if the lady should awake.
The king is summoned to the chamber; he is convinced
of the wife's guilt and cuts off the lad's head, throwing it
to her as a plaything: the lady is banished. After many
trials the conventional ending makes everyone happy except
the mother-in-law.

7. In the *Avowing* (A.) the incident is torn from the
usual setting and is used for humorous effect. Nevertheless
we have in it a close following of the customary program;
the only differences are in the motive of the charge and
in the *dénouement*. The situation, stripped of the humorous
element, is as follows: Arthur, in whose care Baldwin's wife
is left, for some reason plots her ruin. The husband is
on a hunting expedition; shortly before his expected return,
Arthur compels a youth to get into bed with the lady; he
keeps them in this compromising position all night. Early
the next morning, Baldwin returns; he is summoned to his
wife's chamber, and there is confronted by the sight of
another man in her bed. Here the usual order abruptly
changes, the joke is explained, and the husband and wife
are reunited.

8. As to *Cymbeline* (C.), an outline of the story will show
how nearly it corresponds to the usual type; Iachimo hears
the husband of Imogen boasting her beauty and virtue, and
places a wager that he will win her favors. He goes to the
lady's home, makes the customary proposal, and is scornfully
repulsed. He is terrified by the lady's threats to summon
help, and stammers that his whole aim was but to test her.
She forgives him with the usual surprising haste; meanwhile
he plots her ruin. Having won the lady's consent to take

into her room for safe keeping a chest which he alleges contains silver plate, he conceals himself in this chest, and is thus enabled to spend a night in her room. Here he observes the furnishings, takes some jewels, and notes a mole on the lady's breast. Armed with these proofs, he confronts the husband, who readily believes him, and sends orders that the lady be put to death. This punishment becomes practically one of banishment, because the servant charged with her execution permits her to escape. After many perils, she is re-united to her husband, her innocence having been proved.

With these eight important representatives of the cycle in mind, a comparative study of the plot may be made : (1) A lady famous for her beauty and virtue is highly praised in the hearing of a man who lives far from her and has never seen her (T. C.) ; or, in some versions, the lady's beauty inspires with passion the steward or some knight in whose care she is placed (A. G. Ol. Tr.) ; in one version the mother-in-law is the hostile agent (O.). (2) The husband is away, on a hunt (A. Ol.); on a crusade (Tr.) ; on a military expedition (T.); traveling (C.) (3) An effort is made by the suitor to win the lady's favor but is scornfully repulsed (T. Al. G. Ol. Tr. O. C.). (4) In his terror and confusion, the suitor maintains that his sole object was to test the lady's faithfulness to her husband (T. Ol. Tr. C.). (5) He immediately plots the ruin of the woman, either by himself spending the night in her room (C.); or by putting another man in her bed, a loathly leper or knave (T. Al. G. Ol. O.), or a young knight (A.; variations of Ol.). (6) The husband is convinced of his wife's guilt, either by the accuser's proofs that he has spent the night in her room (C.); or by seeing the woman in a compromising position (A. Al. Ol. O.) ; or by the fact that the supposed paramour, having been discovered by the people of the household, has been slain by them (T. G.). (7) The woman is sentenced to death or banishment (T. Al. G. Ol. Tr. O. C.); she suffers many perils and long exile, but is vindicated, either by trial by battle or ordeal (Al. G. T. Ol.), or by confession of the fraud by the accuser (A. C.).

HISTORY OF THE PLOT.

To attempt an elaborate history of the plot which has been considered in the pages immediately preceding would be a task entirely too ambitious for the present work. The immense mass of literature involved, and the large number of variations which different groups show within themselves would make the construction of such a history a very difficult as well as an extremely dangerous task. Even of the group of ballads to which *Sir Aldingar* belongs, the late Professor Child observed, "There is no footing firmer than air for him who would essay to trace the order of the development."[1] But without pressing our inquiry into the ramifications of the plot too far, it may perhaps be safe to call attention to five types which appear to be quite definitely marked and to suggest the possible relations between them. It should be understood that no attempt is made to ascertain the sources, say, of the *Erl of Tolous* or of *Sir Aldingar*. Each of these tales is representative of a large number of others, and may therefore be considered typical. Each contains elements certainly related to elements found in the other romances considered as types, while each also contains elements peculiar to the group, or type, to which it belongs. We may, therefore, classify the great mass of material belonging to the cycle, under such heads as the *Cymbeline* type, the *Erl of Tolous* type, the *Aldingar* type, etc., and may use them for constructing a tentative history of the plot.

[1] *Op. cit.*, II, 43.

A. *The Oriental Type.* The essential element seems to
be the charge that a woman is guilty of sin with a leper or
some other loathly person. Instances have already been
cited to show that lovers of this type were common in the
orient, and the evidence is that even high-born women did
not disdain persons so afflicted. There were two elements
in the construction of what may be called the oriental type

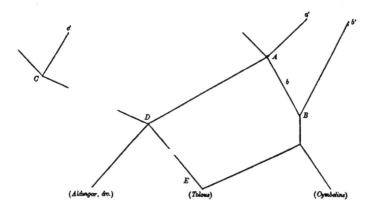

(*Aldingar, &c.*)   (*Tolous*)   (*Cymbeline*)

of the plot: (*a*) A large number of stories in which women
actually loved cripples, lepers, and other repulsive persons;
(*a'*) the existence of stories in which a trusted servant, having vainly attempted to seduce his master's wife, preferred
a false charge against her.[1]   Just when these elements were
united into one story is of course impossible to say.   It
seems safe to suppose that this form of the story is very
old, and that it antedates such types as *Cymbeline* represents.

B. *The Wager Type.* At some point in the development
between type A. and the sources of *Cymbeline*, certain
changes took place in the plot. The article by M. Paris,
already so frequently referred to, seems to show that the

---

[1] For an example of (2) without (1) cf. Bidpai's *Fables*, ed. Keith-
Falconer, p. 104 ff.   An example of (1) without (2) was cited just above.

wager cycle is essentially an Italian and French development. The important characteristics of the type are: (1)
the beauty and virtue of a woman is the subject of wide
report; (2) inspired by lust, or envy, or malice toward a
brother of the woman, a libertine wagers that he will seduce
her; (3) he attempts this and fails; (4) he plots her ruin,
usually by spending a night in her room and noting certain
points to be used as evidence; (5) he is finally put to confusion and the woman is vindicated. It will be seen that
the most important difference between this type and A. is
the introduction of the wager. But there is a group of
stories, to which M. Paris refers in the first division of his
analysis, in which (1) a wager is made; (2) the proposal is
received by the woman with feigned compliance; (3) the
suitor passes a night, as he supposes, with her, and takes as
proof a finger; (4) but it transpires that the woman has
substituted a servant for herself, so that in reality she is
guiltless. M. Paris recognized that this is a primitive form
of the story, but he did not observe that the plot against
the woman, so prominent a feature in the great majority of
the tales belonging to the cycle, is entirely lacking. No
motive for such a plot is given, because the woman feigns
submission, and the gallant supposes that his wager is
easily won.

The conclusion which it seems safe to make at this point
is that two types of tales are united to form the wager type.
Both are oriental in origin; stories involving a mutilation of
the woman by the paramour are not infrequent. In the first
class, which we may call b. and note as a development from
A., the beauty and virtue of a woman prompts an attempt
upon her honor; the proposal is scorned; a plot is laid to
convict her of sin with a porter, a leper, a cripple, etc. In
the second, b'., there is a wager that a certain woman can
be seduced; the attempt is made; the woman feigns com-

pliance but in reality substitutes a servant ; there is no plot
or stratagem. These two elements, united, form B. This
type, as already noted, became extremely popular in Italy
and in France. The numerous examples cited by M. Paris
prove how widely known such tales were, and their popularity continued until the final form was stamped upon the
story by Shakspere. At the same time, the contention that
these stories form not an independent cycle, as M. Paris
seemed to suggest, but a very important branch of the great
cycle of the woman falsely accused, seems justified by the
fact that the wager story as it appears in the *Decamerone,* in
Cymbeline, etc., is developed from two elements (1) the primitive wager story in which the woman feigns compliance and
no other stratagem to convict her of crime is necessary ; and
(2) the story of the hate aroused by a woman's refusal to
yield to a suitor, with the plot to convince her husband that
she entertains a guilty love for a paramour.

The changes made necessary by the fusing of these two
elements are easily explained, since they are due to the
modification of *b.* by the fusing of *b'.* with it. There still
remain, from *b.,* the repulse of the suitor ; his chagrin ; and
the stratagem by which a supposed paramour spends the
night in her chamber. But he cannot rest merely with
bringing to her husband apparent proofs of her infidelity ;
her guilt must be due to her yielding to him, or he must
lose his wager. The putting of a leper or a cripple in
her bed and summoning the husband, the most important
element in *b.,* is accordingly modified by the use of the
stratagem by which the rejected suitor himself passes the
night in her room and is able to prove this to the
husband's satisfaction.

C. *The Northern Type.* It is not to be supposed that all
false charges lodged against women of high position are of
oriental origin. There can be no doubt that such stories

spring from no single source, unless that source be the wickedness of some human hearts no matter what the age or nation. Such stories were no doubt common in the Northern countries from the earliest times. Another element, which seems to me to be more certainly Northern in origin, is the proving of innocence, in tales of this character, by the *judicium dei*. The trial by battle was, as is well known, especially popular among the Germanic nations. Thus two elements, which we may call *c.* and *c'.* united to form a type certainly Germanic and apparently Northern: the false charge (not necessarily of infidelity, but usually so) directed against a woman; and the proving of innocence by *judicium dei*. The result of this union gave a story in which a woman incurs the displeasure of some one high in the husband's favor; is charged by him with infidelity or with some serious crime; protests her innocence, and is subjected to the ordeal or to the trial by battle. Another element almost invariably enters: that of the diminutive champion and the magic sword.[1]

There is a group of Scandinavian ballads which Mr. Child has called cousin to the English *Sir Aldingar*. The subject is *Ravengaard og Memering*, and the story most commonly told is of the hatred conceived for Gunild, wife of king Henry, by Ravengaard, (or Ravnlil).[2] Being repulsed, he plots her ruin, charging her with infidelity with the archbishop. It will be noted that no proof is given or required. The lady protests her innocence, and a trial by battle is decided upon; but although she goes before the nobles with head and feet bare, none ventures to defend her cause save Memering, who is the smallest of men and has least enjoyed the favor of the king. By the aid of the magic sword Adel-

---

[1] Professor Child considered the magic sword a distinctly Northern element (*op. cit.*, II, 35).

[2] Summarized by Child from Gruntvig.

ring, the lady's champion overthrows the false steward, and, in most versions, claims the lady as a reward.[1] This represents the story as told in a Danish ballad preserved in a sixteenth century manuscript. There is no attempt at seduction, but Ravengaard merely asks Gunild for the magic sword Adelring, saying that if she refuses he will tell a great lie about her. This version appears to be nearer the original; it is constructed as follows: (1) hatred for a woman on the part of a high officer; (2) his threat to tell a great lie; (3) the false charge of infidelity, supported only by his own testimony; (4) the trial by battle, in which a diminutive champion wins the victory, by the aid of a magic sword. The substitution, in place of the demand for a sword, of the *motif* of a malice aroused because Gunild refuses to give her favors to Ravnlil (Ravengaard), which is found in all the other versions, is pretty certainly a later development, and it may be that this is an element introduced from the Southern group with which we have been dealing.

However this may be, it seems safe to assume two parallel groups, both very old, which represent early forms of the cycle which we are investigating. The essential elements of A., as we have seen, are (1) the passion of a seneschal or steward for his lord's wife; and his repulse by her; (2) the attempt to fasten a charge of infidelity upon her, by placing in her bed a leper or other loathsome person. In C. we find as the chief characteristics, (1) the hatred of a steward for his lord's wife, a hatred probably not inspired, in the earliest forms, by his failure to seduce her, though it is not safe to be dogmatic on this point; (2) the trial by combat or by ordeal as a means for clearing the lady; (3) the appearance

---

[1] Of course there are a few variations, in the eleven versions, such as the substitution (rare) of ordeal for battle. These are noted by Child, pp. 35–37. Ravengaard is the name of the steward in the sixteenth century Danish poem ; Ravnlil in the other seven.

of a diminutive champion armed with a magic sword. The difference in the mode of vindication should be carefully noted : in A., there is usually a period of exile in which the lady 'suffers many perils and is finally re-united to her husband ; in C., there is the *judicium dei*, while the lady usually becomes the property of her champion, not only as a reward for his prowess, but as a just punishment to a husband entirely too willing to believe false reports about his wife. We shall now note how these two types are combined.

D. *The Composite Type.* By this rather awkward expression is meant, as is suggested above, the union of the principal characteristics of A. with those of C. The result of this union is to be noted in a class of tales in which, (1) a lady famed for her beauty inspires the passion of a knight, a steward, or a seneschal, and he sues for her favors ; (2) he is spurned, and as a result conceives a deep hatred for her ; (3) he places in her bed a leper, a dwarf, a scullion, or a young knight ; (4) the husband is confronted with a proof much stronger than the mere testimony of one man, and is convinced ; (5) a trial by battle or by ordeal proves the lady's innocence. There are three important sets of romances showing these characteristics.

1. *The Oliva group.* The story of Oliva, in its present form, is Norse, but it was translated into that language by a Norseman living in Scotland in the thirteenth century.[1] An abstract of the story has already been given ; it is sufficient here to call attention to the attempt of Milon to seduce Olif (or Oliva) and his repulse ; to his pretended desire for reconciliation and his presentation of the drugged cup ; to the placing of a black beggar, also drugged, in bed with her ; and the summoning of the king. All these are

---

[1] Child, II, 39. The original text is in the Karlamagnus Saga, *Af Fru Olif ok Landres,* Unger, p. 51.

elements originally found in A.; the circumstance that Milon seeks reconciliation on the ground that he was merely trying her virtue, is a curious reminder of the *Cymbeline* group, as already noted in the *Erl of Tolous*. The remainder of the episode shows the indebtedness to originals of the C. type. Olif proposes the trying of her case by ordeal, mentioning in succession several methods. The king is minded to accept this offer, but is each time dissuaded by Milon, who maintains that the woman is a witch and will save herself by the exercise of her art. At last Milon is forced to agree to a trial by battle, and though his adversary is armed only with a wooden wand, is without armor, and has only a mule for a steed, while he himself has full armor and a war horse, the guilty man is overthrown. Strangely enough, he maintains that this is due to the wife's witchcraft, and is again believed by the credulous king. The elements of magic; the trial by combat in which the lady's champion is at a great disadvantage, these are Northern elements. There are numerous versions of the tale.[1]

2. *The Sibilla group.* This group also deals with stories told about Charlemagne.[2] Sibilla is the wife of the great king, and against her a charge of infidelity is preferred, substantiated by the fact that an ugly dwarf is found in bed with her. There are many parallels, according to Mr. Child, in Spanish, Dutch, French, and German tales. It is significant that in all these the dwarf is the instrument of proof; when the story gets into Norse, however, being there told of Sisibe, a Spanish princess married to Sigmundr, the positive evidence is omitted, and the usual means of a slanderous charge of sin with a handsome thrall is substituted.

3. *The Aldingar group.* This version has also been sum-

---

[1] See Child, II, 39, 40.

[2] For references and summaries, cf. Child, 40, 41.

marized in another place. That it belongs to the composite type is proved by the presence of such A. type elements as the desire for revenge inspired by the refusal of the lady to yield to the false steward; the introduction of the lazar into the queen's bed; and the summoning of the king. Type C. is represented by the lady's claim, when charged with the crime, of her right to trial by battle. She is given forty days; no champion appears; the preparations for her execution are made. At this time a child is seen approaching; he demands that Aldingar give him the first stroke. This is granted, and with one blow the child cuts off both the steward's legs at the knee. Confession follows; the lazar becomes whole; the queen is taken back into her husband's affections. Thus the Northern element of magic and the defence by the diminutive or insignificant champion appear again in connection with elements undoubtedly Southern. In some variants of the ballad, such as the Scottish version,[1] the miraculous elements disappear with the exception of the victory of the queen's champion.

E. *The Erl of Tolous Type.*

We come now to the consideration of one of the most interesting of the Middle English romances, the *Erl of Tolous*. At first thought, this belongs to type D.; it presents some very close parallels to such tales as that of *Sir Aldingar*. At the same time, the relations of this romance to the wager group, type B., are so striking as to justify the supposition that some elements came directly from some tale belonging to that type and not through the more primitive line of development from A. to D.

In his critical edition of the romance, Lüdtke[2] lays great stress upon the incident of the trial by battle, presenting a large amount of material in a convincing way. He fails,

---

[1] Child, II, 34.   [2] *The Erl of Tolous*, Berlin, 1881.

however, to treat: I. The curious break in the story, when the earl, having been repulsed by the lady, retreats and the interest is shifted to the two knights. II. The close resemblance between this tale and those of the *Cymbeline* type. III. The introduction of the young knight into the lady's chamber, as evidence of her guilt. The first two of these topics require amplification; the third will be treated incidentally.

I. It will be remembered that the earl, on hearing his captive discourse on the beauty of his lord's wife, is smitten with passion for her, so that he offers the knight his liberty if he may only be conducted to this paragon of womanhood. This is done; the earl finds the lady more adorable than his imagination had conceived; he attempts to induce her to grant him her favors. This she refuses with indignation; he implores her forgiveness; returns to his home and disappears from the story until near the end. Two knights now enter upon the scene; both are smitten with passion for the lady; each makes an attempt to win her love and each is repulsed. In their anger they plot her ruin. During the absence of the husband they induce a young knight to conceal himself in the chamber; the household is aroused and he is found in the room where the lady lies asleep. The young knight is killed and the lady cast into prison. The story ends with the demand of the lady for the trial by battle, with the proclamation for a champion, followed by the coming of the Earl of Tolouse. The lady is reunited to her husband, but he lives only a short time; after his death the earl marries her.

We have here an evident departure from the ordinary type of construction, the object being, it seems to me, to make the earl the hero and to enable him to win the lady. Logically, when he is repulsed, the earl should set about contriving her ruin. Instead of this, he is temporarily withdrawn from the tale, and the more odious work is left to the knights, obviously dragged in to work out the remainder of the story in the orthodox manner. That the author desires to have the earl considered as the hero is manifested not only by the defence in the combat, but by the evident interest which the lady feels for him from the first. We may note, therefore, the following characteristics :

1. The elements belonging to type C. are numerous and interesting : there is the false charge preferred by knights high in the regard of the lady's husband ; the trial by combat ; the appearance of the champion from afar. Again, the champion finally wins the lady's hand, though in a manner much more modern than that by which Memering gained possession of Gunild. One notes, however, the entire absence of the miraculous, indicating entire sophistication.

2. Not less significant is the interference with the stock form of the tale by the withdrawal of the earl after his repulse; we should expect the plot against the lady to be made by him. As it is, the significance of his first effort to win her love is lost; that the incident remains is evidence of not very skilful patchwork, though the artistic instinct of the author led him to seek to show the lady's interest in the earl, and to prove his great love for her, before the incident of the battle.

3. The elements which unite the story to type A. are the attempt at seduction by the knights and the repulse ; the introduction of the concealed knight as a substantial proof of the charge; and the period of exile which the lady suffers before she is vindicated. This last point indicates a radical departure from type D. and leads naturally to our next topic.

II. That there are striking resemblances between this romance and the tales belonging to type B. the following observations will make clear :

1. The man who first makes an attempt upon the lady's

honor is not an officer of the husband's court; he has never seen her. This marks a radical variation from the usual type, and is exactly the situation in *Cymbeline*.

2. He hears her beauty vaunted by another man; in this case a knight belonging to her husband's followers. This is closely parallel to the incident in which the wager has its inception in type B. We might here expect a wager made by the earl that he could seduce this paragon of virtue after two interviews.

3. The lady's character in the scene with the earl Barnard is strangely like that of Imogen, and this characterization is consistently kept throughout the piece. She is forgiving, innocent, unsuspecting, of sterling faith to her husband, while her beauty is celebrated in foreign lands.

4. Passing over the break which transfers the main interest from the earl to the knights, we note not only the usual indignant refusal which the lady gives, but also the same excuse used by Iachimo, that the only object was to test her constancy to her husband.

5. The knight's excuse is accepted at once and he is again received into the lady's favor.

6. The husband is a great way off, and is not summoned to the wife's room in order to see the young knight. The evidence is through testimony apparently based on fact, the supposed paramour having been murdered by the conspirators. Thus the elaborate artifice of inducing the youth to go to the lady's room and unclothe himself is of little effect. It may be noted, in passing, that the youth is merely concealed in the room; he is not placed in the lady's bed.

7. The lady suffers many hardships in a period of exile. Since her vindication is to be by battle, this is not so essential a part of the story as in the representatives of the wager type; it indicates a confusion of sources.

8. After many perils, she is re-united to her husband,

whose confidence in her is completely restored. The means used for vindication constitutes the chief variation from the wager type.

9. Thus the *Erl of Tolous* illustrates the *Cymbeline motif* throughout. What the precise relation is it is hard to say. It seems clear that some relation exists, and that we are therefore justified in concluding that type E. is the result of a combination of stories belonging to types D. and B.

RELATION TO THE MAIN INQUIRY.

This long investigation of the cycle of the Woman Wrongly Accused seems justified by the light which it throws upon the form of the tale preserved in the *Avowing*. It will be noted that the entire interest, in the testing of Baldwin, lies in the presentation to the husband's eyes of seemingly absolute proof of his wife's infidelity. How complete this transference of interest is, may be seen from the fact that we are not even told the lady's name. The following additional conclusions may be drawn:

1. The source of this incident in the *Avowing* is one (or many?) of the tales belonging to the cycle represented by such interesting and varied compositions as *Sir Aldingar*, the *Erl of Tolous*, and *Cymbeline*.

2. The purpose of the author is humorous; there is, therefore, no emphasis on the lady's beauty, no introduction of an attempt upon her honor. Arthur takes the place of the seneschal or the steward, but he is not actuated by malice.

3. The means employed for convincing the husband is the introduction of a strange knight into the wife's bed.[1]

---

[1] It is noticeable that in the later tales a knight was substituted for a leper; this marks the progress of taste. The *Erl of Tolous* is a good

This knight, as usual, is very young, and very innocent. He is frightened half to death by the predicament in which he finds himself.[1]

4. The husband is away at the time of the plot against the wife; this is the usual situation, of course. On Baldwin's return, he is summoned to the chamber, and is there confronted by a sight startling enough to convince any man.

5. The *dénouement*, which consists in the usual confession of the trick by the guilty person, is hurried, since there was no occasion for prolonging what must have been painful for others as well as for the embarrassed woman and the frightened knight. One is thankful, for the sake of the knight at least, that Baldwin showed himself to be a man of such surpassing self-control.

This article is already too long to permit of any discussion of the stories told by Baldwin to illustrate his vows, nor is such discussion necessary in connection with the two special aims of this paper. It has been sought (1) to show the relation of this part of *The Avowing of Arthur* to the large class of popular fictions which I have named the cycle of the Three Counsels, and (2) to discuss the relation of Baldwin's vow against jealousy to other stories in which a false charge is brought against a woman, incidentally contributing something, it is hoped, to the investigation of the plot of *Cymbeline*.   .

EDWIN A. GREENLAW.

example. As already noted, in the Norse variants of the *Sibilla* group a handsome thrall, and not an ugly dwarf, is declared to be the object of the lady's affections.

[1] It will be remembered that Gawain, when placed in a similar situation (Carle of Carelyle) is very far from being embarrassed.

XIV.—THE HISTORY OF *AI* AND *EI* IN FRENCH BEFORE THE DENTAL, LABIAL, AND PALATAL NASALS.

In the following pages the history of the pronunciation in French of accented *ai* and *ei* before *n*, *m* and *ń* is to be investigated in detail. The subject naturally falls into two divisions. On the one hand we have *ai* and *ei* before *n* or *m*, and on the other we have the words in which these diphthongs are followed by *ń*. Both divisions are closely allied and the development of the one is often identical with that of the other. Yet for the better control of the material it will be advisable to separate the history of *ain* or *aim* and *ein* or *eim* from that of *aign* and *eign*.

The various grammars differ in the outline of the history of the sounds in question. Concentrating our attention first upon *ai* and *ei* followed by the dental nasal, and granting that the most direct road from the oldest stage *ãin* to modern *ẽ* is through *ẽin*, what would seem to be the simplest explanation may be found in Nyrop's *Grammaire historique de la langue française*, I, §§ 217 and 222. According to him, *ain* in the 11th century was pronounced *ãin*, and *ein* was *ẽin*. In the 12th century the two sounds coincide with the value of *ẽin*, and remain so until about the 16th century, when the modern pronunciation *ẽ* develops. When both syllables had the same value, one could be written for the other, and hence the well known Old French confusion in the orthography. This view of the question is shared by Meyer-Lübke, *Grammatik der romanischen Sprachen*, I, § 89.

There is, however, evidence that the history of these syllables was not so simple. Many texts and manuscripts present an orthography quite incompatible with the value

637

of *ēin* for graphic *ain*, and rimes can be cited which show
that *āin* remained stationary while *ēin* became *āin*. In
consequence Behrens in the Schwan-Behrens *Altfranzösische
Grammatik*, §§ 257 and 258, admits the history outlined by
Nyrop only for the literary language, while dialectically and
in a region which he describes as lacking accurate delineation he accepts *āin* as the common value of both *ain* and *ein*.

This pronunciation of *āin*, which Behrens believes was dia-
lectic, is looked upon by Suchier, *Altfranzösische Grammatik*,
§ 45, as the regular sound of these syllables in the literary
language ; ' *ēi* ist zu *āi* geworden etwa in der Mitte des XII
Jahrhunderts. Seit dem werden *ein* und *ain* promiscue
geschrieben, und es ist ganz gleichgiltig, ob ein Schreiber
jenes oder dieses bevorzugt.'

It is evident that the question is sufficiently encumbered
to merit a detailed investigation. The arguments available
must be sought in rimes and to a less degree in the orthography. For this purpose a long and representative list of
texts[1] has been studied, extending in chronological order

---

[1] I add here a rough chronological list of the texts that have been most
directly utilized for the present study and I include one or two titles that
are not cited in the discussion, so that others interested in the same problem may be spared the trouble of searching through the same texts again.
If the arguments presented here should not be found convincing, new evidence will have to be sought in different sources.

Karls des Grossen Reise nach Jerusalem und Constantinopel, hrsg. von Koschwitz, Heilbronn, 1883 (*Altfrz. Bibl.*, II) (*Voy. Charl.*).

Li Cumpoz Philipe de Thaün, hrsg. von E. Mall, Strassburg, 1873.

Le Bestiaire de Philippe de Thaün, Texte critique par E. Walberg, Lund,
1900.

Les Voyages Merveilleux de Saint Brandan, Légende .... publiée par Fr.
Michel, Paris, 1878, and by Suchier, *Rom. Stud.*, I, pp. 567–587.
(*Brandan.*)

Le Couronnement de Louis, publié par E. Langlois, Paris, 1888. (*Soc. d.
Anc. Textes.*)

Le Roman de Thèbes, publié par L. Constans, Paris, 1890. (*Soc. d. Anc.
Textes.*)

from the beginning to the 16th century and arranged in
groups according to the dialects. I now present this

Le Roman de Tristan par Béroul, publié par E. Muret, Paris, 1903. (*Soc.
d. Anc. Textes.*)

Eneas, publié par J. S. de Grave, Halle, 1891. (*Bibl. Norm.*, IV.)

Maistre Wace's Roman de Rou et des Ducs de Normandie, hrsg. von H.
Andresen, Heilbronn, 1877–1879. (*R. Rou.*)

Benoît de Sainte-More et le Roman de Troie par A. Joly, Paris, 1871. (*R.
Troie.*)

Le Roman de Troie par Benoît de Sainte-Maure, publié par L. Constans, vol.
I, Paris, 1904. (*Soc. d. Anc. Textes.*)

Chronique des Ducs de Normandie par Benoît, publiée par Fr. Michel, Paris,
1836–1844. (*Coll. d. Doc. Inéd. s. l' Hist. d. France.*)

Adgar's Marienlegenden, hrsg. von C. Neuhaus, Heilbronn, 1886. (*Altfrz.
Bibl.*, IX.)

Aiol et Mirabel und Elie de Saint Gille; Zwei altfranzösische Heldenge-
dichte, hrsg. von W. Förster, Heilbronn, 1876–1882.

Amis et Amiles und Jourdains de Blaivies; Zwei altfranzösische Heldenge-
dichte, hrsg. von C. Hofmann, Erlangen, 1852.

Aucassin und Nicolete, hrsg. von H. Suchier, Paderborn, 1899.

De Saint Laurent, poème anglonormand du XIIe siècle, publié par W.
Söderhjelm, Paris, 1888.

Sainte Catherine—Dvé Verse starofrancouzské Legendy o Sv. Katěrině
vydal U. Jarník, Prague, 1894.

La Vie de Saint Gilles par Guillaume de Berneville, publiée par G. Paris et
A. Bos, Paris, 1881. (*Soc. d. Anc. Textes.*)

Ille et Galeron von Walter von Arras, hrsg. von W. Förster, Halle, 1891.
(*Rom. Bibl.*, VII.)

Christian von Troyes, Sämtliche Werke, hrsg. von W. Förster, Halle, 1884–
1899.

Le Roman de Tristan par Thomas, publié par J. Bédier, Paris, 1901. (*Soc.
d. Anc. Textes.*)

Les Chansons de Gace Brulé, publiées par G. Huet, Paris, 1902. (*Soc. d.
Anc. Textes.*)

Die Lais der Marie de France, hrsg. von K. Warnke, Halle, 1900. (*Bibl.
Norm.*, III.)

Die Fabeln der Marie de France, hrsg. von K. Warnke, Halle, 1898. (*Bibl.
Norm.*, VI.)

Der Roman du Mont Saint-Michel von Guillaume de S. Paier, hrsg. von P.
Redlich, Marburg, 1894. (*Ausg. u. Abh.*, XCII.)

Estienne von Fougiere's Livre des Manières, hrsg. von J. Kremer, Marburg,
1887. (*Ausg. u. Abh.*, XXXIX.)

material, which, though not exhaustive, is yet sufficiently
complete to warrant the drawing of definite conclusions;
and I hope that it may serve to throw light upon one of the

La Vie de Saint Thomas le Martyr par Garnier de Pont-Sainte-Maxence, publiée par C. Hippeau, Paris, 1889.

The Metrical Chronicle of Jordan Fantosme, edited by R. Howlett, London,
1886.

Hue de Rotelande's Ipomedon, hrsg. von E. Kölbing und E. Koschwitz,
Breslau, 1889.

Estoire de la Guerre Sainte par Ambroise, publiée par G. Paris, Paris, 1897.
(*Coll. d. Doc. Inéd. s. l'Hist. d. France.*)

L'Escoufle, publié par H. Michelant et P. Meyer, Paris, 1894. (*Soc. d.
Anc. Textes.*)

Robert le Diable, publié par E. Löseth, Paris, 1903. (*Soc. d. Anc. Textes.*)

Le Roman de la Rose ou de Guillaume de Dole, publié par G. Servois, Paris,
1893. (*Soc. d. Anc. Textes.*)

Chardry's Josaphaz, Set Dormanz und Petit Plet, hrsg. von J. Koch, Heilbronn, 1879. (*Altfrz. Bibl.*, I.)

The Song of Dermot and the Earl, published by G. H. Orpen, Oxford, 1892.

Li Romans de Carité et de Miserere du Renclus de Moiliens, publié par A.-G.
van Hamel, Paris, 1885. (*Bibl. d. l'Éc. d. Hautes Études.*)

*Maistre Elie's Ueberarbeitung der ältesten französischen Uebertragung von
Ovid's Ars Amatoria*, hrsg. von Kuhne und Stengel, Marburg, 1886.
(*Ausg. u. Abh.*, XLVII.)

La Clef d'Amors, hrsg. von A. Doutrepont, Halle, 1890. (*Bibl. Norm.*, v.)

Li Chevaliers as deus Espees, hrsg. von W. Förster, Halle, 1877.

Li Romans de Durmart le Galois, hrsg. von E. Stengel für den litterarischen
Verein in Stuttgart, 1873.

Le Roman de Renart, hrsg. von E. Martin, Strassburg, 1881–1887.

Guillaume de Palerne, publié par H. Michelant, Paris, 1876. (*Soc. d. Anc.
Textes.*)

Le Bestiaire . . . . des Guillaume le Clerc, hrsg. von R. Reinsch, Leipzig,
1892. (*Altfrz. Bibl.*, XIV.)

Le Besant de Dieu von Guillaume le Clerc de Normandie, hrsg. von E.
Martin, Halle, 1869.

*Raoul de Houdenc, Le Songe d'Enfer, Le Songe de Paradis, Li Romans des
Eles*, publiés par A. Scheler, *Trouvères Belges*, Louvain, 1879, vol. II.

La Vie de Saint Grégoire par Frère Angier, publiée par P. Meyer, *Romania*,
XII, pp. 145–208.

Trois Versions rimées de l'Évangile de Nicodème, publiées par G. Paris et A.
Bos, Paris, 1885. (*Soc. d. Anc. Textes.*)

very vexing problems of French Historical Grammar. We shall consider in the first place the history of *ai* and *ei* before *n* or *m*.

L'Histoire de Guillaume le Maréchal, publiée par P. Meyer, 3 vols., Paris, 1891–1901. (*Soc. d. l'Hist. de France*), vol. I.

La Bible Guiot de Provins in *Fabliaux et Contes des Poètes Français*, publiés par Barbazon et Méon, Paris, 1808, vol. II, pp. 307–393.

Le Dit des Rues de Paris, *ibid.*, pp. 238–275.

Les Crieries de Paris, *ibid.*, pp. 276–286.

Les Moustiers de Paris, *ibid.*, pp. 287–292.

Le Roman de Galerent, publié par A. Boucherie, Paris, 1888. (*Soc. pour l'étude des lang. rom.*)

Wistasse le Moine, hrsg. von W. Förster und J. Trost, Halle, 1891. (*Rom. Bibl.*, IV.)

Lyoner Yzopet, hrsg. von W. Förster, Heilbronn, 1882. (*Altfrz. Bibl.*, V.)

Le Roman de la Rose, publié par Fr. Michel, Paris, 1872.

Floris et Liriope des Robert de Blois, hrsg. von W. von Zingerle, Leipzig, 1891. (*Altfrz. Bibl.*, XII.)

Jean Bodel, Le Jeu de Saint Nicolas.

Adam de la Halle, Le Jeu de la Feuillie, both published by Monmerqué et Michel, *Théâtre Français au moyen âge*, Paris, 1885.

Adam de la Halle, Le Jeu de Robin et Marion in Bartsch-Horning, *La Langue et la Littérature Française*, Paris, 1887, col. 523–548.

Trouvères Belges, publiés par A. Scheler, Louvain, 1866–1879.

Rutebeuf, Œuvres Complètes, publiées par A. Jubinal, Paris, 1874–1875. (*Bibl. Elzévirienne.*)

Richars li Biaus, hrsg. von W. Förster, Wien, 1874.

Les Œuvres poétiques de Philippe de Remi, sire de Beaumanoir, publiées par H. Suchier, Paris, 1884–1885. (*Soc. d. Anc. Textes.*) *La Manekine*, vol. I.

Li Dis dou Vrai Aniel, hrsg. von A. Tobler, Leipzig, 1884.

Octavian, hrsg. von K. Vollmöller, Heilbronn, 1883. (*Altfrz. Bibl.*, III.)

Œuvres Complètes d'Eustache Deschamps, publiées par Queux de Saint-Hilaire et G. Raynaud, Paris, 1878–1903. (*Soc. d. Anc. Textes*), vol. I and II.

Miracles de Nostre Dame par personnages, publiés par G. Paris et U. Robert, Paris, 1876–1883. (*Soc. d. Anc. Textes*), vols. I, II and III.

Œuvres poétiques de Christine de Pisan, publiées par M. Roy, Paris, 1886–1896. (*Soc. d. Anc. Textes.*)

Meliador par Froissart, publié par A. Longnon, Paris, 1895–1899. (*Soc. d. Anc. Textes.*)

Poésies Complètes de Charles d'Orléans, publiées par Ch. d'Héricault, Paris, 1896.

I.

AIN—EIN.

The two syllables *ain* and *ein* are not found forming
assonance or riming together in the *Alexis*, the *Roland*, the
Reimpredigt, the French translation of Marbod's *Lapidary*,
the *Comput* and *Bestiaire* of Philippe de Thaon. They are
kept distinct even as late as Guillaume de Berneville's *Vie de
Saint Gilles*.[1] In these texts the pronunciation was *ãin* and
ẽin respectively; cp. *mains*, *Rol.* 3965, in assonance with
-an, *ceinte*, *ibid.* 984, in *ei* assonance, and *peine* 1787, *aleine*
1789, *feindre* 1792 in assonance with *sanglente*, *temples*,
entendent, etc.; cp. also Engelmann, *Ueber die Entstehung der
Nasalvokale*, Halle, 1882, pp. 20 ff.

The earliest[2] definite evidence of a confusion of the two
syllables in rime occurs in the *Brandan*.[3] Here *ain* and *ein*

Œuvres Poétiques de Guillaume Alexis, prieur de Bucy, publiées par A.
    Piaget et E. Picot, Paris, 1896–1899. (*Soc. d. Anc. Textes.*)
L'Amant rendu Cordelier, poème attribué à Martial d'Auvergne, publié par
    A. de Montaiglon, Paris, 1881. (*Soc. d. Anc. Textes.*)
Le Mistère du Viel Testament, publié par le baron James de Rothschild,
    Paris, 1878–1891. (*Soc. d. Anc. Textes.*) Vol. I.
Die Werke Maistre François Villons, hrsg. von W. von Wurzbach, *Roman-
    ische Forschungen*, XVI, pp. 405–584.
Œuvres Complètes de Clément Marot, publiées par B. Saint-Marc, Paris,
    Garnier, without date.

[1] Cp. G. Paris, *ed.* p. xxvii.

[2] In his *Altfrz. Gram.*, p. 72, Suchier cites as earliest instance of the
mingling of *ain* and *ein*, *desteint : refraint*, *Bestiaire* 2865. However, this
rime would be so unique for Philippe de Thaon, that Walberg in his edition
of the text, pp. xlviii and 146, rejects the reading and adopts *restreinte :
desteinte* instead.

[3] To this categorical statement the following note must be added. The
Voyage de Charlemagne in its assonances shows the same pronunciation of
the syllables in question as the *Roland*, cp. Koschwitz, *Rom. Stud.*, II, pp.
38 ff. At the same time this poem contains one *laisse*, ll. 783–802, which

rime freely; cp. *quarenteine : semaine* 133, *cha[e]ines : semaines* 866, *funtaines : pleines* 998, 1586, *meindres : greindres* 1004, and from this poem on, mixture of the two is constant in Old French texts. Suchier suggests, *Altfrz. Gram.*, p. 72, that the process was somewhat slower on the continent than it was in England. Wace in the *Roman de Rou* has 48 pure *ain* and 14 pure *ein* rimes, and only one instance of fusion, *Saint Oain : secrestain* (ANDŒNUM : -ANUM), l. 347. However Pohl, *Rom. Forsch.*, II, pp. 581–2, has shown that while this observation is undoubtedly exact, it is very probably true that the inference that Wace consciously separates the two syllables is not justified, for in the same author's *Brut* mixture of the two is much more frequent, and, at any rate, in other continental texts of the same period, such as *Eneas*, the poems of Marie de France, and Benoît de Sainte-More, the *Livre des Manières*, fusion of the two syllables is quite the rule. In view of these facts it is not at all surprising that in the prose texts of this

---

appears to contradict the accuracy of this assertion. Here the following sequence of assonances is found : *Charlemaignes : compaignes : deplaindre : France : regne : grande : enfraindre : remaignet : Charlemaigne : plaines : pleines : descendre : ente : aimet : regne : France : Charlemaignes : plaigne.* It will be impossible to avoid the conclusion that for this poem *en* and *an* form a correct assonance (cp. *Rom. Stud.*, II, p. 49), though the mixture of the two is not very frequent. That *regne* should be found in the same laisse need not surprise. It had become *rãñe* in pronunciation, and there are numerous other texts giving evidence of a similar pronunciation of the word. However, difficulty is created by the appearance of *pleines*, l. 793, in the series. Since the separation of *ain* and *ein* seems so clearly demanded by the assonances of this text, Koschwitz, *l. c.*, p. 40, suggests that the lines 783–802 should be divided into three laisses as follows : (1) 783–792, *ái : a*, (2) 793–795, *éi : e*, (3) 796–802, *ái : a*. Considering the probable age of the poem and its dialect, this explanation is presumably correct, but whatever the final decision may be, the consideration of the present problem need not concern itself with these lines. Everything depends upon the age of the poem, and if it should be younger than the *Roland*, these assonances would only corroborate what we can observe elsewhere.

period *ain* and *ein* are constantly confused in orthography; cp. for the *Montébourg Psalter*, Harseim, *Rom. Stud.*, IV, pp. 277 and 283; for the *Cambridge Psalter*, Schumann, *Vokalismus und Konsonantismus des Cambridger Psalters*, *Franz. Stud.*, IV, fasc. 4, pp. 17 and 29, and for the *Quatre Livres des Rois*, Schlösser, *Die Lautverhältnisse der Quatre Livres des Rois*, Leipzig, 1887, pp. 13 and 31.

The next point to be discussed is the pronunciation of this syllable written indifferently *ain* or *ein*. To facilitate the control of the available material, we shall divide the examples according to the letter or letters which may follow after the nasal consonant.

1). *ain — ein.*

The union of these two syllables in rime leaves no question that their pronunciation was identical, but it gives no clue as to the nature of the vowel or diphthong that was pronounced. Inasmuch as this was either $\bar{a}in$ or $\bar{e}in$ we may look for imperfect rimes with *an* or *en* as capable of throwing light on the problem. A few examples of *ain : an* occur in the texts which I have examined, and we may add those of *ains : ans* as having the same value. Cp. *Brandan : pan* (PANNUM), *Brandan* 480, *Brandan : an*, *ibid.* 824, *Brandan : vilain*, *ibid.* 163, *Brandan : main*, *ibid.* 658, *Brandans : mains*, *ibid.* 203, *pan* (PANEM): *ahan*, *Mist. Adam* 434, but *pain : Evain*, *ibid.* 786, *Trajan : roman*, Angier, *Grégoire* 2539, but *Traien : paien*, *ibid.* 2715, *derrans : Johans*, Angier, *Dialogues*, 72, rᵒb, cited by Miss Pope, *Langue de Frère Angier*, Paris, 1903, p. 12, *esturman : certan*, *Eneas* 205. For the correct appreciation of these rimes it should be noted that of the words in question, *vilain, main, pan, roman, derrans* and *certan*, involve the Latin vowel *a*, and that *Brandan* is a proper name in which the tonic syllable may have retained its Latin value.[1] When

---

[1] Cp. Suchier, *Zs. f. rom. Phil*, IX, p. 89, note.

we take into account, furthermore, the fact that the texts
from which these few rimes are taken cover a period of a
hundred years, and that *ains*, which certainly had the same
value of vowel as *ain*, occurs in the same texts and in others
of the same period and dialect in rime with *ens* and *iens*
(cp. below, p. 646), it becomes evident that these examples
represent rime licences.   They are either pure Latinisms [1] or
remnants of the earlier practice exemplified by the assonances cited above from the *Roland*, but they have no
argumentative value for the determination of the pronunciation of *ain* in this dialect and during this period.

Rimes of *ain* or *ein* with *en* on the other hand are even
rarer.   It must be borne in mind that *ẹ̃n* in the final syllable of the word exists in Old French only in a few learned
names and in words of the categories of BENE and PAGANUM.
Of the former, as far as I know, only a single instance
occurs in the texts examined, *Jerusalem : Alein, B. Chron.*
36894.   When compared with *Alain : main, ibid.* 36940,
main : frein 16366 and *Jerusalem : huem* 31752, it becomes
evident that both *ain* and *ein* in this text cannot have been
āin and this is also the conclusion of Pohl, *Rom. Forsch.*, II,
p. 554.

Mixture with *ien* points in the same direction.   The
actual rimes that can be cited here are not very numerous,
because the inflected forms of the syllables in question are
more frequent in rime than the uninflected.   Their discussion
may, therefore, be deferred to the succeeding paragraph.

2).   *ains — eins, ainz — einz.*

Several rimes show mixture with *ens* or *enz*; cp. *defens :
mains* (MINUS), *Mist. Adam* 148, *meins : tens, Gaimar* 1811,
ateinz : defenz, B. Chron. 22848, *genz : seinz, ibid.* 32235.
Since checked *e* before a nasal in these texts was certainly *ẹ̃*

---

[1] Cp. Miss Pope, *l. c.*, p. 12.

it will be difficult to avoid the conclusion that *ains* and *eins* tended in the same direction. This inference is emphasized by the existence in the same and similar texts of a certain number of rimes just referred to, beginning with the *R. Troie*, which show fusion of *ains*·and *eins* with *iens*. In the *Eneas* we can observe only mixture of *iens* and *ens*; cp. *Troüens* : *tens* (TEMPUS) 565, 601, 5811, 6319, *anciëns* : *tens* 4127, *Sabiëns* : *cuens* 3949, *cuens* : *Volcens* 5093, and the same is true of Marie de France ; cp. *anciëns* : *tens*, *Milun* 63. The *R. Rou* contains no examples in point, but the *R. Troie* and *B. Chron.* continue the tradition of the *Eneas*, while they add besides rimes of *ain*(*s*) and *ein*(*s*) with *ien*(*s*). Since the latter was *iẹn*(*s*), as shown through the union with *ens* = *ẹns*, there can be little question about the pronunciation of the former. The following are the examples :—

ien(*s*) : *en*(*s*)—*R. Troie.*[1] *Troüen* : *sen* 5813, 6815, *nequeden* : *Troïen* 18641, *Troïens* : *tens* 581, 7179, 20471, : *porpens* 19915, *Atheniens* : *tens* 8489, *Sisiliens* : *buens* 18581, *Paflago-niens* : *suens* 20515 ; *B. Chron. suen* : *bien*, I–1765 (cp. *suens* : *buens*, II–3005), *boens* : *cristiens*, II–24307, *tens* : *Egiptiens*, I–413, *paiens* : *sens*, II–23081, *tens* : *crestiens*, II–39017.

ien(*s*) : *ein*(*s*)—*R. Troie. meins* : *Troiains* 5275 ; *B. Chron. bien* : *Saint Oien*, II–19550 (cp. *Sainz Oieins* : *mains* (MANUS), II–25840, *main* (MANE) : *Oain*, II–7009, 19354).

ien(*s*) : *ain*(*s*)—*R. Troie. primerains* : *Troiains* 13903, 18745, 25273, *germains* : *Indiains* 14091, *Frisains* : *primerains* 15549 ; *B. Chron. cristiens* : *premerains*, I–925, : *parreins*, II–6577, 7988, *bien* : *Saint Oien* 19550 (cp. *Saint Oain* : *main*, II–19354).

Of the same general nature are the rimes *Swein* : *buen* *B. Chron.* 31046, *Sueins* : *buens* 38889 and *seins* (= *suens*)

<hr>

[1] References to the *R. Troie* as far as l. 8292 are given according to the new edition of the poem by Constans, *Soc. d. Anc. Textes*, Paris, 1904.

: *Aleins* 31008 (cp. *Alains* : *seins* (SANUS), *R. Rou* 2735), interesting particulárly for the orthography, for *Suein* is the usual bisyllabic *Soen, Suen*,[1] and *seins* stands for *suens*. The *Chron. Mt. S. Mich.* presents only a single rime *ancieins* : *pens* (PENSO) 3752, interesting also for the orthography, while the *Livre d. Man.* has no rime in point. But the *Beroul Tristan* contains *Brengain* : *bien* 523, : *mien* 553, *Lan*[*ci*]*ën* : *Ivein* 1155, *Uriën* : *Dinoalain* 3487, *suen* : *Denoalen* 4435. Here *Brengain* may stand for *Brangien* and can, therefore, not enter into the argument, éxcept in as much as it shows the value ascribed to the combination *ain* by the copyist. *Frans* : *mains B. Trist.* 3327 is discussed by Muret, edition, p. xliv. On the basis of Gottfried of Strassburg's rime *Isôt als blansche mains* : *Kâedin li frains*, which he probably derived from Thomas, and Heinrich of Freiberg's appellative *li frents* of the same knight he concludes 'nous devons peut-être rétablir au vers 3327 une épithète traditionelle, distincte de l'adjectif franc.' Finally, though the text does not belong strictly to the same dialect, and yet pointing in the same direction as far as the pronunciation of the syllables in question is concerned, there should be cited from the *R. Thèbes* the rimes *ren* : *germain* 6807, and *demen (demain)* : *ben* 8249, 8271, *ben* : *ven* (VANUM) 8487. Here also *ien* rimes with *uen*, as in *rens* : *suens* 4343. The same rime of *ain* : *ien* is probably also involved in the following series from the *Vie de Saint Thomas* of Garnier de Pont-Sainte-Maxence where *prochain* rimes with *main* : *plain* : *sain* : *soverain* on p. 53 and in the form *prosceins* with *biens* : *miens* : *riens* : *fiens* on p. 130.

It seems to me that it will be difficult to avoid what appears to be the evident inference demanded by these

---

[1] Cp. also *Suain* : *plain* (PLENUM), *La Vie de Seint Edmund le Rei* 3703, edited by F. L. Ravenel, Bryn Mawr College Monographs, 1906.

rimes. The fusion of *ien(s)* with *en(s)* on the one hand and
with *ain(s)* and *ein(s)* on the other, together with the rimes
of *ains* or *eins* with *ens* or *enz* in texts where *ens* was pronounced *ẹns*, allows only of one conclusion, viz., that *ain(s)*
and *ein(s)* in the dialect represented by these texts tended
in the direction of their modern value, and had certainly
arrived at least at the stage *ēin(s)*. That *iens* should then
in the pen of a copyist speaking the same dialect become
iains or *ieins* need cause no astonishment. This orthography merely represents his effort to make the rime acceptable to the eye. How far geographically this orthographic
habit extended I am unable to say. Stock, *Rom. Stud.*, II,
p. 468, cites a similar example (*chrestiains : sains*) from
the *Rom. de Mahomet*, l. 1091. Angier writes *premerain* :
Maximiain, *Grégoire* 257, and Miss Pope, *l. c.*, p. 14, adds
arrien : sen, *arriens : tens* but *arrieins : veins* from the *Dialogues* of the same author. There are, no doubt, other
instances of this orthography that might be collected, as
for example *primeraine : meiaine* (*moyenne*) in the *Bestiaire
de Gervaise*,[1] l. 503, but it is evident that the harvest
outside of the manuscripts of *R. Troie* and *B. Chron.* is
limited.

Occasionally a Latinism of the type cited above, p. 644,
may be found; cp. *ancian : an*, *Gaimar* 1682, but *ancien :
mien*, *ibid.* 4319, *Octavian : pan*, *Marie de France, Lanval*
85, *Troïan : oan*, *Eneas* 1699, 2109, *Troians : chans*, *R. Troie*
2299. Suchier, *Altfrz. Gram.*, p. 75, adds some similar
orthographies from the *R. Rou* and the *Ps. Cott.*, but all
such examples are rare and do not affect our problem.

3). *aint — eint, ainte — einte.*

As in the preceding rime-groups the Anglo-Norman and
Norman texts under consideration present little beyond

[1] Cp. *Romania*, I, pp. 426–442.

simple mixture of the two syllables. However, as before, a few isolated rimes show the direction in which the development tended. Suchier, *l. c.*, p. 73, cites *niënt* : *veint* and *niënt* : *desteint* from *Sanson de Nantuil*. We may add, from *B. Chron.*, *ateint* : *destruiement* 17391, *teint* (TENET) : *aimt* 20779, *feint* (FINGIT) : *vient* 21670, *seinte* : *reinte* (REDEMPTA), *Angier*, *Gregoire* 1467 and *ceynt* (CINCTUM) : *torment*, *Évang. de Nicodème*, version C, 767.

4). *aindre — eindre*.

Our texts here show only fusion of the two, but never rime with *ēndre* in such words as *prendre*. Since verbs with this ending are comparatively frequent, it is rather remarkable that this should be the case. Only *mendre — meindre* < MINOR might seem to contradict this rule. However this contradiction does not exist in reality, for *mendre* appears to be the original form of the word and the diphthong in *meindre* is due to the analogy of *meins* < MINUS. As a matter of fact *mendre* is found frequently at the end of the line, but, as far as my observation goes, it rimes only with words like *entendre*, *B. Chron.* 403, 22516, *descendre* 6243, *prendre* 10159 and never with *remaindre*, *feindre* and the like. This is true of all the Norman texts in this study, the *Clef d'Amour* included.[1]

An instance of what indeed might seem to be mixture of *eindre* with *endre* exists in strophes 54 and 111 of the *Livre des Manières*; cp. *raindre* (r. *raeindre*) : *pleindre* : *remeindre* : *ateindre*, str. 54, and *defendre* : *vendre* : *prendre* : *raïendre*,

---

[1] I have noted but one exception to this rule, *meindres* : *greindres*, *Brand.* 1004, which invites construction into an argument for the pronunciation of *greindres* of the type of *eint* : *ent* just noted. However the matter is too doubtful to be pressed; we probably have to do simply with an early sporadic case of the analogy so common later. The old form persisted for a long time. Christine de Pisan rimes *chambre* : *tendre* : *remembre* : *mendre*, *Livre du Dit de Poissy* 280, though elsewhere she joins *meindre* : *remaindre*, *Livre du Duc des Vrais Amants*, 1155.

str. 111. Both *raindre* and *raiendre* represent the same
Latin verb REDIMERE $>$ *raembre*, which on account of its
unique form was drawn over to the *-ndre* verbs, like *tre-
mere* $>$ *oraindre*. But while the stemvowel in both forms,
raeindre and *raiendre* is entirely analogical, it is probably
wrong to consider the two as equivalent. The former, pronounced *raēindre*, could rime with *plēindre*, the latter was
raiëndre, if not *raēndre*, which forms rime with *prēndre*.

Another rime pair with similar bearing stands in Guillaume le Maréchal, l. 2883, *remendre* ($=$*remaindre*) : *attendre*. Unfortunately this rime loses its argumentative
value from the fact that the last six letters of the second
word represent a manuscript correction not written by the
original scribe in the place of something else that has been
erased.

5). *einge.*

As early as the *Brandan* this syllable could rime with
enge as in *prenge*. It is not of frequent occurrence, being
found only in those peculiar Anglo-Norman present sub-
junctives in *-ge* as *meinge* : *prenge*, *Brandan* 119. Since
the second word here certainly contained the nasal *ẹ̃*, cp.
calengent : *prengent*, *ibid.* 1472, *meinge* must have had at
least the value of *mẽinge.*

6). *aine — eine.*

The rimes for the most part show only the usual mixture
of the two syllables. Instances proving the development
of the pronunciation in the direction of *ẹ̃ne* are rather late.
As a matter of fact the combination of *ẹ* $+$ *nasal* $+$ *ẹ* is rare
in Old French. Its main representatives are the French
forms of FEMINA and REGNUM. Rimes between these two
words are well known in Old French texts. Without in any
way aiming to be exhaustive I may cite *Comput* 469, *Eneas*
3, Wace *Brut*, though not the *R. Rou*, cp. Pohl, *Rom. Forsch.*,
II, p. 554, *R. Troie* 3937, *B. Chron.* 1621, *B. Trist.* 287 as

texts where *an* and *en* are not mixed in rime, from which it follows that *femme* : *regne* means *fẽme* : *rẽne* or *rẽ́ne*. Now these same texts in a limited number of rime pairs show these words joined to others in *-aine* or *-eine*; cp. *peine* : *regne, Eneas* 2523, *estreine* (STRENA) : *regne, R. Troie* 8317, *Loherenne* : *femme, B. Chron.* 18052, *regne* : *Loheregne, ibid.* 18066, *vilaine* : *reigne, B. Trist.* 57. The conclusion that in these texts *aine* or *eine* mean at least *ẽine* will be difficult to avoid.[1]

Another combination of rimes pointing in the same direction is that of *aine* or *eine* with *iene*, similar to that of *ain(s)* or *ein(s)* with *ien(s)* already noted. As earliest instance of this fusion might be cited *paaine* : *soltaine, Eneas* 2141, though it is of course possible to regard this rime as a Latinism. It is different, however, with *plataine* : *Egiptaine, R. Troie* 22995, and *B. Chron. vilaine* : *paene*, I-951, *domaine* : *paene*, II-15812, (cp. *anciene* : *paene*, II-57, *paene* : *crestiene*, II-3073, 4383), *mundaines* : *celestienes*, II-20898, *estrienne* (STRENA) : *Bauveisienne*, II-18484, *Rentïëne* (= de Reims) : *plaine, B. Trist.* 3727 and *maenne* (*moyenne*) : *enchaenne* (= *enchaîne*), *Clefi d'Amours* 3419. These words rime only if *aine* or *eine* are pronounced *ẽine* or *ẽne*.

The *Livre des Manières* has three strophes which make some difficulty; cp. the following rimes: *anciennes* : *paiennes* : *sennes* (SYNODQS) : *fames* (FEMINAS), str. 247; *fame* (FEMINA) : *fame* (FAMA) : *raiemme* : *jame* (GEMMA), str. 60; *enteime* : *deraime* : *sorseime* : *feme*, str. 312. It is seen that in strophe 60 *fame* = FAMA seems to oppose the value of *ẽme* for *fame* = FEMINA. Kremer in his edition of the text p. 27 cites the various explanations of this discrepancy that

---

[1] A single rime in Adgar's *Legends, mainent* : *chantent* 4-9, seems to contradict this conclusion. It is so unique that I regard it as erroneous for *hantent* : *chantent*.

have been offered, but they all fail to satisfy. It seems to
have been overlooked that the line containing *fame* = FAMA,
60 b, is too short by one syllable. While this fact tends to
throw doubt on the reading of the line, it does not, however,
prove that the rime is incorrect. · We will have to accept
femme as riming in this text both with *e* and with *a*. The
same phenomenon is not unknown in other texts where *an*
and *en* are kept distinct. Cp. *realme* : *femme*, *Gaimar* 3601,
but *mercenne* : *femme* 2507, *regne* : *femme* 2531, *fame* : *dame*,
R. Troie 18154 ; see also *Rom. Stud.*, II, p. 39, and *Rom.
Forsch.*, II, p. 554.

7). *aime — eime.*

Only very few rimes of this category are available.
Since *ẽime* < EMA does not exist in Old French, *ãime* <
AMA can only rime with itself. Later, however, when *ãime*
had become *ẽime*, a few other words having *ẹme* became
available. This, I believe, is the explanation of *esment*
(ESTIMANT) : *cleiment*, *Angier*, *Grégoire* 645, *aime* : *baptesme*,
Simund de Freine, *Vie de Saint Georges* 1324 and *meime* (=
mesme) : *aime*, *Rom. de Philosophie* 981 of the same author.

Suchier, *Altfrz. Gram.*, p. 71, thinks *esment* stands for
eiment and that the disappearing *s* had called forth a *j* which
formed a diphthong with the preceding vowel. Granting
that this was the case, we should even then have evidence in
these rimes that *ãime* had become *ẽime*. I doubt, however,
whether this explanation is exact. That *s* before *l* and *n*
in the course of disappearance passed through a sound
capable of palatalizing the following consonant seems fairly
reasonable, but this question can not enter into the discussion here. Examples in support are cited by Walberg, *Le Bestiaire de Philippe de Thaün*, p. lxv. It does
not follow, however, that the process was identical before
m. Here it is much more likely that the intervening sound

was a voiceless *m*, such as Wulff[1] has shown to exist under similar circumstances in Andalusian Spanish. When finally all trace of the *s* had disappeared, the vowel in words like *esment, baptesme* was *ę*, and *ei* and *ey* are only graphic variants utilized by the copyist to represent this sound. Then these words were pronounced *ęment, baptęme* and the rimes in question are entirely parallel to those cited above for *ẽine* : *ę̃ne*.

This conclusion is emphasized by the following rimes of *aime* : *ieme* from the *R. Thèbes*; cp. *crement* : *ement* 5077, *creme* : *afeme* (ADFAMAT) 7377, *entrement* : *crement* 8603, *creme* : *eme* 9199.

All the evidence presented so far goes to prove that in the northwest of France and in England *ai* and *ei* with *n* had become *ẽin* about the middle of the 12th century, and that under favorable circumstances the sound could even approximate *ę̃n*.   The evidence of the orthography points in the same direction.   We have to do with a region where for the most part *an* and *en* are kept distinct.   A scribe who pronounced *en* + *cons.* as *ę̃n* would not have written *en* for either *ain* or *ein*, had he pronounced these *ãin*, as *Brandan enz* (*ainz*) 1010, *desclem* 534, *sen* (*saint*) 157, nor would he have introduced *ein* in *mendre* if *meindre* had meant *mãindre* for him as in the rime *tendre* : *meindre*, *Ipomedon* 2651.   A survey of the orthographic habits in Anglo-Norman texts can be found in Stimming's edition of *Boeve de Haumtone*,[2] pp. 185, 196–7, and 201, and in the manuscripts of continental texts similar habits prevail.   Görlich arrives at the same conclusions from the study[3] of the original documents

[1] *Un chapitre de phonétique andalouse*, in *Recueil de Mémoires philologiques présenté a Monsieur Gaston Paris par ses élèves suédois*, 1889, pp. 45 ff.

[2] *Bibliotheca Normannica*, vol. VII.

[3] Görlich, *Die Nordwestlichen Dialekte der Langue d' Oïl, Franz. Stud.*, V, Heft 3, pp. 17–18 and 41.

of the Northwest dialects of the second half of the 13th and the 14th centuries. Besides the noncommittal *ein* he cites *e* in *preschene, prochen, Alen, men, nonen, fren, plen, plene, Magdalene,* *ae* in *maen, daraene, prechaens, prochaenne,* *aei* in *Alaein, prochaein,* *ee* in *dareen,* *oei* in *Moeine* and *oe* in *damoene, demoene.*

We may close this division of our subject with the following passage from the *Orthographia Gallica*[1] which emphasizes the conclusions at which we have arrived; 'item diversitas scripture facit aliquarum diccionum quamvis in voce sint consimiles, verbi gracia . . . . teindre tendre tenir attendre atte[i]ndre . . . . aymer amer,' which can of course only mean *tēndre* and *teindre, attēndre* and *atteindre* are pronounced alike. The rule is found only in MSS. C and O, *i. e.,* in the later version of this earliest grammatical treatise, but even thus it gives valuable evidence of the pronunciation of our syllables in the 14th century, and is entirely in harmony with what we have been able to observe so far.

II.

Leaving the Norman and Anglo-Norman division of Old French texts we may now continue the history of our syllables into the dialect from which the Modern French most directly sprang.

One of the earliest texts to be cited here is the *Roman de l'Escoufle,* written about the year 1200. In this poem *en* and *an + cons.* are kept apart in rime, in spite of the fact that *feme* rimes with *ame,* as l. 125, and *gemme* with *dame,* as l. 5739. But as already pointed out above, p. 652, the same phenomenon can be observed in other texts sepa-

---

[1] Ed. Stürzinger, *Altfrz. Bibl.,* vol. VIII (Heilbronn, 1884), p. 14.

rating *ēn* and *ǎn*.[1] The nasal *ẹ̄n* exists in such rimes as *suens* : *sens* 3189, *vit l'en* : *Julien* 4867, *enmena* : *cil l'en a* 3647, *amena* : *dame en a* 5969. In the light of these *losenge* : *vos ain ge* 2877 can only be interpreted as meaning *lozẹ̄nǵẹ* : *vozẹ̄nǵẹ*. The *Roman de Guillaume de Dole*, which Gaston Paris was inclined to attribute to the same author,[2] shows the same mixture of *feme* : *dame* 1508, 3008, and rimes *maint* (MANET) : *esloint* 4192. This fusion of *ain* : *oin*, which occurs here, as far as I know, for the first time speaks for a pronunciation *ẹ̄n* : *oẹ̄n*. Another isolated early example of the same rime, though of uncertain date, can be found in the *Rom. de Renard*, branch 9, written by the priest of La Croix-en-Brie, *moines* (MONACHUS) : *poines* (PENAS) 505.

From this date forward it is possible to cite an uninterrupted series of texts, including Marot, all showing the same fusion of *ain* and *oin*, which thus present unmistakable evidence that in the dialect centering in Paris both *ain* and *ein* were steadily developing toward their modern value. I copy this list without further comment, and as much as possible in chronological order. The fact that these rimes are few in number in comparison with the *ain* : *ein* rimes probably means that they were felt to be irregularities or rime licences, and this will have to be taken into account in the final estimation of their meaning.

Gaufrey[3] — *hautaine* : *Karlemaine* : *humaine* : *emmaine* : *regne* : *souveraine* : *demouraine* : *demaine* : *essoigne* : *Couloigne* : *entente* : *jenne* (= *jeune*) : *quarantaine*, p. 316.

---

[1] For Picard and Wallonian cp. Haase, *Das Verhalten der pikardischen und wallonischen Denkmäler des Mittelalters in Bezug auf a und e vor gedecktem n.* Halle, 1880, pp. 41 ff.

[2] Cp. *Romania*, XXXII, pp. 487–488. He there suggests 1185 as the date of the *Escoufle* and 1200 as that of *Guillaume de Dole*. The last edition of his *Litt. Franç. au moyen âge* places *Guillaume de Dole* in 1200 and the *Escoufle* in 1210.

[3] Cited by Engelmann, *l. c.*, p. 23.

Roman de la Rose — *paintes* (PINCTAS) : *cointes*, I, pp. 20, 30, 46–47, *paintes* : *pointes* (PUNCTAS) I, p. 31, *maintes* : *ointes*, I, pp. 249–250, *poine* (PENA) : *moine* (MONACHUS) I, p. 100, *saine* : *essoine*, I, p. 73.

Rutebuef — *avaine* : *vaine* : *couvaine*, I, p. 33, *poigne* (PUGNA): *sovraine* : *moine* : *essoine*, I, p. 153, *lainne* : *avainne* : *semainne*, II, p. 57, *demaine* : *moine*, II, pp. 122, 137, *moine* : *emmaine*, II, p. 129, *Jordain* : *enjoin*, II, p. 276, *nonains* : *sains* : *certains* : *mains* (MINUS) II, p. 42, *plaindre* : *joindre* : *poindre*, I, p. 216, *saintes* : *jointes* : *empraintes* : *maintes*, II–253.

Eustache Deschamps — *moins* (MINUS) : *mains* (*MANTI): *mains* : *vains*, I, XXV, *conjoint* : *point* : *vaint* (VINCIT) I–LXXI, *doint* (DONET) : *pourpoint* : *point* : *point* : *faint* (FINGIT): *vaint* : (VINCIT) II–CCXL.

Christine de Pisan — *loings* : *moins* : *besoings* : *froins* (FRENUM) I, p. 26, *moins* : *besoings*, I, p. 56, *mains* : *mains* (MINUS) I, p. 123, III, p. 40.

Miracles de Nostre Dame — *moins* : *chastellains*, IV–178, *lointain* : *soing*, XI–9, *moine* (MONACHUS) : *amaine*, XVIII–1313, *estraine* : *royne*, IV–908, cp. *Guillaume Alexis* and *Villon* below.

Charles d'Orléans — *plains* (PLANGO) : *plains* (PLENUS) : *moins* : *mains*, I–192, *besoing* : *loing* : *baing* : *poing*, II–98, *avoine* : *Touraine* : *paine* : *sepmaine*, II–157.

Guillaume Alexis — *fainctes* (FINCTAS) : *coinctes*, Déb. de *l'Homme et de la Femme* 128, *traine* : *demaine* : *pourmaine* : *chanoine* : *gaine* : *maine*, Blason des Faulses Amours, str. 40, *primeraine* : *essoine* : *Anthoine* : *royne* : *villaine* : *loingtaine*, ibid. 61, *mains* : *mains* (MINUS) : *plains* : *mains* : *poins* : (PUGNUS): *point* (PUNCTUM), ibid. str. 80, *chanoines* : *peines* : *demaines*, Martyrologue des Fausses Langues 254.

L'Amant rendu Cordelier — *mondaines* : *avoynes* : *marjo-*

laines : *certaines* 410, *saindre* (CINGERE) : *estraindre* : *joindre* : *atteindre* 1706, *baings* : *aubefoings* : *poings* : *mains* 1762.

Villon — *fain* (FAMEM) : *foing* (fenum), *Poésies Diverses* 140, *bain* (MS. *boing*) : *poing*, *ibid.* 148, *Anthoine* : *Saine* : *essoine* : *ydoyne*, *Pet. Test.* 226.

Marot—*moindre* : *paindre*, I–104, *moindre* : *joindre*, I–162, *veine* : *Antoine*, I–239, *Antoine* : *souvienne*, I–239, *moins* : *inhumains*, II–313.

In the light of these rimes certain other combinations, which would have little argumentative value by themselves, may be advanced as pointing in the same direction.

Roman de la Rose—*vaine* : *raine* (REGNUM), I–15, *Loheregne* [1] : *regne*, *ibid.*, I–5.

Rutebuef — *raine* (REGNUM) : *chanoine*, II–119, *regne* : *resne* : *saine* : *plaine* : *estraine* : *raisne*, I–127, *raignes* : *raines* (RANAS), II–90, *vilaine* : *raine* (REGNAT), II–206, *amaine* : *raine* (REGNAT), II–254, *tain* (TENEO) : *soucretain*, II–118, 137, 139, *vain* (VENIO) : *vain*, II–139.

Guiot de Provins—*Aquitaine* : *Vienne*, *Bible* 334, *citoien* : *vilein* 998, *Magdalene* : *certene* 2230, *Egipciene* : *Elene* 2248.

Miracles de Nostre Dame—*Estienne* : *maine*, XIV–389.

Eustache Deschamps—*Requiem* : *prouchain* : *moien* : *bien*, I–XLVIII, *certain* : *cappitain* : *tain* (TENEO), I–CLXXIV, *Romains* : *Rains* : *plains* : *restrains* : *tiens* : *certains*, II–CCLIII, *plaine* : *prouchaine*, I–XII, *paine* : *aviengne*, I–XVI, *craime* [2] (*crème*) : *aime*, I–XXXIII.

Christine de Pisan—*Athenes* : *certaines*, I, p. 250, *peine* : *Polixenne* : *vaine* : *prochaine*, *Débat de Deux Amants* 692, *ancienes* : *humaines* : *fontaines* : *mondaines*, *Livre du Dit de*

---

[1] The ending in this word, which can be found elsewhere and earlier, is evidently due to analogy with *regne*, as if the word meant *the kingdom of Lorraine*.

[2] The pronunciation is indicated by the rime *baptesme* : *cresme*, *Mir. d. Nostre Dame*, XX–643.

Poissy 660, *Magdaleine* : *peine*, *Oraison de Nostre Seigneur* 215.

Guillaume Alexis—*penne* (PENNA) : *penne* (PENA) : *penne* (= Mod. Fr. *panne*), *Le a b c des Doubles* 1056. This unique composition, among other peculiarities, is composed entirely in *rimes équivoquées*, whence the spelling of the second rime word. There can be no doubt about its pronunciation.[1]

L'Amant rendu Cordelier—*jenne* (=*jeune*) : *mondaine* 169 ; cp. the same combination cited from *Gaufrey* above, p. 655.

Mistère du Viel Testament—*Damascene* : *regne* 4341.

Villon—*douzaine* : *Estienne*[2] : *paine* : *sepmaine*, *Grant Test.* 1913, *roynes* : *regnes* : *Renes* : *estrenes*, *ibid.* 414, *Neapolitaines* : *Pruciennes* : *Egipciennes* : *Castellaines*, *ibid.* 1524, *villaine* : *Helaine*, *Poésies Diverses* 42, *Magdelaine* : *laine*, *ibid.* 53.

Marot—*veine* : *Antoine*, I–239, *Antoine* : *souvienne*, I–239, *tienne* : *estraine*, I–245, *Magdalaine* : *Helaine* : *souveraine* :

---

[1] In view of the positive evidence of this rime and those cited above, *ayme* (AMAT) : *flamme* : *femme* : *blasme* : *flame* : *enflame*, *Blason des Faulses Amours*, str. 105, and *clame* : *l'ame*, *Passe Temps de tout Homme et de toute Femme* 1083 must be accepted as Latinisms without evidence for the history of our syllables. Similar rimes are cited by Metzke, *Der Dialect von Ile-de-France im* 13. *und* 14. *Jahrhundert*, *Herrig's Archiv*, LXV, p. 61. The same is probably true of *claime* : *aime* : *semme* (SEMINAT) : *reme* (=*rame*) in Christine de Pisan, *Débat de deux Amants*, 484.

[2] Villon rimes also *ien* with *ā* as in *ancien* : *Valerien* : *an*, *Grant Test.* 1552. A similar rime is *anciens* : *sciens* in Guillaume Alexis, *Le a b c des Doubles* 113. The editors Piaget and Picot in a note to this line cite *anciens* : *Cananeans*, *Mist. Viel Test.*, III–23050, and *crestiens* : *ceans*, Montaiglon, *Recueil*, I–53, to emphasize the fact that similar rimes are occasionally found in other authors of this same period. We may add *ancienne* : *Adriane* : *sienne*, Guillaume Alexis, *Martyrologue des Fausses Langues* 198, *Adriane* : *moyenne*, *ibid.* 209, as showing the same liberty also for the feminine form of this ending. Yet the regular pronunciation of this author was *iène*, as shown by the rimes *sienne* : *reviengne*, *Faintes du Monde* 266 and *preigne* : *appartiengne*, *Passe Temps de tout Homme* 3703. Cp. also Nyrop, *Gram.* I, § 218.

seraine, I–337, *Heleine* : *aveine* : *alaine* : *plaine*, I–418, *Philo-mene* : *meine*, I–488, *peine* : *Clymene*, II–175.

We must now face the difficult question how this rather definite evidence of these rimes extending over a period covering several centuries can be harmonized with the statements of the early grammarians [1] in regard to the pronunciation of our syllables. The natural interpretation of the rime of *ain* or *ein* with *oin* as meaning *ēn* : *oēn* appears to be invalidated by the fact that the early grammarians teach that these syllables arrived in the 16th century with a full pronunciation of their diphthong. To harmonize this discrepancy it might be argued that the grammarians were influenced in their statements by the written form of the syllables. Yet this point of view is scarcely tenable in view of the rather positive assertions made by the more accurate among them, who even go so far as to make use of phonetic transcriptions, as Meigret and Baïf; Cp. Thurot, *l. c.*, p. 342. Or it might be maintained that the popular pronunciation differed from the literary. The people said *ēn*, but good taste demanded *ēin*. Here we are met by the fact that the earlier authorities are practically unanimous in their statements, and that we have in general little evidence of such discrimination on their part. There seems no possibility of avoiding the acceptance of their testimony as fairly exact, and if this be so, our problem consists in finding the explanation which will coördinate their assertions with what seems to be the evident history of our syllables. In an article on *The Pronunciation of the French Nasal Vowels in ain ein in the XVI and XVII Centuries* published some years ago in the *Publications of the Modern Language Association*, IX, pp. 451–461, I endeavored to interpret this whole body

---

[1] Cp. Thurot, *De la Prononciation Française*, Paris, 1881, vol. I, pp. 321 and 342.

of evidence from this point of view. I now desire to modify the conclusions reached there to a slight degree, on the basis of the material presented in this study.

The hidden difficulty of the whole problem probably lies in the value of the *n*. The *i* preceding it being originally a glide which developed between the nasalized *ā* or *ę̄* and the dental *n*, as in VANUM > *vāin*, PLENUM > *plę̄in*, it is evident that as long as this *n* kept its original value, which was the case when the syllables in question were final or followed by a consonant, or as long as *eine* was pronounced *ēine*, the conditions which had produced it originally continued to be potent, and *ēin* and *ēine* must have tended to retain the diphthongal value of their vowels. Here we have the explanation why the grammarians almost unanimously speak of a diphthong in this connection. It is perfectly possible, to be sure, to pronounce *ēn* without an intervening *i*, and that this was often done is proved by the rime licences which we have observed in the earlier portions of this study. But it must be borne in mind that, when *ēins* rimes with *ēns*, the dental *n* is still present, and the rime does not represent the modern pronunciation. And similarly the union of *eine* with *oine* or *ienne* means *ē(i)ne* : *oēne* or *iēne*, and not *ę̄ne* : *oęne* or *ięne*.

The fundamental changes, by which the modern value of our syllables was established, took place during the 16th century. At that period the dental *n* disappeared, the diphthong became a simple vowel, and the nasal vowel in the feminine syllable became an oral vowel, *ēï n* developed into *ę̄* and *ēine* into *ęnę*. How this change came about must be a matter of surmise. Probably the diphthong was at first nasalized throughout, *ēin* became *ę̄ïn*, and its second half then passed rapidly through *ę̄ēn* > *ę̄ę̄n* > *ę̄*. In the article cited I suggested a shifting of the accent from *ę̄́ēn* > *ę̄ę̄́n* for the latter half of the century. This presumption was based upon the interpretation of the statements of certain of the grammarians, which seem to demand such an inference. However, their language is obscure and it is not impossible that this interpretation is imperfect. A shift of the accent is certainly not necessary, for $\acute{\xi}\bar{e}n$ can become $\tilde{\xi}$ quite as easily as $\xi\acute{\bar{e}}n$, provided the dental n becomes silent. In the case of $\tilde{\xi}ine$ the process was not quite identical. Here the nasal quality of the vowel disappeared, and in consequence the diphthong ξi was readily reduced to a simple vowel, but the dental n remained; $\bar{e}ine$ become ξne.

If this point of view is accurate, the Old French rimes harmonize perfectly with the evidence of the 16th century grammarians, and it is seen that the growth of our syllables was constantly in a uniform direction toward their Modern French value.

III.

We may now turn to a group of texts in which the development made evident so far has not taken place, and where, on the contrary, *ein* has become *ain*.

Texts in assonances showing this development are enumerated by Engelmann, *l. c.*, pp. 22 ff. The evidence is contained in the *laisses* having *ai* and *ei* + *nasal* in assonance with *a* or *e* + *nasal* + *consonant*. Since *an* and *en* have here undoubtedly the value of *ãn*, it follows that *ain* and *ein* were pronounced *ãin*. Cp. the following assonances:

Aie d'Avignon—comence : Elainne : dame, p. 53.

Aiol—porpensent : Losane : Bretaigne : renge, ll. 8768 ff., *bataille : Chartres : kaine* (CATENA) *: arse*, ll. 8800 ff.

Ogier—demain : grant 2318, *France : atendre* 5970, *gentes : Romaine* 8497, *lantaine : cravente : poissance* 9034.

Renaus de Montauban—Karlesmaine : remaigne : ceigne : ensamble : Flandre : Romaine 142.

Amis et Amiles—parrain : *main* : *desirrans* : *approchant* : *vaillant* : *gaaing* : *sain* : *Romains* : *serjant* 2499, *plains* (PLE-NUS) : *sains* : *mains* : *certain* 3080, *couvent* : *volant* : *gent* : *serjans* : *forment* 1803.

Jourdains de Blaivies—Jordains : *dolàns* : *vans* (VENTUS) 2192, *parrain* : *certain* : *Jordain* 3034.

Very often *aigne* and *eigne* are joined to the words cited. To introduce these into the discussion at this point is contrary to the plan of this study, the object being to establish the pronunciation of *ain(e)* and *ein(e)* as a basis for the further elucidation of the history of *aigne* and *eigne*. It is sufficient therefore for our purpose at this point to note that in the texts cited above both *ain* and *ein* were unquestionably *āin*.

The search for similar proof in the rimed texts has proved rather fruitless. I am able, however, to cite the following pairs of *ain* : *an—Richars li Biaus*, *bans* (= *banc*) : *a(i)ns* 2007, *main* : *Flamain* (= *flamand*) 1607, *Floris et Liriope*, *meshaing* : *awan* 563, *Rom. de Renart*, *vilein* : *Brian* I b, 2981, *Octavian*, *ata*[*i*]*nt* : *garant* 2287.

While these assonances and rimes are few in number, it is interesting to note the rather circumscribed territory to which the majority of these texts belong. All have distinct Picard characteristics. *Aiol* and *Renaut de Montauban* are classified by Gröber, *Grundriss*, as Francian-Picard. *Richars li Biaus* is placed by Förster, ed. p. IX, in the neighborhood of the French-Belgian frontier, and Knauer[1] agrees in the main with this localisation. *Octavian* is a Picard text copied by an Anglo-Norman scribe.

In view of these facts the Picard origin of the trait under consideration becomes a pertinent inquiry. The help of the assonances and rimes being exhausted, our only resource can

---

[1] *Zur altfranzösischen Lautlehre*, Leipzig, 1876.

be the orthography, to be studied primarily in charters and original documents. Here we must move very cautiously, and conclusions can be established only within certain limitations. Yet where we find $e + n$ written constantly *ain, ein* being almost unknown, the inference is certainly justified, that in the opinion of the scribes the pronunciation was rendered more accurately by *ain* than by *ein*. Such is the case in the texts studied by Raynaud, *Le Dialecte Picard dans le Ponthieu*, Paris, 1876. In these original documents extending over the years 1254–1333 the orthography *ein* seems unknown ; cp. p. 67. The same is true of the documents of Champagne examined by Förster as the basis for his study of the language of Chrestien de Troies, cp. *Cliges*, pp. lxi–lxii. The same predominance of *ain* we find in the manuscripts of the following texts examined for the present purpose : *Aucassin et Nicolete, Dis dou vrai Aniel, Richars li Biaus, Ille et Galeron, Trouvères Belges (Beaudouin de Condé, Jean de Condé, Quenes de Béthune, Jacques de Baisieux), Guillaume de Palerne, Jean Bodel (Jeu de Saint Nicolas), Adam de la Halle, (Jeu de la Feuillée, Robin et Marion), Floris et Liriope, Robert le Diable, Durmart, Chevalier as deus Espees, Raoul de Houdenc, Philippe de Beaumanoir, Chronique de Floreffe,*[1] *Froissart*. If the argument of the orthography is of any value the pronunciation *ãin* for both *ain* and *ein* should be ascribed to these texts.

It is possible to control this conclusion to a certain extent by comparison with the modern dialects. Gilliéron's monumental speech atlas [2] (the first 16 fascicules) contains a number of maps of service in this connection. These tabulate the pronunciation of the words *bain, andain, main, essaim, étain, faim, douzaine, chaîne, faîne*. For all of them the pre-

---

[1] Cp. Peters, *Zs. f. rom. Phil.*, **XXI**, p. 12.
[2] *Atlas Linguistique de la France* por Gilliéron et Edmond, Champion, Paris.

10

ponderance of pronunciation in the whole *langue d'oïl*
territory is $\tilde{e}$ or en. However there are two regions where $\tilde{a}$
or $\tilde{a}n$ with various shades of vowel are the rule. These are
the Northern portion of the department of Manche with
sporadic instances in Calvados, and particularly the Northern
portion of Somme and the department of Pas de Calais, going
now and then over into the contiguous territory. The same
pronunciation is cited by Eggert, *Zs. f. rom. Phil.*, XIII,
pp. 375 and 380, for the patois of Val de Saire, La Hague,
Guernsey, and Jersey, and corroborated for the dialect of
Guernsey by Lewis, *Publications of the Modern Language
Association*, X, pp. 18–19 and 27–28. Now it is, of course,
entirely possible that we have here a modern development
of older $\tilde{e}n$ and $\tilde{e}ne$. Yet, if the development of *ein* into
$\bar{i}$ current in Modern Wallonian is taken into consideration,
cp. Gilliéron's *Atlas* and Horning, *Zs. f. rom. Phil.*, IX, pp.
482 and 484, together with that into $\bar{o}n$ as in $v\underset{.}{\bar{o}}n$ (VENA)
$av\underset{.}{\bar{o}}n$ (AVENA) $p\underset{.}{\bar{o}}n$ (PŒNA) in the same region, where an
older *ei* had become *oi* under the influence of a preceding
labial, the conclusion is made rather probable that the basis
of this modern $\tilde{a}$ is an older $\tilde{a}in$.

Now it is striking to note the number of texts in the list
just cited, which fall into the region described in a general
way by the words departments of Pas de Calais, Nord, and
Somme, though to be sure not all of them can be definitely
assigned to this section. This is the territory of the Picard
dialect, and these two facts taken together seem to establish
the conclusion that the development of *ein* to *ain*, made
evident by the overwhelming use of *ain* as the graphic
expression of the sound, is a characteristic of the Picard
dialect extending South into the Francian and Champenois.

The further question of the geographical expansion of
this trait the material at hand does not solve entirely. We
can give, however, some indications. According to Förster's

observations [1] it included the district of Champagne, and in that case the same pronunciation must be assigned to the *Roman de Galeran*, whose home probably lies in the department of Aisne. But its spread was stopped by the Burgundian dialects, where, as is well known, *ein* became *oin*, while *ain* remained, thus showing that the two syllables had not coincided. This is the condition in the *Lyon Yzopet*,[2] though this text contains one rime, *rainne* (RANA) : *poinne* (PŒNA) 165, of *a + n* with *ę + n*. The evidence collected by Görlich, *Der Burgundische Dialekt im xiii und xiv Jahrhundert*,[3] corroborates this statement. In the documents examined by him *a + n* is represented by *ain* and *ein*, very rarely by *oin*, p. 18, while *ę + n* appears regularly as *oin*, *ein*, *ain*, pp. 62 ff. Görlich is inclined to look upon *ain* in the latter case either as a stage in the development of *ein* to *oin*, or as a later secondary alteration of *oin*, but does not at all associate it with *ain* from *a + n*. Further North in Lorraine both *a + n* and *ę + n* are written *ain*, *ein* and *en*, as, for instance, in the *Lorraine Psalter*, and Apfelstedt, the editor [4] of the text attributes the value of *ẹ̄* to these various spellings. Occasionally the more Southern *oin* has crept in, but the former value is confirmed by the modern forms of the words in question. In the patois spoken between Metz and Belfort *a + n* has become *ę̄*, while *ę + n* is *ī*, except after a labial, in which case it has become *ǫ* or *ǫn*; cp. Horning, *Die Ostfranzösischen Grenzdialekte zwischen Metz und Belfort, Franz. Stud.*, v (1887), pp. 9 and 29–30.

Outside of the Burgundian-Lorraine region and yet closely related to it we may cite the *Roman de Fortune et Félicité* of the 14th century by Renaut de Louhans studied by Nagel

---

[1] *Cliges* von Christian von Troyes, p. lxii.
[2] Cp. Förster's edition of this text, *Altfrz. Bibl.*, v, pp. xxvii and xxxi.
[3] *Französische Studien*, xii (1889).
[4] *Lothringischer Psalter*, *Altfrz. Bibl.*, iv, pp. xii–xiii and xxi.

in *Zs. f. rom. Phil.*, XV, pp. 1–24. We there find such rimes
as *plainne* (PLENA) : *encïenne* : *fontainne* : *certainne*, *terrïennes* :
vainnes, *sains* : *fisiciens*, *chastellains* : *gardiens*, *biens* : *mains*
which, though not entirely conclusive, yet seem to point
rather toward the pronunciation *ẹn(e)*. In the direction of
the Wallonian we have the *Poème Moral* and the *Chronique*
of Philippe Mousket. Neither text allows satisfactory conclusions. The former seems to demand *ãin* for both *a* and
ẹ + n, but the argument is based entirely on the orthography,[1] and is unsatisfactory. Philippe Mousket rimes *ain*
and *ein*, and often *ain* is written for both.[2] The present
dialect of Namur, East of Tournai the probable home of
Philippe Mousket, has *ẹ̃* for both syllables ; cp. Nieder-
länder, *Zs. f. rom. Phil.*, XXIV, pp. 7 and 22.

Toward the West and Southwest the *ãin* region also had
its definite limits. We may note the *Roman de Carité et
Miserere* written probably at Molliens-Vidame near Amiens ;
cp. the edition of this text by van Hamel, Paris, 1885,
p. cxcv. Here we find in strophe 41 of the *Miserere* the
rime *pena* : *peine a*, which gives definite evidence for the
pronunciation *pẽine* at least. The modern dialects around
Amiens vary between *ẹ̃* and *ã* ; cp. Sütterlin, *Heutige Pikard-
isch-Französische Mundarten, Zs. f. rom. Phil.*, XXVI, pp. 289
and 297.

Before leaving this portion of our study it is necessary to
discuss briefly the *Estoire de la Guerre Sainte* written soon
after the year 1191 by Ambroise, an ordinary knight of the
third crusade in the army of Richard. Gaston Paris localized
this poem at Evreux. The text shows the usual confusion
in the rimes of *ain(e)* and *ein(e)*, *aindre* and *eindre*, *aint(e)*
and *eint(e)* and no proof for the pronunciation could be

---

[1] Cloetta, *Poème Moral, Rom. Forsch.*, III, pp. 49, 58 and 61.
[2] Link, *Die Sprache der Chronique Rimée*, Erlangen, 1882.

drawn from these, though Gaston Paris, p. xxvii of the edition, accepts *āin* as the common value.   The difficulty arises through the rimes of *aine* and *eine* with *iene*.   We have here such pairs as *Estienes* : *paienes* 10488, *cristiaine* : *paiene* 6353, *teriane* : *cristiane* 41, 3711, 3975, *cristiane* : *paaine* 2323, 3929, *chaane* (CATENA) : *cristiane* 3388, *chaane* : *paiane* 3935. On the basis of the last two pairs Gaston Paris believed (p. xxvii) that a double pronunciation of *iene* must be accepted, viz., on the one hand the normal one in *paiene crestiene*, and on the other *paiaine crestiaine*.   It is certain that the localization of this text at Evreux does not actually conflict with the argument which may be based upon the modern patois of this region; cp. above p. 664.   But on the other hand the evidence for *āin* is absent, except such as may be drawn from the orthography ; and it will be seen that this may be explained otherwise.   It should be noted in the first place that with the exception of *chaane* the ending *ane* is restricted to *teriane*, *cristiane*, and *paiane*, three common mediæval words, whose Latin forms were familiar to every copyist and might readily affect the French form without influencing the pronunciation.   If this point of view be valid, *chaane* would then be merely an adaptation of the word to its mate in rime.   If the scribe said *cristiene* and wrote *cristiane*, he could also write *chaane* and mean *chaaine*, which he couples with *demaine*, l. 9006.   A double pronunciation is imaginable for *cristiene*, but scarcely for *chaeine*.   In the next place it should be observed that *aine* meant *ẹne* for the scribe, which is evident from the following series of rimes : *Avesne* : *regne* 6177, 6637, *Charlemaines* : *regnes* 8479, *regne* : *cheveitaigne* 8607, *cheventaine* : *lointaine* 7087, *cristiaine* : *paiene* 6353. Unless we are much mistaken, therefore, the matter is much less complicated than Gaston Paris imagined, and we have in the language of Ambroise in this particular another example of the type of *R. Troie*, *B. Chron.*, and other texts examined above, p. 651.

The present investigation has shown, I think, two things.
On the one hand a continuous line of assonances and rimes
has been cited proving the development of *ain* in the direction of *ēin* > *ēn*, belonging to the Norman and subsequent
Francian dialect, and on the other evidence has been brought
forward showing that *ēin* had become *āin* and *ān* in a portion of the Picard and neighboring speech forms.

IV.

AIGNE—EIGNE.

While the mingling of *aine* and *eine* in rime is frequent
in French texts after the *Brandan,* the similar fusion of
aigne and *eigne* became customary much more slowly.
Of the Anglo-Norman texts in our list the first to show it
is the *Mist. Adam.* Here we have, ll. 618–621, the following sequence of rimes with partial assonance : *enseigne* :
feigne : *guerre* : *pleigne.* The inference that both *aigne* and
eigne were pronounced *ēñe* it is of course impossible to avoid.

Yet in spite of this long silence of the rimes on this point,
scrutiny of the earlier texts shows that this pronunciation
must have been common since the beginning of the 12th
century. In the *Brandan aigne* rimes with *aine* (*semaine* :
cumpaine 592) and *eigne* with *eine* (*meinet* : *enseignet* 714,
1114 ; cp. also ll. 215, 1110, 1252). Since *aine* and *eine*
are identical in sound, it follows that the absence of the rime
pair *aigne* : *eigne* cannot be due to a difference in pronunciation, and the same inference is legitimate also for the other
texts of this period; cp. *St. Laurent, ovraigne* : *peine* 67,
Adgar, overaigne : *peine* 2–99, 23–237, *desdeign* : *vilain* 30–
151. In the 13th century the fusion of the two syllables
in rime is more frequent; cp. *Angier, Gregoire, gaaingne* :
enseigne 147, *enfreingne* : *destreingne* 911, *enseingne* : *remeingne*

983, *Chardry, Set Dorm.*, *muntainne* : *enseinne* 911, *Guillaume le Maréchal, enseigne* : *remaigne* 2947, *enseigne* : *acompaigne* 3395, *pleingne* : *enseigne* 3823, *plaingne* : *ensenne* 4805, *Bretaingne* : *ensaingne* 6505.

No deductions claiming a conscious separation of the syllables in rime or inferences as to a difference of pronunciation should, however, be drawn from the fact that such rimes even at this time are not more frequent. This proportion is determined entirely by the nature of the words in point. Those with *aigne* are on the whole more frequently employed than those with *eigne*, and this comparative relation is quite well illustrated by the *Ipomedon* of Hue de Rotelande. In the 10578 lines of this poem I have noted only one example of fusion of the two syllables, *desdegne* : *gregne* 2389. At the same time *eigne* occurs only once in rime by itself, l. 5161, and pure *aigne* rimes are frequent.

On the continent the general picture is closely similar. The *Eneas* keeps *aigne* and *eigne* separate. There are 12 rimes in *aigne* (ll. 365, 3147, 4109, 4535, 5003, 5563, 6983, 7099, 7781, 8033, 9509, 10007), 4 in *eigne* (ll. 4523, 5569, 9485, 9897) and one of *aigne* with *regne, regne* : *plaigne* 1427. That *eigne* also might have rimed with *regne* is proved by *enseigne* : *demeine* 4523 and *regne* : *peine* 2523. The *R. Rou* contains 23 pure *aigne* rimes (ll. 25, 427, 515, 661, 671, 1513, 1831, 2597, 2629, 2697, 3931, 3937, 4115, 4481, 5095, 6099, 7593, 7951, 8685, 8715, 8717, 8719, 9143), 2 pure *eigne* rimes (ll. 1629, 3941) and only one instance of fusion, *deigne* : *greigne* 2607. We have seen above, p. 643, that Wace follows the same habit for *ain* and *ein*, but that it would be dangerous to base conclusions upon this fact, because fusion of these two syllables in rime is much more constant in the same author's *Brut*, and we may add here that this same text contains a rime showing mingling of *aigne* with *iegne*, (*vaigne* : *Bretaigne* 6072), a type which we shall presently meet in other texts.

The majority of the Norman texts in our list presents the same appearance as those just considered. The *Chron. Mt. S. Mich.* has 8 rimes in point, all in *aigne* (ll. 49, 501, 565, 783, 1131, 1491, 1649, 2277). The last in this list is *enfregne : maigne*, but here the source of the first word is INFRANGERE in the place of INFRINGERE. The *Liv. d. Man.* has only a single strophe (cciv) in *aigne* (*Espaigne : bargaigne : gaine : ateigne*), Marie de France does not mix these syllables in rime, either in the *Fables* or in the *Lais* with the exception of a single example to be cited presently. Beroul has 3 rimes in *aigne* (731, 2247, 4029), 2 showing fusion,[1] *saine* (*SANGINAT) : *enseigne* 777, *enseigne : Montaigne* 4017 and none in *eigne*. In Guillaume le Clerc's *Besant de Dieu* and *Bestiaire* there are 14 rimes divided as follows: 5 in *aigne*, Bes. Dieu 2355, 3213, Best. 149, 365, 1849 ; 4 in *eigne*, Best. 1247, 2941, 3075, 3601; and 5 showing fusion : Bes. Dieu desdeign : meheign 1767, *enpaigne* (IM-PINGAT) : *plaingne* 1903, *ovraignes : enseignes* 2095, Best. *enseigne : remaigne* 1571, *montaigne : enseigne* 2817. In the *Clef d'Amours* finally we note *aigne* pure 1437, *eigne* pure 2847 and *ouvrengne : ensengne* 2061, *compaignes : enseignes* 3133. That is to say, we have in these texts, taken as a whole, a majority of *aigne* rimes, due to conditions which throw no light on the pronunciation, a very much smaller number of *eigne* rimes, and constant examples of fusion between the two, showing that their pronunciation was identical.

We may now cite the rimes in these texts which aid in determining the pronunciation. These are in the first place *regne : plaigne*, Eneas 1427, *regne : peine*, ibid. 2523, *preigne* (*PRENDEAM) : *feigne*, Marie de France, Lanval 131, *pleig-*

---

[1] In view of this fact *fange : enseigne* 3801 and *enseigne : barnage* 4109 must be looked upon as doubtful readings ; cp. also Muret, *ed.*, p. xliv.

nent,: *blasteignent,* *ibid.* *Fables* 23–25, *entracompaignent* : *espraignent, Best.* 2903.   These must be considered in connection with certain rime pairs in Benoît de Sainte-More. In both poems commonly attributed to this author the commonest rimes are *aigne* : *aigne, eigne* : *eigne* and *aigne* : *eigne,* but in addition there are found a few in *aigne* or *eigne* with *iegne* as follows: *teigne* : *remaigne, R. Troie* 12985, *teigne* : *chastaigne, ibid.* 16851, *teigne* : *enseigne, ibid.* 18407, *teigne* :*maigne, B. Chron.* 17557, and also *aigne* : *PRENDEAM* as *ovraigne* : *preigne, B. Chron.* 19475, *compaigne* : *empreigne, ibid.* 22601.   That is to say we have here more extended evidence of a rime tendency just noted for Wace's *Brut* and Marie de France.   The *Clef d'Amours* points in the same direction with *plengne* : *tiengne* 613, *ensengne* : *contiengne* 2737, *prengnes* : *restraingnes* 401, and *prenge* : *avienge* 1143, *contiengent* :*mesprengent* 2067, *prenge* :*retienge* 2083, *aprenges* : *contienges* 2899, which are probably only variant spellings for the same phonetic value.

Presumably this value was *ēñe,* but of course the rimes themselves contain no evidence and it is quite conceivable that TENEAM and *PRENDEAM were pronounced *tāñe* and *prāñe.*   There is, however, another set of rimes in Benoît showing mixture of *aigne* and *eigne* with *aine* and *eine,* similar to those already noted for the earlier Anglo-Norman texts, and these throw very definite light on our problem; cp. *Seigne* (SEQUANA) : *Bretaigne, B. Chron.* 15044, *Seigne* : *compaigne, ibid.* 39751, *chevetaingne* : *conpainqne, R. Troie* 20419, *Heleine* : *chevetaingne, ibid.* 25863, *estreine* : *Heleine, ibid.* 5069.   Whatever vowel existed in *aine* or *eine* must have been heard also in *aigne* and *eigne,* and since this tended in the direction of *ēne,* cp. above, p. 651, it follows that *aigne* and *eigne* were sounded *ēñe,* and the rime *regne* : *plaigne, Eneas* 1427 agrees with this inference.

We may conclude, therefore, that in the Anglo-Norman

and Norman dialects both *aigne* and *eigne* were pronounced
ēńe, *PRENDEAM was *prēńe* and TENEAM, VENIAM had
become *tiēńe, viēńe* with further development into *tēńe* and
vēńe.

In our study of the history of *ain* and *ein*, after the
determination of the value of these syllables in Anglo-
Norman and Norman, we were led through the *Escoufle* and
Guillaume de Dole into a series of texts where these syllables
rime with *oin*. Only Rutebuef of our list shows the similar
mixture of *aigne* and *eigne* with *oigne*. Since the latter was
pronounced *oēńe*, there can be no question as to the value
of the former. Note the following rimes : *remeigne* : *enseigne*,
I–71, *remeigne* : *preigne*, I–71, *preigne* : *deigne*, I–150, *main-
teingne* : *veingne* : *compeingne* : *esloigne*, I–22, *poingne* : *so-
vrainne* : *moinne* : *essoinne*, I–163, *avaloingnes* : *lontaingnes* :
essoingnes, I–241, *enseigne* : *besoingne*, II–85, *ouvraingne* :
vergoingne, II–176, *coviegne* : *besoingne*, II–184, *souviegne* :
besoingne, II–294, *doingne* : *viengne*, II–376, *praingne* : *besoingne*, II–311. Since REGNUM, written *raine, raigne*, or
règne, rimes with this same class of words, cp. I–101, 127,
II–90, 206, 254, 283, 365, it follows that all were pronounced alike.[1]

The same fusion of the syllables in question with *oigne* is
to be found in the list of assonances from Gaufrey, p. 316,
already cited in part above, p. 655. To the words mentioned

---

[1] Metzke, *Herrig's Archiv*, LXV, p. 60, calls attention to the fact that
proper names like *Champaingne Alemaingne* in the Francian documents
studied by him are never written with *e* or *ei*, and that forms like *Champagne, montagne* are not infrequent. This leads him to accept the modern
pronunciation for the words in question. But the rimes which he cites
from Geffroi de Paris and Gautier de Coincy, in addition to those from
Rutebuef and other authors included in the present study, show such
absolute equivalence of *aigne* and *eigne*, that it follows that their value
must have been identical, and in a note on p. 62 he hesitatingly withdraws
his previous conclusion.

there, add *demaine* : *compegne* : *essoigne* : *ensengne* : *castengne* : *Couloigne* : *Sessoigne* : *grifaingne* : *Espengne* : *vergoigne* : *compengne* : *gaaigne* : *entente* : *jenne* (*=jeune*) : *essoigne* : *quarantaine* : *besongne* : *demouraine*.

The earliest texts ascribed by Suchier, *Altfrz. Gram.*, pp. 2–3, to this region cannot enter into the argument. The *Vie de Saint Thomas* has no rimes in point, and Marie de France, as we have seen, scarcely has either syllable at the end of the line. The still earlier texts, as the *Voyage Charl.* and the *Couron. Louis*, show only *aigne* in assonance with *a*; cp. *Charlemaignes* : *compaignes* : *France* : *remaignet* : *plaigne*, *Voy. Charl.* 783, *Charlemaigne* : *Alemaigne* : *Bretaigne* : *reiames* : *France*, *Couron. Louis* 10, a fact to be expected from the age of these poems. That neither should contain an assonance showing *eigne* : *e* is probably to be explained in a similar way as the relative proportion of *aigne* and *eigne* rimes in the later texts.

If we now look at the texts cited above, pp. 656 ff., in which evidence for the value of *ēn* = *ain* and *ein* can be found, we shall be able to observe some rather definite criteria for our problem in the case of some of them, while we shall find a great deal of obscurity in the case of others. Maistre Elie in his *Art d'Amour* rimes *aigne* : *eigne* and **PRENDEAM*; cp. *remaigne* : *ensaigne* 856, *compaigne* : *preigne* 370, *grevaigne* : *peine* 737, *ensaing* : *desdaing* 785. The author of the *Escoufle* joins *saigne* (SIGNAT) : *montaigne* 5089, *plaigne* (PLANEA) : *prengne* 1125, *daigne* : *prengne* 7839, *compaigne* : *aviegne* 5277, *remaingne* : *aviengne* 1675, *remaigne* : *raigne* (REGNUM) 2221, *Loheraigne* : *raigne* 5477, *i. e.*, *aigne*, *eigne*, *egne*, *iegne* and REGNUM rime in such a way that the conclusion is obligatory that all were pronounced alike either *ãñe* or *ēñe*. Now in this same text *ain* and *ein* are probably *ēn*, cp. above, p. 655, and since *losenge*, which rimes with *vos ain ge* 2877, is coupled with *aveigne* 7459, we are justified in accepting *ēñe* as the pronunciation of the author. *Guillaume de Dole*, which furnishes the earliest example of the fusion of *ain* with *oin* rimes *plaigne* : *Alemaigne* 3771, 5562, *enmainent* : *remaignent* 4085, and *Champaigne* : *apregne* 5, *regne* : *graine* 7, *regne* : *deerraine* 4134. The remaining rimes in point have *a* as tonic vowel, as ll. 972, 1084, 1654, 2560, 3068, 3542, or *ę* as 3582. If *aine* is correctly determined as *ēine*, then *regne* must be *rēñe* or *rēne* and *aigne* was pronounced *ēñe* as is proved by the filiation of *regne* : *aine* : *eine* : *aigne*.

The *R. Rose* also joined *ain* and *oin*. Here we find *aigne* : *eigne* (*Bretaigne* : *enseigne*, I–39), *aigne* : *iegne* (*compaigne* : *tiengne*, I–9), *eigne* : *iegne* (*enseigne* : *tiengne*, I–68), *aigne* : *PRENDEAM* (*refraigne* : *sorpreigne*, I–101, *prengne* : *chastengne*, II–215), *eigne* : *PRENDEAM* (*preigne* : *feingne*, I–321, *prengne* : *faingne*, II–129). Since *saine* rimes with *essoine*, I–73, and *poine* with *moine* (*MONACHUS*), I–100, we may accept *vaine* : *raine* (*REGNUM*), I–15 as meaning *vēne* : *rēne*, and we may infer that *aigne* and *eigne* were pronounced *ēñe*. In support of this conclusion we may cite also *lointaignes* : *taignes* (*TENEAS*), I–59, *lointaingne* : *tiengne*, II–216, and *Loheregne* : *règne*, I–25.

The *Miracles de Nostre Dame* show *maines* : *enseignes*, XII–580, *montaigne* : *ensaingne*, XX–449, *Bretaingne* : *reteingne*, XVII–883, *deigne* : *veigne*, IX–20, *deigne* : *esconveigne*, XIII–408, *viengne* : *enseigne*, XXI–535, XXII–1397, *aprengne* : *tiengne*, VI–392, *appartiengne* : *mesprengne*, VIII–1138. One rime, *compaigne* : *espargne*, III–1079, seems indeed to speak for the pronunciation *āñe*, but *Charles d'Orléans* has *espergne* : *preigne* : *enseigne* : *apreigne*, II–85 showing the correct form. For similar evidence cp. *espergne* : *Auverne*, *B. Chron.* 5039, *espergne* : *cerne*, *ibid.* 16258, *taverne* : *espergne*, *R. Rose*, I–168, *esparne* : *superne*, *Besant Dieu* 3167, and even as late as Marot we can find *espergne* : *Auvergne*, II–14.

The remaining texts[1] of this list present the following examples:

Eustache Deschamps — *paine* : *aviengne* : *empraigne* : *aviengne*, I–XVI, *montaigne* : *souspraingne*, I–LXXXII, *aviengne* : *plaingne* : *demaine* : *maine* and *empraingne* : *souvieingne* : *praingne* : *incertaine*, I–CII, *aviengne* : *Bretaingne* : *souviengne* : *reprangne*, I–CLVII, *foraine* : *Bretaigne*, II–CXCII, *reviengne* : *repraingne* : *maintiengne* : *enseigne*, II–CCXLVIII, *layne* : *apprengne* : *ensaigne* : *craingne* : *aviengne*, II–CCCV.

Guillaume Alexis—*Espaigne* : *peigne*, *Le a b c des Doubles* 485, *attaine* (= *atteigne*) : *hayne*, *Passe Temps de tout Homme et de toute Femme* 2897, *montaigne* : *enseigne*, *ibid.* 3535, *preigne* : *appartiengne*, *ibid.* 3703, *daigne* : *baigne*, *ibid.* 4323.

Villon—*Auvergne* : *Charlemaigne*, *Grant Test.* 382, *Bretaigne* : *enseigne* : *tiengne*, *ibid.* 1629, *paine* : *attaine* (= *atteigne*), *Poés. Div.* 190, *douzaine* : *Estienne* : *paine* : *sepmaine*, *Grant Test.* 1913, *Royne* (= *roẹne*) : *paine*, *ibid.* 1151, *Roynes* : *regnes* : *Renes* : *estrenes*, *ibid.* 414.

Marot—Only *contraignent* : *preignent*, I–146, and *daigne* : *enseigne* : *preigne* : *apprẹigne*, II–47, Epigram CXXII, *Espaigne* : *baigne*, I–259, 345, *montaigne* : *baigne*, I–470, 485, II–165, *baigne* : *gaigne*, II–152 show the older tradition. Most of the rimes in point agree with the modern pronunciation as

---

[1] *Christine de Pisan's* rimes are very unsatisfactory in this connection. The following list includes all those of interest, and no conclusions can be based upon them. The volumes examined contain no *eigne* rimes whatever, and no fusion of *aigne* : *eigne*. All rimes in point are exceedingly rare ; cp. *Alemagne* : *remagne*, *Livre du Duc des Vrais Amants* 717, *remaigne* : *Alemaigne*, *ibid.* 1709, *mahagnent* : *empregnent*, *Epistre au Dieu d'Amours* 645, *prengne* : *Bretaigne* : *compaigne* : *Alemaigne*, *Débat de Deux Amans* 1552. Nyrop, *Gram. Hist.*, I, p. 196, cites *Bretaigne* : *empreigne*, *Chemin de l. Estude* 3695. I may add here, because of similar interest and limited scope, *enseing* : *repreing*, *Guiot de Provins, Bible*, 1440, *praingne* : *Champaigne*, *Orieries de Paris*, 39, *souvienne* : *preingne*, *Mist. du Viel Testament* 1168, *advienne* : *preingne*, *ibid.* 3338.

campaigne : *Espaigne*, ɪ–63, and ɪ–117, 153, 195, 197, 232, 434 and *enseigne* : *enseigne* : *contraigne*, ɪ–82 and 125, 178.

The material presented in the preceding pages lacks without question here and there the precision that one would like to see in an argument of this kind. However, no other criteria are available. The answer to this vexing question must be sought in the rimes, and from the nature of things their meaning must be unraveled with care, and certainly without prejudice. This we have endeavored to do. We have shown that in the Norman dialect *aigne* and *eigne* must have had the value of *ēñe*. Passing into the Francian, we have found evidence of the same pronunciation through the mingling of these syllables with *oigne*, while at the same time they rimed with *iegne* and *PRENDEAM. Then we have seen *oigne* disappearing from this group, but we have noticed the others holding together until Marot's time. The rimes cited from Eustache Deschamps, Guillaume Alexis, and Villon show *aine* and *eine* mixed with them besides, and we have seen these latter in a previous chapter definitely used with the value of *ēne*. The conclusion which is forced upon us is inevitable. From the end of the 12th century until the time of Marot *aigne* and *eigne* in the Francian dialect both had the identical value of *ēñe*. There now remains the problem how the modern readjustment of these syllables into *añe* and *ęñe* is to be explained.

V.

Before taking up the consideration of this question we may study the history of *aigne* and *eigne* in the region where *ain* and *ein* had the value of *ãn*. Engelmann, *l. c.*, pp. 22–23, cites a few assonances showing the value of *ãñe* for both syllables. These are *lances* : *ensaignes* : *grifaigne* : *France*,

Charrois de Nîmes 975 ; *estrange : demande : regne : France : Alemaigne, Prise d'Orenge* 179. We may add *porpensent : Losane : Bretaigne : prendre : lance,* Aïol, CCXXII ; *descendre : ensengne : Franche : Losane : Charlemaine : pendre : feme, ibid.* CCXXV ; *chatainne : demande : mainnes : France, Amis et Amiles* 517 ; *chatainnes : Charlemainne : estraingnes : entrent, ibid.* 2042 ; *demorance : montaingne : lance, Jourdains de Blaivies* 1646.

The rimed texts present no similar evidence. The rime *bangne : espargne, Jacques de Baisieux, Trois Chev.* 247 is of interest mainly on account of the orthography of the first word, but the rime itself is not entirely above suspicion since *espargne* might be a graphic variant for *espergne*, though this is scarcely probable in this dialect. *Demanois : espaignois, Chev. as deus espees* 2767, is also striking for the same reason. The second word is *espanois* < HISPANENSIS, and the syllable *an* could be written *aign* only by a scribe for whom *aign* meant *ãń*.

Nor will the words with which *aigne* and *eigne* are coupled in rime serve to throw light on the problem. We find here, as before, *iegne* and **PRENDEAM*. Only REGNUM seems absent and limited to rimes with *aine* and *eine*. Not all the texts, however, join all these syllables. All four, *aigne : eigne : iegne : *PRENDEAM*, are found in *Ille et Galeron, Guillaume de Palerne, Richars li Biaus* and *Philippe de Beaumanoir* ; *aigne : eigne : *PRENDEAM* rime in the *Chevalier as deus Espees* and the *Roman de Galeran* ; and *aigne : eigne* only are coupled in *Durmart, Robert le Diable* and Froissart's *Meliador.* I do not add examples here to illustrate the nature of these rimes. A few specimens of each type could give no idea of the actual exclusion of the others and their general appearance will become sufficiently clear from the citations given for another purpose below.

. It follows that we have the same groups of rime words to

deal with as before, and the question of their pronunciation
cannot be solved with the evidence which they contain. The
only remaining avenue of approach is the orthography. We
are aware, of course, of the care that must be exercised in
basing an argument on such data. Yet certain orthographic habits can be observed in these texts which are
incompatible with the pronunciation *ēñe*.

1. *Eigne, iegne,* and *PRENDEAM* are constantly written
aigne. Cf. *entresaigne : baigne, Ille et Galeron,* 568, *Bretaigne: taigne* (= *tienne*)*, ibid.* 305, *ouvragne : vaigne* (= *vienne*)*,
Baudoin de Condé,* XXI–503, *empraignent : espaignent, Guill.
de Palerne* 9199, *convaigne : compaigne, ibid.* 5201, *con-
paigne : ensaigne, Robert le Diable* 3115, *chaigne* (= *CINGAT*) :
deschaigne, Chev. as deus Esp. 781, *Bretaigne : praigne, Galeran* 1620, *praigne : remaigne, Manekine* 449, *vaigne* (= *vienne*) :
remaigne, ibid. 2069. A complete list of the available examples would serve no purpose, for it would fail to give
an idea of the proportion of *aigne* outside of the rime in
comparison with the other ways of spelling the syllable, but
the constant recurrence of the *aigne* form in these texts compared with its more restricted employment in the *ēñe* group,
gives it nevertheless the force of a valuable argument at least
for the speech of the scribes who copied the manuscripts.

2. The parasitic *i* is often and in some texts quite regularly omitted. Cf. *Bretagne : adagne, Ille et Galeron* 1683,
remagne : Alemagne, ibid. 2663, *dagne : ensagne, ibid.* 382,
desdang : faing, ibid. 5407, *engagne : gaagne, Rich. li Biaus*
4189, *Espagne : compagne, ibid.* 4899, *Bretagne : estragne
Meliador* 2776.

3. *Eigne* and *PRENDEAM* are written *egne* and *engne.*
Cf. *ensengne : estraigne, Rich. li Biaus,* 3887, *pregne : com-
paigne, Ille et Galeron* 4803, *adengne : daingne, Jean de
Condé,* XXXV–13, *ensengne : mehangne, Jacques de Baisieux,*
V *lettres de Marie* 195, *plaingne : prengne, Guill. de. Pal.*

6697, *ensenges* : *montaignes*, *Rob. le Diable* 637, 1809, *en-senges* : *estranges, ibid.* 899, *ensegne* : *estraigne, ibid.* 2853, *ensengne* : *Bretagne, Meliador* 6799, *ensengne* : *acompagne, ibid.* 7125.

4. These syllables rime with *aine* = *āne.* Cf. *plaine* : *ensenge, Rob. le Diable* 2347, *fontaine* : *plaine* (PLANEA), *ibid.* 2351, *Charlemainne* : *painne, Rich. li Biaus* 15, *vaingne* : *fontainne, ibid.* 1253, *plainnes* (PLENAS) : *compaingnes, ibid.* 4529, *amainne* : *Espaingne, ibid.* 4769, *maine* : *remaigne, Chev. as deus Esp.* 2293, *deschaine* : *remaigne, ibid.* 1461.

5. EXTRANEUS appears as *estrange* and *estragne.* Cf. *estranges* : *blanges* (verbal noun from *blangier*), *Rob. le Diable* 4383, *ensengnes* : *estranges, ibid.* 899, 2123, *ensegne* : *estraigne, ibid.* 2853, *ensengne* : *estraigne, Rich. li Biaus* 3887, *com-paigne* : *estrange, Durmart* 3123, *Montaigne* : *estraigne, ibid.* 5353. Such rimes are incompatible with the pronunciation *ēñe.*

While these points could not in themselves serve as final arguments for the pronunciation, yet taken together they contain a certain cumulative force, which points to the value *āñe* for the texts in question, but the nature of the material on hand does not permit us to draw more definite conclusions.

We refrain from undertaking to determine the geographical limits of this phenomenon. The material for this investigation is here even less satisfactory than in the case of *ain* and *ein.* We may admit that it included Champagne. Chrestien de Troie rimes *aigne* : *eigne* : *iegne* : *PRENDEAM.* Cp. *Bretaigne* : *ansaingne, Yvain* 1, *remaingne* : *praingne, Cliges* 2553, *ansaigne* : *apraingne, Yvain* 4957, *desdaing* : *praing, Erec* 4025. For *aigne* : *iegne* there exists only the isolated rime *plaingne* : *vaingne, Cliges* 3077. Usually *iegne* written *aingne* is kept distinct. Gace Brulé rimes only *aigne* : *eigne* : *PRENDEAM.* Cp. *plaigne* : *ensaigne*, VIII–18, *apraigne* : *remaigne*, VIII–26, *adaigne* : *apraigne*, XVII–32.

11

However, Burgundy, as in the case of *ain* and *ein,* did not share in this development. The *Lyon Yzopet* has *oigne* for *eigne,* while *aigne* has remained; cp. *compaigne : deplaigne* 503, *aplaigne : acompaigne* 859, *complaignent : raignent* (REGNANT) 1121, and *ensoigne : proigne* (*PRENDEAT) 319, 1417, *besoigne : ensoigne* 529, 3007, *doigne* (DIGNAT) : *vergoigne* 999, *ensoigne : cyoigne* 1165, *enproigne : ensoigne* 3387, *besoigne : doigne* 3505. There is no example of fusion of *aigne : eigne* > *oigne.* The material, collected by Görlich, *Burgund. Dial.,* pp. 34 and 63, shows that these examples represent the general habit of this region. *Aigne* is written *aine, ayne, eigne, egne, enne,* very rarely *oigne,* and *eigne* becomes usually *oigne,* though there is occasional interchange with the former group in the orthography.

The *Estoire de La Guerre Sainte,* which on the basis of its development of *ain* and *ein* we were inclined to place with *R. Troie* and *B. Chron.,* agrees with this same group of texts for *aigne* and *eigne.* As in the *R. Rou* the majority of rimes in point show *aigne;* cp. 99, 347, 995, etc., in all 42 rimes. There is one pure *eigne* rime, l. 6225, *regne* rimes with *Charlemaine* 8479, and with *cheveitaigne* 8607, and we must cite besides the isolated *empraine* (IMPREGNAT) : *enpraine* (*IMPRENDEAT) l. 5. With this enumeration the evidence for the pronunciation of our syllables in this text is exhausted, and we believe it should be joined to the rimes of the Norman texts in general, and interpreted together with them.

VI.

We may now endeavor to explain the difference in the modern pronunciation of *montagne, châtaigne, enseigne* and the like. From the preceding pages it has become evident that not one of the long list of texts, Marot included, makes use of the syllables *aigne* and *eigne* with their modern value.

Both rime without distinction during the whole of the Old French period and were pronounced either *ẽñe* or *ãñe*, depending upon the dialect to which the text belongs. Bearing this fact in mind, we may examine the history of *a* and *ẹ* + *ñ* as outlined in the Grammars.

According to Behrens[1] a parasitic *i* developed before *ñ* when it was final or followed by a consonant, but not when it stood in medial position, so that we should have *compaing*, *baing*, *enseint*, but *compagne*, *bagne*, *ensegne*. The *i*, which so constantly appears also in the second group of words, is looked upon as merely graphic. It is evident that this explanation is intended to suit the modern form of the words in question; for if it is correct, *bain*, *gain*, *refrain* are regular as well as *gagner*, *Bretagne*, *Allemagne*, *montagne*, while *baigner*, *plaignons*, *craignons*, and the like can find a ready explanation on the basis of analogy. However, it is overlooked that then *araigne*, *musaraigne* and *châtaigne* are not provided for, and that the rule does not explain the constant union of *a* + *ñ* and *ẹ* + *ñ* in rime in Old French. The further assumed difference between *a* or *ẹ* + *final ñ* and *a* or *ẹ* + *medial ñ* it is difficult to test, since the *i* before *ñ* is usually written in either position. Where it is absent before the medial *ñ*, it may also disappear before the same sound in final position, as *desdang* : *faing*, *Ille et Galeron* 5407, *song* : *beson*, *ibid.* 5780, though it is true that such examples are rather rare, and ordinarily the *i* is written before final *ñ*, even where it is absent in the medial position.

Suchier's explanation[2] differs fundamentally from the preceding. He maintains that in the Francian dialect *ñ* developed a parasitic *i* before it when it preceded the accent as in *plaignons*, *joignons*, *Bourguignon*. The diphthong

---

[1] Schwan-Behrens, *Altfrz. Gram.*, § 203.

[2] *Altfrz. Gram.*, p. 72.

created in this way could enter the tonic syllable (*baigne*), ·
and this happened particularly often in the case of *ēi*. This
new diphthong *ēi* then shared in the common development
of *ēi* > *āi* toward the middle of the 12th century. As
earliest example of this development he cites *ensaignet*,
Mont. Ps. 17–37.

The evidence presented in this study precludes in my
opinion the possibility of accepting this explanation of the
problem. There is no proof that in the Norman and Anglo-
Norman dialect *ein* and *eign* developed in the direction of
āin and *āiń*; on the contrary, all the evidence available
points strongly to the conclusion that *ain* and *aign* became
ēin and *ēiń*. If this be so, *ensaignet* in the *Mont. Ps.* can
only be the earliest evidence of the graphic confusion caused
by the coincidence of the two sounds. Furthermore one is
tempted to ask how Suchier would prove that accented *a*
and *e* followed by *ń* become *āń* and *ēń*, while pretonic *a*
and *e* + *ń* developed into *āiń* and *ēiń*. Certainly the orthography of the *Mont. Ps.*, the *Camb. Ps.*, and the *Q. L. D. R.*
permits of no such conclusion, for in these texts *ń* appears as
ign or *gn* in all positions, regardless of the accent, and the
rimed texts give no evidence for the unaccented syllables.

If *eigne* toward the middle of the 12th century became
aigne, it would have to be shown in the next place when and
where the modern readjustment of the pronunciation of these
syllables was effected, and how *eigne* = *āńe* changed back
to *ēńe* again, while *aigne* = *āńe* retained its Old French value.
We have seen that no evidence of such a division is visible in
the Old French texts. As far as the rimes are concerned,
both syllables are identical in all words of this group from the
end of the 12th century until Marot's time. The pronunciation of both developed in a uniform direction during the
whole of this period, and the conclusion which we have
reached is the only one justified by the evidence before us.

This value of *ēñe* for both *aigne* and *eigne* was slow to disappear. Malherbe still rimes *compagne*:*dedaigne* (*Larmes de Saint-Pierre*); Tabouret[1] in 1584 states that of the words in *eigne* '*la pluspart peuvent rimer avec aigne*', and Lanoue[2] in 1595 reiterates '*ces deux terminaisons n'ont qu'une pronontiation.*'

Yet there is evidence that the modern pronunciation was becoming established during this same period. Meigret[3] writes *accompañé*, *añyao* (*agneau*), *montañes*, *Çharlemañe*, *Çhampañe*, *Hespañol*, *Montañart*, *Hespañe*, *accompañant*, only once *accompaiñé* and *pleñet* (*plaignent*) for words with Latin *a*, and *dedeñans*, *creñans*, *creñet* (*craignent*), *creñez* (*craignez*), *peñons* (*peignons*), *enseñe* (*enseigne*), *enseñé* for words with Latin *e*. Baïf[4] has *gaŋera* (*gagnera*), *montaŋe*, *gaŋer*, *konpaŋ*' (*compagne*), *akonpaŋeront* but *éŋeœs* (*agneaux*), *ŋeleş* (*agnelets*) and *beiŋera* (*baignera*), *deiŋa* (*daigna*), *anseiŋement* (*enseigne*ment), *anséŋér* (*enseigner*), *anseiŋe*, *deiŋe* (*daigne*), and many other examples equally regular from the modern point of view.

Among the various influences which must have been potent in establishing the modern pronunciation we may mention in the first place that of the orthography. Though *aigne* was pronounced *ēñe*, yet the orthography to a very large extent had retained *aigne*, though it is true, as has been shown, that *eigne* is very frequently used in its place. The written form *aigne* might cause a certain hesitation as to the proper pronunciation of the syllable. The *i* might have been looked upon as belonging to *gn*, and just as *aille* was pronounced *al'e* so it might have been felt that *aigne* should be pronounced *añe*. That this sort of reasoning actually did

---

[1] Thurot, *l. c.*, I, p. 330.   [2] Thurot, *ibid.*

[3] Meigret, *Le Tretté de la Grammere Françoeze*, published by Förster, Heilbronn, 1888.

[4] Jean Antoine de Baïf's *Psaultier*, published by Groth, Heilbronn, 1888.

take place seems to follow from the statement of Palliot (1608) cited by Thurot, l. c., I, p. 330. 'Je sçay bien qu'il y a des diphthongues quil vauldroit mieux laisser et n'en retenir que la premiere voyelle plustost que de les écrire ny proferer : tant il s'y donne un mauuois air par des mal-embouchez et mauplaisants prononceurs. Comme celle d'*ai* en *Bretaigne, montaigne, Champaigne, aigneau :* où ils semblent avoir le mords trops serré et se gourmer par trop, à en faire la petite bouche, les prononçantz en *ei, eigneau, Breteigne, monteigne, Champeigne.*'

In the next place it is certain that during the period of reconstruction, when the Old French changed to the modern language, the larger portion of the words in *aigne* fell into disuse. Only a fraction of the Old French rime words in *aigne : eigne* has passed into the modern vocabulary. Of those which remained a certain number readily suggested the Latin word from which they derived, as *Allemagne, Charlemagne, Romagne, Espagne, Pretagne.* The Latin influence which pervaded the language at that time could without difficulty re-establish the original vowel in these words.

Other words with similar ending were introduced at that time from the Italian or the Spanish, as *campagne* < Italian *campagna, pagne* < Spanish *paño.* Both words are interesting for their form. The former occurs first in Marot, cp. *Dict. Gén.* s. v., the first instance of the latter is found in the correspondence of the Père Nacquard in 1650, cp. *ibid.* s. v. In both cases the influence of the traditional orthography is so strong that they are written *campaigne* and *paigne.*

Still other words were influenced by their Italian, Spanish, or Provençal cognates. So *quoquaigne*[1] becomes *cocagne*

---

[1] The word is quite rare in Old French literature. Godefroy cites it, II, p. 164, from *Aimery de Narbonne* (: *remaigne*) and the *Enf. Ogier* (: *engaigne*). Two other references can be found in vol. IX, Suppl. s. v., both in rime

under the influence of Italian *cuccagna*; *champaigne* changes
to *champagne* under the influence of It. *campagna*, Sp. *cam-
paña*, Prov. *campanha*; *compaigne* is affected by It. *com-
pagna*, Sp. *compaña*, Prov. *companha* in spite of the different
gender, and Old French *gaigner* loses its *i* through association
with It. *guadagnare*, in spite of the noun *gain*; and from
these simple words the new pronunciation finds its way
readily into the derivatives, so that we have *compagnie*, *compagnon*, *compagnard* and the like. Similarly *montaigne*
becomes *montagne* under the influence of It. *montagna*, Sp.
montaña. The old orthography has here lived on in the proper
name *Montaigne*, and thereby caused the continuance of the
older pronunciation. Note also the proper name *Champaigne* in rime with *peigne*, *Cyrano de Bergerac*, I, scene 2,
cited by Nyrop, *Gram. Hist.*, I, p. 196.

As far as I know, this list exhausts the modern words[1] in
-*agne*, with the exception of the learned name *Ascagne*, (the
Eneas, 1. 773, has *Ascanius*) and the geographical names
Cerdagne and *Mortagne*.

Other words withstood this influence and retained their
original and regular form. These are in the first place the
nouns *araigne*, *musaraigne*, and *châtaigne*. The reasons for
this isolation remain obscure. It. *aragna* and *castagna*, Sp.
araña and *castaña* might have exercised similar influence
here as in the preceding list. That it was at work is shown
by the rime *compagne* : *aragne* in La Fontaine, *Fables*, III, 8.

The verbs finally have retained their original pronunciation. *Plaignons* is determined by the forms of the paradigm
without *ń*, as *plaindre*; in others the orthography has been

---

with *aigne*. The word occurs also in *Joufroi*, cp. Langlois, *La Société française au XIIIe siècle*, Paris, 1904, p. 42, but the text being beyond my reach
I am not able to verify the reference.

[1] *Bagne* is a comparatively recent importation from the Italian, cp. *Dict.
Gén.* s. v.

changed under the influence of the older confusion, as in *atteindre, atteignons*, or *enfreindre*, O. Fr. *enfraindre*, and *fraindre*. For *saigner* and its derivatives *saignée, saignant, saignement* no apparent reason suggests itself, but *baigner* retains its old vowel because of *bain*.

The words with $ę + \acute{n}$ on the other hand have not varied ·in their pronunciation. The causes which influenced the change of *aigne* to *añe* would have served to strengthen the pronunciation of *ęñe* for *eigne*. Hence we have *enseigne, teigne, peigne*, and all the verbs in *-eindre*, as *astreindre, étreindre, restreindre, teindre, feindre, peindre*, and *éteindre*, which in certain forms of the paradigm contain the syllable *ęñ*. Some words in this group show *ain* or *aign* through orthographic confusion, as *Sardaigne* (SARDINIA) *daigner* (DIGNARE), *dedaigner*, and *contraindre-contraignons*. The whole conjugation of *craindre* is due to analogy with the *aindre* verbs, and similar influence of the *eindre* class has determined the orthography and conjugation of *geindre, empreindre*, and *épreindre*.

JOHN E. MATZKE.

We are told that Louis XIV once submitted a sonnet he
had written to the judgment of Boileau, who said, after
reading it: "Sire, nothing is impossible for your Majesty.
You set out to write some bad verses and you have succeeded." The point of this story for the modern reader lies
not so much in the courage of the critic as in the meekness
of the king. With the progress of democracy one man's
opinion in literature has come to be as good as another's
—a deal better too, the Irishman would add—and such
words as deference and humility are in a fair way to become
obsolete. We can scarcely conceive to what an extent men
once allowed their personal impressions to be overawed and
held in check by a body of outer prescriptions. Only a
century ago an Edinburgh reviewer could write: "Poetry
has this much at least in common with religion, that its
standards were fixed long ago by certain inspired writers
whose authority it is no longer lawful to question."[1] Racine
tells us that the audience did not dare laugh at the first performance of his comedy *Les Plaideurs* for fear that "it
might not laugh according to the rules."

. The revolt came at last from this tyranny of the "rules,"
and the romantic critics opposed to the neo-classic narrowness a plea for wider knowledge and wider sympathy; they
would see before they began to oversee, and be historical
rather than dogmatic; they would neither exclude nor conclude but explain; above all, they would be appreciative, and
substitute the fruitful criticism of beauties for the barren

[1] Article on Southey, *Edinburgh Review*, Oct., 1802.

criticism of faults.   The one weakness of this whole modern
school has been its proneness to forget that knowledge and
sympathy are after all only the feminine virtues of the critic.
Hence the absence of the masculine note in so much recent
criticism, hence the tendency of judgment to be swallowed
up completely in sympathy and comprehension.   "Tout
comprendre, c'est tout pardonner."   Renan one of the most
perfect embodiments of the ideal of wider knowledge and
wider sympathy, says that when anyone was presented to
him he tried to enter into this person's point of view, and
serve up to him his own ideas in advance.   One thinks
almost involuntarily of Dr. Johnson and of how, when
people disagreed with him, he "roared them down;" of how
men like Reynolds and Gibbons and Burke ventured to
present their protest to him only in the form of a Round
Robin so that the awful Aristarch might not know on whom
first to visit his wrath.   It is of course well, and indeed
indispensable, that the critic cultivate the feminine virtues,
but on condition, as Tennyson has put it, that he be man-
woman and not woman-man.   Through neglect of this truth
criticism has tended in its development during the past
century to become first a form of history and then a form of
biography and finally a form of gossip; until of late it seems
to be falling into its "anecdotage."   Sainte-Beuve says that
in studying a writer we should never fail to ask ourselves
such questions as the following: "How did he behave in the
matter of women and of money?   Was he rich or poor?   What
did he eat and drink and what were his daily habits?   Finally
what was his vice or weakness?"[1]   Sainte-Beuve would
have us pursue these inquiries in the name of what he terms
la grande curiosité.   But the danger is manifest that this
"grand" curiosity will degenerate in the hands of critics less

---

[1] *Nouveaux lundis*, t. III, p. 28.

discreet and tactful than Sainte-Beuve into curiosity of the petty or even the prurient type. There has sprung up in this country a whole class of publications that purport to be critical but are in reality only repertories of illustrated gossip. One of the most popular of American periodicals recently advertised the following attractions: "Henry Van Dyke as he lives in the open, in camp with his children; at his favorite sport of fishing; just as he feels a 'bite,'—in separate strikingly new pictures; also Mr. William Dean Howells hoeing corn, mowing the grass; and Mark Twain trying to coax a rabbit, and with his 'porcelain cat.'" Authors who are dealt with in this fashion would have a right to complain with the Rev. Dr. Folliot[1] that they have been "dished up like a savory omelette to gratify the appetite of the reading rabble for gossip;" and sympathize with that gentleman when he adds indignantly: "What business have the public with my nose and wig?" Sainte-Beuve himself is not above commenting on Michaud's finger-nails ("*il les avait fort noirs, les ongles*"),[2] and used occasionally to invite in to dinner the cook of Dr. Véron so that he might gossip with her about the great personages of the Second Empire.[3]

One should hasten to add in the case of Sainte-Beuve that he labored during the latter part of his life to correct, or one might more fairly say to complete, his own earlier method and to assert once more the supremacy of judgment.[4]   It is

---

[1] In T. L. Peacock's *Crotchet Castle.*

[2] *Causeries du lundi*, t. XI, p. 486.   [3] *Nouvelle Correspondance*, p. 226.

[4] For Sainte-Beuve's earlier ideal, which would reduce the critic's rôle to pure comprehension and sympathy, see *Pensées de Joseph Delorme* (*Pensée XVII*). This passage has been appropriately selected by Lemâitre as epigraph for his impressionistic *Contemporains*. Sainte-Beuve's change to a more judicial attitude took place about 1848. For important evidence of this change see *Chateaubriand et son groupe littéraire*, t. II, p. 114 ff. Cf. also *Portraits littéraires*, t. III, p. 550: "En critique, j'ai assez fait l'avocat, faisons maintenant le juge."

curious to trace the transformation of the militant romanticist
of 1830 into the conservative who finally extols as the true
type of the critic Malherbe and Boileau and Dr. Johnson.
He follows these men in founding his own judgments for
the most part on the traditional standards of the classicist,
yet no one knew better than Sainte-Beuve that these standards were doomed. "Soyons les derniers des délicats," he
exclaims. "Let us be the last of our kind before the great
confusion." [1]

The "great confusion" that Sainte-Beuve foresaw is now
upon us. He himself has been correctly defined in his
influence on his successors, not as a defender of standards
and judgment, but as a great doctor of relativity. Now
nearly all recent criticism, so far as it is anything more than
a form of gossip and small talk, may be roughly classified as
either impressionistic or scientific; and it is in this doctrine
of relativity that both impressionistic and scientific critics
unite. To be sure, the doctrine assumes with the impressionist a form closer akin perhaps to true criticism than in
the case of the scientific critic, whose method tends only too
often to dehumanize the study of literature completely.
The impressionist is interested in a book only as it relates
itself to his sensibility, and his manner of praising anything
that makes this appeal to him is to say that it is "suggestive."
The scientific critic for his part is interested solely in the
way a book is related as a phenomenon to other phenomena,
and when it is the culminating point or the point of departure of a large number of these relationships, he says that it
is "significant" (the favorite word of Goethe). If the impressionist is asked to rise above his sensibility and judge by
a more impersonal standard, he answers that there is no such
impersonal element in art, but only "suggestiveness," and is

---

[1] *Portraits littéraires*, t. III, p. 550.

almost ready to define art with a recent French writer as an
"attenuated hypnosis." If the scientific critic in turn is
urged, to get behind the phenomena and rate a book with
reference to a scale of absolute values, he absconds into his
theory of the "unknowable."

We may illustrate by a familiar passage from Taine, who
is easily the most eminent of those who have attempted to
make criticism scientific. "What do we see," he says in
his English Literature, "under the fair glazed pages of a
modern poem? A modern poet who has studied and
travelled, a man like Alfred de Musset, Victor Hugo,
Lamartine or Heine, in a black coat and gloves, welcomed
by the ladies, and making every evening his fifty bows and
his score of *bons mots* in society; reading the papers in the
morning, lodging as a rule on a second floor; not over
gay because he has nerves and especially because in this
dense democracy where we stifle one another, the discredit
of official dignities has exaggerated his pretensions, while
increasing his importance, and because the keenness of his
feelings in general disposes him somewhat to think himself
a god."

Now in the first place the results of this attempt to infer
from a poem the life and personality of the poet are strangely
uncertain. We read in the recently published letters of
John Richard Green that when Taine was in England getting information for the last volume of his English Literature, he began talking about Tennyson with Palgrave, a
great friend of the laureate. "Wasn't he in early youth
rich, luxurious, fond of pleasure, self-indulgent?" Taine
asked. "I see it all in his early poems—his riot, his adora-
tion of physical beauty, his delight in jewels, in the abandonment of all to pleasure, in wine, and . . . ." "Stop! stop!"
said Palgrave out of all patience. "As a young man Tennyson was poor—he had little more than £100 a year, his

habits were as they still are, simple and reserved, he cared then as he cares now for little more than a chat and a pipe, he has never known luxury in your sense." Taine thanked Palgrave for his information—and when the book came out Tennyson was found still painted as the young voluptuary of Taine's fancy.[1]

Even assuming that Taine's inferences could be drawn correctly, he would have us fix our attention on precisely those features of a poem that are least poetical. The very prosaic facts he is looking for would be at least as visible in the writing of some mediocrity as in a work of the first order. It is indeed when Taine starts out to deal in this fashion with a poet of genius like Milton, to reduce Paradise Lost to a mere "sign," that the whole method is seen to be grotesquely inadequate. "Adam," says Taine in his critique of Milton, "is your true pater-familias with a vote, an M. P., an old Oxford man," etc. He listens to the conversation of Adam and Eve, the first pair, only to hear "an English household, two reasoners of the period—Colonel Hutchinson and his wife. Good heavens ! dress them at once ;" and he continues in this vein for pages.

But, says M. Bourget, speaking for the impressionists, there is another way of approaching the volume of verse that Taine would treat solely from the point of view of its "significance;" and in rendering the "suggestiveness" of the volume to the impressionist sensibility, M. Bourget proceeds to employ a luxuriance of epithet that lack of space forbids our quoting. He asks us to imagine a young woman alone in her boudoir on an overcast winter afternoon. A vague melancholy steals upon her as she reclines at ease in her long chair; all a-quiver with ineffable longing, she turns

---

[1] *Letters of John Richard Green*, p. 372. Green's anecdote is perhaps not entirely fair to Taine's account of Tennyson as it finally appeared.

to her favorite poet. She does not surmise behind the delicately tinted pages of the beloved book the prosaic facts of environment, the obscure animal origins of talent that are so visible to Taine. What she does perceive is the dream of the poet—"the inexpressible and mysterious beyond that he has succeeded in throwing like a halo around his verses." For Taine the stanzas are a result; for the young woman "who intoxicates her heart with them so deliciously" they are a cause. "She does not care for the alembic in which the magic philter has been distilled, provided only this magic is operative, provided her reading culminates in an exquisite and trembling exaltation," and "suggests to her dreams either sweet or sad, but always productive of ecstasy." Who does not see, concludes M. Bourget, that entirely different theories of art are implied in the two ways of approaching the volume of verse ?[1]

The two theories are different indeed ; yet they are alike in this, that neither the "significance" of the volume to Taine nor its "suggestiveness" to M. Bourget affords any real means of escape from the quicksands of relativity to some firm ground of judgment. We may be sure that a third-rate bit of contemporary sentimentality will "suggest" more ineffable dreams to the young woman in the long chair than a play of Sophocles. To state the case more generally, how many books there are that were once infinitely suggestive and are still of the highest significance in literary history which yet intrinsically—in their appeal to what Emerson calls the "constant mind of man"—are now seen to be of very inferior value ! This is eminently true of certain writings of Rousseau, to whom much of the peculiar exaggeration of the "sens propre" or individual sense that one finds in

---

[1] Abridged from the chapter on Taine in *Essais de Psychologie contemporaine.*

the impressionists can ultimately be traced.[1] If the special modes of sensibility that impressionism exhibits go back to Rousseau, its philosophical theory may best be considered as a reappearance in modern thought of the ancient maxim that man is the measure of all things. This celebrated dictum became current at a decisive moment in Greek life and would indeed seem to sum up almost necessarily the point of view of any age that has cast off traditional standards. The all-important question is whether one interprets the maxim in the spirit of the sophists or in that of Socrates. The resemblance between the impressionistic and the sophistical understanding of the maxim is unmistakable; not only the individual man, but his present sensations and impressions are to be made the measure of all things. " All of us," says M. Anatole France, "judge everything by our own measure. How could we do otherwise ? since to judge is to compare, and we have only one measure, which is ourselves; and this measure is constantly changing. We are all of us the sport and playthings of mobile appearances." Perhaps no recent writer has shown more of the Socratic spirit in his use of the maxim than Emerson. " A true man," he says, belongs to no other time and place, but is the centre of things. Where he is, there is nature. He measures you and all men and all events." Though Emerson thus asserts the maxim, he has not therefore succumbed like M. France to the doctrine of relativity and the feeling of universal illusion that accompanies it ; on the contrary, he has attained to a new sense of the unity of human nature—a unity founded, not on tradition, but on insight. He says somewhere that he finds such an identity both of thought and sentiment in the best books of the world, that they seem to him to be the

---

[1] " Voici enfin Jean-Jacques, précurseur du xixe siècle, qui dans l'individu, c'est-à-dire dans le Moi affectif et passionnel, voit la mesure unique de toute chose." Pellissier, *Études de Littérature contemporaine.*

work of "one all-seeing, all-hearing gentleman." Now it is evidently this one all-seeing, all-hearing gentleman who is with Emerson the measure of all things, and the individual man only in so far as he has realized in himself this essential human nature. To be sure, the line is often hard to draw in practice between the two types of individualist. There were persons in ancient Athens—for example, Aristophanes in the *Clouds*—who treated Socrates as an ordinary sophist. In the same way, there are persons to-day who fail to see the difference between Emerson and an ordinary impressionist. "The source of Emerson's power," says Professor Santayana, "lay not in his doctrine but in his temperament." [1]

Emerson's language is often undistinguishable from that of the impressionist. "I would write on the lintels of my doorpost, *whim*." "Dream delivers us to dream, and there is no end to illusion." "Life is a flux of moods." But he is careful to add that "there is that in us which changes not and which ranks all sensations and states of mind." The impressionist denies this element of absolute judgment and so feels free to indulge his temperament with Epicurean indolence; at the same time he has the contemptuous indulgence for others that befits beings who are the "sport and playthings of mobile appearances." M. France says that he "despises men tenderly." We would reply in the words of Burke that the "species of benevolence which arises from contempt is no true charity." Impressionism has led to a strange increase in the number of dilettantes and *jouisseurs littéraires*, who have given to the precept *De gustibus non*— developments that would certainly have surprised its author. The Horatian plea for an honest liberty of taste has its necessary corrective in the truth that is very bluntly stated in a Spanish proverb: "There are tastes that deserve the

[1] *Poetry and Religion*, p. 218.

12

cudgel." [1]   We are told that Sainte Beuve was once so offended by an outrageous offense to good taste in a remark of Nicolardot's, that, yielding to an irresistible impulse, he kicked him out of the room.   Dante, in replying to a certain opponent, says with the instinct of a true Italian that he would like to answer such "bestiality not with words but with a knife."   We must remember that "good taste" as formerly understood was made up of two distinct elements: first, one's individual sensibility, and secondly, a code of outer rules by which this sensibility was disciplined and held in check.   The observance of these rules became for the community of well-bred people a sort of *noblesse oblige* and taste in this sense has been rightly defined by Rivarol as a man's literary honor.   Now that the outer code has been abrogated, taste is not therefore delivered over to the caprices of a vagrant sensibility ; taste is attained only when this sensibility is rectified with reference to an inwardly apprehended ideal, and in this sense may be defined as a man's literary conscience ; it is, in short, only one aspect of the struggle between our lower and higher selves.   Some indeed would maintain that taste is not a thing thus to be won by any effort of the will, but is rather an inborn and incommunicable tact, a sort of mysterious election, a free gift of the muses to a predestined few ; that in literature many are called and few are chosen.   In the article *Goût* of the Philosophical Dictionary Voltaire discourses on the small number of the elect in matters of taste, and in almost the next article (*Grâce*) turns all his powers of mockery on those who assert the same doctrine in religion.   Not only individuals but whole nations were once held to be under the reprobation of the muses.   As Voltaire says sadly, *presque tout l'univers est barbare.*   Perhaps even to-day persons might be found who

---

[1] "Hay gustos que merecen palos."

would reply in the negative to the famous query of Father Bouhours whether a German can have wit. There are only too many examples in Germany and elsewhere of how far infinite industry and good intentions are from sufficing for the attainment of taste. However it may be in theology, it remains true in literature, as Gautier remarks, that works without grace are of no avail.

But one may recognize an element of predestination in the problem of taste and not therefore acquiesce in the impressionist's preaching of the fatality and finality of temperament. Everyone, to be sure, has an initial or temperamental taste, but it is hard to say how far this taste may be transformed by subordinating it to the higher claims of our nature. Dr. Johnson says that if he had no duties and no reference to futurity he would spend his life in driving briskly in a post-chaise with a pretty woman. Here then is the temperamental taste of Dr. Johnson, and if he had been a disciple of M. France, he might have accepted it as final. Boswell reports an outburst of Johnson on this very subject: "Do not, Sir, accustom yourself to trust to *impressions*. By trusting to impressions, a man may gradually come to yield to them, and at length be subject to them, so as not to be a free agent, or what is the same thing in effect, to *suppose* that he is not a free agent. A man who is in that state should not be suffered to live ; . . . . there can be no confidence in him, no more than in a tiger."

Johnson would evidently have agreed with the Buddhists in looking on the indolent settling down of a man in his own temperament[1] as the chief of all the deadly sins. A fulmi-

---

[1] This is the full meaning of the Pâli term *Pamâda*. The opposite quality, *appamâda* or strenuousness—the unremitting exercise of the active will—is the chief of the Buddhist virtues ; this oriental strenuousness, one should hasten to add, is directed toward self-conquest and not, like the Occidental variety, toward the conquest of the outer world.

nation like the foregoing is good to clear the air after the
debilitating sophistries of M. France. Yet we feel that
Johnson's point of view implies an undue denial of the individual's right to his own impressions and that therefore it
has become in large measure obsolete. It is well for us after
all to have fresh and vivid and personal impressions; it is
well for us in short to awaken our senses; but we should
"awaken our senses that we may the better judge"—and
not simply that we may the better enjoy. For instance,
Walter Pater continually dwells on the need of awakening
our senses, but when he speaks of "living in the full stream
of refined sensation," when he urges us to gather ourselves
together "into one desperate effort to see and touch," there
is a hedonistic flavor in these utterances that can escape no
one. On the other hand, there should be no ascetic denial
of the value of the impression in itself. M. Brunetière is
reported to have said to another critic, whom he suspected of
intellectual epicureanism : " *You* always praise what pleases
you, *I* never do." [1] This is an asceticism of taste worthy of
the spectator of Racine's comedy who did not laugh for fear
that he might not laugh according to the rules. And so M.
Brunetière has been led naturally into his present reactionary
attitude; seeing only the evil possibilities of individualism,
he would have the modern man forego his claim to be the
measure of all things, and submit once more to outer authority. The seventeenth century critic attempted to establish a
standard that was entirely outside the individual. The
impressionist has gone to the opposite extreme and set up a
standard that is entirely within the individual. The problem
is to find some middle ground between Procrustes and Pro-
teus; and this right mean would seem to lie in a standard
that is in the individual and yet is felt by him to transcend

---

[1] See Lemaître, *Contemporains*, t. VI, p. xi.

his personal self and lay hold of that part of his nature that he possesses in common with other men.

The impressionist not only refuses the individual man any such principle of judgment to which he may appeal from his fleeting impressions; he goes farther and refuses men collectively any avenue of escape from universal illusion and relativity; he denies in short the doctrine embodied in the old church maxim "Securus judicat orbis terrarum," a doctrine so fundamental, we may note in passing, that as recast by Lincoln it has become the cornerstone of democracy : "You cannot fool all the people all the time." M. Anatole France is fond of insisting, like Sainte-Beuve before him, that there inheres in mankind as a whole no such power of righting itself and triumphing over its own errors and illusions. A whole chapter might be made up of passages from Sainte-Beuve on the vanity of fame. "Posterity has allowed three-fourths of the works of antiquity to perish," says M. France in turn ; "it has allowed the rest to be frightfully corrupted. . . . In the little that it has kept there are detestable books which are none the less immortal. Varius, we are told, was the equal of Virgil. He has perished. Aelian was an ass, and he survives. There is posterity for you," [1] etc. Here again the contrast between the two types of individualist is absolute. "There is no luck in literary reputation," says Emerson. "They who make up the final verdict for every book are not the partial and noisy public of the hour, but a court as of angels, a public not to be bribed, not to be entreated, and not to be overawed decides upon every man's title to fame. Only those books come down which deserve to last. Blackmore, Kotzebue or Pollock may endure for a night, but Moses and Homer stand forever. The permanence of all books is fixed by no effort friendly or hostile but by

---

[1] *Vie littéraire,* t. I, p. 111.

their own specific gravity or the intrinsic importance of their contents to the constant mind of man."

We should add, then, in order to define our critical standard completely, that the judgment of the keen-sighted few in the present needs to be ratified by the verdict of posterity.[1]

The keen-sighted few! We can hardly emphasize this part of our definition too strongly. For if it is not possible in literature to fool all of the public all the time, it is only too possible to fool all, or nearly all, the public some of the time, and some of the public all the time. The opposite view, which would value a book according to its immediate effect on the average man, may be called, for want of a better term, the humanitarian fallacy, and is at present one of the chief perils of criticism. Tolstoy, it will be remembered, defends this fallacy with logical thoroughness in his book on Art, and concludes that the crowning masterpiece of nineteenth century literature is *Uncle Tom's Cabin*. Emerson, who has been our guide thus far, can be of little service to us here. He had humanitarian illusions of his own—illusions that he shared with his whole generation—and it is unfortunately this, his weakest side, that has been caught by his disciples and enters as a chief ingredient into most of what passes nowadays for Emersonianism. "We," says Emerson, giving fresh expression to his favorite doctrine that man is the measure of all things, "We are the photometers, we the irritable gold-leaf and tinfoil that measure the accumulations of the subtle element. We know the authentic effects of the true fire through every one of its million disguises." One is naturally prompted to inquire whom Emerson means by this

---

[1] The appeal to the judgment of the keen-sighted few, as opposed to that of the many, first appears in Aristotle, who always assumes an ideal reader, whom he refers to variously as ὁ σπουδαῖος, ὁ φρόνιμος, ὁ εὐφυής. The principle of universal consent as applied to literature, is first clearly stated by Longinus (περὶ ὕψους, cap. VII).

"we." Granting that man is a photometer or measure of light, it is yet absurd to add, as Emerson at times comes dangerously near doing, that this ideal measure exists unimpaired in the average untrained individual. Elsewhere Emerson says of Goethe: "He hates to be trifled with and to repeat some old wife's fable that has had possession of men's faith these thousand years. I am here, he would say, to be the measure and judge of these things. Why should I take them on trust?" This may do very well for Goethe, but when the man in the street thus sets up to be the measure of all things, the result is often hard to distinguish from vulgar presumption. The humanitarian fallacy would be comparatively harmless if it did not fit in so perfectly with a commercialism which finds its profit in flattering the taste of the average man, and an impressionism that has lost the restraining sense of tradition and encourages us to steep and saturate our minds in the purely contemporaneous. As it is, these elements have combined in a way that is a menace to all high and severe standards of taste. To use words as disagreeable as the things they describe, literature is in danger of being vulgarized and commercialized and journalized. There are critics who have founded a considerable reputation on the relationship that exists between their own mediocrity and the mediocrity of their readers. Sainte-Beuve says that in writing "we should ask ourselves from time to time with our brows uplifted toward the hilltops and our eyes fixed on the group of revered mortals: What would they say of us?" We may contrast this advice with the familiar story of the American magazine editor who told his young contributor that there was an old lady out in Oshkosh and that he must always have her in mind and be careful to write nothing that would not be clear to her. It evidently makes a difference whether one write in the ideal presence of the masters or in that of the old lady in Oshkosh.

In Emerson's study at Concord, which remains as at the time of his death, almost the first object that meets one's eyes to the right on entering is a portrait of Sainte-Beuve. Emerson is said to have looked on this portrait as a special treasure. There is scarcely a single mention of Sainte-Beuve in Emerson's writings, and it is interesting to be able to connect even thus superficially men so different as the great doctor of relativity and the philosopher of the oversoul. The *Causeries du lundi* and a book like *Representative Men* are at the opposite poles of nineteenth century criticism ; yet for this very reason and in spite of his humanitarian illusions, —in spite we may add, of his curiously defective feeling for the formal side of art,—Emerson is the necessary corrective of Sainte-Beuve, who has infinite breadth and flexibility but is lacking in elevation. This lack of elevation in Sainte-Beuve is not an accidental defect, but as he himself was aware, bears a direct relation to his method. His own ambition, as he defines it, is to be a *naturaliste des esprits*, yet he never attempted in his moments of real candor to disguise the barrenness and helplessness of naturalism in dealing with the ultimate problems of life.[1] This inadequacy of both the naturalist and romantic points of view has been even more manifest in recent criticism. Sainte-Beuve himself maintained a happy balance between his regard for traditional standards and his aspiration toward wider sympathy and knowledge. This balance has not been preserved by his successors. Knowledge pursued as an end in itself and unsubordinated to any principle of judgment has degenerated into the narrowness of the specialist or into dilettanteism.[2] A too

[1] See, for instance, the striking passage in *Port-Royal* (t. II, p. 442) beginning "Un grand ciel morne, un profond univers roulant, muet, inconnu . . . ; l'homme éclosant un moment, brillant et mourant avec les mille insectes, sur cette île d'herbe flottante dans un marais," etc.

[2] A definition of the word dilettanteism as here used (a use perhaps more French than English) will be found in Bourget, *Essais de psychologie contemporaine*, p. 59.

exclusive emphasis on breadth and keenness of sympathy has led to the excesses of the impressionist. In certain contemporary critics—Mr. Saintsbury for instance—we see the running to seed of the modern critical school in much the same way that we see the running to seed of the classical school in critics like La Harpe. Mr. Saintsbury has extraordinarily wide knowledge and sympathy—all the needful virtues of the critic, in fact, except accuracy and judgment and taste.[1] Sainte-Beuve said of the critics of the First Empire that they were the "small change" of Boileau. If the critics of to-day are to be anything more than the small change of Sainte-Beuve—or rather of one side of Sainte-Beuve—they need to cultivate, as a counterpoise to their use of the historical and biographical method, a feeling for absolute values ; in short, they need to supplement Sainte-Beuve by what is best in a writer like Emerson. The point may be illustrated by two passages, each peculiarly impressive in its own way.

The first passage is from the end of *Port-Royal,* where Sainte-Beuve is commenting on his own efforts to attain the truth : " How little it is after all that we can do ! How bounded is our gaze—how much it resembles a pale torch lit up for a moment in the midst of a vast night ! And how impotent even he feels who has most at heart the knowing of his object, who has made it his dearest ambition to grasp it, and his greatest pride to paint it—how impotent he feels and how inferior to his task on the day when, this task being almost terminated and the result obtained, the intoxication of his strength dies away, when the final exhaustion and inevitable disgust seize upon him, and he perceives in his turn that he is only one of the most fugitive of illusions in the bosom of the infinite illusion !"

---

[1] Mr. Saintsbury is naturally at his worst in his treatment of Boileau (*History of Criticism,* Bk. V, Ch. I). Some of the inaccuracies and absurdities of this chapter were pointed out in a review in the *New York Independent* (January 29, 1903).

And then in contrast to this the last paragraph of Emerson's essay on Illusions: "There is no chance and no anarchy in the universe. All is system and gradation. Every god is there sitting in his sphere. The young mortal enters the hall of the firmament; there he is alone with them alone, they pouring on him benedictions and gifts and beckoning him up to their thrones. On the instant and incessantly fall snow-storms of illusions. He fancies himself in a vast crowd which sways this way and that and whose movements and doings he must obey. . . . Every moment new changes and new showers of deceptions to baffle and distract him. And when by-and-by for an instant the air clears and the cloud lifts for a little, there are the gods still sitting around him on their thrones—they alone with him alone."

In passages like this Emerson furnishes some hint of how it is possible to accept the doctrine of relativity without loss of one's feeling for absolute values, and without allowing oneself to be devoured by the sense of illusion, as Amiel was and Sainte-Beuve would have been if he had not found a sort of oblivion in unremitting toil. So far as Emerson does this, he aids criticism in its search for inner standards to take the place of the outer standards it has lost; he helps it to see in the present anarchy the potentialities of a higher order. What we need, he says, is a "coat woven of elastic steel," a critical canon, in short, that will restore to its rights the masculine judgment but without dogmatic narrowness. With such a canon, criticism might still cultivate the invaluable feminine virtues—it might be comprehensive and sympathetic without at the same time being invertebrate and gelatinous.

Our ideal critic, then, would need to combine the breadth and versatility and sense of differences of a Sainte-Beuve with the elevation and insight and sense of unity of an

Emerson. It might be prudent to add of this critic in particular what Emerson has said of man in general, that he is a golden impossibility. But even though the full attainment of our standard should prove impossible, some progress might at least be made toward tempering with judgment the all-pervading impressionism of contemporary literature and life.

                                                    ·IRVING BABBITT.

XVI.—NEW-MEXICAN SPANISH.

This article is merely a contribution toward a record of popular New-Mexican Spanish. It is incomplete and fragmentary; and, doubtless, it has many errors, since most of the words and expressions it contains were received through the ear. By New-Mexican Spanish is here meant the popular Spanish speech of southern Colorado and northern New Mexico.[1] This region is only a small part of the southwestern States and Territories where Spanish is spoken, and yet it is as large as Italy. Its population may be roughly estimated at 125,000 Spanish-speaking persons, of whom some 40,000 or 50,000 are in Colorado and the remainder in northern New Mexico.

The language spoken throughout this extensive region is nearly uniform. The people, for the most part, are shepherds, drovers, or small "ranchers," or they are day-laborers in the mines, in the sawmills, or on the railways. They are restless and migratory, and move continually to and fro. In certain cultivated valleys and in certain villages one may detect slight differences in vocabulary or in pronunciation— chiefly in accent and intonation; but they are so slight that I have not attempted to record them. In the cities of Santa Fé and Albuquerque certain peculiarities of speech,—for the most part unimportant,—have developed. The speech of these cities, therefore, is not included in this article. Within the region treated, the differences in vocabulary and pronun-

---

[1] I have spent, all told, six months in New Mexico, and three and one-half years in Colorado, and my New-Mexican Spanish note-book has been an inseparable companion.

706

ciation seem to be in the individual or in the family, rather than in the locality.

There are in New Mexico several important private schools, mostly under Roman Catholic control, in which the instruction is given in Spanish, and in the larger towns one meets cultivated persons who speak excellent Spanish. There are also several periodicals published in the Spanish language. But the larger part of the Spanish-speaking people of Colorado and New Mexico are ignorant of Spanish letters. Colorado has had an excellent public school system for many years, but the real development of a public school system in New Mexico dates from 1890. In the public schools of both commonwealths the instruction is given in English. Therefore, the older generation of New Mexicans is, as a rule, illiterate, while the younger generation may read and write English rather than Spanish. Popular New-Mexican Spanish has thus been kept largely free from the leveling-down process of the school-master.

New-Mexican Spanish has been influenced only to a slight extent by English. The speech of the wealthier, more "enlightened" classes shows greater traces of English influence than does that of the common people. A few words and expressions of English origin are in common use; but pronunciation, and inflection and syntax, seem not to have been influenced at all. On the other hand, a strong Indian influence is evident in vocabulary and in pronunciation (cf. the *sh* sound, and an Indian intonation that is common), but not in inflection or construction.

Popular New-Mexican Spanish does not differ greatly from the speech of the rural districts of northern Mexico; nor does it differ from the popular Castilian of central Spain to the extent that the two peoples may not understand each other with little difficulty. Castilian speech, with many

Andalusian characteristics, was carried to Mexico several hundreds of years ago, and thence was carried northward into New Mexico. For generations the New Mexicans have had little intercourse with the people of central and southern Mexico, and almost none with the people of Spain. They have lived in isolation, and they have been ignorant of letters; and yet their speech has not changed greatly since it came from Spain. Probably greater changes have occurred in the popular speech of central Spain than in that of New Mexico during the last century.

In this respect it is interesting to compare the history of Spanish with that of French in America. While French has tended to break up into divergent speech groups that differ considerably one from the other and all from standard French, Spanish has held together with remarkable tenacity, and has, in the main, traveled the same road of phonetic development that the speech of central Spain has followed (cf. x [$= sh$] $> j$, in America and in Spain). Throughout Spanish America the speech of cultivated Castilians is still the standard in literary expression; but, in spoken Spanish, the Americans have certain peculiarities that are recognized standards of speech throughout all Spanish America (cf. $z > s$, $ll > y$,[1] $j >$ a front aspirate, etc.).[2]

---

[1] Dr. Bransby tells me that in central Colombia the l element of ll is retained.

[2] It will be noted that these phenomena are, for the most part, apparently of Andalusian origin. Professor Ford has called my attention to the fact that several of the phonetic peculiarities of New-Mexican Spanish obtain also in the Western and other dialects of the Spanish peninsula (e. g., $e > i$ before a, o, u; $o > u$ before a, e, i; intervocalic n sometimes falls, leaving the preceding vowel nasal; $dije < dice$, etc.; $muncho < mucho$, etc.). These facts would seem to indicate that the Spaniards, from whom New-Mexican Spanish has come, were (1) of Castilian, (2) of Andalusian, and (3) of Western-Spanish (perhaps some of Portuguese), origin.

Thus we have, as it were, a smaller circle within a larger, a general standard for all the Spanish-speaking world, but with certain definite modifications in Spanish America.

I have pleasure in acknowledging my indebtedness to Professor C. C. Ayer of the University of Colorado, Dr. Carlos Bransby of the University of California, Professors C. H. Grandgent and J. D. M. Ford of Harvard University, and Professor C. C. Marden of Johns Hopkins University, who have kindly read parts of this article and have made valuable suggestions and criticisms; and I am especially indebted to Professor Aurelio M. Espinosa[1] of the University of New Mexico, who has not only read and passed judgment on parts of this article, but has also called my attention to many valuable facts.[2]

---

[1] Throughout the article I have marked with an asterisk the facts that Professor Espinosa first called to my attention, although in some cases my explanation of the phenomena differs from that suggested by Professor Espinosa. But, in every case, whether the facts came to me directly, or through another, I have attempted to verify them before incorporating them in this article.

Dr. Bransby has kindly pointed out words in the Vocabulary that are also common to central Colombia. I have marked these by footnotes. There has never been much intercourse between the New Mexicans and the Colombians, and it would therefore seem that those words that are common to both regions were brought over from Spain.

[2] The following statistics, taken from the reports of the census of 1900, may be of interest :—

New Mexico,—total population, 195,310, of whom 143,216 were born in New Mexico, 6,649 in Mexico, 27 in Spain, and 27 in other Spanish-speaking countries. There were 13,144 Indians, 1,610 Negroes, and 349 Mongolians. Illiteracy, amongst those at least ten years of age, was 33.2 % (probably one-half of the Spanish-speaking population was illiterate).

In Colorado the population is composed chiefly of English-speaking people, most of whom were born in the Eastern and Middle-Western States. Most of the "Mexicans" are found in the southern third of the State. Of these 10,222 were born in New Mexico, 274 in Mexico, 41 in Spain, and 235 in other Spanish-speaking countries.

PHONOLOGY.

In this article S. C. denotes the standard speech of Central Spain, and N. M. S. denotes the popular speech of southern Colorado and northern New Mexico.[1] In attempting to write N. M. S. phonetically, certain symbols are used as follows : ˜, over a vowel, indicates that the vowel is nasal ; *b* = voiced bilabial spirant, *B* = voiced bilabial stop ; *d* = voiced interdental spirant, *D* = voiced dental stop ; *g* = voiced guttural or palatal spirant, *G* = voiced guttural or palatal stop ; *n* = voiced dental nasal, *N* = voiced velar nasal ; *sh* = Frènch *ch* ; *z* = voiced *s* ; į = *i* in hiatus ; ų = *u* in hiatus.

Vowels.

Quantity.

In N. M. S. stressed vowels are more prolonged than in S. C., and yet it is rarely true that any vowel is really "long." In exclamations, such as ¡ *bēNGa* ! (*venga*), ¡ *prōto* ! (*pronto*), the final vowel is often long, and it may be prolonged indefinitely ; but, in normal N. M. S., vowels should be classed as " medium long " or " short."

In general, it may be said that stressed vowels are medium long and unstressed vowels are short : *tomó, tomo, tomé, tome.* But, final unstressed *a* or *o* tends to become medium long, and a free vowel immediately preceding or following the

---

[1] The orthography and the pronunciation given by the Spanish Academy are taken as a basis of comparison, although I know full well that even cultivated Castilians do not speak as the Academy wishes them to do. For instance, *oscuro* (*obscuro*), *sétimo* (*séptimo*), *trasparente* (*transparente*), *estender* (*extender*), *amáo* or *amáu* (*amado*), *pa* (*para*), etc., etc., probably occur as commonly in Central Spain as in New Mexico.

stressed syllable of a word of three or more syllables (except final *a* or *o*) tends to become very short: *boca, mã(n)o ; pájaro, artículo, dăDole (dándole)*. It is well to add that a closed syllable, although containing a short vowel, is usually medium long.

a.

(1) Stressed *a*, not final, = French back *a* (approximately) in *vase, pâle*, etc. Before a nasal in the same syllable, it is somewhat farther back than French back *a*, and it is slightly rounded, as in *pãn, tãn* ; before *l* or *r*, in the same syllable, or before a consonant + *l, r*, it seems to be identical with French back *a*, as in *cual, mar, amable* ; in an open syllable before a single consonant, it is usually slightly farther front than French back *a*, as in *cajteyā(n)o (castellano), ejtatua (estatua), casa.*

(2) Stressed final *a* = French front *a* (approximately) in *la*, etc. : *pĩe(d)á (piedad), suidá (ciudad).*

(3) *a*, before *n*, or *m*, + a consonant, is strongly nasal and somewhat rounded, approaching the Parisian French *ã* in *tant, vent*, etc. The *n* or *m* tends to vanish. Ex. : *cãto (canto), cãtar (cantar), ấDale (ándale), cãsar (cansar), ã(m)Boj (ambos).* See *m* and *n*.

(4) Unstressed *a* = French front *a* (approximately) in *patte, salle*, etc. : *rosa, rosaj (rosas), tômãn, abía (había).*

Note :

Unstressed *a* usually falls before a vowel : *asĩ' á (hacia á), (b)amoj aselo (vamos á hacerlo), á caus' e tí* (á causa de tí), ¿l' am' él? (¿la ama él?), p' irse (para irse), ogar * (ahogar), orcar * (ahorcar), pũn or pãn* (para un), p' ojté* or pa ujté (para usted).*

* Espinosa.

13

e.

e is always more or less open : it is never so close as French *e* in *et, cassé,* etc.

(1) Stressed *e* is open and slightly rounded in the diphthong *ue,* approaching the French open *eu* in *seul, neuf,* etc. : *muero, cuĕto (cuento).*

(2) Stressed *e* is medium open in a checked syllable : *tēn, ser, él.*

(3) Stressed *e,* in a free syllable or final, is more nearly close : it is between the English *e* of *met* and the French *e* of *et : meto, temo, café, tomé.*

(4) Unstressed *e,* not final, is open and tends towards the neutral position (cf. the first French *e* of *distinctement* and the English *e* of *battery*) : *temería, metería, ītérprete (intérprete).*

(5) Unstressed final *e* is medium open : *tome, mete, siete.*

Note :

(1) Unstressed *e,* before *a, o, u,* becomes *i : lial (leal), rial (real), desiar* [1] *(desear), peliar (pelear), ti aseite (este aceite), lión (león), pión (peón), pior (peor), ū(m)· Baso di agua (un vaso de agua), di unu i otro* * *(de uno y otro).* [2]

(2) *e,* immediately following a stressed vowel, $>$ *i : trai (trae), caij (caes), lein (leen).*

(3) Final unstressed *e* $>$ *i,* after the palatals *ch, sh, ñ, y* (or *y* $<$ *ll*) : *cochi* * *(coche), lechi* * *(leche), pū(n)shi,* * *sueñi,* * *cai* or *cayi* * *(calle).*

(4) In the radical-changing verbs of the second and third classes, the stem vowel *e* $>$ *i,* when unstressed : *sītir (sentir), pidir (pedir),* etc.

(5) Initial *e,* before a nasal $+$ a dental or labial, some-

---

[1] But *deséu, deseaj,* etc.

[2] Note also, with intervening consonant, *siñor* or *señor, asigŭn (á según).*

* Espinosa.

times becomes the back, slightly rounded, nasal *a*: *ătōsej* *
(*entonces*), *ăDōDe* * (*endonde*), *ātusiazmo* * (*entusiasmo*).

(2) Unstressed *e* falls before *e, i*: *dél* (*de él*), *frir* (*freír**),
*ri̯ir** or *rir* (*reír*), *creo qu'* (*que*) *ibăn, t'* (< *te*) *ibi̯erno* (*este
invierno*); but, note *ler* or *leyer* (*leer*).

<h3 style="text-align:center">i.</h3>

(1) Stressed *i*, in a free syllable and before a single consonant, = French *i* in *bắti*: *comí, ejcrito* (*escrito*).

(2) Stressed *i* is slightly less close in a checked syllable,
or in a free syllable and before two or more consonants:
pidir, tīta (*tinta*), *posible*.

(3) Unstressed *i* is open, approaching English *i* in *sit*:
máquina, petisi̯ón (*petición*).

Note:

(1) Unstressed *i* > *e*, if followed by *i* (usually stressed)
in the same word: *menijtro* (*ministro*), *ēDebi(d)u̯o* * (*indi-
viduo*), *ē(m)Bēsible** (*invencible*), *besita* (*visita*), *me(d)esina*
(*medicina*), *felesidá* (*felicidad*), *prēsipi̯o* * (*principio*).

The radical-changing verbs of the second and third classes
are exceptions to this rule. Cf. *sītir* (*sentir*), *sīti* (*sentí*);
pidir (*pedir*), *pidimoj* (*pedimos* = Pret.). These forms are
by analogy to the other forms with stem vowel *i*.

(2) Final *is* and *iz* > *ej*: *crisej* (*crisis*), *lapej* (*lápiz*).

<h3 style="text-align:center">o.</h3>

o is always somewhat open: it is never so close as French
o in *mot*.

(1) Stressed *o* is open before a consonant in the same
syllable, or if nasal, or in *oi*; this sound of *o* resembles English *o* in *for*, but it is somewhat more rounded: *por, cō(n)*,
tōto (*tonto*), *oi* (*hoy*).

* Espinosa.

(2) Stressed *o* is slightly open in a free syllable : *abló* (*habló*), *toma*.

(3) Unstressed *o* is slightly open : *temo, mã(n)o, tomé, tomaré*.

Note:

(1) Unstressed *o* > *ụ*, before *a, e, i : nụ asej* * (*no haces*), *tụaya* (*toalla*), *almụá* (*almohada*), *qụịẹụ agụa* * (*quiero agua*), *pịasụ é pān* (*pedazo de pan*), *unụ era* * (*uno era*), *esụ ej* * (*eso es*), *dijụ él* (*dijo él*), *ojụ é güei* * (*ojo de buey*). Note also stressed *o* > *ụ*, in *s'ejcapué cai* (*se escapó de caer*), etc.

(2) After a vowel, unstressed *o* usually becomes *u* : *amáu* (*amado*); *cabayu* or *cabáu* (*caballo*); *sētáu* (*centavo*); *beu* (*veo*); *friu* (*frío*).[1]

(3) After the palatals *ch, sh, ñ*, and *y* (including *y < ll*), unstressed *o* usually becomes open *u : ã(n)chu* (*ancho*), *mushu* (*musho*), *añu* (*año*), *suyu* (*suyo*), *gayu* (*gallo*).[2]

(4) Initials *os-, hos-, obs-* > *es* (or *ej < es*) : *ejtētasịón* * (*ostentación*), *ejpital* * (*hospital*), *ejcuro* (*obscuro*), *ejtáculo* (*obstáculo*), *esequịo* * (*obsequio*), *esē(n)o* (*obsceno*).

(5) In the radical-changing verbs of the second class, the stem-vowel *o* > *u*, except under the stress (when it becomes *ụe*, as in S. C.) : *durmir* (*dormir*), *murir* (*morir*).

u.

(1) Stressed *u* is close (but less close than French *ou*) : *tú, único*.

(2) Stressed *u* is less close in a checked syllable, or if nasal : *multa, asũto* (*asunto*), *mũDo* (*mundo*).

(3) Unstressed *u* is open : *mũ(n)chísimo* (*muchísimo*.)

---

[1] *au < ado* is a pure diphthong ; *au < avo, abo, allo*, etc., tends to remain dissyllabic,* and the *u* is open.

[2] The pronunciation of this final *u < o* (except in *au < ado* where *u* ,is close) seems to hesitate between close *o* and open *u*, but I consider it to be usually an open *u* (= approximately English *u* in *full*).

* Espinosa.

Nasal Vowels.

A vowel, before or after a nasal consonant, becomes slightly nasal : a vowel, before *m* or *n* in the same syllable, is strongly nasal (for the loss of *m* and *n*, see these letters): *no, niño, mu(d)o, sĩn, pãn, ū(m) Baso (un vaso), ã(m)Bisi̯õn (ambición)*.

Diphthongs.

(1) *aí, aú* > *ai, au*, respectively : *pai̯ (país), mai̯ (maíz), ai (ahí), baul (baúl)*.

(2) *eí* < *i̯i* or *i: ri̯ir* * or *rir (reír), frir (freír)*.

(3) *oí* > *u̯i* or *oyé : u̯ir* * or *oyer (oír)*; *u̯ido (oído)*.

(4) *aé* > *ai, ayé* or *e : cai(r),* * *cayer*, or *quer* * (*caer*); *trai(r),* * *trayer*, or *trer* * (*traer*) ; *mei̯tro (maestro)*.

(5) *eé* > *e* or *eyé : ler* or *leyer (leer)*. Note also *leyido (leído)*.

Labials.

b, v.

(1) *b* and *v* are usually a voiced bilabial spirant : *abla(b)a (hablaba), bota, binir (venir)*.

(2) After a nasal, *b, v,* > a voiced bilabial stop : *ū(m) Baso (un vaso), cõ(m) Burla (con burla)*.

Note :

(1) *bue, vue,* > *gü̯e : gü̯ē(n)o (bueno), agü̯elo (abuelo), gü̯elta (vuelta), gü̯elbo (vuelvo)*. After a nasal, *B* appears : *ū(m) Bu̯ē(n) õ(m)Bre (un buen hombre), ū(m) Bu̯ei (un buey)*. Cf. *g* and *h*. *u̯e* (< *bue*), instead of *gü̯e*, is heard, but it is rare in N. M. S.

(2) *aul* and *aur* tend to become *abl* and *abr* respectively : *jabla* * (*jaula*), *Abreli̯o* * (*Aurelio*).

* Espinosa.

(3) *b*, final in a syllable, falls : *asurdo* (*absurdo*), *ejcuro* (*obscuro*), *sujcrisi̯ón* (*subscripción*) ; but *amable*, etc.

(4) Intervocalic *b* sometimes falls (chiefly when preceded or followed by unstressed *u*,—including *u* < *o*,—and in the verb ending -*aba*) ; *sẽtáu* (*centavo*) ; *yu̯er* (*llover*) ; *al cau* or even *al co* * (*al cabo*); *nu̯ aj abrilo* * (*no vayas á abrirlo*); *tomaba*, *tomau̯a*, or *tomá*,[1] etc. Note also : *amoj aselo* * (*vamos á hacerlo*) ; and even *ã(m) pa casa* * (*vamos para casa*). *Amoj* (*vamos*) appears to be by analogy to *nu̯ amoj* (*no vamos* < *no vayamos*).

p.

p = S. C. *p*.

Note :

(1) *p*, final in a syllable, falls : *sétimo* (*séptimo*), *sujcrisi̯ón* (*subscripción*).

But :

(2) *apt* and *aps*, before *a*, *o*, *u*, > *aut*[2] and *aus* respectively : *auto* (*apto*), *cáusula* (*cápsula*).

(3) *ept*, before *a*, *o*, *u*, > *eut* or *et* : *aseuto* or *aseto* (*acepto*), *cõseuto* or *cõseto* (*concepto*).

(4) *epc*, before *e*, *i*, > *es* or *aus* : *cõsesi̯ón* or *cõsausi̯ón* * (*concepción*), *esesi̯ón* or *esausi̯ón* (*excepción*).

u̯.

u̯ = S. C. unstressed *u* in hiatus : *gu̯ãte* (*guante*), *güẽ(n)o* (*bueno*).

f.

f = S. C. *f*.

Note :

(1) *f* > *j* before *u̯* + vowel : *ju̯erte* (*fuerte*), *ju̯ego*

---

[1] When *b* falls in *aba*, there seems to be often a trace of a hiatus *u̯* : *amau̯a*, or (in rapid speech) *amá*.

[2] Cf. S. C. *bautismo*, etc.

* Espinosa.

(*fuego*), *juí* (*fuí*), *ajuera* (*afuera*). Sometimes $f > j$ before *u* + consonant, or before *o* : *perjume* * (*perfume*), *jogón* (*fogón*).

(2) Before *e* or *i*, intervocalic $f_ι$ sometimes becomes fj :[1] *cafjé* * (*café*).

Note also *juea* < *fuella* (S. C. *huella*).

m.

m = S. C. *m* : *tomo, mirar*.

Note :

Before *B* or *p*, *m* becomes very indistinct, and may fall, leaving the preceding vowel strongly nasal : *ã(m)Bisiõn* (*ambición*), *ũ(m)Baso* (*un vaso*). Usually a slight trace of consonantal *m* remains.

DENTALS.

d.

(1) *d* is usually a voiced interdental spirant : *berde* (*verde*), *de(d)o*.

(2) After *l* or a nasal, *d* is a voiced dental stop (*D*) : *ejpalDa* (*espalda*), *ãDale* (*ándale*).

Note :

(1) Intervocalic *d* falls regularly in *ada, ado, oda, odo*, and rarely in *ida, ido* : in other cases *d* may usually fall whenever clearness and euphony permit : *amá* (*amada*), *na* (*nada*), *amáu* (*amado*), *toa* (*toda*), *to* (*todo*), *piaso* * (*pedazo*), *mi a* * (*me da*), *deo* or *dedo*, *mieo* or *miedo*, *pue(e)* or *puede* ; but *comida, comido, suidá* (*ciudad*), etc. Note *cõ(m)pá* * (*compadre*).

---

[1] This is as well as I can express it graphically.

* Espinosa.

(2) By analogy, initial *d* may fall : *ĭj* * *que* (*diz que*), *ejpaşįo* (*despacio*), *no quįeų ártelo* * (*no quiero dártelo*), *ame** (*dame*) ; but after *l* or *n*, *d* can not fall : *ãDōDe** (*endonde*), *cõ Dar** (*con dar*), *ĕl Da* (*ĕl da*).

The *d* of *de* usually falls before a consonant : *pįaşụé pãn* (*pedazo de pan*) ; before a vowel, *de* > *di*, or it falls altogether : *ū(m) Baso dį agụa* (un vaso de agua), *tēNGo mįe(d)o aselo* (*tengo miedo de hacerlo*).

t.

t = S. C. *t* : *tío, bota.*

z.

z, and *c* + *e, i,* > *s* (or *j* < *s*) : *casa* (*caza* or *casa*), *nụese* [*j*] (*nueces*), *sapato* (*zapato*), *paj* (*paz*).

l.

l = S. C. *l* : *la, ĕl.*
li + vowel tends to become *y* : *sayēDo* (*saliendo*), *muyēDo* (*moliendo*).

n.

(1) *n* = S. C. *n* : *no, bino* (*vino*).

(2) *n*, before a guttural or palatal consonant, becomes a velar nasal spirant (*N*), as in S. C. : *bãNco* (*banco*), *bēNGo* (*vengo*), *narãNja* (*naranja*), *ũN G* *ẅeso* (*un hueso*).

But :

(1) Before a dental, *n* falls, leaving the preceding vowel strongly nasal : *cãto* (*canto*), *cãtar* (*cantar*), *tēDer* (*tender*), *cãsar* (*cansar*), *cãsáu* (*cansado*)ᵢ Before *f, ch, sh,* it becomes very indistinct, and may fall : *ĩ(n)fįerno* (*infierno*), *ã(n)chu* (*ancho*), *pũ(n)shi* (*punshe*), etc. (Note above in (2) that *n* > *N* before *c, G, j*).

* Espinosa.

(3) Intervocalic *n* sometimes falls (chiefly in *ana, ene*; rarely in *ina, ino*), leaving the preceding and the following vowels nasal: *semã̃* (*semana*); *ermã̃** (*hermana*); *tịẽ[e]** (*tiene*); *bịẽ[e]* (*viene*); *ermano,* or *ermã̃ũ** (*hermano*); *gü̈eno,* or *gü̈ẽo** (*bueno*); but *bino* (*vino*).[1]

(3) *n* falls before *sp* or *st*: *trajparẽte* (*transparente*), *cojtãte* (*constante*).

(4) *ni* + vowel tends to become *ñ*: *ñeto* (*nieto*), *Átoñu** (*Antonio*).

Although they are not properly dentals, *ll* and *ñ* are given here.

ll.

Initial *ll* > *y*: *yamar* (*llamar*), *yubịa* (*lluvia*).

Intervocalic *ll* usually becomes *y*: *gayu* (*gallo*), *cabayu* (*caballo*), *oya* (*olla*), *poyu* (*pollo*), *jụeya* (*huella*).

Note:

(1) *ll* falls in *illa, illo*: *sía* (*silla*), *mãtequía* (*mantequilla*), *potríu* (*potrillo*), *tríu* (*trillo*). Note the analogous forms: *fríu, fría, tenía,* etc.

(2) In *ella, ello*, usage varies between *ea, eu,* and (less commonly) *eya, eyu*: *ea* or *eya* (*ella*), *euj* or *eyuj* (*ellos*), *bea* or *beya* (*bella*), *beu* or *beyu* (*bello*). Note the analogous forms: *beu* or *beyu* (*veo*), *bea* or *beya* (*vea*), *paséu* or *paseyu* (*paseo*)*, *cã(m)Béu* or *cã(m)Beyu** (*cambio*).

(3) Less commonly, *ll* may fall in *alla, allo*: thus, *a** or *ayá* (*allá*), *cate** or *cáyate* (*cállate*), *cabayu* or *cabáu** (*caballo*). Compare *cate* or (more emphatic) *cáyate* with *base* or *báyase* (*váyáse*).

(4) Final *lle* tends to become *i*: *bai** or *bayi* (*valle*), *cai** or *cayi* (*calle*), *mụei* or *mụeyi* (*muelle*). Compare *mụei,*

---

[1] Some New Mexicans retain intervocalic *n* in all positions.
* Espinosa.

*mu̯eij** or *mu̯eyij* (*muelle, muelles*) with *rei, reij** or *reyij*
(*rey, reyes*).

(5). In *llé, llí*, the *y* is indistinct: *poyito* (*pollito*), *caba-
yito* (*caballito*), *siyeta* (*silleta*).[1]

ñ.

ñ = S. C. *ñ* : *añu, niña.*

GUTTURALS.

g.

(1) *g* is usually a voiced guttural or palatal spirant, as
often in S. C.: *gato, aga* (*haga*), *algo, ormiga* (*hormiga*).
Intervocalic *g* is pronounced very softly, and before *u̯* it may
disappear in rapid, careless speech.[2]

(2) After *N, g* = a voiced guttural or palatal stop (*G*):
tēNGo (*tengo*), *bēNGa* (*venga*), *dejtīNGue* (*distingue*).

Note:

(1) *gü̯*, before a vowel, is sometimes confused with *gü̯* <
bu; thus, one hears *ūN Gu̯ăte* or (less commonly) *ū(m) Bwăte**
(*un guante*), *agu̯a* or *abu̯a** (*agua*). Cf. *gü̯ē(n)o*, but
ū(m)Buē(n) ō(m)Bre (*un buen hombre*).

(2) *g*, final in a syllable, falls: *dino* (*digno*), *inorăte*
(*ignorante*), *Inasi̯o** (*Ignacio*) ; but *negro, siglo,* etc. By
exception, *g* falls in *ilesia** (*iglesia*).

(3) *g* is sometimes used between back vowels to avoid
hiatus: *yo go tú** (*yo ó tú*), *uno gu̯otro** (*uno ú otro*).

---

[1] Professor Espinosa holds that *ll* falls in *llé, llí*, but my observation leads
me to believe that a somewhat indistinct hiatus *y* is present.

[2] In American English, *gü̯* in Spanish names is uniformly pronounced *w*,
as in Saguache (*Sah-wátch*), Guanajato (*Wah-nah-háh-to*), etc.

* Espinosa.

c.

$c + a$, *o*, *u*, and $qu + e$, *i*, represent the same sound in N. M. S. and in S. C.: *casa*, *que*.

Note:

(1) *c*, final in a syllable, falls: *asi̯ón* (*acción*), *lesi̯ón* (*lección*), *osidéte* (*occidente*), *cojtrusi̯ón* (*construcción*), *dotor* (*doctor*).

(2) But, *act* > *aut*[1] or *ait* before *a*, *o*, *u*, and *ait* only before *e*, *i*: *cõ(m)pauto* or *cõ(m)paito* (*compacto*), *esauto* or *esaito* (*exacto*), *caráiter* (*carácter*).

(3) *ect*, before *a*, *o*, *u*, > *eit*, *et*, or *eut*:[2] *perfeito*, *perfeto*, or *perfeuto* (*perfecto*).

SIBILANTS.

s.

s (including *s* < *z* or *c*) is pronounced softly and is only slightly sibilant. At the end of a syllable, it usually becomes a soft aspirate, approximating to, but softer and less distinct than German *ch* in *ich*.[3] This sound is here represented by *j*,[4] although it is softer, and is pronounced somewhat farther front than even the soft, palatal N. M. *j*. In the final syllable of a breath group, and especially after *e*, this final *j* tends to vanish, as in *loj árbole(j)* [*los árboles*], *loj Ejpañole(j)*

---

[1] By analogy with *aut* < *apt* (?).

[2] By analogy with *eut* < *ept* (?).

[3] This breathing is made so near the *s* position that an untrained ear would scarcely detect at first the difference between the breathing and the soft final S. C. *s*.

[4] I shall probably be criticised for using *j* to represent two sounds: (1) initial or intervocalic N. M. *j*, in *juta* (*junta*), *jéte* (*gente*), *ojo*, etc.; and, (2) the indistinct front breathing that usually replaces *s* at the end of a syllable in N. M. S. And yet these two sounds probably differ no more than do the two *r*'s in *raro*.

[*los Españoles*], *laj bonitaj muchacha(j)* [*las bonitas muchachas*], *dejpu̯é(j)* [*después*].   When initial or intervocalic, *s* sometimes becomes the regular N. M. *j*, as in *ji* *
(*si*), *nojotroj* * (*nosotros*), *conoje* * (*conoce*).

(1) Initial and intervocalic *s* is usually a voiceless dental
sibilant, softly pronounced : *siglo, casa, sapato* (*zapato*).

(2) *s*, final in a syllable, usually becomes *j*, or vanishes
altogether (see above) : *detrá(j)* [*detrás*], *dejpu̯é(j)* [*después*],
paj (*paz*), *conojco* (*conozco*), *mij cabayuj* (*mis caballos*), *nuejtraj
bacaj* (*nuestras vacas*).   S. C. *reloj, relojes* > N. M. *reloj,
relose(j)*, by analogy with *nu̯ej, nu̯ese(j)* (*nuez, nueces*), etc.

(3) But, before a voiced consonant, *s* usually becomes *z*.
This sound is usually described by observers as equivalent to
English *z* in *daze*; but in N. M. S. I take it to be a voiced
palatal aspirate, differing from the *j* of *dejpu̯é(j)* [*después*]
only in that it is voiced : *loz mizmoj* (*los mismos*), *güe(n)oz díaj*
(*buenos días*), *loz güeyij* (*los bueyes*), *dezde* (*desde*), *durazno*
(*durasno*).

sh.

sh is approximately equivalent to French *ch* in *chat* : it is
made farther front than English *sh*.   This sound is apparently due to Indian influence : *fashico*, 'negro' ; *pū(n)shi*,*
'smoking tobacco' ; *moshca* * (often for *mosca*), etc.

ch.

ch = S. C. *ch* : *muchacho*.

x.

x = *s* (or *j* < *s*) : *esauto* (*exacto*), *esamẽn* (*examen*), *ésito* *
(*éxito*), *ejperiẽsi̯a* (*experiencia*).

* Espinosa.

ASPIRATES.

j.

j, and *g* + *e*, *i*, = a voiceless palatal spirant.   N. M. *j* is made farther front than S. C. *j*, and it is pronounced more softly.

Note:

(1) *f* > *j* in *juego* (*fuego*), *jogón* (*fogón*), etc.[1]

(2) *s* > *j* in *nojotroj* * (*nosotros*), *cõDujen* (*conducen*), *ji* * (*si*), etc.

(3) *h* > *j* in *jerbir* * (*hervir*), *juir* (*huir*), etc.

(4) *j* may be prefixed: *joso* * (*oso*), etc.

h.

h is usually mute, as in S. C.: *ora* (*hora*).

Note:

(1)   *hue-* > *güe-*: *güebo* (*huevo*), *güeso* (*hueso*), *güerta* (*huerta*).   After *N*, this *güe* usually becomes *Güe*: *ūN Güeso* (*un hueso*), *ūN Güebo* (*un huevo*), etc.; but by analogy with *güe(n)o*, *ū(m) Buē(n)o* (*un bueno*), etc., one hears not infrequently *ū(m) Buebo* * (*un huevo*), etc.   Cf. *b* and *g*.   By analogy with *hue-* > *güe-*, we have *sirgüela* * (*ciruela*), etc.

(2)   In a few words, initial *h* > *j*: *jayar* * (*hallar*), *jablar* (*hablar*), *jerbir* * (*hervir*), *jõDo* * (*hondo*), *juir* * (*huir*), etc. One also hears *joso* * (*oso*), etc.

TONGUE-TRILLED CONSONANTS: R AND RR.

r = S. C. *r*: *rato*, *caro*.

rr = S. C. *rr*: *carro*.

---

[1] Some observers consider initial or intervocalic *j* < *f*, *s*, *h*, etc. (as in *jogón*, *nojotroj*, *jõDo*, *joso*), different from the *j* of *jūta* (*junta*), *jēte* (*gente*), etc., but I can detect no difference.

* Espinosa.

Note:

(1) Final *r* is usually sharply trilled, and followed by a slight vocalic resonance due to the dying away of the trill: *tomar, comer, bibir (vivir)*.

(2) In south-eastern Colorado one often hears an *e* post-fixed to final *r*. Amongst New Mexicans living near La Junta, Colo., I observed *e* postfixed to *n* and *l* also. These are some of the expressions noted: *pa cõsiguire la cosa (para conseguir la cosa), tú seráj el bẽsedore (tú serás el vencedor), tratãDụ é bere i ụire laj seremonịaj (tratando de ver y oír las ceremonias), no se parese e na á l'originale (no se parece en nada á lo orijinal), sa carne ole male (esa carne huele mal), l' ejpañole ej máj fásil que l' alemane (el español es más fácil que el alemán)*. There are many Italians in this region, and the final *e* may be due to their influence.

(3) Sometimes *r > j* before *l*: *Cajloj** (*Carlos*), *pejla** (*perla*).

(4) Intervocalic *r* sometimes falls (chiefly in *ara, ere*): *tomara, tomaraj*, etc., or *tomá,** tomáj,*[1] etc.; *comịera, comịeraj*, etc., or *comịea,** comịeaj*, etc.; *tomarõn, tomãun*, or (rarely) *tomõn** (*tomaron*); *comịerõn* or *comịeõn*; *quịero, quịerej*, etc., or *quịeu,** quịe(e)j*, etc.; *quịera*, etc., or *quịea*, etc.; *mía* (*mira*; imperative); *ẽtía qu' ía tõto** (*parecía que era tonto*); *pa* (*para*); *peu* or (rarely) *po** (*pero*); etc.

(5) The final *r* of infinitives falls before a postfixed personal pronoun with initial *l*: *p' aselo (para hacerlo), no quịeu cõ(m)pralo (no quiero comprarlo)*. Note also *poque** (*porque*).

SPIRANT Y.

y (and *y < ll*) usually = S. C. *y*: *yeso, yã(n)o* (*llano*). Note: Initial *y* tends to become a sound between the

---

[1] *Tomá* (*tomara*) has back *a*, while *tomá* (*tomaba*) has front *a*.*

* Espinosa.

French *j* of *juge* and the English *j* of *judge*, as in *yo*,*
yegua,* *yerba*,* *yũNque** (*yunque*).

DOUBLED CONSONANTS.

Doubled consonants are pronounced as one, as usually in
S. C. : *ē na* (*en nada*), *e libro* (*el libro*), *lo sapatoj* (*los
zapatos*), etc.

ORTHOGRAPHY.

Educated New Mexicans use the S. C. orthography ; they
do not use *i* for *y* and *j* for *g*, as do the South Americans of
the Pacific coast. Ignorant New Mexicans, only slightly
acquainted with letters, make amusing mistakes in spelling,
which are mostly due to the non-phonetic value of many S.
C. letters when used to express N. M. S. sounds.

The following were taken from letters and documents :

a verte visto (*haberte visto*). *hise* (*hize*).
baya (*vaya*). *hollendo* (*oyendo*).
ballamos (*vayamos*). *llo* (*yo*).
basayo (*vasallo*). *me nojare* (*me enojaré*).
beo (*bello*). *nabedad* (*navedad*).
berdad (*verdad*). *oya* (*olla*).
confucion (*confusión*). *relles* (*reyes*).
combiene (*conviene*). *ves* (*vez*).
eseso (*exceso*).

MORPHOLOGY.

The inflectional structure of New-Mexican Spanish does
not differ greatly from that of Standard Castilian. As one
would expect, the most highly inflected part of speech, the
verb, shows the greatest divergence. For the most part,

* Espinosa.

only those forms are given in the following notes that differ materially from their standard Castilian equivalents.[1]

It must be borne in mind that the laws of N. M. S. phonology obtain in all inflectional forms, whether the forms be given, or not given, in this article. Of especial importance are the rules governing $e > i$, $o > u$, and $s > j$, as in *sį ō(m)Bre* (*ese hombre*), *tį ama* (*te ama*), *e librų ej īNGléj* (*el libro es inglés*), *dijų él* (*dijo él*), etc.

NOUNS AND ADJECTIVES.

Nouns and adjectives form the feminine and plural as in S. C., except that words ending in *j* ($< s$) form the plural in *se(j)* or *je(j)* : *nųej, nųese(j)* or *nųeje(j)* [*nuez, nueces*]. Note also : *lei, leij* * or *leyij* (*ley, leyes*); *cai* * or *cayi, caij* * or *cayij* (*calle, calles*).

ARTICLES.

The Definite Article is : *el, ľ**; *la, ľ*; *loj, ľj*; *laj, ľj*; *lo, ľ*.

(1) Before or after a vowel, *el > ľ* : *ľ ō(m)Bre, to ľ Día, dijo ľ niñu*.

(2) Before a vowel, *la, lo, > ľ* : *ľermā, ľ orijinal*.

(3) After a vowel, *loj, laj, >* (sometimes) *ľj* : *pa ľj chicoj*.

Note :

á + el > al, as in S. C.

de + el > del, as in S. C.

*con + el > cōel** or *cōl** : *cō(e)l ō(m)Bre, cō(e)l cabayu*.

*en + el > ēel,** *ēl,** or *nel* : *ē(e)l río* or *nel río*.

para + el > pal : *pal tío, pal Amiricā(n)o*.

The Indefinite Article is *un*; *una, un'*.

---

[1] When two or more forms are given, the commoner is given first.

* Espinosa.

un' occurs before a vowel, *una* before a consonant: *un' ora, una niña.*

Note:

$a + un > ãn$ * ; $de + un > d\d{i} \tilde{u}n$; $con + un > c\tilde{u}n$ * or $c\tilde{o}n$ * ; $para + un > p\tilde{u}n$* or $p\tilde{a}n.$*

PERSONAL PRONOUNS.

In N. M. S. there is no personal pronoun of the second person plural: *ojtedej* is the plural of both *tú* and *ojté.*

Singular.

	Nom.	Dat.	Accus.	Prepositional.
1.	*yo*	*me, m'*	*me, m'*	*mí*
2.	*tú, t'*	*te, t'*	*te, t'*	*tí*
3.	*él, l'*	*le, l'*	*lo, l'*	*él*
	ea,[1]	*(le), la, l'*	*la, l'*	*ea*[1]
		se, s'	*se, s'*	*sí*
	eu[1]		*lo,*	*eu*[1]
	*ojté,** *(ujté)*	*le, la, l'*	*lo, la, l'*	*ojté, (ujté)*

Plural.

	Nom.	Dat.	Accus.	Prepositional.
1.	*nosotroj*	*noj,*[2] *n'j*	*noj, n'j*	*nosotroj*
	or *nojotroj**			or *nojotroj**
2.	——	——	——	——
3.	*euj,*[1]	*lej, l'j*	*loj, l'j*	*euj*[1]
	eaj,[1]	*(lej) laj, l'j*	*laj, l'j*	*eaj*[1]
		se, s'	*se, s'*	*sí*
	*ojtedej,** *(ujtedej)*	*lej, laj, l'j*	*loj, laj, l'j*	*ojtedej, (ujtedej).*

* Espinosa.

[1] Or *eya, eyaj, eyuj, eyu.*

[2] In popular New-Mexican Spanish *loj, laj, lej,* or *se*(= *lej*), often replace *noj.** Thus *loj be* may mean "he sees them," or "you," or "us." Note

14

Note:

(1) *l'*, *m'*, *t'*, *s'*, are common before or after a vowel: ¿*õ jtá l?* *yo l' beigo, me l'a dichu.*

(2) After a vowel, *n'j* and *l'j* may occur: *no n'j quie(e), yo lz digo.*

(3) *ojté* and *ojtedej* are common at the beginning of a sentence; after *a*, they may become *ujté, ujtedej*, the *a* and *u* forming a diphthong: ¿*ojté l' crei?* ¿*cómo jtá ujté?* *pa ujté or p' ojté, cõ 'jté.*

POSSESSIVES.

Pronouns: *el mío; el tuyu; el nuejtro; el suyu, d'él.*

Adjectives: *mi, m'; tu, t'; nuejtr(o); su, s'.* Before a vowel, *m'*, *t'*, and *s'*, are common forms. After a vowel, *mi* often becomes *m'*: *pa m' tío,* á *(m') papá.**

DEMONSTRATIVES.

Pronouns: *(é)jte, (é)se, (a)quél [(a)quéa*, etc]. The initial vowel may fall after a vowel: *no creu' so.*

Adjectives: *'jte, te; se; quel (quiá or quea*, etc.).

Note: *'jte* is common after a vowel, and *te* in other positions: *pa 'jti õ(m)Bre, ti õ(m)Br' ej mijicã(n)o, sa niña, cõ quiá mujer.*

SOME OTHER ADJECTIVE-PRONOUNS.

(1) *Nadiẽn* or *naide* = *nadie.*

(2) *Mũ(n)chu* = *mucho.*

the analogous forms: *loj be á euj*, "he sees them"; *loj be á ujtedej*, "he sees you"; *loj be á nosotroj*, "he sees us." Note also *se lo (d)iju á nosotroj*, "he told us so," etc. This usage is widespread, but not universal. In this connection it should be noted that the feminine form *nosotraj* is rare; like other pronouns of the first and second persons, *nosotroj* does not distinguish gender.

(3) In certain expressions, *tụí* * (or *ti*) = *todo y* : *cõ tụí la familịa,** "family and all"; *cõ ti la berdura,* or (more explicitly) *cõ tụitaj claj'e berdura,** "with all sorts of vegetables."

(4) *Mezmo* = *mismo.*

(5) Before *rịale(j)*, *libraj*, etc., *dos, tres, seis,* and *diez,* become *do, tre, se,* and *die.*

(6) Between 16 and 19, *dij* = *diez*: *dij i seij,* etc.

(7) *Sịetesịẽtoj* and *nụebesịẽtoj* = *setecientos* and *novecientos*; and *sịẽn* may replace *sịẽto* in any position.

ADVERBS, PREPOSITIONS, AND CONJUNCTIONS.

a * or *ayá* (*allá*), *ai* (*ahí*), *ãDõDe* * (*en donde*), *ãtõsej* * (*entonces*), *asịá* (*hacia á* < *hacia*), *asigún* (*á según*), *ca* (*acá*), *á causé* * (*á causa de*), *cụasi* (*casi*), *ejpasịo* (*despacio*), *ẽNcõtrẽ* (*en contra de*), *murre* * (*muy re-*[1]), *no máj,** "as soon as," "not even," *õDe* or *õ(n)* (*donde*), *ójala* (*ojalá*), *õnque* or *ãnque* (*aunque*), *ora* (*ahora*), *pa* (*para*), *peu* (*pero*), *puj*, or *poj* (*pues*), *poque* * (*porque*), *qui* (*aquí*), *tamiẽn* (*también*), *tãnre* * or *tãrre* * (*tan re-*[1]), etc.

VERBS.

The following changes have occurred in all verbs, whether regular or irregular :[2]

1. Verbs of the third conjugation are inflected throughout (except in the infinitive) like verbs of the second conjugation. Thus, the pres. ind., 1st person plural, of *abrir* is *abremoj.* This enables the speaker to distinguish the present

---

[1] The *re-* is the intensive prefix.

[2] Whenever, in this article, it is said that a verb is inflected as in S. C., it is meant that the inflection is the same in N. M. S. as in S. C., except for these regularly occurring changes, which are common to all N. M. S. verbs.

* Espinosa.

from the preterite [cf. *abremoj* (pres.) and *abrimoj* (pret.)].

2. Two tenses are lost, viz., the past subjunctive in *-se* and the hypothetical or future subjunctive in *-re*.

3. The second person plural of all verbs is lost, and its place is taken by the third person with *ojtedej* (*ustedes*).

4. The ending *-moj* becomes *-noj*, whenever the stress falls on the antepenult* : *tomá(b)anoj* (*tomábamos*), *tomá-(r)anoj* (*tomáramos*), *tomaríanoj* (*tomaríamos*), *tómenoj* (*tomemos*).

5. In the present subjunctive, first person plural, the stress falls on the antepenult * : *tómenoj* (*tomemos*), *ábranoj* (*abramos*), *sįétanoj* (*sintamos*). This form is not used as an imperative, its place being taken by (*b*)*amoj á* + infinitive : (*b*)*ámonoj á sētar* (*sentémonos*), *no se lo* (*b*)*amoj á disir* (*no se lo dígamos*).[1]

6. The preterite, second person singular, ends in *-tej* (*-ste*): *tomatej* (*tomaste*), *comitej* (*comiste*).

Regular Verbs.

First Conjugation : *tomar.*

tomar, tomăDo, tomáu.
Pres. Ind. : *tomo, tomaj, toma, tomamoj, tomān.*
Pres. Subj. : *tome, tomej, tome, tómenoj, tomēn.*
Imperat. : *toma.*
Imperf. : *toma(b)a, toma(b)aj, toma(b)a, tomá(b)anoj, toma(b)ān.*
Pret. : *tomé, tomatej, tomó, tomamoj, toma(r)ōn.*
Past Subj. : *toma(r)a, toma(r)aj, toma(r)a, tomá(r)anoj, toma(r)ān.*

---

[1] The only imperative (or subjunctive used as an imperative) of the first person plural in N. M. S. is (*b*)*amoj* or (*b*)*ámonoj*. The suffix *-noj* in *tómenoj*, etc., seems to be by analogy to (*b*)*ámonoj*.

*Espinosa.

Fut. Ind.: *tomaré, tomaráj, tomará, tomaremoj, tomarán.*

Cond. Ind. : *tomaría, tomaríaj, tomaría, tomaríanoj, tomarían.*

Note the following :

Pasiar (*pasear*).

pasiar, pasiãDo, pasiáu.

Pres. Ind. : *paséu,*[1] *paseaj, pasea, pasiamoj, paseãn.*

Pres. Subj.: *paséi, paséij, paséi, paséinoj, paseĩn.*

Imperat.: *pasea.*

All other forms have the stem *pasi-.* Thus, all regular verbs in *-iar* (*-ear*). By analogy, verbs with dissylabic stems, that have *-iar* in S. C., are inflected like *pasiar* : e. g., *cã(m)Biar* (*cambiar*): Pres. Ind., *cãmBéu,*[1] *cã(m)Beaj,* etc., (but *fiu, cõ(n)fiu,* etc.).

SECOND CONJUGATION : *comer.*

comer, comiẽDo, comido.

Pres. Ind. : *como, comej, come, comemoj, comēn.*

Pres. Subj.: *coma, comaj, coma, cómanoj, comãn.*

Imperat. : *come.*

Imperf. : *comía, comíaj, comía, comíanoj, comíãn.*

Pret. : *comí, comitej, comió, comimoj, comie(r)ōn.*

Past Subj.: *comie(r)a, comie(r)aj, comie(r)a, comié-(r)anoj, comie(r)ãn.*

Fut. Ind. : *comeré, comeráj, comerá, comeremoj, comerãn.*

Cond. Ind. : *comería, comeríaj, comería, comeríanoj, comerían.*

THIRD CONJUGATION : *bibir* (*vivir.*)

Pres. Ind. : *bibo, bibej, bibe, bibemoj, bibēn.*

Etc., as in the Second Conjugation.

---

[1] Less commonly, *paseyu,** *paseyaj,* etc. ; *cã(m)Beyu,** *cã(m)Beyaj,* etc.

* Espinosa.

VERBS WITH INCEPTIVE ENDINGS.

Conoser (conocer).

conoser, conosi̯ēDo, conosido.

Pres. Ind. : conojco, conosej, conose, conosemoj, conosēn.

Pres. Subj.: conojca, conojcaj, conojca, conójcanoj, conoj-cãn.

Etc.

Note :—The stem conos-tends to become conoj-* throughout the inflection of the verb, by analogy to conojco, conojca, etc.

RADICAL–CHANGING VERBS.

FIRST CLASS: (1) Perder.

perder, perdi̯ēDo, perdido.

Pres. Ind. : pi̯erdo, pi̯erdej, pi̯erde, perdemoj, pi̯erdēn.

Pres. Subj. : pi̯erda, pi̯erdaj, pi̯erda, pi̯érdanoj, pi̯erdãn.

Imperat.: pi̯erde.

Etc.

(2) Morder.

morder, mordi̯ēDo, mordido.

Pres. Ind. : mu̯erdo, mu̯erdej, mu̯erde, mordemoj, mu̯erdēn.

Pres. Subj. : mu̯erda, mu̯erdaj, mu̯erda, mu̯érdanoj, mu̯er-dãn.

Imperat. : mu̯erde.

Etc.

Note : oler is inflected as follows :

oler, oli̯ēDo, olido.

Pres. Ind. : $\left\{ \begin{array}{l} olo,\ olej,\ ole,\ olemoj,\ olēn. \\ gü̯elo,\ gü̯elej,\ gü̯ele,\ olemoj,\ gü̯elēn.^{1} \end{array} \right.$

---

[1] Whenever two forms are given, the commoner is given first.

*Espinosa.

Pres. Subj. : $\begin{cases} ola, olaj, ola, ólanoj, olán. \\ güela, güelaj, güela, güélanoj, güelán. \end{cases}$

Imperat. : *ole* or *güele.*

Etc.

SECOND CLASS: (1) *Sĭtir* (*sentir*).

sĭtir, sĭtįēDo, sĭtido.

Pres. Ind. : *sįēto, sįētej, sįēte, sĭtemoj, sįētēn.*

Pres. Subj. : *sįēta, sįētaj, sįēta, sįétanoj, sįētān.*

Imperat. : *sįēte.*

Pret. : *sĭtí, sĭtitej, sĭtįó, sĭtimoj, sĭtįerōn.*

Etc.

Note : Throughout the inflection of these verbs, the stem vowel is *i* when unstressed.

(2) *Durmir.*

durmir, durmįēDo, durmido.

Pres. Ind. : *dų̆ermo, dų̆ermej, dų̆erme, durmemoj, dų̆ermēn.*

Pres. Subj. : *dų̆erma, dų̆ermaj, dų̆erma, dų̆érmanoj, dų̆er-mān.*

Imperat. : *dų̆erme.*

Pret. : *durmí, durmitej, durmįó, durmimoj, durmįerōn.*

Etc.

Note : Both *durmir* and *murir* have the stem vowel *u* throughout, when the stem is not stressed.

THIRD CLASS : *Siguir* (*seguir.*)

siguir, siguįēDo, siguido.

Pres. Ind. : *sigo, siguej, sigue, siguemoj, siguēn.*

Pres. Subj. : *siga, sigaj, siga, síganoj, sigān.*

Imperat. : *sigue.*

Pret. : *siguí, siguitej, siguįó, siguimoj, siguįerōn.*

Etc.

Note: All verbs of this class have the stem vowel *i* throughout their inflection.

Note : *rịir* or *rir (reír)* is inflected as follows : .

rịir or *rir, rịēDo, rịido* or *rido.*

Pres. Ind. : *ríu, rí(i)ỹ, rí(i), rịemoj, rí(ī)n.*

Pres. Subj. : *ría, ríaj, ría, ríanoj, riān.*

Imperat. : *rí(i).*

Imperf. : *ría* or *rịía,* etc.

Pret. : *rí, ritej, rịó, rimoj, rịerōn.*

–ỤIR VERBS.

Dejtribụir (distribuir).

dejtribụir, dejtribuyēDo or *dejtribụēDo, dejtribụido.*

Pres. Ind. : *dejtrib-ụyu, -ú(y)ỹ, -úyi, -ụ(y)emoj, -ú(y)ịn.*

Pres. Subj. : *dejtrib-ụya, -uyaj, -uya, -úyanoj, -uyān.*

Imperat.: *dejtribú(y)i.*

Pret. :
$$\begin{cases} dejtrib\text{-}ụí, \text{-}ụitej, \text{-}uyó, \text{-}ụimoj, \text{-}uërōn.* \\ dejtrib\text{-}uyí, \text{-}uyitej, \text{-}uyó, \text{-}uyimoj, \text{-}uyerōn. \end{cases}$$

Note: *jụir* * *(huir)* is inflected differently from the other *-ụir* verbs, in that it has *júigo* * in the Pres. Ind., 1st pers. sing., and *júiga, júigaj,* etc., in the Pres. Subj.

IRREGULAR VERBS.

Ser.

ser, sịēDo, sido.

Pres. Ind.: $\begin{cases} soi^1 \\ so \\ ero* \end{cases}$ *erej, ej, semos, sōn.*

Pres. Subj.: *sia,** etc. ; or, *sea,*[2] etc.

Pret.: *jụí, jụitej, jụé, jụimoj, jụerōn.*

Etc.

---

[1] *so, 'jto* or *to, do,* and *bo,* (for *soy, estoy, doy,* and *voy*) are common in south-eastern Colorado.

[2] Less commonly, *seya,* etc.

* Espinosa.

Aber (haber).

haber, ab*įēDo*, abido.
Pres. Ind.: *a, aj, a, amoj, ãn,** or *e, aj, a, emoj, ãn.*
Pres. Subj.: *aiga, aigaj, aiga, áiganoj, ajgãn.*
Pret.: *u(b)e, u(b)itej, u(b)o, u(b)imoj, u(b)įerõn.*
Etc.

Ejtar (estar).

ejtar, ejtãDo, ejtáu.
Pres. Ind.: *ejtoi* or *ejtó, ejtáj, ejtá, ejtamoj, ejtãn.* .
Pres. Subj.: *ejté, ejtéj, ejté, ejtemoj, ejtēn.*
Pret.: *ejtu(b)e, ejtu(b)itej, ejtu(b)o, ejtu(b)imoj, ejtu(b)įerõn.*.
Etc.

Note: After a vowel, or *l, n, r, ejtar* usually becomes
'jtar; at the beginning of a breath-group, it may become
tar; cf. *¿ õ jtá?—él 'jtá qui; él no 'jtá qui; ta güe(n)o.*

Tener.

tener, ten*įēDo*, tenido.
Pres. Ind.: *tēNGo, tįē(ne)j, tįē(ne), tenemoj, tįē(nē)n.*
Pres. Subj.: *tēNGa, tēNGaj, tēNGa, tēNGanoj, tēNGãn.*
Imperat.: *tēn.*
Pret.: *tu(b)e, tu(b)itej, tu(b)o, tu(b)imoj, tu(b)įerõn.*
Etc.

ÃDar (andar).

ÃDar is usually inflected as in S. C., but it may be regular throughout (i. e., Pret.: *ãDé, ãdatej, ãDó,* etc.*). ·

Dar.

As in S. C., (except that both *doi* and *do (doy)* occur),

* Espinosa.

but the initial *d* often falls, except after *l* or *n* : *ame,** *mi a,**
*m' ió,** *él Da, cō Darlo.**

Quirer.

quirer, quiri̯ēDo, quirido.

Pres. Ind. : $\left\{\begin{array}{l} \textit{qui̯e(r)o, qui̯e(r)ej, qui̯e(r)e, quiremoj, qui̯e-} \\ \quad \textit{(r)ēn.} \\ \textit{qui̯ó, qui̯éj, qui̯é, qui̯emoj, qui̯ēn.} \end{array}\right.$

Pres. Subj. : $\left\{\begin{array}{l} \textit{qui̯e(r)a, qui̯e(r)aj, qui̯e(r)a, qui̯é(r)anoj,} \\ \quad \textit{qui̯e(r)ān.} \\ \textit{qui̯á, qui̯áj, qui̯á, qui̯éanoj, qui̯ān.} \end{array}\right.$

Fut : *quedré,* etc. ; or, *querré,* etc.

Pu(d)er (poder).

pu(d)er, pu(d)i̯ēDo, pu(d)ido.

Pres. Ind. : *pue(d)o, pu̯e(de)j, pu̯e(de), pu(d)emoj, pu̯e(dē)n.*

Pres. Subj. : *pu̯e(d)a, pu̯e(d)aj, pu̯e(d)a, pu̯é(d)anoj, pu̯e(d)ān.*

Fut. : *podré,* etc. ; or, *porré,* etc.

Etc.

Caber, saber, and *aser (hacer),* as in S. C.

Ir.

Pres. Ind. : *boi* or *bo, baj, ba, (b)amoj, bãn.*

Pres. Subj. : *ba, baj, ba, bamoj, bãn* ; or *baya, bayaj, baya, báyanoj, bayãn.*

Pret. : *ju̯í, ju̯itej, ju̯é, ju̯imoj, ju̯erōn.*

Etc.

Note : *(b)amoj á + infinitive* is used to form imperatives : *(b)amoj aselo (hagámoslo).*

Binir (venir).

binir, bini̯ēDo, binido.

Pres. Ind.: *bēNGo, bįē(ne)j̦, bįē(ne), bįnemoj, bįē(nē)n.*
Etc.

Poner, Asir, Baler (valer), and *Salir,* as in S. C.

Cai(r),* cayer, or quer * (caer).

cai(r), cayer, or *quer, cayēDo, cai(d)o* or *cayido.*
Pres. Ind. : *caigo, caij̦, cai, caimoj* or *cayemoj, caȋn.*
Imperf. : *caiba,* etc. ; or, *cayía,* etc.
Pret. : *cayí, cayitej, cayó, cayimoj, cayerōn.*
Fut. : *cairé,* etc.

Oyer or ṵir * (oír).

oyer or *ṵir, oyēDo, ṵido* or *oyido.*
Pres. Ind. : *oigo, o(y)ij̦, o(y)i, oyemoj* or *oimoj, o(y)ȋn.*
Imperf. : *oyía,* etc. ; or, *ṵiá,* etc.
Pret. : $\begin{cases} oyí,\ oyitej,\ oyó,\ oyimoj,\ oyerōn. \\ ṵí,\ ṵitej,\ oyó,\ ṵimoj,\ oyerōn. \end{cases}$
Fut. : *oyeré,* etc. ; or, *oiré,* etc.

Trai(r),* trayer, or trer * (traer).

trai(r), trayer or *trer, trayēDo, trai(d)o* or *trayido.*
Pres. Ind. : *traigo, traij̦, trai, traimoj* or *trayemoj, traȋn.*
Imperf. : *traiba,* etc. ; or, *trayía,* etc.
Pret. : *truje, trujitej, trujo, trujimoj, trujerōn*; or, *traje,* etc.
Fut. : *trairé,* etc.

CōDusir (conducir).

As in S. C., except (1) that the stem tends to become
*cōDuj-** throughout, by analogy to *cōDujco, cōDujca,* etc.,
and *cōDuje,* etc. ;ⸯ and (2) that the Pret., 3d pers. plur.,
is usually *cōDujerōn ** (also, *cōDujera,* etc.).

---

[1] *Cai(r)* and *trai(r)* [the *r ** usually falls in these two infinitives] are the
common forms.
* Espinosa.

Disir (decir).

disir, disi̯ēDo, dicho.

Pres. Ind.: *digo, disej, dise, disemoj, disēn.*

Pret.: *dije, dijitej, dijo, dijimoj, dijerōn* or *diji̯erōn.*

Etc.

Note: The stem *dis-* tends to become *dij-*,[*] by analogy to *dije*, etc.

Ber (ver).

ber, bi̯ēDo, bijto.

Pres. Ind.: $\left\{\begin{smallmatrix} b\;\dot{} \\ b^{eugo}\;{}^{*} \\ {}_{eι} \end{smallmatrix}\right\}$ *bej, be, bemoj, bēn.*

Pres. Subj.: *beiga*, etc.; or *bea*,[1] etc.

Imperf.: *bía*, etc.; or, *bi̯ía*, etc.

Pret.: *bí* or *bide, bijte, bió* or *bido, bimoj, bi̯erōn.*

Etc.

EXPRESSIONS.

In this article no attempt has been made to study N. M. S. syntax, but a few common expressions are here given:

asēn (for *ase*) *ciNco añuj,* etc.

¿ *qué oraj sōn* (for ¿ *qué hora ej ?*)

(*ej*)*tá* (for *ase*) *fríu, caliēte,* etc.

(*ej*)*toi biēn* (for *tēNGo rasōn*).

(*ej*)*toi mal* (for *no tēNGo rasōn*).

(*ej*)*toi sųeñoso* (for *tēNGo sųeño*).

The last four, and similar expressions, occur rarely, and chiefly where English is also spoken. There also, *ejtar* tends to replace *aber* in the sense of 'there . . . . to be,' as in *no 'jtaban(abía) máj (d)e trej.*

---

[1] Less commonly, *beyu ; beya, beyaj,* etc.

[*] Espinosa.

In a condition " contrary to fact," the Imperfect Indicative may occur in either the condition or the conclusion, as in *ji'tuyera el tįē(m)po, lo asía,* or *ji tenía el tįe(m)po, lo asía; ji abía ētēdido, uyera preferido*; etc. Note also this use of the conditional: *tomaría yo nụ aberte conosido,* " I wish that I had never known you;" *¿ tomaríanoj el trēn local ?*— " shall we take the local train ? "

VOCABULARY.

Before giving a general list of N. M. S. words, a few expressions are given to illustrate (1) how, to express a given idea, the regular Spanish word may be replaced by one that corresponds in sound with its English equivalent, and (2) how Spanish words and phrases may be made to give expression to American institutions:

(1) *'arribar,* to arrive (*llegar* more common).
carta enregistrada, registered letter.
concilio de suidá (ciudad), town council (also *ayuntamiento*).
coronario, coroner.
ingenio, engine.
mayor, mayor (of a town).
talla, railway tie.
(2) *alguacil,* sheriff.
á prueba de lumbre, fire-proof.
billete por viaje redondo, round-trip ticket.
boleto, (political) ticket.
casa de cortes, court house.
entrada de domicilio, homestead entry.
gavilla, political ring.
junta en masa, mass meeting.
mariscal, (village) marshall.
orden de estafeta, postoffice money order.
paradero colectivo, union railway station.

The following is a list of some N. M. S. words in common use. In this list I have attempted to give only those words that differ (1) in meaning or (2) in form (not including those that differ in form according to regular phonetic laws) from their S. C. equivalents.[1] The list is far from complete. The words are spelled according to the rules of S. C. orthography. If the English equivalent is not given, the word has the same meaning in N. M. S. as in S. C.

*a,** ayá* = *allá.*

abarrotero, m., grocer.

abarrotes, m. pl., groceries.

abrigos, m. pl., underwear (*abrigo,* wrap, as in S. C.).

abuja = *aguja.*

abujero = *agujero.*

agarrar, to catch, take (*coger,* rare);—*el tren,* to catch the train.

*agüelo,** m., bugbear.

aigre = *aire.*

aigro = *agrio.*

álamo, m., cottonwood tree.

alguacil, m., (county) sheriff.

alguacilato, m., office of sheriff.

almario = *armario.*

almendra, f. (any sort of) nut (cf. *nuez*).

amachada, f., balking, resistance.

amacharse, to balk.

amachón, -ona, balky.

amargoso = *amargo.*

---

[1] In a few cases I have given words that have the same meaning in N. M. S. and in S. C., (1) if the word is common in N. M. S. and rare in S. C. (cf. *rasurar*), or (2) if it has in N. M. S. a secondary meaning that does not exist in S. C. (cf. *caldear*).

* Espinosa.

amarrar,[1] to tie (cf. *atar*).

ancina * = *encina*, f., scrub oak.

¡ *ándale!* hurry up !

anque, onque = *aunque.*

antonces * = *entonces.*

antusiasmo * = *entusiasmo.*

apriesa = *aprisa.*

arbolera (< *arboleda*), f., orchard, grove.

ardilla, f., chipmunk.

arrempujar = *empujar.*

arribar, to arrive (also *llegar*).

á según = *según.*

aserrón, m., cross-cut saw.

asistir, to feed.

asistencia :[1] *dar la-*, to give board.

asé ya sau * (< *así y á ese lado*?, or *hacia ese lado*?), this way and that.

atajo, m., train or drove of (pack) animals.

atarque, m., dam (to obstruct flow of water in ditch).

atarse, to be embarrassed, dazed.

atole,* m., fluid Indian corn mush, sweetened.

aveno, m. = *avena*, f.[2]

azúcar(a),* f. = *azúcar*, m.

balear, to wound by shooting.

bandeja, f. (dish-) pan.

bandejita, f., metal cup.

bate (< Eng.), m., bat.

berendo, m., antelope.

betabel, m., beet.

bisbal (< Eng.), m., baseball.

---

[1] Also in Colombia (Bransby).

[2] It has been suggested that *aveno* is by analogy to *heno*, but *heno* is unknown in N. M. S.

* Espinosa.

blanquillo, m., egg (rare : *huevo* is common).

bofes, m. pl., lungs.

bogue (< Eng.), m., " buggy," carriage.

bolsa, f., pocket.

bolsita, f., pocket book.

boquinete, m., " sucker " (a fish).

bota, f., leather legging (also " boot," as in S. C.).

bronco, m., wild, unbroken or poorly broken, horse.

ca * = *acá.*

caballada, f., large drove of horses.

caballerango, m., boy that has charge of cowboys' horses during a " round-up," good horseman.

cabrestante (< *cabestrante*), m., small rope, halter strap (also *látigo*).

cabrestear = *cabestrear.*

cabresto (< *cabestro*), m. (general name for), rope.

*cai(r),** *cayer,* or *quer* * [1] = *caer* : *-agua,* to rain (also *llover*).

cajero, m., clerk (in shop).

cajete, m., wash-tub.

calabaza, f., pumpkin ;—*larga,* squash.

caldear, to heat (as in S. C.), flirt.

caldero, m., flirt.

*caldo,** m., soup.

calor, f. = *calor,* m.

calzones, m. pl., trousers ;—*de lona,* overalls.

camalta (< *cama alta*?), f., bedstead.

camaltilla, f., couch.

cantina, f., barroom.

capulín, m., choke cherry.

carpa, f., tent (also *tenta*).

---

[1] Also in Colombia (Bransby).

* Espinosa.

cartera, f., envelope (*sobre* rare).

carro, m., wagon, (railway) coach (also *coche*).

carroza, f., street car (also *tranvía*).

casa de palos, f., log house.

Caslos * = *Carlos.*

cavador, m., hoe (*azada* and *coa* rare).

cerco, m. = *cerca,* f., fence.

cíbolo, m., buffalo.

cincho, m. = *cincha,* f., saddle-girth.

cobija,[1] f., bed cover.

cócono,[2] m., turkey (also *ganso* or *gallina de la tierra*).

codo de dedo, m., knuckle.

coger, to catch (less common than *agarrar* and *pescar,* but not to be avoided as in Mexico).

coleo, m., cowboys' sport of catching steers by the tail and throwing them.

colorido *, -*a,* red (*colorado* more common); *Colorido,* m., State of Colorado.

compá = *compadre.*

comprender, to hire (a servant).

concilio, m., (town) council.

coronario, m., coroner.

cotensio, m., canvass.

cotón, m., "jumper" (kind of coat), woman's jacket.

cuadrar, to please (more common than *gustar*).

cuartón, m., saw log.

cuartonero, m., logger.

cuasi = *casi.*

---

[1] Also in Colombia (Bransby).

[2] The turkey has many names in American Spanish. I have noted: *guanajo* (Cuba), *guajalote* (central and southern Mexico), *cócono* (northern Mexico and New Mex.), *gallina de la tierra* (New Mex. and Colo.) ; *ganso* * (Colo.), *pisco* (Colombia, Bransby).

* Espinosa.

15

cuates, m. pl., twins.

cubeta, f., bucket, pail.

cute (< Eng. ?), m., overcoat.

cutereano, m. : *á él le dió cute y á mí cutereano,* " I got the worst of it."

chamizo, m., sage brush.

chapa,[1] f., door lock.

chaparreras, f. pl., " chaps," cowboys' leggings.

chapero,* m., old, wornout hat.

chapulín, m., grasshopper.

charola, f., bake pan, vegetable dish, tray.

charro, m., native Mex. costume.

charro, a-, gallant, handsome.

chico, -a, small, as in S. C., (*pequeño* rare).

chicote, m., whip.

chiflón, m., stove pipe, lamp chimney.

chinelas, f. pl., slippers, as in S. C., (*pantuflos* and *zapatillas* rare).

chíquite, m., chewing gum.

chirinola, f., quarrel, row.

chopo, a-, short (referring to persons).

chulo, m., pug dog.

chulo, -a, well formed, well dressed, pretty.

chupa, f., jacket.

chupilote, m., buzzard.

denero = dinero.

descoger* *= escoger.*

deshojar, to husk Indian corn.

desparramar, to spill (*derramar* rare).

destornudar* *= estornudar.*

doctor, m., physician (*médico* rare).

---

[1] Also in Colombia (Bransby).

* Espinosa.

dona, f., gift.

drogas, f. pl., debts : *hacer*—to cheat.

durazno, m., peach, as in S. C., (*melocotón* rare).

efectos secos, m. pl., drygoods.

elote, or *elolote*,* m., ear of green Indian corn.

embutido,* m., embroidery.

embutir,* to embroider.

encontra de = *contra*.

entarime, m., board floor ;—*de calle*, board walk.

enter, to seem.

entrada de domicilio, f., homestead entry.

escalereado, m., stairway.

escarbar, to dig (a ditch, etc.).

escrebir = *escribir*.

eslique (< Eng.), m., " slicker."

espacio = *despacio*.

espauda, f., baking powder (from Eng. " powder ? ").

espinilla,[1] f., pimple.

estampa (*de estafeta* or *de correo*), f., postage stamp.

estecle (< Eng.), m., beefsteak.

estufa, f., stove ;—*de cocina*, kitchen stove ;—*de cuarto*, heating stove.

falda, f., brim (of hat).

fandango, m., (general name for) dance (also *baile*).

fashico, m., negro.

feria, f., change (more common than *cambio*).

fiero,[1] *-a*, homely, ugly (more common than *feo*).

fierro, m., iron, cattle brand (*hierro* rare).

físico, *-a*, foolish.

fistol, m., (large) pin (also *alfiler*).

fletero, m., freighter.

---

[1] Also in Colombia (Bransby).

* Espinosa.

flor, f., wheat flour (but *harina de maíz*).

florear, to grind flour; *máquina de —*, flour mill.

fogón, m., fire-place,* furnace.

fregandera, f., dishwasher.

frezada[1] = *frazada*.

frir * = *freír*.

fuella = *huella*.

gachupín, m., Spaniard.

galón, m., English gallon.

galopear = *galopar*.

gallina de la tierra, f., (wild) turkey.

ganso,* m., (wild) turkey (Colo.), goose.

gegén,[1] m., mosquito.

gogote * = *cocote*.

grandotote,[1] *-a*, very large or tall.

gringo, m., Yankee.[2]

guajalote, m., water dog.

guargüero (< *gargüero*), m., neck.

güisque (< Eng.), m., whiskey.

hacia á = *hacia*.

hijadero (< *ahijadero*), m.: *tiempo de-*, lambing time.

hora[1] = *ahora*.

horquilla, f., pitch-fork (as in S. C.), "hames" (part of horse's harness).

hortaliza, f., vegetable garden.

hueja, f., gourd, dipper;—*de pipa*, pipe bowl.

huerito,* *-a*, dear, beloved.

huero,* *-a*, fair, blond, Yankee.

---

[1] Also in Colombia (Bransby).

[2] The dictionary of the Spanish Academy gives *gringo* < *griego*. I have heard Mexicans say that it comes from the song "Green grows the shamrock," sung upon a certain occasion by a company of Irishmen on the Gulf coast of Mexico.

* Espinosa.

huevón,[1] *-ona,* lazy (vulgar).

ijotes, or *igotes,** m. pl., string beans (cf. Mex. *ejotes*).

ingenio, m., engine (*máquina* rare).

ingüento * = *ungüento.*

íntico * = *idéntico.*

ivierno = *invierno.*

jablar = *hablar.*

jallar * = *hallar.*

jancharse,* to find.

jerga, f., home-spun rug, carpet.

jervir * =[1] *hervir.*

jolas, f. pl., money (*denero* more common).

jololote, m., Indian corn husk.

jondo * =[1] *hondo.*

joso * = *oso.*

juir * =[1] *huir.*

jumate, m., dipper.

lamber[1] = *lamer.*

látigo, m., leather, or horse hair, strap, especially the one to which the girth is fastened.

lavador,* m., washboard.

leche nevada, f., ice cream (also *helados*).

lechón, m., milkweed.

letía * or *aletía,* f., shirt bosom.

leva, f., man's coat.

levetón, m., small overcoat.

levita, f., boy's coat.

leyer = *leer.*

liebre, f., jack rabbit.

luvia,* f., freshet.

ma grande, f., grandmother (also *abuela*).

[1] Also in Colombia (Bransby).

* Espinosa.

maleta, f., pocket book (also hand bag, as in S. C.).

mancuernilla: -de puños, cuff button.

manea, f., brake ;—*de carro,* wagon brake.

mano,[1] *-a,* m. and f., brother, sister ; also friendly term of address to an inferior : * *mano Julio, mana Concha,* etc.

manteca, f., lard (only).

mantequilla,[1] f., butter.

maque, m., (house) paint.

maquear, to paint.

marchante, m., customer (*parroquiano* rare).

mariscal, m., (town) marshall.

martigón (< *almartigón*), m., leather headstall or halter.

mashishe, m., imp.

mayor, m., mayor (of a town).

mecate, m., string, strip of cloth ;—*de zapato,* shoe string.

medio color: de - -, pink.

mero,[1] *-a,** same ; *el merito lugar,* the same place ; *ya mero no dilata,* it will not be long before he comes.

mesmo[1] = *mismo.*

mesteño, -a, wild, untamed.

mestro = *maestro.*

metate, m., Indian mill for grinding corn.

meter : *el sol se mete,* the sun sets (*se pone* rare).

metida del sol, f., sunset.

montera, f., sunbonnet.

mosquito, m., gnat.

mostro[1] = *monstruo.*

mulera, f., bell mule.

muncho = *mucho.*

murre = *muy re-* (intensive prefix).

musharaña (< *musaraña*), f., face made by a child in quarreling.

---

[1] Also in Colombia (Bransby).

* Espinosa.

musho, -*a*, pugnosed.

naide[1] or *nadien* = *nadie.*

naguas[1] = *enaguas.*

nanito, -*a* (< *nana*), dear, beloved.

navaja :—*de bolsa*, pocket knife ;—*de barba*, razor (as in S. C.).

no más,*[1] as soon as, not even.

noria, f., well of water (never *pozo*).

nuez, f., nutmeg (cf. *almendra*).

ñudo[1] = *nudo.*

ójala[1] = *ojalá.*

ololote,* m., Indian corn cob.

olla de hervir, f., pot, kettle.

onde = *donde.*

orden de estafeta, m., postoffice money order.

oriente, m., east, as in S. C., (*este* rare).

oshá, f., medicinal root used for cramps and colic.

¡ *ote!* * come here !

oyer or *uir* * = *oír.*

pa[1] = *para.*

pader = *pared.*

pa grande, m., grandfather (also *abuelo*).

paila,* f., washboard.

palomita, f., butterfly (*mariposa* rare).

pandito, -*a*, vain, conceited.

papa,[1] f., potato ;—*dulce*, sweet potato.

papalina, f., bonnet.

pasando mañana = *pasado mañana.*

pato, m., duck (as in S. C.), teakettle.

pelizcar *[1] = *pellizcar.*

pelo, m., hair (of body, or of animals, only).

pendejo,[1] -*a*, stupid, awkward.

---

[1] Also in Colombia (Bransby).

* Espinosa.

peo or *po* * = *pero*.

perrete del agua, m., water dog (Colo.).

pescador, m., catcher (in game of ball).

pescar, to catch (a ball, etc.).

pesla * = *perla*.

petaquilla, f., trunk (also *baúl*).

pichar (< Eng.), to pitch (a ball).

pinole, m, cornmeal (mush).

platón,[1] m., wash basin (*jofaina* and *palangana* rare).

plaza, f., village, town ; *en-*, down town.

ploga (< Eng.), f., plug (of tobacco).

polvillo, m., toasted bread, ground and steeped.

pollito, -a, prettily dressed (applied to children).

pompa (< *bomba*), f., pump.

poniente, m., west as in S. C. (*oeste* rare).

poque * = [1]*porque*.

pozo, m., hole (in the ground); *este camino tiene pozos muy feos*, there are some bad ruts in this road.

pretales, m. pl., suspenders (also *tirantes* in New Mex.).

privado, m., water closet (also *letrina*).

puela, f., frying pan (cf. French *poêle*).

punshe,* m., smoking tobacco.

pus [1] or *pos* = *pues*.

quel = *aquel*.

quese? * (< *qué se hizo de ?*), what has become of ——? where is (are)?

qui = *aquí*.

rábano, m., turnip.

rabón : pantalones rabones, knee breeches.

raíz quemosa, f., radish.

ranchero, m., farmer.

---

[1] Also in Colombia (Bransby).

* Espinosa.

rancho, m. farm ; *hacer-*, to go into camp.

ratón pardo, m., grey squirrel.

rayar: ¿cuánto rayas? how much do you make? *nos rayan el sábado*, they pay us on Saturday.

reata, f., rope of cowhide or horse hair.

rebozo, m., woman's cotton scarf or, shawl, worn over the head and shoulders.

recordar, to awake, as in S. C. (*despertar* rare),

redibar = *derribar*.

relós [1] = *reloj*.

renegar, to curse, as in S. C. (*maldecir* rare).

reparar, to buck; *el bronco me tumbó reparando*, the " bronco " bucked me off.

resurar (< *rasurar*), to shave, as in S. C. (*afeitar* rare).

riir * or *rir* [1] = *reír*.

rito (dim. of *río*), m., small brook.

rosa, f., wild rose;—*de Castilla*, cultivated rose.

saco, m., man's coat;—*de moda*, evening (" dress ") coat.

salado, -*a*, unhappy, cursed.

salarata, f., baking powder.

salitre, m., alkali.

sarape, m., man's shawl or blanket.

se = *ese*.

semitas, f., pl., poor quality of wheat flour.

señá * [1] = *señora* (also *señora*).

shaguaripa : *sombrero de-*, straw hat.

shaquegüe,* m., Indian corn mush.

silla,[1] f., saddle (as also in S. C.).

silleta,[1] f., chair ;—*mecedora*, rocking chair.

sopalpía,* f., " tortilla " fried in lard.

---

[1] Also in Colombia (Bransby).

* Espinosa.

sopanda, f., spring;—*de cama*, bed spring; *asiento de-*,
spring seat.

sueñoso, -*a*, sleepy.

suidá = ciudad.

tahuré = tahur.

talache, m., pickaxe.

talento, m. ; *sombrero de-*, "derby" hat.

talla, f., (railway) tie.

tamal, m., "tamale."

*tamién * = [1] también.*

tánape (< Eng. turnip), m., turnip.

tanque = estanque.

tanre * = *tan re-* (intensive prefix); *tanre-bueno*, very good.

tápalo, m., shawl.

tato, * m., father, grandfather (term of affection).

te = este.

tecolote, m., little owl.

tegua, f., mocassin (kind of shoe).

tejamanil, m., shingle.

temole, m., chili stew.

tenta (< Eng.), f., tent (also *carpa*).

terno, m., set ; -*de cuarto*, set of furniture ; -*de trastes*, set
of dishes.

tiempo de frío, m., winter (also *ivierno*).

tilma, f., short Indian blanket or apron.

tió, -*á*,* m., f., somewhat contemptuous term of address to
an inferior (somewhat as in S. C.)

tortilla, f., round cake or roll, made from wheat flour, or
from scalded and ground Indian corn ; -*de frijoles*, roll containing beans. The crisp edge of the "tortilla" is sometimes used as a spoon, hence the saying, *comer tuí cuchara*,
"to lick the platter clean."

---

[1] Also in Colombia (Bransby).

* Espinosa.

trai(r), * *trayer,* or *trer* *[1] = *traer.*

tranvía, f., = —, m. (central New Mex.).

tras (de la mano), m., back (of the hand).

trastero, m., cupboard.

trastes, m. pl., dishes.

tripa, f., garden hose.

troncón, m., tree stump.

trotear = trotar.

tuí * = *todo y*; *con tuí libros,* books and all.

túnico, m., woman's gown.

tuso, m., prairie dog.

*tuta,** no, not at all.

víbora, f., (general name for) snake.

vinaigre = vinagre.

vita * (< *vidita*), f., darling.

uir * or *oyer = oír.*

yerba, f., weed (cf. *zacate*).

zacatal, m., haystack.

zacate, m., grass, hay.

zancarrón, m., ankle.

zapato de hule, m., " rubber " overshoe.

zoquete, m.; mud (*lodo* rare).

zoquetoso, -a, muddy.

E. C. Hills.

---

[1] Also in Colombia (Bransby).

* Espinosa.

PUBLICATIONS

OF THE

Modern Language Association of America

1906.

| Vol. XXI, 4. | New Series, Vol. XIV, 4. |

XVII.—PROFESSOR CHILD AND THE BALLAD.

In the course of his insistence upon the necessity of a continued recognition of the popular ballad as a distinct literary type, Professor Gummere points out the value of a collection of Professor Child's critical remarks on the ballad and an attempt to determine their general drift.[1] Such is the purpose of the present paper. Aside from the article in the *Universal Cyclopædia*, Professor Child's comments are mere *obiter dicta*, based upon no underlying principle and forming no part of a set purpose. They are, therefore, not easy to classify; the attempt to reduce them to order can be only partially successful, and any arrangement must appear more or less arbitrary. Yet some arrangement has seemed advisable and they have been roughly grouped under the following headings: (1) Authorship and Transmission; (2) Subject-Matter; (3) Technique; (4) A Comparison of the *Ballads* of 1857–1859 and *The English and Scottish Popular Ballads* of 1882–1898; (5) A Collection of General Comments upon Specific Ballads; (6) Summary.

[1] *Modern Philology*, i, 377 f.

I.

In that article in the *Universal Cyclopœdia* which Professor Child "wished to be neither quoted nor regarded as final,"[1] but which must here be combined with other tentative or fragmentary statements, he defined the *popular ballad* as "a distinct and very important species of poetry. Its historical and natural place," he said, "is anterior to the appearance of the poetry of art, to which it has formed a step, and by which it has been regularly displaced, and, in some cases, all but extinguished. Whenever a people in the course of its development reaches a certain intellectual and moral stage, it will feel an impulse to express itself, and the form of expression to which it is first impelled is, as is well known, not prose, but verse, and in fact narrative verse. The condition of society in which a truly national or popular poetry appears explains the character of such poetry. It is a condition in which the people are not divided by political organization and book-culture into markedly distinct classes, in which consequently there is such community of ideas and feelings that the whole people form an individual. Such poetry, accordingly, while it is in its essence an expression of our common human nature, and so of universal and indestructible interest, will in each case be differenced by circumstances and idiosyncrasy. On the other hand, it will always be an expression of the mind and heart of the people as an individual, and never of the personality of individual men. The fundamental characteristic of popular ballads is therefore the absence of subjectivity and of self-consciousness. Though they do not 'write themselves,' as William Grimm has said, though a man and not a people has composed them, still the author counts for nothing, and it

---

[1] Professor Gummere in *Modern Philology*, I, 378.

is not by mere accident, but with the best reason, that they have come down to us anonymous. Hence, too, they are extremely difficult to imitate by the highly civilized modern man, and most of the attempts to reproduce this kind of poetry have been ridiculous failures.

"The primitive ballad, then, is popular, not in the sense of something arising from and suited to the lower orders of a people. As yet, no sharp distinction of high and low exists, in respect to knowledge, desires, and tastes. An increased civilization, and especially the introduction of book-culture, gradually gives rise to such a division; the poetry of art appears; the popular poetry is no longer relished by a portion of the people, and is abandoned to an uncultivated or not over-cultivated class—a constantly diminishing number."

But "the popular ballad is not originally the product or the property of the lower orders of the people. Nothing, in fact, is more obvious than that many of the ballads of the now most refined nations had their origin in that class whose acts and fortunes they depict—the upper class—though the growth of civilization has driven them from the memory of the highly polished and instructed, and has left them as an exclusive possession to the uneducated. The genuine popular ballad had its rise in a time when the distinctions since brought about by education and other circumstances had practically no existence. The vulgar ballads of our day, the 'broadsides' which were printed in such large numbers in England and elsewhere in the sixteenth century or later, belong to a different genus; they are products of a low kind of *art*, and most of them are, from a literary point of view, thoroughly despicable and worthless.

"Next it must be observed that ballads which have been handed down by long-repeated tradition have always departed considerably from their original form. If the transmission has been purely through the mouths of unlearned people, there is less probability of willful change, but once in the hands of professional singers there is no amount of change which they may not undergo. Last of all comes the modern editor, whose so-called improvements are more to be feared than the mischances of a thousand years. A very old ballad will often be found to have resolved itself in the course of what may be called its propagation into several distinct shapes, and each of these again to have received distinct modifications. When the fashion of verse has altered, we shall find a change of form as great as that in the *Hilde-brandslied*, from alliteration without stanza to stanza with rhyme. In all cases the language drifts insensibly from ancient forms, though not at the same rate with the language of every-day life. The professional ballad-singer or minstrel, whose sole object is to please the audience before him, will alter, omit, or add, without scruple, and nothing is more common than to find different ballads blended together.

"There remains the very curious question of the origin of the resemblances which are found in the ballads of different nations, the recurrence of the same incidents or even of the same story, among races distinct in blood and history, and geographically far separated." It is not necessary to go back to a common ancestry to explain these resemblances. "The incidents of many ballads are such as might occur anywhere and at any time; and with regard to agreements that can not be explained in this way we have only to remember that tales and songs were the chief social amusement of all classes of people in all the nations of Europe during the Middle Ages, and that new stories would be eagerly sought for by those whose business it was to furnish this amusement, and be rapidly spread among the fraternity. A great effect was undoubtedly produced by the crusades, which both brought the chief European nations into closer intercourse and made them acquainted with the East, thus facilitating the interchange of stories and greatly enlarging the stock."

This account of authorship and transmission may be illustrated and supplemented by *obiter dicta* from *The English and Scottish Popular Ballads.* " The author counts for nothing ; " the ballad is essentially anonymous : that Expliceth quod Rychard Sheale means merely that *The Hunting of the Cheviot* (162) "was of course part of his stock as minstrel ; the supposition that he was the author is preposterous in the extreme." [1]

Ballads are at their best when " the transmission has been purely through the mouths of unlearned people," when they have come down by domestic tradition, through knitters and weavers. *Glasgerion* (67, B) " is mainly of good derivation (a poor old woman in Aberdeenshire)." [2] And " no Scottish ballads are superior in kind to those recited in the last century by Mrs Brown, of Falkland." [3] Yet even upon Mrs Brown printed literature may have had some influence : in *Fause Foodrage* (89), " the resemblance in the verse in A 31, 'The boy stared wild like a gray gosehawke,' to one in ' Hardyknute,' 'Norse een like gray goss-hawk stared wild,' struck Sir Walter Scott as suspicious," and ".it is quite possible that Mrs Brown may unconsciously have adopted this verse from the tiresome and affected Hardyknute, so much esteemed in her day." [4] A literary treatment of a ballad theme may affect the traditional versions of that ballad. In the case of *Child Maurice* (83) " the popularity of the play [Home's *Douglas*] seems to have given vogue to the ballad. The sophisticated copy passed into recitation, and may very likely have more or less infected those which were repeated from earlier tradi-

---

[1] III, 303.   [2] II, 136.   [3] I, vii.   [4] II, 296.

tion." [1] A whole ballad may even be completely derived from print, and yet, in the course of time, revert to the popular form. Of this same ballad, *Child Maurice*, "Mr Aytoun considers that E is only the copy printed in the middle of the last century purged, in the process of oral transmission, of what was not to the popular taste, 'and altered more.' There is no doubt that a copy learned from print may be transformed in this way, but it is certain that old tradition does not come to a stop when a ballad gets into print." [2]

Not only the possible influence of print is to be taken into account; much depends on the material to which the reciter was exposed and upon his selection. "It will not .... help the ballad [*Young Bearwell* (302)] much that it was not palmed off on Buchan in jest or otherwise, or even if it was learned from an old person by Mr Nicol in his youth. The intrinsic character of the ballad remains, and old people have sometimes burdened their memory with worthless things." [3] Editors were not the only interpolators; of *The Twa Sisters* (10), A, a, 11–13, need not have been written, but "might easily be extemporized by any singer of sufficiently bad taste." [4] The varying memory of reciters, too, was a cause of unintentional change. Thus "Mrs Brown was not satisfied with A b [of *Bonny Baby Livingston* (222)], which Jamieson had taken down from her mouth, and after a short time she sent him A a. The verbal differences are considerable. We need not suppose that Mrs Brown had heard two 'sets' or 'ways,' of which she blended the readings; the fact seems to be that, at the time when she recited to Jamieson, she was not in good

[1] II, 263. An old woman (the reciter of E) knew *Chield Morice* as a child, but later learned *Gil Morice* which began to be more fashionable. II, 264.

[2] II, 464, n. [3] V, 178. [4] I, 119.

condition to remember accurately."[1]   In general, however, the folk memory is remarkable for its tenacity. "Most of the [Danish] versions [of *Earl Brand* (7)] from recitation are wonderful examples and proofs of the fidelity with which simple people 'report and hold' old tales: for, as the editor has shown, verses which never had been printed, but which are found in old manuscripts, are now met with in recited copies; and these recited copies, again, have verses that occur in no Danish print or manuscript, but which nevertheless are found in Norwegian and Swedish recitations, and, what is more striking, in Icelandic tradition of two hundred years' standing."[2]

The ballad does not remain in the possession of the simple folk, or of reciters of Mrs Brown's instinctive good taste. Its best fortune is then perhaps to fall into the hands of children, like *The Maid Freed From the Gallows* (95), of which " F had become a children's game, the last stage of many old ballads."[3] Again, "it is interesting to find the ballad [*The Twa Brothers* (49)] still in the mouths of children in American cities,—in the mouths of the poorest, whose heritage these old things are."[4] *Sir Hugh* (155) in the form of *Little Harry Hughes and the Duke's Daughter*, was heard, says Mr Newell, "from a group of colored children, in the streets of New York city," and traced "to a little girl living in one of the cabins near Central Park."[5]

Less happy is the fate of the ballad when it falls into the hands of professional singers,—the Minstrel Ballad is to be considered presently,—or when it falls into the hands of amateurs of various sorts, who corrupt and debase it. *Hind Etin* (41) "has suffered severely by the accidents of

[1] IV, 231.

[2] I, 89. See also the comment on Apollodorus and the Cretan fairy-tale, I, 337, quoted, p. 774, below.

[3] II, 346.   [4] I, 435.   [5] Quoted, III, 254.

tradition. A has been not simply damaged by passing
through low mouths, but has been worked over by low
hands. Something considerable has been lost from the story,
and fine romantic features, preserved in Norse and German
ballads, have been quite effaced." [1] Of *The Clerk's Twa Sons
o Owsenford* (72) "D has some amusing dashes of prose,
evidently of masculine origin. [Examples follow]. We
have here a strong contrast with both the blind-beggar and
the housemaid style of corruption ; something suggesting the
attorney's clerk rather than the clerk of Owsenford, but at
least not mawkish." [2] The "blind beggar" is, of course,
Buchan's collector, and whether he or the editor was responsible for the corruptions is not always clear. The blind
beggar himself, however, comes in for special condemnation
in the comment on *The Bent Sae Brown* (71): "The introduction and conclusion, and some incidental decorations, of
the Scottish ballad will not be found in the Norse, but are
an outcome of the invention and the piecing and shaping
of that humble but enterprising rhapsodist who has left his
trail over so large a part of Buchan's volumes." [3] In
Brown Robin (97) "the story undoubtedly stops at the right
point in A, with the escape of the two lovers to the wood.
The sequel in C is not at all beyond the inventive ability
of Buchan's blind beggar, and some other blind beggar may
have contrived the cane and the whale, the shooting and
the hanging, in B." [4] As type of the housemaid style of
corruption may, perhaps, stand *Lizie Lindsay* (226). "Leezie
Lindsay from a maid-servant in Aberdeen," wrote Jamieson
to Scott of A b.[5] And, "in his preface to B, Kinloch
remarks that the ballad is very popular in the North,
'and few milk-maids in that quarter but can chaunt it.'" [6]

---

[1] i, 360.   [2] ii, 173.   [3] ii, 170.   [4] ii, 368.
[5] iv, 255, n.   [6] iv, 255.

"Ballads of this description [a young lord o the Hielands, pretending that he is the son of an auld shepherd and an auld dey, persuades a young lady of Edinburgh to fly with him to the Highlands, where he at length reveals his identity]—ballads of this description are peculiarly liable to interpolation and debasement, and there are two passages, each occurring in several versions, which we may, without straining, set down to some plebeian improver." [1]

Not mere corruption, but serving-man authorship, even, is suggested for *Tom Potts* (109): "Such events [unequal matches] would be celebrated only by fellows of the yeoman or of the foot-boy, and surely in the present case the minstrel was not much above the estate of the serving-man. Lord Jockey's reckless liberality throughout, and Lord Phoenix's in the end, is a mark of the serving-man's ideal nobleman." [2] Again as mere corrupter, rather than author, appears the ostler in one version of *Bewick and Graham* (211). In the 1833 edition of *The Border Minstrelsy* "deficiencies were partly supplied and some different readings adopted 'from a copy obtained by the recitation of an ostler in Carlisle.'" g "is shown by internal evidence to be the ostler's copy. Both copies [g and h] were indisputably derived from print, though h may have passed through several mouths. g agrees with b—f closely as to minute points of phraseology which it is difficult to believe that a reciter would have retained. It looks more like an immediate, though faulty, transcript from print." [3] Contrasting styles are suggested in the comment on *The Broomfield Hill* (43): "The editor [of the broadside, "differing as to four or five words only from F"] remarks that A is evidently taken from F; from which it is clear that the pungent buckishness of the broadside does not necessarily make an impression.

[1] IV, 256. Cf. B 10, D 10, E 19; F 11; E 10, F 6.
[2] II, 441.   [3] IV, 144.

A smells of the broom ; F suggests the groom." [1] Perhaps not to be classed with these non-professional corrupters or interpolaters is the bänkelsänger who is responsible for one of the German versions of *Lady Isabel and the Elf Knight* (4): "M smacks decidedly of the bänkelsänger, and has an appropriate moral at the tail: *animi index cauda!*" [2] Perhaps he is to be regarded as a humble sort of minstrel ; to the comments on this class we may now turn our attention.

It does not appear from Professor Child's remarks whether he thought of the minstrel as composing his ballads,—or making them over,—orally or in writing. Perhaps we are to suppose that he followed now one method, now the other. Rychard Sheale may be supposed to have affixed his "expliceth" to his written copy of Chevy Chase ; yet it is "*quod* Rychard Sheale" as if the manuscript had been written by another from his singing. But whether the ballad passed through the minstrel's mouth or through his hands, it received some peculiar and characteristic modifications. Thus *The Boy and the Mantle* (29), *King Arthur and King Cornwall* (30), and *The Marriage of Sir Gawain* (31) "are clearly not of the same rise, and not meant for the same ears, as those which go before. They would come down by professional rather than by domestic tradition, through minstrels rather than knitters and weavers. They suit the hall better than the bower, the tavern or public square better than the cottage, and would not go to the spinning-wheel at all. An exceedingly good piece of minstrelsy 'The Boy and the Mantle' is, too; much livelier than most of the numerous variations on the somewhat overhandled theme." [3] *Crow and Pie* (111), likewise, "is not a purely popular ballad, but rather of that kind which,

[1] I, 391. [2] I, 34. [3] I, 257.

for convenience, may be called the minstrel-ballad. It has, however, popular features, and markedly in stanzas 13, 14," [1] —the damsel's demanding the name of the man who has wronged her, a feature found in *The Bonny Hind* (50) and its continental parallels.[2] The term *minstrel* may, perhaps, be more loosely used in the passage which describes *The Rising in the North* (175) as "the work of a loyal but not unsympathetic minstrel;" [3] in the statement concerning *Northumberland Betrayed by Douglas* (176), that "the ballad-minstrel acquaints us with circumstances concerning the surrender of Northumberland;" [4] and in the statement to the effect that, in the case of *Tom Potts* (109), "the minstrel was not much above the estate of the serving-man." [5]

We may now attempt to construct an account of the vicissitudes to which the ballad was subject when, in the course of transmission, it sometimes found its way into writing and into print. Version B of *The Hunting of the Cheviot* (162) "is a striking but by no means a solitary example of the impairment which an old ballad would suffer when written over for the broadside press. This very seriously enfeebled edition was in circulation throughout the seventeenth century, and much sung . . . . despite its length. It is declared by Addison, in his appreciative and tasteful critique . . . . to be the favorite ballad of the common people of England." [6] Similarly, in the case of *Sir Andrew Barton* (167), "a collation of A and B will show how ballads were retrenched and marred in the process of preparing them for the vulgar press." [7] "B begins vilely, but does not go on so ill. The forty merchants coming 'with fifty sail' to King Henry on a mountain top . . . . requires to be taken indulgently." [8] Though a broadside differs

---

[1] II, 478.   [2] Cf. I, 444 f.   [3] III, 403.   [4] III, 410.
[5] II, 441.   [6] III, 305.   [7] III, 334.   [8] III, 334, n.

widely from a true ballad, it is not to be supposed that,—
at least in the examples included by Professor Child,—
some general traits or special features peculiar to the popular
or traditional matter or manner did not survive. Thus,
although the ballad of *The Twa Knights* (268) "can have
had no currency in Scotland, and perhaps was known only
through print," yet "a similar one is strictly traditional in
Greece, and widely dispersed, both on the mainland and
among the islands."[1] Again, there are two broadsides of
King John and the Bishop (45), which Professor Child does
not include, "both inferior even to B, and in a far less
popular style."[2] There are, then, degrees of departure
from the popular style. There are degrees of departure from
the popular matter, also, and the broadside preserves sometimes but a single popular feature. Version M of *Young
Beichan* (53) " was probably a broadside or stall copy, and
is certainly of that quality, but preserves a very ancient
traditional feature."[3] The broadside version of *The Broomfield Hill* (43) is distinguished by a "pungent buckishness,"
which is not found in A, and which "suggests the groom."[4]
A broadside may itself become tradition. The English
version of *Lord Thomas and Fair Annet* (73) "is a broadside of Charles the Second's time. . . . This copy has
become traditional in Scotland and Ireland. The Scottish
traditional copy . . . . is far superior, and one of the most
beautiful of our ballads, and indeed of all ballads."[5] The
tradition lives, even after a ballad has found its way into
print, and may influence and modify later versions of the
printed form. Of *Prince Heathen* (104) "the fragment A
. . . . is partly explained by B, which is no doubt some
stall-copy, reshaped from tradition."[6] Of *The Baffled Knight*

---

[1] v, 21. [2] i, 404. [3] i, 455. [4] i, 391.
[5] ii, 180. [6] ii, 424.

(112) "E is, in all probability, a broadside copy modified by tradition."[1] In origin, in any case, the broadsides in *The English and Scottish Popular Ballads* are popular.[2] "There is a Scottish ballad [similar to *The Baffled Knight*] in which the tables are turned. . . . This, as being of comparatively recent, and not of popular, but of low literary origin, cannot be admitted here."[3]

"Last of all comes the modern editor," and from Professor Child's comments and skilful undoing of much of their work one might put together fairly complete accounts of the methods of Percy, Scott, Jamieson, Buchan, and the rest. We are concerned, however, not so much with the editors as with the results of their editing, with the kinds of change that the ballad suffered in their hands. It was often lengthened, in many cases by the combination of several versions. Thus Scott's version of *Tam Lin* (39, I), "as he himself states, was compounded of the Museum copy, Riddell's, Herd's, and 'several recitals from tradition.'"[4] Of this use of materials from recitation examples are very numerous. Ballads were lengthened also by the interpolation of new stanzas. After Scott's edition, in the *Minstrelsy*, of *The Twa Sisters* (10), "Jamieson followed . . . . with a tolerably faithful, though not, as he says, *verbatim*,[5] publication of his copy of Mrs Brown's ballad,

---

[1] ii, 480.

[2] The comparison of broadsides with traditional versions is instructive. See i, A, a, b, c; 10, A, a; 45, B; 53, L, M; 73, D; 104, B, 112, E (and ii, 491); 110, A; 145, C; 151; 152; 153; 162, B; 167, B; 268. Much of the later Robin Hood poetry looks like "char-work done for the petty press" (iii, 42). *Robin Hood Rescuing Will Stutly* (141) "is a ballad made for print, with little of the traditional in the matter and nothing in the style" (iii, 185).

[3] ii, 480.   [4] i, 335.

[5] "Jamieson was not always precise in the account he gave of the changes he made in his texts" (iv, 255). Cf. also i, 138.

somewhat marred, too, by acknowledged interpolations."[1]
King Henry (32) was increased by Jamieson's interpolations
from twenty-two to thirty-four stanzas.[2] Scott's version of
Fair Annie (62, A) "was obtained 'chiefly from the recitation of an old woman,' but we are not informed who supplied
the rest. Herd's fragment, D, furnished stanzas 2–6, 12,
17, 19. A doubt may be hazarded whether stanzas 8–10
came from the old woman."[3] Interpolation and combination are here both illustrated. Scott's later edition of *Tam
Lin* (39) "was corrupted with eleven new stanzas, which
are not simply somewhat of a modern cast as to diction, as
Scott remarks, but of a grossly modern invention, and
as unlike popular verse as anything can be."[4] Of his
version of *Jellon Grame* (90) Scott says: "'Some verses
are apparently modernized.'" "The only very important
difference between Scott's version and Mrs Brown's is its
having four stanzas of its own, the four before the last two,
which are evidently not simply modernized, but modern."[5]

But the editor did not merely combine or interpolate;
more vaguely, he "improved." Version E of *The Fair
Flower of Northumberland* (9), "a traditional version from
the English border, has unfortunately been improved by
some literary pen."[6] Or he "retouched,"[7] or "altered,"[8]
or "emended." Scott confesses to some emendation of
Kinmont Willy (186); "it is to be suspected that a great
deal more emendation was done than the mangling of
reciters rendered absolutely necessary. One would like, for
example, to see stanzas 10–12 and 31 in their mangled
condition."[9] In general, no changes or additions are "in
so glaring contrast with the groundwork as literary emenda-

---

[1] Stanzas 20, 21, 27, etc. I, 119. Cf. II, 83.
[2] I, 297.   [3] II, 63 f.   [4] I, 335.   [5] II, 302.
[6] I, 112.   [7] IV, 5.   [8] I, 138.   [9] III, 472.

tions of traditional ballads." [1]   " Variations," also, are to be
noted : inaccuracies in *The Fire of Frendraught* (196) are
acknowledged by Motherwell ; "the implication is, or should
be, that these variations are of editorial origin." [2]   Of *Sweet
William's Ghost* (77, A and B), " Percy remarks that the
concluding stanza seems modern.   There can be no doubt
that both that and the one before it are modern ; but, to the
extent of Margaret's dying on her lover's grave, they are
very likely to represent original verses not remembered
in form." [3]

Certain general results of transmission, of whatever kind,
are to be noted.   As a ballad passes from one country to
another the nationality of the hero may be changed.   In
Hugh Spencer's Feats in France (158) " Hugh is naturally
turned into a Scotsman in the Scottish version, C." [4]   The
hero's name is not more stable than his nationality.   " In
the course of transmission [of *John Thomson and the Turk*
(266)], as has ever been the wont, names were changed, and
also some subordinate circumstances." [5]   Again, "the actual
name of the hero of a ballad affords hardly a presumption
as to who was originally the hero." [6]   Even the part that
he plays the hero may exchange with another character.
"Robin Hood's rescue of Little John, in Guy of Gisborne,
after quarrelling with him on a fanciful provocation, is a
partial offset for Little John's heart-stirring generosity in
this ballad. [*Robin Hood and the Monk* (119).]   We have
already had several cases of ballads in which the principal
actors exchange parts." [7]   The ballad, again, is not constant
in its attachment to one locality, and " the topography of
traditional ballads frequently presents difficulties, both because it is liable to be changed, wholly, or, what is more

[1] II, 428.   [2] IV, 39. Cf. II, 317.   [3] II, 226.   [4] III, 276.
[5] V, 2.   [6] II, 19.   [7] III, 96.

embarrassing, partially, to suit a locality to which a ballad has been transported, and again because unfamiliar names, when not exchanged, are exposed to corruption." [1] Thus, " in the ballad which follows this [*Rare Willie Drowned in Yarrow* (215)], a western variety of the same story, Willie is drowned in the Clyde." [2]

The corruption of names is but one phase of the change to which all unfamiliar ballad diction is exposed. "At every stage of oral transmission we must suppose that some accidental variations from what was delivered would be introduced, and occasionally some wilful variations. Memory will fail at times; at times the listener will hear amiss, or will not understand, and a perversion of sense will ensue, or absolute nonsense,—nonsense which will be servilely repeated, and which repetition may make more gross. . . . Learned words do not occur in ballads; still an old native word will be in the same danger of metamorphosis. But, though unfamiliarity naturally ends in corruption, mishearing may have the like effect where the original phrase is in no way at fault. . . .

" It must be borne in mind, however, that as to nonsense the burden of proof rests always upon the expositor. His personal inability to dispose of a reading is not conclusive; his convictions may be strong, but patience and caution are his part and self-restraint as to conjectures." [3]

In transmission, then, and even in the best of it, the ballad ordinarily fares but ill, "departs from the original form," becomes less typically ballad; and, generally speaking, the older it is, the earlier it is caught and fixed in print, the better. Professor Child has thus special praise for those Robin Hood ballads which "have come down to us in comparatively ancient form." [4] *Robin Hood's Death* (120, B)

---

[1] IV, 156. [2] IV, 178. [3] V, 309. [4] III, 42.

is "in the fine old strain." [1] *Robin Hood and the Beggar*
(134, II), "by far the best of the Robin Hood ballads of
the secondary, so to speak cyclic, period," is "a composition
of some antiquity," [2] *Thomas Rymer* (37) "is an entirely
popular ballad as to style, and must be of considerable age." [3]
One is not to expect in a late or modern ballad the excellence found in an early or ancient one. *Robin Hood's Chase*
(146) "is a well-conceived ballad, and only needs to be
older." [4] *Walter Lesly* (296) is "a late, but life-like and
spirited ballad." [5] *The Hunting of the Cheviot* (162, B) "is
a striking . . . . example of the impairment which an old
ballad would suffer when written over for the broadside
press." [6] Version M of *Young Beichan* (53) "was probably
a broadside or stall copy, and is certainly of that quality,
but preserves a very ancient traditional feature." [7] The
"ridiculous ballad" of *John Thomson and the Turk* (266)
finds a place in the collection because it is "a seedling from
an ancient and very notable story." [8] *The Knight's Ghost*
(265) "has not a perceptible globule of old blood in it, yet
it has had the distinction of being more than once translated
as a specimen of Scottish popular ballads." [9] Scott's later
edition of *Tam Lin* (39) "was corrupted with eleven new
stanzas, which are not simply somewhat of a modern cast as
to diction, as Scott remarks, but of a grossly modern invention, and as unlike popular verse as anything can be." [10]
Scott's version of *Jellon Grame* (90) has four stanzas of its
own, "which are evidently not simply modernized, but
modern." [11] Certain stanzas in version B b of *Archie o Cawfield* (188) "are indifferent modern stuff." [12] The "modern

[1] III, 103.   [2] III, 159.   [3] I, 320.   [4] III, 206.
[5] V, 168.   [6] III, 305.   [7] I, 455.   [8] V, 1.
[9] IV, 437.   [10] I, 335.   [11] II, 302.   [12] III, 486.

2

ballad" on the subject of *The Heir of Linne* (267) is "an inexpressibly pitiable ditty."[1]

Certain counterfeits, imitations, or "spurious" ballads, wholly or almost wholly the work of editors or modern writers, are included in Professor Child's collection. *Robin Hood and the Tinker* (127) is a "contemptible imitation of imitations."[2] Buchan's version of *Young Waters* (94) is, for the most part, "a counterfeit of the lowest description. Nevertheless it is given in an appendix ; for much the same reason that thieves are photographed."[3] *Young Ronald* (304) is an example of the "spurious" ballad, and the reasons for its inclusion are given at some length. "If any lover of ballads should feel his understanding insulted by the presentation of such a piece as this, I can have no quarrel with him. There is certainly much in it that is exasperating. . . . In this and not a very few other cases, I have suppressed disgust, and admitted an actually worthless and manifestly—at least in part—spurious ballad, because of a remote possibility that it might contain relics, or be a debased representative, of something genuine and better. Such was the advice of my lamented friend, Grundtvig, in more instances than those in which I have brought myself to defer to his judgment."[4] For the same reason is included *The Laidley Worm of Spindleston Heughs :* "This composition of Mr. Lamb's—for nearly every line of it is his [5]—is not only based on popular tradition, but evidently preserves some small fragments of a popular ballad, and for this reason is given in an Appendix."[6]

---

[1] v, 12. Cf. also i, 35, iv, 10, 142, 401, for passages condemned as "modern."

[2] iii, 140.   [3] ii, 342.   [4] v, 182.

[5] Communicated by the Rev. Mr Lamb to Hutchinson "with this harmless preamble : 'a song 500 years old, made by the old Mountain Bard, Duncan Frasier, living on Cheviot, A. D. 1270.'"

[6] i, 308.

II.

From what has been said it is clear that, as a rule, the ballad is at its best, is most typically ballad, when its subject-matter is of purely popular origin. The *Gest* and the earliest Robin Hood ballads "are among the best of all ballads," and Robin Hood "is absolutely a creation of the popular muse. The earliest mention we have of him is as the subject of ballads."[1] "Absolutely a creation of the popular muse" would seem to imply that the ballad is not,—or that these ballads at least are not,—based either upon a formless popular tradition or upon definite prose tales. Local traditions follow the ballad, as attempts to explain it; they do not supply the story. "In places where a ballad has once been known, the story will often be remembered after the verses have been wholly or partly forgotten, and the ballad will be resolved into a prose tale, retaining, perhaps, some scraps of verse, and not infrequently taking up new matter, or blending with other traditions. Naturally enough, a ballad and an equivalent tale sometimes exist side by side."[2]

The existence of foreign traditional parallels is one evidence of popular origin. *The Bent Sae Brown* (71) has close resemblances with Norse ballads; "but the very homeliness of the Scottish ballad precludes any suspicion beyond tampering with tradition. The silliness and fulsome vulgarity of Buchan's versions often enough make one wince or sicken. . . . But such correspondences with foreign ballads as we witness in the present case are evidence of a genuine traditional foundation."[3] Less complete, yet even more striking, are the foreign versions of the theme of *Tam Lin* (39).

[1] III, 42.   [2] I, 46; examples follow.   [3] II, 170, n.

"This fine ballad stands by itself, and is not, as might have been expected, found in possession of any people but the Scottish. Yet it has connections, through the principal feature in the story, the retransformation of Tam Lin, with Greek popular tradition older than Homer."[1] "We come . . . . surprisingly near to the principal event of the Scottish ballad in a Cretan fairy-tale . . . . [1820–1830]." And this "Cretan tale does not differ from the one repeated by Apollodorus from earlier writers a couple of thousand years ago more than two versions of a story gathered from oral tradition in these days are apt to do. Whether it has come down to our time from mouth to mouth through twenty-five centuries or more, or whether, having died out of the popular memory, it was reintroduced through literature, is a question that cannot be decided with certainty; but there will be nothing unlikely in the former supposition to those who bear in mind the tenacity of tradition among people who have never known books."[2] *The Suffolk Miracle* (272) has "impressive and beautiful"[3] European parallels, and therefore finds a place in Professor Child's collection. Other debased or counterfeit or spurious ballads are present for the same reason, or because, like *Tam Lin*, they contain some purely popular or traditional feature. Certain features are expressly declared to be popular or to be common in ballads; among these are the quibbling oaths and the unbosoming oneself to an oven or stove, in *The Lord of Lorn and the False Steward* (271);[4] the miraculous harvest in *The Carnal and the Crane* (55);[5] the childbirth in the wood in *Leesome Brand* (15) and in *Rose the Red and White Lily* (103);[6] the presence of three ladies, "that the youngest may be preferred to the others;" the unpardonable "offence

---

[1] I, 336. [2] I, 337. [3] v, 59. [4] v, 48.
[5] II, 7. [6] II, 416.

given by not asking a brother's assent to his sister's marriage" in *The Cruel Brother* (11);[1] the testament in *The Cruel Brother, Lord Randal, Edward*, etc.;[2] the riddles in *Riddles Wisely Expounded* (1), etc.;[3] and certain stanzas in *Crow and Pie* (111).[4] "Heroic sentiment" is a characteristic of the earlier Robin Hood ballads; in the later it is gone.[5] It may be that in his appreciation of certain other features Professor Child is thinking not merely of their excellence but of their peculiarly popular quality as well. Thus he speaks of "the fine trait of the ringing of the bells without men's hands, and the reading of the books without man's tongue,"[6] in *Sir Hugh* (155); and thinks that "perhaps the original conception [of *The Twa Sisters* (10)] was the simple and beautiful one which we find in English B and both the Icelandic ballads, that the king's harper, or the girl's lover, takes three locks of her yellow hair to string his harp with."[7]

The ballad does not always go to ancient tradition, or draw upon the stock of popular themes and motives; occasionally, in more modern times, it tells the story of some actual occurrence; it is based on fact. But the balladist feels himself under no obligation of loyalty to the fact. "A strict accordance with history should not be expected, and indeed would be almost a ground of suspicion ["or a pure accident"]. Ballad singers and their hearers would be as indifferent to the facts as the readers of ballads are now; it is only editors who feel bound to look closely into such matters."[8] In *Johnie Armstrong* (169) "the ballads treat facts with the customary freedom and improve upon them greatly."[9] *Bonny John Seton* (198) "is accurate as to the date, not commonly a good sign for such things."[10] "A ballad

[1] I, 142.   [2] Examples, I, 143.   [3] I, 1.   [4] II, 478.
[5] III, 159.   [6] III, 235.   [7] I, 121.   [8] II, 19,
[9] III, 366.   [10] IV, 51.

taken down some four hundred years after the event will
be apt to retain very little of sober history." [1] Yet, in the
case of *The Hunting of the Cheviot* (162), at least, "the ballad
can scarcely be a deliberate fiction. The singer is not a
critical historian, but he supposes himself to be dealing with
facts; he may be partial to his countrymen, but he has no
doubt that he is treating of a real event." [2] Part of *The
Earl of Westmoreland* (177) "has an historical substratum,
though details are incorrect." [3] In *Northumberland Betrayed
by Douglas* (176) "the ballad-minstrel acquaints us with
circumstances concerning the surrender of Northumberland
which are not known to any of the historians." [4] Local
tradition would seem to be even less authentic than the
ballad; "in such cases" as *The Coble o Cargill* (242) it
"seldom means more than a theory which people have
formed to explain a preëxisting ballad." [5]

We have already seen how a ballad derived from print
tends to revert to the popular form; the same tendency is
evident in the ballad derived from a romance. Of *Gude
Wallace* (157) "Blind Harry's Wallace . . . . is clearly the
source." "But the portions of Blind Harry's poem out of
which these ballads were made were perhaps themselves
composed from older ballads, and the restitution of the
lyrical form may have given us something not altogether
unlike what was sung in the fifteenth, or even the fourteenth,
century." [6] *Thomas Rymer* (37) is derived from the romance,
yet it is "an entirely popular ballad as to style." [7] These
are the only cases where Professor Child admits without
question the derivation of a ballad from a romance; in other
cases, where ballad and romance tell the same story, he
insists that the possibility of the priority of the ballad must

[1] III, 317.   [2] III, 304.   [3] III, 417.   [4] III. 410,
[5] IV, 359.   [6] III, 265 f.   [7] I, 320.

be considered. Thus the ballad of *Hind Horn* (17) has close affinity with the later English romance, but no filiation. "And were filiation to be accepted, there would remain the question of priority. It is often assumed, without a misgiving, that oral tradition must needs be younger than anything that was committed to writing some centuries ago; but this requires in each case to be made out; there is certainly no antecedent probability of that kind."[1] *Fair Annie* (62) is not derived from the lay; they "have a common source, which lies further back, and too far for us to find."[2] In *Gil Brenton* (5) "the artifice of substituting waiting-woman for bride has been thought to be derived from the romance of Tristan. . . . Grundtvig truly remarks that a borrowing by the romance from the popular ballad is as probable a supposition as the converse."[3] The ballad does sometimes go to the romance for details. Thus, in *The Earl of Westmoreland* (177) "what follows [stanza 15] is pure fancy work, or rather an imitation of stale old romance."[4] *The Kitchie-Boy* (252) is a modern adaptation of King Horn, but, "in the particular of the hero's having his choice of two women, it is more like the *gest* of 'King Horn,' or 'Horn Childe and Maiden Rimnild;' but an independent invention of the Spanish lady is not beyond the humble ability of the composer of 'The Kitchie-Boy.'"[5] In the "worthless and manifestly—at least in part—spurious ballad" of *Young Ronald* (304), "the nicking with nay and the giant are borrowed from romances."[6] Though the *Gest*, finally, "as to all important considerations, is eminently original, absolutely so as to the conception of Robin Hood, some traits and incidents, as might be expected, are taken from what we may call the general stock of mediæval

[1] I, 193.   [2] II, 67.   [3] I, 67.   [4] III, 417.
[5] IV, 401.   [6] V, 182.

fiction." [1] Thus "Robin Hood will not dine until he has
some guest that can pay handsomely for his entertainment.
. . . This habit of Robin's seems to be a humorous imitation of King Arthur, who in numerous romances will not
dine till some adventure presents itself." [2]

Not only from ancient tradition, from fact, from romance
or the sources of romance may the ballad derive its subject-
matter; it may also turn back upon itself, and as late ballads
counterfeit or imitate the style of earlier ones, so late ballads
go to earlier ones for their subject-matter as well. Thus
The Battle of Otterburn (161) "is likely to have been
modernized from . . . . a predecessor." [3] Part of *The King's
Disguise, and Friendship with Robin Hood* (151) "is a loose
paraphrase, with omissions, of the seventh and eighth fits of
the Gest." [4] *The Brown Girl* (295) " recalls ' Lord Thomas
and Fair Annet,' 'Sweet William's Ghost,' 'Clerk Saunders,'
'The Unquiet Grave,' 'Bonny Barbara Allen,' and has
something of all of them. . . . Still it is not deliberately and mechanically patched together (as are some
pieces in Part VIII), and in the point of the proud and
unrelenting character of the Brown Girl it is original." [5]
"Deliberately and mechanically put together" were the
pieces of Part VIII which follow. *Auld Matrons* (249)
"was made by someone who had acquintance with the
first fit of 'Adam Bell.' The anonymous 'old wife' becomes
'auld Matrons;' Inglewood, Ringlewood. The conclusion
is in imitation of the rescues in Robin Hood ballads." [6]
Henry Martyn (250) "must have sprung from the ashes of
'Andrew Barton,' of which name Henry Martyn would be
no extraordinary corruption." [7] *The Kitchie-Boy* (252) is
"a modern 'adaptation' of ' King Horn'. . . . from which

---

[1] iii, 49 f.   [2] iii, 51.   [3] iii, 293.   [4] iii, 220.
[5] v, 166.   [6] iv, 391.   [7] iv, 393.

A 33, 34, B 47, D 7, 8, are taken outright."[1] The first half of *Willie's Fatal Visit* (255) "is a medley of 'Sweet William's Ghost,' 'Clerk Saunders,' and 'The Grey Cock,'"[2] Of *Broughty Wa's* (258), "Stanza 9, as it runs in b, is a reminiscence of 'Bonny Baby Livingston,' and 13 recalls 'Child Waters,' or 'The Knight and the Shepherd's Daughter.'"[3] A large part of *The New-Slain Knight* (263) "is imitated or taken outright from very well known ballads."[4] Like some of these later ballads the *Gest of Robyn Hode* goes back to earlier ballads for its subject-matter. "The Gest is a popular epic, composed from several ballads by a poet of a thoroughly congenial spirit. No one of the ballads from which it was made up is extant in a separate shape, and some portions of the story may have been of the compiler's own invention. The decoying of the sheriff into the wood, stanzas 181–204, is of the same derivation as the last part of Robin Hood and the Potter, No 121, Little John and Robin Hood exchanging parts; the conclusion, 451–56, is of the same source as Robin Hood's Death, No 120."[5] Some of the Middle-English forms "may be relics of the ballads from which this little epic was made up; or the whole poem may have been put together as early as 1400, or before."[6] It is noteworthy that the *Gest* was composed *from*, not *of*, several ballads; it was not made up of unchanged ballads, "deliberately and mechanically put together."

The motives or features characteristic of subject-matter derived from pure popular tradition have already been noted; we may now note those traits which Professor Child declares or implies to be not characteristic of such subject-matter. Extravagance would seem to be one of these: the extravagance of *Hughie Grame* (191, A, 16) "it is to be

1 IV, 401. 2 IV, 415. 3 IV, 423. 4 IV, 434.
5 III, 49. 6 III, 40.

hoped is a corruption." [1] In *Mary Hamilton* (173) "there
are not a few spurious passages. Among these are the
extravagance of the queen's bursting in the door, F 8;
the platitude,[2] of menial stamp, that the child, if saved,
might have been an honor to the mother, D 10, L 3, O 4," [3]
Exaggeration is another non-traditional trait: "It is but
the natural course of exaggeration that the shepherd, having
beaten Robin Hood, should beat Little John. This is
descending low enough, but we do not see the bottom of this
kind of balladry here" [4] [*Robin Hood and the Shepherd*
(165)]. *Robin Hood and Queen Katherine* (145) is "a very
pleasant ballad, with all the exaggeration." [5] The true ballad
is not prosaic: in *Fause Foodrage* (89) "the . . . . king kills
his successful rival on his wedding-day. According to the
prosaic, not at all ballad-like, and evidently corrupted
account in A, there is a rebellion of nobles four months after
the marriage, and a certain False Foodrage takes it upon
himself to kill the king." [6] The true ballad is not over-
refined: in *The Braes of Yarrow* (214, C, 2) "the brothers
have taken offence because their sister was not regarded as
his equal by her husband, which is perhaps too much of a
refinement for ballads, and may be a perversion." [7] The
true ballad is not cynical: *The Twa Corbies* sounds "something like a cynical variation of the tender little English
ballad," [8] and it is not printed as a ballad in Professor Child's
collection. The true ballad is not sophisticated: it was the
influence of the play, Home's *Douglas*, that gave vogue to
the ballad, *Child Maurice* (83), and "the sophisticated copy
passed into recitation." [9] The true ballad is not sentimental:
in *Mary Hamilton* (173), "there are not a few spurious

---

[1] iv, 10.   [2] Cf. iii, 225.   [3] iii, 381.
[4] iii, 165.   [5] iii, 197.   [6] ii, 296.
[7] iv, 161.   [8] i, 253. Cf. also iii, 258.   [9] ii, 263.

passages," among them, "the sentimentality of H 3, 16."[1] Jamieson published *Child Waters* (63, B a) with "the addition of three sentimental stanzas to make Burd Ellen die just as her enduring all things is to be rewarded."[2] The true ballad does not append a moral : a German version of *Lady Isabel and the Elf-Knight* (4) "smacks decidedly of the bänkelsänger, and has an appropriate moral at the tail."[3] A certain degree of probability or naturalness is to be expected of the true ballad story : in *Jellon Grame* (90), "one day, when the boy asks why his mother does not take him home, Jellon Grame (very unnaturally) answers, I slew her, and there she lies : upon which the boy sends an arrow through him."[4] Finally, the plot of the true ballad is not trite. In *Child Owlet* (291) "the chain of gold in the first stanza and the penknife below the bed in the fourth have a false ring, and the story is of the tritest. The ballad seems at best to be a late one, and is perhaps mere imitation."[5]

III.

It is clear that to Professor Child's mind it was necessary that the ballad should tell a story. "The word *ballad* in English signifies a narrative song, a short tale in lyric verse."[6] Thus the English versions of *Geordie* (209) are said to be mere 'goodnights,' whereas "the Scottish ballads have a proper story, with a beginning, middle, and end, and (save one late copy), a good end, and they are most certainly . . . . independent of the English."[7] *Dugall Quin* (294) is a "little ballad, which has barely story enough to be so

---

[1] III, 381.   [2] II, 83.   [3] I, 34.   [4] II, 302.   [5] v, 156 f.
[6] *Universal Cyclopædia*, "Ballad Poetry." The lyrical element is of equal importance ; see p. 790, below.
[7] IV, 126.

called."[1] To the "English 'ditty' (not a traditional ballad) .... there is very little story."[2]

Necessary as the story is, however, it is seldom completely told in the ballad; something is left to the hearers' imagination. Sometimes the close of the story is omitted: "it is not said (except in the spurious portions of E) that the lady was carried back by her husband, but this may perhaps be inferred from his hanging the gypsies. In D and K we are left uncertain as to her disposition."[3] Transitions are usually abrupt,—"abrupt even for a ballad" in *Willie's Lady* (6) from stanza 33 to stanza 34.[4] Jamieson, in printing *The Bonny Birdy* (82), introduced several stanzas 'to fill up chasms.' "But the chasms, such as they are, are easily leapt by the imagination, and Jamieson's interpolations are mere bridges of carpenter's work."[5] Of *Sir Patrick Spens* (58), "Percy's version [A] remains, poetically, the best. It may be a fragment, but the imagination easily supplies all that may be wanting; and if more of the story, or the whole, be told in H, the half is better[6] than the whole."[7] These abrupt transitions do not, then, result in incoherence, which accompanies corruption and is a sign of degeneracy. Thus *The Carnal and the Crane* (55) "had obviously been transmitted from mouth to mouth before it was fixed in its present incoherent and corrupted form by print."[8] *Young Bearwell* (302) is "one of not a few flimsy and unjointed ballads found in Buchan's volumes, the like of which is hardly to be found elsewhere."[9] After an attempt to make the story of *The White Fisher* (264) hang together, Professor

---

[1] v, 165.
[2] iv, 192. [The Broom of Cowdenknows (217)].
[3] iv, 63. [The Gypsie Laddie (200)].
[4] i, 82. [5] ii, 260.
[6] Surely better *as ballad*. Cf. p. 796, below.
[7] ii, 18. [8] ii, 7. [9] v, 178.

Child concludes : " But we need not trouble ourselves much to make these counterfeits reasonable. Those who utter them rely confidently upon our taking folly and jargon as the marks of genuineness." [1] Coherence, on the contrary, is a characteristic of the true ballad, an important phase of ballad excellence. " I am persuaded that there was an older and better copy of this ballad [Bewick and Graham (211)] than those which are extant. The story is so well composed, proportion is so well kept, on the whole, that it is reasonable to suppose that certain passages (as stanzas 3, 4, 50) may have suffered some injury." [2] Introductions, not closely connected with the ballad story, are not characteristic. " The narrator in the Ever Green poem reports at second hand : as he is walking, he meets a man who, upon request, tells him the beginning and the end. Both pieces have nearly the same first line. The borrowing was more probably on the part of the ballad, for a popular ballad would be likely to tell its tale without preliminaries." [3]

Brevity is a characteristic of the true ballad, and it may be, in this respect, profitably contrasted with Buchan's versions. Version C of Brown Adam (98) " has the usual marks of Buchan's copies, great length, vulgarity, and such extravagance and absurdity as are found in stanzas 23, 26, 29." [4] " Buchan, who may generally be relied upon to produce a longer ballad than anybody else, has ' Young Waters' in thirty-nine stanzas, ' the only complete version which he had ever met.' " [5] His version of The Gay Goshawk (96, G) is " vilely dilated and debased," [6] and that of Jellon Grame (90, C) " has nearly the same incidents as B, diluted and vulgarized in almost twice as many verses." [7]

The action is seldom carefully localized : the compiler of

[1] IV, 435. [2] IV, 145. [3] III, 317. [4] II, 373.
[5] II, 342. [6] II, 355. [7] II, 302.

A Gest of Robyn Hode was careless of geography.[1] The New England copy of *Archie o Cawfield* (188, F) " naturally enough, names no places." "The route in C is not described[2] there is no reason, if they start from Cafield (see 23), why they should cross the Annan, the town being on the eastern side. All difficulties are escaped in D by giving no names."[2] The attention given to the setting in some of the Robin Hood ballads is, then, exceptional. Of *Robin Hood and the Monk* (119), "the landscape background of the first two stanzas has often been praised, and its beauty will never pall. It may be called landscape or prelude, for both eyes and ears are addressed, and several others of these woodland ballads have a like symphony or setting: Adam Bell, Robin Hood and the Potter, Guy of Gisborne, even the much later ballad of The Noble Fisherman. It is to be observed that the story of the outlaw Fulk Fitz Warine, which has other traits in common with Robin Hood ballads, begins somewhat after the same fashion."[3]

In dealing with the supernatural the way of the true ballad is to omit description or explanation. In *James Harris* (243), "to explain the eery personality and proceedings of the ship-master, E—G, with a sort of vulgar rationalism, turn him into the devil. . . . D (probably by the fortunate accident of being a fragment) leaves us to put our own construction upon the weird seaman ; and, though it retains the homely ship-carpenter, is on the whole the most satisfactory of all the versions."[4] In *Johnie Scot* (99) "the champion is described in A 31 as a gurious (grugous, gruous?) ghost; in H 27 as a greecy (frightful) ghost; in L 18 he is a fearsome sight, with three women's spans between his brows and three yards between his shoulders; in the Abbotsford copy of A, 29, 30, a grisly sight, with a

---

[1] III, 51. [2] III, 486. [3] III, 95. [4] IV, 362.

span between his eyes, between his shoulders three and
three, and Johnie scarcely reaching his knee. These points
are probably taken from another and later ballad, which is
perhaps an imitation, and might almost be called a parody,
of Johnie Soot." [1] Ghosts, though not thought sufficiently
strange to demand special treatment, should, nevertheless,
"have a fair reason for walking. . . . In popular fictions,
the motive for their leaving the grave is to ask back plighted
troth, to be relieved from the inconveniences caused by the
excessive grief of the living, to put a stop to the abuse of
children by stepmothers, to repair an injustice done in the
flesh, to fulfil a promise; at the least, to announce the
visitant's death." [2]

Turning now from technique,—from treatment of plot,
of setting, of the supernatural,—to style in the narrower
sense, we find that the comments are again largely in the
way of pointing out flaws, or traits which are not characteristic of the true ballad, and which are due to the peculiar
conditions of ballad transmission. From such negative
comments may be inferred, again, the stylistic marks of the
true ballad. Thus, in the first place, ballad style is artless
and homely. In *Andrew Lammie* (233) :

> Her bloom was like the springing flower
>   That hails the rosy morning,
> With innocence and graceful mein
>   Her beauteous form adorning.

and

> ' No kind of vice eer staind my life,
>   Or hurt my virgin honour ;
> My youthful heart was won by love,
>   But death will me exoner' (C, 2, 42).

are " not homely enough." [3]   Moreover,

---

[1] II, 378.   [2] V, 59.   [3] IV, 301, n.

> 'At Fyvie's yetts there grows a flower,
>   It grows baith braid and bonny;
> There's a daisie in the midst o it,
>   And it's ca'd by Andrew Lammie' (A, 1.).

" the mystical verses with which A and B begin are also not quite artless." [1] The ninth stanza of *The New-Slain Knight* (263) "is pretty, but not quite artless." [2] In the true ballad the conceit is out of place. Scott's version (C) of *Thomas Rymer* (37) closes with two satirical stanzas not popular in style. " 'The repugnance of Thomas to be debarred the use of falsehood when he should find it convenient,' may have, as Scott says, 'a comic effect,' but is, for a ballad, a miserable conceit." [3] In *The Mother's Malison* (216), A 8^{1-2}, C 10^{1-2},

> Make me your wrack as I come back,
>   But spare me as I go,

the conceit (from Martial) " does not overwell suit a popular ballad." [4] The literary manner is thus to be contrasted with the popular. In *Edward* (13) " the word 'brand,' in the first stanza, is possibly more literary than popular; further than this the language is entirely fit." [5] Of *Earl Brand* (7) "A a has suffered less from literary revision than . . . . A c." [6] This revision may be illustrated by the following stanza:

> To a maiden true he'll give his hand,
> To the king's daughter o fair England,
> To a prize that was won by a slain brother's hand,

which c substitutes for a 32:

> This has not been the death o ane,
> But it's been that of fair seventeen.

Of *The Fair Flower of Northumberland* (9) " E, a traditional

---

[1] IV, 301, n.   [2] IV, 434.   [3] I, 320, n.
[4] IV, 186.   [5] I, 167.   [6] I, 88.

version from the English border, has unfortunately been improved by some literary pen." [1] These improvements consist in part of descriptions of the lady's states of mind ; [2] for example :

> To think of the prisoner her heart was sore,
> Her love it was much but her pity was more.
>
> The words that he said on her fond heart smote,
> She knew not in sooth if she lived or not.
>
> She looked to his face, and it kythed so unkind
> That her fast coming tears soon rendered her blind.
>
> (Sts. 3, 9, 10.)

Jamie Telfer (190) "was retouched for the Border Minstrelsy, nobody can say how much. The 36th stanza is in Hardy-knute style." [3]

Of *Hughie Grame* (191), B, 3, 8, " are obviously, as Cromek says, the work of Burns, and the same is true of $10^{3\text{-}4}$." [4] *The Famous Flower of Serving-Men* (106), an "English broadside, which may be reasonably believed to be formed upon a predecessor in the popular style, [5] was given in Percy's *Reliques*, . . , 'from a written copy containing some improvements (perhaps modern ones).' These improvements are execrable in style and in matter, so far as there is new matter, but not in so glaring contrast with the groundwork as literary emendations of traditional ballads." [6] Such contrast is found in the "hack-rhymester lines" in *Bewick and Graham* (211, 7^3, 19^2), which are "not up to the mark of the general style." [7] Similarly, *King Henry* (32) "as pub-

---

[1] I, 112.   [2] [The true ballad has little to say of mental states.]
[3] IV, 5. The stanza reads :

> But he's taen aff his gude steel cap,
> And thrice he's waved it in the air ;
> The Dinlay snaw was neer mair white
> Nor the lyart locks of Harden's hair.

[4] IV, 10.   [5] II, 430.   [6] II, 428.   [7] IV, 145.

3

lished by Jamieson . . . . is increased by interpolation to
thirty-four stanzas [from twenty]. 'The interpolations will
be found enclosed in brackets,' but a painful contrast of
style of itself distinguishes them."[1] Editorial changes are,
however, in some cases confined to slight verbal variations,
where the contrast is less evident or painful.[2]

Yet, in spite of its artless, homely, and non-literary style,
the ballad is not without conventions of its own. Most
striking of these is the use of "commonplaces" or passages
which recur in many ballads, like :

> When bells were rung and mass was sung,
> And a' men bound to bed ;

or,

> O whan he came to broken briggs
>   He bent his bow and swam,
> An whan he came to the green grass growin
>   He slackd his shoone and ran.[3]

Another convention is the complete repetition of the
message by the messenger. Thus in *Fair Mary of Walling-
ton* (91, A) "the stanza which should convey . . . . part of
the message is wanting, but may be confidently supplied
from the errand-boy's repetition."[4] Another form of repetition occurs in the narration of similar incidents by different
ballads. "There is a general resemblance between the
rescue of Robin Hood in stanzas 61–81 and that of William
of Cloudesly in Adam Bell, 56–94, and the precaution
suggested by Much in the eighth stanza corresponds to the
warning given by Adam in the eighth stanza of the other
ballad. There is a verbal agreement in stanzas 71 of the
first and 66 of the second. Such agreements or repetitions
are numerous in the Robin Hood ballads, and in other
traditional ballads, where similar situations occur."[5]

---

[1] I, 297.   [2] Cf. II, 83, 317 ; IV, 39.
[3] See the *Index of Matters and Literature*, v, 474 f.
[4] II, 309, n.   [5] III, 96.

In the course of degeneration, ballads retain, but distort, the commonplace. Thus in *Lord Thomas and Lady Margaret* (261) " B 14[3, 4] is a commonplace, which, in inferior traditional ballads, is often, as here, an out-of-place. B 15, 16 is another commonplace, of the silly sort." [1]   " Hacknied commonplaces " occur in *Auld Matrons* (249), stanzas 2–5 ; [2] " frippery commonplaces," in *The White Fisher* (264), stanzas 2, 7, 8, 12.[3]

Turning now to the emotional qualities of ballad style, we find that the ghost ballad, in spite (or perhaps because) of the absence of special treatment noted above, is, at its best, " impressive." The scene at the grave in *Sweet William's Ghost* (77 C 11–13) " may be judged grotesque, but is not trivial or unimpressive. These verses may be supposed not to have belonged to the earliest form of the ballad, and one does not miss them from A, but they cannot be an accretion of modern date." [4]. In *The Wife of Usher's Well* (79) " there is no indication that the sons come back to forbid obstinate grief, as the dead often do. But supplying a motive would add nothing to the impressiveness of these verses. Nothing that we have is more profoundly affecting." [5] *The Suffolk Miracle* (272) is to be contrasted with the continental versions, " one of the most remarkable tales and one of the most impressive and beautiful ballads of the European continent." [6] *Bewick and Graham* (211), in spite of certain defects, " is a fine-spirited ballad as it stands, and very infectious." [7] *Walter Lesly* (296) is " a late, but lifelike and spirited ballad." [8] *The Wee Wee Man* (38) is an " extremely airy and sparkling little ballad." [9] *Andrew Lammie* (233) " is a homely ditty, but the gentleness and fidelity of Annie under the brutal behavior of her family are genuinely pathetic, and justify the remarkable popularity

---

[1] IV, 426.   [2] IV, 391.   [3] IV, 435.   [4] II, 227.   [5] II, 238.
[6] V, 59.   [7] IV, 145.   [8] V, 168.   [9] I, 329.

which the ballad has enjoyed in the north of Scotland." [1] Contrasted with the cynical *Twa Corbies* of Scott's Minstrelsy is *The Three Ravens* (26), a "tender little English ballad." [2] In the *Gest*: "Nothing was ever more felicitously told, even in the best *dit* or *fabliau*, than the 'process' of Our Lady's repaying the money which had been lent on her security. Robin's slyly significant welcome to the monk upon learning that he is of Saint Mary Abbey, his professed anxiety that Our Lady is wroth with him because she has not sent him his pay, John's comfortable suggestion that perhaps the monk has brought it, Robin's incidental explanation of the little business in which the Virgin was a party, and request to see the silver in case the monk has come upon her affair, are beautiful touches of humor, and so delicate that it is all but brutal to point them out." [3] The tales which are cited as parallels to *Queen Eleanor's Confession* (156) all "have the cynical Oriental character, and, to a healthy taste, are far surpassed by the innocuous humor of the English ballad." [4] While we need not question the substantial genuineness of *Fause Foodrage* (89), "we must admit that the form in which we have received it is an enfeebled one, without much flavor or color." [5] *The Suffolk Miracle* (272) preserves the story only in a "blurred, enfeebled, and disfigured shape." [6] Version B of the *Cheviot* (162) is "very seriously enfeebled." [7]

The lyrical quality,—the fact that the ballad was made to be sung,—must not be lost sight of. "Fair Annie's fortunes have not only been charmingly sung, as here [in the ballad of *Fair Annie* (62)]; they have also been exquisitely *told* in a favorite lay of Marie de France." [8] The superior lyrical quality of *The Bonny Birdy* (82) "makes up for its inferiority [to *Little Musgrave* (81)] as a story, so that on

---

[1] IV, 301. [2] I, 253. [3] III, 53. [4] III, 258.
[5] II, 296. [6] V, 59. [7] III, 305. [8] II, 67.

the whole it cannot be prized much lower than the noble English ballad." [1] Thus lyrical quality is to be regarded as no less significant than plot as a trait of the true ballad. *The Queen of Elfan's Nourice* (40), "after the nature of the best popular ballad, forces you to chant and will not be read." [2] Even *The Jolly Pindar of Wakefield* (124) "is thoroughly lyrical, . . . and was pretty well sung to pieces before it ever was printed." [3] "It is not . . . . always easy to say whether an isolated stanza belonged to a ballad or a song ; " [4] and Professor Child speaks even of the whole of *Bessy Bell and Mary Gray* (201) as "this little ballad, or song." [5] Of *Lord Lovel* (75) he says : "It can scarcely be too often repeated that such ballads as this were meant only to be sung, not at all to be recited. . . . 'Lord Lovel' is especially one of those which, for their due effect, require the support of a melody, and almost equally the comment of a burden. No burden is preserved in the case of 'Lord Lovel,' but we are not to infer that there never was one. The burden, which is at least as important as the instrumental accompaniment of modern songs, sometimes, in these little tragedies, foreshadows calamity from the outset, sometimes . . . . is a cheerful-sounding formula, which in the upshot enhances by contrast the gloom of the conclusion. 'A simple but life-like story, supported by the burden and the air, these are the means by which such old romances seek to produce an impression.' " [6] *The Elfin Knight* (2 A) "is the only example, so far as I remember, which our ballads afford of a burden of this kind, one that is of greater extent than the stanza with which it was sung, though this kind of burden seems to have been common enough with old songs and carols." [7]

[1] II, 260.　　　　　[2] I, 358.　　　　　[3] III, 129.
[4] V, 201.　　　　　[5] IV, 75.　　　　　[6] II, 204, n.
[7] I, 7. See the foot-note for Professor Child's longest discussion of the burden.

IV.

The English and Scottish Popular Ballads of 1882–1898 has naturally superseded the *English and Scottish Ballads* of 1857–1859, and Professor Child himself shared the general tendency to underestimate the real value of the earlier collection. It was of course made on a different plan; its limits were not so clearly defined, and it did not attempt to give every version of every known ballad. Many of the sources, moreover, were not yet open. One is, then, surprised to find that, of the three hundred and five ballads printed in the later collection, only ninety are new; and these are, for the most part, unimportant additions to the body of ballad literature. They are distributed as follows: 15 in volume I, 16 in II, 11 in III, 25 in IV, 23 in V. Thus 59 of the 90 occur in the last three volumes; of these there is not one of first importance. Of the remaining 31 not more than 10 can be regarded as really valuable additions, though such an estimate must of necessity be based more or less upon personal impression. Some of these were already accessible, in Buchan's versions, or elsewhere: *Willie's Lyke-Wake* (25), *Lizie Wan* (51), *The King's Dochter Lady Jean* (52), *Brown Robyn's Confession* (57), *Fair Mary of Waltington* (91). These, doubtless, were omitted because of the nature of their subject-matter; it was only in the later collection that Professor Child "had no discretion."[1] Other important ballads were not yet accessible, or not yet discovered: *St. Stephen and Herod* (22), *The Laily Worm and the Machrel of the Sea* (36), *The Queen of Elfan's Nourice* (40), *The Unquiet Grave* (78), *The Great Silkie of Sule Skerry* (113). Of the ten, only four are included in Professor Gummere's collection. The main addition of the later collection is thus rather in the way of

---

[1] *Sheath and Knife* (16), also, was accessible but omitted.

new versions of important ballads, or of more authentic versions based directly upon the manuscripts; in the citation of a larger number of foreign parallels; and, generally, in the matter contained in the introductions.

The *Ballads* contained 115 pieces which do not appear in the later collection. The nature of such material, since it is excluded from the "complete" *English and Scottish Popular Ballads*, is significant as throwing some additional light upon Professor Child's conception. In many cases the reason for exclusion is made clear by Professor Child himself, in comments in the earlier or in the later collection. Of the whole group of lays and romances contained in Book I of the *Ballads*, he says: "Some of the longer pieces in this book are not of the nature of ballads, and require an apology. They were admitted before the limits of the work had been determined with exactness." [1] If such pieces as these do not fulfil the lyrical requirement of the true ballad, others cannot fulfil the requirement of plot, and the songs of the *Ballads*, like *A Lyke Wake Dirge*, *Fair Helen of Kirconnel*, or *The Lowlands of Holland* [2] find no place in the later collection. The *Ballads* contains also translations from the Danish, and the original and translation of a modern Greek parallel of the Lenore story; these are naturally not included in *The English and Scottish Popular Ballads*.

The later collection is much more chary of the admission of broadsides or sheet-ballads: in many cases they are relegated to introductions or appendices; in many more, omitted.

---

[1] *Ballads*, I, xi, n. "Certain short romances which formerly stood in the First Book, have been dropped from this second Edition [1860], in order to give the collection a homogeneous character." *Ballads* [1860], I, xii.

[2] "A song," II, 317. (Where merely volume and page are given the reference is still to the later collection; references to the earlier are preceded by the word *Ballads*.)

William Guiseman is cited merely, under *Brown Robin's Confession* (57), as "a copy, improved by tradition, of the 'lament' in 'William Grismond's Downfal,' a broadside of 1650."[1] *The Lament of the Border Widow*, which occurs in Book VI of the *Ballads*, "shows broader traces of the sheet-ballad," and is quoted in the introduction to No 106 for "those who are interested in such random inventions (as, under pardon, they must be called)."[2] Of *The Lady Isabella's Tragedy* Professor Child says in the later collection: "Though perhaps absolutely the silliest ballad that ever was made, and very far from silly sooth, the broadside was traditionally propagated in Scotland without so much change as is usual in such cases."[3] Even in the *Ballads* one finds this comment: "The three following pieces [*The Spanish Virgin, Lady Isabella's Tragedy, The Cruel Black*] are here inserted merely as specimens of a class of tales, horrible in their incidents but feeble in their execution, of which whole dreary volumes were printed and read about two centuries ago. They were all of them, probably, founded on Italian novels."[4] Although the *Ballads* includes *Macpherson's Rant*, it is declared "worthy of a hangman's pen."[5] A number of tales which employ a highly artificial stanza, such as *The Fray of Suport, The Raid of the Reidswire*, or *The Flemish Insurrection*, do not find their way into the later collection.

Traces of the modern editor or author become less common in the later collection. Versions "modernized and completed by Percy" (Book I, Nos. 1 b and 5 b) are excluded. The cynical *Twa Corbies* appears only in the introduction to *The Three Ravens ;* and Motherwell's edition, declared already in the *Ballads* to be a "modernized version,"[6] does not appear at all. Motherwell's *Bonnie*

---

[1] II, 16.   [2] II, 429.   [3] v, 34, n.
[4] *Ballads*, III, 360.   [5] *Ballads*, VI, 263.   [6] *Ballads*, III, 61.

George Campbell suffers a like fate, and this, we infer, because "Motherwell made up his 'Bonnie George Campbell' from B, C, D."[1] As, no doubt, not merely modernized but modern, *Sir Roland* is excluded. . "This fragment, Motherwell tells us, was communicated to him by an ingenious friend, who remembered having heard it sung in his youth. He does not vouch for its antiquity, and we have little or no hesitation in pronouncing it a modern composition."[2] Similarly, *Lady Anne* "is on the face of it a modern composition, with extensive variations, on the theme of the popular ballad."[3] It is printed in the appendix to No 20. *Earl Richard* is "an entirely modern composition, excepting only the twenty lines of Herd's fragment."[4] Of *Auld Maitland* Professor Child says: "Notwithstanding the authority of Scott and Leyden, I am inclined to agree with Mr Aytoun, that this ballad is a modern imitation, or if not that, a comparatively recent composition. It is with reluctance that I make for it the room it requires."[5] The essential anonymity of the ballad, in Professor Child's final conception, naturally excludes pieces like Henryson's *Robene and Makyne* and *The Bludy Serk*, which had found their way into the *Ballads*.[6]

There are but few instances of definite praise, as ballads, of pieces included in the earlier collection and excluded from the later. *The Children in the Wood* is said to be "perhaps the most popular of all English ballads. Its merit is attested by the favor it has enjoyed with so many generations, and was vindicated to a cold and artificial age by the kindly pen of Addison."[7] We must not forget,

---

[1] iv, 142.   [2] *Ballads*, i, 341.   [3] i, 218, n.   [4] *Ballads*, iii, 293.
[5] *Ballads*, vi, 220. Cf. Mr Andrew Lang's plea for *Auld Maitland*, *Folk-Lore*, xiii, 191 ff.
[6] See also the comments on the Rev. Mr Lamb's *Laidley Worm of Spindleston Heugh*, *Ballads*, i, 386, and cf. p. 772, above.
[7] *Ballads*, iii, 128.

however, that Professor Child was fifty years nearer the kindly pen of Addison. The cold and artificial age, moreover, was also sentimental and moral; and why, with it, this ballad was so popular, a single stanza will show:

> You that executors be made,
>   And overseers eke
> Of children that be fatherless,
>   And infants mild and meek ;
> Take you example by this thing,
>   And yield to each his right,
> Lest God with such like miserye
>   Your wicked minds requite (vv. 153 ff.).

The Blind Beggar's Daughter of Bednall's Green is said to be printed from a modern broadside, yet it is characterized as "this favorite popular ballad."[1] *The Nutbrowne Maid* is "this matchless poem," "this beautiful old ballad."[2] Yet, clearly, it is not a popular ballad at all.

On the whole, it is not difficult to see why the 115 ballads are excluded from the later collection ; and one gets the impression that, had Professor Child chosen to enforce the conception of the ballad which he already had in mind, most of them would have been excluded from the earlier collection as well. This impression is deepened by an examination of the comments scattered through the *Ballads*.

He already regarded the ballad as inimitable:[3] "The exclusion of the 'Imitations'. . . . may possibly excite the regret of a few. . . . Whatever may be the merit of the productions in question, they are never less likely to obtain credit for it, than when they are brought into comparison with their professed models."[4] Again, *Sir Patrick Spence*, "if not ancient, has been always accepted as such by the most skilful judges, and is a solitary instance of a successful

---

[1] *Ballads*, IV, 161.
[2] *Ballads*, IV, 143 f.
[3] Cf. p. 757, above.
[4] *Ballads*, V, iv.

imitation, in manner and spirit, of the best specimens of authentic minstrelsy." [1]

Professor Child had already fallen foul of the editors, and their alterations and interpolations.[2] It is interesting to see how, in many cases, he anticipated the corrections and comments made possible, for the later collection, by access to the manuscripts. Of *The Child of Elle* he says: "So extensive are Percy's alterations and additions, that the reader will have no slight difficulty in detecting the few traces that are left of the genuine composition." [3] Compare: "So much of Percy's 'Child of Elle' as was genuine, which, upon the printing of his manuscript, turned out to be one fifth." [4] Again, Percy acknowledges interpolations, which " might with some confidence be pointed out. Among them are certainly most, if not all, of the last twelve stanzas of the Second Part, which include the catastrophe to the story." [5] In Percy, he says in the later collection, *Sir Cawline* " is extended to nearly twice the amount of what is found in the manuscript, and a tragical turn is forced upon the story." [6] Again : "We have given *Gil Morrice* as it stands in the *Reliques* (iii. 132,) degrading to the margin those stanzas which are undoubtedly spurious." [7] The stanzas thus degraded turned out to be actually spurious.[8] Condemnation of Buchan is scattered throughout the *Ballads*. Thus : "Some resolution has been exercised, and much disgust suppressed, in retaining certain pieces from Buchan's collections, so strong is the suspicion that, after having been procured from very inferior sources, they were tampered with by the editor." [9] Again : "One uncommonly tasteless stanza [41, A, 53], the interpolation of some nursery-maid,[10]

[1] *Ballads*, III, 148–149.   [2] Cf. p. 767, above.   [3] *Ballads*, III, 225.
[4] I, 88.   [5] *Ballads*, III, 173.   [6] II, 56.
[7] *Ballads*, II, 30.   [8] II, 275.   [9] *Ballads*, I, ix, n.
[10] Cf. p. 762, above.

is here omitted. Too many of Buchan's ballads have suffered in this way, and have become both prolix and vulgar."[1] Even in the *Ballads* Professor Child placed "no confidence in any of Allan Cunningham's *souvenirs* of Scottish song,"[2] and his early suspicions[3] of the character of Cunningham's version of Gil Brenton are confirmed in the later collection.[4] *King Henry*, printed in the earlier collection "without the editor's [Jamieson's] interpolations,"[5] appears in the same form in the later, except that stanza 14 is printed in small type, as not being in the Jamieson-Brown MS. Again, in *The Bonny Birdy*, "the lines supplied by Jamieson have been omitted."[6] There is an interesting comment on these lines in the later collection.[7]

Professor Child was already aware that change of nationality was accompanied by change of the scene of action.[8] He quoted Scott's account of the locality of *The Douglas Tragedy* [= *Earl Brand* (7, B)], and added: "After so circumstantial a description of the scene, ... the reader may be amused to see the same story told in various Scandinavian ballads, with a no less plausible resemblance to actual history. This, as has already been pointed out under *Guy of Warwick* and *Kempion*,[9] is an ordinary occurrence in the transmission of legends."[10]

He noted, too, the tendency of ballads to combine: "The natural desire of men to hear more of characters in whom they have become strongly interested, has frequently stimu-

---

[1] *Ballads*, I, 306 n.   [2] *Ballads*, II, 220.   [3] *Ballads*, I, 270.

[4] See I, 62, and, for the omitted couplets, I, 80–81.

[5] *Ballads*, I, 265.   [6] *Ballads*, II, 22.

[7] II, 260. See, also, the comments on Jamieson's *Child Rowland and Burd Ellen*, *Ballads*, I, 416, and *English and Scottish Popular Ballads*, V, 201, n.

[8] Cf. p. 769, above.   [9] *Ballads*, I, 256.   [10] *Ballads*, II, 115.

lated the attempt to continue successful fictions." [1] *Sweet William's Ghost* is often made the sequel to other ballads. [2]

So far as subject-matter is concerned, we find in the *Ballads* the same conception of the relation of ballad and fact. *Jane Shore* "adheres to matter of fact with a fidelity very uncommon," [3] and this is, perhaps, one reason why it does not find a place in the later collection. [4] We may contrast, on the other hand, the two statements in regard to the relation of *Hind Horn* and the romance : "Metrical romances . . . . are known in many cases to have been adapted for the entertainment of humbler hearers, by abridgment in the form of ballads." He regards *Hind Horn* as a case of this sort. [5]

Style and plot, finally, are a test of genuineness : " I cannot assent to the praise bestowed by Scott on *The Outlaw Murray*. The story lacks point and the style is affected— not that of the unconscious poet of the real *traditional* ballad." [6] Though there without comment, it is placed at the very end of the later collection.

From a comment like this it is obvious that Professor Child already had in mind the conception of " a real *traditional* ballad," a " specimen of authentic minstrelsy." [7] Although he admitted to the earlier collection lays, romances, songs, broadsides and sheet-ballads, as well as modern or modernized compositions, yet he was aware that all these differed from the true ballad. This true ballad, he conceived, was inimitable, in matter and manner. In transmission it might suffer, from the invention of a nursery-maid, from Buchan's beggar, from a " hangman's pen," from the modern editors. It drew its subject-matter from fact (to which it

---

[1] *Ballads*, II, 64.   [2] *Ballads*, II, 45.   [3] *Ballads*, VII, 194.
[4] Cf. the comment on *The Hunting of the Cheviot, Ballads*, VII, 25.
[5] *Ballads*, IV, 17.   For the later comment, see p. 777, above.
[6] *Ballads*, VI, 22.   [7] *Ballads*, III, 148–149.

was not loyal), from romances, from other ballads. In quality the subject-matter was not "horrible." In style the true ballad was not feeble in execution, not prolix and vulgar, and not affected. The earlier conception was not as complete as the later, and it was by no means so rigorously enforced. In regard to specific compositions, there was, as is to be expected, some change of opinion. But the significant fact is that for at least forty years Professor Child retained without essential change his conception of the traditional ballad as a distinct literary type.

V.

We may now bring together the passages in which Professor Child declared certain ballads to be of the true "popular" or "traditional" type. The fewness of such passages is at first surprising, yet it clearly formed no part of a set purpose to include in his introductions estimates of this kind, and such "appreciations" seem to have been either spontaneous,—springing, as in the case of *Johnie Cock*, from his delight in the ballad with which he was concerned,—or intended, as in the case of *Edward*, as answer to his predecessors' doubts of authenticity. On ballads like *Lord Randal*, *Babylon*, *Hind Horn*, *Clerk Saunders*, *Fair Margaret and Sweet William*, there is no such comment. It would seem, no doubt, in such cases obviously unnecessary. Nevertheless the list is fairly representative. We have examples of the Domestic Ballad,—tragic, in *Earl Brand* (7), *Edward* (13), *Old Robin of Portingale* (80), *Little Musgrave* (81), *The Bonny Birdy* (82); not tragic, in *Child Waters* (63), *Young Beichan* (53), *Queen Eleanor's Confession* (156): we have examples of the Supernatural Ballad,— transformation, in *The Laily Worm and the Machrel of the Sea* (36); fairy, in *Thomas Rymer* (37); ghost, in *The Wife of Usher's Well* (79) : we have examples of the Border Ballad in *Captain Car* (178 F) and *Jock o the Side* (187) : of the Outlaw Ballad in *Johnie Cock* (114), the Robin Hood ballads, 117–121 : of the Heroic Ballad in *King Estmere* (60), *Sir Aldingar* (59), *Sir Patrick Spens* (58 A).

Johnie Cock (114) : "This precious specimen of the unspoiled traditional ballad." iii, 1.

Edward (13) : "The word 'brand,' in the first stanza, is possibly more literary than popular ; further than this the language is entirely fit. The affectedly antique spelling in Percy's copy has given rise to vague suspicions concerning the authenticity of the ballad, or of the language : but as spelling will not make an old ballad, so it will not unmake one. We have, but do not need, the later traditional copy to prove the other genuine. 'Edward' is not only unimpeachable, but has ever been regarded as one of the noblest and most sterling specimens of the popular ballad." i, 167.

The Laily Worm and the Machrel of the Sea (36) : "Somewhat mutilated, and also defaced, though it be, this ballad has certainly never been retouched by a pen, but is pure tradition. It has the first stanza in common with 'Kemp Owyne,' and shares more than that with 'Allison Gross.' But it is independent of 'Allison Gross,' and has a far more original sound." i, 315.

Earl Brand (7) . . . . "has preserved most of the incidents of a very ancient story with a faithfulness unequalled by any ballad that has been recovered from English oral tradition." i, 88.

The Wife of Usher's Well (79) : "A motive for the return of the wife's three sons is not found in the fragments which remain to us. . . . But supplying a motive would add nothing to the impressiveness of these verses. Nothing that we have is more profoundly affecting." ii, 238.

Thomas Rymer (37) : "B . . . . has been corrupted here and there, but only by tradition." i, 317.

"The fairy adventures of Thomas and of Ogier have the essential points in common, and even the particular trait that the fairy is taken to be the Virgin. The occurrence of this trait again in the ballad, viewed in connection with the general similarity of the two, will leave no doubt that the ballad had its source in the romance. Yet it is an entirely popular ballad as to style,[1] and must be of considerable age, though the earliest version (A) can be traced at furthest only into the first half of the last century." i, 319 f.

---

[1] "Excepting the two satirical stanzas with which Scott's version (C) concludes."

Captain Car (178) : "F is purely traditional and has one fine stanza not found in any of the foregoing :

> Out then spake the lady Margaret,
>   As she stood on the stair;
> The fire was at her goud garters,
>   The lowe was at her hair." III, 429.

Queen Eleanor's Confession (156) : "There is reason to question whether this [F] and the other recited versions are anything more than traditional variations of printed copies. The ballad seems first to have got into print in the latter part of the seventeenth century, but was no doubt circulating orally sometime before that, for it is in the truly popular tone." III, 255.

Robin Hood and the Tanner (126) : "The sturdy Arthur a Bland is well hit off, and, bating the sixteenth and thirty-fifth stanzas, the ballad has a good popular ring. There is corruption at 8^3, 12^3, and perhaps 13^3." III, 137.

The earliest Robin Hood ballads (117–121) "are among the best of all ballads, and perhaps none in English please so many and please so long." III, 42.

Robin Hood and the Monk (119) : "Too much could not be said in praise of this ballad, but nothing need be said. It is very perfection in its kind ; and yet we have others equally good, and beyond doubt should have had more, if they had been written down early, as this was, and had not been left to the chances of tradition. Even writing would not have saved all, but writing has saved this (in large part), and in excellent form." III, 95.

Child Waters (63) : "This charming ballad, which has perhaps no superior in English, and if not in English perhaps nowhere." II, 84. ("Caution is imperative where so much ground is covered, and no man should be confident that he can do absolute justice to poetry in a tongue that he was not born to ; but foreign poetry is as likely to be rated too high as to be undervalued." II, 84, n.)

Jock o the Side (187) : "The ballad is one of the best in the world, and enough to make a horse-trooper of any young borderer, had he lacked the impulse." III, 477.

Sir Patrick Spens (58, A) : "This admired and most admirable ballad." "It would be hard to point out in ballad poetry, or other, happier or more refined touches than the two stanzas in A which portray the bootless waiting of the ladies for the return of the seafarers." II, 17 f.[1]

Young Beichan (53) : "A favorite ballad and most deservedly." I, 455.

King Estmere (60) : "While we cannot but be vexed that so distinguished a ballad, not injured much, so far as we can see, by time, should

---

[1] See also the comment in the *Ballads,* quoted p. 804, below.

not come down to us as it came to Percy, our loss must not be exaggerated. The changes made by the editor, numerous enough, no doubt, cannot be very material until we approach the end. Stanzas 63–66 are entirely suspicious, and it may even be questioned whether the manuscript contained a word that is in them." II, 49.

Little Musgrave and Lady Barnard (81) : "The noble English ballad." II, 260.

The Bonny Birdy (82) : "A fine ballad upon the same theme." II, 243.

Old Robin of Portingale (80) : "This fine ballad." II, 240.

Sir Aldingar (69) ₄ "This ballad, one of the most important of all that the Percy manuscript has saved from oblivion." II, 33.

Robin Hood's Death (120) : "B, though found only in late garlands, is in the fine old strain." III, 103.

Certain ballads are expressly condemned as not "traditional" or "popular" :

Robin Hood Rescuing Will Stutly (141) : "This is a ballad made for print, with little of the traditional in the matter and nothing in the style. It may be considered as an imitation of the Rescue of the Three Squires." III, 185.

Robin Hood's Birth, Breeding, etc. (149) : "The jocular author of this ballad, who would certainly have been diverted by any one's supposing him to write under the restraints of tradition. . . ." III, 214.

The Lovely Northerne Lasse (217, Appendix) : "There is an English 'ditty' (not a traditional ballad) . . . . which was printed in the first half of the seventeenth century. It is here given in an appendix." IV, 192.

To these may be added a few examples of less specific condemnation :

The Earl of Mar's Daughter (270) : A Scandinavian ballad and this "are, perhaps, on a par, for barrenness and folly, but the former may claim some age and vogue, the Scottish ballad neither." V, 39.

The Drunkard's Legacy (267, Appendix) : "The modern ballad . . . . used by Percy was 'The Drunkard's Legacy,' an inexpressibly pitiable ditty." V, 12.

John Thomson and the Turk (266) : "This ridiculous ballad." V, 1.

Robin Hood and the Tinker (127) : "The fewest words will best befit this contemptible imitation of imitations." III, 140.

Robin Hood and Maid Marian (150) : "This foolish ditty." III, 218.

Robin Hood and the Valiant Knight (153) : "Written, perhaps, because it was thought that authority should in the end be vindicated against outlaws, which may explain why this piece surpasses in platitude everything that goes before." III, 225.

4

The Suffolk Miracle (272) : "This piece could not be admitted here on its own merits. At the first look, it would be classed with the vulgar prodigies printed for hawkers to sell and for Mopsa and Dorcas to buy. It is not even a good specimen of its kind." v, 58.

We may add from the *Ballads* half-a-dozen examples of specific praise :

The Lass of Lochroyan [76, D][1] : "This beautiful piece." *Ballads,* II, 98.

The Queen's Marie [173, I] : "Jamieson and Kinloch have each published a highly dramatic fragment of this terrible story." *Ballads,* III, 107.

The Lochmaben Harper [192, A] : "This fine old ballad . . . . has the genuine ring of the best days of minstrelsy. On account of its excellence, we give two versions." *Ballads,* VI, 3.

Earl Richard [68, J] : "This gloomy and impressive romance." *Ballads,* III, 3.

Chevy-Chace [162, A] : "Addison's papers in the *Spectator . . . .* evince so true a perception of the merits of this ballad [162, B], shorn as it is of the most striking beauties of the grand original, that we cannot but deeply regret his never having seen the ancient and genuine copy ('The noble ballad,' 162, A ; *Ballads,* VII, 27), which was published by Hearne only a few days after Addison died." *Ballads,* VII, 43.

Sir Andrew Barton [167, A] : "This noble ballad." *Ballads,* VII, 56.

Sir Patrick Spence [58, A] : "If not ancient, has been always accepted as such by the most skilful judges, and is a solitary instance of a successful imitation, in manner and spirit, of the best specimens of authentic minstrelsy." *Ballads,* III, 149.

VI.

We are now in position to attempt a summary of Professor Child's conception of the popular ballad. He regarded it as a distinct species of poetry, which precedes the poetry of art, as the product of a homogeneous people, the expression of our common human nature, of the mind and heart of the people, never of the personality of an individual man, devoid, therefore, of all subjectivity and self-consciousness.

---

[1] The numbers in brackets are those affixed to the ballads in the later collection.

Hence the author counts for nothing; hence, too, the ballad is difficult to imitate and most attempts in this way are ridiculous failures. In transmission the ballad regularly departs from the original form, least in the mouths of unlearned people, more in the hands of professional singers or editors. It is at its best when it has come down by a purely domestic tradition, yet even so it is sometimes influenced by printed literature; and much depends on the experience and selection of the reciters, and on their varying memory, which is, however, ordinarily remarkable for its tenacity. Less fortunate is the ballad when it passes through low mouths or hands, suffering corruption of various kinds,—in the style of the attorney's clerk, or the housemaid or the serving-man, or ostler, or blind beggar. In the hands of the *bänkelsänger* or of the minstrel, the ballad departs still further from its original form. Or, rewritten for the broadside press, it is seriously enfeebled, or retrenched and marred, though it may retain some original features, and there are thus degrees of departure from the original matter and manner. The broadside may, in turn, become tradition. It is, so far as it appears in Professor Child's later collection, always founded on tradition, and this tradition lives after the composition of the broadside, and may influence the later versions of the printed form. Last comes the modern editor, and by him the ballad is sometimes lengthened,—by combination of different versions, by interpolation of new stanzas, always more or less unlike the popular style; or it is sometimes "improved," or retouched, or emended, or altered,— changed to something in glaring contrast to the groundwork. Some results of the vicissitudes of transmission are, the change of the hero's nationality, of his name, of his rôle; change of the scene of action; corruption of diction resulting in perversion of sense or in nonsense; introduction of learned words. The ballad thus suffers in transmission, and is at its

best when it is early caught and fixed in print.   It is sometimes counterfeited or imitated, and counterfeits are included
in the later collection for contrast, for much the same reason
that thieves are photographed, or because they may contain
relics of something genuine or better. .

Of the Subject-Matter of the ballad, the sources may be,
and in the best instances are, purely popular, consisting of
material which appears only in popular literature. Professor
Child mentions no instance where a prose tale is the source
of a ballad, but the ballad, he says, may sometimes be
resolved into a prose tale. Popular origin is attested by
foreign parallels in folk-literature. Of such literature certain
features or themes are characteristic, such as the quibbling
oath, the miraculous harvest, the childbirth in the wood, the
testament, the riddle, heroic sentiment, etc. The source
may, again, be an actual occurrence, in which case the
ballad, while not deliberate fiction, is yet not loyal to
the fact. Or the source may be a romance, or the source
of a romance, in which case oral tradition may be older than
written, the ballad older than the romance. Or the source
may be earlier ballads, mechanically and deliberately put
together in later ones, made over and assimilated in the *Gest
of Robin Hood*. In the course of transmission certain
features appear which are not characteristic of popular literature ; the subject-matter of the true ballad does not deal in
extravagance, or exaggeration, or platitude; it is not prosaic,
over-refined, cynical, sophisticated, sentimental, unnatural,
trite, or moral, though the "pungent buckishness" of the
broadside, and the gay cynicism of the minstrel, are foreign
to it.

So far as Technique is concerned, the ballad must have
plot. The story may not be completely told ; conclusion,
transitions, and preliminaries may be omitted; but the result
is not nonsense, the ballad is not incoherent. At its best

it is, however, brief. It is careless of geography, and, except in some,—and some of the best,—of the Robin Hood ballads, it touches Setting lightly. In dealing with the Supernatural it does not attempt to explain the action or to describe supernatural figures; ghosts, however, do not walk without reason.

In Style the ballad is artless and homely, and in it the conceit, and literary or learned words and phrases, are out of place. Yet it has certain conventions of its own, such as the "commonplace," the repetition of a message by a messenger, the verbally similar treatment of similar incidents as they occur in different ballads. Emotionally, the ghost ballad is impressive and affecting; and, in general, the ballad may be infectious, or spirited and life-like, or pathetic, or tender, or humorous, or vigorous and not lacking in color or flavor. It is essentially lyrical, and its lyrical quality is not less essential than plot. Often it absolutely requires the support of a melody and the comment of a burden. This burden sometimes foreshadows the calamity, sometimes enhances by contrast the gloom of the conclusion. It is usually less than the stanza with which it was sung; and, unlike the refrain, it was sung, not after the stanza, but with it. It is sometimes of different metre, sometimes not. The absence of the burden is in no case proof that it never existed.

WALTER MORRIS HART.

XVIII.—A LITERARY LINK BETWEEN THOMAS SHADWELL AND CHRISTIAN FELIX WEISSE.

Witchcraft in England in the sixteenth and seventeenth centuries was a subject upon which the dramatists from Marlowe to Shadwell seized with the greatest avidity. There was material of the most pliable sort; it could be moulded into a magnificent tragedy or distorted into the wildest buffoonery. In the sixteenth century it was the darker side of magic which we find in the drama, and though we note as early as 1604 the effort to brighten up Marlowe's tragedy of Doctor Faustus by the introduction of broadly comic scenes taken from the prose tale, yet one can well believe that the theatre audiences from 1590 to 1610 remembered too vividly the cruelties of the witch trials in 1590 to appreciate the buffoonery of Ralph in the comic scenes as deeply as they felt the dark despair of the protagonist Faustus.

> "Ah Faustus,
> Now hast thou but one bare hour to live,
> And then thou must be dam'nd perpetually :
> Stand still, you ever-moving spheres of heaven,
> That time may cease, and midnight never come ;
> Fair Nature's eye, rise, rise again, and make
> Perpetual day ; or let this hour be but
> A year, a month, a week, a natural day,
> That Faustus may repent and save his soul!"

In such lines is found the keynote to the *Stimmung* in which the audiences at the Curtain left a performance of the *Tragical Life and Death of Dr. Faustus*, in 1594. The bibliography of this Faustus story in its prose form from 1592 to 1692 has never been adequately presented, and as it is with the humbler form of the Faust literature, and the

808

lower classes of society, *das Volk*, that this article deals, the following remarks seem in order. Between the years 1592 and 1692 the Faustus legend is referred to seventeen times in English literature (and I do not include the various quarto editions of Marlowe's drama which appeared within those dates). Perhaps a still better criterion of the popularity of the tale is found in the fact that quarto editions of the prose book (English Faust Book of 1592) appeared in 1608, 1618, 1622, 1626, 1636, 1670, 1680, 1682, 1690 and 1700. In 1663 came out a rhymed version of the story, in 1664 another edition of the same, and between 1650 and 1696 a curious little duodecimo prose edition. But this is not all.

Before Marlowe's drama was played at the Curtain by the English actors upon their return from the continent in 1594, the English Wagner Book appeared (licensed in 1593), and in it the common people read a dramatic description of Faustus's death which deserves more notice than has hitherto been accorded it, because of the admirable description therein of the stage hell-mouth. (So far as I know it is not mentioned by any writer upon the pre-Shakesperian stage.) The passage occurs in the tenth chapter, and the latter part of it reads as follows :—

"When *Faustus* hauing long raged, of a soddaine howling lowde, and tearing his haire, laid both his arms uppon his necke, and leapte down headlong of the stage, the whole company immediately vanishing, but the stage with a most monstrous thundering crack followed Faustus hastely,[1] the people verily thinking that they would haue fallen uppon them ran all away, and he was happiest that had the swiftest foote, some leapte into the Riuer and swam away, and all of them with great affright ranne into the Citty and clapt the Citty gates together, streight, and to increase this fear they thought they hard a thing fall into the river as if a thousand houses

---

[1] Cf. Middleton's *Blacke Booke* (1604), page 13 : "he had a head of hayre like one of my Diuells in Doctor Faustus, *when the olde Theater crackt and frighted the Audience.*"

had fallen down from the toppe of Heaven into it. But afterwards this was knowen to be *Wagner's* brauery, who did this to shew the Purceuaunt some point of his skill." [1]

Now this English Wagner Book was printed *twice* [2] in 1593, then nothing more is heard of it for a hundred years. At last we see it pop up again in an edition which appeared sometime between 1670 and 1680 (the date on the quarto is unreadable), as the second part of the 1670 (*circa*) Faust Books, again in 1680 and still again in 1682.

Just at this time (1680–1690), when the legend of Faustus in the prose form was so popular, the handsome young actor, Will Mountfort, took the materials found in Marlowe's drama and the prose tale, and shaped them into a farce which he entitled "*The Life and Death of Doctor Faustus.* Made into a Farce by Mr. Mountford, With the Humours of Harlequin and Scaramouche, As they were several times Acted, By Mr. Lee and Mr. Jevon, . . ." etc. This quarto edition of the farce was printed in 1696; but as the text contains a pointed reference to the Edict of Nantes, and as Jevon died in 1688, it must have been first acted, I judge, about January, 1686. On March 1, 1686, the quarto edition of the farce *The Devil of a Wife* appeared, written (?) by the same Jevon who had played *Harlequin* in his friend Mountfort's farce of *Dr. Faustus.* Some weeks ago the present writer came across a first edition of Jevon's farce, and the striking similarity between the atmosphere of the two farces led him to an investigation of Jevon's and Mountfort's biography; and the first authority consulted was Langbaine, a contemporary of the two actors, who describes Jevon as follows :—

---

[1] Copied from the original 1594 text in the Bodleian. Thoms' reprint of the Wagner Book is inaccurate.

[2] Bibliographers mention only one edition : but I found two in the Bodleian.

"A Person lately dead and one sufficiently known to all that frequent the Theatre, both for his excellency in Dancing and Action. He has writ a Play, or rather Farce, call'd *The Devil of a Wife*, or *A Comical Transformation*. This farce is founded on a Tale as well known as that of *Mopsa*, in Sir Philip Sidney's *Arcadia*; tho' I think if compar'd with our *French* Farces so frequent on our English Stage, it may deserve the Preheminence."[1]

The words, "This farce is founded on a Tale as well known as that of Mopsa, in Sir Philip Sidney's *Arcadia*," have been misquoted by Baker[2] and the *Dictionary of National Biography*, who state that the farce is said to be *founded* on the tale of Mopsa. There is no resemblance between the latter story and the plot of Jevon's farce. What the source of *The Devil of a Wife* was will be brought out a little later. Baker goes on to say that "it was imagined that Mr. Jevon had some assistance in it from his brother-in-law, Thomas Shadwell." This statement, based no doubt upon Whincop's assertion in 1747 of the same fact is, I shall try to show, quite correct and of considerable importance.

Thomas Jevon is first mentioned in the stage records as acting a part in his brother-in-law's comedy, *The Inchanted Island* in 1673.[3] In the same year also he played the rôle of Osrick in *Hamlet*. In 1674 he acted in Settle's *Conquest of Chine by the Tartars*, playing probably Legogim. In this comedy he was to fall on the point of his sword and kill himself, instead of which he laid the sword in the scabbard, placed it on the ground, and fell on it, saying, "Now I am dead," a trick which much enraged Settle, the author of the drama. Other rôles which Jevon impersonated were, Young Bellair, in *The Man of Mode* (1676); Sneak, in Shadwell's

[1] *An account of the English Dramatick Poets*, etc., by Gerard Langbaine, Oxford, 1691.
[2] *Biographia Dramatica*.
[3] Genest : *Some Account of the English Stage*, etc. Vol. I.

Fond Husband (1676); Henry Jollyman, in D'Urfey's
Madam Fickle (1676); Agrippa, in Sedley's *Antony and
Cleopatra* (1677); Don Antonio, in Mrs. Behn's *The Rover*
(1677); Avaritio, in T. P.'s *French Conqueror* (1677);
Eumenes, in Pordage's *Siege of Babylon* (1677); Caper, in
Otway's *Friendship in Fashion* (1678); Poet, in Shadwell's
Timon of Athens (1678); Escalus, in Tate's *Loyal General*
(1680); Cinna, in *The History and Fall of Caius Marius*
(1680); Sir Frolock Whimsey, in D'Urfey's *Virtuous Wife*
(1680); Trickwell, in Mrs. Behn's *Revenge* (1680); Usher,
in Tate's *King Lear* (1681); Fabritius, in Lee's *Lucius
Junius Brutus* (1681); Fourbine, in Otway's *Soldiers of
Fortune* (1671); Foppington, in Mrs. Behn's *City Heiress*
(1682); The Duke of Mayenne, in Dryden and Lee's *Duke
of Guise* (1682); Swordsman, in Fletcher's (?) *King and no
King* (1683); Gillet, in Ravenscroft's *Dame Dobson* (1684);
Furnish, in the *Factious Citizen* (1684); Widgine, in Brome's
Northern Lass (1684); Cinna the Poet, in *Julius Caesar*
(1684); Quicksilver, in Tate's *Alderman no Conjuror* (1685);
Franvil, in D'Urfey's *Commonwealth of Women* (1685);
Harlequin, in Mountfort's *Dr. Faustus* (1686); Jobson, in
The Devil of a Wife (1686); Frisco, in D'Urfey's *Banditti*
(1686); Bearjest, in Mrs. Behn's *Lucky Chance* (1687);
Harlequin, in Mrs. Behn's *Emperor of the Moon* (1687);
The elder Belford, in Shadwell's *Squire of Alsatia* (1688);
a Soldier, in Mountfort's *Injured Lovers* (1688); and lastly
Toby, in D'Urfey's *Fool's Preferment* (1688). Jevon died
December 24, 1688, aged thirty-six.

Jevon, then, began his stage career at the age of twenty-
one with the minor part of Osric in *Hamlet,* and was on the
boards for fifteen years, acting various *rôles,* from Cinna
the Poet to Harlequin the clown; and it is noticeable that
the older he grew the more frequently did he play low

comedy *rôles* (and with great success). *The Devil of a Wife* was the only play Jevon wrote, the biographers say, and the question naturally suggests itself; how did this professional comedian happen to write that one farce at that particular time? It seems to me that the answer is found in these three facts: namely, that his brother-in-law Shadwell had written no play since 1681 and wished to get in another dig at his opponents; secondly, that Shadwell saw his way to do this under the disguise of Jevon's name; and thirdly, that Jevon himself, familiar with the *rôle* of the low comedian and also that of the mischief-making conjuror, decided to emulate his friend Mountfort's success as a writer and try his hand, too, at that most popular of all forms of drama, the farce. The earliest edition of the farce (licensed March 30, 1686) bears the following title-page:—

The | Devil of a Wife, | or A | Comical Transformation. | As it is Acted by their *Majesties |* Servants at the Queens Theatre in | *Dorset* Garden. | Veni, Vidi, Vici. | Licensed March 30th 1686. R. L. S. | *London,* | Printed by *J. Heptinstall,* for *J. Eaglesfield |* at the *Marigold* over against the *Globe-Tavern* in | Fleet-Street. MDCLXXXVI." [1]

The *verso* of the title-page is blank. Then follow two pages devoted to "The Epistle Dedicatory To my Worthy Friends and Patrons at *Lockets* Ordinary," signed "Tho. Jevon." Two pages and a half are then given to the Preface, one and a half to the Prologue, "spoke by Mr. Jevon," and then follows "The Actors Names" in this order:

---

[1] A copy of this text is in the library of Mr. Hiram Bingham, Princeton, N. J., and another in the Harvard Library, while the Boston Public Library possesses copies of the 1693 and 1695 texts.

Men.

Sir *Rich. Lovemore* } An honest Country Gentleman belov'd for good old *Engl.* Housekeeping. { *Mr. Griffin.*

Rowland *Longmore* } Sir Richard's two Friends. { *Mr. Bowman.* *Mr. Peryn.*

Butler *Cook* *Footman* } Servants to Sir *Richard.* { *Mr. Saunders.* *Mr. Percyval.* *Mr. Low.*

Coachm.

The Ladies Father. *Of the old Strain : A Phanatick.* Mr. *Norris.*

Noddy } A Hypocritical Phanatick Parson, loves to eat and cant, Chaplain to my Lady *Lovemore.* { *Mr. Powel.*

Jobson } A Psalm-singing Cobler, Tennant and Neighbour to Sir *Richard.* { *Mr. Jevon.*

Doctor. A Magitian. Mr. *Freeman.*

Nadyr *Abyshog* } Two Spirits.

Countryman.

Blind Fiddler.

Footboy.

Women.

Lady *Lovemore* } Wife to Sir *Richard.* A Proud Phanatick, always canting and brawling. A Perpetual Fixen and a Shrew, (a blessed Wife). { *Mrs. Cook.*

Jane *Lettice* } Lady *Lovemore's* Maids. { *Mrs. Price.* *Mrs. Twyford.*

Nell—Jobson's Wife, a simple innocent Girl. Mrs. *Percyval.*

Tennants, Servants, Dancers, Singers, Wassalers.

The text proper then begins, consisting of fifty-four pages, divided into three acts, and ending with a prologue of two pages, spoken by Mr. Jevon and Mrs. Percyval.

A short summary of the plot now follows. Jobson, the psalm-singing cobbler, tells his wife Nell that he has made an appointment for a convivial evening with the Butler at Sir Richard Lovemore's house. Nell pleads to be taken with him, but he orders her to stay at home, giving her six pence spending' money. Scene 2 shows the servants at the Hall place gathered for the evening's amusement, aud gossiping about the termagant character of their Lady and her disagreeable non-con parson, Noddy. Noddy then enters and orders a hearty meal, as he "feels as it were a strange kind of emptifulness, I have not eat these two houres." Declaiming against Christmas "Pyes" and Christmas customs, the non-con orders a bottle of sack, a bottle of ale, and a bottle of March beer, hoping by this refreshment to hold out till supper. The servants retire, vowing to get even with him that night. A blind fiddler, Jobson, and others enter and commence singing a drinking song, whereupon Noddy attacks the musicians, but in turn is roughly handled by the servants, whereupon he steals out. Scene 3 discovers Lady Lovemore uttering a tirade against her gentle husband for his hospitality toward his neighbors and servants. Noddy complains to the Lady of his rough treatment and my lady abuses the blind fiddler for his music, but Sir Rich. pays the fiddler handsomely and kindly dismisses all. At this juncture the Butler announces the arrival of a "Doctor" who .desires lodging for the night. Sir Richard has to refuse his request for that evening, but directs him to a cobbler's house down the lane. Noddy then comes in and drinks deeply of a huge bowl of strong punch set there purposely for him by the servants. He at once becomes tipsy, and upon the servant announcing supper he staggers out to say grace at the table with my lord and lady. Scene 4 takes place at the cobbler Jobson's house, where the Doctor and Nell are discovered in conversation, the Doctor promising Nell that for her kindness to him she shall on the morrow be wearing silks and purple and be a fine lady. Jobson then enters, thrusts out the "cunning" man, and beats his wife for her neglect of her work. Scene 5 changes to the open country, where the doctor conjures up his two attendant spirits, Nadyr and Abyshog, and says:

> " Praesto, all my charms attend :
> Ere this night shall have an End,
> You shall this Cobler's Wife transform,

And to the Knights the like perform ;
This bed, the Cobler's Wife I'll charm,
The Knights into the Cobler's Arm ;
Let the delusion be so strong,
That none shall know the right from wrong.
The non-con Parson so affright
That he may ever rue this Night ;
Scare him from his little Wits,
And his Hypocritick Fits.''

Nadyr and Abyshog :

" All this, this Night we will perform,
In a whirl-wind, in a Storm,
In Lightning and in Thunder.''

Doctor :

" Fly
And muster all the Clouds i' th' Sky :
Attend me till the Dawn of Day,
And then you may go sport and play.''

The next scene shifts us to the dining room of the Hall
place, where Sir Richard is greeting his friends, Mr. Rowland and Mr. Longmore, who have come for a hunting visit.
Upon asking after Lady Lovemore, Sir Richard informs
them that his wife is a perfect vixen : but that to-night is
her last night's reign, as her father is coming in the morning
to take her away on a separate maintenance agreement.

Act II begins with a meeting of the servants, who relate
how my Lady thought Noddy, the drunken parson, had a fit
of apoplexy and therefore had a hot frying pan held over
Noddy's head, his pate shaved bald, and a caustic plaster
placed between neck and shoulders to raise blisters. Then
the servants dress up in the shape of dogs, bears, etc., hang
iron chains about themselves and in scene 2 enter Noddy's
bedroom, where they frighten the life out of the parson,
handle him roughly, and extract from him a confession of
hypocrisy and gluttony. In the midst of it all, a terrible
storm arises outside, and presently appears in the room one
of the doctor's spirits, who offers Noddy a fried toad to eat.

The servants flee in terror, and Noddy runs roaring out into the arms of Sir Richard and his friends, who lock him up. Upon this the spirits, Nadyr and Abyshog, reenter and tell how the transformation is now complete. my Lady being in the cobbler's hut and Nell occupying her place at the Hall place, after which the spirits disappear. The next scene shows the cobbler's house, Jobson sings the "Wife of Bath," and upon my Lady launching out into a tirade against him, beats her soundly. A countryman then enters and assures Jobson that this is not my Lady but drunken Nell, so he straps my Lady again. The following scene is again at the Hall place, where Nell is in bed, soliloquizing upon her strange but delightful surroundings. The various servants enter to receive their commands for the day, and upon hearing Nell's gentle voice and gracious requests "they run jumping out" overcome with astonishment and delight at the change. Sir Richard and his friends enter and the servants "come jumping in" to tell of the wonderful change in their mistress' temper. Sir Richard is overcome with joy. He asks her if she really will now "go to Church with us, and leave the sniveling Conventicle." (Nell), "Yes, surely Sir, I'll do what ere you please, I'll have nothing to do with Fanaticks, they are a Melancholy ill condition'd People." Sir Richard then tell his joy to his friends and servants and proclaims a "jubilee for three months." Musicians enter and Sir Richard sings a lively song, which he had composed, during the lifetime of his first wife, in praise of married life. In the midst of the rejoicing Noddy comes in, wrapt in his nightcap, and cries out "What meaneth this lewd noise; this most prophane abominable jigging"? He is sternly reprimanded by Sir Richard; then he appeals to Nell (whom he takes for his patroness, my Lady), but gets no encouragement from her, upon which he remarks, "What's this, she is not as she was; *Jampridem*

mulieri ne credas ne mortuae quidem." They then thrust
him out. In the next scene Lady Lovemore's father (a
puritan) enters, and is quite upset by Nell kneeling to ask
his blessing: "What meaneth this, tis Superstitious, and
savors of idolatry"? All then retire to dinner. The
cobbler's house is represented in the next scene, where Lady
Lovemore, deserted and miserable, has to endure Jobson's
rough treatment as best she can until chance offers an
escape, when Jobson goes out to share in the merrymaking
at the Hall. As the guests sit at dinner, my Lady suddenly
bursts in and begins to act the fury and vixen as of old, but
nobody recognizes her, not ever her father and her chaplain
Noddy. Sir Richard is greatly amazed at this strange
mix-up, and doesn't know what to do, suspecting witchcraft
in it all. At last my Lady in despair breaks out—"'What
in the Devil's name was I here before I came hither! that I
should come hither and find that I was here before I came
is the strangest thing to me." This incoherence utterly
dumbfounds the good Sir Richard, and he is not a whit
relieved when Jobson enters and Nell cries out, "O Lord, I
am afraid my husband will beat me that am on yonder
side!" Jobson explains that his wife (as he supposes) has
been drinking with a conjuror at his house' last night, and
has not yet recovered from the effects, so Sir Richard bids
him lead her gently out, saying, "she may be cured of this."
Jobson replies yes, "I will cure her with this strap," upon
which Nell cries out from the other side of the room, "Hold,
hold, pray, do not beat me, Zekel." Sir Richard then thinks
that Nell is crazy also, and the maids leads her out too.
The father of my Lady, disgusted with it all, takes his
departure.

At this juncture the doctor enters and explains the whole
matter. My Lady, repentant, is restored a submissive,
gentle wife to her husband. Noddy is dismissed and Nell

is restored to Jobson, together with a handsome sum of money from Sir Richard. The play ends with all joining in a general rejoicing.

Such is a synopsis of the farce. The *Dictionary of National Biography* is in error in stating the date of the performance of this play. The quarto, indeed, was not licensed until March 30th, 1686; but a reference to the play is found in the preface to D'Urfey's *Banditti* (licensed March 1st, 1686) where the author says: "Jobson's wife is now a much better character than Sempronia or Abigail." Jevon's play, then, must have been on the boards before March 1st, 1686, at the latest. It is now in order to point out that whether Jevon wrote the farce or not, the phraseology contained therein is certainly Shadwell's. Passing over the various classical references found in the dedication and in the preface, (which one would hardly expect to emanate from a comedian of Jevon's type), and bearing in mind that Shadwell wrote no comedy between his *Lancashire Witches* and the *Squire of Alsatia*, it is worth while comparing the phraseology of these two comedies with that of *The Devil of a Wife*. First, the *dramatis personæ* of the *Lancashire Witches* and those of Jevon's farce :—

[*Lan. W.*] "Sir Edward Harfoot, a worthy, hospitable true English Gentleman of good understanding and honest principles."

[*D. of W.*] "Sir Rich. Lovemore, an honest country gentleman, belov'd for good old Engl. Housekeeping."

[*Lan. W.*] "Bellfort, Doubty, two Yorkshire gentlemen of good estates, well bred and of good sense."

[*D. of W.*] "Rowland, Longmore, Sir Richard's two friends."

[*Lan. W.*] "Smerk,[1] Chaplain to Sir Edward, foolish, knavish, popish, arrogant, insolent ; yet for his interest slavish."

[*D. of W.*] "Noddy, a hypocritical fanatic parson, loves to eat and cant, Chaplain to my Lady Lovemore."

---

[1] It was Shadwell's description of this character which excited a great clamor against the whole play and moved the Master of the Revels to strike out a dozen lines of the dialogue.

5

[*Lan. W.*] "Susan, Housekeeper to Sir Edward."
[*D. of W.*] "Jane, Lady Lovemore's maid."
[*Lan. W.*] "Clod, a country fellow, a retainer to Sir Edward's family."
[*D. of W.*] "A countryman."

So much for Jevon's "originality" in the *dramatis personæ*. Next the phraseology found in the two texts:—

(*Lan. W.*) Act I, Sir Edw. "What fatal mischiefs have domestick priests brought on the best of families in England!
Where their dull patrons gave them line enough,
First with the women they insinuate,
(Whose fear and folly make them slaves to you),
And give them ill opinions of their husbands.
Oft ye divide them if the women rule not.
But if they govern, then your reign is sure."

(*D. of W.*) Act I, Sir Richard. "... nay I have married her Chaplain too, who was, I take, a Weaver, and ordain'd himself by virtue of outward *Grace*, and inward Knavery, have a care I warn you of a Bigot or Zealous Woman, for be she never so wicked, she will be always so full of spiritual *Pride*, She'll think you a Limb of Satan."
(Rowl.) "'Tis a just observation."
(Long.) "And for a *Chaplain*, I would as soon have a *Russian* in my house, for he must Govern or the wife will Rage."

(*Lan. W.*) Act I, Sir Edw. "I will advise and teach your master of artship ... to add to your small logick and divinity Two main ingredients, Sir,—sence and good manners."

(*D. of W.*) Act I, Sir Rich. "You deserve it for a meddling, Coxcomb, go to your Book you ignorant Fop and reader and rely more upon good Sence, and less upon your new Light."

(*Lan. W.*) Act II, Sir Edw. "Gentlemen, the storm has obliged me that drove you under my roof; I knew your fathers well: we were in Italy together."

(*D. of W.*) Act I, Sir Rich. "Well my dear Friends, though you have found my House in some disorder, I cannot but rejoyce to see you, the sight of Friends will lighten great afflictions."
(Rowl.) "Some years have passed, since we have been merry together."
(Long.) "We have not met these five years Marriage, Travel, Business, and your Retirement, have thus separated us."

(*Lan. W.*) Act V, Sir Edw. "None but the vilest sports will make their sports their business."

(*D. of W.*) Act I, Sir Rich. "Methinks there's a Pleasure to see 'em hit off at a fault, as there is in a hard riding." . . . "I spare my horses today which made me come home so soon.'

(*Lan. W.*) Act V, Sir Jeff. "Heaven! what a Storm is this! The witches and all their imps are at work."

(*D. of W.*) Act I, Job. "What has the Devil been about to Night? I never heard such Thunder Claps and such a Storm. . . ."

(*Lan. W.*) Act V, Chaplain. "Good sire, continue me your chaplain, and I will do and preach whatever you command me."

(Sir Edw.) "I'll not have a divine with so flexible a conscience. . . . But she has served me well, and I will give her a farm at 40 £ per annum. Go sire, it was an office you were born to."

(*D. of W.*) Act V, Sir Rich. "Go Hypocrite, I discard thee. . . . Give him ten Pound, and in the morning send him packing; here Jobson take thy fine wife."

The reader's attention is now directed to a comparison between passages found in *The Devil of a Wife* (1686), and Shadwell's *Squire of Alsatia* (1688). First the *dramatis personæ* of the two plays :—

(*D. of W.*) "Sir Richard Lovemore, An honest Country Gentleman belov'd for good old *Engl.* Housekeeping. (Mr. Gryffin.)"

(*S. of A.*) "Sir Edward Belfort, A man of great Humanity and Gentleness and Compassion towards Mankind; well read in good Books, possessed with all Gentlemanlike Qualities. (Mr. Griffin.)"

(*D. of W.*) "Noddy, A Hypocritical Phanatick Parson, loves to eat and cant, Chaplain to my Lady *Lovemore*."

(*S. of A.*) "Scrapeall, A hypocriticall, repeating, praying, Psalm singing, precise fellow, pretending to great Piety, a godly knave," etc.

(*D. of W.*) "Lady Lovemore, . . . A Perpetual Fixen and a Shrew, . . ."

(*S. of A.*) "Mrs. Termagant, . . . A furious, malicious, and revengeful Woman, . . ."

The parallel passages from the two texts, which now follow, are, in my opinion, of much significance :—

(*D. of W.*)   Act III, Noddy, "He that wears a brave Soul, and dares
               honestly do,
               Is a Herrald to himself and a Godfather too."
(*S. of A.*)   Act I, Hackum sings, "He that wears a brave Soul, and dares
               honestly do,
               Is a Herald to himself, and a Godfather too."
(*D. of W.*)   Act III, Noddy, . . . "pledge·me all of you, and let every
               Bumper be a facer thus. . . . (They drink off their Glasses
               and Huzzah.)"
Serv.   "Is that a facer, faith 'tis very pretty." [1]
(*S. of Al.*) Act II, Belf. Sen. "Ay, and i faith I'll drink it, pretty
               Rogue."
Sham.   "Let them be *Facers*."
Belf. Sen. "Facers! what are those?"
Sham.   "There's a *Facer* for you. (Drinks the Glass clear off, and
             puts it to his Face.)"
Belf. Sen. "Excellent, acad! Come to our *Facers*." (All do the
             like.) "It is the prettiest way of drinking: Fill
             again, we'll have more *Facers*," etc.
Belf. Sen. "Give the Rogue a Facer to my Mistress. Come fill
             about the *Facers*. Come on my lads, stand to 't.
             Huzza! I vow, 'tis the prettiest way of drinking,
             never stir."
(*D. of W.*)   Act II, Sir Rich. "Here's a Turn; here's a Hypocritical
               Rogue, I think we shall have *Ovid's Metamorphosis* in this
               House. . . ."
(*S. of A.*)   Act II, Belf. Jun. "I am struck with Astonishment! Not
               all *Ovid's Metamorphosis* can shew such a one as this."
(*D. of W.*)   Act I, Sir Rich. "Oh Gentlemen, I would be glad to have
               the Witch of *Endor* were she alive instead of her. . . ."
(*S. of A.*)   Act IV, Tru. . . . "but I had as lieve have had a *Lancashire
               Witch*. . . ."
(*D. of W.*)   Act I, Butler. "I that have lived five and forty year in the
               House, and had for twenty years preserv'd a reverent Beard,
               which made me noted for Wisedom and Discretion through
               all the Countrey, and she to demolish this poor Beard in an
               instant; . . . I saved nothing but this same one Sprig, that
               grew upon a Wart, and that by my Naile. . . . Ay, I am
               become a shame to my Neighbours and dare not show my

---

[1] This instance of the word "facer" is earlier, obviously, than that in the
citation given in the *New English Dictionary*, which is taken from the *Squire
of Alsatia*.

Chin before 'em : Oh that Beard, that poor Beard, what Authority it had amongst them ! ''

(*S. of A.*) Act V, Hack. "I have lost the best Head of Hair in the *Fryers*; and a Whisker worth Fifty Pound, in its intrinsick Value to a Commander. . . . I am as disconsolate as a Bee that has lost his Sting; the other Moiety of Whisker must follow : Then all the Terror of that Face that us'd to fright young Priggs into Submission. I shall now look but like an Ordinary man."

(Epilogue to *D. of W.*, spoken by Mrs. Percyval, who became later Mrs. Mountfort) :

> "Whilst all these lofty Frigots you attacque,
> Pray let in safety pass this little smack.
> Your shot 'gainst us will wast 'ith empty sky,
> The whistling bullets o'er our heads will flye ;
> We lye so low your Cannon mount too high."

(Epilogue to *S. of A.*, spoken by Mrs. Mountfort) :

> "Ye mighty Scowrers of these narrow Seas,
> Who suffer not a Bark to sail in Peace,
> But with your tire of Culverins ye roar,
> Bring 'em by th' Lee, and rummage all their Store :
> Our Poet duck'd and looked as if half dead,
> At every Shot that whistled o'er his Head. . . ."

In conclusion I should like to present the following parallel passages, all of which are chosen from plays of Shadwell which appeared *after* Jevon's *Devil of a Wife*. From these comparisons the reader will see that the phraseology is surely Shadwell's and not Jevon's.

(*B. F.*) Act II, . "He may say as Caesar did, *Veni, Vidi, Vici.*"

(*D. of W.*) Motto on title-page, "Veni, Vidi, Vici."

(*B. F.*) Act II, Bell. "They are Fops, Ned, that make a Business of Sport. I hunt with my Harriers half a dozen Heats in a Morning, for Health and an Appetite : and at Dinner time, let 'em be in never such full cry, I knock off."

(*Lan. W.*) Act V, Sir Edw. (already quoted).

(*D. of W.*) Act I, Sir Rich. (already quoted).

(*B. F.*) Act V, Aldw. "Call in the Fidlers. I am transported ! I am all Air! Sirrah, go you, and set the Bells a going in both Churches. Call in all my Neighbours : I'll have him hang'd thats sober Tonight. Let every Room in my House roar, that it may keep the Whole Town awake. Here are the Fiddlers : fall to dancing presently ; lose no time. Let all this Night be spent in Mirth and Wine."

(*D. of W.*) Act III, Sir Rich. "I am transported beyond my Senses :
        I hear proclaim a Jubilee to all my Family these three
        months : Summon in all the Countrey, I'll keep open house,
        send for my Fidlers, Hoboys, Trumpets, and all Instruments
        of Joy; let all the Bells in the Hundred Ring, let the
        Steeples Rock, and let the Ringers drink enough."
(*The Scowrers.*) Act I, Tope : . . . "Charge a Bill upon me, and I'll
        answer you in a couple of Brimmers of Claret at *Locket's* at
        Dinner. . . ."
        Act II, Tope. "Think on the Turbott and the Calvert Salmon
        at *Lockets.*"
(*The Volunteers*) Act III, M. G. Blunt. "But these plain Fellows in lac'd
        coats, just such as you of the drawing Room and *Lockets*
        Fellows are now, . . ."

In the light of the evidence given in this chapter, the
conclusion is hardly to be avoided that Shadwell, and not
Jevon, was the man behind the pen which wrote *The Devil
of a Wife.*

The second interesting event in the life history of this
little farce occurred in 1730. In that year Charles Coffey,
a stage writer, who had already brought out four or five
musical farces with indifferent success, took hold of *The
Devil of a Wife* and brought it out as a musical farce under
the title of *The Devil to Pay.* Whincop's description of the
play is well worth noting :[1]—

"The Devil to Pay : a Ballad Farce, of one Act ; performed at first with
great Success at the Theatre Royal in *Drury Lane,* and afterwards at every
other Theatre, some times at three together in one Night, and has been
oftener acted than any one Piece on the Stage : Mr. Coffey's name is
printed to it, but it is a difficult Matter to say to whom it properly belongs
to. The Foundation and best Part of it is a Farce of three Acts called,
'A Comical Transformation, or The Devil of a Wife,' wrote by Jevon the
Player ; and some People doubted if that, at the Time it first came out,
was not partly wrote by his Brother-in-law, Shadwell, the Poet Lawreat ;
it was performed in the Year 1686. Forty-four years after, viz., in the
year 1730, Mr. Coffey and Mr. Mottley took each one Act and a half of
this Farce, and altering some parts of the Dialogue, and adding Songs,

---

[1] Whincop, *A Complete List of All the English Dramatic Poets,* etc., 1747.

called it a Ballad Opera, and gave it the name of 'The Devil to Pay.' It was performed in the Summer Season, in three Acts, but some part of it not pleasing, particularly the Part of a Non-conforming Pastor,[1] performed by Mr. *Chark* who had never acted anything before, it was cut shorter, that part left out, and so reduced to one Act, which was done by Mr. *Theophilus Cibber*, one new Song was added by his Father, Mr. Colley Cibber ; another introduced that was wrote by Lord Rochester above fifty years before ;[2] so that we see about six Authors concerned in this one little Piece."

The first quarto of Coffey's opera appeared in 1731,[3] and the following lines are a description of a copy of the original quarto in the Harvard Library :—

(Title-page). "*The Devil to Pay:* or the Wives Metamorphos'd. An Opera, as it is Perform'd at the Theatre Royal in Drury-Lane, By his Majesty's Servants. Written by the Author of the Beggars Wedding, *In nova fert animus mutatas dicere formas corpora . . . . Ovid.* With the *Musick*, prefix'd to each *Song*. London, Printed for J. Watt's, at the Printing Office in *Wildcourt* near Lincoln's-Inn Fields. MDCCXXXI. Price One Shilling and Six Pence."

On the next page is a list of the forty-two songs which are distributed throughout the three acts of the text ; then follows the Prologue, spoken by Theophilus Cibber : and after that the *dramatis personae.* The cast I give in full as it makes an interesting comparison with that of *The Devil of a Wife.*

Men.

Sir John Loverule } An *honest Country Gentleman, belov'd for his Hospitality.* { Mr. *Stopelaer.*

Ranger } His Friends.   { Mr. *Wetherelt*, Jr.
Valentine }   { Mr. *Roberts*

Ananias } An *ignorant* fanatick *Parson, Chaplain* to Lady *Loverule.* { Mr. *Charke*

The Lady's Father, *zealous for the good old* cause.   { Mr. *Wetherelt, Sr.*

---

[1] The *rôle* in the *Lancashire Witches* which brought such a storm against Shadwell, and yet is repeated again in *The Devil of a Wife.*

[2] All the songs contained in the earliest one-act version which I have been able to see (dated 1748) are contained in the original 1731 text except Nos. 3, 4, and 15. I cannot identify these however.

[3] *Gentleman's Magazine*, Aug. 11, 1731.

Butler			Mr. *Berry*
Cook	} Servants to Sir John.		Mr. *Fielding*
Footman			Mr. *Wright*
Coachman			Mr. *Gray*
Jobson, A Psalm-singing *Cobler*, *Tenant to Sir* John.			{ Mr. *Harper*
Doctor			{ Mr. *Oates*
Nadir	} Two Spirits attending the Doctor.		{ Mr. *Fisher Tench*
Abishog			{ Mr. *H. Tench*
Gaffar Dungfork.			{ Mr. *Cibber*, Jr.

Women.

Lady Loverule, Wife to Sir John, a proud, canting, brawling, fanatical Shrew.	{ Mrs. *Mills*
Lucy		
Lettice	} Her Maids.	Mrs. *Oates*
Nell, Jobson's Wife, an innocent country Girl.	{ Mrs. *Clive*

Tennants, Servants, Dancers, etc.
Scene. A Country Village.

Through the kindness of Professor Hiram Bingham of
Princeton, and the authorities of the Harvard and Boston
Public Libraries, I have been able to collate the three
earliest editions of *The Devil of a Wife* (1686, 1693, and
1695) with the original text of Coffey's opera, and from
this collation I judge that Coffey followed the readings of
the earliest text (1686). He sometimes carelessly inserts
the names of "Sir Richard" and "Jane" of the 1686
farce, instead of "Sir John" and "Lucy," the corresponding characters in his own opera, though in one instance
"Jane" is the catchword (page 4 of *The Devil of a Wife*) in
the 1686 text, and would not have been copied by a careful,
original dramatist. In most of his readings Coffey follows
his model very closely, generally word for word: but one
notices a marked tendency in Coffey's lines toward toning
down and sometimes omitting altogether the coarser phrases
found in *The Devil of a Wife*, particularly those referring to
or spoken by the chaplain Noddy. The most striking
innovation, however, is of course the introduction of the
forty-two songs. From a modern musician's point of view

the songs are of a pretty poor quality, and sung at most inopportune moments. The success of the opera, however, was immediate. "Mr. Coffey," says Whincop, "and the other Gentleman concerned with him in altering Jevon's Farce, who did not choose to have his Name appear in it, could not expect the same advantages as from a new Play, and so instead of having the Third, they had not their Benefit till the three and thirthieth Night, and then paid seventy Pounds for it; *but there was a most prodigiously crowded House*, and chiefly in ready money, which shows how ready the Town are to reward those who have the good fortune to please them. I can by no means think that this. Farce is to be put on a level with many others that have pleased very well, but have less Invention and less Wit than is in this, *all Jevon's:* besides it being enlivened by the Music, the Repitition of it shows its Merit, for tho' the Multitude are not always the best Judges of Dramatic Performances yet they are not always mistaken.[1] ... Some severe Critics, but, at the same time ill-judging, have found fault with this Farce for the Improbability of the Fable of two Women being changed into each other, and say it ought not to please because it is so unnatural. ... But the question is whether, upon a Supposition (and it is a Supposition very allowable in Poetry) that if these Women could be so changed, what they say and do then is Natural? And that it is so, the involuntary Applause that always attends them from the Boxes as well as the Upper Gallery sufficiently shews." It may be said in passing that the celebrated actress, Miss Rastor (or Kitty Clive, as she was best known) won her first laurels by her impersonation of the character of Nell in this farce, while Mrs. Jordan, who

---

[1] A remark quite suggestive of Lincoln's epigram a century or more later.

played the same *rôle* fifty years later, achieved no greater applause than when she acted the same part.[1]

The last, and perhaps the most important period in the literary life of the farce, *The Devil of a Wife*, is its entry into the field of German literature. One cannot do better, perhaps, than describe its career in that foreign field in the words of the German scholar, Dr. Jacob Minor, who takes it up at the point where *The Devil of a Wife* has been transformed into *The Devil to Pay* ("*der Teufel ist Los*") : — [2]

"Caspar Wilhelm von Borck, als geheimer Rath (später Minister) in Berlin ansässig, welcher schon während seines Gesandtschaftspostens in London den Julius Cäsar von Shakespere in Versen übersetzt hatte, bearbeitete unter dem Pseudonym Buschmann im Jahre 1743 auch den 'Teufel' von Coffey in ziemlich wörtlicher Uebertragung für die deutsche Bühne. Die Schönemannische Truppe, welcher er das Manuscript zur Verfügung stellte, gab das Singspiel am 24. Januar 1743 zur Feier des Geburtstages König Friederichs II. Die englische Musik des Originals wurde beibehalten, die Arien einstimmig und ohne Musik-begleitung vorgetragen. In Berlin fiel die Operette zwar gänzlich durch, aber in Hamburg scheint sie grossen Beifall gefunden zu haben, und Schönemann gab das Stück zur Michaelismesse 1750 sogar in Leipzig."

In 1752 the theatrical manager Koch came to Christian Felix Weisse and asked him to translate the opera for his troupe. Weisse consented and made a pretty free translation of *The Devil to Pay*, introduced many original songs (or rather the words to the songs), and, finally, the first violinist in Koch's troupe composed entirely new music for Weisse's songs. The first performance took place on October 6, 1752, and its success was enormous, increasing still more the next year on account of the savage attacks made upon it by Gottsched and his party. The opera spread to France,

---

[1] Genest records a performance of the farce as late as 1828.

[2] *Christian Felix Weisse und seine Beziehung zur deutschen Literatur des achtzehnten Jahrhunderts*, von Dr. J. Minor, Innsbruck, 1880.

and in 1756 Sedaine translated it for the French stage.[1] Weisse probably read this French translation during his stay in Paris, and used it for the new edition of his own translation, which appeared in 1766. Hiller wrote the music for this latter text, and the airs became so popular that one heard them sung as far south as Naples. As a result of this popularity, and to protect his work from piracy and corruption, Weisse published the opera in 1768 under the title, *Die verwandelten Weiber oder der Teufel ist Los.*[2] *Eine komische Oper in drey Aufzügen.*

Lack of space forbids giving a complete description of Weisse's opera, but the *dramatis personae* may be of interest for the sake of comparison with that of *The Devil to Pay* and *The Devil of a Wife :*—

"Personen.

Herr von Liebreich, ein Landesedelmann.
Frau von Liebreich, dessen Gemalinn.
Jobsen Zeckel, ein Schuhflicker.
Lene, dessen Frau.
Mikroscop, ein Zauberer.
Kellner,
Koch,
Kutscher, } des Herrn von Liebreich.
Bedienter.
Hannchen, } Mädchen der Frau von Liebreich.
Lieschen.
Andreas, ein blinder Musikante.
Verschiedene Bediente, Unterthanen und Nachbarn des Herrn von Liebreich.
Etliche Geister.
Der Schauplatz ist bald in des Herrn von Liebreichs Hause, bald in des
    Schuhflickers Wohnung.''

---

[1] It appeared in print in 1770 with the title : *Le diable à quatre ou la double métamorphose, Opera comique en trois actes.* An 1829 reprint shows many alterations from the English original.

[2] The earliest text I have seen is that of 1778, although the Leipzig city library possesses a copy of the 1768 edition.

Weisse's translation contains three acts, but they are not divided according to the original 1731 text of *The Devil to Pay*, and the dialogue and songs are materially altered. The *rôles* of the non-conformist parson and the two friends of Sir John Loverule are entirely .omitted,[1] the musician Andreas is given a much more important part, several scenes are inserted which are found only in later editions of Coffey's opera, while other scenes are entirely original with Weisse.

Such is the history of the little Restoration farce, *The Devil of a Wife*. When we recall the noted actors and actresses who played its parts—Will Mountfort, Mrs. Bracegirdle, Kitty Clive, Theophilus Cibber, and Mrs. Jordan— and when we consider that such men as Shadwell, Colley Cibber, Weisse, Gottsched, Nicolai and Lessing all had a share in its history, it hardly seems too much to consider the play as an interesting link between our English Literature of the Restoration period, and that of Germany in the eighteenth century.

ALFRED E. RICHARDS.

---

[1] The parson's *rôle* was first omitted, as already mentioned, by Theophilus Cibber.

XIX.—LEGENDS OF CAIN, ESPECIALLY IN OLD AND MIDDLE ENGLISH.

An examination, some time since, of scattered notes on allusions to Cain in our literature showed that there was still room for a somewhat more thorough investigation of the subject. The results of such leisure as could be given from time to time are here presented. They cover, it is hoped, the main features of the Cain story, though not unlikely some allusions have been missed. Many more references might also be given to notes on various phases of the subject, but I have preferred not to overload the footnotes with comparatively unimportant ones. In general I have intended to give the more important, preferring earlier to later, and original to derived sources when possible. Lack of time to pursue the matter further at present is the excuse for publishing the paper in this form.[1]

The legends connected with Cain may be classed under the following heads: I. Cain's Origin; II. The Sacrifice; III. The Murder of Abel; IV. The Curse and the Mark of Cain; V. The Death of Cain; VI. Cain's Descendants. These will be discussed in order, and especially the allusions to them in our older literature. References to some of them

---

[1] As originally written the paper was read before the Modern Language Association at Philadelphia in 1900. Since that time some additions have been made and the whole has been revised. There has been, however, no essential modification of the principal results of the original study. Yet special mention should be made of a monograph by Dr. Louis Ginzberg, *Die Haggada bei den Kirchenvätern und in der apochryphischen Litteratur*, which has been of special assistance in connection with Hebrew tradition. Though printed in the same year as the reading of this paper I had not seen it when the paper was written. Dr. Ginzberg has also furnished me valuable information in one or two letters.

not directly alluded to in English may be important in explaining passages not here noticed. No special attempt has been made to gather allusions from other literatures, though some such are given when of special value in explaining those of English. In accounting for legendary additions to the Bible story special search has been made of early Christian writings and, so far as possible, of Rabbinical lore when there was reason to believe that source had been drawn upon. In the latter case it is not always easy to prove direct connection. Yet the use of Hebrew tradition in explaining difficult passages of Scripture is so well known, that connection may usually be assumed as fairly certain.

I. Cain's Origin.

The biblical account of Cain as the son of Adam and Eve was much extended by Hebrew tradition. In the first place men felt that something more than human depravity was necessary, to account for such an extraordinary crime as murder in the comparative innocence of the early world. Rabbinical lore even went so far as to assert that Cain was the son, not of Adam, but of the devil. A suggestion of this occurs in *1 John* 3, 12, which reads, "Not as Cain, who was of that wicked one and slew his brother." This passage alone, whether based on Hebrew legend or not, is sufficient to account for many references to the devilish character of Cain. By another account Cain was born in the period of transgression following the fall, and before the repentance of Adam and Eve. Or Cain's character was attributed to that of Eve, who suffered more than her share of opprobrium at the hands of early Christian and medieval commentators.

The tradition that Cain was the son of a devil does not seem to have been used by English writers. If known, it was doubtless felt to be too much at variance with Scripture, though it may have colored later allusions to Cain or his descendants. Indeed, it may almost seem to be implied by a passage in the *Ormulum* :

> Caym Adamess sune toc niþ ӡæn Abæl hiss broþerr,
> Off þatt he sahh þatt he wass god, annd rihhtwis mann annd clene,
> Forr defless þewwess hafenn aӡӡ strang niþ ӡæn Cristess þewwess.[1]

Perhaps there is also a suggestion of it in one of the *Scottish Satirical Poems of the Reformation.* In No. xlv, the *Legend of Bischop of Androis Lyfe,* occur these lines :

> This Adamsone may weill be borne of Eve,
>   Takand his vices of his wicked mother ;
> Likkest to father Adam, I believe,
>   Surpassing Cain cursed or any uther.[2]

The above passage at least emphasizes the evil nature of our first parents after the fall, and thus approaches the idea of Cain's birth in the period of transgression. Such an idea was frequently alluded to. Thus, in the Middle English *Genesis*, Adam and Eve, after leaving Eden, were in sorrow and care, and thought they ought to live apart :

> On sundri ðhenken he to ben,
> And neiðere on oðer sen.[3]

Even when commanded by an angel to live together, they do so

> More for erneste ðan for gamen (l. 411).

The idea is more elaborated in Piers Plowman, allusion being made to it in all the texts. The fullest, in Text A, passus x, 135 f., reads as follows :

---

[1] Holt's ed., ll. 14456 f.
[2] Scot. Text Soc., ed. by Jas. Cranstoun, l. 97.
[3] Early Eng. Text Soc. 7, ll. 393–4.

Fals folk and feiþles,   theoves and lyȝers,
Ben conseyvet in curset tyme,   as Caym was on Eve,
After þat Adam and Eve hedden   eten of þe appel,
Aȝeyn þe heste of him   þat hem of nouȝt made.
An angel in haste   þennes hem tornde
Into þis wrecchede world,   to wonnen and to libben
In tene and in travaile   to here lives ende ;
In þat corsede constellacion   þei knewen togedere,
And brouȝten forþ a barn   þat muche bale wrouȝte ;
Caym men cleped him,   in cursed tyme engendret,
And so seiþ the sauter,   seo hit whon þe likeþ,
     Concepit in dolore, et peperit iniquitatem, etc.[1]

To these may be added one late allusion. Whether Byron
knew of these medieval conceptions or not, he virtually
makes use of the same idea in his *Cain* I, 1, when he makes
Eve say after one of Cain's rebellious speeches,

My boy, thou speakest as I spoke, in sin,
Before thy birth ; let me not see renewed
My misery in thine. I have repented.

The period of transgression following the fall was considerably elaborated by apochryphal writers and these have
influenced English works. In the *Life of Adam and Eve*,
usually called *Canticum Creatione*,[2] there is a full account of
an apochryphal transgression of Eve while both she and
Adam are in penance for the sin of the garden. They have
separated, Adam to stand forty-seven days in the Jordan
river and Eve as many in the Tigris. The devil persuades

---

[1] Early Eng. Text Soc., 28, 117. Upon this passage (EETS. 67, 225)
Prof. Skeat quotes Wright's brief note regarding a popular legend of the
Middle Ages on Cain's birth in the period of transgression, though without showing its connection with Hebrew tradition. He adds, "Petrus
Comestor says : 'Adam cognovit uxorem suam, sed non in paradiso et
ejectus.' " The passage from the C Text of *Piers Plowman* will be found
on p. 900 of this paper.

[2] Horstmann, *Sammlung altenglischer legenden;* Trin. MS., p. 126, l. 140 f. ;
Auch. MS., p. 141, l. 235 f. ; Vern. MS., p. 223.

Eve to leave her place of penance, pretending that he and other angels had prayed for her and obtained remission of further suffering. He goes with her to Adam, who at once exposes the tempter's true character. In grief Eve goes into the wilderness to perform a new penance, is finally received again by Adam, and is told by angels to prepare for the birth of Cain.[1] With this summary the story, which is long and in three forms, need not be quoted.

SOURCES.

That Cain was a son of the devil is directly stated in Pirke Rabbi Eliezar xxi, 6.[1] Bartolocci (*Bibliotheca Magna Rabbinica* I, 291) also quotes Ialkut Sect. Berescith, p. 26, as follows :

"Ingreditur ad Evam (nempe Samael) equitans super serpentem, et gravidavit eam Caino."

In speaking of the demons Bartolocci again says :

"Primus eorum parens assignatur angelus, qui pulchritudine Evae illictus, equitans super serpentem ad eam ingreditur, ex quo concepit Kaim, cuius figuram ut et illius posteritatis non humanum, sed angelicum fuisse autumant."[2]

The general character of these legends may be gathered from Baring-Gould's *Legends of the Patriarchs and Prophets,* ch. vi :

"According to some Rabbis, all good souls are derived from Abel, and all bad souls from Cain. Cain's soul was derived from Satan, his body alone was from Eve; for the evil spirit Samael according to some, Satan according to others, deceived Eve and thus Cain was the son of the evil one."[3]

---

[1] So referred in *Jewish Encyclopædia,* article Cain ; Ginzberg, *Die Haggada bei den Kirchenvätern und in der apochryphischen Litteratur,* p. 59. See also Bayle, *Dict. Hist.,* articles Eve, Cain.

[2] *Bibliotheca Magna Rabbinica,* I, 290.

[3] Based on Eisenmenger, *Entdecktes Judenthum,* II, 8.

6

Such a belief, so baldly stated at least, does not seem to occur in the early Fathers. It was probably felt to be too much at variance with Scripture record, and indeed usually appears as a heresy to be refuted. As the latter it is found in Epiphanius, *Hæres.* 40, 5, and Irenaeus, *Hæres.* I, 30, 7.[1] Philaster also mentions it as a heresy of the Cainites in *Liber de Hæresibus,* cap. ii):

"Caiani . . . . dicentes ex altera vertute, id est diaboli, Cain factum."

On this a note in *Migne* (12, 1115-6) reads as follows:

"In Pirke R. Eliezar dicitur Cain Sammaelis progenies, atque ab aliis Rabbinis apud Gaulminum de morte Moysis, p. 216, traditur ex semine primi serpentis natus Magiae per serpentes auctor."

The devil origin of Cain was also a Manichæan heresy, and this is perhaps an added reason why it was not received by orthodox Christians. Compare Harnack, *History of Dogma,* tr. by Buchanan, III, 125. On the other hand Tertullian seems to state the belief in definite language. In *De Patientia,* cap. 5, he says of Eve:

"Nam statim illa semine diaboli concepta, malitiae fecunditate, iram [read irae] filium procreavit."[2]

Most of the Fathers, however, speak of Cain as a son of the devil only in a metaphorical sense. For this they had Scripture authority in *1 John* iii, 12, already mentioned. Such a passage evoked the following comment of Augustine (*In Epistolam Joannis ad Parthos, Tractatus,* V, cap. iii). After discussing the characteristics of Cain and Abel he says:

"Et hinc apparuit quia filius erat diaboli, et ille [Abel] hinc apparuit justus Dei."[3]

In a similar way comment on *John* 8, 44 makes Cain a

---

[1] References from Ginzberg above.

[2] Reference is by Ginzberg, *Die Haggada,* as above, p. 59.

[3] Cf. also Bede, *Exegetica in Epistolam Joannis* (Migne, 93, 102) ; Martinus Legionensis, *Expositio in Epistolam 1 B. Joannis* (Migne, 209, 270).

son of the devil, as in *Quaestiones ex Novo Testamento* of Augustine :

> ."Diabolus non speciale nomen est, sed commune cum caeteris. . . . Itaque hoc in loco patrem Judaeorum Cain significat. . . . Hoc ergo in loco diabolum Cain esse dixit."[1]

Yet even from such allusions the popular mind might easily have assumed the essential connection of Cain with the devil, if not in the exact sense of Hebrew tradition. It would not be unreasonable to suppose, therefore, a somewhat wider extension of the idea in medieval homilies and more popular works.

That Cain was born after the fall is of course biblical. Yet the Fathers emphasized especially the chastity of our first parents before the transgression. Compare, for example, Jerome, *Adv. Jovinianum*, I, 16 :

> "Ac de Adam quidem et Eva illud dicendum, quod ante offensam in paradiso virgines fuerint; post peccatum autem, et extra paradisum, protinus nuptiae."

Petrus Comestor is equally definite in the *Historia Scholastica, Liber Genesis,* cap. xxv :

> "*Adam cognovit uxorem suam* (*Gen.* iv), sed non in paradiso, sed jam reus et ejectus."

The birth of Cain was, therefore, especially associated with the idea of transgression, and this idea was no doubt emphasized by the new doctrine of celibacy.

That the period of transgression was one of considerable length and filled with much sorrow and many incidents is based upon the apochryphal *Vita Adae et Evae*.[2] On this the Middle English *Life of Adam and Eve*, or *Canticum Creatione*, directly depends. The subject is similarly treated in the Ethiopic *Book of Adam and Eve*. See the translation, edited by Malin, 1882.

---

[1] Appendix to vol. III of *Augustine*, Migne, 35, 2282.
[2] Edited by Meyer, 1879.

II. The Sacrifice.

Legendary allusions to the sacrifice of Cain and Abel are common. These relate to the kind of offering made by Cain, the connection with tithing of later Jewish law, and the manner in which the sacrifice was received. As to the first, the Scripture statement that Cain offered "the fruit of the ground" seemed tame to imaginative minds and was variously extended. In the Chester play of the *Creation* Cain offers poor corn. He says of it.

> Such as the fruite is fallen froe
>   Is good enough for him.

> This corne standing, as mot I thee,
> Was eaten with beastes as men may se;
> God, thou gets non better of me,
>   Be thou never so grim.

> Hit were pittye, by my penne,
> This eared corne for to bren,
> Therefore the divill hang me than
>   And thou of this get ought.

> This earles corne grew nye the waye,
> Of this offer I will todaye;
> For cleane corne, by my faye,
>   Of me getts thou noughte.

> Loe, God, here may thou see
> Such corne as grew to me;
> Part of it I bring to thee
>   Anon withoutten let.

> I hope thou wilt quite me this,
> And send me more of worldlie blisse,
> Els, forsoth, thou doest amisse,
>   And thou be in my debte.[1]

---

[1] *The Chester Plays* ed. by Diemling, EETS. (extra ser.), 62; *The Creation*, ll. 531 f. To this passage Ungemach, *Die Quellen der fünf ersten Chester Plays*, gives a parallel from the Old French *Le Mistere du Viel Testament*. The similarity is only general in the main and can be shown to be common

In the Towneley play of the *Killing of Abel* Càin says of his crop,

> When all mens corn was fayre in feld,
> Then was myne not worth a neld ;
> When I shuld saw and wanted seyde,
> And of corn had full grete neyde,
> Then gaf he me none of his,—
> No more will I gif hym of this.[1]

Later he adds,

> At yere tyme I sew fayre corn,
> Yit was it sich when it was shorne,
> Thystyls and brerys, yei grete plente,
> And all kyn wedis that myght be.[2]

In the Cornish mystery of the *Beginning of the World* Cain objects to burning the good corn, though without indicating what he did offer :

> By my faith a great folly
> It is to go to burn a thing
> Which a man can live upon.[3]

The Middle High German *Genesis* is more explicit as to the badness of the offéring. It says,

> Cain was ein achirman ;   ein garbe er nam,
> Die wolde er opheren do   mit agenen und in dem stro.[4]

The character of Cain's offering is also implied in the *Life of Adam and Eve.* The Trinity MS. version says,

> For he typede of the worste þynge
> And Abel of his beste,

to a large number of sources in other places. For our purpose the main point is that Cain offers "une gerbe meschante, Et une blee non valante," *Des Sacrifices Cayn et Abel*, Société des Anciens Texts Français, p. 95.

[1] *The Towneley Plays*, ed. by England, EETS. (ex. ser.), 71 ; *The Killing of Abel*, ll. 122 f.

[2] *Ibid.*, ll. 200 f.

[3] *Ancient Cornish Drama*, ed. by Norris, l. 473 of translation.

[4] Edition of Diemer, p. 24.

and in the prose of the Vernon MS.,

For he [Cain] wiþheold alway þe beste dole and ȝaf God of þe worste.[1]

The reference to "thystlys and brerys" in the Townely play is close to another form of the legend, in which Cain offered thorns. It occurs in the Cornish mystery of the *Creation*, formerly attributed to William Jordan. There Cain says to Abel,

> Burn it I will not,
> The corn nor the fruits certainly.
> Be silent, Abel, to me, dolt head.
>
> I will gather brambles and thorns,
> And dry cowdung to burn without regret,
> And will make a great bush of smoke.[2]

It is not improbable that this reference in the Cornish play to Cain's offering thorns is connected with such a legend in other parts of England. In other European countries at least it became a part of the moon story, the man in the moon being Cain and his thorns. This latter extension of the story deserves a moment of consideration. It is twice used by Dante in his *Divine Comedy*, as may be sufficiently clear for our purpose from a translation. The *Inferno*, XX, 124 f., in Longfellow's version, reads as follows:

> But come now, for already holds the confines
> Of both the hemispheres, and under Seville
> Touches the ocean wave, Cain and his thorns,
> And yesternight the moon was round already.[3]

To this may be added the lines in *Paradiso*, ii, 51 f.,

[1] Horstmann, *Altenglische Legenden*, p. 130, ll. 482 f; p. 224.

[2] *The Creation*, ed. by Stokes. *Transactions of the Philological Society* (1864), IV, p. 87.

[3] See also a note in Longfellow's edition, mentioning the Italian tradition of Cain though without accounting for it, and suggesting the relation of this passage to two in Shakespeare's *Midsummer Night's Dream*. The latter will be discussed later.

> But tell me what the dusky spots may be
> Upon this body, which below on earth
> Make people tell that fabulous tale of Cain?

The difficulty in connecting this moon legend of Cain with other passages in English writers is that there is another early legend of the man in the moon which differently accounts for the thorns. When, therefore, there is no explicit mention of Cain we can not be sure that this other tale may not have been in mind. According to this second story the man in the moon is one who stole a bundle of thorns and was banished to the moon forever.[1]

Such a legend appears first on English soil, so far as I can learn, in Alexander Neckham's *De Naturis Rerum*, I, XIV ;

Nonne novisti quid vulgus vocet rusticum in luna portantem spinas? Unde quidam vulgariter loquens, ait :

> Rusticus in luna, quem sarcina deprimit una,
> Monstrat per spinas nulli prodesse rapinas.

Quotiens igitur umbram illam dispersam conspicis, revoca ad memoriam transgressionem primorum parentum, et ingemisce.[2]

The earliest allusion in an English work is in a song first printed by Ritson in *Ancient Songs* (1790), and later by Wright in *Specimens of Lyric Poetry* (Percy Society), p. 110. The five stanzas are all interesting and add something to the tale, but the first is all that is necessary for our purpose :

> Mon in þe mone stond ant strit,
> On his[3] bot-forke his[3] burþen he bereþ ;
> Hit is muche wonder þat he na doun slyt,

---

[1] Compare with this the similar legend noted by Grimm in *Deutsche Mythologie*, chap. xxii (Mondsflecken), though there connected with that unfortunate trespasser of *Numbers* 15, 32-36, who was stoned for gathering sticks on the Sabbath. I have found nothing in English which directly connects the moon-man with the trespasser in *Numbers* or with the Sabbath.

[2] Wright's edition in the Rolls Series, 34, p. 54.

[3] MS. is.

> For doute leste he valle he shoddreþ and shereþ.
> When þe forst freseþ muche chele he byd ;
> þe þornes beþ kene, his[1] hattren totereþ.
> Nis no wiht in þe world þat wot wen he syt,
>   Ne, bote hit bue þe hegge, whet wedes he wereþ.[2]

Next in order of time, as bearing upon the legend, is an early seal. This shows the crescent moon surrounding a man bearing, on a stick over his shoulder, a bundle of thorns; he is accompanied by a dog. The inscription about the whole reads, *Te Waltere docebo cur spinas phebo gero.* This seal is upon a deed in the Public Record Office, belonging to the ninth year of Edward III.[3] In the same century is the allusion of Chaucer's *Troilus and Creseide*, I, 1023 :

> Quod Pandarus, 'Thou hast a ful gret care,
> Lest that the cherl may falle out of the mon.'[4]

The fifteenth century furnishes at least two allusions to the moon legend of the stolen thorns. The first is in Pecock's *Repressor*, II, ch. IV. Under "untrewe opinioun of men" he notes,

"As is this opinioun that a man which stale sumtyme a birthan of thornis was sett into the moone, there for to abide forevere."[5]

The second is in Henryson's *Testament of Creseid*, in which the moon is thus described :

---

[1] MS. is.

[2] Böddeker, reprinting this in his *Altenglische Dichtungen*, also refers for the explanation to the German legend given by Grimm, but adds no proof of any sort.

[3] See *Moon Lore*, by Rev. Timothy Hurley (1885), p. 28. For this seal Hurley refers to an article by Hudson Taylor in the *Archæological Journal*, a reference which I have not followed out. Hurley also gives one or two references to this moon legend not found in other places.

[4] Upon this Skeat notes the poem in Ritson above, the passage in Neckham, and those in Shakespeare.

[5] Babington's edition, Rolls Series, p. 155.

Her gyte was gray and full of spottes blake,
And on her brest a chorle paynted full even,
Bearing a busshe of thornes on his bake,
Which for his theft might clyme no ner þe heven.[1]

Upon these various references follow chronologically those from Shakespeare. The two in *Midsummer Night's Dream* supplement each other:

Quince. Ay, or else one must come in with a bush of thorns and a lanthorn, and say he comes to disfigure or to present the person of Moonshine. (III, i, 60.)

Moon. All that I have to say is to tell you that the lanthorn is the moon; I, the man in the moon; this thornbush, my thornbush; and this dog, my dog.

Dem. Why, all these should be in the lanthorn, for all these are in the moon. (v, i, 361.)

To these must be added that in *Tempest*, II, ii, 141:

Ste. . . . I was the man i' the moon when time was.

Cal. I have seen thee in her and I do adore thee; my mistress show'd me thee, and thy dog and thy bush.

There is besides a brief allusion in Dekker's *Landthorne and Candlelight* (ch. viii), which belongs in the same period:

"And as in the moon there is a man that never stirres without a bush of thornes at his backe, so these Moone-men lie under bushes and are indeed no better than hedge creepers." [2]

Ben Jonson agrees with Shakespeare in mentioning both the dog and the thorns. His passage is in *News from the New World discovered in the Moon*. One of the servants of Poetry has just returned from the moon, when the following conversation takes place:

---

[1] Ll. 260–264, as given in the reprint of Thynne's *Chaucer*.

[2] Grosart's *Dekker*, III, 258. Other allusions to the man in the moon are to be found in *Hudibras*, II, iii, 767 f., as noted by Hurley above, and in Wilkins's *Discovery of a New World*, 4th ed., 1684, pp. 77, 94. While Wilkins mentions various suggestions as to the moon's spots they do not bear directly upon our matter.

"*Fact.* Where? Which is he? I must see his dog at his girdle, and the bush of thorns at his back ere I believe it.

1 *Herald.* Do not trouble your faith then; for, if the bush of thorns should prove a goodly grove of oaks, in what case were you and your expectation?

2 *Herald.* These are stale ensigns of the stage's man in the moon, delivered down to you by musty antiquity, and are of as doubtful credit as the makers."

It will be seen that none of these passages makes mention of Cain and, except for two points, may be accounted for by the other legend of the stolen thorns. These two points are first, the dog of the fourteenth century seal and the passages from Shakespeare and Jonson; and second, the shuddering or trembling of the moon-man in Ritson's song and in Chaucer. The dog may easily be connected with the Cain legend for, according to one tradition, a dog was given him to lead him in his wanderings; see foot-note to p. 869 and p. 873. The shuddering or trembling may also be explained as the mark of Cain, according to those who follow a Septuagint reading; see p. 872. These two points, therefore, are strongly in favor of assuming a connection of the moon man with Cain.

There is also one other passage in Shakespeare which, if it could be connected with those above, would show that he had in mind the same legend as that known in Italy. In *Richard II*, v, vi, 43, Bolingbroke banishes from his presence the murderer of the king with these words, among others:

> With Cain go wander thorough shades of night,
> And never show thy head by day nor light.

If now "wander thorough shades of night" be assumed to apply to Cain in the moon, we may reasonably infer that the other references in Shakespeare to the moon and the thorns are also connected with the Cain legend. Such explanation of the passage in *Richard II* is not unlikely, though there is a possibility of another, as we shall show later; see p. 871. Even if this is not connected with the moon story, there still remain the two particulars mentioned above that may be best explained in connection with Cain.

To sum up the evidence, the thorns accompanying the moon figure may be associated with Cain or with a thief of a bundle of thorns, possibly with the Sabbath breaker of *Numbers* 15, 32-36, as that story was told in the middle ages. The dog and the trembling may be best explained in reference to the Cain legend. If we add to these Shakespeare's " With Cain go wander thorough shades of night" as a part of the moon legend, the preponderance of evidence would seem to connect the Elizabethan allusions with the Cain story. Otherwise we must at least assume confusion of the two stories, that of Cain and that of the thief, or possibly the Sabbath breaker.[1]

To return to the Cain legend proper, other allusions to the sacrifice of Cain are connected with the nature of the transgression committed. The Scripture story certainly does not make clear why Cain, "a tiller of the ground," was in error in bringing to sacrifice "of the fruit of the ground."

---

[1] Just as I write this revision there comes to hand the London *Athenæum* of June 23, 1906, with a letter of Paget Toynbee on *Cain as a Synonym of the Moon*. He quotes certain lines from *The Strange Fortune of Alerane*, or *My Ladies Toy* (London, 1605), in which "Cain appears to be used as a synonym of the moon." They read as follows:

> But see how Cupid like a cruel Caine
> Doth change faire daies and makes it frowning weather:
> These Princes joyes, he overcast with paine,
> For 'twas not likely they should match together.

These lines must be regarded, I think, as clinching the argument above in favor of a connection of the moon legend with that of Cain in Elizabethan literature. For completeness of bibliography on this point perhaps I may add reference to my own letter in the *Athenæum* of August 18. This brought no further discussion of the subject.

Various explanations were given as to why the Lord "had not respect" unto Cain's offering. Sometimes the manner of presenting the gift was regarded as the real offence. Thus the *Cursor Mundi* sums it up in the following couplet:

> For Caym gaf him with ivel will;
> Ur Loverd loked noght þartill.[1]

More commonly Cain's offering was connected with the later law of tithing, and Cain was assumed to have been punished for tithing falsely. In the *Life of Adam and Eve* (Trin. MS.) the false tithing is explicitly mentioned:

> Bote such зut was here hap
>
> þat Kaym for his false tidynge,—
> For he typede of þe worste þynge,
> And Abel of his beste.[2]

The last two lines have been already quoted above. Later the same version also adds of Cain,

> And whanne he deyde he зede to helle,
> Evermore þer to dwelle
> For his false typynge.[3]

The prose version is equally explicit:

Abel was tiþer good of alle þinges and þonked God swiþe wel; and Caym tiþed falslich and brak Godes hestes, for he wiþheold alwey þe beste dole and зaf God of þe worste.[4]

In the Towneley play of the *Killing of Abel* this idea of false tithing, together with the evil nature of Cain in other respects, is worked out at length. It may be briefly summarized as follows: A servant of Cain opens the play with a ranting speech in which he tells us that his master would get the better of anyone in a quarrel. Then Cain appears

---

[1] EETS. 57, ll. 1065–6.

[2] Horstmann's *Legenden*, p. 130, ll. 480 f.

[3] *Ibid.*, ll. 487 f.   [4] *Ibid.*, p. 224.

plowing,. complaining of his horse and wrangling with his boy. On coming in Abel is received with no gentle language, but still begs Cain to tithe and make burnt offering. The latter will have none of Abel's sermonizing, and will not leave his plow. He says that God gives him only sorrow and woe, and he complains of his poor crop like a grumbling farmer of to-day. Of tithing he says,

> We, wherof shuld I tend, leif brothere,
> For I am ich yere wars then othere.[1]

Finally Cain gives way to Abel's importunity and begins to tithe, still grumbling and choosing the best for himself:

> Yei, this also shall leif with me,
> For I will chose and best have ;
> This hold I thrift of all this thrafe.
>
> . . . . . .
>
> At yere tyme I saw fayre corn,
> Yit was it sich when it was shorne,
> Thystyls and brerys, yei grete plente,
> And all kyn wedis that myght be.[2]

As he tithes he repeats the count to himself, and Pollard, in his side-notes to the play, conjectures that he doubles the count for his own advantage. When he reaches "ten" he puts aside a sheaf with the remark,

> We, this may we best mys (l. 219),

as if it were the worst of the lot. Abel reproves him and says he is tithing wrongly and of the worst.

In the York play, *Sacrificium Cayme and Abell*, Cain protests against tithing in a similar manner, but the further development of the story has been lost to us. At this point two pages have been cut out of the MS.

The manner in which the sacrifices were received by the

---

[1] *The Killing of Abel*, ll. 108–9. Cf. lines already quoted on p. 839.
[2] *Ibid.*, ll. 195 f.

Lord was also made the subject of legendary extension. A common addition first appears in the prose *Life of Adam and Eve*, where we are told :

> Christ underfong wel fayre þe tiþe of Abel, for þe smoke wente evene upward as hit brende ; and þe smoke of Caym wente dounwart, for he tiþede falsliche.[1]

In the Towneley play the situation is made more dramatic by Cain's sacrifice refusing to burn, and smoking until it almost chokes him.   He exclaims,

> We ! out, haro, help to blaw !
> It will not bren for me, I traw ;
> Puf ! this smoke dos me mych shame—
> Now bren, in the dwilys name.
> A ! what dwill of hell is it ?
> Almost had myne breth beyn dit.
> Had I blawen oone blast more,
> I had beyn choked right thore.[2]

Another turn is given to the scene in the Chester play. There a flame from heaven comes down to the sacrifice of Abel, as in the later story of Elijah.   When Cain sees it he says,

> Out, out, how have I spend my good !
> To se this sight I wax nere wodd ;
> A flame of fire from heaven stode
>   On my brothers offringe.
> His sacrifice, I se, God takes,
> And myne refuseth and forsakes ;
> My semblant for shame shakes,
>   For envie of this thinge.[3]

The story of the flame from heaven was generally adopted by later English commentators, so that it is not strange to find Milton writing of Abel,

> His offering soon propitious fire from heaven
> Consumed with nimble grace and grateful steam.[4]

---

[1] Horstmann, *Legenden*, p. 224.   [2] *The Killing of Abel*, ll. 275 f.
[3] The Chester play of *The Creation*, l. 569.
[4] *Paradise Lost*, XI, 441–2.

The characterization of Cain's offering as merely poorer corn is perhaps based upon Hebrew tradition, perhaps follows naturally from early Christian commentary. Ginzberg shows that Hebrew commentators made Cain offer only that part of his food which was left after eating, rather than newly gathered fruits.[1] On the other hand the early Fathers emphasized that the offering was "of the fruit of the ground," not the "first fruit." Ambrose (*De Cain et Abel*, Lib. II, cap. x) says:

> " *Obtulit*, inquit, *ex fructibus terrae*, non a primis fructibus primitias Deo. Hoc est primitias sibi prius vindicare ; Deo autem sequentia deferre."[2]

The extensions of this idea in later Christian writings may be gathered from the following quotations. Alcuin's *Interrogationes in Genesim* has,

> "Ut quid Abel sacrificium susceptum est et Cain refutatum ? (*Gen.* iv, 4.) Abel Deo optima et naturalia offerebat, Cain vero villora et humana inventione excogitata, ut putatur."[3]

Petrus Comestor explains that Cain's offering was not a proper one, "quia meliora sibi retinuit, spicas vero attritas et corrosas secus viam Domino obtulit."[4] Compare also John a Lapide, *Commentarium in Genesim*, cap. iv :

> " *Ut offeret, etc.* Secundos scilicet et viliores fructus ; hi enim vocantur in Scriptura fructus terrae. Primos ergo et meliores fructus sibi reservabit Cain."

Any more direct statement that Cain offered, thorns in sacrifice I do not find. It is, however, not an unnatural extension of the idea in the passage just quoted. After the curse of the ground in Adam's case, the " fruit of the

---

[1] *Die Haggada*, p. 61 f. [2] Migne, 14, 355.
[3] Migne, 100, 518.
[4] *Hist. Schol.*, *Liber Genesis*, cap. xxvi, Migne, 198, 1077.

ground" might easily be assumed to be the "thorns and thistles" which the Lord had said it should bring forth.

As to Cain's manner of offering his sacrifice the sources are various. The apochryphal *Book of Adam* tells of two sacrifices of the sons of Adam, and of the first says:

"But as to Cain he took no pleasure in offering ; but, after much anger on his father's part, he offered up his gift once, and when he did offer up, his eye was on the offering he made." [1]

The last clause is explained as meaning that Cain offered grudgingly. In the offering preceding the quarrel Cain "behaved haughtily toward his brother and thrust him from the altar." [2] Compare also Augustine (*In Epistolam Joannis ad Parthos*, Tractatus v, cap. iii) in reference to the sacrifices of Cain and Abel :

"Et quem vidit cum charitate offerre, ipsius sacrificium respexit ; quem vidit cum invidia offerre, ab ipsius sacrificio oculos avertit."

The special application to tithing is natural from such interpretation of Cain's offering as that of Ambrose (*De Cain et Abel*) cited above. Otherwise it may depend on a Septuagint reading not found in our modern version. The Latin translation of this (*Septuagint Genesis* 4, 7) is, "Si recte offeras non autem recte dividas, peccasti, quiesce." This was frequently commented upon by various Fathers in such a way as to suggest tithing, though I do not find that specifically mentioned. On the other hand, the explanation of these words as connected with a Hebrew tradition about dividing the world does not seem likely from the use made of them by the Fathers. [3]

Our extracts above give two ways in which the Lord showed his approval and disapproval of the sacrifices. For

---

[1] *Translation* of Malin, Book I, ch. 77.   [2] *Ibid.*, Book I, ch. 78.

[3] This Ginzberg mentions in *Die Haggada*, etc., p. 69, but I think without clear evidence in its favor.

the first, the difference in the way the smoke of the two offerings ascended, I find no source in early Christian writings. The second means of expressing approbation of Abel's offering, the flame from heaven, appears in the *Book of Adam*. In Book I, ch. 78, we read:

"And Abel prayed unto God to accept his offering. Then a divine fire came down and consumed his offering."[1]

This is Hebrew tradition, as shown by Ginzberg, *Die Haggada*, etc., p. 82. It was also commonly adopted by the Church Fathers, appearing first in Theodotion and Cyril of Alexandria, later in many others. Jerome has it in his *Liber Quaestionum in Genesim*, cap. IV, vs. 4:

"Unde scire poterat Cain, quod fratris munera suscipisset Deus et sua repudiasset; nisi illa interpretatio vera est, quam Theodotion posuit: 'Et inflammavit Dominum super Abel, et super sacrificium ejus; super Cain vero, et super sacrificium ejus non inflammavit.'"

So also Alcuin in *Interrogationes in Genesim*:

"Unde noverat Cain Dominum ad munera ejus non respexisse, et ad munera Abel respexisse? Igne misso de coelis, ut creditur, hostiam Abel suscepit, ut saepissimc factum offerentibus viris sanctis legimus; Cain vero ipse sacrificium suum consumere igne debebat."[2]

III. The Murder of Abel.

Several additions to the biblical story of the murder of Abel also occur in various places. In *Genesis* the quarrel arose out of the displeasure of Cain because his offering was not accepted. Hebrew tradition adds jealousy of Abel's handsomer wife as a reason, though to this I find no reference in English. An addition to the story occurs, however, in the *Life of Adam and Eve*, when Eve is made to tell Adam of a dream foreboding evil.

---

[1] See Malin, p. 98.
[2] Migne, 100, 525. Cf. John a Lapide, *Com. in Genesim*, cap. iv.

7

. To Adam þanne þus seyde Eve :
'Sire,' she seyde, 'ȝe mowe me leve,
Slepynge Y say a syȝt.
Me þoȝte Kaym tok Abellis blod,
And sop it op as he were wod.'
þanne seide Adam ful ryȝt :

'I drede me he shel him sle ;
þerfore sondred shel þeȝ be
For drede of afterclap.' [1]

It was then, according to this account, that

þeȝ maden Kaym a tylman,
And Abel a schepherde þan (ll. 478–9),

in order to separate them in occupation and prevent difficulty.   The prose version gives the account in this way :

Eve seide to Adam : 'Ich am sore agast þat Caym wol sle Abel, his
broþer ; þerfore hit bihoveþ, ȝif we wol wel do, to parte hem atwynne.'
þo was Caym maad tilyere, and Abel heerde of scheep and of oþur bestes. [2]

One variation of the biblical narrative, based on the
Septuagint version as we shall see, makes Cain ask Abel to
go into the field with him, the implication being that he
wishes to draw him away to a secret place for the murder.
This appears first in Ælfric's *Translation of the Old Testament :*

þa cwæð Cain to Abel his breðer, ' Uton gan ut.' þa hi ut agane
wæron, etc. [3]

It is also found in the Wyclifite translation of Middle
English :

And Caym seide to Abel his brother, ' Go we out,' etc.

In the *Ormulum* these lines are based upon such a reading :

Annd Caym toc þurrh hete annd niþ Abael hiss aȝhenn broþerr,
Annd ledde himm ut uppo þe feld annd sloh himm outenn gillte. [4]

---

[1] Horstmann, *Legenden*, p. 130, ll. 469 f.   [2] *Ibid.*, p. 224.
[3] *Bibliothek der Angelsächsischen Prosa, Genesis*, 4, 8.
[4] Holt's ed., ll. 14466 f.

In the prose *Life of Adàm and Eve* Cain says,

'Go we now to þe feelde forto witen ur fader bestes.' [1]

This idea explains also a passage in Wiclif's treatise, *The Cler'gy may not hold Property*, chapter iv, in which he says, quoting Bishop Odo.[2]

Syche ben acursid, as Cayme was, þat led owte þe schepe Abel and brynge hym not aȝen, but disseyvyd hym.

In the Towneley play Cain's words are,

> Com furth, Abell, and let us weynd ;
> Me thynk that God is not my freynd,
> On land then will I flyt.[3]

In the Chester play Cain says, after the reproof for his anger,

> Ah well, well, then it is soe,
> Come forth, brother, with me to goe
> Into the feild a lyttle here froe,
> I have an arend to saye.[4]

The instrument which Cain used in murdering his brother is not mentioned in the Bible. To the literal medieval mind this was an unfortunate omission, and it was early supplied by the commentators. In English the earliest reference so far found occurs in the parallels to the *Salomon and Saturn* dialogue cited in the edition of the Ælfric Society. The passage reads,

Saga me forhwam stanas ne sint berende.

Ic ðe secge, forðamðe Abeles blod gefeol ofer stan, ða hine Chain his broðor ofsloh mid anes esoles cinbane.[5]

---

[1] Horstmann, *Legenden*, p. 224.

[2] See Matthew's *Works of Wiclif Hitherto Unprinted*, Early Eng. Text Soc., 74, p. 374.

[3] *The Killing of Abel*, ll. 301 f.   [4] *The Creation*, ll. 593 f.

[5] *Salomon and Saturn*, Ælfric Society, p. 186. This was quoted by Professor Skeat in *Notes and Queries*, 6th ser., II, 143 (1880), later reprinted in *A Student's Pastime*, p. 137, to explain 'Cain's jaw-bone' in *Hamlet*, v, i, 85. He also notes the lines from *Cursor Mundi*, quoted below, but mentions no further allusions in English and does not explain the origin of the tradition.

Tell me why stones do not bear fruit.   I tell you because the blood of Abel, when Cain his brother killed him with an ass's jawbone, fell on a stone.

The next allusion in English seems to be that of the *Cursor Mundi* (ll. 1073–4), where we read of Abel,

> With þe chafte ban of a ded as,[1]
> Men sais þat þarwith slan he was.

The legend is also distinctly stated in the prose *Life of Adam and Eve*:

> And þer Caym slouh Abel ; wiþ þe cheke bon of an asse he smot him on þe hed, and þer he belafte ded in þe feld of Damasse.[2]

Such a legend doubtless explains the allusion to the ' cheke bon ' in the Towneley play.   Cain is speaking :

> We, yei, that shal thou sore abite ;
> With cheke bon, or that I blyn,
> Shal I the and thi life twyn ;
> So lig down ther and take thi rest,
> Thus shall shrewes be chastysed best (ll. 323–27).

The same idea occurs in the Cornish Mystery of *The Creation*.   Cain says to Abel,

> For striving against me
> I will strike thee, rogue, rascal,
> That thou fall on top of thy back.
>
> Take that.
> Thou foul knave,
> On the jowl with bone of the jowl.[3]

The connecting link between the Middle English passages already given and that of Shakespeare is found in the *Master of Oxford's Catechism* of the fifteenth century.   The parallelism to the dialogue illustrating *Salomon and Saturn* will be seen at once.

---

[1] MS. has.   [2] Horstmann, *Legenden*, p. 224.
[3] *Phil. Soc. Trans.*, ll. 1112 f.

Why bereth not stonys froyt as trees?
For Cayme slough his brother Abell with the bone of an asse cheke.[1]

Finally this explains, as Professor Skeat has shown, the allusion in *Hamlet*, v, i, 85 to " Cain's jaw-bone that did the first murder."

It is scarcely to be expected that this story of the jaw-bone should be generally received by serious commentators. They usually follow the Hebrew traditions that the instrument was a stone or a club. Thus Milton says of Cain,

> Whereat he inly raged and, as they talked,
> Smote him into the midriff with a stone
> That beat out life.[2]

Byron, on the other hand, makes Cain strike Abel "with a brand . . . which he snatches from the altar." [3]

The details regarding the exposure of the crime are all additions to the brief Scripture story. According to the *Cursor Mundi* (ll. 1087 f.), when Adam looked upon Cain a sigh escaped the latter, and this made Adam suspicious. He also saw that Cain was angry and questioned him about his brother. It is of him, in this poem, that Cain asks (ll. 1096 f.),

> Quen was I keper of þi child?
> Of him can I sai certain nan
> Bot he to brin his tend bigan.

Then Adam goes to the field and finds the body. Adam and Eve are not inclined to blame Cain, and the dead body would have been hidden, but for the Lord, who calls to Cain as in the Scripture. In the Towneley play Cain is frightened by the deed and would creep into some hole, where he would remain forty days, when he is called by God above.

With additions to the story of the murder must be classed

---

[1] *Salomon and Saturn*, Ælfric Society, p. 219.
[2] *Paradise Lost*, xi, 444–6.
[3] *Cain, A Mystery*, Act III.

one concerning the body of Abel, which when buried refused
to remain hidden. Of it we are told in the *Cursor Mundi*
(ll. 1078 f.) :

> þe bodi moght he nangate hide ;
> For under erth most it nọt rest,
> þe clai ai up þat bodi kest.
> His broþer [1] ded sua wend he dil,
> Bot he moght nouquar [2] it hil.
> Forþi men sais þat to þis tide
> Is na man þat murth mai hide.

This part of the subject may be closed by reference to the
legendary locality of Abel's death in the region of Damascus.
Allusion to it has already been noted in the *Life of Adam
and Eve*, p. 854. It is also found in Trevisa's translation of
Higden's *Polychronicon :*

> Damascus is to menynge schedynge blood, for þere Caym slowh Abel and
> hyd hym in þe sonde. [3]

It is followed in Mandeville's *Travels* (chap. xi), where it
is said,

> And in that place where Damase was founded, Kaym sloughe Abel his
> brother.

Finally we have Shakespeare's allusion in I *Henry VI*, I,
iii, 39. There,

> · This be Damascus, be thou cursed Cain [4]
> To slay thy brother Abel if thou wilt,

---

[1] MS. broiþer.   [2] MS. nourquar.

[3] Higden's *Polychronicon*, I, xv. Rolls Ser. 41, 103.

[4] This legend rests upon that which represented Adam as created outside
of Eden in the region of the later Damascus, and afterward placed in the
garden. Some references are given in Mätzner's *Altenglische Sprachproben*,
(Prosa), 184, as Skeat noted in the article referred to above. That from the
Middle English *Genesis and Exodus* (l. 207) is as explicit as any :

> In feld Damaske Adam was mad,
> And ðeðen fer on londe sad ;

is spoken by the Bishop of Winchester to the Duke of Gloucester.

We may perhaps add Wyntoun's reference to the creation of Adam, in his *Original Chronicle of Scotland*, I, 65 :

> That in þe feild of Damask faire,
> Of nature and of nobill aire,
> Or ellis in þe vale of Ebron,
> As sum men haldis opinioun.

Well known is the allusion in Chaucer's *Monk's Tale* (B. 3197), to which Skeat adds these two lines from Lydgate's *Fall of Princes* :

> Of slyme of the erthe, in Damascene the fielde,
> God made theym above eche creature.

SOURCES.

The first legendary addition under this head, the dream of Eve, is from the *Vita Adae et Evae* :

"Et dixit Eva ad Adam : 'Domine mi, dormiens vidi visum quasi sanguinem filii nostri Abel in manu Cain ore suo deglutientis eum, propterea dolorem habeo.' Et dixit Adam : 'Vae, ne forte, interficiat Cain Abel l Sed separemus eos ab invicem et faciamus eis singulas mansiones.' Et fecerunt Cain agricolam, Abel fecerunt pastorem, ut ita fuissent ab invicem separati." [1]

That variation in the biblical narrative by which Cain invites Abel to go with him to the field is based on the Septuagint version :

> Καὶ εἶπε Κάιν πρὸς ᾿Αβελ τὸν ἀδελφὸν αὐτοῦ,
> Διέλθωμεν εἰς τὸ πεδίον.

This reads in the Latin translation (*Genesis*, 4, 8) "Eamus.

> God bar him into Paradis,
> An erd al ful of swete blis.

[1] Meyer, p. 44. Cf. also the *Revelation of Moses*, Ante-Nicene Fathers, VIII, 565.

in campum," or in the Vulgate, which preserves the Septuagint text in this place, "Dixitque Cain ad Abel fratrem suum : Egrediamur foras."

The idea is much extended in the *Book of Adam.* Thus, after Cain had praised the beauty of the day, he said :

> "To-day, O my brother, I very much wish thou wouldest come with me into the field to enjoy thyself and to bless our fields and our flocks, for thou art righteous and I love thee much, O my brother."[1]

The Septuagint reading is frequently mentioned and commented upon by the Fathers. It is sufficient to note Ambrose (*De Cain et Abel,* Liber II, cap. viii), the heading of which reads :

> "Cain admonitione spreta insolentiam et crimen auget. Ejusdem verbis : *Eamus in campum,* significari ostenditur pravis actionibus deserta loca et sterilia convenire."

Bede, in his *Hexaemeron* (Liber II), has : "Eduxit Cain fratrem suum foras, et occidit, etc."[2]

Legends regarding the instrument used by Cain in the murder are two. That which mentions a stone is Hebrew tradition, as shown by Ginzberg. He translates a Hebrew passage as follows :

> "Die Gelehrten sagen : Er [Cain] hat ihn mit einem Steine getodtet."[3]

Such an explanation of the murder is found in the *Book of Adam.* It should be said that Cain first takes a staff with him, saying to Abel, "Wait for me until I fetch a staff, because of wild beasts." Later Cain "smote him with the staff, blow upon blow, until he was stunned." Abel meanwhile says,

[1] Book I, ch. 78, Malin, p. 99.
[2] Migne, 91, 70.
[3] *Die Haggada,* etc., p. 64.

"If thou wilt kill me, take one of these large stones and kill me outright." Then Cain, the hard-hearted and cruel murderer, took a large stone and smote his brother upon the head until his brains oozed out and he weltered in his blood." [1]

The fathers are for some reason strangely silent as to the instrument of the murder, but later commentators generally made it a stone or a club. I need not quote, but many will be reminded of the pictures in the old family Bible.

For the legend that made the instrument used by Cain the jawbone of an ass, I find nothing beyond the references in English itself.[2] Dr. Ginzberg informs me that it is not Rabbinical in origin. I can suggest only that it may easily have come from some confusion with the story of Samson (*Judges*, 15, 16), but otherwise know of no explanation at present.[3]

Of the extra-biblical incidents connected with the exposure of the crime, I find a source only for that in which the ground refuses to hide Abel's body, as in *Cursor Mundi*. This story appears in the *Book of Adam*, I, ch. 79:

"Then Cain began at once to dig the earth [wherein to lay] his brother. . . . He then cast his brother into the pit and covered him with dust. But the earth would not receive him, but it threw him up at once. Again did Cain dig the earth and hid his brother in it; but again did the earth throw him up on itself, until three times did the earth throw up on itself the body of Abel."

[1] *Book of Adam*, I, 79.

[2] When reading part of this paper before the Philological Club of Western Reserve University, Prof. Borgerhoff informed me that, as a boy, he was taught this legend in a Belgian Sunday School.

[3] This use of one passage of Scripture to explain another, even though not really connected, is characteristic of early commentaries. Thus the "thorns and thistles" of Cain's sacrifice are probably connected with the curse of the ground in the case of Adam; see p. 849. The flame from heaven upon Abel's altar is like that which came upon Elijah's. The ass's jawbone is an interpretation from the story of Samson. Finally the interpretation of the curse of the ground in Cain's case is based on that in the condemnation of Adam; see pp. 864, 871.

The placing of Abel's death near Damascus is Hebrew tradition, early adopted by the Fathers. Ginzberg mentions it in *Die Haggada*, etc., p. 63, and refers to Jerome's use of it in his *Commentarium in Ezechiel*, cap. 27, 18. Jerome's words explain the origin of the tradition as based on etymology :

"Damascus interpretatur sanguinem bibens, et Hebraeorum vera traditio est, campum, in quo interfectus est Abel a parricida Cain, fuisse in Damasco." [1]

Many other passages might be cited to show that this tradition was commonly accepted. For its greater exactness in certain details that from John a Lapide (*Commentarium in Genesim*) may be added:

"*De terra.* Tradunt multi Abel caesum esse in Damasco, et inde dictam Damascum quasi [Hebr.] dam sac, id est sanguinis saccus, qui scilicet bibit et hausit sanguinem Abelis. Intellige Damascum, non Syriae, ut videtur velle S. Hieronymus ; haec enim aliunde suum mortem et originem traxit, ut dicam, cap. xv, vers. 1, sed Damascenum Agrum juxta Hebron, rubra terra confertum (quae hebraice hic vocatur Adama), ubi creatus et vixisse putatur Adam. Ita Burchardius, Adrichomius et alii in Descriptione terrae sanctae, et Abulensis in cap. xiii, Quaes. cxxxviii."

IV. THE CURSE AND THE MARK OF CAIN.

The curse of Cain and the mark set upon him were variously interpreted in medieval times. Especially, the curse was amplified and made more definite by legendary additions. In the Scripture the malediction has three elements. Cain is cursed "from the ground which has opened her mouth to receive thy brother's blood from thy hand." He is told that the ground "shall not henceforth yield unto thee her strength," and he is to be "a fugitive and a wanderer .... in the earth."

---

[1] Migne, 25, 315-16.

The curse of Cain was early represented as being everlasting, and Cain was therefore incapable of regaining God's favor. In the Cædmonian *Genesis* he is "awyrged to widan aldre" 'acursed forever.'[1] In *Cursor Mundi* this part of the curse reads,

> þi derfli dede has liknes nan,
> Of all dedes it es uttan.
> Openlik I tell þe here,
> þou sal it be ful selcuth dere ;
> For þof I wald forgive it þe,
> It is noght worþi forgiven be.[2]

The mystery plays emphasize the same interpretation. *Towneley*, with its usual freedom, does not hesitate to omit much of the curse, and the sign wholly, but introduces Cain and his boy burying the body of Abel. The boy proposes to forsake his master, yet turns the whole scene into comedy by his acts and words. This part is not to our purpose, except at the last. Then Cain bids farewell to the spectators in words which indicate that he understands the severity of his doom :

> Now fayre well, fellows all,
>   For I must nedis weynd,
> And to the dwill be thrall
>   Warld withoutten end ;
> Ordand ther is my stall
>   With Sathanas the feynd.[3]

In the Chester play the curse of the Lord is,

> Cayne cursed on earth thou shalt be aye
> For this dede thou hast done todaye ;
>
> . . . .
>
> And while thou on the earth may goe,
> Of vengeance have thy dole.[4]

Cain himself says of the punishment,

---

[1] L. 1015.
[3] *The Killing of Abel*, l. 462 f.

[2] Ll. 1143 f.
[4] *The Creation*, ll. 625–6, 663–4.

> For my synne so horrible is,
> And I have done so much amisse,
> That unworthy I am, iwis,
> Forgevenes to attayne.[1]

And again,

> Out, out, alas, alas,
> I am damned without grace.
> . . . .
> A lurrell alway I must be,
> For I am escaped thrifte.[2]

In the York play, *Sacrificium Cayme and Abel,* an angel calls Cain to account and says (ll. 86 f.) :

> God hais sent the his curse downe,
> Fro hevyn to hell, maladictio dei ;

and later,

> þou shall be curssed uppon þe grounde,
> God has geffyn þe his malisoune ;
> Yff þou wolde tyll þe erthe so rounde,
> No frute to þe þer shalle be founde.
> Of wikkidnesse sen þou arte sonne,
> þou shalle be waferyng here and þere,
> > þis day.
> In bittir bale nowe art þou boune,
> Outcastyn shall þou be for care,
> No man shal rewe of thy misfare,
> > for þis affraie.

This curse Cain accepts as forever in these words (ll. 117 f.) :

> Allas ! for syte, so may I saye
> My synne it passes al mercie,
> For ask it þe, Lord, I ne maye :
> To have it am I nouȝt worthy.

The interpretation of the curse as everlasting also explains the allusion in the *Parson's Tale* by Chaucer :

" And that a man ne be nat despeired of the mercy of Jesu Crist, as Caym or Judas."[3]

---

[1] *Ibid.*, ll. 641–4.   [2] *Ibid.*, ll. 665–6, 699–700.
[3] *Canterbury Tales,* I, 1013 (Skeat ed.).

Moreover it is highly probable that this character of the curse makes clear certain lines in *Beowulf*, descriptive of Grendel as a descendent of Cain. I refer to lines 168-9 :

> " No he þone gifstol   gretan moste
> maþðum for Metode,   ne his myne wisse."

> Not at all might he approach the throne of grace with gifts for the Creator, nor know his love.

If these lines were written of Cain himself there could be no question that they were a natural expression of the ever-lasting nature of his curse. It is scarcely less probable that they are here extended to one who is regarded in *Beowulf* as a direct descendant of Cain, and fully merits the punishment of the first murderer.

If there were any doubt about the naturalness of the language to express the severity of the curse, it would be set at rest by comparison with the curse of Cain in the fragment of the Old Saxon *Genesis*. The important lines are as follows :

> "Fluhtik scalt thu thoh endi freðig   forwardas nu
> libbean an thesum landa,   so lango so thu thit liaht waros ;
> forhuaton sculon thi hluttra liudi,   thu ni s[c]alt io furthur
>   cuman te thines herron sprako,
> we[h]slean thar mid worðon thinon."

> A fugitive and a wanderer shalt thou now henceforth live in this land, so long as thou shalt endure the light. Good people shall curse thee ; thou shalt not ever again come to the assembly of thy lord, exchange there thy words.[1]

It was probably owing to this interpretation of the curse that Cain came to be called so frequently "cursed Cain," by far the commonest of the general references. It would be almost a waste of time to attempt gathering them all. This interpretation also, gives point to such a jibe as that of Wyclif when he calls a priory "Caymes castle." [2]

---

[1] *Altsächsische Bibeldichtung*, ed. by Zangemeister and Braune, p. 45.
[2] *English Works Hitherto Unprinted*, pp. 129, 211, 420.

The statement in the Bible as to the ground not yielding her strength was also made more specific. In this respect the Cædmonian *Genesis* reads:

> Ne seleð þe wæstmas eorðe
> wlitige to woruldnytte, ac heo wældreore swealh
> halge of handum þinum; forþon heo þe hroðra oftihð
> glæmes grene folde.

Nor shall the earth give goodly fruits for use in this world, but she, holy, swallowed the blood of strife from thy hands; therefore she shall withdraw from thee her comforts, the green earth her beauty.[1]

In the *Cursor Mundi* there is clear influence of the original curse of the ground for Adam's sin. The passage reads:

> þoru þe wark sa ful a plight
> Erth þou sal be maledight,
> þat reseved þi brother blode;
> With pine it sal þe ȝeild þi fode.
> For þe [þi?] mikel felunny
> þi wete sal becom ȝiȝanny;
> Insted o þin oþer sede,
> Ne sal þe growe bot thorne and wede;
> For þi nedeles wickedhede
> þou sal lede ever þi liif in nede.[2]

According to Scripture Cain was to be "a fugitive and a vagabond" on the earth. This idea was emphasised in the Cædmonian *Genesis* as follows:

> þu þæs cwealmes scealt
> wite winnan and on wræc hweorfan
> awyrged to widan aldre.
> . . . .
> þu scealt geomor hweorfan,
> arleas of earde þinum, swa þu Abele wurde
> to feorhbanan; forþon þu flema scealt
> widlast wrecan, winemagum lað.
> . . . .
> Him þa Cain gewat
> gongan geomormod Gode of gesyhðe,
> wineleas wrecca.

<hr>

[1] *Genesis*, ll. 1015 f.   [2] *Cursor Mudin*, ll. 1133 f.

Thou shalt for this murder win punishment, and go into exile acursed forever. . . . Sad thou shalt depart, infamous from thy dwelling place, since thou wast murderer of Abel ; for this reason a fugitive shalt thou tread the track of the wanderer, loathed by thy kinsmen. . . . Then Cain departed, sad in mind, from the sight of God, a friendless exile.[1]

There is another reference, as I believe, to the banishment of Cain and the traditions regarding it in *Beowulf*, 104 f., 1263 f., though one of these depends upon a slightly different interpretation from that ordinarily given. The passages read:

> Fifelcynnes eard
> wonsæli[g] wer   weardode hwile,
> siþðan him Scyppend   forscrifen hæfde ;
> in Caines cynne   þone cwealm gewræc
> ece Drihten,   þæs þe he Abel slog.
> . . . .
> He þa fag gewat,
> morþre gemearcod,   mandream fleon,
> westen warode.

A land of monsters the unhappy man inhabited awhile, after the Creator had condemned him ; on Cain's race the eternal Lord avenged that murder, because he slew Abel. . . . Then he [Cain] guilty departed, marked with murder, fleeing from the joys of men, inhabited a desert place.

The latter passage needs no special explanation. It may be noted, however, that early commentators emphasized the supposed antithesis between Eden, the place of bliss, and the land of Nod, or ' wandering ' to the east of Eden. The land of Nod was naturally the desert, the joyless land.

The former passage seems to have been invariably regarded as referring to Grendel. I suggest that *wonsælig wer* may be easily and naturally explained as anticipating Cain of *Caines cynne*. Cain was the only one directly condemned by the Creator, and the sentence may be connected with the following even better than with the preceding context. In

---

[1] *Genesis*, ll. 1013 f., 1018 f., 1049 f.

other words the beginning of the biblical allusion is with
Fifelcynnes eard, as it certainly should include the whole
reference to the proscription by the Creator. The difficulty
of the present punctuation has often been appreciated. Sievers,
for instance, proposed to better it by including *in Caines
cynne* in the preceding sentence.[1] This, however, requires
reading the next clause as parenthetical, an unfortunate
change at best. These difficulties disappear if we assume
that *wonsælig wer* refers, not to Grendel, but by anticipation
to Cain in line 107. The passage would then read, " A land
of monsters the unhappy man [Cain] inhabited awhile, after
the Creator had condemned him ; on Cain's kin the eternal
Lord avenged that murder, because he slew Abel."

It can not be urged that *wer* is impossible for Grendel,
though it is not elsewhere used for him. He is said to be
on weres wæstum, ' in the form of a man,' in l. 1352, but this
is qualified by *mara þonne ænig man oðer,* ' greater than any
other man.' He is also called *feasceaft guma* in l. 973, but
guma is at least more general than *wer,* the sense of the
expression being nearer ' wretched creature.' The word
which is nearest to *wer* is *rinc* of l. 720 (cf. also 986), but
this poetic term is also applied to the fallen angels in the
Old English *Genesis,* l. 268. Besides, the prevailing terms
applied to Grendel, as we shall show in another place (see
p. 880 f.), emphasize unhuman or superhuman characteristics,
so that *wer* is at least more appropriate for Cain than for his
monster descendant.

Only one expression might seem to be at variance with
this interpretation, the words *fifelcynnes eard* of l. 104. Yet
these words may be regarded as a natural extension of the
idea that Cain was banished to a land full of evil. As there
could be no men in any other part of the world, and animals

---

[1] Paul and Braune's *Beiträge,* IX, 135.

were already created, the place might easily be called 'a land of monsters.' Such an extension of the Scripture story is actually made elsewhere. In the Chester play of *The Creation* Cain emphasizes his banishment by the words,

> For if I out of land[e] flee
> From man[ne]s companye,
> Beastes I wot will werry me.[1]

The Cornish play is even more explicit. As Lamech goes out to hunt he says to his servant,

> And my grandsire Cain yet alive,
> In the desert among beasts
> He is still living.[2]

Later, too, Cain, who was himself taken for a wild beast by Lamech's boy, says,

> I desire not to see a son of man
> With my will at any period,
> But company many times
> With every beast.[3]

Finally, the 'land of monsters' may be inferred from a Hebrew legend. Adam was banished to such a place when he forfeited Eden, and this would be indirectly applicable to Cain. Dr. Ginzberg writes me this is to be found in *Yalkut Reubeni, Bereshit*, I, 88 (ed. Warsaw). Such an interpretation makes clear at once a difficult passage, which is seen to be essentially parallel to that at l. 1263 f. In both, the banishment of Cain is recorded and the place of his exile is described. That the latter is in one place 'a land of monsters,' and in the other 'a desert place' is not contradictory, since each expression supplements the other. It is a place uninhabited by men, Cain's natural companions, but common to wild beasts.

---

[1] *The Creation*, l. 635 f.

[2] *The Creation*, ed. by Whiteley Stokes, l. 1670.   [3] *Ibid.*, l. 1480.

8

Returning to other allusions to Cain as "a fugitive and a vagabond," some emphasize the wandering life of the exile by various additions. In the Chester play (ll. 667–8) Cain says,

> Therefore I will from place to place,
> And loke where is the best;

and in the York play, already quoted (p. 862), the angel condemns Cain with the words:

> Of wikkidnesse sen þou arte sonne,
> Thou shalle be waferyng here and þhere,
>   þis day.

In the *Original Chronicle* of Scotland (I, 173) Wyntoun refers to Cain's punishment in these words:

> Bot will and waverand to be ay
> In dwyle and dred till his end day.

A more significant addition to the legend is made by Shakespeare's allusion in *Richard II*, v, vi, 43. Here Bolingbroke says to Exton, the murderer of Richard,

> With Cain go wander thorough shades of night
> And never show thy head by day nor light.

Attention has already been called to this passage in connection with the moon legend of Cain. We shall show below that the wandering in darkness may possibly be explained without reference to the moon.[1]

It might be expected that the mark set upon Cain would be the subject of much speculation and of various allusions. The Jewish Rabbis, as we shall see, had various interpreta-

---

[1] It is perhaps worth noting that in the Cornish play already referred to Lamech's servant says of Cain,

> It should seem by his favor
> That he is some goblin of night (ll. 1588–9).

tions of this mark.[1] In English, however, allusions are surprisingly few. The *morþre gemearcod* " marked with murder " of *Beowulf* 1265 does not seem to be important. A significant allusion, however, is found in the prose version of *Adam and Eve*, where the sign is mentioned thus :

> And þo sette Crist a mark upon him, þat he waggede alway forþ wiþ his heved.[2]

Further than this the only references I know to the trembling of Cain are the possible ones in Ritson's song and Chaucer ; see pp. 841, 842.

SOURCES.

It is scarcely necessary to suggest any special source for the idea of everlasting punishment for Cain. It follows naturally from the " cursed art thou " of the Lord (*Gen.* 4, 11), and from the heinousness of the crime. Some, it is true, imply that God gave Cain a chance to repent when, instead of smiting him at once, he asked the question "Where is Abel thy brother." But when Cain added falsehood to his other sin there was no hope for him.

That Cain could not appear before the Lord depends not only on the nature of the curse, but upon the guilty one's interpretation of it in *Genesis* 4, 14. " And from thy face shall I be hid." Ambrose, commenting upon the passage in *De Cain et Abel*, II, cap. ix, says,

---

[1] Reference has been made to one Rabbinical tradition, that Cain was given a dog to lead him (see p. 844). According to other Jewish sources the sign was a pair of horns. This does not seem to occur in English, but reference is made to it in the Cornish play of *The Creation*. There Lamech's boy thinks he sees a ' large bullock' (l. 1546), and Cain says,

> God's mark on me is set,
> Thou seest it in (the) horn of my forehead (ll. 1616–17).

[2] Horstmann, *Legenden*, p. 224.

"Qui enim male agit odit lucem, et tenebras et suorum quaerit latibula delictorum."

Bede is even more explicit (*Hexaemeron*, Lib. II) :

"Putet quia ejectus est a facie terrae, id est, a sorte sanctae ecclesiae." [1]

Bruno Astens paraphrases the words of Cain,

" A terra viventium ejiciar, a facie tua abscondar, te ulterius videre non merebor. Insuper et in hac terra peregrinationis vagus ubique et profugus ero, et non solum coelestia, verum etiam nec terrena sine timore et tristitia potero possidere." [2]

With these may be placed some later commentators to show the seriousness with which the view was held. Diodati, *Pious Annotations upon the Holy Bible*, (Ed. 1543) explains " from thy face : "

"That is, from thy church, where thy name is called upon, and where thou dost manifest thyself by spiritual revelations and corporal appari- tions."

Junius, in his *Biblia Sacra* (1603), says of *Genesis* 4, 11 :

"*Maledictus esto*, proinde exclusus a Deo et ecclesia ; quo spectant Kajini verba, a facie tua abscondam me, vs. 14."

Henry, *Exposition of the Books of the Old and New Testament* (third ed., 1725), has this note :

"*Driven out this day from the face of the earth.* As good have no place on earth as not have a settled place. Better rest in the grave than not rest at all. He sees himself excommunicated by it, and cut off from the church and forbidden to attend on public ordinances. His hands being full of blood he must bring no more vain oblations ; Isa., 1, 13, 15. Perhaps this he means when he complains that he was driven out from the face of the earth (for being shut out of the church which none had yet deserted, he was in effect chased out of the world), and that he was *hid* from God's face, being not admitted to come with the sons of God to present himself before the Lord." [3]

---

[1] *Migne*, 91, 71.

[2] *Expositio in Genesim*, Migne, 164, 173.

[3] The special application of these passages to *Beowulf*, 168–9, seems to me to be conclusive. Cf. p. 863.

With regard to Cain's " wandering thorough shades of night" of Shakespeare's *Richard II*, v, vi, 43, the interpretation may possibly be connected with the curse. The words "driven out from the face of the earth" might imply banishment to darkness, though I find no such meaning attributed. Or this may be explained in relation to the moon legend already noted (see p. 844). Still again it might be accounted for indirectly as Hebrew tradition. According to one account Cain's descendants live underground (*Midrash Konen*); according to another, Cain was given a new " mark " after repentance, that is the light of the sun was to shine upon him thereafter (*Genesis Rabbah*, 18).[1] On the whole it seems better to connect the Shakespearean passage above with the moon legend, as already suggested.

The extension of the curse upon the ground to the bearing of thorns occurs in Hebrew tradition and probably comes from that source. The curse as given in the *Talmud* is as follows :

"Cursed be thou from the ground which opened to swallow up thy brother's blood. No longer shall it give thee aught but thorns." [2]

Again the Targums of Onkelos and Ben Uzziel say :

"And it had been, before Cain slew Abel his brother, that the earth multiplied fruits as the garden of Eden, but from the time that he sinned and killed his brother it changed to produce thorns and thistles." [3]

So far I have not found any references to this extension of the curse in medieval Christian writings, but there can be little doubt that some such idea was known in western Christendom.

That Cain was banished to a land of wild beasts or monsters is perhaps nowhere stated explicitly. It is not

---

[1] Dr. Ginzberg has again supplied me with these references, in answer to a question.

[2] *The Talmud: Selections*, trans. by H. Polano, p. 15.

[3] *Targums on the Pentateuch*, ed. by Etheridge, p. 43.

Hebrew tradition, it would seem.[1]   Yet Adam, according to one Hebrew legend, was banished to a land of monsters when he left Eden, and from this Cain's banishment to a similar place might easily be inferred.   The common interpretation of the land of "Nod" was as "a land of wandering," "an unstable place," but it was also a desert, that is uninhabited by men.   The nearest direct reference to wild beasts, and perhaps quite sufficient for our purpose, is in Ambrose, *De Cain et Abel*, Lib. II, cap. x, as follows:

"Repulit enim eum a facie sua, et a parentibus abdicatum separatae habitationis quodam religavit exsilio ; eo quod ab humana mansuetudine transisset ad saevitiam bestiarum."

One might perhaps also note the implications of the following passage from John a Lapide, interpreting the "mark" of Cain :

"Horrorem Cain injiciebant coelestes, pariter et infra coelum positae virtutes : et enim Procopius, praeter fulgura, et corruscationes horrificas, videbat Cain angelos ignis gladiis sibi mortem minantes ; si oculos ad terram dimittebat, serpentes veneno, leones unguibus, caeterasque feras suis armis in se irruentes videbat." [2]

The reference to the mark of Cain, the wagging head of the *Life of Adam and Eve* and probably the trembling of the moon figure, are based on a Septuagint reading of *Genesis* 4, 12.   There, instead of the equivalent of *vagus et profugus*, the reading is $\cdot\sigma\tau\acute{\epsilon}\nu\omega\nu$ $\kappa\alpha\grave{\iota}$ $\tau\rho\acute{\epsilon}\mu\omega\nu$, translated in the Latin version *gemens et tremens*.   This idea is also found in the *Book of Adam* :

"Then Cain trembled and became terrified ; and through this sign did God make an example before all the Creation, as the murderer of his brother." [3]

---

[1] Dr. Ginzberg is again my authority, and he also refers to the following tradition above.

[2] *Commentaria Sacrae Scripturae*, on *Genesis* 4, 15.

[3] Malin's trans., p. 103.

The Septuagint reading is frequently followed by the Fathers. For example Ambrose, in *Epistolae*, Classis I, Epist. ii, 10, says :

"Denique timens et tremens oberrabat Cain parricidalis facinoris luens poenas, ut ei remedio sua mors fuerit, quae vagum exsulem formidato per omnia momente terrore mortis, per mortem exuit." [1]

Alcuin, in *Interrogationes in Genesin*, 89, has,

"Quod est signum Cain, quod posuit [ei] Deus, ut non occideretur? Ipsum videlicet signum, quod tremens et profugus semper viveret; nec audere eum uspiam orbis terrarum sedes habere quietas."

Petrus Comestor, *Historia Scholastica, Liber Genesis*, cap. XXVII, is even more explicit in saying "*Et posuit' Deus signum in Cain, tremorem capitis.*"

The reference to the horn in Cain's forehead in the Cornish play, *The Creation*, is based on Hebrew tradition. Compare Ginzberg, *Die Haggada, etc.*, p. 65. In the same play Cain speaks of himself as covered with hair, a further part of the same Hebrew story. Another Hebrew legend doubtless accounts for the dog which accompanies the man in the moon. Such a dog is the "mark" of Cain in *Genesis Rabbah*, 18.[2] It was given him by God in order to watch over him, and some say it was the dog that watched over Abel's body at his death. The only early Christian reference to this which I now know is in John a Lapide :

"Posuitque Dominum Cain signum. Quaeres quale? Rabbini quidam fabulantur fuisse canem, qui Cainum semper praeibat, et per vias tutas deducebat. Alii fuisse litteram fronte Caini impressam; alii, vultum ferum et truculentum. Verum communior sententia est, signum hoc fuisse tremorem corporis, et mentis ac vultus consternationem, ita ut corpus et vultus peccatum Caini loquerentur." [3]

---

[1] *Migne*, 16, 919.

[2] This reference Dr. Ginzberg furnishes me in a private letter.

[3] *Commentarium in Genesim.* Bayle, *Dict. Histor.*, article Cain, quotes *Saldinum Ot. Theol.*, p. 345, to the effect that "the dog which guarded the flock of Abel was given to Cain for a constant companion in his wandering."

V. The Death of Cain.

The lack of any statement in the Bible regarding the death of Cain was quickly supplied by tradition. In English the influence of such extension of the Scripture story is found as early as the Cædmonian *Genesis*, in which lines 1090-1103 read as follows :

> þa his wifum twæm   wordum sægde
> Lameh seolfa,   leofum gebeddum,
> Adan and Sellan   unarlic spel :
> ' Ic on morðor ofsloh   minra sumne
> hyldemaga ;   honda gewemde
> on Caines   cwealme mine,
> fylde mid folmum   fæder Enoses,
> orbanan Abeles,   eorðan sealde
> wældreor weres.   Wat gearwe
> þæt þam lichryre   on last cymeð
> soðcyninges   seofonfeald wracu,
> micel æfter mane ;   min sceal swiðor
> mid grimme gryre   golden wurðan
> fyll and feorhcwealm,   þonne ic forð scio.'

Then to his two wives Lamech related, to his dear consorts Adah and Zillah, a shameful tale : ' I have struck down in death one of my kinsmen, stained my hands with the murder of Cain, felled with my might the father of Enos, slayer of Abel, given to earth the blood of a man. Truly I know that for that murder shall follow sevenfold vengeance of the King of truth, mighty according to the crime ; more terribly shall it be requited with grim horror, my crime and murder, when I depart hence.'

As we shall see later the poet of *Genesis*, has here incorporated the ordinary medieval interpretation of the song of Lamech, but without adding details of the story. These details occur in the Middle English *Genesis*, as shown by the following passage, lines 471-84 :

> Lamech ledde long lif til ðan
> Ðat he wurð bisne, and haved a man
> Ðat ledde him ofte wudes ner,
> To scheten after ðe wilde der.

Also he mistagte, also he schet,
And Caim in ðe wude is let ;
His knape wende it were a der,
And Lamech droge [h]is arwe ner
An[d] let it flegen of ðe streng ;
Caim unwarde it underfeng,
Grusnede and strekede, and starf wiððan.
Lamech wið wreðe [h]is knape nam,
Unbent [h]is boge, and bet and slog,
Til he fel dun on dedes swog.[1]

There is a bare allusion to the same story in a couplet of the *Cursor Mundi*, (1513-14):

þis Lamech[2] was cald Lamech þe blind :
Caym he slogh wiþ chaunce we find.[3]

The whole story is told in Trevisa's Translation of Higden's *Polychronicon*, Book II, chap. 5, on the basis of the Latin by Petrus Comestor. The passage reads as follows :

(Petrus, 27). Lamech, an archer but somdel blynde, hadde a ȝonglynge þat ladde hym while he honted for pley and likynge, oþer for love of bestes skynnes ; ffor men ete no flesche tófore Noes flood. And hit happe[d] þat he slow Caym þat loted[4] among þe busshes, and wende þat it were a wylde beste ; and for his ledere warned hym noȝt, he slow hym also. And þerfore, siþþe þat Caym his synne was ipunisched sevenfold, þat is in þe sevenþe generacioun,—for Lamech was þe sevenþe from Adam in þat lyne,—Lamech his synne was ipunisched sevene and seventy folde ; ffor seven and seventy children þat come of hym were dede in Noes floode, oþere for so many generacions were bytwene Lamech and Crist þat payed a payne for us alle.[5]

The story is also repeated by Wyntoun, who has this to say of Lamech :

---

[1] *Genesis and Exodus*, EETS., 7, p. 14.

[2] MS. lameth both times.

[3] Version of the Cotton MS. ; *chaunce* of the second line is *chaunge* in the MS.

[4] Another reading is *loyterd*.

[5] Rolls Series, *Higden*, II, 229.

He wes þe first þat schot in bow,
Ouþer with bolt or braid arow.
Sa fell it quhen he falȝeit sycht,
For eild had myrknyt all his mycht.
His [boy] bad him he suld draw neire
Quhare þat he said he saw a deire ;
With þat þe takle up he drew,
And with þat schot he Cayne slew, ⎰
þat lay lurkand þare in a busk.[1]

The story is fully worked out in dramatic form in the
Cornish play of *The Creation*, but does not differ in essential
details from those already quoted. See references on p. 867.

SOURCES.

The story of the death of Cain at the hands of Lamech is
a characteristic Hebrew tradition. The rather unintelligible
song of *Genesis* 4, 23-4, was thus given a meaning, though it
may easily seem at some violence to interpretation. Among
other things it was necessary to assume that Cain had
outlived six generations, but even this did not deter the
imaginative Jewish commentators and the legend became a
highly dramatic narrative. We may quote it as given in
Baring-Gould's *Legends of the Patriarchs and Prophets*, p. 97 :

" Now Lamech became blind in his old age and he was led about by the
boy Tubalcain. Tubalcain saw Cain in the distance and, supposing from
the horn on his forehead that he was a beast, said to his father, 'Span thy
bow and shoot.' Then the old man discharged his arrow and Cain fell
dead. And when he ascertained that he had slain his great ancestor he
smote his hands together, and in so doing by accident struck his son and
killed him." [2]

This legendary account of Cain's death appears in early
Christian literature, though not always accepted by Christian
writers. The *Book of Adam* gives an extended account,

---

[1] *Original Chronicle*, I, 191.
[2] Cf. Ginzberg, *Die Haggada, etc.*, p. 65.

with numerous incidents somewhat different from any other. Yet the facts are essentially the same :

. Then said he [Lamech's boy who guided him], 'O my Lord, is that a wild beast or a robber?' And Lamech said to him, 'Make me to understand which way he looks, when he comes up.' Then Lamech bent his bow, placed an arrow on it, and fitted a stone in a sling, and when Cain came out from the open country, the shepherd said to Lamech : 'Shoot, behold he is coming.' Then Lamech shot at Cain with his arrow and hit him in his side. And Lamech struck him with a stone from his sling, that fell upon his face and knocked out both his eyes ; then Cain fell at once and died. Then Lamech and the young shepherd came up to him and found him lying on the ground. And the young shepherd said to him, 'It is Cain, our grandfather, whom thou hast killed, O Lord.' Then was Lamech sorry for it.[1]

As an example of one who did not accept the story we may cite the *Questiones ex Vetero Testamento* formerly attributed to Augustine. Here the sixth question is, "Si Lamech occidit Cain, sicut putatur?" to which an answer is given against the idea of the legend.[2]

Rabanus Maurus, on the other hand, accepts the story :

"Majorum nostrorum ista est sententia, quod putant in septima generatione a Lamech interfectum Cain. . . . [Lamech] qui septimus ab Adam, non sponte, sicut in quodam Hebraeo volumine scribitur, interfecit Cain. Et ipse postea confitetur : *Quia virum, etc.*" [3]

"Lamech autem percutiens interpretatur. Iste enim percutiens interfecit Cain. Quod etiam ipse postea se perpetrasse uxoribus confitetur." [4]

Other medieval writers might be cited. It will be sufficient to add Petrus Comestor, *Historia Scholastica Liber Genesis*, cap. xxviii :

"Lamech vero vir sagittarius diu vivendo caliginem oculorum incurrit, et habens adolescentem ducem ; dum exerceret venationem, pro delectatione tantum, et usu pellium, quia non erat usus carnium ante diluvium, casu interfecit Cain inter fructeta, aestimans ferum,. quem, quia ad indicium juvenis dirigens sagittam, interfecit."

---

[1] *Malin*, II, ch. xiii.   [2] *Migne*, 35, 2221.
[3] *Commentaria in Genesim*, II, i (Migne, 107, 506).
[4] *De Universo Libri Viginti Duo*, II, 1 (Migne, 111, 33).

VI. Cain's Descendants.

Numerous extra-biblical elements of the Cain story in English are connected with the descendants of the first murderer. We may well begin with what is, in many respects, the most notable of these allusions, that of *Beowulf* 104 f. I quote from what I have already suggested as the beginning of the Christian portion :[1]

> Fifelcynnes eard
> wonsæli[g] wer   weardode hwile,
> siþðan him Scyppend   forscrifen hæfde ;
> in Caines cynne   þone cwealm gewræc
> ece Drihten,   þæs þe he Abel slog.
> Ne gefeah he þære fæhðe,   ac he hine feor forwræc,
> Metod for þy mane,   mancynne fram.

[1] Full credit must here be given to those who have already commented on this *Beowulf* passage. Grimm, in his *Deutsche Mythologie* (1835, third ed. 1854), first called attention to the Hebrew legend of Cain and his posterity, as explaining Grendel's descent from Cain in *Beowulf*. Bouterwek, also, in *Cædmon's des Angelsachsen biblische Dichtungen* (1854) associated the passages connected with the Cain legend and the allusions in *Beowulf*, making some suggestions which will be considered later. Again, in his article *Das Beowulfslied*, Germania, I, 385 f. (1856), he refers to the *Book of Enoch* and rąbbinical lore as explaining Grendel's relationship to Cain. He mentions particularly the tradition that Cain was the son, not of Adam, but of Samael, the chief of the devils, and that after Cain's death two evil spirits were born from his spirit, and from them all evil spirits. Bouterwek also regarded the man-devouring element in the Grendel story as Hebrew folklore, saying "Menschenfressende Riesen kennt das germanische Heidenthum nicht." He emphasized the devil relationship by noting the expressions used for Grendel, but did not do full justice to these, or make any full examination of the origin of the legend. Bugge mentions the Grendel-Cain relationship in *Studien über der Entstehung der nordischen Götter- und Heldensagen*, and in an article in Paul und Braune's *Beiträge*, XII, 81, referring to Bouterwek above. English editors of *Beowulf* have added nothing to the subject. Thorpe barely mentions the Grendel-Cain relationship as "no doubt of Rabbinical origin," a note which may easily have come from Bouterwek. Earle, whose annotations are the most copious that have appeared, passes over it entirely.

Ðanon untydras   ealle onwocon,
eotenas ond ylfe   ond orcneas ;
swylce gigantas,   þa wið Gode wunnon
lange þrage ;   he him ðæs lean forgeald.

A land of monsters the unhappy man inhabited awhile, after the Creator had condemned him ; on Cain's kin the eternal Lord avenged that murder, because he slew Abel. He [Cain] rejoiced not in that feud, but he [the Lord] banished him far from mankind, the Creator, for that crime. Thence arose all monstrous births, etens and elves and spirits of hell ; the giants likewise, that strove against God a long time ; for this he gave them their reward.

There are here noted two classes of beings which sprang from Cain. First are the monsters (*untydras*), further defined as etens,[1] elves, and spirits of hell (*orcneas*). Second are the giants who strove against God. Although the two are closely associated, the division is a convenient one and will be retained in the discussion.

A. *Monsters and Spirits of Evil Descended from Cain.*

It has usually been assumed that the relation of Grendel to Cain is an interpolation and that, by removing a few lines, we can restore the original Teutonic and unchristian character of the Grendel story. But the investigation of the Cain legend throws new light upon this whole idea. Grendel is one of a class of beings well recognized as belonging to the evil progeny of Cain, not only here but elsewhere. As is well known the connection of Grendel with Cain is repeated in what is said of Grendel's mother, *Beowulf*, 1258-66 :

Grendles modor
ides, aglæcwif,   yrmðe gemunde,
se þe wæteregesan   wunian scolde,

---

[1] I can not refrain from retaining this convenient word, which remained in English to modern times, as in Beaumont and Fletcher's *Knight of the Burning Pestle*, I, ii.

cealde streamas,   siþ⸞an Cain wear⸞
to ecgbanan   angan bro⸞or,
fæderenmæge ;   he þa fag gewat,
morþre gemearcod,   mandream fleon,
westen warode.   þanon woc fela
geosceaftgasta ;   wæs þæra Grendel sum.

Grendel's mother remembered her misery, the woman, wife of a
monster, who was compelled to inhabit the terrible sea after Cain
became a murderer of his own brother; he then guilty, marked with
murder, went fleeing from the joys of men, dwelt in the desert.
From him were born many fateful demons; Grendel was one of
them.

Besides, this connection with the evil progeny of Cain
explains effectively many epithets and descriptive phrases
applied to Grendel and his mother.   Grendel, especially, is
called by such names as would be applicable to a monster of
evil birth, or a devil.   He is *feond on helle* 'fiend from hell'
at first (l. 101), and *feond* in twelve other lines (143, 164,
279, 439, 636, 698, 748, 962, 970, 984, 1273, 1276).   In
two of these (164, 1276) he is the more significant *feond
mancynnes*.   Grendel is also *wiht unhælo* (120), *wergan gast*
(133), *ellorgast, ellorgæst* (807, 1349) and possibly in 86
where the MS. has *ellengæst*.   He is also *deorc dea⸞scua*
(160),[1] *helþegn* (142),[2] *helruna* (163), *hellehafta* (788),
hellegast (1274).[3]   He is *Godes ondsaca* twice (786, 1682),
hæ⸞ene sawle (852) and *hæ⸞enes* again (986) ; *mansca⸞a*

[1] For the force of this devil name compare *Crist*, 257, and the note in
Cook's *Christ*.

[2] Ms. *healþegnes*, but I have no hesitation in accepting Ettmüller's conjecture *helþegnes*.

[3] In view of this frequent use of *gast* (*gæst*) for Grendel I question whether
we should not read *gæst* 'spirit, demon' for *gæst* 'guest, enemy' in lines
102, 1331, 1995, 2073.   Possibly also it might be regarded as the correct
reading for *gist* in line 141.   In such case it would be explained as late West
Saxon for Anglian *gest* (i. e. *gēst, gǣst*, WS. *gǣst*), which was misunderstood by the scribe.   The Toller-Bosworth dictionary suggests that *gæst*
means ' spirit ' in *wælgæst* of 1331, and also in 1995.

(712, 737), and he is included among *laðum scuccum* and *scinnum* (938) who had oppressed the land. He is called *eoten* twice (668, 761), a name of one of the other descendants of Cain (112) often associated with the devils elsewhere, and he and his mother are described as *deofla* (1680), *geosceaftgasta* (1266), *dyrna gasta* (1357) *ellorgœstas* (1349). Grendel's mother is also *ellorgast* (*gœst*) in lines 1617, 1621, and *manscaða* in 1339. The close parallelism between these epithets and those used for the devils in such poems as *Genesis*, the *Complaint of the Fallen Angels*, and others is also to be especially regarded. Indeed such comparison shows that many of the terms describing Grendel and his mother are similar to those chosen when devils and demons must be meant. There can be no reasonable doubt, therefore, that the *Beowulf* poet intended them in this sense.

Equally significant are the descriptive phrases used for Grendel and his mother. Grendel is *mane fah* (978), who is to await sentence of God at domesday (*miclan domes*). In addition the following significant expressions are used of him or of his devil mother :

711	Godes yrre bær ;
811	he fag wið God ;
726	him of eagum stod
ligge gelicost	leoht unfæger ;
755	wolde on heolstre fleon,
secan deofla gedræg ;	
801	þone synscaða
ænig ofer eorðan	irenna cyst,
guðbilla nan,	gretan nolde ;
808	ond se ellorgast
on feonda geweald	feor siðian ;
852	þær him hel onfeng ;
2088 glof [of Grendel]	eal gegyrwed
deofles cræftum ;	
2127	hic þæt lic ætbær
feondes fæðmum.	

Grendel is constantly referred to as a monster of darkness.
While this characteristic is not exclusively connected with
Cain and his descendents of course, it was attributed to them
in medieval tradition as we have shown. It may therefore
be noted here as strengthening the argument above. The
passages included are those beginning with lines 87, 115,
134, 161, 166, 193, 275, 410, 646, 683, 702, 707.

Again, the devil relationship of Grendel and his mother
may be emphasized by comparison with the story of the
firedrake. In the latter no single phrase or descriptive
epithet applied to the firedrake can be tortured into any
connection with devils, or creatures of evil in the Christian
sense. The same is in general true of all the episodes in
Beowulf, as of the swimming match, the struggle with the
sea-monsters in the adventure with Grendel's mother, and
the Sigmund story, except that two expressions in the
account of the swimming match, *fah feondscaða* (554) and
manfordœdlan (563), might possibly have such connection
under the influence of the myth concerning Cain's devil
descendants. Besides, the whole story of the adventure
with Grendel's mother, believed by some not to have place
in the original upon which our poem is based, would also
have a new reason for its existence. When the original
story of some monster of the moor was definitely associated
with the devil of Christian writings, it was not unnatural
that the Teutonic conception of the mother of the devil
should be grafted upon the original, in order to emphasize
the completeness of Beowulf's victory. That the latter story
is a late and less artistic imitation of the Grendel-Beowulf
story will perhaps be generally admitted.

Considering all these facts in their relation to the legend
of Cain, with which Grendel is clearly associated at the
beginning, I have no question that the author of the first two
adventures conceived of the monsters as belonging to the
devil descendents of the first murderer. The so-called

interpolation regarding Cain, far from being isolated as often supposed, has an intimate relation to the whole of the first two adventures of the poem. This being true, it confirms the explanation already given of such a passage as that of *Beowulf*, 168–9.[1] If these lines, so long a puzzle to commentators, be assumed as applying to Grendel in his devil relationship to Cain, their natural significance is at once clear and they need no emendation of any kind.[2] They but emphasize the crime of Cain and the punishment to him and his descendants, without hope of pardon, which is quite in accord with medieval tradition and interpretation. Some other passages will also deserve a similar reference, at least by way of conjecture.

Explicit reference to the devil descendants of Cain does not appear in any other Old English poem, or in Old English prose so far as I have been able to discover from general reading. Such a reference is found, however, in a striking passage of the Middle High German poetical *Genesis* which is as old as the first part of the twelfth century. It reads as follows in the text edited by Diemer:[3]

Do ne wolde er in niht vliesen ;   puzze gebot er im chiesen ;
er gap im ein zeichen   daz in er arge nieman dorste anreichen.
Do vloch er als ein wadilære   ze vil manegem iare ;
ubil was sin herzze und sin mut,   diu puzze was im borgut ;
er lerte siniu chint   dei zobir diu hiute sint.
Do wurden die schuzlinge   gelich sinem stamme ;
ubil wuchir si paren,   dem tievil si gehorsam waren.
Adam gebot den chinden bi ir libe   sumeliche wurzzen ze miden ;
dar umbe daz si si niht entarten   an der ir geburte ;
sin gebot si werchurn,   ir geburt si verlurn.
Dei chint dei si gebaren   ungelich si waren ;

---

[1] See p. 863.
[2] Some have even tried to take from the passage any Christian significance whatever. See, for example, Pogatscher's emendation *formetode* instead of *for Metode*, Paul and Braune's *Beiträge*, XIX, 544.
[3] *Genesis und Exodus*, von Joseph Diemer, I, pp. 26–27.

9

sumelich hieten hobet als ein hunt,   sumelich hieten an den brusten munt
an den ahselen ogen,   dei musen sich des hobetes geloben ;
sumelich bedahten sich mit den oren,   wundirlich ist ez ze horen.
Etlicher het einen fuz   der was michel unde groz,
der lief also balde   sam ein tier datzze walde ;
Etlichiu gebar ein chint   daz gie an allen vieren sam ein rint.
Sumelich vluren begarwe   [ir vil] schone varwe,
si werden swarz und eislich,   [dem] do niht was gelich,
dei ogen schinen in alle stunde,   die zene waren lanch in den munde ;
[swenne si] die liezzen plechen   so mahten si den tievil schrechen.
Alsolich leben liezzen die ver[chornen]   al ir aftirchomen
Swie dise [inne] waren [getan]   die geschaft musen dise ozzan han.

> Then he [God] did not wish to destroy him [Cain]; evil punish-
> ment he inflicted upon him. He set a mark upon him that no one
> might touch him with evil intention. Then he fled like a vagabond
> for many years; evil was his heart and his mind, the punishment
> was very good for him. He taught his children the magic that
> exists to-day; then became the offshoots like the parent stem; evil
> fruit they bore, to the devil they became obedient. Adam had com-
> manded his children, upon their lives to avoid certain herbs, that
> they might not thereby degenerate in their nature; his command
> they [these evil descendants of Cain] disregarded, their nature they
> lost. The children which they bore were various (ungelich); some
> had heads like a dog; some had mouths on their breasts, eyes on
> their shoulders, and had to live without heads; some covered them-
> selves with their ears, wonderful it is to hear. Some had one foot
> which was great and large, who straightway ran into the wood like
> a beast; some brought forth children that walked on all fours like
> cattle. Some lost altogether their beautiful complexion; they be-
> came black and terrible, there was nothing like them; their eyes
> were gleaming all the time, the teeth in their mouths were long;
> whenever they showed them they frightened the devil. Such life
> left the abandoned ones to all those who came after them; whatso-
> ever inner nature the former had, such outer nature the latter had
> to have.[1]

The only peculiarity of this passage is the reference to the
magic effect of certain herbs, perhaps an addition from
German folklore. It seems to be introduced to explain the

[1] Cf. p. 895–6. Note also Eschenbach's *Parzival* (ed. of Lachmann), p.
247, a reference given me by Prof. Walz, of Harvard.

transformation which was indirectly, even here, the result of wicked natures.

In Middle English poems[1] there are occasional allusions to the devil kin of Cain, and even to monster descendants similar to Grendel in animal characteristics. The nearest approach to the latter is found in *Ywaine and Gawin*,[2] where a monster of the wood in the form of a man but with some likeness to animals is spoken of as belonging to Cain's race. Thus, in lines 558-561,

> The forest fast than wald he seke,
> And als the karl of Kaymes[3] kyn,
> And the wilde bestes with him.

The description of the monster, in which his likeness to Grendel and the medieval devil in general may be readily seen, is found at line 243 f., as follows;

> Oway I drogh me, and with that
> I saw some whar a man sat
> On a lawnd, the fowlest wight
> That ever yit man saw in syght.
> He was a lathly creatur
> For fowl he was out of mesur;
> A wonder mace in hand he hade,
> And sone my way to him I made.
> His hevyd, methought, was als grete
> Als of a rouncy or a nete;
> Unto his belt hang his hare,
> And efter that byheld I mare;
> To his forhede byheld I than,
> Was bradder than twa large span;
> He had eres als ane olyfant,

---

[1] For some of these references I am indebted to notes by Professor Skeat in his edition of *Piers Plowman*, EETS., 67, 225 (1885), and by Professor Kittredge, PBB., 13, 210 (1887).

[2] Ritson, *Ancient English Metrical Romances*, revised by Goldsmid, I, 133.

[3] This is the ordinary form of the name in Middle English. It is evidently based on Low Latin or Old French Caï(y)m, and has possibly been confused with Cham (Ham).

> And was wele more than geant.
> His face was ful brade and flat,
> His nese was cutted als a cat,
> His browes war like litel buskes,
> And his tethe like bare tuskes ;
> A ful grete bulge opon his bak
> Thar was noght made withowten lac ;
> His chin was fast until his breast ;
> On his mace he gan him rest.

In calling attention to this passage in his note, Professor Kittredge mentions that there is no reference to Cain in the French original. The allusion therefore is not only of English origin but may have some connection with older conceptions of such monsters as Grendel which had been handed down in the lore of the folk. Another passage of similar import to this in *Ywaine and Gawin* occurs in *Kyng Alisaunder*, lines 1932 to 1935 : [1]

> And of Sab, the duk Mauryn
> He was of Kaymes kunrede ;
> His men non kouthe speke no grede,
> Bote al so houndes grenne and berke.

While the legend of monsters as descendants of Cain does not seem to appear in other Middle English works, there is a somewhat natural extension of it in many places. By this, evil men of any description are spoken of as belonging to Cain's kin, though of course without implication of blood relationship. An example is found in *Havelok the Dane*, lines 2044-2046, [2] where those who had persecuted the hero are thus spoken of :

> And yif he livede þo foule theves,
> þat weren of Kaym kin and Eves,
> He scholden hange by þe necke.

The union of Cain and Eve in this place is not strange

---

[1] Weber, *Metrical Romances*, I, 83.   Compare also p. 833.
[2] Edition of Skeat, EETS., 4, p. 57.

considering what an unenviable reputation the poor mother of mankind has borne in all literatures. As already noticed, she was even said to have allowed the devil to usurp the conjugal rights of Father Adam and thus have given birth to the illstarred Cain. It is barely possible that the poet of *Havelok* alluded to this tradition in the line above. Still another allusion to wicked men as Cain's kin occurs in the ballad of *Little John Nobody*, preserved by Percy,[1] one stanza of which contains the line,

> Such caitives count to be come of Cain's kind.

This connection of men of evil with Cain is natural figurative language, but there is also some basis for it in the reference to the descendants of Cain as doing all kinds of wickedness, another extra-biblical idea based on Hebrew and Christian tradition as already noted.[2] It appears especially in those accounts of Cain which mention no devil or monster progeny. Thus, while it is not found in *Beowulf*, it is in *Cædmon*, lines 1255-1257 :

> Ne syndon me on ferhðe   freo from gewitene,
> cneoriss Caines,   ac me·þæt cynn hafað
> sare abolgen.

> They have not departed from me, blameless in life, the children of Cain, but that race hath sorely offended.

The same is true of the Middle English *Genesis*, as in lines 527 to 529,

> Fif hundred ger of ðat ðusent
> Ðat mankin was on werlde sent,
> Caymes sunes wrogten unlage ;

and of *Cursor Mundi*, lines 1223-1232 and 1557-1560. They read,

---

[1] *Reliques of Ancient English Poetry*, Second Series, Book II, iii.
[2] Compare p. 863.

Unseli Caym þat ai was saked,
With God and man þan was he hatted,
He alswa with his oxspring ;
þai luved our Laverd nankin thing,
For þai him warryd with wickud dedis.
He þam forsoke in al þer nedis.
To wrik þare wik[ke] wil þai thoght,
Agh of him na stod þam noght.
þat boght þai siþen wiif and barn,
With water ware þai all forfarn.

.   .   .   .

In Adam time was wrang inogh,
Bot þis tim wex wel mare wogh,
Namlik amang Kaym kin,
þat lited þam noght bot in sin.

Similar passages from *Piers Plowman*, Text A, x, 135 f.; C,
XI, 217 f., need not be quoted here since they will be used,
along with other lines, for another purpose in another part of
this paper. From such as these it would be easy to extend
the use of Cain's name to any evil men, as in the references
already given.

B. *Cain and the Giants.*

The second class of Cain's descendants mentioned in
Beowulf 111 f., are " the giants who strove with God a long
time." The allusion has received slight notice by commentators. Indeed, it has usually been passed over in silence.
Yet it becomes entirely clear in the light of medieval
explanation of certain passages of Scripture. Moreover, it
has intimate connection with the story of Cain. The Cain
story of the fourth chapter of *Genesis* is followed by a chapter
of genealogies. Chapter 6 begins with the apparently disconnected account of the giants who sprang from the union
of the " sons of God " with " the daughters of men." A
modern reader would not closely connect the two, or puzzle
himself to explain this singular progeny of a singular union.

The medieval mind was not so easily satisfied. Here was a tale which excited wonder, and to which some explanation must be made. Both Jewish and Christian commentators, therefore, connected these giants with the preceding historical passages. When this was done it was easy to assume one of the partners in this new union as descended from the wicked Cain.

Besides, the giants of *Genesis* 6 were not only connected with Cain on the one side, but more directly with the flood than is warranted by the Scripture narrative. These giants seduced mankind, opposed God, and by their wickedness brought the flood upon the earth. The full proof of these interpretations will be given hereafter. We may now turn to the embodiment of these legendary additions to Scripture in certain English works.

The legend of the giant descendants of Cain, and their destruction by the flood, may be best considered as it appears in one of its earliest and fullest English forms. This occurs in the Cædmonian *Genesis*, lines 1245–84 :

> Da giet wæs Sethes cynn,
> leofes leodfruman,   on lufan swiðe
> Drihtne dyre   and domeadig,
> oðþæt bearn Godes   bryda ongunnon
> on Caines   cynne secan,
> wergum folce,   and him þær wif curon
> ofer Metodes est   monna eaforan,
> scyldfulra mægð   scyne and fægere.
> þa reordade   rodora Waldend,
> wrað moncynne,   and þa worde cwæð :
> 'Ne syndon me on ferhðe   freo from gewitene,
> cneoriss Caines,   ac me þæt cynn hafað
> sare abolgen.   Nu me Sethes bearn
> torn niwiað,   and him to nimað
> mægeð to gemæccum   minra feonda ;
> þær wifa wlite   onwod grome,
> idesa ansien   and ece feond
> folcdriht wera   þa ær on friðe wæron.'
> Siððan hundtwelftig   geteled rime

wintra on worulde   wræce bisgedon
fæge þeoda,   hwonne Frea wolde
on wærlogan   wite settan,
and on deað slean   dædum scyldige
gigantmæcgas,   Gode unleofe,
micle mansceaðan,   Metode laðe.
þa geseah selfa   sigora Waldend,
hwæt wæs monna   manes on eorðan,
and þæt hie wæron   womma ðriste,
inwitfulle,   he þæt unfægere
wera cneorissum   gewrecan þohte,
forgripan gumcynne   grimme and sare
heardum mihtum.   Hreaw hine swiðe
þæt he folcmægþa   fruman aweahte,
æðelinga ord,   þa he Adam sceop ;
cwæð þæt he wolde   for wera synnum
eall aæðan   þæt on eorðan wæs
forleosan lica gehwilc,   þara þe lifes gast
fæðmum þeahte.   Eall þæt Frea wolde
on þære toweardan   tide acwellan
þe þa nealæhte   niðða bearnum.

Then was the race of Seth, the beloved chieftain, in much esteem, dear to the Lord and blessed with power, until the sons of God began to seek brides from the race of Cain, the cursed folk, and there chose wives for themselves against the wish of the Creator, daughters of men, maids of the guilty race, beauteous and fair.   Then spoke the ruler of the heavens, wroth with mankind, and these words uttered : "They have not departed from me blameless in life, the family of Cain, but me hath that race sorely displeased.   Now the children of Seth are renewing my anger, and are taking for mates daughters of my foes ; there the beauty of women has wickedly influenced the race of men,—beauty of women and the eternal fiend,—which before was at peace."   Afterwards a hundred and twenty winters the fated people were busied in evil, when the Lord wished to inflict punishment on the perfidious and strike down in death the giant race, guilty in deed, hateful to God, mighty evil doers, hostile to the Creator.   When the Lord of victory himself saw what was men's wickedness on earth, and that they were daring in crimes, full of evil, he resolved to avenge that terribly on the race of men, overwhelm mankind grimly and sorely with hard might.   Much it repented him that he had made a beginning of the tribes of men, first of the noble ones when he shaped Adam ; said that he would, for the sins of men, overwhelm all that were on earth, destroy each body that had the spirit of life in its embrace. All that would the Lord overthrow in that toward time which then was drawing near to the children of men.

This account of the giants is immediately followed by the flood in which the giant descendants of Cain are destroyed. In this passage *Sethes cynne* (l. 1249), *Sethes bearn* (l. 1257), and *bearn Godes* (l. 1248) are the same. It is especially important that the "daughters of men" of Scripture are here plainly called *Caines cynne* (l. 1249), and the fruit of the union *gigantmæcgas* (l. 1268), *micle manscea∂an* (l. 1269). The specific period of evil, one hundred and twenty years, comes from *Genesis*, 6, 3: "Yet shall his days be an hundred and twenty years." This was believed by some to refer to the length of life allowed the giants, by others to the period to which man's life had been at this time reduced.

The Cædmonian account of the giant sons of Cain has an interesting parallel in the Old Saxon *Genesis*, with which as we know our Old English *Genesis* has intimate relations in other respects. The passage is in the second of those fragments discovered by Zangemeister in 1894. It breaks off before any account of the flood, but enough is given to show the relation of the giants to Cain.[1]

> Thann quamum eft fan Kaina   kraftaga liudi,
> helidos hardmuoda,   habdun im hugi strangan
> wre∂an willean,   ne weldun waldandas
> lera lestian,   ac habdun im le∂an stri∂;
> wohsun im wrislico;   that was thiu wirsa giburd
> kuman fan Kaina.   Bigunnun im copun thuo
> weros wi∂ undor twisk;   thas war∂ anwer∂it san
> Se∂es gesidi,   war∂ seggio folc
> menu gimengi∂,   endi wur∂un manno barn
> liudi le∂a   them thitt lioht giscuop.

Then descended from Cain a powerful people, hardhearted heroes, who had in them a strong mind, evil purpose; they would

---

[1] *Bruchstücke des altsächsischen Bibeldichtung*, p. 47.

not follow the counsels of the Lord but had in them hostile strife ; grew to giant size ; 'that was the worst offspring that came from Cain. Then began men to marry among them, and by this were Seth's sons at once corrputed, the folk was stained with evil, and the children of men became a hostile people toward him who created light.

There is no allusion to the flood in this fragment as it breaks off, after some lines on Enoch, without returning to the Cain story.

It is now possible to consider what must be regarded as a fairly complete allusion in *Beowulf* to the destruction of the giants by the flood, though one part of it has been differently interpreted. The first part occurs at line 113, where the giants are mentioned as descendants of Cain who strove against God a long time and for that strife received their reward. For the connection the two lines preceding may be quoted :

> Danon untydras   ealle onwocon,
> eotenas ond ylfe   ond orcneas,
> swylce gigantes   þa wið Gode wunnon
> lange þrage ;   he him þæs lean forgeald.

'Thence awoke all monstrous births, etens and elves and spirits of hell, the giants likewise that strove with God a long time; for that he gave them their reward.'

We now know that these giants are none other than those of *Genesis* 6, and that the reward, or retribution given them was the flood. Another passage in the *Beowulf*, lines 1687 to 1693, makes more definite mention of the flood as retribution for this same strife against God and, in the light of the present discussion, must be connected immediately with the legend of Cain. It reads,

> Hroðgar maðelode,   hylt sceawode,
> ealde lafe   on þæm wæs or writen
> fyrngewinnes   syðþan flod ofsloh,
> gifen geotende,   giganta cyn,

frecne geferan ; [1]   þæt wæs fremde þeod
ecean Dryhtne ;   him þæs endelean
þurh wæteres wylm   Waldend sealde.

Hrothgar spoke, looked on the hilt, the old heirloom on which was written the beginning of that old strife when the flood, the overflowing ocean, cut off the race of the giants, the insolent men ; that was a people estranged from the eternal Lord ; for this the Creator, through the fury of waters, gave them their final reward.

It is true that another interpretation has been placed upon this last passage, since it has been regarded as an allusion to the heathen gods of northern mythology, and but slightly changed from an original heathen form. Ettmüller, in his translation of *Beowulf* (1840), has the following note :

"Der alte streit ist wohl die Feindschaft zwischen den Göttern (Ansen, Asen) und den Hrimthursen. Die Völuspa erwähnt gleichfalls diesen ersten Kampf in Strophe 22. Der undichtende Mönch deutete die Sache biblisch auf die vorsintfluchtlichen Menschen, die er gelehrt Giganten nennet, und dadurch auf den griechischen Mythus hinweiset."

Professor Blackburn also, in his article on *The Christian Coloring of Beowulf*,[2] apparently without remembering Ettmuller's note, says :

"A trace of the older heathen version may be seen, I think, in the allusion to the flood, just mentioned. The sinners that lost their lives by the waters are there called giants, and one or two peculiarities of expression lead me to hazard the suggestion that the passage, before it was Christianized, contained an allusion to the Northern tale of the war of the gods with the giants."

But there is nothing in the passage which is not fully explained by the legend of Cain, the giants, and the flood, as already outlined and commonly accepted during the middle ages. The two passages in *Beowulf* simply complete one another, and one is as much Christian as the other. Though

---

[1] Sievers's reading (PBB., 9, 140), for *frecne geferdon* of the MS. Yet it must be said that, except for its abruptness in construction, the textual reading is eminently appropriate to the giants of *Genesis*.

[2] *Publications of Mod. Lang. Association*, 12, 218.

in fragments, they give the whole of the legend as it has already been shown to exist in the Cædmonian and Old Saxon paraphrases of *Genesis*. Of course it need not be urged that this fragmentary allusion, in different places to different parts of the same story . is one of the most characteristic things about the *Beowulf*.[1]

In Middle English poetry the legend of the giants as descendants of Cain appears several times. These are in general derived from later narratives of medieval Latin writers, rather than from Old English literature. Probably the first appearance of the story in this period occurs in the Middle English *Genesis*, ll. 527 to 556, as follows:

> Fif hundred ger of ðat ðusent
> Ðat mankin was on werlde sent,
> Caymes sunes wrogten unlage,
> Wið breðere wifes horeplage ;
> And on ðe sexte hundred ger
> Wimmen welten weres mester,
> And swilc woded wenten on
> Golhed unkinde[2] he gunnen don ;
> And ðe fifte hundred ger
> Wapmen bigunnen quad mester,
> Bitwen hemselven unwreste[3] plage,
> A ðefis kinde, agenes lage.
> Two hundred ger after ðo wunes,
> Miswiven hem gunnen Seðes sunes,
> Agenes ðat Adam forbead,
> And leten Godes frigtihed ;
> He chosen hem wives of Caym,
> And mengten wið waried kin ;

---

[1] I have left this passage as it was in the paper read before the Modern Language Association in 1900. My paper was sent to Professor Bright in 1904 for the use of one of his students, and Dr. James E. Routh, in his dissertation, *Two Studies on the Ballad Theory of the Beowulf*, accepts the above interpretation, as well as some other of my conclusions. See especially p. 28 f. More recently Professor Klaeber has suggested the same interpretation in *Textual Interpretation of Beowulf* (*Mod. Phil.*, III, p. 459).

[2] MS. hunkinde.   [3] hunwreste.

Of hem woren ðe getenes boren,
Migti men, and figti [and] forloren ;
He wrogten manige [sinne] and bale,
Of ðat migt is litel tale ;
For ðat he God ne luveden nogt,
Ðat migt is al to sorge brogt.
For swilc sinful dedes sake,
So cam on werlde wreche and wrake
For to blissen swilc sinnes same,
Ðat it ne wexe at more unframe ;[1]
Ðo wex a flod ðis werlde within,[2]
And overflowged men and deres kin.

The immediate source of this passage, as of so much of the poem, is the *Historia Scholastica* of Petrus Comestor who is closely followed in the details of the narrative, as may be seen by comparing this with the selection on page 926. Special attention need be called only to the direct connection of the giants, ME. *getenes* from OE. *eotenas*, with the flood, which is sent because of their evil lives.

Here may be mentioned also a passage in the Middle High German *Genesis*, which uses this part of Cain legend, as of the demon descendants already noticed. The extract reads as follows, in Diemer's text (I, p. 26):

Den dritten sun gewan Adam,   Set was des chindes nam ;
der ward ein vil gut chnecht,   er minnot niht daz unreht.
Der selbe gewan chint   dei Got hiute liep sint ;
daz Goteswerch si lerten,   ir mut si dar an cherten ;
So liebe dienten si dir trohtin   daz si hiezzen dei chint din ;
mit den werchen und mit dem namen   waren si gecheiden
uon Kain chinden.   Geschriben wir vinden :
der vater hiez Beliali,   daz ist der ubil tievil
der Adam schunte   an die ersten sunte ;
der im des paradises erbunne   und allem manchunne,
den sin selbes ubile   vertreip uon himele ;
der engund uns des niht   daz wir habeten daz ewige lieht
daz er vlos durch ubirmut,   do er sich gelichen wolde Got ;
der geriet och Kain   daz er sluch den brudir sin.
Schoniu wip wurten   von Kain geburte ;

---

[1] hunframe.   [2] widhin.

an grozze ubil wanden si sich,   idoch was in Got genædich ;
er machit si schone und lussam,   Got waren si niht gehorsam.
Do dei Gotes chint   gesahen des tieuels chint
also rehte wolgetan,   ir minne buten si ein andir an.
Von ir beidir minne   michiliu chint si gewunnen,
gigant daz waren,   allez ubil begunde sich meren.
Got gero sere   daz er den mennisc het geschephet.
Do begunde unsir Trohtin   darumbe harte riuich sin
daz er ie geschuf den man   nach sinem bilde getan ;
ez gero in von herzzen,   sere begund ez in smerzzen,
die er geschuf ze den eren   daz die dem tievil solden werden
do wart im ze mute   daz er mit der sinvlute
die werlde wolde vliesen   unde sinen zorn also verchiesen.

Then Adam begot a third son, Seth was the child's name ; he became a very good man, he loved not wrong. He also begot children who are dear to God to-day ; God's work they learned, they turned their minds to it. So lovingly served they thee, Lord, that they were called thy children ; in works and in name were they separated from Cain's children. Of them [the latter] we find written, their father was called Belial, that is the wicked devil, who incited Adam to the first sin ; who begrudged paradise to him and all mankind ; whose own wickedness had driven him from heaven ; who envied us that we should have eternal light which he had lost through his arrogance when he would liken himself to God ; who also advised Cain to kill his brother. Beautiful women were born of Cain's race ; to great wickedness they turned themselves, yet was God merciful to them ; he made them lovely and beautiful, yet to God were they not obedient. When the children of God [that is Seth's children, as in the former selection] saw that the children of the devil [that is of Cain] were so well formed, they offered them their love. From their love they begot children of might, giants they were ; all evil began to increase. Then began our Lord to repent very much that he had ever formed man after his own image ; he repented with all his heart, it pained him greatly that those whom he had created for honor should become the possession of the devil. Then came to him the purpose that he should, with a mighty flood, destroy the world and in this way appease his anger.

The Middle English *Genesis* was written about the middle of the thirteenth century. In the literature of the fourteenth century the legend of Cain's descendants who were destroyed by the flood occurs several times. It is twice mentioned in the *Cursor Mundi*, though in neither case are Cain's sons called giants. They are, however, called foes of God (l. 1593), and they made war upon him (1227). The first passage is a brief one beginning at line 1223 :

Unseli Caym þat ai was saked,
With God and man þan was he hatted,
He als swa with his oxspring ;
þai luved our Lauerd nankin thing,
For þai him warryd with wickud dedis ;
He þam forsoke in al þer nedis.
To wrik þare wikke wil þai thoght,
Agh of him na stod þam noght.
þat boght siþen wiif and barn,
With water ware þai all forfarn,
Als ȝee sal here how hit bifell
Quen I of Noe flod sal tell ;
For all war ille and nan war gode,
þei drunkend all[e] in þe flode.

The second and fuller account is found at line 1557, as follows ;

In Adam time was wrang inogh,
Bot þis tim wex wel mare wogh,
Namlik amang Kaym kyn
þat lited þam noght bot in sin,
Al thoght þam wel þat was þair wil,
And þat was heldand al til il ;
On all thinges was mare þair thoght
þan was on Drightin þat al wroght,
Swa blind þai war in þair insight
þat reckining cuth þai nan o right.
Al þair luf þai gave to lust,
þai did þair saul[i]s all to rust ;
O sothfastnes, als sais te sau,
þai left þe lede of þar lau,
þat es o settnes and o kind,
Withutun mensk þai ar unmind.
Al wex wik, bath an and oþer,
þe toþers wiif lai be þe broþer ;
þair cursnes was noght unkid,
þe lau o kind þai swa fordid.
Wimmen þai forced amang þaim,

Was nan þam moght bring to reclaim.
þe scham, þe sin þat þan was ute
At tel war lang to sett aboute ;
þe find wend witerli with þis
þat al mankind quitli war his ;
Of al and al forsoth he wend
Mankind war til his wil be kend,
Swa forþerli þat God ne might
Bring man into state o right,
Into þe stat þat he had tint ;
Bot God had oþirgates mint.
Of his handwark al for to don,
Wald he noght it war swa fordon,
Forþi in forme of jugement
He thoght a new vengaunce to sent,
Hiis faas to bring al o liif
And waass þat wrang þat was sa riif ;
With his grace to give ham grith
þat he suld restore mankind with.
Qhen he beheld þat foly strang
Drightun þat biden had sa lang,
þof he was wrath it was na wrang ;
þis word out of his hert[e] sprang
And was þe word þat he saiḍ þan :
'Me reus þat ever made I man.'
Bot ilk man þat þis word heris,
Wat noght al þat þar to feris ;
þis word was als a propheci,
þat forsaid was bi his merci,
Of þe reut he siþen kydd,
Quen he to pin himselfen did
For his choslinges on rod[e]tre.
Quat was his reut þan all mai see
Bi þis word þat þan was said ;
His merci had he ferr purveid
To þaim þat wat on his parti,
For to bring þam mightili
Als his auen kyngrik til,
His wiþerwins al for to spil,
Ogains wam he was sa wrath ;
And be his right hand he swar ath
þat þai suld all thole schammes deid,
At sawe þe gode, to give his red
þat all þe feluns war forlorn ;

þe gode allan suld be forborn,
Als it in Noe flod befell,
Quareof I sal yow siþen tell.

It is evident that this account is largely extra-biblical,
and refers to those who in other places are called giants.
Either they are not so called inadvertently, or the author of
Cursor Mundi connected the wicked destroyed by the flood
with the natural descendants of Cain, also wicked according
to tradition. Again the two legends may possibly have
been united, as perhaps in other places to be noted.

There is a brief allusion to the story of Cain's descendants
and the flood in Robert Manning's *Chronicle*, lines 200-5 :

Now of þe story wyl we gynne
When God took wreche of Kaymes synne.
þe erthe was waryed in his werk,
Als yn þe Bible seys þe clerk ;
And þerfore God sente a flood
And fordide al flesche and blood.[1]

A more extended account occurs in *Piers Plowman*, in
which as in the last two passages those destroyed by the flood
are not actually called giants. In other respects, however,
the story by Langland is like that which has gone before.
Allusions occur in both A and C texts,[2] as follows :

Fals folk and feiþles, þeoves and lyȝers,
Ben conseyvet in curset tyme, as Caym was on Eve,
After þat Adam and Eve hedden eten of þe appel
Aȝeyn þe heste of him þat hem of nouȝt made
An angel in haste þennes hem tornde
Into þis wrecchede world to wonen and to libben
In tene and in travaile to here lyves ende ;
In þat corsede constellacion ' þei knewen togedere, '
And brouȝten forþ a barn þat muche bale wrouȝte.
Caym men cleped him, in cursed tyme engendret,
And so seiþ þe sauter, seo hit whon þe likeþ,

---

[1] Ed. of Furnivall, Rolls Series, ll. 201–206.
[2] Text A, x, 135 f.; EETS., 28, 117. Text C, xi, 212 f. ; EETS., 54, 190.

10

concepit in dolore, et peperit iniquitatem, etc.
And alle þat come of þat Caym   Crist hem hatede aftur,
And mony milions mo   of men and of wymmen
þat of Seth and his suster   seþþen forþ coome ;
For þei marieden to corsed men   þat comen of Caymes kuynde.
For alle þat comen of þat Caym   acursed þei weren,
And alle þat couplede hem to þat kun   Crist hem hatede dedliche ;
Forþi he sende to Seth   and seide him bi an angel,
To kepe his cun from Caymes,   þat þei coupled not togedere.
And seþþen Seth and his suster sed   weren spoused to Caymes,
Aȝeyn Godes heste,   gurles þei geeten,
þat God was wroþ with heor werk   and suche wordes seide,
   penitet me fecisse hominem ;
And is þus muche to mene   amonges ȝou alle,
þat I makede man   nou hit me forþinkeþ ;
And com to Noe anon,   and bad him not lette
Swiþe to schapen a schup   of schides and bordes ;
Himself and his sones þre,   and seþþen heore wyves,
Bringen hem to þe bot   and byden þerinne
Til fourti dawes ben folfuld,   þat þe flod have iwassche
Clene awey þe cursede blod   þat Caym haþ imaket.
Beestes þat now ben   mouwen banne þe tyme
þat evere þat cursede Caym com uppon eorþe.

.   .   .   .

þus þorw cursede Caym   com care uppon alle ;
For Seth and his suster children   spouseden eiþer oþer,
Aȝeyn þe lawe of ur Lord   lyȝen togedere,
And weoren maried at mischef,   as men doþ now heore children.

Text C reads,

Caym þe cursed creature   conceyved was in synne,
After þat Adam and Eve   hadden ysynyed ;
Withoute repentaunce   of here rechelesnesse,
A rybaud þei engendrede,   and a gome unryghtful.
As an hewe þat ereþ nat   auntreþ hym to sowe
On a leyelond,   aȝens hus lordes wille,
So was Caym conceyved,   and so been cursed wrecches,
That lichame han aȝen þe lawe   þat oure Lord ordeynede.
Alle þat come of Caym   caytyves were evere,
And for þe synne of Caymes sed   seyde God to Noe,
   penitet me fecisse hominem ;
And bad schape hym a schip   of shides and bordes.
'Thyselve and þy sones þree,   and sitthen ȝoure wyves,
Buske ȝow to þat bot,   and abydeþ þerynne

Tyl fourty dayes be fulfilled   and þe flod have wasshe
Clene away þe cursede blod   þat of Caym ys spronge.
Bestes þat now beeþ   banne shulleþ þe tyme
That evere þat cursed Cayme   cam on this erthe.'

.   .   .   .

Ac whi þe worlde was adrent,   holy writ telleþ,
Was for mariages of mankynde   þat men maden þat tyme.
After þat Caym þe cursede   hadde culled Abel,
Seth, Adames sone,   sitthen was engendred.
And God sente to Seth,   so sone he was of age,
That for no kyne catel,   ne no kyne byheste
Suffren his seed seeden   with Caymes seed hus broþer ;
And for þat Seth suffrede hit   God seide, ' Me forþynkeþ
That I man made,   oþere matrimonye suffrede.'

The special peculiarity of this account in *Piers Plowman* is in making the evil ones who were destroyed by the flood the descendants of wicked sons of Cain and daughters of Seth, another form of the legend.

Another allusion to the giants and the flood occurs in the poem called *Cleanness* by the author of *The Pearl*. In this place, too, just that element of the story omitted in *Cursor Mundi* and *Piers Plowman*, the use of the name giants for the wicked descendants of Cain who were destroyed by the flood, is clearly given. The writer of *Cleanness* is emphasizing for a special purpose the unchastity among men which brought the flood, and the giants are spoken of as the fruit of evil intercourse. The peculiarity of this allusion is that there is no direct reference to Cain, by name at least, but there can be no doubt, in the light of medieval interpretation, that the poet understood his *deȝter of þe douþe* as the daughters of Seth, and the *fende* as the evil descendants of the first murderer. The pertinent part.of the passage, lines 269 to 292, reads as follows :

So ferly fowled her flesch   þat þe fende loked
How þe deȝter of þe douþe   wern derelych fayre,
And fallen in felȝschyp with hem   on folken wyse
And engendered on hem jeauntes   with her japes ille.

þose wern men meþeles   and maȝty on urþe,
þat for her lodlych laykes   alosed þay were.
He was famed for fre   þat feȝt loved best,
And ay þe bigest in bale   þe best was halden ;
And þenne eveles on erþe   ernestly grewen,
And multyplyed monyfolde   inmonges mankynde ;
For þat þe maȝty on molde   so marre þise oþer,
þat þe wyȝe þat al wroȝt   ful wroþly bygynnes.
When he knew uche contre   corupte in hit selven,
And uch freke forloyned   fro þe ryȝt wayes,
Felle temptande tene   towched his hert ;
As wyȝe, wo hym withinne   werp to hym selven :
'Me forþynkes ful much   þat ever I mon made,
Bot I schal delyver and do away   þat doten on þis molde,
And fleme out of þe folde   al þat flesch weres,
Fro þe burne to þe best,   fro bryddes to fysches ;
Al schal doun and be ded   and dryven out of erþe
þat ever I sette saule inne ;   and sore hit me rues
þat ever I made hem myself ;   bot if I may herafter,
I schal wayte to be war   her wrenches to kepe.'

Then follows an extended account of the flood, without
further allusion to the Cain story. A very clear reference
to the giant descendants of Cain is found in Wyntoun's
Original Chronicle of Scotland. It reads,

Intill þis tyme þat I of tell
Wer gyandis wakkand ferss and fell,
That like till men war in figure,
Bot þai were fere maire of stature.
One quhat wiss or quhat manere
This ilk[e] gyantis gotten were,
Sindry haldis opinioune ,
I will mak na conclusioun,
Bot Sethis sonis, as þai say,
Luffit Canys douchteris stout and gay,
And gat upon þaim bodely
Thir gyantis þat were sa forsy.
Or[1] sindry spretis on þare wiss
Slepand women wald suppriss
With maistry, quayntiss or with slicht,
That gat þire gyantis of gret mycht.[2]

---

[1] MS. one.   [2] Scottish Text Society's ed., Book 1, l. 297f .

It will be noticed that Wyntoun gives two possible explanations of the giant births, the second referring them to the medieval *incubi*, rather than to Cain. We are interested only in the first, but the second explanation was often used.

Still one other very clear statement of the medieval tradition is found in the Vernon MS. of the *Life of Adam and Eve*. This MS. dates from the last quarter of the fourteenth century, but the earliest versions of the Adam and Eve story are nearly a century earlier.

And Adam comaunded to Seth þat non of his kuynde schulde felauschupe wiþ Caymes kuynde, ne wedde non wyves in Caymes kuynde; for þo þat coomen of Sethes kuynde ben cleped Godes sones, and Caymes kuynde to men sones. And þenne, at þe fiftene hundred winteres ende, heo bigunnen to don heore lecherie priveliche, and afturward openliche; and þo afturward heo weddeden þet o kuynde into þat oþur and geeten geauns. And þenne God tok wreche, and adreynte al þe world but eihte soules at Noe flood; God was agrevet þereof, and seide þat him forþhouȝte þat he hedde imaad mon, so he nom venjaunce of hem for heore foule synne.[1]

To this may be added a brief yet significant quotation from Trevisa's translation of Higden's *Polychronicon* : [2]

Petrus. Seth his children were good men anon to þe sevenþe generacioun ; bot afterward men mysusede men, and women [mysusede women]. *Genesis.* Godes sones took men douȝteres, þat is to meñynge, Seth his sones took Caym his douȝteres and gete geantis.

Then follows an account of the *incubi*, based on Petrus Comestor. The passage is explicit both as to the connection of "sons of God" with Seth's descendants, and the daughters of men (*men douȝteres*) with Cain.

To show how fully the interpretation we have noted was retained to modern times we may cite Milton's *Paradise Lost*, XI, 573 f. The passage is too long to quote, but every detail of the earlier Christian interpretation is found. "Just men" descended "from the high neighboring hills,"

---

[1] Horstmann, *Sammlung altenglischer Legenden* (1878), p. 225.
[2] Rolls Series, Book II, ch. v.

> When from their tents behold
> A bevy of fair women, richly gay
> In gems and wanton dress ; to harp they sung
> Soft amorous ditties, and in dance came on.

The account then tells how the just men were seduced and
the offspring of their intercourse were

> Giants of mighty bone and bold emprise (1. 642).

The result of their wickedness is the flood, as in the older
writers ; see lines 664 f.

In explaining the vision to Adam, Michael says of the
tents from which the women came,

> Those tents thou saw'st so pleasant were the tents
> Of wickedness, wherein shall dwell his race
> Who slew his brother ;

and he calls the "just men,"

> That sober race of men, whose lives
> Religious titled them the sons of God.

The first are thus the " daughters of Cain " and the second
sons of Seth, called "sons of God" for their righteousness.
Even in minute detail there is here the same conception and
series of conceptions which we have found in the medieval
English writers.[1]

Whether all the references in English have been gathered
or not, enough have been quoted to show that the connection
of the giants with Cain was common medieval tradition.
The light, too, which they throw on the *Beowulf* passages
111 f. and 1687 f. seems to me unmistakable. Whether there
be in the latter especially any influence of Teutonic tradition, as of the runic inscription on the sword, one conclusion

---

[1] There are two other passages in which Milton refers to the giants of
Genesis 6. In the first (*P. L.* III, 463 f.) he places them in Limbo. In
the second (*P. L.* IV, 1. 447 f.) he seems to have in mind the other interpretation, by which the "sons of God," were angels.

seems certain. A Christian writer, or redactor of the Beowulf story, such as could make allusion to Grendel's relation to Cain, would surely understand the passages relating to the giants and the flood as merely a part of Christian tradition. If he added them to an original heathen story, as is usually believed at least, he did so wholly from such Christian sources as were used by the poet of the Cædmonian *Genesis* and other English writers so far mentioned. For my part I have no hesitancy in believing that these two passages supplement each other, and are wholly Christian in origin. This will be even clearer when we consider the numerous Christian writers who used the legend.

C. *The Giants and the Gods of the Heathen*

It remains to mention one of the most significant connections of the legend or group of legends concerning Cain. Even Hebrew commentators who knew Greek literature suggested that the giants who warred against Jove in Greek mythology were the very giants of *Genesis* 6. A hint of this belief among the Jews occurs in a passage from Josephus to be used later; see p. 922. Referring to the giants of Scripture he says, "they did what resembled the acts of those whom the Greeks call giants." Christian writers carried this idea much further. They pointed to the Greek myth as not only confirming Scripture, but explaining in a simple manner the whole basis of the heathen mythologies. The giants who warred against Jove were the giants of Scripture, who opposed God and wrought wickedness. They and their descendants became heathen gods, who were thus not gods at all, but wicked men or devils. The early Fathers connected these heathen gods with the giants of *Genesis* 6, so that they were thus descendants of Cain. This was especially true of those who accepted the Septuagint reading "angels of God," as explained on p. 920. Even though the flood had destroyed their bodies, their spirits were still thought of as existing.

On the other hand, when the reading "angels of God" was given up, and the reading "sons of God" was explained as referring to the sons of Seth, the giants of *Genesis* 6 could no longer be assumed to account for the heathen gods. They, as wholly human, had been entirely destroyed by the deluge. The gods of the heathen were then connected with the descendants of Ham (Cham), the post-diluvian representative of the wicked Cain. When this was done, certain giants of times after the flood were associated especially with Nimrod, who was made a giant by natural interpretation of *Genesis* 10, 8. The war against God, too, was easily associated with the building of the tower of Babel, by an equally natural connection of Babel in *Genesis* 10, 10 and *Genesis* 11, 1-9. This was not strange since Hebrew tradition made Nimrod the builder of the tower of Babel, in order to reach heaven and destroy God himself. Moreover, one third of those who took part with him became devils and evil spirits.

Still a third view of the gods of the heathen connected them with the angels who fell with Lucifer, an explanation familiar from Milton's *Paradise Lost*, Book I, 364 f. This last interpretation, however, we need not now consider, since the others prevailed in the middle ages.

There are frequent allusions in Old and Middle English to the gods of the heathen as giants. Most of these refer to Nimrod and the tower of Babel, as told by Hebrew and Christian commentators. In one sense, therefore, they do not belong here. Yet their close connection with the Cain story makes it best to consider them with the Cain legends.

One of the oldest of these is an interpolation in the Alfredian *Boethius*, Book III, Prose 12. In extension of the reference to the giants of classical mythology by the author, the English translator tells the story of their war against Jove at some length, and then adds :[1]

Dyllica leasunga hi worhton and meahton eaðe seggan soðspell, gif him þa leasungen næren swetran, and þeah swiðe gelic ðisum. Hi meahton seggan hwylc dysig Nefrod se gigant worhte ; se Nefrod wæs Chuses suna ; Chus wæs Chames sunu, Cham Noes. Se Nefrod het wyrcan ænne tor on ðæm felda ðe Nensar hatte, and on ðære ðiode ðe Deira hatte, swiðe neah þære byrig þe mon nu hæt Babilonia. þæt hi dydon for þa ðingum, þe hi woldon witan hu heah hit wære to ðæm heofone, and hu ðicce se hefon wære and hu fæst, oððe hwæt þær ofer wære. Ac hit gebyrede, swa hit cyn was, þæt se godcunda Wald hi to stencte ær hi hit fullwyrcan moston, and towearp ðone tor, and hiora monigne ofslog, and hiora spræce todælde on tu and hund seofontig geþioda.

Such were the false stories they made up ; and they might easily have told true stories, and yet very like to the others, if lies had not been more pleasing to them. They might have told what foolish Nimrod the giant wrought ; this Nimrod was son of Chus, Chus was Cham's son, Cham Noah's. Nimrod ordered built a tower in the plain called Sennar, and among the folk called Deira, very near to the town which men now call Babylon. This they did for the reason that they wished to know how far it was to heaven, and how thick heaven was and how fast, and what was beyond it. But it fell out, as was natural, that the divine power scattered them before they might complete it, and struck down the tower, and slew many of them, and separated their language into two and seventy tongues.

Another passage in the *Boethius* is of like nature. In the elaboration of the allusion to Ulysses and Circe, the English translator says :[2]

þa wæs þær Apollines dohtor, Iobes suna ; se Iob was hiora cyning and licette þæt he sceolde bion se hehsta God, and þæt dysige folc him gelyfde for þa ðe he was cynecynnes. And hi nyston nænne oðerne god on þæne timan, buton hiora cyningas hi weorþodon for godas. þa sceolde þæs Iobes fæder bion eac god, þæs nama wæs Saturnus ; and his suna swa ilce ælcne hi hæfdon for god. þa was hiora an se Apollinus þe we ær ymb spræcon.

Then was there a daughter of Apollo, son of Jove ; this Jove was their king and had feigned that he was the highest God, and the foolish folk

---

[1] Sedgefield's *Boethius*, p. 99. The Latin reads, " Accepisti, inquit, in fabulis lacessentes cælum gigantes ; sed illos quoque, uti condignum fuit, benigna fortitudo deposuit."

[2] *Boethius*, IV., Metre 3. Sedgefield, p. 115.

believed him because he was of royal race, and they knew no other god in that time but worshiped their kings as gods. Then the father of this Jove, whose name was Saturn, had to be a god also, and each of his sons likewise they regarded as a god. Of these one was the Apollo we just now mentioned.

The Old English poetical version of the *Metres of Boethius* also contains a similar interpolation somewhat more extended. After the allusion in the original to Circe as daughter of Apollo, the English translator interpolates an explanation regarding Apollo as follows:

Wæs se Apollinus æþeles cynnes,
Iobes eafora; se wæs gio cyning;
se licette litlum and miclum,
gumena gehwylcum, þæt he God wære
hehst and halgost. Swa se hlaford þa
þæt dysige folc on gedwolan lædde,
oððæt him gelyfde leoda unrim,
forðæm he wæs mid rihte rices hirde
hiora cynecynnes. Cuð is wide
þæt on þa tide þeoda æghwilc
hæfdon heora hlaford for þone hehstan God,
and weorðodon swa swa wuldres cyning
gif he to ðæm rice wæs on rihte boren.
Wæs þæs Iobes fæder god eac swa he;
Saturnus þone sundbuende
heton hæleða bearn. Hæfdon þa mægða
ælcne æfter oðrum for ecne God.
Sceolde eac wesan Apollines
dohtor diorboren dysiges folces
gumrinca gyden, cuðe galdra fela
drifan drycræftas. Hio gedwolan fylgde
manna swiðost manegra þioda,
cyninges dohtor sio Circe wæs
haten for herigum.[1]

This Apollo was of noble race, child of Jove who was formerly king; he feigned to great and small, to every man, that he was God, highest and holiest. So this lord led that foolish folk in deceit, until a multitude of people believed him, because he was rightly the ruler of the kingdom, of their royal race. It is widely known that,

[1] Wülker's *Grein*, III, ii, 46.

in that time, every people regarded their king as the highest God, and worshiped him as the king of glory if he was rightly born to that kingdom. The father of this Jove was a god also as he ; him the sea-dwelling children of men called Saturn. The peoples regarded each after the other as eternal God. Also Apollo's daughter, royal born, had to be a goddess to the foolish folk, proud men, known to exercise magic arts through many sorceries. She, most of men, of many peoples, followed error, daughter of a king, who was called Circe for her oppressions.

There is a covert allusion to the same idea in *Salomon and Saturn*, though this would be by no means clear but for the preceding discussion. Salomon is speaking,

Wa bi𐌸 𐌸onne 𐌸issum modgum monnum   𐌸am 𐌸e her nu mid mane lengest
lifia𐌸 on 𐌸isse lænan gesceafte ;   iu 𐌸æt 𐌸ine leode gecy𐌸don ;
wunnon hy wi𐌸 Dryhtnes mihtum,   for𐌸on hy 𐌸æt weorc ne gedigdon.
Ne sceal ic 𐌸e hwæ𐌸re, bro𐌸or, abelgan ;   𐌸u eart swi𐌸e bittres cynnes,
eorre eormenstrynde,   ne beirn 𐌸u on 𐌸a inwitgecyndo.[1]

Woe, then, shall be to these proud men who here now live longest in evil in this transitory creation ; that, thy people formerly made known ; they strove against the might of the Creator, therefore they did not accomplish that work. Yet should I not vex thee, brother ; thou art come of a' very bitter race, fierce mighty generation ; do not thou incur their guilty nature.

Here Salomon reminds Saturn of his connection with an evil race which strove against God. The Christian poet, in making the allusion, no doubt had in mind the common medieval interpretation of the war of the giants on Jove which connected them with the giants of *Genesis*, probably with Nimrod and the tower of Babel. In that case, the work which they did not accomplish was very likely the tower itself, though possibly the rebellion in general.

Indirectly, also, another passage in the *Metres of Boethius* is explained by a minor part of this same legend regarding heathen gods. It must be premised that the Latin of Metre VII, Book II, was entirely misunderstood by the translator, and he has introduced a most surprising allusion to the

[1] Kemble's *Salomon and Saturn*, Ælfric Society, p. 164.

northern divinity Weland. The writer is discoursing upon
the transitoriness of human fame, and assumes the interroga-
tory form, asking where are various famous Romans. The
first of these interrogations, in the Latin, asks after *ossa
fabricii*; the bones of Fabricius. E$_{vid}$ent$_{ly}$ the English
translator supposed the proper name *Fabricii* meant "artificer,
smith," and at once thought of the great Teutonic artificer
Weland. He therefore translates, interpolating at some
length in explanation,

> Hwær sint nu þæs wisan   Welandes ban,
> þæs goldsmiðes   þe wæs geo mærost?
> Forðy ic cwæð þæs wisan   Welandes ban,
> forðy ængum ne mæg   eorðbuendra
> se cræft losian,   þe him Crist onlænð,
> ne mæg mon æfre þy eð   ænne wræccan
> his cræftes beniman,   þe mon oncerran mæg
> sunnan onswifan   and ðisne swiftan rodor
> of his rihtryne,   rinca ænig.
> Hwa wat nu þæs wisan   Welandes ban,
> on hwelcum hi hlæwa   hrusan þeccen?[1]

Where are now the bones of the wise Weland, the goldsmith, who
was formerly famous? For this reason I said the bones of the wise
Weland because the skill which Christ lends him may not perish
from any of the dwellers on earth; nor may one ever more easily
deprive a hapless wight of his skill, than one may turn the sun backwards, or any man the swift sky from its right course. Who
knows now the bones of Weland, in what mound of earth they may
be covered?

In explanation of the passage[2] it must be noted that a
Christian poet can not be supposed to have made this
extended allusion to a heathen divinity, unless from a
Christian standpoint. And just this is clearly true. For it
is well known that the early Christian Fathers regarded the
finding of large bones in the earth as full proof of the

---

[1] Wülker's *Grein*, III, ii, 16.

[2] The mistake of the translator has of course been pointed out, but without explanation of the underlying conception.

existence of the very giants mentioned in *Genesis*. See, for example, the passage from the *Recognitions of Clement* on page 924 of this paper. Tertullian also, in his treatise *On the Resurrection*, Chapter 42, says,

"These are the carcasses of the giants of the old time; it will be obvious enough that they are not absolutely decayed, for their bony frames are still extant. [1]

It is evident, therefore, that the Christian poet, after his error regarding the Latin, supposed he was using an effective example of transitory fame when he referred to a giant, or heathen god of human origin, whose bones he really thought were buried in some unknown place. His interpolation also implies that the skill of Weland was certainly not derived from the Creator, and he was doubtless thinking of that devil origin of the giants usually accepted in medieval times.

The story of Nimrod and the giants is briefly given in Ælfric's *Homily on the Pentecost*. The reference to the "speaking with tongues" suggested to Ælfric the tower of Babel and the confusion of tongues: [2]

Hit getimode æfter Noes flode, þæt entas woldon aræran ane burh, and ænne stypel swa heahne þæt his hrof astige oð heofon. þa wæs an gereord on eallum mancynne, and þæt weorc wæs begunnen ongean Godes willan. God eac forði hi tostencte swa þæt he forgeaf ælcum ðæra wyrhtena seltcuð gereord, and heora nan ne cuðe oðres spræce tocnawan.

It happened after Noah's flood that giants wished to build a city and a tower so high that its roof should reach to heaven. Then was there one language among all mankind, and that work was begun against the will of God. Therefore God scattered them, so that he gave each of the workmen a different language, and none could understand the other's speech.

A second allusion is found in the *Homily on the Passion of the Apostles Peter and Paul*. Speaking of the false gods which the heathen nations worshipped, Ælfric says, [3]

---

[1] See also Augustine, *City of God*, Book xv, chap. x.

[2] *The Homilies of Ælfric*, ed. by Thorpe, I, 318.

[3] *Ibid.*, I, 366.

Sume hi gelyfdon on deade entas, and him deorwurðlice anlicnyssa
arærdon, and cwædon þæt hi godas wæron for þære micelan strencðe ðe hi
hæfdon ; wæs ðeah heora lif swiðe manfullic and bysmurfull.

Some of them believed in dead giants, and raised costly idols to them
and said that they were gods on account of the great strength which they
had ; yet their lives were criminal and full of ·evil.

The longest passage in explanation of the heathen gods is
in the poetical homily *De Falsis Diis,* formerly attributed to
Ælfric but excluded from his works in the last and excellent
edition of Prof. Skeat.[1] Only part of this homily has been
printed, for a special purpose, in Kemble's edition of *Saloman
and Saturn.* In this portion there is no reference to Nimrod
and the tower of Babel, but comparison with Wulfstan's
homily on the same subject, practically a paraphrase of the
former, shows a distinct allusion to the Nimrod legend.[2]
Following this come the lines quoted by Kemble (p. 120 f.),
some of which may be given, as follows :

> Git ða ðe hæðenan noldon   beon gehealdene
> on swa feawum godum,   ac fengon to wurðigenne
> mislice entas   and men him to godum,
> ða ðe mightige wæron   on woruldlicum geþincðum,
> and egefulle on life,   ðeah ðe hi leofodon fullice.
> An man wæs eardingende   on ðam iglande Creta
> Saturnus gehaten,   swyðlic and wælhreow, etc.
>
> .   .   .   .
>
> Das manfullan men wæron   ða mærostan godas
> ðe ða hæðenan wurðodon   and worhton him to godum.
>
> .   .   .   .

---

[1] Ælfric's *Lives of the Saints,* EETS. 76, 82, 94, 114.

[2] Napier's *Wulfstan,* p. 104 f. The reference to Nimrod reads :
Ac syððan þæt gewearð þæt Nembrod and ða entas worhton þone
wundorlican stypel æfter Noes flode, and him ða swa fela gereorda gelamp,
þæs þe bec secgað, swa ðæra wyrhtena wæs. þa syððan toferdon hy wide
landes and mancyn þa sona swyðe weox, and ða æt nyhstan wurdon hi
bepæhte, þurh ðone ealdan deofol þe Adam ju ær beswac, swa þæt hi worhton
wolice and gedwollice him hæþene godas and ðone soðan God and heora
agenna scyppend forsawan, þe hy to mannum gescop and geworhte.

Monega oðre godas wæron   mislice afundene,
and eac swylce gydenan   on swiðlicum wurðmynte
geond ealne middangeard,   mancynne to forwyrde ;
ac ðas synd ða fyrmestan   ðeah ðe hi fullice leofodon.
Se syrwigenda deofol   ðe swicað embe mancynn
gebrohte ða hæðenan   on ðæt healice gedwyld,
þæt hi swa fule men   him fundon to godum,
ðe ða leahtras lufodon   ðe liciað ðam deofle,
ðæt eac heora biggencgan   heora bysmor lufodon,
and ælfremede wurdon   fram ðam ælmihtigan Gode,
se ðe leahtras onscunað   and lufað ða clænnysse.

Yet still the heathen would not be contented with so few gods, but began to worship as gods various giants and men who had been mighty in worldly dignity and terrible in life, though they had lived foully. One man was dwelling in the island of Crete, called Saturn, strong and ferocious, etc. . . . These guilty men were the mightiest gods which the heathen worshiped, and made gods for themselves. . . . Many other gods there were, variously invented, and also such goddesses in great honor throughout the world, for the ruin of mankind ; but these are the foremost, though they foully lived. The plotting devil who deceives mankind brought the heathen into this great error, that they should set up for gods such foul men, who loved the sins that please the devil, so that their followers loved their shame and became estranged from almighty God, who hates sins and loves purity.

The whole passage, which is too long to quote in full, is noteworthy as showing how early English commentators associated the divinities of the heathen with the giants and with each other, classical deities being made to correspond to those of the northern nations, as in the well-known passage in Layamon's *Brut*, lines 13,897 f. In *Salomon and Saturn*, also in *Adrian and Ritheus*, Mercury the giant is said to be the one who first invented letters.[1]

Slight variations of the Nimrod legend are also found in the Middle English *Genesis*, lines 696, and in *Cursor Mundi*, lines 2195 to 2304, passages which need not be quoted here.

---

[1] In the first, the words are *Mercurius se gigand*, in the second *Mercurius se gigant;* Kemble, *Salomon and Saturn*, pp. 192, 200.

On the other hand Higden, in his *Polychronicon* as translated
by Trevisa, follows the statement of Isidore's *Etymologia*
which he quotes almost exactly. Trevisa's translation reads,

þey þat payenis clepiþ goddes, þey were men ; and as þey bere hem in
her lif, bettre or wers, so þey were iworshipped after her deeþ. Bote by
false lore of fendes men þat come afterward worschipped hem for goddis
þat were first iworschipped onliche for mynde ; and þan, for to make it
more solempne, com feynynges of poetes.[1]

This is followed by a characteristic account of the Greek
divinities, quoting Augustine and others.

Dante combines the Nimrod story with that by which the
gods of the heathen are connected with Lucifer and his fallen
angels. He thus brings together Lucifer, the gods of the
heathen mythologies and Nimrod in his *Purgatorio* XII, 25-
36. I quote from Longfellow's translation :

> I saw that one who was created noble
>> More than all other creatures, down from heaven
>> Flaming with lightnings fall upon one side.
> I saw Briareus smitten by the dart
>> Celestial, lying on the other side,
>> Heavy upon the earth by mortal frost.
> I saw Thymbraeus, Pallas saw, and Mars,
>> Still clad in armour round about their father,
>> Gaze at the scattered members of the giants.
> I saw at foot of his great labour, Nimrod,
>> As if bewildered, looking at the people
>> Who had been proud with him in Senaar.

The question comes whether any English writer connected
heathen gods with the giant descendants of Cain. I suggest
that this is probably true in one respect of the poet of
Beowulf. It will be remembered that the hero, when so
nearly vanquished by Grendel's mother, found a sword in
the cave and with it overcame his foe. The passage at l.
1557 reads as follows :

---

[1] Babington's ed., Rolls Series, Book II, ch. IX.

Geseah ða on searwum   sige-eadig bil,
eald sweord eotenisc,   ecgum þyhtig,
wigena weorðmynd ;   þæt wæs wæpna cyst,
buten hit wæs mare   ðonne ænig mon oðer
to beadulace   ætberan meahte,
god ond geatlic,   giganta geweorc.

The sweord is here called *eald sweord eotenisc* 'old sword of an eten,' and *giganta geweorc* 'the work of giants.' The usual interpretation of such expressions, as by Grimm in *Deutsche Mythologie*, associates them with Teutonic mythology. But I submit that the poet of *Beowulf*, who could connect the giants with Cain as he has done, would have the same giants in mind in this place. The sword is found in the house of a descendant of Cain and presumably belongs to her. On its hilt Hrothgar finds the inscription regarding "the beginning of that old struggle when the flood slew the race of the giants,"[1] a clear allusion to the giant posterity of the first murderer; see p. 893. It can not be that the poet who had so clearly in mind the medieval Cain story could have connected the magic sword with a heathen myth, and placed upon it an inscription of biblical origin.[2]

This supposition becomes a practical certainty, I believe, when we know how fully the working in metals and the making of swords and armor were associated with these same giants of *Genesis* 6. Early apocryphal writings, as, the *Book of Enoch* and the *Book of Adam*, and many of the Fathers emphasized the making of weapons as one of the

---

[1] If *syðþan* of l. 1689 means 'after' instead of 'when,' the passage would doubtless refer to the Nimrod story. Yet the meaning 'when' seems far more likely, owing to the close connection of the 'struggle' with the flood.

[2] This same sword is spoken of in l. 1663 as *eald sweord eacen*, and presumably the same in l. 2140 as having *eacnum ecgum*. In both these places it has been conjectured by Bugge (*Zeitschrift f. d. Philologie*, IV, 206), that the correct reading is *eotenisc* and *eotenum*, though too much must not be made of such a conjecture.

11

evil results of Cain's wickedness. The knowledge of magic
came from the same source. This giant sword of *Beowulf,*
therefore, which also had magical power since it would kill
one whom no human sword would touch, is another evidence
of the poet's acquaintance with the early Christian and
medieval extensions of the Cain story.

If these references to the sword of the cave are to the
biblical giants, rather than to Teutonic mythology, certain
other passages must also be connected with the same. The
sword of Eanmund (l. 2616) is also *eald sweord etonisc,* and
Wulf's sword and helm (l. 2979) are

> eald sweord eotenisc,   entiscne helm.

I see no reason to halt at this conclusion. It seems to
me impossible that the poet of *Beowulf* could have been so
thoroughly Christian as he shows himself in many places, and
make so frequent references to purely heathen conceptions.[1]

Perhaps one late allusion to the derivation of the arts
from Cain may be worth while as showing the long
acceptance of the idea. It is in Donne's *Progress of the Soul,*
stanza lii :

> Wonder with me
> Why plowing, building, ruling and the rest,
> Or most of those arts whence our lives are blest
> By cursed Cain's race invented be.

SOURCES.

A. *Monsters and Spirits of Evil Descended from Cain.*

That Cain was the father of an evil progeny, monsters
and evil spirits, may be accounted for both by Hebrew

---

[1] This is not the usual view, I know, but I have became more and more
inclined toward it. See also Klaeber, *Zum Beowulf, Anglia* xxviii, especially 441 f. If no one forestalls me I hope to take up the matter somewhat
fully in a subsequent paper.

tradition and by Christian interpretation of Scripture. That it should occur in Hebrew tradition is not strange, since some Hebrew commentators gave a supernatural origin to Cain himself; cf. p. 832. From this it would naturally follow that Cain's descendants would be supernatural also. This idea is followed by Bartolocci in a chapter on the origin of demons :

Primus eorum parens assignatur angelus, qui pulcheritudine Evae illectus, equitans super serpentem ad eam ingreditur, ex quo concepit Kain, cujus figuram ut et illius posteritatis non humanum, sed angelicam fuisse autumat, quae (Hebr) generatio diluvii a Kabbinis nominatur, quarum animae daemones factae sint, et modo hominibus nocere aiunt, sed in futuro saeculo, nempne tempore Messiae, annihilabit eos Deus, ne amplius Israelitis neceant. (He refers to R. Eliezer, Pirakim, chap. 34, p. 39). [1]

But Bartolocci also connects demons with Cain through the giant progeny of the murderer. The passage above is followed immediately by these words :

Etiam generatio diluvii in die judicii non resurget, sicut dictum est, gigantes non resurgent, Is. 26, 14. Omnes autem eorum animae factae sunt spiritus et daemones nocentes hominibus, et in futuro saeculo Deus sanctus benedictus perire eos faciet e mundo.

Eisenmenger also quotes Hebrew tradition in respect to demon descendants of Cain :

Von Kain lesen wir in dem Buche Nischmath chajim S. 116, Abs. 1 in dem 12 Kapitel : ' Weiter sagen sie (die Kabbalisten), dass von Kain Teufel und Nachgespenster hergecommen seien, und den deswegen in dem Gesetze (Moses) des Todes seines Samens nicht gedacht werde, wie dessen bei den übrigen Geschlechtern Adams Erwähnung geschicht, weil die vom Samen Kains für ein besonders Geschlecht gehalten worden sind. [2]

But the demon descendants of Cain may also be accounted for by Christian interpretation of Scripture. We have already mentioned the connection assumed by early English

---

[1] *Bibliotheca Rabbinica*, I, 290.
[2] *Entdecktes Judenthum* (ed. of 1893), 589.

writers between the giants of *Genesis,* 6 and Cain. The
descendants of these giants were demons else, so that in this
way we may account for the representation of Grendel and his
mother as being of the posterity of Cain. I quote from
Justin Martyr, *Apologia,* 2, 92   .:

Angeli autem ordinem institutum praetergressi, in stupra cum mulieribus
prolapsi sunt ac filios susceperunt eos, qui daemones appellati ; atque etiàm
postea genus humanum sibi in servitutem addixerunt, partim scriptis
magicis, partim terroribus et suppliciis inferendis, partim sacrificiis,
suffimentis et libaminibus edocendis ; quibus rebus egere coeperunt, ex quo
cupiditatum morbis emancipati sunt ; denique in humanum genus caedes,
bella, adulteria, flagitia atque omne vitiorum genus proseminarunt.[1]

The *Clementine Homilies* give a similar account :

But from this unhallowed intercourse [that of angels who cohabited with
women] spurious men sprang, much greater in stature than men, whom
they afterwards called giants ; not those dragon-footed giants who waged
war against God as those blasphemous myths of the Greeks do sing, but
wild in manners and greater than men in size inasmuch as they were sprung
of angels, yet less than angels as they were born of women. . . . But they,
on account of their bastard natures not being pleased with purity of food
(the manna God has provided), longed after the taste of blood. Wherefore
they first tasted flesh. . . . All things therefore going from bad to worse,
on account of these brutal demons God . . . sent a deluge of water that, all
being destroyed, the purified world might be handed over to him who was
saved in the ark, in order to a second beginning of life. And thus it came
to pass.
    Since, therefore, the souls of the deceased giants were greater than human
souls, . . . they, as being a new race, were called by a new name [*i. e.*
demons]. And to those who survived in the world a law was prescribed of
God through an angel, how they should live. For being bastards in race,
of the fire of angels and the blood of women, and therefore liable to desire
a certain race of their own, they were anticipated by a certain righteous
law. [This law, as given in chapter 19, is that the demons should not
trouble believers, but only those who do not believe.] [2]

This passage is undoubtedly based on the *Book of Enoch.*
In that book the part relating to the birth of evil spirits
from the giants is as follows :

---

[1] Migne, *Patr. Graec.* 6, 451..
[2] *Clementine Homilies,* 8, ch. 14–18 ; Ante-Nicene Fathers, 17, 142 f. .

And now the giants who have been begotten from body and flesh will be called evil spirits on earth, and their dwelling places will be upon earth. Evil spirits proceed from their bodies; because they are created from above, their beginning and first basis being the holy watchers, they will be evil spirits upon the earth and will be called evil spirits.[1]

From Athenagoras, in the translation of the Ante-Nicene Fathers (vol. ii, p. 24) I take the following :

These [angels whose duty it was 'to exercise providence of God over the things created'] fell into impure love of virgins, and were subjugated by the flesh, and became negligent and wicked in the management of the things intrusted to them. Of these lovers of virgins, therefore were begotten those who are called giants. . . . These angels then, who have fallen from heaven and haunt the air and the earth, . . . and the souls of the giants, which are the demons who wander about the earth, perform actions similar, the one to the natures they have received, the other to the appetites they have indulged.[2]

A similar idea is expressed by Lactantius, *De Origine Erroris*, Cap. iv:

Cum ergo numerus hominum coepisset increscere, providens Deus ne fraudibus suis diabolus, cui ab initio terrae dederat potestatem, vel corrumperet homines, vel desperderet, quod in exordio fecerat, misit angelos ad tutelam cultumque generis humani. . . . Itaque illos cum hominibus commorantes dominator ille terrae fallacissimus consuetudine ipsa paulatim ad vitia pellexit, et mulierum congressibus inquinavit. Tum in coelum ob peccata, quibus se immerserant, non recepti, cecederunt in terram. Sic eos diabolus ex angelis Dei suos fecit satellites, ac ministros. Qui autem sunt ex his procreati, quia neque angeli, neque homines fuerunt, sed mediam quamdam naturam gerentes, non sunt ad inferos accepti, sicut in coelum parentes eorum. Ita duo genera daemonum facta sunt, unum coeleste, alterum terrenum.

Perhaps it is worthy of note that some of the derivations of the Hebrew *nephalim*, Greek γίγαντος, come especially near the idea of the *Beowulf* poet. Davis, in *Genesis and Semitic Tradition* p. 106, mentions several. It may mean ' strong, mighty,' or be allied to Hebrew *naphal* in the sense

---

[1] Schodde's *Book of Enoch*, sec. III, ch. 15.
[2] *Plea for the Christians*, ch. 24–25.

(1) of fallen, sinful beings ; or (2) of beings characterized as falling upon others, violent; or (3) bastards, analogous to *nephel,* abortion, miscarriage." The last is the exact idea of the Beowulf *untydras* (l. 111).

No doubt many later medieval writings might be chosen to illustrate this idea of evil descendants of Cain. I quote one more modern source for the connection of Cain with demons. Wierus, in his *Pseudomonarchia Daemonorum,* makes Cain a demon ruler:

Caym magnus Praeses, formam assumens merula ; at quum hominem induit, respondet in favilla ardente, ferens in manu gladium acutissimum. Prae caeteris sapienter argumentare facit ; tribuit intellectum omnium aquarum ; de futuris optime respondet. Fuit ex ordine Angelorum. Praesidet legionis triginta.[1]

B. *The Giants that strove against God.*

We have already shown how the story of the giants in *Genesis,* 6 was connected with the previous historical chapters, and so with Cain. This interpretation is common to early Christian literature as we shall see. Yet different commentators differed somewhat in details of interpretation, and these differences may be best understood at once. I take the clear presentation of Lenormant, in his *Beginnings of History.* Commenting on the Septuagint version of *Genesis,* 6, 2 and 4, which reads " angels of God " instead of " sons of God," he adds :

All the most ancient Fathers of the Church, as St. Justin, Tatian, Athenagoras, Clemens Alexandrinus, Tertullian, St. Cyprian and Lactantius, as well as subsequently St. Ambrose and Sulpicius Severus, reading the Bible in the Greek and therein finding this expression, regard with wonder the circumstances related in Genesis of the culpable unions between

---

[1] *Joannis Wieri Opera Omnia* (1660), p. 659. I am indebted for this reference to John Small's note on *Dunbar's Flyting,* l. 513, Scottish Text Society, 21. Small gives a free paraphrase of the Latin which I quote.

the angels descended upon earth and the daughters of men. This is also the interpretation adopted by Philo (De Gigantibus), Josephus and the author of the Book of Jubilees among the Jews, as well as by the Judaeo-Christian Theodotion. It is developed under the form of a complete and highly poetic narrative in the Book of Enoch, one of the most remarkable of the non-canonical Jewish apocalytic writings. According to this book, the angels to whom God had committed the guardianship of the earth, the Egregors or Vigilants, allowing themselves to be beguiled by the beauty of the women, fell with them into the sin of fornication, which forever shut them from heaven, begetting a race of giants 3000 cubits high, as well as numerous demons. This story of the fall of Egregors is accepted and related with further detail by Tertullian (De Cult. Femin., I, 2, II, 10), Commodian (Instruct., III, Cultus Daemonum), and Lactantius (Div. Inst., II, 14; Testam. Patriarch., 5). And this is not all; at least one positive passage in the New Testament occurs to the Christian in support of a like understanding of the text of Genesis. The Epistle of Jude, which rests upon the Book of Enoch, and clearly borrows from it verses 14 and 15, speaks of the sin of the angels and compares this fornication with the crime of Sodom and Gomorrah, and it is probable that St. Peter alludes to the same story in his second Epistle (II, 4).

But subsequently the Christian doctors were seized with scruples in regard to the consequences which might follow upon the interpretation hitherto accepted in the matter of 'sons of God.' It was supposed to contradict the words of Christ, which deny sex to the angels (Mat. 22, 30). ... The most generally accepted interpretation, beginning with the fourth century, supposes the "sons of God" to be the descendants of Sheth (Seth), upon whom this title was bestowed as belonging to the chosen race which until that period was faithful to a worship of truth, and the "daughters of men" to be the women of the line of Qain (Cain). This view appears for the first time in the romance of the Pseudo-Clementine Recognitions. ... The first orthodox writer who seems to have accepted it is Julius Africanus in his Chronicon, written during the first half of the third century. But subsequently it became the interpretation which counted for its adherents among the orientals St. Ephrem, and the author of the Christian Book of Adam, in the Greek Church Theodoret, St. Cyril, St. John Chrysostom, in the Latin Church St. Augustine and St. Jerome.

For our purpose it is sufficient to note that, whatever interpretation was taken, the children of Cain were included, and the giants were therefore descendants of Abel's murderer. Again, the giants of *Genesis* 6 were connected not only with Cain on the one side, but more directly with the flood than is warranted by the Scripture narrative. These giants were the ones who seduced mankind, induced them to oppose God, and brought the flood as a punishment for their evil deeds.

Both Hebrew and Christian commentators agree in these interpretations. For the first we may quote Josephus, who connects the giants and the flood. In *Antiquities of the Jews*, Book I, ch. 3, we read :

> For many angels of God accompanied with women begat sons that proved unjust, and despisers of all that was good, on account of the confidence they had in their own strength ; for the tradition is that these men did what resembled the acts of those whom the Grecians call giants. . . . Now God loved this man [Noah] for his righteousness. Yet he not only condemned those other men for their wickedness, but determined to destroy the whole race of mankind and make another race that should be pure from wickedness ; and cutting short their lives, and making their years not so many as they formerly lived, but one hundred and twenty years only, he turned the dry land into sea.

The Jewish Rabbis more explicitly mention the connection with Cain. Eisenmenger, in *Entdecktes Judenthum*, quotes Rabbi Eliezer especially :

> Der Rabbi spricht: So sahen die Engel, welche von ihrem heiligen Orte, namlich von Himmel gefallen waren, die Tochter des Kain, welche mit blosses Scham daher gingen und ihre Augen wie Dirnen schminkten. Sie irrten ihnen nach und nahmen Weiber von ihnen, wie (Gen. 6, 2.) gesaget wird : Cumque coepissent homines et cet. Der Rabbi Zadok sagt: Von denselben sind die Riesen, welche in hoher Liebesgrossen dahergehen, gezeugt worden.[1]

Christian commentators, whether directly influenced by Rabbinical lore or not, follow the same interpretation. They cited passages from the Apochrypha which were regarded as bearing upon the subject. Thus Augustine, in his *Civitas Dei*, Book XV, ch. 23, when speaking of the giants of *Genesis* 6, quotes *Baruch* 3, 26-38 :

> Ibi fuerunt gigantes illi nominati, qui ab initio fuerunt staturosi, scientes praelium. Non hos elegit Dominus, nec viam scientiae dedit illis ; et

---

[1] Edition of 1893, p. 47. Cf. also Ginzberg, *Die Haggada, etc.*, p. 75.

interierunt, quia non habuerunt sapientiam, perierunt propter inconsiderantiam.

Augustine also mentions the *Book of Enoch* as quoted by Jude in verse 14 of his Epistle.

The apochryphal *Book of Wisdom* was also cited by early Christian writers for a more direct connection of Cain and the flood. Thus *Wisdom*, 10, 3-4 reads:

> But when the unrighteous went away from her [Wisdom] in his anger, he perished also in the fury wherewith he murdered his brother. For whose cause the earth being drowned with the flood, Wisdom again preserved it and directed the course of the righteous in a piece of wood of small value.

We may quote among other sources the *Book of Adam*, III, ch. iv:

> When the children of Seth went down from the holy mountain and dwelt with the children of Cain, and defiled themselves with their abominations, there were born unto them children that were called Garsina, who were giants, mighty men of valor, such as no other giants were of equal might.
>
> Certain wise men of old wrote concerning them, and say in their sacred books that angels came down from heaven and mingled with the daughters of Cain, who bare unto them these giants. But those wise men err in what they say. God forbid such a thing, that angels who are spirits should be found committing sin with human beings. Never, that can not be. . . . But they were children of Seth, who were of the children of Adam, that dwelt on the mountain high up, while they preserved their virginity, their innocence and their glory like angels, and were then called 'angels of God.'

A selection from numerous other references to the giant progeny of Cain may be given in approximate chronological order. First may stand the *Book of Enoch*, which was so largely followed by the Fathers (cf. the quotation from Lenormant):

> And it came to pass, after the children of men had increased in those days, beautiful and comely daughters were born to them. And the angels, the sons of heaven, saw and lusted after them. . . . And they took unto themselves wives, . . . and they became pregnant and brought forth great giants whose stature was three thousand ells. These devoured all the

acquisitions of mankind till men were unable to sustain themselves. And the giants turned themselves against mankind in order to devour them. And they began to sin against the birds and the beasts, and against the creeping things and the fish, and devoured their flesh among themselves and drank the blood thereof.[1]

Later it is revealed to Enoch in a vision that these giants shall be destroyed :

And the spirits of the giants, who cast themselves upon the clouds, will be destroyed and fall, and will battle and cause destruction upon the earth and do evil.[2]

The *Recognitions of Clement*, Book I, ch. 29, I quote from the translation of the *Ante-Nicene Fathers*, Vol. III, p. 163 ;

All things, therefore, being completed which are in heaven and in earth and in the waters, and the human race also having multiplied, in the eighth generation righteous men who had lived the life of angels, being allured by the beauty of women, fell into promiscuous and illicit connections with them ; and henceforth, acting in all things without discretion and disorderly, they changed the state of human affairs and the divinely prescribed order of life, so that, either by persuasion or force, they compelled all men to sin against God their Creator. In the ninth generation are born the giants so-called from of old, not dragon-footed as the fables of the Greeks relate, but men of immense bodies, whose bones, of enormous size, are still shown in some places for confirmation. But against these the righteous providence of God brought a flood upon the world, that the earth might be purified from their pollutions, and every place might be turned into a sea by the destruction of the wicked.

Sulpicius Severus, in his *Historia Sacra*, I, ii, has a similar account ;

Qua tempestate [of Noah], cum jam humanum genus abundaret, angeli, quibus coelum sedes erat, speciosarum forma virginum capti, illicitas cupiditates appetierunt ; ac naturae suae originisque degeneres, relictis superioribus, quorum incolae erant, matrimoniis se mortalibus miscuerunt. Hi paulatim mores noxios conserentes, humanam corrupere progeniem ; ex quorum coitu Gigantes editi esse dicuntur, cum diversae inter se naturae permixtio monstra gigneret.

Lactantius, *De Origine Erroris*, cap. 15, has :

[1] *The Book of Enoch*, ed. by Schodde, p. 66–7.
[2] *Ibid.*, p. 82.

Itaque illos cum hominibus commorantes dominator ille terrae fallicissi-
mus consuetudine ipsa paulatim ad vitia pellexit, et mulierum congressibus
inquinavit.

Alcuin, *Interrogationes et Responsiones in Genesin*, 96 :

De quibus dixit : *Cum coepissent homines multiplicari super terram et filias
procreassent.* [Et iterum] *videntes Filii Dei filias hominum quod essent pul-
chrae* (Gen. vi, 1, 2) ? Resp. Filias hominum, progeniem Cham ; et filios
Dei sobolem Seth [MS. Sem] appellare Scriptura voluit. Hi avita bene-
dictione religiosi ; illae paterna maledictione impudicae [MS. illi . . .
impudici]; sed postquam filii Seth [MS. Sem] concupiscentia victi ex
filiabus Cham connubia junxerunt, ex tali conjunctione homines immenso
corpore, viribus superbi, moribus [inconditi], quos Scriptura gigantes
nominat, procreati sunt.

This last quotation is especially interesting because the
scribe of the Alcuin MS., or Alcuin himself, has used the
name *Cham* instead of *Cain* in both places. He evidently
refers to the former, as shown by the clause "illae paterna
maladictione impudicae," an allusion to the curse of Noah.
The MS. also has *Sem* instead of *Seth* in the second place. If
such confusion between *Cain* and *Cham* (*Ham*) could be
made in such a place, it is not strange that the earlier
reading of the *Beowulf* MS., *Cames* for *Caines* in line 107,
should have been possible. This is perhaps a better
explanation than that of Bugge (Paul and Braune's *Beiträge*,
XII, 81), who cites only a Celtic parallel to the Beowulf
Cames.

The real explanation of the confusion is that Cham (Ham)
was regarded as the natural successor of Cain after the flood.
This will be clear from a passage in Tertullian's *Liber De
Praescriptionibus*, cap. 47 :

Sed enim illos qui seminis illos prioris instituissent, occulte et latenter, et
ignorante illa matre virtute, cum illis octo animabus in arcam mississe
etiam semen Cham [Cain Fran. Paris], quo semen malitiae non periret, sed
cum caeteris conservatum, et post cataclysmum terris redditum, exemplo
caeterorum excresceret et effunderetur, et totum orbem et impleret et
occuparet.

Finally we may quote Petrus Comestor's *Historia Schol-astica Liber Genesis,* cap. xxxi, which gives the following *De causa diluvii* :

Moyses dicturus de diluvio praemisit causam ejus dicens, *Cumque coepissent homines multiplicari super terram viderunt filii dei,* id est Seth, religiosi, *filias hominum,* id est de stirpe Cain, *et* victi concupiscentia *acceperunt eas uxores,* et nati sunt inde gigantes. Tempore quidem quando factum fuerit hoc utrum sub Noe, vel ante, vel multum vel parum ante, non determinat. Josephus autem dicit quod usque ad septimam genera-tionem boni permanserint filii Seth, post ab mala progressi sunt, recedentes a solemnitatibus paternis, et ob hoc contra se Deum irritaverunt. Nam multi angeli Dei, id est filii Seth, id est qui supra *filii Dei,* cum mulieribus coeuntes injuriosos filios genuerunt, qui propter confidentiam fortitudinis gigantes a Graecis dicti sunt. Methodius causam diluvii. . . . Septingen-tissimo anno secundae chiliadis filii Seth concupierunt filias Cain, et inde orti sunt gigantes. Et incoepta tertia chiliade inundavit diluvium. Sic ordinat Methodius. Potuit etiam esse, ut incubi daemones genuissent gigantes, a magnitudine corporum denominatos, sic dicti a geos, quod est terra, quia incubi vel daemones solent in nocti opprimere mulieres ; sed etiam immanitati corporum respondebat immanitas animorum. [1]

C. *The Giants and the Gods of the Heathen.*

The derivation of the gods of the heathen from the descendants of Cain on the one side, or from Nimrod on the other, seems to be connected with the two views of *Genesis* 6, 2 and 4. This has been already explained on p. 920. The gods of the heathen were thus of angelic origin, or the giant descendants of human beings. We have already noted the passage from Josephus as representing the first view among Hebrew commentators. The Fathers may be illustrated by a quotation from Justin Martyr's *Apologia,* in the translation of the *Anti-Nicene Fathers,* I. 190 :

God, when he made the whole world and subjected things earthly to man, and arranged the heavenly bodies for the increase of fruits and the

---

[1] *Migne,* 198, 1081. On *sic ordinat Methodius* Petrus adds the note : *Hanc opinionem alibi damnat Augustinus.*

rotation of the seasons and appointed this divine law,—for these things also he evidently made for man,—committed the care of men and of all things under heaven to angels whom he appointed over them. But the angels transgressed this appointment, and were captivated by the love of women, and begot children who are those called demons; and besides, they afterwards subdued the human race to themselves, partly by magical writings, and partly by fears and the punishments they occasioned, and partly by teaching them to offer sacrifices, and incense, and libations, of which things they stood in need after they were enslaved by lustful passions; and among men they sowed murders, wars, adulteries, intemperate — deeds, and all wickedness. When also the poets and mythologists, not knowing that it was the angels and those demons who had been begotten of them that did these things to men and women, cities and nations, which they related, ascribed them to God himself and to those who were accounted to be his very ofspring, and to the ofspring of those who were called his brothers, Neptune and Pluto, and to the children again of these their ofspring. For whatever name each of the angels has given to himself and his children, by that name they called them.[1]

The *Instructions of Commodianus*, ch. 3, gives a similar view. In the same translation as the Justin Martyr it reads:

When Almighty God, to beautify the nature of the world, willed that earth should be visited by angels, when they were sent down they despised his laws. Such was the beauty of women that it turned them aside so that, being contaminated, they could not return to heaven. Rebels from God they uttered words against him. Then the Highest uttered his judgment against them, and from their seed giants are said to have been born. By them arts were made known on the earth, and they taught the dying of wool and everything which is done ; and to them, when they died, men erected images. But the Almighty, because they were of evil seed, did not approve that when dead they should be brought back from death. Whence, wandering, they now pervert bodies, and it is such as these especially that ye this day worship and pray to as gods. \

This is followed by definite references to the gods of Roman mythology. Compare also the quotations from the *Clementine Homilies* and the *Recognitions of Clement* on pp. 918, 924. All these are based on such apochryphal writings as the *Book of Enoch*. When the Septuagint reading "angels of God" was given up for "sons of God" in *Genesis* 6, 2

---

[1] See p. 918 for another use of part of this quotation.

and 4, a human origin was assumed for the gods of the heathen. For example Tertullian argues for this in his *Apoligeticus adv. Gentes,* as shown by the arguments of certain chapters. We may quote:

Cap. X. Progreditur jam ad crimen irreligiositatis, aitque Christianos deorum cultum recusare, quia dii non sunt, colendi, si divinitas eorum demonstrari possit. Provocat itaque ad conscientiam gentilium, quae neque non potest omnes illos deos homines olim fuisse, quod jam unius Saturni exemplo liquido demonstrat.

Cap. XI. At cum post mortem homines ob meritorum praesentiam in deos adlecti dicentur, inquirit hoc capite in causas quae hoc exegerint.

Augustine discusses the matter in a similar way in his *City of God,* especially Book VI, though the passage is too long to quote. Perhaps the clearest statement is in the *Etymologia* of Isadore, a work that was so influential during the middle ages. In Book VIII, cap. xi, *De Diis Gentium,* we have the following;

Quos pagani deos asserunt, homines olim fuisse produntur, et pro uniuscujusque vita vel meritis, coli apud suos post mortem coeperunt, ut apud Ægyptum Isis, apud Cretam Jovis, apud Mauros Juba, apud Latinos Faunus, apud Romanos Quirinus. . . . Fuerunt etiam et quidam viri fortes, aut urbium conditores, quibus mortuis, homines qui eos dilexerunt similacra finxerunt, ut haberent aliquod ex imaginum contemplatione solatium, sed paulatim hunc errorem, persuadentibus daemonibus, ita in posteris constat irrepsisse, ut quod illi pro sola nominis memoria honoraverunt successores deos existimaverunt, atque colerent.

These mighty men, who became gods of the heathen, were often referred to as giants and were given characteristics which connect them with the descendants of Cain. For example, they were builders of cities and mighty works, as fortifications. This building of cities was regarded as especially reprehensible. Augustine emphasizes in his *City of God* that the only proper view of life in this world is as transitory to a life hereafter. The building of cities for permanent abiding was therefore a work of the devil.

While they were still conceived of as giants, heathen gods

were also connected more directly with Ham, who was thought to be the first idolator and at least a spiritual descendant of Cain after the flood. These post-diluvian giants were also associated especially with Nimröd, who was made a giant by natural interpretation of *Genesis* 10, 8, and with the tower of Babel by an equally natural connection of Babel in *Genesis* 10, 10 and *Genesis* 11, 1-9; compare p. 906. Without trying to elucidate this legend further, it may be pointed out that Hebrew tradition made Nimrod the builder of the tower of Babel in order to get into heaven and destroy God himself. Moreover, one-third of those who took part with him, those who said "we will climb from it into heaven and strike him [God] down with axes," became devils and evil spirits; see Eisenmenger, *Entdecktes Judenthum*, p. 509 (ed. of 1893).

That the knowledge of weapons and forging in metals are also connected with Cain's descendants is first of all Scripture itself; cf. *Genesis*, 4, 22 on Tubal-Cain. This idea was much extended in medieval works. Tubal-Cain was regarded as a giant, and was thus associated with the giants of *Genesis* 6. That the knowledge of working in metals came first to these monsters may be shown from the *Book of Enoch*:

And Azazel taught mankind to make swords and knives and shields and coats of mail.[1]

With this compare the first working of metals by the the devils in hell, Milton's *Paradise Lost*, Book I. On the other hand, those who associated the gods of the heathen with men made them wicked men who invented instruments of war. Compare Augustine's *City of God*.

OLIVER F. EMERSON.

---

[1] Translation of Schodde, ch. 8.

XX.—GOETHE'S ESSAY, *ÜBER LAOKOON*.

During the year 1906 the four hundredth anniversary of the finding of the marble group of Laocoön and his sons in Rome—"opus omnibus et picturae et statuariae artis praeferendum"—has been duly celebrated. The most conspicuous act in this celebration was undoubtedly Dr. Ludwig Pollak's announcement at a meeting of the German Archeological Institute [1] that he had discovered an ancient copy of the missing right arm of Laocoön, bent backward so that the hand must have been near the head, as has long been supposed. Hardly less noteworthy, however, was the effect of recent additional discoveries of inscriptions [2] in Rhodes that seem to fix the date of the sculptors in the middle of the first century B. C., and Richard Foerster's comprehensive article in the *Jahrbuch des archäologischen Instituts* [3]—the latest and most authoritative exposition of facts and expression of opinions about the statue.

Probably few works of plastic art have given rise to more discussion than the Laocoön, and certainly no other such work has played a more important part in German literature or German esthetic philosophy. From the time when Winckelmann [4] found "den Laokoon eben so unnachahmlich als den Homer" down to our own days the statue has served as a favorite illustration of the ways and means of artistic expression, and, it may be added, has been held to corroborate

---

[1] Jan. 14, 1906. Cf. *Mitteilungen d. kaiserl. deutsch. archäolog. Inst.*, XX, 277, and *The Illustrated London News*, June 23, 1906, p. 902.

[2] F. Hiller v. Gaertringen, *Jahrb. d. arch. Inst.*, IX (1894), 23 and XX (1905), 119.

[3] Vol. XXI (1906), 1 ff.

[4] *Gedanken* (1755), DLD 20, 8.

the most various and conflicting views. Lessing, of course, did most to keep Laocoön in the foreground of esthetic speculation ; but Goethe also gave to a description and interpretation of the statue (*Über Laokoon*) the first place in a magazine by means of which he hoped to convert his fellow-countrymen to the worship of the Greek ideal, the *Propyläen* of 1798.

The apparent settlement of the more important archeological questions connected with the statue, as well as the general disposition to answer the celebrated question " Is Laocoön crying out? " in the negative, now so far assure the student of literature as to the facts that he may profitably pass judgment upon the opinions of Winckelmann, Lessing, or Goethe, and especially, it seems to me, give to Goethe's little essay closer attention than it has hitherto generally received. *Über Laokoon* is, to be sure, neither the most interesting nor the most suggestive of Goethe's essays on art. It is somewhat pompous, somewhat dogmatic; it impresses us from the start with something of an academic character, as the expositor lays down certain first principles to serve as the basis of his discussion ; and in sundry details, indeed in his conception of the whole, Goethe was mistaken. Nevertheless, so eminent a critic as Heinrich Brunn[1] declared, " Goethes Aufsatz .... bildet einen Glanzpunkt in der Laokoon-Literatur." No less instructive in its errors than illuminating in its presentation of many important truths, the essay is an object-lesson in how to see a statue ; and whatever value, great or small, we may attach to it as an interpretation, there can be no doubt of its significance for an understanding of Goethe's attitude towards the plastic arts in general and towards this marble group in particular. It represents Goethe at the height of his Hellenism, and he

---

[1] *Kleine Schriften*, Lpz., 1905, II, 506.

12

thought the Laocoön the masterpiece of Greek sculpture. To define what Hellenism meant for Goethe, and to see how far this statue conformed to his definition, is the purpose of this paper.

That Goethe did not always think as a Greek is well known, and the development of the "Stürmer und Dränger" into the Olympian has been traced by competent hands.[1] No more enlightening commentary on the poetic works of the successive epochs in Goethe's life can be found than the history of the poet's growth in the knowledge and appreciation of the formative arts. *Goetz* and *Werther* belong with the fervent preachments *Von deutscher Baukunst* and *Nach Falconet und über Falconet; Iphigenie, Tasso*, and *Hermann und Dorothea* move in the sphere of the serene and intellectual *Propyläen*. The man of "genius" became a man of rule; the worshipper of nature, feeling, and character became the discoverer and creator of types of humanity. The process of this transformation need not here concern us, but the fact is all-important. The Goethe who wrote[2] in 1772: "Und so modelt der Wilde mit abenteuerlichen Zügen, grässlichen Gestalten, hohen Farben, seine Kokos, seine Federn und seinen Körper. Und lasst die Bildnerei aus den willkürlichsten Formen bestehen, sie wird ohne Gestaltsverhältnis zusammenstimmen, denn e i n e Empfindung schuf sie zum charakteristischen Ganzen. Diese charakteristische Kunst ist nun die einzige wahre "—this same Goethe had discovered

---

[1] A. G. Meyer and G. Witkowski in their edition of *Goethes Werke*, xxx, in Kürschner's DNL; Theodor Volbehr, *Goethe und die bildende Kunst*, Lpz., 1895; L. von Urlichs, *Goethe und die Antike*, G–J, iii, 3 ff; and especially Otto Harnack, *Die Klassische Ästhetik der Deutschen*, Lpz., 1892; *Goethe in der Epoche seiner Vollendung*, 2. Aufl., Lpz., 1901; *Goethes Kunstanschauung in ihrer Bedeutung f. d. Gegenwart*, in *Essais und Studien*, Braunschweig, 1899, p. 170 ff; and most recently in vol. 22 of *Goethes Werke*, in the edition of the Bibliographisches Institut, Lpz.

[2] *Von deutscher Baukunst*, W. A., xxxvii, 149.

in 1788 that there is another kind of art, no less genuine than the frank whimsicalities of the savage, and true in a still more significant sense than because it is the utterance of real feeling : the art whose mode of expression is *style*.[1] The artist always expresses *himself*, but the forms of his expression are forms of nature ; he expresses his ideal, he fills the chosen form with a content of his own conception ; but this content, this ideal, he does not evolve from his inner consciousness, it is the fruit of a penetrating and long-continued study of those natural objects whose form he adopts as a means of expression. The source of both form and content is infinite and inexhaustible nature, but the work of art is no copy of any object existing in nature. It is a free creation, in which the process of nature is imitated, and the product is the representation of a type which the artist has learned to see imperfectly represented in every individual existence in the world of sense. Thus the artist realizes the intentions of nature, which are always good,[2] but are thwarted by the stubborness of material ; and thus the Greeks produced in such a figure as the Venus of Melos not merely the goddess of love, but a more beautiful woman than can perhaps anywhere be actually found in the flesh — feminine beauty in typical form. Art at its best is ideal, is typical, is true. It is the objectivation of a type, true to life and yet transcending the limits of individual form. It is ideal without being unsubstantial ; it is typical without being abstract ; it is individual without being peculiar ; it is true without being demonstrable. The artist strives not for "Naturwirklichkeit" but for "Kunstwahrheit."[3]

It was to illustrate such views as these by a shining

---

[1] *Einfache Nachahmung der Natur, Manier, Stil,* in Wieland's *Teutscher Merkur.,* Feb., 1789, W. A. XLVII, 77 ff.

[2] Eckermann, Apr. 18, 1827.

[3] *Einleitung in die Propyläen,* W. A., XLVII, 23.

example that Goethe wrote his paper *Über Laokoon*. In 1797 Aloys Hirt[1] had contributed to Schiller's *Horen* two articles to prove that the chief merits of the statue were those of *characteristic* art, namely a wealth of peculiar, individual, one might almost say physiological traits. Goethe replied by insisting upon the significance of the figures as *types*, and desired at the same time "auf die Intention der Künstler, die dieses Werk verfertigten, genauer als es bisher geschehen, aufmerksam zu machen."[2]

Accordingly Goethe described the subject here treated as a tragic idyll: a father with his two sons, surprised while asleep, is in danger of being killed by two serpents. These are no divine agents of destruction, but natural creatures, and the victims are human beings shorn of every other characteristic than strength and comeliness of person, and membership in one and the same family. Laocoön is a mere name ; the man so called is not presented to us as a Trojan priest, but as a typical father. The situation is likewise nothing more

---

[1] Cf. G-J, xv, 100 ff., and Harnack, *Klass. Ästhetik*, 177 ff. ; likewise Scholl in these *Publications*, xxi (1906), 118 f. Scholl correctly reports Goethe's attitude before the appearance of Hirt's articles but does not give quite the right impression of the change after their appearance. It is true that Goethe was glad to see the prevalent notions about the lifeless coldness of Greek sculpture dispelled by Hirt; but his references to the "Dogmatiker" in the letter to Meyer of July 14, 1797 (cited by Scholl), are not exactly in a sympathetic tone ; and his subsequent treatment of the "Charakteristiker" in "Der Sammler und die Seinigen," 5. *Brief*, *Propyläen*, *l. c.*, 160 ff., is no less contemptuous than Friedrich Schlegel's in the *Athenäum*. Goethe succinctly formulated his conception of the place of the characteristic in art in the *Sammler* (*l. c.* 163) : "Das Charakteristische liegt zum Grunde, auf ihm ruhen Einfalt und Würde ; das höchste Ziel der Kunst ist Schönheit und ihre letzte Wirkung Gefühl der Anmut" —and to this doctrine Winckelmann himself would have subscribed. Scholl might have adduced O. Harnack's *Klassiker und Romantiker, Essais und Studien*, 270 ff., as well as Minor's article with the same title.

[2] Goethe's own *Anzeige der Propyläen, Allgem. Zeitung*, Apr. 29, 1799, W. A. xlvii, 38.

than a scene in human life : attack, defence, triumph, and defeat in a combat between unequal foes.   The sculptors may be illustrating a myth, but they have represented an action that is complete in itself, with natural causes and effects, and without any suggestion of mythology.   Their statue is a work of art, skilfully composed to secure the maximum of artistic effect, and appealing to the observer with the sensuous charm exercised by every embodiment of an idea in forms of beauty. The artists have proved their wisdom by their choice of the moment to be represented : it is the climax of the action, and can endure in this effectiveness but an instant ; it is a moment when the three victims are discovered at three different stages of danger : the father is being bitten, the younger son is about to be bitten, the elder son is ensnared but as yet unharmed.   The spectator is filled with terror at the plight of the father, he fears a similar fate for the younger boy, he is touched by the sympathetic horror with which the elder boy regards the suffering of his father, but is not without hope that this lad may escape destruction.   The cause of this momentary action is the bite of the serpent in Laocoön's hip, but the effect is not merely physical pain ; Laocoön's feeling is the woe of a father who exerts himself to the utmost but is helpless to defend his sons.   His fate is tragic, as is life itself ; it is not horrible, like that of Milo of Crotona, entrapped in a tree-trunk and devoured by a lion ; and through the hope that remains for the elder son there is even in this sudden and undeserved calamity at least an element of consolation.

Before proceeding to an examination of this interpretation, we may well consider one or two propositions of general purport in the arts which Goethe makes by the way.   He says : [1]   "Wenn ein Werk der bildenden Kunst sich wirk-

---

[1] *Über Laok.*, W. A. XLVII, 107.

lich vor dem Auge bewegen soll, so muss ein vorübergehender
Moment gewählt sein; kurz vorher darf kein Teil des
Ganzen sich in dieser Lage befunden haben, kurz nachher
muss jeder Teil genötigt sein, diese Lage zu verlassen;
dadurch wird das Werk Millionen Anschauern immer wieder
neu lebendig sein." And again:[1] "Hier sei mir eine
Bemerkung erlaubt, die für die bildende Kunst von Wichtig-
keit ist: der höchste pathetische Ausdruck, den sie darstellen.
kann, schwebt auf dem Übergange eines Zustandes in den an-
deren." By "pathetisch" Goethe means "leidenschaftlich,"
that is, passionate, emotional, highly animated; and it might
seem as if he expected "movement" only in the expression of
emotion and passion, having only one sort of subject in mind.
But passion, vivacity, movement, immediate, even momentary effectiveness, were the qualities that he especially admired
in a statue,[2] and he is speaking above of the highest type of
sculpture. Lessing, too, had the highest type of sculpture
in mind when he defined the limits of "painting" and
poetry; he, too, laid stress on the necessity of selecting the
most "fruitful moment" for representation. But Lessing
declared that in plastic art nothing must be expressed which
can be conceived only as transitory.[3] Herder had already[4]
vehemently protested against this attempt to restrict sculpture to the imitation of quiescent, that is, dead bodies;
maintaining that the artist would thereby be deprived of his
best means of expression, and that Lessing's reason for
his rule was derived not from any principle of art, but from

---

[1] *Ibid.*, 110.

[2] "Wenn wir uns genau beobachten, so finden wir, dass Bildwerke uns
vorzüglich nach Massgabe der vorgestellten Bewegung interessieren."
Reizmittel in der bildenden Kunst, W. A. xlix, 32.

[3] *Laokoon*, ed. Blümner, Berlin², 1880, iii, 165.

[4] *Erstes Kritisches Wäldchen* (1769), ix; *Werke*, ed. Suphan, Berlin,
1877 ff., iii, 74 ff.

the limitations of human capacity to enjoy. Lessing argued,
since art gives to a momentary aspect an unnatural perma-
nency, a smile which at first sight is pleasant to behold
becomes, if prolonged, a grimace from which we turn away
in disgust. Herder answered, Yes; but should a smiling
face never be represented because in the long run we become
surfeited with the sight of it? May it not be preserved so
as to give pleasure to thousands who are to see it but once?
Goethe's attitude on this question is evidently similar to
Herder's. He too enjoyed the stimulus of action arrested,
petrified, so to speak, in marble, and yet seeming about to
continue and lead in the next instant to new attitudes and
new expressions.

It is easy to see how Lessing was brought to the exclusion
of the transitory from sculpture and painting. If action is
the domain of poetry and the representation of bodies is the
business of " painting," then movement, transition, belong
to poetry, and immobility, intransitoriness are the qualities
of subjects suitable for the formative arts. Though we may
not accept this precept as a principle,[1] it is none the less
easy to see that a painter or a sculptor does well to avoid
extremes in the use of the privilege of suggesting motion—
a privilege that Lessing by no means denied him.[2] The
rearing horse of Falconet's Petér the Great at St. Peters-
burg is certainly more hazardous in a colossal statue than
the horse with one forefoot raised in Schlüter's statue of the
Great Elector in Berlin—yet one attitude is no more or less
transitory than the other. Upon long acquaintance you may

---

[1] "Man hat der Plastik geraten, Bewegungen möglichst zu vermeiden,
ruhende Stellungen aufzusuchen ; aber die Geschichte lehrt, dass zu allen
Zeiten nicht nur Maler sondern auch Bildhauer ihrem innern Drange
folgend sich daran wagten, lebhaft bewegte Momente darzustellen." Ernst
Brücke, *Die Darstellung der Bewegung durch die bildenden Künste, Deutsche
Rundschau*, XXVI (1881), 39.

[2] *Laok.*, XVI, 251.

easily find the smiling Saskia of Rembrandt "fatal,"[1] and
yet wish to have preserved in a picture the appearance of a
young woman who, standing in the frame of a doorway,
turns half around and is about to speak pleasantly to a
person in the room that she is just leaving—and this
moment is even more fleeting than Saskia's smile. Circumstances evidently govern cases even in such matters and, as
Ziehen points out,[2] so elementary a consideration as the size
of a picture may determine the propriety of suggested motion.
If, however, the suggestion of motion under appropriate
circumstances is admissible, Lessing cannot on principle
exclude the transitory from the formative arts; and if
Theodor Dahmen[3] is right in holding that the effect of all
arts is always to induce in the observer the muscular sensations of motion along the lines of force in a picture, and that
every picture or even diagram has such lines and stimulates
such sensations, then clearly the suggestion of motion by the
representation of transitory states involves a question of
degree and not of kind; and Herder is right in asserting
that Lessing went too far in the direction of rigidity and
lifelessness.

But Goethe went too far in the other direction. Lessing
wrote:[4] "Dasjenige aber nur allein ist fruchtbar, was der
Einbildungskraft freies Spiel lässt. Je mehr wir sehen,
desto mehr müssen wir hinzudenken können. Je mehr wir
dazudenken, desto mehr müssen wir zu sehen glauben. In
dem ganzen Verfolge eines Affekts ist aber kein Augenblick,
der diesen Vorteil weniger hat, als die höchste Staffel des-

---

[1] Cf. Julius Ziehen, *Kunstgeschichtliches Anschauungsmaterial zu Lessings
Laokoon*, Bielefeld und Lpz.[2], 1905, pp. 24, 28.

[2] *L. c.*, p. 30.

[3] *Die Theorie des Schönen. Von dem Bewegungsprinzip abgeleitete Ästhetik*,
Lpz., 1903.

[4] *Laok.*, III, 165.

selben. Über ihr ist weiter nichts, und dem Auge das Äusserste zeigen, heisst der Phantasie die Flügel binden." Goethe says,[1] to be sure, "ein Letztes soll nicht dargestellt werden," meaning that the sculptors would not have chosen to represent the younger son of Laocoön as already at the point of death; but he speaks of "der Gipfel des vorgestellten Augenblicks" as "ein grosser Vorzug dieses Kunstwerks,"[2] declares "die Bildhauerkunst wird mit Recht so hoch gehalten, weil sie die Darstellung auf ihren höchsten Gipfel bringen kann und muss,"[3] and cannot praise too warmly the "Mass, womit das Extrem eines physischen und geistigen Leidens hier dargestellt ist."[4]

Here again, as when speaking of "movement," we must be careful to give no wrench to Goethe's meaning. That the climax of expression and the extreme of suffering which he saw in Laocoön left him abundant scope for the exercise of imagination is apparent from his analysis of the statue. It might seem, therefore, that his doctrine was in no wise inconsistent with Lessing's on this point. Another passage in Goethe's essay proves, however, that he exaggerated the possibility of the plastic expression of passion in the same way that Lessing unduly restricted the possibility of the plastic expression of motion. Goethe writes:[5] "Der Mensch hat bei eignen und fremden Leiden nur drei Empfindungen: Furcht, Schrecken und Mitleiden; das bange Voraussehen eines sich annähernden Übels, das unerwartete Gewahrwerden gegenwärtigen Leidens, und die Teilnahme am dauernden oder vergangenen. . . . Die bildende Kunst, die immer für den Moment arbeitet, wird, sobald sie einen pathetischen Gegenstand wählt, denjenigen ergreifen, der Schrecken erweckt, dahingegen Poesie sich an solche hält, die Furcht und

---

[1] *Über Laok.*, 114.   [2] *Ibid.*, 113.   [3] *Ibid.*, 106.
[4] *Ibid.*, 103.   [5] *L. c.*, 114.

Mitleiden erregen." Lessing, who took such pains[1] to establish the translation " Furcht " for the Aristotelian φόβος, would to some extent at least have sympathized with this distinction between the subjects of sculpture and of poetry; and Goethe's definition of fear, with its implied element of succession of moments in time, marks this emotion as belonging in the realm of that art whose " symbols " are successive words.[2] But the whole trend of Goethe's sentence is in opposition to Lessing. From beginning to end of the *Laokoon* Lessing insists " dass die Poesie die weitere Kunst ist; "[3] Goethe in this sentence holds that the highest degree of fear is proper only for sculpture; and on the same grounds he doubts whether the fate of Laocoön is suitable for literary treatment at all.[4] Be the case as it may with regard to this latter doubt; there are plenty of examples of " terror " at any rate in dramatic poetry: Hamlet, for instance, in the presence of the Ghost—to say nothing of Kleist's Prinz Friedrich von Homburg, cowed by the phantom of ignominious and supposedly undeserved death. And as to sculpture, would a tiger stealthily creeping up to its unsuspecting victim, or crouching and about to spring, be a less suggestive subject than a tiger with a struggling victim in its jaws? Is the struggling Laocoön so fascinating because we see him at the climax of his struggle and his pain? Goethe's answer is clear and positive: " Plastik wirkt eigentlich nur auf ihrer höchsten Stufe."[5] But this answer is too sweeping and is comprehensible only in the light of Goethe's overgreat fondness for the stimulus of emotion and passion. There was a strain of romanticism even in the blood of the classicist.

---

[1] *Hamburgische Dramaturgie*, 74. Stück.
[3] *Laok.*, VIII, 211.
[5] *Maximen und Reflexionen*, W. A., XLVIII, 193.

[2] *Laok.*, XVI, 250 ff.
[4] *Über Laok.*, 117.

In his interpretation of the statue, however, Goethe speaks as an out-and-out classicist—more of a classicist than the sculptors themselves. The group does not, as a matter of fact, represent a "tragic idyll;" it is not a typical scene from human life; it is the very special punishment of the Trojan priest Laocoön for a special offence against Apollo.[1] Laocoön was distinguished as a priest by a laurel-wreath of bronze, traces of which can be seen in a groove about his head,[2] also by the altar upon which he is pressed back, and near which he and his sons would scarcely have chosen to lie down and sleep. His resistance to the serpents is not so much resolute self-defence as it is an instinctive but convulsive and ineffective reaction upon a sudden attack. He knows that he is guilty and realizes whence the punishment comes. The expression of his face is the anguish of physical suffering and remorse. Furthermore, in the composition of their group, which is indeed admirable, the sculptors showed less refinement than Goethe attributed to them. The three victims do in fact appear in three degrees of danger, but not in just the way that Goethe conceived. The father is being bitten, as Goethe says—and he describes the physiological effect of the bite with telling accuracy—but the younger son has already been bitten and his state is "ein Letztes." This is clear from his whole attitude: the hanging head, the relaxation of the muscles of the legs, the probable dropping of the right arm (now incorrectly restored, like the father's) in the direction of his head. Were he not held up by the

---

[1] Servius ad Aen., II, 201, citing Euphorion says of Laocoön : hic piaculum commiserat ante simulacrum numinis cum Antiopa sua uxore coeundo. Cf. Foerster, l. c., p. 13.

[2] Cf. W. Helbig, *Führer durch die öffentlichen Sammlungen klassischer Altertümer in Rom*, Lpz.², 1899, I, p. 87 ; and Karl Sittl, *Empirische Studien über die Laokoongruppe*, Würzburg, 1895, p. 32 ; also Foerster, l. c., p. 23 : "Denn er trägt einen Lorbeerkranz. Auch die Früchte sind an demselben, wie ich am Original feststellen konnte, plastisch gearbeitet."

serpent he would fall to the ground. Goethe's error in his conception of this figure was due partly to his theory of the gradation of danger, but originally and chiefly, no doubt, to the fact that he regarded the head of the serpent biting the boy as an unsuccessful restoration, whereas it is original, but ambiguous.[1] It being more or less concealed under the boy's hand, the sculptors "scamped" it, and trusted that the obvious effect on the boy would indicate that the serpent had already bitten him. In the frontispiece to the first volume of the *Propyläen*, an engraving of the group, Goethe caused this head to be brought farther forward than it really is, so that the serpent's mouth should be seen to be tightly closed: "Keineswegs aber beisst sie."[2] Concerning the elder son and the possibility of his escape, modern opinions have differed and must differ so long as they are based upon the evidence of the statue itself. Heinrich Brunn[3] pointed out that the boy is now turning half away from his father; that only the tail of one serpent encircles his ankle, which, since the serpent is moving in the opposite direction, will soon be freed; and that the boy will then be restrained from flight only by the coil of the other serpent about his right arm, from which also he can quite conceivably extricate himself. Hugo Blümner,[4] on the contrary, called attention to the probability that the serpent now biting Laocoön would in the next instant turn upon the elder son before he could get away, so that he also must perish, and the tragedy which in the scene before us appears in three stages—past (the younger son), present (the father), and future (the elder

---

[1] Cf. Sittl, *l. c.*, p. 35.   [2] *Über Laok.*, 108.

[3] *L. c.*, 502 ff. Brunn wrote two articles on Laocoön: the first the "new interpretation" criticized by Blümner, the second a reply to Blümner and fuller exposition of his own views.

[4] *Eine neue Deutung der Laokoongruppe, Neue Jahrbücher für Philologie und Pädagogik*, LI (1881), 17 ff.

son)—would then be complete. To this argument Brunn replied :[1] the serpents, moving as they do from right to left (from the spectator's point of view) have both passed by the elder son without as yet injuring him. If they were especially sent to punish the father and the younger son, the fruit of his offence, they might disappear as suddenly as they cáme, and leave the elder son, who is now a spectator, then alone a witness to the stern justice of the gods.

When interpreting the statue, we have to reckon, as Brunn did,[2] with the possibility that the sculptors, for all their indebtedness to mythology and tradition, were artists, and as such were free to modify mythological tradition in the interest of their work. To me this seems indeed highly improbable. It is all the more to be regretted that the mythological tradition has come down to us in fragmentary and contradictory forms. There is now no question that the sculptors did not imitate Virgil, as Lessing thought was possible.[3] But whose version of the story is to be regarded as their source? Arctinus in the *Iliupersis* described the death of Laocoön and one of his sons; Sophocles — to mention only one other name—is reported by Dionysius of Halicarnassus to have represented in his lost tragedy the death of all three. Foerster[4] discusses this and other literary evidence, and shows from relics of the lesser arts— a scarab and a vase—that the pictorial representation of the death of all three is as old as the fifth century B. C. It is to be presumed that the sculptors did not depart from this tradition, especially since it had the authority of Sophocles, and the fact that the action takes place before an altar and not, as in some Greek accounts, when Laocoön is among the feasting Trojans, justifies the conclusion that the fault for

[1] *L. c.*, 516 f.　　　　　　　　[2] *L. c.*, 509 f.
[3] *Laok.*, v, 181 ff.　　　　　　[4] *L. c.*, 13 ff.

which he is punished is that attributed to him by Euphorion. The punishment ensued at the scene of the crime. Foerster makes it probable that this *motif* was quite ancient; and that something of the kind must have been Laocoön's tragic guilt in the play of Sophocles. But after all, the one important consideration for us is rather that those for whom the statue was made could have had no doubt as to what it stood for. Every Greek who saw it knew that it illustrated the story of Laocoön, and presumably admired it chiefly for the marvellous technical skill of the sculptors. Pliny, the men of the Renaissance, Goethe, and his contemporaries, admired it for other reasons. The statue has fallen in the estimation of our generation because we have learned more about Greek art than Goethe could possibly know. Friedrich Hebbel was no connoisseur of sculpture, but he with true insight expressed the point of view that is also ours when he wrote:[1]

"Vor dem Laokoon

"Michel Angelo hiess als Wunder der Kunst dich willkommen,
　Weil du als Gegengewicht gegen den schönen Apoll,
Der den Raphael trug und ihn verneinte, ihm dientest ;
　Mancher sprach es ihm nach, aber er sagte zu viel.
Was die Wahrheit vermag, das zeigst du deutlich, o Gruppe,
　Deutlicher zeigst du jedoch, dass sie nicht alles vermag ! "

No man knew better than Goethe the insufficiency of naturalistic methods in the fine arts. He valued the Laocoön because in his opinion it was not merely true to nature. The presuppositions of his admiration are in large measure the criteria of our judgment. But the works that we admire conform to these canons better than the statue by which Goethe thought they were justified and from which he thought they could be derived.

WILLIAM GUILD HOWARD.

---

[1] *Werke,* ed. Werner, Berlin, 1901 ff., vi, 334.

APPENDIX.

Proceedings of the Twenty-Third Annual
Meeting of the Modern Language
Association of America,
held at
Haverford College, Haverford, Pa.,
and at
The University of Wisconsin, Madison, Wis.,
December 27, 28, 29, 1905.

THE MODERN LANGUAGE ASSOCIATION OF AMERICA.

THE ASSOCIATION MEETING.

The twenty-third annual meeting of the MODERN LAN-
GUAGE ASSOCIATION OF AMERICA was held at Haverford
College, Haverford, Pa., December 27, 28, 29, in accordance
with the following invitation :

HAVERFORD COLLEGE, HAVERFORD, PA., *December* 15, 1904.

MODERN LANGUAGE ASSOCIATION OF AMERICA.

Gentlemen:

It would be a great satisfaction to us if you found it agreeable to use the
facilities of Haverford College for your meeting a year hence. We have a
comfortable lecture-hall and library, and the members of the Association
could probably be comfortably accommodated in our dormitories and din-
ing-room, at a moderate expense. If, however, any of the members do not
find this convenient, we are only about fifteen minutes from the heart of
Philadelphia, by steam-car. Drs. Gummere and Comfort, who are your
members, join with me in preferring this request.

Yours very truly,

ISAAC SHARPLESS.

All the sessions were held in Roberts Hall. Professor
Francis B. Gummere, President of the Association, presided
at all.

Reduced rates were secured from the railways.

FIRST SESSION, WEDNESDAY, DECEMBER 27.

The Association met at 3.20 p. m. The session was opened
by an address of welcome from President Isaac Sharpless.

iii

The Secretary of the Association, Professor C. H. Grandgent, submitted as his report the published *Proceedings* of the
last annual meeting and the complete volume of the *Publications* of the Association for 1903.

The report was approved.

The Treasurer of the Association, Mr. W. G. Howard, submitted the following report:

RECEIPTS.

Balance on hand, December 28, 1904, ...					$2,488 27
From Members for 1900, . . . $	3 00				
" " " 1901, . . .	3 00				
" " " 1902, . . .	3 00				
" " " 1903, . . .	18 00				
" " " 1904, . . .	198 00				
" " " 1905, . . .	1,862 90				
" " " 1906, . . .	104 89				
		$2,192 79			
From Libraries for 1903, . . . $	3 00				
" " " 1904, . . .	31 60				
" " " 1905, . . .	154 25				
" " " 1906, . . .	51 35				
		$ 240 20			
For *Publications*, Vol. V, . . $	90				
" " " VIII, . .	5 40				
" " " IX, . .	5 40				
" " X, . .	12 70				
" " XI, . .	7 30				
" " " XII, . .	6 30				
" " " XIII, . .	8 20				
" " XIV, . .	4 60				
" " " XV, . .	2 70				
" " XVI, . .	5 40				
" " " XVII, . .	7 20				
" " XVIII, . .	3 60				
" " " XIX, . .	3 70				
" XX, . .	14 45				
		$ 87 85			

For Reprints from Vol. XX,	.	. . . $		11 50
" Advertising in " XIX,	.	. . .		150 00
From Committee on Inter. Correspondence,	$ 7 80			
Guarantee to R. R. returned,	. . 6 00			
Sale of Reports of Committee of Twelve,	3 40			
" " Postage Stamps,	. . . 40			
		$		17 60
Interest, Cambridge Trust Co.,	. $ 34 91			
" Eutaw Savings Bank,	. . 39 30			
		$		74 21
				$2,774 15
				$5,262 42

EXPENDITURES.

To Secretary for Salary, ...		$200 00	
" " " Postage, Expressage, &c., . .		52 20	
" " " Proof-reading, ...		28 00	
" " " Printing and Stationery, . .		34 45	
		$ 314 65	
To Treasurer for Salary, ...		$100 00	
" " " Postage, ...		1 60	
" " " Clerical Assistance, . . .		11 25	
" " " Printing and Stationery, . .		70 07	
		$ 182 92	
To Secretary, Central Division,			
for Printing and Stationery, 1904, . .		$ 39 25	
" " " " 1905, . .		68 40	
		$ 107 65	
For Printing *Publications*,			
Vol. XX, No. 1, ...		$466 66	
" XX, " 2, ...		526 85	
" XX, " 3, ...		491 39	
" XX, " 4, ...		670 47	
		$2,155 37	
To Printing Program, 23d Annual Meeting, ...		70 54	
Guarantee to R. R. at Providence Meeting, ...		6 50	
Exchange, ...		8 30	
		$2,845 93	
Balance on hand ⎰ Eutaw Savings Bank, . .	$1,350 95		
Dec. 27, 1905, ⎱ Cambridge Trust Co., . .	1,065 54		
		2,416 49	
		$5,262 42	

The President of the Association, Professor Francis B. Gummere, appointed the following committees :

(1) To audit the Treasurer's report : Professors J. D. Bruner and J. F. Coar.

(2) To nominate officers : Professors J. W. Bright and H. Collitz.

The reading of papers was then begun.

1. "A Low German Account of the Voyage of Columbus." By Professor Daniel B. Shumway, of the University of Pennsylvania.

[This work, which contains a description of the voyages of the Portuguese to Africa, India, and America, and of which only one copy is extant, appeared in 1508 under the title : " *Nye unbekande lande unde eine nye werldt in korter vorgangener tyd gefunden.*" It is a translation made by Hans Ghetelen of Ruchamer's *Newe unbekanthe lande*, which in turn is based upon an Italian original. The speaker discussed the relation of the two German editions to the Italian and to each other.—*Twenty minutes.*]

2. "*Patelin* in the Oldest Texts." By Dr. Richard T. Holbrook, of Columbia University.

[Method and luck in finding old editions. Manuscripts and printed books in the 15th century. The known MSS. of *Patelin*. Oldest (Fonds fr. 4723, N. A.) not the source of any known printed book, but nearly identical with Le Roy and Levet. Bigot MS. (MS. 15,080, Bibliothèque Nationale) of early 16th century ; differs widely from other known texts. Ms. fr. 25,467 (Bib. Nat.) perhaps as late as 1540 ; stands by itself. Harvard MS. copied from a printed book.—Methods of determining the age and source of printed books. The editions of Le Roy, Levet, Beneaut, Treperel, Le Caron, etc. Opinions expressed by M. Picot.—*Twenty minutes.*]

3. "On the Date of *King Lear*." By Dr. Robert Adger Law, of Harvard University. [See *Publications*, XXI, 2.]

[Shakspeare's tragedy of *King Lear* was on the stage in December, 1606. Malone suggested that it was written before May, 1605, when the anonymous play of *King Leir* was entered for publication. Though this theory has seemed recently to be growing in disfavor, certain details connected with the printing of both plays render it more plausible.—*Twenty minutes.*]

4. "The Vows of Baldwin in *The Avowing of Arthur.*" By Professor Edwin A. Greenlaw, of Adelphi College. [See *Publications*, XXI, 3.]

[Complex character of the romance : Celtic, English, and Oriental elements. Probable identity of Baldwin. His vows practically *geasa* and related to the widespread cycle in which three counsels form the frame-work for a collection of stories. The tests of Baldwin's self-control : the courage test ; the hospitality test ; the jealousy test. Surprising character of the last-named test and its relation to the widely-known cycle of The Woman Wrongly Accused, of which *Cymbeline* is a representative.—*A twenty-minute abstract.*]

5. "The Raven Banner." By Professor Arthur C. L. Brown, of the University of Wisconsin.

[The *Dream of Rhonobwy*, one of the Welsh tales in the collection commonly called the *Mabinogion*, turns upon Owain's marvelous banner that incited his ravens to victory. Similar standards in Irish, Norse, and English legend, notably Earl Sigurd's raven-banner at the battle of Clontarf, have not heretofore been compared.—*A ten-minute abstract.*]

At 8 p. m. the Association met in Roberts Hall to hear an address by Professor Francis B. Gummere, President of the Association.

After the address, the members and guests of the Association were received by President and Mrs. Sharpless in the Gymnasium.

SECOND SESSION, THURSDAY, DECEMBER 28.

The session began at 9.45 a. m.

6. "Chaucer's Relation to Old French Love-Vision Literature." By Mr. W. Owen Sypherd, of Harvard University.

[A study of Chaucer's four vision-poems—the *Duchesse*, the *Hous of Fame*, the *Parlement of Foules*, and the Prologue to the *Legend*. The purpose of the paper is to show that these visions were composed under the dominating influence of the *genre* of vision literature, to which belong such poems as the *Roman de la Rose*, the *Panthere d'Amours*, and the *Paradys d'Amours*. The present discussion will strengthen the unlikelihood of a definite source for any of Chaucer's visions.—*A twenty-minute abstract.*]

This paper was discussed by Professor J. L. Lowes.

7. "*Beatrijs*, a Netherlandish Romance of the Early Fourteenth Century." By Dr. Harold DeW. Fuller, of Harvard University.

[The purpose of the speaker was merely to call attention to the rare artistic beauties of a romance which has hitherto received but little notice.—*Twenty minutes.*]

This paper was discussed by Professors B. J. Vos, F. E. Schelling, and A. C. L. Brown.

8. "American Speech." By Mr. Leigh R. Gregor, of McGill College.

[Taking Mr. Henry James's *On the Question of our Speech* as text, the speaker discussed possibilities inherent in a *rapprochement* of the two great halves of the Anglo-Saxon world. America's and Americans' contribution to English speech. Traditions and life. Barbarism is precipitate development. Some common phonetic variations met in America.—*Thirty minutes.*]

This paper was discussed by Dr. R. T. Holbrook, Dr. J. D. Spaeth, and Professors T. W. Hunt, F. N. Scott, R. H. Fife, Jr., C. H. Grandgent, and L. F. Mott.

9. "The Chronology of Boccaccio's First Stay in Naples." By Mr. E. H. Wilkins, of Harvard University.

[Boccaccio came to Naples late in 1328. His apprenticeship ended and his study of canon law began in 1332 or 1333. His study of astronomy with Andalò di Negro ended before June, 1334. His rejection by Abrotonia occurred in November or December, 1334. The date to which he assigns the beginning of his love for Fiammetta is March 30, 1336. He began the *Filocolo* in the spring or summer of 1336. His study of canon law ended between June, 1338, and the end of 1339. He left Naples between November, 1339, and March, 1341.—*Twenty minutes.*]

10. "Gismond of Salerne." By Dr. John W. Cunliffe, of McGill College. [See *Publications*, XXI, 2.]

[This tragedy merits more careful examination than it has yet received, not only on account of its early date (1567-68), but because it is the first

English tragedy extant which was based upon an Italian novel. The plot was taken directly from Boccaccio, and not, as has hitherto been assumed, from the English version of the story in Painter's *Palace of Pleasure.* The model chosen was, however, Dolce's *Dido,* to which the English tragedy bears close resemblances, not only in general structure, but in particular passages. There are also extensive borrowings from Seneca.—*A ten-minute summary.*]

Professor E. S. Sheldon presented the report of the Committee of Five, which was appointed (see *Proceedings* for 1904, p. xii) "to examine the Report of the Joint Committee on the subject of a Phonetic English Alphabet, and to report what, if any, amendments are desirable before the Alphabet proposed by the joint Committee shall be submitted to the Association for final action."

The members of the committee have individually examined with care a considerable body of written criticism of the report of the former committee, and they have also had before them opinions from experts connected with a printing establishment and a type foundry. Two meetings were held, at which the various alterations proposed for the alphabet were discussed. At both meetings all the members were present except Professor Weeks, who was unavoidably absent. The others had, however, the benefit of two letters from him, in which his views were set forth at some length, and the committee is able to present a unanimous report.

Only that part of the Joint Committee's Report which is concerned with the alphabet of medium precision, such as is needed for the great pronouncing dictionaries, is here treated, that is, Part III (pp. 17–37). Part V, the proposal for a shorter alphabet (for ordinary phonetic writing and practical spelling reform), offers no difficult problems, but it can hardly claim consideration before the adoption of an alphabet of medium precision. Part VI, the suggestion of a differentiated alphabet (for purposes requiring very great precision) presents a very difficult problem and its discussion now would be premature.

In what follows, the letters of the phonetic alphabet and any words in which that alphabet is employed are in Roman type. Italics designate letters of the ordinary alphabet, as now used, and words cited in the ordinary spelling. Thus, the sign u means the one vowel sound (heard in *bull*) which that letter is to have in the phonetic alphabet, while *u* is the letter of the ordinary alphabet which may have any one of several values, as in *bull, cup, cure, rule, turn,* etc.

It will be most convenient to state first the results of the committee's discussions with only the most necessary explanations, and afterwards to add such further remarks as may be advisable for fuller explanation or justification.

The committee recommends the approval of the alphabet of medium precision proposed by the Joint Committee, with the following amendments :—

1. Omit no. 5, which may be described as a notched ɑ, as the sign for the "intermediate vowel" in *ask, glass, aunt,* etc., and substitute for it no. 1 (ɑ). This latter sign is used in the Oxford English Dictionary as is here proposed, while the Joint Committee used it for the first vowel in *art, artistic,* etc.

2. Use a, â, instead of ɑ and the corresponding long vowel, for the first vowel in *artistic, art,* etc. The Joint Committee used a for the "short a" in *hat, fat,* etc., and â for the corresponding long sound, as in *stare.*

3. Add the ligature æ, to be substituted for no. 4 (a) of the Joint Committee's alphabet, as the sign for the "short a" in *hat, fat,* etc. Use the mark for length over this when needed.

4. Add ɪ (*i. e.,* ɪ with the mark of short quantity lowered so as to touch the letter) for the obscure vowel in some unaccented syllables, heard in *added, honest, carriage, goodness, happily* (second and third syllables), *baby,* etc.

5. For syllabic *l, m, n, r,* use 'l, 'm, 'n, 'r, (*i. e.,* an apostrophe preceding the letter).

6. Use j, not y, for the consonant commonly written *y* in English (as in *you*).

7. Instead of iû, iu write jû, ju, treating the first element as a consonant. But iû, iu, are to be admitted when needed to express a variant pronunciation. This paragraph applies to *union, tube, new, few, feud, Tuesday, mule, pure, Puritan, puristic, mulatto,* etc.

8. Omit the barred c for *tch, ch,* in *catch, chin,* and j for *dg, j, g,* in *edge, join, gem.* These were the alternative signs proposed by the Joint Committee, to be used as well as the preferable tʃ and dʒ.

9. Use the Anglo-Saxon letter ð with a slanting stem instead of the ordinary d with a bar across the upright stem. This can hardly be called an alteration of the sign intended in the former report.

10. The committee does not undertake in general to indicate the close quality of short vowels or the open quality of long vowels, but leaves it to the dictionary maker to employ, if he chooses, the conventional dot under the letter for the close (and short) sound (i, ẹ, ọ, ụ), and the conventional hook under the letter for the open (and long) sound (i̦, e̦, o̦, u̦). Thus *poor* may be written pûᴈr, puᴈr, pu̦ᴈr, pụᴈr, and similarly for *seer* may be written sîᴈr, siᴈr, si̦ᴈr, sjᴈr, and for *react,* riækt′ or ri̦ækt′, if these distinctions seem necessary. It will perhaps be better to add also the mark of long quantity over the letters with the hook, as the conventional dot and hook have properly nothing to do with quantity.

11. The committee recommends ê for "long *a*" (as in *fate*) and ô for "long *o*" (as in *note*), agreeing in practice with the Joint Committee. The diphthongal pronunciation, which is the usual one, though the diphthong is for neither sound always the same, can be more precisely indicated, if any one wishes to do so, by writing ei, ou, or ęę, oǫ, according to the facts. See no. 10, preceding.

12. For foreign sounds which will occasionally need representation the committee suggests the symbols used in the alphabet of the *Association Phonétique Internationale*. This applies, for instance, to the French nasal vowels, French *u*, and German *ch*.

The alphabet as thus changed contains in all forty-one letters ; or, if long and short vowels are not separately counted, the number is thirty-three, for eleven vowels and twenty-two consonants. Of these thirty-three letters ten are new (five vowels and five consonants). The ligature æ is here not counted as new ; though not in the ordinary alphabet it is not a new sign, being in all printing offices. The new signs mentioned in paragraphs 10 and 12 above are also not counted here, for they are not essential parts of the alphabet of medium precision. Of the letters of the ordinary alphabet *c, q, x,* and *y* are not in this one (though *y* would have a slight use under paragraph 12). One letter, *j*, is used with a value uncommon in ordinary English spelling. The alphabet of the Joint Committee has forty-two letters, or thirty-four if long and short vowels are not separately counted.

The whole alphabet, arranged as in the Joint Committee's report, is as follows (see also no. 5, above) :—

Vowels: â a ê̦ æ â̦ ê e î ɪ ə ϴ ô o û u ʊ ʋ ə

Consonants: h k g ŋ j t d l r n s z ʃ ʒ þ ð p b m f v w

Diphthongs : ai au ϴi (iû, iu ; see paragraph 7, above).

The following table, in which the letters are arranged as nearly as possible in the familiar order, with key-words, is taken, with some changes, from the report of the Joint Committee.

Letter.	Key-word.	Letter.	Keyword.
â	art	n	net
a	artistic	ϴ	north
ê̦	air	ϴ	august'
æ	hat	ô	note
â̦	ask	o	poetic
b	be	p	pit
d	do	r	rat
ê	mate	s	set
e	met	ʃ	ship
f	fee	t	ten

Letter.	Key-word.	Letter.	Key-word.
g	*go*	þ	*thin*
ŋ	*sing*	ð	*that*
h	*he*	û	*mood*
î	*marine*	u	*push*
i	*tin*	Û	*urge*
ɪ	*added*	ᴜ	*hut*
j	*hallelujah*	ə	*about*
k	*kin*	v	*vat*
l	*let*	w	*win*
m	*met*	z	*zest*

ʒ as in *azure*

For *tch, ch,* in *catch, chin,* etc., will be written tʃ; for *dg, g, j,* in *edge, gem, join,* etc., will be written dʒ.

It is now necessary to explain and justify the changes made, in so far as this has not been done already.

The first five vowel signs may be conveniently taken together (â, ẳ, æ, ɑ, as compared with the corresponding signs in the former alphabet, â, ɑ, å, a, and the notched ɑ). The general practice outside of English, *i. e.,* the general international usage, agreeing with the original value of the first letter of the alphabet, requires that that letter should have the value heard in *art, artistic,* and should not be used for the peculiarly English sound commonly called "short *a*" (as in *fat, hat,*). Moreover the script form, as we may call it (ɑ), which is a new and unfamiliar sign in printing (at least to most people), is better used for a less important value, one not in universal use among educated and careful speakers either in America or England, namely, the "intermediate sound" sometimes heard in *ask, glass, path,* etc. For the "short *a*" in *fat, hat,* the ligature æ is proposed, which is already much used with this value, as in the Oxford dictionary, the alphabet of the *Association Phonétique Internationale,* the English Dialect Dictionary, and the alphabet of the American Dialect Society. By these changes the signs a, ɑ, æ are all made to designate the same sounds as in the notation of the Oxford dictionary, while the strangest of the new vowel letters proposed by the Joint Committee (no. 5, the notched ɑ) is dispensed with altogether.

The changed values of a and ɑ involve writing ai, au for the diphthongs in *time, house,* instead of ɑi, ɑu.

For the obscure vowel in the second syllable of *added, honest, carriage,* etc., and the first syllable of *except, escape,* etc., a special sign seemed to this committee desirable, though the Joint Committee had not recommended one (see their report, pp. 26, 45). The sound is neither i nor e, but is in natural utterance rather nearer the former. The sign proposed above (paragraph 4) seemed to be a good one for this sound.

The need of symbols for the pronunciation of *l*, *r*, *m*, *n*, as vowels (compare the *l* of *battle* with the *l* of *battling*, the *n* of *button*, *fasten* with the *n* of *fastness*) is met by using these letters with a prefixed apostrophe for this purpose. *Battle* would be written bætl', *battling* is bætliŋ, while *button* would be written with t'n, *fasten* with s'n, but *fastness* with tn.

The sound of the consonant initial in *you*, *yoke*, *year*, had to be considered along with the notation for "long *u*" as in *union*, *mule*, *fuse*, *puma*, and that for the sound after *t*, *d*, *n* in such words as *tube*, *due*, *new*, etc. The Joint Committee used y for the consonant in *you*, *yoke*, etc., and for the "long *u*" it recommended yû (yu when shortened) but actually wrote iû (iu). Moreover the question of j and the barred c for the sounds of *j* in *join* and *ch* in *chin* respectively was also involved. This last question the committee decided first. The Joint Committee had allowed these two signs only as alternates, regarding tʃ and dʒ as the preferable notations. Without considering at length all the objections to the barred c (as that the sound meant is not a simple consonant, a possible lack of sufficient distinctiveness as compared with e, confusing associations with the present very different values of *c*) and to j in this use, it is perhaps enough to say here that for the purposes of the alphabet of medium precision there seems to be in neither of these cases a sufficient reason for alternative symbols meaning the same thing.

The committee after considerable discussion finally agreed unanimously on the recommendations above (nos. 6, 7, 8) though one member voted for no. 6 with some misgivings.

The Anglo-Saxon letter ð with its bent stem seemed more distinctive and more easily recognizable than the upright barred d.

Nos. 10, 11, and 12, make provision for supplementary signs which may be thought necessary or advisable in some dictionaries, though they are not to be considered as necessarily forming a part of the alphabet of medium precision. In connection with no. 10 the following words from the report of the Joint Committee (p. 18) may be quoted here : "The circumflex over a vowel-sign denotes primarily length, but in some cases also a concomitant closeness or roundness. This point is of importance for the proper understanding of the notation. Between e and ê, i and î, o and ô, u and û, there is a difference of quality as well as of quantity. Were we proposing a notation of maximum precision, it would be important to use a quantity-mark which should be nothing else ; but in that case we should need, for example, four signs for the i-sounds ; one for the open short in *pit*, a second for the open long heard sometimes in *fear*, *serious*, a third for the close long in *marine*, and a fourth for the close short in *react*. A similar need would arise in connection with the e-sounds, the o-sounds and the u-sounds. But, as has been seen, the alphabet here described does not aim at maximum precision ; and in a notation where simplicity, economy, and readableness are very urgent considerations, the open long *i*, heard in *serious*, as pronounced by many with an approximation to *Sirius*, may very well be merged with the close long î heard in *seen*; while the close short in *react* may be merged with the open short in *pit*. In this way we reduce the four i-sounds to two and are enabled to denote the two by means of familiar and instantly recognizable signs.'' To this may be added that to many of us the î and the û are often really diphthongs, the end of each sound being somewhat closer than the beginning. But the difference between beginning and end is in neither case noticeable enough to deserve marking. With those of us who have the diphthong it is most easily perceptible when final and stressed before a pause, but it is obviously only an alphabet of great precision that can undertake to mark such occasional deviations from what is commonly felt as the normal sound. With these considerations in view the action of the committee in no. 11 of its recommendations will be also better understood. Here, too, it did not seem important to mark the diphthongal pronunciation, though its existence is beyond doubt and it is more commonly recognized than is the case with î or û. It may be added further that, in general, English has scarcely any really pure (non-diphthongal) vowels except the short vowels.

A few cases where no addition to the alphabet of the Joint Committee has been recommended may here be mentioned. The first concerns the peculiar vowel spoken of in the former report (P. 29) as occurring in the pronunciation of some Americans in certain words where *u* is written in the common orthography. More information is needed as to the words containing the sound in question (which are not the same for all those who have the sound), and also as to the extent of this pronunciation among Americans.

A second case is that of the sign for *wh* in *when*. The Joint Committee used hw, and the present committee has made no change. The notation hw indicates the pronunciation sufficiently well to make it unnecessary to devise a new letter to which some persons would probably object.

A third case is the mark of long quantity. The only objection which seemed to the committee to need consideration was that which came from the printing establishment and specified the letters with the small circumflex over them as bound to suffer from wear or in the process of making the plates. Only the new letters with the circumflex were individually marked as liable to this objection, but it perhaps has force in every case where this mark is used. But its force seems greatly lessened when it is remembered that this is practically the only diacritic used, so that there might be considerable wear without rendering the signs illegible. The greatest risk would perhaps be in î, as distinguished from i. It was the opinion of the superintendent of the printing house that the differentiation between the letters in the small size, or 8-point (common foot-note) type would be clear.

As to the use of diacritics, attention is called to the following extract from the opinion of the type-foundry expert : " All diacritically marked characters should have the distinguishing mark exaggerated for the smaller sizes of types from sizes 6– to 12–point inclusive, that they may be easily recognized in the reading ; otherwise ordinary scanning without magnifying glasses will not separate these characters from similar ones of the regular alphabet."

The types actually used, in the report of the Joint Committee, for the new letters with the circumflex would be decidedly improved if the accent were raised a little higher, as it is for the old letters, so that the top of the letter proper should be more distinctly visible.   The sign ə would be improved if slightly wider open space were left between the top of the letter and the circular part below.   The latter part should be a little smaller.   But it has not seemed necessary to have new types for these letters cut for the present report.

To prevent any misunderstanding on an important point, it may be said here that in cases of varying usage the committee does not wish to be understood as favoring one practice rather than any other.   The decision as to what good usage is in any particular case the committee thinks outside of its province.

E. S. SHELDON,
JAMES W. BRIGHT,
C. H. GRANDGENT,
GEORGE HEMPL,
RAYMOND WEEKS.

The report of the Committee was adopted by a unanimous vote, the Alphabet as amended being approved and the Committee being granted leave to print.   [The report was subsequently printed and distributed.]

[The American Dialect Society held its annual meeting at 12.30 p. m. in Roberts Hall.]

THIRD SESSION, THURSDAY, DECEMBER 28.

The session began at 2.50 p. m.

11.   "Some Notes on the Short Story."   By Mr. H. T. Baker, of Harvard University.

 [The popular idea that all short stories are merely amusing is incorrect. From Poe and Hawthorne, who, more than any other writers, may be said to have invented the short story as a distinct literary form, to Stevenson and Kipling, it has held a high place. It differs from the novel and the mere brief tale in several important particulars ; for example, it generally deals with a single scene, situation, or character, Impressionism—one striking effect, such as that of horror—is sought. Brevity is necessary, but it must be a peculiarly wise brevity—such as Browning illustrates in his dramatic monologues. The element of the artificial in the short story—in the climax, for instance—is so treated that the result is truth to nature. Even in style, the short story seems to be partly or wholly unique, in degree if not in kind. Greater accuracy in choice of word and phrase is essential. The relations of force and clearness are new ; for, though a tale must not be actually obscure, clearness is secondary, because of the inexorable demand for brevity and suggestion. The short story is not a Bureau of Information.—*Twenty minutes.*]

This paper called forth a lively discussion from Dr. K. D. Jessen, Professors F. N. Scott, W. A. Neilson, J. D. Bruner, A. Schinz, and others.

12. "The Structure and Interpretation of the *Widsith*." By Dr. W. W. Lawrence, of Columbia University. [Printed in *Modern Philology*, IV, 2.]

[This paper presented some results of a study of the *Widsith*, with especial reference to previous theories. Although the processes by which the poem reached its present form cannot be traced in detail, it appears possible to discern the nucleus around which other material gathered, and by careful analysis of this nucleus to draw conclusions as to the approximate date of the earlier version. The theory that there is preserved in certain portions of the poem a record of the personal experiences of a Germanic singer is seen in the light of this analysis and of other considerations to be erroneous.—*Fifteen minutes.*]

13. "Jean Paul Friedrich Richter and E. T. A. Hoffmann: A Study in the Relations of Jean Paul to Romanticism." By Professor Robert H. Fife, Jr., Wesleyan University. [To appear in *Publications*, XXII, 1.]

[Many general statements have been made regarding the relations of Richter to certain Romanticists, notably Hoffmann. The paper traced the personal relations of the two writers ; and aimed to show (1) some striking resemblances between Hoffmann's musical hero, Kreisler, and certain of Richter's bizarre characters, (2) a number of minor motives common to both authors, (3) a similarity in the ironical note, and (4) a tendency in

Hoffmann's younger works toward Richter's turgidness of style, "das Jeanpaulisieren." In conclusion, the paper attempted to trace connectedly Richter's influence on Hoffmann's development and work.—*Twenty-five minutes.*]

14. "Furetière as a Satirist." By Professor Isabel Bronk, of Swarthmore College.

[That Furetière was by nature a fighter, a reformer, is apparent both from his life and from his writings. He oftenest chooses satire as a form for his bold attacks upon the society and literature of his time. This paper considered his satirical works, particularly the earliest, *Le Voyage de Mercure* and *Les Satires.* A comparison of Furetière with Régnier and Boileau naturally followed.—*Twenty minutes.*]

This paper was discussed by Professor J. D. Bruner.

15. "Wordsworthian Borrowings in Descriptions of External Nature." By Dr. Lane Cooper, of Cornell University.

[The conventional view of Wordsworth as a poet who at his best depended wholly upon his own senses for the external knowledge upon which his interpretation of nature is based, must be modified somewhat in the light of his borrowings from descriptions found in the literature of travel.—*Ten minutes.*]

In the evening the gentlemen of the Association were entertained by the Local Committee at the Merion Cricket Club.

FOURTH SESSION, FRIDAY, DECEMBER 29.

The session began at 10 a. m.

The Auditing Committee reported that the Treasurer's report was found correct, and recommended its acceptance. The recommendation was adopted.

The Nominating Committee reported the following nominations:

President.

Henry Alfred Todd, of Columbia University.

2

Vice-Presidents.

Frederick Morris Warren, of Yale University.
Fred Newton Scott, of the University of Michigan.
Raymond Weeks, of the University of Missouri.

The candidates nominated were elected officers of the Association for 1906.

[The Executive Council subsequently chose New Haven as the place for the next meeting.]

Professor L. F. Mott offered the following resolution :

Resolved, That the hearty thanks of the Association be tendered to the authorities of the Haverford College and to the gentlemen of the Local Committee for the charm and bounty of their hospitality and for their very successful endeavors to provide for the comfort and entertainment of the visiting members.

The resolution was carried by a rising vote of the Association.

The following resolution was introduced by Professor J. Geddes, Jr. :

Resolved, That the Modern Language Association approves the proposal to hold an international conference of experts in phonetics for the purpose of agreeing on a uniform method of graphic representation of the sounds of speech.

A motion by Professor J. D. Bruner, to refer the resolution to a committee of three, to report at the next meeting, was lost.

At the suggestion of Professor H. Collitz, Professor Geddes agreed to the substitution of "considering" for "agreeing on."

After discussion by Professors Geddes, C. H. Grandgent, H. Collitz, J. D. Bruner, and J. F. Coar, the resolution, as amended, was carried.

On motion of Professor H. Collitz, it was

Voted, That the College Entrance Examination Board be respectfully requested to provide for a revision of the lists of books recommended for preparation in French, German, and Spanish.

On motion of Professor L. A. Loiseaux, it was

Voted, That consideration be given, at the next meeting, to the subject of a uniform terminology in grammars.

The reading of papers was resumed.

16. "The Relation of Dryden's *State of Innocence* to Milton's *Paradise Lost* and Wycherley's *Plain-Dealer :* an Inquiry into Dates." By Professor George B. Churchill, of Amherst College. [Printed in *Modern Philology*, IV, 2.]

[Historic interest of the meeting of Milton and Dryden, and the former's consent to the writing of *The State of Innocence.* The claim that Milton and Marvell saw and criticised Dryden's work. The claim that Wycherley's *Plain-Dealer* was produced in 1674, as evidenced by the reference to it in the "Apology" prefaced to the *The State of Innocence.* Wycherley thus shown to be a slow and painstaking workman. Both these claims dependent upon the assumption that the *State of Innocence* was published in 1674. Proof of this assumption lacking ; no copy to be found ; the evidence of "The Term Catalogues." Saintsbury's copy of the title-page of a supposed 1674 edition ; evidence for this wholly lacking. Conclusion that the *State of Innocence* was first published in 1677.—*Fifteen minutes.*]

17. "The Prosody of Walt Whitman." By Professor F. N. Scott, of the University of Michigan.

[Whitman's departure from the accepted prosodic forms may be accounted for (1) by his belief that prose is a freer and less conventional form of literary art than poetry, (2) by his fondness for the swaying and gliding movements which are characteristic of rhythmical prose. His prosody is an attempt to construct with the units of prose rhythm a pattern similar to that which other poets had constructed with the materials of metre.—*Twenty-five minutes.*]

This paper was discussed by Professors A. C. Thomas, F. B. Gummere, H. E. Greene, R. H. Fife, Jr., J. D. Bruner, W. A. Neilson, Dr. J. W. Cunliffe, and others.

18. "The English *Fabliaux*."   By Mr. Henry S. Canby, of Yale University.   [See *Publications*, XXI, 1.]

[The *fabliau* belongs to a *genus* which differs widely in spirit and origin from the "popular" story. The peculiar qualities which distinguish stories of this order must be studied for the cause and explanation of their propagation through so many ages. Although they constitute the small change of social intercourse, seldom, except when elaborated into *fabliaux*, do they become valuable for the times in which they appear. It is the purpose of this paper to show that Anglo-Saxon is surprisingly poor, early Middle English surprisingly rich, in these stories, and that the few real *fabliaux* have considerable literary merit and a great historical interest.— *Twenty minutes.*]

18. "Ben Jonson's *Alchemist* and Bruno's *Candelaio*." By Professor C. G. Child, of the University of Pennsylvania.

[A main source of the *Alchemist* is probably to be found in one of the chief elements of the plot of Bruno's play. The character of the assumed indebtedness, as regards selection and rejection, accords with the character and the superior gifts of Jonson as a playwright.—*Fifteen minutes.*]

FIFTH SESSION, FRIDAY, DECEMBER 29.

The fifth and last session began at 2.45 p. m.

20. "Margaret Fuller's Criticism of Goethe."   By Dr. Karl D. Jessen, of Bryn Mawr College.

[The existing biographies of Margaret Fuller, by Julia Ward Howe and by Thomas Wentworth Higginson, either barely touch on the side of Margaret Fuller's critical activity or treat it insufficiently if not superficially. While dependent, somewhat, in her estimates of the German poet and man, on Carlyle's and Emerson's attitude towards him, the protagonist of woman's rights in New England and America exhibits remarkable critical judgment of her own, sometimes keener even than Emerson's ; she also overcomes some Puritanic bias in dealing with Goethe's personality in later statements. Her translations from Goethe compare favorably with Carlyle's.—*Twenty minutes.*]

21. "Three 'Lapland Songs.'"   By Professor Frank Edgar Farley, of Simmons College.   In the absence of the

author, this paper was presented by Professor A. E. Hancock. [See *Publications*, XXI, 1.]

[During the period of the romantic revival, certain "Lapland Songs" had a rather extraordinary vogue in England. This paper traces the history of three of these songs and explains their popularity on the ground that they appealed to the taste that encouraged "runic" poetry and "Ossianic" prose. Two of the songs were originally transcribed by Johan Scheffer, to whom they were recited by a Laplander. The third proves to have been a hoax perpetrated upon a local newspaper by a minor poet, George Pickering of Newcastle.—*Five-minute abstract.*]

22. "American Theories of Poetry." By Mr. Clyde B. Furst, of Columbia University.

[A statement of the individual views of poetry, expressed in certain notable critical essays by American poets : Bryant, Poe, Emerson, Lowell, Whitman, Timrod, Lanier, and Stedman ; with a summary and an estimate of their contributions to poetic theory.—*Twelve minutes.*]

23. "Chaucer's *Litel Clergeon.*" By Dr. Carleton F. Brown, Bryn Mawr College. [Printed in *Modern Philology*, III, 4.]

[An attempt to show, in the first place, that the "litel clergeon" of the *Prioresses Tale* was not a choir-boy, as Professor Skeat believes, but merely a young scholar. Proceeding from this, the paper undertook to explain the *Alma Redemptoris* and the "prymer" on the basis of the customs in the schools of the fourteenth century. Finally, the relation of the *Prioresses Tale* to other versions of the story was briefly considered as throwing a sidelight on Chaucer's methods in handling his material.—*Twenty minutes.*]

The Association adjourned at half-past four o'clock.

PAPERS READ BY TITLE.

The following papers, presented to the Association, were read by title only :

24. "The Origin of OE. *neorxna-wang*, 'paradise.'" By Dr. S. N. Hagen.

[The paper gives a brief account of previous attempts to explain *neorxna-wang*, special attention being given to the most recent ones. The author then tries to show that the *crux* may be attacked from another point of view. This point of view is especially favored by the fact that no Germanic dialect has any phonologically similar word for 'paradise,' and also by the fact that it does not seem to be of a popular character, no trace of it being found in Middle English. The isolation of the term in records of a more or less literary character is therefore the starting-point for a view which seeks the origin of the word in foreign material.]

25. "Notes on New-Mexican Spanish." By Professor E. C. Hills, of Colorado College. [See *Publications*, XXI, 3.]

[A large amount of linguistic material collected on the spot.]

26. "A Science of Interpretation." By Professor Theodore W. Hunt, of Princeton University.

[A scientific method. The counter-theory current. Its basis :—(1) Proper point of view; more than one possible; external and internal, dominance of the internal.—(2) True relations of the primary and secondary illustrations. The microscopic method.—(3) The importance of beginnings. Value of the primitive folk-lore.—(4) Emphasis of genuine contrasts. Need of balance and catholicity.—(5) Recognition of the unknown quantity in literature. Examples: complexity, etc. Law of exceptions. Evils of dogmatism.—(6) The absence of pre-judgments. Examples.—(7) Constructive and positive criticism.—(8) Emphasis of the spirit of literature.]

27. "The Diary of a Poet's Mother." By Professor R. Jones, of Vanderbilt University.

[An account of the diary, kept for fifty-three years, by the mother of William Cullen Bryant. The home life of the poet, schooling, preparation for college, time spent at college; his whereabouts during the time that *Thanatopsis* was presumably written, also while he was studying law, and establishing himself in life. Corroborations or corrections of chronology as given by Godwin, Bigelow, and other writers of Lives of Bryant.

28. "Paul Heyse's *Schlimmen Brüder*." By Dr. Emil A. C. Keppler, of the College of the City of New York.

[First printed 1890. According to Paul Heyse, in a letter to the author of this paper, *Die Schlimmen Brüder* was intended merely to symbolize the purification of art through contact with the ideal and the struggle to attain it. The real scope is wider than Heyse intended. The moral problem of Goethe's *Faust* is the redemption of an inherently good soul, gone to the bad, by the good that is in it. It works out merely the promise of Faust's youth. The moral problem of *Die Schlimmen Brüder* is the redemption of a bad soul, striving for the attainment of the bad, by the good that is in it.

Heyse selected Heinz, the poet, to demonstrate this proposition, because the poet is both interpreter of past and present and a seer for the future. Other arts—music and painting (also sculpture)—merely reflect past and, at best, present. The play shows not merely art as moral, but life, which art represents, as moral. Hence art, too, to be genuine, must be moral. Poesy is the most moral of arts ; hence, the poet is the most moral of artists, because the same words may express the artist's meaning differently to different natures. Ideas, however, need speech for expression ; and though painting and music are valuable adjuncts, poetry furnishes the mouthpiece for them. Ideas inevitably move men to advancement. Even though they seem to start on another tack, either by direct furtherance or by combatting of ideas do men advance. The poet chronicles and guides— shapes—this advance. So much for the art theories. The plot is based on the mediæval legend of Satan having a son by a virgin to offset Christ as the virgin-born son of God. Heyse gives Satan three sons. Beyond the purely æsthetic questions involved, the drama humanly shows, in all three (though in greatest degree in Heinz, the Devil's favorite son), the redeeming and purifying effect of moral goodness—really to the point of undermining their hereditary devilishness and of wholly redeeming them by the magic of its purity. Whether other critics will see in this play the elements that in my opinion place it in line for future recognition remains to be seen. But for the present it teaches a much needed lesson both in art and in life.]

29. "Unpublished Italian Fables in Verse." By Professor Kenneth McKenzie, of Yale University. [See *Publications*, XXI, 1.]

[This paper offers the text of seven fables in *terza rima* and eleven in sonnets, together with a discussion of their sources. Only one of the fables in *terza rima* and two or three of those in sonnet form have yet been published (cf. *An Italian Fable, its Sources and its History*, in *Modern Philology*, Vol. I, No. 4.)]

30. "The History of *ai* and *ei* in French before the dental and palatal nasal." By Professor John E. Matzke, of Leland Stanford Jr. University. [See *Publications*, XXI, 3.]

[The paper follows up the history of *ai* and *ei* in French, before the dental and palatal nasal, from the beginning to the 16th century, and is based upon a large and comprehensive collection of rhymes arranged according to dialects and in chronological order. The results are as follows :—(1) In Norman, Anglo-Norman, and Francian, *āin* and *ēin* in the 12th century, later *ēn*.—(2) In a region having Picardy as a centre, *ēin* develops into *āin*.—(3) In both regions the identity of the pronunciation of *ain* and *ein* caused confusion in the orthography, but on the whole *ain* is the rule for both only where *ēin* has become *āin*.—(4) Where *āin* becomes

ẽin, ãigne becomes *ẽigne*.   (5) In the *ãin* region on the other hand *ẽigne*
becomes *ãigne*.— (6) *-Aigne* and *-eigne* rhyme in Norman, Anglo-Norman,
and Francian as late as the 16th century.   The modern differentiation of
the words in these two categories is not therefore the result of Old French
conditions, but is due to Latin, Italian, and Spanish influences potent at
the time of the Renaissance.]

31. "Is the *Pearl* an Elegy?"   By Charles G. Osgood, Jr., of
Princeton University.

[A consideration of Professor Schofield's theory (*Publications*, XIX, 154
ff.) that the *Pearl* is not elegiac, but allegorical.   The varied mediæval
symbolism of the pearl, the poem's content, its analogues, the peculiarities
of the poet's art and thought, indicate that the *Pearl* is an elegy, whose
subject bore the name Margery.]

32. "The Staging of the Spanish *Comedia* in the Time of Lope de Vega.'
By Professor H. A. Rennert, of the University of Pennsylvania.

[The paper attempts to determine what scenic arrangements or other
stage accessories were employed at that time in producing a *comedia* upon
the stage.   This is done by an examination of the stage directions and such
other data as are furnished by the original editions of the comedies of
various dramatists.]

33. "Some Analogues and Probable Originals of the Alchemical Lore
of Ben Jonson."   By Professor Felix F. Schelling, of the University of
Pennsylvania.

[In this paper an attempt is made to ascertain the precise works which
Jonson consulted in his preparation for writing his drama, *The Alchemist*,
and the masque, *Mercury Vindicated from the Alchemists*, and to trace more
surely than has hitherto been attempted the probable originals of those
passages in these works which involve alchemical and hermetic lore.   Two
purposes are held in view : (1) a further illumination of the text of these
two works with a view to the better understanding of them ; and (2) a
determination, so far as possible, of the range and actual sources of Jonson's
alchemical learning.]

34. "Friedrich Schlegel and Goethe, 1790-1802 : a Study in Early
German Romanticism."   By Dr. John W. Scholl, of the University of
Michigan.   [See *Publications*, XXI, 1.]

[A first comprehensive study of the dependence of Friedrich Schlegel
upon Goethe.   It includes a detailed investigation of the years 1790-94,
before his public appearance as an author, a full discussion of the personal
relations, and an attempt to present a complete statement of the Goethean

elements in the *Lucinde.* It follows Schlegel's literary and æsthetic revolution through all its phases, showing in what way each was produced or modified by Goethe's personality, theories, and art-product.]

35. "Parataxis in Provençal." By Professor William P. Shepard, of Hamilton College. [See *Publications*, xxi, 3.]

[An enumeration and comparison of the different types of the paratactic sentence in old Provençal. The classification is not purely functional, as an attempt is also made to discuss the various means employed by the language to suggest the paratactic relation, and the forms of sentence resulting therefrom. Comparison of some of these results with those reached by recent investigations in the classical languages, especially in Early Latin.]

36. "Montaigne : the Average Man." By Mr. Ralph Waldo Trueblood, of Haverford College. [See *Publications*, xxi, 1.]

[Whence Montaigne's popularity? His character seemingly only ordinary ; the essays but the reflex of himself. Literary influence insufficient to explain it. The secret lies in his voluntary typification of average humanity. The essays embody the philosophy of a class hitherto unrepresented in literature. Conceptions of Montaigne frequently erroneous. A passive mediocrity not by nature but by choice. His philosophic defense of this position. Moderation, self-imposed mediocrity, and confessed ignorance the indices of man's highest power. The practical value of such a philosophy.]

37. "English Influence on the German Vocabulary of the Eighteenth Century." By Professor J. A. Walz, of Harvard University.

[The great influence of English writers upon German literature during a large part of the eighteenth century has left distinct traces in the German vocabulary. The attempt will be made to collect such words, figures, and phrases as show English influence and to give their history as far as possible.]

THE CENTRAL DIVISION MEETING.

FIRST SESSION, WEDNESDAY, DECEMBER 27.

The meeting was called to order at 2.30 p. m. by the Chairman, Professor Francis A. Blackburn, in the Lecture Room of the State Historical Society. The Secretary, Professor Raymond Weeks, read his report, which was adopted. The Chairman announced that he would postpone until a later session the appointment of the committees. The reading and discussion of papers was begun at once.

1. "Möser and the doctrine of the Diversity of Nature." By Professor J. A. C. Hildner, of the University of Michigan.

[1. Nature is inexhaustible in its changing forms, therefore the habits and passions of men are diversified, likewise the forms of poetry. 2. The patriarchal life of a country is vindicated by the same theory. 3. Club law is preferable to modern warfare, because it promotes diversity and perfection in individuals. 4. General laws are an affront to humanity and a menace to liberty. 5. A greater diversity in human virtue and a stronger development of soul power are effected not by a state of the individual, but by giving a small community the right to legislate for itself. 6. The theory of the diversity of nature is applied to nations and the conclusion reached that the German should be permitted to move forward in his own characteristic way.—*Fifteen minutes.*]

In the absence of Professor Hildner, the paper was read by Professor A. G. Canfield.

2. "*Los Pastores,* the Mexican Shepherd Plays." By Mr. Arthur Llewellyn Eno, of the University of Illinois.

[This paper offers an account of the Mexican Shepherd Plays as witnessed by the author. These plays were instituted by the Franciscan Friars centuries ago, and are still produced at the Christmas season in commemoration of the birth of Christ. The plays are given by Mexican *rancheros,* in churches, cathedrals, or private houses. In addition to the shepherds, San Miguel, Luzbel (a Spanish edition of Lucifer), with a number of devils, and a grotesque hermit appear. The drama is half chanted, half recited. The various texts, the libretto and music were discussed, and parallels drawn between *Los Pastores* and the Old English plays.—*Twenty minutes.*]

This paper was discussed by Professors R. Weeks, F. H. Chase, H. A. Smith, M. B. Evans.

3. "The Historic Drama before Grabbe." By Miss Louise M. Kueffner, of Lombard College.

[No province in the æsthetics of the drama is as obscure as that of the historic drama. The English Chronicle play, with its height in Shakespeare, represents its first development as a separate species having a nature and laws of its own ; but the lack of historic insight of Shakespeare's age, and the confusion with the Aristotelian individual psychological "tragedy" prevented its development. In Germany, sporadic and crude dramas, historic rather than psychological, precede Lessing's inadequate criticism of the species. Goethe, Schiller, the writers of the "Ritterdrama," to some extent also the Romanticists, give a farther development. Chr. D. Grabbe, however, the child of an age of spreading democracy and of a new insight into history as afforded by Hegel and others, first attempted to present a historic drama whose main interest and point of departure was not an individual psychological problem, but a historic movement of large, mass interest.—*Twenty minutes.*]

This paper was discussed by Professors A. R. Hohlfeld, G. O. Curme.

4. "The Literary Personality of José M. de Pereda." By Professor Ralph Emerson Bassett, of the University of Kansas.

[Pereda's work is preëminently personal, colored by his feelings and affording a first-hand document of his ideas and convictions. It reveals him as a realist who has linked the present with the sound literary traditions of the past. It sets him apart as the most eminent modern representative of all that is distinctively Castilian in sentiments and ideals. It is the product of a mind that typifies Spanish insularity and love of independence from outside influence, that has little or no sympathy with foreign ideas, and that views modern progress with pronounced distrust. It is inspired by a rare sincerity and honesty, presenting a severe arraignment of those who misuse material advantages for greed or sensuality. Its dominant note is a high ethical purpose in the interests, material and moral, of the submerged and disinherited.—*Twenty minutes.*]

This paper was discussed by Professor R. Weeks.

5. "Adam Daniel Richter, Nachricht von J. Wimpflings Deutschland zur Ehre der Stadt Strassburg, etc., mit einigen Anmerkungen zu der teutschen Sprache, 1752." By Professor Ernst Voss, of the University of Wisconsin.

[The author called attention to Wimpfling's *Germania*, which, although ready for the printer in 1501, did not appear until 1648, when it was published by Hans Michel Moscherosch. He reviews at length the book which has been quoted again and again in the controversy about Alsace-Lorraine, but his "Anmerkungen zu der teutschen Sprache," which he adds to his review, are the most interesting part of the essay. His etymologies tell an amusing story of German Philology in those days, *e. g.* : "Dorheit, Thorheit, von dem Gotte Dor. Liberien, Libery, Bibliothec, vielleicht von liber, das Buch, and etwan dem deutschen Worte reyhe, wo die Buecher nach der Reihe stehen.—*Ten minutes.*]

6. "The Language of Tennyson's early Poems, with Reference to the Influence of his Predecessors." By Professor James F. A. Pyre, of the University of Wisconsin.

[This paper aimed to show that in the volumes of 1830 and 1833, we have a studied poetic diction, partly selected from former English poets, and that the poets thus drawn upon are the elder ones, particularly Shakespeare and Milton, rather than Tennyson's immediate predecessors, as, for instance, Coleridge and Keats.—*Twenty minutes.*]

This paper was discussed by Professors F. A. Blackburn, E. H. Lewis.

SECOND SESSION, WEDNESDAY, DECEMBER 27.

The session was called to order at 8 p. m. by Professor Frank G. Hubbard. The address of welcome to the Association was delivered by Edward Asahel Birge, Dean of the College of Letters and Sciences. The Chairman of the Division, Professor Francis Adelbert Blackburn, then delivered an address on "A Neglected Branch of the Teaching of English." [See p. xxxix.]

At the conclusion of the Chairman's address, the members of the Association and their friends were received by Regent and Mrs. Lucien S. Hanks, at their home, 216 Langdon St.

THIRD SESSION, THURSDAY, DECEMBER 28.

The meeting opened at 9 a. m.

The chairman appointed the following committees:

On election of officers: Professors Clarence W. Eastman (Chairman), E. C. Baldwin, M. Batt, F. G. Hubbard, M. Levi.

On place of meeting: Professors Calvin W. Pearson (Chairman), A. R. Hohlfeld, E. H. Lewis, T. A. Jenkins, H. A. Smith.

To audit the accounts of the Secretary: Professors G. O. Curme, A. G. Canfield.

The reading of papers was then resumed.

7. "Paul Bourget, the Novelist." By Professor Moritz Levi, of the University of Michigan.

[The beginnings of Bourget's literary career. His critical essays. Prominent traits of French civilization of the 19th century brought out in the essays. Bourget's own attitude towards the movements described by him. His sympathy with the decadents, with scepticism and dilletantism. His preoccupation with moral problems. His method of bringing about the moral regeneration of his countrymen does not appeal to the English reader. Relation between art and morals. Art should be held responsible, just like any other agency with power for good or evil. Bourget's works are characterized by (1) brilliant power of psychological analysis; (2) skilful depiction of a society abounding in wealth and leisure; (3) fondness for the subdued and soft; (4) love for the mysterious and subtle in art; (5) by cosmopolitanism; (6) by pessimism.—*Twenty minutes.*]

This paper was discussed by Professors E. H. Lewis, T. A. Jenkins.

8. "Friedrich Heinrich Jacobi's Home at Pempelfort." By Dr. Otto Manthey-Zorn, of the University of Illinois.

[Jacobi gathered at Pempelfort a more illustrious number of the greatest talents of the eighteenth century literature than Gleim at his home in Halberstadt. The paper attempted to give a survey of this gathering, and, with the help of an original manuscript as yet unutilized, the most likely reason for Jacobi's popularity is shown.—*Twenty minutes.*]

9. "Symbolism of the early German Romanticists." By Dr. Paul Reiff, of Washington University.

[The period dealt with was that between 1797 and 1807. The conception of the symbol was first touched upon. The extent to which the early German Romanticists believed in the use of symbolism in art was considered, and, finally, certain conclusions as to divergencies of opinion among them were offered.—*Fifteen minutes.*]

10. "Some misinterpreted Passages in *Godefroi de Bouillon.*" By Professor Hugh Allison Smith, of the University of Wisconsin.

[Misinterpretations of two well known passages in Godefroi de Bouillon have been used in support of an important statement about the employment of nurses among the nobility of the Middle Ages in France. In the correction of these interpretations, new relations between the manuscripts of this poem have been noted, and a more complete classification of them established.—*Twenty minutes.*]

This paper was discussed by Professors R. Weeks, F. A. Blackburn, M. Levi, T. A. Jenkins.

11. "German Sources of Ruskin." By Professor Camillo von Klenze, of the University of Chicago.

[Wackenroder's *Herzenergiessungen eines Kunstliebenden Klosterbruders*, by way of protest against the rationalistic attitude towards art (best represented by Raphael Mengs), introduced the principle that the best pictorial art always owes its inspiration to the religious instinct. Independently of him, German artists in Rome, with Tischbein as their leader, formulated the principle that the early masters, like Giotto, Fra Angelico, etc., because of their simplicity and piety, were to be preferred to the more worldly artists of later times. In 1802, Friedrich Schlegel voiced the ideas of Wackenroder and of the Tischbein group in a series of brilliant articles. Rio's *Poesie Chretienne* (1836), spread Schlegel's views in France and especially in England. Ruskin borrowed many of his most striking thoughts from Rio.—*Twenty minutes.*]

This paper was discussed by Professors E. H. Lewis, M. Levi.

The University offered a luncheon at one o'clock in Chadbourne Hall.

FOURTH SESSION, THURSDAY, DECEMBER 28.

The session began at 2.30 p. m.

12. "Some Technical Elements in Donne's Verse." By Professor Henry Marvin Belden, of the University of Missouri.

[An attempt by comparative study of certain seventeenth century poets to ascertain the effect (1) of monosyllabic diction, (2) of symbolic (as distinguished from notional) words in the rhyme place, (3) of logical stress (constituting or crossing the rhythm stress) on symbolic words. The study proceeded from Donne and returned to him, in an endeavor to connect the impression of tenseness which his poetry produces with these three elements of his verse.—*Twenty minutes.*]

This paper was discussed by Professors G. O. Curme, F. A. Blackburn, H. B. Lathrop, J. F. A. Pyre.

13. "Luther's Study of the Social conditions of Germans as a preparation for the Translation of the Bible." By Dr. Warren Washburn Florer, of the University of Michigan.

[Luther began his translation of the Bible in 1521 with the purpose of bringing it to the German people in such a way that'they could understand and appreciate it. A knowledge of the needs and wants of the German people was therefore necessary to accomplish this purpose. For years

before undertaking the translation of the Bible, Luther had been studying
the individual, social, and national needs of the German people. His
famous pamphlet *An den christlichen Adel* was the direct product of this
keen observation. Thus equipped, Luther was prepared to give the
"thoughts right out of the midst of human life" as found in the Bible to
the German people, who were experiencing a social revolution similar to
the revolutions of the Hebrew peoples.—*Fifteen minutes.*]

In the absence of the writer, this paper was not read.

14. "The Source and Composition of *Ille et Galeron.*"
By Professor John E. Matzke, of the Leland Stanford Jr.
University.

[The paper contained a critical study of Foerster's theory that Gautier
d'Arras' poem on the adventures of Ille and Galeron represents a remodel-
ing of the *Eliduc* lay of Marie de France, undertaken for the purpose of
correcting the doubtful moral quality of Eliduc's attitude. The result of
the examination is negative, on account of the numerous discrepancies
which the composition reveals. It was then suggested that, by the side of
the story of the faithless husband (Eliduc), there must have existed the
counterpart, that of the faithful husband, and, as evidence of this fact, an
episode of *Boeve de Haumtone* was cited (ll. 2817-3045), which in its
essential motives shows the closer similarity to the central theme of *Ille et
Galeron.* On the basis of this comparison, the attempt was then made to
give an insight into the method of Gautier d'Arras in the composition of
his poems.—*Read by title.*]

At the conclusion of these papers, the Association separated into three Department Meetings : English, Romance
Languages, and Germanic Languages.

The Chairman of the Department Meeting in English was
Professor Frank G. Hubbard. The discussion was led by
Professor Edward C. Baldwin, who read a paper by
Professor C. S. Baldwin concerning the rhetorical work in
the college "introductory course" in relation to the prepar-
atory study in the high school.

The Chairman of the Department Meeting in Romance
Languages was Professor Arthur G. Canfield. The section
first listened to the report of the committee on desirable

French texts for high school and college use. The Chairman of this committee is Professor T. A. Jenkins, and the Secretary is Professor R. E. Bassett. The Chairman of the committee reported progress, and requested the active coöperation of all interested. The section then passed to the consideration of the publishing of so-called advanced texts in French and Spanish with vocabularies. At the close of a fruitful discussion, the Chairman of the meeting was authorized to appoint a committee of three to report at the next annual meeting. The section then listened to a paper written by Dr. E. J. Dubedout concerning the best French literature for use in modern schools. The paper was read by Mr. E. B. Babcock.

The Chairman of the Department Meeting in Germanic Languages was Professor C. von Klenze. The leader of the discussion was Professor M. B. Evans, who maintained that in German-English vocabularies for elementary texts : (1) The proper accent should be indicated whenever it does not fall upon the radical syllable ; (2) In all cases where sign and sound do not exactly correspond, the correct sound should be clearly indicated ; (3) Every long vowel must be distinctly indicated as long. These suggestions met with general approval.

On Thursday evening the gentlemen in attendance at the meeting were entertained at a smoker at Keeley's Annex. The ladies were entertained at a dinner.

FIFTH SESSION, FRIDAY, DECEMBER 29.

15. "The Thames Fitting." By Professor George Hempl, of the University of Michigan.

[The so-called Thames fitting is a part of an object made in commemoration of the completion of the second year of the archbishopric of Theodorus. —Read by title.]

3

16. "Sebastian Mey's *Fabulario*, a forgotten Collection of Spanish Stories (Valencia, 1613)." By Mr. Milton A. Buchanan, of the University of Chicago.

[In this paper an effort was made to trace the probable sources of the above collection, and references were given to parallel stories.—*Twenty minutes.*]

17. "German Literature in American Magazines from 1800 to 1845." By Dr. S. H. Goodnight, of the University of Wisconsin.

[Educational and cultural conditions during the last half of the eighteenth century. High regard for English and French literature, and ignorance of German literature. A typical magazine article of the period. From 1800 to 1816 ; a period characterized by little first-hand knowledge and by the domination of English opinion in criticism. Great political bitterness and important national issues, favorable to journalistic development, but not to cultural movements. The attitude towards German literature a hostile one, particularly in the case of the drama. An example from a periodical of 1816. From 1817 to 1832, the era of political good feeling. Territorial expansion. Energy displayed in material development, and in education as well. The "Goettingen group." Public sentiment still unfriendly, but less so. An article of 1827-28. From 1833-45: an era of national prosperity and broadening intellectual activity. A marked increase of German influence about 1833. The opposition to it. Journals which played an important rôle. The Dial period, 1845.—*Twenty minutes.*]

This paper was discussed by Professors H. M. Belden and M. Batt.

18. "The relative Dates of the Canterbury Tales." By Dr. Eleanor P. Hammond, of Chicago.

[The improbability that the General Prologue, any more than the Tales and Links, is the result of a single continuous effort on Chaucer's part ; lines 543 ff. as a possible addition, after the first long catalogue of pilgrims was drawn up.—The Tales of the pilgrims then introduced are noticeably the last of the fragments in which they appear, while the first Tales of fragments often show marks of early work. The possibility that Chaucer sketched a ground plan, using some material already in his desk, and composing other Tales, all of which were assigned to pilgrims in his first long list,—the Early Group, including (a) work prior to the Canterbury

Tales, (b) tales written for the Canterbury Tales as first conceived.—The Additional Group: Miller, Reeve, etc.—The Marriage Group of Tales. Conjecture as to the arrangement of Fragments D. E. F.—The Nun's Priest's Tale. The Man of Law's Tale.—Previous conjectures on the relative dates of the Tales. Skeat's grouping before and after the translation of Boethius. The influence of Treveth.—Scanty evidence as yet collected upon the state of the MSS.—Lines of research upon which attempts at dating Chaucer's work should proceed.—*Twenty minutes.*]

19. " English Translations of Modern German Literature, —a statistical Study." By Dr. A. Busse, of Northwestern University.

[The ground covered by the investigation: literary and critical productions of the last twenty-five or thirty years. Authors and works, showing the largest number of translations. A few prominent translators, their literary standing, and the value of their work. Some tests indicating the popularity of certain German authors in America.—*Twenty minutes.*]

This paper was discussed by Professors A. R. Hohlfeld, F. A. Blackburn, M. Batt.

20. "A Study of the Obsolete Words and Grammatical Forms in the Prologues of the French Mysteries of the Fifteenth Century." By Professor David H. Carnahan, of the University of Illinois.

[This study was based on the prologues of the thirty-five mysteries of the fifteenth century which have introductions of the kind under investigation. Examples were given not only of the strictly obsolete words, but also of those which survive in the language, but with a changed meaning.—*Twenty minutes.*]

This paper was discussed by Professor R. Weeks.

21. " The Source of Weisse's *Richard III.*" By Dr. F. W. Meisnest, University of Wisconsin.

[In a prefatory note, Weisse states that he had completed his drama before he read Shakespeare's *Richard III.* Critics have generally doubted this statement. The object of this paper was to prove that Weisse's tragedy is based upon Cibber's *Richard III,* "alter'd from Shakespeare," thus establishing the truth of the poet's assertion.—*Twenty minutes.*]

The Auditing Committee reported that the Secretary's accounts were found correct, and a motion was carried to accept the report of the Committee.

The Nominating Committee reported the following nominations : for Chairman, Professor E. P. Baillot, Northwestern University. For Secretary, Professor Charles Bundy Wilson, University of Iowa. For Members of the Executive Committee: Professors T. Atkinson Jenkins, University of Chicago ; Henry Marvin Belden, University of Missouri ; Marco F. Liberma, University of Cincinnati. A motion was made and carried for the adoption of this report.

The Committee on Place of meeting reported that it favored meeting in Chicago next year, if that could be done without prejudicing the chances for a Union Meeting there in 1907, and suggested that the definite choice of a meeting place be left to the Executive Committee. The report was adopted.

Professor E. H. Lewis offered the following resolution, which was adopted unanimously and with applause.

Resolved, That the Association expresses to all of the ladies and gentlemen who have acted as hosts and hostesses of the Association its appreciation of the gracious hospitality shown it during its stay in Madison, and the perfect arrangements by which this hospitality has been rendered effective.

The following resolution was introduced by Professor E. C. Roedder :—

Resolved, That a committee of three be appointed to report to the Central Division, at its next annual meeting, on some plan to eliminate as far as possible the danger of duplicating work in doctorate theses intended for publication.

The resolution was adopted, and the Chairman appointed Professors E. C. Roedder, F. G. Hubbard, T. A. Jenkins.

In line with a vote adopted at the previous annual meeting, Professor Raymond Weeks moved the following resolution :—

Resolved, That the Central Division of the Modern Language Association approves the proposal to hold an international conference of experts in Phonetics, for the purpose of agreeing on a uniform method of graphic representation of the sounds of speech.

Professor A. R. Hohlfeld moved to amend to read: "approves the idea of holding." The amendment was accepted, and the amended resolution adopted.

There being no further business before the assembly, the Chairman declared the meeting for 1905 adjourned.

OFFICERS OF THE ASSOCIATION FOR 1906

President,

HENRY A. TODD,
Columbia University, New York, N. Y.

Vice-Presidents,

F. M. WARREN,
Yale University, New Haven, Conn.

F. N. SCOTT,
University of Michigan, Ann Arbor, Mich.

RAYMOND WEEKS,
University of Missouri, Columbia, Mo.

Secretary,

C. H. GRANDGENT,
Harvard University, Cambridge, Mass.

Treasurer,

WILLIAM GUILD HOWARD,
Harvard University, Cambridge, Mass.

CENTRAL DIVISION

Chairman,

E. P. BAILLOT,
Northwestern University, Evanston, Ill.

Secretary,

CHARLES BUNDY WILSON,
State University of Iowa, Iowa City, Ia.

EXECUTIVE COUNCIL

JOHN E. MATZKE,
Leland Stanford Jr. University, Palo Alto, Cal.

H. C. G. BRANDT,
Hamilton College, Clinton, N. Y.

CHARLES HARRIS,
Western Reserve University, Cleveland, O.

C. ALPHONSO SMITH,
University of North Carolina, Chapel Hill, N. C.

JOHN B. HENNEMAN,
University of the South, Sewanee, Tenn.

A. R. HOHLFELD,
University of Wisconsin, Madison, Wis.

GEORGE HEMPL,
University of Michigan, Ann Arbor, Mich.

EDITORIAL COMMITTEE

C. H. GRANDGENT,
Harvard University, Cambridge, Mass.

CHARLES BUNDY WILSON,
State University of Iowa, Iowa City, Ia.

CALVIN THOMAS,
Columbia University, New York, N. Y.

JAMES W. BRIGHT,
Johns Hopkins University, Baltimore. Md.

THE CHAIRMAN'S ADDRESS

DELIVERED ON WEDNESDAY, DECEMBER 27, IN MADISON,
WIS., AT THE TENTH ANNUAL MEETING OF
THE CENTRAL DIVISION.
BY FRANCIS ADELBERT BLACKBURN.

A NEGLECTED BRANCH OF THE TEACHING OF ENGLISH.

As a matter of oratory it would perhaps be more skilful
to omit for the present to name this neglected branch and to
lead up to its announcement as a grand climax. But if I
fail to secure your attention and interest by means of the
subject itself and what I have to say about it, I am certain
to fail in the use of any other means. I take occasion
therefore at the beginning to say that the matter which seems
to me to call for more attention is training in talking, in the
oral use of the mother-tongue. I do not refer to public
speaking, sermons, pleas in court, stump speeches, lectures,
etc., tho the training I have in mind will be helpful in these
also, but to common talking, the use of speech in the ordinary events of life.

*   *   *   *

The mastery of a language necessarily includes two
things:

First, understanding it; the ability to recognize its words
and phrases when they are uttered by another and to connect
with them the meanings which they conventionally carry.

Second, speaking it; the skill required to utter its words
and a knowledge of their meanings, so that the speaker may
convey his ideas to others.

It will be noticed that these have in common the knowledge of meanings, that the first has in addition the training
of the ear to distinguish sounds, the second, training of the
vocal organs to utter sounds.   Training the ear calls for no
effort; it takes place under ordinary conditions without our
knowledge or will ; but the organs of speech are trained to
their function by conscious effort.   This difference I need
not dwell on; it has no bearing on my subject.   But I wish
you to note that from the beginning the learning of a
language calls for two things, the memorizing of facts and
the gaining of skill thru practice.

To the two things named as essential may be added as a
corollary a knowledge of the grammar of the language, *i. e.*,
familiarity with the laws of usage that fix the way of putting
words together in connected speech.   How much of this is
necessary depends on the language concerned; often, as in
English, sense may be clearly conveyed in spite of violations
of these laws, yet one who fails to observe them would
hardly be called a master of the language.

I will remind you that I used the word *necessarily* in
saying that mastery of a language includes the matters just
enumerated.   In a large number of the tongues of the earth
no more than these is called for and this was once the case
with all.   Even yet many persons get along very well in
their own spheres of life with these alone.   But in all languages that have received literary development and whose
speakers have shared in civilized progress, something more
is required to entitle one to be called master of a tongue,
viz. :—

Reading and writing ; a knowledge of the conventional
symbols by means of which ideas are conveyed thru the
eye instead of the ear.   This is not a new act; it is merely
another way of doing what is also done by speech, conveying
ideas.   The means used is new ; the sense of sight takes the
place of that of hearing.

After giving this definition of the mastery of a language it is hardly needful to add that such a thing as complete mastery is impossible, since it calls for a knowledge of all the words of a language and of all their various meanings and connotations. When I use the word in this address I have in mind only that degree of mastery which the average individual may hope to attain thru proper instruction and faithful effort.

*　　*　　*　　*

Before a body like this I may assert, I think, without fear of contradiction that the mastery of a language is a valuable accomplishment. But for the ordinary man a partial mastery of at least one language is not a mere social ornament; it is an absolute necessity. The one needed is naturally that used by his associates, those with whom he lives and with whom he must have some means of communication. The average uneducated man masters only a small part of the vocabulary of his mother-tongue, and a still smaller portion of the words of some other language often serves the purpose of the emigrant who finds himself in circumstances that compel him to acquire a second tongue. This little is usually acquired in the same way that he learned his mother-tongue, by hearing and practice.

In the case of one who learns a foreign language by study, the mastery obtained is often only that which enables him to read it. A limited amount of skill in writing may also be obtained in the same way, but speaking and understanding come only thru practice. In the case of the dead languages or the older forms of languages still living, this reading knowledge is all that is usually sought after. There are many languages which no one attempts to write, still less to speak, tho much time is given to the study of them for other ends. It may be a question whether such knowledge should be called mastery, tho its value is beyond question, but it is the only mastery one may hope to attain in the case of many tongues, since they are no longer spoken and the opportunity for practice, which alone can give oral mastery, does not exist.

Now this power of reading and writing a language comes to us in a different way from that of speaking and understanding. The latter is to a great extent a matter of practice; it is like learning to walk or skate or to play ball, while reading is acquired primarily by study of books, and imitation, which plays the chief part in the early stages of speech, is wanting. This distinction is a fundamental one, and the means by which one gains a knowledge of Old Persian or Umbrian is very different from that by which he learned his native speech. I need not elaborate this point or give illustrations, but I wish to emphasize the fact that in these different acquirements different mental processes are used and that they are really different branches of study. Which is the more important is a question that does not call for an answer here; our modern social life makes an absolute demand for both. But do not fail to keep in mind this fact, on which I shall base what I have to say later, that learning to speak and learning to read and write are different branches of study, calling for the exercise of different mental processes and for the use of different methods of instruction. Not totally different, of course, any more than in other related subjects, for the matter is the same, and here as in other teaching, we have the *general* common to both and the *special* peculiar to each.

We who have met here for our annual conference are a small part of a great number of persons engaged in training the youth of the world. We are interested, it is safe to say, in our work and anxious to do it well. Let us consider then how this work of training is done in the one subject which should interest us all, viz.: in the English tongue.

This should interest us all, I say; I have no doubt that it does interest us all to some extent, no matter what kind of work in Modern Language teaching calls for our chief attention and holds our chief interest.

The mother-tongue is the one subject of which every one is a student, and in which the course of study fills the whole life of the student. When the new-born child first opens his eyes to the light he opens his ears also to the sounds of earth, and the first sounds that he hears are those of speech. A little later he begins to utter these sounds and both hearing and speech cease only when life ceases. Moreover, during this whole period the student is under the influence of teachers, tho often both he and the teacher are unconscious of the relation. The teachers are often untrained and unfit, but the training goes on nevertheless with the same result that follows faulty training in other branches of study, defective knowledge and lack of skill to do the work well.

The first teachers of a child are the members of his family, his neighbors, and others with whom he is brought into contact. These remain his teachers, moreover, all his life, and in the simpler, more primitive life they are the only ones. The methods of study, too, and of teaching remain unchanged, being always, as at the beginning, example on the one part and imitation on the other, and skill in the use of language comes to the savage by practice, in the same way as skill in the use of the bow or speed in the race. The whole process of learning his language is simple and is conducted along the same lines as the rest of his life-work. In countries where modern civilized ways have replaced primitive society the same condition persists. We cannot get rid of it, but must still make use of the older way of learning the mother-tongue, tho we have added to it professional teaching, conscious and voluntary study and all the other methods of the schools.

We are apt to forget that tho we speak of the mother-tongue no one is born in possession of one. The law of heredity may give to a child the color, shape of features, mental traits, moral tendencies, etc., of his parents but it does not give him their speech. He gets his mother-tongue in the same way that he gets any other, if so be that he ever does get another. He learns to speak by imitation and practice and he learns to read by study of the printed and written forms. The only reason why he learns one tongue rather than another is that it is the one presented to him by his environment. How then in civilized society does the individual gain such mastery of his mother-tongue as it is his lot in life to gain? As I have already said, perfect mastery of a language is impossible : I may add that it can hardly be considered desirable at the price one would have to pay for it in time and labor. But how does the ordinary man of to-day get that partial mastery or knowledge of his mother-speech that he must have to fill his place in the world and properly play his part in society? And what is our system of education doing to help him gain the needed knowledge?

We all know the order of studies that prevails in this case and must continue under the circumstances, whether pedagogical philosophy gives or withholds its approval. The young child's first task is to learn to understand. He associates certain sounds perceived by the ear with certain things perceived by the sight or some other sense, because the sound and the thing are presented to him together. In time the sound suggests the thing without the presence of the thing itself, and as soon as this is the case with a single word he has made a beginning in learning a language. It may be that the first words he thus learns, or some of them, are not found in the lexicon : they are only "baby-talk," pet words or expressions, but they are words to him and parts of the language of his circle of acquaintances. They serve the same purpose as other words, since they convey ideas. In the course of time the child takes the second step in the mastery of a language, that of conveying thought to others by means of sound : he begins to speak. From this time to the end of his life he does nothing new in these ways of mental activity ; he simply continues to familiarize himself with sound-combinations that serve as signs of ideas, to associate them with the ideas for which they stand, and to communicate them to others by utterance. During his whole life he is a learner, always adding to his stock of words, losing portions by lapse of memory, correcting where he has learned wrongly.

In countries where general education prevails, and it is only with the conditions in such that I am concerned in this address, the child on reaching a certain point in development begins to use a second way of receiving and giving ideas, viz. :—by reading and writing, and this also is continued indefinitely. In regard to this new method I wish at this point only to call attention to the fact that it is entirely artificial, that in spite of its great value it is not essential to social life and progress, that a high civilization may be reached without it. It is in fact only an invention, to be classed with the steam engine and the telephone, tho far outranking them in usefulness. I need not dwell on the difference between this and speech ; you may compare them for yourselves and see how much more valuable to mankind the latter is. Yet strange to say most persons look on reading as the beginning of education. We smile at Dogberry's dictum that reading and writing come by nature : if we thought it worth our while to confute it, our own memories would furnish ample proof that reading and writing come only by hard work. But it is equally ridiculous to suppose that speaking is an outgrowth of nature. Like writing it is acquired by work, as observation clearly shows, tho memory may not reach back to the time of its acquirement. The resemblance goes even further, for the work of learning to speak, like that of learning to read, is under the influence of teachers. The earlier teachers are in general unaware of the fact that they are giving instruction of supreme value, and feel little or no responsibility; in fact most of them care nothing for correctness of speech themselves, and quite as little for the training of their pupils. Conscious effort on the part of the teacher first comes with the beginning of formal study of the written forms. But when this begins most of the pupil's time and energy is demanded by the new work and conscious and intelligent instruction in the oral use of the mother-tongue forms only a small part of the work of the new class of teachers. Even this takes place only during the small portion of the day spent in the school and ceases altogether for the remaining hours. Meanwhile the other teachers are not idle; at home, in the street, on the playground, wherever the child hears or utters words, he is repeating and practising the lessons begun some years earlier. And it goes on all his life, for the grown man, willingly or unwillingly, shapes his speech more or less to that of his associates.

I need not waste time in telling you of the unfitness of these chance teachers. But however unqualified they may be to give instruction it is impossible to eliminate them from our system of training the youth of the land. The relation of children to their parents is a part of the social system, not properly of our modern educational systems, tho it perforce becomes so with the adoption of any system of general teaching. Unfitness to train a child in speech is exactly like moral unfitness or financial inability to do for the child what is best for him. In extreme cases of this kind, to be sure, the state does sometimes interfere to rescue the child, justifying its action by the assumption that a child brought up in moral degradation or kept from proper physical development by poverty is likely to become a burden on the community. But the state anticipates no loss from faulty training in language and has no warrant therefore for taking measures to prevent it. Yet I could show, I think, that the lack of training in speech does cause loss to the community, pecuniary as well as other, but this is only one of many causes of public loss, and does not call for discussion, as there seems to be at present no way of dealing with it. In the golden age of the future when all faults in human nature have been cured and all weaknesses removed we may hope for better things in speech as well as in all else.

But in naming my subject, as you may well assume, I did not have in mind the training of these early years. It is only in the later period of education that anything can be done by us to improve conditions, and therefore only in this period that neglect can be pointed out with any expectation of results of value.

The second period of training in speech covers the years of formal instruction until the pupil enters the High School. It may be characterized as the period of reading and writing, since work in these branches predominates at this time, tho it may begin earlier in the home, and is sometimes continued in the following period. We are warranted in assuming as a general rule, that the teachers charged with this work are competent, but we should not forget that the older kind of teaching goes on still alongside of the newer, and that the same unqualified instructors have it in hand. Now what is done for language training during this period and what share of this training is given to the development in the pupil of skill in speaking ?

Formal training in speech during this time is limited in general to correction of bad habits formed already. This is given by suggestion, as it seems to be needed ; incidentally also in the books on language study. I have never heard of formal classes in speaking, tho there is much formal instruction in writing the language. This instruction is of course of the highest value for training in speech, but is rendered of far less influence by the lack of practice in speech. The result of this lack is a partial divorce of the written language of the individual from his habitual speech. After making due allowance for the more formal style of writing, we still find that such training in speech has a result much like that of training in morals. The knowledge that a certain act is wrong does not at all times keep the one who knows from doing it, and often a perfect knowledge of the rules of the manuals fails to eradicate gross faults of speech. You are all acquainted, I am sure, with persons whose written work is correct, and who are in control of a ready style that runs on of itself without conscious effort, who nevertheless commit errors habitually in conversation. Possibly there may be some present who will be frank enough to join me in the confession that I make, that this statement is based on observation of my own habits as well as of those of certain of my friends.

But the study of the written form does nevertheless give great help in speaking. A knowledge of rules is the first condition for following those rules, and gives a basis for self-help if the learner desires to improve. Reading enlarges the pupil's vocabulary, furnishes models for the construction of sentences and crowds out awkward and faulty forms of speech by making better ways of expressing the same ideas familiar. Practice in written composition acts in the same way and has a special influence moreover in making the new locutions one's own by use, thus increasing not only knowledge but readiness.

The third period covers the High School and College instruction. Special attention is given during this time to practice in writing, but if the pupil gets any training in speech it comes indirectly and incidentally. An exception might be made of declamation, but in this the aim is training in public speaking, a valuable accomplishment, no doubt, but as I have already said, not the kind of speaking that I am now urging. To some extent training is given at this time by voluntary exercise in debating clubs and like organizations, but these are outside of school and college life, and cannot be credited to the teachers or the system of teaching. Moreover, those who get help in this way are as a rule the ones least in need of it. It is the member best trained in talking that does the talking. The pupil that needs practice is apt to remain silent or to remain out of the club altogether.

To sum up, then, the training to talk that the ordinary educated man receives is likely to be about the following :—

First, that which comes from contact with his fellow-men and is given unconsciously and without purpose. This is generally faulty ; the fortunate few in whose homes a purer use of the mother-tongue prevails have the great advantage of having less to unlearn when more formal instruction begins.

Second, that which is given with definite purpose by professional teachers. As has been pointed out, our schools provide almost nothing of this kind.

Third, that which comes thru training in the writing of the language. This is of the highest value, tho it is not the direct object sought. But its value is greatly lessened by the fact that the great majority of the pupils leave school too early to get any real benefit, and go out into the world to act as teachers of their offspring and associates in a subject that they have not learned.

That the part taken by the schools in teaching the pupils to speak is small is no good reason for charging them with neglect, if it can be shown that the omission brings no loss

4

or harm. If men learn to talk without the help of the schools, or if they fail to learn and yet lose nothing thereby, there is no reason why the omission of this particular branch of study should be termed neglect, any more than the omission of formal lessons in base-ball or golf or dancing or any other subject, useful or ornamental. To justify a charge of neglect, one must not only point out that the matter is omitted from the curriculum, but also that it is a necessary or useful thing, that it is not obtained in other ways, that the lack of it is a loss, and that the schools are able to furnish it. I need not discuss further than I have already done the general omission of training in speech or the value of a command of the oral use of language, but it behooves me to consider these questions : whether men and women under the conditions that now prevail do get the training in speech that they need and the lack of which would be a loss, and whether the schools can furnish it. These inquiries should be limited to those that have taken at least a High School course, for it would be unfair to expect the schools to do much in this subject or any other for those that break off their attendance early. How much may be reasonably asked from the lower schools will be spoken of later.

Now what is the result of the prevailing lack of attention to oral English in the schools? Are men and women nevertheless well trained in speech? Ask your own experience and observation. Can you get on your feet when some subject in which you are interested is under discussion and give your opinion in a clear straight-forward manner without halting, stammering, repetition and various other common faults? In your classes can you answer the question of a pupil, if it calls for anything more than a mere word or two of information, in so distinct and exact words that the matter is clear to all those present? If a matter is under debate in your Faculty or Club or Church or Lodge, and you disagree with a fellow-member, can you express your opinion strongly without the fear afterward that you have failed to choose your words properly and have thus given offence where none was intended? Can you engage in a heated political or theological argument and not find yourself fairly choked with the words that wont come? If you can do all this you have gained the mastery of speech which I think so desirable, but which my own observation leads me to regard as an unusual accomplishment. To be sure, coolness of temper or of temperament help very much to such successful speech, but as in all other cases the perfect mastery of the weapons used and the consciousness of that mastery contribute more than any other cause to coolness in the fight. And again to put the question in a less personal form, if you are not willing to admit your dissatisfaction with your own skill, how many of your associates can speak to a question two minutes consecutively without stumbling and repeating, inserting such tags as "it seems to me," "as far as that is concerned," and similar stopgaps that give the speaker time and enable him to "hold the wire" while his mind and memory search for the elusive word or phrase? I do not refer here to cases of lack of knowledge or to persons who try to express an opinion without having a clear one. The remedy in such cases is to be sought elsewhere than in language-study.

Or take the case of those whose formal education is not yet finished, but have got beyond the grade where attention is given to training in English, the higher classes of the undergraduate students. How many of these regularly give answers that express exactly what the speaker intends to express so plainly that no correction or comment is called for? If my own experience is normal, the pupil who does this is rare indeed. Even among graduate students, and that too, among those that have not only completed the course for the bachelor's degree but have spent some years in teaching, a satisfactory presentation of the facts found in the text-book is very rare, and a clear statement of personal opinion, where the words and the phrases of the .books give no help, is almost unknown.   I have been repeatedly imprest in conducting examinations for the higher degrees with this weakness of the candidates.   Only rarely have I met with one that seemed able to state clearly what he apparently knew. It is often the case that the answer is entirely false from the use of wrong words, but is corrected by the student himself when some one of the Committee asks "What do you mean by that"?   Of course the student is under a great strain in such a case and we cannot expect the same skill in choosing words and phrases that one may possibly have at command under less trying circumstances, but as I said before, a conscious mastery of speech is the strongest help to coolness and freedom from nervousness when one is called on to use speech.

If I am right in my statement of conditions in the cases named, I need not enlarge on the state of things among the younger and the uneducated.   We find here naturally the same faults in a greater degree with the addition of gross faults in pronunciation and grammar.   I do not propose to discuss these latter, for they are matters that belong quite as much to reading and writing as to speech, and I have good reason to think that in the teaching of these the schools are already doing all that can reasonably be asked in the effort to correct them.

But what is the remedy?   There is no obligation resting on him who points out a fault to devise a means of curing it, except the general one that rests on all alike to do all that can be done to make the world better in all ways possible, but when any one comes along with denunciations of present conditions in politics or ethics or social usages, we

at once call on him to give us his prescription for a cure.
We assume, it would seem, that an honest man who sees an
evil, or thinks he sees one, will feel it a duty to find a cure,
if possible. I do not claim to be the only one to discover
the evils of which I have been speaking, and I am probably
not the only one who has in mind a plan for removing or
lessening them. But the complaints in general seem to be
directed against the faults and weaknesses of students in
writing English rather than in speaking it, and the cure proposed is of course more training in writing. Complaints of
this kind are so frequent that they seem to have no effect : if
you have not heard enough to satisfy you, read the address
of President Hart before this Association some ten years ago,
in which he sets forth the results of his observation of his
own students. The cure proposed, again, will no doubt be
effective, if only time enough can be found for it. But I am
dealing here with oral use of English, which, as I have
already pointed out, can be made satisfactory only by the
exercise on the part of the student of other mental faculties,
and thru the use by the teacher of other methods of instruction, tho as I have said training in writing is indirectly
very helpful.

In devising any plan for a cure, the first step should be a
correct diagnosis of the disease. I have given you a partial
list of symptoms already ; what is the ailment from which
these symptoms arise? Or, to drop the metaphor, what
faults in knowledge or training lie behind the faults in the
use of speech? Faults in knowledge and training, I say, for
it is these alone that we can hope to make good ; where the
defect springs from some mental peculiarity, as it does in
some cases, the question becomes one for the psychologist or
the pathologist, not for the schools in their general work.

The commonest fault, as you may easily observe, is the
lack of a stock of words so thoroly at command that one can

use them at once. Certain words of our speech become by
constant use so entirely our own, that we never hesitate in
using them: such are the pronouns, many of the prepositions
and conjunctions, verbs and nouns that deal with ordinary
actions and objects, etc. But less usual words, though we
know them well enough, are not at hand when we want them.
This is shown most often and most strongly in the use of
adjectives. Very few have enough of these at hand to give
an appropriate epithet when one is needed, or to employ the
more striking and forcible one instead of a weak and colorless word. The consequences are hesitation while the
memory strives to get hold of the elusive vocable, repetition,
mannerisms, and all the other resorts of the untrained
speaker. In the case of younger persons or of the uneducated this lack of words generally results in the habit of
making certain words or phrases do duty for a great variety
of meanings. A working man ruins a piece of work thru
ignorance or carelessness or haste or mere stupidity, possibly
thru malice outright: what epithet does the foreman use in
censuring him ? There are nine chances to one that he calls
the offender a " damn fool." What is more, it is very probable that the workman will express his anger at the censure
he has received by applying the same epithet to the foreman.
Whether there was folly or not in the action of either, and
whether the profane adjective used properly describes the folly,
does not matter ; the phrase was ready from long habit and
there was no other more appropriate one at hand. In other
circles the same fault shows itself in slang and kindred usage.
To the school-boy all sorts of things are " fierce " or " bum "
or "stunning," while his classmate of the other sex finds
all things in heaven or earth perfectly " lovely " or "horrid."
The reason in both cases is the same as that of the working-
man's profane epithet, a defective stock of words, not mere
silliness as is often supposed. The lack-a-daisical girl would

not describe as perfectly lovely the youth of her latest fancy, or a favorite poem or play, or her friend's new hat, or a box of gum-drops, if she had equally at command more suitable terms of description. As she grows older and her stock of words increases the favorite expressions are disused or restricted to their proper meaning.

A second fault, often associated with the first, is inexactness in the use of words, due to ignorance of their meaning and connotation. This fault is not more marked, perhaps, in the young and the untrained than in others that have a wider range of words, and it springs quite as often from carelessness as from ignorance. It is a fault of written speech also, and it is in more training in writing and in personal efforts for improvement rather than in oral practice that we must seek a cure. It is a besetting sin of extemporaneous preachers and political and social haranguers; in ordinary talk it may be looked for in the mouths of those that try to use a loftier style than they have mastered. Perhaps little harm comes from the talk of such persons, but real loss springs from the habit in other cases. Its results are seen in the continual disputes that come up in business about agreements and promises, where men have different impressions because they attach different meanings to the language used. Even when special care is taken with the wording, as in the statutes, ambiguities are frequent. The courts are often called on to construe a law, a thing, it would seem, that every man bound to obey the law ought to be able to do for himself. Take almost any bill introduced in the legislature and compare it with the finished draft as reported from committee and note the changes made to make it mean what its author supposed it to mean when he submitted it. The direction to put only the address on the front of the U. S. postal card has been changed three or four times to make it say what it ought to say. Now the English language is not so defective that it cannot express ideas, but the users of it are not trained to use it rightly. The instances I have just cited illustrate inexactness in writing it, to be sure, but, as may be expected, inexactness in speaking it is even more frequent and springs from the same causes, ignorance and carelessness. A partial remedy may be found in the lessening of ignorance by more training, but the remedy for carelessness in speech is the same as for carelessness in any other matter. Much can be done in the early training of the child at home and in school to prevent the formation of such a habit, but the adult can find the cure only in his own personal effort.

Of other prevalent faults in speech I need not speak at length. Mispronunciations, grammatical faults and the like are the result of ignorance and are to be cured by instruction with plenty of practice to rub it in. They are exactly analogous to errors in spelling, punctuation, capitalizing, etc., and must be dealt with in the same way. Slovenly utterance and similar habits are the results of faulty training at an early age ; I shall have something to say in regard to their avoidance later ; meanwhile for the adult who finds himself the victim of such a habit I have only one suggestion to make, to wit, that it must be treated like any other bad habit.

After this preliminary description of the trouble, you need hardly be told that the cure must be sought in more practice. Oral practice alone will give the power to speak, just as practice in writing gives skill to write. But if this were all I have to say, it would not be worth while to take so much time as I have already used to talk of unsatisfactory conditions, only to end with so vague a recommendation. That practice in talking is valuable and desirable, you would probably have admitted at the beginning. The troublesome question is how to give it. The present demands on the schools are so many that the curriculum is already overloaded, and it seems impossible to think of adding to the work anything that will call for the expenditure of more time. I have not forgotten this in thinking of the subject, which is by no means a new one to me, but has been before me for many years. I shall offer some suggestions therefore, not as a panacea but only as a palliative. They will not work an entire change at once, even if faithfully followed, and I have no hope that they will be at once accepted and put into practice. A satisfactory command of the mother-tongue will become general, if it ever does become so, only in the way in which all other improvements come, by gradual progress, a slow advance to which each generation adds its portion. But the suggestions are the result of much thought, their value in some cases has been proved by experience, and I ask your careful attention to them. They contain the ideas that I am especially desirous of putting before you and for the sake of which all that I have said thus far has been presented. You may be inclined to say with Chaucer's Friar, "This is a long preamble of a tale," but the tale itself, as in the case of the wife of Bath, will, I hope, be shorter.

I give my suggestions in the order of instruction, for the three periods already spoken of.

For the first period, during which the child's instruction is in the hands of parents and kinsmen, it is plain that little can be done directly by others. We can look to the habits of our own children, of course, and I assume that we who are present feel the importance of doing so and are doing our duty to them, but we must leave to other parents the task of training theirs. But we need not forget that the pupils whom we are now influencing are to be the parents of the next generation, and that any gain they make will not be lost to the general cause.

In the second period, during which the child is brought
under the influence of the teacher, there is work for the
schools and work of the highest importance. It is at this
time that certain habits are definitely formed, which help
greatly in shaping the speech of the adult, and tho no one
perhaps of those present is engaged in teaching in schools of
this grade, I trust that there is enough interest in teaching in
general to warrant me in dealing somewhat fully with this
stage of language study.

The child's entrance into school is an important epoch in
his life for many reasons, but in his acquirement of language
it is peculiar. Up to this time his speech has been under
the direction of parents and other associates only, now, still
keeping these first teachers, he adds new ones. Hitherto he
has dealt only with the spoken tongue, he now adds the study
of the printed symbols and a little later of the written ones.
To a great extent his language thus far has been acquired by
instinct, by the impulse to imitation, as birds learn to fly,
now he begins to make conscious efforts to learn. As yet he
has had little if any help in the way of correction of faults,
now begins the effort on the part of his new teachers to set
him right wherever he is in error from faulty habit. He
learns now for the first time that there is a right and a wrong
in speech as in other things.

It is during this period, moreover, that mental and physical
development are most marked. The pupil begins it a child,
at its end he may be considered an adult, since logical sense,
conscience, and the physical powers that distinguish the adult
have now been acquired; further growth only strengthens
them. This period therefore furnishes the best opportunity
for the formation of the habits of speech. At this time if at
all, the faults of earlier training must be amended, at this
time physical faults, stammering and the like must be cured,
at this time habits of slang, profanity, obscenity, etc., are

generally formed, and it is at this time, accordingly, that special pains should be taken to prevent them.

Training in language forms a large part of the schooling of this period, but the new branch of language study, reading and writing, takes up nearly all the time and must continue to do so as long as our absurd conservatism succeeds in keeping our English methods of misrepresenting our speech to the eye. In view of the strong protests that have been put forth of late years against the faulty writing of advanced students, it is out of the question to think of giving less time to this work, and even from the point of view of one who is urging more attention to oral work, it would be unwise to do so, for the written work is the most helpful of all the work of the period in training in speech. It could not be spared, even if it were not called for as a discipline of great value and an indispensable equipment for modern life.

What I suggest for this period is ;—

First, voice-training. Not what is usually meant by the phrase, which suggests training in declamation or singing, but the cultivation of the habit of clear utterance, proper pitch and pleasing tone. We think it worth while to give instruction, either in school or out of it, in a large number of matters that are supposed to make the learner more attractive to his fellows or more useful to society, and refer to them as accomplishments. Why should not some attention be given to the cultivation of the speaking voice to youth not destined for the stage or the concert hall? A well-modulated, musical utterance, you will all admit, is one of the greatest attractions in either man or woman, and as conversation is to be a part of the life-employment of every pupil, it is surely a wise plan to give some attention to training him to do this work in a pleasing manner. In urging this, please take notice that I do not propose to add a new study to those already pursued; I only wish to impress on the minds of those who have charge of pupils at this stage of their training the importance of the matter, and to induce them to give to it in their daily work the same attention that is now given to emphasis, inflection and the like in the reading lesson.

Second ;—the beginning of the habit of speaking. Do not laugh ; I am well aware that children, especially in America, are charged with the habit of talking far too much, when a little golden silence would better befit their age, but that is not the habit which I desire to have cultivated. It is at times the part of the child to speak and of others to listen, and this duty, which will remain with him all his life, will be better done if he is made to realize that it is a duty and that he ought to look on it as on other duties and use effort to do it as well as possible. Declamation will be of use here, if properly directed, but not the kind that once prevailed in the schools, and probably still prevails, the oratory of the School Speaker, declaimed in wild tones to the accompaniment of wilder gestures. What is needed is the skill to say a simple thing in a clear and simple way, the skill that will be called for in later life from all men and women, not that in which we expect professional speakers to be expert. Now no better opportunity for gaining this can be found than in ordinary recitations and other talk of the school-room. Let the teacher impress on the pupil the fact that his task is not only to master the facts of his lesson, but also to state those facts in the best way possible. Let it be understood that a satisfactory recitation calls not only for a knowledge of the facts, but also for a clear statement of those facts to others. And right here I wish to quote from an authority that at one time was an oracle in such things, and even now will be recognized as deserving of a hearing. I happened on it after I had begun my notes for this address. It is found in Boswell's Life of Johnson. Among other plans for obtaining a livelihood, Johnson at one time thought of starting a private school and drew up a "Scheme for the Classes of a Grammar School." His scheme ends with these words :

"The greatest and most necessary task still remains, to obtain a habit of expression, without which knowledge is of little use. This is necessary in Latin, and more necessary in English ; and can only be acquired by a daily imitation of the best and correctest authors."

In this statement Johnson had in mind expression in writing, but it applies equally well to oral expression, for this too can be acquired only by the imitation of the best models, and my plea is for effort on the part of the teacher to keep the best models before the pupil, to teach him the importance of expression, and to insist that he take pains to follow the models put before him. As I said before, it is sometimes the duty of a child to talk, and one of the occasions when it becomes his duty is when he is called on to recite. The teacher, whether aware of the fact or not, is training him in his mother-tongue, for it is by practice that we all gain mastery in speech as in other crafts. If care is not taken to correct faults and furnish good models, the recitation is a training in faulty speech, whether with the knowledge and consent of the teacher or otherwise.

The third stage of language training may be said to comprise the rest of life. For the great majority this, like the earliest training, is unconscious and due to the influence of one's fellows, in some cases it is also the result of effort on the part of the individual himself. Only a few find further instruction in the High School and still fewer in the College. It is only these few that can be directly influenced by the teacher, but as in other matters this influence reaches the great mass in time. It is with reference to this period that I make a more direct and personal appeal to the teachers present, especially to those whose work includes the earlier part which for convenience I have termed the High School period. To this belongs the chief part of the training in written composition, except for those that have journalism or other literary production in view and take special courses in College. But training in oral speech usually ceases or becomes subordinate and incidental. Yet just here certain phases of it must be developed, if at all.

If the work has been properly done up to the entrance into the High School, a pupil should bring with him a habit of clear utterance, speech freed from the grosser errors of grammar and a fairly good vocabulary of the words of common life. The task of the High School should be to continue the correction of faults, to enlarge his vocabulary, to give enough rhetorical training to enable him to steer clear of the more common errors of style, to cultivate a taste for reading, and to give the practice that will bring a fair fluency in correct speech. Increase of vocabulary comes of itself in the course of his studies, and rhetorical training and study of literature are specifically provided in the curriculum ; it is of the last kind of training named that I wish to treat here.

Ready and fluent speech, without question, has proved an injury to many, leading them to depend on words rather than knowledge. We have all seen it in the pulpit, in the halls of legislation, on the platform, and elsewhere. But the same is true of other qualities. A lawyer may secure an unjust verdict from a jury by his wit and sarcasm, yet a command of these means of influence is certainly desirable and useful. Many a teacher has gained reputation by his management of pupils, his skill in keeping order, his quickness, tho wretchedly deficient in the most important thing, knowledge of his subject. Yet skill in teaching, even if it does sometimes serve the purpose of hiding ignorance, is not to be condemned or despised, and the same is true of skill in the use of speech, tho it may be used to secure ends that should be sought by other means. It should not be over-looked, again, that the influence of these things is due no more to their possession by one party than to their lack by others. The wit and funny stories of a stump speaker would not win him votes if his opponent were his match in the same. So, too, fluent speech would not give reputation and influence if it were not unusual. General training in the use of language would therefore reduce the prestige and power of the merely "tonguey" speaker, by taking away his peculiar advantage and giving to solid argument its proper weight. In the famous Battle of the Books, Bentley's learning has given him the verdict of posterity, but it was his command of a sarcastic wit that put him on a par with his opponents and gained a hearing for his writings. In fact but for a consciousness of this power, it is not probable that he would have ventured to cross swords with the wits of the day.

But with the present clamor for instruction in esthetics, manual training and all else under heaven, how are High Schools to find time for instruction in oral use of speech? This question I shall try to answer, and it is this answer that I consider the most important part of this address, and to which I call special attention. Some of you are in a position to aid directly and all can help thru influence on others.

First: All recitations in any subject are practice in speech. Let them be made practice in good English rather than bad, by the teacher's refusal to be content with any statement from a pupil that is not correct in form as well as in substance. I have already urged this in the case of the lower schools: it is still more important in the High School, since the pupil has now reached a stage at which he can make use of his knowledge of what is good or bad in speech to correct his faults and follow right models. He need not be simply told to replace one form of expression by another on the authority of the teacher : there is now a chance to appeal to the principles that he has learned and to give a reason for correction. It is probable, moreover, that by this time his own personal interest in his habits of speech has been aroused and that we can count on his coöperation.

Second : in the study of foreign tongues, ancient or modern, there is the best opportunity of all for the training I am urging. Translation is oral composition ; the ideas are furnished in the text used and the pupil's task is to express those ideas in English. But it is in the language classes, if my own observation is correct, that English is most sinned against. I have held for many years that the strongest argument for the study of the classics is the old one, that they help to the knowledge of the mother-tongue. But the help they give is not in the grammar, or in the rhetorical or literary models which they were once thought to furnish to the exclusion of all rivals. It is in the practice in English, which is furnished by the daily translation, and this same practice loses its value or even becomes a positive harm, if wrongly used. The pupil who translates is practising English composition and practice fixes habit. It is just as easy to form a bad habit as a good one, and much of the translation work of school and college is doing just this. The injury would no doubt be much greater than it is but for the fortunate circumstance that the other and older practice, which still goes on at home and on the playground serves as a valuable antidote. Foreign idioms find no place there, and the homely speech that prevails is like the fresh air of out-of-doors after the confinement of the school-room. It puts new life into speech, and prevents the loss of health and vigor that would otherwise follow. But after all it is better to have fresh air in the school-house also, if possible, and it is better to have fresh, sound English in the class as well as outside.

I can bear witness from personal experience that it calls for very little effort to secure clear and idiomatic English in translation, if the class is assured from the beginning that no other will pass current without discount. It is a strange anomaly when a teacher of Latin refuses to accept "veni videre" as the equivalent of the English "I have come to see," but will allow the pupil to render "veni ut videam" by "I have come that I may see." Neither rendering is absolutely impossible, but each is rare and unidiomatic, and one is quite as much to be shunned as the other. If we can imagine such a change as would put a class of young Romans in a school studying English, they would be carefully trained, I suppose, to put their Latin sentences into good English, but allowed to say "veni videre" and the like, when they rendered English into Latin.

That I am not setting up a man of straw will be attested, I am sure, by many of you. Complaints of college teachers that their pupils have no command of expression are loud and long, and tho many years of experience in teaching have prepared me to expect almost anything, I am frequently surprised in my classes in Old and Middle English at the wild idioms that my pupils offer as an equivalent for the language of Alfred or Chaucer. Yet they are nearly all graduates and probably three-fourths of them have been teachers of English! Such a complaint in the case of persons of a liberal education and mature mind should be unknown. It is surely not an unreasonable requirement from a candidate for admission to college that he shall be able to speak and write his native language readily and correctly, and if in the earlier work of the lower schools proper attention is given to the matter, there will rarely be cause for complaint. The occasional cases of failure, the pupils who in spite of all their training still remain uncouth and awkward in speech, may be classed with those that fail in any other

5

branch, and the cause will be found to be the same, either a peculiar mental defect or a disinclination to do the work needed to master a subject not attractive to the person concerned. The colleges should enforce this requirement rigorously. If it does not seem advisable to exclude all that cannot pass the test, special classes should be formed for them and they should not be admitted to the regular courses for a degree until they have removed the disability. This is the only way to reach the preparatory schools where the training should be given. These schools, you may be sure, under the present pressure of other demands, will not give proper training in language, as long as their graduates are freely admitted to college without it.

If then candidates for admission to college possess a mastery of English such as I have tried to specify, what work of this character is left for the college course? Manifestly only special and voluntary work, as in the case of other subjects. But every teacher should insist on the use of good English in his classes and thus continue the practice already begun, confirming good habits and helping to root out bad ones, if any still survive, and it will be a long time before the use of the language is universally so correct that there is no danger of one's learning anything faulty. Formal courses in both writing and speaking may be provided for those that have in view the professions that call for special training in these subjects, literary work, journalism, preaching, lecturing, etc. In a word, the work may be put on the same basis as the work in other subjects. But here, as in the lower grades, the greatest opportunity is offered to the teachers of languages. By virtue of the subject, they have a special means of influencing those under their instruction. If a teacher of an advanced class in German makes use of that language in conducting his class, he does so because the teaching is made more effective thereby, and the use of English as the language of the recitation is in the same way a teaching of English. The teacher has no option ; his only choice is between good English and bad, and he should therefore make it a matter of conscience. But it ought to be added that at this stage the correction of faults and the gain of readiness in speech depend mainly on individual attention and effort, as will also be the case after the student days are over. The teacher's influence will be most valuable in showing that he sets a high value on such training, and thus leading the pupil to a proper estimate of it and to personal effort to obtain it.

Now why do I consider this branch of training so important ? Not from any theory of its superiority in mental training and not from an exaggerated estimate of its worth as an accomplishment. Its value in both these ways is unchallenged, but it does not in my opinion give any more help in making either the sage or the gentleman than many other subjects of study. I lay special stress on its worth and advocate it for purely practical reasons. There is a wide difference of opinion as to what branches are practical, but there is little dispute of the dictum that those that are so ought to be given the preference in our courses of study. Opposition to any particular subject is more often based on charges that it is of no practical value, than on any other cause, and the most frequent and as I think the most legitimate argument for the addition of any new study to the course is the proof that it will be of practical value in life.

But anything that increases mental alertness and trains the reason is valuable, and in the broader sense all studies are practical. If we must distinguish any studies as practical in the narrower meaning of the word, it will certainly be those things that one is to do after he leaves school, the branches of activity by which he secures a livelihood. Accepting this definition, we may maintain that for different persons different subjects will prove practical : commercial training for the business man, manual training for the craftsman, science for the scientist, and so on to the end of the list. If any one subject is more practical than another, it must be because it is likely to be used by more persons than the other, and this is the reason for giving to the three R's and related subjects the leading place in the elementary work of the school. The pupil is likely to make use of them later, no matter what work he takes up to earn his living.

Now talking is something that one is likely to do all his life long and it is surely practical to make preparation to do it well. We cannot avoid some preparation for it; we begin practice at a very early age and we keep it up all our lives, but the result of this constant practice under unqualified teachers and with false models before us is that we are very far from doing it well. This address is an appeal to all teachers and others to whom falls the task of correcting the faults of earlier training and furnishing better models, or the opportunity of influencing public opinion and shaping the character of public instruction, to give to pupils faulty in speech the same special attention that they give to other faults, to teach correct language as they teach correct behavior, to use all means to cultivate readiness in speech as they try to cultivate facility in reading or in arithmetical operations, or in any other work in which expertness is desirable. I am not so foolish as to suppose that a satisfactory condition in the use of speech can be gained at once, even if all those who are in a position to promote it give their best efforts to that end; such a condition must grow up slowly in the same way that improvements in social conditions or in morals come. We can do something, nevertheless, in the way I have suggested, and if we do our part, some future age will be able to say of us "other men labored and ye have entered into their labors."

The suggestions that I have made in this address are not intended to be regarded as the only ways in which the mastery of oral use of language may be promoted. They are only a part of the methods which I should like to see put to a practical test by use, and which I should have treated at length if time were sufficient. One other in particular, which has been used in one school to my knowledge, oral composition as a supplement to written work, interests me greatly, but I can give no facts to show how much it can be made to contribute to the facility in speech which it is intended to secure. I have also said nothing of various other ways of help that I might suggest, but have limited myself to methods that may be used without adding subjects to the curriculum and drawing on the pupil's time, already subject to so many demands.

Is it something visionary, or a thing for which we may reasonably hope, if we look forward to the time when every educated man whose mother-tongue is English will be not only a source of intellectual inspiration to others but also a " well of English undefiled " ?

CONSTITUTION OF THE MODERN LANGUAGE ASSOCIATION OF AMERICA.

ADOPTED ON THE TWENTY-NINTH OF DECEMBER, 1903.

I.

The name of this Society shall be *The Modern Language Association of America*.

II.

1. The object of this Association shall be the advancement of the study of the Modern Languages and their Literatures through the promotion of friendly relations among scholars, through the publication of the results of investigations by members, and through the presentation and discussion of papers at an annual meeting.

2. The meeting of the Association shall be held at such place and time as the Executive Council shall from year to year determine. But at least as often as once in four years there shall be held a Union Meeting, for which some central point in the interior of the country shall be chosen.

III.

Any person whose candidacy has been approved by the Secretary and Treasurer may become a member on the payment of three dollars, and may continue a member by the payment of the same amount each year. Any member, or any person eligible to membership, may become a life member by a single payment of forty dollars or by the payment of fifteen dollars a year for three successive years. Distinguished foreign scholars may be elected to honorary membership by the Association on nomination by the Executive Council.

IV.

1. The officers and governing boards of the Association shall be: a President, three Vice-Presidents, a Secretary, a Treasurer; an Executive Council consisting of these six officers, the Chairmen of the several Divisions, and seven other members; and an Editorial Committee consisting of the Secretary of the Association (who shall be Chairman *ex officio*), the Secretaries of the several Divisions, and two other members.

2. The President and the Vice-Presidents shall be elected by the Association, to hold office for one year.

3. The Chairmen and Secretaries of Divisions shall be chosen by the respective Divisions.

4. The other officers shall be elected by the Association at a Union Meeting, to hold office until the next Union Meeting. Vacancies occurring between two Union Meetings shall be filled by the Executive Council.

V.

1. The President, Vice-Presidents, Secretary, and Treasurer shall perform the usual duties of such officers. The Secretary shall, furthermore, have charge of the Publications of the Association and the preparation of the program of the annual meeting.

2. The Executive Council shall perform the duties assigned to it in Articles II, III, IV, VII, and VIII; it shall, moreover, determine such questions of policy as may be referred to it by the Association and such as may arise in the course of the year and call for immediate decision.

3. The Editorial Committee shall render such assistance as the Secretary may need in editing the Publications of the Association and preparing the annual program.

VI.

1. The Association may, to further investigation in any special branch of Modern Language study, create a Section devoted to that end.

2. The officers of a Section shall be a Chairman and a Secretary, elected annually by the Association. They shall form a standing committee of the Association, and may add to their number any other members interested in the same subject.

VII.

1. When, for geographical reasons, the members from any group of States shall find it expedient to hold a separate annual meeting, the Executive Council may arrange with these members to form a Division, with power to call a meeting at such place and time as the members of the Division shall select; but no Division meeting shall be held during the year in which the Association holds a Union Meeting. The expense of Division meetings shall be borne by the Association. The total number of Divisions shall not at any time exceed three. The present Division is hereby continued.

2. The members of a Division shall pay their dues to the Treasurer of the Association, and shall enjoy the same rights and privileges and be subject to the same conditions as other members of the Association.

3. The officers of a Division shall be a Chairman and a Secretary. The Division shall, moreover, have power to create such committees as may be needed for its own business. The program of the Division meeting shall be prepared

by the Secretary of the Division in consultation with the Secretary of the Association.

VIII.

This Constitution may be amended by a two-thirds vote at any Union Meeting, provided the proposed amendment has received the approval of two-thirds of the members of the Executive Council.

MEMBERS OF THE MODERN LANGUAGE ASSOCIATION OF AMERICA

INCLUDING MEMBERS OF THE CENTRAL DIVISION OF THE ASSOCIATION.

Adams, Arthur, Assistant Professor of English, Trinity College, Hartford, Conn.

Adams, Edward Larrabee, Instructor in French and Spanish, University of Michigan, Ann Arbor, Mich. [644 S. Ingalls St.]

Adams, Warren Austin, Professor of German, Dartmouth College, Hanover, N. H.

Alden, Raymond Macdonald, Assistant Professor of English Literature and Rhetoric, Leland Stanford Jr. University, Palo Alto, Cal.

Alder, Eugene Charles, Senior Master of German, William Penn Charter School, Philadelphia, Pa. [The Greystone, 125 School Lane, Germantown, Pa.]

Allen, Edward A., Professor of the English Language and Literature, University of Missouri, Columbia, Mo.

Allen, Philip Schuyler, Assistant Professor of German Literature, University of Chicago, Chicago, Ill. [6132 Kimbark Ave.]

Almstedt, Hermann, Professor of Germanic Languages, University of Missouri, Columbia, Mo.

Armstrong, Edward C., Associate Professor of French, Johns Hopkins University, Baltimore, Md.

Armstrong, Joseph L., Professor of English, Randolph-Macon Woman's College, Lynchburg, Va. [College Park, Va.]

Arrowsmith, Robert, American Book Co., New York, N. Y. [Washington Square.]

Aviragnet, Elysée, Professor of Romance Languages, Bucknell University, Lewisburg, Pa.

Ayer, Charles Carlton, Professor of Romance Languages, University of Colorado, Boulder, Col.

Babbitt, Irving, Assistant Professor of French, Harvard University, Cambridge, Mass. [6 Kirkland Road.]

Babcock, Earle Brownell, Chicago, Ill. [307 E. 56th St.]

Bacon, Edwin Faxon, Teacher of French and German, State Normal School, Oneonta, N. Y. [52 Cedar St.]

Bagster-Collins, Elijah William, Adjunct Professor of German, Teachers' College, Columbia University, New York, N. Y.

Baillot, E. P., Professor of Romance Languages, Northwestern University, • Evanston, Ill. [718 Emerson St.]

Baker, Asa George, G. & C. Merriam Co., Publishers of Webster's Dictionaries, Springfield, Mass. [499 Main St.]

Baker, Franklin Thomas, Professor of English, Teachers' College, Columbia University, New York, N. Y.

Baker, George Merrick, Instructor in German, Yale University, New Haven, Conn. [591 Orange St.]

Baker, George Pierce, Professor of English, Harvard University, Cambridge, Mass. [195 Brattle St.]

Baker, Harry Torsey, Instructor in English Literature and German, Beloit College, Beloit, Wis. [999 Church St.]

Baker, Thomas Stockham, Professor of German, Jacob Tome Institute, Port Deposit, Md.

Baldwin, Charles Sears, Assistant Professor of Rhetoric, Yale University, New Haven, Conn.

Baldwin, Edward Chauncey, Assistant Professor of English Literature, University of Illinois, Urbana, Ill. [704 W. Oregon St.]

Bargy, Henry, Instructor in the Romance Languages and Literatures, Columbia University, New York, N. Y.

Barnes, Frank Coe, Adjunct Professor of Modern Languages, Union College, Schenectady, N. Y.

Bartlett, Mrs. D. L., Baltimore, Md. [16 W. Monument St.]

Bartlett, George Alonzo, Associate Professor of German (retired), Harvard University, Cambridge, Mass. [48 Ware Hall.]

Bassett, Ralph Emerson, Associate Professor of Romance Languages, University of Kansas, Lawrence, Kas.

Batt, Max, Professor of Modern Languages, North Dakota Agricultural College, Fargo, N. D.

Battin, Benjamin F., Professor of German, Swarthmore College, Swarthmore, Pa.

Baur, William F., Instructor in German, University of Cincinnati, Cincinnati, O.

Beam, Jacob, Instructor in German, Princeton University, Princeton, N. J.

Beatley, James A., Master (German and Music), English High School, Boston, Mass. [11 Wabon St., Roxbury, Mass.]

de Beaumont, Victor, Instructor in the Romance Languages, Williams College, Williamstown, Mass.

Becker, Ernest Julius, Instructor in English and German, Baltimore City College, Baltimore, Md.

Belden, Henry Marvin, Assistant Professor of English, University of Missouri, Columbia, Mo.

Bell, Robert Mowry, Instructor in German, Clark University, Worcester, Mass.

Berdan, John Milton, Instructor in Rhetoric, Yale University, New Haven, Conn.

Berkeley, Frances Campbell, Instructor in English, University of Wisconsin, Madison, Wis. [616 Lake St.]

Bernkopf, Anna Elise, Instructor in German, Vassar College, Poughkeepsie, N. Y.

Bernkopf, Margarete, Instructor in German, Smith College, Northampton, Mass.

Béthune, Baron de, Louvain, Belgium. [57 rue de la Station.]

Bevier, Louis, Jr., Professor of the Greek Language and Literature, Rutgers College, New Brunswick, N. J.

Béziat de Bordes, A., Assistant Professor of Romance Languages, University of Michigan, Ann Arbor, Mich.

Bierwirth, Heinrich Conrad, Assistant Professor of German, Harvard University, Cambridge, Mass. [15 Avon St.]

Bigelow, John, Jr., Professor of French and Head of the Department of Modern Languages, Massachusetts Institute of Technology, Boston, Mass.

Bigelow, William Pingry, Associate Professor of German and Music, Amherst College, Amherst, Mass.

Bishop, David Horace, Professor of English, University of Mississippi, University, Miss.

Blackburn, Francis Adelbert, Associate Professor of the English Language, University of Chicago, Chicago, Ill. [383 E. 56th St.]

Blackwell, Robert Emory, President and Professor of English, Randolph-Macon College, Ashland, Va.

Blair, Emma Helen, Historical Editor, State Historical Library, Madison, Wis.

Blaisdell, Daisy Luana, Instructor in German, University of Illinois, Urbana, Ill. [912 W. California Ave.]

Blake, Mrs. Estelle M., Instructor in English and Modern Languages, University of Arkansas, Fayetteville, Ark. [616 Ide Ave.]

Blanchard, Frederic T., Assistant in Rhetoric, Yale University, New Haven, Conn. [633 East Divinity Hall.]

Blau, Max F., Assistant Professor of German, Princeton University, Princeton, N. J.

Bleyer, Willard Grosvenor, Assistant Professor of English, University of Wisconsin, Madison, Wis. [625 Langdon St.]

Bloombergh, A. A., Professor of Modern Languages, Lafayette College, Easton, Pa.

Bohn, William Edward, Instructor in Rhetoric, University of Michigan, Ann Arbor, Mich.

Boll, Helene Hubertine, Instructor in German, Hillhouse High School, New Haven, Conn.

Borgerhoff, J. L., Instructor in Romance Languages, Western Reserve University, Cleveland, O.

Both-Hendriksen, Louise, Professor of the History of Arts and Lecturer in - Literature, Adelphi College, Brooklyn, N. Y. [150 Lefferts Place.]

Bothne, Gisle C. J., Professor of Greek and Norwegian, Norwegian Luther College, Decorah, Ia.

Boucke, Ewald A., Assistant Professor of German, University of Michigan, Ann Arbor, Mich. [808 S. State St.]

Bourland, Benjamin Parsons, Professor of the Romance Languages, Western Reserve University, Cleveland, O. [11170 Euclid Ave.]

Bowen, Benjamin Lester, Professor of Romance Languages, Ohio State University, Columbus, O.

Bowen, Edwin W., Professor of Latin, Randolph-Macon College, Ashland, Va.

Bowen, James Vance, Professor of Foreign Languages, Mississippi Agricultural and Mechanical College, Agricultural College, Miss.

Boysen, Johannes Lassen, Assistant Professor of German, Syracuse University, Syracuse, N. Y. [714 Beach St.]

Bradshaw, S. Ernest, Professor of Modern Languages, Furman University, Greenville, S. C.

Bradsher, Earl L., Assistant in English, University of Missouri, Columbia, Mo.

Brandon, Edgar Ewing, Professor of Romanic Languages and Literatures, Miami University, Oxford, O.

Brandt, Hermann Carl Georg, Professor of the German Language and Literature, Hamilton College, Clinton, N. Y.

Brecht, Vincent B., Professor of the English Language and Literature, Northeast Manual Training High School, Lehigh Ave. and 8th St., Philadelphia, Pa.

Brédé, Charles F., Instructor in German, Northeast Manual Training High School, Lehigh Ave. and 8th St., Philadelphia, Pa.. [4126 Chester Ave.]

Brickner, Edwin S., Instructor in English, College of the City of New York, New York, N. Y.

Briggs, Fletcher, Instructor in German, Harvard University, Cambridge, Mass. [10 Perkins Hall.]

Briggs, Thomas H., Jr., Instructor in English, Eastern Illinois Normal School, Charleston, Ill.

Briggs, William Dinsmore, Instructor in English, Western Reserve University, Cleveland, O. [11170 Euclid Ave.]

Bright, James Wilson, Professor of English Philology, Johns Hopkins University, Baltimore, Md.

Bristol, Edward N., Henry Holt & Co., New York, N. Y. [29 West 23d St.]

Bronk, Isabelle, Professor of the French Language and Literature, Swarthmore College, Swarthmore, Pa.

Bronson, Mrs. Elsie Straffin, Providence, R. I. [232 Brown St.]

Bronson, Thomas Bertrand, Head of the Modern Language Department, Lawrenceville School, Lawrenceville, N. J.

Bronson, Walter C., Professor of English Literature, Brown University, Providence, R. I.

Brooks, Maro Spalding, Head of Modern Language Department, Brookline High School, Brookline, Mass. [25 Waverly St.]

Brooks, Neil C., Assistant Professor of German, University of Illinois, Urbana, Ill.

Brown, Arthur C. L., Professor of English Literature, Northwestern University, Evanston, Ill. [1741 Hinman Ave.]

Brown, Calvin S., Assistant Professor of Modern Languages, University of Mississippi, Oxford, Miss. [University, Miss.]

Brown, Carleton F., Associate in English Philology, Bryn Mawr College, Bryn Mawr, Pa.

Brown, Edward Miles, Professor of the English Language and Literature, University of Cincinnati, Cincinnati, O. [The Auburn Hotel.]

Brown, Frank Clyde, Associate Professor of English, Emory College, Oxford, Ga.

Brown, Frederic Willis, Instructor in French, Collegiate Department, Clark University, Worcester, Mass.

Brownell, George Griffin, Professor of Romance Languages, University of Alabama, University, Ala.

Bruce, James Douglas, Professor of the English Language and Literature, University of Tennessee, Knoxville, Tenn.

Brugnot, Mrs. Alice Gabrielle Twight, Instructor in French, University School for Girls, Chicago, Ill. [22 Lake Shore Drive.]

Brumbaugh, Martin Grove, Professor of Pedagogy, University of Pennsylvania, Philadelphia, Pa. [3224 Walnut St.]

Brun, Alphonse, Instructor in French, Harvard University, Cambridge, Mass. [39 Ellery St.]

Bruner, James Dowden, Professor of Romance Languages and Literatures, University of North Carolina, Chapel Hill, N. C.

Bruns, Friedrich, Fellow in German, University of Wisconsin, Madison, Wis. [623 E. Gorham St.]

Brush, Murray Peabody, Associate in Romance Languages, Johns Hopkins University, Baltimore, Md.

Brusie, Charles Frederick, Principal, Mt. Pleasant Academy, Ossining, N. Y.

Bryant, Frank E., Assistant Professor of English, University of Kansas,, Lawrence, Kas.

Buchanan, Milton Alexander, Lecturer in Italian and Spanish, University of Toronto, Toronto, Canada.

Buck, Gertrude, Associate Professor of English, Vassar College, Poughkeepsie, N. Y. [50 Montgomery St.]

Buck, Philo Meloyn, Jr., Head of the Department of English, McKinley High School, St. Louis, Mo.

Buckingham, Mary H., Boston, Mass. [96 Chestnut St.]

Buffum, Douglas Labaree, Preceptor in Modern Languages, Princeton University, Princeton, N. J. [151 Little Hall.]

Bullinger, Howard Valentine, Instructor in English, Phillips Academy, Andover, Mass. [Phillips Inn.]

Burkhard, Oscar C., Instructor in German, University of Minnesota, Minneapolis, Minn.

Burnet, Percy Bentley, Director of Modern Languages, Manual Training High School, Kansas City, Mo.

Burnett, Arthur W., Henry Holt & Co., New York, N. Y. [29 West 23d St.]

Burton, Richard, Professor of English Literature, University of Minnesota, Minneapolis, Minn.

Bush, Stephen Hayes, Professor of Romance Languages, University of Iowa, Iowa City, Ia.

Busse, Paul Gustav Adolf, Instructor in German, Ohio State University, Columbus, O. [1436 Neil Ave.]

Cabeen, Charles William, Professor of Romance Languages, Syracuse University, Syracuse, N. Y.

Callaway, Morgan, Jr., Professor of English, University of Texas, Austin, Tex. [1104 Guadalupe St.]

Cameron, Arnold Guyot, Princeton, N. J.

Cameron, Susan E , Royal Victoria College, Montreal, Canada.

Campbell, Killis, Instructor in English, University of Texas, Austin, Tex. [2301 Rio Grande St.]

Campion, John L., Kiel, Germany. [370 W. 116th St., New York, N. Y.]

Canby, Henry Seidel, Instructor in English, Sheffield Scientific School, Yale University, New Haven, Conn. [77 Elm St.]

Canfield, Arthur Graves, Professor of Romance Languages, University of Michigan, Ann Arbor, Mich. [909 E. University Ave.]

Capen, Samuel Paul, Assistant Professor of Modern Languages, Collegiate Department, Clark University, Worcester, Mass.

Carnahan, David Hobart, Assistant Professor of Romance Languages, University of Illinois, Champaign, Ill.

Carpenter, Frederic Ives, Assistant Professor of English, University o Chicago, Chicago, Ill. [5533 Woodlawn Ave.]

Carpenter, George Rice, Professor of Rhetoric and English Composition, Columbia University, New York, N. Y.

Carpenter, William Henry, Professor of Germanic Philology, Columbia University, New York, N. Y.

Carr, Joseph William, Professor of Germanic Languages, University of Maine, Orono, Me.

Carruth, William Herbert, Professor of the Germanic Languages and Literatures, University of Kansas, Lawrence, Kas.

Carson, Lucy Hamilton, Professor of English, Montana State Normal College, Dillon, Mont.

Carson, Luella Clay, Professor of Rhetoric and American Literature, University of Oregon, Eugene, Ore. [289 E. 9th St.]

Carteaux, Gustave A., Professor of the French Language, Polytechnic Institute, Brooklyn, N. Y.

Carter, Charles Henry, Instructor in English, Syracuse University, Syracuse, N. Y. [1204 E. Adams St.]

Castegnier, Georges, Civilian Instructor in French, U. S. Military Academy, West Point, N. Y.

Chamberlin, Willis Arden, Professor of the German Language and Literature, Denison University, Granville, O.

Chandler, Frank Wadleigh, Professor of Literature and History, Polytechnic Institute, Brooklyn, N. Y. [22 Orange St.]

Chapman, Henry Leland, Professor of English Literature, Bowdoin College, Brunswick, Me.

Charles, Arthur M., Professor of German and French, Earlham College, Richmond, Ind.

Chase, Frank Herbert, Professor of English Literature, Beloit College, Beloit, Wis. [1005 Chapin St.]

Cheek, Samuel Robertson, Professor of Latin, Central University of Kentucky, Danville, Ky.

Cheever, Louisa Sewall, Instructor in English, Smith College, Northampton, Mass. [Chapin House.]

Chenery, Winthrop Holt, Instructor in Spanish and Italian, Washington University, St. Louis, Mo.

Child, Clarence Griffin, Assistant Professor of English, University of Pennsylvania, Philadelphia, Pa. [4237 Sansom St.]

Churchill, George Bosworth, Professor of English Literature, Amherst College, Amherst, Mass.

Clark, Clarence Carroll, Associate in English Literature, Bryn Mawr College, Bryn Mawr, Pa.

Clark, J. Scott, Professor of the English Language, Northwestern University, Evanston, Ill.

Clark, Thatcher, Instructor in Spanish and French, U. S. Naval Academy, Annapolis, Md. [Hotel Maryland.]

Clark, Thomas Arkle, Professor of Rhetoric, University of Illinois, Urbana, Ill.

Clarke, Charles Cameron, Jr., Assistant Professor of French, Sheffield Scientific School, Yale University, New Haven, Conn. [254 Bradley St.]

Clary, S. Willard, D. C. Heath & Co., Boston, Mass. [120 Boylston St.]

Coar, John Firman, Professor of the German Language and Literature, Adelphi College, Brooklyn, N. Y.

Cohn, Adolphe, Professor of the Romance Languages and Literatures, Columbia University, New York, N. Y.

Colin, Mrs. Thérèse F., Associate Professor of French, Wellesley College, Wellesley, Mass. [Box 293, College Hall.]

Collins, George Stuart, Professor of Modern Languages and Literatures, Polytechnic Institute, Brooklyn, N. Y.

Collitz, Hermann, Professor of Comparative Philology and German, Bryn Mawr College, Bryn Mawr, Pa.

Colville, William T., Carbondale, Pa.

Colvin, Mrs. Mary Noyes, Dansville, N. Y.

Colwell, William Arnold, Instructor in German, Harvard University, Cambridge, Mass. [17 Conant Hall.]

Comfort, William Wistar, Associate Professor of Romance Languages, Haverford College, Haverford, Pa.

Compton, Alfred D., Tutor in English, College of the City of New York, New York, N. Y.

Conklin, Clara, Associate Professor of Romance Languages, University of Nebraska, Lincoln, Neb.

Cook, Albert S., Professor of the English Language and Literature, Yale University, New Haven, Conn. [219 Bishop St.]

Cool, Charles Dean, Decatur, Ill. [511 E. North St.]

Cooper, Lane, Instructor in English, Cornell University, Ithaca, N. Y. [120 Oak Ave.]

Cooper, William Alpha, Assistant Professor of German, Leland Stanford Jr. University, Palo Alto, Cal, [1111 Emerson St.]

Corson, Livingston, Instructor in English, University of Pennsylvania, Philadelphia, Pa.

Corwin, Robert Nelson, Professor of German, Sheffield Scientific School, Yale University, New Haven, Conn. [247 St. Ronan St.] .

Cox, John H., Professor of English Philology, West Virginia University, Morgantown, W. Va. [188 Spruce St.]

Crane, Thomas Frederick, Professor of the Romance Languages and Literatures, Cornell University, Ithaca, N. Y.

Crawshaw, William Henry, Dean and Professor of English Literature, Colgate University, Hamilton, N. Y.

Critchlow, Frank Linley, Instructor in Romance Languages, Princeton University, Princeton, N. J.

Croll, Morris William, Instructor in English, Princeton University, Princeton, N. J.

Cross, Wilbur Lucius, Professor of English, Sheffield Scientific School, Yale University, New Haven, Conn. [306 York St.]

Crow, Charles Langley, Adjunct Professor of Modern Languages, Washington and Lee University, Lexington, Va.

Crowell, Asa Clinton, Associate Professor of Germanic Languages and Literatures, Brown University, Providence, R. I. [345 Hope St.]

Crowne, Joseph Vincent, Instructor in English, College of the City of New York, New York, N. Y.

Cunliffe, John William, Associate Professor of English, McGill University, Montreal, Canada.

Curdy, Albert Eugene, Instructor in French, Yale University, New Haven, Conn. [743 Yale Station.]

Curme, George Oliver, Professor of Germanic Philology, Northwestern University, Evanston, Ill. [2237 Sherman Ave.]

Currell, William Spencer, Professor of English, Washington and Lee University, Lexington, Va.

Cutting, Starr Willard, Professor of German Literature, University of Chicago, Chicago, Ill. [5423 Greenwood Ave.]

Daland, Rev. William Clifton, President and Professor of English and Philosophy, Milton College, Milton, Rock Co., Wis.

Dallam, Mary Therese, Teacher of English, Western High School, Baltimore, Md. [307 Dolphin St.]

Damon, Lindsay Todd, Associate Professor of Rhetoric, Brown University, Providence, R. I.

Daniels, Francis, Professor of Romance Languages, Cornell College, Mt. Vernon, Ia.

Danton, George Henry, Instructor in German, Western Reserve University, Cleveland, O.

Darnall, Henry Johnston, Adjunct Professor of Modern Languages, University of Tennessee, Knoxville, Tenn.

Davidson, Charles, Cambridge, Mass. [16 Linnaean St.]

Davidson, Frederic J. A., Lecturer in Romance Languages, University of Toronto, Toronto, Canada. [22 Madison Ave.]

Davies, William Walter, Professor of the German Language, Ohio Wesleyan University, Delaware, O.

Davis, Charles Gideon, Instructor in German, University of Illinois, Urbana, Ill. [905 W. Green St.]

Davis, Edward Z., Instructor in German, University of Pennsylvania, Philadelphia, Pa. [3223 Powelton Ave.]

Davis, Edwin Bell, Professor of Romance Languages, Rutgers College, New Brunswick, N. J.   [145 College Ave.]

Dawson, Edgar, Professor of the English Language and Literature and of Political Science, Delaware College, Newark, Del.

Deering, Robert Waller, Professor of Germanic Languages and Literature, Western Reserve University, Cleveland, O.   [76 Bellflower Ave.]

De Haan, Fonger, Associate Professor of Spanish, Bryn Mawr College, Bryn Mawr, Pa.

Deister, John Louis, Professor of Latin, French, and German, Manual Training High School, Kansas City, Mo.

De Lagneau, Lea Rachel, Instructor in Romance Languages, Lewis Institute, Chicago, Ill.

Demmon, Isaac Newton, Professor of English, University of Michigan, Ann Arbor, Mich.   [1432 Washtenaw Ave.]

Denney, Joseph Villiers, Professor of Rhetoric and the English Language, Ohio State University, Columbus, O.

Diekhoff, Tobias J. C., Assistant Professor of German, University of Michigan, Ann Arbor, Mich.   [1030 Oakland Ave.]

Dike, Francis Harold, Instructor in Modern Languages, Massachusetts Institute of Technology, Boston, Mass.

Dippold, George Theodore, Brookline, Mass.   [60 Greenough St.]

Dodge, Daniel Kilham, Professor of the English Language and Literature, University of Illinois, Champaign, Ill.

Dodge, Robert Elkin Neil, Assistant Professor of English, University of Wisconsin, Madison, Wis.   [21 Mendota Court.]

Doniat, Josephine C., Instructor in French and German, Lyons Township High School, La Grange, Ill.

Douay, Gaston, Professor of French, Washington University, St. Louis, Mo.

Dow, Louis Henry, Professor of French, Dartmouth College, Hanover, N. H.

Downer, Charles Alfred, Professor of the French Language and Literature, College of the City of New York, New York, N. Y.

Dunlap, Charles Graham, Professor of English Literature, University of Kansas, Lawrence, Kas.

Dunn, Joseph, Assistant Professor of the Celtic Languages, Catholic University, Washington, D. C.

Durand, Walter Yale, Instructor in English, Phillips Academy, Andover, Mass.

Dye, Alexander Vincent, Professor of German and Instructor in French and Spanish, William Jewell College, Liberty, Mo.

van Dyke, Henry, Professor of English Literature, Princeton University, Princeton, N. J.

Eastman, Clarence Willis, Assistant Professor of German, State University of Iowa, Iowa City, Ia.

Easton, Morton William, Professor of English and Comparative Philology, University of Pennsylvania, Philadelphia, Pa. [224 S. 43d St.]

Eaton, Mrs. Abbie Fiske, Redlands, San Bernardino Co., Cal.

Edgar, Pelham, Professor of the French Language and Literature, Victoria College, University of Toronto, Toronto, Canada.

Effinger, John Robert, Junior Professor of French, University of Michigan, Ann Arbor, Mich.

Eggert, Charles A., New Haven, Conn. [338 Orange St.]

Elliott, A. Marshall, Professor of Romance Languages, Johns Hopkins University, Baltimore, Md. [18 E. Eager St.]

Emerson, Oliver Farrar, Professor of Rhetoric and English Philology, Western Reserve University, Cleveland, O. [98 Wadena St., E. Cleveland, O.]

Eno, Arthur Llewellyn, Instructor in English, University of Illinois, Urbana, Ill.

Epes, John D., Professor of English, Washington College, Chestertown, Md.

Erskine, John, Associate Professor of English, Amherst College, Amherst, Mass.

Evans, M. Blakemore, Assistant Professor of German, University of Wisconsin, Madison, Wis. [21 Mendota Court.]

Evers, Helene M., Acting Instructor in Romance Languages, University of Missouri, Columbia, Mo.

Ewart, Frank Carman, Professor of Romance Languages, Colgate University, Hamilton, N. Y.

Fahnestock, Edith, Head of the Modern Language Department, Mississippi Industrial Institute and College, Columbus, Miss. [1104 College St.]

Fairchild, Arthur Henry Rolph, Instructor in the English Language and Literature, University of Missouri, Columbia, Mo. [911 Lowery St.]

Fairchild, J. R., American Book Co., New York, N. Y. [Washington Square.]

Farley, Frank Edgar, Professor of English, Simmons College, Boston, Mass.

Farnsworth, William Oliver, Instructor in French, Yale University, New Haven, Conn. [Asheville, N. C.]

Farr, Hollon A., Associate Professor of German, Yale University, New Haven, Conn. [351 White Hall.]

Farrand, Wilson, Head Master, Newark Academy, Newark, N. J.

Farrar, Thomas James, Professor of Modern Languages, Washington and Lee University, Lexington, Va.

Faurot, Albert Alfred, Head of the Department of Modern Languages, Racine College, Racine, Wis.

Faust, Albert Bernhardt, Assistant Professor of German, Cornell University, Ithaca, N. Y. [406 University Ave.]

Fay, Charles Ernest, Professor of Modern Languages, Tufts College, Tufts College, Mass.

Ferrell, Chiles Clifton, Professor of Modern Languages, University of Mississippi, University, Miss.

Ferren, Harry M., Professor of German, High School, Allegheny, Pa.

Few, William Preston, Professor of English, Trinity College, Durham, N. C.

Fielder, Edwin W., D. Appleton & Co., New York, N. Y. [436 Fifth Ave.]

Fife, Robert H., Jr., Professor of German, Wesleyan University, Middletown, Conn. [240 College St.]

Files, George Taylor, Professor of German, Bowdoin College, Brunswick, Me.

Fiske, Christabel Forsyth, Instructor in English, Vassar College, Poughkeepsie, N. Y.

Fitz-Gerald, John Driscoll, 2d, Tutor in the Romance Languages and Literatures, Columbia University, New York, N. Y.

Fitz-Hugh, Thomas, Professor of Latin, University of Virginia, Charlottesville, Va.

Fletcher, Jefferson Butler, Professor of Comparative Literature, Columbia University, New York, N. Y.

Fletcher, Robert Huntington, Hanover, N. H.

Flom, George T., Professor of Scandinavian Languages and Literatures, State University of Iowa, Iowa City, Ia.

Florer, Warren Washburn, Instructor in German, University of Michigan, Ann Arbor, Mich. [1108 Prospect St.]

Flügel, Ewald, Professor of English Philology, Leland Stanford Jr. University, Stanford University, Cal.

Ford, J. D. M., Assistant Professor of Romance Languages, Harvard University, Cambridge, Mass. [40 Avon Hill St.]

Ford, Joseph S., Head of the German Department, Phillips Academy, Exeter, N. H.

Ford, R. Clyde, Professor of Modern Languages, State Normal College, Ypsilanti, Mich.

Fortier, Alcée, Professor of Romance Languages, Tulane University of Louisiana, New Orleans, La. [1241 Esplanade Ave.]

Fossler, Laurence, Professor of Germanic Languages, University of Nebraska, Lincoln, Neb.

Foster, Irving Lysander, Assistant Professor of Romance Languages, Pennsylvania State College, State College, Pa.

Foulet, Lucien, Associate Professor of French, Bryn Mawr College, Bryn Mawr, Pa.

Fowler, Thomas Howard, Instructor in German, Williams College, Williamstown, Mass.

Fox, Charles Shattuck, Instructor in Modern Languages, Lehigh University, South Bethlehem, Pa. [83 Broad St., Bethlehem].

Francke, Kuno, Professor of German Culture and Curator of the Germanic Museum, Harvard University, Cambridge, Mass. [2 Berkeley Place].

François, Victor Emmanuel, Assistant Professor of French, College of the City of New York, N. Y. [9 Perot St., Kingsbridge, New York, N. Y.]

Fraser, M. Emma N., Head of the Department of Romance Languages, Allegheny College, Meadville, Pa.

Fraser, William Henry, Professor of Italian and Spanish, University of Toronto, Toronto, Canada.

Freeman, J. C., Professor of English Literature, University of Wisconsin, Madison, Wis. [222 Langdon St.]

Froelicher, Hans, Professor of German, Woman's College of Baltimore, Baltimore, Md.

Fruit, John Phelps, Professor of the English Language and Literature, William Jewell College, Liberty, Mo.

Fuller, Harold DeW., Instructor in English, Harvard University, Cambridge, Mass. [44 Brentford Hall.]

Fuller, Paul, New York, N. Y. [71 Broadway.]

Fulton, Edward, Associate Professor of Rhetoric, University of Illinois, Urbana, Ill.

Furst, Clyde B., Secretary of Teachers' College, Columbia University, New York, N. Y.

Galloo, Eugénie, Professor of Romance Languages and Literatures, University of Kansas, Lawrence, Kas.

Galpin, Stanley Leman, Instructor in the Romance Languages, Amherst · College, Amherst, Mass.

Gardiner, John Hays, Associate Professor of English, Harvard University, Cambridge, Mass. [18 Grays Hall.]

Garnett, James M., Baltimore, Md. [1316 Bolton St.]

Garrett, Alfred Cope, Philadelphia, Pa. [525 Locust Ave., Germantown.]

Garver, Milton Stahl, Instructor in French, Yale University, New Haven, Conn. [361 Elm St.]

Gauss, Christian Frederick, Preceptor in Romance Languages, Princeton University, Princeton, N. J.

Gaw, Mrs. Ralph H., Topeka, Kas. [1321 Filmore St.]

Gay, Lucy Maria, Assistant Professor of Romance Languages, University of Wisconsin, Madison, Wis. [216 N. Pinckney St.]

Gayley, Charles Mills, Professor of the English Language and Literature, University of California, Berkeley, Cal. [2403 Piedmont Ave.]

Geddes, James, Jr., Professor of Romance Languages, Boston University, Boston, Mass. [12 Fairmount St., Brookline, Mass.]

Gerig, John L., Lecturer in Romance Languages, Columbia University, New York, N. Y.

Gerould, Gordon Hall, Preceptor in English, Princeton University, Princeton, N. J. [5 S. E. Brown Hall.]

Gilbert, George Clayton, Instructor in English, University of Utah, Salt Lake City, Utah. [1172 E. 1st South St.]

Gillett, William Kendall, Professor of French and Spanish, New York University, University Heights, New York, N. Y.

Glascock, Clyde Chew, Assistant Professor of German, Sheffield Scientific School, Yale University, New Haven, Conn. [Graduates' Club.]

Glen, Irving M., Professor of the English Language and Early English Literature, University of Oregon, Eugene, Ore. [254 E. 9th St.]

Goad, Caroline M., Teacher of German, Wilson College for Women, Chambersburg, Pa.

Goebel, Julius, Lecturer in Germanic Philology and Literature, Harvard University, Cambridge, Mass.

Goettsch, Charles, Associate in German, University of Chicago, Chicago, Ill.

Goodnight, S. H., Instructor in German, University of Wisconsin, Madison, Wis. [619 Harrison St.]

Gould, Chester Nathan, Instructor in German, Dartmouth College, Hanover, N. H.

Gould, William Elford, Flushing, Long Island, N. Y. [189 Madison Ave.]

Grandgent, Charles Hall, Professor of Romance Languages, Harvard University, Cambridge, Mass. [107 Walker St.]

Gray, Charles Henry, Assistant Professor of English, University of Kansas, Lawrence, Kas. [1311 Tennessee St.]

Greene, Herbert Eveleth, Collegiate Professor of English, Johns Hopkins University, Baltimore, Md. [1019 St. Paul St.]

Greenlaw, Edward Almiron, Professor of English, Adelphi College, Brooklyn, N. Y.

Greenough, Chester Noyes, Instructor in English, Harvard University, Cambridge, Mass. [20 Holworthy Hall.]

Gregor, Leigh R., Lecturer on Modern Languages, McGill University, Montreal, Canada. [139 Baile St.]

Griebsch, Max, Director, National German-American Teachers' Seminary, 558–568 Broadway, Milwaukee, Wis.

Griffin, James O., Professor of German, Leland Stanford Jr. University, Stanford University, Cal.

Griffin, Nathaniel Edward, Preceptor in English, Princeton University, Princeton, N. J. [14 N. Dod Hall.]

Grimm, Karl Josef, Professor of the German Language and Literature, Pennsylvania College, Gettysburg, Pa.

Gronow, Hans Ernst, Assistant in German, University of Chicago, Chicago, Ill. [5719 Madison Ave.]

Grossmann, Edward A., Instructor in German, Cutler School, 20 E. 50th St., New York, N. Y. [33 W. 67th St.]

Gruener, Gustav, Professor of German, Yale University, New Haven, Conn. [Box 144, Yale Station.]

Grumbine, Harvey Carson, Professor of the English Language and Literature, University of Wooster, Wooster, O.

Grummann, Paul H., Professor of Modern German Literature, University of Nebraska, Lincoln, Neb. [1930 Washington St.]

Guild, Thacher Howland, Instructor in Rhetoric, University of Illinois, Champaign, Ill. [406 John St.]

Guitéras, Calixto, Professor of Spanish, Girard College and Drexel Institute, Philadelphia, Pa.

Gummere, Francis B., Professor of English, Haverford College, Haverford, Pa.

Gutknecht, Louise L., Teacher of German and French, South Chicago High School, Chicago, Ill. [7700 Bond Ave., Windsor Park, Chicago.]

Haertel, Martin Henry, Instructor in German, University of Wisconsin, Madison, Wis.

Hagen, S. N., Associate Editor, Worcester's Dictionary, Philadelphia, Pa. [616 Bourse Building.]

Hale, Edward E., Jr., Professor of English, Union College, Schenectady, N. Y.

Hall, John Leslie, Professor of the English Language and Literature and of General History, College of William and Mary, Williamsburg, Va.

Ham, Roscoe James, Assistant Professor of Modern Languages, Bowdoin College, Brunswick, Me.

Hamill, Alfred Ernest, Chicago, Ill. [2637 Prairie Ave.]

Hamilton, George Livingstone, Instructor in Romance Languages, University of Michigan, Ann Arbor, Mich. [538 Church St.]

Hamilton, Theodore Ely, Instructor in Romance Languages, University of Illinois, Urbana, Ill. [1007 S. Wright St., Champaign, Ill.]

Hammond, Eleanor Prescott, Chicago, Ill. [360 E. 57 St., Hyde Park.]

Handschin, Charles Hart, Professor of German, Miami University, Oxford, O.

Haney, John Louis, Assistant Professor of English Philology, Central High School, Philadelphia, Pa.

Hanner, James Park, Jr., Professor of Modern Languages, Emory College, Oxford, Ga.

Hansche, Maude Bingham, Teacher of German, Commercial High School for Girls, Broad and Green Sts., Philadelphia, Pa.

Hanscom, Elizabeth Deering, Associate Professor of English Literature, Smith College, Northampton, Mass. [17 Henshaw Ave.]

Hardy, Ashley Kingsley, Assistant Professor of German and Instructor in Old English, Dartmouth College, Hanover, N. H.

Hare, James Alexander, Hamburg-American Line, New York, N. Y. [35 and 37 Broadway.]

Hargrove, Henry Lee, Professor of English, Baylor University, Waco, Texas. [1901 S. 9th St.]

Harper, George McLean, Professor of English, Princeton University, Princeton, N. J,

Harris, Charles, Professor of German, Western Reserve University, Cleveland, O.

Harris, Lancelot Minor, Professor of English, College of Charleston, Charleston, S. C.

Harris, Martha Anstice, Professor of the English Language and Literature, Elmira College, Elmira, N. Y.

Harrison, James Albert, Professor of Teutonic Languages, University of Virginia, Charlottesville, Va.

Harrison, John Smith, Instructor in English, Kenyon College, Gambier, O.

Harrison, Thomas Perrin, Professor of English, Davidson College, Davidson, N. C.

Hart, Charles Edward, Professor of Ethics and Evidences of Christianity, Rutgers College, New Brunswick, N. J. [33 Livingston Ave.]

Hart, James Morgan, Professor of the English Language and Literature, Cornell University, Ithaca, N. Y.

Hart, Walter Morris, Assistant Professor of English, University of California, Berkeley, Cal. [2255 Piedmont Ave.]

Harvey, Rev. A. L., Instructor in English and Modern Languages, University of Arkansas, Fayetteville, Ark.

Hatfield, James Taft, Professor of the German Language and Literature, Northwestern University, Evanston, Ill.

Hathaway, Charles Montgomery, Jr., Instructor in English and Law, U. S. Naval Academy, Annapolis, Md.

Hauschild, George William, Bronx, New York, N. Y. [1031 Macy Place.]

Hausknecht, Emil, Direktor, Reform-Realgymnasium, Kiel, Prussia, Germany.

Head, Walter Dutton, Instructor in French, Phillips Academy, Exeter, N. H.

Heller, Otto, Professor of the German Language and Literature, Washington University, St. Louis, Mo.

Hempl, George, Professor of English Philology and General Linguistics, University of Michigan, Ann Arbor, Mich. [1027 E. University Ave.]

Henneman, John Bell, Professor of English, University of the South, Sewanee, Tenn.

Henning, George Neely, Head Professor of Romance Languages, George Washington University, Washington, D. C.

Herford, Charles Harold, Professor in the University of Manchester, Manchester, England.

Herrick, Asbury Haven, Instructor in German, University School, Cleveland, O.

Hervey, Wm. Addison, Adjunct Professor of the Germanic Languages and Literatures, Columbia University, New York, N. Y.

Heuser, Frederick W. J., Tutor in the Germanic Languages and Literatures, Columbia University, New York, N. Y.

Hewett, Waterman Thomas, Professor of the German Language and Literature, Cornell University, Ithaca, N. Y.

Heyd, Jacob Wilhelm, Instructor in German and French, State Normal School, Kirksville, Mo. [1112 S. Florence Ave.]

Hibbard, Rachel, Teacher of German and English, High School, Marquette, Mich. [325 High St.]

Hills, Elijah Clarence, Professor of Romance Languages and Literatures, Colorado College, Colorado Springs, Col. [1111 Wood Ave.]

Hinsdale, Ellen C., Professor of the German Language and Literature, Mount Holyoke College, South Hadley, Mass.

Hoag, Clarence Gilbert, Instructor in English, University of Pennsylvania, Philadelphia, Pa. [Haverford, Pa.]

Hochdörfer, Karl Friedrich Richard, Professor of Modern Languages, Wittenberg College, Springfield, O. [62 E. Ward St.]

Hodder, Mrs. Mary Gwinn, New York, N. Y. [Hotel San Remo.]

Hodell, Charles Wesley, Professor of the English Language and Literature, Woman's College of Baltimore, Baltimore, Md.

Hohlfeld, A. R., Professor of German, University of Wisconsin, Madison, Wis. [145 W. Gilman St.]

Holbrook, Richard Thayer, Professor of Romance Languages, Bryn Mawr College, Bryn Mawr, Pa.

Holzwarth, Franklin James, Professor of the Germanic Languages and Literatures, Syracuse University, Syracuse, N. Y. [911 Walnut Ave.]

Hopkins, Annette Brown, Assistant in English, Western High School, Baltimore, Md. [232 Laurens St.]

Hopkins, John Bryant, Instructor in Modern Languages, Lafayette College, Easton, Pa. [72 Blair Hall.]

Horning, L. E., Professor of German and Old English, Victoria College, University of Toronto, Toronto, Canada.

Hoskins, John Preston, Assistant Professor of German, Princeton University, Princeton, N. J. [22 Bank St.]

Hospes, Mrs. Cecilia Lizzette, Teacher of German, McKinley High School, St. Louis, Mo. [3001 Lafayette Ave.]

House, Ralph Emerson, Instructor in Romance Languages, University of Chicago, Chicago, Ill.

Howard, Albert A., Professor of Latin, Harvard University, Cambridge, Mass. [12 Walker St.]

Howard, William Guild, Instructor in German, Harvard University, Cambridge, Mass. [25 Conant Hall.]

Howe, George Maxwell, Professor of the German and French Languages and Literatures, Hobart College, Geneva, N. Y.

Howe, Malvina A., Associate Principal, Miss Howe and Miss Marot's School, Dayton, O. [513 W. 1st St.]

Howe, Thomas Carr, Professor of Germanic Languages, Butler College, University of Indianapolis, Indianapolis, Ind. [48 S. Audubon Road, Irvington.]

Howe, Will David, Professor of the English Language and Literature, Indiana University, Bloomington, Ind.

Hoyt, Prentiss Cheney, Assistant Professor of English, Clark College, Worcester, Mass. [940 Main St.]

Hubbard, Frank G., Professor of the English Language, University of Wisconsin, Madison, Wis.

Hughes, Mrs. Charlotte Condé, Grand Rapids, Mich. [18 S. Lafayette St.]

Hulme, William Henry, Professor of English, Western Reserve University, Cleveland, O. [48 Mayfield St.]

Hume, Thomas, Professor of English Literature, University of North Carolina, Chapel Hill, N. C.

Hunt, Theodore Whitefield, Professor of the English Language and Literature, Princeton University, Princeton, N. J.

Hurlbut, Byron Satterlee, Assistant Professor of English, Harvard University, Cambridge, Mass. [32 Quincy St.]

Hutchison, Percy Adams, Instructor in English, Harvard University, Cambridge, Mass.

Hyde, James Hazen, New York, N. Y. [9 E. 40th St.]

Ibbotson, Joseph Darling, Jr., Professor of English Literature, Hamilton College, Clinton, N. Y.

Ilgen, Ernest, Assistant Professor of German, College of the City of New York, New York, N. Y.

Jack, Albert E., Professor of English, Lake Forest University, Lake Forest, Ill.

von Jagemann, H. C. G., Professor of Germanic Philology, Harvard University, Cambridge, Mass.   [113 Walker St.]

Jenkins, T. Atkinson, Associate Professor of French Philology, University of Chicago, Chicago, Ill.   [488 E. 54th Place.]

Jessen, Karl D., Associate in German Literature, Bryn Mawr College, Bryn Mawr, Pa.

Jodocius, Albert, Delancey School, Philadelphia, Pa.   [1420 Pine St.]

Johnson, Henry, Professor of Modern Languages, Bowdoin College, Brunswick, Me.

Johnson, William Savage, Instructor in English, Yale University, New Haven, Conn.   [78 Lake Place.]

Johnston, Oliver Martin, Associate Professor of Romanic Languages, Leland Stanford Jr. University, Stanford University, Cal.

Jonas, J. B. E., Assistant Professor of German, Brown University, Providence, R. I.

Jones, Everett Starr, Instructor in Modern Languages, Jacob Tome Institute, Port Deposit, Md.

Jones, Harrie Stuart Vedder, Instructor in English, University of Illinois, Urbana, Ill.   [605 W. Green St.]

Jones, Jessie Louise, Assistant Professor of German, Lewis Institute, Chicago, Ill.

Jones, Richard, Professor of English Literature, Vanderbilt University, Nashville, Tenn.

Jordan, Daniel, Instructor in the Romance Languages and Literatures, Columbia University, New York, N. Y.

Jordan, Mary Augusta, Professor of the English Language and Literature, Smith College, Northampton, Mass.   [Hatfield House.]

Josselyn, Freeman M., Professor of Romance Languages, Boston University, Boston, Mass.

Joynes, Edward S., Professor of Modern Languages, South Carolina College, Columbia, S. C.

Kagan, Josiah M., Instructor in German, Roxbury High School, Roxbury, Mass.   [19 Trowbridge St., Cambridge, Mass.]

Karsten, Gustaf E., Professor of Modern Languages, University of Illinois, Champaign, Ill.

Keidel, George Charles, Associate in Romance Languages, Johns Hopkins University, Baltimore, Md.

Kellogg, Robert James, Professor of Modern Languages, James Millikin University, Decatur, Ill.

Kent, Charles W., Professor of English Literature, University of Virginia, Charlottesville, Va.

Keppler, Emil A. C., Tutor in Germanic Languages and Literatures, College of the City of New York, New York, N. Y.   [220 W. 107th St.]

Kern, Alfred Allan, Professor of English, Millsops College, Jackson, Miss.

Kern, Paul Oskar, Assistant Professor of Germanic Philology, University of Chicago, Chicago, Ill.

Kerr, William Alexander Robb, Professor of Romance Languages, Adelphi College, Brooklyn, N. Y.

Kinard, James Pinckney, Professor of the English Language and Literature, Winthrop College, Rock Hill, S. C.

Kind, John Louis, Instructor in German, University of Wisconsin, Madison, Wis.

King, Robert Augustus, Professor of French and German, Wabash College, Crawfordsville, Ind.

Kip, Herbert Z., Adjunct Professor of German, Vanderbilt University, Nashville, Tenn.

Kirchner, Elida C., Instructor in German, Central High School, St. Louis, Mo. [1211 N. Grand Ave.]

Kittredge, George Lyman, Professor of English, Harvard University, Cambridge, Mass. [8 Hilliard St.]

Klaeber, Frederick, Professor of English Philology, University of Minnesota, Minneapolis, Minn.

von Klenze, Camillo, Professor of the German Language and Literature, Brown University, Providence, R. I. [125 Lloyd Ave.]

Knoepfler, John Baptist, Professor of German, Iowa State Normal School, Cedar Falls, Ia.

Koren, William, Preceptor in French, Princeton University, Princeton, N. J.

Krapp, George Philip, Instructor in English, Columbia University, New York, N. Y.

Kroeh, Charles F., Professor of Languages, Stevens Institute of Technology, Hoboken, N. J.

Krowl, Harry C., Instructor in English, College of the City of New York, New York, N. Y.

Kueffner, Louise Mallinckrodt, Professor of German and French, Lombard College, Galesburg, Ill.

Kuersteiner, Albert Frederick, Professor of Romance Languages, Indiana University, Bloomington, Ind.

Kuhns, Oscar, Professor of Romance Languages, Wesleyan University, Middletown, Conn.

Kullmer, Charles Julius, Assistant Professor of German, Syracuse University, Syracuse, N. Y.

Kurrelmeyer, William, Instructor in German, Johns Hopkins University, Baltimore, Md.

Lamaze, Edouard, Dean of the School of Languages, International Correspondence Schools, Scranton, Pa.

Lambert, Marcus Bachman, Teacher of German, Boys' High School, Brooklyn, N. Y. [252 Madison St.]

Lancaster, Henry Carrington, Fellow in Romance Languages, Johns Hopkins University, Baltimore, Md.

Lang, Henry R., Professor of Romance Philology, Yale University, New Haven, Conn. [Box 244, Yale Station.]

Lange, Alexis Frederick, Professor of English and Scandinavian Philology, University of California, Berkeley, Cal. [2629 Haste St.]

Lange, Carl Frederick Augustus, Associate Professor of German, Smith College, Northampton, Mass. [83 Massasoit St.]

Langley, Ernest F., Assistant Professor of Romance Languages, Dartmouth College, Hanover, N. H.

Lathrop, Adele, Instructor, Horace Mann School, W. 120th St., New York, N. Y.

Lathrop, Henry Burrowes, Associate Professor of English Literature, University of Wisconsin, Madison, Wis. [311 Park St.]

Law, Robert A., Instructor in English, University of Texas, Austin, Tex.

Lawrence, William Witherle, Instructor in English, Columbia University, New York, N. Y.

Learned, Marion Dexter, Professor of the Germanic Languages and Literatures, University of Pennsylvania, Philadelphia, Pa.

Le Compte, Irville Charles, Instructor in French, Yale University, New Haven, Conn. [115 Ellsworth Ave.]

Le Daum, Henry, Professor of Romance Languages, State University of Iowa, Iowa City, Ia. [330 N. Leim St.]

Le Duc, Alma de L., Assistant Professor of French and Spanish, University of Kansas, Lawrence, Kas.

Lehman, Ezra, Associate Editor of the New Lippincott Dictionary, Elmhurst, Long Island, N. Y. [10th St.]

Lehmann, Gottfried, Professor of Modern Languages, Kentucky University, Lexington, Ky. [181 Mill St.]

Leonard, Arthur Newton, Professor of German, Bates College, Lewiston, Me.

Leonard, Jonathan, Sub-Master (French), English High School, Somerville, Mass. [Sandwich, Mass.]

Levi, Moritz, Junior Professor of Romance Languages, University of Michigan, Ann Arbor, Mich. [928 Olivia Ave.]

Lewis, Charlton Miner, Professor of English Literature, Yale University, New Haven, Conn.

Lewis, Edwin Herbert, Professor of English, Lewis Institute, Chicago, Ill.

Liberma, Marco F., Associate Professor of Romance Languages, University of Cincinnati, Cincinnati, O.

Lieder, Frederick William Charles, Instructor in German, Harvard University, Cambridge, Mass. [46 Holyoke House.]

Lincoln, George, Austin Teaching Fellow in Romance Languages, Harvard University, Cambridge, Mass. [44 Ware Hall.]

Logeman, Henry, Professor of English Philology, University of Ghent, Ghent, Belgium. [343 boulevard des Hospices.]

Loiseaux, Louis Auguste, Adjunct Professor of the Romance Languages and Literatures, Columbia University, New York, N. Y.

Lombard, Mary Joy, Instructor in French and German, Michigan State Normal College, Ypsilanti, Mich. [324 Forest Ave.]

Long, Percy W., Lecturer on English Literature, Bryn Mawr College, Bryn Mawr, Pa. [11 Barrett St.]

Longden, Henry B., Professor of the German Language and Literature, De Pauw University, Greencastle, Ind.

Lotspeich, Claude M., Assistant Professor of German, University of Cincinnati, Cincinnati, O.

Lowes, John Livingston, Professor of English, Swarthmore College, Swarthmore, Pa.

Luebke, William Ferdinand, Instructor in German, Miami University, Oxford, O.

Lutz, Frederick, Professor of Modern Languages and Acting Professor of Latin, Albion College, Albion, Mich.

Lyman, Albert Benedict, M. D., Baltimore, Md. [504 Sharp St.]

Macarthur, John Robertson, Professor of English, New Mexico College of Agriculture and Mechanic Arts, Mesilla Park, New Mex.

McBryde, John McLaren, Jr., Professor of English, Sweet Briar Institute, Sweet Briar, Va.

McClelland, George William, Tutor in English, College of the City of New York, New York, N. Y.

MacClintock, William D., Professor of English, University of Chicago, Chicago, Ill. [5629 Lexington Ave.]

MacCracken, Henry Noble, Harvard University, Cambridge, Mass. [5 Conant Hall.]

McIlwaine, Henry Read, Professor of English and History, Hampden-Sidney College, Hampden-Sidney, Va.

Macine, John, Professor of French and Spanish, University of North Dakota, University, N. D.

McKenzie, Kenneth, Assistant Professor of Italian, Yale University, New Haven, Conn.

McKibben, George F., Professor of Romance Languages, Denison University, Granville, O.

McKnight, George Harley, Assistant Professor of English, Ohio State University, Columbus, O.

McLaughlin, William Aloysius, Instructor in French, University of Michigan, Ann Arbor, Mich. [920 Monroe St.]

McLean, Charlotte Frelinghuysen, Head of the Modern Language Department, Linden Hall Seminary, Lititz, Lancaster Co., Pa.

MacLean, George Edwin, President, State University of Iowa, Iowa City, Ia.

McLouth, Lawrence A., Professor of Germanic Languages and Literature, New York University, University Heights, New York, N. Y.

MacMechan, Archibald, Professor of the English Language and Literature, Dalhousie College, Halifax, N. S.

Magee, Charles Moore, University of Pennsylvania, Philadelphia, Pa. [Conshohocken, Pa.]

Manly, John Matthews, Professor and Head of the Department of English, University of Chicago, Chicago, Ill.

Manthey-Zorn, Otto, Instructor in German, University of Illinois, Urbana, Ill. [905 W. Green St.]

March, Francis Andrew, Professor of the English Language and of Comparative Philology, Lafayette College, Easton, Pa.

Marcou, Philippe Belknap, Assistant Professor of Romance Languages, Harvard University, Cambridge, Mass. [42 Garden St.]

Marden, Charles Carroll, Professor of Spanish, Johns Hopkins University, Baltimore, Md.

Marin La Meslée, A., Civilian Instructor in French, U. S. Military Academy, West Point, N. Y.

Marinoni, Antonio, Adjunct Professor of Romance Languages, University of Arkansas, Fayetteville, Ark. [224 W. Dickson St.]

Marsh, Arthur Richmond, Cambridge, Mass. [13 Hilliard St.]

Marsh, George Linnæus, Instructor in English, University of Chicago, Chicago, Ill. [Box 2, Faculty Exchange.]

Martin, Percy Alvin, Professor of French, Whittier College, Whittier, Cal. [737 Rampart St., Los Angeles, Cal.]

Mather, Frank Jewett, Jr., The Evening Post, New York, N. Y.

Matthews, Brander, Professor of Dramatic Literature, Columbia University, New York, N. Y. [681 West End Ave.]

Matzke, John E., Professor of Romanic Languages, Leland Stanford Jr. University, Stanford University, Cal.

Maynadier, Gustavus H., Instructor in English, Harvard University, Cambridge, Mass. [49 Hawthorn St.]

Mead, William Edward, Professor of the English Language, Wesleyan University, Middletown, Conn.

Meisnest, Frederick William, Instructor in German, University of Wisconsin, Madison, Wis. [1033 W. Johnson St.]

Mensel, Ernst Heinrich, Professor of Germanic Languages and Literatures. Smith College, Northampton, Mass.

Mercier, Louis J., Instructor in French, St. Ignatius College, Chicago, Ill. [199 S. Throop St.]

Meyer, Edward Stockton, Associate Professor of German, Western Reserve University, Cleveland, O. [94 Glenpark Place.]

Meyer, George Henry, Professor of the German Language and Literature, University of Illinois, Urbana, Ill.

Miller, Daniel Thomas, Professor of Languages, Brigham Young College, Logan, Utah.

Mims, Edwin, Professor of English Literature, Trinity College, Durham, N. C.

Montgomery, Maud, Teacher of French, High School, Evansville, Ind. [1049 Upper 2d St.]

Moore, Alfred Austin, Preceptor in Romance Languages, Princeton University, Princeton, N. J.

Moore, Clarence King, Professor of Romanic Languages, University of Rochester, Rochester, N. Y.

Moore, Robert Webber, Professor of German, Colgate University, Hamilton, N. Y.

Morley, Sylvanus Griswold, Newton Centre, Mass. [119 Cedar St.]

Morrill, Clarence B., Instructor in Rhetoric, University of Michigan, Ann Arbor, Mich.

Morrill, Georgiana Lea, Instructor in English, University of Wisconsin, Madison, Wis. [251 Langdon St.]

Morris, Edgar Coit, Professor of English, Syracuse University, Syracuse, N. Y. [University Library.]

Morris, John, Professor of Germanic Languages, University of Georgia, Athens, Ga.

Morton, Asa Henry, Professor of Romance Languages, Williams College, Williamstown, Mass.

Morton, Edward P., Assistant Professor of English, Indiana University, Bloomington, Ind.

Mott, Lewis F., Professor of the English Language and Literature, College of the City of New York, New York, N. Y.

Moyse, Charles E., Dean and Vice-President and Professor of the English Language and Literature, McGill University, Montreal, Canada.

Mulfinger, George Abraham, Professor of German, Allegheny College, Meadville, Pa.

Nason, Arthur Huntington, Instructor in English, New York University, University Heights, New York, N. Y.

Neff, Theodore Lee, Instructor in French, University of Chicago, Chicago, Ill.

Neidig, William J., Instructor in English, University of Wisconsin, Madison, Wis.

Neilson, William Allan, Professor of English, Harvard University, Cambridge, Mass. [2 Riedesel Ave.]

7

Nelles, Walter R., Instructor in English, University of Wisconsin, Madison, Wis.

Nelson, Clara Albertine, Professor of French, Ohio Wesleyan University, Delaware, O.

Nettleton, George Henry, Assistant Professor of English, Sheffield Scientific School, Yale University, New Haven, Conn. [339 Prospect St.]

Nevens, Charles Freeman, Instructor in French and German, Bucknell University, Lewisburg, Pa. [Box 541.]

Newcomer, Alphonso Gerald, Associate Professor of English Literature, Leland Stanford Jr. University, Stanford University, Cal.

Newcomer, Charles Berry, Instructor in Greek and Latin, University of Michigan, Ann Arbor, Mich. [1227 Washtenaw Ave.]

Newell, William Wells, Editor of *The Journal of American Folklore*, 54 Garden St., Cambridge, Mass.

Newman, Carol Montgomery, Associate Professor of English, Virginia Polytechnic Institute, Blacksburg, Va.

Newport, Mrs. Clara P., Teacher of French and German, High School, West Chester, Pa. [107 S. Church St.]

Newson, Henry Dorsey, President of the Newson Publishing Co., 18 E. 17th St., New York, N. Y.

Newton, Walter Russell, Instructor in German, Rutgers College, New Brunswick, N. J.

Nichols, Edwin Bryant, Professor of Romance Languages, Kenyon College, Gambier, O.

Nitze, William Albert, Professor of Romance Languages, Amherst College, Amherst, Mass.

Noble, Charles, Professor of the English Language and Rhetoric, Iowa College, Grinnell, Iowa. [1110 West St.]

von Noé, Adolf Carl, Instructor in German, University of Chicago, Chicago, Ill.

Nollen, John S., Professor of German, Indiana University, Bloomington, Ind.

Norris, Clarence Elnathan, Instructor in German, Brown University, Providence, R. I.

Northup, Clark S., Assistant Professor of the English Language and Literature, Cornell University, Ithaca, N. Y. [107 College Place.]

Ogden, Philip, Assistant Professor of French Literature, Johns Hopkins University, Baltimore, Md.

d'Oleire, E., Trübner's Buchhandlung, Münsterplatz 9, Strassburg i. E., Germany.

Oliver, Thomas Edward, Professor of Romanic Languages, University of Illinois, Urbana, Ill. [912 W. California Ave.]

Olmsted, Everett Ward, Assistant Professor of Romance Languages, Cornell University, Ithaca, N. Y. [730 University Ave.]

Opdycke, Leonard Eckstein, New York, N. Y. [117 E. 69th St.]

Osgood, Charles Grosvenor, Jr., Preceptor in English, Princeton University, Princeton, N. J.

Osthaus, Carl W. F., Junior Professor of German, Indiana University, Bloomington, Ind. [417 S. Tess Ave.]

Ott, John Henry, Professor of the English Language and Literature, College of the Northwestern University, Watertown, Wis.

Owen, Edward T., Professor of French and Linguistics, University of Wisconsin, Madison, Wis.

Padelford, Frederick Morgan, Professor of the English Language and Literature, University of Washington, Seattle, Wash. [University Station.]

Page, Curtis Hidden, Lecturer in the Romance Languages and Literatures, Columbia University, New York, N. Y.

Palmer, Arthur Hubbell, Professor of the German Language and Literature, Yale University, New Haven, Conn. [149 E. Rock Road.]

Palmer, Philip M., Assistant Professor of German, Lehigh University, So. Bethlehem, Pa. [34 N. New St., Bethlehem, Pa.]

Pancoast, Henry Spackman, Hartford, Conn. [78 Vernon St.]

Papot, Bénédict, Teacher of Modern Languages, R. J. Crane High and Manual Training School, Chicago, Ill. [931 Jackson Boulevard.]

Paton, Lucy Allen, Cambridge, Mass. [65 Sparks St.]

Pearson, Calvin Wasson, Harwood Professor of the German Language and Literature, Beloit College, Beloit, Wis.

Pease, Raymond Burnette, University of Wisconsin, Madison, Wis. [216 S. Mills St.]

Peet, Mrs. Julia Dumke, Instructor in German, Lewis Institute, Chicago, Ill.

Pellissier, Adeline, Instructor in French, Smith College, Northampton, Mass. [32 Crescent St.]

Penn, Henry C., Professor of English, Washington University, St. Louis, Mo.

Penniman, Josiah Harmar, Professor of English Literature, University of Pennsylvania, Philadelphia, Pa.

Perrin, Ernest Noël, Instructor in English, College of the City of New York, New York, N. Y.

Perrin, Marshall Livingston, Professor of Germanic Languages, Boston University, Boston, Mass.

Petersen, Kate O., Brooklyn, N. Y. [91 Eighth Ave.]

Phelps, William Lyon, Professor of English Literature, Yale University, New Haven, Conn.

Pietsch, Karl, Associate Professor of Romance Philology, University of Chicago, Chicago, Ill.

Plimpton, George A., Ginn & Co., New York, N. Y. [70 Fifth Ave.]

Poll, Max, Professor of Germanic Languages, University of Cincinnati, Cincinnati, O. [230 McCormick Place, Mt. Auburn, Cincinnati.]

Pope, Paul Russell, Instructor in German, Cornell University, Ithaca, N. Y. [518 Stewart Ave.]

Potter, Albert K., Associate Professor of the English Language, Brown University, Providence, R. I. [220 Waterman St.]

Potter, Murray A., Instructor in Romance Languages, Harvard University, Cambridge, Mass. [191 Commonwealth Ave., Boston, Mass.]

Prettyman, Cornelius William, Professor of the German Language and Literature, Dickinson College, Carlisle, Pa.

Priest, George M., Instructor in German, Princeton University, Princeton, N. J.

Primer, Sylvester, Professor of Germanic Languages, University of Texas, Austin, Tex. [2709 Rio Grande St.]

Prince, John Dyneley, Professor of Semitic Languages, Columbia University, New York, N. Y. [Sterlington, Rockland Co., N. Y.]

Prokosch, Edward, Instructor in German, University of Wisconsin, Madison, Wis.

Pugh, Anne L., Wells College, Aurora, N. Y.

Putnam, Edward Kirby, Davenport, Iowa. [2013 Brady St.]

Putzker, Albin, Professor of German Literature, University of California, Berkeley, Cal.

Quinn, Arthur Hobson, Assistant Professor of English, University of Pennsylvania, Philadelphia, Pa.

Raggio, Andrew Paul, St. Louis, Mo. [4060 Delmar Boulevard.]

Rambeau, A., Instructor in English in the Seminary of Oriental Languages, and Assistant Professor of Romance Languages, University of Berlin, Berlin, Germany. [Bleibtreu-Strasse 10–11, Charlottenburg-Berlin.]

Ramsay, Robert Lee, Assistant in English, Johns Hopkins University, Baltimore, Md.

Rankin, James Walter, Instructor in English, Simmons College, Boston, Mass. [14 Sumner St., Cambridge, Mass.]

Ravenel, Mrs. Florence Leftwich, Biltmore, N. C.

Ray, John Arthur, Instructor in Romance Languages, U. S. Naval Academy, Annapolis, Md. [Hotel Maryland.]

Read, William Alexander, Professor of English, Louisiana State University, Baton Rouge, La.

Reed, Edward Bliss, Assistant Professor of English Literature, Yale University, New Haven, Conn. [Yale Station.]

Reeves, Charles Francis, Seattle, Wash. [University Station.]

Reeves, William Peters, Professor of the English Language and Literature, Kenyon College, Gambier, O.

Remy, Arthur Frank Joseph, Instructor in the Germanic Languages and Literatures, Columbia University, New York, N. Y.

Rendtorff, Karl G., Assistant Professor of German, Leland Stanford Jr. University, Palo Alto, Cal. [1130 Bryant St.]

Rennert, Hugo Albert, Professor of Romanic Languages and Literatures, University of Pennsylvania, Philadelphia, Pa. [4408 Chestnut St.]

Reuther, Frieda, Instructor in German, Wellesley College, Wellesley, Mass. [Ridgeway, Wellesley.]

Reynolds, Minna Davis, Instructor in English, Arundell School, 625 St. Paul St., Baltimore, Md.

Rhoades, Lewis A., Professor of the Germanic Languages and Literatures, Ohio State University, Columbus, O.

Richards, Alfred E., Instructor in German, Princeton University, Princeton, N. J.

Riemer, Guido Carl Leo, Professor of Modern Languages, Bucknell University, Lewisburg, Pa.

Robertson, James Alexander, State Historical Library, Madison, Wis.

Robertson, Luanna, Dean of Girls and Head of the German Department, High School of the School of Education of the University of Chicago, Chicago, Ill. [Kelly Hall, University of Chicago.]

Robinson, Fred Norris, Assistant Professor of English, Harvard University, Cambridge, Mass. [Longfellow Park.]

Roedder, Edwin Carl, Assistant Professor of Germanic Philology, University of Wisconsin, Madison, Wis. [412 Lake St.]

Root, Robert Kilburn, Preceptor in English, Princeton University, Princeton, N. J.

Rosenbach, Abraham S. W., Philadelphia, Pa. [1505 N. 15th St.]

Rosenthal, D. C., Yale University, New Haven, Conn. [70 Whalley St.]

Roy, Rev. James, Niagara Falls, N. Y. [Station A.]

Rumsey, Olive, Instructor in English, Smith College, Northampton, Mass. [Westfield, Chautauqua Co., N. Y.]

Ruutz-Rees, Caroline, Head Mistress, Rosemary Hall, Greenwich, Conn.

de Salvio, Alphonso, Instructor in Romance Languages, Northwestern University, Evanston, Ill. [1928 Sherman Ave.]

Sampson, Martin Wright, Professor of English, Indiana University, Bloomington, Ind. [403 S. College Ave.]

Saunders, Mrs. Mary J. T., Professor of Modern Languages, Randolph-Macon Woman's College, Lynchburg, Va. [College Park, Va.]

Saunderson, George W., Principal of the Saunderson School of Expression and Seattle School of Oratory, Seattle, Wash. · [Holyoke Block.]

Schelling, Felix E., Professor of English Literature, University of Pennsylvania, Philadelphia, Pa. [College Hall, University of Pennsylvania.]

Schevill, Rudolph, Instructor in the Spanish Language and Literature, Yale University, New Haven, Conn. [431 Yale Station.]

Schilling, Hugo Karl, Professor of the German Language and Literature, University of California, Berkeley, Cal. [2316 Le Conte Ave.]

Schinz, Albert, Associate Professor of French Literature, Bryn Mawr College, Bryn Mawr, Pa.

Schlenker, Carl, Professor of German, University of Minnesota, Minneapolis, Minn. [509 River Parkway.]

Schmidt, Friedrich Georg Gottlob, Professor of Modern Languages, University of Oregon, Eugene, Ore.

Schmidt, Gertrud Charlotte, Königs-Strasse 15 III l., Leipzig, Germany. [297 Second Ave., Wauwatosa, Wis.]

Schmidt, Mrs. Violet Jayne, Wellsville, Allegany Co., N. Y.

Schneider, John Philip, Professor of English, Wittenberg College, Springfield, O. [206 Ferncliff Ave.]

Schofield, William Henry, Professor of Comparative Literature, Harvard University, Cambridge, Mass. [23 Claverly Hall.]

Scholl, John William, Instructor in German, University of Michigan, Ann Arbor, Mich. [1017 Vaughn St.]

Schradieck, Helen Elizabeth, Instructor in German, Adelphi Academy, Brooklyn, N. Y.

Scott, Charles Payson Gurley, Yonkers, N. Y.

Scott, Fred Newton, Professor of Rhetoric, University of Michigan, Ann Arbor, Mich. [1351 Washtenaw Ave.]

Scott, Mary Augusta, Professor of English, Smith College, Northampton, Mass.

Sechrist, Frank Kleinfelter, Professor of the English Language and Literature, State Normal School, Stevens Point, Wis. [934 Clark St.]

Segall, Jacob Bernard, Professor of Romance Languages, University of Maine, Orono, Me.

Semple, Lewis B., Teacher of English, Commercial High School, Brooklyn, N. Y. [229 Jefferson Ave.]

Severy, Ernest E., Headmaster, Severy School, Nashville, Tenn. [112 Vauxhall St.]

Shackford, Martha Hale, Associate Professor of English, Wellesley College, Wellesley, Mass. [18 Abbott St.]

Shannon, Edgar Finley, Associate Professor of English and Modern Languages, University of Arkansas, Fayetteville, Ark. [31 Hill St.]

Sharp, Robert, Professor of English, Tulane University of Louisiana, New Orleans, La.

Shaw, James Eustace, Associate in Italian, Johns Hopkins University, Baltimore, Md.

Shearin, Hubert Gibson, Professor of English, Kentucky University, Lexington, Ky. [212 Rand Ave.]

Sheldon, Edward Stevens, Professor of Romance Philology, Harvard University, Cambridge, Mass. [11 Francis Ave.]

Shepard, William Pierce, Professor of Romance Languages, Hamilton College, Clinton, N. Y.

Sherman, Lucius A., Professor of the English Language and Literature, University of Nebraska, Lincoln, Neb.

Sherzer, Jane, President and Professor of English, Oxford College, Oxford, O.

Shillock, Anna Felicia, Senior German Teacher, East Minneapolis High School, Minneapolis, Minn. [425 Twelfth Ave., S. E.]

Shipley, George, Editor of *The Baltimore American*, Baltimore, Md. [University Club.]

Shumway, Daniel Bussier, Assistant Professor of Germanic Languages and Literatures, University of Pennsylvania, Philadelphia, Pa.

Sills, Kenneth Charles Morton, Professor of Latin, Bowdoin College, Brunswick, Me.

Simonds, William Edward, Professor of English Literature, Knox College, Galesburg, Ill.

Simonton, James S., Professor Emeritus of the French Language and Literature, Washington and Jefferson College, Washington, Pa.

Skinner, Macy Millmore, Assistant Professor of German, Leland Stanford Jr. University, Stanford University, Cal.

Skinner, Prescott O., Instructor in Romance Languages, Dartmouth College, Hanover, N. H.

Sloane, Thomas O'Conor, Consulting Engineer and Chemist, New York, N. Y. [76 William St.]

Smith, C. Alphonso, Professor of the English Language and Dean of the Graduate Department, University of North Carolina, Chapel Hill, N. C.

Smith, Edward Laurence, Professor of Modern Languages, Delaware College, Newark, Del.

Smith, Frank Clifton, Professor of Modern Languages, Franklin and Marshall College, Lancaster, Pa.

Smith, Homer, Professor of English, Ursinus College, Collegeville, Pa.

Smith, Hugh Allison, Professor of Romance Languages, University of Wisconsin, Madison, Wis. [504 Madison St.]

Smith, Kirby Flower, Professor of Latin, Johns Hopkins University, Baltimore, Md.

Snow, William Brackett, Master (French), English High School, Boston, Mass.

Snyder, Henry Nelson, President and Professor of English Literature, Wofford College, Spartanburg, S. C.

Spaeth, J. D., Preceptor in English, Princeton University, Princeton, N. J.

Spanhoofd, Arnold Werner, Director of German Instruction in the High Schools, Washington, D. C. [1716 17th St., N. W.]

Spanhoofd, Edward, Head of Department of German, St. Paul's School, Concord, N. H.

Speranza, Carlo Leonardo, Professor of Italian, Columbia University, New York, N. Y. [120 E. 86th St.]

Spieker, Edward Henry, Associate Professor of Greek and Latin, Johns Hopkins University, Baltimore, Md. [915 Edmondson Ave.]

Spingarn, Joel Elias, Adjunct Professor of Comparative Literature, Columbia University, New York, N. Y. [9 W. 73d St.]

Stathers, Madison, Instructor in Romance Languages, West Virginia University, Morgantown, W. Va.

Stearns, Clara M., Chicago, Ill. [5811 Madison Ave.]

van Steenderen, Frederic C. L., Professor of French, Lake Forest University, Lake Forest, Ill.

Steeves, Harrison Ross, Assistant in English, Columbia University, New York, N. Y. [62 W. 130th St.]

Stempel, Guido Hermann, Associate Professor of Comparative Philology, Indiana University, Bloomington, Ind. [400 E. 2nd St.]

Sterling, Susan Adelaide, Assistant Professor of German, University of Wisconsin, Madison, Wis. [109 W. Washington Ave.]

Stevens, Alice Porter, Associate Professor of German, Mt. Holyoke College, South Hadley, Mass.

Stewart, Morton Collins, Cambridge, Mass. [22 Mt. Auburn St.]

Stoddard, Francis Hovey, Professor of the English Language and Literature, New York University, University Heights, New York, N. Y. [22 West 68th St.]

Stoll, Elmer Edgar, Assistant Professor of English, Western Reserve University, Cleveland, O. [9607 Hough Ave.]

Strauss, Louis A., Assistant Professor of English, University of Michigan, Ann Arbor, Mich.

Stroebe, Lilian L., Instructor in German, Vassar College, Poughkeepsie, N. Y.

Sturtevant, Albert Morey, Instructor in German, Harvard University, Cambridge, Mass. [16 Divinity Hall.]

Swearingen, Grace Fleming, Professor of English, Blackburn College, Carlinville, Ill.

Swiggett, Glen Levin, Professor of Modern Languages, University of the South, Sewanee, Tenn.

Sykes, Frederick Henry, Professor and Director of Extension Teaching, Teachers' College, Columbia University, New York, N. Y.

Sypherd, Wilbur Owen, Professor of English and Political Sciences, Delaware College, Newark, Del.

Tatlock, John S. P.; Assistant Professor of English, University of Michigan, Ann Arbor, Mich.

Taylor, George Coffin, Assistant Professor of the English Language, University of Colorado, Boulder, Col. [542 Arapahoe St.]

Taylor, Lucien Edward, Boston, Mass. [839 Boylston St., Suite 3.]

Taylor, Marion Lee, University of Chicago, Chicago, Ill. [Green Hall, University of Chicago.]

Taylor, Robert Longley, Assistant Professor of French, Dartmouth College, Hanover, N. H.

Taylor, Rupert, Joneston, Ark.

Telleen, John Martin, Head of the Department of Rhetoric and English, Case School of Applied Science, Cleveland, O.

Thayer, Harvey Waterman, Preceptor in German, Princeton University, Princeton, N. J.

Thieme, Hugo Paul, Assistant Professor of French, University of Michigan, Ann Arbor, Mich. [1209 E. University Ave.]

Thomas, Calvin, Professor of the Germanic Languages and Literatures, Columbia University, New York, N. Y.

Thomas, May, Instructor in German, Ohio State University, Columbus, O. [233 W. Eleventh Ave.]

Thompson, Elbert N. S., Instructor in Rhetoric, Yale University, New Haven, Conn. [732 Elm St.]

Thorndike, Ashley Horace, Professor of English, Columbia University, New York, N. Y.

Thurber, Charles H., Ginn & Co., Boston, Mass. [29 Beacon St.]

Thurber, Edward Allen, New York, N. Y. [115 W. 71st St.]

Tibbals, Kate Watkins, Instructor in English, Vassar College, Poughkeepsie, N. Y.

Tilden, Frank Calvin, Professor of the English Language and Literature, DePauw University, Greencastle, Ind. [201 Water St.]

Tilley, Morris Palmer, Associate Professor of English, Syracuse University, Syracuse, N. Y. [924 Baldwin Ave.]

Tisdel, Frederick Monroe, President of the University of Wyoming, Laramie, Wyoming.

Todd, Henry Alfred, Professor of Romance Philology, Columbia University, New York, N. Y.

Todd, T. W., Professor of German, Washburn College, Topeka, Kas.

Tolman, Albert Harris, Assistant Professor of English Literature, University of Chicago, Chicago, Ill.

Tombo, Rudolf, Jr., Adjunct Professor of the Germanic Languages and Literatures, Columbia University, New York, N.Y. [628 W. 144th St.]

Tombo, Rudolf, Sr., Instructor in German, Alcuin School, New York, N. Y. [217 W. 111th St.]

Toy, Walter Dallam, Professor of Germanic Languages and Literatures, University of North Carolina, Chapel Hill, N. C.

Trent, William Peterfield, Professor of English Literature, Columbia University, New York, N. Y. [279 W. 71st St.]

Trueblood, Ralph Waldo, Assistant in Chemistry, Haverford College, Haverford, Pa.

Truscott, Frederick W., Professor of Germanic Languages, West Virginia University, Morgantown, W. Va.

Tucker, Alice Blythe, Dean of Women Students and Assistant Professor of English Literature, Adelphi College, Brooklyn, N. Y.

Tufts, James Arthur, Professor of English, Phillips Academy, Exeter, N. H.

Tupper, Frederick, Jr., Professor of Rhetoric and English Literature, University of Vermont, Burlington, Vt.

Tupper, James Waddell, Associate Professor of English Literature, Lafayette College, Easton, Pa.

Turk, Milton Haight, Professor of Rhetoric and the English Language and Literature, Hobart College, Geneva, N. Y. [678 Main St.]

Turrell, Charles Alfred, Professor of Modern Languages, University of Arizona, Tucson, Arizona.

Tuttle, Edwin Hotchkiss, New Haven, Conn. [217 Mansfield St.]

Tweedie, William Morley, Professor of the English Language and Literature, Mount Allison College, Sackville, N. B.

Tynan, Joseph L., Tutor in English, College of the City of New York, New York, N. Y. [Audubon Park, West 155th St.]

Underwood, Charles Marshall, Jr., Instructor in Romance Languages, University of Cincinnati, Cincinnati, O.

Utter, Robert Palfrey, Harvard University, Cambridge, Mass. [43 Grays Hall.]

Vance, Hiram Albert, Professor of English, University of Nashville, Nashville, Tenn. [19 Maple St.]

Viles, George B., Assistant Professor of Germanic Languages and Literatures, Ohio State University, Columbus, O. [229 W. Eleventh Ave.]

Vogel, Frank, Professor of Modern Languages, Massachusetts Institute of Technology, Boston, Mass. [95 Robinwood Ave., Jamaica Plain, Mass.]

Vos, Bert John, Associate Professor of German, Johns Hopkins University, Baltimore, Md.

Voss, Ernst Karl Johann Heinrich, Professor of German Philology, University of Wisconsin, Madison, Wis. [218 W. Gilman St.]

Vreeland, Williamson Up Dike, Professor of Romance Languages, Princeton University, Princeton, N. J.

Wahl, George Moritz, Professor of the German Language and Literature, Williams College, Williamstown, Mass.

Wallace, Malcolm William, Lecturer in English, University College, University of Toronto, Toronto, Canada.

Walter, Hermann, Professor of Modern Languages, McGill University, Montreal, Canada.

Walz, John Albrecht, Assistant Professor of the German Language and Literature, Harvard University, Cambridge, Mass. [13½ Hilliard St.]

Warren, Frederick Morris, Professor of Modern Languages, Yale University, New Haven, Conn.

Wauchope, George Armstrong, Professor of English, South Carolina College, Columbia, S. C.

Weber, Hermann J., Instructor in German, Harvard University, Cambridge, Mass. [19 Wendell St.]

Weber, William Lander, Professor of English, Emory College, Oxford, Ga.

Webster, Kenneth G. T., Iustructor in English, Harvard University, Cambridge, Mass. [19 Ash St.]

Weeks, Raymond, Professor of Romance Languages, University of Missouri, Columbia, Mo.

Weiss, Henry, U. S. Government Intepreter and Translator, Port Townsend, Wash. [Box 556.]

Wells, John Edwin, Professor of English Literature, Hiram College, Hiram, O.

Wendell, Barrett, Professor of English, Harvard University, Cambridge, Mass. [18 Grays Hall.]

Werner, Adolph, Professor of the German Language and Literature, College of the City of New York, New York, N. Y. [339 W. 29th St.]

Wernicke, Paul, Professor of Modern Languages, State College of Kentucky, Lexington, Ky.

Wesselhoeft, Edward Karl, Assistant Professor of German, University of Pennsylvania, Philadelphia, Pa. [College Hall, University of Pennsylvania.]

West, Henry Skinner, Principal and Professor of English, Western High School, Baltimore, Md.

West, Henry T., Professor of German, Kenyon College, Gambier, O.

Weston, George Benson, Instructor in Romance Languages, Dartmouth College, Hanover, N. H.

Weygandt, Cornelius, Assistant Professor of English, University of Pennsylvania, Philadelphia, Pa.

Wharey, James Blanton, Professor of English, Southwestern Presbyterian University, Clarksville, Tenn.

Whitaker, L., Head of the Department of Language and Literature, Northeast Manual Training High School, Lehigh Ave. and 8th St. Philadelphia, Pa.

White, Alain C., New York, N. Y.   [51 E. 57th St.]

White, Horatio Stevens, Professor of German, Harvard University, Cambridge, Mass.   [29 Reservoir St.]

Whiteford, Robert N., Head Instructor in English Literature, High School, Peoria, Ill.

Whitelock, George, Counsellor at Law, Baltimore, Md.   [1407 Continental Trust Building.]

Whiteside, Donald Grant, Instructor in English, College of the City of New York, New York, N. Y.   [430 W. 118th St.]

Whitman, C. H., Associate Professor of English, Rutgers College, New Brunswick, N. J.   [172 College Ave.]

Whitney, Marian P., Professor of German, Vassar College, Poughkeepsie, N. Y.

Whittem, Arthur Fisher, Instructor in Romance Languages, Harvard University, Cambridge, Mass.   [23 Woodbridge St.]

Wightman, John Roaf, Professor of Romance Languages, Oberlin College, Oberlin, O.

Wilkens, Frederick H., Assistant Professor of German, New York University, University Heights, New York, N. Y.

Wilkins, Ernest Hatch, Instructor in Italian and Spanish, Harvard University, Cambridge, Mass.   [399 Broadway.]

Wilson, Charles Bundy, Professor of the German Language, and Literature, State University of Iowa, Iowa City, Ia.

Wilson, Louis Round, Librarian, University of North Carolina, Chapel Hill, N. C.

Winchester, Caleb Thomas, Professor of English Literature, Wesleyan University, Middletown, Conn.

Winkler, Max, Professor of the German Language and Literature, University of Michigan, Ann Arbor, Mich.

Wood, Francis Asbury, Assistant Professor of Germanic Philology, University of Chicago, Chicago, Ill.

Wood, Henry, Professor of German, Johns Hopkins University, Baltimore, Md.   [109 North Ave., W.]

Woods, Charles F., Bethlehem, Pa.   [22 S. High St.]

Woodward, B. D., Professor of the Romance Languages and Literatures, Columbia University, New York, N. Y.

Worden, J. Perry, Professor of Modern Languages, Kalamazoo College, Kalamazoo, Mich.

Wright, Arthur Silas, Professor of Modern Languages, Case School of Applied Science, Cleveland, O.

Wright, Charles Baker, Professor of English Literature and Rhetoric, Middlebury College, Middlebury, Vt.

Wright, Charles Henry Conrad, Assistant Professor of French, Harvard University, Cambridge, Mass.   [7 Buckingham St.]

Wright, Maurice Emerson, Professor of German and French, Grove City College, Grove City, Pa.

Wylie, Laura Johnson, Professor of English, Vassar College, Poughkeepsie, N. Y.

Young, Bert Edward, Adjunct Professor of Romance Languages, Vanderbilt University, Nashville, Tenn.

Young, Mary V., Professor of Romance Languages, Mt. Holyoke College, South Hadley, Mass.

Zdanowicz, Casimir Douglass, Paris, France. [Crédit Lyonnais.]

LIBRARIES

Subscribing for the Publications of the

Association.

Albany, N. Y. : New York State Library.
Amherst, Mass. : Amherst College Library.
Auburn, Ala. : Library of the Alabama Polytechnic Institute.
Aurora, N. Y. : Wells College Library.
Austin, Texas : Library of the University of Texas.
Baltimore, Md. : Enoch Pratt Free Library.
Baltimore, Md. : Johns Hopkins University Library.
Baltimore, Md. : Library of the Peabody Institute.
Baltimore, Md. : Woman's College Library.
Beloit, Wis. : Beloit College Library.
Berkeley, Cal. : Library of the University of California.
Berlin, Germany: Englisches Seminar der Universität Berlin.   [Dorothe-
    enstrasse 94.]
Bloomington, Ind. : Indiana University Library,
Boston, Mass. : Public Library of the City of Boston.
Bryn Mawr, Pa. : Bryn Mawr College Library.
Buffalo, N. Y. : The Buffalo Public Library.
Burlington, Vt. : Library of the University of Vermont.
Cambridge, Mass. : Harvard University Library.
Cambridge, Mass. : Radcliffe College Library.
Chapel Hill, N. C. : Library of the University of North Carolina.
Charlottesville, Va. : Library of the University of Virginia.
Chicago, Ill. : The General Library of the University of Chicago.
Chicago, Ill. : The Newberry Library.
Cincinnati, Ohio : Library of the University of Cincinnati.   [Burnet
    Woods Park.]
Cleveland, Ohio : Adelbert College Library.
Collegeville, Pa : Ursinus College Library.
Columbia, Mo. : Library of the University of Missouri.
Concord, N. H. : New Hampshire State Library.
Decorah, Iowa : Luther College Library.
Detroit, Mich. : The Public Library,
Evanston, Ill. : Northwestern University Library.
Giessen, Germany : Die Grossherzogliche Universitäts-Bibliothek.
Greensboro, Ala. : Library of Southern University.

Halifax, Nova Scotia : Dalhousie College Library.
Hartford, Conn. : Watkinson Library.
Iowa City, Iowa : Library of the State University of Iowa.
Ithaca, N. Y. : Cornell University Library.
Knoxville, Tenn. : University of Tennessee Library.
Lincoln, Neb. : State University of Nebraska Library.
London, England : London Library. [St. James Sq., S. W.]
Madison, Wis. : University of Wisconsin Library.
Middlebury, Vt. : Middlebury College Library.
Middletown, Conn. : Wesleyan University Library.
Minneapolis, Minn. : University of Minnesota Library.
Munich, Germany : Königl. Hof- und Staats-Bibliothek.
Nashville, Tenn. : Library of the Peabody College for Teachers.
Nashville, Tenn. : Vanderbilt University Library.
New Haven, Conn. : Yale University Library.
New York, N. Y. : Columbia University Library.
New York, N. Y. : The New York Public Library (Astor, Lenox, and
    Tilden Foundations). [40 Lafayette Place.]
Oberlin, Ohio : Oberlin College Library.
Painesville, O. : Library of Lake Erie College.
Paris, France : Bibliothèque de l'Université à la Sorbonne.
Peoria, Ill. : Peoria Public Library.
Philadelphia, Pa. : University of Pennsylvania Library.
Pittsburg, Pa. : Carnegie Library.
Poughkeepsie, N. Y. : Vassar College Library.
Princeton, N. J. : Library of Princeton University.
Providence, R. I. : Library of Brown University.
Providence, R. I. : Providence Public Library. [32 Snow St.]
Rochester, N. Y. : Library of the University of Rochester. [Prince St.]
Rock Hill, S. C. : Winthrop Normal and Industrial College Library.
Sacramento, Cal. : State Library of California.
St. Louis, Mo. : Library of Washington University.
Seattle, Wash. : University of Washington Library.
South Bethlehem, Pa. : Lehigh University Library.
Springfield, Ohio : Wittenberg College Library.
Stanford University, Cal. : Leland Stanford Jr. University Library.
Swarthmore, Pa. : Swarthmore College Reading Room.
Urbana, Ill. : Library of the University of Illinois. [University Station.]
Washington, D. C. : Library of Supreme Council of 33d Degree. [433
    Third Street, N. W.]
Wellesley, Mass. : Wellesley College Reading Room Library.
West Point, N. Y. : Library of the U. S. Military Academy.
Williamstown, Mass. : Williams College Library.
Worcester, Mass. : Free Public Library.

[75]

HONORARY MEMBERS.

GRAZIADO I. ASCOLI, Milan, Italy.
K. VON BAHDER, University of Leipsic.
HENRY BRADLEY, Oxford, England.
ALOIS L. BRANDL, University of Berlin.
W. BRAUNE, University of Heidelberg.
SOPHUS BUGGE, University of Christiania.
KONRAD BURDACH, University of Berlin.
WENDELIN FÖRSTER, University of Bonn.
F. J. FURNIVALL, London, England.
GUSTAV GRÖBER, University of Strasburg.
B. P. HASDEU, University of Bucharest.
OTTO JESPERSEN, University of Copenhagen.
FR. KLUGE, University of Freiburg.
MARCELINO MENÉNDEZ Y PELAYO, Madrid.
PAUL MEYER, Collège de France.
W. MEYER-LÜBKE, University of Vienna.
JACOB MINOR, University of Vienna.
JAMES A. H. MURRAY, Oxford, England.
ARTHUR NAPIER, University of Oxford.
FRITZ NEUMANN, University of Heidelberg.
ADOLPH NOREEN, University of Upsala.
H. PAUL, University of Munich.
PIO RAJNA, Florence, Italy.
AUGUST SAUER, University of Prague.
J. SCHIPPER, University of Vienna.
H. SCHUCHART, University of Graz.
ERICH SCHMIDT, University of Berlin.
EDUARD SIEVERS, University of Leipsic.
W. W. SKEAT, University of Cambridge.
JOHANN STORM, University of Christiania.
H. SUCHIER, University of Halle.
HENRY SWEET, Oxford, England.
ANTOINE THOMAS, Sorbonne, Paris.
ADOLPH TOBLER, University of Berlin.
RICHARD PAUL WÜLKER, University of Leipsic.

ROLL OF MEMBERS DECEASED.

J. T. AKERS, Central College, Richmond, Ky.
T. WHITING BANCROFT, Brown University, Providence, R. I. [1890.]
D. L. BARTLETT, Baltimore, Md. [1899.]
W. M. BASKERVILL, Vanderbilt University, Nashville, Tenn. [1899.]
ALEXANDER MELVILLE BELL, Washington, D. C. [1905.]
DANIEL G. BRINTON, Media, Pa. [1899.]
FRANK ROSCOE BUTLER, Hathorne, Mass. [1905.]
CHARLES CHOLLET, West Virginia University, Morgantown, W. Va.
    [1903.]
HENRY COHEN. Northwestern University, Evanston, Ill. [1900.]
WILLIAM COOK, Harvard University, Cambridge, Mass. [1888.]
SUSAN R. CUTLER, Chicago, Ill. [1899.]
A. N. VAN DAELL, Massachusetts Institute of Technology, Boston, Mass.
    [1899.]
EDWARD GRAHAM DAVES, Baltimore, Md. [1894.]
W. DEUTSCH, St. Louis, Mo. [1898.]
ERNEST AUGUST EGGERS, Ohio State University, Columbus, O. [1903.]
FRANCIS R. FAVA, Columbian University, Washington, D. C. [1896.]
L. HABEL, Norwich University, Northfield, Vermont. [1886.]
RUDOLPH HAYM, University of Halle. [1901.]
RICHARD HEINZEL, University of Vienna. [1905.]
GEORGE A. HENCH, University of Michigan, Ann Arbor, Mich. [1899.]
RUDOLPH HILDEBRAND, Leipsic, Germany. [1894.]
JULES ADOLPH HOBIGAND, Boston, Mass. [1906.]
JULIAN HUGUENIN, University of Louisiana, Baton Rouge, La. [1901.]
ANDREW INGRAHAM, Cambridge, Mass. [1905.]
J. KARGÉ, Princeton College, Princeton, N. J. [1892.]
F. L. KENDALL, Williams College, Williamstown, Mass. [1893.]
EUGEN KÖLBING, Breslau, Germany. [1899.]
J. LÉVY, Lexington, Mass.
AUGUST LODEMAN, Michigan State Normal School, Ypsilanti, Mich.
    [1902.]
JULES LOISEAU, New York, N. Y.
JAMES RUSSELL LOWELL, Cambridge, Mass. [1891.]
J. LUQUIENS, Yale University, New Haven, Conn. [1899.]

8

THOMAS McCABE, Bryn Mawr College, Bryn Mawr, Pa. [1891.]
J. G. R. McELROY, University, of Pennsylvania, Philadelphia, Pa. [1891.]
EDWARD T. McLAUGHLIN, Yale University, New Haven, Conn. [1893.]
LOUIS EMIL MENGER, Bryn Mawr College, Bryn Mawr, Pa. [1903.]
CHARLES WALTER MESLOH, Ohio State University, Columbus, O. [1904.]
SAMUEL P. MOLENAER, University of Pennsylvania, Philadelphia, Pa. [1900.]
JAMES O. MURRAY, Princeton University, Princeton, N. J. [1901.]
ADOLPH MUSSAFIA, University of Vienna, Vienna, Austria. [1905.]
BENNETT HUBBARD NASH, Boston, Mass. [1906.]
C. K. NELSON, Brookville, Md. [1890.]
W. N. NEVIN. Lancaster, Pa. [1892.]
CONRAD H. NORDBY, College of the City of New York, New York, N. Y. [1900.]
C. P. OTIS, Massachusetts Institute of Technology, Boston, Mass. [1888.]
GASTON PARIS, Collège de France, Paris, France. [1903.]
W. H. PERKINSON, University of Virginia, Charlottesville, Va. [1898.]
HERBERT T. POLAND, Harvard University, Cambridge, Mass. [1906.]
SAMUEL PORTER, Gallaudet College, Kendall Green, Washington, D. C. [1901.]
F. YORK POWELL, University of Oxford, Oxford, England. [1904.]
RENÉ DE POYEN-BELLISLE, University of Chicago, Chicago, Ill. [1900.]
THOMAS R. PRICE, Columbia University, New York, N. Y. [1903.]
HENRY B. RICHARDSON, Amherst College, Amherst, Mass. [1906.]
CHARLES H. ROSS, Agricultural and Mechanical College, Auburn, Ala. [1900.]
M. SCHELE DE VERE, University of Virginia, Charlottesville, Va. [1898.]
O. SEIDENSTICKER, University of Pennsylvania, Philadelphia, Pa. [1894.]
JAMES W. SHERIDAN, College of the City of New York, New York, N. Y.
MAX SOHRAUER, New York, N. Y.
F. R. STENGEL, Columbia University, New York, N. Y.
H. TALLICHET, Austin, Texas. [1894.]
E. L. WALTER, University of Michigan, Ann Arbor, Mich. [1898.]
KARL WEINHOLD, University of Berlin. [1901.]
CARLA WENCKEBACH, Wellesley College, Wellesley, Mass. [1902.]
HÉLÈNE WENCKEBACH, Wellesley College, Wellesley, Mass. [1888.]
MARGARET M. WICKHAM, Adelphi College, Brooklyn, N. Y. [1898.]
R. H. WILLIS, Chatham, Va. [1900.]
CASIMIR ZDANOWICZ, Vanderbilt University, Nashville, Tenn. [1889.]
JULIUS ZUPITZA, Berlin, Germany. [1895.]